The
Oxford History of
World Cinema

The
Oxford History of
World Cinema

EDITED BY GEOFFREY NOWELL-SMITH

OXFORD

UNIVERSITY PRESS

OXFORD
UNIVERSITY PRESS

Great Clarendon Street, Oxford OX2 6DP

Oxford University Press is a department of the University of Oxford.
It furthers the University's objective of excellence in research, scholarship,
and education by publishing worldwide in

Oxford New York

Auckland Cape Town Dar es Salaam Hong Kong Karachi
Kuala Lumpur Madrid Melbourne Mexico City Nairobi
New Delhi Shanghai Taipei Toronto

With offices in

Argentina Austria Brazil Chile Czech Republic France Greece
Guatemala Hungary Italy Japan Poland Portugal Singapore
South Korea Switzerland Thailand Turkey Ukraine Vietnam

Oxford is a registered trade mark of Oxford University Press
in the UK and in certain other countries

Published in the United States
by Oxford University Press Inc., New York

© Oxford University Press 1996

British Library Cataloguing in Publication Data
Data available

Library of Congress Cataloging in Publication Data
Data available

ISBN 978-0-19-874242-5

19

Printed in Great Britain
on acid-free paper by
Ashford Colour Press Ltd

*I should like to dedicate this book to
the memory of my father,
who did not live to see it finished, and
to my children, for their enjoyment.*

Acknowledgements

This book has been a long time in preparation and in the course of it I have received help from many quarters. I am grateful first of all to my contributors, and in particular to those who, as well as diligently writing their own contributions to the book, also acted as informal advisers on the project—notably Thomas Elsaesser, Charles Musser, Ashish Rajadhyaksha, and A. L. Rees. I also received specialist advice from Stephen Bottomore, Pam Cook, Rosalind Delmar, Hugh Denman, Joel Finler, June Givanni, David Parkinson, Jasia Reichert, and, most valuably of all, from Markku Salmi. I had administrative help in the early stages from my niece Rebecca Nowell-Smith, and editorial assistance—all too briefly—from Sam Cook. For the last two years my Assistant Editor has been Kate Beetham, to whom my debt is indescribable. Lael Lowinstein helped with the bibliography. Picture research was conducted by Liz Heasman, whose knowledge and judgement are unrivalled in this tricky field. The tiresome work of tracing picture permissions devolved on Vicki Reeve and Diana Morris. For this normally thankless task they deserve particular thanks. And thanks, too, to my editors at the Oxford University Press, Andrew Lockett and Frances Whistler, especially for their patience.

Translations are by Robert Gordon (*Italy: Spectacle and Melodrama*, *The Scandinavian Style*, *Italy from Fascism to Neo-Realism*, *Italy: Auteurs and After*); Gerald Brooke (*The Soviet Union and the Russian Émigrés*); Timothy Seaton (*Cinema in the Soviet Republics*); and Nina Taylor (*Yiddish Cinema in Europe*, *East Central Europe before the Second World War*, *Changing States in East Central Europe*).

G.N.-S.

Contributors

Richard Abel (USA)
Rick Altman (USA)
Roy Armes (UK)
John Belton (USA)
Janet Bergstrom (USA)
Chris Berry (Australia)
Hans-Michael Bock (Germany)
David Bordwell (USA)
Royal Brown (USA)
Edward Buscombe (UK)
Michael Chanan (UK)
Paolo Cherchi Usai (USA)
Donald Crafton (USA)
Stephen Crofts (Australia)
Chris Darke (UK)
Rosalind Delmar (UK)
Karel Dibbets (Netherlands)
Michael Donnelly (USA)
Phillip Drummond (UK)
Michael Eaton (UK)
Thomas Elsaesser (Netherlands)
Cathy Fowler (UK)
Freda Freiberg (Australia)
David Gardner (USA)
Douglas Gomery (USA)
Peter Graham (France)
David Hanan (Australia)

Phil Hardy (UK)
John Hawkridge (UK)
Susan Hayward (UK)
Marek and Małgorzata
    Hendrykowski (Poland)
Michèle Hilmes (USA)
Vida Johnson (USA)
Anton Kaes (USA)
Yusuf Kaplan (UK)
Philip Kemp (UK)
Peter Kenez (USA)
Vance Kepley (USA)
Marsha Kinder (USA)
Hiroshi Komatsu (Japan)
Antonia Lant (USA)
Li Cheuk-to (Hong Kong)
Jill McGreal (UK)
Joe McElhaney (USA)
P. Vincent Magombe (UK)
Richard Maltby (UK)
Martin Marks (USA)
Morando Morandini (Italy)
William Moritz (USA)
Charles Musser (USA)
Hamid Naficy (USA)
James Naremore (USA)
Kim Newman (UK)

Natalia Nussinova (Russia)
Ed O'Neill (USA)
Roberta Pearson (UK)
Duncan Petrie (UK)
Graham Petrie (Canada)
Jim Pines (UK)
Jean Radvanyi (France)
Ashish Rajadhyaksha (India)
A. L. Rees (UK)
Mark A. Reid (USA)
Eric Rentschler (USA)
David Robinson (UK)
Bill Routt (Australia)
Daniela Sannwald (Germany)
Joseph Sartelle (USA)
Thomas Schatz (USA)
Ben Singer (USA)
Vivian Sobchack (USA)
Gaylyn Studlar (USA)
Yuri Tsivian (Latvia)
William Uricchio (Netherlands)
Ruth Vasey (Australia)
Ginette Vincendeau (UK)
Linda Williams (USA)
Brian Winston (UK)
Esther Yau (USA)
June Yip (USA)

Contents

① SILENT CINEMA 1895–1930

SOUND CINEMA 1930–1960

THE MODERN CINEMA 1960–1995

CONTENTS

CONCLUSION

Special Features

List of Colour Illustrations

(Between pages 362 and 363)

General Introduction

GEOFFREY NOWELL-SMITH

The cinema, wrote the documentarist Paul Rotha in the 1930s, 'is the great unresolved equation between art and industry'. It was the first, and is arguably still the greatest, of the industrialized art forms which have dominated the cultural life of the twentieth century. From the humble beginnings in the fairground it has risen to become a billion-dollar industry and the most spectacular and original contemporary art.

As an art form and as a technology, the cinema has been in existence for barely a hundred years. Primitive cinematic devices came into being and began to be exploited in the 1890s, almost simultaneously in the United States, France, Germany, and Great Britain. Within twenty years the cinema had spread to all parts of the globe; it had developed a sophisticated technology, and was on its way to becoming a major industry, providing the most popular form of entertainment to audiences in urban areas throughout the world, and attracting the attention of entrepreneurs, artists, scientists, and politicians. As well as for entertainment, the film medium has come to be used for purposes of education, propaganda, and scientific research. Originally formed from a fusion of elements including vaudeville, popular melodrama, and the illustrated lecture, it rapidly acquired artistic distinctiveness, which it is now beginning to lose as other forms of mass communication and entertainment have emerged alongside it to threaten its hegemony.

To compress this complex history into a single volume has been, needless to say, a daunting task. Some developments have to be presented as central, while others are relegated to the margins, or even left out entirely. Certain principles have guided me in this work. For a start, this is a history of the cinema, not of film. It does not deal with every use of the film medium but focuses on those which have concurred to turn the original invention of moving images on celluloid into the great institution known as the cinema, or 'the movies'. The boundaries of cinema in this sense are wider than just the films that the institution produces and puts into circulation. They include the audience, the industry, and the people who work in it—from stars to technicians to usherettes—and the mechanisms of regulation and control which determine which films audiences are encouraged to see and which they are not. Meanwhile, outside the institution, but constantly pressing in on it, is history in the broader sense, the world of wars and revolution, of changes in culture, demography, and life-style, of geopolitics and the global economy.

No understanding of films is possible without understanding the cinema, and no understanding of the cinema is possible without recognizing that it—more than any other art, and principally because of its enormous popularity—has constantly been at the mercy of forces beyond its control, while also having the power to influence history in its turn. Histories of literature and music can perhaps be written (though they should not be) simply as histories of authors and their works, without reference to printing and recording technologies and the industries which deploy them, or to the world in which artists and their audiences lived and live. With cinema this is impossible. Central to the project of this book is the need to put films in the context without which they would not exist, let alone have meaning.

Secondly, this is a history of cinema as, both in its origins and in its subsequent development, above all popular art. It is popular art not in the old-fashioned sense of art emanating from the 'people' rather than from cultured élites, but in the distinctively twentieth-century sense of an art transmitted by mechanical means of mass diffusion and drawing its strength from an ability to connect to the needs, interests, and desires of a large, massified public. To talk about the cinema at the level at which it engages with this large public is once again to raise, in an acute form, the question of cinema as art and industry—Paul Rotha's 'great unresolved equation'. Cinema is industrial almost by definition, by virtue of its use of industrial technologies for both the making and the showing of films. But it is also industrial in a stronger sense, in that, in order to reach large audiences, the successive processes of production, distribution, and exhibition have been industrially (and generally capitalistically) organized into a powerful and efficient machine. How the machine works (and what happens when it breaks down) is obviously of the greatest importance in understanding the cinema. But the history of the cinema is not just a history of this machine, and certainly cannot be told from the point of view of the machine and the people who control it. Nor is industrial cinema the only sort of cinema. I have tried to give space in this volume not only for cinema as industry but also for divergent interests, including those of film-makers who have worked outside or in conflict with the industrial machinery of cinema.

This involves a recognition that in the cinema the demands of industry and art are not always the same, but neither are they necessarily antithetical. It is rather that they are not commensurate. The cinema is an industrial art form which has developed industrialized ways of producing art. This is a fact which traditional aesthetics has had great difficulty in coming to terms with, but it is a fact none the less. On the other hand, there are many examples of films whose artistic status is dubious to say the least, and there are many examples of films whose artistic value is defined in opposition to the values of the industry on which they depended in order to be made. There is no simple answer to Rotha's equation. My aim throughout the book has been to maintain a balance between the values expressed through the market-place and those which are not.

Thirdly, this is a history of world cinema. This is a fact of which I am particularly proud and which is true in two senses. On the one hand the book tells the history of the cinema as a single global phenomenon, spreading rapidly across the world and controlled, to a large degree, by a single set of interlocking commercial interests. But it also, on the other hand, tells the history of many different cinemas, growing in different parts of the world and asserting their right to independent existence often in defiance of the forces attempting to exercise control and to 'open up' (that is to say, dominate) the market on a global scale.

Finding a way to relate the two senses of the phrase 'world cinema', and to balance the competing claims of the global cinema institution and the many different cinemas which exist throughout the world, has been the biggest single challenge in planning and putting together this book. The sheer diversity of world cinema, the number of films made (many of which do not circulate outside national borders), and the variety of cultural and political contexts in which the world's cinemas have emerged, means that it would be foolish or arrogant, or both, for any one person to attempt to encompass the entire history of cinema single-handed. This is not just a question of knowledge but also of perspective. In presenting a picture of world cinema in all its complexity, I have been fortunate in being able to call upon a team of contributors who are not only expert in their own fields but are in many cases able to bring to their subject a 'feel' for the priorities and the issues at stake which I, as an outsider, would never be able to replicate—even if I knew as much as they do, which I do not. This has been particularly

valuable in the case of India and Japan, countries whose cinemas rival Hollywood in scale but are known in the west only in the most partial, fragmentary, and unhistorical fashion.

Giving space to multiple perspectives is one thing. It is also important to be able to bring them all together and to give a sense of the interlocking character of the many aspects of cinema in different places and at different times. At one level the cinema may be one big machine, but it is composed of many parts, and many different attitudes can be taken both to the parts and to the whole. The points of view of audiences (and there is no such thing as 'the' audience), of artists (and there is no single prototype of 'the artist'), and of film industries and industrialists (and again there is not just one industry) are often divergent. There is also the problem, familiar to all historians, of trying to balance history 'as it happened'—and as it was seen by the participants—with the demands of present-day priorities and forms of knowledge (including present-day ignorance). No less familiar to historians is the question of the role of individuals within the historical machine, and here the cinema offers a particular paradox since unlike other industrial machineries it not only depends on individuals but also creates them—in the form, most conspicuously, of the great film stars who are both producers of cinema and its product. In respect of all these questions I have seen my task as editor as one of trying to show how different perspectives can be related, rather than imposing a single all-encompassing point of view.

HOW THE BOOK IS ARRANGED

An editor's chief weapon is organization, and it is through the way the book is organized that I have attempted to give form to the interrelation of different perspectives as outlined above. The book is divided chronologically into three parts: the Silent Cinema, the Sound Cinema from 1930 to 1960, and the Modern Cinema from 1960 to the present. In each part the book looks first at aspects of the cinema in general during the period in question, and then at cinemas in particular parts of the world. The general essays cover subjects such as the studio system, technology, film genres, and a range of developments in both mainstream and independent cinema in America, Europe, and elsewhere.

As far as possible I have tried to ensure that each development is covered from a broad international perspective, in recognition of the fact that from the earliest times the cinema has developed in remarkably similar ways throughout the industrial world. But it is also a fact that, from the end of the First World War onwards, one film industry—the American—has played a dominant role, to such an extent that much of the history of cinema in other countries has consisted of attempts by the indigenous industries to thwart, compete with, or distinguish themselves from American ('Hollywood') competition. The American cinema therefore occupies a central position throughout the 'general' sections of the book, and there is no separate consideration of American cinema as a 'national cinema' along with the French, Japanese, Soviet, and other cinemas.

Coverage in the 'national', or 'world cinema', sections extends to all the major cinemas of Europe, Asia, Africa, Australasia, and the Americas. With some regret, however, I decided that in the area of Asian cinema (the world's largest) it was preferable to concentrate on a study in depth of the most important and representative national cinemas rather than attempt an overview of every film-producing country. The areas focused on are the three major Chinese-language cinemas (those of the People's Republic of China, Hong Kong, and Taiwan), and the cinemas of Japan, Indonesia, India, and Iran. I also soon realized that almost any way of grouping world cinemas, and especially forms of grouping based on notions like First, Second, and Third World, was highly prejudicial; the 'national' or 'world cinema' sections are therefore simply strung out in a roughly west to east geographical order. This sometimes means that cinemas that show political or cultural similarities are grouped together. For example, East Central Europe, Russia, and the Soviet Republics of the Caucasus and Central Asia are both geographically adjacent and shared a common political system in the period 1948–90, and are covered in succession in Part III. But mainland China, which also shared that system (and whose cinema was shaped by similar ideological imperatives), is grouped with the other Chinese-speaking cinemas of Hong Kong and Taiwan. In all three parts of the book the journey starts in France, but in Part I it ends in Japan, and in Parts II and III in Latin America. While the decision to start in France may be taken to imply a certain priority, the form taken by the journey thereafter emphatically does not.

The various world cinemas are also dealt with in terms of the time of their emergence on the world stage. In Part I there are relatively few; there are more in Part II, and a lot more in Part III. This means that a number of essays in Part II and even more in Part III also delve back into the earlier history of the cinema in the country concerned. This minor violation of the chronological structure of the book seemed to me better than pedantically assigning, say, Iranian silent films to the silent cinema section, rather than to a single, coherent essay on Iran.

For reasons made clear at the beginning of this introduction, many of the essays in the book focus on institutional factors—on industry and trade, on censorship, and so on—and on the conditions surrounding the activity of film-making, as much as they do on films and film-makers. It is also sadly the case that it is simply not possible, in a book of this size, to do justice to all the many individuals who have played noteworthy roles in the history of cinema. But the lives and careers of individual artists, technicians, or producers are not only interesting in their own right, they can also illuminate with particular clarity how the cinema works as a whole. In a way the story of Orson Welles, for example, who spent his career either in conflict with the studio system or in attempts to make films outside it entirely, can tell one more about the system than any number of descriptions of how life was lived within it. To help provide this illumination, as well as for intrinsic interest, the text of the book is interspersed with 'insets' devoted to individual film-makers—actors, directors, producers, and technicians—who have contributed in various ways to making the cinema what it has become.

The choice of individuals to feature has been inspired by a number of overlapping criteria. Some have been chosen because they are obviously important and well known, and no history of the cinema would be complete without some extended treatment of their careers. Examples in this category—taken more or less at random—include D. W. Griffith, Ingmar Bergman, Marilyn Monroe, and Alain Delon. But there are other people—the Indian 'megastars' Nargis or M. G. Ramachandran, for instance—who are less well known to western readers but whose careers have an equal claim to be featured in a history of world cinema. The need for different perspectives has also dictated the inclusion of independent women film-makers (Agnès Varda, Chantal Akerman) and documentarists (Humphrey Jennings, Joris Ivens) alongside more mainstream directors. All these examples can be seen as illustrative or typical of something about the cinema which a more orthodox account of film history might not adequately reflect. But I have been tempted to go further, and have also chosen for 'inset' treatment one or two individuals whose careers can hardly be described as typical but which throw light on some of the rich diversity and occasional oddity of cinema, and the place it occupies in the world. The result, needless to say, is that alongside the individuals who are featured there are also many whom readers might expect to be on the list, but for whom a place was not found. This will no doubt lead to disagreements and occasional disappointments, particularly where personal favourites are not among the list of those accorded 'inset' treatment. But it is not possible to accommodate all tastes, and, more to the point, the purpose of the insets (as I hope I have made clear) is not to be a pantheon of 150 great names but to illuminate the cinema across the board.

In the first century of its existence the cinema has produced works of art worthy to stand comparison with the masterworks of painting, music, and literature. But these are only the tip of the iceberg of an art form whose growth to pre-eminence has been without precedent in the history of world culture. Even more than that, the cinema is ineradicably embedded in the whole history of the twentieth century. It has helped to shape, as well as to reflect, the reality of our times, and to give form to the aspirations and dreams of people the world over. More than anything else, this book aims to give a sense of this unique achievement and to illuminate not only the richness of cinema itself but the place it occupies in the wider world of culture and history.

REFERENCES

Each essay in the book is followed by a short list of books either referred to as sources by the author or recommended as further reading. Priority has been given to works which are easily accessible in English; but where (as sometimes happens) no adequate source exists in English or other major western languages, more recondite sources may be cited. Full bibliographical references for all works cited are given in the general bibliography at the end of the book. Besides a list of books, the insets are also followed by a selected filmography.

In the matter of foreign film titles, no single rule has been applied. Films which have a generally accepted release title in English-speaking countries are usually referred to under that title, with the original title in parentheses the first time the film is mentioned. For films which have no generally accepted English title the original title is used throughout, followed by an English translation in parentheses and quotation marks on first occurrence. But in the case of some European and Asian countries, translated titles are used throughout. The Pinyin transcription has been used for Chinese names, except in the case of Taiwanese and Hong Kong artists who themselves use other transcriptions. Russian personal names and film titles have been transcribed in the 'popular' form. thus Eisenstein, rather than the more correct but pedantic Eizenshtein; *Alexander Nevsky* rather than *Aleksandr Nevskii*. Every effort has been made to render accents and diacriticals correct in Scandinavian and Slavic languages, in Hungarian and in Turkish, and in the transcription of Arabic, but I cannot promise that this has been achieved in every case.

Silent Cinema

1895–1930

ERIC GRAY

Introduction

GEOFFREY NOWELL-SMITH

The history of the cinema in its first thirty years is one of unprecedented expansion and growth. Beginning as a novelty in a handful of big cities—New York, Paris, London, and Berlin—the new medium quickly found its way across the world, attracting larger and larger audiences wherever it was shown and displacing other forms of entertainment as it did so. As audiences grew, so did the places where films were shown, culminating in the great 'picture palaces' of the 1920s which rivalled theatres and opera-houses for opulence and splendour. Meanwhile films themselves developed from being short 'attractions', only a couple of minutes long, to the feature length that has dominated the world's screens up to the present day.

Although French, German, American, and British pioneers have all been credited with the 'invention' of cinema, the British and the Germans played a relatively small role in its world-wide exploitation. It was above all the French, followed by the Americans, who were the most ardent exporters of the new invention, helping to implant the cinema in China, Japan, and Latin America as well as in Russia. In terms of artistic development it was again the French and the Americans who took the lead, though in the years preceding the First World War Italy, Denmark, and Russia also played a part.

In the end it was the United States that was to prove decisive. The United States was—and has remained—the largest single market for films. By protecting their own market and pursuing a vigorous export policy, the Americans achieved a dominant position on the world market by the eve of the First World War. During the war, while Europe languished, the American cinema continued to develop, pioneering new techniques as well as consolidating industrial control.

Meanwhile, in the United States itself, the centre of film-making had gravitated westwards, to Hollywood, and it was films from the new Hollywood studios that flooded on to the world's film markets in the years after the First World War—and have done so ever since. Faced with the Hollywood onslaught, few industries proved competitive. The Italian industry, which had pioneered the feature film with lavish spectaculars like *Quo vadis?* (1913) and *Cabiria* (1914), almost collapsed. In Scandinavia, the Swedish cinema had a brief period of glory, notably with the powerful sagas of Victor Sjöström and the brilliant comedies of Mauritz Stiller, before following Denmark into relative

Annette Benson in the British comedy *Shooting Stars* (1928), directed by A. V. Bramble and (uncredited) Anthony Asquith

obscurity. Even the French cinema found itself in a precarious position. In Europe, only Germany proved industrially resilient, while in the new Soviet Union and in Japan the development of the cinema took place in conditions of commercial isolation.

Hollywood took the lead artistically as well as industrially. Indeed the two aspects were inseparable. Hollywood films appealed because they had better-constructed narratives, their effects were more grandiose, and the star system added a new dimension to screen acting. Where Hollywood did not lead from its own resources it bought up artists and technical innovations from Europe to ensure its continued dominance over present or future competition. Sjöström, Stiller, and the latter's young protégé Greta Garbo were lured away from Sweden, Ernst Lubitsch and F. W. Murnau from Germany; Fox acquired many patents, including that of what was to become CinemaScope.

The rest of the world survived partly by learning from Hollywood and partly because audiences continued to exist for a product which corresponded to needs which Hollywood could not supply. As well as a popular audience, there were also increasing audiences for films which were artistically more adventurous or which engaged with issues in the outer world. Links were formed with the artistic avant-garde and with political groupings, particularly on the left. Aesthetic movements emerged, allied to tendencies in the other arts. Sometimes these were derivative, but in the Soviet Union the cinema was in the vanguard of artistic development—a fact which was widely recognized in the west. By the end of the silent period, the cinema had established itself not only as an industry but as the 'seventh art'.

None of this would have happened without technology, and cinema is in fact unique as an art form in being defined by its technological character. The first section of Part I of this book, 'The Early Years', therefore begins with the technical and material developments that brought the cinema into being and helped rapidly to turn it into a major art form. In these early years this art form was quite primitive, and uncertain of its future development. It also took some time before the cinema acquired its character as a predominantly narrative and fictional medium. We have therefore divided the history of the first two decades of cinema into two: an early period proper (up to about 1905); and a transitional period (up to the emergence of the feature film shortly before the First World War), during which the cinema began to acquire that character as a form of narrative spectacle which has principally defined it ever since.

The watershed came with the First World War, which definitively sealed American hegemony, at least in the mainstream of development. The second section, 'The Rise of Hollywood', looks first at Hollywood itself in the 1910s and 1920s and the way the Hollywood system operated as an integrated industry, controlling all aspects of cinema from production to exhibition. The international ramifications of America's rise to dominance are considered next. By 1914 the cinema was a truly world-wide business, with films being made and shown throughout the industrialized world. But it was a business in which the levers of power were operated from afar, first in Paris and London, and then increasingly in New York and Hollywood, and it is impossible to understand the development of world cinema without recognizing the effect that control of international distribution had on nascent or established industries elsewhere.

As far as European cinema was concerned, the war provoked a crisis that was not merely economic. Not only did European exporters such as France, Britain, and Italy lose control over overseas markets, and find their own markets opened up to increasingly powerful American competition, but the whole cultural climate changed in the aftermath of war. The triumph of Hollywood in the 1920s was a triumph of the New World over the Old, marking the emergence of the canons of modern American mass culture not only in America but in countries as yet uncertain how to receive it.

Early cinema programmes were a hotch-potch of items, mingling actualities, comic sketches, free-standing narratives, serial episodes, and the occasional trick or animated film. With the coming of the feature-length narrative as centrepiece of the programme, other types of film were relegated to a secondary position, or forced to find alternative viewing contexts. This did not in fact hinder their development, but tended rather to reinforce their distinct identities. The making of animated cartoons became a separate branch of film-making, generally practised outside the major studios, and the same was true of serials. Together with newsreels, both cartoons and serial episodes tended to be shown as short items in a programme culminating in the feature, though some of Louis Feuillade's serials in France could fill a whole programme and there were occasional attempts at feature-length animation. Of the genres emerging out of the early cinema, however, it was really only slapstick comedy that successfully developed in both short and feature format. While Charlie Chaplin and Buster Keaton made a successful transition to features in the early 1920s, the majority of silent comedians, including Stan Laurel and Oliver Hardy, built their careers in the silent period almost entirely around the short film.

The section 'The Silent Film' looks at the kinds of film, like animation, comedy, and serials, which continued to thrive alongside the dramatic feature in the 1920s, and also at the factual film or documentary, which acquired an increasing distinctiveness as the period progressed, and at the rise of avant-garde film-making parallel (and sometimes counter) to the mainstream. Both documentary and the avant-garde achieved occasional commercial successes (Robert Flaherty's *Nanook of the North* ran for several months in a cinema in Paris; and works by French 'impressionist' film-makers like Jean Epstein and Germaine Dulac also attracted substantial audiences). On the whole, however, documentary and the avant-garde were non-commercial forms, with values distinct from the mainstream and a cultural and political role that cannot be assessed in commercial terms. The film avant-garde had an important place in the modernist art movements of the 1920s, especially in France (with Fernand Léger, Marcel Duchamp, and Man Ray), but also in Germany (Hans Richter) and the Soviet Union, and this modernist impulse was to animate documentary both in the 1920s (Dziga Vertov in the Soviet Union, Walter Ruttmann in Germany) and after.

Of the countries which developed and managed to sustain distinctive national cinemas in the silent period the most important were France, Germany, and the Soviet Union. Of these, the French cinema displayed the most continuity, in spite of the crisis provoked by the war and the economic uncertainties of the post-war period. The German cinema, by contrast, relatively insignificant in the pre-war years, exploded on to the world scene with the 'expressionist' *Cabinet of Dr Caligari* in 1919 and throughout the Weimar period succeeded in harnessing a wide spectrum of artistic energies into new cinematic forms. Even more spectacular was the emergence of the Soviet cinema after the Revolution of 1917. The new Soviet cinema resolutely turned its back on the past, leaving the style of the pre-war Russian cinema to be perpetuated by the many *émigrés* who fled westwards to escape the Revolution. The section on National Cinemas gives separate treatment to all three elements: the pre-revolutionary Russian cinema, recently rediscovered; the Soviet cinema; and the Russian *émigrés*.

The other countries whose cinemas merit an article of their own in this Part are: Britain, which had an interesting but relatively undistinguished history in the silent period; Italy, which had a brief moment of international fame just before the war; the Scandinavian countries, mainly Denmark and Sweden, which played a role in the development of silent cinema quite out of proportion to their small populations; and Japan, where a cinema developed based on traditional theatrical and other art forms and only gradually adapted to western influence. Space is also given to the unique phenomenon of the transnational Yiddish cinema, which flourished in eastern and central Europe in the inter-war years.

For most of these articles the period covered is from the earliest days up to the introduction of synchronized sound at the end of the 1920s. For the German cinema, however, the cut-off point is the Nazi takeover in 1933. For similar reasons the story of Yiddish cinema is carried up to 1939, when it was brutally terminated by the Holocaust. In the case of Japan, only the years up to the great Kanto earthquake of 1923 are covered in this part, and the later development of silent cinema in Japan, which went on well into the 1930s, is dealt with in Part II.

Silent cinema is strictly speaking a misnomer, for although films themselves were silent, the cinema was not. The showing of early films, particularly non-fiction, was often accompanied by a lecturer or barker, and in Japan there developed the remarkable institution of the *benshi*, who both commented on the action and spoke the dialogue. It was largely because of the *benshi* that silent film survived in Japan long after other countries had converted to sound. Universal throughout the 'silent' cinema, however, was musical accompaniment, which ranged from improvisations on an out-of-tune piano to full orchestral scores by composers of the calibre of Saint-Saëns (*L'Assassinat du Duc de Guise*, 1908) or Shostakovich (*New Babylon*, 1929). Music was an integral part of the silent film experience. The final section of this part looks first at the extraordinary development of film music and its role in shaping the audience's perception, before proceeding to an overview of what the silent cinema was like in its heyday in the 1920s.

THE EARLY YEARS

Origins and Survival

PAOLO CHERCHI USAI

PRE-CINEMA, FILM, TELEVISION

The history of cinema did not begin with a 'big bang'. No single event—whether Edison's patented invention of the Kinetoscope in 1891 or the Lumière brothers' first projection of films to a paying audience in 1895—can be held to separate a nebulous pre-cinema from cinema proper. Rather there is a continuum which begins with early experiments and devices aimed at presenting images in sequence (from Étienne Gaspard Robertson's *Phantasmagoria* of 1798 to Émile Reynaud's *Pantomimes lumineuses* of 1892) and includes not only the emergence in the 1890s of an apparatus recognizable as cinema but also the forerunners of electronic image-making. The first experiments in transmitting images by a television-type device are in fact as old as the cinema: Adriano de Paiva published his first studies on the subject in 1880, and Georges Rignoux seems to have achieved an actual transmission in 1909. Meanwhile certain 'pre-cinema' techniques continued to be used in conjunction with cinema proper during the years around 1900–5 when the cinema was establishing itself as a new mass medium of entertainment and instruction, and lantern slides with movement effects continued for a long time to be shown in close conjunction with film screenings.

Magic lantern, film, and television, therefore, do not constitute three separate universes (and fields of study), but belong together as part of a single process of evolution. It is none the less possible to distinguish them, not only technologically and in terms of the way they were diffused, but also chronologically. The magic lantern show gradually gives way to the film show at the beginning of the twentieth century, while television emerges fully only in the second half of the century. In this succession, what distinguishes cinema is on the one hand its technological base—photographic images projected in quick succession giving the illusion of continuity—and on the other hand its use prevailingly as large-scale public entertainment.

THE BASIC APPARATUS

Films produce their illusion of continuous movement by passing a series of discrete images in quick succession in front of a light source enabling the images to be projected on a screen. Each image is held briefly in front of the light and then rapidly replaced with the next one. If the procedure is rapid and smooth enough, and the images similar enough to each other, discontinuous images are then perceived as continuous and an illusion of movement is created. The perceptual process involved was known about in the nineteenth century, and given the name persistence of vision, since the explanation was thought to lie in the persistence of the image on the retina of the eye for long enough to make perception of each image merge into the perception of the next one. This explanation is no longer regarded as adequate, and modern psychology prefers to see the question in terms of brain functions rather than of the eye alone. But the original hypothesis was sufficiently fertile to lead to a number of experiments in the 1880s and 1890s aimed at reproducing the so-called persistence of vision effect with sequential photographs.

The purposes of these experiments were various. They were both scientific and commercial, aimed at analysing movement and at reproducing it. In terms of the emergence of cinema the most important were those which set out to reproduce movement naturally, by taking pictures at a certain speed (a minimum of ten or twelve per second and generally higher) and showing them at the same speed. In fact throughout the silent period the correspondence between camera speed and projection was rarely perfect. A projection norm of around 16 pictures ('frames') per second seems to have been the most common well into the 1920s, but practices differed considerably and it was always possible for camera speeds to be made deliberately slower or faster to produce effects of speeded-up or slowed-down motion when the film was projected. It was only with the coming of synchronized sound–tracks, which had to be played at a constant speed, that a norm of 24 frames per second (f.p.s.) became standard for both camera and projector.

First of all, however, a mechanism had to be created which would enable the pictures to be exposed in the camera in quick succession and projected the same way. A roll of photographic film had to be placed in the camera and alternately held very still while the picture was exposed and moved down very fast to get on to the next picture, and the same sequence had to be followed when the film was shown. Moving the film and then stopping it so frequently put considerable strain on the film itself—a problem which was more severe in the projector than in the camera, since the negative was exposed only once whereas the print would be shown repeatedly. The problem of intermittent motion, as it is called, exercised the minds of many of the pioneers of cinema, and was solved only by the introduction of a small loop in the threading of the film where it passed the gate in front of the lens (see inset).

FILM STOCK

The moving image as a form of collective entertainment—what we call 'cinema'—developed and spread in the form of photographic images printed on a flexible and semi-transparent celluloid base, cut into strips 35 mm. wide. This material—'film'—was devised by Henry M. Reichenbach for George Eastman in 1889, on the basis of inventions variously attributed to the brothers J. W. and I. S. Hyatt (1865), to Hannibal Goodwin (1888), and to Reichenbach himself. The basic components of the photographic film used since the end of the nineteenth century have remained unchanged over the years. They are: a transparent *base*, or *support*; a very fine layer of *adhesive substrate* made of gelatine; and a light-sensitive *emulsion* which makes the film opaque on one side. The emulsion generally consists of a suspension of silver salts in gelatine and is attached to the base by means of the layer of adhesive substrate. The base of the great majority of 35 mm. films produced before February 1951 consists of *cellulose nitrate*, which is a highly flammable substance. From that date onwards the nitrate base has been replaced by one of *cellulose acetate*, which is far less flammable, or increasingly by *polyester*. From early times, however, various forms of 'safety' film were tried out, at first using cellulose diacetate (invented by Eichengrun and Becker as early as 1901), or by coating the nitrate in non-flammable substances. The first known examples of these procedures date back to 1909. Safety film became the norm for non-professional use after the First World War.

The black and white negative film used up to the mid-1920s was so-called orthochromatic. It was sensitive to ultraviolet, violet, and blue light, and rather less sensitive to green and yellow. Red light did not affect the silver bromide emulsion at all. To prevent parts of the scene from appearing on the screen only in the form of indistinct dark blobs, early cinematographers had to practise a constant control of colour values on the set. Certain colours had to be removed entirely from sets and costumes. Actresses avoided red lipstick, and interior scenes were shot against sets painted in various shades of grey. A new kind of emulsion called *panchromatic* was devised for Gaumont by the Eastman Kodak Company in 1912. In just

The Loop and the Maltese Cross

The cinema did not really come into being until films could be projected. In this respect the Kinetoscope, patented by Thomas Alva Edison and W. K. L. Dickson in 1891 and marketed from 1893, cannot properly be considered cinema, since it consisted only of a peepshow device through which short films could be viewed by one person at a time. In the Kinetoscope the film ran continuously past a small shutter, as in Victorian optical toys such as the Zoetrope, and the flow of light was constructed by the viewer's perceptual apparatus to form an image of objects in motion—a form of viewing only possible if the spectator was peering directly into the device. By 1895, however, a number of inventors were ready with devices in which the film ran intermittently, both in the camera and in a projector, so that an image was held stably in front of the spectator before passing on to the next one. In the Lumière brothers' Cinématographe, for example (in some versions of which the same machine doubled as both camera and projector), a metal claw jerked the film down frame by frame in front of the gate and the film was held steady for the duration of each image. Since the Lumière films were very short, this form of intermittent motion did not strain the film too severely.

For longer films, however, or for the regular projection of a sequence of short films, a method had to be found to ease the passage of the film in front of the gate. By 1896–7, thanks to the pioneering inventions of Woodville Latham in the United States and R. W. Paul in Britain, projectors had been developed in which a loop of film was formed at the gate between two continuously-running sprocket wheels, and only the piece of film held in the loop was given intermittent motion, thus protecting the film from undue strain. What then attracted attention was how to find a smoother way of turning the continuous motion of the camera/projector motor into intermittent motion as the film passed the gate. The solution, again pioneered by R. W. Paul, took the form of a device known as the Maltese cross. A pin attached to a cam engaged with the little slots between the arms of the cross as it rotated, and each time it did so the film was drawn forward one frame. This method, perfected around 1905, remains in use for 35 mm. projection to this day.

GEOFFREY NOWELL-SMITH

over a decade it became the preferred stock for all the major production companies. It was less light-sensitive in absolute terms than orthochrome, which meant that enhanced systems of studio lighting had to be developed. But it was far better balanced and allowed for the reproduction of a wider range of greys.

In the early days, however, celluloid film was not the only material tried out in the showing of motion pictures. Of alternative methods the best known was the Mutoscope. This consisted of a cylinder to which were attached several hundred paper rectangles about 70 mm. wide. These paper rectangles contained photographs which, if watched in rapid sequence through a viewer, gave the impression of continuous movement. There were even attempts to produce films on glass: the Kammatograph (1901) used a disc with a diameter of 30 cm., containing some 600 photographic frames arranged in a spiral. There were experiments involving the use of translucent metal with a photographic emulsion on it which could be projected by reflection, and films with a surface in relief which could be passed under the fingers of blind people, on a principle similar to Braille.

FORMATS

The 35 mm. width (or 'gauge') for cellulose was first adopted in 1892 by Thomas Edison for his Kinetoscope, a viewing device which enabled one spectator at a time to watch brief segments of film. The Kinetoscope was such a commercial success that subsequent machines for reproducing images in movement adopted 35 mm. as a standard format. This practice had the support of the Eastman Company, whose photographic film was 70 mm. wide, and therefore only had to be cut lengthwise to produce film of the required width. It is also due to the mechanical structure of the Kinetoscope that 35 mm. film has four perforations, roughly rectangular in shape, on both sides of each frame, used for drawing the film through the camera and projector. Other pioneers at the end of the nineteenth century used a different pattern. The Lumière brothers, for example, used a single circular perforation on each side. But it was the Edison method which was soon adopted as standard, and remains so today. It was the Edison company too who set the standard size and shape of the 35 mm. frame, at approximately 1 in. wide and 0.75 in. high.

Although these were to become the standards, there were many experiments with other gauges of film stock, both in the early period and later. In 1896 the Prestwich Company produced a 60 mm. film strip, an example of which is preserved in the National Film and Television Archive in London, and the same width (but with a different pattern of perforations) was used by Georges Demenÿ in France. The Veriscope Company in America introduced a 63 mm. gauge; one film in this format still survives—a record of the historic heavyweight championship fight between Corbett and Fitzsimmons in 1897. Around the same time Louis Lumière also experimented with 70 mm. film which yielded a picture area 60 mm. wide and 45 mm. high. All these systems encountered technical problems, particularly in projection. Though some further experiments took place towards the end of the silent period, the use of wide gauges such as 65 and 70 mm. did not come into its own until the late 1950s.

More important than any attempts to expand the image, however, were those aimed at reducing it and producing equipment suitable for non-professional users.

In 1900 the French company Gaumont began marketing its 'Chrono de Poche', a portable camera which used 15 mm. film with a single perforation in the centre. Two years later the Warwick Trading Company in England introduced a 17.5 mm. film for amateurs, designed to be used on a machine called the Biokam which (like the first Lumière machines) doubled as camera, printer, and projector; this idea was taken up by Ernemann in Germany and then by Pathé in France in the 1920s. Meanwhile in 1912 Pathé had also introduced a system that used 28 mm. film on a non-flammable diacetate base and had a picture area only slightly smaller than 35 mm.

The amateur gauge *par excellence*, however, was 16 mm. on a non-flammable base, devised by Eastman Kodak in 1920. In its original version, known as the Kodascope, this worked on the reversal principle, producing a direct positive print on the original film used in the camera. Kodak launched their 16 mm. film on the market in 1923,

An alternative to celluloid film, the Kammatograph (*c*.1900) used a glass disc with the film frames arranged in a spiral

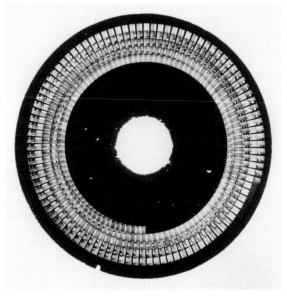

Filoteo Alberini, unidentified 70 mm. film (1911). Frame
enlargement from a negative in the film collection at George
Eastman House, Rochester, NY

and around the same time Pathé brought out their 'Pathé-
Baby', using 9.5 mm. non-flammable stock. For many years
9.5 was a fierce competitor with 16 mm., and it survived
for a long time as a reduced projection gauge both for
amateur film-making and for the showing of films originally made on 35 mm.

There were also more exotic formats, using film divided
into parallel rows which could be exposed in succession.
Of these only Edison's Home Kinetoscope, using 22 mm.
film divided into three parallel rows with an image-width
of just over 5 mm., each of them separated by a line of
perforations, had any significant commercial application.

COLOUR

As early as 1896, copies of films which had been hand-
coloured frame by frame with very delicate brushes were
available. The results achieved by this technique were
often spectacular, as in the case of Georges Méliès's *Le
Royaume des fées* (1903), whose images have the glow of
medieval miniatures. It was very difficult, however, to
ensure that the colour occupied a precise area of the
frame. To achieve this, Pathé in 1906 patented a mechanical method of colouring the base called Pathécolor.
This method, also known as 'au pochoir' in French and
stencil in English, allowed for the application of half a
dozen different tonalities.

A far less expensive method was to give the film a
uniform colour for each frame or sequence in order to
reinforce the figurative effect or dramatic impact. Basically there were three ways of doing this. There was *tinting*,
which was achieved either by applying a coloured glaze
to the base, or by dipping the film in a solution of coloured
dyes, or by using stock which was already coloured. Then
there was *toning*, in which the silver in the emulsion was
replaced with a coloured metallic salt, without affecting
the gelatine on the film. And finally there was *mordanting*,
a variety of toning in which the photographic emulsion

was treated with a non-soluble silver salt capable of fixing
an organic colouring agent. Tinting, toning, mordanting,
and mechanical colouring could be combined, thus mul-
tiplying the creative possibilities of each technique. A
particularly fascinating variation on tinting technique is
provided by the Handschiegl Process (also known as the
Wyckoff–DeMille Process, 1916–31), which was an elaborate system derived from the techniques of lithography.

The first attempts (by Frederick Marshall Lee and
Edward Raymond Turner) to realize colour films using the
superimposition of red, green, and blue images date back
to 1899. But it was only in 1906 that George Albert Smith
achieved a commercially viable result with his Kinemacolor. In front of the camera Smith placed a semi-transparent disc divided into two sectors: red and blue-green.
The film was then projected with the same filters at a
speed of 32 frames per second, and the two primary
colours were thus 'merged' in an image which showed
only slight chromatic variations but produced an undeniable overall effect. Smith's invention was widely imitated and developed into three-colour systems by
Gaumont in 1913 and the German Agfa Company in 1915.

The first actual colour-sensitive emulsion was invented
by Eastman Kodak around 1915 and shortly afterwards
marketed under the trademark Kodachrome. This was still
only a two-colour system, but it was the first stage in a
series of remarkable developments. Around the same time
a company founded by Herbert T. Kalmus, W. Burton
Westcott, and Daniel Frost Comstock—the Technicolor
Motion Picture Corporation—began experimenting with a
system based on the additive synthesis of two colours;
disappointed by the results thus obtained, the three
changed tack in 1919 and began exploring (still with two
colours only) the possibility of using the principle of subtractive synthesis first elaborated by Duclos du Hauron in
1868. This worked by combining images each of which
had filtered out light of a particular colour. When the
images were combined, the colour balance was restored.
Using the subtractive principle the Technicolor team were
ready within three years to present a colour film—*The Toll*

of the Sea (Chester M. Franklin, Metro Pictures, 1922)—created on two negatives and consisting of two sets of positive images with separate colours printed back to back.

The late 1910s and early 1920s saw many other inventions in the field of colour, but by the end of the decade it was clear that Kalmus and his associates were way ahead of the field, and it was their system that was to prevail for professional film-making throughout the 1930s and 1940s. Meanwhile the great majority of films during the silent period continued to be produced using one or other of the methods of colouring the print described above. Literally black and white films were in the minority, generally those made by smaller companies or comic shorts.

SOUND

Almost all 'silent' films had some sort of sound accompaniment. Early film shows had lecturers who gave a commentary on the images going past on the screen, explaining their content and meaning to the audience. In a number of non-western countries this practice continued long beyond the early period. In Japan, where silent cinema remained the rule well into the 1930s, there developed the art of the *benshi*, who provided gestures and an original text to accompany the image.

Along with speech came music. This was at first improvised on the piano, then adapted from the current popular repertoire, and then came to be specially commissioned. On big occasions this music would be performed by orchestras, choirs, and opera singers, while a small band or just a pianist would play in less luxurious establishments. Exhibitors who could not afford the performance of original music had two choices. The first was to equip a pianist, organist, or small band with a musical score, generally consisting of selections of popular tunes and classics in the public domain ('cue sheets'), which provided themes suitable to accompany different episodes of the film. The second, more drastic, was to fall back

on mechanical instruments, from the humble pianola to huge fairground organs powered by compressed air into which the 'score' was inserted in the form of a roll of punched paper.

Music was sometimes accompanied by noise effects. These were usually obtained by performers equipped with a wide array of objects reproducing natural and artificial sounds. But the same effects could be produced by machines, of which a particularly famous and elaborate example was the one in use at the Gaumont Hippodrome cinema in Paris.

From the beginning, however, the pioneers of the moving image had more grandiose ambitions. As early as April 1895, Edison put forward a system for synchronizing his twin inventions of phonograph and Kinetoscope. Pathé also seems to have attempted the synchronization of films and discs around 1896. All such systems, however, were hampered by the lack of amplification to project the sound in large auditoriums.

The alternative to synchronizing films and discs was to print the sound directly on the film. The first experiments in this direction took place at the beginning of the century, and in 1906 Eugène-Auguste Lauste patented a machine capable of recording images and sound on the same base.

It was only after the First World War that the decisive steps were taken towards the achievement of synchronized sound film. The German team of Vogt, Engel, and Massolle established a method of recording sound photographically by converting the sounds into light patterns on a separate film strip and their TriErgon system was premièred in Berlin in 1922. Kovalendov in the Soviet Union and Lee De Forest in the United States were also working in the same direction. De Forest's Phonofilm (1923) involved the use of a photoelectric cell to read a sound-track printed on the same strip of film as the image. Meanwhile the introduction of electric recording and the thermionic valve as an offshoot of radio technology solved

An early example of split-screen technique in an unidentified documentary on Venice. Title on print *Santa Lucia, c.*1912

the problem of amplifying the sound to make it audible in theatres.

In 1926 the Hollywood studio Warner Bros. presented *Don Juan*, with John Barrymore, using the Vitaphone system of sound synchronization. This was a sound-on-disc system, linking the projector to large discs, 16 in. in diameter, which ran at a speed of $33\frac{1}{3}$ r.p.m., with the needle starting at the centre and going outwards. The Vitaphone system was used again the following year for the first 'talking' picture, *The Jazz Singer* with Al Jolson, and continued in being for a few more years. Meanwhile a rival studio, Fox, had bought up the rights on the Tri-Ergon and Photophone patents, using them to add sound to films that had already been shot. Fox's Movietone sound-on-film system proved far more practical than Vitaphone, and became the basis for the generalized introduction of synchronized sound in the early 1930s.

ASPECT RATIO

The size and shape of the 35 mm. film frame remained virtually unchanged throughout the silent period, at about 23 mm. (just under 1 in.) wide and 18 mm. (0.75 in.) high. The spacing of the frames meant each foot of film contained 16 frames. This too has remained unaltered, and continues to be the standard today. When projected, the ratio between width and height worked out at between 1.31 and 1.38 to 1. With the coming of sound the frame size was altered slightly to accommodate the sound-track, but the projection ratio remained roughly the same—at approximately 4 : 3—until the arrival of widescreen processes in the 1950s. In the silent and early sound periods there were a few attempts to change the size and shape of the projected picture. The sides of the frame were occasionally masked out, to produce a square picture, as in the case of Murnau's *Tabu* (1931). In 1927 the Frenchman Henri Chrétien presented the first anamorphic system, known as Hypergonar, in which the image was 'squeezed' by the camera lens to accommodate a wider picture on the frame, and then 'unsqueezed' in the projector for presentation on a wide screen. This was an early fore-runner of CinemaScope and the other anamorphic systems which came into commercial use in the 1950s. Other experiments included Magnascope (1926), which used a wide-angle projector lens to fill a large screen, and devices for linking multiple projectors together. As early as 1900 Raoul Grimoin-Sanson attempted to hitch up ten 70 mm. projectors to produce a 360-degree 'panorama' completely surrounding the spectator. More famous (though equally ephemeral) was the Polyvision system used in the celebrated 'triptych' sequence in Abel Gance's *Napoléon* (1927), where three strips of film are simultaneously projected alongside each other to produce a single image.

PROJECTION

The normal method of projection from the earliest times involved placing the projector at the back of the hall and projecting the image on to the screen in a cone of light over the heads of the audience. Occasional attempts were made to devise alternative spatial arrangements. In 1909, for example, the German Messter Company experimented with showing its 'Alabastra' colour films through a complex system of mirrors on to a thin veiled screen from a projection booth placed under the theatre floor. It was also possible to project on to the screen from behind, but this process (known as back-projection) took up a lot of space and has rarely been used for public presentation. It came into use in the sound period as a form of special effect during film-making allowing actors to perform in front of a previously photographed landscape background.

Throughout the silent years projectors, whether hand-cranked or electrically powered, all ran at variable speeds, enabling the operator to adjust the speed of the projector to that of the camera. For its part, camera speed varied according to a number of factors: the amount of available light during shooting, the sensitivity of the film stock, and the nature of the action being recorded. To keep the movements of the characters on the screen 'natural', projectionists in the years before 1920 showed films at various speeds, most often between 14 and 18 frames per second. (The flicker effect that these relatively slow speeds tended to produce was eliminated by the introduction early in the century of a three-bladed shutter which opened and closed three times during the showing of each frame.) The average speed of projection increased as time went on, and by the end of the period it had regularly reached a norm of 24 frames per second, which became the standard for sound film. Faster and slower speeds were occasionally used for colour film experiments or in some amateur equipment.

The quality of projection was greatly affected by the type of light source being used. Before electric arc lights became standard, the usual method of producing light for the projector was to heat a piece of lime or a similar substance until it glowed white hot. The efficacy of this method (known as 'limelight') was very dependent on the nature and quality of the fuel used to heat the lime. The usual fuels were a mixture of coal-gas and oxygen or of ether and oxygen. Acetylene was also tried, but soon abandoned as it produced a weak light and gave off a disagreeable smell.

FROM PRODUCTION TO EXHIBITION

It is not known (and probably never will be known) exactly how many films of all types were produced during the silent period, but the figure is almost certainly in the order of 150,000, of which not more than 20,000 to 25,000 are known to have survived. With the rapid growth of the film business, films soon came to be printed in large numbers. For *Den hvide slavehandel II* ('The white slave trade II', August Blom, 1911) the Danish company Nordisk made no fewer than 260 copies for world–wide distribution. On the other hand many early American films listed in distributors' catalogues seem to have sold not more than a couple of copies, and in some cases it may be that none at all were printed, due to lack of demand.

Since the cinema was from the outset an international business, films had to be shipped from one country to another, often in different versions. Films might be recorded on two side-by-side cameras simultaneously, producing two different negatives. Intertitles would be shot in different languages, and shipped with the prints or a duplicate negative of the film to a foreign distributor. Sometimes only one frame of each title would be provided, to be expanded to full length when copies were made, and some films have survived with only these 'flash titles' or with no titles at all. Sometimes different endings were produced to suit the tastes of the public in various parts of the world. In eastern Europe for example, there was a taste for the 'Russian' or tragic ending in preference to the 'happy end' expected by audiences in America. It was also common to issue coloured prints of a film for show in luxury theatres and cheaper black and white ones for more modest locales. Finally, censorship, both national and local, often imposed cuts or other changes in films at the time of release, and many American films in particular have survived in different forms as a result of the varied censorship practices of state or city censorship boards.

DECAY

In the early years of the cinema films were looked on as essentially ephemeral and little attempt was made to preserve them once they reached the end of their commercial life. The appeal of the Polish scholar Bolesław Matuszewski in 1898 for a permanent archive of film images to be created to serve as a record for future generations fell on deaf ears, and it was not until the 1930s that the first film archives were created in a number of countries to preserve surviving films for posterity. By that time, however, many films had been irretrievably lost and many others dispersed. The world's archives have now collected together some 30,000 prints of silent films, but the lack of resources for cataloguing them means that it is not known how many of these are duplicate prints of the same version, or, in the case of what appear to be duplicates, whether there are significant differences between versions of films with the same title. While the number of films collected continues to rise, the number of surviving films is still probably less than 20 per cent of those thought to have been made.

Meanwhile, even as the number of rediscovered films

rises, a further problem is created by the perishable nature of the nitrate base on which the vast majority of silent (and early sound) films were printed. For not only is cellulose nitrate highly flammable, which may in some cases lead to spontaneous combustion: it is also liable to decay and in the course of decay it destroys the emulsion which bears the image. Even in the best conservation conditions (that is to say at very low temperatures and the correct level of humidity), the nitrate base begins to decompose from the moment it is produced. In the course of the process the film emits various gases, and in particular nitrous anhydride, which, combined with air and with the water in the gelatine, produces nitrous and nitric acids. These acids corrode the silver salts of the emulsion, thereby destroying the image along with its support, until eventually the whole film is dissolved.

RESTORATION

The decomposition of nitrate film can be slowed down, but not halted. For this reason film archives are engaged in a struggle to prolong its life until such time as the image can be transferred to a different support. Unfortunately the cellulose acetate base on to which the transfer is made is itself liable to eventual decay unless kept under ideal atmospheric conditions. Even so, it is far more stable than nitrate and infinitely preferable to magnetic (video) tape, which is not only perishable but is unsuitable for reproducing the character of the original film. It may be that some time in the future it will prove possible to preserve film images digitally, but this has not yet been demonstrated to be a practical possibility.

The aim of restoration is to reproduce the moving image in a form as close as possible to that in which it was originally shown. But all copies that are made are necessarily imperfect. For a start, they have had to be duplicated from one base on to another, with an inevitable loss of some of the original quality. It is also extremely difficult to reproduce colour techniques such as tinting and toning, even if the film is copied on to colour stock, which, given the expense, is far from being universal practice. Many films which were originally coloured are now only seen, if at all, in black and white form.

To appreciate a silent film in the form in which it was originally seen by audiences, it is necessary to have the rare good luck of seeing an original nitrate print (increasingly difficult because of modern fire regulations), and even then it has to be recognized that each copy of a film has its own unique history and every showing will vary according to which print is being shown and under what conditions. Different projection, different music, the likely absence of an accompanying live show or light effects, mean that the modern showing of silent films offers only a rough approximation of what silent film screening was like for audiences at the time.

Bibliography
Abramson, Albert (1987), *The History of Television, 1880 to 1941*.
Cherchi Usai, Paolo (1994), *Burning Passions: An Introduction to the Study of Silent Cinema*.
Hampton, Benjamin B. (1931), *A History of the Movies*.
Liesegang, Franz Paul (1986), *Moving and Projected Images: A Chronology of Pre-cinema History*.
Magliozzi, Ronald S. (ed.) (1988), *Treasures from the Film Archives*.
Rathbun, John B. (1914), *Motion Picture Making and Exhibiting*.

Early Cinema

ROBERTA PEARSON

In the first two decades of its existence the cinema developed rapidly. What in 1895 had been a mere novelty had by 1915 become an established industry. The earliest films were little more than moving snapshots, barely one minute in length and often consisting of just a single shot. By 1905, they were regularly five to ten minutes long and employed changes of scene and camera position to tell a story or illustrate a theme. Then, in the early 1910s, with the arrival of the first 'feature-length' films, there gradually emerged a new set of conventions for handling complex narratives. By this time too, the making and showing of films had itself become a large-scale business. No longer was the film show a curiosity sandwiched into a variety of other spectacles, from singing or circus acts to magic lantern shows. Instead specialist venues had been created, exclusively devoted to the exhibition of films, and supplied by a number of large production and distribution companies, based in major cities, who first sold and then increasingly rented films to exhibitors all over the world. In the course of the 1910s the single most important centre of supply ceased to be Paris, London, or New York, and became Los Angeles—Hollywood.

The cinema of this period, from the mid-1890s to the mid-1910s, is sometimes referred to as 'pre-Hollywood' cinema, attesting to the growing hegemony of the California-based American industry after the First World War. It has also been described as pre-classical, in recognition of the role that a consolidated set of 'classical' narrative conventions was to play in the world cinema from the 1920s onwards. These terms need to be used with caution, as they can imply that the cinema of the early years was only there as a precursor of Hollywood and the classical style which followed. In fact the styles of film-making prevalent in the early years were never entirely displaced by Hollywood or classical modes, even in America, and many cinemas went on being pre- or at any rate non-Hollywood in their practices for many years to come. But it remains true that much of the development that took place in the years from 1906 or 1907 can be seen as laying the foundation for what was to become the Hollywood system, in both formal and industrial terms.

For the purposes of this book, therefore, we have divided the period into two. The first half, from the beginnings up to about 1906, we have simply called early cinema, while the second half, from 1907 to the mid-1910s, we have designated transitional since it forms a bridge between the distinctive modes of early cinema and those which came later. Broadly speaking, the early cinema is distinguished by the use of fairly direct presentational modes, and draws heavily on existing conventions of photography and theatre. It is only in the transitional period that specifically cinematic conventions really start to develop, and the cinema acquires the means of creating its distinctive forms of narrative illusion.

INDUSTRY

Various nations lay claim to the invention of moving pictures, but the cinema, like so many other technological innovations, has no precise originating moment and owes its birth to no particular country and no particular person. In fact, one can trace the origins of cinema to such diverse sources as sixteenth-century Italian experiments with the camera obscura, various early nineteenth-century optical toys, and a host of practices of visual representation such as dioramas and panoramas. In the last decade of the nineteenth century, efforts to project continuously moving images on to a screen intensified and inventors/entrepreneurs in several countries presented the 'first' moving pictures to the marvelling public: Edison in the United States; the Lumière brothers in France; Max Skladanowsky in Germany; and William Friese-Greene in Great Britain. None of these men can be called the primary originator of the film medium, however, since only a favourable conjunction of technical circumstances made such an 'invention' possible at this particular moment: improvements in photographic development; the invention of celluloid, the first medium both durable and flexible enough to loop through a projector; and the application of precision engineering and instruments to projector design.

In spite of the internationalization of both film style and technology, the United States and a few European countries retained hegemony over film production, distribution, and exhibition. Initially, French film producers were arguably the most important, if not in terms of stylistic innovation, an area in which they competed with the British and the Americans, then certainly in terms of market dominance at home and internationally. Pride of place must be given to the Lumière brothers, who are frequently, although perhaps inaccurately, credited with projecting the first moving pictures to a paying audience. Auguste and Louis Lumière owned a photographic equipment factory and experimented in their spare time with designing a camera that they dubbed the Cinématographe. It was first demonstrated on 22 March 1895 at a meeting of the Société d'Encouragement à l'Industrie Nationale. Subsequent to this prestigious début, the Lumières continued to publicize their camera as a scientific instrument, exhibiting it at photographic congresses and conferences of learned societies. In December 1895, however, they executed their most famous and influential demonstration, projecting ten films to a paying audience at the Grand Café in Paris.

Precisely dating the first exhibition of moving pictures depends upon whether 'exhibition' means in private, publicly for a paying audience, seen in a Kinetoscope, or projected on a screen. Given these parameters, one could date the first showing of motion pictures from 1893, when Edison first perfected the Kinetoscope, to December 1895 and the Lumières' demonstration at the Grand Café.

The Lumières may not even have been the 'first' to project moving pictures on a screen to a paying audience; this honour probably belongs to the German Max Skladanowsky, who had done the same in Berlin two months before the Cinématographe's famed public exhibition. But despite being 'scooped' by a competitor, the Lumières' business acumen and marketing skill permitted them to become almost instantly known throughout Europe and the United States and secured a place for them in film history. The Cinématographe's technical specifications helped in both regards, initially giving it several advantages over its competitors in terms of production and exhibition. Its relative lightness (16 lb. compared to the several hundred of Edison's Kinetograph), its ability to function as a camera, a projector, a film developer, and its lack of dependence upon electric current (it was hand-cranked and illuminated by limelight) all made it extremely portable and adaptable. During the first six months of the Lumières' operations in the United States, twenty-one cameramen/projectionists toured the country, exhibiting the Cinématographe at vaudeville houses and fighting off the primary American competition, the Edison Kinetograph.

The Lumières' Cinématographe, which showed primarily documentary material, established French primacy, but their compatriot Georges Méliès became the world's leading producer of fiction films during the early cinema period. Méliès began his career as a conjurer, using magic lanterns as part of his act at the Théâtre Robert-Houdin in Paris. Upon seeing some of the Lumières' films, Méliès immediately recognized the potential of the new medium, although he took it in a very different direction from his more scientifically inclined countrymen. Méliès's Star Film Company began production in 1896, and by the spring of 1897 had its own studio outside Paris in Montreuil. Producing hundreds of films between 1896 and 1912 and establishing distribution offices in London, Barcelona, and Berlin by 1902 and in New York by 1903, Méliès nearly drove the Lumières out of business. However, his popularity began to wane in 1908 as the films of the transitional cinema began to offer a different kind of entertainment and by 1911 virtually the only Méliès films released were Westerns produced by Georges's brother Gaston in a Texas studio. Eventually, competitors forced Méliès's company into bankruptcy in 1913.

Chief among these competitors was the Pathé Company, which outlasted both Méliès and the Lumières. It became one of the most important French film producers during the early period, and was primarily responsible for the French dominance of the early cinema market. Pathé-Frères was founded in 1896 by Charles Pathé, who followed an aggressive policy of acquisition and expansion, acquiring the Lumières' patents as early as 1902, and the Méliès Film Company before the First World War. Pathé also expanded his operations abroad, exploiting markets ignored by other distributors, and making his firm's name practically synonymous with the cinema in many Third World countries. He created subsidiary production companies in many European nations: Hispano Film (Spain); Pathé-Russe (Russia); Film d'Arte Italiano; and Pathé-Britannia. In 1908 Pathé distributed twice as many films in the United States as all the indigenous manufacturers combined. Despite this initial French dominance, however, various American studios, primary among them the Edison Manufacturing Company, the American Mutoscope and Biograph Company of America (after 1909 simply the Biograph Company), and the Vitagraph Company of America (all founded in the late 1890s) had already created a solid basis for their country's future domination of world cinema.

The 'invention' of the moving picture is often associated with the name of Thomas Alva Edison, but, in accordance with contemporary industrial practices, Edison's moving picture machines were actually produced by a team of technicians working at his laboratories in West Orange, New Jersey, supervised by the Englishman William Kennedy Laurie Dickson. Dickson and his associates began working on moving pictures in 1889 and by 1893 had built the Kinetograph, a workable but bulky camera, and the Kinetoscope, a peep-show-like viewing machine in which

An early poster for the 'Cinématographe' with, on screen, the Lumiére film *Watering the Gardener* (*L'Arroseur arrosé*, 1895)

a continuous strip of film between 40 and 50 feet long ran between an electric lamp and a shutter. They also developed and built the first motion picture studio, necessitated by the Kinetograph's size, weight, and relative immobility. This was a shack whose resemblance to a police van caused it to be popularly dubbed the 'Black Maria'. To this primitive studio came the earliest American film actors, mainly vaudeville performers who travelled to West Orange from nearby New York City to have their (moving) pictures taken. These pictures lasted anywhere from fifteen seconds to one minute and simply reproduced the various performers' stage acts with, for example, Little Egypt, the famous belly-dancer, dancing, or Sandow the Strongman posing.

As with the Lumières, Edison's key position in film history stems more from marketing skill than technical ingenuity. His company was the first to market a commercially viable moving picture machine, albeit one designed for individual viewers rather than mass audiences. Controlling the rights to the Kinetograph and Kinetoscope, Edison immediately embarked upon plans for commercial exploitation, entering into business agreements that led to the establishment of Kinetoscope parlours around the country. The first Kinetoscope parlour, a rented store-front with room for ten of the viewing machines each showing a different film, opened in New York City in April 1894. The new technical marvel received a promotional boost when the popular boxing champion Gentleman Jim Corbett went six rounds against Pete

Courtney at the Black Maria. The resulting film gained national publicity for Edison's machine, as well as drawing the rapt attention of female viewers, who reportedly formed lines at the Kinetoscope parlours to sneak a peek at the scantily clad Gentleman Jim. Soon other Kinetoscope parlours opened and the machines also became a featured attraction at summer amusement parks.

Until the spring of 1896 the Edison Company devoted itself to shooting films for the Kinetoscope, but, as the novelty of the Kinetoscope parlours wore off and sales of the machines fell off, Thomas Edison began to rethink his commitment to individually oriented exhibition. He acquired the patents to a projector whose key mechanism had been designed by Thomas Armat and C. Francis Jenkins, who had lacked the capital for the commercial exploitation of their invention. The Vitascope, which projected an image on to a screen, was advertised under Edison's name and premièred in New York City in April of 1896. Six films were shown, five produced by the Edison Company and one, *Rough Sea at Dover*, by the Englishman R. W. Paul. These brief films, 40 feet in length and lasting twenty seconds, were spliced end to end to form a loop, enabling each film to be repeated up to half a dozen times. The sheer novelty of moving pictures, rather than their content or a story, was the attraction for the first film audiences. Within a year there were several hundred Vitascopes giving shows in various locations throughout the United States.

In these early years Edison had two chief domestic rivals. In 1898 two former vaudevillians, James Stuart Blackton and Albert Smith, founded the Vitagraph Company of America initially to make films for exhibition in conjunction with their own vaudeville acts. In that same year the outbreak of the Spanish–American War markedly increased the popularity of the new moving pictures, which were able to bring the war home more vividly than the penny press and the popular illustrated weeklies. Blackton and Smith immediately took advantage of the situation, shooting films on their New York City rooftop studio that purported to show events taking place in Cuba. So successful did this venture prove that by 1900 the partners issued their first catalogue offering films for sale to other exhibitors, thus establishing Vitagraph as one of the primary American film producers. The third important American studio of the time, the American Mutoscope and Biograph Company, now primarily known for employing D. W. Griffith between 1908 and 1913, was formed in 1895 to produce flipcards for Mutoscope machines. When W. K. L. Dickson left Edison to join Biograph, the company used his expertise to patent a projector to compete with the Vitascope. This projector apparently gave better-quality projection with less flicker than other machines and quickly replaced the Lumières as Edison's chief competitor. In 1897 Biograph also began to produce films but the Edison Company effectively removed them from the market by entangling them in legal disputes that remained unresolved until 1902.

At the turn of the century, Britain was the third important film-producing country. The Edison Kinetoscope was first seen there in October 1894, but, because of Edison's uncharacteristic failure to patent the device abroad, the Englishman R. W. Paul legally copied the non-protected viewing machine and installed fifteen Kinetoscopes at the exhibition hall at Earl's Court in London. When Edison belatedly sought to protect his interests by cutting off the supply of films, Paul responded by going into production for himself. In 1899, in conjunction with Birt Acres, who supplied the necessary technical expertise, Paul opened the first British film studio, in north London. Another important early British film-maker, Cecil Hepworth, built a studio in his London back garden in 1900. By 1902 Brighton had also become an important centre for British film-making with two of the key members of the so-called 'Brighton school', George Albert Smith and James Williamson, each operating a studio.

At this time, production, distribution, and exhibition practices differed markedly from those that were to emerge during the transitional period; the film industry had not yet attained the specialization and division of labour characteristic of large-scale capitalist enterprises. Initially, production, distribution, and exhibition all remained the exclusive province of the film manu-facturers. The Lumière travelling cameramen used the adaptable Cinématographe to shoot, develop, and project films, while American studios such as Edison and Biograph usually supplied a projector, films, and even a projectionist to the vaudeville houses that constituted the primary exhibition sites. Even with the rapid emergence of independent travelling showmen in the United States, Britain, and Germany, film distribution remained non-existent. Producers sold rather than rented their films; a practice which forestalled the development of permanent exhibition sites until the second decade of the cinema's history.

As opposed to the strict division of labour and assembly-line practices that characterized the Hollywood studios, production during this period was non-hierarchical and truly collaborative. One of the most important early film 'directors' was Edwin S. Porter, who had worked as a hired projectionist and then as an independent exhibitor. Porter joined the Edison Company in 1900, first as a mechanic and then as head of production. Despite his nominal position, Porter only controlled the technical aspects of filming and editing while other Edison employees with theatrical experience took charge of directing the actors and the *mise-en-scène*. Other American studios seem to have practised similar arrangements. At Vitagraph, James Stuart Blackton and Albert Smith traded off their duties in front of and behind the camera, one acting and the other shooting, and then reversing their roles for the next film. In similar fashion, the members of the British Brighton school both owned their production companies and functioned as cameramen. Georges Méliès, who also owned his own company, did everything short of actually crank the camera, writing the script, designing sets and costumes, devising trick effects, and often acting. The first true 'director', in the modern sense of being responsible for all aspects of a film's actual shooting, was probably introduced at the Biograph Company in 1903. The increased production of fiction films required that one person have a sense of the film's narrative development and of the connections between individual shots.

STYLE

As the emergence of the film director illustrates, changes in the film texts often necessitated concomitant changes in the production process. But what did the earliest films actually look like? Generally speaking, until 1907, film-makers concerned themselves with the individual shot, preserving the spatial aspects of the pro-filmic event (the scene that takes place in front of the camera). They did not create temporal relations or story causality by using cinematic interventions. They set the camera far enough from the action to show the entire length of the human body as well as the spaces above the head and below the feet. The camera was kept stationary, particularly in exterior shots, with only occasional reframings to follow the action, and interventions through such devices as editing or lighting were infrequent. This long-shot style is often referred to as a tableau shot or a proscenium arch shot, the latter appellation stemming from the supposed resemblance to the perspective an audience member would have from the front row centre of a theatre. For this reason, pre-1907 film is often accused of being more theatrical than cinematic, although the tableau style also replicates the perspective commonly seen in such other period media as postcards and stereographs, and early film-makers derived their inspiration as much from these and other visual texts as from the theatre.

Concerning themselves primarily with the individual shot, early film-makers tended not to be overly interested in connections between shots; that is, editing. They did not elaborate conventions for linking one shot to the next, for constructing a continuous linear narrative, nor for keeping the viewer oriented in time and space. However, there were some multi-shot films produced during this period, although rarely before 1902. In fact, one can break the pre-1907 years into two subsidiary periods: 1894–1902/3, when the majority of films consisted of one shot and were what we would today call documentaries, known then, after the French usage, as actualities; and 1903–7, when the multi-shot, fiction film gradually began to dominate, with simple narratives structuring the temporal and causal relations between shots.

Many films of the 1894–1907 period seem strange from a modern perspective, since early film-makers tended to be quite self-conscious in their narrative style, presenting their films to the viewer as if they were carnival barkers touting their wares, rather than disguising their presence through cinematic conventions as their successors were to do. Unlike the omniscient narrators of realist novels and the Hollywood cinema, the early cinema restricted narrative to a single point of view. For this reason, the early cinema evoked a different relationship between the spectator and the screen, with viewers more interested in the cinema as visual spectacle than as story-teller. So striking is the emphasis upon spectacle during this period that many scholars have accepted Tom Gunning's distinction between the early cinema as a 'cinema of attractions' and the transitional cinema as a 'cinema of narrative integration' (Gunning, 1986). In the 'cinema of attractions', the viewer created meaning not through the interpretation of cinematic conventions but through previously held information related to the pro-filmic event: ideas of spatial coherence; the unity of an event with a recognizable beginning and end; and knowledge of the subject-matter. During the transitional period, films began to require the viewer to piece together a story predicated upon a knowledge of cinematic conventions.

1894–1902/3

The work of the two most important French producers of this period, the Lumières and Méliès, provides an example of the textual conventions of the one-shot film. Perhaps the most famous of the films that the Lumières showed in December 1895 is *A Train Arriving at a Station* (*L'Arrivé d'un train en gare de la Ciotat*), which runs for about fifty seconds. A stationary camera shows a train pulling into a station and the passengers disembarking, the film continuing until most of them have exited the shot. Apocryphal tales persist that the onrushing cinematic train so terrified audience members that they ducked under their seats for protection. Another of the Lumières' films, *Workers Leaving the Lumière Factory* (*Sortie d'usine*), had a less terrifying effect upon its audience. An eye-level camera, set far enough back from the action to show not only the full-length figures of the workers but the high garage-like door through which they exit, observes as the door opens and disgorges the building's occupants, who disperse to either side of the frame. The film ends roughly at the point when all the workers have left. Contemporary accounts indicate that these and other Lumière films fascinated their audiences not by depicting riveting events, but through incidental details that a modern viewer may find almost unnoticeable: the gentle movement of the leaves in the background as a baby eats breakfast; the play of light on the water as a boat leaves the harbour. The first film audiences did not demand to be told stories, but found infinite fascination in the mere recording and reproduction of the movement of animate and inanimate objects.

However, the Lumières did include a story film of sorts in the public début of the Cinématographe, *Watering the Gardener* (*L'Arroseur arrosé*). Unlike most of the Lumières'

Edwin S. Porter's *The Great Train Robbery* (1903)

work, which depicted events that might have taken place even in the camera's absence, this famous film stages action specifically for the moving pictures. A gardener waters a lawn, a boy steps on the hose, halting the flow of water, the gardener peers questioningly at the spigot, the boy removes his foot, and the restored stream of water douses the gardener, who chases, catches, and spanks the boy. The film is shot with a stationary camera in the standard tableau style of the period. At a key point in the action the boy, trying to escape chastisement, exits the frame and the gardener follows, leaving the screen blank for two seconds. A modern film-maker would pan the camera to follow the characters or cut to the off-screen action, but the Lumières did neither, providing an emblematic instance of the preservation of the space of the pro-filmic event taking precedence over story causality or temporality.

Unlike the Lumières, Georges Méliès always shot in his studio, staging action for the camera, his films showing fantastical events that could not happen in 'real life'. Although all Méliès's films conform to the standard period tableau style, they are also replete with magical appearances and disappearances, achieved through what cinematographers call 'stop action', that is, stopping the camera, having the actor enter or exit the shot, and then starting the camera again to create the illusion that a character has simply vanished or materialized. Méliès's films have played a key part in film scholars' debates over the supposed theatricality of early cinematic style. Whereas scholars had previously thought that stop action effects required no editing and hence concluded that Méliès's films were simply 'filmed theatre', examination of the actual negatives reveals that substitution effects were, in fact, produced through splicing or editing. Méliès also manipulated the image through the superimposition of one shot over another so that many of the films represent space in a manner more reminiscent of photographic devices developed during the nineteenth century than of the theatre. Films such as *L'Homme orchestre* (*The One-Man Band*, 1900) or *Le Mélomane* (*The Melomaniac*, 1903) showcased the cinematic multiplication of a single image (in these cases of Méliès himself) achieved through the layering of one shot over another.

Despite this cinematic manipulation of the pro-filmic space, Méliès's films remain in many ways excessively theatrical, presenting a story as if it were being performed on a stage, a characteristic they have in common with many of the fiction films of the pre-1907 period. Not only does the camera replicate the proscenium arch perspective, but the films stage their action in a shallow playing space between the painted flats and the front of the 'stage', and characters enter or exit either from the wings or through traps. Méliès boasted, in a 1907 article, that his studio's shooting area replicated a theatrical stage

'constructed exactly like one in a theatre and fitted with trapdoors, scenery slots, and uprights'.

For many years film theorists pointed to the Lumière and Méliès films as the originating moment of the distinction between documentary and fiction film-making, given that the Lumières for the most part filmed 'real' events and Méliès staged events. But such distinctions were not a part of contemporary discourse, since many pre-1907 films mixed what we would today call 'documentary' material, that is, events or objects existing independently of the film-maker, with 'fictional' material, that is, events or objects specifically fabricated for the camera. Take, for example, one of the rare multi-shot films of the period, *The Execution of Czolgosz with Panorama of Auburn Prison* (Edison, 1901), a compilation of four self-contained individual shots dealing with the execution of the assassin of President William McKinley. The first two shots are panoramas of the exterior of the prison, the third shows an actor portraying the condemned man in his cell, and the fourth re-enacts his electrocution. Given films of this kind, it is more useful to discuss very early genres in terms of similarities of subject-matters rather than in terms of an imposed distinction between fiction and documentary.

Many turn-of-the-century films reflected the period's fascination with travel and transportation. The train film, established by the Lumières, practically became a genre of its own. Each studio released a version, sometimes shooting a moving train from a stationary camera and sometimes positioning a camera on the front of or inside the train to produce a travelling shot, since the illusion of moving through space seemed to thrill early audiences. The train genre related to the travelogue, films featuring scenes both exotic and familiar, and replicating in motion the immensely popular postcards and stereographs of the period. Public events, such as parades, world's fairs, and funerals, also provided copious material for early cameramen. Both the travelogue and the public event film consisted of self-contained, individual shots, but producers did offer combinations of these films for sale together with suggestions for their projection order, so that, for example, an exhibitor could project several discrete shots of the same event, and so give his audience a fuller and more varied picture of it. Early film-makers also replicated popular amusements, such as vaudeville acts and boxing matches, that could be relatively easily re-enacted for the camera. The first Kinetoscope films in 1894 featured vaudeville performers, including contortionists, performing animals, and dancers, as well as scenes from Buffalo Bill's Wild West show. Again, the shots functioned as self-contained units and were marketed as such, but exhibitors had the option of putting them together to form an evening's entertainment. By 1897 the popular filmed boxing matches could potentially run for an hour. The same was true of another of the most popular of early genres, Passion plays telling the life of Christ, which were often filmed recordings of theatrical companies' performances. A compilation of shots of the play's key events could last well over an hour. A third group of films told one-shot mini-narratives, most often of a humorous nature. Some were gag films, resembling the Lumières' *Watering the Gardener*, in which the comic action takes place in the pro-filmic event, as for instance in *Elopement by Horseback* (Edison, 1891), where a young man seeking to elope with his sweetheart engages in a wrestling match with the girl's father. Others relied for their humour upon trick effects such as stop action, superimposition, and reverse action. The most famous are the Méliès films, but this form was also seen in some of the early films made by Porter for the Edison Company and by the film-makers of the English Brighton school. These films became increasingly complicated, sometimes involving more than one shot. In Williamson's film *The Big Swallow* (1901), the first shot shows a photographer about to take a picture of a passer-by. The second shot replicates the photographer's viewpoint through the camera lens, and shows the passer-by's head growing bigger and bigger as he approaches the camera. The man's mouth opens and the film cuts to a shot of the photographer and his camera falling into a black void. The film ends with a shot of the passer-by walking away munching contentedly.

1902/3–1907

In this period, the multi-shot film emerged as the norm rather than the exception, with films no longer treating the individual shot as a self-contained unit of meaning but linking one shot to another. However, film-makers may have been using a succession of shots to capture and emphasize the highpoints of the action rather than construct either a linear narrative causality or clearly establish temporal-spatial relations. As befits the 'cinema of attractions', the editing was intended to enhance visual pleasure rather than to refine narrative developments.

One of the strangest editing devices used in this period was overlapping action, which resulted from film-makers' desire both to preserve the pro-filmic space and to emphasize the important action by essentially showing it twice. Georges Méliès's *A Trip to the Moon*, perhaps the most famous film of 1902, covers the landing of a space capsule on the moon in two shots. In the first, taken from 'space', the capsule hits the man in the moon in the eye, and his expression changes from a grin to a grimace. In the second shot, taken from the 'moon's surface', the capsule once again lands. These two shots, which show the same event twice, can disconcert a modern viewer. This repetition of action around a cut can be seen in an American film of the same year, *How They Do Things on the Bowery*, directed by Edwin S. Porter for the Edison Manufacturing Company. An irate waiter ejects a customer unable to pay his bill. In an interior shot the waiter throws the man out and hurls his suitcase after him. In the following exterior shot, the customer emerges from the restaurant followed closely by his suitcase. In a 1904 Biograph film *The Widow and the Only Man*, overlapping action is used not to cover interior and exterior events but to show the same event a second time in closer scale. In the first shot a woman accepts her suitor's flowers and smells them appreciatively. Then, rather than a 'match cut', in which the action picks up at the beginning of the second shot from where it left off at the end of the first, as would be dictated by present-day conventions, a closer shot shows her repeating precisely the same action.

While overlapping action was a common means of linking shots, film-makers during this period also experimented with other methods of establishing spatial and temporal relations. One sees an instance of this in *Trip to the Moon*: having landed on the moon, the intrepid French explorers encounter unfriendly extraterrestrials (who remarkably resemble those 'hostile natives' the French were encountering in their colonies at this very time!). The explorers flee to their spaceship and hurry back to the safety of Earth, their descent covered in four shots and twenty seconds of film time. In the first shot, the capsule leaves the moon, exiting at the bottom of the frame. In the second shot, the capsule moves from the top of the frame to the bottom of the frame. In the third the capsule moves from the top of the frame to the water, and in the fourth the capsule moves from the water's surface to the sea-bed. This sequence is filmed much as it might be today, with the movement of the spaceship following the convention of directional continuity, that is, an object or a character should appear to continue moving in the same direction from shot to shot, the consistent movement serving to establish the spatial and temporal relationships between individual shots. But while a modern film-maker would cut directly from shot to shot, Méliès dissolved from shot to shot, a transitional device that now implies a temporal ellipsis. In this regard, then, the sequence can still be confusing for a modern viewer.

Linking shots through dissolves was not in fact unusual in this period, and one can see another example in *Alice in Wonderland* (Hepworth, 1903). However, another English film-maker, James Williamson, a member of the Brighton school, made two films in 1901, *Stop Thief!* and *Fire!*, in which direct cuts continue the action from shot to shot. *Stop Thief!* shows a crowd chasing a tramp who has stolen a joint from a butcher, motivating connections by the diagonal movement of characters through each of the individual shots; the thief and then his pursuers entering the frame at the back and exiting the frame past the camera. The fact that the camera remains with the scene until the last character has exited reveals how character movement motivates the editing. Film-makers found this

Early editing: two adjacent shots from G. A. Smith's *As Seen through a Telescope* (1900). The view through the telescope (achieved by using a mask) shows a girl's ankle being stroked, thereby 'explaining' the previous shot

editing device so effective that an entire genre of chase films arose, such as *Personal* (Biograph, 1904), in which would-be brides pursue a wealthy Frenchman. Many films also incorporated a chase into their narratives, as did the famous 'first' Western *The Great Train Robbery* (Edison, 1903), in which the posse pursues the bandits for several shots in the film's second half.

In *Fire!*, Williamson uses a similar editing strategy to that employed in *Stop Thief!*, the movement of a policeman between shots 1 and 2 and the movement of fire engines between shots 2 and 3 establishing spatial-temporal relations. But in the film's fourth and fifth shots, where other film-makers might have used overlapping action, Williamson experiments with a cut on movement that bears a strong resemblance to what is now called a match cut. Shot 4, an interior, shows a fireman coming through the window of a room in a burning house and rescuing the inhabitant. Shot 5 is an exterior of the burning house and begins as the fireman and the rescued victim emerge through the window. Although the continuity is 'imperfect' from a modern perspective, the innovation is considerable. In his 1902 film *Life of An American Fireman*, undoubtedly influenced by *Fire!*, Porter still employed overlapping action, showing a similar rescue in its entirety first from the interior and then from the exterior perspective. A year later, however, Williamson's compatriot G. A. Smith also created an 'imperfect' match cut, *The Sick Kitten* (1903), cutting from a long view of two children giving a kitten medicine to a closer view of the kitten licking the spoon.

During this period, film-makers also experimented with cinematically fracturing the space of the pro-filmic event, primarily to enhance the viewers' visual pleasure through a closer shot of the action rather than to emphasize details necessary for narrative comprehension. *The Great Train Robbery* includes a medium shot of the outlaw leader, Barnes, firing his revolver directly at the camera, which in modern prints usually concludes the film. The Edison catalogue, however, informed exhibitors that the shot could come at the beginning *or* the end of the film. Narratively non-specific shots of this nature became quite common, as in the British film *Raid on a Coiner's Den* (Alfred Collins, 1904), which begins with a close-up insert of three hands coming into the frame from different directions, one holding a pistol, another a pair of handcuffs, and a third forming a clenched fist. In Porter's own one-shot film *Photographing a Female Crook*, a moving camera produces the closer view as it dollies into a woman contorting her face to prevent the police from taking an accurate mug shot.

Even shots that approximate the point of view of a character within the fiction, and which are now associated with the externalization of thoughts and emotions, were then there more to provide visual pleasure than narrative information. In yet another example of the innovative film-making of the Brighton school, *Grandma's Reading Glasses* (G. A. Smith, Warwick Trading Company, 1900), a little boy looks through his grandmother's spectacles at a variety of objects, a watch, a canary, and a kitten, which the film shows in inserted close-ups. In *The Gay Shoe Clerk* (Edison/Porter, 1903) a shoeshop assistant flirts with his female customer. A cut-in approximates his view of her ankle as she raises her skirt in tantalizing fashion. This close-up insert is an example not only of the visual pleasure afforded by the 'cinema of attractions' but of the early cinema's voyeuristic treatment of the female body. Despite the fact that their primary purpose is not to emphasize narrative developments, these shots' attribution to a character in the film distinguishes them from the totally unmotivated closer views in *The Great Train Robbery* and *Raid on a Coiner's Den*.

The editing strategies of the pre-1907 'cinema of attractions' were primarily designed to enhance visual pleasure rather than to tell a coherent, linear narrative. But many of these films did tell simple stories and audiences undoubtedly derived narrative, as well as visual, pleasure. Despite the absence of internal strategies to construct spatial-temporal relations and linear narratives, the original audiences made sense of these films, even though modern viewers can find them all but incoherent. This is because the films of the 'cinema of attractions' relied heavily on their audiences' knowledge of other texts, from which the films were directly derived or indirectly related. Early film-makers did learn how to make meaning in a new medium, but were not working in a vacuum. The cinema had deep roots in the rich popular culture of the age, drawing heavily during its infant years upon the narrative and visual conventions of other forms of popular entertainment. The pre-1907 cinema has been accused of being 'non-cinematic' and overly theatrical, and indeed film-makers like Méliès were heavily influenced by non-dramatic theatrical practices, but for the most part lengthy theatrical dramas provided an inappropriate model for a medium that began with films of less than a minute, and only became an important source of inspiration as films grew longer during the transitional period. As the first Edison Kinetoscope films illustrate, vaudeville, with its variety format of unrelated acts and lack of concern for developed stories, constituted a very important source material and the earliest film-makers relied upon media such as the melodrama and pantomime (emphasizing visual effects rather than dialogue), magic lanterns, comics, political cartoons, newspapers, and illustrated song slides.

Magic lanterns, early versions of slide projectors often lit by kerosene lamps, proved a particularly important influence upon films, for magic lantern practices permitted the projection of 'moving pictures', which set precedents for the cinematic representation of time and space. Magic lanterns employed by travelling exhibitors often had elaborate lever and pulley mechanisms to produce movement within specially manufactured slides. Long slides pulled slowly through the slide holder produced the equivalent of a cinematic pan. Two slide holders mounted on the same lantern permitted the operator to produce a dissolve by switching rapidly between slides. The use of two slides also permitted 'editing', as operators could cut from long shots to close-ups, exteriors to interiors, and from characters to what they were seeing. *Grandma's Reading Glasses*, in fact, derives from a magic lantern show. Magic lantern lectures given by travelling exhibitors such as the Americans Burton Holmes and John Stoddard provided precedents for the train and travelogue films, the lantern illustrations often intercutting exterior views of the train, interior views of the traveller in the train, and views of scenery and of interesting incidents.

In addition to mimicking the visual conventions of other media, film-makers derived many of their films from stories already well known to the audience. Edison advertised its *Night before Christmas* (Porter, 1905) by saying the film 'closely follows the time-honored Christmas legend by Clement Clarke Moore'. Both Biograph and Edison made films of the hit song 'Everybody Works but Father'. Vitagraph based its Happy Hooligan series on a cartoon tramp character whose popular comic strip ran in several New York newspaper Sunday supplements. Many early films presented synoptic versions of fairly complex narratives, their producers presumably depending upon their audiences' pre-existing knowledge of the subject-matter rather than upon cinematic conventions for the requisite narrative coherence. *L'Épopée napoléonienne* ('The Epic of Napoleon', 1903–4 Pathé) presents Napoleon's life through a series of tableaux, drawing upon well-known historical incidents (the coronation, the burning of Moscow) and anecdotes (Napoleon standing guard for the sleeping sentry) but with no attempt at causal linear connection or narrative development among its fifteen shots. In similar fashion, multi-shot films such as *Ten Nights in a Barroom* (Biograph, 1903) and *Uncle Tom's Cabin* (Vitagraph, 1903) presented only the highlights of these familiar and oft-performed melodramas, with shot connections provided not by editing strategies but by the audiences' knowledge of intervening events. The latter film, however, appears to be one of the earliest to have intertitles. These title cards, summarizing the action of the shot which followed, appeared at the same time as the multi-shot film, around 1903–4, and seem to indicate a recognition on the part of the producers of the necessity for internally rather than externally derived narrative coherence.

EXHIBITION

Cinema initially existed not as a popular commercial medium but as a scientific and educational novelty. The cinematic apparatus itself and its mere ability to reproduce movement constituted the attraction, rather than any particular film. In many countries, moving picture machines were first seen at world's fairs and scientific expositions: the Edison Company had planned to début its Kinetoscope at the 1893 Chicago World's Fair although it failed to assemble the machines in time, and moving picture machines were featured in several areas of the 1900 Universal Exposition in Paris.

Fairly rapidly, cinema exhibition was integrated into pre-existing venues of 'popular culture' and 'refined culture', although the establishment of venues specifically for the exhibition of films did not come until 1905 in the United States and a little later elsewhere. In the United

States, films were shown in the popular vaudeville houses, which by the turn of the century catered to a reasonably well-to-do audience willing to pay 25 cents for an afternoon or evening's entertainment. Travelling showmen, who lectured on educational topics, toured with their own projectors and showed films in local churches and opera-houses, charging audiences in large metropolitan areas the same $2 that it cost to see a Broadway show. Cheaper and more popular venues included tent shows, set up at fairs and carnivals, and temporarily rented store-fronts, the forerunners of the famous nickelodeons. Early film audiences in the United States, therefore, tended to be quite heterogeneous, and dominated by no one class.

Early exhibition in Britain, as in most European countries, followed a similar pattern to the United States, with primary exhibition venues being fairgrounds, music halls, and disused shops. Travelling showmen played a crucial role in establishing the popularity of the new medium, making films an important attraction at fairgrounds. Given that fairs and music halls attracted primarily working-class patrons, early film audiences in Britain, as well as on the Continent, had a more homogeneous class base than in the United States.

Wherever films were shown, and whoever saw them, the exhibitor during this period often had as much control over the films' meanings as did the producers themselves.

Until the advent of multi-shot films and intertitles, around 1903–4, the producers supplied the individual units but the exhibitor put together the programme, and single-shot films permitted decision-making about the projection order and the inclusion of other material such as lantern slide images and title cards. Some machines facilitated this process by combining moving picture projection with a stereopticon, or lantern slide projector, allowing the exhibitor to make a smooth transition between film and slides. In New York City, the Eden Musée put together a special show on the Spanish–American War, using lantern slides and twenty or more films from different producers. While still primarily an exhibitor, Cecil Hepworth suggested interspersing lantern slides with films and 'stringing the pictures together into little sets or episodes' with commentary linking the material together. When improvements in the projector permitted showing films that lasted more than fifty seconds, exhibitors began splicing twelve or more films together to form programmes on particular subjects. Not only could exhibitors manipulate the visual aspects of their programmes, they also added sound of various kinds, for, contrary to popular opinion, the silent cinema was never silent. At the very least, music, from the full orchestra to solo piano, accompanied all films shown in the vaudeville houses. Travelling exhibitors lectured over the films and lantern

An early travelling cinema: Green's Cinematograph Show, Glasgow, 1898

slides they projected, the spoken word capable of imposing a very different meaning on the image from the one that the producer may have intended. Many exhibitors even added sound effects—horses' hooves, revolver shots, and so forth—and spoken dialogue delivered by actors standing behind the screen.

By the end of its first decade of existence, the cinema had established itself as an interesting novelty, one distraction among many in the increasingly frenetic pace of twentieth-century life. Yet the fledgeling medium was still very much dependent upon pre-existing media for its formal conventions and story-telling devices, upon somewhat outmoded individually-driven production methods, and upon pre-existing exhibition venues such as vaudeville and fairs. In its next decade, however, the cinema took major steps toward becoming *the* mass medium of the twentieth century, complete with its own formal conventions, industry structure, and exhibition venues.

Bibliography

Balio, Tino (ed.) (1985), *The American Film Industry*.

Barnes, John (1976). *The Beginnings of the Cinema in England*.

Bordwell, David, Staiger, Janet, and Thompson, Kristin (1985), *The Classical Hollywood Cinema*.

Chanan, Michael (1980), *The Dream that Kicks*.

Cherchi Usai, Paolo, and Codelli, Lorenzo (eds.) (1990), *Before Caligari*.

Cosandey, Roland, Gaudreault, André, and Gunning, Tom (eds.) (1992), *Une invention du diable?*

Elsaesser, Thomas (ed.) (1990), *Early Cinema: Space, Frame, Narrative*.

Fell, John L. (1983), *Film before Griffith*.

——(1986), *Film and the Narrative Tradition*.

Gunning, Tom (1986), 'The Cinema of Attractions'.

Holman, Roger (ed.) (1982), *Cinema 1900–1906: An Analytic Study*.

Low, Rachael, and Manvell, Roger (1948), *The History of the British Film, 1896–1906*.

Musser, Charles (1990), *The Emergence of Cinema*.

——(1991), *Before the Nickelodeon*.

Transitional Cinema

ROBERTA PEARSON

Between 1907 and 1913 the organization of the film industry in the United States and Europe began to emulate contemporary industrial capitalist enterprises. Specialization increased as production, distribution, and exhibition became separate and distinct areas, although some producers, particularly in the United States, did attempt to establish oligopolistic control over the entire industry. The greater length of films, coupled with the unrelenting demand from exhibitors for a regular infusion of new product, required this standardization of production practices, as well as an increased division of labour and the codification of cinematic conventions. The establishment of permanent exhibition sites aided the rationalization of distribution and exhibition procedures as well as maximizing profits, which put the industry on a more stable footing. In most countries, early cinemas held fairly small audiences, and profits depended upon a rapid turnover, necessitating short programmes and frequent changes of fare. This situation encouraged producers to make short, standardized films to meet the constant demand. This demand was enhanced through the construction of a star system patterned after the theatrical model which guaranteed the steady loyalty of the newly emerging mass audience.

The films of this period, often referred to as the 'cinema of narrative integration', no longer relied upon viewers' extra-textual knowledge but rather employed cinematic conventions to create internally coherent narratives. The average film reached a standard length of a 1000-foot reel and ran for about fifteen minutes, although the so-called 'feature film', running an hour or more, also made its first appearance during these years. In general, the emergence of the 'cinema of narrative integration' coincided with the cinema's move toward the cultural mainstream and its establishment as the first truly mass medium. Film companies responded to pressures from state and civic organizations with internal censorship schemes and other strategies that gained both films and film industry a degree of social respectability.

INDUSTRY

Before the First World War, European film industries dominated the international market, with France, Italy, and Denmark the strongest exporters. From 60 to 70 per cent of all the films imported into the United States and Europe were French. Pathé, the strongest of the French studios, had been forced into aggressive expansion by the relatively small domestic demand. It established offices in major cities around the world, supplemented them with travelling salesmen who sold films and equipment, and, as a result, dominated the market in countries that could support only one film company.

US producers faced strong competition from European product within their own country for, despite the proliferation of relatively successful motion picture manufacturers during the transitional years, a high percentage

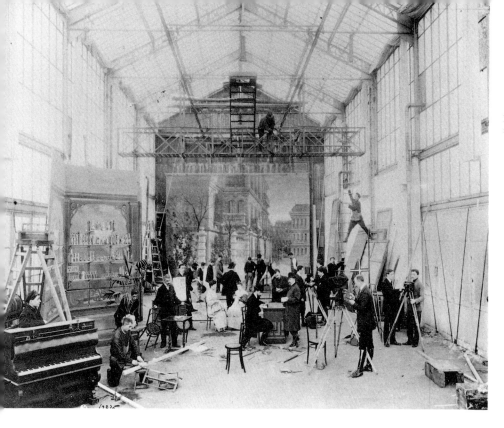

Pathé Frères' glass-topped studio at Vincennes, in 1906

of films screened in the USA still originated in Europe. Pathé opened a US office in 1904, and by 1907 other foreign firms, British and Italian among them, were entering the US market on a regular basis. Many of these distributed their product through the Kleine Optical Company, the major importer of foreign films into the United States during these years and a company that played a prominent role in the transition to the longer feature film. In 1907 French firms, particularly Pathé, controlled the American market, sharing it with other European countries: of the 1,200 films released in the United States that year only about 400 were domestic. The American film industry took note of this, and the trade press, established in this year with *Moving Picture World*, often complained about the inferior quality of the imports, criticizing films that dealt with contemporary topics for their narrative incomprehensibility and, worse yet, un-American morals.

Paradoxically, an earlier move to rationalize film distribution had resulted in a maximization of profits, and as a result US manufacturers initially concentrated on the domestic market. However, during these years they began a campaign of international expansion that resulted in their being well placed to step into the number one position in 1914, when European film industries were reeling from the effects of the outbreak of war. In 1907 Vitagraph became the first of the major US firms to establish overseas distribution offices, and in 1909 other American producers established agencies in London, which remained the European centre for American distribution until 1916. As a result the British industry tended to concentrate

on distribution and exhibition rather than production, conceding American dominance in this area. American films constituted at least half of those shown in Britain with Italian and French imports making up a substantial portion of the rest. Germany, which also lacked a well-established industry of its own, was the second most profitable market for American films. In the pre-war years, however, American firms lacked the strength to compete with the powerful French and Italian industries in their own countries. American films were distributed outside Europe, but often not to the financial benefit of the production studios, who granted their British distributors the rights not only to the British Isles and some Continental countries but to British colonies as well.

During this period American film production took place mainly on the east coast, with an outpost or two in Chicago and some companies making occasional forays to the west coast and even to foreign locations. New York City was the headquarters of three of the most important American companies: Edison had a studio in the Bronx, Vitagraph in Brooklyn, and Biograph in the heart of the Manhattan show-business district on Fourteenth Street. Other companies—Solax and American Pathé among them—had studios across the Hudson in Fort Lee, New Jersey, which also served as a prime location for many of the New York based companies. *The Great Train Robbery* (Edison, 1903) was only one of the many 'Jersey' Westerns shot in the vicinity. So over-used were certain settings that a contemporary anecdote claimed that two companies once shot on either side of a Fort Lee fence, sharing the same gate. Chicago served as headquarters for the Selig and Essanay studios and for George Kleine's distribution company. Many studios sent companies to California during the winter to take advantage of the superior locations and shooting conditions, and Selig established a permanent studio there as early as 1909. However, Los Angeles did not become the centre of the American industry until the First World War.

Around 1903, the rise of film exchanges led to a crucial change in distribution practices, which in turn created a radical change in modes of exhibition. The rise of permanent venues, the nickelodeons that began to appear in numbers in 1906, made the film industry a much more profitable business, encouraging others to join Edison, Biograph, and Vitagraph as producers. Until this time the companies had sold rather than rented their product to exhibitors. While this worked well for the travelling showmen who changed their audiences from show to show, it acted against the establishment of permanent exhibition sites. Dependent upon attracting repeat customers from the same neighbourhood, permanent sites needed frequent changes of programme, and so long as this involved having to purchase a large number of films it was prohibitively expensive. The film exchanges solved this problem by buying the films from the manufacturers and renting them to exhibitors, making permanent exhibition venues feasible and increasing the medium's popularity. Improvements in projectors also facilitated the rise of permanent venues, since exhibitors no longer had to rely on the production companies to supply operators.

By 1908 the new medium was flourishing as never before, with the nickelodeons—so called because of their initial admission price of 5 cents—springing up on every street corner, and their urban patrons consumed by the 'nickel madness'. But the film industry itself was in disarray. Neighbouring nickelodeons competed to rent the same films, or actually rented the same films and competed for the same audience, while unscrupulous exchanges were likely to supply exhibitors with films that had been in release so long that rain-like scratches obscured the images. The exchanges and exhibitors now threatened to wrest economic control of the industry from the producers. In addition civil authorities and private reform groups, alarmed by the rapid growth of the new medium and its perceived associations with workers and immigrants, began calling for film censorship and regulation of the nickelodeons.

In late 1908, led by the Edison and Biograph companies, the producers attempted to stabilize the industry and protect their own interests by forming the Motion Picture Patents Company, or, as it was popularly known, the Trust. The Trust incorporated the most important American producers and foreign firms distributing in the United States, and was intended to exert oligopolistic control over the

industry. Along with Edison and Biograph, members included Vitagraph, the largest of American producers, Selig, Essanay, Méliès, Pathé and Kleine, the Connecticut-based Kalem, and the Philadelphia-based Lubin. The MPPC derived its powers from pooling patents on film stock, cameras, and projectors, most of these owned by the Edison and Biograph companies. These two had been engaged in lengthy legal disputes since Biograph was founded, but their resolution now enabled them to claim the lion's share of the Trust's profits despite the fact that they were at the time the two least prolific of the American production studios.

The members of the MPPC agreed to a standard price per foot for their films and regularized the release of new films, each studio issuing from one to three reels a week on a pre-established schedule. The MPPC did not attempt to exert its mastery through outright ownership of distribution facilities and exhibition venues, but rather relied upon exchanges' and exhibitors' needs for MPPC films and equipment that could only be obtained by purchasing a licence. The licensed film exchanges had to lease films rather than buy them outright, promising to return them after a certain period. Only licensed exhibitors, supposedly vetted by the MPPC to ensure certain safety and sanitation standards and required to pay weekly royalty on their patented projectors, could rent Trust films from these exchanges. The Trust's arrangements had an immediate impact on the market, freezing out much foreign competition so that by the end of 1909 imports constituted less than half of released films, a percentage which continued to decline. The prejudice against foreign films manifested in the Trust's exclusionary tactics may have encouraged European studios to produce 'classic' subjects, literary adaptations and historical epics for example, which were more acceptable to the American market. Pathé, whose 1908 position as a primary supplier of product to American exchanges made it a prominent member of the MPPC, pioneered this approach through the importation of European high culture in the form of the *film d'art*.

In 1910 the MPPC began business practices that presaged those of the Hollywood studios, establishing a separate distribution arm, the General Film Company. This instituted standing orders (an early form of block booking) and zoning requirements that prevented unnecessary competition by prescribing which exhibitors within a certain geographical area could show a film. Higher rental rates for newly released films, versus lower ones for those that had been in circulation, encouraged the differentiation of first-run venues from those showing the older and less expensive product, another hallmark of the coming studio system.

The Motion Picture Patents Company survived as a legal entity until 1915, when it was declared illegal under the

Asta Nielsen
(1881–1972)

After *Joyless Street* (1925), Asta Nielsen was called the greatest tragedienne since Sarah Bernhardt. However, her fame was established fifteen years earlier with her first screen appearance in *The Abyss* (*Afgrunden*, 1910), a film of sexual bondage and passion featuring the erotic 'gaucho' dance in which Nielsen, a respectable girl led astray, ties up her lover with a whip on stage as she twists her body around his provocatively. *The Abyss* was an explosive success and Nielsen became, overnight, the first international star of the cinema, celebrated from Moscow to Rio de Janeiro. Her performance brought people to the cinema who had never before taken it seriously as an art form. Her personal appearances drew crowds around the world.

Born in Denmark to a working-class family, Nielsen began acting in the theatre. There she met Urban Gad, who produced and directed *The Abyss* and became her husband. The couple moved to Berlin, where Nielsen became one of the greatest stars of the German cinema, making nearly seventy-five films in two decades.

Between 1910 and 1915, Nielsen and Gad collaborated on over thirty films, establishing the signature style of her first period. In these early films, Nielsen's sensuality is matched by her intelligence, resourcefulness, and a boyish physical agility. Her expressive face and body seem immediate and modern, especially when compared with the exaggerated gestures that were common in early cinema. Her powerful, slim figure and large, dark eyes, set off by dramatic, suggestive costumes, allowed her to cross class and even gender lines convincingly. She became, in turn, a society lady, a circus performer, a scrubwoman, an artist's model, a suffragette, a gypsy, a newspaper reporter, a child (*Engelein*, 1913), a male bandit (*Zapatas Bande*, 1914), and Hamlet (1920). She excelled at embodying individualized, unconventional women whose stories conveyed their entanglement within, and their resistance to, an invisible web of confining class and sex roles. She surpassed all others in her uniquely cinematic, understated manner of expressing inner conflict. Nielsen's celebrated naturalness was the result of careful study: in her autobiography, she described how she learnt to improve her acting by watching herself magnified on the screen.

Nielsen was a key influence on the shift away from naturalism that characterized German cinema after the First World War. Her techniques for conveying psychological conflict became stylized gestures emphasizing a sense of claustrophobia and limitations. Nielsen's spontaneity slowed, her contagious smile rarely in evidence except as a bitter-sweet reminder of her past. Close-ups now emphasized the mask-like quality of her face. Her enactments of older women doomed and self-condemning in their passionate attachment to shallow, younger men (*Joyless Street*; *Dirnentragödie*, 1927) only take on their proper resonance when contrasted to Nielsen's earlier embodiment of young women struggling against social constraints.

JANET BERGSTROM

Asta Nielsen

SELECTED FILMOGRAPHY

(All films directed by Urban Gad unless otherwise indicated) Afgrunden (The Abyss) (1910); Der fremde Vogel (1911); Die arme Jenny (1912); Das Mädchen ohne Vaterland (1912); Die Sünden der Väter (1913); Die Suffragette (1913); Der Filmprimadonna (1913); Engelein (1914); Zapatas Bande (1914); Vordertreppe und Hintertreppe (1915); Weisse Rosen (1917); Rausch (dir. Ernst Lubitsch, 1919; no surviving print); Hamlet (dir. Svend Gade, 1921); Vanina (dir. Arthur von Gerlach, 1922); Erdgeist (dir. Leopold Jessner, 1923); Die freudlose Gasse (Joyless Street) (dir. G. W. Pabst, 1925); Dirnentragödie (dir. Bruno Rahn, 1927)

BIBLIOGRAPHY

Allen, Robert C. (1973), 'The Silent Muse'.
Bergstrom, Janet (1990), 'Asta Nielsen's Early German Films'.
Seydel, Renate, and Hagedorff, Allan (eds.) (1981), *Asta Nielsen*.

provisions of the Sherman Anti-Trust Act, but even as early as 1912, several years before its *de jure* decline, the Trust had *de facto* ceased to exert any significant control over the industry. Indeed, its members at this point represented the old guard of the American film industry and many would cease to exist soon after the court's unfavourable ruling. Their place was taken by the companies of the nascent Hollywood moguls, many of whom had initially strengthened their position in the industry through their resistance to the Trust's attempt to impose oligopolistic control.

The MPPC's short-sighted plan to drive non-affiliated distributors and exhibitors out of the business ironically sowed the seeds of its own destruction, for it gave rise to a vigorous group of so-called 'independent' producers who supplied product to the many unlicensed exchanges and nickelodeons. In late 1909, Carl Laemmle, who had entered the business as a distributor, founded the Independent Moving Picture Company, known as IMP, to produce films for his customers, since he could not purchase films from the MPPC. By the end of the year IMP released two reels a week of its own as well as two Italian reels from the Itala and Ambrosio companies, an output that rivalled the most powerful of the Trust companies. Not only did Laemmle spearhead the opposition, but IMP eventually expanded to become Universal, one of the major studios of the Hollywood silent period. By this time several other independent producers had gone into business, some of the more significant being the Centaur Film Manufacturing Company, the Nestor Company, and New York Motion Picture Company, which first employed Thomas Ince. In 1910 Edwin Thanhouser founded the Thanhouser Company, using the stock company from his theatre and specializing in literary and theatrical adaptations. Also in 1910, the same year the MPPC established the General Film Company, the independents formed their own combination to resist the Trust. Their distribution arm, the Motion Picture Distributing and Sales Company, mimicked the Trust's practices, regulating release dates and the price per foot, and also instituting standing orders from exchanges to the studios and from the exhibitors to the exchanges.

With this move, the independents ceased to be independent in anything but name, and by 1911 two rival oligopolies controlled the United States film industry. It is wrong to assume, as have some historians, that the Trust met its demise because of its conservative business practices and resistance to new ideas such as the feature film and the star system. It was an MPPC company, Vitagraph, which made many of the first American multireel films. Similarly, while Carl Laemmle of IMP has been credited with forcing other producers to emulate the theatrical star system through his promotion of Florence Lawrence in 1910, MPPC companies had previously publicized their use of theatrical stars and showed no reluctance to tout their own home-grown products.

Before 1908, several factors had militated against the development of a cinematic star system. Initially, most moving picture actors were transient, working on the stage as well, and did not remain with any particular company long enough to warrant promotion as a star. This situation changed in 1908 as studios began to establish regular stock companies. Also, until around 1909, film action was usually staged too far away from the camera for audiences to recognize actors' features, a precondition for fan loyalty. At the outset of the nickelodeon period audience loyalty was to the studio trademark rather than the actors, and so most companies, both Trust and independent, resisted a star system until about 1910, fearing it would shift the economic balance of power (as indeed it did to some extent). For this reason, the Biograph Company, which had some of the most popular actors under contract, would not reveal its players' names until 1913. Other members of the MPPC, however, did experiment, as early as 1909, with publicizing their use of theatrical stars; the Edison Company advertising Miss Cecil Spooner in its adaptation of Twain's *The Prince and the Pauper*, and Vitagraph inserting a title into its *Oliver Twist* stating that Miss Elita Proctor appeared as 'Nancy Sikes'. By the next year, the mechanics of star publicity were set in motion, as Kalem made lobby cards of its stock company for display in nickelodeons. Other companies followed suit, distributing photographs to fans as well as exhibitors and sending their stars out on personal appearances. The biggest American stars of this period were Florence Lawrence of IMP (formerly of Biograph), Florence Turner and Maurice Costello of Vitagraph, and, of course, Mary Pickford of Biograph. Other countries also gave prominence to leading actors and, more commonly, actresses in this period. The Danish actress Asta Nielsen was a leading light of both the German and Danish cinema, while in Italy divas such as Francesca Bertini and Lyda Borelli starred in films which they also produced.

Like the American industry, the French industry came into its own in 1907–8. Film was no longer considered a poor cousin of photography but rather a major entertainment which threatened the popularity of more traditional forms, such as the theatre. The increased importance of the medium was shown by the remarkable increase in the number of Parisian cinemas, from only ten in 1906 to eighty-seven by the end of 1908, as well as the appearance in that year of the first regular newspaper column devoted to the moving pictures. Pathé remained the most important of the studios, its only serious domestic competition coming from the Gaumont Company, founded by Léon Gaumont in 1895. Although less significant than Pathé in terms of output and international presence, from 1905 to 1915 Gaumont had the largest studio in the world. The company also had the distinction of employing the first woman director, Alice Guy Blache, who later founded the Solax Company with her husband Herbert Blache. Gaumont's most important director was Louis Feuillade, who specialized in the detective serial, the most popular of which was *Fantômas*, produced between 1913 and 1914, and based on a series of popular novels about a master criminal and his detective nemesis. The box-office success of Feuillade's serials enabled Gaumont to overtake Pathé as the country's most powerful studio, but it achieved this position on the eve of the World War which caused the end of French domination of international markets.

The Italian film industry had a relatively late start, dominated as it was by Lumières in the early years. The Cines Company, founded by the Italian aristocrats Marchese Ernesto Pacelli and Barone Alberto Fassini, built the country's first studio in 1905 and became one of the most important producers of the silent period. Cines set the pace for the industry as a whole by producing the first Italian costume film, *La presa di Roma* (*The Capture of Rome*, 1905), starring the famous theatrical actor Carlo Rosaspina. During its initial years, Cines concentrated mostly on comedies, contemporary melodramas, and actualities, in 1906 producing sixty fiction films and thirty actualities. 1907 saw the real take-off of the Italian industry, with both production and exhibition flourishing. Cines had built its studio in Rome, another important company, Ambrosio, operated from Turin, and several other producers built studios in Milan. In this year there were 500 cinemas in the country with total box-office receipts of 18 million lire.

By 1908, then, the Italian industry was able to compete on the international market with France and the United States, the Italian studios strengthening their position through the production of historical spectaculars. Ambrosio's first version of *Gli ultimi giorni di Pompei* (*The Last Days of Pompeii*) began a rage for the costume drama, many of which dealt with Roman history or adapted Italian literary masterpieces: *Giulio Cesare* (1909), *Bruto* (1909), and *Il Conte Ugolino* (1908, from Dante's *Inferno*). The relatively low costs of building the massive sets and hiring the large casts of extras necessary for these spectacle-intensive films enabled the Italians to differentiate their product from that of their foreign rivals and break into the international market without massive expenditure. This strategy succeeded so well that Pathé, concerned about Italian rivalry, established a subsidiary, Film d'Arte Italiano, to produce costume films of its own. It took advantage of location shooting amidst the splendours of Italian Renaissance architecture to produce films like the 1909 *Othello*.

FILM PRODUCTION

In all the major producing countries, film production during this period was marked by an increasing spe-

cialization and division of labour that brought the film industry into line with other capitalist enterprises. In the early period film-making was a collaborative enterprise, but the emergence of the director coincided with the appearance of other specialists, such as script-writers, property men, and wardrobe mistresses, who worked under his direction. Soon, the bigger American studios employed several directors, giving each his own cast and crew and requiring him to turn out one reel a week. This led to the creation of yet another job category, the producer, who oversaw the whole process, co-ordinating between the individual units. In 1906 Vitagraph, the largest of the American studios, had three separate production units headed by the company's founders, James Stuart Blackton and Albert E. Smith, and their employee James Bernard French. These men operated the cameras and had an assistant responsible for the staging of the action. Vitagraph reorganized its production practices in 1907, putting a director in charge of each unit and making Blackton the central producer. At Biograph, D. W. Griffith was the sole director from June 1908 until December 1909. By the time Griffith left in autumn 1913, six directors were shooting Biograph films under his supervision, while he also continued to direct his own unit.

With the exception of certain films designed to lend the new medium cultural respectability, the American film industry during this period emphasized speed and quantity. The studio front offices for the most part disdained 'artistry', since all films, whether 'artistic' or not, sold for the same standard price per foot. In 1908 the average film was shot in a single day at a cost of $200–$500, and averaged one reel, or 1,000 feet, in length. The introduction of artificial lighting in the form of mercury vapour lights in 1903 facilitated interior shooting but the studios still tended to film outdoors as much as possible. Interiors were filmed in what were initially fairly small studios (the Biograph studios were simply a converted New York City brownstone house) on theatrical sets with painted backdrops.

Looking in more detail at the best documented of all the American studios, the Biograph Company, permits us to follow the production of individual films through each step of the process. In 1908 the Biograph Company hired one of their actors, David W. Griffith, as a director, intending that he should simply rehearse the actors. But, as Griffith's cameraman Billy Bitzer reported in his memoirs, the new director soon became responsible for much more.

Before his [Griffith's] arrival, I, as cameraman, was responsible for everything except the immediate hiring and handling of the actor. Soon it was his say whether the lights were bright enough or if the make-up was right.... A cameraman had enough to do watching the rapidity of the action and keeping the hand-cranked camera going at a steady pace to prevent the film from buckling.

Until Griffith's institution as director, the Biograph Company had depended upon transient actors, but the new director developed his own stock company, integral to the period's ensemble style of film-making and, incidentally, presaging the Hollywood studios' practice of keeping actors under exclusive contract. While Griffith had the primary responsibility for hiring and casting, by the time he arrived at the studio Biograph had a story department that had been producing scripts, perhaps since 1902. By the nickelodeon period, it was standard practice for staff writers to prepare a script, often without consulting the director, although in the case of Biograph Griffith seems to have worked closely with the story department.

In most studios, although Biograph again may have been an exception, the principal actors received scripts before the shooting occurred in order to prepare themselves for rehearsals, which became increasingly important as stories grew more intricate. Rehearsal time seems to have varied from one studio to another, although by 1911 a trade press writer indicated that on average each scene was rehearsed from five to ten times. When Griffith arrived at Biograph, the front office emphasized the rapid production of films, and discouraged lengthy rehearsals, the directors simply ensuring that the actors remained within camera range. By mid-1909, however, Griffith was already willing to devote half a day or more to rehearsal, and by 1912 he averaged a week's rehearsal for each one-reeler.

At Biograph, little remained to be done by the time of the actual shooting. The cameraman's assistant put down the 'lines', using nails and cord to surround the area that would be in the frame, and there would be a quick, final rehearsal for positioning. When the camera began to crank, the actors were expected to do exactly what had been agreed upon in rehearsals. Griffith did, however, coach from the sidelines, telling actors to tone it down or give more. The tight schedule, with films taking only from one to three days to shoot, prohibited retakes, requiring actors and technicians to get everything right first time. In the days before sound and elaborate special effects, the post-production process was fairly simple; the out-of-order shots were assembled according to the pre-existing script, and intertitles added. Numerous positive prints were then run off by the laboratory and the film was ready for sale to the exchanges.

THE BEGINNING OF NARRATIVE

There was a 'crisis' in transitional cinema around 1907, signalled by complaints in the trade press about lack of narrative clarity, as well as by exhibitors' increased use of lectures in an attempt to make films understandable to their audiences. Films were poised between an emphasis upon visual pleasure, 'the cinema of attractions', and

story-telling, 'the cinema of narrative integration', but conventions for constructing internally coherent narratives had not yet been established. In the transitional years, between 1907–8 and 1917, the formal elements of film-making all became subsidiary to the narrative, as lighting, composition, editing were all increasingly designed to help the audience follow a story. Integral to these stories were psychologically credible characters, created through performance style, editing, and dialogue intertitles, whose motivations and actions seemed realistic and helped to link together a film's disparate shots and scenes. These 'well-rounded', believable characters, resembling those of the then fashionable realist literature and drama, contrast sharply with the earlier period's one-dimensional stock characters drawn from the melodrama and vaudeville comedy skits.

The increased use of editing and the decreased distance between camera and actors most obviously distinguish the films of the transitional period from their predecessors. The tableau or proscenium arch shot, showing the actors' entire bodies as well as the space above and below them, characterized the early cinema. However, towards the beginning of the transitional period the Vitagraph Company began using the so-called '9-foot line', staging the action about 9 feet from the camera, a scale that showed the actors from the ankles up. At around the same time in France, Pathé and companies under its influence, Film d'Art and SCAGL, also adopted the 9-foot line. By 1911 the camera had moved yet closer, producing the three-quarter shot that became the predominant scale of the transitional cinema and indeed of the entire silent period. In addition to moving the camera closer to the actors, film-makers also moved the actors closer to the camera. In chase films the actors had exited the shots in close proximity to the camera, but during the transitional period the practice became standardized, deliberately employed to enhance dramatic effects, as in a shot from *The Musketeers of Pig Alley* (Griffith, 1912) in which a gangster slinks along a wall until he is seen in medium close-up.

The decreased distance between action and camera not only enabled identification of the actors and the development of the star system, but also contributed to the increased emphasis upon individualized characters and facial expression. Editing was also developed for this end; both to emphasize moments of psychological intensity and to externalize characters' thoughts and emotions. The three-quarter scale already permitted audiences to see the actors' faces more clearly than before, but film-makers often cut even closer at climactic points. This was designed to encourage fuller viewer involvement in the characters' emotions, and not, as in early films like *The Great Train Robbery*, simply for shock value. For

David Wark Griffith

(1875–1948)

Born in Kentucky on 23 January 1875, the son of Civil War veteran Colonel 'Roaring Jake' Griffith, David Wark Griffith left his native state at the age of 20 and spent the next thirteen years in rather unsuccessful pursuit of a theatrical career, for the most part touring with second-rate stock companies. In 1907, after the failure of the Washington, DC, production of his play *A Fool and a Girl*, Griffith entered the by then flourishing film industry, writing brief scenarios and acting for both the Edison and Biograph companies. In the spring of 1908 the Biograph front office, facing a shortage of directors, offered Griffith the position and launched him, at the age of 33, on the career which most suited him.

Between 1908 and 1913 Griffith personally directed over 400 Biograph films, the first, *The Adventures of Dollie*, released in 1908 and the last, the four-reel biblical epic *Judith of Bethulia*, released in 1914, several months after Griffith and Biograph had parted company. The contrast between the earliest and latest Biograph films is truly astonishing, particularly with regard to the aspects of cinema upon which Griffith seems to have concentrated most attention, editing and performance. In terms of editing, Griffith is perhaps most closely associated with the elaborate deployment of cross-cutting in his famous last-minute rescue scenes, but his films also exerted a major influence upon the codification of other editing devices such as cutting closer to the actors at moments of psychological intensity. With regard to acting, the Biograph films were recognized even at the time as most closely approaching a new, more intimate, more 'cinematic' performance style. Several decades after they were made, the Biograph films continue to fascinate not only because of their increasing formal sophistication, but also because of their explorations of the most pressing social issues of their time: changing gender roles; increasing urbanization; racism; and so forth.

Increasingly chafing under the conservative policies of Biograph's front office, particularly the resistance to the feature film, Griffith left Biograph in late 1913 to form his own production company. First experimenting with several multi-reelers, in July 1914 Griffith began shooting the film that would have assured him his place in film history had he directed nothing else. Released in January 1915, the twelve-reel *The Birth of a Nation*, the longest American feature film to date, hastened the American film industry's transition to the feature film, as well as showing cinema's potential for great social impact. *The Birth* also had a profound impact upon its director, for in many ways Griffith spent the rest of his career trying to surpass, defend, or atone for this film.

His next feature, *Intolerance*, released in 1916, was a direct response to the criticism and censorship of *The Birth of a Nation*, as well as an attempt to exceed the film's spectacular dimensions. *Intolerance* rather unsuccessfully weaves together four different stories all purporting to deal with intolerance across the ages. The two most prominent sections are 'The Mother and the Law', in which Mae Marsh plays a young woman attempting to deal with the vicissitudes of modern urban existence, and 'The Fall of Babylon', dealing with the Persian invasion of Mesopotamia in the sixth century and featuring massive, elaborate sets and battle scenes with hundreds of extras. In an editing *tour de force*, the film's famous ending weaves together last-minute rescue sequences in all four stories. The third of the important Griffith features, *Broken Blossoms*, is by contrast a relatively small-scale effort focused on three protagonists, an abused teenager, played by Lillian Gish in one of her most impressive performances, her brutal stepfather, Donald Crisp, and the gentle and sympathetic Chinese who befriends her, this role, as enacted by Richard Barthelmess, clearly intended to prove that Mr Griffith was no racist after all.

After the release of *Broken Blossoms* in 1919, Griffith's career began a downward trajectory, both artistically and financially, which he never managed to reverse.

D. W. Griffith on set, with cameraman Billy Bitzer and Dorothy Gish

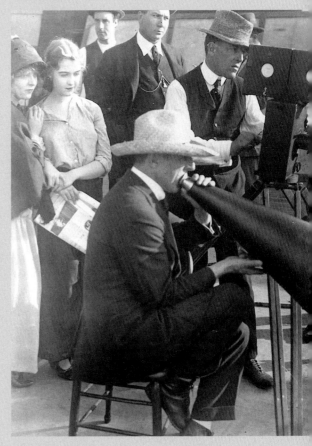

Plagued to the end of his life by the financial difficulties attendant upon an unsuccessful attempt to establish himself as an independent producer-director outside Hollywood, perhaps more importantly Griffith never seemed able to adjust to the changing sensibilities of post-war America, his Victorian sentimentalities rendering him out of sync with the increasingly sophisticated audiences of the Jazz Age. Indeed, the two most important Griffith features of the 1920s, *Way Down East* (1920) and *Orphans of the Storm* (1921), were cinematic adaptations of hoary old theatrical melodramas. While these films have their moments, particularly in the performances of their star Lillian Gish, they none the less look determinedly back to cinema's origins in the nineteenth century rather than demonstrate its potential as the major medium of the twentieth century. Making a series of increasingly less impressive features throughout the rest of the decade, Griffith did survive in the industry long enough to direct two sound films, *Abraham Lincoln* (1930) and *The Struggle* (1931). The latter, a critical and financial failure, doomed Griffith to a marginal existence in a Hollywood where you are only as good as your last picture. He died in 1948, serving occasionally as script-doctor or consultant, but never directing another film.

ROBERTA PEARSON

SELECT FILMOGRAPHY

Shorts
The Song of the Shirt (1908); A Corner in Wheat (1909); A Drunkard's Reformation (1909); The Lonely Villa (1909); In Old Kentucky (1910); The Lonedale Operator (1911); Musketeers of Pig Alley (1912); The Painted Lady (1912); The New York Hat (1912); The Mothering Heart (1913); The Battle of Elderbush Gulch (1914)
Features
Judith of Bethulia (1914); The Birth of a Nation (1915); Intolerance (1916); Broken Blossoms (1919); Way Down East (1920); Orphans of the Storm (1921); Abraham Lincoln (1930)

BIBLIOGRAPHY

Gunning, Tom (1991), *D. W. Griffith and the Origins of American Narrative Film.*
Pearson, Roberta E. (1992), *Eloquent Gestures: The Transformation of Performance Style in the Griffith Biograph Films.*
Schickel, Richard (1984), *D. W. Griffith: An American Life.*

example, in *The Lonedale Operator* (Griffith, Biograph, 1911) burglars menace a telegraph operator (Blanche Sweet) and attempt to break into her office. As Sweet desperately telegraphs for help, the film cuts from a three-quarter to a medium shot, allowing a closer view of her fearful expression.

Editing was also used more directly to convey characters' subjectivities. In the earlier period, film-makers had adopted the theatrical 'vision scene', using double exposure to put the character and a literal embodiment of externalized thoughts in the same frame. *Life of an American Fireman* (Edison, 1902), for example, uses this device to show a fireman thinking of an imperilled family, who appear in a balloon slightly above him and to his right. This convention continued in the transitional period, as in *The Life Drama of Napoleon Bonaparte and the Empress Josephine of France* (Vitagraph, 1909), in which the divorced and distraught Empress reaches out to a superimposed vision of her erstwhile husband. But the film's companion reel, *Napoleon, the Man of Destiny*, approaches the conventional flashback structure of the Hollywood cinema, in which a 'present-day' shot of the character authorizes the film's presentation of the 'past'. Napoleon returns to Malmaison shortly before his exile to Elba and, as he 'thinks' of his past, the film cuts from him to re-enactments of battles and other events in his life.

The transitional period also saw the emergence of the editing pattern that is most closely associated with character subjectivity: the point-of-view shot, in which a film cuts from a character to what the character sees and then back to the character. This pattern did not become fully conventionalized until the Hollywood period, but film-makers during the transitional period experimented with various means of 'showing' what characters saw. In an early example, *Francesca da Rimini* (Vitagraph, 1907), there is a cut from a tableau-scale shot of a character looking at a locket to an insert close-up of the locket. In *The Lonedale Operator*, *Enoch Arden* (1911), and other films, Griffith cuts between characters looking through a window to what they see, although the eyeline match seems 'imperfect' by today's standards.

This last kind of editing, of course, not only externalized characters' thoughts but helped establish the spatial and temporal relations crucial to narrative coherence, both in the same scene (roughly, actions occurring at the same place and time) and between scenes taking place at the same time in different locations. In the earlier period film-makers occasionally broke down the space of a shot, selecting details for closer examination, as in *Grandma's Reading Glasses*. While not as prevalent as it was later to become, this analytical editing was sometimes used in the transitional period to highlight narratively important details rather than, as in the earlier period, simply to provide visual pleasure. In *The Lonedale Operator*, for example, when the burglars eventually break into the telegraph operator's office, she holds them at bay with what appears to be a revolver but a cut-in reveals to be a wrench. While analytical editing was comparatively rare, conventions for linking the different spaces of one scene together, to orientate the viewer spatially, became established practice. In fact, part of the suspense in *The Lonedale Operator* depends upon the viewer having a clear idea of the film's spatial relations. When the telegraph operator first arrives at work, she walks from the railway office's porch into an outer room and then into an inner room. Following the principle of directional continuity, the actress exits each shot at screen right and re-enters at screen left. When the burglars break through the outermost door, the viewer knows exactly how much further they must go to reach the terrified woman. Here, character movement links the shots, but various other conventions, many relating to the relative position of the camera in successive set-ups, also arose for establishing spatial relations.

The Lonedale Operator also provides an example of an editing pattern primarily associated with the name of its director, D. W. Griffith. He became famous for the cross-cutting, parallel action, or parallel editing through which he constructed his spine-tingling last-minute rescues. Several pre-Griffith films, however, show that, while the Biograph director may have conventionalized parallel editing, he did not invent it. Two 1907 Vitagraph films, *The Mill Girl* and *The Hundred-to-One-Shot*, cross-cut between different locations, the latter even featuring a somewhat attenuated last-minute rescue. Several Pathé films from 1907–8 also contain fairly brief parallel editing sequences, the plot and editing of one, *A Narrow Escape* (1908), prefiguring Griffith's *The Lonely Villa* (1909). But from his earliest films, Griffith experimented with cutting between pursued, pursuer, and potential rescuer, and he and other American directors soon developed parallel editing beyond the fairly elementary form seen in French films. The climax of *The Lonedale Operator*, for example, cuts from the menaced heroine, to the menacing burglars breaking down doors, to the hero in the cab of a speeding locomotive, to an exterior tracking shot of the onrushing train.

When Griffith first began directing at Biograph in 1908 his films averaged about seventeen shots, increasing fivefold to an average of eighty-eight by 1913. The later Griffith Biographs probably feature more shots per film than those produced by other American studios, such as Vitagraph, during the same years, but American film-makers as a general rule tended to rely more heavily on editing than did their European counterparts, who were concerned more with the *mise-en-scène* and the possibilities of staging in depth. American films tended to stage the action on a shallow plane, with actors entering and exiting from the

sides. Particularly toward the beginning of the transitional period, they even used painted flats, making no attempt to disguise their theatricality. By contrast, European films, particularly the French and Italian, began to create a sense of deep space not possible in the theatre. Lowering the camera to waist level from its previous eye level facilitated shooting in depth; the reduction of the empty space above the actors' heads produced both a larger, closer view of the characters and much more contrast between characters closer to and further from the camera, permitting the staging of action in the foreground, midground, and background. Convincing three-dimensional sets for interior scenes, often with doors that gave glimpses of an even deeper space behind the set, added to the illusion of depth. The use of doorways and contrasting light and shadows often enhanced the feeling of deep space in exterior shots, as seen in *Romeo and Juliet* (Film d'Arte Italiana, 1909). In one shot, Romeo returns to Verona and walks through the dark shadow under an arch into the well-lit deep space behind. The next shot, Juliet's funeral procession, is a graphic match cut to the shadowy arched doorway of a vast church out of which pours a huge cast. The film holds the shot long enough for the many gorgeously costumed extras to wind past the camera, the lengthy procession drawing the eye back to the church door.

The American cinema's emphasis on editing rather than *mise-en-scène* was coupled with the development of a new 'cinematic' performance style that contributed to the creation of credible, individualized characters. Film acting began increasingly to resemble that of the 'realist' drama and to reject the codified conventions of an older performance style, associated primarily with the melodrama. The earlier or 'histrionic' style was predicated upon the assumption that acting bore no relation to 'real' or everyday life. Actors expressed themselves through a pre-established lexicon of gestures and poses, all corresponding to pre-specified emotions or states of mind. Movements were broad, distinct, and forcefully performed. By contrast, the newer or 'verisimilar' style assumed that actors should mimic everyday behaviour. Actors abandoned the standard and conventionalized poses of the 'histrionic' style and externalized characters' thoughts and emotions through facial expression, small individuated movements, and the use of props. Two Griffith Biographs made three years apart, *A Drunkard's Reformation* (1909) and *Brutality* (1912), illustrate the differences between the histrionic and verisimilar styles. In both films a wife despairs over her husband's affection for the bottle. In the earlier film, the wife (Florence Lawrence) collapses into her chair and rests her head on her arms, extended straight out in front of her on the table. Then she sinks to her knees and prays, her arms fully extended upward at about 45 degrees. In the later film the wife (Mae Marsh) sits down at the dining-room table, bows her head, and begins to collect the dirty dishes. She looks up, compresses her lips, pauses, then begins to gather the dishes again. Once more she pauses, raises her hand to her mouth, glances down to her side, and slumps a little in her chair. Slumping a little more, she begins to cry.

The changing use of intertitles during the transitional period also related directly to the construction of credible, individualized characters. Initially, intertitles had been expository, often preceding a scene and providing fairly lengthy descriptions of the upcoming action. Gradually, shorter expository titles dispersed throughout the scene replaced these lengthy titles. More importantly, dialogue titles began to appear from 1910. Film-makers experimented with the placement of these titles, first inserting them before the shot in which the words were uttered, but by about 1913 cutting in the title just as the character spoke. This had the effect of forging a stronger connection between words and actor, serving further to individuate the characters.

If the formal elements of American film developed in this period, its subject-matter also underwent some changes. The studios continued to produce actualities, travelogues, and other non-fiction films, but the story film's popularity continued to increase until it constituted the major portion of the studios' output. In 1907 comedies comprised 70 per cent of fiction films, perhaps because the comic chase provided such an easy means for linking shots together. But the development of other means of establishing spatio-temporal continuity facilitated the proliferation of different genres.

Exhibitors made a conscious effort to attract a wide audience by programming a mix of subjects; comedies, Westerns, melodramas, actualities, and so forth. The studios planned their output to meet this demand for diversity. For example, in 1911 Vitagraph released a military film, a drama, a Western, a comedy, and a special feature, often a costume film, each week. Nickelodeon audiences apparently loved Westerns (as did European viewers), to such an extent that trade press writers began to complain of the plethora of Westerns and predict the genre's imminent decline. Civil War films also proved popular, particularly during the war's fiftieth anniversary, which fell in this period. By 1911 comedies no longer constituted the majority of fiction films, but still maintained a significant presence. Responding to a prejudice against 'vulgar' slapstick, studios began to turn out the first situation comedies, featuring a continuing cast of characters in domestic settings; Biograph's Mr and Mrs Jones series, Vitagraph's John Bunny series, and Pathé's Max Linder series. In 1912 Mack Sennett revived the slapstick comedy when he devoted his Keystone Studios to the genre. Not numerous, but none the less significant, were the 'quality' films: literary adaptations, biblical epics, and

historical costume dramas. Contemporary dramas (and melodramas), featuring a wide variety of characters and settings, formed an important component of studio output, not only in terms of sheer numbers but in terms of their deployment of the formal elements discussed above.

These contemporary dramas display a more consistent construction of internally coherent narratives and credible individualized characters through editing, acting, and intertitles than do any of the other genres. In these films, producers often emulated the narrative forms and characters of respectable contemporary entertainments, such as the 'realist' drama (the proverbial 'well-made' play) and 'realist' literature, rather than, as in the earlier period, drawing upon vaudeville and magic lanterns. This emulation resulted partially from the film industry's desire to attract a broader audience while placating the cinema's critics, thus entering the mainstream of American middle-class culture as a respectable mass medium. Integral to this strategy were the quality films, which brought 'high' culture to nickelodeon audiences just at the moment when the proliferation of permanent exhibition venues and the 'nickel madness' caused cultural

Warner's first cinema, 'The Cascade', in New Castle, Pennsylvania, 1903

Cecil B. DeMille

(1881–1959)

Cecil B. DeMille was born in Ashfield, Massachusetts, the son of a playwright and a former actress. He tried his hand at both his parents' professions, without much success, until two tyro producers, Jesse L. Lasky and Sam Goldfish (later Goldwyn), invited him to direct a film. This was *The Squaw Man* (1914), the first American feature-length movie and one of the first films to be made in the small rural township of Hollywood. A thunderously old-fashioned melodrama, it was a huge hit. By the end of 1914 DeMille, with five more pictures under his belt and hailed as one of the foremost young directors, was supervising four separate units shooting on the Lasky lot, later to become Paramount Studios.

DeMille's prodigious energy was matched, at this stage of his career, by an enthusiasm for innovation. Though relying for his plots mainly on well-worn stage dramas by the likes of Belasco or Booth Tarkington, he actively experimented with lighting, cutting, and framing to extend narrative technique. *The Cheat* (1915), much admired in France (notably by Marcel L'Herbier and Abel Gance), featured probably the first use of psychological editing: cutting not between two simultaneous events but to show the drift of a character's thoughts. 'So sensitive was DeMille's handling', observes Kevin Brownlow, 'that a potentially foolish melodrama became a serious, bizarre and disturbing fable.'

The Whispering Chorus (1918) was even more avant-garde, its sombre, obsessive story and shadowy lighting anticipating elements of film noir. But it was poorly received, as was DeMille's first attempt at a grand historical spectacular, the Joan of Arc epic *Joan the Woman* (1917). Aiming to recapture box-office popularity, DeMille changed course—for the worse, some would say. 'As he lowered his sights to meet the lowest common denominator,' Brownlow maintains, 'so the standard of his films plummeted.' With *Old Wives for New* (1918) he embarked on a series of 'modern' sex comedies in which alluring scenes of glamour and fast living—including, wherever possible, a coyly titillating bath episode—were offset by a last-reel reaffirmation of traditional morality. Box-office receipts soared, but DeMille's critical reputation took a dive from which it never recovered.

This increasingly didactic pose—preaching virtue, while giving audiences a good long look at the wickedness of vice—found its logical outcome in DeMille's first biblical epic, the $1m *The Ten Commandments* (1923). Despite misgivings at Paramount, now run by the unsympathetic Adolph Zukor, the film was a huge success. Two years later DeMille quit Paramount and set up his own company, Cinema Corporation of America, to make an equally ambitious life of Christ, *King of Kings* (1927). This was an even bigger hit, but CCA's other films flopped and the company folded. After a brief, unhappy stay at MGM DeMille swallowed his dislike of Zukor and rejoined Paramount, at a fraction of his former salary.

To consolidate his position, DeMille shrewdly merged his two most successful formulas to date, the religious epic and the sex comedy, in *The Sign of the Cross* (1932): opulent debauchery on a lavish scale (with Claudette Colbert's Poppaea in the lushest bath scene yet) and a devout message to tie it all up. Critics sneered, but the public flocked. When they stayed away from his next two films, both smaller-scale, modern dramas, DeMille drew the moral: grandiose and historical was what paid off. From

Cecil B. DeMille on set, c.1928

then on, in Charles Higham's view (1973), he abandoned 'the artistic aspirations which had driven him as a young man. He would simply set out to be a supremely successful film-maker.'

Cleopatra (1934) dispensed with religion, but made up for it with plenty of sex and some powerfully staged battle scenes. With *The Plainsman* (1937) DeMille inaugurated a cycle of early Americana, leavening his evangelical message with the theme of Manifest Destiny. The brassbound morality and galumphing narrative drive of films like *Union Pacific* (1942) or *Unconquered* (1947) were calculated, Sumiko Higashi suggests, 'to reaffirm audience belief in the nation's future, especially its destiny as a great commercial power'.

The one-time innovator had now become defiantly old-fashioned. His last biblical epics, *Samson and Delilah* (1949) and the remake of *The Ten Commandments* (1956) are lit and staged as a series of pictorial tableaux with the director himself, where needed, providing the voice of God. DeMille had always been known as an autocratic director; in his later films the hierarchical principle informs the whole film-making process, casting the audience in a subservient, childlike role. Yet audiences did not stay away. For all his limitations, DeMille retained to the end the simple, compulsive appeal of the born storyteller.

PHILIP KEMP

SELECT FILMOGRAPHY

The Squaw Man (1914); The Virginian (1914); Joan the Woman (1917); The Whispering Chorus (1918); Old Wives for New (1918); The Affairs of Anatol (1921); The Ten Commandments (1923); King of Kings (1927); The Sign of the Cross (1932); Cleopatra (1934); The Plainsman (1937); Union Pacific (1939); Unconquered (1947); Samson and Delilah (1949); The Greatest Show on Earth (1952); The Ten Commandments (1956).

BIBLIOGRAPHY

Brownlow, Kevin (1968), *The Parade's Gone By.*
DeMille, Cecil B. (1959), *The Autobiography of Cecil B DeMille.*
Higashi, Sumiko (1985), *Cecil B DeMille: A Guide to References and Resources.*
Higham, Charles (1973), *Cecil B DeMille.*

arbiters to fear the potential deleterious effects of the new medium.

Although the peak period of quality film production coincided roughly with the first years of the nickelodeon (1908–9), film-makers had already produced 'high-culture' subjects such as *Parsifal* (Edison, 1904) and *L'Épopée napoléonienne* (Pathé, 1903–4). In 1908 the French *films d'art* provided a model that would be followed by both European and American film producers as they sought to attain cultural legitimacy. The Société Film d'Art was founded by the financial firm Frères Lafitte for the specific purpose of luring the middle classes to the cinema with prestige productions; adaptations of stage plays or original material written for the screen by established authors (often members of the Académie Française), starring well-known theatrical actors (often members of the Comédie-Française). The first and most famous of the *films d'art*, *L'Assassinat du Duc de Guise* (The Assassination of the Duke of Guise), derived from a script written by Académie member Henri Lavedan. Although based on a historical incident from the reign of Henry II, the original script constructed an internally coherent narrative intended to be understood without previous extra-textual knowledge. Reviewed in the *New York Daily Tribune* upon its Paris première, the film made a major impact in the United States. Further articles on the *film d'art* movement appeared in the mainstream press, while the film trade press asserted that the *films d'art* should serve to inspire American producers to new heights. The exceptional coverage accorded *film d'art* may have served as an incentive for American film-makers to emulate this strategy at a time when the industry badly needed to assert its cultural bona fides.

The Motion Picture Patents Company encouraged the production of quality films, and one of its members, Vitagraph, was particularly active in the production of literary, historical, and biblical topics. Included in its list of output between 1908 and 1913 were: *A Comedy of Errors*, *The Reprieve: An Episode in the Life of Abraham Lincoln* (1908); *Judgment of Solomon, Oliver Twist, Richelieu; or, The Conspiracy, The Life of Moses* (five reels) (1909); *Twelfth Night, The Martyrdom of Thomas à Becket* (1910); *A Tale of Two Cities* (three reels), *Vanity Fair* (1911); *Cardinal Wolsey* (1912); and *The Pickwick Papers* (1913). Biograph, on the other hand, concentrated its efforts on bringing formal practices in line with those of the middle-class stage and novel, and its relatively few quality films tended to be literary adaptations, such as *After Many Years* (1908) (based on Tennyson's *Enoch Arden*) and *The Taming of the Shrew* (1908). The Edison Company, while not as prolific as Vitagraph, did turn out its share of quality films, including *Nero and the Burning of Rome* (1909) and *Les Misérables* (two reels, 1910), while Thanhouser led the independents in their bid for respectability with titles such as *Jane Eyre* (1910) and *Romeo and Juliet* (two reels, 1911).

EXHIBITION AND AUDIENCES

During the early years of film production, the dominance of the non-fiction film, and its exhibition in 'respectable' venues—vaudeville and opera-houses, churches and lecture halls—kept the new medium from posing a threat to the cultural status quo. But the advent of the story film and the associated rise of the nickelodeons changed this situation, and resulted in a sustained assault against the film industry by state officials and private reform groups. The industry's critics asserted that the dark, dirty, and unsafe nickelodeons showed unsuitable fare, were often located in tenement districts, and were patronized by the most unstable elements of American society who were all too vulnerable to the physical and moral hazards posed by the picture shows. There were demands that state authorities censor films and regulate exhibition sites. The industry responded with several strategies designed to placate its critics: the emulation of respectable literature and drama; the production of literary, historical, and biblical films; self-censorship and co-operation with government officials in making exhibition sites safe and sanitary.

Permanent exhibition sites were established in the United States as early as 1905, and by 1907 there were an estimated 2,500 to 3,000 nickelodeons; by 1909, 8,000, and by 1910, 10,000. By the start of 1909, cinema attendance was estimated at 45 million per week. New York rivalled Chicago for the greatest concentration of nickelodeons, estimates ranging from 500 to 800. New York City's converted store-front venues, with their inadequate seating,

Sir Herbert Beerbohm-Tree playing the title role in the first US version of *Macbeth* (John Emerson, 1916). This was one in a series of quality dramas, often adaptations of Shakespeare, that Beerbohm-Tree starred in following the success of the 1910 British film *Henry VIII*

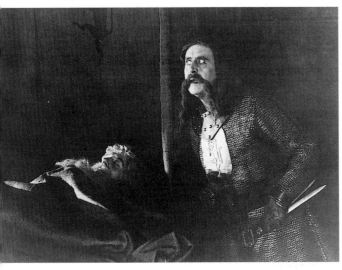

insufficient ventilation, dim lighting, and poorly marked, often obstructed exits, posed serious hazards for their patrons, as confirmed by numerous police and fire department memos from the period. Regular newspaper reports of fires, panics, and collapsing balconies undoubtedly contributed to popular perceptions of the nickelodeons as deathtraps. Catastrophic accidents aside, the physical conditions were linked to ill effects which threatened the community in more insidious ways. In 1908 a civic reform group reported: 'Often the sanitary conditions of the show-rooms are bad; bad air, floors uncleaned, no provision of spittoons, and the people crowded closely together, all make contagion likely.'

There is no accurate information on the make-up of cinema audiences at this time, but impressionistic reports seem to agree that, in urban areas at least, they were predominantly working class, many were immigrants, and sometimes a majority were women and children. While the film industry asserted that it provided an inexpensive distraction to those who had neither the time nor the money for other entertainments, reformers feared that 'immoral' films—dealing with crimes, adultery, suicide, and other unacceptable topics—would unduly influence these most susceptible of viewers and, worse yet, that the promiscuous mingling of races, ethnicities, genders, and ages would give rise to sexual transgressions.

State officials and private reform groups devised a variety of strategies for containing the threat posed by the rapidly growing new medium. The regulation of film content seemed a fairly simple solution and in many localities reformers called for official municipal censorship. As early as 1907, Chicago established a board of police censors that reviewed all films shown within its jurisdiction and often demanded the excision of 'offensive' material. San Francisco's censors enforced a code so strict that it barred 'all films where one person was seen to strike another'. Some states, Pennsylvania being the first in 1911, instituted state censorship boards.

State and local authorities also devised various ways of regulating the exhibition sites. Laws prohibiting certain activities on the Christian Sabbath were invoked to shut the nickelodeons on Sundays, often the wage-earners' sole day off and hence the best day at the box-office. Authorities also struck at box-office profits through state and local statutes forbidding the admission of unaccompanied children, depriving exhibitors of a major source of income. Zoning laws were used to prohibit the operation of nickelodeons within close proximity to schools or churches. In counter-attacking, the industry attempted to form alliances with influential state officials, educators, and clergymen by offering evidence (or at least making assertions) that the new medium provided information and clean, amusing entertainment for those otherwise bereft of either education or diversion. The more powerful

Vitagraph's *The Life of Moses* (1909), one of the first 'feature' films.

members of the industry, such as the Motion Picture Patents Company, often encouraged the incorporation of health and safety requirements into local ordinances dictating the construction of new exhibition venues and the upgrading of old ones. The New York City ordinance of 1913, specifying in detail such matters as the number of seats, aisle width, and air flow, represented the culmination of efforts to make exhibition venues more salubrious, that is, bearing a stronger resemblance to legitimate theatrical houses. In fact, in that year and in that city, the first 'movie palaces' appeared. These large and well-appointed theatres contrasted strongly with the nickelodeons. With seats for up to 2,000 patrons, architecture mimicking Egyptian temples or Chinese pagodas, large orchestras, and uniformed ushers, these theatres provided environments nearly as fantastic as those projected on to their screens.

It was not only in the United States that film houses faced criticism and opposition in this period. Permanent exhibition sites appeared in Germany in 1910, a few years later than in the United States, but the rapid growth and increasing popularity of the new medium attracted the attention of state officials and private reform groups concerned about film's possible malign influence upon susceptible audiences and the nation's culture. The Berlin Police Commission instituted an official pre-censorship plan in 1906, a year earlier than their Chicago counter-

parts. As in the United States, children were perceived as particularly vulnerable and in need of protection. Teachers and clergymen produced several studies testifying to cinema's deleterious effect upon the young while teachers' associations and other groups for popular and continuing education denigrated the use of the cinema for amusement and urged increased production of scientific films for teaching purposes. In 1907 reformers joined together in the cinema reform movement (*Kinoreformbewegung*) and touted the new medium's potential both for child and adult education. Supported in their efforts by the trade press, who saw co-operation as a way to avoid more official censorship, the cinema reformers were successful in persuading the German industry to produce educational films, or *Kulturfilme*, that dealt with natural sciences, geography, folklore, agriculture, industry, technology and crafts, medicine and hygiene, sports, history, religion, and military affairs.

In 1912, literary intellectuals became interested in the by then predominant fiction film, urging adherence to aesthetic standards to elevate the story film to art rather than 'mere' amusement. The industry responded with the *Autorenfilm*, or author film, the German version of the *film d'art*. The first *Autorenfilm*, *Der Andere* (*The Other One*), was adapted from a play by Paul Lindau about a case of split personality and starred the country's most famous actor, Albert Bassermann. The prestigious theatre director Max

Reinhardt followed with filmed versions of two popular plays, *Eine venezianische Nacht* ('A Venetian night', 1913) and *Insel der Seligen* ('Island of the blessed', 1913).

Britain had no real equivalent to the American nickelodeon period, although debates about cinema's cultural and social status paralleled those taking place across the Atlantic. By 1911, when film rental and permanent exhibition sites became standard, most cinemas mimicked the up-market accoutrements of the legitimate theatre. Before this, films were exhibited in a variety of locations—the music halls and fairgrounds that had constituted the primary venues of the early period as well as the so-called 'penny gaffs'. Although never as numerous and often more transient than the nickelodeons, these store-front shows were equivalent to their American counterparts in being unsanitary and unsafe. The first theatre devoted entirely to film exhibition seems to have been established in 1907, and, between the following year and the advent of the World War, films were increasingly exhibited in 'picture palaces', the equivalent of the American 'movie palaces', replete with uniformed ushers and red plush seating for up to 1,000 or even 2,000 customers. While prices remained low enough to permit former patrons to continue to attend, all these amenities served to distance the cinema from its previous associations with the music halls and the working class, to attract, as the trade press fervently hoped, a 'better' class of customer.

Like their transatlantic counterparts, British filmmakers also pursued respectability through more positive tactics. In 1910 producer Will Barker paid the eminent theatrical actor-manager Sir Herbert Beerbohm-Tree £1,000 for appearing in a film version of Shakespeare's *Henry VIII*. Rather than selling the film outright to distributors, as was still the dominant practice, Barker gave one distributor exclusive rights to rent, but not to sell, the film, claiming that its high production costs and high cultural status required special treatment. Barker produced other films of a similar nature, establishing the 'exclusive' or 'quality' picture, the adjectives referring to both the films and their distribution. Hepworth and other producers followed Barker's lead, adapting contemporary plays and literary classics that would appeal to the customers now patronizing the up-market theatres. In 1911 the Urban Company issued a catalogue of films suitable for use in schools. In the same year, the trade paper *Bioscope* urged the industry to persuade government authorities to recognize the educational value of film, even arranging a film screening for members of the London County Council.

French *films d'art* provided the model for film producers in other countries, in their quest for cultural respectability. French film-makers also emulated the narrative strategies of more respectable entertainments, imitating the stories in popular illustrated family magazines such as *Lectures pour tous*. Upon taking the position as chief producer-director at Gaumont in 1907, Louis Feuillade wrote an advertisement for the studio's new serial, *Scènes de la vie telle qu'elle est* (*Scenes from Real Life*), claiming that the films would elevate the position of the French cinema by affiliating it with other respectable arts. 'They represent, for the first time, an attempt to project a realism on to the screen, just as was done some years ago in literature, theatre, and art.'

EPILOGUE: TRANSITION TO FEATURE FILMS

By about 1913 the American film industry's strategies for attaining respectability—emulating respectable entertainments, internal censorship, and improved exhibition venues—had begun to pay off. Conditions were very different from what they had been in 1908 when the medium had been the centre of a cultural crisis. Now a mass audience sat comfortably ensconced in elaborate movie palaces, watching the first true mass medium. And the films they watched were beginning to change as well, telling longer stories through a different deployment of formal elements than had been the case in 1908 or even 1912. A few years later, by 1917, the situation had changed yet again. The majority of important and powerful studios were located in Hollywood, by now the centre not only of American film-making but of world film-making, largely as a result of the First World War disruption of the European industries. Hollywood production and distribution practices now set the norm for the rest of the world. The films themselves had grown from one reel to an average length of sixty to ninety minutes, as film-makers mastered the demands of constructing lengthier narratives and codified into standard practices the formal conventions experimented with during the transitional years.

The industry called these lengthier films 'features', adopting the vaudeville term referring to a programme's main attraction. They were descended from the multiple reel films produced by the members of the Motion Picture Patents Company and the independents during the transitional period, as well as from foreign imports. Although film historians have characterized the MPPC's business practices as somewhat retrograde, the honour of producing the first American multi-reeler goes to Trust member Vitagraph. In 1909 and 1910 Vitagraph released the biblical blockbuster *The Life of Moses*; a five-reel film depicting the story of the Hebrew leader from his adoption by the Pharaoh's daughter to his death on Mount Sinai. Vitagraph continued to produce multi-reelers, and the other studios adopted the policy. Biograph, for example, released the two-reel Civil War story *His Trust* and *His Trust Fulfilled*, in 1911. Clearly, then, elements within the American film industry had begun to chafe at the 1,000-foot or fifteen-minute limit, finding it increasingly impossible to tell a story within these constraints.

Existing distribution and exhibition practices, however, militated against conversion to the multi-reel film. The limited seating of most nickelodeons dictated short programmes featuring a variety of subjects in order to ensure rapid audience turnover and a profit. The studios, therefore, treated each reel of the multi-reelers separately, releasing them to the exchanges according to the agreed schedule, sometimes weeks apart, and the nickelodeons, except in rare instances, showed only one reel in any specific programme, charging the same admission price as they did for all their other films. For this reason, the impetus for the transition to the feature film came from the European, and specifically Italian, films imported into the country. Multi-reel foreign imports were distributed outside the control of the Trust and the independents, with rental prices keyed to both negative costs and box-office receipts. Instead of playing the nickelodeons, these features were 'roadshowed' as a theatrical attraction, shown in legitimate theatres and opera-houses.

Films from other countries, such as *Queen Elizabeth* (Louis Mercanton, 1912), played a part in establishing feature films as the norm, but it was the spectacular Italian costume films whose profits and popularity persuaded the American industry to compete with longer films of its own. In 1911 three Italian productions, the five-reel *Dante's Inferno* (Milano Films, 1909), the two-reel *Fall of Troy* (1910, Giovanni Pastrone), and the four-reel *The Crusaders or Jerusalem Delivered* (1911), treated American audiences to a pictorial splendour seldom seen in domestic productions—elaborate sets and huge casts enhanced through the use of deep space. Released in the United States in the spring of 1913, the nine-reel *Quo vadis?* (Enrico Guazzoni, Cines, 1913), running for more than two hours and exhibited exclusively in legitimate theatres, really sparked the craze for the spectacular feature film. Adapted from the best-selling novel by Henryk Sienkiewicz, the film boasted 5,000 extras, a chariot race, and real lions, as well as clever lighting and detailed set design. The 1914 *Cabiria* (Giovanni Pastrone, Italia) capped the trend. The twelve-reel depiction of the Second Punic War contained such visually stunning scenes as the burning of the Roman fleet and Hannibal's crossing of the Alps. Pastrone enhanced the film's spectacle through extended tracking shots (unusual at this time) that created a sense of depth through movement rather than through set design.

Quo vadis? inspired a host of imitators, not least D. W. Griffith's own multi-reel biblical spectacular, *Judith of Bethulia* (1913), which was made against the wishes of a Biograph front office still committed to the one-reel film. But Griffith's own historical costume drama epic, *The Birth of a Nation* (1915), excelled all previous features in length and spectacle, while dealing with a truly American subject, the Civil War and Reconstruction. It was this film

that began to establish the feature as the norm rather than the exception. Prior to the film's January 1915 release, Griffith's publicity department had hyped its expense, huge cast, and historical accuracy, creating great public anticipation for the famous director's most ambitious project. Griffith exercised as much care with the film's exhibition. Premièred in the largest movie palaces in Los Angeles and New York, *The Birth of a Nation* was the first American film to be released with its own score, played by a forty-piece orchestra. The admission price of $2, the same as that charged for Broadway plays, ensured that the film would be taken seriously, and it was widely advertised and reviewed in the general press rather than the film trade press. All these factors showed that film had come of age as a legitimate mass medium. Of course, the film attracted attention for other reasons as well, its reprehensible racism eliciting outrage from the African-American community and their supporters, and offering an early insight into the social impact that this new mass medium could have.

The narrative structures, character construction, and editing patterns of the first multi-reel films, both American and Italian, strongly resembled those of the one-reel films of the time. This was particularly apparent in terms of narrative structure: one-reelers tended to follow a pattern of an elaborated single incident or plot device intensifying toward a climax near the end of the reel. The first multi-reel American films, intended to stand on their own, adopted this structure but, even after distribution channels became available, longer films often continued to appear more like several one-reelers strung together than the lengthy integrated narratives that we are accustomed to today. However, film-makers quickly realized that the feature film was not simply a longer version of the one-reel film, but a new narrative form, demanding new methods of organization, and they learned to construct appropriate narratives, characters, and editing patterns. As they had in 1908, producers again turned to the theatre and novels for inspiration, not only in terms of screen adaptations but in terms of emulating narrative structures. Feature films, therefore, began to include more characters, incidents, and themes, all relating to a main story. Instead of one climax or a series of equally intense climaxes, features began to be constructed around several minor climaxes and then a dénouement that resolved all the narrative themes. *The Birth of a Nation* provides an extreme example of this structure, its (in)famous last-minute rescue, as the Ku-Klux-Klan rides to secure Aryan supremacy, capping several reels of crisis (the death of 'Little Sister', the capture of Gus, and so forth) and resolving the fates of all the important characters.

However, the basic elements of the earlier films remained unchanged—credible individual characters still served to link together the disparate scenes and shots, the

Lillian Gish
(1893–1993)

Dorothy Gish
(1898–1968)

Lillian and Dorothy Gish were born in Ohio, daughters of an actress and her absentee drifter husband. Stage juveniles being in constant demand, both girls were acting professionally before they were 5. They were enticed into movies by their friend Mary Pickford, who was already working for D. W. Griffith, and they made their screen début together in his *An Unseen Enemy* (1912).

Over the next two years the sisters played numerous roles for Griffith's company, both together and separately. At first Griffith had trouble telling them apart (tying coloured ribbons in their hair, he addressed them as 'red' and 'blue') but their very different characters, and screen personae, soon emerged. Dorothy was effervescent, gregarious, a natural comedienne. Lillian was serious, intense, with a toughness belied by her delicate looks. 'When Dorothy arrives the party begins,' Lillian once remarked, adding wryly, 'When I arrive it usually ends.'

Dorothy, Griffith noted, 'was more apt at getting the director's idea than Lillian, quicker to follow it, more easily satisfied with the result. Lillian conceived an ideal and patiently sought to realize it.' Since this dedicated approach appealed more to Griffith's own workaholic temperament, Lillian generally got the better parts, and was awarded the lead in his epoch-making Civil War epic *The Birth of a Nation* (1915). As Elsie Stoneman, daughter of a family split by the conflict, she transcended the hearts-and-flowers, virgin-in-jeopardy elements of the role with a performance of sustained emotional truth. The film made her a major star, as Griffith acknowledged in casting her as the iconic cradle-rocking Mother linking the four stories of his next epic, *Intolerance* (1916).

There seems to have been no rivalry between the sisters. Lillian suggested Dorothy as a rowdy French peasant girl in their first major film together, the First World War drama *Hearts of the World* (1918), and was amused when Dorothy stole the picture. Even so, Dorothy continued to work for other directors, while Griffith reserved Lillian ('She is the best actress I know. She has the most brains') for his own films.

Lillian's supreme performance for Griffith was as the abused child of *Broken Blossoms* (1919), terrorized by a brutal father and finding tenderness with a lonely young Chinaman in nineteenth-century Limehouse. It was pure Victorian melodrama, dripping with sentiment, but transmuted by the subtlety of Gish's acting and the power—for all her ethereal looks—with which she could convey raw emotion. *Way Down East* (1920), no less melodramatic, made equally good use of her blend of physical frailty and inner tenacity.

Dorothy continued to specialize in comedies, including one directed by Lillian, *Remodelling her Husband* (1920). It did well, but Lillian found directing 'too complicated' and refused to try it again. Dorothy's range reached far beyond comedy, as shown by their finest film together, *Orphans of the Storm* (1921). They played sisters caught up in the French Revolution; Dorothy's performance as the blind sister, moving but not for a moment mawkish, is in no way overshadowed by Lillian's.

It was their last film for Griffith, who could no longer afford Lillian's salary. They parted from him amicably and moved to the Inspiration Company, where they made *Romola* (1924) together—from George Eliot's

novel—before Lillian signed a contract with MGM. Dorothy went to London for four films for Herbert Wilcox, of which the most successful was *Nell Gwynne* (1926).

Lillian was now one of the highest paid ($400,000 p.a.) actresses in Hollywood, able to approve her own scripts and directors. She chose Victor Sjöström to direct her in two of her greatest roles: a passionate, wayward Hester Prynne in Hawthorne's *The Scarlet Letter* (1926), and the gentle wife whipped into desperation by the elements in *The Wind* (1928), a performance of awesome physicality.

But fashions were changing. Garbo's star was in the ascendant, and Lillian was too identified with virginal virtues and the silent cinema. Irving Thalberg offered to fabricate a scandal for her; she coolly declined, and returned to the live stage. Dorothy did the same, her film career virtually over. Lillian, though, appeared in a dozen or so films after 1940, of which the finest was Laughton's Gothic fable *The Night of the Hunter* (1955). In it she portrays, as Simon Callow (1987) comments, 'the spirit of absolution and healing... with a kind of secular sanctity which cannot be forged'. Gish relished making the film: 'I have to go back as far as D. W. Griffith to find a set so imbued with purpose and harmony.' Coming from her, there could be no greater praise.

Lillian outlived her sister by a quarter-century, ageing gracefully and still acting in her mid-nineties. Well before her death, she saw herself securely reinstated as the supreme actress of the silent cinema. Dorothy, a fine actress if not a great one, still awaits fair reassessment.

PHILIP KEMP

SELECT FILMOGRAPHY

Lillian
The Birth of a Nation (1915); Intolerance (1916); Broken Blossoms (1919); True Heart Susie (1919); Way Down East (1920); La Bohème (1926); The Scarlet Letter (1926); The Wind (1928); Duel in the Sun (1946);The Night of the Hunter (1955); The Cobweb (1955); The Unforgiven (1955); A Wedding (1978); The Whales of August (1987)

Dorothy
Remodelling her Husband (1920); Nell Gwynne (1926)

Lillian and Dorothy
Hearts of the World (1918); Orphans of the Storm (1921); Romola (1924)

BIBLIOGRAPHY

Gish, Lillian (1969), *The Movies, Mr Griffith and Me.*
—— (1973), *Dorothy and Lillian Gish.*
Slide, Anthony (1973), *The Griffith Actresses.*

Opposite: Lillian and Dorothy Gish in D. W. Griffith's *Orphans of the Storm* (1921)

difference being that character motivation and plausibility became yet more important as films grew longer and the number of important characters increased. Films now had the space to flesh out their characters, endowing them with traits that would drive the narrative action. Often entire scenes served the sole purpose of acquainting the audience with the characters' personalities. *The Birth of a Nation* devotes its first fifteen minutes or so, before the outbreak of the Civil War occurs, to introducing its major characters, seeking to engender audience identification with the Southern slave-holding family, the Camerons. In scenes that establish the plantation owners' kindly and tolerant natures, we see the pater familias surrounded by puppies and kittens and his son Ben shaking hands with a slave who has just danced for Northern visitors.

Feature films also deployed their formal elements to further character development and motivation. Dialogue intertitles had first appeared around 1911, but their use increased so that by the mid-1910s dialogue titles outnumbered the expository titles that revealed the presence of a narrator; the responsibility for narration being accorded more and more to the characters. Although the standard camera scale remained the three-quarter shot that had become dominant during the transitional period, film-makers increasingly cut closer to characters at moments of psychological intensity. In *The Birth of a Nation*, closer views of terrified white women supposedly intensify audience identification with these potential victims of a fate worse than death. Point-of-view editing also became standardized in the feature films of this time. Although Griffith actually used this pattern fairly sparingly, in two key scenes in *The Birth* we get Ben's point of view of his beloved Elsie, the first time as he looks at a locket photograph of her and the second as he actually looks at her, an irised shot of Elsie mimicking the photograph's composition.

The transition to features served to codify many of the devices that film-makers had experimented with during the transitional period. This is particularly related to moves to create a unified spatio-temporal orientation. Analytical editing became more common as film-makers sought to highlight narratively important details. In the scene in *The Birth* where Father Cameron plays with the puppies and kittens, a cut-in to a close-up of the animals at his feet emphasizes the alignment of the Southern family with these appealing creatures. Most features included some parallel editing, *The Birth* of course being the *locus classicus* of the form, not only in the climactic last-minute rescue that cuts among several different locations, but throughout the film where alternation between Northern and Southern families and the home front and the battlefield reinforces the film's ideological message. Devices such as the eyeline match and the shot/reverse-shot became standard conventions for linking disparate spaces together, and devices such as the dissolve, fade, and close-up became clear markers of any deviations from linear temporality such as flashbacks or dreams.

After a decade of profound upheaval, by 1917, the end of the 'transitional' period, the cinema was poised on the brink of a new maturity as *the* dominant medium of the twentieth century. Films, while continuing to reference other texts, had freed themselves from dependence upon other media, and could now tell cinematic stories using cinematic devices; devices which were becoming increasingly codified and conventional. A standardization of production practices, consonant with the operations of other capitalist enterprises, assured the continuing output of a reliable and familiar product, the so-called 'feature' film. The building of ever larger and more elaborate movie palaces heralded the medium's new-found social respectability. All was ready for the advent of Hollywood and the Hollywood cinema.

Bibliography

Abel, Richard (1988), *French Film Theory and Criticism.*
Balio, Tino (ed.) (1985), *The American Film Industry.*
Bitzer, Billy (1973), *Billy Bitzer: His Story.*
Bordwell, David, Staiger, Janet, and Thompson, Kristin (1985), *The Classical Hollywood Cinema.*
Bowser, Eileen (1990), *The Transformation of Cinema, 1907–1915.*
Cosandey, Roland, Gaudreault, André, and Gunning, Tom (eds.) (1992), *Une invention du diable?*
Elsaesser, Thomas (ed.) (1990), *Early Cinema: Space, Frame, Narrative.*
Fell, John L. (1986), *Film and the Narrative Tradition.*
Gunning, Tom (1991), *D. W. Griffith and the Origins of American Narrative Film.*
Jarratt, Vernon (1951), *The Italian Cinema.*
Koszarski, Richard (1990), *An Evening's Entertainment.*
Low, Rachael (1949), *The History of the British Film, 1906–1914.*
Pearson, Roberta E. (1992), *Eloquent Gestures.*
Thompson, Kristin (1985), *Exporting Entertainment.*
Uricchio, William, and Pearson, Roberta E. (1993), *Reframing Culture: The Case of the Vitagraph Quality Films.*

THE RISE OF HOLLYWOOD

The Hollywood Studio System

DOUGLAS GOMERY

Around the year 1910 a number of film companies set up business in and around the small suburb of Hollywood to the west of Los Angeles. Within a decade, the system they created came to dominate the cinema, not only in the United States but throughout the world. By concentrating production into vast factory-like studios, and by vertically integrating all aspects of the business, from production to publicity to distribution to exhibition, they created a model system—the 'studio system'—which other countries had to imitate in order to compete. But attempts at imitating the American system were only partially successful, and by 1925 it was the 'Hollywood' system, rather than the studio system as such, which dominated the market from Britain to Bengal, from South Africa to Norway and Sweden. By that time, Hollywood had not only seized control of the majority of world markets but had made its products and its stars, such as Charlie Chaplin and Mary Pickford, the most famous cultural icons in the world.

Throughout the period of its inexorable rise, Hollywood fashioned the tools of modern business, from economics of scale to vertical integration, to give it the edge over all possible competitors. It developed cost-effective methods of production, extended the market for its product to cover the entire globe, and ensured the flow of films from producer to consumer by acquiring ownership of key theatres in major cities, not just in the United States but in other countries as well. European nations tried various protectionist measures, such as special taxes, tariffs, quotas, and even boycotts, to keep Hollywood's domination at bay, but to no avail. Although the Japanese market remained hard to penetrate, and the Soviet Union was able to close its frontiers against foreign imports in the mid-1920s, as far as the rest of the world was concerned it was only a matter of time before the Hollywood film became standard fare on the nation's screens.

The emergence of Hollywood as the centre of this all-powerful industry can be found in the failures of the Motion Picture Patents Company's attempt to monopolize the film business. This was a combination of ten leading American and European producers of movies and manufacturers of cameras and projectors, who in 1908 combined to form a 'Trust' to inflate the prices of equipment they alone could manufacture. The Trust pooled patents and made thousands of short films. Only co-operating companies, licensed by the Trust, could manufacture 'legal' films and film equipment. The Trust extracted profits by charging for use of its patents. To use a projector legally an exhibitor needed to hand over a few dollars; to make movies, producers paid more.

However, the Trust found it difficult to maintain control, and in the space of half a dozen years (1909–14) independents such as Carl Laemmle and William Fox rose in opposition to the Trust, sowing the seeds of what we now know as Hollywood. Adolph Zukor put together Paramount; Marcus Loew created what was to become MGM; William Fox fashioned his movie empire.

These and other independent exhibitors and movie-makers differentiated their products, making longer and more complicated narratives while the Trust tended to stick with two-reel, fifteen-minute stories. The independents raided pulp magazines, public domain novels, and successful plays for plots. Westerns supplied the most popular of these 'new' movie genres and helped spark interest in shooting on location 'out West'. In time the independents found their home in southern California, 2,000 miles away from the New York headquarters of the Trust and, with its temperate climate, cheap land, and lack of unions, an ideal place to make their new low-cost 'feature-length' motion pictures.

By 1912 the independents were producing enough films to fill theatrical bills. Each movie became a unique product, heavily advertised. With more than 20,000 cinemas open in the USA by 1920, the ever-increasing number of feature-length 'photoplays' easily found an audience. Distribution into foreign markets proved a bonus; in this era of the silent cinema, specialists quickly translated intertitles, and produced foreign versions for minimal added production costs.

The independents also began to take control of exhibition in the USA. They did not attempt to buy up all the 20,000 existing movie houses, concentrating instead on the new movie palaces in the largest cities. By 1920 these 2,000 picture palaces, showing exclusive first-runs, were capturing over three-quarters of the revenue of the average film. From these chains of movie palaces from New York City to Chicago to Los Angeles, the major Hollywood

Rudolph Valentino

(1895–1926)

On 18 July 1926, the *Chicago Tribune* published an unsigned editorial that railed against a pink powder machine supposedly placed in a men's washroom on Chicago's North Side. Blame for 'this degeneration into effeminacy' was laid at the feet of a movie star then appearing in the city to promote his latest film: Rudolph Valentino. The muscular star challenged the anonymous author of the 'Pink Powder Puff' attack to a boxing match, but the editor failed to show. Nevertheless, the matter would be settled, in a way, the following month. On 23 August the 31-year-old star died at New York City's Polyclinic of complications from an ulcer operation.

Following Valentino's unexpected death, the vitriolic response of American men to Valentino was temporarily put aside as women, long regarded as the mainstay of the star's fans, offered public proof of their devotion to the actor. The *New York Times* reported a crowd of some 30,000, 'in large part women and girls', who stood in line for hours to glimpse the actor's body lying in state at Campbell's Funeral Church. These mourners caused, noted the *Times,* 'rioting . . . without precedent in New York'. The funerary hysteria, including reports of suicides, led the Vatican to issue a statement condemning the 'collective madness, incarnating the tragic comedy of a new fetishism'.

Valentino was not the first star constructed to appeal to women, but in the years that followed his death his impact on women would be inscribed as Hollywood legend. The name of Rudolph Valentino remains one of the few from the Hollywood silent era that still reverberates in the public imagination; a cult figure with an aura of exotic sexual ambiguity. Valentino's masculinity had been held suspect in the 1920s because of his former employment as a paid dancing companion, because of his sartorial excess, and because of his apparent capitulation to a strong-willed wife, the controversial dancer and production designer Natasha Rambova. To many, Valentino seemed to epitomize the dreaded possibilities of a 'woman-made' masculinity, much discussed and denounced in anti-feminist tracts, general interest magazines, and popular novels of the time.

Valentino came to the United States from Italy in 1913 as a teenager. After becoming a professional dancer in the cafés of New York City, he ventured out to California in 1917, where he entered the movies in bit parts and graduated to playing the stereotype of the villainous foreign seducer. Legend has it that June Mathis, an influential scriptwriter for Metro, saw his film *Eyes of Youth* (1919), and suggested him for the role of the doomed playboy hero in Rex Ingram's production of *The Four Horsemen of the Apocalypse* (1921). The film became a huge hit; by some reports it was Hollywood's biggest box-office draw of the entire decade.

Through the films that followed Valentino came to

represent, in the words of Adela Rogers St Johns, 'the lure of the flesh', the male equivalent of the vamp. Valentino's exotic ethnicity was deliberately exploited by Hollywood as the source of controversy, as was the 'Vogue of Valentino' among women, discussed in the press as a direct threat to American men. The hit movie *The Sheik* (1921) made Valentino a top star and sealed his seductive image, but he was not satisfied with playing 'the sheikh' forever, and began to demand different roles. After a sensitive performance in *Blood and Sand* (1922) and his appearance in other, less memorable films (like *Beyond the Rocks* and *Moran of the Lady Letty*, both 1922), Valentino was put on suspension by Famous Players–Lasky because of his demand for control over his productions. During his absence from the screen, Valentino adroitly proved his continuing popularity with a successful dance tour for Mineralava facial clay. He returned to the screen in a meticulously produced costume drama, *Monsieur Beaucaire* (1924), in which he gives a wonderfully nuanced performance as a duke who masquerades as a fake duke who masquerades as a barber.

Valentino's best performances, as in *Monsieur Beaucaire* and *The Eagle* (1925), stress his comic talents and his ability to move expressively. These performances stand in contrast to the clips that circulate of Valentino's work (especially from *The Sheik*) that suggest he was an over-actor whose brief career was sustained only by his beauty and the sexual idolatry of female fans. However, the limited success of *Monsieur Beaucaire* outside urban areas would prove (at least to the studio) that Madam Valentino's control over her 'henpecked' husband was a danger to box-office receipts. After a couple of disappointing films and separation from his wife, a Valentino 'come-back' was offered with the expertly designed and directed *The Eagle,* cleverly scripted by frequent Lubitsch collaborator Hans Kräly. Ironically, Valentino's posthumously released last film, *The Son of the Sheik,* would be a light-hearted parody of the vehicle that had first brought 'The Great Lover' to fame only five years before.

GAYLYN STUDLAR

SELECT FILMOGRAPHY

The Four Horsemen of the Apocalypse (1921); The Sheik (1921); Blood and Sand (1922); Monsieur Beaucaire (1924); The Eagle (1925); The Son of the Sheik (1926)

BIBLIOGRAPHY

Hansen, Miriam (1991), *Babel and Babylon.*
Morris, Michael (1991), *Madam Valentino.*
Studlar, Gaylyn (1993), 'Valentino, "Optic Intoxication" and Dance Madness'.
Walker, Alexander (1976), *Valentino.*

Opposite: The tango from Rex Ingram's *Four Horsemen of the Apocalypse*

companies, led by Paramount, Fox, and MGM, were able to collect millions of dollars per year in profit.

By this time the independents were independents no longer. They had become the system. The most successful of these former independents succeeded at what the well-financed members of the Trust had failed to accomplish—control of the production, distribution, and exhibition of movies. From this massive base they moved to dominate the world. With any one film costing $100,000 or more to produce, the extra few thousand dollars to make prints and send them around the world proved relatively small.

This world-wide popularity in turn created a demand which required non-stop production. To meet this requirement, the Los Angeles basin offered year-round sunshine and thus long working days outdoors, in addition to all possible combinations of locations for filming. Nearby farmland (now swallowed up by suburbs) fronted for the Midwest; the Pacific Ocean stood in for the Caribbean and Atlantic; mountains and desert, just a day away, gave Westerns an authentic feel.

By the early 1920s the social impact of Hollywood's glamorous image was enormous. As early as 1920, the Hollywood Chamber of Commerce was obliged to run advertisements begging aspiring actors and actresses to stay at home, pleading: 'Please Don't Try to Break into the Movies.'

THE PRODUCTION SYSTEM

During the late 1910s and early 1920s, the successful companies, led by Adolph Zukor's Famous Players–Lasky corporation, developed a system by which to manufacture popular films on a large scale. This system was much admired abroad, and film industries the world over sent their representatives over to Hollywood to study and, if possible, copy it. As well as visitors from France, Germany, and Britain, Hollywood was to play host in the 1930s to Luigi Freddi, head of the Italian Fascist film industry, and to Boris Shumyatsky, Stalin's henchman in charge of the industry in the Soviet Union.

The centrepiece of the product offered by the Hollywood companies was the feature film, generally about ninety minutes long. Ten-minute newsreels or animated subjects might provide a complement, but it was the feature that sold the show. The feature film had to be a story of unusual interest, produced at a cost of about $100,000, sometimes up to $500,000. Ironically, inspiration for this had come from Europe. Through the 1910s foreign features repeatedly demonstrated that longer films could draw sizeable audiences. The then independents imported epics from European film-makers who did not care to book through the Trust. The success of prestigious Italian productions such as *Dante's Inferno* (1911) not only proved there existed a market for longer fare, but helped to give the new medium much-needed respectability in the eyes of the traditional middle class.

In 1911 *Dante's Inferno* enjoyed successful extended engagements in New York and Boston. Where the average two-reel Trust film may have played two days, *Dante's Inferno* was held over for two weeks. Where the average Trust film was shown in a 200-seat 'odeon' for 10 cents, *Dante's Inferno* was presented in 1,000-seat rented legitimate theatres for $1. Indeed, the most influential of early feature films, D. W. Griffith's *The Birth of a Nation* (1915), opened a few years later in a noted New York City legitimate theatre and ran for a year at an unheard of admission price of $2. In less than two decades the industry had moved from selling movies as a novelty to developing a finely-honed publicity machine to promote an entire system and its nationally advertised products.

Hollywood centred its promotional efforts on the star system. Publicists had to acquire the art of manipulating the new techniques of mass advertising and mass communication to create something special in the minds of the growing middle-class public. Stars provided an effective means of differentiating feature films, making each individual title an unmissable attraction. In 1909, for example, Carl Laemmle lured Florence Lawrence from Biograph, and named her his 'IMP Girl'—the letters representing his Independent Motion Picture Company (later Universal). Laemmle then sent his star on tour and planted story after story in the newspapers, including one falsely reporting her death.

Others plucked their stars from the legitimate stage. Adolph Zukor's pioneering company Famous Players (later Paramount), whose slogan was 'Famous Players in Famous Plays', achieved early successes with *The Count of Monte Cristo* (1912) starring James O'Neill, *The Prisoner of Zenda* (1913) starring James Hackett, *Queen Elizabeth* (1912) starring Sarah Bernhardt, and *Tess of the D'Urbervilles* starring Minnie Maddern Fiske.

Zukor soon saw the need to develop his own stars, not simply buy up already established names. Mary Pickford saw her salary increase from $100 a week in 1909 to $10,000 per week in 1917 as Zukor made her the biggest star of her day. Zukor's rivals developed their own 'Little Marys', and 'inked' them to exclusive, long-run contracts. The Hollywood companies then fashioned elaborately prepared scenarios as centrepieces for their stars. But the stars were quick to realize that, if they were so important to the studios, they had bargaining power of their own. Although many remained tied to exploitative contracts, some of the most successful broke loose from the system. On 15 January 1919, major luminaries Charlie Chaplin, Douglas Fairbanks, and Mary Pickford joined with director D. W. Griffith to create United Artists, and issued a declaration of independence from their former studio bosses. United Artists announced it would distribute star-produced features so their makers could extract the riches their star power had generated.

United Artists achieved great success with, for example: *The Mark of Zorro* (1920, Fairbanks), *Robin Hood* (1923, Fairbanks), *Little Lord Fauntleroy* (1921, Pickford), and *The Gold Rush* (1925, Chaplin). Unfortunately, however, the studio did not regularly release enough star-laden films. Theatre owners called for three Chaplin, Fairbanks, and Pickford films per year, but the company was able to deliver only one every twenty-four months. Theatre owners could not afford to go dark to wait for biennial inspirations, and turned back to the majors. Thus, in the long run, United Artists simply became a haven for independent producers (some good, some bad) fleeing from the strict confines of the major Hollywood studios.

United Artists was an anomaly. The standard Hollywood system of feature film-making sought to guarantee the shipment of attractive films to theatres on a weekly basis, and the studios developed efficient and cost-effective production methods to produce films that filled theatres. This factory system would prove the best method by which to provide a regular supply of films.

In the days before the feature film, there had been two standard methods of production. For 'reality' subjects, a camera operator would journey to the subject, record the action, and then edit it together. For films inspired by vaudeville acts or taken from literary sources, movie companies employed a director to stage 'scenes' and a camera operator to record them. Gradually during the 1910s, as the demand for narrative films increased, specialists were trained to assist the director to make movies faster. Writers thought up story lines, scenic artists painted backgrounds, and designers fashioned appropriate costumes.

Soon film-makers realized that it was less expensive to shoot the story out of order, rather than chronologically record it as it might be staged in a theatre. Once all planned scenes were filmed, an editor could reassemble them, following the dictates of the script. All this required a carefully thought out, prearranged plan to calculate the minimum cost in advance. Such a plan became known as the shooting script.

The Hollywood studio had to fashion shooting scripts which would turn out to be popular at the box-office. Gradually, as feature films became longer, stories became more complicated, requiring more complex shooting scripts. Paying careful attention to script preparation meant faster and cheaper feature film-making. One could make a careful estimate of the necessary footage for each scene, and film-makers developed techniques to minimize the need for retakes.

William Cameron Menzies's sets for *The Thief of Bagdad* seen from the air in 1924.

The typical script immediately proclaimed its genre (comedy or drama, for example), listed the cast of characters, and sketched a synopsis of the story, and only then went on to a scene-by-scene scenario. From this plan, the head of the film company could decide whether he wanted to make the movie. The producer could, once the project was approved by the studio boss, redo the shooting script to fashion the actual order of production.

The Hollywood production system was not invented, but evolved in response to a number of felt imperatives, of which the most important was the need for regular and consistent profit. A pioneering role, however, can be ascribed to producer Thomas Ince, working at Mutual in 1913. The standard studio working procedure, as devised by Ince, involved a studio boss, the film's director, and a continuity script. Once Ince as head producer had approved a project, he assigned available buildings for filming, and commissioned writers and production artists to create the necessary script, sets, and costumes. Back-up systems, such as an internal police force to keep out crowds, or fire-fighters to assist when wooden sets burned, meant that by the early 1920s studio lots, covering many acres, operated as veritable subcities within the urban environs of Los Angeles.

Studio bosses planned a programme of films a year in advance. Sets were efficiently used over and over again, and adapted for different stories. Art directors designed and constructed sets; casting directors found the talent; make-up artists perfected the glamorous movie look; and cinematographers were picked to shoot scripts as written.

Time was of the essence, so actors were shuttled from film to film. Often multiple cameras were used for complicated shots (for example, a battlefield sequence) to avoid having to stage them twice. And always present was the continuity clerk, who checked that, when shooting was completed, the film could be easily reassembled.

DISTRIBUTION AND CONTROL OF THE MARKET

If Ince pioneered this Hollywood studio 'factory' production system, it was Adolph Zukor who taught Hollywood how fully and properly to exploit it. By 1921 Zukor had fashioned the largest film company in the world—his Famous Players. Five years earlier he had merged twelve producers and the distributor, Paramount, to form the Famous Players–Lasky Corporation. By 1917 his new company included stars such as Mary Pickford, Douglas Fairbanks, Gloria Swanson, Pauline Frederick, and Blanche Sweet. Two years later, about the time Pickford and Fairbanks left to form United Artists, a quarter of the cinemas in the USA were regularly presenting Famous Players films.

Famous Players began to block book its yearly output of 50 to 100 feature films, which meant that the theatre owner who sought to show the films of Mary Pickford had also to take pictures featuring less well-known Famous Players stars. In turn, Famous Players used these guaranteed bookings to test and develop new stars, and to try new story genres. When major theatre owners began to baulk at the risks involved, Zukor stepped in, acquired theatres, and set up his own theatre chain.

Such a large real estate venture needed more investment than could be financed with the cash on hand. Zukor therefore turned to the Wall Street investment banking firm of Kuhn Loeb for the necessary $10 million. At that time Kuhn Loeb was an outsider on Wall Street, a small Jewish-run business in a world of WASP-dominated institutions. In time, however, the company would grow into a financial giant, partly on the basis of deals with expanding film companies from the west coast like Famous Players. Hollywood may have been over 2,000 miles from New York City, but to gain crucial financing not available from conservative west coast bankers, Zukor showed the industry that eastern money was there to be tapped.

During the 1920s Famous Players became a high-flyer on the New York Stock Exchange. Others soon followed. Marcus Loew put together Metro-Goldwyn-Mayer. William Fox expanded his film company as did Carl Laemmle with his Universal Studios. Even stalwart independents United Artists built a theatre chain. Thus a handful of major, vertically integrated companies came to dominate and define Hollywood.

It was not enough, however, that this small handful of companies controlled all the movie stars and theatres. They sought to expand their markets beyond the US border, to establish distribution all over the world. The First World War offered a crucial opening. While other national cinemas were constrained, the leading Hollywood companies moved to make the world their marketplace. Although the average cost for Hollywood features of the day rarely ranged beyond $500,000, expanding distribution across the globe meant revenues regularly topped $1,000,000. Adolph Zukor, ever aggressive, led the way with a series of spectacular foreign deals, and was able during the years prior to the coming of sound to effect a stranglehold on the world-wide market-place.

To maintain conditions for maximizing profits abroad, the major Hollywood companies formed an association, the Motion Picture Producers and Distributors Association of America (MPPDA), and hired former Postmaster-General Will H. Hays to keep these international markets open. With Hays as an unofficial ambassador, assisted by a willing US State Department under Presidents Harding, Coolidge, and Hoover, the MPPDA fought to make sure that foreign countries permitted Hollywood corporations to operate with an absence of constraint.

By the mid-1920s, Hollywood dominated not only the major English-speaking markets of Great Britain, Canada, and Australia, but most of continental Europe except for

Joseph M. Schenck

(1877–1961)

Among the figures who rose to power as Hollywood moguls during the studio period, Joseph M. Schenck and his younger brother Nicholas had perhaps the most remarkable (if chequered) careers. In their heyday the two brothers between them ran two major studios; while Joe Schenck operated from behind the scenes as first the head of United Artists and later that of Twentieth Century–Fox, Nick ran Loew's Inc. and its world famous subsidiary, Metro-Goldwyn-Mayer.

Like most movie moguls, the Schencks were immigrants—in their case from Russia. They came to the USA in 1892 and grew up in New York City, where they built up a successful amusement park business. They prospered and in time merged with vaudeville act supplier Loew's.

Nick Schenck rose to the presidency of Loew's, a position he held for a quarter of a century. Joe, on the other hand, was more independent and struck out on his own. By the early 1920s he had relocated to Hollywood and was managing the careers of Roscoe (Fatty) Arbuckle, Buster Keaton, and the three Talmadge sisters.

Joe married Norma Talmadge in 1917 while Keaton married Natalie, and through the 1920s the Schenck–Keaton–Talmadge 'extended family' ranked at the top of the Hollywood pantheon of celebrity and power. After his divorce in 1929 Schenck played the role of the bachelor of Hollywood's golden era, acting as mentor to, and having rumoured affairs with, stars from Merle Oberon to Marilyn Monroe.

Through the 1920s Joe Schenck formed a close association with United Artists, through which many of the stars he managed distributed their films. He joined in November 1924 as president. Even as company head, however, he continued to work with the artists he had sponsored, producing a number of their films, including Buster Keaton's *The General* (1927) and *Steamboat Bill Jr.* (1928).

In 1933 he created his own production company Twentieth Century Pictures, partnered with Darryl F. Zanuck and backed financially by brother Nick at Loew's Inc. When Twentieth Century merged with Fox two years later, Joe retained control, thanks again to his brother's financial support. Thereafter, as Zanuck cranked out the pictures, Joe Schenck worked behind the scenes, co-ordinating world-wide distribution and running Twentieth Century–Fox's international chain of theatres.

Through the late 1930s Schenk and other studio heads (including brother Nick) paid bribes to Willie Bioff of the projectionists' union to keep their theatres open. In time government investigators unearthed this racketeering, and convicted Bioff. One movie mogul had to go to gaol, to take the fall for the others. Convicted of perjury, Schenk spent four months and five days in a

Joe Schenck (right) posing with D. W. Griffith before the making of *Abraham Lincoln* (1930)

federal prison in Danbury, Connecticut; in 1945 he was pardoned and cleared on all charges by President Harry Truman.

The Schenk brothers hung on, through the bitter economic climate of the 1950s; through a period where the methods that they had employed for nearly thirty years were mocked as obsolete. With new audiences and new competition from television, the Schencks ungracefully lost their positions of power. Ever the deal-maker, during the 1950s Schenck and longtime friend Mike Todd signed up a widescreen process called Todd-AO, and produced *Oklahoma!* (1955) and a number of other top-drawer films. Yet, at the end, old age finally slowed Schenck, and he died in Hollywood a bitter old man, living at the edge of an industry he had helped to create.

More than the bribery conviction, this woeful ending to their magisterial careers has robbed the brothers Schenck of their proper due in histories of film. Both deserve praise for building Hollywood into the most powerful film business in the world during the 1920s and 1930s.

DOUGLAS GOMERY

SELECT FILMOGRAPHY

As producer
Salome (1918); The Navigator (1924); Camille (1927); The General (1927); Eternal Love (1929); Abraham Lincoln (1930); DuBarry: Woman of Passion (1930)

Germany and the Soviet Union, and had successfully expanded into South America, Central America, and the Caribbean. This crippled the development of rival studio systems, except in isolated locations. For example, Japan at the time was not an international trader, but a nation that kept to itself. Although Hollywood films were popular with Japanese audiences, a native studio system was able to grow and rival Hollywood in a way a British or French industry never could. Germany also retained some degree of autonomy, though even this began to be undermined by the end of the 1920s, with Hollywood companies tempting away many leading German artists, and striking deals with the major German company, Ufa.

In an attempt to limit Hollywood penetration, a number of nations enacted governmental protection for their film industries. The Germans, followed by the French, devised the 'contingent system', whereby Hollywood imports were restricted to a certain number per year. The British quota system, set up in 1927, was designed to set aside a certain proportion of screen time for British films on the home market, but it was framed in such a way that Hollywood companies were able to open up a production facility in Britain and make films that would qualify as 'British'.

Indeed Hollywood's continued international monopoly forced film entrepreneurs in other countries to struggle to please their native audiences, somehow to 'better' Hollywood. But with their control of international distribution, the Hollywood corporations could and would define appropriate standards of film style, form, content, and money-making. Imitation would not work, however competitive the product.

THE PICTURE PALACE

The production and distribution of films constituted only two of the three essential pegs of institutional Hollywood power. Movie moguls knew that money came through the theatrical box-office and thus sought some measure of control over exhibition, the third crucial sector of the film business. If 'Hollywood' was initially a group of California studios and offices for distribution throughout the world, it also came to include a cluster of movie palaces situated on main streets from New York to Los Angeles, Chicago to Dallas, and, within a short time, London and Paris as well.

The modern movie palace era commenced in 1914 with Samuel 'Roxy' Rothapfel's opening of the 3,000-seat Strand in 1914 in New York. Roxy combined a live vaudeville show with movies. His vaudeville 'presentation' offered a little something extra that attracted audiences away from more ordinary movie houses down the street. Roxy's shows opened with a house orchestra of fifty musicians playing the national anthem. Then came a newsreel, a travelogue, and a comic short, followed by the live stage show. Only then came the feature film.

The movie palace itself was far more than just a theatre.

The splendour of its architecture and the 'touch of class' lent by the ubiquitous ushers evoked a high-class fantasyland. Adolph Zukor soon caught on to Roxy's innovations and swooped in to purchase a string of movie palace theatres, thus gaining control of a fully integrated system of motion picture production, distribution, and exhibition.

Roxy was never able to sustain his economic enterprise and sold out. Chicago's Balaban & Katz, however, developed an economic system for making millions of dollars from their movie palace empire and, in the period immediately after the First World War, pioneering exhibitors took their cue for maximizing profits from the extraordinary success of this Chicago corporation. Indeed, Adolph Zukor approached Balaban & Katz and the two operations merged and created Paramount Pictures in 1925, marking the true affirmation of the Hollywood studio system in its three-part strategy of domination.

Balaban & Katz's success began when their Central Park Theatre opened in October 1917. This mighty picture palace became an immediate success, and Sam Katz, as corporate planner and president, put together a syndicate of backers who had all been wildly successful with their own Chicago-based businesses: Julius Rosenwald, head of Sears–Roebuck; William Wrigley, Jr., the chewing-gum magnate; and John Hertz, Chicago's taxi king and later innovator of the rental car network. With this support, Balaban & Katz expanded rapidly, leading the nascent movie exhibition business from a marginal leisure-time industry to centre stage in the economy of entertainment.

Balaban & Katz devoted strategic care to the location of theatres. Until then, theatre owners had chosen sites in the prevailing entertainment district. Balaban & Katz, however, constructed their first three movie palaces in outlying business centres on the edge of Chicago, away from the centre of town, selecting points at which the affluent middle class could be expected to congregate. For them it was not enough simply to open a movie house anywhere; one had to take the show to a transportation crossroads. Rapid mass transit had enabled the middle class and the rich to move to the edge of the city to the first true suburbs. It was this audience, able and willing to pay high prices for luxurious shows, that Balaban & Katz set out to cultivate.

The architecture of the movie palace insulated the public from the outside world and provided an opulent stage for the entertainment. The Chicago architectural firm headed by the brothers George and C. W. Rapp designed the new-style theatres by mixing design elements from nearly all past eras and contemporaneous locales, among them classic French and Spanish designs and contemporary art deco renderings. Film-goers soon came to expect triumphal arches, monumental staircases, and grand, column-lined lobbies (inspired by the Hall of

Mirrors in Versailles). Façades were equally dramatic. Strong vertical lines were accentuated by ascending pilasters, windows, and towers, sweeping high above the tiny adjacent shop-fronts. The actual theatre building was made from a rigid, steel shell, on which plaster-made decorations hung in brilliant purples, golds, azures, and crimsons. Massive steel trusses supported thousands of people in one or two balconies.

Outside, colossal electric signs could be seen for miles. The upright signs towered several storeys high, flashing forth their messages in several colours. Behind them, stained-glass windows reflected the lights into the lobby, evoking an ecclesiastical atmosphere and linking the theatre to the traditional, respected institutional architecture of the past.

Once inside, patrons weaved through a series of vestibules, foyers, lobbies, lounges, promenades, and waiting rooms designed to impress and excite. The lobbies and foyers were, if anything, more spectacular than the architectural fantasy outside. Decorations included opulent chandeliers, classical drapery on walls and entrances, luxurious chairs and fountains, and grand spaces for piano or organ accompaniment for waiting crowds. And since there always seemed to be a queue, keeping newly arriving customers happy was as important as entertaining those already seated. Inside the auditorium, everyone had a perfect view of the screen, and careful acoustical planning ensured the orchestral accompaniment to the silent films could be heard even in the furthest reaches of the balcony.

One commentator compared these Balaban & Katz theatres to baronial halls or grand hotels in which one might have tea or attend a ball. Balaban & Katz sought to make its upwardly mobile patrons feel as if they had come home to the haunts of a modern business tycoon.

Balaban & Katz offered free child care, rooms for smoking, and picture galleries in the foyers and lobbies. In the basement of each movie palace a complete playground included slides, sand-pits, and other objects of fun for younger children left in the care of nurses while their parents upstairs enjoyed the show.

Ushers maintained a constant quiet decorum within the auditorium proper. They guided patrons through the maze of halls and foyers, assisted the elderly and small children, and handled any emergencies. Balaban & Katz recruited their corps from male college students, dressed them in red uniforms with white gloves and yellow epaulettes, and demanded they be obediently polite even to the rudest of patrons. All requests had to end with a 'thank you'; under no circumstances could tips be accepted.

The Balaban & Katz stage shows outdid even Roxy by developing local talent into 'stars' to equal Mary Pickford or Charlie Chaplin. The shows were elaborate mini-musicals with spectacular settings and intricate lighting

effects. They celebrated holidays, fads of the day, heroic adventures, and all the highlights of the Roaring Twenties from the Charleston to the exploits of Charles Lindbergh to the new medium of radio. For their orchestras and organists, who provided music for the silent films, Balaban & Katz also depended on a star system. Jesse Crawford became an organist as well known as any Chicagoan of the 1920s. In 1923 his wedding to fellow organist Helen Anderson was the talk of Chicago's tabloids. When Sam Katz took the pair to New York, the Chicago newspapers mourned the loss in the same way they would the departure of a sports hero.

Most of the features described above could be easily copied by any theatre chain willing to make the necessary investment. One part of the Balaban & Katz show, however, was unique. Balaban & Katz offered the first air-conditioned movie theatres in the world, providing summertime comfort no middle-class citizen in the sweltering Midwestern states could long resist. After 1926 most important movie palaces either installed air conditioning or built the new theatre around it.

There had been crude experiments with blowing air across blocks of ice, but prior to Balaban & Katz's Central Park Theatre most movie houses simply closed during the summer or opened to tiny crowds. The movie palace air-conditioning apparatus took up an entire basement room with more than 15,000 feet of heavy-duty pipe, giant 240-horsepower electric motors, and two 1,000-pound flywheels.

Soon summer became the peak movie-going season. With its five-part strategy—location, architecture, service, stage shows, and air conditioning—Balaban & Katz set the scene for a redefinition of movie-going in the USA. The rest of the world followed cautiously, adopting or adapting some features of the new system as circumstances permitted. In most European cities prime sites for movie theatres continued to be in the traditional entertainment districts, though in Britain at least a number of well-equipped and opulent theatres were opened in the developing suburbs of major cities. In poorer countries and those with more equable climates air conditioning was an expensive luxury, and summer film-going never became as popular elsewhere as it did in North America. Hollywood took advantage of this to phase the release of major films, bringing them out on the domestic market in the summer and elsewhere in the world in the autumn.

With the merger with Famous Players, Sam Katz successfully transferred the Balaban & Katz system to Paramount's national chain of theatres. Other companies quickly followed suit: Marcus Loew with MGM, and Warner Bros. with their First National chain. But none could rival the success of Adolph Zukor and Paramount. As the silent era drew to a close, it was Zukor and Paramount who had the top stars, the most world-wide

Sid Grauman

(1879–1950)

During the 1920s there was no single movie exhibitor in the United States more famous than Sid Grauman and no theatre more famous than Grauman's Chinese on Hollywood Boulevard. Sidney Patrick Grauman revelled in his status as movie palace mogul, flamboyant in every respect, right down to his courtyard of world famous impressions in cement.

According to legend, Norma Talmadge stepped into a block of wet cement while visiting the Chinese Theatre during its construction, and thus was born the greatest of theatrical publicity tools. In time Gene Autry brought his horse Champion to imprint four hooves alongside cement impressions of Al Jolson's knee, John Barrymore's profile, Tom Mix's ten-gallon hat, and Harold Lloyd's glasses.

Grauman should also be remembered for his innovation of the stage show prologue; live shows, preceding silent films, thematically linked to the narrative of the feature. During the late 1920s Grauman was justifiably world famous for these prologues. Before Cecil B. DeMille's *King of Kings* (1927), Grauman had a cast of more than 100 play out five separate biblical scenes to fascinate and delight the audience.

Sid Grauman first tasted show business working with his father in tent shows during the 1898 Yukon Gold Rush. Temporarily rich, David Grauman moved the family to San Francisco and entered the nascent film industry during the first decade of the twentieth century. Father and son turned a plain San Francisco store-front into the ornate and highly profitable Unique Theatre. The 1906 San Francisco earthquake destroyed the competition and from a fresh start the Graumans soon became powers in the local film exhibition business.

Young Sid moved to Los Angeles to make his own mark on the world, and a decade later, in February 1918, opened the magnificent Million Dollar Theatre in downtown Los Angeles. The Million Dollar stood as the first great movie palace west of Chicago, an effective amalgamation of Spanish colonial design elements with Byzantine touches to effect an almost futurist design. In 2,400 seats citizens of Los Angeles could witness the best screen efforts nearby Hollywood companies were producing. Four years later Grauman followed up this success with his Egyptian Theatre on Hollywood Boulevard.

But the Chinese Theatre was Sid Grauman's crowning personal statement. At the grand opening on 19 May 1927, D. W. Griffith and Mary Pickford were present to praise Grauman's achievement. Outside a green bronze pagoda roof towered some 90 feet above an entrance that mimicked an oriental temple. Inside a central sunburst pendant chandelier hung 60 feet above 2,000 seats in a flame red auditorium with accents of jade, gold, and classic antique Chinese art reproductions.

Even Grauman's considerable theatrical skills proved inadequate as the Hollywood film industry acquired control of the exhibition arm of the movie business. During the Great Depression Hollywood needed managers who followed orders from central office, not pioneering entrepreneurs, and the coming of sound made Grauman's prologues *passé*. By 1930 the powerful Fox studio, located only a few miles closer to the Pacific Ocean, owned the Chinese Theatre, and Sid Grauman, showman extraordinary, friend of silent picture stars, was just another employee.

Through the 1930s and 1940s Grauman grew more and more famous in the eyes of the movie-going public, but his heyday was over. Grauman was like the stars uptown, under contract, taking orders from the studio moguls, helping promote the latest studio project. The rise—and fall—of Sid Grauman parallels the history of the motion picture industry in the United States, from its wild free-for-all beginnings to the standardized control by the Hollywood corporate giants.

DOUGLAS GOMERY

BIBLIOGRAPHY

Gomery, Douglas (1992), *Shared Pleasures*.

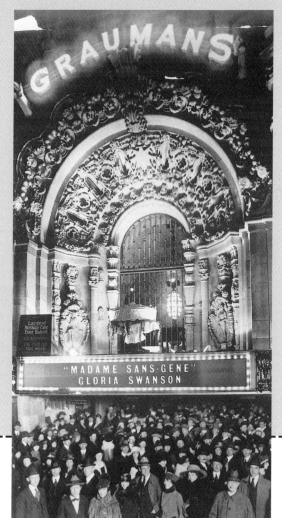

Sid Grauman and Gloria Swanson (in foreground) attending the Hollywood premiere of Léonce Perret's *Madame Sans-Gêne* at Grauman's Chinese Theatre in 1925

distribution, and the most extensive and prestigious theatre chain—the very model of the integrated business through which Hollywood's power was asserted.

This Hollywood system crested in the heady days prior to the Great Depression. Hollywood as an industrial institution had come to dominate the world of popular entertainment as no institution had before. The coming of sound simply eliminated competition from the stage and vaudeville. But change was on its way, precipitated by the Depression and by the rise of the new technologies of radio and television. Hollywood at the end of the 1920s and throughout the 1930s was faced by a series of shocks—falling audiences, the loss of some overseas markets, threats of censorship, and anti-monopoly legislation. But it adjusted and survived, thanks to the solid foundations laid by its pioneers.

Bibliography
Balio, Tino (ed.) (1985), *The American Film Industry*.
Bordwell, David, Staiger, Janet, and Thompson, Kristin (1985), *The Classical Hollywood Cinema*.
Gomery, Douglas (1986), *The Hollywood Studio System*.
—— (1992), *Shared Pleasures*.
Hampton, Benjamin B. (1931), *A History of the Movies*.
Jobs, Gertrude (1966), *Motion Picture Empire*.
Koszarski, Richard (1990), *An Evening's Entertainment*.

The World-Wide Spread of Cinema

RUTH VASEY

The world-wide spread of cinema has been dominated by the distribution and exhibition of Hollywood movies, despite the fact that film production has taken place around the world since the turn of the century. The first means of film production and projection were developed virtually simultaneously in France, Germany, and the United States in about 1895, with the earliest films typically comprising single shots of single scenes or incidents. Many of these early movies delighted audiences with their authentic rendering of snippets of 'reality', and French innovators Auguste and Louis Lumière seized upon the commercial possibilities inherent in the documentary capacities of the new medium. They trained a team of cameramen/projectionists to demonstrate their Cinématographe internationally, recording new footage as they went. By the end of July 1896 they had carried the invention to London, Vienna, Madrid, Belgrade, New York, St Petersburg, and Bucharest, creating widespread interest with their cinematic revelations of both the exotic and the familiar. By the end of the year they had been around the world, introducing the phenomenon of cinema to Egypt, India, Japan, and Australia. In the mean time Thomas Edison's projector, the Vitascope, was also popularizing the medium in the United States and Europe.

At the turn of the century motion picture production was essentially a cottage industry, accessible to any enthusiastic entrepreneur with a modicum of capital and know-how. The world's first feature film of over an hour's duration was made not in France or America but in Australia, where *The Story of the Kelly Gang* was produced in 1906; the theatrical company J. & N. Tait made the film without the benefit of any industrial infrastructure whatsoever. By 1912 Australia had produced thirty features, and feature-length productions had also been made in Austria, Denmark, France, Germany, Greece, Hungary (with fourteen features in 1912 alone), Italy, Japan, Norway, Poland, Romania, Russia, the United States, and Yugoslavia.

Despite the energy and commitment represented by this early flurry of film-making, singular achievements in the area of production were to prove less important than innovations in business organization in determining the shape of international film commerce. Again France was the first to seize the initiative in terms of foreign distribution. By 1908 the production company Pathé-Frères had established a network of offices to promote its products—mainly short dramas and comic scenarios—in areas including western and eastern Europe, Russia, India, Singapore, and the United States itself. In fact, in 1908 Pathé was the largest single supplier of films for the American market. Films by other French companies, as well as British, Italian, and Danish productions, were also circulating internationally at this time. By contrast, relatively scant foreign business was conducted by American production houses. Although the American companies Vitagraph and Edison were represented in Europe, their agents were more interested in buying European films for circulation in America than in promoting their own products abroad.

HOLLYWOOD'S RISE TO DOMINANCE

If there was little early sign of America's future dominance in the foreign field, the streamlining of the American industry's business organization in its home market

53

Erich von Stroheim

(1885–1957)

The actor and director known as 'Von' to his friends was born Erich Oswald Stroheim on 22 September 1885 in Vienna, to a middle-class Jewish family. In 1909 he emigrated to the United States, giving his name on arrival as Erich Oswald Hans Carl Maria von Stroheim. By the time he directed his first film *Blind Husbands* in 1919 he had converted to Catholicism and woven various legends about himself, eagerly seized on and elaborated by the Hollywood publicity machine. In these legends he was always an aristocrat, generally Austrian, with a distinguished record in the imperial army, but he also passed himself off as German, and an expert on German student life. His actual military record in Austria seems to have been undistinguished, and it is not known if he had ever been to university, let alone in Germany.

The 'German' version seems to have been merely, though bravely, opportunist, helping him to an acting career as an evil Prussian officer in films made during the anti-German fever of 1916-18, and contributing to his screen image as 'the man you love to hate'. But the Austrian identity struck deeper. He became immersed in his own legend, and increasingly assumed the values of the world he had left behind in Europe, a world of decadence but also (in both senses of the word) nobility.

As an actor he had tremendous presence. He was small (5' 5") but looked larger. His gaze was lustful and his movements were angular and ungainly, with a repressed energy which could break out into acts of chilling brutality. Both his charm and his villainy had an air of calculation—unlike, say, Conrad Veidt, in whom both qualities seemed unaffectedly natural.

His career as a director was marked by excess. Almost all his films came in over-long and over budget, and had to be salvaged (and in the course of it often ruined) by the studio. He had fierce battles with Irving Thalberg, first at Universal and then at MGM, which ended in the studio asserting control over the editing. To get the effects he wanted he put crew and cast through nightmares, shooting the climactic scenes in *Greed* on location in Death Valley in midsummer 1923, in temperatures of over 120° F. Some of this excess has been justified (first of all by Stroheim himself) in the name of realism, but it is better seen as an attempt to give a extra layer of conviction to the spectacle, which was also marked by strongly unrealistic elements. Stroheim's style is above all effective, but the effect is one of a powerful fantasy, drawing the spectator irresistibly into a fictional world in which the natural is indistinguishable from the grotesque. The true excess is in the passions of the characters—overdrawn creations acting out a mysterious and often tragic destiny.

On the other hand, as Richard Koszarski (1983) has emphasized, Stroheim was much influenced by the naturalism of Zola and his contemporaries and followers. But this too is expressed less in the representational technique than in the underlying sense of character and destiny. Stroheim's characters, like Zola's, are what they are through heredity and circumstance, and the drama merely enacts what their consequent destiny has to be.

Belief in such a theory is, of course, deeply ironic in Stroheim's case, since his own life was lived in defiance of it. Unlike his characters, he was what he had become, not what fate had supposedly carved him out to be.

What he had become, by 1925 if not earlier, was the unhappy exile, for ever banished from the turn-of-the-century Vienna which was his imaginary home. A contrast between Europe and America is a constant theme in his work, generally to the disadvantage of the latter. Even those of his films set in America, such as *Greed* (1924) or *Walking down Broadway* (1933) can be construed as barely veiled attacks on America's myth of its own innocence. Most of his other films are set in Europe (an exception is the monumental *Queen Kelly*, set mostly in Africa). Europe, and particularly Vienna, is a site of corruption, but also of self-knowledge. Goodness rarely triumphs in Stroheim's films, and love triumphs only with the greatest difficulty. Nostalgia in Stroheim is never sweet and he was as savage with Viennese myths of innocence as with American. His screen adaptation of *The Merry Widow* (1925) turned Lehar's operetta into a spectacle in which decadence, cruelty, and more than a hint of sexual perversion cloud the fantasy Ruritanian air.

The Merry Widow was a commercial success. Most of his other films were not. Stroheim's directing career did not survive the coming of the synchronized dialogue film, and he had increasing difficulty finding roles as an actor in the changed Hollywood climate. In his later years he moved uneasily between Europe and America in search of work and a home. In the last, unhappy decades of his life he created two great acting roles, as the camp commandant Rauffenstein in Renoir's *La Grande Illusion* ('The great illusion', 1937), and as Gloria Swanson's butler in Wilder's *Sunset Boulevard* (1950). It is for his acting that he is now best remembered. Of the films he directed, some have been lost entirely, while others have survived only in mangled versions. This tragedy (which was partly of his own making) means that his greatness as a filmmaker remains the stuff of legend—not unlike the man himself.

GEOFFREY NOWELL-SMITH

SELECT FILMOGRAPHY

As director
Blind Husbands (1919); The Devil's Pass Key (1920); Foolish Wives (1922); Merry-Go-Round (1923); Greed (1924); The Merry Widow (1925); Wedding March (1928); Queen Kelly (1929); Walking down Broadway (1933)

BIBLIOGRAPHY

Curtiss, Thomas Quinn (1971), *Von Stroheim*.
Finler, Joel (1968), *Stroheim*.
Koszarski, Richard (1983), *The Man You Loved to Hate: Erich von Stroheim and Hollywood*.

Opposite: Erich von Stroheim (as 'Eric von Steuben') turns his amorous attentions to Francellia Billington ('the wife') in *Blind Husbands* (1919)

was laying the foundations of its economic strength in the first fifteen years of the century. The motion picture market within the United States was, and has remained, by far the most lucrative in the world. In the years prior to the First World War American producers concentrated on consolidating that market under their own control. As Kristin Thompson (1985) points out, the relatively late entry of the Americans into serious international film commerce can be put down to the more ready profits waiting to be exploited in the domestic arena; the French market, by contrast, was relatively small, so it did not take French producers long to look abroad for new audiences for their products. The sheer size of the American exhibition field encouraged the application of standardized business practices, including increasingly systematic and efficient methods of production and distribution. Although a fully vertically integrated system of industrial organization did not emerge until the 1920s, the various branches of the industry were already tending towards combination in the 1910s. With the majority of economic power concentrated in the hands of relatively few players, the larger companies could afford to act as an exclusive oligopoly, collectively protecting the interests of existing corporations at the expense of newcomers—either domestic or international—with the result that after 1908 it became increasingly difficult for foreign companies to gain access to the American exhibition field. The implications of this situation for the subsequent history of world cinema were extremely far-reaching. It meant that the American producers eventually had consistent and virtually exclusive access to their own exceptionally lucrative market, enabling them to recoup most of the costs of expensive productions, or to go into profit, even before entering overseas distribution. As a result, the American industry could produce highly capitalized productions that outperformed their international rivals in terms of both production values and reliability of supply. Moreover, with costs largely being recovered in the domestic sphere, even the most lavish American productions could be offered to foreign exhibitors at affordable prices. In retrospect, it is apparent that the effective control of the domestic market by American producers was the factor that resulted in much of the world's motion picture commerce becoming a one-way affair.

Nevertheless, in the years prior to the First World War the inevitability of this outcome was by no means clear, either to American producers or to the Europeans, who were enjoying considerable success in the international arena. Frenchman Max Linder, working for Pathé, was probably the world's most popular comedian, not yet facing competition from Hollywood clowns such as Chaplin or Keaton. The Danish company Nordisk was distributing 370 films a year by 1913, making it second only to Pathé in terms of international sales; its star, Asta Nielsen,

Mary Pickford

(1893–1979)

Born Gladys Louise Smith in Toronto, Canada, in 1893, Pickford and her two siblings went on the stage at an early age to support their widowed mother. As Mary Pickford, Gladys made her New York stage début in 1907. Two years later she was hired by the American Mutoscope and Biograph Company to play a bit part in a D. W. Griffith one-reeler, *Her First Biscuits* (1909). Her screen presence and well-developed acting talent ensured her a central place in Griffith's troupe, and under his direction she appeared in virtually a film a week during 1909 and 1910. Biograph did not credit their actors by name, for fear that they would become too powerful. However, Pickford became famous as an innocent and engaging heroine; the 'Biograph Girl with the Curls'.

In late 1910 she left Biograph in search of greater control and a larger salary. After periods at various companies she settled at Adolph Zukor's Famous Players in 1913. She was touted in publicity as 'America's Foremost Film Actress'. Her professional stamina was legendary; she made seven features in 1914, eight in 1915. These films, particularly *Tess of the Storm Country* (Porter, 1914), cemented her screen image and the public's affection for her, and elevated her to the position of first female screen superstar.

Her Botticelli-esque blonde beauty sent American critics into barely suppressed erotic rapture. Yet her aura of dainty Victorian delicacy, so often emphasized in still photographs, was complicated on screen by a quality of independent asexuality. She was expert at playing the adolescent on the verge of womanhood, the good-natured tomboy posing as street tough, and the neglected working-class daughter. The success of these portrayals depended upon her extraordinary ability to capture natural details of everyday behaviour and to project an engaging, mischievous energy.

'America's Sweetheart' sold war bonds, gently preached the virtues of female equality, and scrupulously hid her grown-up failings, including several adulterous affairs. Nothing could touch her popularity, not even a divorce from her first husband to marry actor Douglas Fairbanks in 1920. In fact, her marriage to Fairbanks was a publicist's dream come true, and sealed the popularity of both stars. The couple became the royalty of Hollywood, reigning from their palatial mansion Pickfair. Their fame was not limited to America. In 1926 the couple received a rapturous welcome from crowds in Moscow. Pickford had become 'The World's Sweetheart'.

Pickford's success had much to do with her skills as an astute businesswoman, who carefully controlled her own image. At her peak, she assembled production teams, chose her co-stars, wrote scenarios, occasionally directed herself (without credit), or hired directors who would do what she told them.

In 1917 she began to produce her own Artcraft Pictures

for Paramount/Famous Players–Lasky. She made enormous amounts of money for the studio with films like *Poor Little Rich Girl* (Tourneur, 1917) and *Rebecca of Sunnybrook Farm* (1917) until she reputedly told Zukor she could no longer 'afford to work for $10,000 a week'. The unprecedented control she had over her career culminated in 1919 with the founding of United Artists with Fairbanks, Chaplin, and Griffith. This allowed her to oversee the production and the distribution of her films.

However, Pickford did not use her extraordinary professional freedom to increase the diversity of her roles until it was too late. UA films like *Pollyanna* (1920) and *Little Lord Fauntleroy* (1921) continued to portray her as the sweet adolescent. This conservatism was broken only once, in a daring (for her) collaboration with director Ernst Lubitsch, the costume drama *Rosita* (1923). The film was a critical and financial success, but Pickford could not break with her established image and, although now over 30, reverted back to sentimental adolescent girl roles in *Little Annie Rooney* (1925) and *Sparrows* (1926). The silent film audience never seemed to tire of this image.

However, under the pressure of talkies and changing cultural mores, she made a decisive transition to adult roles in her first sound film *Coquette* (1929); the film brought her profits and an Oscar, but Pickford's screen persona seemed increasingly out of step with the modern sexual ideals promulgated by the Jazz Age. She was, as Alistair Cooke has suggested, the woman every man wanted—for a sister.

Pickford retired from the screen in 1933 after her fourth talkie. The success of *Coquette* was never repeated, and her career did not recover from *The Taming of the Shrew* (1929), a disastrously unpopular talkie in which she had starred with Fairbanks; their first and last film together. She retreated to the legendary Pickfair and, it is said, to the dubious consolations of the bottle.

Fearful of public ridicule of her adolescent screen persona she bought the rights to her silent films with the apparent intention of having them destroyed on her death. Although she later relented, her films are still difficult to see, and this has contributed to the fixing of her image as the eternal innocent girl.

GAYLYN STUDLAR

SELECT FILMOGRAPHY

The Lonely Villa (1909); The New York Hat (1913); Tess of the Storm Country (1914/1922); The Poor Little Rich Girl (1917); Stella Maris (1918); Daddy Long Legs (1919); Little Lord Fauntleroy (1921); Rosita (1923); Little Annie Rooney (1925); My Best Girl (1927); Coquette (1929); The Taming of the Shrew (1929); Secrets (1933)

BIBLIOGRAPHY

Eyman, Scott (1990), *Mary Pickford: From Here to Hollywood.*
Pickford, Mary (1955), *Sunshine and Shadow.*

Opposite: Mary Pickford in *Little Annie Rooney* (1925)

enjoyed widespread international success. Italy was producing the most notable spectaculars on the world scene, making grand historical epics such as *Quo vadis?* (Enrico Guazzoni, 1913). Even when the war disrupted film industries across western Europe, and closed all but domestic markets to French production, the Americans were slow to expand their foreign sales: rather than dealing directly with the majority of their foreign customers, they allowed most of their overseas business to be conducted by foreign sales agents who re-exported American movies from London to destinations around the world. It was not until 1916, when the British imposed tariffs on foreign film trade, that the centre of movie distribution shifted from London to New York. The consequent increase in American control over foreign sales and rentals encouraged producers and distributors to take a more active and involved stance in foreign trade.

Between 1916 and 1918 the extent of the American industry's representation overseas increased markedly. Some companies preferred to sign agents overseas to act on their behalf, while others formed subsidiary branches to handle foreign distribution. Universal, which had established distribution facilities in Europe before the war, initiated new branches in the Far East, while Fox established a combination of agencies and branches in Europe, South America, and Australia. Famous Players–Lasky and Goldwyn both worked through agencies in South Africa, South America, Australia, Scandinavia, Central America, and Europe. While these patterns of expansion involved a measure of competition, particularly in Europe, it is notable that between them these four companies managed to encircle virtually the entire globe with regional networks. In 1920 American exports of exposed film stood at 175,233,000 feet, five times the pre-war figure. From this time onward the industry could depend on at least 35 per cent of its gross income arising from foreign sources. With the formerly powerful industries of France and Italy greatly reduced, the American companies found themselves in an unaccustomed position of international supremacy.

Throughout the silent period the American industry received assistance in its foreign operations from the Departments of State and Commerce. US consular offices co-operated in gathering a wealth of information relevant to motion picture trade, including audience preferences, conditions affecting exhibition, and activities of competitors. In 1927 Will Hays, president of the industry's trade association (the Motion Picture Producers and Distributors of America), successfully lobbied Congress for the establishment of a Motion Picture Department within the Department of Commerce, on the grounds that movies acted as 'silent salesmen' of American goods to audiences world-wide. Rewriting the nineteenth-century imperialist slogan that trade followed the flag, Hays proclaimed that now 'Trade Follows the Films'. Indeed, it seems likely that Hollywood's conspicuous display of material affluence was itself a factor attractive to audiences, both at home and abroad.

PROTECTIONISM

While Hollywood's flair for unofficial advertising may have won it friends amongst popular audiences and the US Congress, it also stirred up opposition to the American product amongst foreign governments. In 1927 the British government expressed concern that only 5 per cent of films shown in the British Empire were of Empire origin, while the vast majority were American, reflecting American values and showcasing American goods. A parliamentary inquiry concluded that the Empire would be better served by films reflecting values and products of an Imperial stamp. Arguments about the cultural influence of Hollywood were part of a pervasive discourse of anti-Americanism among European cultural élites. Bourgeois cultural nationalists feared the homogenizing influence of American mass culture, in which previously clear representations of class and nationality, such as costume and gesture, became increasingly undifferentiated. Ironically, the pervasiveness of Hollywood itself served as an impetus behind government initiatives to support film-making in Britain, as was equally the case in many other countries. Quite apart from ideological issues, large profits were at stake in box-office revenues: Britain constituted the most lucrative market in the world outside the United States, generating $165 million at the box-office in 1927. Its own level of film production in that year stood at forty-four features (4.85 per cent of films shown), compared to the 723 (81 per cent) that were imported from the USA. In France, the proportion of domestically produced product exhibited was slightly higher, with 74 French features being shown (12.7 per cent) compared with 368 American imports (63.3 per cent).

The only European nation in which domestic production exceeded imports in the late 1920s was Germany. Commercial film production had begun to develop in Germany from about 1911, but it was not conspicuous amongst early European producers. During the World War the country's isolation from French, British, Italian, and American sources of film supply encouraged domestic production. With an eye to both the entertainment and the propaganda values of the medium, the German government helped to underwrite the development of the local industry. A merger of several companies brought about the formation of the large combine Universum-Film Aktiengesellschaft, or Ufa, which was secretly funded by the State. In addition to its studio facilities (which included a state-of-the-art complex that was constructed in 1921 at Neubabelsberg near Potsdam) it also served as a distributor, handling the products of other German

studios in addition to its own output. In the 1920s it continued to make capital acquisitions, including the Danish company Nordisk and its foreign cinema circuits: unlike France, which by now concentrated mainly on production for domestic consumption, Germany remained committed to expansion in the foreign field. Indeed, it needed receipts from foreign markets to support its level of production. The number of features produced peaked at 646 in 1921 (compared to 854 produced by Hollywood in that year), and thereafter declined to about 200 films a year, or roughly a third of Hollywood's output, at the end of the decade.

Germany was at the forefront of initiatives that were designed to counter Hollywood's hegemony in Europe. In 1925, when the American share of the German market was on the increase, the government responded by instituting a 'contingent' plan that was designed to limit the proportion of foreign films that were exhibited in the German domestic market. In effect, the new regulation stated that only as many films could be imported each year as were produced within Germany. In 1927 German studios produced a total of 241 features, which amounted to 46.3 per cent of the total number of films exhibited in that year. American imports amounted to only 36.8 per cent, with the remainder being drawn from a variety of other foreign sources. The 'contingent' paved the way for many similar kinds of protective legislation by the film-producing nations of Europe: Austria, Hungary, France, Britain, and Australia all introduced quota legislation of some kind in the late 1920s. The British Films Act of 1928, for example, specified a gradual increase in the proportion of domestically produced film to be distributed in the British market, beginning with 7.5 per cent in the first year.

There were many difficulties inherent in making such regulations work smoothly, especially in countries where infrastructure for film-making was less advanced than it was in Germany. In trying to formulate appropriate protectionist measures, governments were forced to perform delicate balancing acts between the economic and cultural imperatives of production, distribution, exhibition, and consumption. Probably the most intransigent problem was that exhibitors in most countries favoured American movies, for obvious reasons: they arrived like clockwork and they made profits. In every country (including the United States) investment in sites of exhibition amounted to more than total investment in production. The culturally based protectionist arguments of producers therefore had to contend with weighty resistance from exhibitor lobbies which sought to retain unrestricted access to American material. Another problem was that quotas could result in the production of rapid, substandard films (often funded by national subsidiaries of Hollywood studios) designed simply to meet the regulations and allow for the concomitant importation of the maximum number of American products. 'Quota quickies', as they were known in Britain, simply had the effect of eroding the prestige of the local product.

BRITAIN AND THE EMPIRE

Australia, Canada, and New Zealand were hopeful that British quota legislation could lead to a 'film-buying' group amongst the film-producing members of the British Empire, perhaps countering some of the advantages of America's exclusive home market. The requirement that Empire films should be afforded certain minimum amounts of screen time in Britain raised the possibility that countries throughout the Empire would benefit first through the exhibition of their films in the British Isles and secondly through their mutual distribution throughout the other countries of the Empire. In practice, however, this arrangement favoured the products of the relatively highly capitalized British industry, and did very little to boost production in other countries. Empire countries remained overwhelmingly dependent upon imported films, most of which were American. In 1927, 87 per cent of Australian and New Zealand film imports originated in Hollywood, compared with 5 per cent from Britain and 8 per cent from other countries. In Canada the proportion of American product was even higher, possibly reaching over 98 per cent. Hollywood's Canadian business was integrated into the domestic US distribution network to the extent that American distributors typically classified Canadian revenue as domestic income. In India at least 80 per cent of films shown in the late 1920s were American, even though twenty-one studios manufactured local films, eight or nine of them in regular production. (Although its narrow range of distribution restricted its cinematic and social influence, Indian film production later burgeoned, with production levels exceeding those of any other country, including the United States, from the 1970s on.)

Australia had the remarkable distinction of being the world's leading importer of Hollywood film footage in 1922, 1926, 1927, and 1928. However, this does not imply that Australia was the American industry's most lucrative customer nation during those years. The relative importance of markets as generators of revenue for Hollywood's coffers depended upon a range of factors including population size, per capita income, distribution costs, and rates of foreign exchange. In the final analysis, Britain was always Hollywood's most important foreign market, generating approximately 30 per cent of foreign income in the late 1920s. In 1927 it was followed in importance by Australasia (15 per cent), France (8.5 per cent), Argentina and Uruguay (7.5 per cent), Brazil (7 per cent), and Germany (5 per cent).

FILM EUROPE

The idea of countering America's dominance abroad through co-operative international action gained some currency in Europe in the 1920s. The so-called 'Film Europe' movement consisted of various European initiatives, carried out between 1924 and 1928, aimed at joint production and reciprocal distribution of films in the European sphere. Film production on a small scale was carried out all over Europe in the 1920s: for example, in 1924 feature films were made in Austria (30 films), Belgium (4), Denmark (9), Finland (4), Greece (1), Hungary (9), the Netherlands (6), Norway (1), Poland (8), Romania (1), Spain (10), Sweden (16), and Switzerland (3). However, the major participants in Film Europe were the principal producers of western Europe: Germany (228), France (73), and Great Britain (33). The general idea was to create a kind of cinematic Common Market by breaking down sales barriers to European movies within Europe, allowing a larger base for production than any nation could manage individually. Ideally, the movement would give European producers dominance within their own region as a prelude to a renewed push into the wider global market. In 1924 an arrangement for mutual distribution between Ufa and the French company Établissements Aubert raised hopes that co-operative ventures would gather momentum, but other deals were slow to eventuate. In 1925 the solidarity of the movement was shaken when Ufa ran into financial difficulties and was bailed out by American studios; part of the settlement of the loan required that a specified number of films by Paramount and MGM be given exhibition in Germany, while Ufa films were given reciprocal distribution in the United States. Production and distribution within Europe did increase at the expense of Hollywood as a result of the 'contingent' and quota arrangements of the late 1920s, but the change was never dramatic. As Thompson (1985) shows, France benefited least: when American imports fell in any of the participating countries the difference was made up mainly with German films, and a few from Britain.

If silent films had remained the norm, perhaps Film Europe would have continued to gain ground, but it could not survive the introduction of sound. The effect of talking pictures was to splinter this incipient unity into its component language groups. Any sense of cohesion that had arisen from the shared determination to resist the American industry was undermined by the local cultural imperative of hearing the accents of one's own language. In Italy, for example, a law was passed in 1929 prohibiting the projection of a movie in any language other than Italian, and similar strictures were temporarily instituted in Portugal and Spain. Disastrously for the producers in France and Germany, they found themselves alienated from the highly lucrative British market, leaving that field

Douglas Fairbanks
(1883–1939)

In the autumn of 1915 a Broadway actor named Douglas Fairbanks made his first appearance on the screen. Although Triangle Pictures' expectations for him were modest, Fairbanks's début film, *The Lamb* (1915), was a smash hit. Audiences loved him in the role of Gerald, a 'mollycoddle' whose genteel, old-money ways were corrected by tapping his pioneer heritage through proper Western adventure. Soon Fairbanks was starring in one 'athletic comedy' a month. The standard formula for these was established on his third film, *His Picture in the Papers* (1916), a clever urban satire penned by scenarist Anita Loos and directed by John Emerson. These films earned him the nicknames of 'Dr Smile', 'Douggie', and 'Mr Pep'. He was Hollywood's primary cinematic exponent of optimism and a bouncing, exuberant masculinity that made the world a playground to be scaled, leapt over, and swung through.

It was clear to critics and audiences that Fairbanks was bringing the same character into every film, but it left few complaining: he was virtually unrivalled in popularity. During the late 1910s, Fairbanks gained increasing control over his productions. He moved from Triangle to Artcraft, a prestigious, artist-controlled division of Paramount. There, he continued his collaboration with Loos and Emerson with more clever satires of modern American life. Quack psychology, food faddism, the peace movement, even Rooseveltian nostalgic primitivism, all became fodder for good-humoured kidding. In one of his most successful pictures of this period, *Wild and Woolly* (1917), Fairbanks plays a childish New York railway heir who is sent out West to supervise a paternal project. To gain the railway's business, Bitter Creek accommodates him by turning their modern-day community into an 1880s boom town complete with Wild West shoot-outs (with blanks) and a 'prairie flower' of a girl.

Like his hero Theodore Roosevelt, Fairbanks became a cultural icon of the 'strenuous life' so touted in American discourse as the antidote to 'over-civilization', to urban life, and to feminine influence. Fairbanks, however, drained this masculine ideal of its bellicose quality and substituted a boyish charm. Audiences found him the perfect balance between Victorian gentility and modern vitality.

In 1919, Fairbanks joined other top box-office draws Charles Chaplin, wife-to-be Mary Pickford, and director D. W. Griffith in the formation of United Artists. There he had greater control of his films, and they began to change. He turned from contemporary comedies to costume dramas like *The Mark of Zorro* (1920), an epic that played off Fairbanks' penchant for transmutation between masculinities, here between the effete Spaniard Don Cesar Vega and Zorro, the vigorous masked hero. Fairbanks repeatedly turned to stories drawn from literature either written for boys or popular with them, like Dumas's *The Three Musketeers* (1921) with its youthful romantic hero D'Artagnan.

Fairbanks's artistic independence at UA led to more technically and aesthetically ambitious films: *Robin Hood* (1922), *The Thief of Bagdad* (1924), and *The Black Pirate* (1926), which are the epitome of the humorous adventure epic. By the end of the silent period, however, Fairbanks's exuberance was beginning to wane as he entered his late forties, and he decisively ended his silent film career with an elegantly produced swan-song to boyish fantasy, *The Iron Mask* (1929), a film that ends, notably, with D'Artagnan's death.

Like Mary Pickford, Fairbanks had a youthful image that was linked in the public imagination with the heyday of the silent cinema. Neither of these great silent stars managed to re-establish their careers after the coming of sound. Fairbanks starred in a number of unsuccessful talkies before his premature death in 1939.

GAYLYN STUDLAR

SELECT FILMOGRAPHY

The Lamb (1915); His Picture in the Papers (1916); Wild and Woolly (1917); The Mollycoddle (1920); The Mark of Zorro (1920); The Three Musketeers (1921); Robin Hood (1922); The Thief of Bagdad (1924); Don Q, Son of Zorro (1925); The Black Pirate (1926); The Iron Mask (1929); The Private Life of Don Juan (1934)

BIBLIOGRAPHY

Cooke, Alistair (1940), *Douglas Fairbanks: The Making of a Screen Character*.
Schickel, Richard, and Fairbanks, Douglas, Jr. (1975), *The Fairbanks Album*.

Douglas Fairbanks in Raoul Walsh's *The Thief of Bagdad* (1924)

wide open for the Americans. British manufacturers themselves adopted sound film production with enthusiasm, but were now more interested in the ready-made English-speaking market of the British Empire than in the problematic European arena. They were also quick to recognize new potential for trade in the American market, and were inclined to enter into deals across the Atlantic rather than across the English Channel. Several Hollywood companies, including Warner Bros., United Artists, Universal, and RKO, organized tie-ups with producers in England or entered into production there themselves, encouraged by the need to secure product to satisfy the British quota.

The USSR was not directly involved in Film Europe, although some Soviet films found their way into European circulation through the agency of a German Communist organization (the Internationale Arbeitershilfe). The relationship of the Soviet film industry to Hollywood output was quite different from that of the western Europeans: for a few years in the early and mid-1920s American product was welcomed for its revenue-raising potential. Since the whole industry was nationalized, profits earned at the box-office could be put straight back into Soviet film production. The stream of imports was reduced to a trickle after 1927 when Soviet films first generated more revenue than imported products, and in the 1930s imports virtually ceased altogether. For their part, Soviet movies gained very limited exposure in the United States in the 1920s and 1930s through the New York office of the distributor Amkino.

Japanese films did not generally receive any international exposure at all. Yet, amazingly, in the years 1922–32 Japan was the world's leading producer of feature films. Interest in film had been strong amongst the Japanese since the inception of the medium, and domestic business was profitable. Japanese studios reputedly manufactured 875 features in 1924—some 300 more than the USA in the same year—marketing them all exclusively within its own domestic sphere. The five major companies were vertically integrated, and so wielded decisive control over their industry much as the major studios did in the United States. Cinemas tended to show either Japanese or foreign products but not both, and the majority of theatres catered to the less expensive local product. Although Hollywood companies were well represented in Japan, the Americans probably only enjoyed about 11 per cent of the market in the late 1920s, with European movies comprising a considerably smaller share.

HOLLYWOOD AND THE WORLD MARKET

The Japanese motion picture, designed for an audience conspicuous in its cultural homogeneity, may never have had a future as a product for export. On the other hand, the American product seems to have been universally well received.

Will Hays liked to explain the movies' popularity in terms of their historical appeal to the polyglot immigrant communities of the large American cities; he claimed that American producers necessarily developed a style of filmic communication that was not dependent upon literacy or other specific cultural qualifications. Perhaps popular audiences were attracted by fast-paced action and the optimistic, democratic outlook that had always characterized American films, as well as by their unusually high production values. The structure of the American domestic market itself supported the high capitalization of American movies, since controlled distribution practices discouraged overproduction and led to relatively high levels of investment in each individual project. At the same time, foreign receipts were an integral part of Hollywood's economic structure in the 1920s, and the studios therefore consciously tailored aspects of their output to the tastes of foreign consumers. The higher the budget of the movie, the more comprehensively the foreign market needed to be taken into account. Smaller films did not have to be shown everywhere to make their money back, and consequently had to make fewer allowances for foreign sensibilities. The most obvious concession to foreign tastes in 'prestige' productions lay in the selection and promotion of stars with international drawing power. Foreign audiences often responded particularly warmly to their own compatriots when they appeared in the full international context of the Hollywood industry. When Hollywood producers 'poached' acting talent from other national industries it not only weakened their competitors, it also recruited the affections and loyalties of foreign populations. Examples of European actors who were to be contracted to Hollywood studios include Charles Laughton, Maurice Chevalier, Marlene Dietrich, Charles Boyer, Robert Donat, Greta Garbo, and many others. Garbo constitutes a particularly conspicuous example of the influence of foreign tastes. Although she is remembered today as the quintessential screen goddess of the late 1920s and 1930s, she was never overwhelmingly popular in the United States. Her reputation depended upon her immense following abroad, and her films consistently depended upon the foreign market to take them into profit.

It was not just actors who were recruited from foreign industries, but also technical workers of all kinds, notably directors and cameramen. It was a logical business move for an industry that could afford it to buy up the best staff in the world. As a tactic, there was a capitalist elegance about it: only the strongest national industries could offer the training and experience that would make a technician attractive to Hollywood. Once the acquisition had been made not only was the American industry inherently strengthened but its most immediate competitors were proportionately weakened. The industry's explanation for this policy was that it allowed producing companies to make products best fitted for international consumption. For example, Hays talked about 'drawing into the American art industry the talent of other nations in order to make it more truly universal', and this explanation is not wholly fatuous. Whether or not it was the original intention behind Hollywood's voracious programme of acquisition, the fact that the studios contained many émigrés (predominantly European) probably allowed a more international sensibility to inform the production process. Whatever the reasons, Hollywood's particular achievement was to design a product that travelled well. Even considering the studios' corporate might, without this factor American movies could not have become the most powerful and pervasive cultural force in the world in the 1920s.

In addition to the explosion of film commerce that characterized the first three decades of the century, the silent period was also marked by the widespread circulation of cinematic ideas. No national cinematic style developed in isolation. Just as the Lumières' apprentices carried the fundamentals of the art around the globe within a year, new approaches to filmic expression continued to find their way abroad, whether or not they were destined for widespread commercial release. The German and French industries may not have been able to compete with the Americans abroad, but their products nevertheless circulated in Europe, Japan, China, and many other markets. The Soviets professed their admiration for Griffith even as they developed their theories of montage, while Mary Pickford and Douglas Fairbanks were held spellbound by Eisenstein's *Battleship Potemkin* (1925). By the time sound arrived, cinema all around the world was already capable of speaking many languages.

Bibliography
Jarvie, Ian (1992), *Hollywood's Overseas Campaign*.
Thompson, Kristin (1985), *Exporting Entertainment*.
Vasey, Ruth (1995), *Diplomatic Representations: The World According to Hollywood, 1919–1939*.

The First World War and the Crisis in Europe

WILLIAM URICCHIO

The summer of 1914 witnessed the opening of the Panama Canal, the start of production on D. W. Griffith's *The Birth of a Nation*, and the assassination of Archduke Ferdinand of Austria. Each of these events, in its own way, would tangibly influence the course of film history. The canal would stimulate the development of the US shipping industry, providing the film industry with an infrastructure for greater international distribution. Griffith's film would contribute to the transformation of film production practices and distribution techniques, all of which helped the US industry to triumph over its European competitors. And the Archduke's fate triggered the Great War, realigning the global political economy and helping to destroy the once internationally prominent film industries of France, England, and Italy.

The contours of international political, economic, and cultural power emerged from the war fundamentally transformed. Changes of a magnitude almost unthinkable before the war appeared on the political front in the form of a republic in Germany, a revolutionary government in Russia, and women voters in the USA and Britain. The USA grew from a pre-war parochial and introspective giant, lacking the vision and shipping resources for world trade, into an assertively international dynamo, armed with ample product and the means to deliver it. The balance of international political power, banking, trade, and finance had decisively turned in the USA's favour. The cultural upheaval created by the war was equally profound. Simply put, the war hurled Europe into the twentieth century. Social hierarchies, epistemological and ethical systems, and representational conventions all changed radically between 1914 and 1918. The very concepts of time, space, and experience, recast by the writings of Einstein and Freud, found something close to mainstream tolerance in the form of Cubism, Dada, and Expressionism. But just as significantly, the old, élite cultures of Europe gave way in many sectors to the new mass culture dominated by the United States.

The motion picture industry came out of the war as both emblem and instrument of the cultural and economic realignment that would characterize the remainder of the century.

In broad terms, the pre-1914 domination of international production and distribution by the French, Italians, and English gave way by 1918 to the expansionist interests of the US studios and a very different vision of the cinema. The war not only disrupted the trade patterns so crucial to the traditional European powers, it also exacted a heavy price in terms of the lives, material, and ongoing experimentation so vital to film production. And, in very different ways, it assisted in the successful transformation of the US, German, and ultimately Russian industries.

Despite the best attempts of the Motion Picture Patents Company (MPPC—popularly known as 'the Trust') to limit competition within the USA in the pre-war era by licensing domestic producers and restricting imports, the US market proved extremely attractive to leading European producers whose industries were predicated upon international distribution. Pathé-Frères, for example, had penetrated the market long before its membership in the MPPC, and by 1911 opened its own US production studios and led fellow Trust members in profits, while Urban-Eclipse, Gaumont, and later Cines product appeared on American screens thanks to MPPC member George Kleine. Many of the other large European producers, however, offered their films to the quickly growing independent movement. Constant litigation and shifting organizational alliances encouraged companies such as Denmark's Nordisk Kompagni (Great Northern Film Company) and Italy's Ambrosio (Ambrosio America Co.) to open their own US offices, and sometimes, as in the case of Éclair, even laboratories and studios. The pre-war assault upon the American market was not unique; nations such as Germany, Austria, Hungary, Russia, and the Netherlands found themselves the targets of the same internationally oriented production companies, without the organized resistance offered by America's Trust. Reflecting larger trade patterns, French, Italian, and British films also dominated the import markets of countries in South and Central America, Asia, Africa, and Australia.

Despite the prominence of Pathé-Frères in the USA, and of French product world-wide, the situation would soon shift dramatically. A war-induced production slump, changes in industry practice, direct government intervention into film affairs, and disrupted international trade, all provided American producers with a market opening. The US industry, however, largely insulated from the ravages of war by the nation's neutrality until April 1917, was anything but peaceful. The years 1912 to 1915 saw the demise of the MPPC, the fatal weakening of many of its members, and the simultaneous rise of an oligopoly engineered by entrepreneurs such as Zukor, Fox, and Laemmle. By standardizing production practices through strict divisions of labour and elaborate organizational hierarchies, by seizing market advantage through such tactics as the systematic exploitation of the star system, and by controlling film distribution and exhibition through techniques such as direct theatrical competition and block booking, the oligopoly transformed the character of the industry and its products.

The war would contribute to the growth of the studios by weakening foreign competition both domestically and internationally, opening the way for post-war US domination. But in many cases, the seeds of change could

already be found in the immediate pre-war years. In the summer of 1914, as Europe's leaders shuttled diplomatic briefs and its people prepared to mobilize, America's MPPC neared the end of its long legal battles and prepared to abandon its protectionist barriers. The US film market would never again be so open to imports, but meanwhile old Trust members such as Eastman Kodak and Vitagraph had themselves already launched an increasingly effective export counter-offensive. For example Vitagraph, the leading American film exporter prior to the war, opened its main European offices in Paris in 1906 and by 1908 had built a complete film laboratory there from which it sent prints to its distribution offices in Italy, England, and Germany. French domination of the international industry in the pre-war period notwithstanding, American films competed for space on Paris screens before 1914. As Richard Abel (1984) points out, increasing competition from American and Italian producers, together with a series of legal and financial pressures, weakened France's grip on some of its traditional markets.

Shortly before the declaration of war, as the French economy braced for an intense but short conflict, its film industry ground to a temporary halt. General mobilization would empty the studios of their personnel, the idle spaces instead finding use as temporary barracks, and Pathé's film stock factory at Vincennes would be converted to the production of war materials. Despite these adverse conditions, within a few months of the war's declaration production quickly resumed in France, although not at pre-war levels, with Pathé (shooting in the USA) and Gaumont, for example, creating extremely successful serials such as *Les Mystères de New York* ('The Mysteries of New York', Pathé, 1915–16) and Feuillade's *Les Vampires* ('The Vampires', 1915–16). But as the war dragged on and Charles Pathé sought to supply his far-flung empire with films, his company increasingly took on the character of a distribution agency for other companies despite its continued support of independent productions. In so restructuring, Pathé led the French industry to the same fate as the British, emphasizing distribution at the expense of regularized production.

The cultural presence of the United States in French life increased thanks in part to Pathé's reliance on its American studios for film production. But more directly, American products in the form of Chaplin and Lloyd comedies and William S. Hart Westerns not only filled the gaps left by domestic producers, they generated a positive enthusiasm among French audiences and served as signs of the erosion of pre-war cultural value systems. The remarkable popularity of the action-adventure female protagonist in many of the wartime French serials, and the eager acceptance of America's 'new' culture (displacing audiences' recent infatuation with Italian classical spectacles), points to the transformation of popular taste

Frank Borzage

(1894–1962)

The son of an Italian stone mason, Frank Borzage was born in Salt Lake City. One of fourteen children, he left home at fourteen to join a travelling theatrical troupe and soon became a member of Gilmour Brown's stock company, playing character parts in mining camps throughout the West. In 1912 Borzage went to Los Angeles, where producer-director Thomas Ince hired him as an extra, then leading man in two and three-reel Westerns. In 1916, he began directing films in which he starred; two years later, he gave up acting for directing.

Borzage's early films as actor/director explore characters and situations that recur in his later work. As Hal, the dissolute son of a millionaire in *Nugget Jim's Partner* (1916), a drunk Borzage argues with his father and hops a freight car which bears him to a western mining town. Here he encounters Nugget Jim, rescues Jim's daughter from her dreary life as a dance hall girl, and creates with them an idyllic world of their own. Slightly-built and curly-headed, Borzage conveys the innocence, energy, and optimism that became the trademark of Charles Farrell's performances for the director in *7th Heaven* (1927), *Street Angel* (1928), *Lucky Star* (1929) and *The River* (1929).

Borzage's origins inform a number of his films set in lower and working class milieux. His first major success was an adaptation of Fannie Hurst's *Humoresque* (1920), which describes the rise to fame of a young violinist from the teeming Jewish ghetto on New York's lower east side and his efforts, as wounded war veteran, to recover his ability to play again. The love story of *Seventh Heaven*,

which earned Borzage the first Academy Award for Best Director and which *Variety* labelled the 'perfect picture', involves the rescue of a gamine of the Parisian streets by a sewer worker. *Bad Girl* (1931), another Oscar winner, was a work of tenement realism, favourably compared to Vidor's *Street Scene* (1931) by contemporary critics, exploring the mundane routines of courtship, marriage, pregnancy, and birth, and celebrating the triumphs and tragedies of an average young couple.

Borzage specialized in narratives dealing with couples beset by social, economic, and/or political forces which threaten to disrupt their romantic harmony. The hostile environments of war and social and economic turmoil function both as an obstacle to his lovers' happiness and the very condition of their love, against which they must affirm their feelings for one another. In many of his films, the context of war obstructs the efforts of young lovers to establish a space for themselves apart from that of the more cynical and worldly characters around them.

Throughout his career, Borzage denounced war and violence; *Liliom* (1930) condemns domestic abuse; a profound pacifism underlies *A Farewell to Arms* (1932), and *No Greater Glory* (1934); and he emerged as one of Hollywood's first and most confirmed anti-fascists, dramatizing the evils of totalitarian movements in post-war Germany in *Little Man, What Now?* (1934), and openly attacking fascism well before American entry into World War II in *The Mortal Storm* (1940).

Borzage's vision is genuinely Romantic in its emphasis upon the primacy and authenticity of feeling. His lovers emerge as nineteenth-century holdovers in a dehumanized and nihilistic modern world. The form which Borzage's romanticism most often takes is a secularized religious allegory. In *7th Heaven*, *Street Angel*, *Man's Castle*

(1933), and *Little Man, What Now?*, his edenic lovers transform their immediate space into a virtual heaven on earth. Chico, the hero in *7th Heaven*, dies and is mysteriously reborn; Angela, the heroine in *Street Angel*, becomes an angel, a transformation mirrored in the hero's madonna-like portrait of her. *Strange Cargo* (1940), which was banned by the Catholic church in several American cities, provides perhaps the most overt religious allegory. In it, a group of escaped convicts and other outcasts follow a map, written inside the cover of a Bible, through a tropical jungle. Their 'exodus' concludes with a hazardous sea voyage in a small open boat and with the miraculous apotheosis of their Christ-like guide. Borzage's purest lovers appear in *Till We Meet Again* (1944) in which the director fashions an unstated, repressed romantic liaison between an American aviator shot down behind enemy lines and the novice from a French convent who poses as his wife in order to escort him to safety.

According to Hervé Dumont (1993), Borzage's basic narrative pattern in his romantic melodramas was that of Mozart's *Magic Flute*, and involved a symbolic struggle resembling the rites of passage embodied in the initiation ceremonies of Freemasonry. Borzage joined the Masons in 1919, eventually rising to the 32nd grade ('Master of the Royal Secret') in 1941. Like Mozart's Sarastro, Borzage oversees the passage of young lovers through a series of trials and ordeals to achieve a state of spiritual enlightenment and transformation.

Borzage's repudiation of contemporary reality in favour of an emotional and spiritual inner world proved to be out of step with post-war American culture. After 1945 he made only four films, and his attempt to retell the great love story of *7th Heaven* to a new generation of filmgoers in *China Doll* (1958) failed to find a receptive audience. Though various revivals of his films in the United States, Britain, and France in the 1970s attempted to re-establish his status as a major force in film melodrama, his work, unlike the more sophisticated and 'modern' cinema of Douglas Sirk, has yet to achieve the critical recognition it deserves.

JOHN BELTON

SELECT FILMOGRAPHY

Humoresque (1920); Lazybones (1925); 7th Heaven (1927); Street Angel (1928); Lucky Star (1929); Bad Girl (1931); A Farewell to Arms (1932); Man's Castle (1933); Little Man, What Now? (1934); History Is Made at Night (1937); Three Comrades (1938); Strange Cargo (1940); The Mortal Storm (1940); I've Always Loved You (1946); Moonrise (1948); China Doll (1958); The Big Fisherman (1959)

BIBLIOGRAPHY

Belton, John (1974), *The Hollywood Professionals*.
Dumont, Hervé (1993), *Frank Borzage: Sarastro à Hollywood*.
Lamster, Frederick (1981), *Souls Made Great Through Love and Adversity*.

Opposite: Charles Farrell ('I'm a very remarkable fellow') with Janet Gaynor in a scene from *Seventh Heaven* (1927)

which would reinforce America's market advantage in the post-war era.

The British film industry, in contrast to the French, experienced a steady production decline well before the war, but, as Kristin Thompson points out in her analysis of trade patterns (1985), England enjoyed a strong distribution and re-export business. With its large domestic exhibition market, the world's most developed shipping and sales network, a system of dependent colonial and commonwealth trading partners, and until 1915 tariff-free imports, Britain served as the heart of pre-war international export. On the eve of the war, however, although England had traditionally provided the USA's largest export market (with Germany a distant second), elaborate French and Italian productions successfully competed for an increased share of the business. This momentary deviation would more than be rectified as the USA went on to command the allegiance of wartime British viewers as never before.

The events of the summer of 1914 and growth of the US studio system would profoundly alter the character of the British industry. The disruption of Continental markets (the loss of Germany to British trade, for example), difficulties in shipping generated by insurance requirements and reallocation of cargo space to war-essential materials, and an import duty on films, all proved disastrous to an industry predicated upon distribution and re-export. Film seemed a particularly troublesome commodity since the raw material of film stock, cellulose nitrate, was both highly flammable (a potential threat to war-essential shipping) and capable of being used in the manufacture of explosives (and, given Germany's total reliance on imported nitrates, of natural interest to Britain's enemy). But the rise of the USA's aggressively entrepreneurial studio system compounded Britain's problems. Prior to the war, with the exception of Vitagraph, American Trust members had been content to carry on the vast majority of their trade with England, which in turn re-exported US films to Continental and world-wide markets. Thompson credits the examples set by the international marketing of *The Birth of a Nation* (1915) and *Civilization* (1916), both of which required country-by-country negotiations, with a wider change in US industry practice. By 1916, companies such as Fox, Universal, and Famous Players–Lasky opened their own offices or negotiated through their own agents in locations around the world. Fortunately for the studios, the boom in the US shipping industry triggered in part by the Panama Canal (evident in increased shipbuilding and the development of a world-wide network of US banks) greatly facilitated their expansionist policies.

Italy, the site of Europe's other major film industry, eventually suffered much the same fate as its French and British allies. The Italian government entered the conflict some nine months after the principals and was initially spared the disruption facing its neighbours. In the years leading up to the war, the Italian industry experienced growing momentum thanks in part to its spectacle films. With casts numbering in the thousands and lavish, often authentic, sets, films such as *Quo vadis?* (1913), *The Last Days of Pompeii* (1913), and *Cabiria* (1914) captured the attention of viewers around the world, often at the expense of American competition. The depressed economic conditions which permitted such labour-intensive productions, however, also required the Italian studios to generate export sales in order to survive. In the context of France's dropping production levels and Britain's growing neglect of many former markets, Italy's delay in entering the war both stimulated its already prominent market position and at least through 1916 provided the exports it so badly needed. From that point on, however, Italy faced the same array of obstacles as most of the belligerent nations: inadequate supplies of film stock, military priorities in shipping, and redeployment of the work-force, to which Italy could add a slowly collapsing economy.

Not surprisingly, the war stifled the emerging film industries of German-occupied nations such as Belgium and belligerent powers such as Austria-Hungary. Their screens reflected the proximity of military action and the consequent disruption of distribution patterns, both of which resulted in a growing percentage of German films. By contrast, nations which sought to remain above the fray, such as the Netherlands, Denmark, and Sweden, used their neutrality to take advantage of the war-created reconfiguration of distribution, and, through 1916 at least, to increase production levels. Despite the modest levels of success they achieved, all three industries felt the constraints of shrinking markets, reduced availability of stock, and shipping difficulties. In the Netherlands, opportunistic distribution practices stimulated the film industry generally and production in companies such as Hollandia-Film reached new levels. In Sweden's case, Charles Magnusson carefully developed a production infrastructure which would be sustained in the post-war period, while encouraging the work of directors such as Victor Sjöström and Mauritz Stiller. Denmark, a self-sufficient film market and home to the internationally active Nordisk Kompagni, enjoyed initial success, but fell victim to a series of pre-war industrial difficulties (from ever-expanding budgets to stylistic rigidity). More dramatically, however, a 1917 German buy-out of Nordisk's substantial holdings in Germany, and with them rights to Nordisk's films in much of Europe, effectively neutralized Denmark as an international producer.

In sharp contrast to the film industries of Europe's Allied and neutral nations, Germany's industry consolidated its domestic market and expanded its influence rapidly in both occupied and neutral lands. As Germany had shown with its deployment of gas and submarines,

where sensitivity to the potentials of modern warfare joined with a vigorous plan of action, a fresh vision together with centralized authority could lead to tremendous advances. Thanks to the efforts of several leading industrialists and General Erich Ludendorff, the nation was able to move from a pre-war reliance on imported French, Danish, and American films, to control of its own screens by the war's end.

The rapid changes in the German market resulted from two major factors. First, the declaration of war interrupted the flow of imports from England, France, and eventually Italy, forcing Germany to rely increasingly upon trade with neutrals such as Denmark and the USA. This experience underscored the problems of trade dependencies. Secondly, as early as 1914 industrialists such as Krupp's Alfred Hugenberg realized the positive advantages to be gained by film as a medium of political influence. Hugenberg, later to control Universum-Film AG (Ufa), formed the Deutsche Lichtbild Gesellschaft, effectively provoking competing representatives from the electrical and chemical industries to forge an alliance with the government. In a grand plan secretly orchestrated by General Ludendorff and partially financed by the government, existing companies such as Messter, Union, and Nordisk were purchased and reorganized in 1917 into Ufa, which overnight became Germany's most important producer, distributor, and exhibitor of films. Government and industrial capital, the new markets provided by territorial conquest and Nordisk's rights, and an acute awareness of film's propaganda potential, all in a virtually competition-free environment, led to continued theatre construction and increased film production until the end of the war.

The experience of the Russian film industry until the government's collapse in 1917 appeared somewhat closer to the German than the Allied model. With a pre-war dependence on imports for up to 90 per cent of its films, war-related transportation problems, and declining production levels among its French, British, and Italian trading partners, the Russian industry had to fend for itself. Toeplitz (1987) claims that by 1916, despite difficult economic conditions, domestic production levels reached some 500 films. Under these circumstances, the Russian market, characterized by among other things its demands for films with tragic endings and a high degree of formal stasis, helped to develop a distinctly national cinema as evident in the work of Yevgeny Bauer and Yakov Protazanov. From late 1917 onwards, however, the Bolshevik revolution and the civil war which followed it, together with extreme privation in many parts of the nation, temporarily halted the progress of the film industry.

The war, regardless of its impact on the various national cinemas, encouraged a series of common developments. Film played an explicit role in shaping public sentiments towards the conflict and in informing the public of the

A scene from *Maudite soit la guerre* ('A curse on war'), a pacifist drama made for Pathé's Belgian subsidiary by Alfred Machin in 1913, and released just before the outbreak of the War in 1914

war's progress. From Chaplin's *The Bond* (1918) or Griffith's *Hearts of the World* (1918) to *The Universal Animated Weekly* or *Annales de guerre*, film served the interests of the State, and in so doing demonstrated its 'good citizenship'. Such demonstrations of civic responsibility helped to placate the film industry's lingering enemies from the pre-war era—concerned clergy, teachers, and citizens who perceived motion pictures as a threat to established cultural values—and to reassure those progressive reformers who held high hopes for film as a medium with uplifting potentials. National governments and the military, too, took an active role in the production and often regulation of film. Germany's BUFA (Bild- und Film Amt), the USA's Committee on Public Information, Britain's Imperial War Office, and France's Service Photographique et Cinématographique de l'Armée variously controlled photographic access to the front, produced military and medical training films, and commissioned propaganda films for the public. And, legitimizing strategies aside, tent cinemas on the front and warm theatres in European cities short of fuel drew new audiences to the motion picture. In this regard, the unusually high levels of organization and support provided by the German government to BUFA and Ufa were matched by its efforts on the front, with over 900 temporary soldiers' cinemas.

Europe's first major military conflict in the modern era obviously proved attractive as a motion picture subject, as the rapid development of atrocity and war films in each of the combatant nations suggests. These films often cut across existing forms, as Chaplin's *Shoulder Arms* (1918), Winsor McKay's animated *The Sinking of the Lusitania* (1918), and Gance's *J'accuse* (*I Accuse*, 1919) attest. And the interest both in the new war genre and in explorations of the horrors and heroism of the First World War continued well beyond it, from Vidor's *The Big Parade* (1925) and Walsh's *What Price Glory* (1926), to Kubrick's *Paths of Glory* (1957). Beyond permeating the period's realist films, often in as muted a form as character reference, it would echo particularly loudly during the economic crisis of the late 1920s and early 1930s, when reappraisal of the war could serve the causes of pacifism (Milestone's 1930 *All Quiet on the Western Front* and Renoir's 1937 *La Grande Illusion*) or militarism (Ucicky's 1933 *Morgenrot* ('Dawn')).

The war, then, served not only to dismantle Europe's dominant pre-war industries, but, ironically, to construct a tacit consensus regarding the national importance of cinema. The latter point underwent a curious permutation which assisted the US penetration of markets such as England, France, and Italy, and meanwhile stimulated the distinctive national identities of the German and Russian cinemas. As the specifically 'national' character of the European allies' cinema became increasingly associated with the gruelling war effort and pre-war national identities, the US cinema increasingly appeared as a morale booster and harbinger of a new internationalism. Chaplin's appeal to French children, workers, and intellectuals alike outlined the trajectory which American feature films would follow by the war's end, as US films

William S. Hart
(1865–1946)

Although born in New York, William Surrey Hart spent his childhood in the Midwest, at a time when it still retained much of the feel of the frontier. A career on the stage offered him only a meagre living until he landed the part of Cash Hawkins, a cowboy, in Edwin Milton Royle's hit play *The Squaw Man* in 1905. Parts in other Western dramas followed, among them the lead in the stage version of Owen Wister's *The Virginian* in 1907. Touring California in 1913, he decided to look up an old acquaintance, Thomas Ince, who was busy developing the studio at Santa Ynez which would soon be known as Inceville.

Ince recognised Hart's potential and offered him work at $175 a week. For the next two years Hart appeared in a score of two-reel Westerns and a couple of features, working with the script-writer C. Gardner Sullivan. Typically, as in *The Scourge of the Desert*, Hart is cast as a 'Good Badman', frequently an outlaw moved to reform by the love of a pure woman. In 1915 Ince and Hart joined Triangle Films, and Hart, by now a hugely successful Western star, graduated finally to feature-length pictures.

One of his most successful Triangle films was *Hell's Hinges*, released in 1916. Hart plays Blaze Tracy, a gunman hired by the saloon owner to ensure that the newly arrived preacher does not ruin his trade by civilizing the town. But Blaze is moved by the radiance of the preacher's sister. When a mob sets light to the church, he arrives to rescue the girl, and then takes on the whole town single-handed and burns it to the ground. Hart's tall, lean figure and his angular, melancholy face projected a persona imbued with all the moral certainties of the Victorian age which formed him. To villains and to other races, especially Mexicans, he is implacably hostile. But he is courteous, even diffident, around women. Hart is a loner, his only companion his horse Fritz.

In 1917 Hart moved to Famous Players–Lasky when Adolph Zukor offered him $150,000 a picture. Distribution of his films under Paramount's Artcraft label ensured great success in the years immediately after the First World War. Not all Hart's films were Westerns, but it was the Western to which he returned time and again. Of Hart's later films still extant, *Blue Blazes Rawden* (1918), *Square Deal Sanderson* (1919), and *The Toll Gate* (1920) are among the best. Production budgets increased, and more time and trouble were taken. Those which Hart did not direct himself were entrusted to the reliable Lambert Hillyer.

But as the 1920s progressed, Hart's films began to appear dated. The pace grew ponderous; Hart, never one for the lighter touch, took himself more and more seriously, and his tendency towards sentimentality grew more pronounced. Hart liked to think that his films presented a realistic picture of the West, and *Wild Bill Hickok* (1923) was an attempt at a serious historical reconstruction. But Paramount were unhappy with it. Hart was by now 57 years old, and could no longer present a convincing action hero to the Jazz Age audience. His next picture, *Singer Jim McKee* (1924), was a flop and his contract was terminated.

His last film, *Tumbleweeds* (1925), released through United Artists, had $100,000 of his own money in it. It contained some spectacular land rush scenes, but it was another failure and Hart was forced to retire. *Tumbleweeds* was reissued a decade later, with a sound-track on which Hart delivered a spoken introduction: 'My friends, I loved the art of making motion pictures. It is, as the breath of life to me . . .'. It is an extraordinary moment, fascinating for the glimpse it offers of a Victorian stage actor in full, faintly ludicrous rhetorical flight, yet undeniably moving in its evocation of the world of the silent Western which Hart embodied.

EDWARD BUSCOMBE

SELECT FILMOGRAPHY

In the Sage Brush Country (1914); The Scourge of the Desert (1915); Hell's Hinges (1916); The Return of Draw Egan (1916); The Narrow Trail (1917); Blue Blazes Rawden (1918); Selfish Yates (1918); Square Deal Sanderson (1919); The Toll Gate (1920); Wild Bill Hickok (1923); Tumbleweeds (1925)

BIBLIOGRAPHY

Koszarski, Diane Kaiser (1980), *The Complete Films of William S. Hart: A Pictorial Record*.

W. S. Hart featured on the cover of *Picture-Play* magazine in 1917

Tom Mix
(1880–1940)

The most popular Western star of the 1920s, Tom Mix was the epitome of a Jazz Age movie hero. In place of the moral fervour of William S. Hart, a Tom Mix picture provided non-stop entertainment, a high-speed melange of spectacular horse-riding, fist-fights, comedy, and chases. Usually the stunts were performed by Mix himself. In his early twenties he had worked as a wrangler at the famous Miller Brothers 101 Ranch, a Wild West show based in Oklahoma. Mix was working with another show in 1909 when the Selig Company used its facilities to make a film entitled *Ranch Life in the Great Southwest*, in which he was featured briefly as a bronco-buster. Over the next seven years Mix appeared in nearly a hundred Selig one- and two-reel Westerns, shot first in Colorado and then in California.

In 1917 the Fox studio promoted Mix to feature-length films, with high-quality production values, much of the filming being done on location at spectacular western sites such as the Grand Canyon. Mix's star persona was a fun-loving free spirit, adept at rescuing damsels in distress. On screen Tom was clean-living, with no smoking or drinking, and little actual gun-play. Villains were more likely to be captured by a clever ruse than dispatched by a bullet.

Mix made the occasional foray outside the Western, for example in *Dick Turpin* (1925), but it was the Western that made him, and he in turn made the Fox studio the most successful Western producer of the age. Many of his sixty or so features are no longer extant. Only a few sequences survive of *North of Hudson Bay*, one of two Mix films under the direction of Fox's premier Western director at the time, John Ford. Fortunately, several good examples of his work do remain. *The Great K & A Train Robbery* (1926) gives a typical impression of Mix in his prime. It opens with a spectacular stunt in which Tom slides down a cable to the bottom of a gorge, and ends, after skirmishes on top of moving trains, with an epic fist-fight in an underground cavern between Tom and about a dozen villains. He captures them all.

The Fox publicity machine worked hard at constructing a biography which was as colourful as Mix's screen performance. It was variously claimed that his mother was part-Cherokee, that he fought with the army in Cuba during the Spanish–American War, taking part in the famous charge up San Juan Hill with Teddy Roosevelt's Rough Riders, and also fought in the Boxer Rebellion in Peking. None of these things was true. Mix did not leave the United States during his brief army service, which ended ignominiously with his desertion when he got married.

By all accounts Mix often found it difficult to separate out fact from fiction. He followed the show-business tradition of Western heroes initiated by Buffalo Bill Cody. Both on and off screen he became an increasingly flamboyant figure, with his huge white hat, embroidered western suits, diamond-studded belts, and hand-tooled boots. Though, unlike Hart, Mix had been a genuine working cowboy, his roots were in the Wild West show and the rodeo, and at periodic points in his career he returned to touring in live shows, including circuses.

Mix's career was past its peak by the time sound came to the Western, but the singing cowboys of the 1930s, with their fanciful costumes and Arcadian vision of western ranch life, were his direct descendants. His last film, the serial *The Miracle Rider*, was a rather sad affair. Five years later, short of money, he tried to persuade Fox to finance a come-back. His old friend John Ford had to explain that the picture business had passed him by. Later that year his car overturned at a bend outside Florence, Arizona, killing him instantly.

EDWARD BUSCOMBE

Select Filmography

Ranch Life in the Great Southwest (1909); The Heart of Texas Ryan (1917); The Wilderness Trail (1919); Sky High (1922); Just Tony (1922); Tom Mix in Arabia (1922); Three Jumps Ahead (1923); The Lone Star Ranger (1923); North of Hudson Bay (1923); Riders of the Purple Sage (1925); The Great K & A Train Robbery (1926); Rider of Death Valley (1932)

Bibliography

Brownlow, Kevin (1979), *The War, the West and the Wilderness*. Mix, Paul E. (1972), *The Life and Legend of Tom Mix*.

Riders of the Purple Sage (1925)

served the cultural functions of social unification and entertainment while expressing the emphatically modern *Zeitgeist* of the post-war era.

The German experience differed considerably. The perceived cultural distinctions which in part provoked the war and which lurked behind the government's active support of Ufa would continue to drive the film industry in the post-war era. Although US film penetration of the German market increased until late in 1916, the taste for American product acquired by the French, British, and Italians failed to take hold. And the post-war *Aufbruch*, or break with the past, also failed to resonate with the cultural values of the USA, at least as manifest in its films. The late date of US resumption of trade with Germany, and the extremity of German inflation (which led to an exchange rate of over 4 trillion marks to the dollar in 1923) effectively precluded US interest in the film market and prolonged Germany's isolation. National cultural needs would be met by national film production. The Russian situation, although quite different and compounded by a lingering civil war and economic boycott, shared the same basic dynamic as a revolutionary culture set out to produce its own revolutionary films.

Europe emerged from the war ridden by debt (mostly to the USA) and physically traumatized. France, Italy, and Germany faced the additional ordeals of social unrest, political turmoil, severe inflation, and an influenza epidemic which swept across Europe killing more people than the war itself. With the exception of Germany, where the film industry enjoyed relative stability, Europe's motion picture business emerged from the war in a state of shock. For example, its sometimes successful attempts to produce films notwithstanding, the French industry turned increasingly to distribution, while Italy attempted to return to the glories of the spectacle film, but found that international taste had changed considerably. As the leaders of the pre-war industry attempted to shake off several years of relative inactivity and re-enter the world of production and international distribution, they found conditions very much changed by the American studios. The linkage of big-budget features, new studio technologies and production practices, expensive stars, and the consequent need to assure investors of large international markets was difficult to break, especially in the face of ravaged domestic economies and a still splintered and impoverished Europe. America, by contrast, came out of the war with a massive and relatively healthy domestic market, and an aggressive and well-oiled studio system. Moderately sensitive to the needs of the foreign market, and armed with an international infrastructure of shipping, banking, and film offices, the US industry was in a position to enjoy the post-war shift in the balance of power. Although the weakened film industries of several European nations attempted to have protective tariffs erected, such efforts initially had little effect since the American studios could simply exploit the advantages of the USA's diplomatic and financial power and block legislation.

But the triumph of American films in the post-war period also reflects the changed position of cinema within the cultural hierarchy, and, in turn, the broader fabric of cultural transformations which helped give rise to and took form through the war. The often brutal disruption of lives, families, work, and values served to shatter lingering nineteenth-century sensibilities. The differences between Sennett's conception of comedy and Harold Lloyd's, or between Mary Pickford's embodiment of feminine identity and Theda Bara's, or between the value systems of *The Birth of a Nation* (1915) and DeMille's *Male and Female* (1919), suggest the dimensions of the change that had occurred within sectors of the American public.

An emphatic break with (and often critique of) the past and a self-conscious embrace of the modern characterized the post-war scene. But the 'modern' itself was a vexed category. Post-war Europe quickly defined the modern within an older, élitist, and highly intellectualized aesthetic sensibility, as the institutional histories of the various '-isms' in painting, music, and avant-garde film suggest. But the modern as manifest in American mass culture, and nowhere more apparent than in the Hollywood feature, embodied democratic appeal, instant gratification, and seamless illusionism. The promise of a ready-made, one-size-fits-all culture reinforced the economic inroads made by the US film industry in Europe, evident in the rise to western dominance of what has been dubbed the classical Hollywood cinema. In contrast to a European modernism predicated upon the self-conscious use of image and cutting patterns, Hollywood's modernism inhered in the industrialized creation of products driven by the project of telling stories as efficiently and transparently as possible, deploying such techniques as 'invisible editing' to that end. Although these divergent senses of the modern would fuel endless cultural debates, the post-war dominance experienced by the US film industry and the persistence throughout the west of the signifying practices associated with Hollywood would characterize the decades to come.

Bibliography

Abel, Richard (1984), *French Cinema: The First Wave, 1915–1929*.

Bordwell, David, Staiger, Janet, and Thompson, Kristin (1985), *The Classical Hollywood Cinema*.

Cherchi Usai, Paolo, and Codelli, Lorenzo (1990). *Before Caligari*.

Koszarski, Richard (1990), *An Evening's Entertainment*.

Monaco, Paul (1976), *Cinema and Society*.

Reeves, Nicholas (1986), *Official British Film Propaganda During the First World War*.

Thompson, Kristin (1985), *Exporting Entertainment*.

THE SILENT FILM

Tricks and Animation

DONALD CRAFTON

Contrary to popular belief, the history of animation did not begin with Walt Disney's sound film *Steamboat Willie* in 1928. Before then there was a popular tradition, a film industry, and a vast number of films—including nearly 100 of Disney's—which pre-dated the so-called classic studio period of the 1930s.

The general history of the animated film begins with the use of transient trick effects in films around the turn of the century. As distinct genres emerged (Westerns, chase films, etc.) during 1906–10, there appeared at the same time films made all or mostly by the animation technique. Since most movies were a single reel, there was little programmatic difference between the animated films and others. But as the multi-reel film trend progressed after around 1912, with only a handful of exceptions, animated films retained their one-reel-or-less length. At the same time they began to be associated in the collective mind of producers and audiences with comic strips, primarily because they adapted already-existing heroes from the popular printed media and 'signed' the films in the cartoonists' names, although the artists generally had no involvement in the production. Until the First World War, animation was a thoroughly international phenomenon, but after about 1915 the producers in the United States dominated the world market. Although there were many attempts at indigenous European production, the 1920s remained the dominion of the American character series: Mutt and Jeff, Koko the Clown, Farmer Al Falfa, and Felix the Cat. Of all the ways in which the formation of the animated film paralleled feature production, the most notable was the cartoon's assimilation of the 'star system' in the 1920s, during which animation studios created recurring protagonists who were analogous to human stars.

DEFINITIONS

The animated film can be broadly defined as a kind of motion picture made by arranging drawings or objects in a manner that, when photographed and projected sequentially on movie film, produces the illusion of controlled motion. In practice, however, definitions of what constitutes animation are inflected by a variety of technical, generic, thematic, and industrial considerations.

Technique

Animated images were being made long before cinematography was invented in the 1890s; as David Robinson (1991) has shown, making drawings move was a prototype for making photographs move and has a history that diverges from that of cinema. If we restrict our discussion to theatrical animated films, then 1898 is a possible starting-point. Although there is no acceptable evidence to verify either claim, the animation technique might have been discovered independently by J. Stuart Blackton in the United States and by Arthur Melbourne-Cooper in England. Each claimed to have been first to exploit an alternative way of using the motion picture camera: manipulating objects in the field of vision and exposing only one or a few frames at a time in order to mimic the illusion of motion created by ordinary cinematography. In projection, it makes no difference whether the individual frames have been exposed 16–24 times per second or exposed with an indefinite interval; the illusion of motion is the same. So the traditional technologically based definition of animation as constructing and shooting frame by frame is clearly inadequate. *All* movies are composed, exposed, and projected frame by frame (otherwise the image would be blurred). The defining technical factor seems to be in the intended effect to be produced on the screen.

Genre

It was not until about 1906 that the animated film became a recognizable mode of production. *Humorous Phases of Funny Faces* (Blackton, 1906) depicted an artist's hand sketching caricatures which then moved their eyes and mouths. This was done by exposing a couple of frames, erasing the chalk drawing, redrawing it slightly modified, then exposing more frames. The impression was created that the drawings were moving by themselves. Émile Cohl's *Fantasmagorie* (1908) also showed an artist's drawings moving on their own, achieving independence from him. Gradually these conventions were consolidated into characteristic themes and iconography which set this kind of film-making apart from other novelty productions. Before about 1913, the items that were animated tended to be objects—toys, puppets, and cut-outs—but slowly the proportion of drawings to objects increased until, after 1915, 'animated cartoons', that is, drawings (especially comic strips), were understood as constituting the genre.

Themes and conventions

Should animation be defined by characteristic themes? Some commentators have identified 'creating the illusion of life' as animation's essential metaphor. Another recurring motif is the representation of the animators (or their symbolic substitutes) within the films. The confusion between the universe represented in the films and the 'real' world of the animator and the film audience is another persistent theme.

Animated films can also be defined culturally. It is often imagined that animation is a humorous genre, aimed mainly at children, and indeed children have always been (and continue to be) a large part of the audience for the cartoon film. But animation consists of more than cartoons, and it should not be forgotten that even the classic cartoon was made for general audiences, not a juvenile audience alone. A cultural definition of animation would therefore need to take into account the kind of humour it represents but also its association (particularly in the early period) with magic and the supernatural, and its ability to function as a repository of psychological processes such as fantasy or infantile regression.

Industry

Produced in specialized units (whether in studios or in artisanal workshops), animated films soon came to have a particular place in the film programme. The cartoon was the moment in the programme which foregrounded neither 'reality' (newsreel or documentary) nor human drama (the feature), but humour, slapstick spectacle and narrative, animal protagonists, and fantastic events, produced by drawings or puppets.

PRECURSORS

The 'trick film' was one of the earliest film genres. While identified primarily with the work of the French magician

A precursor of the animated film: a shot from Georges Méliès's 'trick film' *The Man with the Rubber Head* (*L'Homme à la tête en caoutchouc*, 1902)

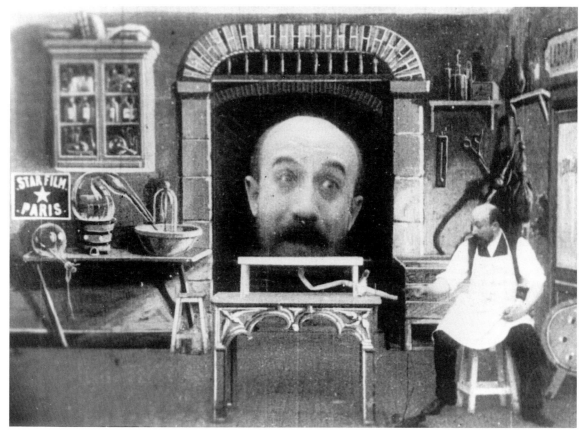

turned film-maker Georges Méliès, many such films were made in several countries between 1898 and 1908. During photography the camera would be stopped, a change made (for example, a girl substituted for a skeleton), then photography resumed.

Méliès himself apparently did not make extensive use of frame-by-frame animation. For that one must turn to James Stuart Blackton, one of the founders of the Vitagraph Company and maker of what is usually taken to be the first true animated cartoon, *Humorous Phases of Funny Faces*. In 1906–7, Blackton made half a dozen films which employed animated effects. His most influential was *The Haunted Hotel* (February 1907), which was a smash hit in Europe, primarily because of its close-up animation of tableware. Among film-makers profoundly influenced by Blackton's Vitagraph work were Segundo de Chomón of Spain (working in France), Melbourne-Cooper and Walter R. Booth (England), and, in the United States, Edwin S. Porter at Edison and Billy Bitzer at Biograph.

In these trick films animation was basically—a trick. Like the sleight of hand in a magic film, the animated footage in these short films was a way to thrill, amuse, and incite the curiosity of the spectators. As the novelty wore off, some producers—notably Blackton himself—abandoned this kind of film. Others expanded and modified it, leading to the creation of the new autonomous film genre.

ARTISANS: COHL AND McCAY

Émile Cohl had been a caricaturist and comic strip artist before discovering cinema around the age of 50. From 1908 to 1910 he worked on at least seventy-five films for the Gaumont Company, contributing animated footage to most of them. A rather obsessive artist, Cohl quickly devised numerous animation procedures which remain fundamental, such as illuminated animation stands with vertically mounted electrically driven cameras, and charts for calculating movement duration and lens depth of field. He placed various media under the camera, including drawings, models, puppets, photographic cut-outs, sand, stamps, and assorted objects. What Cohl's films did *not* exhibit was a traditional linear plot; instead his background as a graphic artist became a source for ever-changing scenes of fantastic drawings that metamorphosed into each other with irrational logic and obscure symbolism. Bizarre though they seem today, Cohl's films were apparently extremely popular. He worked for the Pathé and Éclair companies, the latter of which assigned him to its American branch in Fort Lee, New Jersey, in 1912. He adapted a cartoon series based on George McManus's comic strip 'The Newlyweds and their Baby'. The success of these fourteen films inspired many other newspaper cartoonists to produce or commission animated versions of their own works.

One interested graphic artist was Winsor McCay, unquestionably the most brilliant newspaper cartoonist of the day. In 1911 he screened a short untitled film in which he animated some characters from his 'Little Nemo in Slumberland' strip. The drawings were meticulously retraced on cards, photographed by Vitagraph, and then the release print was coloured by McCay frame by frame. In the live-action prologue McCay proudly displayed the thousands of drawings and the flipping apparatus for testing the movements. In addition to providing narrative integration for the animation, the prologue also vividly showed how to draw and photograph animated cartoons to all who watched—and there were many. In 1912 McCay made *The Story of a Mosquito*, in which static backgrounds were used, retraced in each drawing. There were some ambitious experiments in moving perspective. *Gertie*, presented on stage in 1914 and also released as a one-reel feature, was the most accomplished animated film to date (and for many years thereafter). We see McCay call Gertie the dinosaur out of hiding in her cave and put her through some circus-like tricks. The film was rightly hailed as a masterpiece and contributed to the increasing popularity of the genre. His *The Sinking of the Lusitania: An Amazing Moving Pen Picture* was released in 1918. It depicted the wartime tragedy with a combination of 'objective' and 'cartoon' graphic styles. McCay conceived many film projects and managed to finish several before his death in 1934.

INDUSTRIALIZATION: BRAY AND BARRÉ

From the popularity of 'The Newlyweds', McCay's extravaganzas, and the sporadic releases by novice animators it was clear that audiences were delighting in these films. The problem was that the craft was so labour-intensive that the rental return was insufficient to offset production costs. Cohl and others had tried to use cut-outs to replace some of the time-consuming drawing, but this compromised the graphic interest of the films.

John Randolph Bray invented a way to alleviate much of the retracing which the older methods required. A comic strip artist and fledgeling animator (having released one film in 1913), Bray developed the use of transparent overlays made of sheets of cellulose nitrate. It was through his encounter with another animator, Earl Hurd, who already held patents on celluloid use, that he perfected what became called the cel system. This involved separating the moving from the static elements in the picture. The background and other non-moving parts were drawn on a paper sheet; moving figures were drawn in their proper sequential poses on the transparent cels. These were laid over and photographed individually to obtain the illusion of a figure moving across a stationary background. This process remained standard in the animation industry until the advent of xerography and computer-aided design. Bray and Hurd aggressively protected their proprietary claim to the process. Most animation studios from 1915 to the early 1930s obtained licences from the Bray–Hurd patent company and paid royalties.

Bray was good at adapting techniques developed by others. This was also the case with a competitor, Raoul Barré, a talented comic strip artist from Montreal who, in collaboration with William Nolan, began making cartoons for the Edison studio in 1915. Barré, rather than attempting to turn out films single-handedly, introduced the concept of a division of labour, rather like a car assembly line with a hierarchy of jobs. Another valuable contribution was the use of pegs on the drawing board which fitted precisely into punched alignment holes on the tracing sheets. (McCay and Bray had used printer's cross-marks for registering drawings.) Barré and Nolan invented their own way of streamlining the animation chore, but without using cels (and not patentable). The slash system, as it is now called, also divided the composition into moving and static elements but, ingeniously, the drawing was planned so that the background could be placed *over* the foreground (the inverse of the cel system). Both elements were drawn on the same kind of white paper. Holes were cut in the background sheet where the moving foreground figures needed to show through. During photography the moving sheet was placed first on the pegs, and the 'slashed' background was placed on top. For the next exposure the same background sheet was used, but with the next moving sheet under it.

Borrowed by the Bray studio, Barré's assembly-line concept and his perf.-and-peg system became integral to United States animation production practice.

Another labour-saving practice patented by Bray, but probably pioneered by Barré, was 'in-betweening'. The animator would sketch the beginning and end poses of a sequence, then the intervening poses would be drawn by lower-paid assistants known as in-betweeners.

ANIMATION STUDIOS

Besides the studio Barré founded at Edison, he also worked briefly at the International Film Service and for the Mutt and Jeff series in 1916. He formed a partnership with Charles Bowers, who had contracted to make the series based on Bud Fisher's comic strip. Bowers and Fisher eased Barré out of the business in 1919, but the Mutt and Jeff series, despite changes in studios, staff, and distributors, continued throughout the silent era.

The International Film Service studio was started by William Randolph Hearst in December 1916. Since Hearst had contractual control over his newspaper cartoonists, it was a natural business move to exploit their characters in movies. Gregory La Cava, formerly a minor staffer at Barré's, was hired to supervise the operation. One of his first moves was to engage his former boss, Raoul Barré. Though there were frequent changes in personnel, the

studio thrived. It ceased operation in 1918, not because it was unprofitable, but because of political and financial difficulties in the parent company, Hearst's International News Service. The animators migrated to other studios, including Bray, which acquired the rights to animate Hearst comic strips in August 1919.

Former Hearst cartoonist Paul Terry, who claimed to have his own cel patents, resisted Bray's attempts to extract licensing fees. After years of trials and negotiations, an agreement was finally reached in 1926. Meanwhile Terry had cranked out more than 200 weekly cartoons in his Fables Pictures studio. Though originally the films were whimsical adaptations of Aesop's fables, the literary conceit was quickly exhausted. Farmer Al Falfa and other original characters cavorted in the series. In 1928 Terry's partner Amadee Van Beuren bought a controlling interest in the business, renamed it after himself, and it became a leading studio in the early 1930s. Terry went on to found Terrytoons, which he supervised until 1955.

MAX AND DAVE FLEISCHER

The Fleischer brothers broke into the movie business by way of Dave Fleischer's invention, the rotoscope. The device projected single frames from a strip of movie film one at a time on to the back of a glass drawing surface. The images could be traced on to paper or cels and then rephotographed by the normal animation process to obtain drawings that moved 'realistically' when projected. J. R. Bray put Max and Dave Fleischer in charge of instructional film production, much of it exploiting the clarity of rotoscoped images. In April 1920, the 'Out of the Inkwell' series featuring a rotoscoped clown began appearing irregularly on the Bray programme. Rave reviews in trade journals and even the *New York Times* emboldened the animators and they set up their own studio in 1921. Yet it was not until around 1923 that the clown was given a name: Koko. The premiss of each 'Out of the Inkwell' was that a cartoonist, played by Max, would bring Koko out of the ink bottle and place him on the sketch pad whereupon the figure would 'come to life'. Koko became one of the most important early cartoon stars.

Unfortunately the Fleischers were not as good at business as they were at making films, and their Red Seal studio foundered in 1926. They settled at Paramount, releasing more 'Out of the Inkwells' with 'Ko-Ko' renamed to secure copyright. In the early 1930s the Fleischers' Betty Boop and Popeye the Sailor eclipsed the clown's stardom.

WALTER LANTZ

The future creator of Woody Woodpecker began his career in animation washing cels for reuse at the International Film Service, but soon became a director for La Cava. He joined the Bray studio in 1919, first designing posters and advertisements and then, after Max Fleischer left in 1921, becoming general supervisor of the animation studio. The first series he directed for Bray, beginning in 1924, was 'Dinky Doodles', which superimposed an animated boy character over photographed backgrounds. 'Unnatural Histories' started in 1925, and 'Hot Dog' (with Pete the Pup) in 1926 (until the studio closed in 1927). In all these series, Lantz appeared as a congenial actor. He joined Universal in 1928 and one of his first assignments was to direct 'Oswald the Lucky Rabbit', a character which had been originated by Disney.

WALT DISNEY

Walter Elias Disney had the good fortune to grow up in Kansas City, Missouri, where most of the distributors had exchanges for the Midwest region. The owner of one of the large theatres contracted with Disney and his partner, Ubbe (nicknamed Ub) Iwerks, for a series of 'Laugh-O-Grams', short combinations of cartoon jokes and advertisements. When the series proved to be a financial failure, Disney moved to California in 1923 in order to be closer to the film industry. His 'Alice Comedies' were distributed by pioneer cartoon businesswoman Margaret J. Winkler. Alice was a live character who acted out her adventures in an animated world. Her companion Julius was a Felix look-alike. Between 1923 and 1927 there were over fifty 'Alices' released. In 1927 Disney and Iwerks created Oswald the Lucky Rabbit and received enthusiastic praise in the trade press. But Charles Mintz, Margaret Winkler's husband and by then business manager, had secretly set up his own Oswald studio in New York and hired some of Disney's staff to produce the films (until Mintz was replaced by Lantz and the series returned to Hollywood).

Disney's response to losing the rights to Oswald was to compete with another animal character, a black mouse which Iwerks imbued with a Buster Keatonesque personality. Two Mickey Mouse cartoons were completed in early 1928, but no national distributor was interested. Disney and his brother Roy decided to plan a sound cartoon. *Steamboat Willie* was recorded on the Powers Cinephone (a sound-on-film system with a rather dubious legal pedigree). It was not the first sound cartoon (the Fleischers and Paul Terry had beaten Disney to this milestone), but it was the first one with singing, whistling, and audiovisual percussive effects (such as cats miaowing when their tails were pulled) specifically designed for sync sound. After the film opened in November 1928, silent cartoon production was obsolete. The economics of sound film-making caused a realignment of the industry, with many independents and one major studio—Sullivan's—failing to make the change-over.

SULLIVAN AND MESSMER

Otto Messmer was a neophyte cartoonist at the Universal Weekly newsreel in 1915 when comic strip artist and animator Pat Sullivan walked in to arrange to have some drawings of his own photographed. Sullivan's personal problems (he was gaoled for raping a minor) and Messmer's service during the war delayed them but in 1919 they were releasing cartoons for the Paramount Screen Magazine. One of these, *Feline Follies*, featured a mischievous backyard cat—soon to be known as Felix. In 1921 Margaret Winkler began to distribute the series and continued to do so until 1925. Despite constant bickering and lawsuits with Sullivan, Winkler successfully promoted the cat to national prominence.

The studio was run by Otto Messmer, who was in charge of all the details, large and small. Long before, Sullivan had withdrawn completely from the creative side of Felix production, focusing only on travel and business arrangements. Increasingly his alcoholism impaired his ability.

Felix the Cat in *Pedigreedy* (1927) by Pat Sullivan, directed by Otto Messmer. Character © Felix the Cat Productions, Inc.

The Felix of this early period was drawn in an angular style and moved in jerky motions rather like the walk of Chaplin's Tramp character. He was distinguished by a strong personality which remained consistent from film to film; audiences could identify with him and would return to see his next cartoon. Animator Bill Nolan, from 1922 to 1924, redesigned Felix's body to make him more rounded and cuddly—more like the Felix dolls that Sullivan so successfully marketed.

The Sullivan studio was based on Barré's model (Sullivan had worked at Barré's briefly; many of the animators came from there; Barré himself worked on Felix from 1926 to 1928). Though cels were employed, they were background overlays, placed over sheets of animated drawings on paper. This saved both the expense of cels and Bray–Hurd licensing. Variations of the slash system were also used sporadically.

Ladislas Starewitch
(Władysław Starewicz)
(1882–1965)

Władisław Starewicz was born in Vilnius—now the capital of Lithuania but then part of Poland—and started his film career making documentaries for the local Ethnographic Museum. His first animated film was *Valka zukov rogachi* ('The Battle of Stag-Beetles', 1910), a reconstruction (using preserved specimens) of the nocturnal mating rituals of this local species, which could not be filmed 'live-action' in the dark.

For his first entertainment film, *Prekrasnya Lukanida* ('The fair Lucanida', 1910), Starewitch developed the basic technique he would employ for the rest of his life: he built small puppets from a jointed wooden frame, with parts such as fingers that needed to be flexible rendered in wire, and parts that need not change cut from cork or modelled in plaster. His wife Anna, who came from a family of tailors, padded them with cotton and sewed leather and cloth features and costumes. He designed all the characters and built the settings.

Starewicz moved to Moscow, making animations which range from the impressively grim *The Grasshopper and the Ant* (*Strekozai i muraviei*, 1911) in which the literalness of the insects reinforces the cruel message, to the enchanting *The Insects' Christmas* (*Rozhdyestvo obitateli lyesa*, 1912). His most astonishing early film, *The Cameraman's Revenge* (*Miest kinooperatora*, 1911), shows Mrs Beetle having an affair with a grasshopper-painter, while Mr Beetle carries on with a dragonfly cabaret-artiste, whose previous lover, a grasshopper-cameraman, shoots movies of Mr Beetle and Dragonfly making love at the Hotel d'Amour. The cameraman screens these at the local cinema when Mr and Mrs Beetle are present, and the resulting riot lands both Beetles in jail. This racy satire of human sexual foibles gains a biting edge from the ridiculousness of bugs enacting what humans consider their most serious (even tragic) passions—as when Mrs Beetle reclines like an odalisque on the divan awaiting the absurd embrace of her lover, which involves twelve legs and two antennae in lascivious motion. The reflexive representation of the cinematic apparatus, reaching its apotheosis in the projection of previous scenes before an audience of animated insects, adds a metaphysical dimension to the parable.

After the Revolution, Starewicz left Russia and settled in France in 1920, changing his name to Ladislas Starewitch. Here he made 24 films which combine witty sophistication and magical naïveté, including moral fables such as the splendid *The Town Rat and the Country Rat* (*Le Rat de ville et le Rat des champs*, 1926) or the lovely *La voix du rossignol* ('The nightingale's voice', 1923), adventure epics like *The Magic Clock* (*L'Horloge magique*,1928), a bitter rendering of Anderson's *The Steadfast Tin Soldier* (*La Petite Parade*, 1928), and a feature-length *Reynard the Fox* (*Le Roman de Renard*, shot 1929/30, released 1937) which renders the gestures and emotions of the animals (in sophisticated period costumes) with great subtlety.

His 1933 masterpiece *The Mascot* (*Fétiche mascotte*) begins with a live-action sequence starring the Starewitch daughters Irène and Jeanne (who assisted and acted in most of the films) as a mother who supports herself making toys, and her sick daughter who longs for an orange. A stuffed dog, Fétiche, sneaks out at night to steal an orange for the girl, but gets caught at the Devil's ball, where all the garbage of Paris comes to life in a dissolute orgy at which drunken stemware suicidally crash into each other, and re-assembled skeletons of eaten fish and chickens dance. The dog escapes with the orange, pursued home by a motley gang of torn-paper and vegetable people, dolls and animals. Starewitch nods homage to René Clair's Dada short *Entr'acte* in his use of speeding live-action street traffic, the saxophone player with a balloon head that inflates and deflates as he plays, and the climactic mad, weird pursuit. Starewitch matches his brilliant visual details with witty use of sound, making the voices of Fétiche and the Devil whining musical instruments, or playing the Devil's words backwards to sound like unearthly gibberish.

WILLIAM MORITZ

SELECT FILMOGRAPHY

Valka zukov rogachi (The Battle of Stag-Beetles) (1910); Strekozai i muraviei (The Grasshopper and the Ant) (1911); Miest kinooperatora (The Cameraman's Revenge) (1911); Rozhdyestvo obitateli lyesa (The Insects' Christmas) (1912); L'Épouvantail (The Scarecrow) (1921); Les grenouilles qui demandent un roi (Frogland) (1922); La voix du rossignol (The Nightingale's Voice) (1923); Le Rat de ville et le Rat des champs (The Town Rat and the Country Rat) (1926); L'Horloge magique (The Magic Clock) (1928); La Petite Parade (The Steadfast Tin Soldier) (1928); Le Roman de Renard (The Tale of the Fox) (shot 1929/30, released April 1937); Fétiche mascotte (The Mascot) (1933)

BIBLIOGRAPHY

Holman, L. Bruce (1975), *Puppet Animation in the Cinema, History and Technique*.
Martin, Léona Béatrice and Françoise Martin (1991), *Ladislas Starewitch*.

Charlie Chaplin with other puppet figures in Ladislas Starewitch's *Amour noir, Amour blanc* (*Love in Black and White*, 1928)

Felix became the first animated character to gain the attention of the cultural élite, as well as huge popularity with audiences. He was the subject of praise from Gilbert Seldes, an American cultural historian, from Marcel Brion, a member of the French Academy, and from other intellectuals; Paul Hindemith composed a score for a 1928 Felix film. Thanks to Sullivan's aggressive marketing, the character also became the most successful movie 'ancillary' (until knocked aside by Mickey). Felix's likeness was licensed for all kinds of consumer products.

In 1925 Sullivan arranged to distribute through the Educational Film Corporation. Its national network combined with the increasingly creative stories and superb draughtsmanship of the Felix studio to generate the richest period, both in picture quality and in revenue. The Felix craze became a world-wide phenomenon.

But the cat's bubble burst at its height of popularity. The demise of the series can be traced to several factors: the coming of sound, competition from Mickey Mouse, and Sullivan's draining the organization of its capital (while Disney was channelling every cent back in). Despite the excellence of such films as *Sure-Locked Homes* (1928), Educational did not renew its contract and the series went steadily downhill.

HARMAN, ISING, AND SCHLESINGER

When Mintz and Winkler took over Oswald the Rabbit in 1928, they hired Hugh Harman and Rudolph Ising from Disney's studio to animate it. After Universal retrieved the series and gave it to Walter Lantz, Harman and Ising formed a partnership and produced a pilot film called *Bosko the Talk-ink Kid* in 1929. Entrepreneur Leon Schlesinger saw the potential of tying in sound films with popular music and obtained backing from Warner Bros. The film company would pay Schlesinger a fee to 'plug' its sheet music properties by animating cartoons around the songs. In January 1930 the partnership began producing 'Looney Tunes' (then, in 1931, 'Merrie Melodies'), the kernel of what would become the Warner Bros. cartoon studio with its memorable stars, beginning with Porky Pig.

ANIMATION IN OTHER NATIONAL CINEMAS

Every country with a significant silent film industry also had a local animation industry. With the economic advantage gained during the 1914–18 war, the United States film industry's financial impact on international cinema was reflected in the dissemination of American cartoons. Cohl's 'Newlyweds' series, for example, was exported to France, where it was distributed by the parent company, Éclair. Chaplin's successful short films were accompanied by US-made animated versions. Barré's Edison films were distributed by Gaumont. Margaret Winkler contracted with Pathé to distribute 'Out of the Inkwell' and 'Felix the Cat' in Great Britain.

Despite foreign competition, there were two areas in which Europeans had the market to themselves: topical sketches and advertising. The British sketchers, notably Harry Furniss, Lancelot Speed, Dudley Buxton, George Studdy, and Anson Dyer, entertained wartime audiences with their propaganda cartoons. Dyer went on to make some successful short cartoons in the early 1920s, including *Little Red Riding Hood* (1922), and would become an important producer in the 1930s. Studdy, in 1924, launched a series of Bonzo films starring a chubby dog. Advertising was a familiar component of the film programme. Among the notable names producing animated ads were O'Galop and Lortac in France, Pinschewer, Fischinger, and Seeber in Germany. In a category by itself are the productions of the State Film Technicum in Moscow. A regular series of entertainment cartoons (with a social message) appeared from 1924 to 1927, supervised by Dziga Vertov. The most important animator was Ivan Ivanov-Vano.

Other specialities were puppet and silhouette films. Ladislas Starewitch began his career in Russia in 1910 and soon was releasing popular one-reel films with puppets and animated insects for the Khanzhonkov Company. In 1922 he moved to France, where the puppet film became his life's work. *Le Roman du renard*, completed in 1930, was the first animated feature in France.

The important pioneer of the silhouette film was Lotte Reiniger. Her feature *Die Abenteuer des Prinzen Achmed* (*The Adventures of Prince Ahmed*) was released in Berlin in 1926 and gained world-wide acclaim. Its Arabian Nights story, lively shadow-puppets, and complicated moving backgrounds took three years to photograph.

Also worth mentioning are Quirino Cristiani and Victor Bergdahl. The former worked in Argentina and released a political satire, *El apóstol* ('The apostle'), in 1917. About an hour in length (about the same as *Prince Achmed*), it has been called the first feature-length cartoon. Bergdahl, from 1916 to 1922, animated a Swedish series featuring Kapten Grogg which was distributed in Europe and in the United States.

As Giannalberto Bendazzi (1994) has documented, animation was practised in many countries throughout the 1920s, both by avant-garde artists and commercially. But despite the popularity of animation films, the economic realities of the film industry in the 1920s, and the great cultural diversity in popular graphic humour traditions, made it extremely difficult for other countries to compete on the world market with the output of the American studios.

Bibliography

Bendazzi, Giannalberto (1994), *Cartoons: One Hundred Years of Cinema Animation*.

Cabarga, Leslie (1988), *The Fleischer Story*.
Canemaker, John (1987), *Winsor McCay: His Life and Art*.
—— (1991), *Felix: The Twisted Tale of the World's Most Famous Cat*.
Cholodenko, Alan (ed.) (1991), *The Illusion of Life: Essays on Animation*.
Crafton, Donald (1990), *Émile Cohl, Caricature and Film*.
—— (1993), *Before Mickey: The Animated Film, 1898–1928*.
Gifford, Denis (1987), *British Animated Films, 1895–1985: A Filmography*.

—— (1990), *American Animated Films: The Silent Era, 1897–1929*.
Maltin, Leonard (1980), *Of Mice and Magic: A History of American Animated Cartoons*.
Merritt, Russell, and Kaufman, J. B. (1994), *Walt in Wonderland: The Silent Films of Walt Disney*.
Robinson, David (1991), 'Masterpieces of Animation, 1833–1908'.
Solomon, Charles (1987), *Enchanted Drawings: The History of Animation*.

Comedy

DAVID ROBINSON

In a bare quarter of a century, the silent cinema created a tradition of film comedy as distinctive and as self-contained as the *commedia dell'arte*—from which, however remotely, it seemed to derive something of its character.

The cinema arrived at the end of a century that had witnessed a rich flowering of popular comedy. Early in the century, both in Paris and in London, archaic theatrical regulations had forbidden spoken drama in certain theatres, and thus provided unintended stimulus for the inspired mime of Baptiste Debureau at Les Funambules in Paris, and for the English burletta, with its special combination of music, song, and mime. Later, the new proletarian audiences of the great cities of Europe and America found their own theatre in music hall, variety, and vaudeville. With these popular audiences, comedy was in constant demand. When life was bad, laughter was a comfort; when it was good, they wanted to enjoy themselves just the same. Famous comedy mime troupes of the music halls, like the Martinettis, the Ravels, the Hanlon-Lees, and Fred Karno's Speechless Comedians, can be seen as direct forerunners of one-reel slapstick films. Karno, in fact, was to train two of the greatest film comedians, Charlie Chaplin and Stan Laurel.

BEFORE THE WAR: THE EUROPEAN ERA

The earliest comic films—still only a minute or less in length—were generally one-point jokes often inspired by newspaper cartoons, comic strips, comic postcards, stereograms, or magic lantern slides. The world's first film comedy, the Lumières' *L'Arroseur arrosé* (*Watering the Gardener*, 1895), was directly derived from a comic strip showing a naughty boy stepping on a garden hose and then releasing his foot as the unwitting gardener peers into the nozzle.

By the turn of the century, however, films were growing longer, and film-makers began to discover the specific qualities of the medium. Georges Méliès and his imitators used cinematic tricks, like stop action and accelerated movement, for comic effects. In the years 1905–7 the chase film—which typically featured an ever-growing crowd of eccentrics in escalating pursuit of a thief or other malefactor—became very popular with audiences. The best-known exponents of the genre were the directors André Heuze in France and Alfred Collins in England.

The year 1907 brought a revolution, when the Pathé Company launched a series of comedies featuring the character Boireau played by the comedian André Deed (André Chapuis, born 1884). Deed was the cinema's first true comic star, and achieved international popularity with his grotesque, infantile, comic character. From Méliès, with whom he probably worked as an actor, Deed learnt much about the craft of film-making, and particularly trick effects.

When in 1909 Deed was wooed away from Pathé by the Itala Company of Turin (he was to return to France two years later), Pathé already had an even greater comic star to take his place. This comedian, Max Linder, possessed an apparently inexhaustible comic invention, and was a performer of exquisite skill. The most durable and prolific of Pathé's stable of comic stars was Charles Prince (born Charles Petit-demange Seigneur), who made nearly 600 films in the course of ten years, in the character of Rigadin. Other Pathé comedians included Boucot (Jean-Louis Boucot), the established variety star Dranem, Babylas, Little Moritz, the stout Rosalie (Sarah Duhamel), Cazalis, and the comic detective Nick Winter (Léon Durac).

The Boireau and Max series proved an incomparable draw at the box-office and Pathé's rivals strove to compete. Gaumont poached the comedian Romeo Bosetti from Pathé, and he directed a Romeo series and a Calino series (starring Clément Migé) before returning to head Pathé's new Comica and Nizza comedy studios on the Côte d'Azur. Bosetti's successor at Gaumont was Jean Durand, whose greatest innovation was to create a whole comic troupe, called Les Pouics, whose orgies of slapstick and destruction were particularly admired by the surrealists. Out of the group emerged Onésime (Ernest Bourbon), who starred in at least eighty films which sometimes rose to truly surreal fantasy: in *Onésime contre Onésime*, for instance, he plays his own wicked *alter ego* whom he ultimately dismembers and devours. As Léonce, Léonce Perret, subsequently to become a significant director, specialized in a more sophisticated style of situation comedy. A plump, cheerful, clubbable man, his comic disasters generally involved social or amorous mix-ups rather than slapstick farce.

Gaumont's prolific star director, Louis Feuillade, personally directed two comedy series featuring charming and clever little boys, Bébé (Clément Mary) and Bout-de-Zan (René Poyen). The Éclair Company's child star, a precocious English boy called Willie Saunders, had little of their charm but enjoyed brief success in an era when the audience's appetite for comedy seemed inexhaustible, and led every French film company to develop its own, albeit often ephemeral, comedy stars.

The Italian cinema developed a parallel but distinctive school of film comedy, which produced forty comic stars and more than 1,100 films in the six years between 1909 and 1914. At the start of this period Italian cinema was undergoing great industrial expansion. Giovanni Pastrone, energetically building the fortunes of the Itala Company, recognized the commercial success of the French comedies which were being imported into Italy, and lured André Deed to his studio in Turin. Deed's new Italian character of Cretinetti proved as successful as Boireau, and the hundred or more films he made for Itala assured the company's prosperity.

Deed's transformation from Boireau to Cretinetti was not unusual in the comedy production of this era. The character names were regarded as the property of the company, so that when a comedian changed his allegiance, he had to find a new name. Moreover, every country where the films were shown tended to rename the character. Thus Deed's Cretinetti became Foolshead in England and America, Muller in Germany, Lehman in Hungary, Toribio in the Spanish-speaking countries, and Glupishkin in Russia. In France, the former Boireau now became Gribouille, only to revert to his original name when he returned to Pathé in 1911, the change being formally acknowledged with the film *Gribouille redevient Boireau*.

The success of the Cretinetti series launched a frantic competition between the companies to recruit comic stars wherever they could be found—in circuses, music halls, or the legitimate theatre. Pastrone launched the Coco series with the actor Pacifico Aquilano. At the rival Turin studio of Arturo Ambrosio there were Ernesto Vaser as Frico, Gigetta Morano as Gigetta, and the Spanish Marcel Fabre as Robinet. In Milan, the Milano Company launched the French comedian E. Monthus as Fortunetti, shortly afterwards changing his name to Cocciutelli. In Rome, however, Cines discovered the greatest native comedian of the period, Ferdinand Guillaume, who adopted the successive comic identities of Tontolini and—after defecting to the Turin company Pasquali—Polidor. Cines also boasted another of the best comics of the period, Kri-Kri, personified by Raymond Fran, who like Fabre had trained as a clown in the French circus and music hall. Italian producers took note of the popularity of Bébé and Bout-de-Zan, and groomed their own child stars, Firuli (Maria Bey) at Ambrosio and Frugolino (Ermanno Roveri) at Cines. Cines's most charming and enduring child star was Cinessino, played by the nephew of Ferdinand Guillaume, Eraldo Giunchi.

The films and their subjects were often repetitive, but this is hardly surprising, given that they were turned out at the rate of two or more a week. Characteristically, each film established a particular setting, occupation, and problem for the comedian. Every clown in turn would be a boxer, a house-painter, a policeman, a fireman, a flirt, a hen-pecked husband, a soldier. Novelties, fashions, and foibles of the day were all grist to the mill—motor-cars, aeroplanes, gramophones, the tango craze, suffragettes, temperance campaigns, unemployment, modern art, the cinema itself. Yet, even in their short, simple films, the best comedians brought the vitality of their own personality and peculiarities. Deed/Boireau/Cretinetti was frenetic, with the over-enthusiasm of a child (quite often he chose to adopt infantine clothes, like sailor suits). More often than not the chains of comic catastrophe were provoked by his own eagerness to fulfil his chosen role whether as insurance salesman, paper-hanger, or Red Cross volunteer. In contrast, Guillaume/Tontolini/Polidor was quaint, sweet, and innocent, the passive victim of comic holocausts, often finding himself obliged to disguise himself, with delirious and delightful effect, as a woman. Kri-Kri excelled in gag invention. The handsome Robinet's disasters generally arose from the manic enthusiasm with which he threw himself into every new undertaking, whether cycling or ballroom dancing.

Although the Italian school of comedy was originally inspired by the French example and the immigrant Deed, these films possess something indigenous and inimitable. The streets and houses and homes, the life and manners of the petty bourgeoisie whose well-ordered existence our heroes so carefully observe and so recklessly disrupt, convey the world and concerns of pre-war urban Italy. Although some basic forms of the one-reel comedy may have been imported, the films of the Italian comics drew heavily and profitably on earlier native lines of popular comedy—circus, vaudeville, and an ancient tradition of *spettacolo da piazza* which provides a link with the *commedia dell'arte*.

Other countries enjoyed their smaller share of this brief, prolific period of European film comedy. In Germany the clown-stars included Ernst Lubitsch and the infant

Buster Keaton

(1895–1966)

Of all the great silent comedians, Buster Keaton is the one who suffered the worst eclipse with the coming of sound but whose reputation has recovered the best. He was born Joseph Francis Keaton, in Piqua, Kansas, where his parents were appearing in a medicine show. Nicknamed Buster by fellow artist Harry Houdini, he joined his parents' act while still a baby. By the age of 5 he was already an accomplished acrobat and was soon billed as star of the show. In 1917 the family act broke up. Buster went to work with Roscoe (Fatty) Arbuckle at his Comique film studios in New York and then followed Arbuckle and producer Joe Schenck to California at the end of the year. He worked with Arbuckle for a couple of years, learning filmcraft with the same dedication as he had given to stagecraft, but struck out on his own, with Schenck's backing, in 1921. Between then and 1928, with Schenck as his constant mentor and producer (and also brother-in-law, since each had married one of the Talmadge sisters), he starred in some twenty shorts and a dozen features, almost all of which he directed himself and on which he enjoyed total creative freedom. To this period belong such classics as *The Navigator* (1924), *The General* (1926), and *Steamboat Bill, Jr.* (1928). The coming of sound brought an even more abrupt end to his career than to those of many other artists of the silent period. Losing Schenck's patronage, he joined MGM as a salaried contract artist with no creative control. His marriage to Natalie Talmadge broke up definitively in 1932. In the last twenty-five years of his life, which was plagued with personal problems, he struggled to keeep his career alive. Throughout the early sound years and into the 1940s he appeared in numerous second-rate films which gave little scope for his unique silent persona. But he was largely forgotten by the public until invited to play opposite Chaplin in a brilliant cameo in the latter's *Limelight* (1951). His career began to pick up and his financial and personal difficulties lessened. His last film appearance was in Richard Lester's *A Funny Thing Happened on the Way to the Forum* in 1965.

Keaton was above all a consummate professional. A brilliant and extremely courageous acrobat, he devised the most elaborate gags and performed them with extraordinary aplomb. Only rarely did he have recourse to tricks and special effects, and when he did the effects often constitute gags of their own, almost as ingenious as his own performances. Sometimes the effects are transparent, as in the transitions between reality and fantasy in *Sherlock Jr.* (1924); sometimes they are concealed, as with the mechanism that controls the mysterious behaviour of the doors in *The Navigator*. In *Our Hospitality* (1923), where the rescue of the heroine intercuts shots which really are on the raging rapids with studio mock-ups, the basic effect remains one of realism. The sense of being in a real world, full of real, if recalci-

trant, objects, provides an essential context for those moments in Keaton films in which objects—as in the much imitated gag of the sinking lifebelt—do not behave in realistic ways.

Keaton's mastery of timing—the natural comedian's stock-in trade—was extraordinary. From very early on, however, he extended it from the field of acting performance into that of extended *mise-en-scène*. He developed running gags and constructed comic scenes which lasted for several minutes and deployed extensive resources, often centred around moving objects such as trains or motor-bikes. Control of the architecture of these scenes was as important as the comic business carried by his performance. When the house in *One Week* (1920) is demolished, not by the train the audience expects to destroy it, but by another one steaming in from a different angle, and the hero is left bemused and forlorn among the wreckage, it is hard to say whether it is Keaton the director or Buster the performer who is most to be admired. The saddest feature of his later films, from *Spite*

Marriage (1929) onwards, is not the loss of his performing talent but the fact that he could no longer construct entire films in which to develop it.

But Keaton's gags would be mere pyrotechnics were it not for the personality of Buster himself. A slight figure, with a seemingly impassive face, generally equipped with a straw hat placed (to borrow T. S. Eliot's phrase about Cavafy) at a slight angle to the universe, Buster was the perennial innocent plunged into ridiculous and impossible situations and emerging unscathed through a mixture of obstinacy and unexpected resource. Unlike Chaplin or Lloyd, the Buster persona makes no appeal to the audience. He is a blank sheet, on whom testing circumstances and awakening sexual desire gradually impose a character. At the outset the Buster character tends to be a dreamer or a fantasist, blissfully unaware of the gap between reality and fantasy or the obstacles that might stand in the path of realizing his desire. Faced with recalcitrant objects or hostile fellow-beings, he remains unfazed, tackling each obstacle with grim determination and expedients of greater and greater daring and extremity. By the end when he (usually) wins the girl, he has become wiser to the world, but his innocence remains.

In September 1965, Keaton, now nearly 70, made a personal appearance at the Venice film Festival, where he was tumultuously applauded. He died of cancer a few months later.

GEOFFREY NOWELL-SMITH

SELECT FILMOGRAPHY

Short films
The Butcher Boy (with Roscoe Arbuckle) (1917); Back Stage (with Roscoe Arbuckle) (1919); One Week (1920); Neighbors (1920); The Goat (1921); The Playhouse (1921); The Paleface (1921); Cops (1922); The Frozen North (1922)
Keaton–Schenck features
Three Ages (1923); Our Hospitality (1923); Sherlock Jr. (1924); The Navigator (1924); Seven Chances (1925); Go West (1925); Battling Butler (1926); The General (1926); College (1927); Steamboat Bill, Jr. (1928)
MGM productions (silent period)
The Cameraman (1928); Spite Marriage (1929)

BIBLIOGRAPHY

Blesh, Rudi (1967), *Keaton*.
Keaton, Buster (1967), *My Wonderful World of Slapstick*.
Robinson, David (1969), *Buster Keaton*.

Opposite: Buster Keaton in *The Navigator* (1924)

Curt Bois. The insatiable cinema audiences of Russia had the ever love-lorn Antosha (the Pole, Antonin Fertner), Giacomo, Reynolds, the fat Djadja Pud (V. Avdeyev), the simple peasant Mitjukha (N. P. Nirov), and the urbane, silk-hatted Arkasha (Arkady Boitler). Despite a strong music hall tradition, which contributed a number of stars to American film comedy, Britain's star comics, Winky, Jack Spratt, and the most talented, Pimple (Fred Evans), showed little of the verve or invention of the French and Italians.

This era of European comedy nevertheless made its own distinctive contribution to the development of film style. While the cultural pretensions of more prestigious dramatic and costume films led their makers to borrow style as well as respectability from the stage, the comedians were unfettered by such inhibitions or ambitions. They ranged freely; much of the time they shot in the streets, catching the atmosphere of everyday life; yet at the same time they were employing and exploring all the artifices of camera trickery. The rhythm of talented mimes was imposed upon the films themselves.

Europe's golden age of comedy was brief, and was ended by the First World War. Many of the young artists went off to the war and did not return, or never retrieved their pre-war glory after service and war injuries. Film tastes and economies were changing. The Italian cinema's immediate pre-war boom burst like a bubble when the old markets were disrupted. Meanwhile, the old comedies were made to seem archaic overnight, in the blaze of new competitors from the other side of the Atlantic. The American film industry, already migrating to the open spaces and spectacular natural décors of the West, was poised to dominate the world cinema industry.

AMERICAN COMEDIES AND MACK SENNETT

America had lagged behind continental Europe in developing name comedians who could sustain regular series of one-reel films. The first true American comic star of the type was John Bunny (1863–1915), a fat, genial man who had been a successful stage actor and producer before recognizing the potential of films, and offering himself to the Vitagraph Company. Although today his films, generally revolving around social mix-ups and marital spats, seem woefully unfunny, his success with audiences before the First World War was phenomenal, and encouraged other American companies to try comedy series. Essanay's Snakeville Comedies introduced 'Alkali Ike' (Augustus Carney) and 'Mustang Pete' (William Todd). Another Essanay series introduced a future star, Wallace Beery, as Sweedie.

The transformation and pre-eminence of American screen comedy, however, may be dated from the formation of the Keystone Comedy Studio under Mack Sennett, in 1912. Keystone was the comedy arm of the New York Motion Picture Company, whose other Hollywood studios were 101 Bison, producing Thomas Ince's Westerns and historical films, and Reliance, specializing in dramas. Sennett was Irish-Canadian, an unsuccessful stage actor who in 1908 had been reduced to working in movies. He was fortunate to be recruited to the Biograph Studios, where his natural curiosity led him to observe and absorb the discoveries of Biograph's principal director D. W. Griffith. Along with Griffith's revolutionary techniques, Sennett studied the comedies coming from France, and by 1910 had acquired enough skill to be appointed Biograph's principal comedy director, a post which led to his appointment to run Keystone. He brought with him to Keystone some of his former Biograph collaborators including Fred Mace, Ford Sterling, and the beautiful and witty Mabel Normand.

Sennett was uneducated, intelligent, and tough, with an instinctive sense of comedy. Because he was easily bored himself, he could tell what would hold the audience's attention and what would not. Having mastered film craft at Biograph, he passed on his lessons. The Keystone cameramen were dextrous in following the free flight of the clowns; and the fast Keystone editing was adapted from Griffith's innovatory methods.

Keystone stars and films derived from vaudeville, circus, comic strips, and at the same time from the realities of early twentieth-century America. Keystone pictures depicted a world of wide, dusty streets with one-storey clapboard houses, hardware stores and groceries, dentists' surgeries and saloon bars. The clowns inhabited a familiar world of kitchens and parlours, seedy hotel lobbies, bedrooms with iron cots and rickety wash-stands, bowler hats and wild beards, feathered hats and harem skirts, Model-Ts and horses-and-buggies. Comedy at Keystone was a wild caricature of the ordinary joys and terrors of everyday life, and the guiding rule was to keep things moving, to allow the audience no pause for breath or critical reflection. Sennett built up a stock company of outrageous grotesques and fearless acrobats, including Roscoe 'Fatty' Arbuckle—a fat man with great comedy style and dexterity—cross-eyed Ben Turpin, walrus-whiskered Billy Bevan and Chester Conklin, giant Mack Swain, obese Fred Mace. Other comedians who emerged from the Keystone Studio included the future stars Harold Lloyd and Harry Langdon, Charlie Chase, who became a notable director as Charles Parrott, Charles Murray, Slim Summerville, Hank Mann, Edgar Kennedy, Harry McCoy, Raymond Griffith, Louise Fazenda, Polly Moran, Minta Durfee, and Alice Davenport. At least two Keystone Kops, Eddie Sutherland and Edward Cline, as well as two Sennett gagmen, Malcolm St Clair and Frank Capra, later became notable comedy directors in their own right.

The Keystone comedies remain a monument of early twentieth-century popular art, transmuting the evident surfaces of the life and times of the 1910s and 1920s into a comedy that is basic and universal. The Keystone shorts were uncompromisingly anarchic. In an era of determinedly materialistic values, the Sennett films celebrated orgiastic destruction of goods and possessions, of cars and houses and china ornaments. As in all the best comedy, authority and dignity were tumbled and ridiculed.

Sennett's greatest year was 1914, when his most famous star, Charlie Chaplin, won world fame for himself and the studio in a few months of phenomenal discovery, innovation, and comedy creation. When his one-year Keystone contract expired, Chaplin, recognizing his immense commercial value, asked for a large raise on his $150 a week salary. Sennett, short-sightedly perhaps, was unwilling to meet his demands. Chaplin was to move in turn to the Essanay Studios and contracts with Mutual and First National which gave him the increased independence of operation which he craved. Keystone survived the loss, but the Chaplin year had been the studio's apogee.

Sennett's success at Keystone spurred many rival studios, some short-lived, to set up in comedy production. His most serious rival was Hal Roach, who teamed up with a fellow film extra, Harold Lloyd, to make a comedy series starring Lloyd as Willie Work, a pale imitation of Chaplin's Tramp. Subsequent collaborations fared better, and the creation of Lloyd's bespectacled 'Harold' character launched their careers to joint success. After the parting with Lloyd, Roach was inspired to team two comedians who had been working solo for years. Laurel and Hardy were to pass into universal mythology, the sublime partnership of the tiny, diffident, tearful Stan with the large, pompous, unwisely over-confident Ollie.

The style of the Roach stars over the years—Lloyd, Laurel and Hardy, the troupe of child comedians Our Gang, Thelma Todd and ZaSu Pitts, Charlie Chase, Will Rogers, Edgar Kennedy, Snub Pollard—exemplify the difference between Roach and Sennett. The latter's films tended to frenetic action and slapstick. Roach preferred well-constructed stories and a more restrained, realistic, and ultimately more sophisticated style of character comedy. Harold Lloyd and Stan and Ollie are recognizably human, sharing the foibles, feelings, and anxieties of an audience which is also engaged in the permanent battle with the perilous uncertainties of the contemporary world.

THE HEYDAY OF SILENT COMEDY

At least until 1913 the standard length of a film was one reel; multi-reel feature films were at first resisted in many quarters of the film trade. It was, then, a dramatic revolution when Sennett announced the first multi-reel comedy at the end of 1914. *Tillie's Punctured Romance* (1914) was designed to star the famous comedienne Marie Dressler in an adaptation of one of her stage successes. Charlie Chaplin was cast as her leading man. Despite the success of this film, it was to be several years before the

Harold Lloyd in *For Heaven's Sake* (1926)

feature-length comedy was established. Chaplin made his first two-reeler, *Dough and Dynamite* (1914), at Keystone, but not until 1918 and *A Dog's Life* did he embark on feature-length films. Keaton made his first feature in 1920, Lloyd in 1921, Harry Langdon in 1925.

Chaplin, Keaton, Lloyd, and Langdon—the four giants of American silent film comedy—all emerged from the one- and two-reeler period to reach the apogee of their careers in the 1920s. Chaplin trained in the British music hall and, in the manipulation of the image at Keystone, created in his Tramp character the most universal fictional human image in history. Like Chaplin, Keaton was above all a highly accomplished actor, who gave each of the characters he played—they ranged from millionaires to cowhands—its own validity. The myth of 'The Great Stone Face' misrepresents his startlingly expressive face and still more eloquent body. A lifetime of creating comedy and solving stage problems (he was working professionally from the age of three) gave him an impeccable sense of comic structure and *mise-en-scène*. The characteristic, escalating Keaton gag enchainments make him the equal of any director working in 1920s Hollywood.

Harold Lloyd was exceptional among the silent film comedians since his background and training were not in vaudeville. Stage-struck from youth, he had worked in little stock companies before landing a job as a $5-a-day extra at Universal Studios, where he met Hal Roach. Lloyd joined Sennett after the Willie Work films and a disagreement with Roach; but they reunited to make a new series, with Lloyd as a hayseed, Lonesome Luke. The films proved successful enough; but in 1917 Lloyd put on a pair of horn-rim glasses for a film called *Over the Fence* (1917), and discovered a far better character which was to bring him lasting fame. The Harold character evolved through a series of shorts, and was fully formed by the time of his first feature *A Sailor-Made Man* (1921). Harold was always aspiring to be the all-American boy, the Horatio Alger hero, an enthusiastic go-getter. The drive for social or economic betterment that always motivates the plot of a Lloyd comedy probably represented a sincere moral belief: Lloyd was in real life the embodiment of his own success stories.

With *Safety Last* (1923) Lloyd introduced the special style of comedy of thrills with which his name is always associated. The plot somehow called upon the innocent Harold to take the place of a human fly; and the last third of the picture is a rising crescendo of gags as Harold encounters ever more horrible hazards in attempting to scale the side of a skyscraper. Lloyd's eleven silent features, including *Grandma's Boy* (1922), *The Freshman* (1925), and the

83

Charlie Chaplin
(1889–1977)

At the age of 24, after only a few days in pictures and a single film appearance, Charles Chaplin created the comic character that was to bring him world fame, and which even today remains the most universally recognized fictional representation of human kind—an icon both of comedy and the movies themselves.

Chaplin's little Tramp appears to have been a spontaneous, unpremeditated creation. On or about 5 January 1914, deciding that he needed a new comic persona for his next one-reel film, he went into the wardrobe shack at the Keystone Studios, and emerged in the costume, make-up and character more or less as we still know it. He had invented many stage characters before, and he would continue to experiment with others on the screen; but no figure that he or any other comedian created would ever be so potent.

Chaplin's first ten years had witnessed more tribulation than most human beings ever encounter in long lifetimes. His father, a moderately successful singer on the London music halls—apparently exasperated by his wife's infidelities—abandoned his family, and succumbed to alcoholism and early death. His mother, a less successful music hall artist, intermittently struggled to maintain Charles and his half-brother Sydney. As her health and mind broke down—she was eventually permanently confined to mental hospitals—the children spent extended periods in public institutions. By his tenth year Charles Chaplin was familiar with poverty, hunger, madness, drunkenness, the cruelty of the poor London streets and the cold impersonality of public institutions. Chaplin survived, developing his self-reliance.

At ten years old he went to work first in a clog-dance act and then in comic roles; and by the time he joined Fred Karno's Speechless Comedians in 1908 he was well versed in every kind of stage craft.

Karno was a London impresario who had built his own comedy industry, maintaining several companies, with a 'fun factory' to develop and rehearse sketches, to train performers, and to prepare scenery and properties. An inspired judge of comedy, Karno groomed several generations of talented comedians, including Stan Laurel and Chaplin himself. In length, form and knockabout mime, Karno's sketches closely anticipated the classic one-reel comedy of the early cinema.

While touring the United States as the star of a Karno sketch company, Chaplin was offered a contract by the Keystone film company. Mack Sennett, its chief, was very much the Hollywood equivalent of Karno—an impresario with a special gift for broad comedy. After a tentative first film, *Making a Living*, Chaplin devised his definitive role (the costume was first seen in 1914 in *Kid Auto Races at Venice*) and embarked on a series of one-reel films that within months made him a household name. The po-

tency of the Tramp was that in creating this character, Chaplin used all the experience of humanity he had absorbed in his first ten years, and transformed it into the comic art he had so completely mastered in the apprenticeship of the years that had followed.

Dissatisfied with the breakneck Keystone pace that give him no chance to develop his subtler comedy style, Chaplin quickly persuaded Sennett to let him direct, and after June 1914 was always to be his own director. He left Sennett at the end of the year's contract, moving from company to company in search of greater rewards and also, more important in his view, greater creative independence.

The Little Tramp prospecting in the harsh conditions of the Yukon: *The Gold Rush* (1925)

The one- and two-reel films he made at Keystone (1914, 35 films), Essanay (1915, 14 films) and for distribution by the Mutual Company (1916-17, 12 films) show a continuous progression: many feel that he never surpassed the best of the Mutual films, which include *One A.M.*, *The Pawnshop*, *Easy Street* and *The Immigrant*. Chaplin revealed qualities that were then quite new to film comedy— mime that achieved the highest level of acting art, pathos, and daring commentary on social issues.

In 1918 he built his own studio, where he was to work for the next 33 years in conditions of unparalleled independence. A brilliant series of short features for distribution by First National included *Shoulder Arms* (1918), a comedic vision of the First World War, *The Pilgrim* (1923), which tilts at religious bigotry, and *The Kid* (1921), a unique, rich sentimental comedy in which more than anywhere else Chaplin exposes the lingering pain of his own childhood experience of poverty and public charity.

With Douglas Fairbanks, Mary Pickford and D.W.Griffith, Chaplin co-founded United Artists, in 1919, and all his subsequent American-made features were to be released through this concern. His first UA picture *A Woman of Paris* (1923), a brilliant and innovative social comedy, was rejected by the public at large since Chaplin himself did not appear, apart from an uncredited walk-on. In *The Gold Rush* (1925) he made high comedy out of the privations of the Klondyke prospectors. No less inspired, *The Circus* (1928), a troubled production that coincided with divorce proceedings by his second wife, also had bitter undertones.

Knowing that speech would mark the end of the Tramp, Chaplin temporized throughout the 1930s with two more silent films, with music and effects as concessions to the sound era. *City Lights* (1931) is an unfailingly effective sentimental comedy-melodrama; *Modern Times* (1936), in which the Tramp made his farewell, is a comic commentary on the machine age, whose satire still retains its bite.

Chaplin felt increasing responsibility to use his comic gifts for critical commentary on his times. He courted grave unpopularity in isolationist America with his satire on Hitler and Mussolini, *The Great Dictator* (1940); and risked even more, in the first days of Cold War paranoia, with *Monsieur Verdoux* (1946), in which he ironically compared the activities of a Landru-style mass murderer with the wholesale killing licensed by war.

Chaplin's situation in America was already insecure. His outspoken liberal views, his appeal to leftish thinkers and his refusal to take American nationality had long made him anathema to the FBI, which had files on him stretching back to the 1920s. The Bureau pushed an unstable young woman, Joan Barry, into bringing a series of charges, including a paternity claim, against Chaplin. The paternity claim was later proved to be false; but the mud stuck, and the FBI went on to manipulate a smear campaign charging Chaplin with Communist sympathies.

Limelight (1952), a dramatic film set in the theatrical London of Chaplin's childhood, and dealing with the difficulties of making comedy and the fickleness of the public, seemed at once a reflection on his own impaired reputation and a retreat into nostalgia.

When Chaplin left for Europe for the London premiere of *Limelight*, the FBI persuaded the Attorney General to rescind the re-entry permit that, as an alien, he required. He was to spend the rest of his life in Europe, returning only briefly in 1972 to accept an honorary Oscar and fulsome eulogies that seemed to be Hollywood's atonement. His home from 1953 was in Vevey, Switzerland, where he lived with his wife, the former Oona O'Neill, and a family that eventually numbered eight children.

He continued to work in exile. The uneven *A King in New York* (1957) ridiculed America's McCarthyist paranoia. Though hurt by the poor press for his last film, *A Countess from Hong Kong* (1967), starring Marlon Brando and Sophia Loren, Chaplin worked, almost to the end, on a new project *The Freak*. In addition he produced two autobiographical volumes, and composed musical scores for his old silent films. Knighted in 1975, Sir Charles Chaplin died on Christmas Day 1977.

In recent years Chaplin's achievement has sometimes been underestimated by critics without historical perspective, or perhaps influenced by the public smears of the 1940s. His popularity contributed much to Hollywood's prosperity and rise to worldwide pre-eminence in the period of the First World War. The sophisticated intelligence and skills he brought to slapstick comedy forced intellectuals to recognise that art could reside in a wholly popular entertainment, and not just in those self-consciously 'artistic' products with which the cinema first tried to court respectability. In the 1910s and 20s Chaplin's Tramp, combating a hostile and unrewarding world with cheek and gallantry, afforded a talisman and champion to the underprivileged millions who were the cinema's first mass audience.

DAVID ROBINSON

SELECT FILMOGRAPHY

Kid Auto Races at Venice (1914); Tillie's Punctured Romance (1914); The Champion (1915); The Tramp (1915); A Woman (1915); A Night at the Show (1915); Police (1915); One A.M. (1916); The Pawnshop (1916); Behind the Screen (1916); Easy Street (1917); The Cure (1917); The Immigrant (1917); A Dog's Life (1918); Shoulder Arms (1918); The Kid (1921); The Pilgrim (1923); A Woman of Paris (1923); The Gold Rush (1925); The Circus (1928); City Lights (1931); Modern Times (1936); The Great Dictator (1940); Monsieur Verdoux (1946); Limelight (1952); A King in New York (1957); A Countess From Hong Kong (1967).

BIBLIOGRAPHY

Chaplin, Charles (1964), *My Autobiography*.
Huff, Theodore (1951), *Charlie Chaplin*.
Lyons, Timothy J. (1979), *Charles Chaplin, A Guide to References and Resources*.
McCabe, John (1978), *Charlie Chaplin*.
Robinson, David (1985), *Chaplin, His Life and Art*.

culminating *The Kid Brother* (1927) and *Speedy* (1928), were among the biggest-earning comedies of the 1920s, even outgrossing Chaplin's films.

Harry Langdon's output was smaller and more uneven than the others; but he merits his place in the pantheon of great clowns on the strength of three features, *Tramp, Tramp, Tramp*, *The Strong Man* (both 1926), and *Long Pants* (1927)—the first scripted by Frank Capra, the others directed by him. Langdon's screen character is quiet, cute, and rather weird. His round, white face and podgy figure, his tight-fitting clothes, and his stiff slightly uncontrolled movements give him the look, as James Agee pointed out, of an elderly baby. This childlike, guileless quality gives an eerie edge to his encounters with the grown-up world of sexuality and sin.

In this enchanted age of comedy, the reputation of other comedians has been unjustly eclipsed. Raymond Griffith emulated the sartorial elegance of Max Linder and encountered catastrophes and peril with insouciant ingenuity; his masterpiece *Hands Up!* (1926) cast him as a Civil War spy. Marion Davies's fame as the mistress of William Randolph Hearst has eclipsed her contemporary celebrity as a comedienne of particular charm whose fun was seen at its best in the films in which King Vidor directed her, *Show People* and *The Patsy* (both 1928). The Canadian-born entertainer Beatrice Lillie left her mark in a single wonderful silent comedy, *Exit Smiling* (1927). Migrants from Europe, the Italian Monty Banks (Monte Bianchi) and the English Lupino Lane enjoyed successful if brief starring careers; Banks subsequently turned director. Larry Semon, with his distinctive white mask like a Pierrot lunaire started the 1920s as Hollywood's highest-paid comedian, but his later features met with diminishing success, and hardly bear revival today. W. C. Fields and Will Rogers made sporadic forays into silent films, though their essentially verbal style of comedy was only to come into its own in the era of talking pictures.

The extraordinary flowering of silent film comedy in Hollywood was not to any great extent reflected anywhere else in the world—perhaps indeed because American comedies enjoyed such huge international distribution and popularity that there was no chance of competing with them. In Britain, Betty Balfour, who made two feature films in her character of Squibs, was the nearest to a star comedienne: attempts to put popular music hall comedians on the screen lacked both skill and success. In Germany the child star of 1909, Curt Bois, grew up to be the bright star of a few comedies, the best of them *The Count from Pappenheims*. In France René Clair brought the comedy style of the French stage vaudeville to the screen with *The Italian Straw Hat* (*Un chapeau de paille d'Italie*, 1927) and *Les Deux Timides* (1928). But screen comedy was distinctly an American art form.

It was to remain so, although the golden age of silence was abruptly extinguished with the coming of sound. The causes were manifold. Some comedians were disoriented by the fact of sound itself (Raymond Griffith was an extreme case, having a severe throat defect which restricted his power of speech). The new techniques—the microphones and the cameras enclosed in sound-proof booths—suddenly restricted the freedom of film-makers. More important the escalating costs and profits of film-making led to much closer production supervision, which generally proved inimical to the independence which had been vital to the working methods of the best comedians. Rare ones, like Chaplin and Lloyd, were able to win themselves freedom of operation for a few more years, but others, including Keaton and Langdon, found themselves employees of huge film factories which had no place or concern for individualists. After 1929 Keaton never directed another film, and Langdon vanished into obscurity. A new art had been born, had flowered, and died in little more than a quarter of a century.

Bibliography
Kerr, Walter (1975), *The Silent Clowns*.
Lahue, Kalton C. (1966), *World of Laughter*.
—— (1967), *Kops and Custard*.
McCaffrey, Donald W. (1968), *Four Great Comedians*.
Montgomery, John (1954), *Comedy Films: 1894–1954*.
Robinson, David (1969), *The Great Funnies: A History of Film Comedy*.

Documentary

CHARLES MUSSER

The term 'documentary' did not come into popular use until the late 1920s and 1930s. It was initially applied to various kinds of 'creative' non-fiction screen practice in the post-First World War, classical cinema era. Originating films in the category have typically included Robert Flaherty's *Nanook of the North* (1922), various Soviet films of the 1920s such as Dziga Vertov's *The Man with the Movie Camera* (*Chelovek s kinoapparatom*, 1929), Walter Ruttmann's *Berlin: Symphony of a City* (*Berlin: die Sinfonie der Großstadt*, 1927), and John Grierson's *Drifters* (1929). Yet 'documentary' cinema has roots that lie further back in the reworking of a vital and long-established form that had flourished throughout the second half of the nineteenth century—the illustrated lecture. Early documentarians used the magic lantern to create complex and often sophisticated programmes out of a succession of projected photographic images accompanied by a live narration, with an occasional use of music and sound effects. By the turn of the century, films were gradually replacing slides while intertitles usurped the function of the lecture—changes that eventually gave rise to the new terminology. The documentary tradition preceded film and has continued into the era of television and video, thus being redefined in the light of technological innovations, as well as in the context of shifting social and cultural forces.

ORIGINS

The use of projected images for documentary purposes can be traced back to the mid-seventeenth century, when the Jesuit Andreas Tacquet gave an illustrated lecture about a missionary's trip to China. In the first decades of the nineteenth century, the magic lantern was often used to give audio-visual programmes on science (particularly astronomy), current affairs, travel, and adventure.

The ability to transfer photographic images on to glass and project them with the lantern was a crucial leap forward in documentary practice. Lantern slide images not only achieved a new ontological status but became much smaller and easier to produce. Frederick and William Langenheim, German-born brothers then residing in Philadelphia, achieved this result in 1849 and showed examples of their work at the Great Exhibition in London in 1851. By the mid-1860s the use of these slides in travel lectures had become popular in eastern cities of the United States, with an evening's programme typically focusing on a single foreign country. In June 1864, for instance, New York audiences could see *The Army of the Potomac*, an illustrated lecture on the Civil War using photographs taken by Alexander Gardner and Mathew Brady. Although the magic lantern had been used primarily to evoke the mystical or fantastic in the late eighteenth and early nineteenth centuries, by the late 1860s it was being used predominantly for documentary purposes and was assigned new names as a result—the 'stereopticon' in the United States and the 'optical lantern' in England.

These documentary-like illustrated lectures flourished in western Europe and North America. In the United States, several exhibitors toured the principal cities, giving a series of four or five programmes which changed from year to year. In the last three decades of the nineteenth century, many noteworthy documentary-like programmes were given by adventurers, archaeologists, and explorers. Programmes on the Arctic were particularly popular from 1865 onward, and often displayed an ethnographic bent. Lieutenant Robert Edwin Peary inter-

rupted his efforts to reach the North Pole by presenting travelogue-style lectures in the early and mid-1890s. Displaying 100 lantern slides in his 1896 lecture, Peary not only recounted his journey from Newfoundland to the Polar ice cap in heroic terms but offered an ethnographic study of the Inuit or 'Esquimaux'.

Similar kinds of programme were offered in Europe. Magic lantern activities flourished particularly in Britain, where the colonial agenda was strong: Egypt was a favourite topic, and illustrated lectures such as *War in Egypt and the Soudan* (1887) were big money-makers. Victorian audiences also savoured lantern shows featuring local towns and countryside unaffected by the industrial revolution, including several series of slides made by photographer George Washington Wilson (*The Road to the Isles*, c. 1885).

Illustrated lectures about seemingly primitive, impoverished peoples in distant locales had their counterpart in lantern shows on the urban poor. In Britain programmes such as *Slum Life in our Great Cities* (c. 1890) treated poverty in a picturesque fashion, often attributing it to alcoholism. In the United States the social issue documentary began with Jacob Riis, who gave his first programme, *How the Other Half Lives and Dies*, on 25 January 1888. It focused on recent immigrant groups, particularly Italians and Chinese, who lived in poverty and germ-infested slums.

By the early 1890s highly portable 'detective' cameras allowed amateur and professional photographers to take candid pictures, often without the knowledge or permission of their subjects. Alexander Black used pictures he took of his Brooklyn neighbourhood to give an illustrated lecture he alternatively titled *Life through a Detective Camera* and *Ourselves as Others See Us*.

Most of the basic genres of documentary—covering travel, ethnography and archaeology, social issues, science, and war—were in place before the arrival of cinema. Many were evening-length single-subject programmes, while others were much shorter, designed to occupy a twenty-minute slot on a vaudeville bill or as part of a multi-subject, magazine-style format. Ethical issues about the relationship between documentarians and their subjects had been encountered, though rarely given much attention. In short, documentary screen practice had become an important part of middle-class cultural life in Europe and North America during the second half of the nineteenth century.

FROM SLIDES TO FILM

As film-making spread rapidly through Europe and North America in 1894–7, non-fiction subjects predominated, for they were easier and generally less expensive to produce than fiction films using sets and performers. The Lumières sent cameramen such as Alexandre Promio to countries

British cameraman J. B. McDowell in the trenches

in Europe, North and Central America, Asia, and Africa, where they shot groups of films that appropriated subject-matter and even compositions from earlier lantern views designed for travel lectures. Cameramen in other countries followed the Lumières' lead. In England Robert Paul sent cinematographer H. W. Short to Egypt in March 1897 (producing *An Arab Knife Grinder at Work*) and took a dozen films himself in Sweden that July (*A Laplander Feeding his Reindeer*). James H. White of the Edison Manufacturing Company toured through Mexico (*Sunday Morning in Mexico*), the western United States, Hawaii, China, and Japan (*Japanese Sampans*) over ten months in 1897–8.

News films were also frequently taken; seven were made of the Tsar's coronation in Russia, including the Lumières' *Czar et Czarine entrant dans l'église de l'Assomption* ('Tsar and Tsarina entering the Church of the Assumption', May 1896), and sporting events were also a popular subject, Paul filming *The Derby* in 1895. In smaller or less developed countries, local film-makers quickly emerged to take these 'actualities': in Italy, Vittorio Calina shot *Umberto e Margherita di Savoia a passeggio per il parco* ('King Umberto and

Margherita of Savoy strolling in the park', 1896); in Japan Tsunekichi Shibata took films of the Ginza, Tokyo's fashionable shopping district, in 1897; in Brazil, Alfonso Segreto began to take news and actuality films during 1898.

The very earliest motion pictures, whether *Sandow* (Edison, 1894), *Bucking Broncho* (Edison, 1894), *Rough Sea at Dover* (Paul–Acres, 1895), *The German Emperor Reviewing His Troops* (Acres, 1895), or *Sortie d'usine* (*Workers Leaving the Lumière Factory*, Lumière, 1895), had 'documentary value' but did not necessarily function within 'the documentary tradition'. Exhibitors often projected these non-fiction films in a variety format, interspersed with fiction films. The location of a given view was usually well labelled either in the programme or by a lecturer, but narrative and a sustained treatment of a specific subject were thwarted.

This 'cinema of attractions' approach continued to be popular, but it rapidly began to be balanced by the efforts of exhibitors to sequence films of related subject-matter, in many instances through an extended narrative. In England, for example, exhibitors routinely grouped together five or six films of Queen Victoria's Jubilee (June 1897) in an effort to cover the event. Each 'film' was generally one shot long and in an increasing number of instances each film was introduced by a title slide; often a lecturer or 'spieler' accompanied the screening with verbal explanations as well.

By 1898, exhibitors in different countries had begun to integrate slides and films into full-length documentary-like programmes. At the Brooklyn Institute of Arts and Science (New York) in April 1897, Henry Evans Northrop interspersed Lumière films through his lantern show *A Bicycle Trip through Europe*. Dwight Elmendorf gave a popular illustrated lecture, *The Santiago Campaign* (1898), which supplemented his own slides with Edison films of the Spanish–American War. Many programmes on the Spanish–American War combined actuality views with staged or 're-enacted' events as well as fictional vignettes, posing the problem of generic specificity that continues to this day. In England, Alfred John West produced a full-length show of slides and films, *West's Our Navy* (1898), which ran for many years and proved effective propaganda for the British Admiralty.

By the turn of the century, production companies shot groups of short films on a single theme that were then exhibited together, either as a short subject or as part of a longer slide-film presentation. The Charles Urban Trading Company (London) supplied news films of the Russo–Japanese War: in the United States, Burton Holmes acquired and used them for his full-length slide-film lecture *Port Arthur: Siege and Surrender* (1905), while Lyman Howe showed the same films but as one portion of his two-hour, magazine-style format. In the United States at least, professional illustrated lecturers were regularly combining slides and films into full-length documentary programmes by 1907–8.

With the rise of the story film between 1901 and 1905, non-fiction film lost its domination of the world's movie screens. Increasingly it was relegated to the margins of industrial practice. News films posed a particular problem. Unlike fiction films, they quickly became dated, losing their commercial value and their attraction for exhibitors and distributors. Only films showing events of earth-shaking importance tended to sell. This problem was solved when Pathé-Frères began to distribute a weekly newsreel, *Pathé Journal*, in 1908, first in Paris and, by the following year, throughout France, Germany, and England. *Pathé Weekly* débuted in the United States on 8 August 1911, and was rapidly followed by several American imitations.

Documentary-type programmes continued to appeal to middle-class and genteel audiences, and performed a range of significant ideological functions. They were frequently employed as propaganda for the colonial agenda of industrialized nations. The Anglo-Boer war was extensively photographed and filmed from a British perspective in 1899–1900. After 1905 numerous films were taken in the British, French, German, and Belgian colonies of Central Africa, including *Chasse à l'hippopotame sur le Nil Bleu* ('Hunting hippopotamus on the Blue Nile', Pathé, 1907), *Matrimonio abissino* ('Abyssinian marriage', Roberto Omenga, 1908), and *Leben und Treiben in Tangka* ('Life and events in Tangka', Deutsche-Bioskop, 1909). Many non-fiction films, such as *Making of a Newspaper* (Urban, 1904), depicted work processes which celebrated the technology of production, while showing workers as peripheral to these achievements. Innumerable depictions of royalty, activities of the rich, and military forces on parade or manœuvres all tended to offer a reassuring picture of the world scene. On the eve of World War, these non-fiction programmes generally lacked both critical perspective and any awareness of the catastrophe that loomed.

Many of the earliest feature films were full-length illustrated lectures using only motion pictures. These included *Coronation of King George V* (Kinemacolor, 1911), although the majority were still 'travelogues'. By the end of the 1910s no major expedition was complete without a film cameraman, and many produced popular films: *Roping Big Game in the Frozen North* (1912), taken on the Carnegie Alaska–Siberian Expedition by Captain F. E. Kleinschmidt; *Captain Scott's South Pole Expedition* (Gaumont, 1912). Others featured underwater photography (*Thirty Leagues under the Sea*, George and Ernest Williamson, 1914) or returned to Africa (*Through Central Africa*, James Barnes, 1915) and the poles (*Sir Douglas Mawson's Marvelous Views of the Frozen South*, 1915). For all of these programmes, lecturers stood by the screen and delivered their talk. They had generally

participated in the events and expeditions, or at least were eyewitnesses or acknowledged experts, and so they shared their personal understanding or insights with the audience. Often several prints of a given title would be in circulation at the same time, with each lecturer's personalized narration varying considerably. Frequently a programme would initially be presented by the chief film-maker or even the expedition head; then lesser figures would gradually take over these responsibilities. While often shot in exotic locales, these programmes always featured the adventures of Europeans or European Americans. In a remark about popular fiction that is equally applicable to the documentary Stuart Hall (1981) has observed, 'In this period, the very idea of adventure became synonymous with the demonstration of the moral, social and physical mastery of the colonisers over the colonised.'

Non-fiction film played a crucial role as propaganda during the First World War, although governments and their top military officers at first barred cameramen from the front lines. More or less rapidly they came to recognize that documentary materials could not only inspire or reassure their own civilian populations but be shown in neutral countries, where they could influence public opinion. In the United States fiction films depicting the war were barred because they violated America's claims to neutrality, but documentaries were seen as informational, and were allowed to be shown. Films made by the belligerent nations and screened in the United States included *Britain Prepared* (US title: *How Britain Prepared*; Charles Urban, 1915), *Somewhere in France* (French government, 1915), *Deutschwehr War Films* (Germany, 1915). These 'official war films' served as precedents for documentaries such as *America's Answer* (1918) and *Pershing Crusaders* (1918), which were produced by the Committee on Public Information, a section in the United States government headed by George Creel, when the United States finally entered the conflict in April 1917. Shown in a wide range of situations, these feature-length films generally relied on intertitles rather than a lecturer—though someone associated with the sponsoring organization commonly introduced each screening. Documentaries of this kind continued being made and screened throughout the war, and beyond, including Alexandre Devarennes's *La Femme française pendant la guerre* ('The Frenchwoman during the War', 1918), Percy Nash's *Women Who Win* (GB, 1919), and Bruce Woolf's *The Battle of Jutland* (GB, 1920).

FROM 'ILLUSTRATED LECTURE' TO 'DOCUMENTARY'

After the war, illustrated lectures continued to be widespread, but many were eventually turned into straight documentaries with intertitles replacing the lecturer. Former President Theodore Roosevelt had given a slide-film lecture, *The Exploration of a Great River*, in late 1914, and in 1918 this material was given a more general release as *Colonel Theodore Roosevelt's Expedition into the Wilds*. Martin E. Johnson, who had begun his career giving illustrated lectures, released his documentary *Among the Cannibal Isles of the South Pacific* (1918), which played S. F. Rothapfel's Tivoli Theater. Robert Flaherty had filmed the Inuit of northern Canada between 1914 and 1916 and subsequently used this material in an illustrated lecture *The Eskimo* (1916). When the possibility of turning it into an intitled documentary was lost when the negative went up in flames, Flaherty, with sponsorship from the French furriers Revillon Frères, returned to northern Canada and filmed *Nanook of the North* (1922).

The term 'illustrated lecture' had obviously become an inadequate label for the many non-fiction films that were being distributed and shown with intertitles rather than live narration. But critics and film-makers initially applied

Robert Flaherty's *Nanook of the North* (1922)

the term 'documentary' to those programmes that displayed a marked cultural shift, rather than simply to all non-fiction programmes that embraced a shift in production and representational practices. The illustrated lecture typically took the western explorer or adventurer (who was often also the presenter standing by the screen) as its hero. *Nanook of the North* switched its centre of attention from the film-maker to Nanook and his Inuit family. To be sure, Flaherty was guilty of romanticization and salvage anthropology (western influence was effaced as the Eskimos were dressed in traditional clothing they no longer used). The Eskimos he depicted as naïve primitives mystified by a simple record player actually fixed his camera, developed his film, and actively participated in the film-making process.

Nanook is a highly contradictory film: it exhibits strong elements of participatory film-making that has been celebrated by innovative and progressive film-makers of the present day. In many respects it was an inter-cultural

collaboration, but a collaboration between two men for whom the daily life of women is of marginal interest. The desperate search for food, synonymous with male hunting activities, provides the most elaborate scenes, which are woven throughout the film. Confining the film-maker's voice to the intertitles and keeping him behind the camera made the film appear more 'objective' than earlier practices, even though the film-maker had, in fact, become more assertive in shaping his materials. In many respects *Nanook* appropriated the techniques of Hollywood fiction film-making, operating on the borderline between fiction and documentary, and turning ethnographic observations into a narrativized romance. Flaherty constructs an idealized Inuit family and gives us a star (Allakariallak both 'plays' and 'is' Nanook—an attractive personality the equal of Douglas Fairbanks) and a drama (man versus nature). Despite this evident fictionalization, however, its long-take style was subsequently applauded by André Bazin for the respect Flaherty gave to his subject and phenomenological reality.

The transformation of the adventure-travel film is inscribed within *Grass* (1925), made by Merian C. Cooper and Ernest B. Schoedsack. The documentary starts out by focusing on the film-makers, but then shifts its attention to the Bakhtiari people as they struggled to cross the rugged mountains and Karun River of south-western Persia (Iran) during their annual migration. Despite the shift that *Nanook* and *Grass* represented, conventional travel films, with the white men as protagonists, continued to be made throughout the 1920s.

For his second feature-length documentary, *Moana* (1926, shot on the South Sea island of Samoa), Robert Flaherty kept his small American crew behind the camera. To provide the necessary drama in a land where survival was easy, Flaherty induced the local inhabitants to revive the ritual of tattooing—a male puberty rite. Less participatory and more opportunistic as film-making than *Nanook of the North*, *Moana* also lacked a comparable success at the box-office.

Cooper and Schoedsack followed *Grass* with *Chang: A Drama of the Wilderness* (1927), a story of a farmer and his family's struggle to survive at the end of a jungle in Siam (Thailand). Here the documentary impulse gave way to Hollywood story-telling, pointing towards the film-makers' later success *King Kong* (1933).

THE CITY SYMPHONY FILM

The shift in cultural outlook associated with documentary is also evident in the cycle of city symphony films, which, beginning with Charles Sheeler and Paul Strand's *Manhatta* (1921), took a modernist look at metropolitan life. *Manhatta* rejected the assumptions of social reform photography and cinematography as well as the touristic vision that had previously dominated depictions of the city. The film focuses on the business district of Lower Manhattan, ignoring city landmarks such as the Statue of Liberty and Grant's Tomb. Human bodies are dwarfed by the area's skyscrapers, and many scenes were shot from the tops of buildings, emphasizing the sense of abstract patterning produced by modern architecture. *Manhatta* conveys the sense of scale and impersonality experienced by city dwellers. The film loosely follows the course of a single day (starting with commuters leaving the Staten Island Ferry for work and ending with a sunset), a structural form that became characteristic of the city film. The film enjoyed little attention in the United States but was more widely shown in Europe, where it may have encouraged Alberto Cavalcanti to make *Rien que les heures* ('Only the hours', 1926) and Walter Ruttmann to undertake *Berlin: Symphony of a City*.

Rien que les heures focuses on cosmopolitan Paris, often contrasting rich and poor even as it combines non-fiction sequences with short staged or fictional vignettes. *Berlin*, shot by Karl Freund, expresses a profound ambivalence toward the city that is consistent with the ideas articulated by the influential Berlin sociologist Georg Simmel (1858–1918), in such writings as 'The Metropolis and Mental Life' (1902). From the film's opening sequence, in which a train races through the quiet countryside into the metropolitan centre, city life produces an intensification of nervous stimuli. The film depicts a suicide: a woman is overwhelmed (her desperation depicted in the film's only close-up) and jumps off a bridge into the water. Yet no one in the crowd of casual spectators tries to rescue her. Urban life is shown to require exactness and minute precision, evident in the depiction of certain production processes as well as the way work halts abruptly at noon. As the absence of close-ups emphasizes, all this coalesces 'into a structure of the highest impersonality'.

Berlin: Symphony of a City refuses either to humanize the city or to respect its geographic integrity. Yet Ruttmann's organization of shots and abstract images also emphasizes a heightened subjectivity made possible by urban culture. This tension is evident in the film's English title: 'Berlin'— a concrete, impersonal designation—and 'Symphony of a City', which asks the spectator to view the film abstractly and metaphorically. As with Simmel, Ruttmann's dialectics underscore the contradictions of city life. The city allows unprecedented freedom and this freedom 'allows the noble substance common to all to come to the fore', but the city also requires a specialization, which means 'death to the personality of the individual'. On one hand there is the mass—suggested by shots of feet and the intercutting of soldiers and cattle. On the other there are the people who try to assert their individuality by dressing in highly eccentric clothing. As the film's almost relentless cataloguing of urban activities suggests, the personality of the individual cannot readily maintain itself under the

Walking advertisements for stomach salts in Walter Ruttmann's *Berlin: Symphony of a City* (1927)

Dziga Vertov

(1896–1954)

Denis Arkadevich (David Abramovich) Kaufman, later to become famous under the name Dziga Vertov, was born in Bialystok (now in Poland), where his father was a librarian. His younger brothers both became cameramen: Mikhail (born 1897) worked with Vertov until 1929, while the youngest, Boris (born 1906), emigrated first to France (where he shot Jean Vigo's films) and then to America (where he won an Academy Award for *On the Waterfront*).

Starting his career with the conventional newsreel *Kino-Nedelia* ('Film-Weekly', 1918-19), Vertov rapidly absorbed ideas shared by left-wing and Constructivist artists (Alexander Rodchenko, Vladimir Tatlin, Varvara Stepanova) and Proletkult theorists (Alexander Bogdanov, Alexei Gan). The documentary and non- or anti-fictional character of his cinema was conceptualized in the context of the 'mortification of art' in the future proletarian culture, and the 'kinoki' (cine-eye) group, with Kaufman, Vertov, and his (second) wife Elizaveta Svilova as its core, saw themselves as the Moscow headquarters of a national network (which never materialized) of local cine-amateurs providing continuous flow of newsreel footage. Later the network was supposed to be supplemented by a 'radio-ear' component to finally merge into the 'radio-eye', a global TV of the future socialist world with no place for fictional stories. Vertov's crusade against the fiction film was intensified after 1922 when Lenin's New Economic Policy led to an increase in fiction film imports, but he was equally scathing about the new Soviet cinema of Kuleshov and Eisenstein, describing it as 'the same old crap tinted red'.

The polar tenets of Vertov's theory were 'life caught unawares' and 'the Communist deciphering of reality'. The 'kinoki' worked on two series of newsreels at the same time: *Kino-pravda* ('Cine-truth') grouped facts in a political perspective, while the more informal *Goskinokalendar* ('State film calendar') arranged them in a casual home-movie style. Gradually the orator in Vertov took the upper hand: between 1924 and 1929 the style of his feature-length drifted from the diary style towards 'pathos', while *Kino-glaz* ('Cine-eye', 1924) foregrounded singular events and individual figures. In accordance with the trend at the time towards the monumental, *Shagai, Soviet!* ('Stride, Soviet!', 1926) was conceived as a 'symphony of work', and the poster-style *The Eleventh Year* (1928) as a 'hymn' celebrating the tenth anniversary of the Revolution.

Despite the self-effacing 'we' of the manifestos, the film practice of the 'kinoki' was largely defined by Vertov's own highly individual amalgam of interests in music, poetry, and science. Four years of music lessons followed by a year of studies at the Institute of Neuropsychology in Petrograd (1916) led him to create what he later called the 'laboratory of hearing'. Inspired by the Italian Futurist Manifestos (published in Russia in 1914) and the trans-sense poetry (*zaum*) practised by Russian and Italian futurist poets, Vertov's acoustic experiments ranged from mixing fragments of stenographically registered speech and gramophone records to verbal rendering of environmental noises such as the sound of a saw-mill. After 1917, the futurist cult of noises was given a revolutionary tinge by Proletkult as part of the 'art of production', and urban cacophonies remained significant for Vertov throughout the 20s. He took part in the citywide 'symphony of factory whistles' (with additional sound effects of machine-guns, marine cannons, and hydroplanes) staged in Baku in 1922, and his first sound film, *Enthusiasm* (1930) employed a similar noise symphony for its soundtrack.

No less important was his suppressed passion for poetry. All his life Vertov wrote poetry (never published) in the style of Walt Whitman and Vladimir Mayakovsky, and in his films of 1926-28 Vertov the poet emerges through profuse titling, particularly convoluted in *One Sixth of the World* (1926) with its editing controlled by Whitmanesque intertitles: 'You who eat the meat of reindeer [image] Dipping it into warm blood [image] You sucking on your mother's breast [image] And you, high-spirited hundred-years-old man', etc. While some critics declared that such editing inaugurated a new genre of 'poetic cinema' (Viktor Shklovsky went so far as to see in the film traditional forms of the 'triolet'), others found it inconsistent with the LEF (Left Front) doctrine of 'cinema of facts' to which the 'kinoki' formally subscribed.

In response to these criticisms, Vertov ruled out the use of all intertitles from his filmic manifesto *The Man with the Movie Camera* (*Chelovek s kinoapparatom*, 1929), a *tour de force* which results in what appears to be the most 'theoretical' film of the silent era self-confined to the image alone. Documentary in material but utopian in essence (its setting was a nowhere city, a composite location of bits of Moscow, Kiev, Odessa, and a coal-mining region of the Ukraine), *The Man with the Movie Camera* summarized the thematic universe of the 'kinoki' movement: the image of the worker perfect as the machine, that of the film-maker as socially useful as the factory worker, together with that of the super-sensitive spectator reacting to no matter how complicated a message the film offers to his or her attention. In 1929, however, all these Quixotic images were hopelessly out of date—including the master image of the film, that of the ideal city in which private life and the life of the community are harmonized and controlled by the infallible eye of the movie camera.

More personal in style but less original in imagery, Vertov's post-'kinoki' films of the sound period revolved around songs and music, images of women, and cult figures, past and present. In *Lullaby* (1937) liberated women sing praise to Stalin, much in the spirit of the earlier *Three Songs of Lenin* (1934), while *Three Heroines* (1938) shows women mastering 'male' professions as engineer, pilot, and military officer. These three films stem back to a project of 1933 carrying the generic title 'She', a film that was supposed to 'trace the working of the brain' of a fictional composer as he writes an eponymous symphony of womanhood across the ages.

Under Stalin, Vertov's feature-length documentaries were largely suppressed: although never arrested, he was blacklisted during the anti-Semitic campaign of 1949. He died of cancer on 12 February 1954.

YURI TSIVIAN

SELECT FILMOGRAPHY

Kinonedelia (1918–19); Boi pod Tsaritsynym ('The Battle of Tsaritsyn'); Istoriya grazdanskoi voiny ('History of the Civil War') (1921); Kino-Pravda (1922–25); Goskinokalendar (1923–25); Kino-glas (1924); Shagai, Soviet! ('Stride, Soviet!') (1926); Shestaya chast sveta (One Sixth of the World) (1926); Odinnadsatyi (The Eleventh Year) (1928); Chelovek s Kinoapparatom (The Man with the Movie Camera) (1929); Entuziazm—simfoniya Donbassa (Enthusiasm—Symphony of the Donbas) (1930); Tri pesni o Lenine (Three Songs of Lenin) (1934); Kolybelnaya ('Lullaby') (1937); Sergo Ordzonikidze (1937); Tri geroini (Three Heroines) (1938); Tebe, front ('To you, front') (1941); Novosti dnia ('News of the day'; separate issues) (1944–54)

BIBLIOGRAPHY

Feldman, Seth (1979), *Dziga Vertov: a guide to references and resources.*
Petric, Vlada (1987), *Constructivism in Film.*
Vertov, Dziga (1984), *Kino-eye.*

Opposite: Original poster for *The Man with the Movie Camera* (1929)

assault of city life. The city is where money reigns and money is the leveller, expressing qualitative differences in the term 'how much?' The film thus does not emphasize class distinctions; if they are sometimes apparent, it is only to suggest how eating and drinking (the oldest and intellectually most negligible activity) can form a bond among heterogeneous people.

Many short city symphony films were made in the late 1920s and early 1930s. Joris Ivens made *The Bridge* (*De brug*, 1928), a meticulous portrait of a Rotterdam railway bridge that opened and closed so ships could travel the Maas River. Influenced by a machine aesthetic, Ivens saw his subject as 'a laboratory of movements, tones, shapes, contrasts, rhythms and the relationship between all of these'. His film *Rain* (*Regen*, 1929) is a film poem that traces the beginning, progress, and end of a rain shower in Amsterdam. Henri Storck's *Images d'Ostende* (1930), László Moholy-Nagy's *Berliner Stillleben* ('Berlin still life', 1929), Jean Vigo's *À propos de Nice* ('About Nice', 1930), Irving Browning's *City of Contrasts* (1931), and Jay Leyda's *A Bronx Morning* (1931) all functioned within the genre. In contrast to *Berlin*, Leyda's film begins with an *underground* train leaving (rather than entering) the central city for one of New York's outer boroughs. Once in the Bronx, Leyda captures an array of quotidian activities (children's street games, vegetable sellers, and mothers with prams) that counter Ruttmann's views of the city. Mikhail Kaufman made a city symphony film in the Soviet Union, *Moscow* (*Moskva*, 1927), but a more important and internationally renowned one was made by his brother Denis Kaufman, known as Dziga Vertov. Vertov's *The Man with the Movie Camera* (*Chelovek s kinoapparatom*, 1929) is a city symphony film that fuses a futurist aesthetic with Marxism. The cameraman and his team help to create a new Soviet world. This is literalized on the screen by the building up of an imaginary, artificial city through the juxtaposition of sites and scenes taken in different locations. Alcoholism, capitalism (via the New Economic Policy), and other pre-revolutionary problems are shown to persist next to more positive developments. The cinema's role is to show these truths to the new Soviet citizen and so bring about understanding and action. *The Man with the Movie Camera* thus constantly draws attention to the processes of cinema—film-making, editing, exhibiting, and film-going. In this regard, Vertov's film is a manifesto for the documentary film and a condemnation of the fiction feature film that Vertov railed against in his various manifestos and writings.

DOCUMENTARY IN THE SOVIET UNION

Although Vertov and others often felt that non-fiction films were unfairly marginalized in the Soviet Union, thousands of workers' clubs provided a unique and unparalleled outlet for documentaries. Moreover, the Soviet film industry produced numerous industrials and short documentaries for these venues, such as *Steel Path* on the activities of the rail workers' union and *With Iron and Blood* on the construction of a factory. Soviet documentary as a whole also provided the most radical and systematic break with previous non-fiction screen practices.

For Vertov, *The Man with the Movie Camera* was the culmination of a decade of work in non-fiction film-making. He sought to build up a group of trained film-makers, whom he referred to as the 'kinoks'. Their films celebrated electrification, industrialization, and the achievements of workers through hard labour, and even in the early *Kinopravda* (*Cine-Truth*, 1922–5) newsreels, subject matter and treatment reveal a modernist aesthetic. Vertov's films grew more audacious and controversial as the decade progressed. In *Stride, Soviet!* (1926), work processes are shown in reverse and bread and other products are taken from bourgeois consumers and repossessed by those who made them.

A radically new ethnographic impulse can be found in certain Soviet documentaries of this period. *Turksib* (Victor Turin, 1929) looks at the different, potentially complementary lives of people in Turkestan and Siberia as a way to explain the need for a railroad linking these two parts of the Soviet Union. The film then shows the planning and building of the railway with a final exhortation to finish it more quickly. A similar narrative is evident in *Sol Svanetii* ('Salt for Svanetia', 1930), based on an outline by Sergei Tretaykov and made by Mikhail Kalatozov in the Caucasus. The film engages in a kind of salvage anthropology but not, as was the case for Flaherty, for purposes of romanticization. Religion, custom, and traditional power relations are shown to be oppressive, blocking even the simplest improvements in people's lives. Among their many problems, the people and animals of Svanetia suffer from a lack of salt. After depicting the problem, the film offers a solution: roads. The point was easy for relatively unsophisticated viewers to grasp, but the increasing pressures of Stalinism are palpable in the film's hysterical enthusiasm and its reductive solutions. Significantly, the Svanetians do not experience an awakening of revolutionary consciousness—it is the State that recognizes the problem and determines the solution.

Another genre to which the Soviets made important contributions was the historical documentary, a genre that relied heavily on the compilation of previously shot footage. The most accomplished maker of compilation documentaries was Esfir Shub, a former editor of fiction films. Her impressive panorama of Russian history consisted of three feature-length productions: *The Fall of the Romanov Dynasty* (*Padeniye dinasti Romanovikh*, 1927), which covered the period from 1912 to 1917; *The Great Road* (*Veliky put*, 1928), about the first ten years of the Revolution (1917–27); and *The Russia of Nikolai II and Lev Tolstoy* (*Rossiya Nikolaya*

II i Lev Tolstoy, 1928), made for the centennial of Tolstoy's birth and using film from the 1897–1912 era. *The Fall of the Romanov Dynasty* displays a Marxist analysis attuned to the social and economic conditions that culminated in the First World War and the overthrow of the Tsar. Through the powerful juxtapositions of images, it initially explicates the functionings of a profoundly conservative society by examining class relations (landowning gentry and peasants, capitalists and workers), the role of the State (the military, subservient politicians in the Duma, appointed governors and administrative personnel, with Tsar Nikolai perched at the top), and the mystifying role of the Russian Orthodox Church. The international struggle for markets unleashes the forces of war leading to devastating slaughter, and ultimately to the February 1917 Revolution that brought Alexander Kerensky to power. The images are often striking in their composition or subject-matter, but Shub's framework attaches significance to even the most clichéd scenes, such as marching soldiers.

POLITICAL DOCUMENTARY IN THE WEST

Non-fiction film-making of an overtly political nature also went on in the United States and western Europe after the First World War. Short news and information films on strikes and related activities were made by unions and leftist political parties in many countries. In the United States, Communist activist Alfred Wagenknecht produced *The Passaic Textile Strike* (1926), a short feature that combined documentary scenes with studio re-enactments, while the American Federation of Labor produced *Labor's Reward* (1925). In Germany, Prometheus, formed by Willi Münzenberg, produced such documentaries as *The Document of Shanghai* (*Das Dokument von Shanghai*, 1928), which focused on the March 1927 revolutionary uprisings in China. The German Communist Party subsequently produced a number of short documentaries, including Slatan Dudow's *Zeitproblem: wie der Arbeiter wohnt* ('Contemporary problem: how the worker lives', 1930). Large corporations, right-wing organizations, and government also used non-fiction film for purposes of propaganda.

In contrast to these breaks with pre-First World War non-fiction screen practices, the new documentary appeared late in Britain, and in a modest form—John Grierson's *Drifters* (1929), a fifty-eight-minute silent documentary about the fishing process. It focuses on a fishing boat that drifts for herring, and the people who pull in the nets and pack the fish in barrels for market. It combines a Flaherty-style plot of man versus nature with partially abstracted close-ups and a rhythmic editing pattern learned from careful scrutiny of Eisenstein's *Potemkin* (1925). As Ian Aitken has remarked, Grierson was seeking to express a reality that transcended specific issues of exploitation and economic hardship. Nevertheless, Grierson relegated the people who did the actual work to his film's periphery, even as he synthesized the familiar narrative of a production process with modernist aesthetics. The film enjoyed a strong critical success, suggesting the extent to which the British documentary had lost its way in the years since the First World War, but also the potential for renewal in the 1930s and beyond.

During the 1920s, documentary film-makers struggled either at the margins of commercial cinema or outside it altogether. Despite the comparatively inexpensive nature of documentary production, even the most successful films did little more than return their costs. The general absence of profit motive meant that documentarians had other reasons for film-making, and often had to rely on sponsorship (as Flaherty did with *Nanook*), or self-financing. Although conventional travelogues had a long-standing niche in the market-place, outside the Soviet Union there was little or no formal or institutional framework to support more innovative efforts at production.

Despite their low returns, in the industrialized nations non-fiction programmes were shown in a wide range of venues. In the United States, films such as *Nanook of the North*, *Berlin: Symphony of a City*, and *The Man with the Movie Camera* enjoyed regular showings at motion picture theatres in a few large cities and so were reviewed by newspaper critics, with varying degrees of perspicacity (*Berlin* was considered to be a disappointing travelogue by New York critics). Films such as *Manhatta* were sometimes shown as shorts within the framework of mainstream cinema's balanced programmes, and avant-garde documentaries were often shown at art galleries. In Europe, the network of ciné clubs provided an outlet for many artistically and politically radical documentaries. Cultural institutions and political organizations of all types screened (and occasionally sponsored) documentaries as well. Even in the Soviet Union, prominent documentaries quickly departed town-centre theatres for extended runs at workers' clubs. Because most non-fiction programmes generally had some kind of educational or informational value, they penetrated into all aspects of social life and were shown in the church, the union hall, the school, and cultural institutions like the Museum of Natural History (New York). By the end of the 1920s, then, documentary was a broadly diffused if financially precarious phenomenon, characterized by its diversity of production and exhibition circumstances.

Bibliography

Aitken, Ian (1990), *Film and Reform: John Grierson and the Documentary Film Movement.*

Barnouw, Erik (1974), *Documentary.*

Brownlow, Kevin (1979), *The War, the West and the Wilderness.*

Calder-Marshall, Arthur (1963), *The Innocent Eye: The Life of Robert J. Flaherty.*

Cooper, Merian C. (1925), *Grass.*

Flaherty, Robert J. (1924), *My Eskimo Friends.*

Hall, Stuart (1981), *The Whites of their Eyes.*

Holm, Bill, and Quimby, George Irving (1980), *Edward S. Curtis in the Land of the War Canoes.*

Jacobs, Lewis (ed.) (1979), *The Documentary Tradition.*

Musser, Charles, with Nelson, Carol (1991), *High-Class Moving Pictures: Lyman H. Howe and the Forgotten Era of Traveling Exhibition, 1880–1920.*

Vertov, Dziga (1984), *Kino-Eye: The Writings of Dziga Vertov.*

Cinema and the Avant-Garde

A. L. REES

Modern art and silent cinema were born simultaneously. In 1895 Cézanne's paintings were seen in public for the first time in twenty years. Largely scorned, they also stimulated artists to the revolution in art that took place between 1907 and 1912, just as popular film was also entering a new phase of development. Crossing the rising barriers between art and public taste, painters and other modernists were among the first enthusiasts for American adventure movies, Chaplin, and cartoons, finding in them a shared taste for modern city life, surprise, and change. While the influential philosopher Henri Bergson criticized cinema for falsely eliding the passage of time, his vivid metaphors echo and define modernism's attitude to the visual image: 'form is only the snapshot view of a transition.'

New theories of time and perception in art, as well as the popularity of cinema, led artists to try to put 'paintings in motion' through the film medium. On the eve of the First World War, the poet Guillaume Apollinaire, author of *The Cubist Painters* (1913), explained the animation process in his journal *Les Soirées de Paris* and enthusiastically compared *Le Rythme coloré* ('Colour rhythms', 1912–14), an abstract film planned by the painter Léopold Survage, to 'fireworks, fountains and electric signs'. In 1918 the young Louis Aragon wrote in Louis Delluc's *Le Film* that cinema must have 'a place in the avant-garde's preoccupations.

They have designers, painters, sculptors. Appeal must be made to them if one wants to bring some purity to the art of movement and light.'

The call for purity—an autonomous art free of illustration and story-telling—had been the cubists' clarion-cry since their first public exhibition in 1907, but the search for 'pure' or 'absolute' film was made problematic by the hybrid nature of the film medium, praised by Méliès in the same year as 'the most enticing of all the arts, for it makes use of almost all of them'. But for modernism, cinema's turn to dramatic realism, melodrama, and epic fantasy was questioned, in terms reminiscent of the classical aesthetics of Lessing, as a confusion of literary and pictorial values. As commercial cinema approached the condition of synaesthesia with the aid of sound and toned or tinted colour, echoing in popular form the 'total work of art' of Wagnerianism and art nouveau, modernism looked towards non-narrative directions in film form.

ART CINEMA AND THE EARLY AVANT-GARDE

The early avant-garde followed two basic routes. One invoked the neo-impressionists' claim that a painting, before all else, is a flat surface covered with colour; similarly, the avant-garde implied, a film was a strip of transparent material that ran through a projector. This issue was debated among the cubists around 1912, and opened the way to abstraction. Survage's designs for his abstract film were preceded by the experiments of the futurist brothers Ginna and Corra, who hand-painted raw film as early as 1910 (a technique rediscovered in the 1930s by Len Lye and Norman McLaren). Abstract animation also dominated the German avant-garde 1919–25, stripping the image to pure graphic form, but ironically also nurturing a modernist variant of synaesthesia, purging the screen of overt human action while developing rhythmic interaction of basic symbols (square, circle, triangle) in which music replaces narrative as a master code. An early vision of 'Plastic Art in Motion' is found in Ricciotto Canudo's 1911 essay *The Birth of a Sixth Art*, an inspired if volatile amalgam of Nietzsche, high drama, and futurist machine dynamism.

A second direction led artists to burlesque or parody films which drew on the primitive narrative mainstream, before (as many modernists believed) it was sullied by realism. At the same time, these films are documents of the art movements which gave rise to them, with roles played by—among others—Man Ray, Marcel Duchamp, Erik Satie, and Francis Picabia (*Entr'acte*, 'Interlude', 1924), and Eisenstein, Len Lye, and Hans Richter (*Everyday*, 1929). The ironic humour of modernism was expressed in such films (some now lost) as *Vita Futurista* (1916), its Russian counterpart *Drama of the Futurist Cabaret* (1913), its successors in *Glumov's Diary* (Eisenstein, 1923) and Mayakovsky's comic-Guignol films, and such later elaborations of cultural slap-

stick as Clair's classic *Entr'acte* (1924) and Hans Richter's dark comedy *Ghosts before Noon* (1928). This genre was explored mostly in the Dada and surrealist tradition, which valued dream-like 'trans-sense' irrationality as the key trope of film montage and camera image.

An alternative route to the cinema as an art form (the specific meaning of which overrides the general sense in which all cinema is an art) ran parallel to the artists' avant-garde from c. 1912 to 1930 and sometimes overlapped with it. The art cinema or narrative avant-garde included such movements as German Expressionism, the Soviet montage school, the French 'impressionists' Jean Epstein and Germaine Dulac, and independent directors such as Abel Gance, F. W. Murnau, and Carl Theodor Dreyer. Like the artist-film-makers, they resisted the commercial film in favour of a cultural cinema to equal the other arts in seriousness and depth. In the silent era, with few language barriers, these highly visual films had as international an audience as the Hollywood-led mainstream they opposed. Film clubs from Paris to London and Berlin made up a non-commercial screening circuit for films which were publicized in radical art journals (*G*, *De stijl*) and specialist magazines (*Close-Up*, *Film Art*, *Experimental Film*). Conference and festival screenings—pioneered by trade shows and expositions such as the 1929 'Film und Foto' in Stuttgart—also sometimes commissioned new experimental films, as in the light-play, chronophotography, and Fritz Lang clips of *Kipho* (1925, promoting a 'kine-foto' fair) by the veteran cameraman Guido Seeber. Political unions of artists like the November Group in Weimar Germany also supported the new film, and French ciné-clubs tried to raise independent production funds from screenings and rentals.

For the first decade there were few firm lines drawn by enthusiasts for the 'artistic film' in a cluster of ciné-clubs, journals, discussion groups, and festivals, as they even-handedly promoted all kinds of film experiment as well as minor, overlooked genres such as scientific films and cartoons which were similarly an alternative to the commercial fiction cinema. Many key figures crossed the divide between the narrative and poetic avant-gardes; Jean Vigo, Luis Buñuel, Germaine Dulac, Dziga Vertov, and Kenneth McPherson of the aptly named *Borderline* (1930—starring the poet H.D., the novelist Bryher, and Paul Robeson).

The idea of the avant-garde or 'art film' in Europe and the USA linked the many factions opposed to mass cinema. At the same time, the rise of narrative, psychological realism in the maturing art cinema led to its gradual split from the anti-narrative artists' avant-garde, whose 'cine-poems' were closer to painting and sculpture than to the tradition of radical drama.

Nowhere was this more dramatically the case than in a series of Chinese-style scroll-drawings made in Swit-

Marcel Duchamp's *Anémic cinéma*

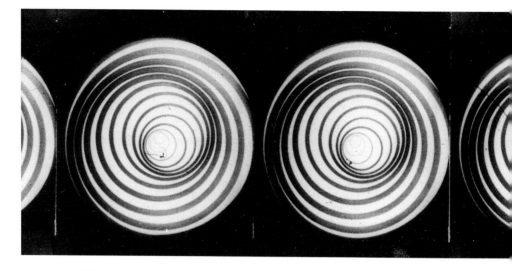

zerland by the Swedish artist and dadaist Viking Eggeling in 1916–17. These sequential experiments began as investigations of the links between musical and pictorial harmony, an analogy Eggeling pursued in collaboration with fellow dadaist Hans Richter from 1918, leading to their first attempts to film their work in Germany around 1920. Eggeling died in 1925 shortly after completing his *Diagonal Symphony*, a unique dissection of delicate and almost art deco tones and lines, its intuitive rationalism shaped by cubist art, Bergson's philosophy of duration, and Kandinsky's theory of synaesthesia. It was premièred in a famous November Group presentation (Berlin, 1925) of abstract films by cubist, Dada, and Bauhaus artists: Hans Richter, Walter Ruttmann, Fernand Léger, René Clair, and (with a 'light-play' projection work) Hirschfeld-Mack.

The division between the narrative and poetic avant-gardes was never absolute, as seen in the careers of Buñuel, Vigo (especially in the two experimental documentaries *Taris* (1931), with its slowing of time and underwater shots, and the carnivalesque but also political film *À propos de Nice* ('About Nice', 1930)), and even Vertov, whose *Enthusiasm* (1930) reinvokes the futurist idea of 'noise-music', has no commentary, and is unashamedly non-naturalistic despite its intended celebration of the Soviet Five-Year Plan.

Artists' films were underpinned by the flourishing of futurist, constructivist, and dadaist groups between 1909 and the mid-1920s. This 'vortex' of activity, to use Ezra Pound's phrase, included the experiments in 'light-play' at the Bauhaus, Robert and Sonya Delaunay's 'orphic cubism', Russian 'Rayonnisme' and the cubo-futurism of Severini and Kupka, and its Russian variants in the 'Lef' group. In turn, all of these experiments were, at least in part, rooted in the cubist revolution pioneered by Braque and Picasso from 1907 to 1912. Cubism was an art of

fragments, at first depicting objects from a sequence of shifting angles or assembling images by a collage of paper, print, paint, and other materials. It was quickly seen as an emblem of its time—Apollinaire in 1912 was perhaps the first to evoke an analogy between the new painting and the new physics—but also as a catalyst for innovation in other art forms, especially in design and architecture. The language of visual fragmentation was called by the Fauve painter Derain (Eggeling's mentor) in 1905 the art of 'deliberate disharmonies' and it parallels the growing use of dissonance in literature (Joyce, Stein) and music (Stravinsky, Schoenberg).

CUBISM

While cubism sought a pictorial equivalent for the newly discovered instability of vision, the cinema was moving rapidly in the opposite direction. Far from abandoning narrative, it was encoding it. The 'primitive' sketches of 1895–1905 films were succeeded by a new and more confidently realist handling of screen space and film acting. Subject-matter was expanded, plot and motivation were clarified through the fate of individuals. Most crucially, and in contrast to cubism's display of artifice, the new narrative cinema smoothed the traces of change in shot, angle of vision, and action by the erasure effect of 'invisible editing' to construct a continuous, imaginary flow.

Nevertheless cubism and cinema are clearly enough products of the same age and within a few years they were mutually to influence each other: Eisenstein derived the concept of montage as much from cubist collage as from the films of Griffith and Porter. At the same time, they face in opposite directions. Modern art was trying to expunge the literary and visual values which cinema was equally eager to incorporate and exploit (partly to improve its respectability and partly to expand its very language).

These values were the basis of academic realism in painting, for example, which the early modernists had rejected: a unified visual field, a central human theme, emotional identification or empathy, illusionist surface.

Cubism heralded the broad modernism which welcomed technology and the mass age, and its openly hermetic aspects were tempered by combining painterly purism with motifs from street life and materials used by artisans. At the same time, cubism shared with later European modernism a resistance to many cultural values embodied in its own favourite image of the new—the cinema, dominated then as now by Hollywood. While painters and designers could be fairly relaxed in their use of Americana, because independent at this time of its direct influence, the films of the post-cubist avant-garde are noticeably anti-Hollywood in form, style, and production.

The avant-garde films influenced by cubism therefore joined with the European art cinema and social documentary as points of defence against market domination by the USA, each attempting to construct a model of film culture outside the categories of entertainment and the codes of fiction. Despite frequent eulogies of American cinema, of which the surrealists became deliberately the most delirious readers (lamenting the growing power of illusionism as film 'improved'), few surviving avant-garde films resemble these icons. Only slapstick, as in *Entr'acte* (1924), was directly copied from the American example, but this has its roots tangled with Méliès.

ABSTRACTION

The abstract films of Richter, Ruttmann, and Fischinger were based on the concept of painting with motion, but also aspired towards the visual music implied in such titles as Richter's *Rhythmus* series (1921–4) and Ruttmann's *Opus I–IV* (1921–5). This wing of the avant-garde was strongly idealist, and saw in film the utopian goal of a universal language of pure form, supported by the synaesthetic ideas expressed in Kandinsky's *On the Spiritual in Art*, which sought correspondences between the arts and the senses. In such key works as *Circles* (1932) and *Motion Painting* (1947), Fischinger, the most popular and influential of the group, tellingly synchronized colour rhythms to the music of Wagner and Bach.

Fischinger alone pursued abstract animation throughout his career, which ended in the USA. Other German film-makers turned away from this genre after the mid-1920s, partly because of economic pressure (there was minimal industrial support for the non-commercial abstract cinema). Richter made lyric collages such as *Filmstudie* (1926), mixing abstract and figurative shots in which superimposed floating eyeballs act as a metaphor for the viewer adrift in film space. His later films pioneer the surrealist psychodrama. Ruttmann became a documentarist with *Berlin: Symphony of a City* in 1927 and later worked on state-sponsored features and documentaries, including Leni Riefenstahl's *Olympia* (1938).

SURREALISM

In France, some film-makers, such as Henri Chomette (René Clair's brother and author of short 'cinéma pur' films), Delluc, and especially Germaine Dulac, were drawn to theories of 'the union of all the senses', finding an analogue for harmony, counterpoint, and dissonance in the visual structures of montage editing. But the surrealists rejected these attempts to 'impose' order where they preferred to provoke contradiction and discontinuity.

The major films of the surrealists turned away equally from the retinal vision of form in movement—explored variously by the French 'impressionists', the rapid cutting of Gance and L'Herbier, and the German avant-garde—towards a more optical and contestatory cinema. Vision is made complex, connections between images are obscured, sense and meaning are questioned. Man Ray's emblematic 1923 Dada film—its title *Le Retour à la raison* ('Return to reason') evoking the parody of the Enlightenment buried in the name Cabaret Voltaire—begins with photogrammed salt, pepper, tacks, and sawblades printed on the film strip to assert film grain and surface. A fairground, shadows, the artist's studio, and a mobile sculpture in double exposure evoke visual space. The film ends, after three minutes, in a 'painterly' shot of a model filmed 'against the light', in positive and negative. Exploring film as indexical photogram, iconic image, and symbolic pictorial code, its Dada stamp is seen in its shape, which begins in flattened darkness and ends in the purely cinematic image of a figure turning in 'negative' space.

Man Ray's later *Étoile de mer* ('Star of the sea', 1928), loosely based on a script by the poet Robert Desnos, refuses the authority of the 'look' when a stippled lens adds opacity to an oblique tale of doomed love, lightly sketched in with punning intertitles and shots (a starfish attacked by scissors, a prison, a failed sexual encounter). Editing draws out the disjunction between shots rather than their continuity, a technique pursued in Man Ray's other films, which imply a 'cinema of refusal' in the evenly paced and seemingly random sequences of *Emak Bakia* (1927) or repeated empty rooms in *Les Mystères du Château de Dés* ('The mysteries of the Chateau de Dés', 1928). While surrealist cinema is often understood as a search for the excessive and spectacular image (as in dream sequences modelled on surrealist theory) the group were in fact drawn to find the marvellous in the banal, which explains their fascination with Hollywood as well as their refusal to imitate it.

Marcel Duchamp cerebrally evoked and subverted the abstract image in his ironically titled *Anémic cinéma* (1926), an anti-retinal film in which slowly rotating spirals imply

Artists Marcel Duchamp and Man Ray playing chess in a scene from René Clair's *Entr'acte* (1924)

sexual motifs, intercutting these 'pure' images with scabrous and near-indecipherable puns that echo Joyce's current and likewise circular 'Work in Progress', *Finnegans Wake*. Less reductively than Duchamp, Man Ray's films also oppose 'visual pleasure' and the viewer's participation. Montage slows or repeats actions and objects (spirals, phrases, revolving doors and cartwheels, hands, gestures, fetishes, light patterns) to frustrate narrative and elude the viewer's full grasp of the fantasies film provokes. This austere but playful strategy challenges the rule of the eye in fiction film and the sense of cinematic plenitude it aims to construct.

FROM *ENTR'ACTE* TO *BLOOD OF A POET*

Three major French films of the period—Clair's *Entr'acte* (1924), Léger's *Ballet mécanique* ('Mechanical Ballet', 1924) and Buñuel's *Un chien andalou* ('An Andalusian dog', 1928)—celebrate montage editing while also subverting its use as rhythmic vehicle for the all-seeing eye. In *Entr'acte*, the chase of a runaway hearse, a dizzying roller-coaster ride, and the transformation of a ballerina into a bearded male in a tutu all create visual jolts and enigmas, freed of narrative causality. *Ballet mécanique* rebuffs the forward flow of linear time, its sense of smooth progression, by loop-printing a sequence of a grinning washerwoman climbing steep stone steps, a Daumier-like contrast to Duchamp's elegantly photo-cinematic painting *Nude Descending a Staircase* of 1912, while the abstract shapes of machines are unusually slowed as well as speeded by

montage. Léger welcomed the film medium for its new vision of 'documentary facts'; his late-cubist concept of the image as an objective sign is underlined by the film's Chaplinesque titles and circular framing device—the film opens and closes by parodying romantic fiction (Madame Léger sniffs a rose in slow motion). Marking off the film as an object suspended between two moments of frozen time was later used by Cocteau in *Blood of a Poet* (*Le Sang d'un poète*, 1932), in this case shots of a falling chimney. The abrupt style of these films evokes earlier, 'purer' cinema; farce in *Entr'acte*, Chaplin in *Ballet mécanique*, and the primitive 'trick-film' in *Blood of a Poet*.

These and other avant-garde films all had music by modern composers—Satie, Auric, Honegger, Antheil—except *Un chien andalou*, which was played to gramophone recordings of Wagner and tangos. Few avant-garde films were shown silently, with the exception of the austere *Diagonal Symphony*, for which Eggeling forbade sound. According to Richter they were even shown to popular jazz. The influence of early film was added to a Dada spirit of improvisation and admiration for the US cinema's moments of anti-naturalistic excess. Contributors to a later high modernist aesthetic of which their makers—like Picasso and Braque—knew nothing at the time, these avant-garde films convey less an aspiration to purity of form than a desire to transgress (or reshape) the notion of form itself, theorized contemporaneously by Bataille in a dual critique of prose narrative and idealist abstraction. Their titles refer beyond the film medium: *Entr'acte*

('Interlude') to theatre (it was premièred 'between the acts' of a Satie ballet), *Ballet mécanique* to dance, and *Blood of a Poet* to literature; only *Un chien andalou* remains the mysterious exception.

The oblique title of *Chien andalou* asserts its independence and intransigence. Arguably its major film and certainly its most influential, this stray dog of Surrealism was in fact made before its young Spanish director joined the official movement. A razor slicing an eye acts as an emblem for the attack on normative vision and the comfort of the spectator whose surrogate screen-eye is here assaulted. Painterly abstraction is undermined by the objective realism of the static, eye-level camera, while poetic-lyrical film is mocked by furiously dislocated and mismatched cuts which fracture space and time, a post-cubist montage style which questions the certainty of seeing. The film is punctuated by craftily inane intertitles to aim a further blow at the 'silent' cinema, mainstream or avant-garde, by a reduction to absurdity.

The widely known if deliberately mysterious 'symbolism' of the film—the hero's striped fetishes, his yoke of priests, donkeys, and grand pianos, a woman's buttocks that dissolve into breasts, the death's head moth and ants eating blood—for long dominated critical discussion, but recent attention has turned to the structure of editing by which these images are achieved. The film constructs irrational spaces from its rooms, stairways, and streets, distorting temporal sequence, while its two male leads disconcertingly resemble each other as their identities blur.

For most of its history, avant-gardes have produced the two kinds of film-making discussed here; short, oblique films in the tradition of Man Ray, and the abstract German films, which broadly set up a different space for viewing from narrative drama, in which stable perception is interrupted and non-identification of subject and image are aimed for. *Chien andalou* sets up another model, in which elements of narrative and acting arouse the spectator's psychological participation in plot or scene while at the same time distancing the viewer by disallowing empathy, meaning, and closure; an image of the dissociated sensibility or 'double consciousness' praised by Surrealism in its critique of naturalism.

Two further French films expand this strategy, which came with the sound film era and the end of the first phase of avant-garde film-making before the rise of Hitler; *L'Age d'or* ('The golden age', 1930) and *Blood of a Poet* (1932). Almost feature length, these films (privately funded by arts patron the Vicomte de Noailles as successive birthday presents to his wife) link Cocteau's lucid classicism to Surrealism's baroque mythopoeia. Both films ironize visual meaning in voice-over or by intertitles (made on the cusp of the sound era, they use both spoken and written text). Cocteau's voice raspingly satirizes his Poet's

obsession with fame and death ('Those who smash statues should beware of becoming one'), paralleled in the opening of *L'Age d'or* by an intertitle 'lecture' on scorpions and an attack on Ancient and modern Rome. Buñuel links the fall of the classical age to his main target, Christianity (as when Christ and the disciples are seen leaving a chateau after a Sadean orgy). The film itself celebrates 'mad love'. A text written by the surrealists and signed by Aragon, Breton, Dalí, Éluard, Peret, Tzara and others was issued at the first screening: *L'Age d'or*, 'uncorrupted by plausibility', reveals the 'bankruptcy of our emotions, linked with the problem of capitalism'. The manifesto echoes Vigo's endorsement of *Un chien andalou*'s 'savage poetry' (also in 1930) as a film of 'social consciousness'. 'An Andalusian dog howls,' wrote Vigo; 'who then is dead?'

Unlike Buñuel's film, Cocteau's is not overtly anti-theocratic, but even so his Poet-hero encounters archaic art, magic and ritual, China, opium, and transvestism before dying in front of an indifferent stage audience while he plays cards. Cocteau's film finally affirms the redemptive classic tradition, but the dissolution of personal identity opposes the western fixation on stability and repetition, asserting that any modern classicism was to be determinedly 'neo'.

THE 1930S

Experimental sound-tracks and minimal synchronized speech in these films expanded the call for a non-naturalistic sound cinema in Eisenstein's and Pudovkin's 1928 manifesto and explored by Vertov's *Enthusiasm* (1930). This direction was soon blocked by the popularity and realism of the commercial sound film. Rising costs of film-making and the limited circulation of avant-garde films contributed to their decline. The broadly leftist politics of the avant-garde—both surrealists and abstract constructivists had complex links to Communist and socialist organizations—were increasingly strained under two reciprocal policies which dominated the 1930s; the growth of German nationalism under Hitler from 1933 and the Popular Front opposition to Fascism which rose, under Moscow's lead, a few years later. The attack on 'excessive' art and the avant-garde in favour of popular 'realism' were soon to close down the international co-operation which made possible German–Soviet co-productions like Piscator's formally experimental montage film *Revolt of the Fishermen* (1935) or Richter's first feature film *Metall* (abandoned in 1933 after the Nazi take-over). Radical Soviet film-makers as well as their 'cosmopolitan' allies abroad were forced into more normative directions.

The more politicized film-makers recognized this themselves in the second international avant-garde conference held in Belgium in 1930. The first more famous congress in 1929 at La Sarraz, Switzerland, at which Eisenstein, Balázs, Moussinac, Montagu, Cavalcanti, Richter, and

Ruttmann were present, had endorsed the need for aesthetic and formal experiment as part of a still growing movement to turn 'enemies of the film today' into 'friends of the film tomorrow', as Richter's optimistic 1929 book affirmed. One year later the stress was put emphatically on political activism, Richter's social imperative: 'The age demands the documented fact,' he claimed.

The first result of this was to shift avant-garde activity more directly into documentary. This genre, associated with political and social values, still encouraged experiment and was ripe for development of sound and image montage to construct new meanings. In addition, the documentary did not use actors; the final barrier between the avant-garde and mainstream or art-house cinema.

The documentary—usually used to expose social ills and (via state or corporate funding) propose remedies—attracted many European experimental film-makers including Richter, Ivens, and Henri Storck. In the United States, where there was a small but volatile community of activists for the new film, alongside other modern developments in writing, painting, and photography, the cause of a radical avant-garde was taken up by magazines such as *Experimental Film* and seeped into the New Deal films made by Pare Lorentz and Paul Strand (a modernist

photographer since the age of *Camerawork* and New York Dada).

In Europe, notably with John Grierson, Henri Storck, and Joris Ivens, new fusions between experimental film and factual cinema were pioneered. Grierson's attempt to equate corporate patronage with creative production led him most famously to the GPO, celebrated as an emblem of modern social communications in the Auden–Britten montage section of *Night Mail* (1936), which ends with Grierson's voice intoning a night-time hymn to Glasgow— 'let them dream their dreams . . .'.

Alberto Cavalcanti and Len Lye were hired to open the documentary cinema to new ideas and techniques. Lye's uncompromising career as a film-maker, almost always for state and business patrons, showed the survival of sponsored funding for the arts in Europe and the USA in the depression years. His cheap and cheerfully hand-made colour-experiments of the period treat their overt subjects (parcel deliveries in the wholly abstract *A Colour Box* (1935), early posting in *Trade Tattoo* (1937)) with a light touch; the films celebrate the pleasures of pure colour and rhythmic sound-picture montage. The loss of both Grierson and Lye to North America after the 1940s marked the end of this period of collaboration.

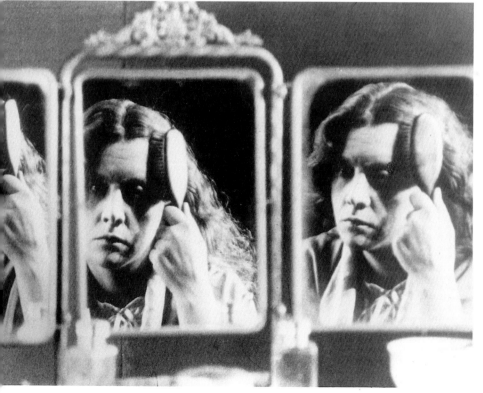

Germaine Dermoz as the bored wife in Germaine Dulac's *Smiling Madame Beudet* (*La Souriante Madame Beudet*, 1923)

Carl Theodor Dreyer

(1889–1968)

The illegitimate son of a maid and a factory-owner from Sweden, Dreyer was born and brought up in Copenhagen, where his adoptive family subjected him to a miserable and loveless childhood. To earn a living as soon as possible, he found work as theatre critic and air correspondent for a Danish newspaper. He also began to write film scripts, the first of which was made into a film in 1912. The following year he began an apprenticeship at Nordisk, for whom he worked in various capacities and wrote some twenty scripts. In 1919 he directed his first film, *The President* (*Præsidenten*), a melodrama with a rather clotted Griffithian narrative structure which nevertheless showed a strong visual sense. This was followed by the striking *Leaves from Satan's Book* (*Blade af Satans bog*), an episode film partly modelled on *Intolerance*, shot in 1919 but not released until 1921.

The young Dreyer proved to be something of a perfectionist in matters of *mise en scène* and in the choice and direction of actors. This provoked a break with Nordisk and the director embarked on a independent career which led him to make his remaining silent films in five different countries. *The Parson's Widow* (*Prästänkan*, 1920) was shot in Norway for Svensk Filmindustri. While owing a stylistic debt to Sjöström and Stiller, it shows a marked preference for character analysis at the expense of narrative development. This impression is confirmed by *Mikael*, made in Germany in 1924, the story of an emotional triangle linking a painter, his male model, and a Russian noblewoman who seduces the boy away from the master, depriving him of his inspiration. Although heavy with symbolist overtones (derived in large part from the original novel by Hermann Bang), *Mikael* represents Dreyer's first real attempt to analyse the inner life of characters in relation to their environment.

Dreyer fell out with Erich Pommer, the producer of *Mikael*, and returned to Denmark where he made *Master of the House* (*Du skal ære din hustru*, 1925), a drama about a father whose egotistical and authoritarian behaviour wreaks terror on his wife and children. Here the close-ups on faces take on a crucial role. 'The human face', Dreyer wrote, 'is a land one can never tire of exploring. There is no greater experience in a studio than to witness the expression of a sensitive face under the mysterious power of inspiration.' This idea is the key to *The Passion of Joan of Arc* (*La Passion de Jeanne d'Arc*, 1928), in which the close-up reaches its apotheosis in the long sustained sequence of Joan's interrogation against a menacing architectural backdrop—all the more oppressive for seeming to lack precise spatial location.

Dreyer's last silent film, *Joan of Arc* was shot in France with massive technical and financial resources and in conditions of great creative freedom. It was instantly acclaimed by the critics as a masterpiece. But it was a commercial disaster, and for the next forty years Dreyer was only able to direct five more feature films. *Vampyr* (1932) fared even worse at the box office. Using only non-professional actors, *Vampyr* is one of the most disturbing horror films ever made, with a hallucinatory and dreamlike visionary quality intensified by a misty and elusive photographic style. But it was badly received, and Dreyer found himself at the height of his powers with the reputation of being a tiresome perfectionist despot whose every project was a failure.

Over the next ten years Dreyer worked on abortive projects in France, Britain, and Somalia, before returning to his former career as a journalist in Denmark. Finally, in 1943, he was able to direct *Day of Wrath* (*Vredens dag*), a powerful statement on faith, superstition and religious intolerance. *Day of Wrath* is stark and restrained, its style pushing towards abstraction, enhanced by high-contrast

photography. Danish critics saw in the film a reference to Nazi persecution of the Jews, and the director was persuaded to escape to Sweden. When the war was over, he returned to Copenhagen, scraping together enough money from running a cinema to be able to finance *The Word* (*Ordet*, 1955) the story of a feud between two families belonging to different religious sects, interlaced with a love story between members of the opposing families.

Ordet takes even further the tendency towards simple and severe decors and *mise en scène*, intensified by the use of long, slow takes. Even more extreme is *Gertrud* (1964), a portrait of a woman who aspires to an ideal notion of love which she cannot find with her husband or either of her two lovers, leading her to renounce sexual love in favour of asceticism and celibacy. While the restrained classicism of *Ordet* won it a Golden Lion at the Venice Festival in 1955, the intransigence of *Gertrud*, with its static takes in which neither the camera nor the actors seem to move at all for long periods, was found excessive by the majority of critics. A storm of abuse greeted what deserved to be seen as Dreyer's artistic testament, a work of distilled and solemn contemplation. Dreyer continues to be admired for his visual style, which, despite surface dissimilarities, is recognized as having a basic internal unity and consistency, but the thematic coherence of his work—around issues of the unequal struggle of women and the innocent against repression and social intolerance, the inescapability of fate and death, the power of evil in earthly life—is less widely appreciated. His last project was for a Life of Christ, in which he hoped to achieve a synthesis of all stylistic and thematic concerns. He died shortly after he had succeeded in raising the finance from the Danish government and Italian state television for this project, on which he had been working for twenty years.

PAOLO CHERCHI USAI

SELECT FILMOGRAPHY

Præsidenten (The President) (1919); Prästänkan (The Parson's Widow) (1920); Blade af Satans bog (Leaves from Satan's Book) (1921); Die Gezeichneten (Love One Another) (1922); Der var engang (Once upon a Time) (1922); Mikael (Michael / Chained / Heart's Desire / The Invert) (1924); Du skal ære din hustru (The Master of the House) (1925); Glomdalsbruden (The Bride of Glomdale) (1926); La Passion de Jeanne d'Arc (The Passion of Joan of Arc) (1928); Vampyr der Traum des Allan Gray (Vampyr / Vampire) (1932); Vredens dag (Day of Wrath) (1943); Två människor (Two People) (1945); Ordet (The Word) (1955); Gertrud (1964)

BIBLIOGRAPHY

Bordwell, David (1981), *The Films of Carl Theodor Dreyer*.
Drouzy, Maurice (1982), *Carl Th. Dreyer né Nilsson*.
Monty, Ib (1965), *Portrait of Carl Theodor Dreyer*.
Sarris, Andrew (ed.) (1967), *Interviews with Film Directors*.
Schrader, Paul (1972), *Transcendental Style in Film*.

Opposite: Ordet (1955)

HARMONY AND DISRUPTION

The now legendary conflict between director Germaine Dulac and poet Antonin Artaud, over the making of *The Seashell and the Clergyman* (*La Coquille et le clergyman*, 1927) from his screenplay, focuses some key issues in avant-garde film. Dulac made both abstract films such as *Étude cinégraphique sur une arabesque* ('Cinematic study of a flourish', 1923) and stylish narratives, of which the best known is the pioneering feminist work *Smiling Madame Beudet* (*La Souriante Madame Beudet*, 1923). These aspects of her work were linked by a theory of musical form, to 'express feelings through rhythms and suggestive harmonies'. But Artaud opposed this vehemently, along with representation itself. In his 'Theatre of Cruelty', Artaud foresaw the tearing down of barriers between public and stage, act and emotion, actor and mask. In film, he wrote in 1927, he wanted 'pure images' whose meanings would emerge, free of verbal associations, 'from the very impact of the images themselves'. The impact must be violent, 'a shock designed for the eyes, a shock founded, so to speak, on the very substance of the gaze'. For Dulac too, film is 'impact', but typically its effect is 'ephemeral . . . analogous to that provoked by musical harmonies'. Dulac fluently explored film as dream state (expressed in the dissolving superimpositions in *La Coquille*) and so heralded the psychodrama film, but Artaud wanted film only to keep the dream state's most violent and shattering qualities, breaking the trance of vision.

Here, the avant-garde focused on the role of the spectator. In the abstract film, analogies were sought with non-narrative arts to challenge cinema as a dramatic form, and this led to 'visual music' or 'painting in motion'. In Jean Coudal's 1925 surrealist account, film viewing is seen as akin to 'conscious hallucination', in which the body—undergoing 'temporary depersonalization'—is robbed of 'its sense of its own existence. We are nothing more than two eyes rivetted to ten meters of white screen, with a fixed and guided gaze.' This critique was taken further in Dalí's 'Abstract of a Critical History of the Cinema' (1932), which argues that film's 'sensory base' in 'rhythmic impression' leads it to the *bête noire* of harmony, defined as 'the refined product of abstraction', or idealization, rooted in 'the rapid and continuous succession of film images, whose implicit neologism is directly proportional to a specifically generalizing visual culture'. Countermanding this, Dalí looks for 'the poetry of cinema' in 'a traumatic and violent disequilibrium veering towards concrete irrationality'.

The goal of radical discontinuity did not stop short at the visual image, variously seen as optical and illusory (by Buñuel) or as retinal and illusionist (by Duchamp). The linguistic codes in film (written or spoken) were also scoured, as in films by Man Ray, Buñuel, and Duchamp which all play with intertitles to open a gap between word, sign, and object. The attack on naturalism continued into the sound era, notably in Buñuel's documentary on the Spanish poor, *Las Hurdes* (*Land without Bread*, 1932). Here, the surrealist Pierre Unik's commentary—a seemingly authoritative 'voice-over' in the tradition of factual film—slowly undermines the realism of the images, questioning the depiction (and viewing) of its subjects by a chain of *non sequiturs* or by allusions to scenes which the crews—we are told—failed, neglected, or refused to shoot. Lacunae open between voice, image, and truth, just as the eye had been suddenly slashed in *Un chien andalou*.

Paradoxically, the assault on the eye (or on the visual order) can be traced back to the 'study of optics' which Cézanne had recommended to painters at the dawn of modernism. This was characteristically refined by Walter Benjamin in 1936, linking mass reproduction, the cinema, and art: 'By its transforming function, the camera introduces us to unconscious optics as does psychoanalysis to unconscious impulses.'

The discontinuity principle underlies the avant-garde's key rhetorical figure, paratactic montage, which breaks the flow—or 'continuity'—between shots and scenes, against the grain of narrative editing. Defined by Richter as 'an interruption of the context in which it is inserted', this form of montage first appeared in the avant-garde just as the mainstream was perfecting its narrative codes. Its purpose is counter-narrative, by linking dissonant images which resist habits of memory and perception to underline the film event as phenomenological and immediate. At one extreme of parataxis, rapid cutting—down to the single frame—disrupts the forward flow of linear time (as in the 'dance' of abstract shapes in *Ballet mécanique*). At the other extreme, the film is treated as raw strip, frameless and ageless, to be photogrammed by Man Ray or hand-painted by Len Lye. Each option is a variation spun from the kaleidoscope of the modernist visual arts.

This diversity—reflected too in the search for non-commercial funding through patronage and self-help co-operatives—means that there is no single model of avant-garde film practice, which has variously been seen to relate to the mainstream as poetry does to prose, or music to drama, or painting to writing. None of these suggestive analogies is exhaustive, in part because of the avant-garde's own insistence that film is a specific if compound medium, whether basically 'photogenic' (as Epstein and others believed) or 'durational' (film was first defined as 'time-based' by Walter Ruttmann in 1919). The modernist credo that art is a language brought the early avant-gardes close to Kuleshov ('the shot as a sign'), to Eisensteinian montage, and to Vertov's 'theory of intervals' in which the gaps between shots—like silences in post-serial music—are equal in value to the shots themselves.

Even the supposedly unified constructivist movement (itself made up of both rationalist and spiritualist traits) included 'cinematology' (Malevich), the Dada-flavoured films of Stefan and Franciszka Themerson (whose *Adventures of a Good Citizen*, made in Poland in 1937, inspired Polanski's 1957 surreal skit *Two Men and a Wardrobe*), the abstract film *Black-Grey-White* (1930) by László Moholy-Nagy as well as his later documentary shorts (several, like a portrait of Lubetkin's London Zoo, made in England), the semiotic film projects of the young Polish artist and political activist Mieczysław Szczuka and the light-play experiments of the Bauhaus. For these and other artists film-making was an additional activity to their work in other media.

FROM EUROPE TO THE USA

The inter-war period closes emblematically with Richter's exile from Nazi-occupied Europe to the USA in 1940. Shortly before, he had completed his book *The Struggle for the Film*, in which he had praised both the classic avant-garde as well as primitive cinema and documentary film as opponents of mass cinema, seen as manipulative of its audience if also shot through (despite itself) with new visual ideas. In the USA, Richter became archivist and historian of the experimental cinema in which he had played a large role, issuing (and re-editing, by most accounts) his own early films and Eggeling's. The famous 1946 San Francisco screenings, Art in Cinema, which he co-organized, brought together the avant-garde classics with new films by Maya Deren, Sidney Peterson, Curtis Harrington, and Kenneth Anger; an avant-garde renaissance at a time when the movement was largely seen as obsolete.

Richter's influence on the new wave was limited but substantial. His own later films—such as *Dreams that Money can Buy* (1944–7)—were long undervalued as baroque indulgences (with episodes directed by other exiles such as Man Ray, Duchamp, Léger, and Max Ernst) by contrast to the 'pure'—and to a later generation more 'materialist'—abstract films of the 1920s. Regarded at the time as 'archaic', *Dreams* now seems uncannily prescient of a contemporary post-modernist sensibility. David Lynch selected extracts from it, along with films by Vertov and Cocteau, for his 1986 BBC *Arena* film survey. Stylish key episodes include Duchamp's reworking of his spiral films and early paintings, themselves derived from cubism and chronophotography, with sound by John Cage. Man Ray contributes a playful skit on the act of viewing, in which a semi-hypnotized audience obeys increasingly absurd commands issued by the film they supposedly watch. Ernst's episode eroticizes the face and body in extreme close-up and rich colour, looking ahead to today's 'cinema of the body' in experimental film and video. Richter's own classes in film-making were attended by, among others, another recent immigrant Jonas Mekas, soon to be the energetic magus of the 'New American Cinema'.

Two decades earlier, the avant-garde had time-shifted cubism and Dada into film history (both movements were essentially over by the time artists were able to make their own films). By the 1940s, a new avant-garde again performed a complex, overlapping loop, reasserting internationalism and experimentation, at a time as vital for transatlantic art as early modernism had been for Richter's generation. Perhaps the key difference, as P. Adams Sitney argues, is that the first avant-garde had added film to the potential and traditional media at an artist's disposal, while new American (and soon European) film-makers after the Second World War began to see film-making more exclusively as an art form that could exist in its own right, so that the artist-film-maker could produce a body of work in that medium alone. Ironically, this generation also reinvented the silent film, defying the rise of naturalistic sound which had in part doomed its avant-garde ancestors in the 'poetic cinema' a decade before.

Bibliography
Curtis, David (1971), *Experimental Cinema*.
Drummond, Phillip, Dusinberre, Deke, and Rees, A. L. (eds.) (1979), *Film as Film*.
Hammond, Paul (1991), *The Shadow and its Shadow*.
Kuenzli, Rudolf E. (ed.) (1987), *Dada and Surrealist Film*.
Lawdor, Standish (1975), *The Cubist Cinema*.
Richter, Hans (1986), *The Struggle for the Film*.
Sitney, P. Adams (1974), *Visionary Film*.

Serials

BEN SINGER

I am the serial. I am the black sheep of the picture family and the reviled of critics. I am the soulless one with no moral, no character, no uplift. I am ashamed.... Ah me, if I could only be respectable. If only the hair of the great critic would not rise whenever I pass by and if only he would not cry, 'Shame! Child of commerce! Bastard of art!'

('The Serial Speaks', *New York Dramatic Mirror*, 19 August 1916)

It is rare indeed for a promotional article in the 1910s to lapse, however briefly, from the film industry's perennial mantra, 'We are attracting the better classes; We are uplifting the cinema; We are preserving the highest moral and artistic standards ...' Probably few readers ever took such affirmations as anything more than perfunctory, and dubiously sincere, reassurances to a cultural establishment that approached the cinema with an unpredictable mixture of hostility and meddlesome paternalism. Nevertheless, it is unusual—and telling—that a studio mouthpiece (in this case, George B. Seitz, Pathé's serial tsar) should see fit to abandon the 'uplift' conceit altogether. Clearly, it was impossible even to pretend that the serial played any part in the cinema's putative rehabilitation. The serial's intertextual background doomed it to disrepute. Growing directly out of late nineteenth-century working-class amusements—popular-priced stage melodrama (of the buzz-saw variety), and cheap fiction in dime novels, 'story papers', *feuilletons*, and penny dreadfuls—the serial was geared to a decidedly lowbrow audience.

As early titles like *The Perils of Pauline*, *The Exploits of Elaine*, *The House of Hate*, *The Lurking Peril*, and *The Screaming Shadow* make obvious, serials were packaged sensationalism. Their basic ingredients come as no surprise: as Ellis Ober-

holtzer, Pennsylvania's cranky head censor in the 1910s, described the genre, 'It is crime, violence, blood and thunder, and always obtruding and outstanding is the idea of sex.' Elaborating every form of physical peril and 'thrill', serials promised sensational spectacle in the form of explosions, crashes, torture contraptions, elaborate fights, chases, and last-minute rescues and escapes. The stories invariably focused on the machinations of underworld gangs and mystery villains ('The Hooded Terror', 'The Clutching Hand', etc.) as they tried to assassinate or usurp the fortunes of a pretty young heroine and her hero-boyfriend. The milieu was an aggressively non-domestic, 'masculine' world of hide-outs, opium dens, lumber mills, diamond mines, abandoned warehouses—into which the plucky girl heroine ventured at her peril.

Serials were a hangover from the nickelodeon era. They stood out as mildly 'shameful' at a time when the film industry was trying to broaden its market by making innocuous middlebrow films suitable for heterogeneous audiences in the larger theatres being built at the time. Rather than catering to 'the mass'—a homogeneous, 'classless' audience fancied by the emerging Hollywood institution—serials were made for 'the masses'—the uncultivated, predominantly working- and lower-middle-class and immigrant audience that had supported the incredible 'nickelodeon boom'. Oberholtzer again offers a sharp assessment:

The crime serial is meant for the most ignorant class of the population with the grossest tastes, and it principally flourishes in the picture halls in mill villages and in the thickly settled tenement houses and low foreign-speaking neighborhoods in large cities. Not a producer, I believe, but is ashamed of such an output, yet not more than one or two of the large manufacturing companies have had the courage to repel the temptation to thus swell their balances at the end of the fiscal year.

Serials were also a proletarian product in Britain (and probably everywhere else). A writer in the *New Statesman* in 1918 observed that British cinema-goers paid much higher ticket prices than the Americans, but he notes an exception to this rule:

Only in those ramshackle 'halls' of our poorer streets, where noisy urchins await the next episode of some long since antiquated 'Transatlantic Serial' does one notice the proletarian invitation of twopenny and fourpenny seats.

Almost never screened in large first-run theatres, serials were a staple of small, cheap 'neighbourhood' theatres (for all intents and purposes, these theatres were simply nickelodeons that had survived into the 1910s). Although the serious money was in big first-run theatres, small theatres still constituted the large majority in terms of sheer numbers, and the studios, despite their uplift proclamations, were reluctant to give up this lowbrow market.

WHY SERIALS?

The film industry turned to serials for a number of reasons, aside from the ease of tapping into an already established popular market for sensational stories. It saw the commercial logic of adopting the practice of serialization, already a mainstay of popular magazines and newspapers. With every episode culminating in a suspenseful cliffhanger ending, film serials encouraged a steady volume of return customers, tantalized and eager for the fix of narrative closure withheld in the previous instalment. In this system of deliberately prolonged desire punctuated by fleeting, intermittent doses of satisfaction, serials conveyed a certain acuity about the new psychology of consumerism in modern capitalism.

Serials also made sense, from the studios' perspective, because, at least in their earliest years, they represented an attractive alternative for manufacturers who were incapable or unwilling to switch over to five- and six-reel feature films. Released one or two reels at a time for a dozen or so instalments, serials could be pitched as 'big' titles without overly daunting the studios' still relatively modest production infrastructure and entrenched system of short-reel distribution. For several years, serials were, in fact, billed as 'feature' attractions—the centrepiece of a short-reel 'variety' programme. Later, as real feature films became the main attraction, serial instalments were used to fill out the programme, along with a short comedy and newsreel.

Serials appeared at a pivotal moment in the institutional history of film promotion: producers were just realizing the importance of 'exploitation' (i.e. advertising), but were still frustrated by brief film runs that kept advertising relatively inefficient. As late as 1919, only about one theatre in a hundred ran films for an entire week, one in eight ran them for half a week, and over four out of five changed films daily. In this situation, serials were ideal vehicles for massive publicity. They allowed the industry to flex its exploitation muscle, since each serial stayed at a theatre for three to four months. Serial producers invested extremely heavily in newspaper, magazine, trade journal, billboard, and tram advertising, as well as grandiose cash-prize contests. Serials helped inaugurate the 'Hollywood' system of publicity in which studios paid more for advertising than for the production of the film itself.

The emergence of serials was linked to one form of publicity in particular. Until around 1917, virtually every film serial was released in tandem with prose versions published simultaneously in newspapers and national magazines. Movies and short fiction were bound together as two halves of what might be described as a larger, multi-media, textual unit. These fiction tie-ins—inviting the consumer to 'Read it Here in the Morning; See it on the Screen Tonight!'—saturated the entertainment market-place to a degree never seen since. Appearing in major newspapers in every big city and in hundreds (the studios claimed thousands) of provincial papers, the serials' publicity engaged a potential readership well into the tens of millions. This practice exploded the scope of film publicity, and paved the way for the cinema's graduation to a truly mass medium.

THE FILMS AND THEIR FORMULAS, 1912-1920

Although series films (narratively complete but with continuing characters and milieu) had appeared as early as 1908, or earlier if one counts comedy series, the first serial film proper (with a story-line connecting separate instalments) was Edison's *What Happened to Mary*, released in twelve monthly 'chapters' beginning in July 1912. Recounting the adventures of a country girl (and, needless to say, unknowing heiress) as she discovers the pleasures and perils of big-city life while eluding an evil uncle and sundry other villains, the story was published simultaneously (along with numerous stills from the screen version) in *Ladies' World*, a major women's monthly magazine. Although critics derided the serial as 'mere melodrama of action' and 'a lurid, overdrawn thriller', it was popular at the box-office, making the actress Mary Fuller, playing Mary Dangerfield, one of the cinema's first really big (if rather ephemeral) stars. The commercial success of *What Happened to Mary* prompted the Selig Polyscope Company and the *Chicago Tribune* syndicate to team up in the production and promotion of *The Adventures of Kathlyn*, exhibited and published fortnightly throughout the first half of 1914. In keeping with the early star system's trope of eponymous protagonists, Kathlyn Williams played

Kathlyn Hare, a fetching American girl who, in order to save her kidnapped father, reluctantly becomes the Queen of Allahah, a principality in India.

When it became clear that *Kathlyn* was a huge hit, virtually every important studio at the time (with the notable exception of Biograph) started making action series and twelve- to fifteen-chapter serials, almost all connected to prose-version newspaper tie-ins. Kalem produced *The Hazards of Helen*, a railway adventure series that ran for 113 weekly instalments between 1914 and 1917, as well as *The Girl Detective* series (1915), *The Ventures of Marguerite* (1915), and a number of other 'plucky heroine' series. Thanhouser had one of the silent era's biggest commercial successes with *The Million Dollar Mystery* (1914), although its follow-up *Zudora (The Twenty Million Dollar Mystery)* was reportedly a flop. By far the biggest producers of serials in the 1910s were Pathé (its American branch), Universal, Mutual, and Vitagraph. Pathé relied heavily on its suc-

cessful Pearl White vehicles—*The Perils of Pauline* (1914), *The Exploits of Elaine* (1915—and two sequels), *The Iron Claw* (1916), *Pearl of the Army* (1916), *The Fatal Ring* (1917), *The House of Hate* (1918) (which Eisenstein cites as an influence), *The Black Secret* (1919), and *The Lightning Raider* (1919)—as well as numerous serials starring Ruth Roland and various lesser-known 'serial queens'. Universal, like Pathé, had at least two serials running at any time throughout the decade. Several were directed by Francis Ford (John Ford's older brother) and starred the duo of Ford and Grace Cunard: *Lucille Love, Girl of Mystery* (1914) (the first film Luis Buñuel recalled ever seeing), *The Broken Coin* (1915), *The Adventures of Peg o' the Ring* (1916), and *The Purple Mask* (1916). Mutual signed up Helen Holmes (of *Hazards of . . .* fame) and continued in the vein of railway stunt thrillers with *The Girl and the Game* (1916), *Lass of the Lumberlands* (1916–17), *The Lost Express* (1917), *The Railroad Raiders* (1917), and others. Vitagraph at first claimed it was offering a 'better

Pearl White in vigorous mode in *Plunder* (1923), her last serial for Pathé in America

Louis Feuillade

(1873–1925)

The youngest son of a devoutly Catholic, anti-republican family from Languedoc, Louis Feuillade arrived in Paris with his wife in 1898. He worked as a journalist before becoming an assistant editor for the right-wing *Revue-mondiale*. Engaged by Gaumont in December 1905 as a scenario writer and first assistant to Alice Guy, by 1907 he had advanced to head of film production and was active in writing and directing all of the genres produced by Gaumont, from trick film (*L'Homme aimanté*, 1907), to domestic melodrama (*La Possession de l'enfant*, 1909).

The popularity of the film series had been established in France by Éclair's Nick Winter crime series (1908). In 1910 Feuillade introduced the *Bébé* comic series, starring René Dary, which ran to nearly seventy films over the course of two years. In 1911, he wrote and directed *Les Vipères* as the first of the successful *Scènes de la vie telle qu'elle est* series, which merged the popular traditions of melodrama and realism. The *Bout-de-Zan* series, starring René Poyen, replaced *Bébé* in 1912, eventually running to forty films by the time of the war.

During these first six years, Feuillade's films were marked by sober, restrained acting, solid narrative construction, a flexible editing style, and, together with his cameraman Albert Sorgius, he created a masterful sense of composition and lighting. Many films in the *Vie telle qu'elle est* series exposed the tragic, or at least pathetic, consequences of unjustifiable social and sexual stereotyping.

In 1913 came the film for which Feuillade is best remembered, *Fantômas*, based on the crime novels of Marcel Allain and Pierre Souvestre and starring Navarre as an elusive figure of amazing power and *savoir-faire*. The first of five feature-length films, *Fantômas* skilfully established the 'fantastic realism' that Feuillade and his new cameraman Guérin would make characteristic of the series before it was interrupted by the war: the master criminal circulated freely through all kinds of actual landscapes and social milieux, particularly in and around Paris, his incredible, sometimes bloody exploits deftly masked by the reassuringly mundane façade of daily life.

When Gaumont resumed film production, in 1915, Feuillade returned to the crime series with *Les Vampires*, ten feature-length episodes released monthly to July 1916. Here it was Musidora, as the *femme fatale* Irma Vep, who emerged as the film's most powerful, repeatedly deceptive figure, infatuating the reporter hero (Édouard Mathé) on the track of her black-clad criminal band and deflecting his plans to revenge his kidnapped wife. Partly in reaction to provincial bannings of *Les Vampires*, Feuillade enlisted the popular novelist Arthur Bernède (and another cameraman, Klausse) to create more conventional adventure stories for his next two serials, the hugely successful *Judex* (1917) and *La Nouvelle Mission de*

Judex (1918). Wrapped in a black cape and accompanied by a sidekick (Marcel Lévesque), the detective Judex (René Cresté) performed like an updated chivalric hero, protecting the weak and righting wrongs in order to revenge his father and reclaim the honour of his name.

After the war, Gaumont's production began to decline and Feuillade made fewer but more diverse films. Serials continued to be his trademark, but they went through several changes. In *Tih-Minh* (1919), he resurrected the Vampire gang as displaced 'colonial' antagonists to a French explorer (Cresté) in search of buried treasure and the love of an Indo-Chinese princess; in *Barrabas* (1920) he loosed a devious criminal gang to operate behind the façade of an international bank. *Les Deux Gamines* (1921), *L'Orpheline* (1921), and *Parisette* (1922), however, turned to the very different formula of the domestic melodrama, focusing on an orphaned *ingénue* heroine (Sandra Milowanoff) who, after long suffering, married the 'sentimental hero' (in one series, René Clair). The last of Feuillade's serials took another turn towards historical adventure (soon to become the trademark of Jean Sapène's Cinéromans), best illustrated in the spectacular action of *Le Fils du flibustier* (1922). Around this time some of Feuillade's films reverted to the 'realist' tradition that he had worked in before the war. Using a topical story of German spies among refugees displaced by the war, *Vendémiaire* (1919), made with his last cameraman, Maurice Champreux, documented boat traffic on the Rhone River and the life of the Bas-Languedoc peasant community during the grape harvest. *Le Gamin de Paris* (1923), by contrast, achieved an unusual sense of charm and poignancy through 'naturalistic' acting (by Milowanoff and Poyen), location shooting in the Belleville section of Paris, skilful studio lighting and set décor (by Robert Jules-Garnier), and American-style continuity editing.

In February 1925, on the eve of shooting another historical serial, *Le Stigmate* (which would be completed by Champreux), Feuillade was taken ill, and died of acute peritonitis.

RICHARD ABEL

SELECT FILMOGRAPHY

Serials
Bébé (1910); Scènes de la vie telle qu'elle est (1911); Bout-de-Zan (1912); Fantômas (1913); Les Vampires (1915); Judex (1917); La Nouvelle Mission de Judex (1918); Tih-Minh (1919); Vendémiaire (1919); Barrabas (1920); Les Deux Gamines (1921); L'Orpheline (1921); Parisette (1922); Le Fils du flibustier (1922); Le Gamin de Paris (1923)

BIBLIOGRAPHY

Abel, Richard (1993), *The Ciné Goes to Town: French Cinema, 1896–1914.*
Lacassin, Francis (1964), *Louis Feuillade.*
Roud, Richard (ed.) (1980), *Cinema: A Critical Dictionary* (entry on Louis Feuillade).

Opposite: Judex (1917)

grade' of serials for a 'better class of audience', but in truth its serials are hardly distinguishable from the sensational melodramas of its competitors.

The 1910s was the era of the serial queen. In their stunt-filled adventures as 'girl spies', 'girl detectives', 'girl reporters', etc., serial heroines demonstrated a kind of toughness, bravery, agility, and intelligence that excited audiences both for its novelty and for its feminist resonance. Serial queens defied the ideology of female passivity and domesticity, and instead displayed traditionally 'masculine' attributes, competences, and interests. They tapped into a larger cultural fascination with the 'New Woman', a revised model of femininity floated by the media (if not entirely adopted in practice) during the rise of metropolitan modernity and the disintegration of the Victorian world-view. While still fulfilling classic melodrama conventions of female imperilment, serial heroines in the 1910s were not simply objects to be saved by the hero. To be sure, they still needed to be rescued with some regularity, but they also got out of plights using their own wits and daring. And in the serial's system of polymorphous prowess, one is almost as likely to see the heroine rescue the hero tied-to-the-railroad-tracks as the reverse.

In every serial, the conflict between villain and hero/heroine expresses itself in a back-and-forth struggle both for the possession of the heroine (whom the villain constantly kidnaps or tries to kill) and also for the possession of a highly prized object—what Pearl White called the 'weenie'. The weenie took many forms: a blueprint for a new torpedo; an ebony idol containing the key to a treasure trove; a secret document outlining the defence of the Panama Canal; a special fuel to power a machine that disintegrates people; the secret formula for turning dirt into diamonds, and so on. The capture and recapture of the weenie afforded a sufficiently loose structure on which to hang a series of thrills.

Another constant in serial stories relates to the pivotal position of the heroine's father, along with the total non-existence of any mother characters (and, for that matter, most other female figures as well). The heroine is always the daughter (often an adopted one) of a powerful man (rich industrialist, army general, fire chief, explorer, inventor, or newspaper mogul) who is assassinated by the villain in the first episode or (less frequently) abducted and blackmailed. The serial hinges on the daughter's fight to gain her inheritance while the villain and sundry henchmen try to kill her and usurp it. Alternatively, the serial involves the daughter's fight to save her father from the clutches of the villain, redeem his tarnished name, or simply aid the father (independent of his supervision) in thwarting his, and the nation's, enemies.

Although when they hit they hit resoundingly, American serials had an erratic commercial history. Information on box-office receipts is hard to come by, but trade-journal surveys of film exchanges (rental offices) may tell us something about the serial's popularity among audiences. Between 1914 and 1917, *Motion Picture News* conducted a number of in-depth polls of exchangemen. In October 1914, to the question 'Do serials continue popular?', 60 per cent said 'yes', while about 20 per cent said 'no' (the rest saying 'fairly'). A year later, however, the 'noes' had swelled to 70 per cent. But a year after that, at the end of 1916, the serial's popularity had rallied again, with about a 65 : 35 percentage split between 'yes' and 'no' responses. By the summer of 1917 the responses had levelled out to exactly 50 : 50. A number of factors explain the serial's mixed popularity among distributors and (presumably) exhibitors and audiences. At least in part it reflected the growing rift, on many levels, between a residual 'nickelodeon' cinema, geared toward small-time exhibitors and lower-class audiences, and an emergent Hollywood model of mass entertainment. It is also likely that many audiences simply tired of the serial's highly formulaic stories, dubiously thrilling thrills, and low production values.

INTERNATIONAL SERIES AND SERIALS

Although an international history of series and serials has yet to be written, series and serials were far from being just an American phenomenon. France's considerable investment in series and serials is well covered in Richard Abel's history of silent French cinema. Éclair pioneered the genre with the extremely popular series *Nick Carter, le roi des détectives* ('Nick Carter, king of the detectives', 1908), followed by *Zigomar* (1911) and various sequels, all directed by Victorin Jasset. Louis Feuillade directed a number of celebrated underworld crime serials for Gaumont: *Fantômas* (1913–14), *Les Vampires* ('The Vampires', 1915–16), *Judex* (1917), and *La Nouvelle Mission de Judex* ('Judex's new mission', 1918).

While these and other domestically produced serials enjoyed considerable popularity, it was Pathé's American-made serials that caused the biggest sensation among French audiences. Released, as in America, in conjunction with massive newspaper tie-ins, *Les Mystères de New York* (1916) (a repackaging of twenty-two episodes from *The Exploits of Elaine* and its two sequels) was a smash hit and began a trend in *ciné-romans* (or 'film-novels').

In Britain leading serials were, among others, *The Adventures of Lieutenant Rose* (1909), *The Adventures of Lieutenant Daring* (1911), *The Exploits of Three-Fingered Kate* (1912). Films Lloyds in Germany made the Detective Webb series (1914), which, like Feuillade's *Fantômas*, was comprised of feature-length instalments. In Russia, a few serials followed after the huge success of imported American and French serials: Jay Leyda briefly cites Drankov's *Sonka, the Golden Hand*, Bauer's *Irina Kirsanova*, and Gardin and Protazanov's

Petersburg Slums. Italy had *Tigris* and *Za la Mort*; Germany had *Homunculus* (an early instance of the silent German cinema's fascination with stories about man-made supermen); and Austria *The Invisible Ones*.

Third World cinemas also made serials, although extremely little is known about this topic. A particularly fascinating implementation of the serial-queen formula is a group of Hindi serials starring 'Fearless Nadia', an Australian actress of Welsh–Greek extraction. Inspired by imported American serials, director Homi Wadis also made the feature *Hunterwali* (*The Lady with the Whip*) with Fearless Nadia in 1935. Bombay's Kohinoor Studios produced numerous follow-up serials, as did other Indian studios. *The Diamond Queen* (1940) is among those still available from Indian distributors.

THE 1920S AND AFTER

In the United States, film serials lived out the 1920s, and survived to the rise of television, as a low-budget 'B' product with limited distribution and an appeal primarily to hyperactive children. To some degree this had been the case from the very start, but after the 1910s it became more obvious that serials were slapdash juvenile movies for 'Saturday afternoon at the Bijou'. With the phasing out of prose-version tie-ins in the late 1910s, serials never again enjoyed wide publicity and distribution. Furthermore, the disappearance of the classical blood-and-thunder stage melodrama, and a generational shift that caused adult audiences to view overwrought sensational melodrama as ridiculous and old-fashioned rather than exhilarating, solidified the serial's decline into a cartoonish children's genre. The serial's essential formula (hero and heroine fight villain for possession of weenie) remained unchanged throughout, but the genre underwent some key transformations. The 'serial-queen' cycle faded away in the late 1910s and early 1920s as emphasis shifted toward the adventures of traditional beefy heroes like Elmo Lincoln (*Elmo, the Mighty*, 1919; *Elmo, the Fearless*, 1920; *The Adventures of Tarzan*, 1921), Eddie Polo (*King of the Circus*, 1920; *Do or Die*, 1921), and Charles Hutchinson (*Hurricane Hutch*, 1921; *Go Get 'Em Hutch*, 1922). Evidently, the plucky New Woman's novelty had worn off and it was incumbent upon serial heroines to resume the role of damsel in distress.

The serial's intertextual links also changed. Serials became much more closely associated with pre-existing characters in the Sunday comics, comic books, radio, and pulp magazines. In 1936 Universal bought the rights to many comic strips owned by the King Features Syndicate, and other studios made similar deals. Serials now fleshed out heroes like Flash Gordon, Superman, Captain Marvel, Dick Tracy, Batman, Buck Rogers, The Phantom, Captain America, Deadwood Dick, the Lone Ranger, and so on.

There could be little question that serial producers were after the nickels and dimes of America's children.

With Mutual's dissolution in 1918 and the purchase of the already hapless Vitagraph by Warner Bros. in 1925, Pathé and Universal remained as the key serial producers in the 1920s. Pathé got out of the serial-producing business in 1928, when Joseph P. Kennedy came in and reorganized the studio. An upstart company, Mascot Pictures, filled the void left by Pathé's departure, and then in 1935 merged with a few other concerns to form Republic Pictures. The quintessential 'poverty row' studio, Republic nevertheless made the best serials, according to most collectors and nostalgia buffs. In terms of output, Universal, Republic, and Columbia Pictures were the undisputed 'big three' in sound-era serials, each studio offering three or four a year. Running weekly for between twelve and fifteen weeks, serials filled up an entire exhibition 'season', one leading directly into the next. An assortment of minor independent producers made one or two serials in the 1930s, but none at all ventured into this field thereafter. With serials falling even lower in reputation and commercial importance, Universal bowed out for good in 1946, while Republic and Columbia plodded along making serials until around 1955, when television became the chosen medium for weekly adventure series.

In all, Mascot and Republic made ninety serials between 1929 and 1955; Columbia made fifty-seven between 1937 and 1956; and Universal made sixty-nine between 1929 and 1946. Independents account for fifteen serials between 1930 and 1937. In addition to these 231 sound serials, just under 300 serials were made in the silent era. All told, this adds up to over 7,200 episodes. If serials are a minor footnote in the history of film as art, they deserve recognition as an important phenomenon in the history of cinema as a social and institutional commodity.

Bibliography

Barbour, Alan G. (1977), *Cliffhanger: A Pictorial History of the Motion Picture Serial*.

Kinnard, Roy (1983), *Fifty Years of Serial Thrills*.

Lahue, Kalton C. (1964), *Continued Next Week: A History of the Moving Picture Serial*.

Oberholtzer, Ellis P. (1922), *The Morals of the Movies*.

Singer, Ben (1993), 'Fictional Tie-ins and Narrative Intelligibility, 1911–18'.

Stedman, Raymond William (1977), *The Serials: Suspense and Drama by Instalment*.

NATIONAL CINEMAS

French Silent Cinema

RICHARD ABEL

In 1907, the French press repeatedly erupted in astonishment over the speed with which the cinema was supplanting other spectacle entertainments like the *café-concert* and music hall and even threatening to displace the theatre. As a song from the popular revue, *Tu l'as l'allure*, put it:

> So when will the Ciné drop and die?
>   Who knows.
> So when will the Café-conc' revive?
>   Who knows.

Whatever the attitudes taken—and they ranged from exhilaration to resigned dismay—there was no doubt that, in France, 1907 was 'the year of the cinema' or, as one writer enthused, 'the dawn of a new age of Humanity'. So limitless seemed the cinema's future that it set off an explosion of entrepreneurial activity.

PATHÉ-FRÈRES INDUSTRIALIZES THE CINEMA

At the centre of that activity was Pathé-Frères as it systematically industrialized every sector of the new industry. Two years before, Pathé had pioneered a system of mass production (headed by Ferdinand Zecca) which soon had the company marketing at least half a dozen film titles per week (or 40,000 metres of positive film stock per day) as well as 250 cameras, projectors, and other apparatuses per month. By 1909, those figures had doubled across the board, and the Pathé studio camera and projector had become the standard industry models. This production capacity enabled Pathé to construct one cinema after another in Paris and other cities, beginning in 1906-7, shifting film exhibition away from the fairgrounds to permanent sites in urban shopping and entertainment districts. By 1909 Pathé had a circuit of nearly 200 cinemas throughout France and Belgium, probably the largest in Europe. In order better to regulate distribution of its product within that circuit, in 1907-8 the company also set up a network of six regional agencies to rent, rather than sell, its weekly programme of films. This network augmented the dozens of agencies Pathé had opened across the globe, beginning as early as 1904, and through which it quickly dominated the world-wide sale and rental of films. By 1907, one-third to one-half of the films making up American nickelodeon programmes were Pathé's—as a general rule, the company shipped up to 200 copies of each film title to the United States. As the 'empire' of this first international cinema corporation began to stabilize (and eventually contract in the USA because of MPPC restrictions) and film distribution and exhibition became its most secure sources of revenue, Pathé gradually shifted film production to a growing number of quasi-independent affiliates. By 1913-14, Pathé-Frères had become a kind of parent company (Charles Pathé himself invoked the analogy of a book publisher) to a host of production affiliates, from France (SCAGL, Valetta, and Comica) to Russia, Italy, Holland, and the USA.

The other French companies engaged in the cinema's expansion either followed Pathé's lead or found a profitable niche in one or more sectors of the industry. Léon Gaumont's company, Pathé's closest rival, was the only other vertically integrated corporation active in every sector, from manufacturing equipment to producing, distributing, and exhibiting films. Its 1911 renovation of the Gaumont-Palace (seating 3,400 people), for instance, not only anchored its own circuit of cinemas but spurred the construction of more 'palace' cinemas in Paris and elsewhere. Unlike Pathé, however, Gaumont steadily increased direct investment in production so that it too could release at least half a dozen film titles per week. Under the management of Charles Jourjon and Marcel Vandal, Éclair operated within a slightly narrower sphere, having never established a circuit of cinemas to present its product. Instead, to fuel its aggressive expansion between 1910 and 1913, Éclair concentrated on producing and distributing films as well as manufacturing various kinds of apparatuses. Along with Pathé, it was the only French company with the capital and foresight to open its own production studio in the USA. Most smaller French companies either confined their efforts to production (Film d'Art, Eclipse, and Lux) or concentrated on distribution (AGC). The most important independent distributor, Louis Aubert, embarked on a somewhat different trajectory, much as Universal, Fox, and Paramount would slightly later in the USA. Aubert's company prospered through its exclusive contracts to release films by the major Italian and Danish producers in France, including *Quo vadis?*; by

112

1913 Aubert was reinvesting his profits in a circuit of 'palace' cinemas in Paris as well as a new studio for producing his own films.

What kinds of films dominated French cinema programmes during this period, and what specific titles could be singled out as significant? The *actualités*, trick films, and *féeries* which once characterized the early 'cinema of attractions' had, by 1907, given way to a more fully narrativized cinema, especially through Pathé's standardized production of comic chase films and what its catalogue advertised as 'dramatic and realist' films, often directed by Albert Capellani. The latter category covered domestic melodramas such as *La Loi du pardon* ('The law of pardon', 1906), in which families were threatened with dissolution and then securely reunited, and Grand Guignol variants such as *Pour un collier!* ('For a necklace!', 1907), in which the resolution was anything but secure. Within such films there coalesced a system of representation and narration that relied not only on long-take tableaux (recorded by Pathé's 'trademark' waist-level camera), bold red intertitles, inserted letters, and accompanying sound effects but on changes in framing through camera movement, cut-in close shots, point-of-view shots, and reverse-angle cutting as well as on various forms of repetition and alternation in editing. This system achieved remarkable effects in melodramas as diverse as *The Pirates* (1907), *A Narrow Escape* (1908) (which D. W. Griffith remade in 1909 as *The Lonely Villa*), and *L'Homme aux gants blancs* ('The man with white gloves', 1908) as well as in comic films like *Ruse de mari* ('The husband's trick', 1907) and *Le Cheval emballé* ('The wrapped-up horse', 1908). In other words, Pathé films were deploying most of the elements so basic to the system of narrative continuity, all of which historians still often attribute to slightly later Vitagraph or Biograph films.

Another instance of increasing standardization within the French cinema was the continuing series, a marketing strategy in which one film after another could be organized around a central character (identified by name) and a single actor. As early as 1907, Pathé began releasing a comic series entitled Boireau, named after a recurring character played by André Deed. Boireau's success soon led to other comic series (especially after Deed left France to work in Italy as Cretinetti). In 1909 Gaumont introduced its Calino series, with Clément Migé often playing a bumbling civil servant; the following year there was the Bébé series, with René Dary; two years later came the incredibly wacky Onésime series, with Ernest Bourbon, and Bout-de-Zan, with René Poyen as an even more threatening *enfant terrible*. As for Pathé itself, among the half-dozen comic series it regularly distributed, two stood out above the rest. One was Rigadin, starring Charles Prince as a parodic white-collar Don Juan; *Le Nez de Rigadin* ('Rigadin's Nose', 1911), for instance, ruthlessly mocks his large upturned

nose, one of the comic's singular assets. The other starred Max Linder, usually as a young bourgeois dandy, and quickly made him 'the king of the cinematograph'. Skilful, cleverly structured gags distinguish Linder's work from *La Petite Rosse* ('The little nag', 1909) through *Victime du quinquina* ('Quinine victim', 1911) to *Max pédicure* ('Max the pedicure', 1914). So popular was the comic series that Éclair, Eclipse, and Lux all made them a regular part of their weekly programmes. The one variation on this strategy came from Éclair. Victorin Jasset's Nick Carter series (1908–10) drew its formula from the American detective dime novels just being translated into French and proved such a success that Éclair soon adapted others, making the male adventure series a trademark of its production.

Together with these standardization practices came a concerted attempt to legitimize the cinema as a respectable cultural form. Here, the trade press was unusually active, especially *Phono-Ciné-Gazette* (1905–9), edited by Pathé's collaborator, the Paris lawyer Edmond Benoît-Lévy, and *Ciné-Journal* (1908–14), edited by Georges Dureau. Yet these efforts at legitimization were most visible in the production of literary adaptations or *films d'art*, led by Film d'Art and SCAGL, new companies with close ties to prestigious Paris theatres. The earliest and best known of these was Film d'Art's *L'Assassinat du Duc de Guise* ('The assassination of the Duc de Guise', 1908), whose deep-space *mise-en-scène* (including 'authentic' décors), economical acting style (particularly that of Charles Le Bargy), and succinct editing had a considerable influence, at least in France. That influence can be seen, in conjunction with the system of narrative continuity earlier developed by Pathé, in subsequent historical films, many based on nineteenth-century plays and operas. Although most clearly evident in those dealing with an indigenous French history, such as SCAGL's *La Mort du Duc d'Enghien* ('The death of the Duc d'Enghien', 1909) and Gaumont's *Le Huguenot* ('The Huguenot', 1909), it is also apparent in films as disparate as Film d'Art's *La Tosca* (1909) and *Werther* (1910). Generally, those running counter to this pattern were 'oriental' films such as Pathé's *Cléopâtre* and *Sémiramis* (both 1910), whose privileged moments of spectacle (accentuated by the company's trademark stencil colour) and 'exotic' characters served to reinforce the mandate for France's colonial empire.

Until 1911, nearly all French films were released in a single reel whose length depended on certain rules. A single reel of 200–300 metres (ten to fifteen minutes) had become the standard fiction film format, particularly for the more 'serious' genres, while the half-reel of 100–150 metres (five to seven minutes) was standard for the comic series. Those rules continued to hold for many films over the next several years and sometimes proved an excellent means of concentrated story-telling—as in Louis Feuillade's *Les Vipères* ('The vipers', 1911), the first of

Gaumont's 'realist' *Scènes de la vie telle qu'elle est* ('Scenes from Real Life') series, the same company's bleak railyard melodrama, *Sur les rails* ('On the rails', 1912), directed by Léonce Perret, or Pathé's intricately choreographed bourgeois melodrama *La Coupable* ('The guilty one', 1912), directed by René Leprince. At least two short films from Pathé and Gaumont respectively—Georges Monca's astonishing *L'Épouvante* ('The terror', 1911), starring Mistinguett, and Henri Fescourt's *Jeux d'enfants* ('Children's games', 1913)—even used extensive cross-cutting with a skill that rivalled Griffith's. Finally, the best of the comic series increased to a full reel, a length perfectly suited for Perret's sophisticated Léonce series (1912–14). Films such as *Les Épingles* ('The pins'), *Léonce à la campagne* (Léonce in the country'), and *Léonce cinématographiste* ('Léonce the cinematographer') (all 1913) reveal that this series deftly exploited the social situations in which Perret himself, as a solidly assured bourgeois type, either outsmarted or was outsmarted by his wife (usually Suzanne Grandais) in a perpetual battle for domestic dominance.

It was also in 1911 that 'feature' films of three or more reels began appearing on cinema programmes. Pathé introduced the first of these that spring: Capellani's historical melodrama *Le Courrier de Lyon* ('The courier of Lyons'), and Gérard Bourgeois's 'social drama' *Victimes d'alcool* ('Victims of alcohol'). Not until the autumn, however, was there a clear sense that such lengthy films would prove acceptable and profitable. Every major production company invested in the new format, with films that spanned the spectrum of available genres. Pathé and Film d'Art drew on the cultural capital of familiar literary adaptations with, respectively, *Notre Dame de Paris* ('The hunchback of Notre-Dame'), starring Henry Krauss and Stacia Napierkowska, and *Madame Sans-Gêne*, in which Réjane reprised her celebrated performance in Victorien Sardou's play of twenty years before. Gaumont contributed a film from Feuillade's *Vie telle qu'elle est* series, *La Tare* ('The fault'), starring Renée Carl, which headlined the programme inaugurating the Gaumont-Palace. Based on its past success, Éclair banked on Jasset's adaptation of Léon Sazie's popular serial crime novel *Zigomar*, starring Arquillière as a master criminal who could also be read as a ruthless capitalist entrepreneur.

Over the next few years, feature-length films became the principal weekly attraction on French cinema programmes. Film d'Art, for instance, convinced Sarah Bernhardt to reprise one of her more famous roles in *La Dame aux camélias* ('The lady of the camellias', 1912), which led to her performance in Louis Mercanton's independent production of *Queen Elizabeth* (1912) and to a hugely successful roadshow presentation in the USA. Whereas these two films relied on an old-fashioned tableau style of representation, Capellani skilfully integrated a wide range of representational strategies in perhaps the best, and

certainly the most exhibited, French historical film, SCAGL's twelve-reel *Les Misérables* ('The wretched', 1912), again with Krauss. Most feature-length films, however, now took on contemporary subjects. A former playwright and theatre director, Camille de Morlhon proved adept at imitating the pre-war boulevard melodrama, as in his Valetta production of *La Broyeuse des cœurs* ('The breaker of hearts', 1913). Éclair, by contrast, continued to trade on its crime series, in Jasset's *Zigomar contre Nick Carter* ('Zigomar against Nick Carter', 1912) and *Zigomar, peau d'anguille* ('Zigomar the eelskin', 1913), until Gaumont seized control of the genre with Feuillade's famous *Fantômas* series (starring René Navarre), which ran to five separate films between 1913 and 1914. For Gaumont, Perret also directed two 'super-productions', *L'Enfant de Paris* ('The child of Paris', 1913) and *Roman d'un mousse* ('A midshipman's tale', 1914), which neatly combined features of the crime series with others from the domestic melodrama in narratives involving a lost, threatened child. In fact, *L'Enfant de Paris* became one of the first French films to occupy an entire Paris cinema programme.

THE GREAT WAR: COLLAPSE AND RECOVERY

The general mobilization orders in early August 1914 brought all activity in the French cinema industry to an abrupt halt. Until recently, it has been customary to use the war to explain the decline of the French *vis-à-vis* the American cinema industry. Although there is some truth to that claim, the French position had been weakening before the war began. By 1911, for instance, under pressure from MPPC restrictions and the 'independent' companies' expansion, Pathé's portion of the total film footage released in the USA had dropped to less than 10 per cent. By the end of 1913, in both numbers of film titles and total footage in distribution, the French were losing ground to the Americans on their own home territory. The war simply accelerated a process already well under way, and its most devastating effect, other than cutting off production, was severely to restrict the export market on which the French companies so heavily depended for distributing their films.

Although Pathé, Gaumont, Éclair, and Film d'Art all resumed production in early 1915, wartime restrictions on capital and material forced them to operate at a much reduced level and to rerelease popular pre-war films. Furthermore, they faced an 'invasion' of imported American and Italian films which quickly filled French cinemas, one of the few entertainment venues to reopen and operate on a regular basis. And many of those films were distributed by new companies, some with American backing. First came a wave of Keystone comedies, most of them distributed by Western Imports/Jacques Haik, which had become a crucial foreign distributor just before the war. By the summer and autumn, through Western Imports

114

The 'tableau': Sarah Bernhardt
in Louis Mercanton's *Queen
Elizabeth* (1912)

and Adam, the films of Charlie Chaplin (nicknamed Charlot) were the rage everywhere. Next came *Les Mystères de New York* ('The mysteries of New York'), a compilation of Pearl White's first two serials, produced by Pathé's American affiliate and distributed by Pathé in France, and its only rival in popularity was the Italian spectacular *Cabiria* (1914). By 1916, through Charles Mary and Monat-Film, it was the turn of Triangle films, especially the Westerns of William S. Hart (nicknamed Rio Jim), and Famous Players adaptations such as Cecil B. DeMille's *The Cheat* (1915), which ran for six months at the Select cinema in Paris.

Despite contributing to the onslaught of American films, as well as losing critical personnel like Capellani and Linder to the USA, Pathé remained a major distributor of French product. Not only did the company support feature-length productions from SCAGL (Leprince, Monca) and Valetta (Morlhon), but it sought out new film-makers, notably the famous theatre director André Antoine. Pathé also provided financial backing to Film d'Art, where Henri Pouctal was joined by young Abel Gance. Gaumont, by contrast, had to cut back its production schedule, especially after Perret left to work in the USA. Yet it maintained a strong presence in the industry, largely through Feuillade's popular, long-running serials as well as its circuit of cinemas (the second largest after Pathé's). Although continuing to produce films, Éclair never fully recovered from the double blow of the war and a fire that destroyed its American studio and laboratories in April 1914. Eventually, the company reorganized into smaller components, the most important devoted to processing

film stock and manufacturing camera equipment: Éclair's camera, for instance, competed with Debrie's 'Parvo' and Bell & Howell's for dominance in the world market. Eclipse survived largely on the strength of its new film-making team, Mercanton and René Hervil. In spite of the odds, independent production companies actually increased in number, and some (those of André Hugon, Jacques de Baroncelli, and Germaine Dulac) even flourished. That they could succeed under such conditions was due, in large part, to the relatively widespread distribution their films had in France, through AGC or especially Aubert, whose circuit of cinemas continued to expand.

The French films available to spectators between 1915 and 1918 were somewhat different from before. Perhaps because it was now difficult for the French to laugh at themselves, at least as they had been accustomed to, the once prolific comic series almost disappeared. Pathé kept up the Rigadin series, but with fewer titles; Gaumont went on making Bout-de-Zan films and then concocted a series with Marcel Levesque. Production of large-scale historical films was also curtailed, unless they were conceived within a serial format, as was Film d'Art's *Le Comte de Monte-Cristo* ('The Count of Monte-Cristo', 1917–18), directed by Pouctal and starring Léon Mathot. Given French budget restrictions and the success of Pearl White's films, the serial became a staple of production, especially for Gaumont. There, Feuillade turned out one twelve-episode film per year, returning to the crime serial in *Les Vampires* ('The Vampires', 1915–16), then shifting to focus on a detective hero (played by René Cresté) in *Judex* (1917) and *La*

Nouvelle Mission de Judex ('Judex's new mission', 1918). Otherwise, patriotic melodramas were *de rigueur*, at least for the first two years of the war: perhaps the most publicized were Pouctal's *Alsace* (1915), starring Réjane, and Mercanton and Hervil's *Mères françaises* ('French mothers', 1916), which posed Bernhardt at Joan of Arc's statue before the ruined Rheims cathedral. Soon these gave way, however, to more conventional melodramas and adaptations drawn from the pre-war boulevard theatre of Bataille, Bernstein, and Kistemaeckers. Many of these films were now devoted to women's stories, in acknowledgement of their dominant presence in cinema audiences and of their ideological significance on the 'home front' during the war. Moreover, they gave unusual prominence to female stars: to Mistinguett, for instance, in such Hugon films as *Fleur de Paris* ('Flower of Paris', 1916), Grandais in Mercanton and Hervil's Suzanne series, and Maryse Dauvray in Morlhon films such as *Marise* (1917). But most prominent of all, between 1916 and 1918, in more than a dozen films directed by Monca and Leprince for SCAGL, was the boulevard actress Gabrielle Robinne.

Out of such melodramas developed the most advanced strategies of representation and narration in France, particularly in what Gance polemically called 'psychological' films. Some, like Gaumont's one-reel *Têtes de femme, femmes de tête* ('Women's heads, wise women', 1916), directed by Jacques Feyder exclusively in close shots, nearly passed unnoticed. But others were celebrated by Émile Vuillermoz in *Le Temps* and by Colette and Louis Delluc in a new weekly trade journal, *Le Film*. The most important were Gance's own *Le Droit à la vie* ('The right to life', 1916) and especially *Mater Dolorosa* (1917), both much indebted to *The Cheat* and starring Emmy Lynn. Through unusual lighting, framing, and editing strategies, *Mater Dolorosa* seemed to revolutionize the stylistic conventions of the domestic melodrama, perhaps most notably in the way everyday objects, such as a white window curtain or a fallen black veil, took on added significance through singular framing (or magnification) and associational editing. These strategies were shared by a related group of 'realist' melodramas which Delluc saw as influenced by certain Triangle films but which also derived from an indigenous French tradition. Here, Antoine's adaptations of *Le Coupable* (1917) and *Les Travailleurs de la mer* ('Workers of the sea', 1918) were exemplary, especially in their location shooting (one on the outskirts of Paris, the other on the coast of Brittany). But Delluc also drew attention to the *photogénie* of the peasant landscapes in Baroncelli's *Le Retour aux champs* ('Return to the fields', 1918) as well as certain factory scenes in Henri Roussel's *L'Âme du bronze* ('The bronze soul', 1918), one of Eclair's last films. Both kinds of melodrama would provide the basis for some of the best French films after the war.

'LES ANNÉES FOLLES': FRENCH CINEMA REVIVED

By the end of the war, the French cinema industry confronted a crisis aptly summed up by posters advertising Mundus-Film (distributors for Selig, Goldwyn, and First National): a cannon manned by American infantrymen fired one film title after another into the centre of a French target. According to *La Cinématographie française* (which soon became the leading trade journal), for every 5,000 metres of French films presented weekly in France there were 25,000 metres of imported films, mostly American. Sometimes French films made up little more than 10 per cent of what was being screened on Paris cinema programmes. As Henri Diamant-Berger, the publisher of *Le Film*, bluntly put it, France was in danger of becoming a 'cinematographic colony' of the United States. How would the French cinema survive and, if it did, Delluc asked, how would it be French?

The industry's response to this crisis was decidedly mixed over the course of the next decade. The production sector underwent a paradoxical series of metamorphoses. The established companies, for instance, either chose or were forced to beat a retreat. In 1918 Pathé-Frères reorganized as Pathé-Cinéma, which soon shut down SCAGL and sold off its foreign exchanges, including the American affiliate. Two years later, another reorganization made Pathé-Cinéma responsible for making and marketing apparatuses and film stock and set up a new company, Pathé-Consortium (over which Charles Pathé lost control), which rashly began investing in big-budget 'super-productions' that soon resulted in staggering financial losses. After briefly underwriting 'Séries Pax' films, Gaumont gradually withdrew from production, a move that accelerated with Feuillade's death in 1925. Film d'Art also reduced its production schedule as its chief producers and directors left to set up their own companies. Only the emergence of a 'cottage industry' of small production companies during the early 1920s provided a significant counter to this trend. Joining those film-makers already having quasi-independent companies of their own, for instance, were Perret (returning from the USA), Diamant-Berger, Gance, Feyder, Delluc, Léon Poirier, Julien Duvivier, René Clair, and Jean Renoir. Even larger companies were established by Louis Nalpas, who left Film d'Art to construct a studio at Victorine (near Nice), by Marcel L'Herbier, who left Gaumont to found Cinégraphic as an alternative atelier for himself and other independents, and by a Russian *émigré* film colony which took over Pathé's Montreuil studio, first as Films Ermolieff and then as Films Albatros. The two other principal producers were the veteran Aubert and a newcomer, Jean Sapène. Based on an alliance with Film d'Art, Aubert built up a consortium which, by 1923–4, included half a dozen quasi-independent film-makers. Sapène, the publicity editor at *Le Matin*, took over a small company named Cinéromans,

Max Linder

(1882–1925)

Max Linder was one of the most gifted comic artists in the history of the performing arts. Inscribing a photograph to him in the early 1920s, Charlie Chaplin called him 'The Professor—to whom I owe everything'; and there is no doubt that Linder's style and technique were a great influence on Chaplin, as indeed upon practically every other screen comedian who followed him, whether or not they were aware of it.

Born Gabriel Leveille to a farming family near Bordeaux, Linder was stage-struck from childhood. He studied at the Bordeaux Conservatoire, and acted in Bordeaux, and later in Paris with the company of Ambigu. In 1905 he began to augment his salary by working by day at the Pathé studios. The shame of working in moving pictures was concealed by using the *nom d'art* Max Linder. In the course of two years he made his mark as a light comedian; and when Pathé's first great comedy star André Deed defected to the Itala Studios in Turin, Linder starred in his own series. The first of these films were tentative, but during 1910 the eventual Max character evolved rapidly.

While the other comic stars of the period were generally manic and grotesque, Linder adopted the character of a svelte and handsome young *boulevardier*, with sleek hair, trimmed moustache, and impeccably shiny silk hat which survived all catastrophes. Max was resourceful and generally discovered some ingenious way out of the many scrapes in which he found himself, usually as a result of his incorrigible gallantry to pretty ladies. Linder perceived the comedy in the contrast between Max's debonair elegance and the ludicrous or humiliating adventures which befell him.

Despite his stage training Linder was acutely conscious of the specific nature of the cinema, recognizing the possibility it provided for subtlety of expression. He had the gift of naturalness. Every action was in essence true to life. We laugh at his predicaments because we know just how he feels.

Inexhaustibly inventive, Linder had a talent for devising endless variations upon some basic theme. In the sublime *Max prend un bain* (1910), the apparently simple process of taking a bath brings problems that escalate until Max, still in his bath, is carried through the streets shoulder high by a solemn cortège of policemen. With exquisite sang-froid Max leans out and proffers his hand to two passing ladies of his acquaintance.

Max reached the peak of his popularity in the years just preceding the First World War, when his international tours to make personal appearances became royal progresses. His health was permanently impaired by grave injuries he received fighting at the front during the war. He accepted a contract from the Essanay Company to go to America to replace Chaplin. The failure of his films there (largely due to Essanay's ugly attempts to use him to denigrate Chaplin, with whom he was personally friendly) was a further blow to his spirits.

Encouraged by Chaplin he returned to America in 1921, and made three features which remain his masterpieces: *Seven Years' Bad Luck* (1921), *Be my Wife* (1921), and a genial parody of Douglas Fairbanks's *The Three Musketeers*, *The Three Must-Get-Theres* (1922). When these films too were coolly received, Max returned to France only to find his reputation even there eclipsed by Chaplin. He fell victim to the comedian's traditional melancholia.

Despite this he continued to work. He made an eerie horror-comedy, *Au secours!* (1923) with Abel Gance, and went to Vienna to shoot *Le Roi du cirque* (1924). His comic brilliance was undiminished, but his life was rapidly moving into tragedy.

In 1922 he had become infatuated with a 17 year old, Ninette Peters, whom he eventually married. Gravely disturbed, with periods in a sanatorium, Max became prey to a pathological jealousy. He and Ninette were both found dead in a hotel room on the morning of 1 November 1925. His daughter Maud Linder concludes that he persuaded Ninette to take a soporific, and then cut her veins and his own.

DAVID ROBINSON

SELECT FILMOGRAPHY

La Première Sortie d'un collégien (1905); Les Débuts d'un patineur (1907); Max prend un bain (1910); Les Débuts du Max au cinéma (1910); Max victime de quinquina(1911); Max veut faire du théâtre (1911); Max professeur du tango (1912); Max toréador (1912); Max pédicure (1914); Le Petit Café (1919); Au secours! (1923)
In USA
Max in a Taxi (1917); Be my Wife (1921); Seven Years Bad Luck (1921); The Three Must-Get-Theres (1922)

BIBLIOGRAPHY

Linder, Maud (1992), *Les Dieux du cinéma muet: Max Linder*.
Mitry, Jean (1966), *Max Linder*.
Robinson, David (1969), *The Great Funnies: A History of Film Comedy*.

hired Nalpas as his executive producer, and set up an efficient production schedule of historical serials to be distributed by Pathé-Consortium. So successful were those serials that Sapène was able to assume control of and revitalize Pathé-Consortium, with Cinéromans as its new production base.

Although French production increased to 130 feature films by 1922, that figure was far below the number produced by either the American or German cinema industries, and French films still comprised a small percentage of cinema programmes. To improve its position, the industry embarked on a strategy of co-producing 'international' films, especially through alliances with Germany. This came after earlier repeated failures to create alliances with the American cinema industry or to exploit American stars such as Sessue Hayakawa and Fanny Ward; it was also impelled by Paramount's bold move to launch its own production schedule in Paris, resulting in such box-office hits as Perret's 'Americanized' version of *Madame Sans-Gêne* (1925), starring Gloria Swanson. Pathé, for instance, joined a new European consortium financed by the German Hugo Stinnes and the Russian *émigré* Vladimir Wengeroff (Vengerov), which initially backed Gance's proposed six-part film of *Napoléon* and, through Ciné-France, managed by Noé Bloch (formerly of Albatros), underwrote Fescourt's four-part adaptation of *Les Misérables* (1925) and Victor Tourjansky's *Michel Strogoff* (1926). That consortium collapsed, however, when Stinnes's sudden death exposed an incredible level of debt. Further French–German alliances were then curtailed by heavy American investment, through the Dawes Plan, in the German cinema industry. The results of this co-production strategy were mixed. Although generally profitable, such films required huge budgets which, coupled with a high rate of inflation in France, reduced the French level of production to just fifty-five films in 1925—drying up funds for small production companies and driving most independent film-makers into contract work with the dominant French producers.

During the last half of the decade, every major French production company went through changes in management and orientation. After losing its Russian *émigré* base, Albatros secured the services of Feyder and Clair to direct films (especially comedies) that were more specifically French in character. Although Aubert himself began to take a less active role, his company's production level remained strong, especially through contracts with Film d'Art, Duvivier, and a new film-making team, Jean Benoît-Lévy and Marie Epstein. Cinéromans launched a series of 'Films de France' features (by Dulac and Pierre Colombier, among others) to complement its serials; but when Sapène himself took over Nalpas's position as executive producer, the company's output generally began to suffer. Joining these companies were four others, all either financed by

Russian *émigré* money or associated with Paramount. In 1923 Jacques Grinieff provided an enormous sum to the Société des Films Historiques, whose grandiose scheme was 'to render visually the whole history of France'. Its first production, Raymond Bernard's *Le Miracle des loups* ('The miracle of the wolves'), premièred at the Paris Opéra and went on to become the most popular film of 1924. In 1926–7 Bernard Natan, director of a film-processing company and publicity agency with connections to Paramount, purchased an Éclair studio at Épinay and constructed another in Montmartre in order to produce films by Perret, Colombier, Marco de Gastyne, and others. At the same time, Robert Hurel, a French producer for Paramount, founded Franco-Film, wooing Perret away from Natan after *La Femme nue* ('The naked woman', 1926) to deliver a string of hits starring Louise Lagrange, the new 'Princess of the French Cinema'. Finally, out of the ashes of Ciné-France arose the Société Générale des Films, which drew on Grinieff's immense fortune to complete Gance's *Napoléon* (1927) and finance Alexandre Volkoff's *Casanova* (1927) and Carl Dreyer's *La Passion de Jeanne d'Arc* ('The Passion of Joan of Arc', 1928). Against this tide of consolidation, a few lone figures maintained a tenacious, but marginal, independence, among them Jean Epstein and especially Pierre Braunberger (the former publicity director for Paramount), whose Néo-Film offered a 'laboratory' for young film-makers.

During the 1920s the distribution sector of the industry faced an even more severe challenge. One after another, the major American companies either set up their own offices in Paris or strengthened their alliances with French distributors. In 1920 came Paramount and Fox-Film; in 1921 it was the turn of United Artists and First National; in 1922 they were joined by Universal, Metro, and Goldwyn, the latter two signing exclusive distribution contracts, respectively, with Aubert and Gaumont. That this could happen so easily was due not only to the Americans' economic power but also to the French government's inability either to impose substantial import duties on American films or to legislate a quota system restricting their numbers *vis-à-vis* French films. The American success stood in stark contrast to the French film industry's failure to rebuild its own export markets lost in the war. In the United States, for instance, no more than a dozen French films were exhibited annually from 1920 to 1925, and few reached cinemas outside New York. By the end of the decade, the number had increased only slightly. The situation was different in Germany, where a good percentage of French production was distributed between 1923 and 1926, in contrast to the far fewer German films imported into France. That too changed, however, when ACE began distributing German films in Paris, bypassing French firms altogether. By 1927 the number of German titles released in France surpassed the total production of the French cinema industry.

That the French distribution market did not capitulate completely to the Americans and Germans was due in large part to Pathé-Consortium. Whatever its internal problems and shifts in production, Pathé served, much as it did before and during the war, as the major outlet not only for its own product but also for that of smaller companies and independent producers. Cinéromans serials played a decisive role precisely at the moment when, in 1922–3, fresh from their conquest of the British cinema market and just before their intervention in Germany, American companies seemed ready to impose a block-booking system of film distribution within France. According to Fescourt, the serials functioned as a counter system of block booking in that, for at least nine months, they guaranteed exhibitors 'a long series of weeks of huge returns from a faithful public hooked on the formula'. Having taken over the contracts of AGC and negotiated others with Film d'Art and independents such as Feyder and Baroncelli, by 1924–5 Aubert complemented Pathé efforts as the second largest French distributor. Yet, even though other companies emerged, such as Armor (to distribute Albatros films), there were never enough independent French distributors, nor was there a consortium or network which could distribute the great number of independent French films. As the decade wore on, the French resistance to foreign domination began to weaken: Gaumont came under the control of MGM, while Aubert and Armor gradually moved within the orbit of ACE. However successful Pathé, Aubert, and others had been, the Americans and Germans secured a foothold within the French cinema industry at the crucial moment of the transition to sound films.

Compared to the rest of the industry, the exhibition sector remained relatively secure throughout the 1920s. The number of cinemas rose from 1,444 at the end of the war to 2,400 just two years later and nearly doubled again to 4,200 by 1929. At the same time, box-office receipts increased exponentially, even taking into account a short period of high inflation, going from 85 million francs in 1923 to 230 million in 1929. This occurred despite the fact that the vast majority of French cinemas were independently, even individually, owned (the figure was perhaps as high as 80 per cent), few of those had a capacity of 750 seats or more, and less than half operated on a daily basis. That the exhibition sector did so well was due partly to the enormous popularity of American films, from *Robin Hood* (with Douglas Fairbanks) to *Ben-Hur*. Yet French films, and not only the serials, also contributed: Feyder's costly *L'Atlantide* (1921), for instance, played at the prestigious Madeleine cinema for a whole year. Equally important, however, the luxury cinemas or palaces, most of them constructed or renovated by Aubert, Gaumont, and Pathé

as 'flagships' for their circuits, generated an unusually high volume of receipts. There were Aubert-Palaces in nearly every major French city as well as the 2,000-seat Tivoli in Paris. As its interests shifted to distribution and exhibition, Gaumont acquired control of the Madeleine, which, with the Gaumont-Palace, served to anchor its Paris circuit. Pathé renovated the Pathé-Palace into the Caméo, constructed the Empire and Impérial, and formed an alliance with a new circuit in the capital, Lutetia-Fournier. Only a few Paris palaces remained independent: the Salle Marivaux, constructed in 1919 by Edmond Benoît-Lévy, and the Ciné Max-Linder. Yet even the exhibition sector was not safe from American intervention. In 1925 Paramount began buying or building luxury cinemas in half a dozen major cities, culminating in the 2,000-seat Paramount-Palace, which opened in Paris for the 1927 Christmas season. By that time, the major French cinemas had long established a programme schedule which featured a single film *en exclusivité* along with a serial episode and/or a newsreel or short documentary. The Paramount-Palace introduced the concept of the double-bill programme. Furthermore, it was prepared to spend lavishly on advertising; within less than a year it was taking in nearly 10 per cent of the total cinema receipts in Paris.

Although Delluc abhorred them, serials were a distinctive component of the French cinema, remaining popular well into the late 1920s. Initially, they followed the pattern established by Feuillade during the war. In *Tih-Minh* (1919) and *Barrabas* (1920), Feuillade himself returned to criminal gangs operating with almost metaphysical power in a world described by Francis Lacassin as a 'tourist's nightmare of exotic locales'. Volkoff's adaptation of Jules Mary's *La Maison du mystère* ('The house of mystery', 1922) focused instead on a textile industrialist (Ivan Mosjoukine) falsely imprisoned for a crime and forced to exonerate himself in a series of deadly combats with a devilish rival. Another pattern began to develop out of films like Diamant-Berger's *Les Trois Mousquetaires* ('The three musketeers', 1921) and Fescourt's *Mathias Sandorf* (1921): the costume or historical adventure story which Sapène and Nalpas seized on as the basis for the Cinéromans serials. War heroes and adventurer-brigands from the period either before or after the French Revolution were especially popular. Fescourt's *Mandrin* (1924), for instance, depicted the exploits of a Robin Hood figure (Mathot) against the landowners and tax collectors of the Dauphiné region, while Leprince's *Fanfan la Tulipe* (1925) staged one threat after another to an orphan hero (nearly executed in the Bastille) who finally discovered he was of 'noble blood'. By resurrecting a largely aristocratic society and celebrating a valiant, oppositional hero, who both belonged to a supposedly glorious past and figured the transition to a bourgeois era, the Cinéromans serials also played a significant role, after the war, in addressing a

Saccard (Alcover) and
Sandorf (Brigitte
Helm) in Marcel
L'Herbier's *L'Argent*
(1929)

Séverin-Mars in Abel
Gance's *La Roue* (1921)

collective ideological demand to restore and redefine France.

That ideological project also partly determined the industry's heavy investment in historical films. Here, too, the often nostalgic resurrection of past moments of French glory—and tragedy—contributed to the process of national restoration. *Le Miracle des loups*, for instance, returned to the late fifteenth century, when a sense of national unity was first being forged. Here, the bitter conflict between Louis XI (Charles Dullin) and his brother Charles the Bold was mediated and resolved, according to legend, by Jeanne Hachette—and ultimately by a code of suffering and sacrifice. Espousing a similar code, Roussel's *Violettes impériales* ('Imperial violets', 1924) transformed the singer, Raquel Meller, from a simple flower-seller into a Paris Opéra star and a confidante of Empress Eugénie, all within the luxurious splendour of the Second Empire.

Later French films tended to focus either on one of two periods of French history or else on subjects involving tsarist Russia. Some took up the same era favoured by the Cinéromans serials, as in *Les Misérables* or Fescourt's remake of *Monte Cristo* (1929). Others followed the example of *Le Miracle des loups*, as in Gastyne's *La Merveilleuse Vie de Jeanne d'Arc* ('The marvellous life of Joan of Arc', 1928), starring Simone Genevois, or Renoir's *Le Tournoi* ('The tournament', 1928). The most impressive of the French subjects were *Napoléon* and *La Passion de Jeanne d'Arc*. In *Napoléon*, Gance conceived young Bonaparte (Albert Dieudonné) as the legendary fulfilment of the Revolution, a kind of Romantic artist in apotheosis, which others like Léon Moussinac read as proto-Fascist. Everyone agreed, however, on the audacity of Gance's technical innovations—the experiments with camera movement and multiple screen formats, most notably in the famous triptych finale. *La Passion de Jeanne d'Arc*, by contrast, deviated radically from the genre's conventions. Dreyer focused neither on medieval pageantry nor on Joan's military exploits, showcased in *La Merveilleuse Vie de Jeanne d'Arc*, but on the spiritual and political conflicts marking her last day of life. Based on records of the Rouen trial, Dreyer's film simultaneously documented Falconetti's ordeal playing Jeanne and created a symbolic progression of close-up faces, all within an unusually disjunctive space–time continuum.

Several of the most successful historical productions, however, permitted the Russian *émigrés* to celebrate—and sometimes criticize—the country from which they had fled. *Michel Strogoff*, the Impérial cinema's inaugural film, adapted Jules Verne's adventure novel about a tsarist courier who successfully carries out a dangerous mission in Siberia. By contrast, Bernard's *Le Joueur d'échecs* ('The chess player', 1926), which set box-office records at the Salle Marivaux, represented the triumph of Polish independence from the Russian monarchy, just prior to the

French Revolution. More fantastical in style than either was *Casanova*, one of whose episodic series of adventures had Casanova meet and befriend Catherine the Great. All three of these films showcased magnificent set décors and costumes (by either Ivan Lochakoff and Boris Bilinsky or Robert Mallet-Stevens and Jean Perrier) as well as marvellous location shooting (by L.-H. Burel, J.-P. Mundviller, and others), whether in Latvia, Poland, or Venice.

The boulevard melodrama continued to serve as an important asset to the industry for several years after the war. Tristan Bernard's plays, for instance, helped to secure his son Raymond's initial reputation as a film-maker. The more 'artistically' inclined film-makers also continued to work within the bourgeois milieu of the domestic melodrama, extending the advances made during the war, often by means of original scenarios, in what Dulac was the first to call 'impressionist films'. In *J'accuse* ('I accuse', 1919) and *La Roue* ('The wheel', 1921), Gance experimented further with elliptical point-of-view shot sequences, different forms of rhythmic montage (including rapid montage), and patterns of rhetorical figuring through associational editing. Dulac did likewise in a series of films which focused predominantly on women, from *La Cigarette* (1919) to *La Mort du soleil* ('The death of the sun', 1922) and especially *La Souriante Madame Beudet* ('Smiling Madame Beudet', 1923), whose central character was inescapably trapped in a provincial bourgeois marriage. Perhaps the high point of this experimentation came in L'Herbier's 'exotic' *El Dorado* (1921), which deployed a remarkable range of framing and editing strategies (along with a specially composed score) to evoke the subjective life of a Spanish cabaret dancer, Sybilla (Eve Francis), and culminated backstage in a stunning 'dance of death'.

By the middle of the decade, the bases for film melodrama had shifted from the theatre to fiction, and across several genres. Some followed the path of *L'Atlantide*, drawn from a popular Pierre Benoît novel, by adapting either 'exotic' Arabian Nights tales or stories of romance and adventure in the French colonies, usually in North Africa. The latter were especially popular in films as diverse as Gastyne's *La Châtelaine du Liban* ('The chatelaine of the Lebanon', 1926) and Renoir's *Le Bled* ('The wasteland', 1929). Others exploited the French taste for fantasy, particularly after the success of 'Séries Pax' films such as Poirier's *Le Penseur* ('The thinker', 1920). These ranged from Mosjoukine's satirical fable *Le Brasier ardent* ('The burning brazier', 1923) or L'Herbier's modernist fantasy *Feu Mathias Pascal* ('The late Mathias Pascal', 1925), to refurbished *féeries*, Clair's *Le Fantôme du Moulin Rouge* ('The ghost of the Moulin Rouge', 1925), or tales of horror, Epstein's *La Chute de la maison Usher* ('The Fall of the House of Usher', 1928).

The major development in the melodrama genre, however, was the modern studio spectacular, a product of the cultural internationalism which now characterized the urban *nouveau riche* in much of Europe and a new target of French investment in international co-productions. According to Gérard Talon, these films represented the 'good life' of a new generation and helped establish what was modern or à la mode in fashion, sport, dancing, and manners. Perfectly congruent with the ideology of consumer capitalism, this 'good life' was played out in milieux which tended to erase the specificity of French culture. Elements of the modern studio spectacular can be seen as early as Perret's *Koenigsmark* (1923), but the defining moment came in 1926 with a return to theatrical adaptations in L'Herbier's *Le Vertige* ('Vertigo') and Perret's *La Femme nue*, with their fashionable resorts and chic Paris restaurants. Thereafter, the modern studio spectacular came close to dominating French production. Yet some films cut against the grain of its pleasures, from L'Herbier's deliberately 'avant-garde' extravaganza, *L'Inhumaine* ('The inhuman one', 1924) to his updated adaptation of Zola, *L'Argent* ('Money', 1928), whose highly original strategies of camera movement and editing helped to critique its wealthy characters and milieux. A similar critique marked Epstein's $6\frac{1}{2}$ x 11 (1927) and especially his small-budget film *La Glace à trois faces* ('The three-sided mirror', 1927), which intricately embedded four interrelated stories within just three reels.

The 'realist' melodrama, by contrast, sustained its development throughout the decade and remained decidedly 'French'. Two things in particular distinguished these films. First, they usually celebrated specific landscapes or milieux, as spatial co-ordinates delineating the 'inner life' of one or more characters and, simultaneously, as cultural fields for tourists. Second, those landscapes or milieux were divided between Paris and the provinces, privileging the picturesque of certain geographical areas and cultures, often tinged with nostalgia. The Brittany coast provided the subject for films from L'Herbier's *L'Homme du large* ('The man of the high seas', 1920) and Baroncelli's *Pêcheur d'Islande* ('Iceland Fisherman', 1924) to Epstein's exquisite 'documentary' *Finis terrae* (1929), and Jean Grémillon's extraordinarily harrowing *Gardiens du phare* ('Lighthouse keepers', 1929). The French Alps dominated Feyder's exceptional *Visages d'enfants* ('Children's faces', 1924), while the Morvan provided a less imposing backdrop for Duvivier's *Poil de carotte* ('Ginger', 1926). Barge life on French canals and rivers was lovingly detailed in Epstein's *La Belle Nivernaise* ('The beautiful Nivernaise', 1924), Renoir's *La Fille de l'eau* ('Water girl', 1925), and Grémillon's *Maldone* (1928). The agricultural areas of western, central, and southern France were the subject of Feuillade's *Vendémiaire* (1919), Antoine's *La Terre* ('The land', 1920), Robert Boudrioz's *L'Âtre* ('The hearth', 1922), Delluc's *L'Inondation* ('The flood', 1924), and Poirier's *La Brière* (1924).

Another group of 'realist' films focused on the 'popular' in the socio-economic margins of modern urban life in Paris, Marseilles, or elsewhere. Here, for *flâneurs* of the cinema, were the iron mills and working-class slums of Pouctal's *Travail* ('Work', 1919), the claustrophobic sailor's bar of Delluc's *Fièvre* ('Fever', 1921), the street markets of Feyder's *Crainquebille* (1922), and the bistros and cheap amusement parks of Epstein's *Cœur fidèle* ('Faithful heart', 1923). Although their numbers decreased during the latter half of the decade, several achieved a remarkable sense of verisimilitude, notably Duvivier's *Le Mariage de Mlle Beulemans* ('The marriage of Mlle Beulemans', 1927), shot in Brussels, and the Benoît-Lévy/Epstein production of *Peau de pêche* ('Peach-skin', 1928), which juxtaposed the dank, dirty streets of Montmartre to the healthy air of a Charmont-sur-Barbuise farm. Perhaps the most 'avant-garde' of these later films were Dmitri Kirsanoff's brutally poetic *Ménilmontant* (1925), with Nadia Sibirskaia, and Alberto Cavalcanti's documentary-like stories of disillusionment and despair, *Rien que les heures* ('Only the hours', 1926) and *En rade* ('Sea fever', 1927).

One last genre, the comedy, also remained solidly grounded in French society. The 1920s at first seemed no less inauspicious for French film comedy than had the war years. *Le Petit Café* ('The little café', 1919), Bernard's adaptation of his father's popular boulevard comedy, starring Max Linder (recently returned from the USA), was a big success, yet failed to generate further films. There was Robert Saidreau's series of vaudeville comedies, of course, and Feuillade's charming adaptation *Le Gamin de Paris* ('The Parisian boy', 1923), but not until 1924 did a significant renewal of French film comedy get under way, ironically from the Russian *émigré* company Albatros. The initial model of comedy construction was to update the figure of the naïve provincial come to the sophisticated capital, as in Volkoff's *Les Ombres qui passent* ('Passing shadows', 1924). Another was to transpose American gags and even characters into an atmosphere of French gaiety, as in the Albatros series starring Nicholas Rimsky, or in Cinéromans's *Amour et carburateur* ('Love and carburettor', 1926), directed by Colombier and starring Albert Préjean. The real accolades, however, went to Clair for his brilliant Albatros adaptations of Eugène Labiche, *Un chapeau de paille d'Italie* (*The Italian Straw Hat*, 1927) and *Les Deux Timides* ('The timid ones', 1928), with ensemble casts featuring Préjean, Pierre Batcheff, and Jim Gerald. Accentuating the original's comedy of situations, Clair's first film thoroughly mixed up a wedding couple and an adulterous one to produce an unrelenting attack on the *belle époque* bourgeoisie through a delightful pattern of acute visual observations. Almost as successful was Feyder's *Les Nouveaux Messieurs* ('The new gentlemen', 1928), which provoked the ire of the French government, not for its satire of a labour union official (played by Préjean), but for its so-called disrespectful depiction of the National Chamber of Deputies. Finally, there was Renoir's adaptation of *Tire au flanc* ('Laze about', 1928), financed by Braunberger, which transformed a vaudeville comedy of army barracks life into an exuberant social satire, pitting a blithely assured but ineffectual bourgeois master against his big-hearted, bumbling servant, played with grotesque audacity by Michel Simon.

By the end of the decade, the French cinema industry seemed to evidence less and less interest in producing what Delluc would have called specifically French films. Whereas the historical film was frequently reconstructing past eras elsewhere, the modern studio spectacular was constructing an international no man's land of conspicuous consumption for the *nouveau riche*. Only the 'realist' film and the comedy presented the French somewhat *tels qu'ils sont*—if not as they might have wanted to see themselves—the one by focusing on the marginal, the other by invoking mockery. With the development of the sound film, both genres would contribute even more to restoring a sense of 'Frenchness' to the French cinema. Yet would that 'Frenchness' be any less imbued with nostalgia than was the charming repertoire of signs, gestures, and songs that Maurice Chevalier was about to make so popular in the USA?

Bibliography

Abel, Richard (1984), *French Cinema: The First Wave, 1915–1929*.

—— (1988), *French Film Theory and Criticism: A History/Anthology, 1907–1929*.

—— (1993), *The Ciné Goes to Town: French Cinema, 1896–1914*.

Bordwell, David (1980), *French Impressionist Cinema: Film Culture, Film Theory and Film Style*.

Chirat, Raymond, and Icart, Roger (eds.) (1984), *Catalogue des films français de long métrage: films de fiction, 1919–1929*.

—— and Le Roy, Eric (eds.) (1994), *Le Cinéma français, 1911–1920*.

Clair, René (1972), *Cinema Yesterday and Today*.

Delluc, Louis (1919), *Cinéma et cie*.

Epstein, Jean (1921), *Bonjour cinéma*.

Guibbert, Pierre (ed.) (1985), *Les Premiers Ans du cinéma français*.

Hugues, Philippe d', and Martin, Michel (1986), *Le cinéma français: le muet*.

Mitry, Jean (1967), *Histoire du cinéma*, i: *1895–1914*.

—— (1969), *Histoire du cinéma*, ii: *1915–1923*.

—— (1973), *Histoire du cinéma*, iii: *1923–1930*.

Moussinac, Léon (1929), *Panoramique du cinéma*.

Sadoul, Georges (1951), *Histoire générale du cinéma*, iii: *Le cinéma devient un art, 1909–1920 (l'avant-guerre)*.

—— (1974), *Histoire générale du cinéma*, iv: *Le cinéma devient un art, 1909–1920 (La Première Guerre Mondiale)*.

—— (1975a), *Histoire générale du cinéma*, v: *L'Art muet (1919–1929)*.

—— (1975b), *Histoire générale du cinéma*, vi: *L'Art muet (1919–1929)*.

Italy: Spectacle and Melodrama

PAOLO CHERCHI USAI

Film production in Italy began relatively late in comparison with other European nations. The first fiction film—*La presa di Roma, 20 settembre 1870* ('The capture of Rome, 20 September 1870'), by Filoteo Alberini—appeared in 1905, by which time France, Germany, Britain, and Denmark already had in place well developed production infrastructures. After 1905, however, the rate of production increased dramatically in Italy, so that for the four years preceding the First World War it took its place as one of the major powers in world cinema. In the period 1905–31 almost 10,000 films—of which roughly 1,500 have survived—were distributed by more than 500 production companies. And whilst it is true that the majority of these companies had very brief life-spans, and that almost all entrepreneurial power was concentrated in the hands of perhaps a dozen firms, the figures nevertheless give a clear indication of the boom in this field in a country which, though densely populated (almost 33 million in 1901), lagged behind the rest of Europe in terms of economic development.

The history of early film production in Italy can be divided into two periods: a decade of expansion (1905–14) during which up to two-thirds of the total number of films in the silent era were made, followed by fifteen years of gradual decline after the sudden collapse in output, in common with the whole of Europe, during the war. In 1912 an average of three films a day were released (1,127 in total, admittedly many of them short); in 1931 only two feature films in the entire year.

BEGINNINGS

The tradition of visual spectacle has deep historical roots in Italy. Aspects of it which are particularly important to the prehistory of cinema include entertainments in travelling shows—from the 'Mondo Niovo' of the late eighteenth century to the nineteenth century 'Megaletoscopio'—and scientific curiosities (documented by A. Riccò in his 1876 study *Esperienze cromostroboscopiche*, 'Chromostroboscopic experiments'). It is in this context that the first appearance of the 'Cinématographe Lumière' in the Roman photographic atelier Le Lieure, on 13 March 1896, provoked an excited reaction and this new French invention spread to Naples, Turin, and gradually to several other cities. Markedly less success awaited the

'Chronophotographe Demenÿ', Robert W. Paul's 'Theatrograph', and the Edison apparatus.

As local distribution initiatives multiplied, the Société Lumière made its presence felt thanks to four cameramen: Vittorio Calcina, Francesco Felicetti, Giuseppe Filippi, and Albert Promio. As well as actualities and scenes from real life, there were also the brief narrative films of Italo Pacchioni, who built his own camera in 1896 along with his brother Enrico, and of the variety artist Leopoldo Fregoli, who used the Cinématographe (renamed the 'Fregoligraph') to reproduce the quick-change impressions that had made him famous throughout Europe. But these were isolated efforts, which did very little to contribute towards the setting up of stable, commercially viable projects. For almost ten years, therefore, the diffusion of cinema in Italy was dependent on sporadic initiatives taken by travelling performers, by photographers who became amateur managers, and by owners of variety or café-concert clubs.

It was not until nearly a decade after 1896 that such fragmented elements came together to create a number of production companies constructed on a more solid base. Some of these very quickly acquired a pioneering role in their field. In Rome, there was the Alberini & Santoni studio (1905), which changed its name to Cines in April 1906; in Milan, companies owned by Adolfo Croce and Luca Comerio (the latter became SAFFI–Comerio in 1908 and then Milano Films in late 1909); in Turin, which was the real capital of Italian cinema in the period of its creation, Ambrosio (1905), Aquila Film founded by Camillo Ottolenghi (1907), Pasquali and Tempo (1909), and Carlo Rossi & Co., formed in 1907 and renamed Itala Film in May 1908 at the behest of Giovanni Pastrone and Carlo Sciamengo.

NON-FICTION, COMEDY, AND ANCIENT ROME

The French domination of the Italian film market led to a serious crisis in the nascent home industry as early as 1907. The recently formed companies struggled to find adequate distribution outlets for their work, and responded by adopting a strategy which aimed to exploit the popularity enjoyed by three particular genres: historical films, documentaries, and, above all, comedies, for which demand from exhibitors was growing at a remarkable pace. Comerio, Ambrosio, Itala, and Cines all developed an aggressive policy of documentary and real-life film-making, sending specialized film-makers to areas of natural beauty which had not yet been covered by Pathé, Éclair, and Gaumont, as well as to areas struck by natural disasters (such as Calabria and Sicily after the 1909 earthquake). Of particular note were Giovanni Vitrotti, who worked for Ambrosio in Italy and abroad, and Roberto Omegna, who began with Milano Films a career in scientific documentaries which lasted for several decades. It is not unusual to find in these non-fiction films interesting elements of technical innovation. In *The Island of Rhodes* (*Tra le pinete di Rodi*, Savoia, 1912) the final view of a shooting cannon transforms this travelogue into a pretext for colonial propaganda when the film is suddenly flooded with red, white, and green, the colours of the Italian flag. An unidentified film made by Ambrosio probably around 1912, and known by the apocryphal title *Santa Lucia*, has shots with a split screen divided into several different-sized sectors.

In the field of comedy, the Italian response to the overwhelming influence of the French was initiated by Giovanni Pastrone, who travelled to Paris in 1908 in order to entice a well-known actor back to Turin. The two principal candidates, both employed by Pathé, were Max Linder, who was already on the way up, even if not yet arrived at stardom, and André Deed (pseudonym of André Chapuis), who had served a brief apprenticeship under Georges Méliès before moving on to Pathé and immense success in the role of Boireau. Pastrone chose Deed, changed his nickname to Cretinetti (or Foolshead in Britain and America), and, from January 1909 onwards, produced a series of around 100 short comedies, interrupted only by the actor's temporary return to France (1912–15), and closed with the 1921 feature *L'uomo meccanico* ('The mechanical man', Milano Films).

The main ingredients of the phenomenal world-wide success enjoyed by Deed from 1909 to 1911 were the surreal use of visual tricks and the acceleration of the hectic rhythm typical of chase comedies. With its madcap, almost hysterical pace, its systematic destruction of whatever surrounded the action, and its upturned logic, André Deed's work constitutes an anarchic paradigm of transformation, in the nihilistic sense, of everyday, urban comedy. His example was followed by every one of the major companies of the time, creating a gallery of around forty characters of varying talent and fortune. The most interesting personalities amongst them were the circus artists Ferdinand Guillaume (as Tontolini for Cines, 1910–12, and as Polidor for Pasquali, 1912–18), Marcel Fabre (as Robinet for Ambrosio, 1910–15) and Raymond Fran (Ovaro) (as Kri-Kri for Cines, 1912–16). They drew heavily on their repertoire of clownery in making film comedies. Some, such as Kri-Kri, created visual novelties and original situations which were occasionally upgraded to more complex forms of *mise-en-scène*.

The development of the third strand in Italian production of this period was based on the reconstruction of historical settings and characters, from Ancient Greece and Rome to the Middle Ages to the Renaissance, and, to a lesser extent, the eighteenth century and the Napoleonic era. The trend towards this sort of production, partly derived from French models (the company Film d'Arte Italiana was founded by Pathé in 1909), was immediately successful with Italian audiences, and also encountered favourable reactions abroad. The success of the new genre became an important cultural phenomenon with the release of *The Fall of Troy* (*La caduta di Troia*, 1911), directed by Giovanni Pastrone and Romano L. Borgnetto for Itala Film. Despite its hostile reception by Italian critics, the film was greeted with unprecedented public approval in Europe and America, inspired by its spectacular monumental reconstructions of classical architecture, filmed using depth of field rather than two-dimensional backdrops, and by its unashamed aspiration to artistic grandeur.

THE POWER AND THE GLORY

Such aspiration to the status of art formed the basis of the most successful period in the history of Italian silent cinema, which, despite the relatively modest resources available to its creators, managed to secure a deserved place amongst the great powers of international production nations between 1911 and 1914. Progress was aided by the support forthcoming from a new generation of entrepreneurs, with its roots in the aristocracy or in the world of high finance and big business, who in part took over the role of the pioneers who had laid the foundations for a stable production system only a few years earlier.

These members of the privileged classes could call upon immense resources in order to pursue such a prestigious hobby as film-making. But their contribution was not solely economic in nature. They also brought a certain instinct for patronage and philanthropy, insisting on the potential of the moving image as an instrument for the moral and cultural education of a nation which was still in large part illiterate. For good or ill, they provided the Italian film industry with the entrepreneurial backing which had been strikingly absent thus far from the spontaneous, dilettante approaches of the first practitioners.

Encouraged by the didactic mission of its backers, the full-length feature film emerged earlier in Italy than in most other countries. *La Gerusalemme liberata* (*The Crusaders*, Cines, 1911) by Enrico Guazzoni was 1,000 metres long; *L'Inferno* (*Dante's Inferno*, Milano Films, 1911), directed by Francesco Bertolini and Adolfo Padovan, in collaboration with Giuseppe De Liguoro, was two years in the making and was announced as measuring 1,300 metres.

In a short period of time, the trend towards grand spectacle produced two costly films, both set in Ancient Rome, which were destined to have an enormous impact on the development of film production: *The Last Days of Pompeii* (*Gli ultimi giorni di Pompei*, Ambrosio, 1913), directed by Eleuterio Rodolfi, 1,958 metres, with, literally, a cast of hundreds; and *Quo vadis?* (Cines, 1913), by Enrico Guazzoni, whose length (2,250 m.) had only ever been surpassed by the Danish film *Atlantis* (Nordisk, 1913) by August Blom

(2,280 m. excluding intertitles). *The Last Days of Pompeii* repeated and by far exceeded the sensational success in America of *The Fall of Troy*, so that one American distributor, George Kleine, was even tempted to start up a production company of his own—Photodrama of Italy—along with a large studio at Grugliasco, near Turin. His courageous venture failed on the outbreak of war, but it illustrates eloquently the power of attraction exercised by Italian cinema outside Italy in the years leading up to 1914.

The apotheosis of the historical genre was reached with *Cabiria* (Itala Film, 1914), by Giovanni Pastrone, a film which symbolizes the zenith of achievement of silent cinema in Italy. The majestic drama set against the background of the Punic wars between Rome and Carthage was by a wide margin the most lavish film made in that era. Pastrone, a gifted but reclusive figure, was the first producer to grasp the need for a sound managerial attitude to film production. Unlike other producers of the time, his background was modest: he had started out on a career in bookkeeping, but he came to combine his businesslike style with genuine artistic vision. He tried out new technical possibilities, such as a camera for amateurs designed to shoot four separate films using a single length of 35 mm. film divided into four segments; and 'stereoscopic' and 'natural colour' shooting which were tried, without success, for *Cabiria*. He acquired a fund of technical knowledge for his company by hiring an expert from Pathé whose forte was special effects, Segundo de Chomón. He reorganized his company in 1910 with the adoption of a rigorous and efficient set of internal regulations, written out in detail and distributed to all employees. And finally, he secured a sound financial base thanks to the success of André Deed's comedies and to a number of 'sensational' films such as *Tigris*, by Vincenzo C. Dénizot, produced in 1913 and inspired by the success of the French *Fantômas* series by Louis Feuillade. All these elements created for Pastrone the opportunity to develop and extend formal and expressive fields of research.

One of the first results of this ambition was *Padre* ('Father', Gino Zaccaria and/or Dante Testa, 1912), in which Ermete Zacconi, a great theatre actor, appeared in front of the camera for the first time. The even grander aim of *Cabiria* was to obtain the collaboration and support of the most famous intellectual figure of the era, Gabriele D'Annunzio. D'Annunzio agreed to write the intertitles for the film, and was even credited as its author. However, beyond its literary echoes and its weighty architectural apparatus, *Cabiria* offers stylistic and technological solutions which make it a pioneering, avant-garde work. Above all, it repeatedly uses long tracking shots which move across the scene. Although these had already been seen in earlier films, such as, among others, *Le Pickpocket mystifié* ('The pickpocket bewildered', Pathé, 1911), *Sumerki*

zenskoi dushi ('Twilight of a woman's soul', Star (Khanzhonkov/Pathé), 1913) by Yevgeny Bauer, and *Metempsicosi* ('Metempsychosis', Cines, 1913) by Giulio Antamoro, the tracking shots of *Cabiria* perform a crucial narrative and descriptive function, and were filmed on a sophisticated system of tracks which allowed for remarkably complex camera movements.

With the emergence of the full-length feature, the Italian film industry underwent a further transformation. In order to make a profit on a smaller number of film shows, the exhibitors enlarged their halls, ticket prices went up, and so, in turn, did the directors' pretensions. From a popular spectacle, designed in large part for working-class audiences, cinema became a middle-class form of entertainment. This new situation accentuated the competition between companies, whose number grew to excess after 1915, shifting the centre of production from the north (Turin and Milan) to Rome and Naples, challenging the monopoly of the bigger companies, and hampering any further consolidation of the newly formed production base. The embryonic 'studio system' of the years after 1910 was thus replaced by a growing fragmentation of the industry.

One effect of this new situation, as in all the other major film-making countries, was the decline of the documentary and the comic short, which from this moment on became mere programme-fillers. Conversely, there was a sharp increase in grandiose productions, which aimed to develop what were held to be the highest of ideals, such as the promotion of the nationalist spirit or of religious values. In the wake of the success of *Quo vadis?*, Enrico Guazzoni emerged as a specialist in historical reconstruction through a series of monumental dramas set in Ancient Rome, such as *Antony and Cleopatra* (*Marcantonio e Cleopatra*, Cines, 1913), *Julius Caesar* (*Cajus Julius Caesar*, Cines, 1914), and *Fabiola* (Palatino Film, 1918), or in the Middle Ages (a new version of *La Gerusalemme liberata*, Guazzoni Film, 1918), or in the period of the Napoleonic Wars (*Scuola d'eroi*, Cines, 1914; UK title *How Heroes are Made*; US title *For Napoleon and France*). The same direction was followed by Luigi Maggi, Mario Caserini, Ugo Falena (*Giuliano l'apostata* ('Julian the Apostate'), Bernini Film, 1919), and Nino Oxilia. Some of the most significant expressions of Catholic orthodoxy in this context were *Christus* (Cines, 1916) by Giulio Antamoro, *Frate Sole* ('Brother Sun', Tespi Film, 1918) by Ugo Falena, and *Redenzione* ('Redemption', Medusa Film, 1919) by Carmine Gallone.

REALISM: THE FIRST WAVE

Alongside the trend towards a cinema aimed at highbrow audiences, the more popular forms, out of which cinema

Ancient Rome as grand spectacle: Enrico Guazzoni's *Quo vadis?* (1913)

had originally developed, also flourished. However, in this area, Italy remained dependent on vogues and developments brought in from abroad. The line of 'sensational' crime dramas which had begun with *Tigris* found its greatest exponent in the eccentric, and, given the gossip surrounding his private life, also somewhat romantic figure of Emilio Ghione. In *Nelly la gigolette* (Caesar Film, 1914) Ghione created the character of Za la Mort—a French-looking scoundrel living among apache gangsters—who starred in serials such as *La banda delle cifre* ('The numbers gang', Tiber-Film, 1915), *Il triangolo giallo* ('The yellow triangle', Tiber-Film, 1917), and above all *I topi grigi* ('The grey rats', Tiber-Film, 1918), which all exploited the restrictions imposed by a low-cost production to produce a tight, nervous narrative pace while making full use of the visual resources provided by the landscapes of the Roman countryside.

The stamp of realism which is clearly identifiable in *I topi grigi* is also evident in another undoubtedly significant, although marginal, trend towards realism which runs through Italian cinema of the 1910s. The most accomplished exemplar of this trend was *Sperduti nel buio* ('Lost in the dark', Morgana Films, 1914), by Nino Martoglio and Roberto Danesi, which has acquired an air of legend owing to the mysterious circumstances surrounding its disappearance. Many other works made between 1912 and 1916 bear witness to a marked taste for the observation of everyday life, often intertwined with elements of melodrama—as in *L'emigrante* ('The emigrant', Itala Film, 1915), by Febo Mari, which was Ermete Zacconi's second film, or light comedies such as *Addio giovinezza!* ('Farewell youth!', Itala Film, 1913), directed by Nino Oxilia and remade twice by Augusto Genina in 1918 and 1927. Other films present examples of straightforward naturalism: such as *Assunta Spina* (Caesar Film, 1915) by Gustavo Serena and Francesca Bertini—adapted from a play by Salvatore Di Giacomo—and *Cenere* ('Ash', Ambrosio, 1916) by Febo Mari and Arturo Ambrosio, Jr., from a book by Sardinian novelist Grazia Deledda. The latter was the only film made by the great theatre actress Eleonora Duse.

FROM DECADENTISM TO DECADENCE

The outbreak of the First World War and the growing power of American cinema in the European market put an abrupt end to dreams of expansion of the Italian industry. The heavy commitment to the war effort required of the weak national economy diverted energies from other activities, and this draining of resources would only get worse in the aftermath of the disastrous defeat by the Austrians at Caporetto in 1917. A substantial part of the films which were made were dedicated to the theme of war, thus producing a brief resurgence of the documentary genre. Propaganda efforts even extended into

127

comedy, as evinced in André Deed's *La paura degli aero-mobili nemici* ('The fear of enemy flying-machines', Itala Film, 1915) and Segundo de Chomón's children's animation *La guerra e il sogno di Momi* ('The war and Momi's dream', Itala Film, 1917). Unlike in France, however, Italian cinema was wholly unprepared for the demands thrown up by this new situation. The geographical and financial dispersal of production centres, the lack of any co-ordinated exhibition circuit, and the endemic disorganization of much of the production system meant that, at the first signs of difficulty, the industry was brought to its knees.

After the end of the war, in 1919, one late and doomed salvage attempt was made when a group of bankers and producers, with the support of two powerful financial institutions, set up the Unione Cinematografica Italiana (UCI), a trust under whose aegis were gathered the eleven largest production companies in the country. But the initiative did more harm than good. The poorly improvised attempt to create a production monopoly to control the market destroyed all competition. The number of films made annually grew initially from 280 in 1919 to more than 400 in 1921, but on the whole the films were mediocre, worryingly similar to each other in their constant reprise of well-worn ideas and, worst of all, hopelessly inadequate in the face of the American onslaught, whether at home or abroad. Already by December 1921, the failure of one of the major backers of the scheme—the Banca Italiana di Sconto—had seriously wounded the consortium, and from 1923 its constituent companies plunged one by one into a fatal crisis. From that moment onwards, rates of output decreased rapidly, and Italian cinema sank into a mire from which it was not to re-emerge until after the end of the silent period.

One of the genres which may be seen as partly responsible for the decline had been born in the period before the war. Its protagonists were a set of actresses whose personalities and acting style gave rise to the cult of the diva, which permeated all social classes and for a certain time even spread to other European countries and to the United States (with the short-lived meteoric career of

A studio portrait of the Italian 'diva' Pina Minichelli

Theda Bara). *Ma l'amor mio non muore!* 'Love Everlasting', Film Artistica 'Gloria', 1913), by Mario Caserini, was the signal forerunner of the genre, with its simplified and exaggerated appropriation of symbolism and decadentism. In the following decade, its influence was felt throughout Italian society. Lyda Borelli, the diva *par excellence*, set the standard of a style based more on the charismatic presence of the actress than on any technical or aesthetic qualities of the production. In her films the expressivity of the body was assigned a determining role. The characters played by Borelli—and by other divas such as Maria Carmi, Rina De Liguoro, Maria Jacobini, Soava Gallone, Helena Makowska, Hesperia, Italia Almirante Manzini—are sensual, tormented figures, caught between frail melancholia and anxiety, expressed through mannered poses. They live in luxuriant and at times oppressively opulent surroundings, where excited glances and sharp movements mirror the excess of the costumes and scenery.

The perverse, sometimes evil nature of the divas was reinforced by the screenplays, which were tailor-made for each actress, thereby diminishing the power and significance of the director. *Rapsodía satanica* ('Satanic rhapsody') by Nino Oxilia (with an orchestral score composed for the film by Pietro Mascagni) and *Malombra* by Carmine Gallone—both made by Cines in 1917—are the most striking examples of the aesthetic of 'borellismo', the cinematic equivalent of the Italian taste for neo-classical and Pre-Raphaelite academic imagery. Some performers, however, did manage to create distinctive styles. Francesca Bertini, who starred in *Sangue blu* ('Blue blood') by Nino Oxilia (Celio Film, 1914), had a somewhat more sober, and at times even naturalistic, acting style; and Pina Menichelli achieved a 'D'Annunzian' morbid dramatic intensity in two Giovanni Pastrone films, *Il fuoco* ('The flame', Itala Film, 1915) and *Tigre reale* ('Royal tiger', Itala Film, 1916, from the story by Giovanni Verga).

The narrative world built up around the divas amounted to a compendium of love and intrigue in upper bourgeois and aristocratic circles, a world marked by rigid social conventions and uncontainable passions, so detached from any sense of reality as to constitute a closed universe, dominated by sex and death. A remarkable exception to this rule seems to have been the work of Lucio d'Ambra (1879–1939), whose films such as *L'illustre attrice cicala formica* ('The famous actress cicada ant', 1920) and *La tragedia su tre carte* ('Tragedy on three cards', 1922) were characterized by an eccentric but rich figurative elegance. Unfortunately most of them appear to be lost.

Exceptions apart, in the 1920s melodrama of this kind became the staple fare of Italian cinema. Both quality and quantity suffered and the industry turned in on itself, confusing the ruins of its former glories with potential new directions. The last vestiges of the aspiration to artistic grandeur were stamped out by a series of yet more historical genre films: another *Quo vadis?*, directed by Gabriellino D'Annunzio and Georg Jacoby (UCI, 1924); another *Last Days of Pompeii* (Società Anonima Grandi Film, 1926), directed by Amleto Palermi and Carmine Gallone; a suggestive, perturbing return to (Gabriele) D'Annunzio in *La nave* ('The ship', Ambrosio/Zanotta, 1921) by Gabriellino D'Annunzio and Mario Roncoroni. The avant-garde futurist movement dabbled in film, but had little impact. The most significant evidence of their involvement to have survived is *Thaïs* (Novissima Film/Enrico De Medio, 1917) by Anton Giulio Bragaglia and Riccardo Cassano, a pale shadow of the aggressive declarations of futurist theoreticians.

TWILIGHT: STRONG MEN AND NEAPOLITANS

Of course, some of these relics were also notable commercial successes. The exceptional demand for *Cabiria* had led to its being rereleased several times after 1914. Pastrone even made a synchronized version in 1931, which was the version best known to audiences until a restored version of the original appeared in 1995. The success of *Cabiria* was due to the character of the slave Maciste (Bartolomeo Pagano), whose athletic prowess made him a favourite with audiences and spawned a long series of films devoted to him, from *Maciste* (Itala Film, 1915), by Vincenzo C. Dénizot and Romano L. Borgnetto, to the war propaganda film *Maciste alpino* ('Maciste in the Alpine Regiment', Itala Film, 1916), by Luigi Maggi and Romano L. Borgnetto, to the apotheosis of kitsch in *Maciste all'inferno* (Fert-Pittaluga, 1926) by Guido Brignone. These were the first in the tradition of 'strong-man' films, an athletic variant on the adventure film, whose protagonists are endowed with extraordinary physical strength and untarnished simplicity of emotion. Pagano's lead was followed in the first half of the 1920s by several other champions of the athlete-cum-acrobat-cum-actor: Sansone (Luciano Albertini), Saetta (Domenico Gambino), Galaor (Domenico Boccolini) and the Graeco-Roman wrestling champion Giovanni Raicevich.

Elsewhere, the fading fortunes of cinema on a national scale contributed to a spontaneous renaissance in a formerly minor area of film-making, the Neapolitan dialect melodrama. The companies behind this strange phenomenon were in some cases organized on a family basis. The films were distributed mainly in southern Italy and in the larger northern cities, although on occasion they were exported to wherever emigrant communities had settled. The Dora Film Company, owned by Elvira and Nicola Notari, which had been founded shortly after 1910, succeeded in infusing its films with a simplicity and authenticity which was far removed from the anodyne 'modernity' of the commercial films being made for nation-wide audiences. 'A santanotte ('Holy Night') and E'piccerella ('The little girl', Film Dora, 1922), both directed by Elvira Notari, are two of the most important films in a genre which has its roots in the Neapolitan popular theatre form, the sceneggiata (a simple, powerful drama interspersed with popular songs), which was directed and acted by non-professionals, with no artistic or technical training, and yet which managed to strike a chord with the audiences' feelings.

Still in Naples, Gustavo Lombardo had set up his own production company in 1918 which emerged unscathed from the collapse of UCI. Hence, in the second half of the 1920s, when directors, actors, and technicians were leaving in droves for France and Germany, Lombardo Film continued to produce a steady stream of relatively good-quality films, including a number starring the talented actress Leda Gys. Gys had performed with outstanding results alongside Francesca Bertini in the pantomime Histoire d'un pierrot ('A pierrot's story', Italica Ars/Celio Film, 1914) by Baldassarre Negroni. For Lombardo, she made a trilogy entitled I figli di nessuno ('Children of nobody', 1921), directed by Ubaldo Maria Del Colle, which combined populist drama with a significant degree of polemical social critique. Lombardo Film changed its name to Titanus, and some years later moved to Rome to join forces with a new organization founded by the Genoese producer Stefano Pittaluga in a move which radically transformed the distribution system throughout Italy.

In the desolate panorama of the national film industry at the end of the 1920s, there are some signs of renewal. The influence of the Fascist regime was still only marginal: it had set up the Istituto Nazionale LUCE (acronym of L'Unione Cinematografica Educativa—the Union of Cinema and Education) in 1924 with the aim of exploiting cinema for propagandist and didactic ends, but it generally refrained from direct intervention in the affairs of the industry. Aldo De Benedetti demonstrated in La grazia ('Grace', Attori e Direttori Italiani Associati, 1929) how

even a traditional story-line could give rise to a style of filming of extraordinary purity.

The first Italian sound film to be released was a sentimental comedy by Gennaro Righelli, La canzone dell'amore ('The love song', Cines, 1930), which came out also in French and German versions. It was shortly followed by Sole ('Sun', Società Anonima Augustus, 1929) by Alessandro Blasetti, a film about the draining of the Pontine marshes which showed the influence of German and Soviet cinema. Another young director, Mario Camerini, who had already shown himself capable of injecting new energy into the worn formulas of adventure films and bourgeois comedies through a more smooth and technically sophisticated style—as in Voglio tradire mio marito! ('I want to betray my husband!', Fert Film, 1925) and Kif tebby (Attori e Direttori Italiani Associati, 1928)—now took a further step forwards with Rotaie ('Rails', SACIA, 1929), which was shot as a silent film, but came out two years later in a sound version. The Sole and Rotaie are marked by clearly differing intentions, but both are inclined towards experimentation with new forms which refashion with vision and authority the Italian vocation for realism.

Bibliography
Bernardini, Aldo (1980–82), *Cinema muto italiano, 1896–1914*.
—— (ed.) (1991), *Archivo del cinema italiano*, Vol.i: *Il cinema muto, 1905–1931*.
—— and Gili, Jean A. (eds.) (1986), *Le Cinéma italien*.
—— and Martinelli, Vittorio (1979), *Il cinema italiano degli anni Venti*.
Brunetta, Gian Piero (1980), *Storia del cinema italiano*, Vol. i: *1905–1945*.
Dall'Asta, Monica (1992), *Un Cinéma musclé: le surhomme dans le cinéma muet italien (1913–1926)*.
Leprohon, Pierre (1972), *The Italian Cinema*.
Martinelli, Vittorio (1980–91), 'Il cinema muto italiano, 1915–1931'.
Masi, Stefano, and Franco, Mario (1988), *Il mare, la luna, i coltelli: per una storia del cinema muto napoletano*.
Redi, Riccardo (1986), *Ti parlerò ... d'amor: cinema italiano fra muto e sonoro*.

British Cinema from Hepworth to Hitchcock

JOHN HAWKRIDGE

The tendency among film historians has always been to represent the British cinema as having had influential and innovative beginnings—the so-called British pioneers—but then to have fallen into decline and stagnation. From this perspective, as expressed for example by Georges Sadoul (1951), *Rescued by Rover* (Cecil Hepworth, 1905) is the high point. Films produced after that date, particularly in the period (1908–13) when one-reel dramatic narrative was dominant, have been neglected. Even writers like Barry Salt (1992), who has done a careful formal analysis of films from the early years, have focused perhaps unduly on fictional dramatic narrative, at the expense of the comic film and—even more important—the various forms of actuality film.

As a result of these historiographical biases, a certain injustice has been done to British films of the immediately post-'pioneer' period. Where there was innovation, it has been overlooked, or interpreted in the light of later developments, notably those that came to be part of the dominant Hollywood mode from 1913 onwards. In fact British films of the period were often quite sophisticated, particularly in the comic and actuality fields. Narrative editing, too, was often innovative—but, unfortunately, the innovations tended to be in directions which went against the grain of what was to prove the dominant approach.

EARLY FORMAL DEVELOPMENTS

Before 1907–8, it was the actuality (in its broadest generic sense) and the comic film that dominated British production output. Producers were geographically widespread, although in the period after 1906 most of the production companies were located in or around London. Thousands of titles were produced; before 1902 most consisted of only one shot, but by 1905 lengthier films had led to the development of some reasonably complex editing strategies. For example, the point-of-view shot pair came into relatively early usage in British film. A particularly early example of this narrational strategy can be found in the Gaumont (British) film *The Blacksmith's Daughter* (1904). Here the second shot of the point-of-view shot pair is cued by having an old man lift a child up to look over a fence, into a garden which a couple (the daughter of the title and her lover) have just entered. The second shot shows the field of vision; it lacks the presence in shot of the looker(s), but is taken from the space occupied by the man and the child in the previous shot. That this is intended as a point-of-view perspective is shown by the fact that the camera has been placed so as to shoot the scene through the fence, with the railings clearly visible in the second shot.

The Blacksmith's Daughter is not the only early British film that displays innovative shooting and editing strategies. The 1906 actuality *A Visit to Peek Frean and Co.'s Biscuit Works* (Cricks and Sharp, 1906) is remarkable not only for its relative length—in excess of 2,000 feet when most fictional subjects were less than 500 feet—but also because of its use of high-angle camera shots, panning, and tilt movement, and its use of scene dissection to give a more complete view of specific factory processes.

Despite the attention that has been paid by film historians to the development of early editing practices, one particular technique, which has relevance to comic, actuality, and fictional film narratives, has been largely overlooked; the jump cut in the context of shots which maintain a continuity of framing. For example, in *The Missing Legacy; or, The Story of a Brown Hat* (Gaumont Film Company, 1906), when a fight develops between the protagonist and three men, there is a cut at the point where the protagonist is wrestled to the ground. This is not 'lost footage' but a jump cut which allows the man's clothing to be reduced to tatters during the 'absent time' of the cut. The film-maker disguised this lack of clothing continuity by having the action staged largely out of frame, and by having the protagonist partially obscured by his attackers. Similarly, the jump cut is important in the narrative construction of some of the actuality films of the period. Thus in *Building a British Railway—Constructing the Locomotive* (Urban, 1905) the jump cut (keeping continuity of framing) is used to create the temporal ellipsis that allows various stages in the process to be shown, including both initial and final stages of construction.

Film-makers of this period in fact showed considerable ingenuity in developing editing and shooting practices which ensured the effect they desired, whether in comic and actuality films or dramatic narrative films. For example, the device of the 'ingenious cheat' (Salt, 1992), whereby actor movement is used to simulate camera movement, has been noted in the case of *Ladies Skirts Nailed to a Fence* (Bamforth, 1900). However, this practice was not restricted to such comic sketches, but clearly also had a function in fictional dramatic narratives.

Cecil Hepworth's *Rescued by Rover* (1905) was a major commercial success, and in order to produce enough prints to meet demand, Hepworth's company remade the film twice. From a narrative perspective all three films are the same, but at the level of film form there are some small yet significant differences. In the first version of the film the scene in which the remorse-stricken nurse bursts into the room and confesses to the loss of the child is handled differently from the two later versions. The first version breaks this scene down into two shots, the second being filmed from a closer camera position and at a slightly different angle to the action. The other two versions, however, simply use one shot—the second camera set-up. Thus, on the face of it, the earliest version makes use of scene dissection, whilst the later versions do not. If we view scene dissection as a development in film form, then here we have a seeming regression. What has happened, however, is rather that the film-maker has learnt from the 'mistake' in the staging of the scene in the first version, in which the two shots of this scene register perceptually as a change of camera position when it is actually the actors who have moved. Thus by 1905 Hepworth had a clear idea of how close the camera should be to the staged action, and was prepared to move the actors forward to accommodate. When confronted by a similar problem in a scene in *Falsely Accused*, produced the same year, Hepworth moved the camera forward, since the staging of the action (with an attempted exit through a window being dramatically important) precluded the possibility of moving the actors.

THE MAIN FILM GENRES

The fact that British films in the period up to 1906–7 were successful and influential, nationally and internationally, has been well documented. Even contemporary critical writing confirms the view of the superiority of British films *vis-à-vis* their American counterparts. An editorial in the *Projection Lantern and Cinematograph* of July 1906 states, 'The cinematograph trade seems to be booming in the States. The demand for films is exceptionally heavy, with the result that very inferior subjects are being produced, many of which would not be tolerated at British halls'. The British success was derived from both innovative film-making (*Fire!*, *Daring Daylight Burglary*, *Desperate Poaching Affray*) and the fact that international markets were open. However, by 1912 the situation had reversed. The *Moving Picture World* of 20 January 1912 commented, 'English films in this country are a hopeless drug on the market and cannot even please the Canadians.' So why the fall? Hepworth himself, in his autobiography, refers to being 'not sufficiently alive to the many changes which were occurring in the industry', and such Hepworth films as *Dumb Sagacity* (1907) and *The Dog Outwits the Kidnappers* (1908) do show a remarkable similarity (in story and film form) to the earlier *Rescued by Rover*. Added to the perceived lack of quality of British films, and not unrelated, was the effective closure of the American market to British producers with the formation of the Motion Picture Patents Company in 1908.

It was around this time that the series film first appeared on British screens. The British and Colonial Kinematograph Company (hereafter B. & C.) moved into the production of series films at an early date. *The Exploits of Three-Fingered Kate* (First Series) was reviewed in the *Bioscope* in October 1909, and a number of series were to follow in the years leading up to the First World War. In terms of popular success none was more important than the Lieutenant Daring series, which first appeared in 1911; the *Bioscope* of 28 March 1912 published an interview (and photograph) of Lieutenant Daring, 'the famous English film actor'. However, since the interview was conducted with references solely to Daring the fictional character, and not to Percy Moran, the actor who played the role, then it would be more correct to refer to the notion of a picture personality rather than a star. From the perspective of film form these B. & C. series films are also interesting because of their use of emblematic shots (of the eponymous hero/heroine) at the end (or, less often, at the beginning) of the films. Their inclusion might be seen in terms of a generic code, since shots of this type are relatively rare in other film genres, with the exception of the comic film, where again emblematic shots can be found at the beginning or end of the film in productions from various British companies.

The importance of the Daring series can also be gauged by the fact that, when B. & C. undertook a production trip to the West Indies in 1913 (something of a first for a British company to take its artists such a distance), Percy Moran was in the party, and at least one series entry was shot in Jamaica; *Lt. Daring and the Dancing Girl*. Although the West Indies was its most far flung and exotic shooting location, this company often made use of scenic location shooting, a fact that its publicity emphasized. For example, the first in the Don Q series of films (1912) was advertised as having been filmed 'amidst Derbyshire's rugged and picturesque' hills, and this strategy of foregrounding scenic pleasure is structured into the film itself in *The Mountaineer's Romance* (1912), when an introductory title card announces, 'This Photo-Play Was Enacted Around The Beautiful Peak District, Derbyshire'.

The parodic film appeared relatively early in British film production. In the same year as Charles Urban first produced his *Unseen World* series of films, the Hepworth Company made a parody of it. The format of the Urban series was based on combining the technologies of the microscope and the movie camera, to produce magnified views of the 'natural world'. Hepworth's *The Unclean World* (1903) has a man place a piece of the food he has been eating under a microscope. A circular mask shot then reveals two beetles, but the joke is realized when two hands enter the frame and turn the beetles over, revealing their clockwork mechanisms.

It was with the series film, however, that the parody almost developed into a genre in its own right. B. & C.'s 'Three-Fingered Kate', who is continually eluding the hapless Detective Sheerluck, may well be a direct parody of Éclair's 'Nick Carter—le roi des détectives'. The sending up of current events, and particularly current film releases, was the stock-in-trade of Fred Evans, the most successful screen comic in Britain around 1913–14, who in the latter year produced a number of spoof 'Lieutenant Pimple' films, including *Lieutenant Pimple and the Stolen Invention*. The Hepworth Company was also producing spoofs of B. & C.'s and Clarendon's naval heroes. The prevalence of these cheap-to-produce parodies is an indicator both of the lack of any comic star in the British cinema in the pre-war period and of the still largely artisanal nature of British film production, with the concomitant lack of finance, since much of the comic pleasure of these film parodies resides in cheapness of production. The only requirement was that the audience could make the necessary link back to the parodied film(s), and most often this was clearly signalled in the titles themselves.

Although good at producing popular and cheap series and parodies for the home market, British companies were slow at exploiting their own cultural heritage, unlike the American competitors such as Vitagraph, who produced *A Tale of Two Cities* (1911) to celebrate the centenary of Dickens. British producers concentrated heavily on

Clive Brook and Betty Compson in the successful British melodrama *Woman to Woman* (1923), directed by Graham Cutts from a script by Alfred Hitchcock

comedy production in this period, when the dramatic narrative had become the staple of the industry. For example, of the films released in Britain in January 1910, the only British company with a significant number of fictional drama releases is Hepworth, and these were considerably shorter than comparable films from European and American producers (three of the four dramas released by Hepworth in that month were less than 500 feet, whereas European and American dramas were closer to 1,000).

None the less by 1912 there was a degree of optimism in the British trade press, and the view expressed by both Cecil Hepworth (1951) and George Pearson (1957) was that by 1911–12 British companies had largely caught up lost ground. This was particularly true for companies like Hepworth and B. & C., who began to produce a more attractive product through, for example, the good dramatic use of scenic locations and a more restrained and naturalistic acting style, notably in films like *A Fisherman's Love Story* (Hepworth, 1912) and *The Mountaineer's Romance* (B. & C., 1912). Some of these films also display a remarkable degree of filmic sophistication. For example, in *Lt. Daring and the Plans for the Minefields* (B. & C., 1912), a scene in which Daring prepares to pilot a plane is broken down into a series of four shots, involving axial cut-ins and a reverse-angle shot.

COMPETITION FROM AMERICA

However, if British film-makers had 'caught up' in 1911–12, the rise to dominance of the multi-reel film shortly afterwards, and the distribution practices of American film companies, would again leave the British trailing behind. The home industry suffered from the way a

133

number of American companies 'tied in' British exhibitors. For example, the *Gaumont Weekly* of 28 August 1913 complained, 'Many theatres have exclusive contracts with the American manufacturers—a cheap way of supplying the theatre'. Almost coincident with the shift to multi-reel films as the industrial norm was the emergence of a star system in America. This was not the case in Britain, where even in the 1920s the only actresses who could be called British film stars were Chrissie White and Alma Taylor (particularly through their work with Hepworth) and Betty Balfour. Stars in general and male film stars in particular were significantly lacking, in a period when they were so central to the rise to dominance of the American film. Indeed, writing as late as 1925, Joseph Schenck commented brutally on British film productions: 'You have no personalities to put on the screen. The stage actors and actresses are no good on the screen. Your effects are no good, and you do not spend nearly so much money' (*Bioscope*, 8 January 1925). Related to the lack of male stars in the British film industry was an accompanying lack of any action genre equivalent to the Western, and the lack of light comedy, genres which established so many American male stars in the 1910s and 1920s.

Despite the low esteem in which most British film productions were held, particularly in the international market-place, optimism remained high in the immediate post-war years in the British trade press, though the idea of a protection system, for example by the imposition of import quotas, was beginning to gain ground. The London Film Company had made use of American personnel (producers and actors) as a means of differentiating its products from other British producers as early as 1913, and continued with this strategy through the war years. A similar strategy was adopted by B. & C. after the war, although with the quite specific aim of breaking into international markets, particularly the American. Despite some initial success, the American market remained as elusive for this company as it proved for other British producers, and by the mid-1920s the company went out of business. In terms of production and exhibition, 1926 can be seen as the nadir of the British film industry; according to the Moyne Report not more than 5 per cent of films exhibited that year in Britain originated from British studios.

But it was not only American distribution practices and lack of capitalization or a star system which hampered the potential success of the British film. At a time when American films were clearly beginning to exhibit the dynamic traits associated with continuity editing, British films were often marked by narrational uncertainty and the inability to construct a unified spatio-temporal narrative logic (the hallmarks of what we now call the classical Hollywood style). For example, the distinction between fade and cut shot transitions, which had become clearly established in the American cinema in the 1910s, was often lacking in British films. Thus in *The Passions of Men* (Clarendon, 1914) the temporal logic of the narrative is at times disrupted when shot transitions are made by fades rather than cuts, and vice versa. Hepworth, idiosyncratic even in the context of British film-making, used the fade as the general mode of shot transition, even into the 1920s. The fact that Hepworth used the fade transition not for temporal ellipsis, but simply to link shots together, posed a number of narrational problems. Most obviously, compared to Hollywood films, with their slick continuity editing, the films appeared slow and ponderous. More specifically, the constant use of the fade transition tended to emphasize the discontinuous nature of narrative space, and the films, albeit often of beautiful pictorial quality, become a series of 'views'. Regarded by Hepworth as his best and most important film, *Comin' thro' the Rye* (1916) did not find a distributor in America. As Hepworth somewhat poignantly states in his autobiography, regarding his attempts to find an American distributor, 'I was told that it might not be so bad if it was jazzed up a bit, and I came home.'

Although Hepworth's films of the 1910s and 1920s were admittedly idiosyncratic, other British films from this period exhibited varying degrees of narrational uncertainty. A lengthy part of the narrative in Barker's melodrama *The Road to Ruin* (1913) is devoted to a dream sequence. However, clearly uncertain as to the audience's ability to follow the narrative logic of the story, the film-makers twice remind the spectator of the dream status of the events unfolding; once through a return to a shot of the protagonist dreaming, and once through the interpolation of an intertitle, which simply states, '—and dreaming still …'. Similarly, the use of the point-of-view shot pair, although increasingly common in films of the 1910s, was sometimes used with a degree of equivocation. Many of the films of the early 1910s did not use a true optical point of view, but moved the camera 180 degrees in relation to the character looking off screen, so that the second shot reveals not only the object of the look, but also the 'looker' as well. At a key point in *The Ring and the Rajah* (London Film Co., 1914), the film makes use of point-of-view shots. One of these has the rajah looking intently off screen, through some open French windows. This is followed by a shot of the rajah's rival in love, from a camera placement that approximates to the rajah's optical viewpoint. The relationship between these shots was clearly not regarded as self-explanatory, and an intertitle is introduced, with the words 'What the Rajah saw'. The next shot, which has both the looker (the rajah's servant) and the object of the look in shot is then in turn preceded by an intertitle which states, 'What the servant saw', suggesting a distinct lack of confidence in the audience's ability to read point-of-view articulations, in spite of the fact that they had been in use in both the American and British cinema for nearly a decade.

Thus it was not only under-capitalization, or the lack of a star system, but also aspects of film form that made British films so uncompetitive with those of the United States. Reference to British films in the American trade press as 'soporific' can in large part be linked to issues of film form—lack of scene dissection and degrees of narrational uncertainty. Indeed, a film such as *Nelson* (1918), produced by Maurice Elvey for International Exclusives, can fairly be described as primitive—whether in terms of its cheap and poorly designed backdrops, its wooden acting, or a mode of narrative construction that makes minimal use of continuity editing. It is mainly the film's length (seven reels), that distinguishes it from films produced a decade before.

THE 1920S: A NEW GENERATION

By the mid-1920s most of the pre-war production companies had gone out of business, and with them such 'pioneers' as Cecil Hepworth. A new generation of producers or producer-directors entered the industry during this period. Both Michael Balcon (producer) and Herbert Wilcox (producer-director) adopted similar strategies to develop the indigenous industry. One such strategy was the importation of Hollywood stars. This was not a total novelty, but in the past it had met with only limited success. However, Wilcox successfully utilized the talents of Dorothy Gish, and in doing so also established a deal with Paramount. More important was the development of co-production agreements by both Balcon and Wilcox, and other British producers. Co-productions, particularly with Germany but also with other countries such as Holland, would become a significant factor in the development of the British film industry in the mid- and late 1920s. It was as a result of this practice that the young Alfred Hitchcock acquired experience of German production methods when he was sent to work at the Ufa studios in Neubabelsberg early on in his career with Gainsborough.

For Herbert Wilcox, the agreements he signed with Ufa were important not only as a way of opening up the market but also because the contracts gave him access to the

Ivor Novello and Mae Marsh in *The Rat* (1925), the story of a Parisian jewel thief, directed by Graham Cutts and produced by Michael Balcon

better-equipped German studios. His *Decameron Nights* (1924) was shot in Germany, co-financed by Ufa and by Graham–Wilcox, and employed English, American, and German actors. With its large, well-designed and well-executed sets, and story of sexual intrigue, *Decameron Nights* was a commercial success both in Britain and the United States. However, this success was in large part attributable to spectacle (adequately financed) and the sexual dynamic of the narrative; but Wilcox, unlike Hitchcock and some other young directors, seems to have learnt little from the encounter with German cinema, and, from the perspective of film form, *Decameron Nights* is a film still marked by the relatively long scale of most of its shots and a general lack of scene dissection.

Michael Balcon was an important figure in the British film industry for a number of reasons. Although he produced only a relatively small number of films in the 1920s, most of them, including *The Rat* (Gainsborough, 1925), were big commercial successes. Further, Balcon's career was a clear signpost to that division of labour that came rather late in the British film industry: that is, between producing and directing. Balcon was a producer, rather than a producer-director, and it was only the separation of these roles that allowed the development of skills specifically associated with each function.

Although in the context of British culture film-making was generally held in low esteem, a number of university graduates were to enter the film industry towards the end of this period, including Anthony Asquith, the son of the Liberal Prime Minister. Asquith had not only developed a considerable knowledge of European cinema during his university days, but his privileged background enabled him to meet many Hollywood stars and directors during his visits to the United States. The importance of these factors became evident when he began his film career. On *Shooting Stars* (British Instructional Films, 1928) Asquith

was assistant director, but he had also written the screenplay, and was involved with the editing of the film. *Shooting Stars* was self-reflexive, in so far as it was a film about the film industry, film-making, and stars, although the reference was more to Hollywood than England, with Brian Aherne featuring as a Western genre hero. The lighting (by Karl Fischer), the use of a variety of camera angles, and the rapid editing of some sequences linked the film more to a German mode of expression. These elements, combined with the fact that the screenplay was not developed from a West End theatre production, unlike so many British productions in the 1920s, produced a film that was pure cinema.

By the end of the 1920s the British film industry was transformed. The shift to vertical integration established a stronger industrial base, and, despite its negative aspects, the protective legislation introduced in 1927 did also lead to an expansion of the industry. The new generation who entered the industry in the mid-1920s had a greater knowledge and understanding of developments taking place in both European cinema and Hollywood, and this was also to play its part in the transformation of the British cinema, making it better prepared to face the introduction of sound at the end of the decade.

Bibliography
Hepworth, Cecil (1951), *Came the Dawn: Memories of a Film Pioneer.*
Low, Rachael (1949), *The History of the British Film, ii: 1906–1914.*
—— (1950), *The History of the British Film, iii: 1914–18.*
—— (1971), *The History of the British Film, iv: 1918–29.*
—— and Manvell, Roger (1948), *The History of the British Film, i: 1896–1906.*
Pearson, George (1957), *Flashback: The Autobiography of a British Filmmaker.*
Sadoul, Georges (1951), *Histoire générale du cinéma*, vol. iii.
Salt, Barry (1992), *Film Style and Technology.*

Germany: The Weimar Years

THOMAS ELSAESSER

'German Cinema' recalls the 1920s, Expressionism, Weimar culture, and a time when Berlin was the cultural centre of Europe. For film historians, this period is sandwiched between the pioneering work of American directors like D. W. Griffith, Ralph Ince, Cecil B. DeMille, and Maurice Tourneur in the 1910s, and the Soviet montage cinema of Sergei Eisenstein, Dziga Vertov, Vsevolod Pudovkin in the late 1920s. The names of Ernst Lubitsch, Robert Wiene, Paul Leni, Fritz Lang, Friedrich Wilhelm Murnau, and Georg Wilhelm Pabst stand, in this view, for one of

the 'golden ages' of world cinema, helping—between 1918 and 1928—to make motion pictures an artistic and avant-garde medium.

Arguably, such a view of film history is no longer unchallenged, yet surprisingly many of the German films from this period are part of the canon: *The Cabinet of Dr Caligari* (*Das Cabinet des Dr. Caligari*, Robert Wiene, 1919), *The Golem* (*Der Golem, wie er in die Welt kam*, Paul Wegener, 1920), *Destiny* (*Der müde Tod*, Fritz Lang, 1921), *Nosferatu* (F. W. Murnau, 1921), *Dr Mabuse* (Lang, 1922), *Waxworks* (*Das*

Wachsfigurenkabinett, 1924), *The Last Laugh* (*Der letzte Mann*, Murnau, 1924), *Metropolis* (Lang, 1925), *Pandora's Box* (*Die Büchse der Pandora*, G. W. Pabst, 1928). Even more surprisingly, they have also entered popular movie mythology and now live on, parodied, pastiched, and recycled, in very different guises, from pulp movies to post-modern video-clips. In their time, the films were associated with German Expressionism, mainly because of their self-conscious stylization of décor, gesture, and lighting. Others regarded the same pre-eminence of stylization, fantasy, and nightmare visions as evidence of the inner torment and moral dilemmas in those for whom the films were made. Equivocation was not confined to the films: did the films reflect the political chaos of the Weimar Republic, or did the parade of tyrants, madmen, somnambulists, crazed scientists, and homunculi anticipate the horrors that were to follow between 1933 and 1945? But why not assume that the films, even in their own time, look back, cocking a snook at Romanticism and neo-Gothic? The standard works on the subject, Lotte Eisner's *The Haunted Screen* (1969) and Siegfried Kracauer's *From Caligari to Hitler* (1947), resolutely do not consider this last possibility, but opt, as their somewhat lurid titles indicate, for seeing the films as symptoms of troubled souls.

Eisner's and Kracauer's powerful portraits left much else about the early German cinema in the shadows. In some respects, the spotlight they cast on the early and mid-1920s only deepened the darkness into which prejudice and physical destruction had already plunged the first two decades of German film history. One point to make when reassessing the earliest period is that Germany could boast, in the field of film technology, optics, and photographic instruments, of a fair share of inventors and 'pioneers': Simon Stampfer, Ottomar Anschütz, the Skladanowsky brothers, Oskar Messter, Guido Seeber, the Stollwerck and Agfa works connote innovators of international stature, but also a solid manufacturing and engineering basis. Yet Wilhelmine Germany was not a major film-producing nation. Cultural resistance as much as economic conservatism caused film production up to about 1912/13 to stagnate at a pre-industry stage. While the Skladanowsky brothers' first public presentation of their Bioskop projector in November 1895 at the Berlin Wintergarten narrowly precedes the Lumière brothers' first public demonstration of the Cinématographe, the lead in exhibition did not translate into production.

THE WILHELMINE YEARS

Of the companies that established themselves mainly in Berlin, Hamburg, and Munich, the firms of Messter, Greenbaum, Duskes, Continental-Kunstfilm, and Deutsche Mutoskop und Biograph stand out. They were often family businesses, manufacturing optical and photographic equipment, which entered into film production mainly as a way of selling cameras and projectors. Oskar Messter appears to have been interested in the scientific and military uses of the cinema as much as he was in its entertainment potential. By contrast, the strategy of Paul Davidson, the other important German producer of the 1910s, was entirely entertainment-oriented. Originally successful in the Frankfurt fashion business, Davidson built his Allgemeine Kinematographen Gesellschaft Union Theater (later: PAGU) bottom-up, from the films to the sites and the hardware. In 1909 he opened a 1,200-seater cinema at the Berlin Alexanderplatz, and took up production, to complement his supply of films from foreign companies, notably Pathé in Paris and the Nordisk Film Kompagni in Copenhagen. While Messter was still experimenting with his 'Tonbilder' (arias from *Salome*, *Siegfried*, *Tannhäuser* filmed in the studio and synchronized with sound cylinders for projection), Davidson, in 1911, took under contract one of the Nordisk's major assets, Asta Nielsen and her husband-director Urban Gad.

By the outbreak of the war, no more than 14 per cent of the total films shown in German cinemas were German-produced. The films that have survived from before 1913 reflect this haphazard growth quite accurately. For the first decade, actuality films (Berlin street scenes, military parades, naval launches, the Kaiser reviewing troops), vaudeville and trapeze acts (a boxing kangaroo, tumbling acrobats, cycle tricks), fashion shows, and erotic bathing scenes make up the bulk of the films, along with comic sketches in the Pathé manner, magic lantern or zoetrope slides transferred to film, trick films, and mother-in-law jokes.

From 1907 onwards, one begins to recognize a certain generic profile: dramas featuring children and domestic animals (*Detected by her Dog*, 1910; *Carlchen und Carlo*, 1912), social dramas centred on maid-servants, governesses, and shopgirls (*Heimgefunden*, 1912; *Madeleine*, 1912), mountain films (*Wildschützenrache* ('A poacher's revenge'), 1909; *Der Alpenjäger* ('Alpine hunter'), 1910), love triangles at sea (*Der Schatten des Meeres* ('The shadow of the sea'), 1912), and marital dramas in time of war and peace (*The Two Suitors*, 1910, *Zweimal gelebt* ('Two lives'), 1911). On the whole, the titles are indicative of an ideologically conservative society, conventional in its morality, philistine in its tastes, but, above all, family-oriented. Yet the films themselves, while often ponderous and predictable, show that much care was taken over the visual *mise-en-scène*.

A number of films have the cinema itself as subject: *Der stellungslose Photograph* ('The unemployed photographer', 1912), *Die Filmprimadonna* ('The film star'), and *Zapata's Bande* ('Zapata's gang') (both with Asta Nielsen, 1913). They are almost the only suggestion that German pre-war films, too, could communicate some of the modernity, the zany energy, and raffish bohemianism to which the cinema

A scene from Paul Leni's 'Expressionist' *Waxworks* (*Das Wachsfigurenkabinett*, 1924)

owed its mass appeal and which was so typical of French, American, and especially Danish films of the period.

As to German film stars, there is no doubt that the first one was Kaiser Wilhelm II himself, always shown strutting with his generals and admirals. Asta Nielsen was soon rivalled by Henny Porten (a discovery of Messter) as Germany's major female star of the pre-war period, though she remained much less well known internationally. Messter, who had begun to make longer films by 1909, proved adept at taking actors from stage and vaudeville under contract, giving many later stars their début, among them Emil Jannings, Lil Dagover, and Conrad Veidt.

The year 1913 was a turning-point for the German cinema, as it was in other film-making countries. By then, the exhibition situation had stabilized around the three- to five-reel feature film, premièred in luxury cinemas. German film production increased, developing a number of genres that were to become typical. Outstanding among them were suspense dramas and detective films, some of them (*Die Landstrasse* ('The highway'), *Hands of Justice*, *Der Mann im Keller* ('The man in the cellar')), showing a quantum increase in cinematic sophistication, with remarkable use of outdoor locations and period interiors. Lighting, camera movement, and editing began to be deployed as part of a recognizable stylistic system, which compares interestingly with the handling of space and narration in American or French films of the time.

Adapted from Danish and French serials, the crime films often featured a star detective with an Anglicized name, such as Stuart Webbs, Joe Deebs, or Harry Higgs. As private detective and master criminal try to outwit each other, their cars and taxi-rides, railway pursuits and telephone calls convey the drive and energy of the new medium. The films cast a fascinated eye on modern technology and urban locations, on the mechanics of crime and detection, while the protagonists revel in disguise and transformation, motivating spectacular stunts, especially in the frequent chase scenes.

A distinct vitality and wit exudes from the cinema of Franz Hofer (*Die schwarze Kugel* ('The black ball')) and Joseph Delmont, whose feeling for the excitement of the metropolitan scene makes him depict Berlin, in *Das Recht auf Dasein* ('The right to live'), gripped by a construction and housing boom. Henny Porten and Asta Nielsen were no match in popularity for the first matinee idol superstar, Harry Piel, specializing in daring adventure and chase films. An exception to the rule that Germans have no film humour is the comedies of Franz Hofer (*Hurrah! Einquartierung* and *Das rosa Pantöffelchen*), which prove worthy antecedents of Ernst Lubitsch's farces from the mid-1910s, with their tomboyish, headstrong heroines.

These popular genres and stars have often been neglected in accounts of the period, because of the more commented-on aspect of 1913, namely, the emergence of the so-called *Autorenfilm* ('author's film'). Initiated under the impact of the French *film d'art*, the aim was to profit from the established reputation of published or performed authors, and to persuade the leading names of Berlin's theatres to lend cultural prestige to the screen.

Not only were popular but now forgotten writers such as Paul Lindau and Heinrich Lautensack signed on, but also Gerhard Hauptmann, Hugo von Hofmannsthal, and Arthur Schnitzler. Because of an acrimonious union dispute in 1911, actors had been contractually forbidden to appear in films, but when in 1913 Albert Bassermann agreed to star in Max Mack's adaptation of the Lindau play *Der Andere* ('The other one', 1913), others followed suit. Davidson took under contract the star-maker *par excellence*, Max Reinhardt, who directed two films, *Eine venezianische Nacht* ('A Venetian night', 1913) and *Insel der Seligen* ('The island of the blessed', 1913), full of mythological and fairy-tale motifs which were liberally borrowed from Shakespeare's comedies and German *fin-de-siècle* plays.

The most militant advocate of the author's film was the cinema owner and novelist Hanns Heinz Ewers, who with Paul Wegener and Stellan Rye made *The Student of Prague* (*Der Student von Prag*, 1913), which, because of the motif of the double, has often been compared to *Der Andere*. The Danish influence is no accident, since Nordisk was one of the prime forces behind the *Autorenfilm*, producing two of the genre's most costly ventures, *Atlantis* (1913, based on a Hauptmann novel) and *Das fremde Mädchen* ('The foreign girl', a 'dream play' specially written by Hoffmannsthal). Another firm specializing in literary adaptations was Heinrich Bolten-Baeckers's BB-Literaria, founded as a joint venture with Pathé, in order to exploit Pathé literary rights in Germany. Such moves underscore the international character of the German cinema in 1913, with actors and directors from Denmark (Viggo Larsen, Valdemar Psilander) undoubtedly exercising the strongest influence on domestic production, while France, Britain, and America supplied the majority of non-German films shown in the cinemas.

GERMAN CINEMA AND THE FIRST WORLD WAR

The upturn and consolidation of German film production was thus already well under way when war broke out, and the immediate effect of hostilities on the film business was mixed. With an import embargo in force, some firms, such as PAGU, suffered substantial losses before they were able to organize new sources of film supply. But there were also winners for whom the confiscation of property from the foreign firms operating in Germany, and the soaring demands for films, signalled a unique opportunity. A new generation of producers and producer-directors made their breakthrough, after the government had lifted the initial ban on cinema-going. Erich Pommer, a young sales representative for the French firms Gaumont and Éclair, seized his chance and formed Decla ('Deutsche Éclair'), which was to become the key producer of German quality cinema after the war. Among the new firms which flourished was that of producer-director Joe May, soon the

market leader in detective serials and highly successful with his 'Mia May films', melodramas featuring his wife. In his case, too, it was the war years which laid the foundation of his post-war fame as Germany's chief producer of epics and spectaculars. Similarly, the director-producer Richard Oswald, one of the most competent professional film-makers of the 1910s, was later epitomized as 'war profiteer', when after the abolition of censorship in 1918 he spotted a niche for his highly successful 'enlightenment films' (moralizing sex melodramas). To give an indication of the scale on which the German film industry expanded during the war: in 1914, 25 German firms competed with 47 foreign ones; by 1918, the relation was 130 to 10.

The quality of German films from the war years has rarely been assessed impartially. Some featuring the war, and often dismissed as patriotic propaganda films or 'field-grey kitsch', turn out to be major surprises. Thus, the films of Franz Hofer (e.g. *Weihnachtsglocken* ('Christmas bells'), 1914) are stylistically sophisticated, projecting a feel both distinctively German and free of jingoism, as they plead for self-sacrifice and peace between the social classes. An unusual blend of melodrama and lyricism can be found in *Wenn Völker streiten* ('When nations quarrel', 1914) as well as several other films which take the war as subject (such as Alfred Halm's *Ihr Unteroffizier* ('Their non-commissioned officer', 1915)). Among the melodramas, the most extraordinary is *Das Tagebuch des Dr. Hart* ('The diary of Dr Hart', 1916), directed by Paul Leni and funded by BUFA, the government-owned film propaganda unit. The story of two families with split political loyalties and crossed love interests, *Das Tagebuch* is an anti-tsarist propaganda film in the guise of championing Polish nationalism. But it also makes a strongly pacifist statement through the realistic battle scenes, the depiction of the wounded in field hospitals, and images of rural devastation.

However, films on war subjects were the exception. Serials featuring male stars made up the bulk of the production, with the then-famous actors Ernst Reicher, Alwin Neuss, and Harry Lambert-Paulsen enjoying a following that allowed them single-handedly to keep their respective companies in profit. Female serial queens like Fern Andra and Hanni Weisse were also prolific, while directors like Joe May, Richard Oswald, Max Mack, and Otto Rippert would make an average of six to eight films a year, moving effortlessly between popular films (*Sensationsfilme*) and art films (*Autorenfilme*). Rippert's six-part *Homunculus*, starring yet another Danish import, Olaf Fons, was the super-hit of 1916, and Oswald's *Hoffmanns Erzählungen* ('Hoffmann's tales'), an adaptation of three E. T. A. Hoffmann stories, used outdoor locations most spectacularly. Both films have been seen as forerunners of that prototypical art cinema genre, the fantastic or 'expressionist' film, but

Conrad Veidt

(1893–1943)

Conrad Veidt started his career in 1913, at Max Reinhardt's acting school. After a short period of employment in the First World War as a member of different front theatre ensembles, he returned to the Deutsches Theater Berlin, and then, in 1916, began working in the movies. In 1919, in the first homosexual role on screen in *Anders als die Andern*, and above all as the somnambulist Cesare in *Das Cabinet des Dr. Caligari*, he created an expressionist acting style that made him an international star. In the early 1920s he starred in several of Richard Oswald's *Sittenfilme* dealing with sexual enlightenment, and went on to work with many of the best-known directors of the time. Veidt moved to the USA in the second half of the decade, but returned to Germany on the introduction of sound, starring in some of the early Ufa sound successes and their English versions. In 1932 Veidt started work in Britain, shooting a pro-Semitic version of *Jew Süss* (1934) and the more equivocal *Wandering Jew* (1933), after which he became *persona non grata* in Nazi Germany. With his Jewish wife Lily Preger he remained in London, gaining British citizenship in 1939. He continued to work, incarnating Prussian officers for Victor Saville and Michael Powell. In 1940 he moved to Hollywood, where he was cast mainly as a Nazi—most famously, Major Strasser in *Casablanca* (1942).

From Cesare to Major Strasser, Veidt's portrayals of dark figures reach beyond the scope of the familiar scoundrel cliché. His characters are burdened with the knowledge that they are doomed, and so have an introverted and stoic edge, accepting their fate and never compromising in order to save their own lives. They always remain true to their mission and often border on the fanatical in their sense of duty and singleness of vision. However, Veidt's characters are also enveloped in an aura of melancholy which is made distinguished by their good manners and cosmopolitan elegance.

Veidt's face reveals much of the inner life of his characters. The play of muscles beneath the taut skin, the lips pressed together, a vein on his temple visibly protruding, nostrils flaring in concentration and self-discipline. These physical aspects characterize the artists, sovereigns, and strangers of the German silent films, as well as the Prussian officers of the British and Hollywood periods.

The intensity of Veidt's facial expressions is supported by the modulation of his voice and his clear articulation. His tongue and his slightly irregular teeth become visible when he speaks, details which allow his words to flow carefully seasoned from his wide mouth—in contrast to the slang-like mutterings of Humphrey Bogart who played opposite him in two US productions of the 1940s. Veidt's German accent is a failing which he turns into a strength; it becomes the means of structuring the flow of speech. The voice, which can take on every nuance from

Conrad Veidt as the German Lieutenant Hart in Michael Powell's *The Spy in Black* (1939)

an ingratiating whisper to a barking command, is surprising in its abrupt changes in tone. Once heard, it is easy to imagine the voices of his silent film characters. Veidt's late film roles reflect back on the early silent ones, enriching them retrospectively with a sound-track.

DANIELA SANNWALD

SELECT FILMOGRAPHY

(with directors)
Der Weg des Todes (Robert Reinert, 1916–17); Anders als die Andern (Richard Oswald, 1918–19); Das Cabinet des Dr Caligari (1919–20); Das indische Grabmal (Joe May, 1921); Die Brüder Schellenberg (Karl Grune, 1925); Der Student von Prag (Henrik Galeen, 1926); The Man who Laughs (USA, Paul Leni, 1927); Die letzte Kompagnie (Kurt Bernhardt, 1929); Der Kongress tanzt (Erik Charell, 1931); Jew Süss (Lothar Mendes, 1934); The Spy in Black (Michael Powell, 1939); Casablanca (Michael Curtiz, 1942); Above Suspicion (Richard Thorpe, 1943)

BIBLIOGRAPHY

Allen, Jerry C. (1987), *From Caligari to Casablanca*.
Jacobsen, Wolfgang (ed.) (1993), *Conrad Veidt: Lebensbilder*.
Sannwald, Daniela (1993), 'Continental Stranger: Conrad Veidt und seine britischen Filme'.

they belong more properly to the multi-episode *Sensationsfilme*, not so different from Joe May's *Veritas vincit* (1916), which was Italian-inspired, and later parodied by Ernst Lubitsch, who himself acted in and directed about two dozen comedies, before he had his first international success with *Madame Dubarry* in 1919.

To find the origins of the fantastic film, one has to return to the *Autorenfilm*, whose outstanding figure was neither Hans Heinz Ewers nor Stellan Rye, but Paul Wegener. A celebrated Max Reinhardt actor before he came to make films, between 1913 and 1918 Wegener created the genre of the Gothic-Romantic fairy-tale film. After *The Student of Prague* he acted in and co-directed *The Golem* (1920), based on a Jewish legend and the prototype of all monster/Frankenstein/creature features. There followed *Peter Schlemihl*, *Rübezahl's Wedding*, *The Pied Piper of Hamlin*, and several other films exploiting the rich vein of German Romantic legend and fairy-tales.

Wegener's work in the 1910s is crucial for at least two reasons: he was attracted to fantastic subjects because they allowed him to explore different cinematic techniques, such as trick photography, superimposition, special effects in the manner of the French detective *Zigomar* series, but with a sinister rather than comic motivation. For this, he worked closely with one of the early German cinema's most creative cameramen, Guido Seeber, himself a somewhat underrated pioneer whose many publications about the art of cinematography, special effects, and lighting are a veritable source-book for understanding the German style of the 1920s. But Wegener's fairy-tale films also promoted the ingenious compromise which the *Autorenfilm* wanted to strike between countering the immense hostility shown towards the cinema by the educated middle class (manifested in the so-called 'Kino Debatte') and exploiting what was unique about the cinema, its popularity.

The prevalence of the fantastic in the German cinema may thus have a simpler explanation than that given by either Lotte Eisner or Siegfried Kracauer, who enlist it as proof of the nature of the German soul. Reviving gothic motifs and the romantic *Kunstmärchen*, the fantastic film achieved a double aim: it militated for the cinema's aesthetic legitimacy by borrowing from middlebrow Wilhelmine 'culture', but it also broke with the international tendency of early cinema, by offering nationally identifiable German films. Up until the *Autorenfilm*, film subjects and genres were quasi-universal and international, with very little fundamental difference from country to country: film-makers were either inspired by other popular entertainments, or they copied the successful film subjects of their foreign rivals and domestic competitors. With the *Autorenfilm*, the notion of 'national cinema' became construed in analogy to 'national literature', as well as a certain definition of the popular, in which the rural-*völkisch* and the national-romantic played an important role.

The Wegener tradition thus set a pattern which was to repeat itself throughout the 1920s: conservative, nostalgic, and national themes contrasting sharply with the experimental and avant-garde outlook film-makers had with regard to advancing the medium's technical possibilities. Seeking to define a national cinema by blending a high-culture concept of national literature with a popular pseudo-folk culture, the Wegener tradition tried to take the wind out of the establishment's critical sails. It is the combination of both these objectives in the fantastic film that makes it such a mainstay of the German cinema for at least a decade (from 1913 until about 1923), suggesting that the celebrated 'expressionist film' is the tail end of this truce between highbrow culture and a lowbrow medium, rather than a new departure. What breathed new life into the vogue was, of course, *The Cabinet of Dr Caligari*, mainly because of its extraordinary reception in France (and subsequently in the United States), which in turn made producers and directors self-consciously look for motifs that the export market would recognize as German.

The conjunction of a boom in demand and a war economy had, by the end of the war, led to an unsustainable number of small, undercapitalized production firms competing with each other, some of which had tried to gain an advantage via mergers or takeovers. The first such association of small producers was the Deutsche Lichtbild A.G. (Deulig), formed in 1916, backed by heavy industry interests in the Ruhr, and headed by Alfred Hugenberg, then a director of Krupp, and also owner of a newspaper and publishing empire. One of Hugenberg's chief lieutenants, Ludwig Klitzsch, saw the advantage of diversifying into a potentially profitable medium. He also had a veritable mission to use the cinema as a promotional tool for both commerce and lobby politics. Klitzsch occupied a leading function in the German Colonial League, one of the two nationally organized initiatives—the other being the German Navy League—which had, from about 1907 onwards, relied heavily on the cinematograph in order to promote its aims. The Navy League especially provoked the anger of cinema exhibitors, since it provided unfair competition by getting free advertising for its shows in the local press, and captive audiences from school officials or local army commandants.

UFA, DECLA, AND THE WEIMAR CINEMA

The Deulig initiative led to a counter-offensive by a consortium of firms from the electrical and chemical industries, headed by the Deutsche Bank. They were able to persuade military circles to use the government-owned film propaganda unit, the Bild und Film Amt (BUFA), to front a large-scale merger operation. Under considerable secrecy, the Universum-Film Aktiengesellschaft (Ufa) was founded in December 1917, combining the Messter GmbH, PAGU, Nordisk, along with a handful of smaller firms. The Reich provided funds to buy out some of the owners, while others were offered shares in the new company, with Paul Davidson becoming the new firm's first head of production. The establishment of a horizontally and vertically integrated company of this size meant not only that Deulig was dwarfed, but that a great many other middle-size companies became increasingly dependent on Ufa as Germany's chief domestic exhibitor and export distributor.

Neither the strategy of such a merger, nor the use of a special interest group for the purposes of creating a film propaganda instrument, were the invention of Ufa's backers. Both obeyed a certain commercial logic, and both belonged to the political culture of Wilhelmine society, making Ufa an expression not so much of the war, as of a new way of thinking about public opinion and the media in general. By the time Ufa became operational, however, Germany had been defeated, and the new conglomerate's goal was to dominate the domestic as well as the European film market. Its chief assets were in real estate (extensive studio capacity, luxury cinemas all over Germany, laboratories and prime office space in Berlin), while owning Messter brought Ufa horizontal diversification into film

equipment, processing, and other cinema-related service industries, and the Nordisk stake both extended the exhibition basis already present from PAGU and gave Ufa access to a world-wide export network.

Production at first continued under the brand names of the merged firms: PAGU, Messter, Joe May Film, Gloria, BB-Film, some using the new purpose-built studios in Babelsberg, soon to become the heart of Ufa and the German film industry. The PAGU team around Davidson and Lubitsch rose to international fame with a series of historical spectaculars and costume dramas, often based on operettas (e.g. *Madame Dubarry*, 1919). Specializing in exotic *Großfilme* (*Das indische Grabmal* ('The Indian Tomb'), 1920), Joe May's multi-episode serials like *Die Herrin der Welt* ('The mistress of the world') proved particularly popular to Germany's war-exhausted spectators, not least because each episode featured a different continent, with the heroine travelling from China to Africa, from India to the United States.

Among the firms which initially did not form part of the Ufa conglomerate, the most important was Decla, headed by Erich Pommer. Decla's first major films after the war were *Die Spinnen* ('The spiders', 1919), an exotic detective serial written and directed by Fritz Lang, and *Die Pest in Florenz* ('The plague in Florence', 1919), a historical adventure directed by Rippert and scripted by Lang.

Louise Brooks with Kurt Gerron in G. W. Pabst's *Diary of a Lost Girl* (*Das Tagebuch einer Verlorenen*, 1929)

Together with *The Cabinet of Dr Caligari*, directed by Robert Wiene and written by Carl Mayer and Hans Janowitz, these three films made up a production programme which defined the course that the German cinema was to take in the early 1920s. Popular serials, with exotic locations and improbable adventures, historical spectaculars, and the 'stylized' (or 'expressionist') film were the backbone of a concept of product differentiation, carried by such directors as Lang and Wiene, Ludwig Berger and F. W. Murnau, Carl Mayer, Carl Froelich, and Arthur von Gerlach.

Given the decisive role of *Caligari* in typecasting the German cinema, it is remarkable how unrepresentative it is of the films made during the years of the Weimar Republic. Its explicitly 'expressionist' décor remained almost unique, and the few German films that were able to repeat its international commercial success were each very different: *Madame Dubarry, Variete* (1925), *The Last Laugh, Metropolis*. Yet in one respect *Caligari* does illustrate a common pattern for the period. For in so far as one production strand, strongly though not exclusively identified with Pommer and the Decla–Bioskop label, has an identity as an 'art cinema', its films have a remarkably similar narrative structure. The 'lack' which, according to narratologists, drives all stories, centres in the Weimar cinema almost invariably on incomplete families, jealousies, overpowering father figures, absent mothers, and often is not remedied by an attainable or desired object choice. If one takes a dozen or so of the films still remembered, one is struck by their explicitly Oedipal scenarios, by the recurring rivalry between fathers and sons, by jealousy between friends, brothers, or companions. Rebellion, as Kracauer has already pointed out, is followed by submission to the law of the fathers, but in such a way that the rebels are haunted by their shadow, their double, their phantom selves. This cluster of motifs can be found in Fritz Lang's *Destiny* and *Metropolis*, in Arthur Robison's *Schatten* ('Shadows', 1923) and *Manon Lescaut* (1926), in E. A. Dupont's *Das alte Gesetz* ('The old law', 1923) and *Variete* (1925), in Paul Leni's *Waxworks* (1924) and *Hintertreppe* ('Backstairs', 1921), Lupu Pick's *Scherben* ('Fragments', 1921) and *Sylvester* (1923), Murnau's *The Last Laugh* and *Phantom*, in Karl Grune's *Die Strasse* ('The road', 1923), and Robert Wiene's *Orlacs Hände* ('The hands of Orlac', 1925).

These obliquely symbolic conflicts correspond to indirect forms of narration via flashbacks, framing devices, and nested narratives, as in *Caligari, Destiny* (1921), *Variete, Nosferatu, Zur Chronik von Grieshuus* ('The chronicle of Grieshuus', 1925), and *Phantom*. This often makes the films' temporal structure difficult, if not impossible, to reconstruct, changing by that very fact the viewer's understanding of character and motivation. At the same time, the editing often obscures rather than expresses continuity and causal links between segments or even between shots. Hence the impression of interiority, of the uncanny and the mysterious, since so much of the action and the protagonists' motivation has to be guessed, presumed, or otherwise inferred.

For many of the stories of Weimar cinema one can identify sources and intertexts from other media. Besides the folk-tales and legends already mentioned in connection with Wegener—to which one could add Lang's *Destiny* and *The Nibelungen* (1923), Ludwig Berger's *Der verlorene Schuh* ('The lost shoe', 1923), and Leni Riefenstahl's *Das blaue Licht* ('The blue light', 1932)—the sources are serialized novels from newspapers (*Dr Mabuse, Schloss Vogelöd, Phantom*), middlebrow entertainment literature (*Der Gang in die Nacht* ('The walk in the night'), *Variete*) and adaptations of authors identified with Germany's national literature (Goethe, Gerhard Hauptmann, Theodor Storm). These cross-media influences are indicative of the vertical links already at that time existing between film production and the publishing industries, suggesting that choice was determined by economic factors, exploiting the popularity and notoriety of the material. Yet they also continue the middlebrow, consensus-fostering, canon-forming notion of a national cinema, borrowing from literature and a common stock of cultural references.

A particularly striking feature is that among the films most often cited as symptomatic for the inner state of Germany, a surprising number were written by just two script-writers: Carl Mayer and Thea von Harbou. With regard to genre and story material, it is almost entirely their films that define the 'identity' of Weimar cinema, in particular for the period up to 1925: Mayer's *Kammerspiel*-films (*Genuine, Hintertreppe, Scherben, Sylvester, The Last Laugh, Tartüff, Vanina*), and Thea von Harbou's racy adaptations of classics, bestsellers, and national epics (all of Fritz Lang's and three Murnau films, as well as ten by other directors).

The inordinate influence of a few individuals indicates the existence of a fairly close-knit creative community, with the same names turning up repeatedly among the directors, the set designers, the producers, the cameramen, and script-writers. Barely two dozen people seem to have made up the core of the German film establishment of the early 1920s. Largely formed around Ufa and a few other Berlin-based production companies, the groups can be traced directly to the formation of producer-director units around Joe May, Richard Oswald, Fritz Lang, Friedrich W. Murnau, and the PAGU-Davidson group.

This focuses attention once more on Ufa, and Erich Pommer, who, after taking over as Head of Production, seemed unwilling to impose the kind of central-producer system practised by that time in Hollywood. Pommer's production concept had two salient features. With his background in distribution (Gaumont, Éclair) and export

(Decla), Pommer—like Davidson—conceived of production as driven by exhibition and export. He recognized the importance that export had for the domestic market itself, as shown in his efforts as deputy director of the Export-verband der deutschen Filmindustrie, founded in May 1920, to put pressure on 'the internal organisation of the market, if necessary by sidestepping the people who currently feel themselves to be in charge of the German film business' (Jacobsen 1989).

Madame Dubarry in the USA and *Caligari* in Europe were the two export successes which broke the international boycott of German films. On their basis, Pommer developed his concept of product differentiation, trying to service two markets: the international mass audiences, firmly in the hands of Hollywood, and the international art-cinema outlets, where what he called the 'stylized film' generated the prestige which became linked to the German cinema. Yet the initial export successes were greatly facilitated by hyperinflation, since depreciation automatically amortized a film's production cost: in 1921, for instance, the sale of a feature film to a single market like Switzerland earned enough hard currency to finance an entire new production. But with the stabilization of the Mark in 1923, this trading advantage disappeared for German production, and Pommer's twin strategy became increasingly precarious.

In response Pommer tried to establish a common European film market dominated by Germany and Ufa. He entered into a number of distribution and co-production agreements under the banner 'Film Europe', demonstrating his awareness that, despite its size and concentration, Ufa on its own was in no position to brave Hollywood even in Europe, not to mention penetrating the US market. Despite its ultimate failure, the Film Europe initiatives laid the groundwork for the very extensive contacts that were to exist throughout the late 1920s and lasting well into the 1940s, between the German and French and British film-making communities.

Until 1926, when he left for the United States, Pommer's original production system at Ufa remained the director-unit system, giving his teams, most of which dated from the Decla–Bioskop period, great creative freedom. The benefits of this policy are well known: they made up the grandeur of the so-called Ufa style, with scope for technical and stylistic experimentation and improvisation at almost every stage of a project. This led to heavy reliance on studio-work, which Ufa's admirers thought 'atmospheric', and others merely 'claustrophobic'.

There were drawbacks, too: often it seemed that, with perfectionism and the craft ethos permeating all departments, time and money were no object. Furthermore, the refusal to divide and control the labour processes of film production as was standard practice in Hollywood often came into conflict with a production policy geared towards exhibition schedules. Given the German film industry's chronic over-production, few of Ufa's more expensive films could be fully exploited, making Pommer's production concept deficit-prone, and, as illustrated by the loan and distribution agreement concluded with US majors (the Parufamet Agreement), ultimately fatal to Ufa's fortunes as a manufacturing company run on industrial lines with commercial imperatives. The aesthetic and stylistic results of Pommer's concept, on the other hand, were more lasting: revolutionary techniques in special effects (*Destiny, Faust, Metropolis*), new styles of lighting (*Phantom*, the *Kammerspiel* films), camera movement and camera angles (*Variete* and *The Last Laugh*), and set design fully integrated into style and theme (as in *Die Nibelungen*). These achievements gave Ufa film technicians and directors their high professional reputation, making the German cinema of the 1920s, paradoxically, both a financial disaster and a film-makers' Mecca (Hitchcock's admiration for Murnau, Buñuel's for Lang, not to mention the influences on Joseph von Sternberg, Rouben Mamoulian, Orson Welles, and on Hollywood film noir of the 1940s).

Yet fending off American competition was not the only front on which the German cinema did battle in the 1920s, and, while it dominated exhibition, Ufa did not make up much more than 18 per cent of the national production. The smaller firms not distributing via Ufa, such as Emelka, Deulig, Südfilm, Terra, and Nero, tried to maintain their own exhibition network by entering into agreements with American and British firms, thus further splitting the German market, to the ultimate advantage of Hollywood.

As a capitalist conglomerate, Ufa was the target of critics on the left, foremost among them writers from the liberal and social-democratic press, whose cultural distrust of the cinema was hardly less pronounced than that of their conservative colleagues, but for whom Ufa was clearly a tool in the hands of the nationalist right. The *feuilleton* critics also showed a somewhat contradictory attitude to the popular: denouncing 'artistic' films as 'Kitsch', they despised popular or genre films as 'Schund', thus operating a concept of film art where in the mid-1920s only Chaplin and in the late 1920s only the Soviet cinema could pass muster.

The predominantly critical attitude of the intelligentsia towards both the nation's art cinema and commercial cinema led to another paradox: discussions about the cinema, its cultural function, and aesthetic specificity as an art form were conducted at a high level of intellectual and philosophical sophistication, giving rise to theoreticians and critics of distinction: among them Béla Balázs, Rudolf Arnheim, and Siegfried Kracauer. Even daily journalism produced outstanding essays by Willy Haas, Hans Siemsen, Herbert Jhering, Kurt Tucholsky, and Hans Feld.

Erich Pommer

(1889–1966)

Erich Pommer was the most important person in the German and European film industries of the 1920s and 1930s. He worked in Berlin, Hollywood, Paris, and London—discovering talents, and forming technical and artistic teams which created some of the most important films of Weimar cinema. He also introduced Hollywood production systems to the European film industry, and was responsible for attempts to rebuild the West German film after the Second World War.

Pommer entered the film industry in 1907. By 1913 he had become general representative of the French Éclair company for central Europe. When war broke out, Éclair was put under forced administration by the German government. To rescue his business interests Pommer founded Decla (derived from 'Deutsche Eclair'). While Pommer served in the Prussian army, the new company, managed in Berlin by his wife Gertrud and his brother Albert, successfully produced comedies and melodramas for the booming German movie business.

After Pommer's return, the films became more artistically ambitious. At the end of 1919 a mixture of commercial thrift, artistic daring, simple décor, and clever advertising strategy resulted in the creation of a film legend: *Das Cabinet des Dr Caligari* (1919).

In March 1920 Decla merged with Deutsche-Bioscop. Pommer concentrated his activities on export—a crucial aspect of film production in a period of economic crisis and booming inflation. A year later the company was taken over by Ufa but continued to produce under the brand name 'Decla–Bioscop'. In 1923 he became head of Ufa's three production companies at the studios in Neubabelsberg. There he tried to realize his vision of creative production, combining art and business to create a total art form. Acting as executive producer, he initiated big prestige productions aimed at the international market. Directors F. W. Murnau, Fritz Lang, Ludwig Berger, Arthur Robison, and E. A. Dupont, writers Carl Mayer, Thea von Harbou, and Robert Liebmann, cinematographers Karl Freund, Carl Hoffmann, Fritz Arno Wagner, and Günther Rittau, art directors Robert Herlth and Walter Röhrig, Otto Hunte, and Erich Kettelhut formed the reservoir of manpower from which Pommer formed lasting artistic teams. They created film classics such as *Destiny* (*Der müde Tod*, 1921), *Dr. Mabuse* (1922), *Phantom* (1922), *Die Nibelungen* (1924), *Die Finanzen des Grossherzogs* (1923), *The Last Laugh* (*Der letzte Mann*, 1924), *Tartüff* (1925), *Variete* (1925), *Metropolis* (1925), and *Manon Lescaut* (1926).

Employing foreign talent, such as Carl Theodor Dreyer, Robert Dinesen, Benjamin Christensen, and Holger-Madsen from Denmark, and Herbert Wilcox, Alfred Hitchcock, and Graham Cutts from Great Britain, Pommer tried to strengthen international co-operation in what he called 'Film Europe'—a European force working against the American domination of the world film market.

Pommer's way of allowing his production teams great creative freedom to perform their artistic and technical experiments led to over-extended budgets and contributed to Ufa's growing financial crisis. When Pommer left Ufa in January 1926, Lang's *Metropolis* was in its sixth month of production and would take another year to be ready for release. Pommer went to Hollywood, where he produced two films for Paramount with former Ufa star Pola Negri. But he had problems adapting to the Hollywood system, and argued with the studio bosses.

In 1928 Ufa's new studio head Ludwig Klitzsch lured Pommer back to Babelsberg, where his production group was given top priority to produce sound films. Combining his European and American experience, he hired the Hollywood director Josef von Sternberg to direct Emil Jannings in *The Blue Angel* (*Der blaue Engel*, 1930): an international film for the world market. Pommer employed new talents such as the brothers Robert and Kurt Siodmak, and Billie (later Billy) Wilder. He pioneered the genre of film operetta with films like Erik Charell's *The Congress Dances* (*Der Kongress tanzt*, 1931).

When the Nazis took power in 1933 and Ufa ousted most of its Jewish employees, Pommer emigrated to Paris, where he set up a European production facility for Fox, for which he produced two films—Max Ophuls's *On a volé un homme* (1933) and Fritz Lang's *Liliom* (1934). After a brief period in Hollywood he moved to London to work with Korda. In 1937 he founded Mayflower Pictures with actor Charles Laughton, whom he directed in *Vessel of Wrath* (1938). Hitchcock's *Jamaica Inn* (1939) was their last production before the Second World War broke out and Pommer went to Hollywood for the third time. He produced Dorothy Arzner's *Dance, Girl, Dance* for RKO but his studio contract was cancelled following a heart attack.

In 1946 Pommer (an American citizen since 1944) returned to Germany as Film Production Control Officer. His tasks were to organize the re-establishment of a German film industry and the rebuilding of destroyed studios, and to supervise the denazification of film-makers. But Pommer found his position difficult, caught between the interests of the American industry and his desire to reconstruct an independent German cinema. In 1949 his duties on behalf of the Allies ended. He stayed in Munich, working with old colleagues from Ufa such as Hans Albers, and new talents such as Hildegard Knef. He produced a few films until the failure of the anti-war picture *Kinder, Mütter und ein General* (1955) led to the collapse of his Intercontinental-Film. In 1956 Pommer, whose health was declining, retired to California, where he died in 1966.

HANS-MICHAEL BOCK

BIBLIOGRAPHY

Bock, Hans-Michael, and Töteberg, Michael (eds.) (1992), *Das Ufa-Buch*.
Hardt, Ursula (1993), *Erich Pommer: Film Producer for Germany*.
Jacobsen, Wolfgang (1989), *Erich Pommer: Ein Produzent macht Filmgeschichte*.

Friedrich Wilhelm Murnau
(1888–1931)

One of the most gifted visual artists of the silent cinema, F. W. Murnau made twenty-one films between 1919 and 1931, first in Berlin, later in Hollywood, and finally in the South Seas. He died prematurely in a car accident in California at the age of 42. Born Friedrich Wilhelm Plumpe in Bielefeld, Germany, Murnau grew up in a cultured environment. As a child, he immersed himself in literary classics and staged theatrical productions with his sister and brothers. At the University of Heidelberg, where he studied art history and literature, he was spotted by Max Reinhardt in a student play and offered free training at Reinhardt's school in Berlin. When the war began in 1914, he enlisted in the infantry and fought on the Eastern Front. In 1916 he transferred to the air force and was stationed near Verdun, where he was one of the few from his company to survive.

In *Nosferatu* (1921), Murnau created some of the most vivid images in German expressionist cinema. Nosferatu's shadow ascending the stairs towards the woman who awaits him evokes an entire era and genre of filmmaking. Based on Bram Stoker's *Dracula*, Murnau's *Nosferatu* is a 'symphony of horror' in which the unnatural penetrates the ordinary world, as when Nosferatu's ship glides into the harbour with its freight of coffins, rats, sailors' corpses, and plague. The location shooting used so effectively by Murnau was rarely seen in German films at this time. For Lotte Eisner (1969), Murnau was the greatest of the expressionist directors because he was able to evoke horror outside the studio. Special effects accompany Nosferatu, but because no effect is repeated exactly, each instance delivers a unique charge of the uncanny. The sequence that turns to negative after Nosferatu's coach carries Jonathan across the bridge toward the vampire's castle is quoted by Cocteau in *Orphée* and Godard in *Alphaville*. Max Schreck as Nosferatu is a passive predator, the very icon of cinematic Expressionism.

The Last Laugh (*Der letzte Mann*, 1924), starring Emil Jannings, is the story of an old man who loses his job as doorman at a luxury hotel. Unable to face his demotion to a menial position, the man steals a uniform and continues to dress with his usual ceremony for his family and neighbours, who watch him come and go from their windows. When his theft is discovered, his story would end in tragedy were it not for an epilogue in which he is awakened, as if from a dream, to news that he has inherited a fortune from an unknown man he has befriended. Despite the happy ending required by the studio, this study of a man whose self-image has been taken away from him is the story of the German middle class during the ruinous inflation of the mid-1920s. Critics around the world marvelled at the 'unbound' (*entfesselte*), moving camera expressing his subjective point of view. Murnau used only one intertitle in the film, aspiring to a universal visual language.

For Eric Rohmer, *Faust* (1926) was Murnau's greatest artistic achievement because in it all other elements were subordinated to *mise-en-scène*. In *The Last Laugh* and *Tartüff* (1925), architectural form (scenic design) took precedence. *Faust* was the most pictorial (hence, cinematic) of Murnau's films because in it form (architecture) was subordinated to light (the essence of cinema). The combat between light and darkness was its very subject, as visualized in the spectacular 'Prologue in Heaven'. 'It is light that models form, that sculpts it. The film-maker allows us to witness the birth of a world as true and beautiful as painting, the art which has revealed the truth and beauty of the visible world to us through the ages' (Rohmer 1977). Murnau's homosexuality, which was not acknowledged publicly, must have played a role in aestheticizing and eroticizing the body of the young Faust.

Based on the phenomenal success of *The Last Laugh*, Murnau was invited to Hollywood by William Fox. He was given complete authority on *Sunrise* (1927), which he shot with his technical team in his accustomed manner, with elaborate sets, complicated location shooting, and experiments with visual effects. *Sunrise: A Song of Two*

Humans is about sin and redemption. A *femme fatale* from the city (dressed in black satin like the arch-tempter Mephisto in *Faust*) comes to the country, where she seduces a man and nearly succeeds in getting him to drown his wife before he recovers himself and tries to recreate the simplicity and trust of their lost happiness. *Sunrise* overwhelmed critics with its sheer beauty and poetry, but its costs far exceeded its earnings and it was to be the last film Murnau made within a production system which allowed him real control. His subsequent films for Fox, *Four Devils* and *City Girl*, were closely supervised by the studio. Murnau's decisions could be overridden by others, and in his eyes both films were severely damaged. None the less, *City Girl* should be appreciated on its own terms as a moral fable in which the landscape (fields of wheat) is endowed with exquisite pastoral beauty that turns dark and menacing, as in *Nosferatu*, *Faust*, and *Tabu*.

In 1929 Murnau set sail with Robert Flaherty for the South Seas to make a film about western traders who ruin a simple island society. Wanting more dramatic structure than Flaherty, Murnau directed *Tabu* (1931) alone. It begins in 'Paradise', where young men and women play in lush, tropical pools of water. Reri and Matahi are in love. Nature and their community are in harmony. Soon after, Reri is dedicated to the gods and declared tabu. Anyone who looks at her with desire must be killed. Matahi escapes with her. 'Paradise Lost' chronicles the inevitability of their ruin, represented by the Elder, who hunts them, and by the white traders, who trap Matahi with debt, forcing him to transgress a second tabu in defying the shark guarding the black pearl that can buy escape from the island. In the end, Matahi wins against the shark but cannot reach the boat carrying Reri away. It moves across the water as decisively as Nosferatu's ship, its sail resembling the shark's fin. Murnau died before *Tabu*'s première.

JANET BERGSTROM

FILMOGRAPHY

Note: Starred titles are no longer extant.
*Der Knabe in Blau (Der Todessmaragd) (1919); *Satanas (1919); *Sehnsucht (1920); *Der Bucklige und die Tänzerin (1920); *Der Januskopf (1920); *Abend—Nacht—Morgen (1920); Der Gang in die Nacht (1920); *Marizza, genannt die Schmugglermadonna (1921); Schloss Vogelöd (1921); Nosferatu: Eine Symphonie des Grauens (1921); Der brennende Acker (1922); Phantom (1922); *Die Austreibung (1923); Die Finanzen des Großherzogs (1923); Der letzte Mann (The Last Laugh) (1924); Herr Tartüff / Tartüff (1925); Faust (1926); Sunrise: A Song of Two Humans (1927); *Four Devils (1928); City Girl (1930); Tabu (1931)

BIBLIOGRAPHY

Eisner, Lotte (1969), *The Haunted Screen*.
—— (1973), *Murnau*.
Göttler, Fritz, et al. (1990), *Friedrich Wilhelm Murnau*.
Rohmer, Eric (1977), *L'Organisation de l'espace dans le 'Faust' de Murnau*.

Opposite: Faust (1926)

Another group to interest themselves ideologically in the cinema were professional pedagogues, lawyers, doctors, and the clergy of both Protestant and Catholic denominations. As early as 1907 they promoted debates about the dangers of the cinema for youth, work-discipline, morals, and public order, the so-called 'anti-dirt-and-smut campaign'. The aim was not to ban the cinema, but to promote 'cultural' films, that is, educational and documentary cinema, as opposed to fictional film narratives.

POST-WAR FERMENT

After the war, the strict Wilhelmine censorship was abolished, but, given the climate of revolutionary ferment and sexual licence, the industry soon found itself under fire once more, and film-makers had few friends who defended their freedom of expression when parliament reimposed partial censorship in May 1920: even Bertolt Brecht thought that the 'capitalist smut-merchants' had to be taught a lesson. What caused more serious divisions inside the film industry were the local entertainment taxes levied on cinemas and depressing their economic viability. At the same time, legislation adopted to protect national producers from Hollywood competition was as ingenious as it was ultimately ineffectual: if import restrictions and quota regulations (the so-called *Kontingentsystem*) helped boost production of 'quota-quickies', they also not only hurt distributors wanting American films for their audiences, but aggravated the glut of films generally. In other respects, too, politicians wielded only a blunt instrument: although the government occasionally banned uncomfortable films on the grounds that their showing might threaten public order (as happened in Berlin in the case of *Battleship Potemkin*, 1925, and *All Quiet on the Western Front*, 1930), it could do little to foster a prosperous and united national film business, since import restrictions and the entertainment tax invariably played one section of film industry (the producers) off against another (the exhibitors).

There is, then, a Weimar intellectual legacy which, although hostile to German films, none the less helped to foster an informed, discriminating, and heavily politicized film culture, implied in the term 'Weimar cinema'. Although the film business was ideologically and economically embattled, it was also a political fact, not only because it appealed to the government for assistance, but because both the intellectual-liberal and the anti-democratic forces took the cinema seriously.

The organized radical left was, throughout most of the decade, almost uniformly hostile towards the cinema, lambasting Ufa for poisoning the minds of the masses with reactionary celebrations of Prussia's glory (e.g. *Die Tänzerin Barberina* ('The dancer Barberina') by Carl Boese,

Robert Herlth

(1893–1962)

Robert Herlth, the son of a brewer, studied painting in Berlin before the First World War. Drafted into the army in 1914, he was befriended by the painter and set designer Hermann Warm, who helped him spend the last two years of the war at the army theatre in Wilna and away from the front.

After the war, Warm became head of the art department at Erich Pommer's Decla-Bioscop, and in 1920 he invited Herlth to join his team. Together with Walter Reimann and Walter Röhrig, Warm had just created the 'expressionist' décors of *Das Cabinett des Dr Caligari* (1919). When working on F. W. Murnau's *Schloss Vogelöd* (1921) and the Chinese episode of Fritz Lang's *Destiny* (*Der müde Tod*, 1921), Herlth was introduced to Röhrig, and the two were to form a team lasting nearly fifteen years, mainly at the Decla-Bioscop studios that were expanded by Ufa into the most important production centre in Europe.

This was the time when, under the guidance of producer Erich Pommer, teams of set designers and cinematographers laid the foundations on which the glory of Weimar cinema was based.

The oppressive, dark, medieval interiors for Pabst's *Der Schatz* (1922-3) were among the first collaborations of Herlth and Röhrig, who went on to design three films that form the peak of German film-making in the 1920s: Murnau's *The Last Laugh* (*Der letzte Mann*, 1924), *Tartüff* (1925), and *Faust* (1926). They were involved with the productions from the early planning stages with Murnau, 'Film-Dichter' Carl Mayer, and cinematographer Karl Freund. Together they created the concept of the 'camera unbound' (*entfesselte Kamera*) and cinematic mixture of actors, lighting, and décor that is typical of these films. Léon Barsacq (1976) writes: 'The sets are reduced to the essential, sometimes to a ceiling and a mirror. In his initial sketches Herlth, influenced by Murnau, began by roughing in characters as they were positioned in a particular scene; then the volume of the set seemed to create itself. Thus interiors became simpler and simpler, barer and barer. Despite the simplification, all the tricks of set design and camera movements were utilized, and sometimes invented, for this film [*The Last Laugh*]. Scale models on top of actual buildings made it possible to give a vertiginous height to the façade of the Grand Hotel.'

Towards the end of the silent period Herlth and Röhrig joined forces for one of Ufa's best films, Joe May's *Asphalt* (1928). They built a Berlin street crossing complete with shops, cars, and buses, using the former Zeppelin hangar-turned-film-studio at Staaken. After the introduction of sound they stayed with the Pommer team at Ufa, working with some of his young talents such as Robert Siodmak and Anatole Litvak and also creating the lavish period sets for the opulent and very successful

145

multilingual versions of operettas such as Erik Charell's *Der Kongress tanzt* (1931) and Ludwig Berger's *Walzerkrieg* (1933).

In 1929 they started a collaboration with the director Gustav Ucicky which afforded them a smooth transition into the Ufa of the Nazi period. Ucicky, a former cinematographer and reliable craftsman, specialized in entertainment with a nationalistic touch, and Herlth and Röhrig were able to avoid the hard propaganda films by working on popular entertainment. In 1935 they designed the Greek temples for Reinhold Schünzel's satirical comedy *Amphitryon* (1935), which mocked the pseudo-classical architecture of Albert Speer's Nazi buildings. Michael Esser describes their concept: 'Set design doesn't create copies of real buildings; it brings found details into a new context. Their relation to the originals is a distancing one, often even an ironic one.'

In 1935 Herlth and Röhrig wrote, designed, and directed the fairy-tale *Hans im Glück*. Shortly afterwards the collaboration ended.

After constructing the technical buildings for Leni Riefenstahl's *Olympia* (1938), Herlth (whose wife was Jewish) worked for Tobis, then Terra, designing mainly entertainment films. His first production in colour was Bolvary's operetta *Die Fledermaus*, which was shot in winter 1944–5 and released after the war by DEFA.

After the war Herlth first worked as stage designer for theatres in Berlin. In 1947 he designed the ruins of a Grand Hotel for Harald Braun's *Zwischen gestern und morgen* (1947). Throughout the 1950s he was again mainly involved with entertainment films made by the better directors of the period such as Rolf Hansen and Kurt Hoffman. For one of his last big productions, Alfred Weidenmann's two-part adaptation of Thomas Mann's *Die Buddenbrooks* (1959) (designed in collaboration with his younger brother Kurt Herlth and Arno Richter) Robert Herlth was awarded a 'Deutscher Filmpreis'.

HANS-MICHAEL BOCK

SELECT FILMOGRAPHY

Der Schatz (1923); The Last Laugh (Der letzte Mann) (1924); Tartüff (1925); Faust (1926); Asphalt (1928); The Congress Dances (Der Kongress tanzt) (1931); Amphitryon (1935); Hans im glück (1936); Olympia (1938); Kleider machen Leute (1940); Die Fledermaus (1945); Die Buddenbrooks (1959)

BIBLIOGRAPHY

Barsacq, Léon (1976), *Caligari's Cabinet and Other Grand Illusions*.
Herlth, Robert (1979), 'Dreharben mit Murnau'.
Längsfeld, Wolfgang (ed.) (1965), *Filmarchitektur Robert Herlth*.

Opposite: Set design by Robert Herlth for the Ufa production *Amphitryon* (1935), directed by Reinhold Schünzel

1921 and *Fredericus Rex* by Arzen von Czerepy, 1922), while chiding the masses for preferring such films to party meetings and street demonstrations. Only after the successful screening of the so-called 'Russenfilme' in 1925 did Willi Münzenberg, the left's most gifted propagandist, find support for his slogan 'Conquer the Cinemas', the title of a pamphlet in which he argued that films were 'one of the most effective means of political agitation, not to be left solely in the hands of the political enemy'. Münzenberg's International Workers' Aid set up a distribution company, Prometheus, to import Russian film and also finance its own productions. Apart from documentaries, Prometheus made features such as the comedy *Überflüssige Menschen* ('Superfluous men', 1926) by the Soviet director Alexander Razumny, and Piel Jutzi's proletarian melodrama *Mutter Krauses Fahrt ins Glück* ('Mother Krause's journey to fortune', 1929). Not to be outdone by the Communists, the Social Democrats also financed feature films, among them Werner Hochbaum's *Brüder* ('Brothers', 1929) and several documentaries dealing with housing problems, anti-abortion legislation, and urban crime. Earlier, the trade unions had sponsored *Die Schmiede* by Martin Berger ('The forge', 1924), who also made *Freies Volk* ('Free people'), in 1925 and *Kreuzzug des Weibes* ('Woman's crusade'), in 1926. However, Prometheus' best-known film was *Kuhle Wampe* (1932), directed by Slatan Dudow from a script by Bertolt Brecht, which opens with the suicide of an unemployed adolescent, and follows the fortunes of a young working-class couple as they try to find jobs and a home in order to found a family, finally realizing that only when marching with their fellow workers can they change the world, and thus improve their own fate.

Very rarely did films with a party-political affiliation succeed in providing what critics missed in almost all Ufa productions: 'realism', and a commitment to topics taken from everyday life. Such a demand, comprehensible from a critical establishment still under the impact of literary naturalism, was none the less not always compatible with the export objectives pursued by Pommer. Abroad, the reality of Germany was still too much associated with the World War for subjects with a contemporary setting to appeal to international audiences. While before 1918 the German cinema extensively utilized locations, realistic décor, and contemporary themes, after the war it was mainly productions intended for the domestic market (comedies, social dramas, or Harry Piel adventure films) which resorted to realist settings. Most of the prestige productions that later became associated with the realism known as 'Neue Sachlichkeit', whether those by G. W. Pabst (*Joyless Street* (*Die freudlose Gasse*), 1925; *Die Liebe der Jeanne Ney* ('The love of Jeanne Ney'), 1927; *Pandora's Box*) or Joe May (*Asphalt*), remained, until the coming of sound, wedded to the Ufa studio look, regardless of the period in which the action was set.

THE END OF WEIMAR CINEMA

In the United States, by contrast, the complaint against German films was the absence of strong plots, clear conflicts, but, above all, the absence of stars. The star system has always been fundamental for international film-making, partly because the qualities and connotations of a star transcend national boundaries in a way that setting and subject-matter often do not. One of the problems Ufa encountered in this respect was that, as soon as it developed stars, they tended to be wooed to Hollywood, following the example of Lubitsch's first international discovery, Pola Negri. The only truly international star in the 1920s who also worked in Germany was Emil Jannings, and he was indeed a commanding presence in a disproportionate number of Germany's American successes: *Madame Dubarry*, *Variete*, *The Last Laugh*, *The Blue Angel*. Attempts to launch international stars by importing American actresses in the latter part of the 1920s were only intermittently successful. Louise Brooks never became popular in the 1920s, Anna May Wong (directed by E. A. Dupont and Richard Eichberg) failed to catch the attention of American audiences, nor did Betty Amann—Pommer's American 'discovery' for May's *Asphalt*—develop her star potential. The cast of Murnau's *Faust* (1926, with Emil Jannings, Yvette Guilbert, Gösta Ekman) was deliberately international, but the fact that Camilla Horn was given the role of Gretchen, originally offered to Lillian Gish (to echo her success in Griffith's *Way down East*, 1920, and *Broken Blossoms*, 1919), did not help these transatlantic ambitions. It is even more remarkable that none of Fritz Lang's leading men or women (including Brigitte Helm) ever became an international star. When he and Pommer visited Hollywood, Lang was apparently irritated by Douglas Fairbanks insisting that what mattered in American picture-making was the performer, not the set, nor the originality of the subject. Only with the coming of sound—and when importing an American director like Josef von Sternberg—did Ufa develop successful stars, such as Marlene Dietrich, Hans Albers, Lilian Harvey, Willy Fritsch, or Marika Rökk, all of them closely modelled on American stars of the early 1930s.

By that time, the fortunes of the German cinema as a national and international cinema had become even more closely allied to the fate of Ufa. Following severe losses in 1926 and 1927, the company's major creditor, Deutsche Bank, was prepared to force Ufa into receivership, unless new outside capital could be found. Alfred Hugenberg, thwarted in his ambitions when Ufa was first set up in 1917, seized his chance and acquired majority holdings. His new director, Ludwig Klitzsch, set about restructuring the company, following the Hollywood studio system. He introduced American management principles, separating the finance department from production, reorganizing

distribution, and hiving off some of the subsidiary companies. Klitzsch thus brought to Ufa the central producer system, overseen by Ernst Hugo Correll, who divided production up between different heads of production (*Produktionsleiter* such as Günther Stapenhorst, Bruno Duday, and Erich Pommer), thereby achieving both greater central control and greater division of labour. If the Hugenberg take-over sealed the fate of Ufa ideologically, as most commentators have argued, it is equally true that, from a business perspective, it was thanks to Klitzsch that for the first time Ufa was run along strictly commercial lines.

The Klitzsch regime allowed Ufa, with remarkable speed, to catch up with the major international developments, such as the introduction of sound, which the previous management had been very slow to take an interest in. Ufa converted to sound production within little more than a year, while the company was also able to avoid costly competition by agreeing terms with its major domestic rival, Tobis Klangfilm. From 1930–1 onwards, Ufa once more began to show profit, not least because it proved a successful exporter, aggressively marketing its foreign-language versions in France and Great Britain, in addition to exploiting its gramophone and sheet music interest. However, it was not with its star directors of the 1920s that Ufa achieved financial recovery: Murnau had left for Hollywood early in 1927, Lang and Pabst were working for Seymour Nebenzahl's Nero Film, while Dupont was working in Britain, as was Carl Mayer, who after following Murnau to Hollywood had settled in London in 1931. Efficient genre directors such as Karl Hartl, Gustav Ucicky, and above all Hanns Schwarz put Ufa back in the black, the latter with six films, among them some of the biggest box-office successes until then: *Bomben auf Monte Carlo* ('Bombs on Monte Carlo', 1931), *Einbrecher* ('Burglar', 1930), *Ungarische Rhapsodie* ('Hungarian rhapsody', 1928), and *Die wunderbare Lüge der Nina Petrowna* ('Nina Petrowna's wonderful lie', 1929).

Musicals and comedies became the mainstay of the internationally minded German cinema, with super-productions like *Der Kongress tanzt* ('The Congress Dances', 1931), star vehicles like *Die Drei von der Tankstelle* ('Three from the petrol station', 1930), screwball comedies like *Viktor und Viktoria* (1933), and domestic melodramas like *Abschied* ('Departure') conveying quite a different image of the German cinema from that of the 1920s. Even before the Nazi take-over in 1933 the transformations of the German film industry from a twin-track 'artistic film'/prestige production cinema to a mainstream entertainment cinema were well under way, forced by economic necessity and technological change even more than by political interference. While the migration of personnel to Hollywood, begun with Ernst Lubitsch in 1921 and followed by Murnau, Dupont, and

Leni, had also gathered pace by 1927–8, its motives were, at least until 1933, personal and professional as much as political.

The German cinema on the eve of Hitler's rise to power confronts one with a paradox: the narrative which attributes the rise of this cinema to the flourishing of talent in the creative ferment of the Weimar Republic must perforce see its cinema enter into decline, as the Republic disintegrates under the blows of the nationalist and Fascist right. The evidence, however, does not bear this out, since if decline there was, it was due to the drain of talent away to the richer pastures of Hollywood. If, on the other hand, one takes economic performance as an indicator of success, it was only during the political upheavals of the Republic's final years that the German film industry matured into a financially viable business. Elsewhere in Europe, too, the days of an innovative art cinema were strictly limited; what is remarkable about the German cinema is how long these days lasted right at the heart of a commercial enterprise, which by its very nature should not have been able to afford them at all.

Bibliography

Bock, Hans-Michael, and Töteberg, Michael, (eds.) (1992), *Das Ufa-Buch.*

Cherchi Usai, Paolo, and Codelli, Lorenzo (eds.) (1990), *Before Caligari.*

Eisner, Lotte (1969), *The Haunted Screen.*

Jacobsen, Wolfgang (1989), *Erich Pommer.*

——, Kaes, Anton, and Prinzler, Hans Helmut (eds.) (1993), *Geschichte des deutschen Films.*

Kracauer, Siegfried (1947), *From Caligari to Hitler.*

Kreimeier, Klaus (1992), *Die Ufa-Story.*

Lamprecht, Gerhard (1976–80), *Deutsche Stummfilme, 1903–1931.*

Murray, Bruce (1990), *Film and the German Left.*

Petley, Julian (1979), *Capital and Culture.*

Petro, Patrice (1989), *Joyless Streets.*

Plummer, T., *et al.* (1982), *Film and Politics in the Weimar Republic.*

Rentschler, Eric (ed.) (1986), *German Film and Literature.*

The Scandinavian Style

PAOLO CHERCHI USAI

For a brief period after 1910, the countries of Scandinavia, despite their low population (less than 2.5 million in Denmark in 1901; around 5 million in Sweden in 1900) and their marginal place in the western economic system, played a major role in the early evolution of cinema, both as an art and as an industry. Their influence was concentrated into two phases: the first centred on Denmark in the four-year period 1910–13, which saw the international success of the production company Nordisk Film Kompagni; and the second on Sweden between 1917 and 1923. And, far from consisting of an isolated blossoming of local culture, Scandinavian silent cinema was extensively integrated into a wider European context. For at least ten years the aesthetic identity of Danish and Swedish films was intimately related to that of Russian and German cinema, each evolving in symbiotic relation to the others, linked by complementary distribution strategies and exchanges of directors and technical expertise. Within this network of co-operation only a marginal role was played by the other northern European nations. Finland, which did have a linguistically independent cinema, remained largely an adjunct of tsarist Russia until 1917. Iceland—part of Denmark until 1918—only saw its first film theatre opened in 1906, by the future director Alfred Lind. And Norway produced only seventeen fiction titles, from its first film *Fiskerlivets farer: et drama på havet* ('The perils of fishing: a drama of the sea', 1908) until 1918.

ORIGINS

The first display of moving pictures in Scandinavia took place in Norway on 6 April 1896 at the Variété Club in Oslo (or Christiania as it was then called) and was organized by two pioneers of German cinema, the brothers Max and Emil Skladanowsky. Such was the success of their show, and of their Bioskop projection equipment, that they stayed on until 5 May. In Denmark, the earliest documented moving picture show was put on by the painter Vilhelm Pacht, who installed a Lumière Cinématographe in the wooden pavilion of the Raadhusplasen in Copenhagen on 7 June 1896. The equipment and the pavilion were both destroyed in a fire started by a recently sacked electrician out for revenge, but the show was relaunched on 30 June to a fanfare of publicity. Even the royal family had visited Pacht's Kinopticon on 11 June.

The arrival of cinema in Finland followed a few weeks on from its first appearance in St Petersburg on 16 May. Although the Lumière Cinématographe remained in the Helsinki town hall for only eight days after opening on 28 June, owing to the high prices of seats and the relatively small size of the city, the photographer Karl Emil

A scene from *Häxan* (*Witchcraft through the Ages*), made in Sweden in 1921 by the Danish director Benjamin Christensen

Ståhlberg was inspired to take action. He took on the distribution of Lumière films from January 1897, and outside Helsinki the 'living pictures' were made available through the exhibitor Oskar Alonen. In 1904, Ståhlberg set up in Helsinki the first permanent cinema in Finland, the Maailman Ympäri ('Around the world'). In the same year were produced the first 'real-life' sequences, but it is not clear whether or not Ståhlberg was also responsible for these.

On 28 June 1896 the Industrial Exhibition at the Summer Palace in Malmö hosted the first projection in Sweden, again with Lumière material, organized by the Danish showman Harald Limkilde. The Cinématographe spread north a few weeks afterwards, when a correspondent of the Parisian daily *Le Soir*, Charles Marcel, presented films with the Edison Kinetoscope on 21 July at the Victoria Theatre, Stockholm, in the Glace Palace of the Djurgården. They were not a great success, however, and the Edison films were soon supplanted by the Skladanowsky brothers, who shot some sequences at Djurgården itself: these were the first moving pictures to be shot in Sweden.

FINLAND

The first Finnish film company, Pohjola, began distributing films in 1899 under the direction of a circus impresario, J. A. W. Grönroos. The first location officially designated for the projection of films was the Kinematograf International, opened at the end of 1901. But, like the two other cinemas which opened shortly afterwards, it survived for only a few weeks, and it was not until Karl Emil Ståhlberg's initiative in 1904 that film theatres were definitively established on a permanent basis. In 1911 there were 17 cinemas in Helsinki, and 81 in the rest of the country. By 1921, the figures had risen to 20 and 118 respectively.

The first Finnish fiction film, *Salaviinanpolttajat* ('Bootleggers'), was directed in 1907 by the Swede Louis Sparre assisted by Teuvo Puro, an actor with Finland's National Theatre, for the production company Atelier Apollo, run by Ståhlberg. In the following ten years, Finland produced another 27 fiction films and 312 documentary shorts, as well as two publicity films. Ståhlberg's near monopoly on production—between 1906 and 1913 he distributed 110 shorts, around half the entire national production—was short-lived. Already in 1907 the Swede David Fernander and the Norwegian Rasmus Hallseth had founded the Pohjoismaiden Biografi Komppania, which produced forty-seven shorts in little more than a decade. The Swedish cameraman on *Salaviinanpolttajat*, Frans Engström, split with Ståhlberg and set up—with little success—his own production company with the two protagonists of the film, Teuvo Puro and Teppo Raikas. An extant fragment of *Sylvi* (1913), directed by Puro, constitutes the earliest example of Finnish fiction film preserved today. Greater success awaited Erik Estlander, who founded Finlandia Filmi (forty-nine films between 1912 and 1916, including some shorts shot in the extreme north of the country), and the most important figure of the time, Hjalmar V. Pohjanheimo, who from 1910 onwards began to acquire several film halls, and soon turned to production. The films distributed by Pohjanheimo under the aegis of Lyyra Filmi were documentaries (1911), newsreels (from 1914), and comic and dramatic narratives, made with the help of his sons Adolf, Hilarius, Asser, and Berger, and the theatrical director Kaarle Halme.

The First World War brought the intervention of the Russian authorities, who in 1916 banned all cinematographic activity. The ban lapsed after the Revolution of February 1917 and was definitively removed in December when Finland declared its independence. The post-war period was dominated by a production company founded by Puro and the actor Erkki Karu, Suomi Filmi. Its first important feature-length film was *Anna-Liisa* (Teuvo Puro and Jussi Snellman, 1922), taken from a work by Minna Canth and influenced by Tolstoy's *The Power of Darkness* (1886): a young girl who has killed her child is overwhelmed by remorse and confesses to expiate her crime. The actor Konrad Tallroth, who had already been active in Finland before the war but had then emigrated to Sweden following the banning of the film *Eräs elämän murhenäytelmä* ('The tragedy of a life'), was taken on in 1922 by Suomi for *Rakkauden kaikkivalta—Amor Omnia* ('Love conquers all'), an uneven and isolated attempt to adapt Finnish cinema to the mainstream features emerging from western Europe and the United States. Production in the following years was limited in quantity, and tended to return to traditional themes of everyday life, in the line of contemporary Swedish narrative and stylistic models. Judging by accounts written at the time, only the documentary *Finlandia* (Erkki Karu and Eero Leväluoma/ Suomi Filmi, 1922) achieved a certain success abroad. Around eighty silent feature films were produced in Finland up to 1933. About forty fiction films, including shorts, are conserved at the Suomen Elokuva-Arkisto in Helsinki.

NORWAY

The first Norwegian film company of any significance was Christiania Film Co. A/S, set up in 1916. Before then, national production—represented by Norsk Kinematograf A/S, Internationalt Film Kompagni A/S, Nora Film Co. A/S, and Gladtvet Film—had been in an embryonic stage. Fewer than ten fiction films had been produced between 1908 and 1913, and no record exists of important productions for the two following years.

For the entire period of silent cinema, Norway boasted no studio to speak of, and thus the affirmation of a 'national style' particular to it derived in large part from the exploitation of the Nordic landscape. The first sign of the end of a semi-amateur phase in production came in 1920 with the appearance of two films: *Kaksen på Øverland* ('The braggarts of Overland'), directed by G. A. Olsen, and *Fante-Anne* ('The lady-tramp'), acted by Asta Nielsen and directed by Rasmus Breistein. The following year saw the first important adaptation of a work by Knut Hamsun, *Markens grøde* ('The growth of the soil', Gunnar Sommerfeldt, 1921), but, significantly, the film was directed by a Dane and photographed by a Finn, George Schnéevoigt, who was resident in Denmark at the time and who had been the cameraman for Carl Theodor Dreyer's *Pränkästan* (*The Parson's Widow*, 1920), filmed in Norway for Svenska Biografteater. Another film—*Pan* (Harald Schwenzen, 1922), produced by the newly formed Kommunernes Films-Central—was also taken from a work by Hamsun.

After an interval of a year, the first film to be considered at the time as worthy of an international audience appeared: *Till Sæters* ('In the mountains', 1924), the first film directed by the journalist Harry Ivarson. *Den nye lensmanden* ('The new commissar', Leif Sinding, 1926), produced by a new company, Svalefilm, achieved equal acclaim. The brief flourishing of Norwegian silent cinema reached its peak with *Troll-elgen* ('The magic leap', Walter Fürst, 1927), a grandiose natural fresco whose worth is in part due to the photography of the Swede Ragnar Westfelt, and with *Laila* (1929), dedicated to the Lapps in the north of the country. Even here however, it is worth noting the foreign input, from the Finno-Danish director Schnéevoigt to the acting of the Swedish Mona Mårtenson and the Danish Peter Malberg.

The somewhat limited extent of Norwegian silent cinema is today represented by about thirty titles available at the Norsk Filminstitutt, Oslo.

DENMARK

On 17 September 1904 Constantin Philipsen opened the first permanent film exhibition hall in Copenhagen. Danish fiction film production had already got under way a year earlier when the photographer to the royal family, Peter Elfelt, had made *Henrettelsen* ('The execution'), which still survives today. In 1906 an exhibitor, Ole Olsen, set up the Nordisk Film Kompagni, which was to play a fundamental role in Danish cinema throughout the silent period, and indeed in international cinema for a good part of the 1910s. By 1910, Nordisk was considered the world's second largest production company after Pathé; its first studio, built by the company in 1906, is the oldest surviving film studio in the world. Most of the fiction films of the early period were directed by ex-staff sergeant Viggo Larsen, and shot by Axel Sørensen (renamed Axel Graatkjær after 1911). Of the 248 fiction films produced between 1903 and 1910, 242 were made by Nordisk. Only after 1909 did other companies extend the panorama of Danish cinema: Biorama of Copenhagen and Fotorama of Aarhus, both founded in 1909; and Kinografen in 1910.

In 1910 a Fotorama film called *Den hvide slavehandel* ('The white slave trade') marked a turning-point in the evolution of fiction films not only in Scandinavia but throughout the world. The film dealt with the theme of prostitution in previously unheard of explicit terms, and thereby inaugurated a new genre—the 'sensational' film, set in the world of crime, vice, or the circus. On the basis of the success of the Éclair film *Nick Carter, le roi des détectives* ('Nick Carter, King of the detectives', Victorin Jasset, 1908), Nordisk began a series in 1910 whose protagonist was a brilliant criminal, Dr Gar el Hama: Eduard Schnedler-Sørensen directed both *Dødsflugten* (UK title: *The Flight from Death*; US title: *The Nihilist Conspiracy*, 1911) and *Dr. Gar el Hama II | Dr. Gar el Hama Flugt* (*Dr. Gar el Hama: Sequel to A Dead Man's Child*, 1912), and to some extent these films inspired the most famous films of criminal exploits, made in France by Jasset (*Zigomar*, 1911) and later by Louis Feuillade (*Fantômas*, 1913).

One important consequence of the move towards 'sensational' drama was the development of new techniques in lighting, in camera-positioning and in set design. The case of *Den sorte drøm* ('The black dream'), by Urban Gad (Fotorama, 1911), is particularly noteworthy in this regard. For the high anxiety of the most intense scenes, the reflectors were taken down from their usual stands and laid on the ground, so that the actors threw long, dark shadows on to the walls. The use of a hand-held lantern, clutched by the protagonists as they struggled forward in the dark, was deployed to great effect after 1914, in *Gar el Hama III: Slangøn* (*The Abduction*, or *Dr. Gar el Hama's Escape From Prison*, 1914) by Robert Dinesen, and in *Verdens undergang* (*The Flaming Sword*, or *The End of the World*, 1916) by August

Blom. A variant on this effect was to have a character enter a dark room and turn on the light. The shooting was suspended and the actor blocked as the lamp in shot was about to be turned on; the scene was then lit as if by the lamp in question and shooting recommenced. Often the two segments of the shot were tinted in different colours, usually in blue for darkness and ochre for light. Another powerful effect, hardly seen outside Denmark before 1911, was the silhouette outline, shot from an interior with the lens pointing towards an open or half-open door, or a window. These ideas, which characterize two films directed by August Blom for Nordisk—*Ungdommens ret* (*The Right of Youth*, 1911) and *Exspeditricen* (*In the Prime of Life*, 1911)—are taken to an extreme in *Det hemmelighedsfulde X* (*Sealed Orders* or *Orders under Seal*, 1913), the first film by the greatest Danish director of the silent period besides Carl Theodor Dreyer, Benjamin Christensen (1879–1959). Christensen developed techniques and figures already used by the French director Léonce Perret in *L'Enfant de Paris* ('The child of Paris'), and *Le Roman d'un mousse* ('A midshipman's tale', Gaumont, 1913), and arrived at extraordinary results using silhouettes and half-lit images. His aggressive experimentalism reached its peak in the thriller *Hævnens nat* (*Blind Justice*, 1915).

Another frequent trick was to show a character who was out of range of the camera's field in a mirror: for example, in *Ved fængslets port* (*Temptations of a Great City*, 1911) by August Blom—starring the most famous male lead actor of the time, Valdemar Psilander—and in *For åbent Tæppe | Desdemona* (1911). In all probability, the mirror was used as an expedient to avoid the need for montages of several shots in a scene (since Danish directors seem not to have been keen on elaborate editing techniques), but nevertheless, its allusive and symbolic impact enriched the treatment of sexuality in films such as the frank and open *Afgrunden* by Urban Gad (*The Abyss*, Kosmorama, 1910), which saw the début of the greatest actress of Danish silent film, Asta Nielsen.

Early Danish film-makers paid relatively little attention to the narrative dynamic of their films: before 1914 tracking shots, flashbacks, and close-ups were very rarely used. They thus fell well short of the fluidity and naturalism typical of American cinema of the same period. However, the Danes had a profound and lasting influence on film production on an international scale. On a general level, their most significant contribution was in the development away from short-length narrative films to films of three, four, or even more reels—August Blom's *Atlantis* (Nordisk, 1913), with a huge budget, ran to 2,280 metres of film, excluding intertitles—and in the cultural legitimization of cinema, which was encouraged by the appearance of established actors and actresses from classical theatre.

On a more specific level, Danish cinema had an enormous impact on its neighbours. The first works by the Swedish directors Mauritz Stiller and Victor Sjöström, along with almost all Swedish films before 1916, bear the technical imprint of Denmark, and only in the following two years was an autonomous identity developed in Sweden. Danish films were also widely distributed in pre-revolutionary Russia, leading some companies to shoot alternative endings designed to satisfy the Russian taste for tragic denouements. Films shot in Russia in the earlier 1910s, and especially the first dramas by Yevgeny Bauer from 1913, display techniques of lighting (back- and multiple-lighting) and framing (doors and windows shot from within) which clearly derive from methods current in Danish cinema.

The most lucrative foreign market for Nordisk was Germany—at least until 1917, when the German government took control of the national film industry. Profits were so high that the company could invest in a huge chain of cinemas. The close relationship between Danish and German cinema in the 1910s and 1920s becomes apparent if one compares the 'sensational' themes (criminal geniuses, white slave trade, extreme passions)

and the markedly expressionist camera techniques (oblique shots, half-light effects) of pre-1914 Danish dramas with the work of German directors such as Joe May, Otto Rippert, and early Fritz Lang. Vilhelm Glückstadt, whose extraordinary work as a director has remained almost unexplored to this day, was the author of three films which reveal profound affinities with the expressionist aesthetic: *Den fremmede* ('The benefactor', 1914); *Det gamle spil om enhver / Enhver* ('Anyone', 1915), a complex tangle of flashbacks, parallel story-lines, and strongly metaphorical imagery; and the impassioned *Kornspekulanten* ('The wheat speculators', 1916), whose attribution to Glückstadt is not entirely certain, but which looks forwards to Carl Theodor Dreyer's *Vampyr* (1932).

Dreyer is a towering figure in the pantheon of Danish cinema. His work represents the most complete synthesis of its expressionist tendencies with its meticulous figurative sobriety. His interest in psychology and in the conflicts between the unconscious and the rational elements in human actions was already apparent in his first film *Præsidenten* (*The President*, 1919), and in the episode film *Blade af Satans bog* (*Leaves from Satan's book*, 1921), and

Karin Molander as the reporter in Mauritz Stiller's brilliant comedy *Kärlek och journalistik* ('Love and journalism', 1916)

Victor Sjöström

(1879–1960)

In 1880 Sjöström's parents—a lumber merchant and a former actress—emigrated from Sweden to the United States, taking their seven-month-old baby Victor with them. But the mother soon died, and the son, to escape an unwelcome stepmother and an increasingly authoritarian father, returned to Sweden, where he was brought up by his uncle Victor, an actor at the Royal Dramatic Theatre in Stockholm. Fired by enthusiasm for the stage, the young Victor also became an actor, and at the age of 20 was already renowned for his sensitive performances and powerful stage presence.

In 1911 Charles Magnusson was busily reorganizing the Svenska Biografteatern film studio, where he was head of production, aiming to give cinema more cultural legitimacy by bringing in leading technical and artistic personnel from the best theatre companies in Sweden. He hired the brilliant cameraman Julius Jaenzon (later to be responsible for the distinctive look of many of Sjöström's most famous Swedish films), then in 1912 Mauritz Stiller and, shortly afterwards, Victor Sjöström. Sjöström was by then running his own theatre company in Malmö, but he eagerly accepted Magnusson's offer, driven (he wrote later) 'by a youthful desire for adventure and a curiosity to try this new medium of which then I did not have the slightest knowledge'.

After acting in a couple of films directed by Stiller, Sjöström turned to direction, making his mark with the crisp realism applied to the controversial social drama *Ingeborg Holm* (1913). But it was with *Terje Vigen* in 1917 that his creativity came into full flower. The film shows a profound feeling for the Swedish landscape of his maternal origins and achieves an intimate correspondence between natural events and the inner and interpersonal conflicts of the characters. This symbiosis of inner and outer is even more prominent in *Berg-Ejvind och hans hustru* (*The Outlaw and his Wife*, 1918), the tragedy of a couple seeking refuge—but finding death—in the mountains, in a vain attempt to escape an unjust and oppressive society. 'Human love', said Sjöström, 'is the only answer to fling in the face of a cruel nature.'

Partly out of her admiration for Sjöström's films, the novelist Selma Lagerlöf had granted all her film rights to Svenska Bio. Sjöström found in her work the ideal expression of the active role played by nature in the destiny of characters torn between good and evil. In his adaptation of *The Sons of Ingmar* (*Ingmarssönerna*, 1919) this vision finds expression in a family saga of monumental scope. But it is at its most intense in *The Phantom Carriage* (*Körkarlen*, 1921), a drama of the supernatural with a complex structure of interlaced flashbacks, set on a New Year's Eve dominated by remorse and a desperate search for redemption.

Swedish cinema had profited from the country's neutrality during the First World War to make an impact on the European market and to challenge American supremacy. But after the war it lost its precarious privileged position. With the industry in crisis, both Stiller and Sjöström accepted offers to go to Hollywood. Sjöström arrived there in 1923, with a contract from Goldwyn and his name changed to Seastrom. After some

difficulty settling in, he scored a success with *He Who Gets Slapped* (1924), in which he applied his merciless analysis of character to the melodramatic masochism of the Lon Chaney character—a scientist who decides to become a clown after a false friend has gone off not only with his wife but with his most important research discovery.

Triumphant in Hollywood, Sjöström made *The Divine Woman* (1928) with his even more famous compatriot, Greta Garbo. But more important and characteristic were two films with Lillian Gish, *The Scarlet Letter* (1927) and *The Wind* (released in 1928). The former is a free adaptation of Hawthorne's novel in which he was able to develop the theme of intolerance and social isolation explored in *Berg-Ejvind*. Then, in *The Wind* he achieved the ultimate tragic fusion of the violence of the elements and of human passions in a story set in an isolated cabin in the midst of a windswept desert.

A high point of the silent aesthetic, *The Wind* was distributed in a synchronized version, allegedly with the ending changed. Shortly after its release, Sjöström returned to Sweden. Although, in a letter to Lillian Gish, he later referred to his time in the United States as 'perhaps the happiest days of my life', it is possible that he felt apprehensive about his future role in Hollywood after the coming of sound. After making one more film in Sweden and one in England, he went back to his former career as an actor and in the 1940s became 'artistic adviser' to Svensk Filmindustri. He acted in nineteen films—by Gustaf Molander, Arne Mattsson, and (most notably) Ingmar Bergman, his protégés at Svensk Filmindustri; his final role was in Bergman's *Wild Strawberries* (1957), a film which can be seen as a moving autobiographical reflection of Sjöström's ideas on dreams and on the failings of mankind, and an expression of his wonderment in face of the role of nature in shaping human feeling.
                                              PAOLO CHERCHI USAI

SELECT FILMOGRAPHY

Trädgårdsmästeren (The Gardener) (1912); Ingeborg Holm (1913); Judaspengar (Judas Money / Traitor's Reward) (1915); Terje Vigen (A Man there Was) (1917); Tösen från Stormyrtorpet (The Girl from Stormy Croft / The Woman He Chose) (1917); Berg-Ejvind och hans hustru (The Outlaw and his Wife) (1918); Ingmarssönerna I-II (The Sons of Ingmar) (1919); Klostret i Sendomir (The Monastery of Sendomir / The Secret of the Monastery) (1920); Mästerman (Master Samuel) (1920); Körkarlen (The Phantom Carriage / The Stroke of Midnight) (1921); Name the Man (1924); He Who Gets Slapped (1924); The Scarlet Letter (1927); The Divine Woman (1928); The Wind (1928); A Lady to Love / Die Sehnsucht jeder Frau (1930); Markurells i Wadköping (The Markurells of Wadköping) (1931); Under the Red Robe (1937)

BIBLIOGRAPHY

Forslund, Bengt (1980), *Victor Sjöström: His Life and Work*.
Jeanne, René and Ford, Charles (1963), *Victor Sjöström*.
Roud, Richard (ed.) (1980), *Cinema: A Critical Dictionary*.
Pense, Hans (1969), *Seastrom and Stiller in Hollywood*.

Opposite: Tösen från Stormyrtorpet (The Girl from Stormy Croft, 1917).

reached a new level of excellence in *Du skal ære din hustru* (*The Master of the House*), produced in 1925 by a new, fierce competitor of Nordisk, Palladium, run by Lau Lauritzen. Danish cinema went into gradual decline after the First World War, and Dreyer remained an isolated figure of genius in his home country. He was driven to continue his career abroad, in Norway, Sweden, Germany, and France. Danish cinema responded to its inexorable loss of influence by turning in on itself. In the early 1920s, in a last-ditch effort to stop the rot, Nordisk offered huge sums of money to the director Anders Wilhelm Sandberg to adapt a number of Dickens's novels, but the genuine success of the results in Denmark struggled to transfer abroad. A similar fate awaited the first Danish animation film, *De tre smaa mænd* ('Three little men', Robert Storm-Petersen and Carl Wieghorst, 1920), and experiments in sound cinema carried out by Axel Petersen and Arnold Poulsen after 1922. The only significant exception to the rule was the series of comedies 'Fyrtaanet og Bivognen' ('Long and short'), produced between 1921 and 1927 by Carl Schenstrøm and Harald Madsen. *Klovnen* ('Clowns', Anders Wilhelm Sandberg, 1926) was the last great drama film made by Nordisk to be distributed in America, but its success was not sufficient to prevent the virtually total eclipse of Denmark in the arena of the great producing nations.

Around 2,700 fiction and non-fiction titles were produced in Denmark between 1896 and 1930. Most of the films of which copies have survived (including about 400 fiction films) are to be found at Det Danske Filmmuseum in Copenhagen.

SWEDEN

The first entrepreneur to dedicate himself full-time to cinema in Sweden was Numa Peterson, a photographer who had begun his activity by showing Lumière films. In 1897 a Lumière agent, Georges Promio, taught an employee of Petersen's, Ernest Florman, how to film events live and how to stage short comic episodes. However, foreign companies remained the dominant force in the Swedish market until 1908, when an accountant who was also an amateur photographer, Charles Magnusson, was offered the chance to join Svenska Biografteatern, a company which had been formed at Kristianstad in February of the year before. He had some success with a series of films synchronized with gramophone recordings, and then moved on to dedicate his energies to productions which reflected the themes and personalities of Swedish theatre. He was assisted in his task by Gustaf 'Munk' Linden, the author of an ambitious and popular version of the historical drama *Regina von Emmeritz and King Gustaf II Adolf* (1910), and by the first female director in Scandinavia, Anna Hofman-Uddgren, who was given permission by August Strindberg to adapt his plays *Miss Julie* and *The Father* for the screen. Both appeared in 1912. The modest success of these films and the growing competition from Denmark induced the owners to transfer production to Stockholm, where a larger studio set could be built and where the chain of cinemas throughout Sweden could be better co-ordinated.

Magnusson demanded and was given absolute control over the move. He planned the new studios at Lidingö, near Kyrkviken, and acquired the support of a group of artists and technicians who were to define the course of silent cinema in Sweden: Julius Jaenzon, appointed chief cameraman and director of the studios at Lidingö; Georg af Klercker, head of production and director; Victor Sjöström, 'the best director on the market today' according to the magazine *Scenisk Konst*, 6–7 April 1912; and Mauritz Stiller, a Russian–Jewish theatre actor and director whose uneven stage career had led him back and forth between Sweden and Finland for many years. Magnusson himself directed a number of films between 1909 and 1912, but he soon settled into a role as producer-patron, offering his formidable intuition and energy in support of the most risky ideas put to him by his directors, but also ensuring the collaboration of high-calibre intellectuals, such as Selma Lagerlöf, whose novels were filmed by Stiller and Sjöström. In 1919 a new young financier, Ivan Kreuger, appeared on the scene and engineered the merger of Magnusson's company with its rival Film Scandia A/S to form a new company, Svenska Filmindustri. New studios were built, new cinemas were opened, and old ones restored. By 1920 Svenska Filmindustri had become a world power, with subsidiaries across the globe. The 'golden age' of Swedish cinema, stretching from 1916 to 1921, was in part due to Sweden's neutrality in the Great War. At a time when almost all the other great film industries in Europe (including that of Denmark) were threatened by embargoes and serious financial difficulties, Sweden continued to export films without hindrance, and, by the same token, took full advantage of the drastic reduction in imports. However, even these favourable conditions would have had little impact were it not for the creative contribution of a number of exceptionally talented directors.

The first in chronological order—before Stiller and Sjöström joined Svenska Biografteatern—was Georg af Klercker, whose films are characterized by an extreme figurative precision, a meticulous attention to acting, and by a restrained and rigorous reinterpretation of the canons of bourgeois drama, social realism, and the 'circus' genre, initiated in Denmark by Robert Dinesen and Alfred Lind with the seminal *De fire djævle* ('The four devils', Kinografen, 1911) and characterized by sentimental plots, spectacular clashes, and vendettas amongst riders and acrobats. After *Dödsritten under cirkuskupolen* (*The Last Performance*, 1912), the company's first international success, Klercker moved briefly to Denmark. He returned to Sweden on the invitation of a new company, F. V. Hasselblad Fotografiska AB of Göteborg, for whom he directed twenty-eight films between 1915 and 1917. One of the best was *Förstadsprästen* ('The suburban vicar', 1917), the story of a priest working to help society's rejects, filmed on location in the poor districts of Göteborg.

Mauritz Stiller (1883–1928) specialized in comedies with a carefully controlled pace and a subtle vein of social satire which verged on the burlesque, in which the construction and articulation of events took precedence over psychological analysis and description. Two typical examples of his style are provided by *Den moderna suffragetten* ('The modern suffragette', 1913) and *Kärlek och journalistik* ('Love and journalism', 1916). He moved on with *Thomas Graals bästa film* (*Wanted: A Film Actress*, 1917) and *Thomas Graals bästa barn* (*Marriage à la mode*, 1918) to a set of 'moral tales' marked by a disillusioned perspective on the precarious nature of relations between the sexes and on the inconstancy of passion. This tendency in Stiller's work reached a peak of cynicism and disrespect in *Erotikon* (*Just like a Man*; also known as *After We are Married* or *Bonds that Cheat*, 1920), but is offset at the turn of the decade by his growing penchant for treatments of themes such as ambition and guilt. *Herr Arnes pengar* (UK title: *Snows of Destiny*; US title *Sir Arne's Treasure*, 1919) and *Gösta Berlings saga* (UK title: *The Atonement of Gösta Berling*; US title: *The Legend of Gösta Berling*, 1923), both taken from novels by Selma Lagerlöf, elaborate such themes with a figurative intensity and epic energy which no director in Europe had thus far achieved. *Gösta Berlings saga* also introduced a talented young actress, Greta Garbo, whose inseparable companion and mentor Stiller was to become. Invited to Hollywood by Louis B. Mayer, Stiller insisted on bringing Garbo with him; but whereas their departure from Sweden was the first step in her meteoric rise to stardom, for Stiller it coincided with a creative crisis from which he never recovered.

With the departure to America of Sjöström (1923), Stiller and Garbo (1925), the actor Lars Hanson, and the Danish director Benjamin Christensen who had made his most ambitious film in Sweden, the perturbing documentary drama *Häxan* (*Witchcraft through the Ages*, 1921), Swedish cinema entered a phase of steep decline. Instead of deciding on a renewal of the themes and styles which had brought them such glory, directors of not negligible talent such as Gustaf Molander, John W. Brunius, and Gustaf Edgren were forced to ape their conventions in a wan attempt to adapt characteristics of their national cinema to the genres and narrative models of 1920s Hollywood. 'We can now say', wrote Ture Dahlin in 1931 in

L'Art cinématographique, 'that the great silent cinema of Sweden is dead, dead and buried.... It would take a genius to resurrect it from its present, routine state.'

The fiction films made in Sweden in the silent period are estimated to have been about 500 (including shorts synchronized with phonograph recordings). About 200 are at present preserved at the Svenska Filminstitutet in Stockholm.

Bibliography
Engberg, Marguerite (1977), *Dansk stumfilm*.
Film in Norway (1979).
Forslund, Bengt (1988), *Victor Sjöström: His Life and his Work*.
Schiave bianche allo specchio: le origini del cinema in Scandinavia (1896–1918), (1986).
Uusitalo, Kari (1975), 'Finnish Film Production (1904–1918)'.
Werner, Gösta (1970), *Den svenska filmens historia*.

Pre-Revolutionary Russia

YURI TSIVIAN

Original as it may seem in style and subject-matter, film production in Russia started as an offshoot of international trade. Because neither cameras nor film stock were manufactured in Russia in the 1910s, Russian production companies developed in a very different way from the major film companies in the west. Rather than being a corollary of the equipment industry, national film-making in Russia was actuated by importers (in the first place), distributors, and (in rare cases) theatre owners.

With the notable exception of the ex-photographer Alexander Drankov, the importer was the key to the first production companies in Russia. The importer was a go-between linking foreign film producers and local exhibitors; the more companies an importer was able to enlist, the more chances he had to launch his own production. Alexander Khanzhonkov's production company started as a small commission agency selling films and projection equipment manufactured by Théophile Pathé, Urban, Hepworth, Bioscope, and Itala Film. Companies like Gaumont (until 1909), Warwick, Ambrosio, Nordisk, and Vitagraph were represented by Pavel Thiemann, another powerful figure in the pre-revolutionary film industry. Because it took a lot of travelling between Russia and the exporting countries, the share of early American films on the Russian market was relatively small. Pathé-Frères preferred to send their own representatives engaged in equipment sales (from 1904), laboratory services, or production (1908–13). Gaumont followed Pathé's example, but on a more modest scale.

Around 1906–7, film theatres in Moscow and St Petersburg started renting used prints to the provinces, and the system of importers purchasing films from production companies to resell to exhibitors began to be replaced. Specialized distribution agencies in Moscow supplied prints to the city's theatres and regional agencies. Each regional agency controlled several provinces, known as their 'distribution district' (*prokatnyi rayon*), renting prints to local cinemas.

Incidentally or otherwise, the first home-produced films appeared when the distribution system was fully established on the Russian film market. Combining production with distribution in this way was the only hope of success for a film-producing company in Russia in the 1910s. A vertically semi-integrated system allowed Russian studios to invest the money they earned from distributing foreign films into native productions—a system that would be used, with variable success, by the stock-holding company Sovkino in the mid-1920s.

STRATEGIES

Two types of strategy—disruptive and competitive—were employed by studios competing for the Russian market. Disruption (*sryv*), was a notorious gimmick whereby a competitor's production was undermined by a cheaper (and sloppier) version of the same subject (story, title) released earlier or on the same day. Borrowed from the theatre entrepreneur F. Korsh (who used the method to rob competitors' first productions of their novelty value), disruption was systematically employed in the film industry by financially insecure companies like Drankov or Perski in order to tempt regional renting agencies with a low-price alternative to Khanzhonkov's or Pathé's hits. This policy achieved little beyond hectic production races and a pervasive atmosphere of paranoid secrecy. Distinct from disruption, a strategy of competition (developed by studios with solid financial backing: first Khanzhonkov, Pathé-Frères, Thiemann, and Reinhardt, later Yermoliev and Kharitonov) consisted of promoting the idea of 'quality pictures' and turning a recognizable studio style into a marketable value.

STYLE

In terms of style, Russian pre-revolutionary film-making falls into two periods, before and after 1913. From 1908 and the first Russian-made movie (Drankov's *Stenka Razin*) until 1913, the two main competitors were Khanzhonkov & Co. and Pathé-Frères. However, in 1913 all foreign production in Russia was curtailed, and the

Yevgeny Bauer

(1867–1917)

Regarded in Russia in the 1910s as his country's most important film-maker, only to be condemned as a 'decadent' by official Soviet histories, Yevgeny Frantsevich Bauer was internationally rediscovered in 1989 as a major director. His work was informed by Art Nouveau aesthetics and a Symbolist sensibility characteristic of the silver age of Russian culture as a whole.

Born on 20 January 1867, into the family of a well-known Austrian zither-player and his Russian wife, Bauer kept Austrian citizenship, but was baptized into the Orthodox religion.

Yevgeny Bauer attended (but never graduated from) the Moscow College of Painting, Sculpture, and Architecture, and became known as a set designer for operetta and farcical comedies at Charles Aumont's winter garden Aquarium in Moscow, Mikhail Lentovsky's vaudeville theatre, Hermitage, and the Theatre of Miniatures, Zon. During this time, he also occasionally performed as an amateur actor. In 1912 he was hired as a contract set designer for the Pathé Frères Moscow Department assisted by the future leading Soviet set designer Alexei Utkin. In 1913 he designed sets for Drankov and Taldykin's super-production *The Tercentenary of the Rule of the House of Romanov*, and later the same year began his career as a director at Pathé's and Drankov and Taldykin's studios.

Bauer's unique directorial achievements were singled out as early as 1913, as 'being above praise in their artistic taste and intuition—something rarely found in cinema'. When Bauer joined the Khanzhonkov company in January 1914, his fame was boosted by the company's trade press; however, despite attempts to rank him among the biggest names of contemporary theatre, Bauer's name remained largely unknown outside the circles of film fans and film-makers.

Of the eighty-two films firmly accredited to Bauer, twenty-six remain—enough to evaluate his original style in terms of set design, lighting, editing, and camera movement. Referring to the unusually spacious interiors in Bauer's films, contemporaries noted their affinity with Art Nouveau interior architecture associated in Russia with the name of Fedor Shekhtel. Bauer's genius as a set designer reached its apex in 1916 in an ambitious high-budget production *A Life for a Life* with lavish interiors filmed in very long shots with overhead space sometimes twice the height of the characters. As a reviewer remarked about these sets (designed in collaboration with Utkin), 'Bauer's school does not recognize realism on the screen; but even if no one would live in such rooms . . . this still produces an effect, a feeling, which is far better than the efforts of others who claim to be directors.'

When in 1916 the craze for close-ups hit Russian film-making, many directors opposed it on the grounds that the actors' faces covered the background space and thus diminished the artistic effect of the settings. Although Bauer was excited by the narrative possibilities provided by the close-up, it was not a simple change to make for a director whose reputation (and, indeed, whose genius) was based on extraordinary set design.

However, despite Bauer's fame as a set designer, his achievements as a director were not limited to this area. As early as 1913 his tracking shots display a sympathy towards the 'inner life' of the characters rather than merely stressing the vastness of the décor. In marked contrast to the Italian style (as evidenced for example in Pastrone's 1914 *Cabiria*) in which the camera scans the scene's space laterally without entering into it, Bauer's camera darts in and out, mediating between the viewer and the actor.

Bauer's interest in original lighting effects was further encouraged in 1914 by analogous Danish and American experiments. This is how the actor Iran Perestiani remembered Bauer's work with light: 'His scenery was alive, mixing the monumental with the intimate. Next to a massive and heavy column—a transparent web of tulle sheeting; the light plays over a brocade coverlet under the dark arches of a low flat, over flowers, furs, crystal. A beam of light in his hands was an artist's brush.'

Bauer died of stagnant pneumonia on 9 June 1917, in a hospital in Crimea. There is no way to tell what he would have achieved had he lived into the 1920s. Many of his associates made impressive careers in the Soviet cinema: Bauer's permanent cameraman Boris Zavelev shot Alexander Dovzhenko's *Zvenigora* (1927); Vasily Rakhal designed sets for Sergei Eisenstein and Abram Room, and Bauer's youngest disciple Lev Kuleshov was declared the founding father of the montage school.

YURI TSIVIAN

SELECT FILMOGRAPHY

The Twilight of a Woman's Soul (1913); Child of the Big City / The Girl from the Streets (1914); Silent Witnesses (1914); Daydreams / Deceived Dreams (1915); After Death / Motifs from Turgenev (1915); One Thousand and Second Ruse (1915); A Life for a Life / A Tear for Every Drop of Blood (1916); Dying Swan (1916); Nelly Raintseva (1916); After Happiness (1917); The King of Paris (1917); The Revolutionary (1917).

BIBLIOGRAPHY

Robinson, David (1990), 'Evgenii Bauer and the Cinema of Nikolai II', *Sight and Sound*, Winter 1990.
Tsivian, Yuri (1989), 'Evgenii Frantsevich Bauer'.

Opposite: Singed Wings (1915)

exiting Pathé lent support to the rising studios of Thiemann & Reinhardt and Yermoliev. Promptly followed by Khanzhonkov, they began redefining old standards of quality by creating (and selling) films in the so-called 'Russian style'.

From its very beginning, early Russian film-making was marked by dependence on non-cinematic culture. This can be explained partly by the belated start of Russian production. Because the first Russian film, *Stenka Razin*, was made in the same year as *L'Assassinat du Duc de Guise* ('The assassination of the Duc de Guise'), Russian film skipped the entire period of tricks and chases which formed the basis of all other key national cinemas, and started by trying to match the success of the *film d'art*.

Aside from forays into the sensationalist Grand Guignol style internationally practised in European cinema in 1908–10 (and up to 1913 in Russia), *film d'art* style exercised complete sway over the first period of Russian film-making. This tendency coincided with (and was maintained by) the foreign policy of Pathé-Frères, which, as Richard Abel has suggested, was to produce culturally specific art pictures, mainly historical costume dramas and ethnographic pictures from peasant life. Because the Moscow production department of Pathé was primarily concerned with the international market, the cultural specificity of their films usually boiled down to touches of local colour: reportedly, no one was able to talk the Pathé director Kai Hansen out of having a *de rigueur* samovar in every frame, even in a film set in the sixteenth century, or having actors taking low 'boyard bows' instead of hat tipping in modern dramas. Khanzhonkov on the other hand aimed its product at the domestic market, boasting cultural and ethnic authenticity in the form of screen versions of Russian classical literature, directed by the studio's leading director Pyotr Chardynin. The literary orientation of Khanzhonkov's style was the trump card in their game against Pathé, to which the latter responded with live tableaux staged after famous Russian paintings.

From 1911 the influence of the *film d'art* style on Russian film-making began to wane. With Pathé and Gaumont production removed from the Russian scene, Russian film-making found itself under the influence of the Danish and Italian salon melodrama. The scene of action shifted from past to present and from the countryside to the city; serious costume drama gave way to sophisticated melodrama with a decadent flavour. The shift was epitomized by Vladimir Gardin's and Yakov Protazanov's 5,000-metre-long (about three hours) hit *The Keys to Happiness* (1913), which pushed into prominence Thiemann & Reinhardt, a studio hitherto overshadowed by Khanzhonkov and Pathé-Frères. This film introduced a characteristic pause-pause-pause manner of acting (initially called 'the braking school', later known simply as 'Russian style'), originally conceived as a cinematic counterpart to

Stanislavsky's method used on stage. This acting technique soon evolved into a specific melancholy mood that is particularly pervasive in Yevgeny Bauer's films shot for the Khanzhonkov Company.

The First World War, which closed so many borders to film imports, was the golden age of the Russian film industry. Never before or since have Russian productions so dominated the Russian film market. During 1914–16 an introverted, slow manner was consciously cultivated by Russian directors and formulated by the trade press as a national aesthetic credo. The style was crystallized at Yermoliev's studio, which developed typical characters—the *femme fatale*, the victimized woman, the neurotic man—and a typical *mise-en-scène*—the motionless tableau with each character deep in thought. The tableau image became more important than the development of the plot.

'Psychological' mannerisms and slow action became obsolete in the radical change Russian film-making style was to undergo after 1917. In tune with the more general process of cultural reorientation taking place in Soviet Russia, the notion of a well-made plot (*syuzhet*) and rapid narrative became important in literature and film. The age of Lev Kuleshov with his accelerated editing and obsessive action was heralded by *Engineer Prait's Project* (1918)—a film reflecting not so much changes in Russian society as film-makers' reaction to the past decade of film production.

PERSONALITIES

The best years of private production in Russia (1914–19) were marked by the increasing role of film fandom. Initially promoted as local counterparts of foreign stars ('our Psilander' Vladimir Maximov, or Vera Kholodnaya as 'Bertini of the North'), Russian names were soon found to be winning over the public. This led to fresh strategies in studio competition: some new studios emerged (like Kharitonov's) built entirely around enticing stars with established reputations. Alongside the trade journals, fan

magazines started to appear. One titled *Pegas*, financed by Khanzhonkov and shaped like the 'thick' literary magazines, regularly offered aesthetic discussions of cinema as art and the contribution of individual film-makers. Thus the concept of a 'film director' with his or her individual career was formed. Pyotr Chardynin had the reputation of an 'actor's director'; after quitting Khanzhonkov's company for Kharitonov's in 1916 (with several major actors joining him), Chardynin directed an all-star box-office hit *The Tale of my Dearest Love* (1918), which saw a number of successful rereleases well into the Soviet era. Yakov Protazanov was acclaimed for *The Queen of Spades* (1916), whose elaborate costumes and set design imitated Alexander Benois's drawings; his reputation as 'high art director' was confirmed by the success of *Father Sergius* (1918). Though less known among the general public, the 'wizard' of animated insects Ladislas Starewitch was the film-maker most in demand by the studios. However, among Russian directors he was the only one who managed to preserve partial independence; he had a small studio of his own and a free hand in his choice of subjects. In the eyes of their Soviet successors their pre-revolutionary reputations turned directors into 'bourgeois specialists' (*spetsy*). With the notable exception of the protean Protazanov, not one of them was able to make a comparable career in the new Russia.

Bibliography
Ginzburg, Semion (1963), *Kinematografiya dorevolyutsionnoy Rossii* ('The cinema of pre-revolutionary Russia').
Hansen, Miriam (1992), 'Deadly Scenarios: Narrative Perspective and Sexual Politics in Pre-revolutionary Russian Film'.
Leyda, Jay (1960), *Kino: A History of Russian and Soviet Film*.
Likhachev, Boris (1926), *Kino v Rossii*.
Cherchi Usai, Paolo, Codelli, Lorenzo, Montanaro, Carlo, and Robinson, David (eds.) (1989), *Silent Witnesses: Russian Films, 1908–1919*.
Tsivian, Yuri (1989), 'Some Preparatory Remarks on Russian Cinema'.

The Soviet Union and the Russian Émigrés

NATALIA NUSSINOVA

CINEMA AND THE REVOLUTION

The Soviet cinema was officially born on 27 August 1919, when Lenin signed the Council of People's Commissars of the RSFSR Decree 'On the transfer of the photographic trade and industry to Narkompros [The People's Commissariat of Education]', nationalizing private film and photographic enterprises. But the struggle for power in film had already begun in 1917, when film workers banded

together in three professional organizations: the OKO (a federation of distributors, exhibitors, and producers); the Union of Workers in Cinematographic Art (creative workers—the 'film aristocracy'); and the Union of Film-Theatre Workers (the grass roots or proletariat, largely projectionists). The last of these, asserting workers' control over cinemas and film enterprises, soon came to determine the line taken by the Moscow and Petrograd

Cinema Committees, which had been set up in 1918 and had already begun nationalizing parts of the film industry. By the end of 1918 the Petrograd Committee had nationalized sixty-four non-functioning cinemas and two film studios abandoned by their previous owners, while in Moscow, where most film enterprises were concentrated, a process of nationalization was carried out between November 1918 and January 1920.

In this early phase only large companies were subject to nationalization, and the biggest film studio (that of the Khanzhonkov Company) had no more than 100 people on its staff, so during the first years of Soviet cinema private and state film companies coexisted. Certain pre-revolutionary film companies (Drankov, Perski, Vengerov, and Khimera) went out of business even before nationalization. The basis of Soviet film production was therefore laid by half a dozen film enterprises, which after nationalization came under the Photography and Film section of Narkompros. These were the former Khanzhonkov studio (which became First Enterprise 'Goskino'), the Skobolev Committee (Second Enterprise), Yermoliev (Third Enterprise), Rus (Fourth Enterprise), Taldykin's 'Era' (Fifth Enterprise), and Kharitonov (Sixth Enterprise). New studios also began to be constructed, of which the first was Sevzapkino in Petrograd (later Leningrad).

The process of restructuring continued throughout the 1920s. The former Khanzhonkov and Yermoliev studios were merged in 1924, then in 1927 construction began in the village of Potylikha outside Moscow of new premises for this studio, which it was decided should become the largest in the country. Construction continued until the beginning of the 1930s and in 1935 the new combined studio became known as Mosfilm.

Meanwhile private companies subsisted. The most resilient private owners adopted a parallel policy of merging individual studios into larger enterprises, sometimes handing over to Soviet power in so doing an element of their financial autonomy, sometimes acquiring it in a new form. A prime example was Moisei Aleinikov, owner of Rus film enterprise, which had been in existence since 1915. In 1923 Rus merged with the film bureau Mezhrabpom and formed the company known as Mezhrabpom-Rus, which was reorganized in 1926 as a joint-stock company. Two years later it changed the composition of its shareholders and reorganized itself again as Mezhrabpom-Film, becoming part of the German distribution organization Prometheus and obtaining from the Council of People's Commissars special rights to export and import films. In this guise Mezhrabpom was to play a central role in the diffusion of Soviet film in the west.

Pressure from film workers also continued to play a role in shaping the new situation. In 1924 a group of film-makers, led by Sergei Eisenstein and Lev Kuleshov, came together in Moscow to form the Association of Revolutionary Cinematography (ARC). The objective of ARC (whose members came to include Vsevolod Pudovkin, Dziga Vertov, Grigory Kozintsev, Leonid Trauberg, Georgi and Sergei Vasiliev, Sergei Yutkevich, Friedrich Ermler, Esfir Shub, and many other leading film-makers) was to reinforce ideological control over the creative process. Branches were formed in practically every studio, and the organization had its own publications, including the weekly newspaper *Kino* and (later) the magazines *Sovietsky ekran* and *Kino i kultura*. In 1929 ARC was renamed ARRC (Association of Workers of Revolutionary Cinematography). At the end of the decade, the All-Russian Association of Proletarian Writers (RAPP) had a strong influence on ARRC, and a new aim was adopted of '100 per cent proletarian ideological film', as part of the 'cultural revolution' being imposed throughout the arts.

During the 1920s regional studios came into being in the republics of the newly formed USSR—in the Ukraine, Armenia, Georgia, Azerbaijan, Uzbekistan, and elsewhere. The aim of these studios was to produce films relating to the local nationality in those areas, and they enjoyed a certain measure of autonomy.

It was not long before the aim of concentrating and centralizing film production in order to bring the cinema under social and state control led to the idea of establishing a single national film industry. The first step in this direction came with the creation in December 1922 of the film enterprise Goskino, which was given a monopoly over film distribution. In this form, Goskino turned out to be a useless bureaucracy, and it was axed at the Twelfth Party Congress. A commission was set up to consider ways of 'uniting the film industry on an all-Union basis' and merging all state film enterprises in each of the Union republics in a single joint-stock society. The Thirteenth Party Congress in May 1924 confirmed this direction, adding the demand for reinforced ideological monitoring in film-making and the appointment of 'tested Communists' to senior positions in the industry. From December 1924 this became the role of Sovkino in the Russian Federation, while similar organizations were set up in the Union republics—VUFKU in the Ukraine, AFKU in Azerbaijan, Bukhkino in Central Asia, and Goskinprom in Georgia. Sovkino and its clones had a full monopoly of distribution, import, and export of films, and gradually took over production functions as well. Although it managed to lose a lot of money in its early years, the Sovkino system survived to the end of the decade without significant alteration and provided the infrastructure for the great Soviet films of the late silent period.

THE RUSSIAN ÉMIGRÉS

With the Revolution, the Russian cinema split into two camps. One section of the industry remained in the USSR, zealously dedicated to destroying the pre-revolutionary

A scene from the science fantasy *Aelita* (1924), directed by the returning *émigré* Yakov Protazanov, with constructivist sets by Exter

experience, and creating the art of a new epoch unencumbered by the heritage of a bygone age. Another section went into exile, endeavouring to preserve abroad the cinema which had come into being during the pre-revolutionary years.

The emigration started with a group of film-makers who in the summer of 1918 had gone down to the Crimea to film on location. Convinced that it would be impossible to 'sit out the Revolution' there, they embarked on a tortuous journey westward. Most found their way to Paris, but some went to Italy, and other centres of *émigré* film-making activity were Germany, Czechoslovakia, and, later in the 1920s, Hollywood.

In February 1920 Iosif Yermoliev, together with his enterprise, emigrated to Paris, where he adopted the spelling Ermolieff and organized a studio called Ermolieff-Film. After 1922 he handed it over to producers Alexander

Kamenka and Noé Bloch and it was renamed Albatros. Among artists who worked there were directors Yakov Protazanov (who later returned to the Soviet Union), Alexander Volkov, Vladimir Strizhevsky, and Vyacheslav Turzhansky (or Victor Tourjansky, as he became known in the west), and actors Ivan Mozzukhin (Mosjoukine) and Natalia Lissenko. Also in France were the Russian-Polish animator Władysław Starewicz (in French Ladislas Starewitch), with his own studio at Fontenay-sous-Bois, and the producer Pavel Thiemann, who settled at Joinville.

Ermolieff moved to Berlin, where a sizeable *émigré* community soon developed. He brought with him Strizhevsky and Protazanov and drew Georgi Azagarov, who was already there, into working with him. Another major Russian producer, Dmitri Kharitonov, also emigrated, and in 1923 the major film company of Vladimir Vengerov and Hugo Stinnes was created, bringing together many

Russians who had settled in Germany. Among the most important Russian actors working in Germany in the 1920s were Vladimir Gaidarov, Olga Gsovskaya, and Olga Chekhova (Tschekowa)—the latter also a producer and director. Many film people moved between the two major centres of Russian emigration, including Tourjansky, Volkov, and Mosjoukine.

The director Alexander Uralsky, the actresses Tatiana and Varvara Yanova, and the actors Osip Runich and Mikhail Vavich became the centre of a film community that settled in Italy. In Czechoslovakia the Russian diaspora was represented in the early 1920s by Vera Orlova, Vladimir Massalitinov, and others, joined later in the decade by the famous Soviet actress Vera Baranovskaya, who moved to Prague and established a new reputation for herself there.

Hollywood became a centre of Russian film *émigrés* in the second half of the 1920s. Besides Tourjansky and Mosjoukine (who did not stay long), Russians who came to seek their fortune in America included actresses Anna Sten and Maria Uspenskaya (Ouspenskaya), actors Vladimir Sokolov and Mikhail (Michael) Chekhov, nephew of the playwright, and directors Ryszard Bolesławski (Richard Boleslawsky), Fyodor Otsep, and Dmitri Bukhovetsky (Dimitri Buchowetzki). America created a powerful Russian myth in the cinema, and at the same time, according to the recollections of contemporaries, was capable of swallowing the *émigrés* and absorbing them into itself. The overriding idea of the Russian emigration, to preserve Russian culture abroad intact in order to bring it back to Russia when the Bolsheviks were overthrown, was impossible in practice in America. Hollywood harshly imposed its own standards, and the most authentically Russian films produced by the emigration were those of the *émigré* colony in France, clustered around the most intensely Russian studio, Ermolieff-Film (Albatros).

The style of the Russian cinema in France could be defined as 'conservationist', attempting to preserve the traditions of Russian pre-revolutionary cinema but gradually giving ground to the demands of its western context. A number of films were direct remakes of pre-revolutionary works. Protazanov remade his 1915 film *The Prosecutor* in 1921 as *Justice d'abord* ('Justice above all'), while Tourjansky remade Yevgeny Bauer's *Song of Triumphant Love* under the same title in 1923. But there were also 'indirect remakes', covering the same subjects and using the thematic structures of pre-revolutionary films, such as Tourjansky's *Le XVme Prélude de Chopin* (*Chopin's Fifteenth Prelude*, 1922), which repeats motifs from his earlier *The Gentry's Ball* (1918). It is interesting that in both his French films Tourjansky uses Bauer's frame composition and his method of articulating space by splitting the action in several layers at various degrees of distance from the camera. The theme of visions appearing to characters who are poised between the real and unreal worlds and expressive of the mystical consciousness of the Russian intelligentsia of the early 1900s, which was widely used in pre-revolutionary cinema, is transformed in *émigré* cinema into a subject-based unreality. This may take the form of hallucinations, as in Tourjansky's *Song of Triumphant Love*, or delirium, as in the same director's *Michel Strogoff* (1926). More often, however, it is represented as dream—as in *Angoissante Aventure* ('Dreadful adventure', 1920) or Mosjoukine's *Le Brasier ardent* ('The burning brazier', 1923)—and is used by the *émigrés* as a persistent metaphor of their post-revolutionary existence as something temporary and transitory, which can only end with a happy awakening. Thus one of the major canons of the pre-revolutionary film is broken—the obligatory tragic finale, or 'Russian ending'. For western audiences such an ending was acceptable only in the case of the classic melodrama, such as Volkov's *Kean, ou désordre et génie* ('Kean, or disorder and genius', 1923). Increasingly the *émigré* film-makers were forced to surrender this position—though to varying degrees in different countries. Hollywood categorically demanded a happy ending. For example, Dimitri Buchowetzki, working in 1925 on a film version of *Anna Karenina*, felt obliged to prepare a version of the screenplay in which Anna turns out to have thrown herself under the train only in dream and in actual fact she marries Vronsky. In France the film-makers surrendered their position only after a longer struggle. Distortion of the Russian classics was seen as a sacrilege, which was only conceded in the 1930s, as in Tourjansky's adaptation of Pushkin's story 'The Stationmaster' (under the title *Nostalgie*) in 1937. More often a compromise was reached. For example, in *Song of Triumphant Love*, Turgenev's story is simply left incomplete; it breaks off on a happy note, creating for western film-goers the sensation of a happy ending, while directing Russians to the mystical tragic finale of the literary source. Alternatively use is made of a double ending, with a happy end tacked on to the 'Russian finale', so that in *Angoissante Aventure* the hero is shown awakening from a nightmare, while in *Chopin's Fifteenth Prelude* the heroine's suicide is forestalled by chance.

Wedded as they were to the values of a conservative consciousness, and unwilling to give up the traditions of pre-revolutionary cinema with its slowed-down rhythm and pace of action, the *émigrés* showed themselves unreceptive to the avant-garde experiment that typified western cinema of the 1920s, particularly in France. The only exception was Mosjoukine's *Le Brasier ardent*, which in this respect sets itself apart from the rest of *émigré* cinema. The traditional approach, the lack of interest in experiment with montage, the centrality of the actor, all distinguish the style of *émigré* cinema from its contemporary Soviet counterpart in the 1920s. It is significant that, according to contemporary testimony, *Le Brasier*

Ivan Mosjoukine (Ivan Ilich Mozzhukhin)
(1889–1939)

Born in Penza on 26 September 1889, the young Ivan Ilich Mozzhukhin went to law school in Moscow for two years, but gave up his studies and left for Kiev, to pursue a theatrical career. After two years touring the provinces, he returned to Moscow, where he worked at several theatres including the Moscow Dramatic Theatre. He made his film debut in 1911 in *The Kreutzer Sonata*, directed by Pyotr Chardynin, the first of many films he was to make for the powerful Khanzhonkov Company. At first he was cast in a variety of roles, from the comic in *Brothers* (1913), to the tragic hero of *In the Hands of Merciless Fate* (1913). It was in 1914, while working with the director Yevgeny Bauer on *Life in Death* (1914), that he developed what was to become his artistic trademark—a steady, direct, tear-filled gaze turned full on the cinema audience. From this was born the myth about the mystical power of Mozzhukhin's gaze. His role as a key dramatic and melodramatic actor was confirmed in such films as Chardynin's *Chrysanthemums* (1914), and *Idols* (1915), again with Bauer.

In 1915 he left Khanzhonkov and transferred to the Yermoliev studio. Here, under the direction of Yakov Protazanov, the mystical element of his image was enhanced, while a demonic edge entered into his richest characterizations—for example in *The Queen of Spades* (1915) or *Father Sergius* (1917).

The ideas of the playwright A. Voznesensky helped Mozzhukhin to form a conception of cinema which depended on the expressiveness of the actor's gaze, his gestures, his use of pauses, and his ability to hypnotize his partner. Speech was to be avoided as much as possible, and the ideal film would be devoid of all commentary and intertitles.

In 1919 Yermoliev and his troupe left Russia and set up in Paris. Mozzhukhin went with them, adopting the spelling Mosjoukine under which he was to become famous throughout Europe. His ideas on acting found reinforcement in theories of cinema current in France at the time, most notably the idea of *photogénie*.

Towards the end of his Russian period an important new theme had emerged in his work; the double or split personality. In the two-part epic *Satan Triumphant* (1917), directed by Ch. Sabinsky, he played multiple roles, an experiment he repeated in *Le Brasier ardent* (1923), with himself as director. Doubles and *doppelgängers* surface many times in his French films, most spectacularly in *Feu Mathias Pascal* (1925) adapted by Marcel L'Herbier from a Pirandello story about a man believed dead who invents a new life for himself.

Mosjoukine was also a poet, and in his poems he compares himself, as actor and as *émigré*, to a werewolf, many sided and restless. From this sprang the figure of the eternal wanderer (*Casanova*, 1927) and the Tsar's courtier (*Michel Strogoff*, 1926). But what most preoccupied him during his French period was a constant wish to rid himself of the 'mystical' film star persona. He attempted this in various ways—by infantilizing and thus caricaturing heroic roles, by a return to comedy, or by bringing opposing character types together in one film. This conscious eclecticism was reinforced by his discovery of the French avant-garde and of American cinema—notably Griffith, Chaplin, and Fairbanks. His interest in America aroused, he moved there in 1927, appearing in just one film, Edward Sloman's *Surrender*. Later that year he returned to Europe. In Germany he rejoined some of his fellow *émigrés*, and himself played the role of the Russian *émigré* in two major films, *Der weisse Teufel* (1929) and *Sergeant X* (1931). However, as he had always feared, speech in film proved to be a problem and in a foreign language even more so. His last roles were few and of little consequence. On 17 January 1939 he died of acute tuberculosis in a hospital for the poor.

NATALIA NUSSINOVA

Ivan Mosjoukine in the film he directed himself, *Le Brasier ardent* (1923)

SELECT FILMOGRAPHY

The Kreutzer Sonata (1911); Christmas Eve (1912); A Terrible Vengeance (1913); The Sorrows of Sarah (1913); Satan Triumphant (1917); Little Ellie (1917); Father Sergius (1917); Le Brasier ardent (also dir.) (1923); Feu Mathias Pascal (1925); Michel Strogoff (1926); Casanova (1927); Surrender (1927); Der weisse Teufel (1929); Sergeant X (1931); Nitchevo (1936)

ardent was the only *émigré* film to exercise any influence on the young directors of the Soviet cinema.

THE SOVIET STYLE

In contrast to the *émigrés*, the young Soviet directors strove to break the link with their pre-revolutionary heritage completely. Their desire to create a new cinema reflected an idea of renouncing the old world which was widespread in Russia in those years.

A commitment to reality in the cinema—and particularly to the rapidly changing reality of the Revolution—came through the use of montage to transform cinematic representation. In part this came about through economic necessity, coupled with a certain unconscious aggression towards the past. With raw film in short supply, one way for the cinema to develop was through the re-editing of old films, sometimes even on the negative. With this in view, a special 'Re-editing Department' was created in the production section of the Moscow Film Committee. According to film historian Veniamin Vishnevsky, Vladimir Gardin was the first Soviet theoretician of montage. On 10 February 1919 Gardin delivered a lecture to the Re-editing Department on montage as one of the fundamentals of film art. This lecture had a great impact on his colleagues, notably on Lev Kuleshov. Kuleshov, whose famous 'experiments' are traditionally considered the origin of the Soviet concept of montage, was, according to Vishnevsky, developing ideas put forward by Gardin.

The best known of these experiments—the 'Kuleshov effect'—took the form of a still close-up of the face of the actor Ivan Mozzhukhin, juxtaposed to three different frames: a plate of soup, a dead woman in a coffin, and a child playing. As a result of the juxtaposition the audience had the impression that the expression on the actor's face altered, while the background (taken from an unknown pre-revolutionary film) remained unchanged. With this experiment Kuleshov sought to confirm one of the laws of montage that he had discovered: that the meaning of a montage sequence in cinema is determined not by the content of the montage elements, but by their juxtaposition. This experiment, known in the west from the lecture 'Model instead of actor' given in London by Vsevolod Pudovkin in 1929 (and therefore often incorrectly referred to as the Pudovkin effect), was sometimes seen by contemporaries not as a manifestation of the avantgarde thinking of the new epoch, but as evidence of the vandalism of the Soviet cinema towards its predecessors. Thus Moisei Aleinikov (head of the Rus film studio and later of Mezhrabpom-Film) describes in his memoirs how Kuleshov's 'montage people', wearing leather jackets and carrying revolvers, used to 'arrest' old film negatives in the studio, in order to re-edit this 'rubbish . . . filmed by the bourgeoisie' into new revolutionary film—there being no raw film in the country from which new films could be made.

In the early days, the embryonic Soviet cinema was heavily dependent on the principle of creation through destruction. The smashing of the old commercial structures of the genre film began almost at once. In 1919 a wave of propaganda films appeared, with titles like *Daredevil*, *Their Eyes were Opened*, *We Are above Vengeance*, or *For the Red Banner*, dedicated to the first anniversary of the Revolutionary Army. These *agitki* (agitational pieces), which were to become a regular feature of early Soviet cinema, were shown throughout the country with the aid of specially equipped mobile cinemas and of the famous 'Agit-trains', the first of which set out for the countryside under the direction of M. I. Kalinin in April 1919.

On 7 November 1920 shooting began on a mass-action film of the storming of the Winter Palace. The concept of the action combined the principle of the play-film and the 'unplayed film' which was fundamental to the idea of the filmed chronicle. The film also introduced the concept of group authorship (the production was the work of thirteen directors headed by Nikolai Yevreinov), the de-individualizing of the actor (10,000 people took part in the filming), a heightened concept of the audience (the performance was played out in the presence of 100,000 people), and, finally, a blurring of the dividing line between theatre and cinema (theatre was being enacted in the square, but being shot on film).

Stage-screen hybrids were generally typical of Soviet cinema in the early 1920s. Grigory Kozintsev's and Leonid Trauberg's theatrical productions of *The Marriage* (*Zhenit'ba*) included screen projection in their structure, as did Eisenstein's show *The Wise Man* (*Mudrets*), with its film interlude 'Glumov's Diary', and Gardin's production *The Iron Heel* (*Zheleznaya pyata*). This technique goes back to pre-revolutionary experiments in the theatre, but the Soviet directors seem to have been unaware of this and to have assumed that here too they were the destroyers of tradition.

The idea of collective authorship was also important in the 1920s. The first group to be formed (in 1919) was Kuleshov's and included Pudovkin, Boris Barnet, V. P. Fogel, and others. Its work was based on the rejection of the pre-revolutionary 'psychological drama' and it introduced a new concept of acting: the notion of the 'model' (a term suggested by Turkin in 1918) in which psychological embodiment of character is replaced by the study of reflexes and the automating of the acting.

Kuleshov's group was followed by one headed by Dziga Vertov (pseudonym of Denis Arkadevich Kaufman), including among its members Vertov's wife Elisaveta Svilova and his brother Mikhail, as well as A. M. Rodchenko and others. In its manifestos, published in the magazines *Kinofot* and *LEF*, Vertov's group totally rejected the very concept of the

Sergei Eisenstein

(1898–1948)

At age 25 Eisenstein was the *enfant terrible* of Soviet theatre; *The Wiseman*, his irreverent, circus-style production of an Ostrovsky classic, marked a high point of experimentation in the post-revolutionary stage. After two more productions Proletkult invited Eisenstein to make a film. It became *The Strike* (1925), and Meyerhold's pupil soon became the most famous Soviet film-maker. 'The cart dropped to pieces', he noted some years later, 'and the driver dropped into cinema.'

Eisenstein brought his theatrical training into all his films. His version of Soviet typage relied on the de-psychologized personifications he found in *commedia dell'arte*. His later films unashamedly invoked the full resources of stylized lighting, costume, and sets. Above all, Eisenstein's conception of expressive movement, exceeding norms of realism and aimed at the direct excitation of the spectator, emerged again and again. In *The Strike*, the workers' struggle with a foreman to blow a steam whistle becomes a calisthenic exercise. In *The Old and the New* (1929), a woman's despairing act of flinging down a plough transforms itself into a fierce gesture of defiance. The two-part *Ivan the Terrible* (1944, 1946) acquires its majestic pace through an instant-by-instant modulation of the actor's movement.

A drawing by Eisenstein for *Ivan the Terrible* (1944)

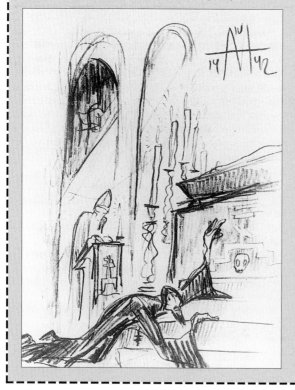

Cinema was not only the next step in the development of theatre; Eisenstein considered cinema the synthesis of all the arts. He found in the cinematic technique of montage analogies to the juxtapositions of images in verse, to the inner monologue of Joyce's *Ulysses*, to the rich 'intercutting' of action and dialogue in Dickens and Tolstoy. In *The Battleship Potemkin* (1925) a sailor furiously smashes a plate he is washing; the fragmentation of the action parallels him to Myron's Discus-Thrower. Eisenstein posited a 'polyphonic' montage in cinema that would interweave pictorial motifs. And the arrival of sound technology led him to posit a 'vertical' montage between image and sound which would create the inner unity achieved in Wagnerian music drama.

Expressive movement and montage, the cornerstones of Eisenstein's aesthetic, could find fulfilment in cinema as in no other art. He argues that in *Alexander Nevsky* (1938) vertical montage brings out the emotional dynamic latent in both image and musical score, intensifying the suspenseful anticipation of Alexander's troops awaiting the Teutonic Knights' attack. Earlier in his career, he had suggested that *The Wiseman*'s 'montage of attractions', its assembly of perceptual 'shocks', could rouse the audience to emotion and, eventually, reflection. Making *October* (1928), he speculated that, like haiku poetry and Joycean stream of consciousness, the juxtapositions of shots can create purely conceptual associations. *October*'s most famous passage of 'intellectual montage', the little disquisition on God and Country, uses images and titles to demonstrate the mystification surrounding religion and patriotism. Montage, Eisenstein believed, would allow him to make a film of Marx's *Capital*.

Throughout the silent era Eisenstein assumed that his aesthetic experimentation could be harmonized with the propaganda dictates of the State. Each of his silent films begins with an epigraph from Lenin, and each depicts a key moment in the myth of Bolshevik ascension: the pre-revolutionary struggles (*The Strike*), the 1905 revolution (*Potemkin*), the Bolshevik coup (*October*), and contemporary agricultural policy (*The Old and the New*). The world-wide success of *Potemkin* won sympathy and respect for the regime; who could not be moved by Eisenstein's shocking portrayal of the tsarist troops massacring innocents on the Odessa Steps? After a stay in Hollywood in 1930 and an attempt to make an independent film in Mexico (1930-2), Eisenstein returned to a Soviet Union in the grip of Stalin. The film industry was in the process of repudiating the montage experiments of the silent era, and soon a conception of 'Socialist Realism' became official policy. Eisenstein's teaching at the State Film Academy allowed him to explore ways of reconciling his own interests with the new standards, but his efforts to put his ideas into practice in *Bezhin Meadow* (1935-7) ran into opposition and the film was halted.

He had more success with *Nevsky*, which coincided with Stalin's Russophilia and served as timely propaganda against German invasion. Eisenstein won the

Order of Lenin. The first part of *Ivan the Terrible* also enhanced his stature. Stalin had encouraged a 'progressive' reading of certain tsars, and Eisenstein portrayed his hero as a decisive ruler bent on unifying Russia.

But the second part of the projected *Ivan* trilogy fell afoul of policy-makers. Ivan, hesitating to kill his enemies, was now judged too 'Hamlet-like', and the film was banned by the Central Committee. It is likely that this action was part of a general reassertion of Party control of the arts, which had enjoyed considerable latitude during the war. The attack on *Ivan* Part Two led Eisenstein, already in poor health, to greater isolation. He died in 1948, under a cloud of criticism which would not be lifted for a decade. Ironically, his films and writings were far more visible in the west than in the USSR, and, although his reputation has undergone periodic reappraisals, he has remained the most celebrated and influential representative of Soviet film culture.

DAVID BORDWELL

SELECT FILMOGRAPHY

Stachka (The Strike) (1925); Bronenosets 'Potemkin' (The Battleship Potemkin) (1925); Oktyabr (October / Ten Days that Shook the World) (1928); Staroe i novoe (The Old and the New); Generalnaya Liniya ('The general line') (1929); Bezhin lug (Bezhin Meadow) (1935–7); Alexander Nevsky (1938); Ivan Grozny (Ivan the Terrible) Part I (1944); Ivan Grozny (Ivan the Terrible) Part II (1946)

BIBLIOGRAPHY

Bordwell, David (1993), *The Cinema of Eisenstein*.
Eisenstein, Sergei (1949), *Film Form: Essays in Film Theory*.
—— (1992), *Towards a Theory of Montage*.
—— (1988), *Writings, 1922-34*.
Leyda, Jay, and Voynow, Zina (eds.) (1982), *Eisenstein at Work*.
Nizhny, Vladimir (1962), *Lessons with Eisenstein*.
Seton, Marie (1952), *Sergei M. Eisenstein: A Biography*.

Below: A scene from *Bezhin Meadow* (1935-7). The film itself is lost, and all that survive are a couple of frames of each shot

actor ('a danger', 'an error'), and the idea of play-films with a story-line. The aim of the Kino-Eye group was to capture 'life taken unawares', *kino-pravda* (cine-truth), 'revolution by newsreel'—based on the *LEF* idea of the 'literature of fact', in response to the call of the constructivists to eliminate 'art itself'. However the transformation of reality by means of the new language of cinema when it was transferred to the screen was permitted, and the 'kino eye' was endowed with the ability to manipulate time and space.

Eisenstein's cine-collective 'The Iron Five' (G. V. Alexandrov, M. M. Shtraukh, A. I. Levshin, M. I. Gomorov, A. A. Antonov) came into being in 1923. In his very first theoretical work Eisenstein proposed replacing the plot in the cinema by a montage of attractions, and in his first full-length film, *The Strike* (*Stachka*, 1925), he put forward the masses as hero as an alternative to the Russian pre-revolutionary and contemporary western system of stars. The frame for Eisenstein was an independently significant unit of montage, an 'attraction'—that is, a shock for the audience's perception—and the 'montage of attractions' was a sequence of shocks having an effect on the spectator and provoking a response reaction in such a creatively productive way that the spectator became, as it were, the director's co-author in creating the film text. Herein lay the chief difference between Eisenstein's concept of montage and that of Kuleshov, within whose system the spectator was allotted a passive role and was simply the recipient of prepared information. According to Kuleshov's theory the role of the frame in a montage sequence was equivalent to that of the letter in a word and it was not the content of each frame which was significant but their juxtaposition.

Eisenstein was indebted to Kuleshov for the idea itself of the frame as a unit of montage. According to the recollections of eyewitnesses, Eisenstein learnt to construct mass scenes from the example of Kuleshov's *The Death Ray* (*Luch smerti*, 1925). He also acknowledged his indebtedness to the re-editing school, mainly via the re-editing of foreign films for Soviet distribution, in which he was involved working for Esfir Shub. As for the idea of attractions, Grigory Kozintsev and Leonid Trauberg recollect that it was suggested to Eisenstein by their show *The Marriage*, which represented a sequence of attractions. Eisenstein first combined attractions into a montage series in his stage production of *The Wise Man* in 1923.

FEX (The Factory of the Eccentric Actor) came into being in Leningrad under the leadership of Grigory Kozintsev and Leonid Trauberg in 1921 as a theatrical workshop and from 1924 became a cinematographic collective. The emphasis on 'eccentrism' put forward by FEX testified on the one hand to their orientation towards 'low' genres (circus, vaudeville, the variety stage) and their rejection of the traditions of the 'serious' art of the salon. On the other hand it encoded the self-perception of the artists of the Leningrad school as new provincials, after the capital was moved to Moscow. On the cover of the manifesto *Eccentrism* (1922, with articles by Kozintsev, Kryzhitsky, Trauberg, and Yutkevich) the place of publication was indicated as 'Ex-centropolis'—that is, Leningrad (formerly Petrograd), now no longer the centre and therefore literally 'eccentric'. The composition of the FEX acting troupe changed over time, as did its direction, and from 1926 it continued in being in name only.

Also based in Leningrad was a rival group, KEM (Experimental Cinema Workshop), led by Friedrich Ermler, Edward Johanson, and Sergei Vasiliev. Unlike FEX, KEM was purely a film group. Rejecting the Stanislavsky system, it modelled itself on the ideas of Vsevolod Meyerhold, stressing professionalism above inspiration in the actor's craft. In 1927, at the height of the montage period, Ermler declared, 'the actor and not the frame makes films', but this provocative statement was belied by his own formally subtle *Oblomok imperii* ('Fragment of an empire', 1929).

'Eccentric' techniques, based on circus and vaudeville, were particularly prominent in short films, including Ermler's *Skarlatina* ('Scarlet fever', 1924), Pudovkin and Shpikovsky's *Chess Fever* (*Shakhmatnaya goryachka*, 1925), and Yutkevich's *Radiodetektiv* ('The radio detective', 1926). The quintessence of the new genre, however, was Kozintsev and Trauberg's *Adventures of Oktyabrina* (*Pokhozdeniya Oktyabriny*, 1924), which sought, in Trauberg's words, to combine the theme of an *agitka* with political features from the Soviet satirical press, the tricks of American comics, and a headlong montage rhythm that could outdo the French avant-garde.

What united all tendencies was a shared cult of Charlie Chaplin. Constructivists such as Alexei Gan and Dziga Vertov saw Chaplin as a model to counterpoise to the pre-revolutionary tradition. For the FEX group, he was the embodiment of the Eccentric view of the world. Eisenstein wrote of the 'attractional qualities of the specific mechanics of [Chaplin's] movements'. For Kuleshov as well as for the FEXes, he was the embodiment of America.

The 'America' celebrated by the Soviet avant-garde was not so much a real place as an emblem of the machine-age rhythm of the twentieth century. For Kuleshov this America functioned as a kind of notional montage space, which he made the subject of one of his early experiments in 'creative geography', *Tvorimaya zemnaya poverkhnost* ('The earth's surface created', 1920), where Khoklova and Obolensky 'emerge' from Gogol Boulevard in Moscow on to the steps of the Capitol in Washington. In another experiment around the same time, *Tvorimiy chelovek* ('The person being created') applied the same abstract notion to the human body, putting together 'the back of one woman', 'the eyes of another', and 'the legs of a third'.

This idea of the film author as demiurge was shared by other film-makers. In his 1923 manifesto Dziga Vertov spoke of the ability of the 'kino eye' to put together in montage a person 'more perfect than the creation of Adam', while Kozintsev and Trauberg in their unfilmed scenario *Zhenshchina Edisona* ('Edison's woman', 1923) envisaged the creation of a new Eve, the daughter of Edison and the primogenitrix of the new world.

Parallel with the avant-garde tendency, an academic and traditional cinema also survived in the Soviet Union, practised largely by directors such as A. Ivanovsky, C. Sabinsky, and P. Chardynin who had already been working in Russia before the Revolution. Needless to say, this cinema was not entirely conservative. Rather it tended to mix traditional technique with artificially introduced 'revolutionary' subject-matter. An interesting example of this is Gardin's *Prizrak brodit po Yevropie* ('A spectre is haunting Europe', 1923). Inspired by Edgar Allan Poe's 'The Masque of the Red Death', this film has a subtly conceived montage but

traditional narration, with a double-exposure nightmare scene in which the masses rising in revolution confront the Emperor, who is in love with a shepherdess. The masses are victorious, the Emperor and his shepherdess are consumed by fire, but the ending is implausible, since the film is made in the melodramatic genre leading the audience to sympathize with the 'hero' and 'heroine' rather than with the depersonalized masses. Less ambiguous was *Aelita* (1924), made by Yakov Protazanov on his return to the Soviet Union and based on the revolutionary science-fiction fantasy by Alexei Tolstoy, but incorporating all the staple elements and poetic conventions of the *émigré* film.

Constructing new genres was in fact a major problem of Soviet film-makers in the 1920s. An implicit model early in the decade, according to Adrian Piotrovsky (1969), was the Griffith melodrama, both at the level of plot ('disaster-pursuit-rescue') and at that of expressive technique (montage of details, exploitation of emotional attractions, symbolism of objects). Plot features of the early Soviet film include the creation of the role of the new Soviet

By the Law (*Po zakonu*, 1926), adapted by Viktor Shklovsky from a story by Jack London, and directed by Lev Kuleshov

detective—as in Kuleshov's *The Extraordinary Adventures of Mr West in the Land of the Bolsheviks* (*Neobychainiye priklucheniya mistera Vesta v stranie bolshevikov*, 1924)—while at the micro-level there developed techniques of 'montage of attractions' (Eisenstein) and 'rhythmically regulated montage' (the 'Kino-Eye' group).

A fusion of new techniques, to some degree transcending the polemics over the 'played' and 'unplayed' film, is found in the development in the mid-1920s of the 'historical revolutionary epic'. Films in this category were distinguished by non-traditional plot structure and narration, intensive montage, and rich use of metaphor and experiments in film language, while fulfilling a social and ideological requirement by their treatment of revolutionary themes. They include such classics as Eisenstein's *The Strike* and *The Battleship Potemkin* (*Bronenosets Potëmkin*, 1925), Pudovkin's *Mother* (*Mat*, 1926), *The End of St Petersburg* (*Koniets Sankt-Peterburga*, 1927), and *The Heir of Genghis Khan* (*Potomok Chingis-Khana*, 1928—also known as *Storm over Asia*), and Alexander Dovzhenko's *Zvenigora* (1927) and *Arsenal* (1929).

The 'standardization' of film genres which (according to Piotrovsky) took place after 1925 also led to the production of historical epics of a more academic type, such as Ivanovsky's *Dekabritsky* ('The Decembrists', 1927) or Yuri Tarich's *Krylya kholopa* ('Wings of the serf', 1926), made under the influence of the Moscow Arts Theatre. The continuing battle between traditionalists and innovators spurred Kozintsev and Trauberg and the FEX group to abandon their commitment to purely contemporary subjects and to make their own film about the Decembrist movement, *The Club of the Big Deed* (*Soyuz velikova dela*, or *SVD*), later in 1927.

SVD had as script-writers the formalist theoreticians Yuri Tynyanov and Yuli Oksman, and from 1926 the Soviet silent cinema enters what Eisenstein was to call its 'second literary period'. Intense debates took place about the role of the scenario. At one extreme were Vertov, who rejected the idea of the played film entirely, and the writer Osip Brik, who went so far as to propose writing the scenario after the film had been shot. At the other were Ippolit Sokolov and the proponents of the 'iron scenario' in which every shot was numbered and pre-planned in advance. Against the iron scenario, Eisenstein proposed an 'emotional' scenario, a 'stenographic record of the impulse', which would assist the director in finding a visual incarnation for the idea.

On the whole the intervention of the formalist writers and critics led to at least a partial reintegration of literary values into Soviet cinema. This is evident in Tynyanov's script for *The Overcoat* (*Shiniel*, 1926), adapted from Gogol and directed by Kozintsev and Trauberg, and Viktor Shklovsky's for Kuleshov's *By the Law* (*Po zakonu*, 1926), based on Jack London's story 'The Unexpected'. But Shklov-

sky also contributed to the transfer of some of the cinematic and anti-literary values of Vertov's 'fact films' to the fiction film, as in his work on Abram Room's *Bed and Sofa* (*Tretya Meshchanskaya*, 1927), a film showing careful attention to the detail of everyday life.

The everyday genre, with its interest in the detail of surrounding reality, including industry, gradually began to occupy a dominating position in Soviet cinema, with films like Petrov-Bytov's *Vodororot* ('The whirlpool') and Ermler's *Dom v sugrobakh* ('The house in the snowdrifts', 1928), not to mention Eisenstein's *The General Line* (1929). Everyday life is also central to the comedies of Boris Barnet, such as *The Girl with the Hatbox* (*Devushka s korobkoi*, 1927) and *The House on Trubnaya Square* (*Dom na Trubnoi*, 1928), where it merges with another important trend in Soviet cinema—the urbanist film. Here the theme is the counterpoising of the city and the provinces, with the city as a new world opening up before the new arrival from the provinces, as in Ermler's *Katka bumazhny ranet* ('Katya's reinette apples'), Room's *V bolshom gorodie* ('In the big city'), Y. Zhelyabuzhsky's *V gorod vkhodit nelzya* ('No entry to the city'), and also Pudovkin's *The End of St Petersburg*.

By the end of the decade a contradictory situation had arisen in Soviet cinema. The montage cinema had reached a peak, or rather several peaks, since there were divergent tendencies within it. On the one side was the theory of intellectual cinema, which Eisenstein had begun to develop at the time when he was working on *October* (*Oktyabr*, 1927), and which took definitive shape in 1929 with his article 'The Fourth Dimension in the Cinema' and came to exercise an important influence on the avant-garde. And on the other side stood the so-called 'lyrical' or 'emotional' cinema, functioning through image-symbols and typified by Dovzhenko's films *Zvenigora* (1927) and *Arsenal* (1929), Nikolai Shengelai's *Elisso* (1928), and Yevgeni Chervyakov's *Girl from the Distant River*, *My Son* (*Moi syn*, 1928), and *Golden Beak* (*Zolotoi klyuv*). Trauberg recalls that, under the influence of Eisenstein's article on the Fourth Dimension, he and Kozintsev completely altered the montage principle of their film *New Babylon* (*Novy Vavilon*, 1929), abandoning 'linkage of the action' in plot development in favour of what Eisenstein called the 'conflicting combination of overtones of the intellectual order'. They then saw Pudovkin's freshly released *The End of St Petersburg*, which stood at the midway point between the intellectual and emotional poles, and under its influence nearly remade the film all over again.

This period, which was the high point of the development of the intellectual and lyrical-symbolic montage cinema and the cinema of the implied plot, created at the same time a parallel system in the commercial genre

New Babylon (*Novy Vavilon*, 1929), Grigory Kozintsev and Leonid Trauberg's epic story of the Paris Commune

film—notably in the work of Gardin (*The Poet and the Tsar*), Chardynin (*Behind the Monastery Wall*), and Konstantin Eggert (*The Bear's Wedding* (*Medviezhya svadba*), 1926). But by the end of the decade articles began to appear in the critical literature which censured both the innovators ('left-wing deviation') and the traditionalists ('right-wing deviation'). In the spring of 1928 an All Union Party conference on the cinema was called and the demand for 'a form which the millions can understand' was put forward as the main aesthetic criterion in evaluating a film. But the rejection of the commercial cinema, which furthermore was largely being created by film-makers of the old school, bore witness to the fact that more than formal questions were at stake. 'Purges' began in the cinema, and the images of the White Guard, the kulak, the spy, or the White *émigré* wrecker who had insinuated himself into Soviet Russia began to crop up in films with increasing frequency. Films like Protazanov's *Yego prizyv* ('His call', 1925), Zhelyabuzhsky's *No Entry to the City*, Johanson's *Na dalyokom beregu* ('On the far shore', 1927), and G. Stabova's *Lesnoi cheloviek* ('Forest man', 1928) bear disturbing witness to this new trend. The increasingly powerful role of RAPP in literature began to create a situation of ideological pressure of which the cinema too became a target.

Besides the change in the political climate, the arrival of sound played a significant part in the sequence of epochs in Soviet cinema. Already in 1928–9, before the new invention had been introduced in the Soviet cinema, Soviet film-makers began to discuss its likely implication. In 1928 Eisenstein, Pudovkin, and Alexandrov put forward the concept of audio-visual counterpoint in a statement 'The Future of the Sound Film'. The engineers Shorin (Leningrad) and Tager (Moscow) were working at that time to create a sound-recording system for Soviet film studios. The introduction of sound into the cinema becomes in a certain sense state policy. Pudovkin's film *Prostoi sluchai* ('A simple case'), also known as *Ochen' khorosho zhivyotsya* ('Life is very good', 1932), and Kozintsev and Trauberg's *Odna* ('Alone', 1931), conceived as silent, were on orders from above 'adapted for sound', as a result of which they reached the screen after a one- to two-year delay. Probably those in charge saw in the talking picture one of the ways of bringing the cinema to the masses which the 1928 conference had urged. And although for several more years, because of the absence of sound projectors in country areas, silent films continued to be made alongside talkies (notably Mikhail Romm's *Boule de suif* and Alexander Medvedkin's *Happiness* (*Shchastie*), both of 1934), one can say that the silent film as an art form reached its zenith in Soviet cinema by 1929, in which year it ceased to progress, yielding place to its successor.

Bibliography
Christie, Ian, and Taylor, Richard (eds.) (1988), *The Film Factory.*
Leyda, Jay (1960), *Kino: A History of Russian and Soviet Film.*
Piotrovsky, Adrian (1969), *Teatr, Kino, Zhizn* ('Theatre, cinema, life').
Istoriya sovietskogo kino v chetyryokh tomakh ('A history of the Soviet cinema in 4 volumes'), Vol. i: *1917–1931.*
Lebedev, Nikolai (1965), *Ocherk istorii kino SSSR. Nemoe kino (1918–1934)* ('An outline history of cinema in the USSR. Silent cinema').
Margolit, Yevgeny (1988), *Sovietskoie kinoiskusstvo* ('Soviet film art'). Moscow, 1988.

Yiddish Cinema in Europe

MAREK AND MAŁGORZATA HENDRYKOWSKI

No panorama of early European cinema can be complete without mention of the unique phenomenon of the transnational Yiddish cinema, which flourished in eastern and central Europe throughout the silent period and into the 1930s. This Yiddish cinema derived from the extra-territorial tradition of European Jewish culture and literature rooted in the Yiddish language. Yiddish is a language of exceptional expressiveness, highly developed idiom, and rich vocabulary, which by the turn of the century had become the mother tongue of over 10 million Jews, living mostly in central and eastern Europe but also as part of the Jewish diaspora in the United States, Mexico, Argentina, and elsewhere in the New World.

THE YIDDISH CULTURAL TRADITION

Throughout eastern and central Europe Yiddish had a full-fledged literature, comparable with other European national literatures. Alongside élite works aspiring to the rank of canonical literature, more popular prose was also printed in instalments in cheap pamphlet form. Leading representatives of Yiddish literature at the turn of the century include Avrom Goldfadn, father of the Jewish theatre, Yankev Gordin, An-ski (Shloyme Zaynvil Rapoport), Yitskhok Leyb Perets, Sholem Ash, Yoysef Opatoshu (Yoysef Meyer Opatovski), and Sholem Aleykhem (Sholem Rabinowicz), and it was often to the works of these authors that the nascent Yiddish cinema turned for inspiration in the 1910s and 1920s.

Yiddish cinema has its roots in Jewish drama and theatre of the late nineteenth and early twentieth centuries, stemming from the tradition of the Purim-Shpil and incorporating elements of the so-called 'shund-roman' or popular fiction. It was in 1892 that the actress Ester Rokhl Kaminska, 'the Jewish Eleonora Duse', first appeared in the Eldorado theatre in Warsaw. By 1911 three Jewish theatres were open in that city: Kaminski's Literary Troupe at the Dynasy, the Elizeum, and the Orion, while the famous Vilner troupe was started in Vilna (now Vilnius) by Mordkhe Mazo in 1916. In 1918, on the other side of the Atlantic, Yankev (Jacob) Ben-Ami, together with Moris Shvarts, founded the even more famous Yiddish Arts Theatre in New York.

The Yiddish theatrical repertoire consisted of biblical tales, eastern European legends, and Jewish folk customs. Scenes generating a religious aura were often interwoven with dances and songs. Their changing atmosphere betrayed a permanent sense of dread, and combined drama and tragedy with tearful, melodramatic scenes and a devastating wit that triggered off contagious laughter. The performances owed their unique character and expressiveness to their (sometimes satirical) borrowing from Hasidic tradition, and Yiddish theatrical plays and films cannot be fully understood without reference to eastern European Hasidism, with its own specific brand of mysticism and philosophy, and recurrent interest in themes of individual Romantic rebellion of the individual and the conflict of tradition and assimilation.

SILENT FILM

From the outset Yiddish films enjoyed considerable popularity not only with Jewish audiences but among spectators of other nationalities in search of the exotic. They were made in Poland, Russia, Austria, Germany, Czechoslovakia, and Romania. In Russia they were produced by the S. Mintus Company in Riga (Latvia), the Mizrakh and Mirograf Company in Odessa, and by the Kharitonov, Khanzhonkov, and Pathé production companies in Moscow, and elsewhere. But the majority originated from Poland, whose Jews, characterized by a particularly strong feeling of their own national identity, accounted for some 10 per cent of the population. In the early years of this century, more than 80 per cent of the more than 400,000-strong Jewish population of Warsaw spoke and read Yiddish.

In Poland the main centre of Yiddish film production was Warsaw, where the first production company, Siła, was founded by Mordkhe (Mordka) Towbin. Among the films produced by Siła before the outbreak of the First World War were four adapted from plays by leading Yiddish playwright Yankev (Jacob) Gordin, starting in 1911

with *Der vilder Foter* (*The Cruel Father*) with Herman Sieracki in the title-role and Zina Goldshteyn in the role of the daughter. Siła also engaged the services of members of the theatrical Kaminski family. Avrom Yitskhok Kaminski directed *Destitute Murder* (1911) and the mystical drama *God, Man and Devil* (1912), while *Mirele Efros* (1912), directed by Andrzej Marek (Marek Arnshteyn or Orenshteyn), starred both Ester Rokhl Kaminska and Ida Kaminska, who made her début in the role of the boy Shloymele.

In 1913 a dynamic new Yiddish film enterprise called Kosmofilm was founded in Warsaw by Shmuel Ginzberg and Henryk Finkelstein. In 1913–14 Kosmofilm produced screenings of further plays by Gordin: *Der Umbakanter* (*Love and Death* or *A Stranger*), *Gots Shtrof* (*God's Punishment*), *Dem Khagzns Tokhter* (*The Cantor's Daughter*), and *Di Shkhite*, and a new version of *Di Shtifmuter* (*The Stepmother*), already filmed by Siła a couple of years earlier. The last film to be made by Kosmofilm with captions in Yiddish before the German invasion of Warsaw on 5 August 1915 was *Di farshtoysene Tokhter* (*The Repudiated Daughter*), based on the play by Avrom Goldfadn, with the participation of Ester Rokhl Kaminska.

Jewish themes also attracted the attention of film-makers in Germany before and during the First World War. *Shylock von Krakau* (*Kol Nidre*, 1913) was based on the novella by Felix Salten, directed by Carl Wilhelm, and designed by Hermann Warm, with the well-known actor Rudolf Schildkraut in the title-role, and *Der gelbe Schein* (*The Yellow Ticket*, 1918) was filmed for Ufa in occupied Warsaw by Victor Janson, with Polish actress Pola Negri in the main role.

Indigenous production revived after the war. Three outstanding Yiddish films made in Poland in the 1920s were: *Tkies Kaf* (*The Oath*, 1924), directed by Zygmunt Turkow; *Der Lamedvovnik* (*One of the Thirty-six*, 1925) by Henryk Szaro; and *In Poylishe Velder* (*In Polish Woods*, 1929), directed by Jonas Turkow, an adaptation of Yoysef Opatoshu's best-selling novel of the same title, with both Polish and Jewish actors playing the roles. Like *The Oath*, this film addressed the fundamental question of Jewish assimilation in nineteenth-century Poland and participation alongside the Poles in the January Uprising of 1863 against Russia. Yiddish films continued to be made in the USSR. *Yidishe Glikn* (*Jewish Luck*, 1925), by Alexander Granovski, was based on the famous *Menakhem-Mendl* story-cycle by Sholem Aleykhem, and was made with the participation of actors from the Habima Theatre and the great Soviet Yiddish actor Shloyme Mikhoels. *Blondzhende Shtern* (*Wandering Stars*, 1927), directed by Grigory Gricher Cherikover, was a story about a Jewish boy who runs away from the parental home and years later becomes a famous violinist. It too was based on a story by Aleykhem and had a script by Isaac Babel. Babel changed Aleykhem's story considerably in order to make it ideologically acceptable—an effort that

A classic of Yiddish cinema: *Yiddle with his Fiddle* (*Yidl mitn fidl*, 1936), produced and directed by Joseph Green and starring Molly Picon

proved ultimately vain, since this great writer and friend and confidant of Sergei Eisenstein was to die in the purges not many years later. Gricher Cherikover also made a number of other Yiddish films, including *Skvoz Slezy* (1928) which enjoyed worldwide fame under its American title *Laughter through Tears*.

SOUND CINEMA

The introduction of sound at the beginning of the 1930s resulted in a brief hiatus, but the second half of the decade proved to be a golden age for the Yiddish cinema, with synchronized dialogue now able to capture the richness of the language. Two Polish companies specialized in Yiddish films, Joseph Green's Green-Film, and Shaul and Yitskhok Goskind's Kinor. Aleksander Ford created fictionalized documents such as *Sabra Halutzim* (1934) with the participation of actors from the Jewish Theatre, and *We're on our Way* (*Mir kumen on*, 1935). Together with Jan Nowina-Przybylski, the enterprising producer and director Joseph Green (Yoysef Grinberg, a native of Łódź) made *Yiddle with his Fiddle* (*Yidl mitn Fidl*, 1936) with music by Abraham Ellstein and with Molly Picon in the title-role, and *The Purim Player* (*Der Purim-spiler*, 1937) with Miriam Kressin and Hymie Jacobson. With Konrad Tom he then directed

Little Mother (*Mamele*, 1938) with the participation of Molly Picon. Then, in association with Leon Trystan, he filmed *A Little Letter to Mother* (*A Brivele der Mamen*, 1938) with Lucy and Misha Gehrman. The talented director Henryk Szaro (Szapiro) did a sound remake of *The Oath* (*Tkies Kaf*, 1937) with Zygmunt Turkow as the prophet Elijah and with the participation of the choir of the Great Synagogue in Warsaw. In 1937 Leon Jeannot directed *Jolly Paupers* (*Di Freylekhe Kabtsonim*) with the participation of two famous Jewish comic actors, Shimen (Szymon) Dzigan and Yisroel Shumakher. But the most important artistic event of Yiddish cinema is rightly considered to be *The Dybbuk* (*Der Dibek*, 1937), adapted from the play (and ethnographic survey materials) by An-ski and directed by Michał Waszyński (Misha Wachsman). In this story, based on the old legend about the unhappy love of a poor Talmud scholar for Lea, the daughter of a rich man, Hasidic mysticism and symbolism come fully to the fore. The last Yiddish film to be produced in Poland before the outbreak of war was *Without a Home* (*On a Heym*, 1939), directed by Aleksander Marten (Marek Tennebaum, born in Łódź, and a refugee from Hitler's Germany), based on the play by Yankev Gordin, with Shimen Dzigan, Yisroel Shumakher, Adam Domb, and Ida Kaminska in the leading roles.

As life for European Jewry became increasingly threatened, the centre of Yiddish film production shifted to the United States, where the Austrian-born *émigré* Edgar G. Ulmer co-directed the popular success *Green Fields* (*Grine Felder*) with Yankev Ben-Ami. Ulmer's varied and prolific career (he had been the assistant of F. W. Murnau and went on to make numerous Hollywood B pictures) was interspersed with a number of other Yiddish films including *The Singing Blacksmith* (*Yankl der Shmid*, 1938) and *American Matchmaker* (*Amerikaner Shadkhn*, 1940). Gordin's *Mirele Efros* was remade by Josef Berne in 1939, while Moris Shvarts of the Yiddish Arts Theatre crossed over to film production to direct and act in *Tevye der Milkhiker* (1939).

The Holocaust took a cruel toll of Yiddish film-makers. Directors Henryk Szaro and Marek Arnshteyn, actors Klara Segalowicz, Yitskhok Samberg, Dora Fakel, Abram Kurc, and many others died in the Warsaw ghetto. Yiddish films continued to be made after the war, but in the aftermath of the final solution the glorious past of Yiddish cinematography assumed the special dimension of a value irredeemably lost.

Bibliography

Goldberg, Judith N. (1983), *Laughter through Tears: The Yiddish Cinema.*

Goldman, Eric A. (1988), *Visions, Images and Dreams: Yiddish Film Past and Present.*

Hoberman, Jim (1991), *Bridge of Light: Yiddish Film between Two Worlds.*

Shmeruk, Chone (1992), *Historia literatury jidisz* ('A history of Yiddish literature').

Japan: Before the Great Kanto Earthquake

HIROSHI KOMATSU

The apparatus of moving images, such as Edison's Kinetoscope, Lumière's Cinématographe, Edison's Vitascope, and the Vitascope copied by Lubin, were first exhibited in Japan in the latter half of 1896. By the autumn of 1897, the British motion picture camera, the Baxter and Wray Cinematograph, was imported by Konishi Photographic Store. Using these imported cameras, the first cameramen, such as Shiro Asano, Tsunekichi Shibata, and Kanzo Shirai, filmed street scenes and geisha dances, and, as early as 1898–9, were making skit films exploiting trick effects, like *Bake Jizo* ('Jizo the spook', 1898) and *Shinin no sosei* ('The resurrection of a corpse', 1898). However, by the turn of the century there was still no established film industry in Japan, and French, American, and British films dominated the Japanese market.

Following the tradition of the magic lantern show, or *utsushie*, early films were shown at variety halls, rental halls, or ordinary theatres, alongside presentations in different media. Many of the first Japanese films recorded scenes from kabuki: in 1899, *Momijigari* ('Viewing scarlet maple leaves') and *Ninin Dojoji* ('Two people at Dojo temple') were filmed by Tsunekichi Shibata, and Tsuneji Tsuchiya made *Nio no ukisu* ('The floating nest of the little grebe'). *Momijigari*, a film of the kabuki play, featuring the legendary actors Danjuro Ichikawa IX and Kikugoro Onoe V, consisted of three shots and already showed a primitive form of film narrativity. *Ninin Dojoji* was the first tinted film ever made in Japan. It was coloured by the Yoshizawa Company, manufacturers of magic lantern apparatus and slides, who later became one of the first Japanese film production companies. When *Ninin Dojoji* was projected at the kabuki theatre in August 1900, the sponsor created a mock-up of a valley in front of the screen, with a fish-filled pond between the rocks, and a cool breeze generated by an electric fan wafting over the audience. Such extra-filmic devices were an important feature of early Japanese cinema.

In addition to the Konishi Photographic Store, Asanuma & Co. and Tsurubuchi Photographic Store dabbled with film production at the turn of the century, but soon turned exclusively to the sale of film stock and equipment. Japanese audiences were hungry for domestic subjects, but even as late as 1904 there were no production companies to fulfil their needs. The Komatsu Company, established in 1903, made some subjects for travelling exhibitions in the provinces, but even Yoshizawa Company, the most active, filmed only news subjects, landscapes, and geisha dances, and foreign films, especially from France, still dominated the market.

It was the outbreak of the Russo–Japanese War in 1905 that vitalized domestic production. A number of journalists and cameramen were sent to the Asian mainland to report on the war, among them motion picture cameramen Tsunekichi Shibata and Kozaburo Fujiwara, whose war films, along with those shot by British cameramen, became extremely popular in Japan. The popularity of war films led to the production of Japanese-made fake documentaries, and, in a similar vein, in 1905–6 a number of French 'reproduction of war' films were released. These fake documentaries of the Russo–Japanese War drew audiences' attention to the differences between fiction and non-fiction films, a distinction that had not been visible in the Japanese film industry up until that point.

Until 1908 there was no film studio in Japan, and all films were shot in the open air, including the kabuki films that required painted backdrops. However, after visiting the Edison studio in the USA, Kenichi Kawaura, the head of Yoshizawa Company, built a glass studio in Meguro, Tokyo, completed in January 1908. Soon afterwards, Pathé built a film studio in Okubo, Tokyo, the Yokota Company followed suit in Kyoto, and a year later the Fukuhodo Company started film-making in the Hanamidera studio, also in Tokyo. From 1909, then, systematic film-making, particularly of fiction films, could begin, and these four companies formed the mainstream of that production in the early years.

In October 1903 Japan's first cinema (Denki-kan or Electric Theatre) was established in Asakusa, Tokyo, and from this point the number of cinemas gradually increased, slowly replacing the vaudeville halls. The Japanese developed a unique way of showing films, borrowed from the traditions of the staged kabuki and Noh, which lasted throughout the silent period; a *benshi*, who explained the filmic image to the audiences, attended each performance. In the primitive era they introduced the films and told their outlines to the audience before the show began. But, as the films became longer and increasingly complex, the *benshi* explained the scenes and spoke the dialogue, accompanied by Japanese music, while the silent images flickered on the screen. The system of one or sometimes several players narrating from outside the filmic image prevented Japanese cinema's complete assimilation to the western form of film practice. The narrative function of the intertitles and the shot organization tended to be simplified as much as possible to emphasize the skill of the *benshi* in describing the narrative development of the film, the meaning of the scene,

177

the atmosphere, and the feelings of the characters. There were few intertitles in Japanese films even in the late 1910s, and in most cases they functioned only as captions to each chapter of the story. Similarly, the dominance of the *benshi*'s voice obliged the exclusion of the short take and any rapid action by the actors. By the 1910s, the popularity of the *benshi* became so enormous that they exerted as much power over the finished look of a film as any of the production companies, if not more.

This is not to say, however, that Japanese films did not adopt any western influences. By 1912, inspired by the French films that flooded the domestic market, the powerful Yoshizawa Company was making dramas with contemporary subjects (known as Shinpa), and filming in diverse genres such as comedy, trick film, scenery, and travelogue, alongside more traditional kabuki. However, similarities with western cinema were superficial, and Japanese films preserved a unique flavour throughout the 1910s. The existence of the *benshi* as a narrator 'outside' the film meant that the primary purpose of the *mise-en-scène* of Japanese cinema was representing the characters' interactions and changes of feeling and mood within each scene, rather than constructing an illusion of a smoothly developing story. There were some, however, who did attempt to assimilate western filmic forms into early Japanese film; *Shin hototogisu* ('The cuckoo—new form', Pathé, 1909), directed by Shisetsu Iwafuji, used flashbacks, and *Matsu no midori* ('The green of the pine', Yoshizawa, 1911) used a film-within-a-film as the climax of the narrative. Even these works, however, adopted the traditional theatrical rule that the female role was to be played by an *oyama*, the special male actor who always played the women's roles. Until the early 1920s, there were very few actresses in Japanese cinema, because it was believed that femininity could be rendered more effectively by an *oyama* than by a real woman.

In 1912, aiming to monopolize the market, Yoshizawa, Yokota, Pathé, and Fukuhodo consolidated into the trust Nippon Katsudoshashin Co. (Nikkatsu). This company built the Mukojima studio in Tokyo, where they produced scores of Shinpa (New School) films. These dealt with contemporary subjects, often adapted from newspaper serials or foreign fiction, in a melodramatic style. In Kyoto they used the former Yokota studio, and produced Kyuha (Old School) films; *samurai* films with historical backgrounds. As soon as Nikkatsu was established, several anti-trust companies were also formed. Among them, Tenkatsu, established in March 1914, became the most competitive rival to Nikkatsu. Before being absorbed into Nikkatsu, Fukuhodo had bought the rights to Charles Urban's Kinemacolor for the purpose of releasing Urban's Kinemacolor films and producing Japanese films shot by the process. Taking over these rights, Tenkatsu was established to make Kinemacolor films to compete with Nikkatsu films.

Tenkatsu, who imitated Nikkatsu by making both Old School and New School films, also produced *rensageki*, or chain drama, a combination of stage play and cinema using films for the scenes that were difficult to represent live on the stage. The live action and filmic images alternated in a 'chain' fashion. After one scene was played by actors on the stage, the screen descended and the next scene was projected on to it for several minutes, and then the actors played on the stage again. Tenkatsu was unusual in employing actresses for these films as early as 1914.

The distinction between the Old School and New School was borrowed from the concept of genre chiefly established in stage plays of the Meiji period. The Old School, which was later called *jidaigeki* (period drama), was constituted, in most cases, by sword-play films in which people in historical costume appeared, set in the periods before the Meiji restoration. The New School, which was later called *gendaigeki* (modern drama), consisted of films set in contemporary circumstances. The Old School was always based around a superstar: Matsunosuke Onoe was Nikkatsu's most famous star, while Tenkatsu had the very popular Shirogoro Sawamura. The cinema of stars was thus established first and foremost by the period drama in Japan. In such films, stereotyped stories were repeated again and again, and played by the same actors. This tradition of repetition became one of the most particular traits in the history of Japanese cinema. Such stories as *Chushingura* ('The loyal forty-seven retainers') have been made many times and continue to be made to this day.

By 1914 there were nine film-producing companies in Japan. The largest one was Nikkatsu, which released fourteen films a month from their two studios. Tenkatsu had studios in Tokyo and Osaka and made fifteen films a month. The oldest company, Komatsu, established in 1903, had ceased film production for a while, but began to produce films again in a studio in Tokyo in 1913. In 1914 this company made six films a month. The ephemeral company Nippon Kinetophone made a few sound films in the same year. Tokyo Cinema and Tsurubuchi Lantern & Cinematograph were making news films. In Osaka, there were some small companies like Shikishima Film, Sugimoto Film, and Yamato On-ei. By 1915, when M. Kashii Film, the company that took over Pathé, joined these anti-trust companies, Nikkatsu's aspirations to monopolize the market were dashed.

Masao Inoue's *Taii no musume* ('The daughter of the lieutenant', 1917), made at the newly established Kobayashi Co., was quite different from the traditional New School films in using westernized techniques. Adapted from the German film *Gendarm Möbius* (Stellan Rye, 1913), *Taii no musume* was inspired by its stylistically static direction, but Masao Inoue used a flashback that the German film had not, and utilized close-ups that were unusual in

Japanese cinema at the time. In the period when the filmic image was for the most part constituted as a kind of illustration for the *benshi*'s vocal skills, Inoue showed the rhetorical sense in the picture itself. The image of the bride's trousseau being carried for the wedding ceremony is reflected on the surface of a river, while the camera pans slowly to catch the faces of people in the frame. Such westernized direction was rare in Japanese cinema even in 1917. Inoue again used close-ups in his next film *Dokuso* ('The poisonous herb', 1917), but in most Japanese films of this period, where *oyama* still played the female roles, the close-up of the 'woman' was not effective.

There had been partial and sporadic attempts to westernize Japanese cinema even before 1910. For example, in the Yoshizawa Company's comedy films, which were heavily influenced by French cinema, the main actor was a Max Linder imitator. But it was in the late 1910s that some companies attempted to change the highly codified organization of primitive Japanese cinema into the constitution of westernized reality; incorporating realist settings, rapid shot development, and a move away from stereotyped subjects. This was also the period when the role of director attained a new importance. In 1918 directors like Eizo Tanaka and Tadashi Oguchi made changes to the dominant form of Nikkatsu's New School films.

Although stereotypes could not be avoided totally in modern drama, films of the New School did show more artistic ambition, particularly those produced in Nikkatsu's Mukojima studio in the late 1910s. In Japanese arts in the post-Meiji period, artistic ambition was widely considered to be a western concept, so that the value of art in Japan could be made highbrow by conforming to the norms of western art. The westernization of style was easier in modern drama than in period drama, and so it was here that the developments took place.

The process of westernization in Japanese cinema, which included the phasing out of *oyama* in favour of actresses, began in earnest in the late 1910s, spearheaded by the ideas of the young critic and film-maker Norimasa Kaeriyama. Kaeriyama asserted that Japanese cinema, which was only the illustration of the *benshi*'s voice impersonations, had to find a way for the narrative to be automatically formed by the filmic image, as seen in the dominant form of European and American cinema. In 1918, when Nikkatsu allowed Eizo Tanaka and Tadashi Oguchi to make westernized films on this principle, Tenkatsu, accepting Kaeriyama's idea of the 'pure film drama', gave him the opportunity to make two films: *Sei no kagayaki* ('The glow of life') and *Miyama no otome* ('Maid of the deep mountains', both 1918). These films were set in imaginary westernized circumstances, avoiding the highly codified comportment of the actors employed in traditional Japanese cinema, and manufacturing naturalism that was in complete opposition to the prevalent

Japanese style. They were the first Japanese films actively, if very naïvely, to adopt western concepts of art.

Slowly other film companies took up this trend, and by the early 1920s the traditional form of Japanese cinema had become completely old-fashioned. The period between 1920 and the first half of 1923 (just before the Great Kanto Earthquake) witnessed a change of form in Japanese cinema. The New School became established as modern drama, and the Old School as the period drama. There was a transition from the traditional theatrical form to the studio system, and film style, as well as the production process, began to follow the western model. The earliest form of Japanese cinema, which avoided rapid changes of images, used intertitles only for the chapters of a story, or used filmic images for discrete segments of a stage play as seen in the chain drama, was obliged to change in this period, even within the most conservative companies, like Nikkatsu. The company resisted assimilating to the western form for a long time and attempted to preserve tradition, but finally the audience's changing demands prompted change in company policy.

In this short period, two ephemeral companies made some interesting films. One of the two was Kokkatsu, which absorbed Tenkatsu in 1920, and gave Norimasa Kaeriyama the opportunity to make films. This company not only produced period dramas directed by Jiro Yoshino, but also began actively employing actresses in the place of *oyama*. It allowed some directors to experiment with making realist films, such as *Kantsubaki* ('Winter camellia', Ryoha Hatanaka, 1921), or films which partially employed expressionist settings, for example *Reiko no wakare* ('On the verge of spiritual light', Kiyomatsu Hosoyama, 1922).

Eizo Tanaka's *Kyoyo erimise* ('Kyoka, the collar shop', 1922), one of the last Japanese films to feature *oyama* (male actors in female roles)

Daisuke Ito
(1898–1981)

Largely forgotten today, Daisuke Ito was regarded in the late 1920s and early 1930s, by Japanese audiences and critics alike, as one of Japan's foremost directors. Most of his films from that period are unfortunately now lost, and, except for a few fragments and the miraculously surviving *Oatsurae Jirokichi goshi* ('The chivalrous robber Jirokichi', 1931), all his silent films were known after the war only by repute. But in December 1991 his most famous silent film was rediscovered, and some of the second part and most of the third part of the great trilogy *Chuji tabi nikki* ('A diary of Chuji's travels', 1927) became available for modern audiences to enjoy.

Ito made his first film in 1924 and thereafter worked consistently as a director until 1970. But it is on his silent films that his reputation is founded, and except for one or two works such as *Oosho* ('The chess king', 1948) his sound films, particularly post-war, have been undervalued. The main reason for this is that critics have tended to judge them (rather as happened in the case of Abel Gance in France) against a fading memory of his innovative silent style. The energetic style of his late 1920s films was indeed unique in the world. The camera roamed in every direction, *samurai* dashed across the screen, a row of lanterns swirled around in the deep dark of night, and the rhythm of the films reached vertiginous speeds through accelerated montage. Intertitles that stressed the dialogue were synchronized to the rhythm of the images, and the rhythm of the words was inspired by Japanese poetry and other forms of story-telling.

Above all, a spirit of Romanticism, sentimentalism, nihilism, and a despairing rebellion against power penetrated all of Ito's films of the period. He raised the jidaigeki (period drama) to the level of avant-garde cinema, even competing with the so-called tendency film (expressing proletarian ideology). Some of his jidaigeki borrowed materials from German or French novels. Elsewhere, he repeatedly tried to break out of the established formula for jidaigeki films, including an attempt to conjure up images inspired by Chopin's music in *Ikiryo* ('Evil spirit', 1927). In the early 1930s, like Alfred Hitchcock, he experimented with sound. In his first sound film, *Tangesazen* (1933), he deliberately restricted the use of dialogue and sound, and he used Schubert's Unfinished Symphony in a jidaigeki—*Chusingura* ('The loyal forty-seven Ronin', 1934).

Ito always saw himself as an artisan, and his work of the sound period contains its fair share of mediocre entertainment films made to the orders of producers. His wartime work, such as *Kurama Tengu* (1942) or *Kokusai mitsuyudan* ('International smugglers', 1944), provided an escape from the reality of war as well as from the propaganda film.

He returned to the front rank of Japanese cinema in 1948 with the highly acclaimed *Oosho*, but apart from a few films, such as *Hangyakuji* ('The conspirator', 1961), his post-war work remains largely unrecognized. Among his lesser-known films *Yama wo tobu hanagasa* ('The hat adorned with flowers flying over the mountain',1949) is undoubtedly, from a modern standpoint, a masterpiece, as is *Harukanari haha no kuni* ('The motherland far far away', 1950), with its contrapuntal editing of image and sound and use of metaphorical montage.

Throughout the 1950s and 1960s Ito made many jidaigeki, and came to be regarded as a director of a single genre of film. His early career as maker of highly prized silent films became forgotten, as did the films themselves. But he is now beginning to be rediscovered and valued, both for his masterly silent films and for the qualities of *mise-en-scène* in his sound films.

HIROSHI KOMATSU

SELECT FILMOGRAPHY

Jogashima (1924); Ikiryo (1927); Oatsurae Jirokichi goshi (1931); Tangesazen (1933); Chusingura (1934); Kokusai mitsuyudan (1944); Oosho (1948); Yama wo tobu hanagasa (1949); Harukanari haha no kuni (1950); Hangyakuji (1961)

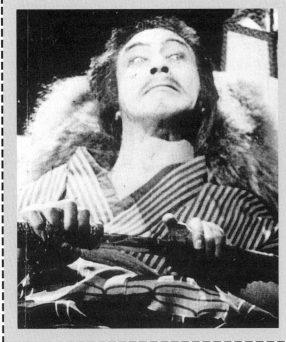

A shot from Daisuke Ito's recently rediscovered masterpiece *Chuji tabi nikki* ('A diary of Chuji's travels', 1927)

The Taikatsu Company was established to produce intellectual films. This company did not, unlike Nikkatsu and Kokkatsu, draw the audience in by making Old School sword-play films with popular stars, and neither was the company interested in the already codified form of New School films. Taikatsu's intention was to produce cinematic Japanese films inspired by, but not directly imitating, European and American cinema. For this purpose, the company invited Junichiro Tanizaki to be their adviser. Their first production was *The Amateur Club* (Kisaburo Kurihara, 1920), in which elements of American cinema—bathing beauties, chase scenes, slapstick—were adapted to Japanese circumstances, attaining a visual dynamism absent from other traditional Japanese films of the time. This was one of the first Americanized films produced in Japan, and its director, Kurihara, went on to make *Katsushika sunago* (1921), *Hinamatsuri no yoru* ('The night of the dolls' festival', 1921), and *Jyasei no in* ('The lasciviousness of the viper', 1921) at Taikatsu, and expand this aesthetic.

The early 1920s also saw the establishment of Shochiku Kinema, a company which relinquished archaic filmmaking from the outset, and introduced American formulas in film direction. Shochiku used actresses who adopted facial expressions found in American films in order to represent psychological complexity, and tried to render the more natural movement of the everyday world. Shochiku built a studio in Kamata, Tokyo, and immediately began to produce Americanized films under the advice of George Chapman and Henry Kotani from Hollywood studios. The tendency to represent the naïve imaginary world, as seen in the works of Kaeriyama, and a blatant desire to rebuff the traditional Japanese style, were the hallmarks of the Shochiku films. The forthright Americanism of the studio was decried by critics at first, but such criticism ceased in the mid-1920s, when Japanese cinema as a whole assimilated a studio system based on the model of the United States.

In 1920 such American methods in Japanese filmmaking would still have seemed strange to the audiences, but the situation changed rapidly, and the system was transformed virtually within a year. At Shochiku, Kaoru Osanai, the innovator of the theatre world, turned to filmmaking, supervising the revolutionary *Rojo no reikon* ('Soul on the road', Minoru Murata, 1921), the very apotheosis of the studio's desire to produce a new Japanese aesthetic. In this film, plural stories were narrated in parallel, a new practice, inspired by D. W. Griffith's *Intolerance* (1916). By this time even Nikkatsu, which had been making the most traditional films, could not resist the current. In January 1921 the company founded a special section for 'intellectual' film-making, dominated by the director Eizo Tanaka, who made three films that year: *Asahi sasu mae* ('Before the morning sun shines'), *Shirayuri no kaori* ('Scent of the white lily'), and *Nagareyuku onna* ('Woman in the stream'). These were, for Nikkatsu, attempts at innovation. They were released in theatres that specialized in screening foreign films to an intellectual audience. Their intertitles were written in both Japanese and English. The New School films employed several *benshi* and the intertitles were traditionally felt to disturb the flow of the filmic image. However, foreign films were narrated by a solitary *benshi*, so Nikkatsu inserted bilingual intertitles into these 'intellectual' films to avoid the resistance of the traditional film fans and to establish an affinity with the similarly titled foreign films.

Nevertheless, as the acting style in these films remained traditional, the attempts at innovation were not wholly successful, especially in the face of competition from Shochiku. Although Tanaka's films did feature actresses, in the main Nikkatsu, the last film company to give up the *oyama*, continued to make films with them up until 1923.

So, despite this general shift towards westernized cinematic styles, traditional Japanese forms were not totally abandoned. Indeed in 1922 Eizo Tanaka made the masterpiece *Kyoya erimise* ('Kyoya, the collar shop') employing *oyama*. Unlike the contemporary directors at Shochiku, Tanaka did not simply follow American cinematic trends. This was a film about an old collar shop, Kyoya, in which the downfall of one family, and, by implication, of old Japan, is described through the passing of the four seasons. The distinction of the seasons in this film corresponds to seasonal words in haiku, traditional Japanese poetry, which, added to the poetic background and atmosphere of downtown Tokyo, made this the most refined form of Japanese traditional art achieved by the cinema to date. As one of the last Nikkatsu films that employed *oyama*, *Kyoya erimise* was the final swan-song of archaism in the vanishing old style of Japanese cinema. Without demolishing the concepts of conservative film, Nikkatsu was able to preserve the pure Japanese plastic beauty in this masterpiece. For the film, Tanaka constructed the Kyoya shop in its entirety in the Mukojima studio. The partition walls could be removed according to the camera position, and for natural representation of actors' movement from room to room and from the verandah to the garden.

After this, Nikkatsu was to make a series of high-quality films, before the Great Kanto Earthquake of September 1923. Tanaka made *Dokuro no mai* ('Dance of the skull', 1923), using actors and actresses who belonged to the Association of Stage Players. It was a portrayal of the asceticism of a Buddhist priest and, at eleven reels, was highly ambitious. Critics compared it to classic foreign works, in particular Stroheim's *Foolish Wives* (1922). Japanese films were finally being received on the same level as foreign, especially American, films.

Together with Tanaka, Kensaku Suzuki was the first

auteur in the history of Japanese cinema. In addition to these two, younger directors emerged in this period, like Osamu Wakayama and, youngest of all, Kenji Mizoguchi, Tanaka's protégé and assistant on *Kyoya Erimise*. Some of the most important achievements in Japanese film are found in the works of Suzuki. In a short period of activity, he realized a film form akin to the European avant-garde, and anticipated a wholly new trend of film-making that would arise suddenly in the aftermath of the Earthquake. The extremely pessimistic style and content of his films were feverishly applauded by the young audience of the time. *Tabi no onna geinin* ('The itinerant female artiste', 1923) portrays the parallel lives of two desperate souls, a man and a woman who only meet by chance in the final scene to part again and go on their gloomy ways. In the Stroheimian *Aiyoku no nayami* ('Agony of lust', 1923) an old man is tragically besotted with a younger woman. The bleakest realism came in *Ningen-ku* ('Anguish of a human being', 1923), in which Suzuki rejected conventional narrativity, and demonstrated his ideology of pessimism in a new form. The first reel of this four-reel film shows the fragmented existences of various assorted low-life characters: a starved old man, a group of tramps, bad boys, and prostitutes. The lives of these poor and ill-fated people is paralleled by the glittering images of an aristocratic ball. Following this, a poor man sneaks into the home of a rich man and witnesses the master of the house, who is bankrupt, committing suicide after killing his wife. The film depicts events from about 10 p.m. to 2 a.m., so that all the scenes are shot at night, with a grim *mise-en-scène*

of rainy streets, gas lamps, flowing muddy water, and dilapidated buildings. Suzuki, insisting on extreme realism, made the actor who played the 'shadowy old man' fast for three days. Other innovations in *Ningen-ku* include frequent close-ups, dialogue intertitles, and, notably, rapid editing that was not to be the norm in Japan until the late 1920s.

By 1923 Japanese cinema had virtually demolished the long-standing traditional form, on the one hand by assimilating American cinema, and on the other through the inspiration of avant-garde film forms such as German Expressionism and French Impressionism. Nevertheless, Japanese cinema had not only assimilated and imitated. For example, the point-of-view shot was extremely scarce in Japanese cinema even in the mid-1920s. This resulted from the fact that Japanese cinema depended on the force of narrative illusionism constituted by the voice of the *benshi*, and from the long-standing tradition of the distance kept between the object and the lens of the camera. The archaic form of Japanese art and culture still exerted influence on Japanese cinema beyond the early period.

Bibliography
Anderson, Joseph L., and Richie, Donald (1982), *The Japanese Film: Art and Industry*.
Burch, Noël (1979), *To the Distant Observer*.
Nolletti, Arthur, Jr., and Desser, David (eds.) (1992), *Reframing Japanese Cinema: Authorship, Genre and History*.
Sato, Tadao, *et al.* (eds.) (1986), *Koza Nihon Eiga*, i and ii.
Tanaka, Junichiro (1975), *Nihon Eiga Hattatsu Shi*, i and ii.

THE SILENT CINEMA EXPERIENCE

Music and the Silent Film

MARTIN MARKS

Silent films were a technological accident, not an aesthetic choice. If Edison and other pioneers had had the means, music would probably have been an integral part of film-making from the very start. But because such means were lacking, a new type of theatrical music rapidly developed; the wide variety of films and screening conditions in Europe or America between 1895 and the late 1920s came to be matched by an equally wide range of musical practice and musical materials. With the coming of synchronized sound this variety disappeared and a whole past experience was lost from view. Since the 1980s, however, with the renewed interest in reviving silent performance, film musicians and historians have begun to rediscover the field and even to find new forms of accompaniment for silent film.

MUSICAL PRACTICE

Music in silent cinema has long been of interest to film theorists, and a number of explanations have been proposed to account for its apparently indispensable presence right from the start. These have tended to concentrate on the psycho-acoustic functions of music (well summarized by Gorbman 1987), and only recently have historians begun to pay close attention to the theatrical context of film presentations and in particular to the debt owed by film music to long-standing traditions of music for the theatre, adapted as necessary to suit the new medium.

Consider, for example, the remarkable variety and richness of so-called 'incidental' music for stage plays throughout the nineteenth century (a variety that becomes still richer if one looks further to the past). At one end, lavish incidental works by Beethoven, Mendelssohn, Bizet, and Grieg, though somewhat atypical, proved highly useful for film accompaniment—or so we can presume, since excerpts from these works were repeatedly published in film music anthologies and inserted into compiled scores (often for scenes quite unlike their original contexts). But most theatre music was the work of minor figures, who, like their successors in the field of film music, continually had to compose, arrange, conduct, or improvise functional bits and pieces—'mélodrames', 'hurries', 'agits', and so on—on the spur of the moment, for one ephemeral production after another.

Relatively little of this music is known today, but what has been seen (like the collection of Victorian-period examples published by Mayer and Scott) bears a strong family likeness to the seemingly 'new' music later published in film anthologies. Thus, the practitioners of incidental music supplied a triple legacy—of pre-existent repertoire, stylistic prototypes, and working methods—just as did those who specialized in the genres of ballet and pantomime. The latter genres sometimes came very close to anticipating the peculiar requirements of scores for silent films, owing to their absence of speech and need for continuous music, some of it consisting of closed forms suitable for patterned choreography, some of it open-ended and fragmentary, intended to mirror the smallest details of stage action.

Paradoxically, the theatrical genre with perhaps the most powerful influence on film music was the one with which its affinity was the weakest, namely opera. Instrumental arrangements from many hundreds of popular works (Italian, French, German, English) were called for in silent-film cue sheets of the 1910s and 1920s; moreover, by that time Wagner's development of a symphonic approach (the orchestra supplying a continuous commentary), characterized by the use of symbolic themes, long-range thematic transformations, opulent tone colours, and romantic harmonies, was so much admired that many leading composers of film scores (including Joseph Carl Breil, Gottfried Huppertz, and Mortimer Wilson, all discussed below) either explicitly acknowledged his influence or implicitly imitated his style, albeit with less than Wagnerian results.

As was true of film music's antecedents, accompaniments to silent films were of many types, so the popular image of the lone pianist improvising (badly, on an out-of-tune relic) to whatever appeared on the screen is only the smallest and darkest part of a much broader and brighter panorama. All told, musical ensembles fell into four distinct categories, determined largely by the time period and theatrical milieu.

1. Vaudeville/music hall orchestras accompanied films when seen as part of variety shows during the early years

Ernst Lubitsch

(1892–1947)

The son of a Jewish tailor, Lubitsch joined Max Reinhardt's Deutsches Theater in 1911 as supporting actor, and had his first starring part in a film farce, *Die Firma heiratet* (1914). The role, an absent-minded, accident-prone, and over-sexed assistant in a clothing shop, established him as a Jewish comedy character. Between 1914 and 1918 he acted in about twenty such comedies, the majority of which he also directed (among the ones to have survived are *Schuhpalast Pinkus*, 1916; *Der Blusenkönig*, 1917; and *Der Fall Rosentopf*, 1918).

Lubitsch was the most significant German film talent to emerge during the war, creating a type of visual and physical comedy familiar from pre-war Pathé films, but situated in a precise ethnic milieu (the German-Jewish lower middle class) and mostly treating the staple theme of much early German cinema: social rise. After 1918, Lubitsch specialized in burlesque spoofs of popular operettas (*Die Austernprinzessin*, 1919), of Hoffmannesque fantasy subjects (*Die Puppe*, 1919), and of Shakespeare (*Romeo und Julia im Schnee* and *Kohlhiesels Töchter*, both 1920). Centred on mistaken identities (*Wenn vier dasselbe tun*, 1917), doubles (*Die Puppe*, *Kohlhiesels Töchter*), and female cross-dressing (*Ich möchte kein Mann sein*, 1918), his comedies feature foppish men and headstrong women, among them Ossi Oswalda (*Ossis Tagebuch*, 1917) and Pola Negri (*Madame Dubarry*, 1919).

Working almost exclusively for the Projections-AG Union, Lubitsch became the preferred director of Paul Davidson, who from 1918 onwards produced a series of exotic costume dramas (*Carmen*, 1918; *Das Weib des Pharao*, 1922), filmed plays (*Die Flamme*, 1923), and historical spectacles (*Anna Boleyn*, 1920) which brought both producer and director world success. The 'Lubitsch touch' lay in the way the films combined erotic comedy with the staging of historical show-pieces (the French Revolution in *Madame Dubarry*), the *mise-en-scène* of crowds (the court of Henry VIII in *Ann Boleyn*), and the dramatic use of monumental architecture (as in his Egyptian and oriental films). But one could also say that Lubitsch successfully cross-dressed the Jewish *schlemihl* and let him loose in the grand-scale stage sets of Max Reinhardt.

Lubitsch's stylistic trademark was a form of visual understatement, flattering the spectators by letting them into the know, ahead of the characters. Already in his earliest films, he seduced by surmise and inference, even as he built on the slapstick tradition of escalating a situation to the point of leading its logic *ad absurdum*. Far from working out this logic merely as a formal principle, Lubitsch, in comedies like *Die Austernprinzessin* (1919) or *Die Bergkatze* (1921), based it on a sharply topical experience: the escalating hyperinflation of the immediate post-war years, nourishing starvation fantasies about the American way of life, addressed to a defeated nation wanting to feast on exotic locations, erotic sophistication, and conspicuous waste. What made it a typical Lubitsch theme was the *mise-en-scène* of elegant self-cancellation, in contrast to other directors of exotic escapism, who dressed up bombastic studio sets as if to signify a solid world. Lubitsch, a Berliner through and through, was also Germany's first, and some would say only, 'American' director. He left for the United States in 1921, remaking himself several times in Hollywood's image, while, miraculously, becoming ever more himself.

If his first calling card was *Rosita* (1923), an underrated vehicle for Mary Pickford's ambitions to become a *femme*

fatale, Lubitsch cornered the market as the definitive Continental sophisticate with comedies that not so much transformed as transfigured the slapstick theme of mistaken identities. *The Marriage Circle* (1923), *Forbidden Paradise* (1924), *Lady Windermere's Fan* (1925), and *So This is Paris* (1926) are gracefully melancholy meditations on adultery, deceit, and self-deception, tying aristocratic couples and decadent socialites together to each other, in search of love, but settling for lust, wit, and a touch of malice. After some Teutonic exercises in sentimentality (*The Student Prince*, 1927; *The Patriot*, 1928), the coming of sound brought Lubitsch new opportunities to reinvent his comic style. Prominent through his producer-director position at Paramount Studios, and aided by the script-writing talents of Ernest Vajda and Samson Raphaelson, Lubitsch returned to one of his first inspirations; operetta plots and boulevard theatre intrigues, fashioning from them a typical 1930s Hollywood *émigré* genre, the 'Ruritanian' and 'Riviera' musical comedies, starring mostly Maurice Chevalier, with Jeanette MacDonald, or Claudette Colbert (*The Love Parade*, 1929; *The Smiling Lieutenant*, 1931; *The Merry Widow*, 1934). Segueing the songs deftly into the plot lines, and brimming with sexual innuendoes, the films are bravura pieces of montage cinema. But Lubitsch's reputation deserves to rest on the apparently just as frivolous, but poignantly balanced, comedies *Trouble in Paradise* (1932), *Design for Living* (1933), *Angel* (1937), and *Ninotchka* (1939). Invariably love triangles, these dramas of futility and *vanitas* between drawing room and boudoir featured, next to Melvyn Douglas and Herbert Marshall, the screen goddesses Marlene Dietrich and Greta Garbo, whom Lubitsch showed human and vulnerable, while intensifying their erotic allure. During the 1940s, Lubitsch's central European *Weltschmerz* found a suitably comic-defiant mask in films like *The Shop around the Corner* (1940) and *To Be or Not to Be* (1942), the latter a particularly audacious attempt to sabotage the presumptions not only of Nazi rule, but of all tyrannical holds on the real: celebrating, as he had always done, the saving graces and survivor skills of make-believe.

THOMAS ELSAESSER

SELECT FILMOGRAPHY

Schuhpalast Pinkus (1916); Ich möchte kein Mann sein (1918); Die Austernprinzessin (1919); Madame Dubarry (1919); Anna Boleyn (1920); Die Bergkatze (1921); Das Weib des Pharao (1922); The Marriage Circle (1923); Lady Windermere's Fan (1925); So This is Paris (1926); The Love Parade (1929); Trouble in Paradise (1932); Design for Living (1933); The Merry Widow (1934); Angel (1937); Ninotchka (1939); The Shop around the Corner (1940); To Be or Not to Be (1942)

BIBLIOGRAPHY

Carringer, Robert, and Sabath, Barry (1978), *Ernst Lubitsch: A Guide to References and Resources.*
Prinzler, Hans Helmut, and Patalas, Enno (eds.) (1984), *Lubitsch.*
Weinberg, Herman G. (1977), *The Lubitsch Touch: A Critical Study.*

Opposite: Marie Prevost and Monte Blue in Ernst Lubitsch's *The Marriage Circle* (1923)

(mid-1890s into the early 1900s), and there is considerable evidence to suggest that the music played during such presentations was as carefully prepared as it was for all other portions of the show.

2. When films moved into theatres of their own (nickelodeons, etc., beginning *c.*1905), music came with them, principally on pianos or mechanical equivalents. This phase marks the beginning of film music as a distinct profession, but for a time many theatre owners neglected the musical end of their operations: some of these pianos *were* out of tune, some of the performers quite unskilled. Still, the trade periodicals regularly mentioned certain theatres featuring music to praise rather than blame; and the importance of music even in these modest arenas is further attested by the widespread custom of enhancing programmes with 'illustrated songs' (as in small-time vaudeville houses).

3. From about 1910 theatres tended to be built larger, with more impressive facilities and increased budgets for music: chamber ensembles of anything from three players (comprising a melody instrument, piano, and drums) to fifteen became common. This development coincided with radical changes in film production and distribution, as well as the length and nature of individual films, and led to a growing market for musical arrangements suitable for film-playing. From 1910 onwards, therefore, there was a great flowering of film music publications, which continued until the end of the period.

4. The final phase is that of the grand movie 'palaces', built during the late 1910s and 1920s. There one heard spectacular theatre organs (the earliest models date from about 1912, but they became far more impressive a decade later), sharing the spotlight with large orchestras and colourful conductors some of whom (William Axt, Giuseppe Becce, Carli Elinor, Louis Levy, Hans May, Erno Rapée, Hugo Riesenfeld, Marc Roland, and others) also became prominent as film composers. At least one such palace could be found in every town of even moderate size, while metropolitan centres like New York, London, and Berlin boasted several. The shows became lavish, mingling concert overtures, vaudeville stars, classical performers, and skits intended as prologues to the actual films, and these too comprised a rich array, from cartoon and travelogue to the main feature.

Of course accompaniments were as diverse as the musicians who played them, but circumstances pressed toward the middle of the spectrum—between improvisation at one end and full original scores at the other. A keyboard soloist can improvise and play with expressive subtleties of rhythm not possible for an ensemble, but the quality of improvisation is apt to flag, the soloist's store of ideas exhausted, when playing for new films day after day. (Moreover, as witnesses attest, improvisation can be

185

dangerous when you do not know what is coming next in the film.) On the other hand, complete original scores were simply not practical or feasible: there were special cases from the very earliest years, but most films were too short-lived, the distribution system too far-flung, and performers too varied in ensemble and too uneven in talent to justify commissioned scores.

Since most soloists and all ensembles needed something written out to play, the practical solution was to rely on compiled/composed mixtures of music, much of it ready-made or familiar to the performers. Compiled scores for feature films thus became the great tradition of film music, especially after the appearance of Breil's landmark score for *The Birth of a Nation* in 1915. The Breil score, after first being played by orchestras on tour with the film, was made available to theatres in printed copies, and the policy of 'publication' of a score for distribution with its film was adopted for many subsequent important American films. Scores survive for many of these films, including: *The Battle Cry of Peace* (J. Stuart Blackton, 1915; S. L. Rothapfel, with Ivan Rudisill and S. M. Berg), *Joan the Woman* (Cecil B. DeMille, 1916; William Furst), *Civilization* (Thomas Ince, 1917; Victor Schertzinger), *Where the Pavement Ends* (Rex Ingram, 1922; Luz), *The Big Parade* (Vidor, 1925; Axt and David Mendoza), *Beau Geste* (Herbert Brenon, 1926; Riesenfeld), *Wings* (William Wellman, 1927; J. S. Zamecnik); and four films by D. W. Griffith: *Hearts of the World* (1917, Elinor), *The Greatest Question* (1919, Pesce), *Broken Blossoms* (1919, Louis Gottschalk), *Way down East* (1920, Louis Silvers and William F. Peters). Griffith in fact commissioned scores for almost all of his silent features from *The Birth of a Nation* on (so long as his finances allowed), but few Hollywood directors or producers showed a similar interest in music. The majority of feature films were not supplied with scores for distribution; instead performers were left to devise accompaniments of their own, aided by cue sheets, anthologies, and catalogues.

MUSICAL MATERIALS

The first and most succinct aids for performers were what came to be called cue sheets: that is, brief lists of specific pieces and/or types of music to accompany particular films, with cues and supplementary instructions. At first these lists were relatively crude and perhaps not all that reliable, but like other aids they became steadily more apt, sophisticated, and commercially valuable during the second half of the silent period, reflecting changes in cinema itself. It is interesting to compare the anonymous cue sheet for the Edison Company's one-reel *Frankenstein* (1910) and the 'Thematic Music Cue Sheet' prepared by James C. Bradford for Paul Leni's popular feature *The Cat and the Canary* (1927). The former is a typical specimen

from the pioneering series published between 1909 and 1912 in the American edition of the *Edison Kinetogram* and offers merely the barest outline of an accompaniment, comprising fourteen cues beginning as follows:

At opening: Andante–'Then You'll Remember Me'
  Till Frankenstein's laboratory: Moderato—'Melody in F'
  Till monster is forming: Increasing agitato
  Till monster appears over bed: Dramatic music from *Der Freischütz*
  Till father and girl in sitting room: Moderato
  Till Frankenstein returns home: 'Annie Laurie'
[etc.]

In sharp contrast, the *Canary* cue sheet was issued as a lavish eight-page brochure in a coloured cover (apparently an exceptional format), and spells out sixty-six explicit cues, using three dozen pieces by more than two dozen composers. It also contains, on the front and back covers, detailed description of the score's recurring themes, together with useful 'suggestions for playing', cue by cue.

The differences are significant, but there is one key point of resemblance: both lists feature monuments of nineteenth-century repertoire for crucial scenes. In *Frankenstein*, 'dramatic music' from Weber's *Freischütz* is called for five times (vague cues indeed, probably indicating eerie excerpts from the Overture or the 'Wolf's Glen Scene', to be performed ad lib), whenever the monster appears; in *Canary*, the beginning of Schubert's 'Unfinished' Symphony appears four times and is identified as the 'Mammy Theme'. (The music, according to Bradford, indicates 'the uncertainty and questionable position of this woman who is distrusted'.) Both scores also mix their classical fragments with morsels in varied lighter styles: *Frankenstein* includes a sentimental salon piece and an old-fashioned parlour song (Rubinstein's 'Melody in F', 'Annie Laurie'); *Canary* brings together many comic *misteriosos* and up-to-date popular numbers, all suitable for the film's tongue-in-cheek tone. Such jumbles were the norm (though Bradford claims that his suggested music offers 'a perfect sequence of modulations from one selection to another'), because they were seen as the most appropriate way to follow the films; and one finds the same sort of odd but functionally efficient hodge-podge within the period's anthologies and catalogues.

By the 1920s, the latter materials had become just as elaborate as cue sheets (which, as in the Bradford example, drew from them extensively for repertoire), after similarly modest beginnings. Early anthologies were made up of not-too-difficult piano pieces usually running to no more than a single page, as in Zamecnik's collections of *Sam Fox Moving Picture Music* (seventy original pieces in three volumes, 1913–14; a fourth volume appeared in 1923) and the *Witmark Moving Picture Album* (an in-house compilation of 101 pieces which had been previously published, 1913). The range of categories was hit or miss, though there was a recurrent emphasis on music for 'national scenes' and ethnic groups (especially patriotic songs and exotic pieces of 'Indian' or 'Oriental' music), along with basic moods (comic, mysterious, pathetic, etc.) and types of action (funeral, hurry, storm, wedding, etc.). Later anthologies were intended to be more comprehensive and systematic. For example, all but two of the fourteen volumes of the *Hawkes Photo-Play Series* (1922–7) contained half a dozen expansive pieces, each by a different English composer; and, as was then typical, each volume could be obtained in a piano album and/or in arrangements for small or full orchestra.

The most impressive single book of piano music, however, was Erno Rapée's *Motion Picture Moods* (1924), which contained 370 pieces, many of them of great difficulty, indexed under fifty-three headings. In a unique format these headings are listed alphabetically on the margin of every page to facilitate 'rapid reference', but the contents of the book are really too vast for such an index to do more than steer pianists in the right direction. The group of 'National' pieces alone extends over 150 pages, beginning with the USA (for which there is the lengthiest subsection, including patriotic hymns, college songs, and Christmas carols), and then proceeding alphabetically from Argentina to Wales, with a huge assortment of anthems, dances, and traditional songs. Rapée followed this the next year with an *Encyclopedia of Music for Pictures* aimed at directors of ensembles: the book offered more than 5,000 titles of published arrangements under 500 headings, plus a great deal of space for additional numbers to be added to the lists, allowing for each theatre to build its own customized music library. (In recent years, some of these libraries—for example the Balaban & Katz collection in Chicago and the Paramount library in Oakland—have turned up virtually intact, and while each is organized differently, all tend to follow a system similar to Rapée's.) As a compendium of repertoire, the *Encyclopedia* was superseded only by the thematic index in Hans Erdmann and Giuseppe Becce's two-volume *Allgemeines Handbuch der Film-Musik* (1927), one of the period's last and most valuable sources.

By the mid-1920s, then, the spectrum of film music publications encompassed tens of thousands of pieces, some of them arrangements of pre-existent material, some newly composed for film accompaniment, and some nominally new but clearly based on existing themes. New or old, the music was then indexed according to the purpose it could serve in film accompaniment. It would seem that almost any piece was suitable for more than one context, or at least could be rendered so by changing the style of performance, no matter how it was marked. Rapée's anthology contains an item called 'Agitato No. 3', by Otto Langey, whose first strain is obviously modelled on Schubert's 'Erlkönig', and the piece is described as 'suitable for gruesome or infernal scenes, witches, etc.'. But Rapée indexes it under 'Battle', and elsewhere in the anthology, even more confusingly, the actual beginning of Schubert's own song is categorized as a 'misterioso' (despite its tempo marking of 'presto'). The more the repertory grew, therefore, the more it seems to have fundamentally stayed the same, dictated by functional requirements. Most pieces were expected to communicate their essential messages within the space of a few bars, and often had to be broken off for the next cue. (In Bradford's list, the shortest items are timed at thirty seconds, the longest three minutes.) Under the circumstances, too much stylistic variety was suspect, but clichés were not (and they made the music easier to play); moreover, familiar music (like the text that sometimes went with it) might be valued highly for its allusive power, even if the reference was imprecise.

Similar considerations apply when evaluating compiled scores. As mixed in their repertoire as cue sheets, many were stereotyped and seemingly haphazard, and all were liable to be altered greatly from performance to performance. However, in several cases both the selection and the synchronization of the music were carefully planned, and led to results well above the norm. Three examples can serve to illustrate the range of possibilities, as determined by types of films and circumstances of their production/distribution.

1. Walter C. Simon's music for the 1912 Kalem film *The Confederate Ironclad*: this concise piano score, from an impressive series Simon created for Kalem in 1912 and 1913, was written for an advanced example of film narrative at that time. It fits the film exceptionally well, and even though much of it is 'original', it is very much like a written out cue-sheet score, with several pre-existent tunes.

2. Breil's orchestral score for *The Birth of a Nation* can be seen as a Simon score writ large, with the added interest of extensive original music involving more than a dozen key leitmotivs, plus effective varieties of orchestral colour. By this time too, the repertoire has been opened up to include a large number of nineteenth-century symphonic and operatic works, more suitable for orchestral than piano accompaniments, and necessary for such a film epic. There is no doubt that Griffith wanted music to be an integral part of the film experience and, although the degree of his involvement cannot be known precisely, he certainly played a role in encouraging Breil's ambitious efforts.

3. The Axt–Mendoza score for Vidor's *Big Parade* follows the Breil model and is no less a major piece of work, though with neither the same amount of original music nor the personal stamp of the Griffith scores. Indeed, just as this later epic displays a smoother style than Griffith's, the score shows how, by the mid-1920s, film music had

become a polished 'studio' product. In this case, the studio was inside a New York theatre, where Riesenfeld created the score and gave it its première; the city, like Berlin, had become a prime locale for the manufacture of scores, thanks to co-operative partnerships between film producers, theatres, and music publishers.

Alongside compiled scores, original scores also increased in number in the 1920s, often with remarkable results. A significant American example is Mortimer Wilson's music for Raoul Walsh's 1924 *The Thief of Bagdad*: richly worked out in terms of both thematic structure and orchestration, its lavish design is fitting for so opulent a film and presages the achievements of Erich Korngold and the great composers of Hollywood scores in the sound period. But the most impressive centres of original work were not in New York or Hollywood, but in France, Germany, and Russia, where the fascination of artists and intellectuals with the new medium led to unique collaborations.

An important precedent had been set in Europe much earlier, with Camille Saint-Saëns's score for the 1908 *film d'art*, *L'Assassinat du Duc de Guise*. As one might expect given the composer's many years of experience and mastery of his craft, this score displays impressive thematic unity and harmonic design, and is as polished as his many previous essays in ballet, pantomime, and tone poem. Yet because it serves the film so well, the score has come to share the fate of his other incidental pieces: mentioned in surveys but rarely studied, regarded more as a fascinating transitional effort than as a convincing work of art.

Of the many innovative scores by composers who gravitated toward film in the 1920s, three in particular deserve mention, each successful in attaining different goals.

1. Eric Satie's score for *Entr'acte* (1924) shines as an anti-narrative, proto-minimalist gem; like Clair's film, it is designed both to dazzle and to disorient the audience, partly by parodying the medium's customary product, partly by following a subtle formal logic beneath a deceptively random surface.

2. The Huppertz score for *Metropolis* (1927), commissioned for the Berlin première, is one of the most peculiar examples known to survive of music following Wagner's leitmotiv system, within an elaborate symphonic framework. Apparently following Lang's original tripartite structure for the film, Huppertz divides his score into three independent 'movements' with the unusual names of 'Auftakt', 'Zwischenspiel', and 'Furioso'. Like the film, the music intermixes elements of nineteenth-century melodrama and twentieth-century modernism, and that is an essential part of its fascination: it strives

Mood music: an orchestra playing on the set to create the right atmosphere for a scene from Warner Bros.' *The Age of Innocence* (1924)

to reinforce Lang's messages, and, while showing similarities to the American compilations discussed above, employs a far more complex and varied musical vocabulary.

3. Dmitri Shostakovich's score for Kozintsev and Trauberg's *New Babylon* (1929) ranks among the greatest examples of film music by a leading avant-garde composer of any generation. Like the film, and somewhat like Satie's score for *Entr'acte*, the music is in large part satirical, and depends for its effects on the distortion of well-known tunes, especially the 'Marseillaise', as well as the use of French-style 'wrong-note' harmonies and persistent motor rhythms—all designed to offer both counterpoint and continuity to the film's energetic montage. But the score (now available in a complete recording by the Berlin Radio Symphony) also makes strong ideological points and attains tragic stature. One great example occurs at the end of part vi, for scenes of the despair, desperate resistance, and massacre of the Communards. While an old revolutionary pauses to play a piano abandoned on the barricades, and while his comrades listen, visibly moved, the orchestra pauses too, for the pit pianist's poignant fragment of 'source music' (Tchaikovsky's 'Chanson triste'); this trails off, and when the final battle begins, the orchestra commences a prolonged agitato, which finally resolves into a thumpingly banal waltz. Thus Shostakovich emphasizes the brutality of the French bourgeoisie, who are seen applauding at Versailles, as if presiding over the scenes of carnage. No less pointed is the music for the film's end, though it aims in an opposite direction: here Shostakovich combines a noble horn theme for the Communards with the melody of the Internationale in rough, dissonant counterpoint. The double purpose is to honour the martyrdom of the film's heroes, and, more generally, to convey hope without clichéd sentiment. In a final symbolic gesture, he ends the score virtually in mid-phrase, a fitting match to the film's open-ended final three shots of the words 'Vive' | 'la' | 'Commune', seen scrawled as jagged graffiti pointing dynamically past the edges of the frame.

Each of these three scores offers a unique solution to the challenging compositional problems posed by an unusual film. Together, they crown the silent film's 'golden age', and show that the medium had found ways to tap music's expressive potential to the highest degree.

SILENT FILMS AND MUSIC TODAY

Even as Shostakovich completed his score, silent films were rapidly becoming obsolete. It did not take long for many of the practices and materials of the period to be forgotten or lost, but there have been efforts ever since to revive them. Cinematheques and other venues where silent films continued to be screened went on providing piano accompaniments, but often in a mode that was neither musically inspiring nor historically accurate. At

Greta Garbo

(1905–1990)

Born Greta Gustafsson, daughter of a Stockholm sanitary worker, Garbo had an unhappy, impoverished childhood. She entered films via advertising, and after making a comedy short was discovered by Mauritz Stiller, who renamed her and cast her in *Gösta Berlings saga* (1924). He also remoulded her. Her advertising films had shown a plump, bouncy teenager, but Stiller drew from her something cool and remote. She was touchingly vulnerable as a middle-class girl reduced to prostitution in Pabst's *Die freudlose Gasse* (1925), after which she left for Hollywood. Louis B. Mayer had seen *Berling* and wanted Stiller; reluctantly he signed the director's young protégée as well.

At a loss what to make of Garbo, MGM dubbed her 'the Norma Shearer of Sweden' and put her into *The Torrent* (1926), a trashy melodrama that Shearer had turned down. With the first rushes they realized what they had—not just an actress but a mesmerizing screen presence. Stiff, bony, and awkward in everyday life, Garbo was transformed on screen into an image of graceful eroticism. Stiller, his Hollywood career a disaster, returned to Sweden and an early death while Garbo, distressed by the loss of her mentor, was propelled to the heights of stardom.

Flesh and the Devil (1926), directed by Clarence Brown

and co-starring John Gilbert, confirmed her unique quality. The urgency of her love scenes with Gilbert (with whom she was involved off-screen) conveyed a hunger bordering on despair, an avid, mature sexuality never before seen in American films, and a revelation to audiences used to the vamping of Pola Negri or the coy flirtings of Clara Bow. Brown's cinematographer was William Daniels, who shot nearly all Garbo's Hollywood films and devised for her a subtle, romantic lighting, rich in expressive half-tones, that did much to enhance her screen image.

Garbo's combination of sexual need and soulful resignation defined her as the archetypal Other Woman, fated to play sirens and adulteresses. She twice portrayed one of the greatest, Anna Karenina, the first time in *Love* (1927) with Gilbert as Vronsky. The rest of her silent films were unworthy of her, though she had already proved her ability to transcend the shoddiest material. 'To see, in these early films, Garbo breathe life into an impossible part', comment Durgnat and Kobal (1965), 'is like watching a swan skim the surface of a pond of schmaltz.'

MGM, having seen the careers of European-accented stars like Negri ruined by sound, nervously delayed Garbo's first talkie. *Anna Christie* (1930), a pedestrian version of O'Neill, showed they had no cause for concern. Her voice was deep, vibrant, and melancholy, her accent exotic but musical. With her status assured as Metro's top female star, the legend began to grow: the asceticism, the shyness, the reclusiveness. 'I vahnt to be alone',

a line from her role as a ballerina in *Grand Hotel* (1932), became a catch-phrase. All this was cultivated by the studio press office, but by no means wholly invented. The image and the woman were hard to disentangle—which made her all the more fascinating.

Costume dramas figured largely in Garbo's 1930s films, not always to advantage. 'A great actress', wrote Graham Greene, reviewing *Conquest* (1937), 'but what dull pompous films they make for her.' Here as elsewhere the austerity of her acting was smothered in period fustian and stilted dialogue, the direction entrusted to sound journeymen like Brown (who also handled the remade *Anna Karenina*, 1935). Cukor's *Camille* (1936) was an improvement, with Garbo heartbreaking in her doomed gaiety, but in Mamoulian's *Queen Christina* (1933) she gave the performance of her career, passionate and sexually ambiguous—and, in the final scene, hugging her grief to her like a concealed dagger.

The mystery of Garbo, the haunting aloofness and sense of inner pain, had made her (and still make her) the object of cult adoration. MGM, as if puzzled what to do with this enigma, decided she should be funny. 'Garbo laughs!' they announced for *Ninotchka* (1939), apparently never having noticed the full-throated abandonment of her laugh before. Acclaimed at the time, the film now looks contrived and, for Lubitsch, surprisingly heavy-handed. *Two-Faced Woman* (1941), an attempt at screwball comedy, was a catastrophe.

Garbo announced a temporary retirement from film-making—which became permanent. From time to time, even as late as 1980, come-backs were mooted—*Dorian Gray* for Albert Lewin, *La Duchesse de Langeais* for Ophuls—but never materialized. A legendary recluse, she retreated into inviolable privacy—confirmed in her status as the greatest of movie stars, because the most unattainable. The woman and the myth had become indissolubly merged.

PHILIP KEMP

SELECT FILMOGRAPHY

Gösta Berlings saga (The Atonement of Gösta Berling) (1924); Die freudlose Gasse (Joyless Street) (1925); Flesh and the Devil (1926); Love (Anna Karenina) (1927); A Woman of Affairs (1928); The Kiss (1929); Anna Christie (1930); Susan Lenox: Her Fall and Rise (The Rise of Helga) (1931); Mata Hari (1932); Grand Hotel (1932); As You Desire Me (1932); Queen Christina (1933); The Painted Veil (1934); Anna Karenina (1935); Camille (1936); Conquest (Marie Walevska) (1937); Ninotchka (1939); Two-Faced Woman (1941)

BIBLIOGRAPHY

Durgnat, Raymond, and Kobal, John (1965), *Greta Garbo*.
Greene, Graham (1972), *The Pleasure-Dome*.
Haining, Peter (1990), *The Legend of Garbo*.
Walker, Alexander (1980), *Greta Garbo: A Portrait*.

Opposite: Greta Garbo with Lars Hanson in Victor Sjöström's *The Divine Woman* (1928)

the Museum of Modern Art in New York between 1939 and 1967, however, Arthur Kleiner maintained the tradition of using original accompaniments, availing himself of the Museum's collection of rare scores; where scores were lacking, he and his colleagues created scores of their own, which were reproduced in multiple copies and rented out with the films.

In recent years scholarly work (particularly in the USA and Germany) has greatly increased our knowledge of silent film music; archives and festivals (notably Pordenone in Italy and Avignon in France) have provided new venues for the showing of silent films with proper attention to the music; and conductors such as Gillian Anderson and Carl Davis have created or re-created orchestral scores for major silent classics. This initially specialist activity has spilled over into the commercial arena. In the early 1980s two competing revivals of Abel Gance's *Napoléon* vied for public attention in a number of major cities—one, based on the restoration of the film by Kevin Brownlow and David Gill, with a score composed and conducted by Carl Davis, and the other with a score compiled and conducted by Carmine Coppola. Even wider diffusion has been given to silent film music with the issue of videocassettes and laser discs of a wide range of silent films, from Keystone Cops to *Metropolis*, all with musical accompaniment.

Both because of and despite these advances, however, the current state of music for silent films is unsettled, with no consensus as to what the music should be like or how it should be presented. (There was a lack of consensus during the silent period, too, but the spectrum was not as broad as it is today.) Discounting the option of screening a film in silence, an approach now generally held to be undesirable except in the very rare cases of films designed to be shown that way, we can distinguish three basic modes of presentation currently in use: (1) film screened in an auditorium with live accompaniment; (2) film, video, or laser disc given a synchronized musical sound-track and screened in an auditorium; (3) video or laser disc versions screened on television at home. Obviously, the second and third modes, while more prevalent and feasible than the first, take us increasingly further from the practices of the period. To show a silent film or its video copy with a synchronized score on a sound-track is to alter fundamentally the nature of the theatrical experience; indeed, once recorded, the music hardly seems 'theatrical' at all. As for home viewing, whatever its advantages it forgoes theatricality to the point that any type of continuous music, and especially thunderous orchestras and organs, can weigh heavily on the viewer.

As for the scores themselves, they too can be divided into three basic types: (1) a score that dates from the silent era, whether compiled or original (Anderson has made this type of score her speciality); (2) a score newly created (and/or improvised) but intended to sound like 'period' music—the approach usually taken by Kleiner, by the organist Gaylord Carter, and more recently by Carl Davis; (3) a new score which is deliberately anachronistic in style, such as those created by Moroder for *Metropolis* in 1983, and by Duhamel and Jansen for *Intolerance* in 1986. Thus, altogether there now exist nine possible combinations of music and silent cinema (three modes of presentation, three types of score), and all of them have yielded results both subtle and obtrusive, both satisfying and offensive.

Particularly interesting in this respect are the cases where different versions have recently been prepared of the same film. For *Intolerance*, for example, there now exist four different versions. There is Anderson's, which is based on the Breil score and has been performed in conjunction with a restoration of the film (by MOMA and the Library of Congress) in a version as close as possible to that seen at the 1916 New York première. There is a Brownlow–Gill restoration with Davis score, which has been screened both live and on television. There is the 'modernist' Duhamel and Jansen version. And a laser disc also exists of a further restoration with a recorded organ score by Carter. In the case of *Metropolis* popular attention has been grabbed by the Moroder version with its synthetic mix of disco styles and new songs performed by various pop artists, but the film has been presented several times with a version of the original Huppertz score adapted and conducted by Berndt Heller, and with semi-improvisatory scores performed live by avant-garde ensembles. It is not possible to make hard-and-fast choices between the different approaches taken in these cases. Anderson has argued persuasively in favour of the presentation of a film like *Intolerance* in proper viewing conditions with the music originally designed for it, but even she has admitted that

such meticulous restorations can have more historical than aesthetic interest. Meanwhile a case can also be made for the enlivening use of 'anachronistic' music, particularly for unconventional films, though the case of *Metropolis* shows that the use of trendy pop-music scores can make the film itself look dated when the music itself begins to date and progressive styles of jazz and minimalism can provide a more effective counterpoint to the film.

It is good to face so many possibilities, even if they stand in such confusing array. The simple fact is that music for silent films was ever-changing, because live, and to be truly 'authentic' must continue to change. Moreover, it is probably futile to expect that the musical traditions of silent cinema will ever be fully restored; for one thing, we simply cannot watch the films in the same way as our ancestors, after so many decades of experience with sound films, and after so much of the original repertoire has either been forgotten or has lost any semblance of freshness. The best that can be hoped for, perhaps, is that from time to time we will be able to return to the theatre to hear a live accompaniment, whether old or new, that makes an effective match to the film and is sensitively performed; when this happens, we are better able to imagine the silent cinema's past glories, and to experience it as an art still vital, a century after it all began.

Bibliography
Anderson, Gillian (1990), 'No Music until Cue'.
Erdmann, Hans, and Becce, Giuseppe (1927), *Allgemeines Handbuch der Film-Musik*.
Gorbman, Claudia (1987), *Unheard Melodies*.
Marks, Martin (1995), *Music and the Silent Film*.
Rapée, Erno (1924), *Motion Picture Moods*.
—— (1925), *Encyclopedia of Music for Pictures*.

The Heyday of the Silents

GEOFFREY NOWELL-SMITH

By the middle of the 1920s the cinema had reached a peak of splendour which in certain respects it would never again surpass. It is true that there was not synchronized sound, nor Technicolor, except at a very experimental stage. Synchronized sound was to be introduced at the end of the decade, while Technicolor came into use only in the mid 1930s and beyond. Nor, except in isolated cases like Abel Gance's *Napoléon* (1927), was there anything approaching the wide screen that audiences were to be accustomed to from the 1950s onwards. It is also the case that viewing conditions in many parts of the world, par-

ticularly in rural areas, remained makeshift and primitive.

But there were many compensations. Audiences in cities throughout the developed world were treated to a spectacle which only twenty years earlier would have been unimaginable. In the absence of on-screen sound there were orchestras and sound effects. Film stocks using panchromatic emulsion on a nitrate base produced images of great clarity and detail enhanced by tinting and toning. Flicker effect had been eliminated, and screens up to 24 × 18 feet in size showed images brightly and without distortion, large enough to give physical embodiment to the grand scale of the action.

Many of these qualities were to be lost with the coming of sound. Live music disappeared from all but a handful of auditoriums. Tinting and toning effects were abandoned because the colour on the film interfered with the sensors for reading the sound-track. The focus of investment moved from visual effects to the problems of sound recording and, on the exhibition side, to the installation of playback equipment. Sound also encouraged a loss of scale, as emphasis shifted to the kind of scenes that could be shot with dialogue. The spectacular qualities that had distinguished many silent films were reduced as the new dialogue pictures took over, with musicals as the only significant exception.

The scale of the action projected into the large spaces which film-makers designed films to be seen in was perhaps the most striking feature of the silent cinema in its heyday. There was grandeur and a larger-than-life quality both in the panoramic long shots incorporating landscapes, battles, or orgies, and in the close-ups magnifying details of an object or a face. It was rare for a film to miss out on opportunities to aggrandize its subject, whether this was the conquest of the West or life on a collective farm. The houses of the rich tended to be mansions and those of the poor teeming tenements. Heroes and heroines were beautiful, villains ugly, and dramatic values were projected on to the bodies of the performers, enhanced by effects of shot scale and camera angle.

For this concatenation of effect to be achieved, many techniques had to be developed and made concordant with each other. Film-makers proceeded blindly, with little to guide them in the way of either precedent or theory. They did not exactly know what effects they wanted, nor, to the extent that they knew, did they all want exactly the same effects. As a result there were many experiments—in technology, in dramaturgy, in narrative, in set design—some of which proved to have no sequel. A number of distinct styles developed, notably in Hollywood, but also in Germany, France, the Soviet Union, India, Japan, and elsewhere. On the whole it was American—'Hollywood'—styles which provided at least a partial model for film-making throughout the world, but German models were also influential, even in America, while the Russian 'montage' style was more admired than imitated.

The style developed in America from about 1912 onwards and consolidated throughout the silent period has sometimes been called 'classical', to distinguish it on the one hand from the 'primitive' style which preceded it and on the other hand from other, less consolidated styles which cropped up elsewhere and on the whole had less historical success. Although it allowed for effects on a large scale, it was straightforward in the way effects were marshalled. It was above all a narrative style, designed to let a story unfold in front of the audience, and it organized its other effects under the banner of narrative entertainment. Underlying this style, however, were other deep-seated characteristics, including a more generalized 'realistic-illusionist' aesthetic, developed in the industrial context which increasingly determined the practice of film-making and viewing in the age of the silent feature.

INDUSTRY

The key to the spectacular development of the silent cinema (and to its rapid transition to sound at the end of the 1920s) lay in its industrial organization. This was not an incidental characteristic—as maintained for example by writer, film-maker, and (twice) French Minister of Culture André Malraux, who once airily described the cinema as being 'par ailleurs' ('furthermore') an industry. Rather, the potential for industrial development was built into the cinema from the very beginning, both through its intrinsic dependence on technology (camera, film stock, projector) and through its emergence in the early period as, literally, 'show business'. The early cinema should not really be dignified with the name of industry. It was a ramshackle business, conducted on a small scale, using equipment and technology which (with the exception of the film stock itself) could be put together in an artisanal workshop. But as films became more elaborate, and the level of investment necessary to make them and ensure their distribution increased, so the cinema came to acquire a genuinely industrial character—in the scale of its operations, in its forms of organization, and in its dependence on capital.

The definitive industrialization of cinema was not achieved until the coming of sound at the end of the 1920s, which consummated its integration into the world of finance capital and its links (via the electric companies) to music recording and radio. But already in the years after the end of the First World War the cinema had acquired its character as a prototype of what has since come to be called a culture industry. Like radio and music recording it was technological by definition, but unlike them it was not just a technology used to transmit a pre-existing content. The content itself was created by means of the technology. Having been technologically created, films then also had to be distributed to places where a related technology could be used for showing them. The quantity of investment, the time scale over which it was deployed, and the need to match supply and demand imposed on the cinema not only industrial organization at the point of production, but related business practice at every level. Films were produced for the market, and operations designed to manage market demands had a great influence on film production. This was to have unprecedented consequences for every aspect of the medium.

THE STUDIO

Films were produced in studios. Although the American film companies had moved to southern California in the 1910s partly for the sake of the abundant sunlight and the variety of locations, by the 1920s a majority of scenes had come to be shot in artificial settings, either indoors under electric light or outdoors on constructed sets. Film-makers ventured on to locations only for scenes (or single shots) which could not be simulated in the studio. Studio shooting not only gave more control of filming conditions, it was also more economical. The twin needs of economy and control also gave rise to simplified methods of constructing sets and ever more sophisticated ways of putting shots and scenes together with the aid of special effects of one kind or another.

Although in common parlance the term special effects is generally reserved for techniques which simulate fantastic events, many of the same techniques were in practice more often used for the portrayal of realistic scenes—as an easier and cheaper way of shooting them than if the scene had to be reproduced in actual real settings. The enormous expense of constructing the actual-size sets for the Babylonian sequence of Griffith's *Intolerance* (1916) spurred film companies to research simpler ways of making it appear as if the action was taking place in actual three-dimensional space. Within a scene studio shots (for example close-ups) would be matched to location shots, while a single shot could be composed of heterogeneous elements carefully merged to look as if it represented a single reality. A simple device was to paint part of a scene on a glass plate, with the action being shot through the clear portion of the glass. But there were also more complicated techniques, such as the one devised by the German cinematographer Eugen Schüfftan in the mid-1920s and used, among other films, on Fritz Lang's *Metropolis* (1927). This involved constructing miniature sets which were located to the side of the action to be filmed. A partially scraped mirror was then placed in front of the camera, at an angle of forty-five degrees. The action was shot through the scraped part of the mirror, while the sets were reflected through the unscraped part. Alternatively part of the scene could be obscured by a matte, and inserted into the shot later in the laboratory. Or a background (shot on location by a second film unit) could be projected on a screen at the back of the studio, while the characters performed in front of it, though this did not come into widespread use until the early sound period, when dialogues needed to be recorded in studio conditions.

The effect of these developments in studio production techniques was to push the cinema of the late silent period more and more in the direction of realistic illusion, blurring the boundaries between the obviously illusionistic (the films of Georges Méliès for example), the theatrical, and the unquestionably real. Fiction films aspired to a reality effect whether their content was realistic events or fantastic and implausible ones. Only at the margins were films made which either played on effects for their own sake (or for the audience to wonder at) or which depended on unmediated authenticity in portraying real events. Occasionally, as in comedy, these two extremes would be joined and the audience would be left marvelling both at the fantastic things that were happening (or appeared to be happening) and at the real physical achievement of the gag taking place in real time in a real place. More often, however, the resources at the disposal of the studio were deployed for purposes of a generic verisimilitude; the action had a sufficient 'ring of truth' for the means of its enactment to pass largely unnoticed.

The idea that cinema could use artifice of many kinds to create a self-sufficient cinematic reality emerged slowly, and continued to be felt as something of a paradox. The first person really to get to grips with this paradox was probably the Soviet film-maker and theoretician Lev Kuleshov, whose famous 'experiments' in the early 1920s were devoted to showing how the narrative content of single shots was determined by their juxtaposition rather than by their intrinsic 'real-life' properties. But Kuleshov's experiments focused almost entirely on montage (the editing together of shots) rather than on the potential for artifice present in the making of the shot itself, and it was in Germany and in Hollywood, where the techniques of studio production were most highly developed, that realist illusionism (more realist in the Hollywood case, more illusionist in the German) really came into its own as the dominant aesthetic of the silent film.

MELODRAMA, COMEDY, MODERNISM

During the silent period most of the genres emerged that were to characterize the cinema throughout the studio period—crime films, Westerns, fantasies, etc. Of the classic genres only the musical, for obvious reasons, was absent, though many films were made for non-synchronized musical accompaniment. Overarching the generic categories into which films were grouped for marketing purposes, however, the films of the silent period (and to a great extent thereafter) can be categorized under two main 'modes', the comic and the melodramatic.

The term melodrama is used by film scholars to designate two types of film in particular—those (particularly in the very early period) which show a clear historical descent from nineteenth-century theatrical melodrama, and the sagas of love and family life (often overlapping with so-called 'women's pictures') that had such a powerful presence in Hollywood in the 1930s, 1940s, and 1950s. These uses are not strictly compatible, since the two types of film have few particular features in common. Early film melodrama was highly gestural and involved the accent-

The MGM costume department in 1928

uating of moral and dramatic values around characteristic motifs—heroes spurred to action by revelations of unspeakable villainy, leading to last-minute rescues of innocent heroines, *deus ex machina* endings, and the like. These features are all somewhat attenuated in the so-called melodramas of the later period, and are instead to be found more often in action films (such as Westerns) than in the increasingly psychological dramas of the 1930s and after. Links between the two are to be found in the work of D. W. Griffith, who formalized the means for inserting melodramatic values into the flow of cinematic narrative and (by his use of the close-up as both a narrative and an emotive device) gave the conventional melodrama a measure of psychological depth; and in that of Frank Borzage, who, in *Humoresque* (1920), *7th Heaven* (1927), and other films, turned stock figures of melodrama into characters driven by preternatural inner strength.

More generally, the American cinema in the 1920s had great difficulty in liberating itself from the narrative schemas of theatrical melodrama and its Griffithian con-

tinuation in the cinema. With the steady increase in the length of films from about 1913 onwards—from three or four reels to six or even more in the post-war period—film-makers were able to turn to stories of broader scope and greater complexity, often in the form of adaptations of novels. Despite the refinement of narrative technique, however, it was rare for this opportunity to be translated in the direction of realistic and nuanced character development. Rather (and this is as true if not truer of the bulk of European production as it was of American) narratives became clotted with incident, while the characters to whom the incidents happened continued to be drawn in schematic terms. In Rex Ingram's acclaimed *Four Horsemen of the Apocalypse* (1921), for example, the main characters and the values they represent are proclaimed in the intertitles early in the film and typified in appearance and gesture throughout the action, which is spread over several decades. Although the moral values of Griffith's melodramas, and their embodiment in scowling villains, luckless heroes, and perennially threatened

Fritz Lang
(1890–1976)

Born in Vienna, the son of a municipal architect, Fritz Lang began studying architecture, but in 1911 set out on a two-year journey around the world which ended in Paris, where he learnt painting while supporting himself by selling painted postcards and drawings. When war broke out he enlisted in the Austrian army. He served at the front and was wounded several times. In 1918 he moved to Berlin to write scripts, becoming a director in 1919. In 1920 he married the well-known screen-writer and novelist Thea von Harbou. All of Lang's subsequent German films were made in collaboration with her.

With Murnau and Lubitsch, Lang was one of the giants of the German silent cinema. His films helped to win a strong international audience for German films and maintain an aesthetic distinctiveness that offered a serious alternative to Hollywood. His fascination with the parallels between criminal psychology and ordinary psychological processes is already evident in *Dr Mabuse, der Spieler* (*Dr Mabuse, the Gambler*, 1922), in which an evil genius attempts to gain total control over society. Mabuse manipulates the stock market as easily as a private poker game, using hypnosis, seductive women, and psychological terror to drive his wealthy victims to self-destruction. Fittingly, it is a woman who causes Mabuse's inevitable downward spiral into a madness so profound that his once omnipotent vision is turned against himself as he hallucinates his victims returning from the dead to accuse him.

Die Nibelungen (1924) and *Metropolis* (1926) were lavish super-productions designed for international audiences.

They were remarkable for the persuasiveness of their artificial, monumental worlds and their superb pictorial beauty in which dramatic contrasts in architectural scale and graphic composition convey their principal themes. *Siegfried*, the first part of *Die Nibelungen*, is characterized by strong geometrical patterns in contrast to the asymmetrical confusion that dominates Part 2, *Kriemhilds Rache* (*Kriemhild's Revenge*). The imbalance in visual composition correlates with the inhuman brutality of Kriemhild's revenge against her own family for Siegfried's murder, ultimately destroying two civilizations. In *Metropolis*, the rhythmic, forced march of the workers at the beginning is contrasted with their chaotic attempts later to escape the flood they have let loose on their own homes. As in *Die Nibelungen*, a woman is the vehicle for the destruction of an entire society: the 'bad' Maria (Brigitte Helm), a sexy, hypnotic robot created to wreak havoc on the workers, is a replica of the 'good' Maria, who unites the workers through their blind faith in her as their saviour. The tyrant's son falls in love with the virginal Maria only to be deceived by her deceitful, evil twin, much as the workers are. In the end, brotherly love unites the tyrant with the workers and, unconvincingly, everyone seems to win.

In Lang's first sound film, *M* (1931), Peter Lorre portrays a serial child murderer whose crimes terrorize an entire city. The twin forces of the police and the underworld, at times deliberately juxtaposed through editing to emphasize the similarities between their organizations and motives, race against each other to capture the person responsible for disrupting both spheres of business. If the underworld is the dark mirror of the police, the murderer's unconscious compulsion to repeat his crime is the dark side of his rational self, and he is helpless to control it.

Nazi censors did not approve the release of Lang's next film, *Das Testament des Dr Mabuse* (1932). According to Lang, he was then summoned to a meeting with Goebbels who, rather than discuss the film, announced that Hitler wanted him to head the Nazi film industry. Lang, however, promptly left Germany for Paris and ended his marriage with Thea von Harbou, who was sympathetic to the new regime. In 1934 he moved on to Hollywood with a one-year contract from MGM. Between 1936 and 1956, Lang was to make twenty-two American films, changing studios almost continuously.

While waiting for his assignment from MGM, Lang took steps to gain fluency in American popular culture so he could understand his new audience. Above all, he was told, Americans expect characters to be ordinary people. With this lesson in mind, Lang convinced the studio to let him make *Fury* (1936), a film in which an ordinary man is mistakenly arrested on suspicion of kidnapping and possibly murdering a child and eventually succeeds in wreaking revenge on his accusers while sacrificing his family and sweetheart in the process. One of Lang's most powerful films, *Fury* shows the inhabitants of a small town turning into a lynch mob under instigation from the media, but it also shows (as do other of Lang's films, from *Kriemhild's Revenge* to *The Big Heat*, 1953) how revenge dehumanizes people—not only the mob, but also the hero himself.

In Lang's German films, the spectator is in a superior position of knowledge to the characters. This omniscience is undermined in the American films, where circumstantial evidence plays a large role, and where appearances are often deceptive for the spectator as well as the characters. In *You Only Live Once* (1936), circumstantial evidence and Lang's framing, lighting, and point-of-view editing lead the audience to believe that the ex-convict committed another robbery, despite his fiancée's trust in his innocence. As in *Fury*, at the end of the film romantic love is wholly believable and social change still seems possible. In the films Lang was to make twenty years later, this is no longer the case.

After some unusual Westerns and a series of suspenseful anti-Nazi films (including *Hangmen Also Die!* (1942), with Brecht collaborating on the script), Lang went on to make three films starring Joan Bennett. The success of the dream-like suspense drama *The Woman in the Window* (1944) led to a partnership with Bennett's husband, producer Walter Wanger, in two further films which portray the fatalistic dreamscape of film noir in explicitly psychoanalytic terms: *Scarlet Street* (1945), a remake of Renoir's *La Chienne* (1931), and *Secret beyond the Door . . .* (1947).

Lang's films during the 1950s are sharply critical of the American media, particularly *While the City Sleeps* (1955) and *Beyond a Reasonable Doubt* (1956). He presents his characters in an increasingly distant manner, discouraging audience identification in the usual sense and communicating instead through structure, repetition, editing, and effects of *mise-en-scène*. His most successful film of this period, *The Big Heat*, escapes depersonalization through the exceptional performances of Gloria Grahame and Lee Marvin.

At the end of his career Lang returned briefly to Germany to shoot two films based on his adventure scripts from the 1920s: the two-part *Der Tiger von Eschnapur/Das indische Grabmal* (1959) and a third Mabuse film set in the age of surveillance cameras (the paranoid icon par excellence), *Die tausend Augen des Dr Mabuse* (1960). These films show an extreme stylization and distillation of Lang's preoccupations and incorporate references to many of his earlier films.

In the eyes of some critics, there are two Fritz Langs: the mighty genius of the German period, and the American refugee who became a cog in the wheels of the Hollywood film industry and was never again able to achieve mastery over his art. In the 1950s this received opinion was challenged, particularly in the French magazine *Cahiers du cinéma*. Lang's American films were seen as enactments of a personal vision that articulated a deeply moral view of the individual's place within society. His pessimism and his return to individuals who are caught by accident in a series of events that spiral out of their control is consistent throughout his career, as is his preoccupation with structures of doubling and reversal, processes of psychological manipulation, and the limits of rationality and social institutions. In 1963, Lang played himself in Godard's *Contempt* (*Le Mépris*), a director persisting in articulating his own vision in the cinema with seriousness and dignity despite the depersonalizing conditions of the international co-production.

JANET BERGSTROM

SELECT FILMOGRAPHY

Die Spinnen, Part 1: Der goldene See (1919); Die Spinnen, Part 2: Das Brillantenschiff (1920); Der müde Tod (Destiny) (1921); Dr Mabuse, der Spieler (Dr Mabuse, the Gambler, 1922); Die Nibelungen Part 1: Siegfried; Part 2: Kriemhilds Rache (Kriemhild's Revenge) (1924); Metropolis (1926); Spione (Spies) (1927); M (1931); Das Testament des Dr. Mabuse (1932); Fury (1936); You and Me (1938); The Return of Frank James (1940); Western Union (1940); Man Hunt (1941); Hangmen Also Die! (1942); Ministry of Fear (1944); The Woman in the Window (1944); Scarlet Street (1945); Secret beyond the Door . . . (1947); Rancho Notorious (1951); The Blue Gardenia (1953); The Big Heat (1953); Human Desire (1954); Moonfleet (1955); While the City Sleeps (1955); Beyond a Reasonable Doubt (1956); Der Tiger von Eschnapur (Part 1): Das indische Grabmal (Part 2) (1959); Die tausend Augen des Dr Mabuse (The Thousand Eyes of Dr Mabuse) (1960)

BIBLIOGRAPHY

Bogdanovich, Peter (1969), *Fritz Lang in America*.
Eisner, Lotte (1976), *Fritz Lang*.
Grafe, Frieda, Patalas, Enno, Prinzler, Hans Helmut, and Syr, Peter (1976), *Fritz Lang*.
Jenkins, Stephen (ed.) (1980), *Fritz Lang*.

Opposite: A scene from *Siegfrieds Tod* (1923), Part I of Fritz Lang's *Die Nibelungen*

Lon Chaney
(1883–1930)

Lon Chaney became a major star for Metro-Goldwyn-Mayer in the 1920s, in spite of the fact that his stardom would seem to run counter to every convention of the cult of personality surrounding film actors, especially in the glamour-crazed 1920s. Even though a Hollywood career based on self-effacing impersonation is not an impossibility, Chaney's stardom seems particularly peculiar. It has often been explained in terms of mimetic gifts honed in Chaney's childhood attempt to communicate with his deaf-mute parents, but Chaney's was a histrionic style of acting that was quickly passing away from the screen in the 1920s. The talents of the 'Man of a Thousand Faces' were not used to address a wide range of roles as the epithet suggests, but a surprisingly narrow range that exploited his face and body as a spectacle of grotesque possibilities.

After a knock-about career in regional theatre, Chaney started out in Hollywood in 1912 as a bit player at Universal. In seventy-five films over five years he increasingly foregrounded his ability to change his appearance through the application of make-up and distortion of his body. Chaney's breakthrough role came in *The Miracle Man* (now lost except for partial scenes), one of the biggest critical and popular hits of 1919. Chaney was featured as 'The Frog', a con artist who pretends to be contorted by paralysis. He followed this success by playing the double role of pirate and blind man in Paramount's version of *Treasure Island* (1920). Later that year he appeared in *The Penalty* (1920) for Goldwyn in which he starred as 'Blizzard', a piano-playing criminal mastermind who seeks revenge against the doctor who mistakenly cut off his legs as a cure for a blow to the head. Burns Mantle, writing in *Photoplay*, declared the film to be 'about as cheerful as a hanging', but it was a box-office success, and it can still draw gasps of astonishment, particularly for the displays of grotesque physicality achieved by Chaney, who harnessed his legs behind him and walked on wooden pegs strapped to his knees.

Although 'The Star Sinister' is best remembered for his roles in two epic productions, *The Hunchback of Notre Dame* (Universal, 1923) and *Phantom of the Opera* (Universal, 1925), the majority of his films were modestly conceived, often part exploitation film, part family-revenge melodramas. Chaney specialized in characters who, through misfortune of birth or circumstance, were disfigured, mutilated, or faked these conditions. The *New York Times*

reviewer of *The Black Bird* (1926) attributed Chaney's repeated appearance as a 'twisted and crippled character' to the actor's own 'penchant' for the bizarre rather than to the demands of the studio.

That penchant was particularly evident in his collaborations with director Tod Browning. Their films together included *The Black Bird* (1926), *London After Midnight* (1927), *The Unknown* (1927), *The Big City* (1928), *West of Zanzibar* (1928), as well as the first of two successful versions of *The Unholy Three* (1925/1930) in which Chaney plays a side-show ventriloquist who masquerades as an old lady. Many of the other Browning/Chaney films also depended on sideshow or circus settings and curious plots. In *The Unknown* Chaney plays Alonzo, a circus knife thrower who has his arms surgically removed to please a girl-friend (Joan Crawford) who already believes him to be armless. Reviewers were critical of such vehicles, and increasingly responded most positively to Chaney's appearances in films when he wasn't 'all hunched up, legless' or deformed. In spite of this, Chaney repeatedly returned to the more grotesque roles in films aimed at his established audience of primarily male viewers.

A Chaney cult was sustained for decades through male fans and magazines like *Famous Monsters of Film Land*. Chaney's appeal was linked to his ability to capture a certain romantic agony, one associated with the transformative male body. The cult around Chaney was also fuelled by the melodramatic ironies of the star's personal life. Rumours circulated that his second wife had been married to a legless cigar vendor, and studio publicity emphasized the suffering Chaney underwent in his various cinematic disguises. The final irony occurred when, after filming his long delayed talking film debut, a remake of *The Unholy Three* (1930), Chaney was struck with a fatal throat cancer. In his last hours he was forced to mime his wishes, as he had so many years before with his parents.

GAYLYN STUDLAR

SELECT FILMOGRAPHY

The Miracle Man (1919); The Penalty (1920); The Hunchback of Notre Dame (1923); He Who Gets Slapped (1924); The Phantom of the Opera (1925); The Unknown (1927); West of Zanzibar (1928); The Unholy Three (1925/1930).

BIBLIOGRAPHY

Blake, Michael F. (1993), *Lon Chaney: The Man Behind the Thousand Faces*.

Opposite: Lon Chaney preparing his make-up for *The Penalty* (1920)

heroines, no longer fitted the changed atmosphere of the Jazz Age and the post-war world in general, narrative and psychological schemas were slow to adapt. Some of the complexities and ambiguities of late nineteenth-century literary and theatrical realism appear in the films of Erich von Stroheim in America and those of German and Scandinavian directors such as G. W. Pabst, Carl Theodor Dreyer, and Victor Sjöström, but on the whole a broadly melodramatic approach to both character and plot prevailed on both sides of the Atlantic—whether in action films or in those purporting to be more psychological in intent.

Relief from the melodramatic mode in the silent period was found mainly in comedy, which came in two types. On the one hand there was what is generally thought of as silent film comedy, a uniquely brilliant genre centred on comic performance (often of a knockabout type) and typified by the names of Charlie Chaplin, Buster Keaton, Harold Lloyd, and Stan Laurel and Oliver Hardy. This type of comedy exploited to the full the mimic and action potential of the silent cinema and although it more or less died with the arrival of the talkies it continues to be appreciated and enjoyed. But the silent cinema also possessed a different type of comedy, whose destiny has been exactly the opposite. This was the attempt to realize in the silent medium a form of comedy, based on the stage play, which in its original form was heavily dependent on verbal wit and repartee. Comedy of this type was severely hampered by the absence of spoken dialogue but it came into its own again as a genre with the arrival of the talkies. Silent examples of the genre have consequently tended to be forgotten, but the genre was in fact quite popular and engaged the talents of some of the greatest artists of the period, including Mauritz Stiller, Ernst Lubitsch, and even Chaplin. It was Chaplin's *A Woman of Paris* in 1923 which launched the career of Adolphe Menjou as the archetypal suave and debonair hero of many society comedies, beginning with Lubitsch's *The Marriage Circle* later that year, while in 1925 Lubitsch himself exceeded the bounds of what would be thought possible in silent film with a scintillating adaptation of Oscar Wilde's *Lady Windermere's Fan* in which every wicked nuance is conveyed by subtle touches of look and gesture.

Much of the appeal of the society comedy for popular audiences lay in the opportunity to enjoy and at the same time ironize over the lives of the idle rich. But even more it gave the opportunity to ironize over the values of the melodrama. Many of the situations and devices of the society comedy (and indeed of comedy of other types) are identical with those of the melodrama—confusion of identities, the character forced into an unwelcome marriage, the letter that goes astray. It is the manner in which they are treated, and the emotional response provoked in the audience, that is antithetical.

James Wong Howe

(1899–1976)

Howe was born Wong Tung Jim in Kwantung, China. He arrived in America aged 5 and grew up in Pasco, Washington. Short (5'1") but stocky, he trained as a boxer and fought professionally as a teenager, but he was fascinated by photography. Making his way to Los Angeles, he landed a job with DeMille's unit at the Lasky Studios and worked his way up to camera assistant.

Howe owed his breakthrough to a happy chance. Assigned to shoot stills of the star Mary Miles Minter, he delighted her by making her eyes appear dark. (The orthochromatic film of the time lightened blue eyes into blankness.) Puzzled at first, Howe realized that black velvet drapes behind him had created the effect. Minter insisted he should shoot all her films, and rumours spread that she had imported her own Chinese cameraman who hid behind black velvet to work his magic. Howe was soon widely in demand.

Luckily, the magician had more than one trick up his sleeve. Imaginative and experimental, Howe was never content to rely on accepted techniques. He believed that a good cinematographer 'should be willing to gamble a little more. . . The normal thing is not really interesting; it's the unusual and sometimes even accidental things that are.' Right to the end of his career he went on taking chances.

Reacting against the flat, shadowless photography preferred by his directors, Howe set about exploring the creation of mood through the camera. To suggest the fantasy world of *Peter Pan* (1924) he used low-key lighting (a technique which for a while became so characteristic that he gained the nickname 'Low-Key Howe'). He seized eagerly on devices to increase camera mobility: *Mantrap* (1926) was one of the first films to make extensive use of dolly-shots.

When sound hit Hollywood Howe was in China trying to set up a film to direct. The project fell through, and when he returned to America he found himself tagged 'silent-era'. Work was scarce until Howard Hawks chose him for *The Criminal Code* (1930). This earned him a two-year contract with Fox where he lent *The Power and the Glory* (1933), a tycoon's life-saga, a quasi-newsreel look that may have influenced Welles's *Citizen Kane* (1941). There followed a stint at MGM, creating dark, opulent interiors for *Manhattan Melodrama* (1934) and *The Thin Man* (1934), but Howe came under constant pressure from Cedric Gibbons, the studio's design head, to over-light. Quitting, he visited England, where two costume dramas, *Fire over England* (1936) and *Under the Red Robe* (1937), were flattered by his warm, romantic treatment.

Returning to Hollywood, Howe freelanced for a while. *The Prisoner of Zenda* (1937) and *Algiers* (1938), moody and atmospheric, mark the culmination of his 1930s black and white work; *The Adventures of Tom Sawyer* (1938) was his first colour feature. Rejecting the brash tones beloved

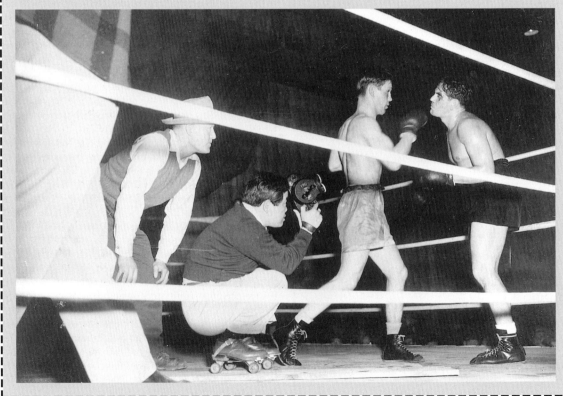

of Technicolor, Howe went for subdued, earthy colours befitting the poor rural setting, to the alarm of Technicolor's house cameraman Wilfred Cline. Howe simply ignored Cline, and was banned from Technicolor films for the next twelve years.

In 1938 Howe signed with Warners. The studio style, grainy and downbeat, should have suited his penchant for realism, but in the event he found Warners as restrictive as MGM. Their cut-price, fast-shooting methods outraged the perfectionist Howe, who liked to prepare meticulously and take time to get things right. Even so he achieved some fine work, often in an expressionistic vein—all high contrast and oppressive shadows—to match melodramas like *Kings Row* (1942) or *Passage to Marseille* (1944), besides the near-documentary look of *Air Force* (1943) and *Objective Burma!* (1945). Released from Warners, the ex-boxer captured some sweatily vivid fight scenes for *Body and Soul* (1947) by having himself pushed round the ring on roller-skates.

For the rest of his career Howe freelanced. Most of his colour films date from this period, from the picture-book fantasy of *Bell, Book and Candle* (1958) to the muted subterranean shades of *The Molly Maguires* (1969). There was never a uniform Howe look; the style, he insisted, 'should conform to the story', but he preferred black and white, and his late masterpieces are all in monochrome: *Hud* (1962), with its flat white Texan skies; the tormented distortions of *Seconds* (1966); and the slick, glitzy nightworld of *Sweet Smell of Success* (1957).

Howe was never easy to work with. Tireless and dedicated, he demanded equal dedication from his crews and, perhaps in reaction to the racial slurs he suffered all his life, adopted an autocratic approach that risked alienating colleagues. Given an inexperienced director Howe would virtually take over, sometimes to the point of directing the actors, and even strong directors knew better than to cross him. But few doubted that whatever he did was for the sake of the story—nor that he was, as Alexander Mackendrick put it, 'quite simply, the best'.

PHILIP KEMP

Select Filmography

Mantrap (1926); The Criminal Code (1930); Manhattan Melodrama (1934); The Thin Man (1934); Fire over England (1936); The Prisoner of Zenda (1937); Algiers (1938); Strawberry Blonde (1941); Kings Row (1942); Objective Burma! (1945); Body and Soul (1947); Sweet Smell of Success (1957); Hud (1962); Seconds (1966); The Molly Maguires (1969)

Bibliography

Eyman, Scott (1987), *Five American Cinematographers*.
Higham, Charles (1970), *Hollywood Cameramen: Sources of Light*.
Rainsberger, Todd (1981), *James Wong Howe, Cinematographer*.

Opposite: James Wong Howe with improvised dolly, shooting *Body and Soul* (1947)

Comedy brought to the cinema an element of modernity, which the melodrama generally lacked. This is true both of the comedy of manners, with its ironic view of the moral dilemmas of modern life, and of the knockabout kind, which regularly foregrounded motor cars, machinery, and similar emblems of modernity. Comedy was also a route through which artistic modernism entered the silent cinema, both through the conscious efforts of the avant-garde (as in René Clair's *Entr'acte* ('Interlude') and Eisenstein's *Glumov's Diary*) and in less obvious ways. Though there were attempts to exploit melodrama in a modernistic vein, from Anton Giulio Bragaglia's *Thaïs* (1917) to Marcel L'Herbier's *L'Inhumaine* (1924), they rapidly degenerated into a rather sterile decorativism and soon dissolved back into more conventional approaches.

The most systematic attempt to develop a cinema around the tenets of artistic modernism, however, came in the Soviet Union, where in the early years of the Revolution artists enjoyed a relative freedom from commercial (and even political) constraint and experimented with the cinema as an art of the machine, involving a new concept of vision (Vertov's 'camera-eye') and of the mechanization of the human body. Editing (the famous 'Soviet montage'), acting (the 'Factory of the Eccentric Actor'), and narrative (centred on the mass as opposed to the individual hero) were the object of concerted experiment to a degree unparalleled elsewhere.

Soviet modernism was facilitated by the fact that in the early years the State was prepared (not always enthusiastically) to risk substantial resources on experiments which had no guarantee of immediate popular success. In the rest of Europe and in Japan, by contrast (and even more in the United States), the introduction of potentially unpopular modernist elements into feature film-making was restricted by commercial considerations. The radical modernism which flourished in avant-garde circles in France in particular was therefore expressed more on the fringes than in the mainstream of film production. In Germany, Expressionism spread from painting and theatre to enter parts of the film world, and was also influential in Japan. But it tended to be the more conservative aspects of Expressionism—those most easily assimilated to Romantic tradition—that found a home in German studios; the more radical side of Weimar culture was politically as well as aesthetically risky, and had little impact on the mainstream. What was very strong in Germany, however, was the cult of art as a quasi-transcendent value. In film terms, this sometimes meant the tacking on to film of signifiers of artistic quality, but there were also attempts, of which F. W. Murnau's *The Last Laugh* (1924) is the most striking example, to create an artistic language of film based purely on the expressive qualities of the image.

NARRATIVE

While the broad lines of film narrative in the silent period were dictated by the demands of dramaturgy and plot, which tended to remain crude, the detail of scene construction underwent rapid development, particularly in the American cinema. The transitional period saw the emergence of specifically cinematic means of cueing changes of scene and creating narrative continuity within scenes by means of editing. The techniques which emerged in the middle and late 1910s were formalized and refined in the 1920s to create a system which has come to be known variously as 'invisible', 'continuity', and 'analytic' editing and has survived, with remarkably few modifications, until the present day. More than anything, it was these techniques of editing and scene construction which provided the hallmark of what, since the ground-breaking work of Bordwell, Thompson, and Staiger (1985), has come to be known as the classical Hollywood style.

The terms invisible and continuity editing refer to the fact that, at least within the scene, action was supposed to appear continuous and the joins between shots invisible. In practice, however, editing within the scene was never perfectly invisible, and dramatic effects were often achieved by cuts which were not only visible but actively presented to the spectator as narrative devices—for example in order to show that a character was being observed by another, previously unseen character and that more was going on than initially met the eye. An alternation of continuity and discontinuity was also important, to alert the spectator to the significance of scene changes without recourse to intertitles.

More significant than the question of visibility and continuity was the analytic aspect. In order for scenes to function, they had to be broken down into components which were pre-planned in the light of a notion of what the action was supposed to be and how it should be presented. Although pictorial effects entered into consideration in the planning of scenes, primacy went to the way the action was articulated and how an idea of the action could be most effectively and economically embodied. Staging, or *mise-en-scène*, therefore, tended to function as the fleshing out of a narrative idea, rather than as a value in its own right.

Analytic editing also consummated the move away from frontality in the presentation of scenes. The scene was no longer assembled in front of the camera, to be staged in a more or less theatrical manner. Instead the camera could enter inside the scene, acting as a mobile narrator directing the spectator's view now this way, now that. To ensure that the spectator was stably oriented within the spaces demarcated by the sequence of camera angles, a '180-degree rule' came into use in the Hollywood cinema. An imaginary line was drawn across the scenic space in front of the action and so long as the camera did not cross this line, but adopted varied positions just in front of it, the characters remained in recognizably similar places and the scene remained legible. (If the camera did, physically, cross the line—for example by tracking forward or moving in for a close-up—its angle of view still had to be from beyond the line.) The result was the creation of an artificial, but realistic, scenic space within which the camera could alternate objective and quasi-subjective viewpoints.

One particularly common device, which came into increasingly regular use from 1913 onwards, was the eyeline match and reverse shot, in which a character's glance is followed by a shot from a different angle of what the character is looking at. The systematic use of this and related devices had the effect of annulling the spectator's sense of distance from the actions and presumed thoughts and feelings of the characters and 'stitching over' the gap between spectator and spectacle to create an imaginary fusion between the two.

The development of narrative-through-editing followed a different course in Europe than in America. Analytic editing was certainly in use in most European cinemas in the 1920s, though the degree to which it was borrowed from American example as opposed to independently invented remains unclear. But European film-makers remained attached to frontality for a longer time, and with it to longer-held shots modelled in depth. Meanwhile a totally different concept of editing also developed, based more on the juxtaposition of images than on the linking of the components of the action.

The juxtaposition—or 'montage'—of images was not, of course, totally absent from American cinema (where it was used spectacularly by Griffith in the 1910s), just as continuity editing was not absent from the European. But it is safe to say that for the most part the use of montage in Hollywood was subordinated to the needs of continuity, and it was mainly in Europe (though also in Japan) that montage effects were regularly used to override narrative functions or reshape them on different lines.

Examples of montage not subordinated to continuity can be found all over European cinema in the 1920s, from the rapid sequences of shots in Abel Gance's La Roue ('The wheel', 1921) to the interpolation of threatening images in Hitchcock's Blackmail (1929), passing through the barrage of dramatic devices associated with German Expressionism. But it was in the Soviet Union, with the work of Kuleshov and Eisenstein in particular, that montage as such was elevated to the status of a constitutive principle of cinema.

Eisenstein's theories of montage are notoriously complicated, and became even more so in the 1930s, when he extended them to cover the counterpointing of image and sound. There are also important differences between the main practitioners and theorists of montage cinema—Eisenstein himself, Kuleshov, Pudovkin, and Vertov. Common to all approaches, however, was the idea that montage was not a linear process; it was not simply a way of articulating the narrative, but introduced values of its own by the juxtaposition and dramatic collision of semantic elements.

Looking back in the 1950s over the history of cinema, the French critic André Bazin discerned two main lines: the montage school, typified by Eisenstein, in which the putting together of elements to create a predetermined meaning was all important, and a less clearly identifiable tendency, connected among others with Murnau and Stroheim, in which the reality inherent in each shot was allowed to speak for itself. Bazin's insight into one of the fundamental questions of film aesthetics—the film's relation to visible reality—remains pertinent, but the way he framed the question is misleading. For it was not only Soviet montage but the rival Hollywood system of continuity editing that set out to predetermine meaning and limit the power of the image to express reality. Each system was, in its way, profoundly artificial, and used its artifice to direct the spectator's attention along preset lines.

ACTING AND THE STAR SYSTEM

Acting in the silent cinema was always to some degree gestural, since it was mainly by action and gesture that meaning had to be conveyed. With the development of analytic editing and increasing use of medium and close shots in the transitional period, acting in the American cinema became on the whole much more naturalistic than in the early period, and the same was generally true elsewhere. A strongly gestural style survived in Italy in particular throughout the 1910s, reaching a histrionic extreme in performances by 'divas' such as Lyda Borelli and (to a lesser extent) the men who played opposite them. It was also a major component of German Expressionism, in which inner states were 'expressed' and given form by dramatic gesture. More significant, however, was a divergence between techniques based on internalization of the role and those based on various forms of screen presence with no necessary mental correlative on the part of the actor.

The idea of an actor's performance emerging from a minute internalization of the role is generally associated with the work of Constantin Stanislavsky at the Moscow Arts Theatre in the 1910s and 1920s. Stanislavsky's ideas greatly influenced the early Russian cinema and were imported into America by the Russian émigrés, finding their way into cinema via the famous Actors' Studio founded by Elia Kazan and directed by Lee Strasberg in the 1940s. In between, however, they enjoyed mixed fortunes and were decisively rejected by many of the revolutionary Soviet film-makers in the 1920s.

In the theatre the 'Stanislavsky system' was contested by Brecht and Piscator in Germany as well as by film and theatre groups such as FEX in the Soviet Union. Neither Brecht nor Piscator was able to put his ideas into practice in the silent cinema, and (isolated experiments apart) a specifically Brechtian influence was not felt in the cinema until the work of Godard, Straub, Fassbinder, and Wenders in the 1960s and 1970s. In the Soviet Union, however, the montage cinema called for, and received, approaches to actorial performance diametrically opposed to the internalization inherent in the Stanislavsky method.

Alternative Soviet ideas on film acting varied between the demand for a high degree of professionalism (but based on mechanized movements and circus routines rather than psychology) and the rejection of the values of professional acting. Pudovkin's 'typage' called for actors to be chosen on the basis of physical features appropriate to what the character was meant to represent; screen acting, therefore, consisted in the ways this appearance could be put to use. Actors did not prepare for scenes, but were prepared (by the director) for each shot.

The American cinema also type-cast, but in a different way. Both melodrama and comedy required types, partially at least defined on the basis of appearance. In these conditions, an actor's ability to be an emblem of a particular role was often as valuable as the ability to create one. (This is not to say that roles and even types were not occasionally created by performers: the personalities of the great comics and also of some melodramatic actors were all the object of conscious creation.) Generic recognition was also very important, and films were promoted not only according to their type of plot but according to the characters they contained, and who performed them. It was not enough for an actor to 'be' a role in a particular film or group of films, and increasingly the status of the actor came to exceed that of the role that he or she played. Films became vehicles for the presence of their stars, and the stars' screen images and what was known or believed about them in their off-screen existence not only drew people in to see the film but inflected their enjoyment and understanding of what was portrayed.

The 'star system' which evolved in Hollywood in the 1920s was an elaborate mechanism to enable the studios to exploit the physical attributes of the actors and actresses they had under contract, and to organize the acting function and real-life existence of those who performed it around the creation and maintenance of an image. As such it differed radically from the practices in use in other performing arts and in less industrially developed cinemas. It was not the phenomenon of stardom that was new: Caruso could be considered a star, or Sarah Bernhardt; Asta Nielsen has been called the first international film star. The system, however, was, and the industrial logic that lay behind it.

The contract binding star to studio was on the face of it an innocent document, obliging the actor to supply a certain service exclusively to one purchaser in exchange for money and the promise of fame. Its basic similarity to contracts prevalent in other branches of business made it hard to challenge in the courts, as actors were to find out to their cost. What the actor was supplying, however, was not really a service (nor was it labour, or a manufactured object); rather actors and actresses supplied themselves, their physical body, beauty, and talent, to be concocted into an image that became a commodity for public consumption. So long as an actor's career went well, this was not experienced as oppressive. But when actors found themselves miscast, or not cast at all, or put out on loan, metaphors of slavery and prostitution were invoked to describe their lot. Of these, the prostitution metaphor is the more apposite, since stars were often chosen (and marketed) on the basis of their sex appeal, and rented out their bodies to the studio to be turned into sexually desirable images.

If modernity and industrialism in the Soviet cinema meant mechanizing the actor's body, in Hollywood it meant commodifying it. The star system was the *ne plus ultra* of the fetishism of commodities analysed by Marx in *Capital*. Audiences, however, demanded more than just the two-dimensional images they saw on the screen. They wanted to know who the lovers kissing on the screen were, and what they did in real life. This desire was fed, but also frustrated, by a constant flow of information (much of it fabricated) about the off-screen lives and loves of the stars. So far from adding a dimension of truth behind the image, the activities of the publicity departments and gossip columnists served to commodify the actors even further, making their private lives a managed spectacle almost as enthralling as the films themselves.

AUDIENCES

Much dispute reigns as to who the audiences were who so thrilled to the silent cinema in its heyday. If one thing is certain, it is that throughout the world they were primarily urban. Concentration of population, the availability of transport, and a supply of mains electricity were an essential pre-condition of the cinema as a viable mass entertainment. But the evidence about the class and gender composition of the audience remains fragmentary and contradictory. Audiences in North America in the 1920s seem to have been increasingly middle-class, as the industry systematically targeted the affluent white suburban population. But while this may have been Hollywood's strategy, in practice audiences were quite varied in composition. In America itself there were separate black and other ethnic audiences, while in Britain the audience is almost always described as prevailingly working-class. Real cultural and demographic differences between countries undoubtedly played a role in determining the composition of audiences, but differences of perception affected how they were described. Whoever they were originally aimed at, Hollywood films certainly reached the majority of the urban population throughout the industrial world and filtered through to rural and undeveloped areas as well, giving to all alike a shared mythology of adventure and romance.

Women were an important component of the film audience. The First World War brought women into the labour market, and the loss of a whole generation of men in the trenches meant that after the war many single women found themselves living independent lives. Even in countries which had not experienced the carnage of war, female emancipation and new possibilities of employment gave women a changed social position. The post-war generation of women was a large part not only of the audience for films but of the readership of magazines which celebrated the cinema and its heroes and heroines. Rarely acknowledged in the context of an industry and a culture where few women attained positions of power and obvious influence, it was the desires of this generation which helped to form, and in turn were formed by, the social imaginary of the silent cinema in its heyday.

Bibliography
Bazin, André (1967) 'Montage interdit'.
Bordwell, David, *et al.* (1985), *The Classical Hollywood Cinema*.
Eisenstein, Sergei (1991), *Towards a Theory of Montage*.
Koszarski, Richard (1990), *An Evening's Entertainment*.
Morin, Edgar (1960), *The Stars*.

Sound Cinema

1930–1960

Introduction

GEOFFREY NOWELL-SMITH

At the end of the 1920s the cinema underwent a revolution. The centre of this revolution was the introduction of synchronized sound dialogue, but it affected other areas as well, leaving very few untouched. It was a revolution that began in America and spread inexorably to the rest of the world, though certain aspects of it had a specific European inflection and some remote corners of the world did not feel the effects of any of it for some time.

The revolution can be conveniently dated from 6 October 1927, with the New York première of Warner Bros.' *The Jazz Singer* in which Al Jolson pronounces the immortal line 'You ain't heard nothin' yet' with more or less perfect synchronization between his lips in the film and his voice recorded in parallel on a disc. But that was only a beginning. By 1930 the sound-on-disc technology pioneered by Western Electric was replaced by a simpler and more reliable sound-on-film system devised by the rival corporation General Electric. A European consortium led by the German companies Siemens and AEG entered the fray and successfully seized a sizable corner of the growing market for sound equipment. Within a few years thousands of theatres in Europe and America were wired for sound using technology licensed from the powerful patents holders. Only in the Soviet Union and Japan was the conversion to sound slow to take effect.

Sound affected film form and the structure of the industry in equal measure. The old silent comedy was replaced by the wisecracking of Mae West and the Marx Brothers. Playwrights and script-writers assumed a new importance. An entirely new genre, the musical film, came into being. The integration of music on to the sound-track brought massive redundancies among theatre musicians but it also meant that exhibition conditions became standardized since the film was now the same wherever it was shown. Visual styles became cramped by the inflexible new technology. Hollywood suffered a temporary set-back in overseas markets because audiences demanded dialogue in their own language. Since in the early years of sound all dialogue had to be recorded live, the practice grew up of making films in multilingual versions, with different actors, until the institution of dubbing in the mid-1930s made it superfluous.

The main effect of the coming of sound was a consolidation of the studio system, both at the level of production and at that of the overall organization of the industry. Films became an increasingly industrial product, while the boundaries of the industry extended to overlap with the burgeoning music recording business.

While the coming of sound can be seen as a phenomenon internal to the cinema and music industries, it coincided with important events in the world outside. The Soviet montage cinema fell victim to Stalinist accusations of formalism as much as to technological developments. The rise of Fascism in Europe affected not only the Fascist countries themselves but the political culture of resistance in western Europe. Experimental film-makers turned increasingly to documentary and to themes of social and international struggle. In the late 1930s the Japanese attack on China was followed by Germany's invasion of successively Czechoslovakia, Poland, the Low Countries, and France, until by the end of 1941 the whole world was engulfed in the Second World War.

The end of the war in 1945 meant a new beginning for the cinema in a number of countries. In east central Europe and in China the cinema revived rapidly after the devastation of war, but it was also subject to bureaucratic control by the newly installed Communist regimes. In Germany, Italy, and Japan the problem was one of creating a new cinema that would not be tainted by the legacy of complicity with Fascism. Indian independence, followed by a steady decolonization throughout Asia and Africa, aligned the cinemas of the emerging nations firmly with the struggle for national self-affirmation.

After the war Hollywood acted quickly to regain the overseas markets it had lost during the conflict. But it found its hegemony threatened on two fronts. Artistically, the Italian neo-realist movement, arising from the ashes of Fascism, demonstrated the possibility of a freer, less studio-bound type of cinema. More significant from an industrial point of view, however, was the decline in audiences which set in after the war, first in Britain and the United States, and then in other industrialized nations. This coincided with the introduction in the United States of anti-trust legislation, forcing the major studios to divest themselves of the theatre chains which provided a near-captive audience for the studio's product. As well as the end of war, 1945 also marks the beginning of the end for the studio system, with Hollywood conducting a rear-guard action to retain its markets at home and abroad, and with the emergence of competing forms of cinema elsewhere in the world.

Rhett Butler (Clark Gable) and Scarlet O'Hara (Vivien Leigh) in David O. Selznick's epic *Gone with the Wind* (1939)

The period 1930–60 thus falls broadly into two halves. In the first half, up to the Second World War, the studio

The Jazz Singer at the Warners' Theatre in New York City

system reached its apogee, not only in the United States but elsewhere as well. After the war, the system survived, but weakened, and in an environment which increasingly threatened its stability.

The structure of this part of the book aims to reflect the world-wide importance of the coming of sound, as a factor both of change and of consolidation. It also tries to respect the complex interlacing of aesthetic, industrial, and political developments and the different temporalities in which they were expressed in different parts of the world.

After an initial look at the coming of sound itself, and its world-wide implications, the first focus is on the world of the studios, how the system operated—particularly in Hollywood—and how different aspects of the cinema were meshed together during the studio period. The section 'The Studio Years' deals first with industrial organization in the Hollywood studios in their heyday, with what sorts of film were produced, and how market influences made themselves felt. The studios, however, were not entirely free to make films simply for the market. The system also encountered problems of how to regulate itself to take account of political, social, and moral concern. While other countries experienced political censorship of varying degrees of severity, the Hollywood cinema suffered relatively little interference from central government and was instead faced with carefully orchestrated demands for a moral clean-up and the risk of intervention by local censor boards. To obviate the problem, which had severe economic implications, the industry engaged in a rigorous programme of self-regulation, culminating in the setting up of the Production Code Administration in 1934.

Along with spoken dialogue, the major innovation of the sound cinema was synchronized music. This rapidly developed into a highly sophisticated art, musically and dramatically as well technically. Composition, performance, and recording were all subject to studio control, and the production of musical tracks of high quality can be counted one of the greatest achievements of the system. Outside Hollywood music tracks were often less polished, but directors were more often free to work with composers of their own choice, and Sergei Prokofiev's music for Eisenstein's *Alexander Nevsky* (1938) provides an interesting contrast to two classic Warner Bros. scores of the same period—Erich Korngold's *The Adventures of Robin Hood* (1938) and Max Steiner's *Casablanca* (1943).

Technologically, the main innovations of the studio years, apart from sound itself, were colour (beginning in the 1930s) and new widescreen formats (in the early 1950s). Although developed outside the studios, Technicolor was very much a studio phenomenon, being both expensive and cumbersome. It was not until after the war that simplified colour systems (Agfacolor, Eastman Color) found their way on to the market, allowing colour to be used in cheaper films and even in documentary. Likewise, the arrival of widescreen needs to be seen in the context of the attempts by the studios to woo back audiences from television by restoring a sense of spectacle to the cinema experience. One other innovation, however, magnetic sound, introduced into the mainstream cinema to provide stereo sound-tracks for widescreen films, proved to have much wider applications and helped to initiate a revolution in documentary film-making at the end of the 1950s.

The first area of film-making to make extensive use of Technicolor was animation, in the person of Walt Disney. It was Disney, too, who turned animation from a cottage industry into a form of mainstream studio production, as highly specialized as the making of live-action films. In the late 1930s and the 1940s animation became almost synonymous with mass-circulation Warner Bros. and MGM cartoons on the one hand and Disney's cartoons and animated features on the other. Marginalized during much of the studio period, independent animation nevertheless survived and came into its own again in the changed circumstances of the post-war years.

The next section, 'Genre Cinema', examines the role of genre categories in the production and reception of films, and looks at some of the major genres that flourished during the studio period. While the majority of films can be seen to belong in some sort of genre category and a division of films into genres is as old as the cinema itself (and indeed older, since early cinema inherited its categories from other art forms), genre cinema in the strong sense of the word is very much an industrial phenomenon, in both production and marketing terms. Genre cinema can flourish either as a specialist fringe of an industry, as with 'Hammer horror' in Britain in the late 1950s and 1960s and 'spaghetti Westerns' in Italy in the 1970s, or at the very heart. In Hollywood in the studio period, it was at the heart of the system. Of the genres under consideration here, only the musical was specific to the years 1930–60. The Western dates back almost to the beginning of cinema, although, like the musical, it has been in never-quite-terminal decline since the 1960s; the chapter on the Western deals with the whole history of the genre, from *The Great Train Robbery* in 1903 to *Unforgiven* in 1992, taking in German and Italian Westerns *en route*. In the case of crime films, on the other hand, it has been necessary to be restrictive, and the chapter on the crime movie confines

itself to Hollywood cinema, concentrating on the gangster film of the 1930s and the 'film noir' of the 1940s. We have also grouped together under the general heading of 'Fantasy' three popular genres—horror, science fiction, and fantasy adventure—which, although normally considered distinct, all base their appeal on a stretching of the boundaries of the normal, verisimilar world.

Documentary film flourished in the 1930s, absorbing within it much of the energy of the avant-garde. In 'Engaging with Reality' we look at the impulses, many of them political, behind the impressive development of the documentary cinema in the early sound period, before opening up into the wider issues raised by political events in the inter-war, wartime, and immediately post-war years, from the Russian Revolution, through Fascism and anti-Fascism, to the onset of the Cold War. During this period politics provided more than just a context for the development of the cinema. The strongest effects, of course, were felt in countries under totalitarian rule, but nowhere, not even Hollywood, was exempt from the political ebb and flow.

The 'National Cinemas' section is wider than in Part I. As before, there are chapters on France, Italy, Britain, Germany, the Soviet Union, and Japan, but not on Scandinavia, where the earlier glories of Denmark and Sweden were never recaptured. There are chapters on east central Europe (principally Poland, Hungary, and Czechoslovakia), India, China, Australia, and Latin America, each of which also deals with the silent period. Many of the chapters finish earlier than 1960. The chapter on east central Europe goes up to 1945, that on China to the Communist victory in 1949, that on the Soviet Union to the death of Stalin in 1953. The chapter on Germany deals with the Nazi period and with the post-war Federal Republic, but not with East Germany, whose post-war history is considered (along with other countries in the eastern bloc) only in Part III.

The fact that different *termini* have been chosen for particular countries is a reminder of how different each country's history is—in cinematic terms as well as more generally. It is noteworthy that in France, for example, the cinema rapidly forged links with both mass and high culture and became an expression of both. In Italy, on the other hand, where a modern mass culture did not really exist in the early part of the twentieth century, it was the cinema that created one—as an ironic by-product of the Fascist regime's need to find forms of popular entertainment competitive with Hollywood. The contrast between Germany and Italy is also striking: both countries geared their cinemas in the 1930s largely to the production of harmless entertainment, but it was only in Nazi Germany that this was part of a programme of stage management of reality, linking entertainment to the most noxious forms of nationalistic propaganda. In Italy, in spite of all the posturing and parading promoted by Mussolini, the cinema never fulfilled such a role, nor did it in the Soviet Union under Stalin.

World cinema culture in the 1920s and 1930s had been shaped (as it is today) by the omnipresence of the Hollywood film. This was interrupted by the Second World War, when the supply of American films was blocked off in German- and Japanese-occupied countries, and by the post-war extension of the Communist bloc. Hollywood films returned to continental Europe in 1946 and a new cultural contest developed, pitting Hollywood not only against national cinemas, both established and emerging, but against what was to become international art cinema. Meanwhile Hollywood itself began to change. The system became less monolithic, and independent producers played a larger role. European attitudes to Hollywood changed as well. While opposition to Hollywood's power grew more vociferous, American movies were appreciated more than ever, not only for their entertainment value but for their artistic qualities overall. Significantly this happened when Hollywood itself was entering a long-drawn-out crisis and many of the most appreciated American films were produced on the fringes of the system and displayed qualities which, in its heyday, the system would have suppressed. The final section of this part, 'The Post-War World', looks first at the immediate aftermath of war and then at the tendencies at work in the late 1940s and 1950s which were to gather force as the period progressed and lead to the radically new developments that characterized the 1960s.

SOUND

The Introduction of Sound

KAREL DIBBETS

The transition from silent to sound film marks a period of grave instability as well as great creativity in the history of cinema. The new technology produced panic and confusion, but it stimulated experiments and expectations too. While it undermined Hollywood's international position for several years, it led to a revival of national film production elsewhere. It is a period with specific features that differentiate it from the years before and after. This chapter will focus on these special characteristics, without losing track of some important continuities. Though the conversion to sound did not follow the same path everywhere, and while every country has its own history, most attention will be paid here to the main line of developments.

To understand the impact of sound, it should not be forgotten that silent cinema was not silent at all. Silent films have plenty of references to all kinds of sounds; they deliberately put the viewer in the position of a listener. Moreover, these films were presented in a cinema with live music performed by a pianist or an orchestra, and often the musicians would add sound effects to the action on the screen. In Japanese cinemas a voice was added to the images by a lecturer or *benshi*, who actually dominated the film show with his verbal interpretations.

DIFFUSION PROBLEMS

Long before the introduction of talking pictures, inventors on both sides of the Atlantic had developed a range of technical devices to synchronize sound with moving images. The oldest method was to link a phonograph to a film projector. Thomas Edison himself built the prototype of this sound-on-disc apparatus in the early days; it was still a viable system in the 1920s. Another method, more inspired by modern electro-technics, did away with the discs and recorded sound directly on film. This sound-on-film system would prevail and become the standard of the international film industry in the 1930s.

The conversion to sound did not depend completely on technology, nor would its effects be restricted to technological matters. Software, not hardware, would become the deciding factor of the innovation process in the USA as well as in Europe, although this was not immediately obvious. Hollywood took its first step towards conversion in the 1926–7 season when Warner Bros. and Fox Film began wiring their theatres for sound. Both studios hoped to earn an extra profit by investing in new technology, but the roads they followed were different.

Warners presented its first synchronized programme in August 1926 using a sound-on-disc system called Vitaphone. Warners' main intention was to offer the cinema owners a substitute for the live performers in their programme, in particular the cinema orchestra and the stage show. Because of this, their first feature film with sound, *Don Juan* (1926), was not a talking picture at all; it only used a musical score recorded on discs to accompany the silent images. The studio was more interested in Vitaphone's shorts: lipsync-recorded performances of popular vaudeville and opera stars, who could now bring their act to even the smallest theatres. Fox did not believe in talking feature films either. In April 1927 the studio launched sound newsreels as its alternative, using a sound-on-film system. Fox Movietone News, as it was called, became a big attraction immediately. The success of these innovations was temporary, however, as the novelty appeal wore off.

The real breakthrough came during the 1927–8 season when Warners released a second feature film, this time with lipsync recordings of songs as well as some dialogue. *The Jazz Singer*, directed by Alan Crosland and starring the popular vaudeville star Al Jolson, was really a silent picture incorporating a few inserts with sound. This hybrid form, in which two technological eras come together, corresponds well to the melodramatic theme of the film. A conflict of generations finds expression in a clash of two musical traditions that seem to be mutually exclusive: religious songs and profane jazz. In this way, the film gave birth to a new film genre, the musical.

The success of *The Jazz Singer* proved that sound could come off well if presented as a full-fledged feature film with lipsync acting. As soon as this fact was recognized, the other Hollywood studios rushed to convert to sound. Their hurry was not unmotivated: the new technique would save the costs of live musical accompaniment in their main theatres, and the savings would exceed the costs of conversion considerably (an advantage that did not apply to small cinemas). Cinema musicians were fired

and replaced by hardware. By 1930 most American cinemas had been wired for sound and Hollywood had stopped making silent films. However, this was by no means the only effect of the conversion process.

In May 1928, after thorough examination of the different sound techniques, almost all studios decided to adopt Western Electric's sound-on-film system. This meant the imminent end of Warners' Vitaphone productions on discs. It also meant the sudden creation of a new major studio, Radio–Keith–Orpheum or RKO. This was established by RCA, one of America's biggest radio companies, who were unwilling to leave the motion picture industry to their major competitor, Western Electric. Once the studios had decided to convert, the innovation process entered a new phase. The rest of the world would feel the consequences as Hollywood, Western Electric, and RCA began to prepare for export. The 1928–9 season would become the year of the international diffusion of talking pictures.

What interest there was in sound film outside the USA in the 1920s was to be found with engineers of the radio and phonograph industry. European inventors like Berglund in Sweden, the TriErgon trio in Germany, or Petersen and Poulsen in Denmark had been experimenting for years with sound-on-film technology. They had given demonstrations of their inventions in the early 1920s, but the European film industry had shown little interest in their work. The transition period in Europe, Japan, and Latin America, then, really begins in the 1928–9 season with the first public screening of American talking feature films.

The arrival of American sound films provoked reaction from electronic companies in Europe, who immediately began to organize resistance. Patents were now seen as the keys to the box-office of the European cinemas, worth hundreds of millions of dollars. This lucrative prospect appealed to the imagination of financial and industrial businessmen, and in 1928 two powerful companies were rapidly established. The first, Ton-Bild Syndikat AG, or Tobis, owned the very important TriErgon patents as its main asset; it was created with Dutch and Swiss venture capital and a minor German participation. The other company, Klangfilm GmbH, was backed by the industrial capacity of two major German electrical firms, AEG and Siemens. In March 1929 Tobis and Klangfilm agreed to form a cartel with the aim of fighting off the American invasion and bringing the entire European film industry under its control. They used patent suits to slow down their opponents, while taking advantage of language bar-

The multilingual film. E. A. Dupont's *Atlantic* (1929) was shot simultaneously in English, French, and German. Above, a scene from the English version, with John Stuart and Madeleine Carroll, and below the same scene in the German version, with Francis Lederer and Lucie Mannheim

riers and import restrictions. The patents war that followed would last until July 1930.

The struggle for industrial control alone was enough to rock the foundations of the international film world, but this instability was increased by the language barrier. A silent picture could be exhibited in all countries of the world. A talking picture, however, became the prisoner of its own language. A translation technique did not yet exist and it would take some years before dubbing was developed and generally adopted. Moreover, most pictures were English speaking, and this hurt the self-respect of audiences in non-English-speaking countries, and aroused nationalist feelings. Italy banned talking pictures that used languages other than Italian, and Spain, France, Germany, Czechoslovakia, and Hungary took similar protectionist measures.

As a result, the international film market, dominated by Hollywood for more than a decade, suddenly began to disintegrate: it split into as many markets as there were languages. At first, these language barriers were bridged with songs; the musical film did not rely on dialogue alone and could be enjoyed all over the world without translation. Since musicals were new and very popular, Hollywood was happy to make them in great quantities for its international clients. However, talking pictures with lots of dialogue posed a real problem. Dialogue jeopardized the concept of Hollywood as the centre of the international film industry. For some time, a decentralization of American film production appeared to be the only answer to the language problem, and in 1930 several American studios began to invest extensively in Europe's film industry. Paramount built a giant studio in Joinville, France, to produce multilingual films: they would shoot the same film in different languages, using the same set and costumes over again. Warners set out to co-produce a multilingual film in Germany, *Die 3-Groschenoper* (G. W. Pabst, 1930; the French version was called *L'Opéra de quat' sous*), before securing an important share in Europe's most promising venture in sound film production, Tobis. MGM approached the problem from the opposite end: it invited foreign actors to the USA to play the different language versions in its Hollywood studios. MGM could also employ some of its own stars to this end, as in *Anna Christie* (1930), in which Greta Garbo, born in Sweden, played a Swedish immigrant who speaks both English and German with a foreign accent. This method of producing multilingual films had been invented and tried out first in Great Britain in 1929 when E. A. Dupont directed *Atlantic* in English-, German-, and French-speaking versions, but it remained a very expensive solution.

The future looked gloomy for the American studios in 1929–32, and not only because the economic depression had broken out at the same time. Sound had unleashed forces that undermined Hollywood's international

Joseph P. Maxfield

Joseph P. Maxfield was one of a small group of multi-talented individuals privileged to oversee the development of new sound technologies and their application to Hollywood film-making. Having cut his teeth on the design of Western Electric's state-of-the-art public address system in the early 1920s, Maxfield was given the task of developing a new phonograph at AT&T's newly formed research facility, Bell Laboratories. The resulting 1925 invention, the first phonograph to exploit the possibilities of electric recording and the technology of matched impedance, was licensed for marketing by Victor (as the Orthophonic Victrola) and by Brunswick–Balke–Collender (as the Panatrope), and subsequently became the basis for the Vitaphone sound-on-disc system.

Appointed head of the Western Electric subsidiary responsible for installing the new film sound system, Electric Research Products, Inc. (ERPI), Maxfield published widely on recording techniques appropriate to the new film sound technology. One of the first to recognize the aesthetic importance of controlling reverberation, he was instrumental in devising practical methods of manipulating the acoustics of recording spaces and exhibition spaces alike. An early champion of single microphone use and the matching of sound scale to image scale, Maxfield had a direct and substantial influence on Hollywood's accommodation to the new technology.

A long-term association with Leopold Stokowski, principal conductor of the Philadelphia Orchestra, permitted Maxfield to make signal contributions in the field of music recording as well. Collaborating with Stokowski throughout the 1930s, Maxfield pioneered Hollywood's (and the rest of the recording industry's) use of volume compression and the control of reverberation and aesthetic emphasis through the mixing of two radically different ('dead' and 'live') sound recordings. In the late 1930s he was one of the early supporters of multiple-track and stereo techniques as methods of assuring maximum volume and frequency range as well as enhanced acoustic perspective.

While other important contributors to Hollywood sound technology and technique confined their careers either to the research and development area (A. C. Wente and Harvey Fletcher at Bell Labs, Harry F. Olson at RCA) or to the Hollywood studio domain (Carl Dreher and James G. Stewart at RKO, Douglas Shearer at MGM), Maxfield spanned the full range of technological development and aesthetic technique. From his experience at Bell Labs he learnt to apply engineering formulas to technique, and from his regular contact with the cinema and music industries he learnt the importance of practical solutions. To him we owe not only the technology that made sound film possible but also many of the techniques and conventions that give Hollywood studio era films their particular sound.

RICK ALTMAN

leading role. Exports stagnated not only because of language barriers and patent disputes abroad, but also because Western Electric's policies did not square with Hollywood's.

Their European competitors, on the other hand, had more reason to be optimistic. They hoped to improve their position thanks to the disintegration of Hollywood. Among them was the Tobis–Klangfilm cartel mentioned above, which demanded an international sharing of power with Western Electric. Film-makers dreamed of new national film industries, protected by language barriers, and indeed, sound did stimulate film production in countries like France, Hungary, and the Netherlands. Even the Roman Catholic Church made plans to create its own Catholic sound film monopoly, the International Eidophon Company, based on the patents of a clergyman. 'This is a magnificent opportunity,' a Catholic newspaper wrote in 1931, 'a gift of God to intervene in the world's mighty film industry. It is now or never.' Europe abounded with illusions.

The challenge of Tobis–Klangfilm was eventually met in Paris in July 1930. Here, the electronic companies involved on either side of the Atlantic held a conference that resulted in the foundation of a new cartel. According to their agreement, Europe's mainland became the exclusive territory of Tobis–Klangfilm. The latter could now collect all royalties on sound equipment and films in Europe. (Denmark proved to be an exception since Petersen and Poulsen successfully challenged the cartel with their own patents.) The rest of the world either became American territory or was open to both parties. Western Electric and RCA also agreed to the principle of interchangeability: they allowed Hollywood films to be played on European equipment, and vice versa. Tobis and Klangfilm left Paris in triumph.

In 1932 there was a major breakthrough in solving the language problem, when dubbing was introduced as the standard method of translating talking pictures in major languages, while subtitling became the solution for minor language regions. The dubbing technique had taken four years to develop. In 1933 and thereafter the Hollywood companies would recover from the initial set-back, although import quotas and the Depression would still take their toll. By that time, European film-makers had lost their illusions and stopped dreaming. Hollywood could produce its films at home again, and Paramount's Joinville studio was transformed into a huge dubbing centre, the world's biggest ventriloquist.

REVISION IN THE MOVIE THEATRE

The consequences of the coming of sound are usually evaluated with respect to the production of films, though the changes at the level of film exhibition and reception are of no less importance. Sound changed not only the

film, but also the film's presentation and its relation to the viewer. In fact, the roots of silent film culture had to be demolished to give room to the rise of talking pictures. In the first place, the transferral of the orchestra from the pit to the sound-track marked the end of the cinema as a multimedia show with live performance, giving way to the cinema as a single-medium event. Musical accompaniment by a local orchestra was made superfluous; nor was it necessary any longer for the exhibitor to support his programmes with a live stage show. Secondly, films no longer came to the theatre as semi-manufactured goods, but as final products. The new technology put an end to local variations in presentation. Sound films could offer a complete show in themselves, independent of local performers, and this show would be the same in every theatre all over the world. Thirdly, the definition of film changed drastically when music and sound effects, formerly a live element of the viewing context, became an integral part of the recorded film text. As a result of this 'textualization' of the context, the film text as an independent, autonomous artefact came into being. This would lead, among other things, to new concepts in film theory and criticism. Finally, the conversion to sound did not only change the conditions, but also the rules of film viewing. Audiences no longer visited a multimedia show that was primarily staged at this side of the screen, now they entered a cinema just to see what happened *on* the screen, or at the other side of the screen, as one might say. Without the mediation of a live orchestra, the thrill of watching a movie was transformed from a communal happening between four walls into an exclusive relation between the film (-maker) and the individual viewer. The capacity of the exhibitor or the audience to intervene in the communication process had been reduced to a minimum.

The Cinema Act in the Netherlands provides an illustration of these shifts. The Act had been drafted in the silent period and drew a fine distinction between silent films and their exhibition. While the pictures themselves were to be supervised by the central government, their verbal and musical presentation had to be controlled by local administrations. However, when the new technology transferred the production of sounds from the theatre to the studio, the control of sounds tended to shift from local to central government, as the latter was now in a position to check all elements of the presentation. However, the Act did not sanction this interference with local authority. The consequences of this transfer of powers were debated at the highest political levels of government and Parliament in the Netherlands in 1930.

The elimination of the cinema orchestras was first of all a social tragedy. In the 1920s the cinema had become the world's largest employer of musicians. Thousands of musicians were sacked while many vaudeville artists lost an important source of employment. Only the most luxurious movie theatres maintained a reduced orchestra and a side-show with live entertainment; a few even continued this tradition even into the 1960s. The greatest musical talents could find a job on the radio, but the majority had no alternative. Their wholesale dismissal could not have come at a worse time since it coincided with the outbreak of the economic depression and the spread of unemployment.

The wiring of cinemas also affected the competition between movie houses. A luxurious theatre could take advantage of the innovation since the conversion led to important savings. In doing so, however, it lost a characteristic attraction that had distinguished it from smaller theatres. Talking pictures made it possible to offer the same show in every cinema on earth. This levelling of differences would undermine the old theatre hierarchy and increase the competition in exhibition.

In all countries film critics, particularly the advocates of film as art, had great difficulties in accepting the new technology and integrating it in their aesthetic views. This reaction is understandable though paradoxical. Sound had increased the autonomy of the film by banning local influences on the presentation, thereby contributing to the ideal of film as an autonomous art, a central issue in the critical discussion of the 1920s. The champions of this view rejected the talking picture, however, for to them the end of silent cinema meant the death of the seventh art. It took some time before they had adapted their aesthetic views to the new conditions. And some, like the German film theorist Rudolf Arnheim, never did.

The revolution in the movie theatre also introduced the new experience of foreign languages to the public. It should be noted that the protests against foreign languages were not directed exclusively against American pictures. Czech audiences, for example, got very annoyed about the glut of German talking pictures in 1930. The release of Gustav Ucicky's *Der unsterbliche Lump* provoked anti-German demonstrations of such magnitude that the Czech government installed a temporary ban on German films (it has been rumoured that American film companies instigated the protest actions to harm the German competition). Retaliation was inevitable, and German theatres began a boycott against Czech playwrights, eight opera-houses cancelling the works of composer Leoš Janáček, while German radio refused to broadcast Czech music. It was clear that the world needed translation techniques urgently, but it took several years before subtitling and dubbing were universally accepted as standard solutions.

ADJUSTMENTS IN THE STUDIO

The introduction of sound marked a period of artistic experimentation in modernist as well as in classical filmmaking. Formal experiments could be found in Europe, particularly in the avant-garde movement, though its output remained small. Interesting examples are Walter Ruttmann's *Melodie der Welt* (Germany, 1929), Dziga Vertov's *Enthusiasm* (Soviet Union, 1930), and Joris Ivens's *Philips Radio* (the Netherlands, 1931). These pictures have a few traits in common. The avant-gardists edited sounds like images, creating aural worlds parallel to visible worlds. A special feature of their films is the absolute

A retrospective look at the coming of sound: Gene Kelly (as Don Lockwood) and Jean Hagen (as Lina Lamont) being rehearsed for the microphone in a scene from *Singin' in the Rain* (1952)

Josef von Sternberg
(1894–1969)

On seeing *The Salvation Hunters* in 1925, Charlie Chaplin declared its tyro director, Josef von Sternberg, to be a genius. In 1932, advertising *Blonde Venus*, Paramount also called him a genius. French critics freely used the term to explain why his silent films *Underworld* and *The Docks of New York* so easily acquired a cultish admiration among Parisian audiences. In the 1930s, his discovery and protégée Marlene Dietrich vociferously reconfirmed his genius, and her willing submission to it. Geniuses, however, are not always welcome, especially in Hollywood. By 1939, Sternberg would be declared 'a menace to the business'.

In his autobiography Sternberg noted of his experience in Hollywood: 'I proved to be an outsider and as such I remained.' The industry's rejection of him was justified in the press by accounts of his personality. He was depicted as petulantly arrogant and unreasonably dictatorial, even for a director. Legend has it he would sit on a boom and throw silver dollars to actors who pleased him, but Dietrich's daughter describes him as a shy little man with sad eyes and more than a measure of self-abnegating sensitivity.

Born in Vienna, Sternberg emigrated to the United States with his family shortly after the turn of the century. He was apprenticed to a millinery shop, but ran away from home. In New York City, he found a job working for a motion picture film repairer, and in his spare time he started observing film production at the studios in Fort Lee, New Jersey. After non-combat service in the First World War, he drifted to Hollywood, where he be-

came an assistant director. In 1924, with $5,000, he made *The Salvation Hunters*, whereupon Chaplin offered to produce his second film, *A Woman of the Sea* (1926), only to withdraw the film after one public screening. Sternberg was hired briefly by MGM, but was replaced on his first assignment *The Exquisite Sinner* (1926) and found himself again demoted to assistant director. His attempts to achieve what he regarded as filmic perfection were seen as outrageous, and columnist Walter Winchell publicly ridiculed him as an 'out of work' and, therefore, 'genuine' genius.

Paramount–Famous Players Lasky, however, were willing to take a chance and in 1927 assigned Sternberg to direct a minor gangster film *Underworld*, which proved a huge success, with memorable performances (from George Bancroft, Clive Brook, and Evelyn Brent), psychologically fascinating characters in a love triangle, and evocative images, including a gorgeous, confetti-filled gangsters' ball. Two further successes followed in 1928: *The Docks of New York* (with Victor McLaglen) and *The Last Command* (with Emil Jannings). In 1930 he went to Germany to direct a Ufa–Paramount co-production to be made in both German and English versions. This film, *The Blue Angel*, was planned as a starring vehicle for Jannings, but it was Sternberg's casting of Marlene Dietrich as the *femme fatale* Lola Lola that would create a sensation. It would also begin their seven-film collaboration that would earn the director the epithet of 'Svengali Joe'.

Sternberg returned to Hollywood, with Dietrich. Their pictures together at Paramount over the next five years would be marked by variations on the theme of the sexual humiliation of a masochistic male: *Morocco* (1930), *Dishonored* (1931), *Blonde Venus* (1932), *Shanghai Express* (1932), *The Scarlet Empress* (1934), and *The Devil Is a Woman*

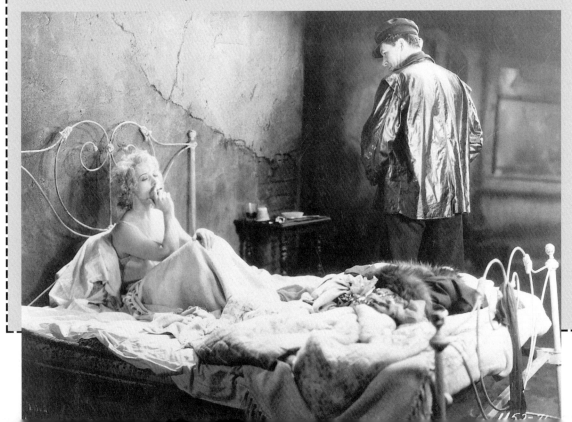

(1935). At first critics and public responded enthusiastically to the films' ornate visual style, their ambiguous insinuations of sexual abnormality and melodramatic exoticism, but after *Shanghai Express* (1932), poor box-office returns and unfavourable reviews became the rule rather than the exception. While Dietrich's star rose, Sternberg's fell. The director was blamed for creating 'tonal tapestries, two-dimensional fabrications valuable only for their details', of making that 'beautiful creature', Marlene Dietrich, a mere 'clothes-horse'. But it was precisely through his attention to detail and his apparent obsession to fill what he termed 'dead space' that Sternberg was able to create a visual poetry of unusual pictorial expressivity. He was not a genius merely because he used soft focus or elaborately artificial scenic effects, but because his films achieved uncommon structural unity and thematic complexity through their unique visual style.

After the release of *The Devil Is a Woman*, Paramount no longer required Sternberg's services. Other than the remarkably decadent film *The Shanghai Gesture* (1942), the rest of Sternberg's career in Hollywood would be marked by assignments either embarrassingly unworthy of his talents (*The King Steps out*, *Sergeant Madden*) or with a promise only fitfully realized, as in the case of *Crime and Punishment* (1935, with Peter Lorre). His attempt to make *I, Claudius* for Alexander Korda in England was aborted after one of the stars (Merle Oberon) was incapacitated. Sternberg's last feature film would be a Japanese production, *The Saga of Anatahan* (1953). Sternberg himself was disappointed with the film, but defiantly reaffirmed his work's primary and continuing virtue: his films were visual experiences without need for the encumbrance of dialogue or even, he once asserted, narrative.

Sternberg recounts that he was warned that 'so much talent will always be punished', but his talent would ultimately be vindicated. Before his death in 1969, he had the satisfaction of seeing a new generation of critics restore to him the title of genius first granted and then torn away by Hollywood early in his career.

GAYLYN STUDLAR

SELECT FILMOGRAPHY

The Salvation Hunters (1925); Underworld (1927); The Docks of New York (1928); The Last Command (1928); Der blaue Engel / The Blue Angel (1930); Morocco (1930); An American Tragedy (1931); Dishonored (1931); Blonde Venus (1932); Shanghai Express (1932); The Scarlet Empress (1934); The Devil Is a Woman (1935); Crime and Punishment (1936); I, Claudius (1937–unfinished); The Shanghai Gesture (1941); Macao (1952); The Saga of Anatahan (1953)

BIBLIOGRAPHY

Baxter, Peter (1993), *Just Watch! Sternberg, Paramount and America.*
Sternberg, Josef von (1965), *Fun in a Chinese Laundry.*
Studlar, Gaylyn (1988), *Von Sternberg, Dietrich and the Masochistic Aesthetic.*

Opposite: George Bancroft and Betty Compton in Josef von Sternberg's *The Docks of New York* (1928)

equivalence of all sounds: there is no hierarchical relation between music, voices, noises, and silences, as is usually the case in narrative sound films. (This treatment of the sound-track demonstrates an affinity with Bruitism, or the Art of Noise, advocated by the Italian futurist Luigi Russolo.) They avoided the use of dialogue and stuck to the principle of speechlessness as the essence of film art.

The avant-garde cinema proved, however, to have a very restricted future, and it declined with the arrival of sound. This decline was not simply a consequence of the new technology, as critics suggested at the time; the artistic malaise had set in earlier and was certainly not restricted to film. Sound rather accelerated the demise, and ensured that it was irreversible.

During this period traditional film-makers also made a real effort to innovate their artistic practice. Big studios in Hollywood and Berlin explored the possibilities of sound within the old narrative framework. To this end, they had to adapt the technical infrastructure. For example, building walls had to be made sound-proof, and the hissing arc lamps and the humming camera had to be silenced. To control the sound-recording process, the studio had to employ personnel of a different kind (notably electrical engineers), and to edit the film, new equipment had to be designed.

These and other investments in technology went hand in hand with extensive artistic experimentation. However, these experiments were not intended to develop new styles, as the avant-garde had done; on the contrary, all creative efforts were mobilized to bring sound into line with the existing practice of film-making to serve classical story-telling. In this way, the expressive qualities of the microphone were tested and compared to those of the camera. The microphone would become the ear, as the camera had been the eye of the imaginary observer. Visual point of view could be matched with aural point of view, camera distance with sound distance, visual depth with sound perspective. The vocabulary of film-making and criticism was extended with a set of concepts that sprang from this analogy of sound and image.

The French film critic André Bazin stressed the continuity of style in a well-known essay from 1958, asking: 'Did the years from 1928 to 1930 actually witness the birth of a new cinema?' (Bazin 1967). To answer his question, Bazin returns to silent cinema. According to him, two styles had coexisted in the silent period: one that privileged editing, and one that privileged staging or *mise-en-scène*. The former had dominated silent film-making, but the latter would become more prominent after the introduction of sound. This emphasis on continuity in the transition from silent to sound cinema seems to be confirmed in later studies. Sound stimulated stylistic innovation, but within narrow limits. For example, talking pictures tended to have longer shots, and (contrary to what earlier historians used to say) they often showed more camera mobility than silent films did. Reframings, pannings, trackings, and a quicker succession of scenes compensated for a slackening of the tempo caused by the spoken word. This can be observed in American movies, but also in German and French films of the 1930s. In general, however, the shift in style did not alter the basic rules of realist story-telling that had come into being during the silent era.

The practice of musical illustration, almost perfected during the silent period, was more or less transplanted to the sound era. An important difference was, of course, that music could now become a part of the fictional world, for example when the film showed an orchestra or a singer in action. Further, sound film would subordinate music not only to the image, but to dialogue as well, turning it into pure background. Also, the big band with its brass and percussion instruments that had become popular in so many of the luxurious cinemas of the west, in imitation of American jazz, was replaced by a symphonic orchestra, a European invention from the nineteenth century. Studios now preferred strings and woodwinds, and Hollywood contracted composers with a training in classical European music, like Erich Korngold and Max Steiner. It would take a long time before the big band was accepted to play a film score again. The memory of the cinema orchestra in the mean time was reduced to a stereotype honky-tonk piano accompaniment of silent slapstick films.

The art of writing dialogue was new to the film and had to be imported from the stage. More than ever before, talented playwrights were employed in the film industry. The spoken word did not only enhance verbal communication in the screenplay, but an actor received a voice that would help to determine his character. In the early 1930s stars came to be identified by their voice as much as by their face. Hollywood developed a wide diversity of speaking styles, from tough-talking gangsters like James Cagney to the *double entendres* of Mae West, and the absurd puns of Groucho Marx. This quality was lost in foreign countries where voices were dubbed; dubbing damaged the star system. Dialogue also had the effect of enhancing the cultural specificity of a film in a way that could not be repressed by dubbing. This can best be seen in American films, for while Hollywood's silent pictures had a strong European bias, the spoken word urged them to give a more realistic impression of American society. Dialogue would make characters, scenes, and events thoroughly American.

CONCLUSION

The end of the transition period did not arrive in all countries at the same time. While the wiring of American theatres had almost been completed as early as 1930, the rest of the world would follow with a delay of at least three years. North European countries like Great Britain, Germany, Denmark, and the Netherlands finished the conversion process in 1933; France and Italy followed two or three years later, and eastern Europe needed even more time to catch up. In Japan, the innovation was delayed for several years since the film lecturers, or *benshi*, successfully opposed it. During this gradual diffusion process silent and sound films coexisted side by side in the cinemas.

Though sound had interrupted the process of internationalization that characterized the film industry from its beginnings, it could not bring it to a halt. Hollywood's world empire was shaken, but it survived the transition period. The American film industry would dominate the world again in 1933 as it had done in 1928, with the exception of countries like Germany, Italy, and the Soviet Union that had imposed severe import restrictions on American films. In fact, sound ultimately stimulated internationalization, for the more films were produced as self-contained and final products, the more easily they could be distributed internationally as complete commodities. Sound brought an end to local differences in exhibition, and guaranteed uniform presentations all over the world. It also reduced the differences in style internationally, making films look more homogeneous. In brief, sound marked a new phase in a long-term integration process.

Some peculiar discontinuities should be pointed out too. Since 1932 the world has been divided into nations that prefer dubbing and those that hate it and favour subtitling of films. These preferences have become deeply rooted in national viewing habits, and eventually were transferred to television. It is not always clear, however, on what grounds these choices were made at the time. Though dubbing is more expensive and can be processed profitably only in major language regions, the economic motive was not always decisive. Japan opted for subtitles, though dubbing would have been economically feasible in this densely populated country. On the other hand, the choice in favour of dubbing was influenced by nationalist considerations in many countries, although the fear that the sounds of foreign languages in the cinema might corrupt the mother tongue as well as national culture appears to be unfounded in retrospect. The opposite might be the case since it can be argued that foreign languages in the cinema and on television lead to an intensified awareness of cultural identity. Subtitles are a continuous signal for the viewer that there is a gap between the country of production and the place of reception. This signal is missing in dubbing. Dubbing facilitates the process of acculturation that goes hand in hand with the international diffusion of films, since culture is not only transmitted by words but by images as well. That is why there is little reason to suppose that cultural identity can be defended by excluding foreign languages from the screen. The production of films and television programmes in the native tongue is a better means to this end.

An important effect of the new technology was the revival of film production in many countries in response to the sudden demand for talking pictures in native languages. French cinema peaked with 157 feature films in 1932 after an all-time low of 52 in 1929, though the introduction of dubbing would bring the number down again. Small nations like Hungary, the Netherlands, and Norway, formerly dependent on film imports altogether, enjoyed an unexpected renaissance of national film production in their own languages. Most impressive, however, was the recovery of Czech cinema. Protected by language barriers and import restrictions, Czechoslovakia witnessed a boom in film-making, cinema attendance, and theatre-building. Czech talking pictures were received enthusiastically in the home market, and the new demand for films would lead to the recruitment of authentic talents like Martin Frič and Otakar Vávra. The success of Czech cinema was surpassed only by India, where local film production benefited immensely from the transition to sound, integrating musical numbers with action scenes, thus reconciling cinema with long-standing popular traditions. Without sound, India might not have become the world's largest producer of motion pictures.

The initial fear that the introduction of sound might cause a catastrophe aroused a greater sense of film history.

Silent film art was discovered as an endangered heritage worth preserving for future generations. The importance of film archives was recognized, as a source of historical evidence and for aesthetic reasons. Nostalgia for the silent era came into being. Special cinemas were opened where one could see the masterpieces of the past, and the first histories of film as art were written: early attempts to define the canon of silent film, evaluating what belonged to the classical heritage and what did not. Here also begins the selection process that is typical of every historical enterprise: the tendency to forget what one did not want to see or hear in the past. For example, it was fifty years before it became possible to show a silent film as it had been presented originally in the cinema: accompanied by a live orchestra.

Bibliography
Altman, Rick (ed.) (1992), *Sound Theory, Sound Practice.*
Arnheim, Rudolf (1983), *Film as Art.*
Bazin, André (1967), 'The Evolution of the Language of Cinema'.
Geduld, Harry M. (1975), *The Birth of the Talkies.*
Neale, Stephen (1985), *Cinema and Technology: Image, Sound, Colour.*
Salt, Barry (1992), *Film Style and Technology: History and Analysis.*
Walker, Alexander (1987), *The Shattered Silents: How the Talkies Came to Stay.*
Weis, Elisabeth, and Belton, John (eds.) (1985), *Film Sound: Theory and Practice.*

THE STUDIO YEARS

Hollywood: The Triumph of the Studio System

THOMAS SCHATZ

The 1920s had been a decade of tremendous growth and prosperity for the American motion picture industry, with all phases of production, distribution, and exhibition expanding rapidly as movie-going became the nation's—and indeed much of the world's—preferred form of entertainment. Following the industry's conversion to sound films in 1927–8, the so-called 'talkie boom' capped this halcyon period, providing an additional market surge at the decade's end and further solidifying the dominant position of Hollywood's major studio powers. The talkie boom was so strong, in fact, that Hollywood was touting itself as 'Depression-proof' in the wake of Wall Street's momentous collapse in October 1929, and the American movie industry enjoyed its best year ever in 1930 as theatre admissions, gross revenues, and studio profits reached record levels.

The Depression caught up with the movie industry in 1931, however, and its delayed impact was devastating. Between 1930 and 1933, theatre admissions fell from 90 million per week to only 60 million, gross industry revenues fell from $730 million to about $480 million, and combined studio profits of $52 million became net losses of some $55 million. Thousands of the nation's 23,000 theatres closed their doors in the early 1930s, leaving only about 15,300 in operation by 1935. Among the Hollywood powers, the Depression hit the Big Five integrated major studios especially hard because of the massive debt service on their theatre chains. Three of the Big Five—Paramount, Fox, and RKO—suffered financial collapse in the early 1930s, and Warner Bros. survived only by siphoning off roughly one-quarter of its assets. MGM, meanwhile, not only survived but prospered during the Depression due to its relatively limited chain of first-class metropolitan theatres, the deep pockets of powerful parent company Loew's Inc., and the quality of product turned out by its Culver City studio.

Hollywood's three 'major minor' studios—Columbia, Universal, and United Artists (UA)—fared somewhat better in the early 1930s. These companies produced top product and had their own nation-wide and overseas distribution operations, like the Big Five, but they did not own theatre chains. While this had been a tremendous disadvantage during the 1920s, it proved to be a blessing during the Depression, since these studios avoided the related mortgage commitments. The major minors also adjusted their production and market strategies more effectively than the integrated majors. UA, which was essentially a releasing company for the A-class productions of its active founders (Charlie Chaplin, Mary Pickford, and Douglas Fairbanks) and for major independent producers like Sam Goldwyn and Joe Schenck, simply limited its output to about a dozen A-class pictures per annum. Columbia and Universal pursued a very different course, gearing their factories to low-cost, low-risk features which fell into a new and significant 1930s product category: the 'B movie'.

The rapid rise of the B movie and the 'double feature' was a direct result of the Depression. To attract patrons in those troubled economic times, most of the nation's theatres began showing two features per programme, and changed programmes two or three times per week. The increased product demand was met largely via B movies—that is, quickly and cheaply made formula fare, usually Westerns or action pictures, which ran about sixty minutes and were designed to play on double bills in subsequent-run theatres outside the major urban markets. Not surprisingly, this period saw the emergence of many companies which specialized in B pictures. Referred to as 'independents', these were straight production companies without distribution set-ups; they released through the states' rights system, farming out their films to small-time independent distributors on a regional basis. A few of these B-picture studios, notably Monogram and Republic, not only survived the Depression but became relatively important companies by the late 1930s.

B-movie production was scarcely confined to the 'poverty row' outfits, but in fact became an important element in the studio system at large. All of the integrated majors produced Bs during the 1930s, with up to half of the output of Warners, RKO, and Fox falling into that category as the decade wore on. While most of the major studios' revenues came from A-class features, the production of B movies enabled them to keep their studio operations running smoothly and their contract personnel working regularly, to develop new talent and try new genres, and to ensure a regular supply of product.

While Bs and double bills helped the studios and exhibitors weather the early Depression years, the real key to Hollywood's survival—as well as its tremendous late-1930s success—was the intervention of both Wall Street and Washington, DC. In fact, one might argue that Hollywood's classical era could not have occurred without the financial support of Wall Street and the government's economic recovery programme. New York financiers and banking firms had been involved with the movie industry's development since the early 1920s, particularly in the studios' theatre chain expansion and conversion to sound. Wall Street's involvement increased significantly during the early 1930s, as various firms engineered and financed the reorganization of foundering studios and became more directly involved in their management and operations as well.

The federal government, meanwhile, initiated an economic recovery programme during the Depression which enabled the major Hollywood powers to solidify their control of the industry. The crucial factor here was the election of Franklin D. Roosevelt to the presidency in late 1932, and the impact of FDR's National Industrial Recovery Act (NIRA), which went into effect in June 1933. The NIRA strategy, basically, was to promote recovery by condoning certain monopoly practices by major US industries—including motion pictures. The studios now enjoyed what Tino Balio (1985) has termed 'government sanction for the trade practices that [the majors] had spent ten years developing through informal collusion'. Hollywood's own trade association, the Motion Picture Producers and Distributors Association (MPPDA), drafted the Code of Fair Competition required by the NIRA. This formally codified trade practices such as block booking, blind bidding, and a run-zone-clearance, which minimized the studios' financial risks and maximized the profitability of their top features.

Another significant effect of the NIRA on the industry, and particularly on studio production, was the rise of organized labour. To mitigate the potential for worker exploitation and abuse inherent in the recovery programme, the NIRA authorized labour organizing and collective bargaining—an effort reinforced by Congress via the Wagner Act in 1935 and the creation of the National Labor Relations Board. Thus Hollywood evolved from essentially an 'open shop' to a 'union town' in the 1930s, with the division and specialization of film-making labour now mandated by the government and codified by the various unions and guilds.

Beyond the government-mandated regulation of the industry, the 1930s saw increasingly heavy regulation of movie content by the MPPDA. In 1930 MPPDA president Will Hays authorized the drafting of the Production Code,

a doctrine of ethics designed, according to its preamble, to safeguard 'the larger moral responsibility of the motion pictures'. Code enforcement was somewhat lax and inconsistent until 1933, when widespread public criticism of sex and violence in movies, especially by the newly created Catholic Legion of Decency, led Hays and the MPPDA to devise a means of formal self-censorship. The result was the Production Code Administration (PCA), an MPPDA agency which, under director Joseph Breen, regulated movie content. Beginning in 1934, PCA approval was required on all scripts before production and then on the finished film, which was assigned a PCA seal prior to release.

The extensive codification and regulation of the movie industry during the 1930s enhanced economic recovery, stabilized film-making operations, and solidified the major studios' control of virtually every phase of the industry. By the late 1930s the eight major studios produced about 75 per cent of the features released in the USA, which generated 90 per cent of all box-office revenues. As distributors they took in 95 per cent of all rental receipts. Hollywood films also accounted for an estimated 65 per cent of all films exhibited world-wide, and roughly one-third of studio revenues throughout the 1930s came from foreign markets—predominantly Britain, which supplied nearly half of Hollywood's overseas revenues.

The five integrated majors, meanwhile, had solidified their dominant position via command of the crucial first-run market. Taken together, the Big Five owned or controlled about 2,600 'affiliated' theatres in 1939; this was only 15 per cent of the nation's total, but it comprised over 80 per cent of metropolitan first-run theatres—that is, the de luxe town-centre houses in the largest cities with seating in the thousands which ran only top features, operated day and night, and generated the lion's share of industry revenues. While the majors' theatre holdings had been a severe financial burden during the darkest Depression years, by the late 1930s they again were keying the Big Five's utter domination of the movie market-place. As Mae Huettig stated (1944) in her study of industry economics in the late 1930s: 'As a control device, the development of strategic first-run theaters as the showcase of the industry proved remarkably effective. Ownership of these relatively few theaters gave [the integrated major studios] control over access to the market.'

STUDIO MANAGEMENT IN THE 1930S

Given the changing economic fortunes of the studios during the 1930s, as well as the changes in industry trade practices, there were significant changes in management at virtually all levels: the executive control of the motion picture companies themselves, the operation of the studio-factories in Los Angeles, and the supervision of

Bette Davis

(1908–1989)

In 1930 Bette Davis, a young actress with a growing reputation on the Broadway stage, was spotted by a Hollywood talent scout looking for new screen actors for the 'talkies'. Davis was signed by Universal, but after a year spent playing minor roles moved to Warner Bros., where she would remain for nearly twenty years, becoming Queen of the Lot and the most respected actress in Hollywood.

Her rise to stardom was slow and difficult. She neither relished nor suited the pin-up image in which the studio initially cast her, and she later characterized her roles in these early films as 'vapid blondes and silly ingenues'. However, they provided the training ground for her to develop her screen acting skills, and her strong performances began to attract attention from critics and audiences.

Her breakthrough came in 1934 with *Of Human Bondage*. In Mildred, the bitter vampish waitress, Davis recognized a part that would suit her ability and her style, and she delivered a *tour de force* performance that justified her demands for central roles. *Of Human Bondage* established the Bette Davis image—the aggressive, independent, and driven woman. Davis proved that this role could dominate a film, and hold an audience as fascinated as they were by the glamour queens and sentimental lovers traditionally at the centre of Hollywood's women's narratives. Her performances in *Bordertown* (1935) and *Dangerous* (1935) consolidated her image, and her popularity. Warners, however, did not seem able or willing to capitalize on her success, and in February 1936 Davis walked off the lot, demanding better roles and a new contract.

At that time all the studios signed actors to restrictive seven-year contracts, but Warners were notorious for keeping stars on low wages, making cheap, quick films, for as long as possible. Throughout the 1930s and 1940s they were challenged in court by some of their top stars, including Cagney and Bogart. When Davis, suspended without pay, accepted film work in London, Warners filed a lawsuit to stop her. After a battle watched with bated breath by stars and studios alike, the court ruled that Davis must confine her services exclusively to Warner Bros. She returned to the studio, but did not moderate her demands for better roles. She continued to struggle, largely unsuccessfully, against the limitations of her contract for the rest of her career at Warners.

The court battle had important implications for Davis, Warners, and Hollywood. The Davis case, along with that of Cagney several years previously, set a precedent which led to the studios' suspension practices being outlawed in 1943, and began a slow shift towards star power in Hollywood. The court battle had kept Davis in the public eye and seemed to validate her screen image as a strong woman. Warners had been without one of their leading actresses for over a year, and so, despite losing in court, Davis found her hand considerably strengthened. The studio bought the rights to *Jezebel*, a property Davis had long been requesting, and it was the success of this film, with audiences and critics, that confirmed Davis's stardom and her position at the studio. It also signalled a shift in Warners' production policy, which moved towards prestige pictures that could compete with the best that Hollywood could offer (in this case *Gone with the Wind*, 1939). Davis was central to this policy, and over the next ten years starred in some of the most successful quality Hollywood costume dramas and melodramas, helping to confirm Warners as a top flight studio.

Jezebel (1938) provided the model for the mature Davis heroine; Julie Marsden wilfully becomes an outcast from New Orleans society by wearing a red dress to a ball, instead of the white dictated for unmarried women. Her sacrifice at the end of the film redeems her, but is itself an act of wilfulness and bravery. Although Davis played a

Bette Davis in her Oscar-winning role as the wayward Julie Marsden in William Wyler's *Jezebel* (1938)

wide diversity of roles at Warners, from waitress to queen, they can be divided in to two types; the strong, bitter, almost evil woman of *The Little Foxes* (1941), *The Letter* (1940), *Of Human Bondage*; and that staple of the women's picture, the tragic heroine of *Dark Victory* (1939), *Now, Voyager* (1942), *The Old Maid* (1939). What linked these disparate roles was the powerful Davis persona, which revealed the suffering beneath the hard surface of the 'wicked', and the strength beneath the suffering of the romantic.

Davis's enormous popularity with female audiences in the 1930s and 1940s was largely due to this ability to unite apparently contradictory visions of a woman's role. She represented both the glamour of a movie star, and the ordinary woman, who faced crisis alone, and struggled to survive in a world dominated by men. Her sacrifices and disappointments never erased her sense of self, or her streak of selfishness.

She was capable of producing remarkably controlled performances, even in overblown roles. In *The Letter* she delivers a powerful study of repressed passion, as the apparently respectable wife of a Singapore planter who empties her gun into her lover, and then lies and lies again to cover up her crime. Her portrayal of Margo Channing in *All about Eve* (1950), as an ageing actress professionally and sexually challenged by a younger woman, is a study of bitchiness covering vulnerability.

All about Eve proved to be her last great role. In the 1950s and 1960s Davis continued to work, generally for television and low-budget movies. Due to lack of quality material, the subtleties of her performance and persona disappeared. She proved she could deliver the best Bette Davis caricature in *Whatever Happened to Baby Jane?* (1962), playing the aggressive and selfish woman as grotesque and mad. Davis vowed that she would never retire, and continued working up to her death.

Carl Laemmle, after seeing her in *Bad Sister* (1931) in her Universal days, is reputed to have been horrified by what his studio had signed; 'Can you imagine some poor guy going through hell . . . in a picture and ending up with her at the fade out.' Davis went through hell, and frequently put other people through hell, but she is enduringly popular precisely because she did not wait around for the fade out, or for some man to validate her struggle.

KATE BEETHAM

SELECT FILMOGRAPHY

Of Human Bondage (1934); Dangerous (1935); Jezebel (1938); Dark Victory (1939); The Private Lives of Elizabeth and Essex (1939); The Letter (1940); The Little Foxes (1941); Now, Voyager (1942); Mr Skeffington (1944); All about Eve (1950); Whatever Happened to Baby Jane? (1962)

BIBLIOGRAPHY

Davis, Bette (1962), *The Lonely Life: An Autobiography*.
Higham, Charles (1981), *Bette*.
Leaming, Barbara (1992), *Bette Davis: A Biography*.

actual film production. The Depression-era collapse of five of the Big Eight studios gave several Wall Street firms the opportunity, usually through the trustees or boards of directors of these salvaged companies, directly to control particular studios and to impose their own notions of efficiency and sound business practices. These efforts had relatively little real impact, however, which is instructive in terms of studio ownership and management. As film historian Robert Sklar has pointed out in his analysis of studio control during the 1930s:

The ultimate issue is not who owns the movie companies but who manages them. When several studios began to founder in the early Depression years, the outside interests who took them over were determined to play a direct role in running them, to demonstrate how practical business and financial minds could make money where movie men could not. By the end of the 1930s, however, all the studios were back under the management, if not the ownership, of men experienced in the world of entertainment. (Sklar 1976)

This latter distinction is crucial, as has been demonstrated by film historians applying the tenets of neoclassical economic theory. Balio, for example, argues that the ownership–management split which took hold in the 1930s indicated that the studios had developed into modern business enterprises. 'As they grew in size', writes Balio, the studios 'became managerial, which is to say, they rationalized and organized operations into autonomous departments headed by a professional manager'. The studio founders themselves either became 'full-time career managers'—as with the Cohns (at Columbia) and the Warners—or, as was more often the case, they relinquished direct control to salaried executives. And as Balio notes, most of the chief executives appointed during the 1930s who successfully managed the studios had backgrounds in either distribution or exhibition; management of actual film-making operations was invariably left to salaried executives with direct production experience.

These refinements in top management of the motion picture companies during the 1930s were accompanied by equally important adjustments in production supervision. During the early studio era, executive management of the major motion picture companies involved a classic 'top-down' procedure which well indicated the commercial imperatives of the vertically integrated industry. The New York office was the site of ultimate power and authority; there the chief executives managed the direction of capital, marketing and sales, and, for the Big Five, theatre operations. The New York office also set the annual budget and determined the general production requirements of the studio-factory. The Hollywood plant, in turn, was managed by one or two corporate vice-presidents who were responsible for day-to-day studio operations and the overall output of pictures.

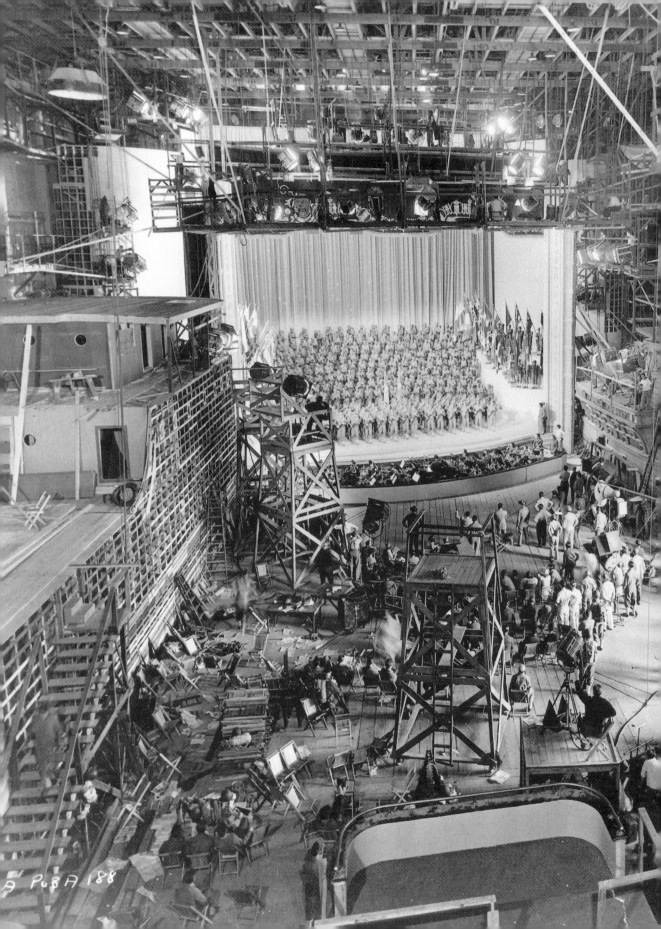

Generally, the West Coast studios were run by a two-man team comprised of a 'studio boss' and a 'production chief'—Louis B. Mayer and Irving Thalberg at MGM, Jack Warner and Darryl Zanuck at Warner Bros., Jesse Lasky and B. P. Schulberg at Paramount, and so on. And in every case, there was a clear chain of command extending from the New York office, through the 'front office' at the studio, and into the production arena itself—usually via 'supervisors' who oversaw production and acted on behalf of the higher corporate executives.

This type of 'central producer' system, wherein one or two studio executives supervised all production, typified the mass-production mentality and factory-oriented operations of the studio system in the early years. This approach gradually gave way to a more flexible 'unit' system during the 1930s. As Janet Staiger has noted (Bordwell *et al.* 1985), 'In 1931 the film industry moved away from the central producer management system to a management organization in which a group of men supervised six to eight films per year, usually each producer concentrating on a particular type of film.' This shift to a 'unit-producer system' occurred gradually in the course of the decade, and was fairly pervasive by the late 1930s. By then the only widespread remnant of the factory-oriented, assembly-line approach to production was in the B-picture realm, where production was still managed by a foreman: J. J. Cohn at MGM, Bryan Foy at Warners, Sol Wurtzel at Fox, Harold Hurley at Paramount, and Lee Marcus at RKO.

While the shift to unit production involved a variation of sorts on the United Artists model, UA itself faced increasingly severe management problems in the 1930s and early 1940s. These problems invariably centred on conflicts between UA's board of directors and its top management executive—that is, independent producers Joe Schenck, Sam Goldwyn, and David Selznick, who, in succession, managed UA's production and release programme during this period. Each was crucial to UA's feature output as well as its overall operations, and each left UA due to difficulties with its still-active founding partners, Chaplin and Pickford. Thus while UA's film-makers enjoyed more autonomy as unit producers than their counterparts at the major studios, the company itself was in almost constant turmoil at the management level—and particularly in 1940–1 during Goldwyn's bitter battle (and much-publicized lawsuit) with Chaplin and Pickford, which resulted in Goldwyn releasing through RKO.

One notable exception to this shift to a production-unit system in the 1930s was 20th Century–Fox. In 1933 independent producer Joe Schenck convinced Warners' production chief, Darryl Zanuck, to leave the studio and

Shooting a scene from the wartime musical *This is the Army* (1943) on the lot at the Warner Bros. studio

join him in creating Twentieth Century Pictures. Twentieth released through UA and provided roughly half its output in 1934–5, but Schenck and Zanuck broke with UA in 1935 when Chaplin and Pickford refused to make them full partners. Twentieth then merged with the (previously bankrupt) Fox Film Corporation, with Schenck and Zanuck forming a two-man studio management team and Zanuck reverting to the role he had played at Warners of central producer.

In fact Zanuck, having risen through the writers' ranks at Warners, was the only 'creative executive' running a studio in the late 1930s, and the only top studio executive with an active hand in actual production—a practice he would continue well into the 1950s. Zanuck personally supervised all of Fox's A-class pictures, from such revenue-generating 'hokum' (Zanuck's own term) as the Tyrone Power adventure-romances to its acclaimed 'John Ford pictures' with contract star Henry Fonda: *Drums along the Mohawk* (1938), *Young Mr. Lincoln* (1939), and *The Grapes of Wrath* (1940). At Warner Bros., meanwhile, Zanuck had been replaced by Hal Wallis, who along with Jack Warner orchestrated a steady shift to unit production in the late 1930s, although at Warners top directors like Michael Curtiz and William Dieterle (and later John Huston and Howard Hawks) rather than producers were the key unit personnel.

Columbia Pictures was also a notable exception in terms of studio management in the 1930s, although here the distinction involved the owners and top executives. Until the early 1930s Columbia's ownership and executive control operated much like Warners, in that the company was owned and operated by brothers—Jack and Harry Cohn (along with founding partner Joe Brandt)—and the siblings' executive roles reflected the relations of power within the industry. As with Warners, the older brother (in this case, Jack Cohn, along with Joe Brandt) ran the New York office as the senior executive, while vice-president and younger sibling Harry Cohn ran the studio. When Brandt retired in 1931, however, a power struggle ensued; Harry prevailing, thanks largely to the support of A. H. Giannini of the Bank of America. Thus Columbia, with Harry Cohn as president and Jack as vice-president handling marketing and sales out of New York, was the only major producer-distributor whose studio boss was also the chief executive of the company.

STUDIO FILM-MAKING IN THE 1930S

While the 'creative control' and administrative authority of studio film-making in the 1930s steadily dispersed throughout the producers' ranks, the industry remained as market-driven and commercially motivated as ever. Indeed, in that era of well-regulated block booking, blind bidding, and run-zone-clearance, each studio's film-making set-up was attuned to market conditions and to

Judy Garland
(1922–1969)

An important fixture of the MGM Freed unit musicals, Judy Garland was an unforgettable icon of both the triumphs and casualties of the Hollywood studio system. Signed by L. B. Mayer when she was barely a teenager, she made nearly thirty films during the fifteen-year run of her MGM contract. Only 28 years old when the studio with 'more stars than there are in the heavens' declined to renew her contract, Garland, by then debilitated by drug addiction, depression, and alcoholism, turned her attention to public concerts and a series of 'come-backs' which built upon the mythology and turmoil of her life and screen work, elevating her star image and popularity to a level that few have rivalled.

She made her first stage appearance at the age of 3 and at 5 was touring the vaudeville circuit with her sisters under the billing of 'Baby' Gumm. After a while, the family settled in Los Angeles, where her ambitious mother hoped to launch Judy's film career at a time when child stars such as Shirley Temple and Jackie Coogan were at the height of their commercial appeal. Garland's precocious voice brought her to the attention of lyricist Arthur Freed, who convinced Mayer to hire her.

Garland's image and talent were not easily reconciled; the studio had difficulty type-casting her blend of innocent 'ordinariness' with her mature, torchy singing voice. Paired with Mickey Rooney, she often featured as a film's principal commentator through song, yet found herself relegated to the role of wholesome 'girl-next-door' rather than love interest. Garland suffered in comparisons with Lana Turner and Hedy Lamarr, despite the persistent and near-oppressive efforts of MGM's 'Special Services' department to slim her down through diet and Dexedrine.

Eventually her engaging, manic sincerity and emotionally persuasive singing convinced Freed that she had both the charm and vulnerability to carry a film. In spite of this, her breakthrough role in *The Wizard of Oz* (1939) found her once again disguised as a pre-pubescent farmgirl, a feat which required the 17-year-old actress to hide her figure beneath constricting bindings and an innocuous gingham dress.

After that, however, Garland was rewarded with romantic leading roles. Freed's influence here was crucial, for he was beginning his bid to become a producer, and hoped that Garland's appeal would propel the projects he envisioned. Much has been written about the Freed unit at MGM, but what has rarely been recognized is the extent to which Freed's recognition of Garland's potential enabled him to win Mayer's support for his experimental venture. Behind the ambition and foresight of assembling a prodigious team of writers, composers, designers, and choreographers was Freed's practical desire to construct the ideal vehicle for Judy Garland's diverse talents.

That ideal was attained in collaboration with Vincente Minnelli, who eventually married Garland. In films as varied as *Meet Me in St. Louis* (1944), *The Clock* (1945), and *The Pirate* (1948), Freed, Minnelli, and Garland displayed moments of excessive fantasy, hysteria, even neurosis which were uncharacteristic of previous Hollywood musicals, yet provided a remarkable common ground for Minnelli's innovative style and the Garland persona. Her performance of 'Have Yourself a Merry Little Christmas' in *Meet Me in St. Louis*, or the wedding dinner in *The Clock*, reveal a dark, uneasy pathos first evident in Garland's portrayal of Dorothy in Oz. Meanwhile in films by other directors (such as Charles Walters's *Easter Parade* (1948), where she plays opposite Fred Astaire and Peter Lawford)

she showed herself still capable of projecting the uncomplicated *ingénue* charm for which the studio had originally hired her.

Garland's dependence on stimulants, brought on by the intense pressure of growing up at Metro, took its toll. She acquired a difficult reputation and was often physically unable to fulfil her film commitments. Shortly after MGM severed ties with Garland, her marriage to Minnelli disintegrated. (This, the second of her five marriages, left her with a daughter, future star Liza Minnelli; her third, to Sid Luft, produced two more daughters, one of whom, Lorna, went on to become a singer.) Although she made fewer than five films in the remaining twenty years of her life, she worked steadily on recordings, concert performances, and television appearances. Failed suicide attempts and continued struggles with drug addiction gave way to a new image, that of fragile survivor.

Garland's most memorable screen performances seemed now to be informed by the obvious difficulties of her life and studio career. The 'Born in a Trunk' sequence of her first 'come-back' film, George Cukor's *A Star is Born* (1954), perfectly illustrates how the mature Garland communicated both pain and endurance in the mythology of her stardom. The more her voice and appearance seemed to deteriorate, the greater the effect of her theatrical pathos. In Britain and the USA she became a powerful icon of gay sub-culture, where her androgynous charisma seemed to fulfil a fantasy of both alienation and acceptance. Her identification as a tragic, victimized, and yet cherished entertainer was a significant part of the subtext of Garland's stardom. Her death from a drug overdose at the age of 47 only added to her legend, and was seen as a catalyst for the Stonewall rebellion which launched the gay rights movement less than a month after.

DAVID GARDNER

SELECT FILMOGRAPHY

Broadway Melody of 1938 (1937); Love Finds Andy Hardy (1938); Babes in Arms (1939); The Wizard of Oz (1939); Strike up the Band (1940); Ziegfeld Girl (1941); For Me and my Gal (1942); Meet Me in St. Louis (1944); The Clock (1945); The Harvey Girls (1946); Easter Parade (1948); The Pirate (1948); Summer Stock (1950); A Star is Born (1954); Judgment at Nuremberg (1961); A Child is Waiting (1963)

BIBLIOGRAPHY

DiOrio, Al, Jr. (1973), *Little Girl Lost.*
Dyer, Richard (1986), *Heavenly Bodies: Film Stars and Society.*
Frank, Gerold (1975), *Judy.*
Minnelli, Vincente, with Acre, Hector (1975), *I Remember it Well.*

Opposite: Judy Garland as Esther, singing to the boy next door in Vincente Minnelli's MGM musical *Meet Me in St. Louis* (1944)

the industry's vertically integrated structure. The co-ordination of market strategies, management structure, and production operations was in fact the essential feature of the Hollywood studio system—it was the basis for what Tino Balio has termed the 'grand design' of 1930s Hollywood, and for what André Bazin has aptly termed the 'genius of the system' of classical Hollywood film-making.

The primary studio product was the feature film, of course, which accounted for over 90 per cent of the $150 million invested in Hollywood film production in 1939. Feature production at the eight major studios included both A-class pictures and B movies, with the proportion of As to Bs dependent on the company's resources, theatre holdings (or lack thereof), and general market strategy. The majors also turned out occasional 'prestige pictures'— that is, bigger and more expensive features, usually released on a 'roadshow' basis in select first-run theatres with increased admission prices and reserved seating. As the economic recovery took hold and as market conditions improved in the late 1930s, prestige output increased— best exemplified by major independent productions like Disney's *Snow White and the Seven Dwarfs* (1938) and Selznick's *Gone with the Wind* (1939), along with ambitious studio productions such as MGM's *The Wizard of Oz* (1939) and Paramount's Cecil B. DeMille epics like *Union Pacific* (1939) and *North West Mounted Police* (1940).

Actually, these occasional high-cost, high-risk pictures were fundamentally at odds with the market structure and trade practices of the studio era. The most crucial commodity in classical Hollywood, without question, was the A-class feature, and particularly the routine 'star vehicle'. Each studio's 'star stable' was its most visible and valuable resource, an inventory of genre variations which drove its entire operation. Indeed, there was a direct correlation between a studio's assets and profits, its stable of contract stars, and the number of star-genre formulas in its repertoire—ranging from the talent-laden MGM, which boasted 'all the stars in the heavens', to companies like RKO, Columbia, and Universal, which had only one or two top stars under contract and turned out only a half-dozen or so A-class pictures per year. Each company constructed its entire production and marketing strategy around its established star-genre formulations, which dominated the first-run market and generated the majority of studio revenues. A-class star vehicles also provided veritable insurance policies not only with the public but also with the unaffiliated theatres that were subject to block booking, in that a company's top features 'carried' its entire annual programme of pictures.

Each studio's A-class star-genre formulations also keyed its distinctive 'personality' or 'house style' during the classical era. The Warners style in the 1930s, for instance, coalesced around its steady output of crime dramas and gangster films with James Cagney and Edward G.

Robinson, crusading bio-pics with Paul Muni, backstage musicals with Dick Powell and Ruby Keeler, epic swash-bucklers with Errol Flynn and Olivia de Havilland, and, in a curious counter to its male ethos, a succession of 'women's pictures' starring Bette Davis. These pictures were the key markers in Warners' house style, the organizing principles for its entire operation from the New York office to the studio-factory. They were a means of stabilizing marketing and sales, of bringing efficiency and economy into the production of some fifty features per annum, and of distinguishing Warners' collective output from that of its competitors.

The contract talent and resources necessary to sustain these formulas extended well beyond a studio's star stable, of course. In fact, with the development of the unit-production trend during the 1930s, the studios tended to form collaborative 'units' around these star-genre formulas. And while a studio's stars were crucial to the formulation of its house style, the chief architects of that style were its production executives and top producers. As Leo Rosten noted in his landmark 1941 study,

Each studio has a personality; each studio's product shows special emphases and values. And, in the final analysis, the sum total of a studio's personality, the aggregate pattern of its choices and its tastes, may be traced to its producers. For it is the producers who establish the preferences, the prejudices, and the predispositions of the organization and, therefore, of the movie which it turns out.

In some cases, production units were informal and fluid, changing somewhat from one star-genre formulation to the next, while in other cases the units were remarkably consistent, particularly in terms of directors, writers, cinematographers, composers, and other key creative roles. Not surprisingly, studio-based production units (and the pictures they turned out) tended to be most consistent in the realm of low-budget film-making, especially on the series pictures which comprised roughly 10 per cent of Hollywood's total feature output in the 1930s and early 1940s. These were produced with ruthless, factory-like efficiency, invariably under the supervision of a particular producer.

Some A-class star-genre formulas attained series or quasi-series status in the 1930s, as well, and also were turned out by relatively consistent units—Paramount's Marlene Dietrich films via the Josef von Sternberg unit, for instance, or Universal's Deanna Durbin musicals via its Joe Pasternak unit. But while unit production brought economy and efficiency even to high-end studio output, it was not necessarily a rigid or mechanical process—an important concern regarding A-class pictures, given the demand for product differentiation. Indeed, under the right circumstances and given adequate resources, unit production proved to be remarkably flexible, and quite responsive to changes in both audience tastes and studio personnel.

For an illuminating example of studio-based unit production and star-genre formulation at the A-class feature level, consider the late-1930s emergence at MGM of the so-called 'Freed unit' and of a new musical cycle featuring two emerging contract stars, Mickey Rooney and Judy Garland. Rooney's star was already in rapid ascent at the time, due largely to yet another unit-based star-genre formula, MGM's Hardy Family pictures. In 1937 Rooney was cast as the son of a middle-class, middle-American couple (Lionel Barrymore and Spring Byington) in a modest comedy-drama, *A Family Affair*. Audiences responded and exhibitors clamoured for more, so Mayer replaced Barrymore and Byington with two lesser stars, Lewis Stone and Fay Holden, and assigned J. J. Cohn's low-budget unit to develop a series. Cohn assembled a specialized unit around associate producer Lou Ostrow, director George B. Seitz, writer Kay Van Riper, cinematographer Lew White, *et al.*, which turned out a new Hardy instalment every few months from 1938 to 1941. The Hardy pictures qualified as As in terms of budget, running time, and release schedule, and they were by far the most profitable pictures on MGM's schedule.

With each Hardy instalment, Rooney's character took greater command of the series. By 1939 every picture carried the name 'Andy Hardy' in the title, and Rooney was the nation's top star. While an ideal vehicle for Rooney, the series also provided a context for trying out new talent, particularly contract *ingénues* who could serve as a friend or 'love interest' for Andy. Besides Ann Rutherford, who became a regular in 1938, the series enjoyed guest appearances from such emerging Metro stars as Lana Turner, Ruth Hussey, Donna Reed, Kathryn Grayson, and most significantly (and most frequently) Judy Garland. While these *ingénues* had an obvious dramatic value in terms of Andy's male adolescent rites of passage, Garland also introduced a musical dimension to the series and thus brought out quite another facet of Rooney's character and talent.

The first real Hardy musical was *Love Finds Andy Hardy* in 1938. A surprisingly strong box-office hit, even for a Hardy film, it suggested that MGM might have a new musical team on its roster. Garland's success in the Hardy musical also confirmed Mayer's decision to give her the lead in *The Wizard of Oz* (in a role initially conceived for Shirley Temple, whom MGM planned to borrow from Fox). *Oz* was MGM's biggest risk and most expensive picture of the decade, costing $2.77 million to produce and tying up five sound stages and hundreds of personnel for twenty-two weeks of shooting. But remarkably enough, considering the film's subsequent success as a perennial television event in the USA, *Oz* was not a big commercial hit on its initial release. The picture did gross over $3 million, but due to its high production and marketing costs it actually lost about $1 million.

The disappointing revenues on *Oz* were offset by its prestige value and by the emergence of Judy Garland as a bona fide star, and also by the ascent of Arthur Freed to the producer ranks at MGM. Freed had worked uncredited on *Oz* as an assistant to producer Mervyn LeRoy on the assurance that he could produce a musical of his own once *Oz* was completed. Freed convinced Mayer to purchase the rights to a 1937 Rogers and Hart stage hit, *Babes in Arms*, and to bring Busby Berkeley over from Warner Bros. to direct and choreograph the film. He also convinced Mayer to let him team Rooney and Garland as co-stars. Freed hoped to combine the energy and appeal of the Hardy pictures with the 'backstage musical' formula that Berkeley had refined at Warners in pictures like *42nd Street* and *Gold Diggers of 1933* (both 1933). The Rodgers and Hart musical was one of those 'Hey kids, let's put on a show!' types, which Freed and Berkeley redesigned as a showcase for Rooney and Garland. Kay Van Riper rewrote the script to add some of the Hardy series flavour, while musical director Roger Edens revamped the song-and-dance numbers.

Shot in only ten weeks for just under $750,000, a remarkably low figure for a major musical, *Babes in Arms* grossed well over $3 million. One of MGM's biggest hits in 1939, it surpassed not only the high-stakes *Wizard of Oz* but a number of other more reliable star vehicles as well. Indeed, Mayer could gamble on pictures like *Oz* or *Babes in Arms* knowing that MGM's release schedule included such bankable products as *Ninotchka* with Greta Garbo, *The Marx Brothers at the Circus*, *Another Thin Man* with William Powell and Myrna Loy, *The Women* with Joan Crawford, Norma Shearer, and Rosalind Russell, *Northwest Passage* with Spencer Tracy, and three more Hardy Family pictures.

While it may have lacked the critical cachet of *Oz* or other top features, *Babes in Arms* also underscored what the studio system did best: it was an economical, efficiently produced star vehicle, an A-class genre amalgam with just enough novelty to satisfy audiences and ensure its success in the lucrative first-run market, and a prime candidate for reformulation. Immediately after *Babes in Arms*, Freed, Berkeley, Roger Edens, *et al.* set to work on a cycle of Rooney–Garland show musicals—*Strike up the Band* (1940), *Babes on Broadway* (1942), *Girl Crazy* (1943), etc.—marking the birth of MGM's Freed unit, which produced many of Hollywood's greatest musicals during the 1940s and 1950s.

INTO THE 1940S: THE APPROACH OF WAR

MGM's 1939 output contributed heavily to what many critics and film historians consider Hollywood's greatest year ever, a view underscored by the Oscar contenders for best picture of 1939: *Mr. Smith Goes to Washington*, *The Wizard of Oz*, *Stagecoach*, *Dark Victory*, *Love Affair*, *Goodbye,*

Mr. Chips, *Of Mice and Men*, *Ninotchka*, *Wuthering Heights*, and *Gone with the Wind*. The view of 1939 as Hollywood's peak year was reinforced in quite another way by the industry's rapid transformation and decline in the 1940s, a decade-long process that began in 1940–1 during the odd, intense interval between the Depression and America's entry into the Second World War.

While a range of factors and events were involved in that process, two were of principal importance in 1940–1: the US government's anti-trust campaign against the studios, and the outbreak of war overseas. The antitrust campaign actually had been brewing for several years, beginning in earnest in July 1938 when the US Justice Department filed suit against the Big Eight studios on behalf of the nation's independent theatre owners for monopolizing the movie industry. The government's objectives in the so-called 'Paramount case' (named after the first defendant cited) were extensive trade reforms and the 'divorcement' of the integrated majors' theatre chains. The studios managed to keep the US attorneys at bay until early 1940, when the case was ordered to trial. At that point the Big Five (MGM, Warners, Paramount, Fox, and RKO) signed a consent decree—essentially a plea of no contest and a compromise with the government. The studios agreed to limit block booking to groups of no more than five pictures, to end blind bidding by holding trade screenings of all features, and to modify their run-zone-clearance policies. The 1940 Consent Decree scarcely satisfied either the independent exhibitors or the Justice Department; both vowed to keep the Paramount case alive through appeals, and to continue the anti-trust campaign.

Meanwhile, the outbreak and escalation of war overseas threatened to devastate Hollywood's vital overseas trade. The studios' exports to the Axis nations—principally Germany, Italy, and Japan—had declined to almost nil in 1937–8, but still Hollywood derived roughly one-third of its total revenues from overseas markets. The primary overseas client was Europe, which supplied about 75 per cent of the studios' foreign income in 1939, and the United Kingdom in particular, alone providing 45 per cent. Those markets were severely disrupted by the outbreak of war in September 1939, and they went into free fall as the fighting on the Continent intensified. The Nazi blitzkrieg across Europe eliminated one key foreign market after another in 1940, culminating in the fall of France in June. By late 1940 Britain stood virtually alone against Germany in the west—and it stood alone as Hollywood's only significant remaining overseas market as well.

The war in Europe induced the US government to initiate a massive military and defence buildup, which had tremendous impact on the movie industry. While the buildup promised an eventual boost to Hollywood's domestic market, the short-term effects were primarily negative. The government financed its defence pro-

Ingrid Bergman
(1925–1982)

Following on the heels of Garbo and Dietrich, Ingrid Bergman achieved a phenomenal success and popularity as a Hollywood star born outside the USA. At the height of her studio career in the 1940s, Bergman's box-office strength and prestige placed her among the ranks of actresses such as Joan Crawford, Bette Davis, and Katharine Hepburn. Her film roles combined a rare blend of worldliness with a transcendent purity that seemed to emanate from her considerable beauty. Bergman's complex screen persona carried over into her personal life, where she tested the limits of public sympathy by abandoning both Hollywood and her family to pursue an artistic and romantic association with the Italian neo-realist director Roberto Rossellini. She garnered three Academy Awards in the course of her forty-year career, working actively in six countries and four languages.

By the time producer David O. Selznick 'discovered' Bergman she had already established herself as a promising film actress in her native Sweden. Her work was praised by American critics who predicted that Bergman would soon be lured to Hollywood. In films such as *Intermezzo* (1936) she displayed a radiant sensitivity even when caught in a doomed love triangle. Her ability to render a melancholic, morally ambiguous role as a poignant, almost heroic study of human endurance was a crucial aspect of her appeal; her presence alone transformed mediocre tear-jerkers into something which seemed far more profound to audiences and critics alike.

Although Bergman's ambitions no doubt lay in the direction of California, she worked steadily throughout her career to build upon her international appeal, eventually making films for Ingmar Bergman and Jean Renoir. She made only one film for Ufa in Germany before the Second World War broke out, but hoped to return after the conflict was resolved. Some, including her husband Petter Lindström, criticized her judgement in working under the Nazi regime in 1938, but Bergman deftly managed to distance herself from the politics of the day. She expressed concern about the anti-German sentiments of her first major American success, *Casablanca* (1942), perhaps out of sympathy for German relatives (her mother was from Hamburg), but more likely to avoid souring her deal with Ufa.

She agreed to a seven-year contract with Selznick, whose small stable of prestige talent and properties boasted Alfred Hitchcock, Joseph Cotten, and *Gone with the Wind*. Although his meticulous management and detailed memoranda were legendary, Selznick's independent outfit could hardly match the output of the major studios. Bergman, like Hitchcock, grew impatient of waiting for him to find the 'perfect' vehicle for her, and resented the huge profits Selznick reaped by farming her out to other studios in the interim. She made only two films for Selznick, but was loaned out nine times.

Equally confident playing a barmaid or nun, she could alternate within one portrayal between enigmatic aloofness, easy warmth, and pained compassion. Hitchcock, fascinated by her cool assurance and inscrutable longings, cast her in three of his films.

Her most memorable roles in Hollywood exploited this ambivalence: in *Casablanca*, conflicting reports in the narrative paint Bergman's Ilsa as an *aventurière* who has deeply wounded Rick (Humphrey Bogart). Even so, Bergman's striking beauty and fundamental nobility read plainly in sustained close shots; her face explains what the story cannot—that Rick has judged her hastily, and she is in fact virtuous. Her moral indecision comes across as understated strength, a passive grace which allows Rick to act honourably.

When her obligation to Selznick had been fulfilled, Bergman hoped once more to expand her career on an international stage. She felt stifled by the limits of what she had already achieved in Hollywood, and she was in love. Her collaboration with Rossellini provoked a major scandal with the American public and press, and the films proved unpopular at first. In retrospect, they offer a rare view of a Hollywood star in an entirely unfamiliar setting. While films such as *Stromboli* (1949) and *Viaggio in Italia* ('Journey to Italy', 1954) attest to Bergman's courage and ability as an actress, they reveal an insecurity she had always disguised in the past. Rossellini documents in these films her struggles to acclimatize to an alien culture, her ambivalence towards deserting her family and mainstream career, even the complexities of their difficult relationship together. In the end, Rossellini forced Bergman to reconcile her Hollywood persona with her driving personal ambition and apolitical self-interest. Bergman knew her accomplishments with Rossellini were enduring works of visual and psychological poetry, even if less gratifying to her than her Hollywood triumphs.

Yet it was to Hollywood production that she returned in 1956 with *Anastasia*. She was rewarded with her second Oscar, a sign that she had been forgiven.

DAVID GARDNER

SELECT FILMOGRAPHY

Intermezzo (1936); Intermezzo (1939, US remake); Casablanca (1942); For whom the Bell Tolls (1943); Gaslight (1944); The Bells of St. Mary's (1945); Spellbound (1945); Notorious (1946); Joan of Arc (1948); Under Capricorn (1949); Stromboli (1949); Viaggio in Italia (Journey to Italy) (1954); Elena et les hommes (Paris Does Strange Things) (1956); Anastasia (1956); Indiscreet (1958); Autumn Sonata (1978)

BIBLIOGRAPHY

Bergman, Ingrid (1980), *My Story*.
Leamer, Lawrence (1986), *As Time Goes By*.
Quirk, Lawrence J. (1970), *The Films of Ingrid Bergman*.
Steele, Joseph H. (1959), *Ingrid Bergman: An Intimate Portrait*.

Opposite: Ingrid Bergman in *Stromboli* (1949), the first of five films she made with Italian director Roberto Rossellini

gramme mainly via tax increases, which hit the industry particularly hard, while pressure from the White House to support the buildup also put Hollywood in a delicate position politically. President Roosevelt lobbied for industry support in 1940, even though the USA was still officially neutral and public sentiment was split into isolationist and interventionist camps. Not surprisingly, Hollywood played it safe, producing a few war-related features in 1940 but confining its treatment of the war mainly to newsreels and documentary shorts.

By 1941 both Hollywood and the nation had shifted into a more pronounced 'pre-war' mode, as Axis aggression solidified US support of Britain and rendered American intervention against Germany and Japan all but inevitable. On the domestic front, the defence buildup went into high gear, signalling the definitive end of the Depression and the onset of a five-year 'war boom' for the American movie industry. Hollywood stepped up its war-related production in 1941, including features with clear interventionist and 'preparedness' themes. The public was clearly buying; five of the top ten box-office hits in 1941 were war related, topped by *Sergeant York* (Warner Bros., 1941) and Charlie Chaplin's late-1940 UA release *The Great Dictator*. Hollywood's war-related efforts provoked America's dwindling isolationist contingent, including several US Senators who demanded an inquiry into the movies' pro-war, anti-German bias. The Senate 'propaganda hearings' of September 1941 became a major media event, with public and press support swinging solidly behind the movie industry.

While the anti-trust campaign and the war involved external forces well beyond the industry's direct control, the Hollywood studio powers faced a number of serious internal threats as well in 1940–1. Many of these were related to the unprecedented demand for top product, which resulted from both the 1940 Consent Decree (with its blocks-of-five and advance-screening provisions) and the defence buildup (with its overheated first-run markets).

To meet the increased demand for top features, the studios either turned to independent producers, whose ranks grew rapidly in the early 1940s, or granted their own contract talent greater freedom and authority over their productions. This not only accelerated the unit-production trend already under way, but gave it a strong independent impetus as well. Indeed, by 1940–1 UA's strategy of distributing major independent productions had been adopted by four other studios: RKO, Warners, Universal, and Columbia.

Actually, each of these studios developed a significant variation on the UA model, depending on whether production facilities and financing were provided as well as distribution. The number of these 'outside' productions also varied considerably. Warners, for instance, was quite

William Cameron Menzies

(1896–1957)

William Cameron Menzies is among the most undervalued talents in American film history. His career spanned Hollywood's classical era and effectively defined the role and status of the art director (and later, the 'production designer') within the studio production system. Menzies' success also gave him the opportunity to direct and even to produce, but his most significant work was in the visual design of motion pictures.

Born in New Haven, Connecticut, in 1896, Menzies learnt his craft during the 1910s at the Pathé studio in Fort Lee, New Jersey. A crucial early influence was Anton Grot, who took Menzies as his assistant and taught him the art of storyboarding as well as set design. Working at Pathé and then in Hollywood in the 1920s, Grot and Menzies steadily refined the pre-production practice of creating charcoal illustrations not only of the sets required for a picture but of virtually every camera set-up as well. This greatly enhanced production efficiency, since only those portions of the sets actually photographed had to be built; moreover, the camera angles, lenses, lighting, and cutting continuity could be planned in advance of actual shooting.

Menzies quickly established himself in Hollywood during the 1920s, working as art director on twenty-one pictures during the decade, with such top film-makers as Ernst Lubitsch, D. W. Griffith, Lewis Milestone, and Raoul Walsh. His reputation was secured with the success of *The Thief of Bagdad* (1924), on which Grot served as his assistant, and in 1928 he was awarded the first Academy Award for 'Interior Decoration' for his work on both *Tempest* (1927) and *The Dove* (1928). While few outside the industry were aware of his contributions, Menzies was widely recognized in Hollywood as an innovative visual stylist, particularly adept at creating lavish, imaginative sets in the baroque style.

By 1930 the position of art director was well established within the Hollywood system, with the major studios developing entire departments around top art directors, many of whom had enormous impact on the studio's 'house style' and on the 'look' of particular productions. For instance, Anton Grot, art director at Warners, designed sixteen pictures for Michael Curtiz and ten for William Dieterle, and he was a crucial contributor to the 'Warners style' that coalesced in the 1930s.

Menzies, meanwhile, maintained his autonomy as a free-lance artist, and diversified into other film-making areas. Beginning in 1931 he combined the roles of director and art director. From 1931 to 1937 he directed and designed seven pictures, the most important for Alexander Korda in England, notably *Things to Come* (1936), a futuristic spectacle and genuinely 'visionary' production which stands as a remarkable testament to Menzies' diverse talents.

In 1937 Menzies returned to Hollywood at the behest of David O. Selznick, who was preparing his own ambitious spectacle, *Gone with the Wind* (1939). Selznick's goal during pre-production was to create 'a pre-cut picture' with up to '80 percent on paper before we grind the cameras'. Menzies devoted roughly two years to the visualization of the Technicolor epic, earning the unprecedented screen credit: 'Production Designed by William Cameron Menzies.' The Motion Picture Academy also recognized Menzies' unique contribution on *Wind*. Menzies received a Special Academy Award 'for outstanding achievement in the use of color for the enhancement of dramatic mood in the production'.

Menzies concentrated on art direction during the 1940s and did some of his best work, especially in tandem with director Sam Wood on *Our Town* (1940), *The Devil and Miss Jones* (1941), *Kings Row* (1942), and *For whom the Bell Tolls* (1943). All were critical and commercial hits, and all were heavily indebted to Menzies, who by then routinely produced over 1,000 shot-by-shot storyboards for each film. James Wong Howe, the director of photography for *Kings Row*, stated in *American Cinematographer* that Menzies, via his storyboards, specified the camera position, appropriate lenses, and lighting schema for each set-up, as well as the set design. 'Menzies created the whole look of the film', said Howe. 'I simply followed his orders. Sam Wood just directed the actors; he knew nothing about visuals.'

Menzies returned to directing with *Address Unknown* in 1944, and he also worked on two Selznick projects, designing and directing the Dali-inspired dream sequences in *Spellbound* (1945), and directing (uncredited) portions of *Duel in the Sun* (1947). He slowed down considerably after the war, when his only notable achievements were the production design on *Arch of Triumph* (1948), and the direction and design of two 3-D science-fiction pictures in 1953: *Invaders from Mars* and *The Maze*. He served as associate producer on *Around the World in Eighty Days* in 1956, and died the following year.

By the time of Menzies' death in 1957, the terms 'art director' and 'production designer' had become common in Hollywood, thanks largely to his efforts and talents. Menzies' career demonstrates the crucial role of the art director in preparing a visual 'blueprint' for production to complement the shooting script, and so underscores the complexities of accounting for film authorship and film style.

THOMAS SCHATZ

SELECT FILMOGRAPHY

As art director
Rosita (1923); The Thief of Bagdad (1924); Tempest (1927); The Dove (1928); Abraham Lincoln (1930); Gone with the Wind (1939); Foreign Correspondent (1940); The Devil and Miss Jones (1941); For whom the Bell Tolls (1943); Spellbound (1945); Arch of Triumph (1948)
As director
Things to Come (1936); Address Unknown (1944); Invaders from Mars (1953)

BIBLIOGRAPHY

Balio, Tino (1993), *Grand Design: Hollywood as a Modern Business Enterprise, 1930-1939.*
Barsacq, Léon (1976), *Caligari's Cabinet and Other Grand Illusions.*
Hambley, John, and Downing, Patrick (1978), *The Art of Hollywood: Fifty Years of Art Direction.*
Higham, Charles (1970), *Hollywood Cameramen: Sources of Light.*

Opposite: A scene from the futuristic fantasy *Things to Come*, the film version of H. G. Wells's 'The Shape of Things to Come', designed and directed by William Cameron Menzies and produced by Alexander Korda

tentative in its foray into independent production, entering only two such deals in 1940: Frank Capra's *Meet John Doe* and Jesse Lasky's *Sergeant York* (directed by freelancer Howard Hawks). The most aggressive of the four companies was RKO, which had over a dozen independent unit productions under way in 1940 and was relying on outside units for virtually all of its A-class product.

Meanwhile, all of the studios also saw a marked increase in the number of 'hyphenates' under contract in 1940–1—notably writers and directors who attained producer status. The most aggressive studio in this regard was Paramount, which elevated director Mitchell Leisen to producer-director and writer Preston Sturges to writer-director, while the writing team of Billy Wilder and Charles Brackett was recast as a writer-producer (Brackett) and writer-director (Wilder) unit. And in perhaps the most significant—and most forward-looking—move along these lines, Paramount not only granted Cecil B. DeMille the status of an 'in-house independent' producer, but gave him a profit-participation deal on his pictures as well.

The growing power of independent film-makers and top contract talent in the early 1940s was reinforced by the concurrent rise of the talent guilds—that is, the Screen Actors Guild (formally recognized by the studios in 1938), the Screen Directors Guild (recognized in 1939), and the Screen Writers Guild (recognized in 1941). The top talent guilds represented yet another serious challenge to studio control, particularly in terms of film-makers' authority over their work. Moreover, top contract talent was 'going freelance' in unprecedented numbers in 1940–1 due to the demand for A-class product and the shift to independent production, as well as the considerable tax advantages involved in avoiding salaried income and creating independent production companies. This further undermined the long-standing contract system, a crucial factor in studio hegemony and in efficient studio production.

Thus Hollywood was on the verge of a sea-change in late 1941, with the studios' control of both production and exhibition facing serious challenges. The crisis mentality was underscored by sociologist Leo Rosten in *Hollywood: The Movie Colony*, an influential, in-depth industry analysis published in November 1941. Lamenting what he termed the 'end of Hollywood's lush and profligate period', Rosten surveyed the range of concerns and crises facing the studios at the time:

Other businesses have experienced onslaughts against their profits and hegemony; but the drive against Hollywood is just beginning. No moving picture leader can be sanguine before the steady challenge of unionism, collective bargaining, the consent decree (which brought the Department of Justice suit to a temporary armistice), the revolt of the independent theater owners, the trend toward increased taxation, the strangulation of the foreign market, and a score of frontal attacks on the citadels of the screen.

WAR BOOM

Rosten's assessment is notable for two principal reasons: first, its accurate inventory of the deepening industry crises in 1940–1, and second, how completely those crisis conditions would change within only weeks of the book's publication, following the US entry into the Second World War. With America suddenly engaged in a global war, Hollywood's social, economic, and industrial fortunes changed virtually overnight. Among the more acute ironies of the period—and there were many—was Hollywood's sudden rapport with a government that now saw the 'national cinema' as an ideal source of diversion, information, and propaganda for citizens and soldiers alike. In the months after the USA entered the war, Hollywood's film-making operations, from its studio-factories to its popular genres and cinematic forms, were effectively retooled for war production. Within a year of Pearl Harbor nearly one-third of Hollywood's feature films were war related, as were the vast majority of its newsreels and documentaries.

Thus the war was a period of massive paradox for the movie industry, and especially for the Hollywood studios. Granted a reprieve of sorts by the Justice Department 'for the duration', the studios reasserted their control of the movie market-place during the war and enjoyed record revenues, while playing a vital role in the US war effort. The nation's wholesale conversion to war production sustained Hollywood's 'war boom' for five years, with millions of defence plant workers concentrated in major urban-industrial centres pushing weekly theatre attendance to its record pre-Depression levels. Hollywood's overseas trade was limited primarily to the UK and Latin America, but with Britain undergoing an industrial and movie-going boom of its own during the war—and relying more than ever on Hollywood product, given the severe cut-backs of film production in Britain—Hollywood's foreign revenues also reached record levels. Indeed, the degree of integration between the US and British markets and film-making efforts during the Second World War was not only unprecedented but altogether unique in motion picture annals, and was crucial to the war effort in each nation.

Hollywood's studio production system saw some modification during the war, as the unit-production trend continued and as A-class output was increased to accommodate the overheated first-run market. The Big Five radically reduced their overall output (from an average of fifty films per year for each studio to about thirty), concentrating on 'bigger' pictures which played longer runs and enjoyed steadily increasing revenues. The studios readily adapted to changing social conditions, developing two government-mandated genres, the combat film and home-front melodrama, and a new crop of wartime stars—notably Bob Hope, Betty Grable, Greer Garson, Abbott and Costello, and Humphrey Bogart. Traditional genres (particularly the musical) were converted to the war effort, while Hollywood's long-standing bias for 'love stories' was adjusted to favour couples who separated at film's end to perform their respective patriotic duties. There were significant stylistic adjustments during the war as well. Hollywood's war-related features, particularly the combat film, employed quasi-documentary techniques which were altogether distinctive for American cinema. And in something of a stylistic and thematic counter to the realism and enforced optimism of the war films, Hollywood also cultivated a darker and more 'anti-social' vision in urban crime films and 'female Gothic' melodramas steeped in a style which post-war critics would term film noir.

The war boom continued through 1945 and into 1946, fuelled by returning servicemen, the lifting of wartime restrictions, and a wide-open global market-place starved of Hollywood product. But as box-office revenues and studio profits reached staggering levels in 1946, the 'drive against Hollywood' that Rosten had described in 1941 resumed with a vengeance. In fact, the mood in Hollywood grew decidedly downbeat in 1946 due to deepening labour strife, the renewed anti-trust campaign, and the threats of 'protectionist' policies in major foreign markets. Moreover, the studios faced a host of distinctly post-war woes at home, from suburban migration and the rise of commercial television, to the Cold War and anti-Communist crusades. With each passing month in the post-war era it became more evident that the Hollywood studio system and the classical cinema that it had engendered were rapidly coming to an end.

Bibliography
Balio, Tino (1976), *United Artists*.
—— (ed.) (1985), *The American Film Industry*.
—— (1993), *Grand Design: Hollywood as a Modern Business Enterprise, 1930–1939*.
Bordwell, David, Staiger, Janet, and Thompson, Kristin (1985), *The Classical Hollywood Cinema*.
Finler, Joel (1988), *The Hollywood Story*.
Gomery, Douglas (1986), *The Hollywood Studio System*.
Huettig, Mae D. (1944), *Economic Control of the Motion Picture Industry*.
Jacobs, Lea (1991), *The Wages of Sin*.
Jowett, Garth (1976), *Film: The Democratic Art*.
Kindem, Gorham (ed.) (1982), *The American Movie Industry*.
Rosten, Leo (1941), *Hollywood: The Movie Colony*.
Schatz, Thomas (1988), *The Genius of the System*.
Sklar, Robert (1976), *Movie-Made America*.
Staiger, Janet (1983), 'Individualism versus Collectivism'.

Censorship and Self-Regulation

RICHARD MALTBY

When applied to cinema, the term 'censorship' often conflates two distinct practices: governmentally administered systems of control over the expression of political ideas in film; and systems of self-regulation operated by entertainment cinema industries to ensure that the content of films conforms to the moral, social, and ideological mores of their national culture. Except in periods of national emergency, such as wartime, authoritarian forms of censorship, exercised through the monopoly power of the State, have not been prominent features of twentieth-century liberal democracies, and the explicit, routine supervision of film content by state institutions—censorship as a form of official criticism—has been largely the preserve of totalitarian regimes. Self-regulation, on the other hand, can be understood as a form of market censorship, in which those forces in control of the production process determine what may and may not be produced. The most effective form of market censorship prevents movies from being made rather than suppressing them after production, but in either guise, censorship is a practice of power, a form of surveillance over the ideas, images, and representations circulating in a particular culture. Because cinema has been an international industry almost from its inception, the two forms of censorship have constantly interacted to reinforce each other. But Hollywood's international dominance has also meant that its form of self-regulation has been the most important censorship practice in cinema history.

THE ORIGINS OF FILM CENSORSHIP

Although film has always been more closely regulated than other forms of communication, cinema censorship cannot be directly equated with censorship of the press or other publications, because, for most of their history, films have not been granted a legally protected status as speech. In a 1915 decision that established the legal status of cinema in the United States, the US Supreme Court declared the exhibition of motion pictures to be 'a business pure and simple, originated and conducted for profit', and not to be regarded 'as part of the press of the country or as organs of public opinion'. They were thus not protected by the First Amendment's guarantee of free speech, but liable to prior censorship by state and municipal authorities. This legal definition of cinema as outside the spheres of politics and art is itself an implicit form of censorship. As a result debates over the regulation of cinema have been primarily concerned with questions of whether the entertainment it provided had harmful

effects on its individual viewers. In practice, the great majority of film censorship, at least in the English-speaking world, has been concerned more with the cinema's representations, particularly of sex and violence, than with its expression of ideas or political sentiments.

Both the basis on which the censorship of cinema was justified and the mechanisms by which it would be practised were already well established by the time of the Supreme Court's judgement. Although the details of censorship procedures varied from nation to nation, there was a striking similarity in the evolution of those mechanisms in the countries of Europe, the Americas, and Australasia. In the nineteenth century most of these countries divided public entertainment performances into two categories for regulative purposes. What was often called 'legitimate theatre' was distinguished from what was known in France as *spectacles de curiosité*, a category of commercialized amusement that included marionettes, *cafés-concerts*, magic shows, panoramas, animal exhibitions, and 'all travelling shows which lack either a permanent site or a solid structure'. In France, for example, theatrical censorship ceased in 1906, but because cinema was classed as a spectacle, its performances were still subject to the control of local authorities.

By 1906, as cinema exhibition began to move into dedicated buildings, municipal governments determined that it was necessary to license the 'nickelodeons' or 'penny gaffs' on grounds of public safety, since they were seen as firetraps and health hazards. The regulation of content was something of an afterthought to these environmental concerns. The principal anxieties were created by the fact that nickelodeons were hot, dark places, where children in particular might be 'influenced for evil by the conditions surrounding some of these shows'.

The proliferation of local controls over cinema exhibition led to the establishment of national institutions of industrial self-regulation in the United States, Britain, and other European countries. By 1908, municipal public safety regulations were being widely used as the pretext for local film censorship, a practice which was strongly opposed by the emerging national distribution industries, because such regulations interfered with the circulation of their product. The symbiotic relationship between the regulation of film content and the development of monopoly structures within the industry is best illustrated by the creation of the American National Board of Censorship (NBC) in 1909.

Just before Christmas 1908, New York's Mayor George B. McClellan closed all New York's movie theatres because of alleged fire hazard. In response, New York exhibitors formed an association to protect themselves from both the closures and the Motion Picture Patents Company (MPPC), whose formation had been announced only days before McClellan's action. In alliance with anti-monopoly reformers (and in the hope of displacing the reform movement's concern with the 'movie problem' from the theatres themselves to the movies shown in them), they called for censorship to 'protect them from the film manufacturers who foisted improper pictures' on them, and for the establishment of a Board of Censorship. The MPPC, however, saw in the Board an instrument for the imposition of a nationally standardized product over which it could have control, and the trade press and reform journals alike advocated that the Board become a national organization, to obviate the need for local censorship.

The institutional function of the National Board was to develop standardized formulas of acceptable content: not only prohibiting the representation of particular actions but encouraging the construction of narratives relying on a regulated set of conventions. For example, the Board's Standards on Crime declared:

The results of the crime should be in the long run disastrous to the criminal, so that the impression carried is that crime will inevitably find one out, soon or late, and bring on a catastrophe which causes the temporary gain from the crime to sink into insignificance. The results should spring logically and convincingly from the crime, and the results should take a reasonable proportion of the film.

Such narrative strategies demonstrated the 'respectability' of moving pictures as an instrument for both ordering and explaining a dominant ideology, and there was an implicit political censorship in insisting on the triumph of virtue. *Moving Picture World* objected to a 1912 movie that ended with 'the villain unrepentant and unpunished and the poor in their same, sad situation', because 'subjects of this character are calculated to arouse class prejudices unless treated in the most delicate manner and it is open to question if good can result from accentuating the social differences of the people'.

Although the NBC lost its authority after the outcry over *The Birth of a Nation*, by 1915 the industry had developed its essential strategy for avoiding external censorship: a system of containment, overseen by an internal regulation more subtly compulsory and pervasive than any legal prior censorship might be.

The American pattern was repeated elsewhere. In Britain the 1909 Cinematograph Act required local authorities to issue licences to cinemas as evidence that they met safety standards, but this power was rapidly used as the basis for local censorship. In 1912 representatives of the industry asked the government to approve the establishment of the British Board of Film Censors (BBFC), which, like the NBC, had no statutory power of enforcement. These industry bodies did not replace local censorship, but their purpose was to make it unnecessary by anticipating its prescriptions, and in this they were generally successful. A different pattern evolved in France, where in 1916 the Ministry of the Interior established a Commission to examine and regulate films shown throughout the country, by issuing a visa to films that had been approved. French constitutional law, however, determined that the visa did not pre-empt local authorities from taking further censorship action.

Most of the countries of Europe, South America, and the French and British Empires enacted censorship legislation between 1911 and 1920, and extended government control on grounds of national security during the First World War. The Soviet Union abolished film censorship in 1917, but reinstated it in 1922, in order to exercise ideological control over films imported from abroad. In Germany, the national censorship established by the imperial administration collapsed in November 1918, but it was re-established by the Weimar government in 1920, when two censor boards were set up in Berlin and Munich.

The justification for censorship was invariably paternalist. Cinema was held to exert a powerful influence over its viewers, particularly over those susceptible groups which comprised the bulk of its audience: children, workers, and those described by colonial rhetoric as 'subject races' (or, in the USA, immigrants). Legislation usually regulated the attendance of children, but only in Belgium were censors restricted to determining which films were 'calculated to trouble the imagination of children, to upset their equilibrium and moral well-being'. From its inception, British censorship classified the films it approved, initially either as 'U' (suitable for universal exhibition), or 'A' (restricted to adults only). The BBFC classifications served only as guidelines, but after 1921 most local authorities accepted the London County Council rules that banned children under 16 from 'A' movies unless they were accompanied by a guardian. In 1932 the BBFC added a further category, 'H' (for horror), from which children were excluded altogether. State-enforced schemes followed similar procedures, prohibiting children's attendance at certain films. Exhibitors, however, resisted such arrangements when they could, in part because they were themselves usually required to police the law while also being liable for any breaches of it. Moreover, they objected to the loss of custom, and to the way in which the classification of the movie being shown randomly changed the public space that their cinema provided, from a family environment to one for adults only. In the United States, these arguments were sufficient to outweigh the demands of reformers for classification, and the occasional argument from producers that classification would improve the quality or sophistication of the movies they could make. The American industry's machinery of self-regulation resisted introducing classification until 1968.

In the early days, the preoccupations of censors varied: the Dutch and Scandinavian boards were more concerned by violence than by sexual themes, while Australian and South African censors tended to be noticeably more puritanical than the British Board. Agendas of cultural or political nationalism operated more or less overtly. In 1928 France required its Commission to take 'national interests' into consideration, 'especially the interest in preserving the national customs and traditions, as well as (in the case of foreign films) the facilities given to French films in the countries of origin'. In countries with a substantial indigenous production industry, censorship legislation was frequently used as a form of protectionism, particularly after the American industry achieved its global hegemony. In general, censors' decisions showed a greater degree of sensitivity to matters of foreign policy—in seeking to avoid offence to other nations, for instance—than they did to domestic issues. While France banned all Soviet films in 1928, the Weimar government actively encouraged their exhibition as a way of promoting German–Soviet relations.

HOLLYWOOD AND SELF-REGULATION

Although in most countries the function of censorship was undertaken by a government-appointed agency, there was invariably a large element of industry participation in the process. The aim of censorship was to police exhibition rather than to prohibit it, and both distributors and exhibitors recognized that it was in their economic interest to co-operate with established censorship practices. Self-regulation was thus justified as an anticipatory form of co-operation, as well as a means of circumventing demands for more extensive governmental regulation of the industry.

Between 1911 and 1916 Pennsylvania, Kansas, Ohio, and Maryland established state censor boards, and in the early 1920s almost every state legislature considered a censorship bill. The increased vigour of this pro-censorship campaign had less to do with the more explicit sexuality of movies such as Cecil B. DeMille's *Why Change your Wife?* (1920) than it did with larger social factors: the establishment of prohibition, and the post-war depression, which intensified middle-class anxieties about the potentially disruptive condition of the working class.

In 1921 the National Association of the Motion Picture Industry (NAMPI) unsuccessfully attempted to prevent

Clara Bow (the 'It' girl) with the young Gary Cooper in *Children of Divorce*, produced and directed by Frank Lloyd for Famous Players–Lasky (Paramount) in 1927, just before the introduction of the first Production Code

Will Hays

(1879–1954)

Will Hays's name is perpetuated in cinema history through the Hays Code, the popular name for the Motion Picture Production Code. But censorship was only the most conspicuous aspect of Hays's role. As the industry's most prominent public representative, he exercised a determining influence over the organization and products of Hollywood.

As chairman of the Republican National Committee Hays organized Warren Harding's presidential campaign in 1920, and became Postmaster General. He was then approached by film industry leaders looking for a prominent figure to become president of their new trade association, the Motion Picture Producers and Distributors of America (MPPDA). The financial scandals that discredited the Harding administration ended Hays's chances of gaining high elective office, but he remained influential in the Republican Party throughout the 1920s and 1930s.

Hays was selected for the job partly because he was the most respectable Protestant politician industry leaders could buy, but also because of his political connections and organizational skills. *Variety* gave Hays the grandiloquent title of 'czar of all the Rushes', but Hays presented the MPPDA as an innovative trade association at the forefront of corporate development, largely responsible for the industry's maturation into respectability, standardizing trade practices and stabilizing relationships between distributors and exhibitors through Film Boards of Trade, arbitration, and the Standard Exhibition Contract. Its stated object, to establish 'the highest possible moral and artistic standards of motion picture production', was in one sense simply an extension of this practice, but it also implicitly accepted that 'pure' entertainment—amusement that was not harmful to its consumer—was a commodity comparable to the pure meat guaranteed by the Food and Drug Administration.

The MPPDA's central concern was that legislation or court action might impose a strict application of the anti-trust laws on the industry, and force the major vertically integrated companies to divorce production, distribution, and exhibition from each other. Throughout the 1920s and 1930s, the industry was subject to a constant barrage of municipal and state legislation, proposed by politicians who saw the fabled riches of Hollywood as a potential source of local revenue. The MPPDA maintained an extensive network of local political alliances to prevent the passage of such legislation, as well as conducting the industry's dealings with the federal government and its foreign policy in negotiations over treaties and quotas with other countries.

Hays's political influence secured the industry's favourable treatment by the Coolidge administration, permitting the smooth expansion of the 1920s. Although the Association was attacked by Protestant religious groups who viewed its manipulation of public opinion as symptomatic of the crimes of the 1920s 'business civilization', Hays's gift for the resonant platitude and his adept political organization piloted the industry through the legislative uncertainties of the early Depression. One of Hays's great political skills was his ability to stage-manage and manipulate a crisis such as that created by the Legion of Decency in 1934.

Although the MPPDA was initially implicated in the Department of Justice's 1938 anti-trust suit, which did eventually break up the vertically integrated structure of the industry, Hays helped to engineer the consent decree that postponed resolution of the case until 1948. He also ensured that the federal government recognized Hollywood as an 'essential industry' during the Second World War. He retired two weeks after the end of the war, and was replaced by Eric Johnston, who changed the MPPDA's name to the Motion Picture Association of America.

Will Hays was a conventional man. Small with large ears, a Presbyterian Church elder who neither smoked nor drank, to many he seemed a Babbitt in Babylon on a 'Charlie Chaplin salary', an easy figure to caricature. But he had a gift for compromise, a faith in the principle of arbitration, and an enthusiasm for communicating; he was rumoured to have the largest telephone bill in the United States. His 'deepest personal convictions', he averred, were 'faith in God, in folks, in the nation, and in the Republican party'. Paradoxically, his profoundly conventional public persona has almost effaced him from most histories as other more flamboyant figures, including Production Code Administration director Joseph Breen, have been accorded greater prominence. But Hays did more than any other individual to preserve Hollywood for oligopoly capital, and his comment on his role in bringing the Production Code into being might summarize his career achievement of maintaining the industry's status quo: 'I give Providence the glory, but I did the engineering.'

RICHARD MALTBY

BIBLIOGRAPHY

Hays, Will H. (1955), *The Memoirs of Will H. Hays*.
Gomery, Douglas (ed.) (1986), *The Will Hays Papers*.

Will Hays (left) on a visit to the Talmadge studios

the passage of the New York state censorship bill. Discussions began about replacing NAMPI with a more effective body to serve the mutual interests of the major companies, which were then under attack from anti-trust reformers. In August 1921 the Federal Trade Commission charged Famous Players–Lasky with monopolizing first-run exhibition, and there were calls for the Senate Judiciary Committee to conduct an investigation into the political activities of the motion picture industry. These events led to the creation, in March 1922, of the Motion Picture Producers and Distributors of America, Inc. (MPPDA), with former Postmaster-General Will Hays as its president.

Resisting the spread of state censorship and regulating movie content was only one aspect of the MPPDA's overall task of internally reorganizing the industry's affairs. The disputes between distributors and exhibitors during the process of vertical integration had been exploited by reform groups and had also undermined the confidence of Wall Street in the competence of industry management. The Hollywood scandals of 1920 and 1921 led the industry to be regarded as a site of moral as well as economic extravagance. Hays persuaded industry leaders that they needed a much more effective public relations operation to reorient the industry's image, and he constructed the MPPDA as the instrument to resolve the contradictions of efficiently restricting Hollywood's extravagance.

Hays sought to persuade his employers that they could not 'ignore the classes that write, talk, and legislate': their movies had not merely to provide a satisfactory level of entertainment for their diverse audiences, but also to offend as small a proportion of the country's cultural and legislative leadership as possible. His public relations policy affiliated the MPPDA with nationally federated civic and religious organizations, women's clubs, and parent–teacher associations, aiming to contain the legislative threat posed by their political lobbying power. To establish self-regulation as a form of industrial self-determination, the industry had to demonstrate that, as Hays put it, 'the quality of our pictures is such that no reasonable person can claim any need of censorship'. In part he achieved this by conceding that there was no dispute over the need to regulate entertainment or over the standards by which it should be regulated, only over who possessed the appropriate authority to police the apparatus of representation.

In addition to municipal censorship, state censor boards now operated in seven of the forty-eight states, and the MPPDA estimated that more than 60 per cent of domestic exhibition, together with virtually the entire foreign market, was affected. This meant that the Association's self-regulation comprised an additional, rather than a replacement, censorship structure.

In 1924 Hays established a mechanism for vetting source material, known as 'the Formula', in order 'to exercise

Don'ts and Be Carefuls

Hollywood's first self-regulating code, 1927 (see p. 241)

(see p. 241)

It is understood that those things included in the following list shall not appear in motion pictures irrespective of the manner in which they are treated:

1. Pointed profanity — this includes the words, God, Lord, Jesus Christ (unless they be used reverently in connection with proper religious ceremonies), S.O.B., Gawd, and every other profane and vulgar expression.
2. Any licentious or suggestive nudity — in fact or in silhouette; and any lecherous or licentious notice thereof by other characters in the picture.
3. The illegal traffic in drugs.
4. Any inference of sexual perversion.
5. White slavery.
6. Miscegenation (sex relationships between the white and black races).
7. Sex hygiene and venereal diseases.
8. Scenes of actual childbirth — in fact or in silhouette.
9. Children's sex organs.
10. Ridicule of the clergy.
11. Willful offense to any nation, race, or creed.

It is also understood that special care be exercised in the manner in which the following subjects are treated, to the end that vulgarity and suggestiveness may be eliminated and that good taste may be emphasized:

1. The use of the Flag.
2. International relations (avoid picturing in an unfavorable light another country's religion, history, institutions, prominent people and citizenry).
3. Religion and religious ceremonies.
4. Arson.
5. The use of firearms.
6. Theft, robbery, safe-cracking and dynamiting trains, mines, buildings, et cetera (having in mind the effect which a too-detailed description of these may have upon the moron).
7. Brutality and possible gruesomeness.
8. Technique of committing murder by whatever method.
9. Methods of smuggling.
10. Third degree methods.
11. Actual hangings or electrocutions as legal punishments for crime.
12. Sympathy for criminals.
13. Attitude toward public characters and institutions.
14. Sedition.
15. Apparent cruelty to children or animals.
16. Branding of people or animals.
17. The sale of women, or a woman selling her virtue.
18. Rape or attempted rape.
19. First night scenes.
20. Man and woman in bed together.
21. Deliberate seduction of girls.
22. The institution of marriage.
23. Surgical operations.
24. The use of drugs.
25. Titles or scenes having to do with law enforcement or law enforcement officers.
26. Excessive or lustful kissing, particularly when one character or the other is a 'heavy'.

Marlene Dietrich
(1901–1992)

An aura of sexual fascination surrounds the star persona of Marlene Dietrich. More than half a century after she sprang to prominence in the films directed by her mentor Josef von Sternberg her image continues to circulate as a cinematic fetish for gay and straight fans alike, and the androgynous glamour and sexual ambiguity that marked her star persona are more fashionable than ever.

Her career began on the German stage of the 1920s, with small parts in dramas and musical reviews. She rapidly became a figure of adoration in Berlin's raucous post-war cabaret scene. Within that enclave, she was renowned for stylish donning of male evening wear and her ability to attract a myriad assortment of lovers of both sexes. In her professional life, Dietrich became a promising performer with film, recording, and stage experience, but she possessed no definitive screen image until Sternberg hired her to play Lola Lola in the Ufa/Paramount co-production *Der blaue Engel | The Blue Angel* (1930). It was the 'Sternberg touch' and Dietrich's performance in the film as a *femme fatale* insolently indifferent to male sexual debasement that would bring her instant international fame and suggest the beginnings of the Dietrich legend.

With a two-film contract with Paramount Pictures, Dietrich went to Hollywood in 1930 as Sternberg's pro-

tégée. The Paramount publicity machine promoted her as an alluring Continental rival to MGM's Greta Garbo. *Morocco* (1930), co-starring Gary Cooper and Adolphe Menjou, was a hit even before *The Blue Angel* was released in the United States. With a single exception, Dietrich continued to make films only with Sternberg over the next five years: *Dishonored* (1931), *Shanghai Express* (1932), *Blonde Venus* (1932), *The Scarlet Empress* (1934), and *The Devil is a Woman* (1935). Distinguished by a heady visual eroticism centred around their star, the Sternberg–Dietrich films again and again return her to the role of an enigmatic and sensual woman who inspires masochistic behaviour in the men subject to her fatal and provocative charm.

Dietrich's success in Hollywood was immediate. She gained an Academy Award nomination for her portrayal of Amy Jolly in *Morocco*; *Shanghai Express* drew raves. But as the Sternberg–Dietrich films became more insular in their depiction of a fantastic world in which desire is everything and nothing, they also became increasingly problematic at the box-office and with critics, who regarded them as odd if not wilfully perverse. Their failure was blamed on Sternberg, who was let go by the studio.

Although the director was publicized as having a Svengali-like hold over his Teutonic Trilby, Dietrich was capable of scrutinizing and exercising a measure of control over her own image, even to the point of influencing her films' lighting and costuming. Her 'collaborations' with Travis Banton became exemplars of Hollywood fashion

design at its best. Thus, Dietrich was able to maintain her glamorous on-screen image, but her Paramount films after Sternberg's departure did not always have those qualities of insolence, sophistication, and sexual ambiguity that Sternberg's films had exploited as being uniquely and mysteriously 'Dietrich'. Although she was amusing as a jewel thief in Frank Borzage's light-hearted romance *Desire* (1936), her career faltered in the late 1930s.

Dietrich's come-back occurred with the unlikely role of 'Frenchy' in George Marshall's comedy Western, *Destry Rides Again* (1939). Bolstered by songs written for her by *Blue Angel* composer Frederick Hollander, she gave a memorably wry performance as a dance hall singer. A short string of successful films (mainly at Universal) followed, with Dietrich often playing a sassy cabaret singer with a heart of gold, as in Tay Garnett's charming *Seven Sinners* (1940). She was declared box-office poison in 1942 after the release of *Pittsburgh*. As a recently naturalized American citizen, she sold war bonds, then joined a USO tour in 1944–5. Dietrich toured the European front, where she entertained troops with numbers played on a musical saw delicately perched between her gorgeous gams.

After the war, Dietrich often worked with talented directors (Wilder, Hitchcock, Lang, Leisen), but with mixed results. She was most effective in the roles with those qualities of detachment and unsentimentality that Sternberg had often emphasized; as the Nazi-sympathizing songstress in Billy Wilder's *A Foreign Affair* (1948), and in a cameo role as a world weary prostitute in Orson Welles's *Touch of Evil* (1958). Apart from other occasional cameos in the 1960s and 1970s, 'the world's most glamorous grandmother' devoted her time to a touring one-woman stage show until the physical toll of drugs, alcohol, and age drove her to retreat to her Paris apartment. There, she would spend the last decade of her life as a bedridden recluse who refused to be photographed.

GAYLYN STUDLAR

SELECT FILMOGRAPHY

Der blaue Engel / The Blue Angel (1930); Morocco (1930); Dishonored (1931); Shanghai Express (1932); Blonde Venus (1932); The Scarlet Empress (1934); The Devil is a Woman (1935); The Garden of Allah (1936); Destry Rides Again (1939); Seven Sinners (1940); Kismet (1944); A Foreign Affair (1948); Stage Fright (1950); Rancho Notorious (1952); Witness for the Prosecution (1958); Touch of Evil (1958); Judgement at Nuremberg (1961)

BIBLIOGRAPHY

Riva, Maria (1993), *Marlene Dietrich by her Daughter*.
Spoto, Donald (1992), *Blue Angel: The Life of Marlene Dietrich*.
Sternberg, Josef von (1965), *Fun in a Chinese Laundry*.

Opposite: Marlene Dietrich with Clive Brook in Josef von Sternberg's *Shanghai Express* (1932)

every possible care that only books or plays which are of the right type are used for screen presentation'. In 1927, the Association published a code to govern production, administered by its Studio Relations Committee (SRC) in Hollywood. The 'Don'ts and Be Carefuls', as this code was familiarly known, was compiled by a committee chaired by Irving Thalberg, and synthesized the restrictions and eliminations applied by state and foreign censors. Films were modified after production but before release in order to assuage the concerns of civic, religious, or manufacturing interests, but until 1930 the SRC's function was only advisory.

The technological complexities of sound production necessitated a more exact arrangement. Unlike silent film, talkies could not be altered by local censors, regional distributors, or individual exhibitors without destroying synchronization. Producers began to demand something firmer than advice from the SRC, but at the same time they wanted to establish a more permissive code for sound. But their desire to 'bring Broadway to Main Street' ran counter to the hostility of an increasingly insecure Protestant provincial middle class. Combining opposition to monopoly with a barely concealed anti-Semitism, provincial Protestantism saw movies threaten the ability of small communities to exercise control over the cultural influences they tolerated.

In the autumn of 1929 the Association was the subject of heavy criticism for reasons only tangentially connected to movie content. Its relationship with the federal government had been strained by a wave of mergers and theatre-buying among the major companies. At the same time, the public relations edifice Hays had constructed disintegrated in the wake of the Association's failure to establish a co-operative relationship with the Protestant churches similar to that they enjoyed with organized Catholicism. In the aftermath of the Wall Street Crash, the movie industry provided a highly conspicuous target for critics of the business culture of the 1920s, and the Protestant campaign gave independent exhibitors the chance to combine their attack on the majors' trade practices with a morals charge. Confronted with criticism about the moral standards of the movies they showed, small exhibitors defended themselves by arguing that the majors' insistence on block booking forced exhibitors to show 'sex-smut' regardless of their own or their communities' preferences. They insisted that the only way to secure decency on Main Street was through extensive federal regulation of the industry.

Under attack from several directions, Hays seized on the regulation of film content as an area where the Association might be able to demonstrate its usefulness to both the public and its members. In September 1929 he initiated the revision of the 1927 code, and a committee of producers presented a draft code in November. A quite separate document emanated from Chicago, where Martin Quigley, a prominent Chicago Catholic involved in the Association's work, proposed a much more elaborated Code enunciating the moral principles underlying screen entertainment. He recruited a Jesuit, Father Daniel Lord, to draft it.

The director of the SRC, Colonel Jason Joy, spent January 1930 attempting to compromise the two drafts and their differing ambitions. After much discussion, a producers' committee wrote a 'condensed' version, and Lord and Hays rewrote Lord's draft as a separate document entitled 'Reasons Underlying the Code'. With the consent of both parties, Catholic involvement in the Code remained secret, as did its implementation procedure, the Resolution for Uniform Interpretation, which placed responsibility for making changes in finished films with the companies concerned. It also appointed a 'jury' composed of the heads of production of each of the member companies as final arbiters of whether a film conformed 'to the spirit and the letter of the Code'. This caution in publicly committing the Association to the Code's enforcement had as much to do with recognition of the practical problems of the Code's application as it did with a scepticism about producers' intentions.

The text of the Code provided a list of prohibitions rather than the moral arguments of Lord's original draft. Its 'Particular Applications' elaborated the 'Don'ts and Be Carefuls', and added clauses on liquor, adultery, vulgarity, and obscenity. Lord's contribution was most visible in the three 'General Principles' that preceded the 'Particular Applications':

1. No picture shall be produced which will lower the moral standards of those who see it. Hence the sympathy of the audience shall never be thrown to the side of crime, wrongdoing, evil or sin.
2. Correct standards of life, subject only to the requirements of drama and entertainment, shall be presented.
3. Law, natural or human, shall not be ridiculed, nor shall sympathy be created for its violation.

Although a growing chorus of voices denounced the moral evils of the movies, it would be wrong to conclude that movies became more salacious or vicious between 1930 and 1934. With occasional exceptions, the reverse is the case. The early 1930s was a period of moral conservatism in American culture and elsewhere, and both the SRC and state censors applied increasingly strict standards. The industry's most vociferous critics tended to judge the movies on their advertising, which was far less strictly controlled than their contents, and a small number of visible infringements were sufficient to fuel the flames of their righteousness.

Joy's approach to the improvement of content was gradualist. He thought the 'small, narrow, picayunish fault-finding' of censor boards inhibited his attempts to negotiate strategies of representation that permitted producers 'to paint the unconventional, the unlawful, the immoral side of life in order to bring out in immediate contrast the happiness and benefits derived from wholesome, clean and law-abiding conduct'. He recognized that, if the Code was to remain effective, it had to allow the studios to develop a system of representational conventions 'from which conclusions might be drawn by the sophisticated mind, but which would mean nothing to the unsophisticated and inexperienced'. Particularly in the early years of its operation, much of the work of the Production Code lay in the creation and maintenance of this system of conventions. Like other Hollywood conventions, the Code was one of several substitutes for detailed audience research. Having chosen not to differentiate its product through a ratings system, the production industry had to find ways of appealing to both 'innocent' and 'sophisticated' sensibilities in the same object without transgressing the boundaries of public acceptability. This involved devising systems and codes of representation in which 'innocence' was inscribed into the text while 'sophisticated' viewers were able to 'read into' movies whatever meanings they pleased to find, so long as producers could use the Production Code to deny that they had put them there. As Lea Jacobs (1991) has argued, under the Code 'offensive ideas could survive at the price of an instability of meaning . . . there was constant negotiation about how explicit films could be and by what means (through the image, sound, language) offensive ideas could find representation'.

Censors, however, continued to identify some disturbing developments in movie content. The crime film had been the subject of the municipal censorship as early as 1907, and the genre was regarded as the most threatening to public order. Beginning in late 1930, the brief cycle of gangster films inspired by press coverage of Al Capone revived charges that the movies were encouraging young audiences to view the gangster protagonist as a 'hero-villain', and proved a public relations calamity for the Association. In September 1931 Code procedures were considerably tightened, submission of scripts was made compulsory, and further production of gangster films was prohibited. But every time the Association responded to one kind of complaint, it was replaced by another. As soon as Joy was provided with the means to ensure the overall morality of a movie's narrative, reformers argued that the stories Hollywood told were not the primary source of its influence. The cinema's power to corrupt was now assumed to lie in the seductive pleasure of its spectacle, exemplified in the screen careers of Jean Harlow, Mae West, and the actress Father Lord described as 'the unspeakable Constance Bennett'.

In January 1932 Joseph Breen arrived in Hollywood to oversee its publicity for the Association. His abrasive style constituted a significant shift away from Joy's attempts at consensus. In September Joy left to become a producer at Fox, and his replacement, James Wingate, proved unable to establish a rapport with any of the studio heads, and paid too much attention to details of elimination rather than wider thematic concerns. Joy's resignation coincided with the first publication of extracts from the Payne Fund Studies, a research programme investigating children's attendance at and emotional responses to motion pictures, undertaken by the Motion Picture Research Council (MPRC), which had become the focal point of Protestant and educational concerns about the cultural effects of the movies. A widely circulated sensationalized digest of the Studies, Henry James Forman's *Our Movie Made Children*, made the MPRC's demands for federal regulation a profound threat to the industry. By the end of 1932 nearly forty religious and educational organizations had passed resolutions calling for federal regulation of the industry.

The early months of 1933 comprised the low point of the industry's fortunes. Many studios were facing bankruptcy, and Hays insisted that more than economic action was required to deal with the crisis. Only a more rigid enforcement of the Code, he argued, could maintain public sympathy and defeat the pressure for federal intervention. He persuaded the Board to sign a Reaffirmation of Objectives acknowledging that 'disintegrating influences' threatened 'standards of production, standards of quality, standards of business practice', and pledged them to the maintenance of 'higher business standards'. The Reaffirmation became the implement with which Hays began to reorganize the SRC. The tone of its correspondence changed: as one studio official explained to his producers, 'prior to this time, we were told "it is recommended", but recently letters definitely state, "it is inadmissible", or something equally definite'. Breen relinquished his other work to concentrate full-time on self-regulation, and established his usefulness to the companies by doing what Wingate apparently could not: providing practical solutions to a studio's problem in applying the Code, and thus protecting its investment. From August 1933 he was in effect running the SRC.

Breen was also in almost constant conspiratorial correspondence with Quigley and other prominent Catholics, attempting to involve the Church hierarchy in a demonstration of Catholic cultural assertiveness. By November 1933 they had persuaded the Catholic bishops to establish an Episcopal Committee on Motion Pictures, and in April 1934 the Committee announced it would recruit a Legion of Decency, whose members would sign a pledge promising 'to remain away from all motion pictures except those which do not offend decency and Christian morality'. The Legion was not a spontaneous expression of public feeling. Its campaign was delicately orchestrated

to achieve a precise objective: the effective enforcement of the Production Code by the existing machinery. Although its principal weapon appeared to be the economic one of a threatened boycott of films or theatres, its real power lay in its capacity to generate publicity. It was designed to intimidate producers, not to inflict major economic damage. It was, indeed, vital to its success that it separate the question of Code enforcement from issues of industry trade practice like block booking, in order to differentiate the Legion from the MPRC and make it clear that the bishops had 'no purpose or desire to tell the picture people how to run their business'. It was a complete success. In June the MPPDA Board revised the Resolution for Uniform Interpretation. The SRC was renamed the Production Code Administration (PCA), with Breen as its director and an augmented staff. The producers' jury was eliminated, leaving appeal to the MPPDA Board as the only mechanism for questioning Breen's judgement. Each film passed by the PCA would be given a seal, displayed on every print. All member companies agreed not to distribute or release a film without a certificate. A penalty clause imposed a $25,000 fine for violation of the new Resolution.

Given the public attention being paid to the campaign, it was in the industry's best interests to make a show of atonement. Industry publicity emphasized the scale of the 1934 crisis in order to create a dividing line between 'before', when the SRC had been unable to control production, and 'now', when PCA 'self-regulation' had really become effective. As a result of this need for a public act of contrition, the history of the SRC's gradual implementation of the Production Code was concealed behind a more apocalyptic account. The immediate purpose behind this exaggeration was less to flatter the Catholics (although the Legion of Decency remained a powerful influence at the PCA) than to outmanoeuvre those still demanding federal regulation of the industry. But in fact, Breen had largely won the internal battle by March, when most of the studios were showing 'a definite willingness to do the right thing'. Only Warners, always the most recalcitrant of the major companies in their attitude to the Code and the MPPDA, had to be brought into line. With the implementation of the agreement in mid-July, conditions tightened further. As in March 1933, a number of films were withheld from release, and drastic reconstruction undertaken: the conversion of Mae West's *It Ain't no Sin* into *Belle of the Nineties* (1934) being the most prominent. A number of films then in circulation were withdrawn before the end of their release cycle: many more were refused certification over the next few years when companies attempted to rerelease them. In another important respect production policy had changed dramatically in early 1934. The wave of Hollywood's adaptation of high-budget literary classics and historical

Hedy Kiesler (later known as Hedy Lamarr) in the nude bathing scene from Gustav Machatý's *Extase* (1933). Shortly after the film was made, she married Austrian millionaire Fritz Mandl, who attempted—unsuccessfully—to buy up all prints of the film to prevent its circulation

biographies resulted directly from the requirements of the industry's public relations.

The establishment of the PCA did not end discussion over what constituted satisfactory material for films. Writers and producers commonly left material that they knew would be cut in scripts sent to the PCA, often in hopes of using it as a bargaining tool to get something else through, and frequently shots or sequences that the PCA initially objected to survived into the final film. In 1935 disputes over the representation of crime resurfaced with the attempt by several studios to circumvent the prohibition on gangster films in the G-Men cycle, until British censors objected to the trend. On the whole, however, these questions of Code enforcement were relatively minor: the studios had acquiesced to the PCA machinery and, with occasional displays of resistance, acquiesced to its decisions. More importantly, public opinion had generally recovered from its moral panic and accepted the Association's or the Legion's account of the industry's rescue from the abyss in 1934.

Breen's insistence that the PCA was 'regarded by producers, directors, and their staffs, as participants in the processes of production' was perfectly accurate. Beyond the shared assumption that the PCA functioned as an aid, not a hindrance, to production, there were two underlying considerations that governed its working operation. 'Compensating moral values', as understood by Breen, ensured not only that 'No picture shall be produced which will lower the moral standards of those who see it', but also that a calculus of retribution would invariably be deployed to punish the guilty. Plots had to be morally unambiguous in their development, dialogue, and conclusion, so the site of textual ambiguity shifted from narrative to the representation of incident; matters of sex, particularly, were represented in such a way that a pre-existent knowledge was required to gain access to them. As screen-writer Elliott Paul pithily observed, 'A scene should give full play to the vices of the audience, and still have a technical out.'

The difficulties the Association faced over film content in the late 1930s were largely the results of its success. As his dealings with the studios became more assertive after 1934, Breen's correspondence made fewer distinctions between a decision under the Code, advice regarding the likely actions of state or foreign censors, and the implementation of 'industry policy' in response to pressure groups, foreign governments, and corporate interests. Industry policy was, like self-regulation, designed to prevent the movies becoming a subject of controversy or giving offence to powerful interests, but events such as MGM's decision in 1936 not to produce a film version of

Sinclair Lewis's *It Can't Happen Here*, and Catholic protest over *Blockade* (1938), set in the Spanish Civil War, led to accusations from liberals within the industry and outside that 'self-regulation … has degenerated into political censorship'. However, the PCA case that received most public attention in the late 1930s was as trivial as most publicized instances of moral censorship: the inclusion of the usually prohibited word 'damn' in Clark Gable's last line in *Gone with the Wind* (1939).

INTO AND AFTER THE WAR

Distinctly less trivial were the issues raised by the increasing political tensions in Europe and the world at large. In the United States itself directly political censorship was mostly confined to the banning of some Soviet films by state or local censor boards. Newsreels were generally exempted from state censorship, but they were made with a firm degree of self-regulation, avoiding the coverage of crime as well as political controversy. Meanwhile Nazi Germany and Fascist Italy had instituted severe censorship, aimed not only at regulating the (mainly escapist) content of domestic production but at controlling the content of American and other imports, while Japan and the Soviet Union not only practised internal censorship but had become effectively closed markets. Throughout most of the 1930s Hollywood's reaction to the rise of Fascism was one of economically motivated appeasement, aimed at ensuring that its films would not attract the attention of foreign censors and so lead to the further closure of the market. In 1936, for instance, MGM acquired the screen rights to Robert E. Sherwood's play *Idiot's Delight*, which took place during the outbreak of a new European war brought about by an Italian invasion of France. Recognizing the dangers such a project posed to their European distribution, both the studio and the PCA engaged in protracted negotiations with Italian diplomats in the USA to devise a storyline that contained nothing that would offend the Italian government. The movie's generalized anti-war theme lost the play's specific indictment of Fascist aggression, and the natives of what producer Hunt Stromberg called the 'nondescript' European country in which the movie was set spoke Esperanto, not Italian. Production delays, caused in part by these negotiations, meant that *Idiot's Delight* was not released until early 1939.

By that time, however, the worsening crisis meant that markets were closed anyhow, and the resulting loss of revenue eroded the economic logic behind the industry's earlier policies of appeasement to the Nazi and Fascist regimes. David O. Selznick, among others, argued that the industry should abandon the 'insane and inane and outmoded' Code, but the PCA's censorship of the movies became a political issue primarily as a result of the anti-trust suit filed against the major companies by the Department of Justice in July 1938. Implicating the PCA in the majors' restrictive practices, the suit alleged that they used the Code to exercise a practical censorship over the entire industry, restricting the production of pictures treating controversial subjects and hindering the development of innovative approaches to drama or narrative by companies that might use innovation as a way of challenging the majors' monopoly power. In 1939 the PCA's jurisdiction was restricted so that there was a clear distinction between its administration of the Code and its other advisory functions. One effect of this was to acquiesce in the use of politically more controversial content as a way of demonstrating that the 'freedom of the screen' was not hampered by the operations of the PCA. Although PCA officials continued to voice concern over whether such subjects as *Confessions of a Nazi Spy* (1939) constituted appropriate screen entertainment, they were much more circumspect in expressing their opinions.

In Britain, too, liberal criticism of the BBFC in the late 1930s had resulted in some relaxation of its earlier rigidity over politically controversial subjects. During the war government agencies in both Britain and the USA worked in parallel with the industry's self-regulatory bodies rather than replacing them. In Britain, the Ministry of Information (MOI) had a Censorship Division, but it delegated its 'security' film censorship of both feature films and newsreels to an augmented BBFC, which also retained responsibility for 'moral' censorship. The MOI had the power to suppress movies, although it never used it. In the USA, the Office of War Information (OWI) set up a Bureau of Motion Pictures, which had no powers of censorship over Hollywood, but sought to establish a parallel system of script supervision to the PCA's, in order to insert themes promoting the war effort. Under Joe Breen, the PCA remained politically as well as morally conservative, but his dislike of the pro-Soviet propaganda of *Mission to Moscow* was brushed aside by the liberal OWI. The studios co-operated with the propaganda programme so long as it did not put their profits at risk. They were, however, unsympathetic to the OWI's complaint that Hollywood over-represented both frivolity and 'the sordid side of American life'; government reviewers objected to the Preston Sturges comedy *The Palm Beach Story* (1942) as 'a libel on America at war', as strongly as they did to movies in which gangster heroes joined up. The OWI achieved its greatest influence after 1943, when military victories began to open up overseas markets again, and studios needed the approval of the government's separate Office of Censorship to export their product. As in many other wartime industries, government and business found a mutually beneficial way of combining patriotism and profit. The studios' relationship with the OWI also repeated the history of the Production Code: after some initial skirmishes to establish a basis for their dealings,

Maurice Chevalier

(1888–1972)

Maurice Chevalier was, for a long time, the world's stereotype of 'the Frenchman', thanks to his Hollywood films of the early 1930s. As a singer and music hall artist, he dominated French entertainment for the first half of the century.

Chevalier was born in Ménilmontant, a popular district of Paris. After an impoverished childhood, young Maurice ('Momo') started performing in cheap local *cafés-concerts*. Around 1907 he left his neighbourhood for luxury music halls like the Folies Bergère, where Mistinguett became his partner, on and off stage. Not endowed with a particularly remarkable voice, Chevalier relied, for his cocky *gavroche* persona, on his gift of the gab, Parisian accent, and a set of gestures: shrugging shoulders, hands in pockets, and the famous protruding lower lip; to this he gradually added the identity of the boulevard dandy, in dinner jacket, bow tie, and straw hat. His career took off spectacularly: from the end of the First World War to 1928 he was the toast of Paris, leading countless stage revues, and creating hit songs like 'Dans la vie faut pas s'en faire' (1921) and 'Valentine' (1924). Inevitably, he attracted Hollywood's attention and was signed by Paramount in 1928.

Chevalier—who had already appeared in several short French films—made sixteen American movies between 1928 and 1935, mostly features, many of them multi-language versions. *Innocents of Paris* (1929) was his first hit, in both the USA and France, and it was followed by many others. The best were directed by Ernst Lubitsch (*The Love Parade*, 1929; *The Smiling Lieutenant*, 1931; *One Hour With You*, 1932; *The Merry Widow*, 1934) and co-starred Jeanette MacDonald (except *The Smiling Lieutenant* in which his partners are Claudette Colbert and Miriam Hopkins). These films were delightful sophisticated comedies, set in a fantasy Paris or countries like 'Sylvania'. In this make-believe universe, Chevalier epitomized, in a comic mode, the frivolous and sexy Parisian, underlined by exaggerated gestures and caricatural accent, a novelty in early talkies (rumour had it that he was prevented from taking English lessons while in Hollywood). Characters and settings were clichéd, but Chevalier's accomplished skills as a performer came through, especially in the musical numbers, dovetailing with Lubitsch's wicked humour.

Back in Europe from 1935, Chevalier made a few films which, given his Hollywood success and his continuing popularity on stage, had a surprisingly lukewarm reception. *Break the News*, directed in Britain by René Clair in 1938, and co-starring Jack Buchanan, turned out to be less funny than its French original (*Le Mort en fuite*). In France Chevalier starred in the populist *L'Homme du jour* (1936, directed by Julien Duvivier), as well as *Avec le sourire* (1936), a cynical backstage comedy by Maurice Tourneur, and the thriller *Pièges* (1939), Robert Siodmak's last French film. The interest of these films, and probably the reason for their semi-failure, lies in their uneasy attempts at reconciling the image of Chevalier, the glamorous international star, with the down-to-earth populist milieu of the French films of the period.

Chevalier went on working during the war, like many other French performers, but his compliance with the occupying forces and his endorsement of the Vichy ideology led to problems at the Liberation (although he was not, strictly speaking, a collaborator and used his connections to help many Jews, including the family of his lover, Nita Raya). Nevertheless, alongside his singing career, he went on making films in France and Hollywood, the two most notable being René Clair's *Le Silence est d'or* (1947) and Vincente Minnelli's *Gigi* (1958). Both are nostalgia pieces; Clair's film is an affectionate tribute to silent cinema, and Minnelli's a lavish musical version of Colette's story about the education of a young woman (Leslie Caron) in turn-of-the-century Paris. In both cases, Chevalier incarnates an ageing beau, a persona occasionally bordering on the suspect, as evidenced by his rendering of 'Thank Heavens for Little Girls' in *Gigi*. His presence in these two films, however, has other, less uncomfortable resonances. Evoking his own earlier career, his characters also epitomize an era of popular entertainment then on the brink of vanishing for ever.

GINETTE VINCENDEAU

SELECT FILMOGRAPHY

Innocents of Paris (1929); The Love Parade (1929); The Smiling Lieutenant (1931); One Hour with You (1932); The Merry Widow (1934); Break the News (1938); L'Homme du jour (1936); Pièges (1939); Le Silence est d'or (1947); Gigi (1958)

BIBLIOGRAPHY

Ringgold, Gene, and Bodeen, De Witt (1973), *Chevalier*.

Maurice Chevalier in Ernst Lubitsch's *The Merry Widow* (1934)

the OWI had found a way of demonstrating that censorship was 'smart showmanship'. According to historians Clayton Koppes and Gregory Black (1987), the OWI's involvement in Hollywood was 'the most comprehensive and sustained government attempt to change the content of a mass medium in American history', since it told the industry not only what material should be omitted but also what should be included.

The censors' rigid standards over sex and violence gave ground during the war, partly because of the imperatives of other agendas: the BBFC refrained almost entirely from making cuts in British, American, or even Soviet propaganda films, even when they transgressed the principles applied before 1939. Some of Hollywood's wartime productions, including *Double Indemnity* (1944), *Duel in the Sun* (1946), and *The Postman Always Rings Twice* (1946), required significant concessions from the PCA's pre-war standards not simply in the details of what they showed, but also in their thematic preoccupations. In other respects, however, the war saw little change. The OWI was unwilling for Hollywood to represent social problems unless it showed a solution for them, and this coincided with PCA standards and studio practice. Studios had, for example, always staged the performances of black musical artists in such a way that their routines could be deleted by local censors in Southern states without disrupting the continuity of the movie.

The war's end, however, brought rapid changes. Germany and Japan were subject to a military censorship imposed by the occupying forces, and, along with Italy, to a heavy influx of American movies, as Hollywood sought opportunities to continue to profit from its patriotism. A Fox executive expressed the widely-held opinion that 'the motion picture must continue as an articulate force in the post-war world so that it can contribute vitally to the development of permanent peace, prosperity, progress and security on a global basis'. Increasingly, producers complained at the thematic restrictions imposed on them by the Production Code. After the PCA withdrew its seal from *The Outlaw* in 1946, Howard Hughes's legal challenge to its authority delayed the liberalization of Hollywood's censorship, but it was clear that even in the reactionary political climate of the early Cold War the ground gained during the war would not be surrendered. As well as the more explicit representations of sexual and psychological variation and psychopathic violence in film noir, movies dealing with racial prejudice challenged the legitimacy of municipal censorship in the Southern states. Local bans on *Pinky* and *Lost Boundaries* (both 1949) were overturned by the Supreme Court, which declared in its ruling on the Paramount anti-trust case in 1948 that it now regarded movies as 'included in the press whose freedom is guaranteed by the First Amendment'. It was not, however, until 1952 that the Court reversed its 1915 ruling on the constitutional status of cinema, in a case in which Rossellini's *The Miracle* (1948) had been banned by the New York censor board on the grounds of its being 'sacrilegious'. Over the next three years the Supreme Court ruled state and municipal censorship unconstitutional on any grounds other than that of 'obscenity'.

In Britain the changing attitude to cinema was embodied in the 1952 Cinematograph Act, which placed greater emphasis on regulation in the interests of children, and coincided with the introduction of the 'X' category to replace the 'H' certificate. The 'X' certificate permitted the exhibition of movies with more sexually daring themes, generally of European origin. State censorship in most of continental Europe had always evidenced more concern with violence than with sex, and this distinction became more pronounced after 1950. In Britain and the USA, the growth of the 'art-house' circuits provided exhibition outlets for these products in a context that challenged the appropriateness of censorship for adults. The liberalization of censorship standards in the 1950s had much to do with the precipitous decline in attendance: as cinema came to be viewed as something other than a form of mass entertainment for an undifferentiated audience, many of the fundamental justifications of its censorship lost their persuasive power.

In the United States, the Supreme Court's decision in *The Miracle* case weakened the authority of the Production Code, but did not destroy it, although in 1953 a Maryland court observed that 'if the Production Code were law, it would be plainly unconstitutional'. The PCA had relied on the sanction of 'political censorship', and the liberalization of standards in both America and Europe eroded that sanction. However, the Court's decision in the

A familiar sight to generations of British film goers: the X Certificate preceding Jean Dréville's *La Ferme du pendu* (*Hanged Man's Farm*), made in 1945 and released in Britain in 1951

Paramount case was actually of greater consequence. The PCA's effective power came from the major companies' agreement that they would not exhibit any movie that did not have a seal; thus PCA approval was vital to a movie's profitability in the American domestic market. The divorcement of exhibition from production and distribution that followed the Paramount decision meant that the PCA could no longer enforce exclusion. In 1950 independent distributor Joseph Burstyn refused to make two minor cuts in *Bicycle Thieves* (1948) to accommodate Breen's PCA, and the movie, which won the Best Foreign Film Oscar that year, was exhibited in first-run theatres without a seal. Three years later, United Artists refused to modify Otto Preminger's comedy *The Moon Is Blue* (1953) as Breen demanded. It became the first major company production to be exhibited without a seal, and was the fifteenth-highest grossing movie of 1953.

The PCA's authority had depended on vertical integration and the majors' oligopoly. Without constitutional sanction, a market censorship as rigid as Breen had imposed was no longer viable. As movie attendance declined in the 1950s, production and exhibition strategies changed so that fewer movies were targeted at an undifferentiated audience. A new genre of 'adult' movies emerged, often adapted from bestsellers and drawing audiences by their sensational treatment of serious social subject-matter that television would not handle. Movies such as *The Man with the Golden Arm* (1955) and *Baby Doll*

(1956) led to revisions in the Production Code in 1954 and 1956, after which 'mature' subjects such as prostitution, drug addiction, and miscegenation could be shown if 'treated within the limits of good taste'. Concerns about the cinema's influence on behaviour persisted, however; one source of anxiety being the treatment of juvenile delinquency in movies like *The Wild One* (1953) and *Blackboard Jungle* (1955).

In 1954 Joe Breen retired as director of the PCA. He was replaced by his long-serving deputy, Geoffrey Shurlock, who would oversee the increasing liberalization of Code procedures and practices. Under Breen, the PCA had been among the most powerful influences on Hollywood production for more than twenty years, and although his personal control over the PCA's standards has often been exaggerated, the classical Hollywood of the studio system would have been unrecognizable without the determining market censorship the PCA exercised.

Bibliography
Hunnings, Neville March (1967), *Film Censors and the Law*.
Jacobs, Lea (1991), *The Wages of Sin*.
Koppes, Clayton R., and Black, Gregory D. (1987), *Hollywood Goes to War*.
Leff, Leonard J., and Simmons, Jerold L. (1990), *The Dame in the Kimono*.
Maltby, Richard (1993), 'The Production Code and the Hays Office'.
Moley, Raymond (1945), *The Hays Office*.

The Sound of Music

MARTIN MARKS

The history of music for sound films falls into two distinct periods: the first extending from 1925 to 1960, the second from 1960 to the present. In terms of style, there are great differences between them, owing to changing personnel, aesthetic goals, economic conditions, and production techniques. If the division is somewhat arbitrary, it does reflect the fact that certain approaches to film-scoring were consistently followed from the 1930s to the 1950s, only to be challenged and replaced by more 'modern' practices from the 1960s to the 1980s. Moreover, within the earlier period one finds three linked phases of development: wide-ranging experiment in the late 1920s and early 1930s, stylistic and technological standardization from the mid-1930s to the mid-1940s, and, in the decade and a half that followed, a steady broadening of film music's functional and expressive potential.

THE SPECTRUM OF INNOVATION 1926–1935

In the beginning was not the word but music, and initially it seemed as if feature sound films would be little different from silents, save for their fixed, synchronized accompaniments. The earliest example, Warner Bros.' *Don Juan* (1926), was given an orchestral score by two experienced hands, William Axt and David Mendoza of the Capitol Theater in New York, and like their previous scores this one was a compilation, intermixed with some original music. What set it apart was that it was recorded (in performance by the New York Philharmonic under Henry Hadley) and played back on discs coupled to projectors by means of the 'Vitaphone' process. Moreover, in place of the customary live performances that often preceded the presentation of important films, this première included a one-hour programme of Vitaphone shorts, plus a brief filmed speech promising 'a new era in music and motion pictures'. The promise came closer to fulfilment with a subsequent, phenomenally popular Vitaphone feature, *The Jazz Singer* (1927). Though it was given much the same kind of accompaniment (skilfully arranged by Louis Silvers, who had prepared scores for some of Griffith's films), what excited audiences the most were the songs performed by Jolson, enlivened as usual by his colloquial ad libs (notably, the now immortal 'You ain't heard nothin' yet').

The success of *The Jazz Singer* pointed the way toward three parallel developments in Hollywood over the next few years: the demise of the silent film, the emergence of a new genre (the musical), and the rush by other studios to develop their own recording technologies (some using sound recorded on film, which ultimately became the standard process). Yet, seen from outside Hollywood, the direction film music was taking—or ought to take—was by no means clear. In Europe as well as America, these were years of enormous excitement and debate over the advantages and drawbacks of the new technology, and not everyone rushed to embrace either synchronized sound in general or 'canned' music in particular. Even as late as 1932, in a characteristically succinct, insightful, and perverse essay, Virgil Thomson could dismiss the music that had been composed expressly for sound films, remembering fondly the days of hearing 'better-known movements from the symphonic repertory' performed live, and asserting that 'the best union of movies and music that has ever been made' was still to be found in René Clair's short film *Entr'acte* (1924) with its score by Erik Satie. Thomson's position may have been unique (and reflected his interest in modern French music), but he had raised a question which needed to be addressed by avant-garde and mainstream film-makers alike: what roles and types of music worked best in a medium which had once been purely visual but could now be heard as well as seen?

EXPERIMENTAL SOUND-TRACKS

Despite Thomson's assertion, experimental collaborations between avant-garde directors and composers in Europe did not cease with *Entr'acte* or with the coming of sound. Indeed, Paris itself continued to be a key site for their production: it was home, for example, to three delightfully unconventional 'musical' comedies by Clair himself (*Sous les toits de Paris*, 1930; *Le Million*, 1931; and *À nous la liberté*, 1931). The last of these was graced by a particularly charming score by Georges Auric, who in 1930 had composed stranger music for Cocteau's exercise in surrealism, *Blood of a Poet* (this being the only sound film which Thomson acknowledged to contain some 'fine music'). After Auric the most original film musician to appear in Paris was Maurice Jaubert, who early on composed remarkable scores for films of Painlevé, Storck, Clair,

Cavalcanti, and—most notably—for Vigo's *Zéro de conduite* and *L'Atalante* (in 1933 and 1934).

In Britain and Germany some of the most impressive collaborations originated in the documentary genre, as in Basil Wright and Walter Leigh's *Song of Ceylon* (1934). This film was conceived for purposes of social analysis and propaganda, and Leigh made use of (inexpensive) chamber ensembles, and anti-Romantic textures and tunes through the imitation of Far Eastern idioms. (Moreover, like Thomson and Jaubert, and Eisler in Germany, Leigh explained his approach in various writings, and thereby became a spokesman for 'modernist' theories of film music.) *Song of Ceylon* is notable, too, for the complexity of its sound-track, which exemplifies what came to be called 'sound montage': that is, the music overlaps with other auditory fragments (narration taken from a 1680 travelogue, conversational voices, machine sounds, etc.). Leigh's intention was apparently to create a musical style based on the dictates of the new technology. 'Every sound in a film,' he wrote, 'must be a significant one'; and he praised the 'canned' quality of film music as its 'most important characteristic and greatest virtue'. No less important is the sound-track's 'contrapuntal' effect, where what is heard often bears only an indirect correspondence to what is seen. Thus was realized one of the key goals of avant-garde film-making throughout the early sound period: somehow to preserve the silent film's highly developed art of montage, which was for a time impeded by the cumbersome nature of the new technology, and threatened more generally by the impact of popular films offering sound-tracks that were simply literal in nature.

THE 'TALKIES'

What concerned creative film-makers most was the dominance of 'talkies': an apt name for early sound films which combined dialogue, naturalistic sound effects, and purely diegetic uses of music. At first these sound-tracks were recorded live, and, owing to technological constraints, many of the earliest examples were very dull (e.g. Warners' first '100 per-cent all-talkie', *The Lights of New York*, 1928); but, after a few years, developments in camera technology and techniques of post-synchronization allowed for increased fluidity of both sights and sounds. Even so, in the interest of greater realism most of these films broke with tradition and dispensed with continuous accompaniment, thus pointing up a key paradox: only the advent of the sound film enabled the medium to claim moments of silence as part of the narrative. Given this new cinematic universe, film-makers discarded the traditional silent-film score and learnt to rely on ways of making small scraps of music count. One famous example is Fritz Lang's *M* (1931), which makes narrative use of diegetic music, notably Grieg's 'In the Hall of the Mountain King', which is obsessively whistled by the murderer. The piece had long been used in silent-film scores (for example, it accompanied the segment of Griffith's *The Birth of a Nation* (1915) showing the burning of Atlanta); but here it functions as much more than a glorified *agitato*: in addition to signalling the murderer's presence (off screen), its qualities of obstinate repetition and implacable menace become a chilling index of his compulsive yet childlike character; also, like an emblem of fate, it leads to his being recognized, caught, and destroyed. Moreover, Lang's film is filled with spiralling visual motifs that are matched by the very shape of the music. For these reasons it would be difficult to imagine a more effective musical 'score' for the film than this, though no composer was required to create it.

ANIMATED FILMS AND MUSICALS

Two Hollywood genres which did require major contributions from composers and abundant amounts of music were musicals and Disney's animated films; and they also gave rise to far-reaching developments in techniques of recording and (post-)synchronization. Cartoons needed virtually continuous music to bring the flat drawings to life, and, for the illusion to be sustained, had to be precisely synchronized from start to finish. So, too, did each musical number in a feature, and by the mid-1930s the common procedure was to record the number first, and then to film it using the 'playback' method, which enabled the actors to move freely about the set, or dance upon it, while mouthing the words. (Post-production 'dubbing' allowed for additional refinements to the process as necessary.) Thus, pioneers in both genres solved technological problems, while creating many films that display considerable artistry.

To Disney is due part of the credit for such small-scale masterpieces as *Skeleton Dance* (1928) and *Three Little Pigs* (1933); at least an equal amount should go to the men who composed their scores, Carl Stalling and Frank Churchill respectively. Both can be seen as prototypes for cartoon scores ever since: the former is a parody of silent-film music styles and links five distinct segments into a tightly organized whole, each containing symmetrical patterns suitable for dance; the latter is more loosely organized owing to the shape of the film's narrative, but is centred on the simple title song's verse and chorus tunes in a kind of free rondo structure. Being a more expansive score, the range of parody extends from nineteenth-century melodrama to opera and piano concerto, and, happily, such 'silly symphonies' have endured as another long-standing tradition of cartoon scores. Stalling came up with the 'Silly Symphony' label and was Disney's principal composer between 1928 and 1930; he proved even more inventive and witty at Warner Bros., where he was Music Director for cartoons from 1936 to 1958.

Hollywood musicals flourished from 1929 on. Although as mixed in musical idioms as cartoons (which often resembled musicals in miniature), they owed their musical essentials to Broadway, which supplied the Hollywood studios with a continual influx of performers, composers, arrangers, and conductors. As in Broadway shows, moreover, most songs in movie musicals followed two basic forms, which consisted of an introductory verse and a chorus of thirty-two bars in one of two patterns, either A A' or A A B A'. But most films had fewer numbers than Broadway shows: musical numbers on film carried more weight than their stage counterparts, and were often distributed less evenly. *Broadway Melody* (1929), for example, contains only two important songs ('Broadway Melody' and 'You Were Meant for Me', by Nacio Herb Brown and Arthur Freed), each representing a key theme of the narrative. The first is sung three times, the second only once. (Both, however, are heard at other points as underscoring.) What removed film musicals even further from their stage cousins was that each number was shaped by camera movement and cutting: as a result, the observer's point of view might shift freely, from distant views of the proscenium, to intimate close-ups, to overhead or even under-leg shots, as in the fantastic choreography of Busby Berkeley. Berkeley was one of the genre's three greatest founding figures, along with Fred Astaire, and Irving Berlin, whose songs display a perfect balance of lyric and musical expression.

Berlin's first and finest original film score was for *Top Hat* (1935), which brought him together with Astaire, in one of the most satisfying examples of the genre ever made. The plot's breezy style is consistent with the film's gentle satire of high-class speech, manners, and dress, and serves as a perfect backdrop for five skilfully constructed songs ('No Strings', 'Isn't this a Lovely Day', 'Top Hat', 'Cheek to Cheek', and 'The Piccolino'); of these the second and fourth, duets in dance, evoke the film's deepest feeling (especially the latter, one of Berlin's most unusually structured and passionate numbers, given stunning choreography). Unusually, the songs are spaced evenly through the film (one every ten to fifteen minutes), and at least the first four function beautifully to crystallize character and advance plot. What makes the score still more significant is that it is the result of a triple collaboration, between Berlin, Astaire, and Max Steiner as music director. *Top Hat* succeeds so well because the three men were perfectly matched in their ability to negotiate a range of idioms: Berlin bridged jazz and classical styles of melody and harmony, Astaire (co-choreographer with Hermes Pan) moved easily from vaudeville tap to ballet, and Steiner from the pit band to the symphony orchestra. Steiner, moreover, was one of the pioneers of synchronization techniques, and of the so-called background score, including those he had previously composed for such landmark RKO films as *King Kong* (1933) and *The Lost Patrol* (1934).

Composer Brian Easdale recording the music track of Michael Powell and Emeric Pressburger's *Black Narcissus* (1947) with the London Symphony Orchestra

STEINER, KORNGOLD, AND OTHERS

By the mid-1930s, music for Hollywood features occupied one of two contrasting positions: in the diegetic foreground (of musicals), or in the non-diegetic background (of all other films). In the one, the music came first into the production, or nearly so; in the other, it came last, at the end of the studio 'assembly line'.

Within this system, composers served as subordinates under contract to studio music departments, and faced serious constraints. For one thing, a feature usually required more than an hour of music, but time was almost always short—sometimes as little as three weeks—since the major studios turned out from thirty to fifty films a year. For another, the music was to be composed in short segments ('cues'), following detailed timing charts ('cue sheets'), and these were normally decided upon and prepared by someone other than the composer. Moreover, composers were usually assigned to films by the studio's

music director, who might ask for two or more to work on one film (sometimes simultaneously, sometimes in succession), the cues divided between them according to their specialities. (To save time, certain cues were recycled from film to film, as in accompaniments to silent films.) Finally, recording engineers (or music editors) presided over the final sound-track 'mix', whereby cues could be altered in volume, replaced, shortened, or eliminated altogether.

Offset against these unpleasant circumstances were various advantages for the composers, including financial security, a position in a circle of highly talented musicians, and the knowledge that their music would be heard by millions. Certain individuals throve within the system, because it was stable enough to allow them to gain abundant experience and polish their craft. Such was the case with Max Steiner (between 1936 and 1965 he was on the staff at Warners and composed about 185 scores), Alfred

Max Ophuls
(1902–1957)

Born in Saarbrücken, in western Germany, to a well-to-do Jewish family, the young Max Oppenheimer took the stage name Max Ophüls when he went to work in the theatre in 1919. On his Hollywood films his name is spelt Opuls (or Opals). On his French films it is Ophuls (without the *umlaut*), and this is the form he came to prefer and is also the one adopted by his son, the French documentarist Marcel Ophuls.

After ten years working all over Germany as (it would appear) a rather innovative theatre director, Ophuls came to Berlin in 1930, at the time of the introduction of sound, to begin a second career as a film-maker. In Berlin he made five films including *The Bartered Bride* (*Die verkaufte Braut*, 1932—from Smetana's opera, with Karl Valentin) and *Liebelei* (also 1932—from the play by Arthur Schnitzler). But in 1933 he fled Germany with his family, returning there only in 1954. In the 1930s he made films mainly in France, but also in Holland, and in Italy (*La signora di tutti*, 1934). In 1940 he was forced to flee again, this time to Hollywood. There he had great difficulty finding work, until in 1947 he was engaged by the actor Douglas Fairbanks, Jr., to make a swashbuckler, *The Exile*. John Houseman then took him on for *Letter from an Unknown Woman* (1948), adapted from the story by Stefan Zweig. After two more films in Hollywood—*Caught* (1948) and *The Reckless Moment* (1949)—he returned to Europe. He made three films in France—*La Ronde* (1950, another Schnitzler adaptation), *Le Plaisir* (1951, based on three stories by Maupassant), and *Madame de . . .* (1953). In 1954 he moved to Germany, where he made his last film, the sumptuous *Lola Montès* (1955); cut by the producers before release, it was cut further by its British distributors and released there as *The Fall of Lola Montes*.

Ophuls's films are almost all love stories, and in almost all of them love is thwarted, or impermanent, or brings disaster to one or both of the lovers. Though happy ends are few, the films are never depressing. This is due in the first place to the *mise-en-scène*. The camera glides smoothly through lavish décors, evoking a world of pleasure and risk-taking. This world is immensely seductive; characters are drawn on to the carousel and occasionally (and these are the characters Ophuls is most interested in) thrown off. Out of exuberance or weakness, or a mixture, characters make mistakes, often disastrous. But, whatever their flaws, neither the seducers nor the seduced are morally judged. There are no out-and-out villains or out-and-out heroes. Most of the focus is on the heroines, and Ophuls has been widely admired (though also disparaged) for his loving concentration on the psychology of women caught in doomed love affairs. What

has been less noticed is the acuteness of his portrayal of male psychology. The characters who bring destruction on others are mostly men, and all deeply narcissistic. Those who risk self-destruction—mostly women—do so because the object of their passion is, in the last analysis, deeply self-regarding and impervious to love. But the quest for love is always worth it. If there is moral judgement in Ophuls's films, it is that risks are worth taking, since it is only in risk that there is any possibility of fulfilment. On the whole it is the women who, because of their more precarious social position, run the greater risk. But Ophuls does not fix character within sex roles, and it can be either men (as in *Letter from an Unknown Woman*) or women (as in *La signora di tutti* or *Lola Montès*) whose self-regard or need for the regard of others brings disaster in its wake.

A recurring feature of Ophuls's films is the use of framing devices. Stories are told in flashback (*La signora di tutti*), or with the aid of on- or off-screen narrators (*La Ronde, Le Plaisir*), or using both devices. In *Letter from an Unknown Woman*, Lisa tells her story in voice-over. In *Lola Montès*, Lola's story is told as a series of flashbacks introduced by the circus master for whom she now performs. The characters' destiny is thus always already known to the audience. The character has already made the fatal mistake leading to destruction, or missed the moment when the mistake could have been averted. This gives the films an elegiac quality and a sense of loss and regret for the might-have-been, the pleasure aspired to but never enjoyed.

Ophuls was a consummate stylist. The flowing camerawork, the glittering surfaces, the superbly managed changes of mood, the care lavished on building up character through detail, all these have been widely (if grudgingly) admired. Seeing only the surface, socially minded critics have often dismissed Ophuls's work as trivial or unimportant. But Ophuls's films are not only beautiful to look at and psychologically acute, they also strike to the heart of a society in which beauty, pleasure, and self-fulfilment are in strict dependence on the contrasting values of wealth and power.

GEOFFREY NOWELL-SMITH

BIBLIOGRAPHY

Beylie, Claude (1984), *Max Ophuls*.
Willemen, Paul (ed.) (1978), *Ophuls*.
Williams, Alan (1980), *Max Ophüls and the Cinema of Desire*.

Opposite: Max Ophuls with Martine Carol on the set of *Lola Montès* (1955)

Newman (only about twenty complete scores, but a very productive career as conductor and music director at Fox), Franz Waxman (about sixty scores, first at Universal, later principally at Paramount), and Erich Korngold (a special figure at Warner Bros.). Each of them found imaginative ways to adapt Romantic idioms to the dictates of film scoring. This was in part due to their training and musical inclinations, in part a response to the demands of executives and the public; most importantly, their styles were well suited to a number of very good films.

Such is the case with Korngold's score for *The Adventures of Robin Hood* (1938), Newman's for *Wuthering Heights* (1939), Waxman's for *Rebecca* (1940), and Steiner's for *Casablanca* (1943), among many others. The Steiner and Korngold scores are two of the finest examples, and a highly instructive pair for comparison. Like virtually all other Romantic scores of the period, they have some fundamental stylistic elements in common, including lush orchestrations (Hugo Friedhofer, then one of the best arrangers at Warners, was assigned to do both), contrasting leitmotifs, and complex harmonic progressions and modulations. They also have some common functional procedures. For example, as can be seen in the diagram, the music for the opening of each film (the 'main title') reinforces the introductory credits with a series of distinct segments designed to indicate something about the setting and narrative; and each 'overture' continues into the film proper, moving the audience completely into the film's world:

Casablanca

WB logo	main title (credits)	music by M.S.	narration + montage	action
WB fanfare→	frenzied exotic dance→	'Marseilleise' (phrase)→	impassioned lament→	'Deutschland über Alles' (phrase)

Robin Hood

WB logo	main title (credits)	music by E.K.	narrative titles	1st shot
2-bar intro→	theme 1 ('Merry Men')→	theme 2 ('Danger')→	theme 3 ('Loyalty')→	fanfare = coda

Yet despite some evident parallels, the two main titles are enormously different in terms of musical material. In *Casablanca*, there is an underlying simplicity to each of Steiner's opening themes, the simplest being the two borrowed from familiar anthems (the 'Marseillaise' and 'Deutschland über Alles'), intended to symbolize the narrative struggle between the Nazis and their heroic opponents. These reappear as leitmotifs throughout the score, while the rest of the music, having served its function, is discarded. The remaining leitmotifs, four in all, are every bit as simple. Two are borrowed from other familiar songs: 'Watch on the Rhine', a second German tune transposed to a minor key, symbolizes the Nazi menace, and the opening phrase from 'As Time Goes by' serves as the theme of Rick and Ilsa's remembered love.

Two are Steiner originals: a warm hymn-like melody associated with Victor Laszlo, and a slowly descending fragment of a chromatic scale, threatening the lovers with doom. In short, all six themes use concise melodic material that is easily recognized and ideal for manipulation. By contrast, Korngold's score for *Robin Hood* contains at least eleven primary themes, all of them original and more elaborate than Steiner's. Of the three introduced in the main title, the first is a jaunty march of sixteen bars enlivened by some very unconventional harmonies and inner-voice counterpoint; the second sounds like the kind of distorted folk tune heard in symphonies by Mahler; and the third is a long-breathed Romantic melody that spans almost two octaves. Moreover, in the middle of this theme one hears a phrase that anticipates the beginning of the score's soaring love theme, which does not actually appear until much later in the film. Such thematic inter-

relationships and long-range transformations were favourite devices of Korngold, part of his interest in achieving complex musical structures. That interest is already evident in the shape of his main title. Like Steiner, his is through-composed, and ends with new material; but whereas Steiner's opening music gradually subsides under other elements of the sound-track, and ends by pausing in suspense in mid-phrase, Korngold's comes to a rousing close that fits the film with split-second precision. Indeed, he uses the pretext of the film's opening shot (with drummers signalling an announcement) to supply a thumping coda that both finishes the piece and launches us into the story via diegetic music.

Steiner had a genius for making his music move ahead in linear fashion from moment to moment. In the main title, for example, the links between the dance, the 'Marseillaise', and the subsequent lament are handled with

The Adventures of Robin Hood (1938): the climactic sword fight between Robin (Errol Flynn) and the evil Guy of Gisbourne (Basil Rathbone) is given added drama by Erich Korngold's score

exemplary smoothness. And a much more telling example occurs with the Paris flashback: the bridge from present to past—from the close-up of Rick in his darkened café, listening to Sam 'play it' (again), through a dissolve to a shot of the Arc de Triomphe in Paris, then to one of Rick and Ilse riding together in the French countryside—the sequence being accompanied by a fluid series of transformations of 'As Time Goes by', punctuated by a single phrase of the 'Marseillaise' when the arch comes into view. Without music the sequence, which includes some process shots that now appear quite crude, must seem utterly artificial; and for such reasons it became obligatory for Hollywood composers to supply music for all flashbacks and other special devices, such as voice-overs and newspaper montages. Here, the key point is that Steiner could do it so well, constructing this cue (and several others) with a theme not his own, and one that he claimed not to like. 'As Time Goes by' was a 1931 ballad by a minor Broadway composer, Herman Hupfeld, and, though Steiner asked if he could compose a love theme of his own for the score, his request was denied, if only because Hupfeld's song was written into the story.

Making a virtue of necessity, Steiner withholds the song from his score until after Ilse enters the café and asks Sam to sing it, 'for old time's sake'. But almost immediately after it *is* introduced, Steiner begins to use it frequently in a number of contrasting variations. These culminate in a passionate waltz, when the lovers say goodbye ('We'll always have Paris' . . . 'Here's looking at you, kid'), capped by a grandly tragic cadence. Yet the cadence does not hold, but melts instead into the next culminating segment of the score, based on other themes, most notably the 'Marseillaise'. As Rick and Renault walk off together into the fog, this song, in variations ethereal and triumphant, provides the film with a satisfying conclusion—and, as such, it precludes our worrying about the details of the plot, or the implausibly quick resolution. (It brings us back out of the film's world just as efficiently as the main title brought us in.) Thus, from beginning to end, Steiner's method is to subordinate his music to key aspects of the narrative, catching as many cinematic details as he can, often at the expense of coherent form. Indeed, at times his music follows a film's action so literally (in the manner of a score for a cartoon) that the style has been described with the derogatory term 'Mickey-Mousing'. All the same, Steiner's scores often move us deeply; just as the writers of *Casablanca* understood that we can be overwhelmed by nostalgia when we hear certain songs from our past (no matter whether they are actually any good), so Steiner knew that very simple themes, skilfully connected and repeated in deft transformations, could work both intellectually and subliminally on an audience, and make the melodramatic convincing.

Like Steiner, Korngold made every effort to achieve parallels between musical and cinematic details, but he also sought to create film scores as rich in substance as a symphony or an opera. Moreover, because he was a special figure at Warner Bros.—treated as a European master, who brought the studio prestige—he was required to compose no more than two scores a year. He worked at each score for many months, sitting at the piano and playing segments repeatedly while he watched the film over and over; and the results could be dazzling in their harmonic richness and contrapuntal splendour, as in his music for the scenes of the archery tournament and coronation procession in *Robin Hood*. These are the score's great set pieces (coming amid others almost as worthy, including the dance music that emulates old English styles for the scene of the banquet at Nottingham castle). If they are surpassed, it is only by the score's ending, which offers a gorgeous series of modulations and transformations of Robin Hood's theme (in its third, noblest version), culminating in a truly Romantic apotheosis, whereby melody and harmony come together to suggest both trumpet fanfares and the glorious pealing of wedding bells. *Robin Hood* is as entertaining a fantasy as Hollywood knew how to make, and no other music could do more to enhance the pleasure it provides. The scores of 'classical' Hollywood cinema—films of the studio era, of which *Robin Hood* qualifies as a prime example—must be heard as a brilliant descendant of the 'romantic' century's musical art.

NEW TENDENCIES TO 1960

Even in the early 1940s, however, some composers were undermining the established form of Hollywood scoring. In a lucid essay published in 1941, Aaron Copland questioned the need for film composers to be restricted to a nineteenth-century symphonic style. A sympathetic outsider, Copland visited Hollywood periodically and produced important scores for four major independent films: *Of Mice and Men* (1939), *Our Town* (1940), *The Red Pony* (1948), and *The Heiress* (1949). In all of them he wrote in his own distinctively modern idiom, without benefit of leitmotifs. Yet this did not seem to diminish his influence in or out of Hollywood; in fact in 1949 he was awarded both a Pulitzer Prize for his *Red Pony Suite*, and an Academy Award for his score for *The Heiress*.

Copland's case is roughly parallel to that of three other composers active during the same period: Virgil Thomson (also a lucid essayist on film music), Sergei Prokofiev, and William Walton. Like Copland, each of them had undergone rigorous classical training that led to careers primarily as concert composers; and each developed an idiosyncratic style that was considered conservative for its use of tonality and (neo-)classical forms, nationalistic for its use of native tunes, and modernistic in terms of harmony, orchestration, and emotional tone. As for their film scores, each is best known for a handful written in

Marilyn Monroe

(1926–1962)

Born Norma Jean Mortenson on 1 June 1926 in Los Angeles, Marilyn Monroe spent her childhood in a succession of foster homes and orphanages. She never knew her father, and her mother was committed to a mental institution when Norma Jean was 5. At 16 she left school to marry. It was while working in a defence plant in 1944 that she was discovered by an army photographer, and became a model and pin-up. Two years later she realised her childhood ambition by signing a movie contract, with Twentieth Century–Fox. She dyed her hair blonde, and changed her name to Marilyn Monroe.

Competition was fierce for even the smallest film roles, but Monroe exhibited great determination to succeed, turning up at the studio even when not assigned to a film, and paying for her own acting tuition. Over the next four years she did have numerous walk-on roles, as the 'blonde girl', but it was in *The Asphalt Jungle* (1950) that her progression from model to actress was revealed. She played the part of the bent lawyer's mistress, and in a few minutes of screen time delivered a detailed characterization of a naïve and trapped woman.

In 1953 three films were released that raised Monroe to stardom, and which remain among her most popular; *Niagara*, *Gentlemen Prefer Blondes*, and *How to Marry a Millionaire*. Her physique, her wiggle, and her breathless, sensual voice established her as Hollywood's biggest blonde bombshell, although the latter two films allowed Monroe to demonstrate her comic talent, and reveal the complexity of her erotic image. The female sexuality that Monroe embodies and celebrates is raised to the level of cliché, and made the subject of humour. However, Monroe's own enjoyment of her body and its effects is essentially guileless and guiltless, and so her exaggerated sexuality appears disarmingly natural. Humour lies in this gap between the effect she has on men, and her own lack of awareness of this effect. Unlike her many later imitators she managed to appear totally erotic, and yet innocent at the same time. Monroe's appeal lies in the ability to unify these contradictions, and to naturalize and purify a constructed vision of female sexuality, until she became, as Lee Strasberg said at her funeral, 'for the entire world . . . a symbol of the eternal female'.

Gentlemen Prefer Blondes (directed by Howard Hawks) contradicts the dominant Monroe image that was developing through her films and studio publicity. As Lorelei Lee she is, for once, in control of her sexuality, using it to get what she wants; a millionaire for a husband. This makes her powerful, and therefore threatening. This aggressive sexuality, and the strength of the film's central female friendship, provide a contrast to Monroe's later roles, where her pure and passive femininity are inevitably linked to fragility and victimhood.

By the première of *How to Marry a Millionaire* in November 1953, critics and audiences were focusing on Mon-

roe, rather than her co-stars, Bacall and Grable. She was Fox's biggest star, and continued to develop sexual-comedy roles for the studio. The material was not always up to her talent, but like Garbo she had a presence on screen that made poor films worth watching. Monroe, however, was increasingly unhappy with the scripts she was offered, and was keen to develop her acting in more demanding and varied roles. In 1954 she withdrew to New York to work at the Actors Studio with Lee Strasberg. Her 'pretensions' were derided by critics at the time; the same commentators who dismissed her famous witticisms as unconscious refused to see any evidence of talent in her screen performances. There is still controversy today about her abilities as an actress. The reason her talent is not recognized is, ironically, the same reason why she continues to fascinate audiences; her ability to ap-

pear totally natural on screen. As McCann (1988) said, 'she succeeded in stripping away the top layer of personality, encouraging us to believe that we were seeing through to some essential quality of love or loneliness, pleasure or pain'. The screen seems to give us direct access to her as Monroe, even as she gives life to her characters. It is debatable to what extent this could be learnt. Monroe's rigorous training in the Strasberg method, using her own experiences, particularly of her childhood, in her acting, probably adds to the exposed quality of the emotion that can be seen in her later films.

Bus Stop (1956), her first film on her return to Hollywood, silenced many critics' doubts about her acting talents. In the role of Cherie, the down-at-heel night-club singer, she delivered a subtle performance that combined sexuality, comedy, and pathos, and which led the director, Joshua Logan, to proclaim her 'as near genius as any actor I ever knew'.

However, from this point on Monroe's career began to be soured by a reputation as unreliable, and by illness and personal problems played out in the glare of media attention. She struggled through the production of *Some Like it Hot* (1959), and produced a touching comic performance as Sugar. A singer with an all-girl band, she falls in love with the penniless Tony Curtis, who is masquerading as a millionaire. The opposite of Lorelei Lee, Sugar is an emotionally vulnerable woman; her attempts to find a rich husband are appealing but unsuccessful, and she is herself the victim of scheming and trickery.

Monroe's death of a drug overdose in August 1962, weeks after being fired from the set of *Something's Got to Give*, sealed her status as a screen legend. She would remain young and beautiful forever, and her star persona was fixed as the tragic victim who could not cope with her own stardom. More than thirty years after her death Marilyn Monroe's image is everywhere, and her legend is as powerful as ever. Even more than with other stars, there is an obsession to understand and possess the 'real Marilyn', but every true story of her life, or new revelation about her death, only add to the layers of her myth. Ultimate screen goddess and apotheosis of Hollywood stardom, it seems fitting that Monroe and the studio system expired together.

KATE BEETHAM

SELECT FILMOGRAPHY

The Asphalt Jungle (1950); All about Eve (1950); Niagara (1953); Gentlemen Prefer Blondes (1953); How to Marry a Millionaire (1953); River of no Return (1954); There's no Business like Show Business (1954); The Seven Year Itch (1955); Bus Stop (1956); The Prince and the Showgirl (1957); Some Like it Hot (1959); Let's Make Love (1960); The Misfits (1961)

BIBLIOGRAPHY

McCann, Graham (1988), *Marilyn Monroe*.
Spoto, Donald (1993), *Marilyn Monroe. The Biography*.

Opposite: Marilyn Monroe entertaining U.S. troops in Korea in 1954. She was later to describe this as the most important work of her life.

close collaboration with special directors (Copland with Milestone, Prokofiev with Eisenstein, Thomson with Lorentz and Flaherty, Walton with Olivier); finally and most importantly, each reshaped his music into concert works that have become staples of the modern repertory. Thomson was the first to do so, creating suites for both *The Plow that Broke the Plains* and *The River* (documentaries released in 1936 and 1937); and he, too, received the Pulitzer Prize, a year before Copland, for his orchestral suite from *Louisiana Story*. Prokofiev's Cantata from *Alexander Nevsky* (1938) is probably the most widely performed of these works; indeed, on several recent occasions the original version has even been presented like a silent-film score, in live accompaniment to screenings of the film. (One reason for this is that the sound-track of the film suffers from the inferior state of Soviet recording technology at that time; another is that, except for the music, most of Eisenstein's epic *is* silent, the spoken lines and sound effects being sparse.) Recordings of suites from Walton's scores for Olivier's three main Shakespeare films—*Henry V* in 1944, *Hamlet* in 1948, and *Richard III* in 1955—are numerous: particularly of *Henry V*, for which there exist multiple versions, reflecting the extensive scope and vitality of the score. The *Nevsky* and *Henry V* scores rank among the greatest for sound films, and are emblematic of the privileged position given to film music by important directors outside Hollywood. Eisenstein wrote more than once about the give and take of his working relationship with Prokofiev, and described occasions when he re-edited sequences so as to adjust them to the music. Probably the most celebrated example is the 'battle on the ice' from *Nevsky*, and one sign of its impact is that it was closely imitated by Olivier and Walton when creating the Battle of Agincourt for *Henry V*. Of equal importance is the way Eisenstein honoured Prokofiev in an analytical essay devoted entirely to the opening of this scene: though problematic, it offers us the first careful study of detailed relationships between music and the filmed image. Such relationships may also be observed in *Henry V* right from the start: a flute solo accompanies the first shot of a fluttering playbill, solemn choral music is heard as the camera pans over a model of London up to the Globe theatre, a march with an Elizabethan flavour represents the 'Overture' being performed by the gallery musicians inside. Overall, the effect is one of great originality: though full of allusions to traditional English music, the score sounds modern, and appropriate for this innovative treatment of Shakespeare. Olivier's gratitude to the composer is evident at the film's end: accompanied by an all-stops-out choral arrangement of the Agincourt carol, the credits scroll by and culminate with these words: 'Music | by | William | Walton | Conducted by | Muir Mathieson | Played by | The London Symphony.' Thus was enshrined a composer who had participated in a lavish patriotic effort in wartime, and who, taking his cue from Prokofiev, treated the project like cinematic opera (with frequent vocal music by performers off screen). The nationalistic and epic qualities of these films may date them somewhat; but their innovative treatment of music remains fresh.

INNOVATION INSIDE AND OUTSIDE HOLLYWOOD

In the 1940s and 1950s, many other influential directors outside Hollywood likewise sought to transcend the clichés of 'movie music' in a number of ways. Perhaps the most radical was to dispense with it as much as possible; in several films by Buñuel and Bergman, for example, the absence of music contributes to the general desolation. Another was to use very simple music for soloist(s), an effective means of saving money, and either suggesting a particular locale or providing a poignant atmosphere. Two of the films best known for this approach are *The Third Man* (1949), scored entirely with zither solos by Anton Karas, and *Jeux interdits* (1952), with haunting guitar music by Narciso Yepes. Some directors took an alternative route to the same destination by introducing quotations from a single piece in the classical repertoire (following Lang's method in *M*): though this practice became more common after 1960 than before, one finds important instances in every decade, including such divergent films as *Brief Encounter* (1945) and *Un condamné à mort s'est échappé* (*A Man Escaped*, 1956), which feature Rachmaninov's Second Piano Concerto and Mozart's Mass in C Minor respectively. Still, most directors continued to depend on living composers for large amounts of music. If these scores seem to differ in style or function from the norms of Hollywood, the reason is that the film *auteurs* had direct control of their work, trust in their composers (often sustained through collaborations of long standing), and an appreciation for new musical styles. Examples abound in the films of Powell and Pressburger, Mackendrick (and other directors of Ealing comedies), Ophuls, Fellini, Wajda, and Mizoguchi: all made great films during these decades, and all deserve attention for their sensitivity to the power of music as a crucial component of innovative cinema.

So, too, do Welles, Preminger, Wilder, Hitchcock, Wyler, and Sturges, among others: directors of great films *within* Hollywood in the 1940s, they favoured composers who were willing to take risks and scores that challenged prevailing styles. Thus, for example, Welles brought Bernard Herrmann from New York to RKO to score *Citizen Kane* (1941), as part of his Mercury Theatre team; and, like the film, his score abounds in brilliant ideas, especially impressive from someone scoring a film for the first time. Another brilliant first occurred when Preminger gave David Raksin, until then mainly a staff arranger at Fox, the opportunity to write the score for *Laura* (1944). Wilder

and Hitchcock, with Selznick their producer, brought Miklós Rózsa to *Double Indemnity* (1944) and *Spellbound* (1945), thus launching him on a new career as a master of contemporary psychological drama and film noir. Wyler took a chance on Friedhofer, at that time employed mostly as an orchestrator; and, as a result, *The Best Years of our Lives* (1946) was given one of Hollywood's most perfect scores, very much in the Copland manner. Finally, Sturges—this time with Newman himself as both conductor and composer—brought off *Unfaithfully Yours*, in which Rossini, Wagner, and Tchaikovsky are parodied with great wit. Moreover, the comedy is brilliantly self-reflexive, and subtly makes a point about the purposes of 'movie music'. Blurring distinctions between the diegesis and the external, the film demonstrates, in its presentation of dreams 'conducted' by music, that the latter has the power to control our imagination and to make even the most outlandish fantasy seem real.

The power of fantasy, and self-reflexiveness, also contribute to the substance and style of Wilder's *Sunset Boulevard* (1950), a film which signals the growing appeal of modernism in the 1950s, with important consequences for music. Most of Waxman's score for *Sunset Boulevard* is wonderfully subtle. Particularly effective is the music which accompanies the scene near the end when Joe Gillis attempts to walk out on Norma Desmond and is murdered. Waxman composed a repeat of music from the main title, commencing with the D minor 'Fate Theme' (his own label). But, unlike the strident original, here the music is barely audible and proceeds in 'slow motion' throughout, the effect being unsettling, seeming to suggest that Joe is trapped in a dream without knowing it. For the film's climaxes—especially at the end, as Norma descends into madness—Waxman shifts to deliberately intrusive music, with exaggerated power, first with a deliberate parody of Strauss's *Salomé*, finally with a shockingly abrupt close in a surprise major key. This is music in the expressionist style, which had its roots in film noir scores of the 1940s and which thereafter flourished in numerous dark American 'problem films'.

By 1950, even in Hollywood, the traditional Romantic styles no longer exclusively occupied centre stage; and developments such as the breakup of the studio theatre chains, the steady growth of independent productions, the introduction of widescreen processes, and the parallel adoption of stereophonic sound and magnetic tracks did much to broaden the range of available styles. New styles came into play, alongside the tried and tested: a brilliant new series of musicals (from MGM), atonal music, jazz idioms, 'authentic' modal styles for biblical epics, and folk-like ballads for Westerns. Yet no matter what the idiom, the 1950s were definitely the 'golden age' of the Hollywood symphonic score: Steiner, Newman, Waxman, and other elder statesmen continued to compose alongside their younger colleagues, among them André Previn, Alex North, Leonard Rosenman, Elmer Bernstein, and Henry Mancini, all of whom began their careers during this decade.

To crown these lists, it is both chronologically fitting and aesthetically crucial to remember the collaboration of Alfred Hitchcock and Bernard Herrmann, which began with *The Man who Knew Too Much* in 1955 and ended eleven years later amid the ruins of the rejected score for *Torn Curtain*. In between, from 1958 to 1960, came the peaks of achievement for director and composer, in *Vertigo*, *North by Northwest*, and *Psycho*. Here were three symphonic scores unmistakably by Herrmann, but stylistically worlds apart. In succession they offer an intensely Romantic tragedy reminiscent of Wagner's *Tristan*, exuberantly comic dance music with fantastic rhythmic drive, and a disturbingly complex and modernistic score for string orchestra alone. All three continue to fascinate because they begin with dazzling 'overtures' to Saul Bass titles, because the music develops continuously through the films in fascinating structures, and because the scores provide psychological depth and passion as a balance to Hitchcock's tendency

toward voyeuristic detachment. The balance is a delicate one indeed, of a sort rare in film music's history, and ought to remind us of Herrmann's remark (which he in turn attributes to Cocteau) that in a good film score 'one is not aware whether the music is making the film go forward or whether the film is pushing the music forward'. This maxim may well serve to guide us as we push forward into film music's future.

Bibliography
Copland, Aaron (1941), *Our New Music*.
Eisenstein, Sergei (1992), *Towards a Theory of Montage*.
Gorbman, Claudia (1987), *Unheard Melodies*.
Kalinak, Kathryn (1992), *Settling the Score: Music and the Classical Hollywood Film*.
Karlin, Fred (1994), *Listening to Movies: The Film Lover's Guide to Film Music*.
Palmer, Christopher (1990), *The Composer in Hollywood*.
Prendergast, Roy M. (1992), *Film Music, a Neglected Art: A Critical Study of Music in Films*.
Thomas, Tony (1991), *Film Score: The Art and Craft of Movie Music*.
Thomson, Virgil (1932), 'A Little about Movie Music'.

Technology and Innovation

JOHN BELTON

The transition to sound at the end of the 1920s initiated a transformation in basic motion picture technology that extended beyond the unique innovation of sound itself. The sound revolution set in motion a series of other experiments in the area of motion picture presentation. These experiments would ultimately lead to a second major technological revolution in the 1950s, to the introduction of widescreen movies, filmed in colour and recorded in stereophonic, magnetic sound. Of course, colour had been in more or less continuous use for filming spectacles throughout the 1930s and 1940s. However, the number of colour films made during this period remained quite small, and it was not until the 1950s that colour was extensively used by the entire film industry.

Indeed, what remains so fascinating about this 'second' technological revolution is how long it took to occur. Given that its origins lay in the late 1920s, why was its full realization delayed until the 1950s? The transition to sound took place in less than four years, but the shift to widescreen and colour, as new standards for production and exhibition, did not occur for over twenty years. All three inventions had been adequately innovated by the early to mid-1930s to permit their adoption by the motion picture industry, but the first widescreen revolution had

already failed by the end of 1930 and colour film-making, which found use in only a handful of films each year, emerged during the 1930s and 1940s as a minor variation on the norm of black and white.

The 1930–60 period also witnessed a number of other major technological developments, such as the innovation of deep focus cinematography and the shift from nitrate-based to acetate-based film stock, as well as several minor ones, such as the advent of the zoom lens and 3-D. Ironically, all of these techniques and technologies also trace their origins back to the 1920s and early 1930s, though only the zoom and 3-D exploit a similar principle of novelty to that which drove the development of sound, colour, and widescreen.

THE TRANSITIONAL PERIOD

Since their inception in the 1890s, motion pictures have routinely been part of a larger entertainment programme which featured other attractions, such as live stage shows. In the late 1910s and 1920s, movie palaces included live prologues, comedy acts, dancers, and singers. Films were accompanied by orchestras or organists, which also performed separately in individually billed 'concerts.' Early sound films, especially Warner Bros.' Vitaphone shorts, which presented popular vaudeville routines, and Fox's Movietone newsreels, which headlined topical events or well-known personalities, served to duplicate the attractions featured by vaudeville theatres and movie palaces for playback in the average neighbourhood theatre.

Even the first full-length sound films drew upon this mode of presentation, introducing sound segments or 'acts' into otherwise silent narratives. *The Jazz Singer* (1927), for example, intersperses short synchronous dialogue and song sequences with long stretches of musically underscored, melodramatic action that is essentially 'silent'. Much of the thrill of these early films came from the sudden and dramatic switch from silence to sound. Even today, these shifts to sound function as a kind of spectacle, foregrounding the medium of sound, while the reversions to silence behave as anti-climactic interruptions of the spectacle.

This concept of spectacle in presentation informs the experimentation that takes place with new technologies other than sound. Widescreen and large-screen projection of the period regularly drew upon sensational alterations in image size. Thus Abel Gance's *Napoléon* (1927), which was partially filmed in Polyvision, expands at climactic moments of the narrative from one-screen to three-screen projection, tripling the width of the projected image. Gance filmed certain sequences with three interlocked 35 mm. cameras, which were mounted side by side and which recorded a panoramic view on three separate strips of film. In other sequences, Gance juxtaposed the central image with different flanking images, creating a mosaic of separate shots across the surface of the three screens.

At around the same time, Paramount experimented with a new projection process called Magnascope. Magnascope involved the use of a special, wide-angle projection lens, which magnified the image, blowing it up in projection from a standard 15- by 20-foot screen size to an overwhelming 30- by 40- foot dimension. In December 1926 the Rivoli Theatre used the Magnascope lens to project two sequences of the silent naval epic *Old Ironsides*. As with Polyvision, the sense of spectacle depended, in large part, on the abrupt and quite striking enlargement of the projected image.

COLOUR

By the same token, early experiments in colour cinematography resulted in the production of both colour sequences in black and white features, and colour shorts, reinforcing the notion of the new technology as a novelty. Between 1926 and 1932, over thirty films were made which included one or more colour sequences. The majority of these sequences were musical numbers, such as those in *The Broadway Melody* (1929), *The Desert Song* (1929), and *King of Jazz* (1930); fashion shows, as in *Irene* (1926); ceremonial

displays, such as the military procession in *The Wedding March* (1928); and action sequences, such as aerial combat footage in *Hell's Angels* (1930).

Walt Disney enjoyed the exclusive rights to make animated films in Technicolor from 1932 to 1935, producing Academy Award winning shorts such as *Flowers and Trees* (1932) and *The Three Little Pigs* (1933). In 1933 Pioneer Productions, which owned stock in Technicolor, began to make films in colour, commencing with *La Cucaracha*, a live-action, three-colour film which won an Academy Award for Best Comedy Short Subject.

Filming was accomplished with a special camera, containing a beam-splitting prism behind the lens. The beam-splitter directed part of the light which entered the lens to the left, where it passed through an aperture on to two strips of film held together (emulsion to emulsion) in a bi-pack. The front film of the bi-pack recorded blue information; the back film recorded red. The remainder of the light passed directly through the lens to a green-sensitive negative at the rear of the camera. In this way, each negative recorded the black and white record of a different colour and could be used, together with the other two, to reconstruct the original colour of the scene that had been filmed.

By the mid-1930s, colour as a novelty had given way somewhat to more normative patterns of colour usage. Black and white films no longer featured colour sequences, though occasional transitions from black and white to colour, as in *The Wizard of Oz* (1939), continued to function as signifiers of spectacle and fantasy. Indeed, the majority of colour films tended to be animated films (*Snow White and the Seven Dwarfs*, 1938), musicals (*The Goldwyn Follies*, 1938), Westerns (*Ramona*, 1936; *Trail of the Lonesome Pine*, 1936), and costume pictures and/or epics (*Becky Sharp*, 1935; *The Adventures of Robin Hood*, 1938; *Gone with the Wind*, 1939).

By 1929 a similar attempt to provide a more uniform usage of widescreen had also been introduced in the form of various wide film processes, such as Grandeur, Realife, Vitascope, Magnafilm, and Natural Vision. Magnascope merely enlarged standard 35 mm. film, making the granular structure of the image increasingly visible. However, these other widescreen processes relied on wide film, ranging from 56 mm. (Magnafilm) to 65 mm. (Grandeur), which provided a better image when projected on a large screen in the theatre. Unlike colour, however, wide film quickly disappeared, largely because it involved tremendous costs on the part of exhibitors, who would be required to install new projectors and screens, and because its use was restricted to a small number of urban movie palaces which could accommodate it without an extensive and costly redesign of their theatres. Whatever funds exhibitors had for capital improvement had already been spent on the installation of new sound equipment;

Early sound technology: the Vitaphone sound studio, showing the camera in its soundproof box, or 'blimp'

few could afford the additional costs of widescreen technology.

The appearance of colour and widescreen during the transition-to-sound period stems not only from that era's interest in novel forms of presentation in the theatre but from technological considerations as well. Prior to sound, colour was frequently achieved on the screen by tinting and toning motion pictures. Tinting involved immersing the entire film or parts of the film in a dye bath to give it a single colour cast; night scenes would routinely be tinted blue, day scenes yellow, sunsets yellow-orange, and so forth. Toning enabled film-makers to add a second colour to the original tint. It relied on chemicals which interacted with the silver content of the image itself, resulting in a change of colour. However, both of these processes affected black and white optical sound-tracks adversely, interfering with their ability to transmit sound information which was optically encoded alongside the image. Tinting and toning posed particular problems for variable density sound-tracks, which relied on subtle variations in the blackness of the sound-track to control its amplitude.

Technicolor's two- and three-colour processes solved this problem, relying on a printing process that preserved the integrity of the original black and white sound-track information. Technicolor used separate black and white negatives—one for each colour record—to produce matrices, or relief images similar to printing blocks or rubber stamps. Each of these matrices was dipped in a different colour dye and was then used to transfer this dye on to blank film stock bearing the black and white sound-track. This process was known as 'imbibition' (or IB) printing because the blank film stock 'drank up' the colour dyes; it was also referred to as the 'dye transfer' process.

The addition of an optical sound-track alongside the film image also prompted experimentation with wide film. The addition of a sound-track diminished the space on the film left for image information. When this reduced image area was blown up to fill the standard theatre screen, the quality of the projected image suffered from increased grain, much as in the Magnascope process. One solution to this problem lay in wide film, which dramatically expanded the area occupied by image

Gregg Toland
(1904–1948)

Perhaps the most important of all Hollywood cinematographers during the classical era, Gregg Toland was certainly among the most influential and innovative. He was the only Hollywood cameraman to be associated with his own distinctive photographic 'style' and his innovative camera work was a crucial factor, perhaps the crucial factor, in the development of the highly stylized realism that emerged during the peak years of Hollywood's golden age just prior to the Second World War.

Gregg Toland was a 'boy wonder'. Born on 24 May 1904 in Charleston, Illinois, Toland broke into films at age 15 as an office boy, and within a year was working as an assistant cameraman. At 22 he became an assistant to cinematographer George Barnes, who served as his mentor for several years, and by 27 Toland was the youngest 'first cameraman' in Hollywood. He was admitted to the American Society of Cinematographers (ASC) in 1934 at 30, and by then was widely recognized as one of Hollywood's most efficient and innovative cameramen, a supreme technician who was equally adept at dealing with practical, technological, and artistic challenges.

The key figure in Toland's career was independent producer Sam Goldwyn, for whom he shot a total of thirty-seven pictures in the 1930s and 1940s, most of them 'prestige' projects involving top film-making talent. Goldwyn had Toland under contract during most of this period, and allowed him considerable creative freedom, funding his technical research and experiments with different lights, lenses, lens coatings, and so on. He also enabled Toland to maintain his own photographic 'unit', including camera assistants and equipment.

Most important, perhaps, Toland's relationship with Goldwyn enabled him to work regularly with William Wyler, with whom he collaborated on *These Three* (1936), *Come and Get it* (1936), *Dead End* (1937), *Wuthering Heights* (1939, for which he received an Oscar), *The Westerner* (1940), *The Little Foxes* (1941), and *The Best Years of our Lives* (1946). It was in his work with Wyler in the late 1930s that Toland began to develop his style, working systematically with compositions in depth, multiple planes of action, 'ceiled' sets (interiors with the ceiling visible), and chiaroscuro lighting (pools of light illuminating portions of an otherwise dark set). This required extensive experimentation with 'faster' film stock, innovative lighting techniques, and camera lenses capable of maintaining a huge focus range.

Toland further refined his distinctive photographic style in two films for John Ford, *The Grapes of Wrath* (1940) and *The Long Voyage Home* (1940), but it is on *Citizen Kane* (1941) that the Toland style is most pronounced, most systematically and effectively employed, and most widely recognized. Although he had been refining his methods in the films with Wyler and Ford, Toland had yet satisfactorily to combine his technical and stylistic interests within a single picture. He saw *Citizen Kane* as a chance to experiment on a large scale. In a June 1941 article in *Popular Photography* entitled 'How I Broke the Rules on Citizen Kane', Toland related that 'the photographic approach . . . was planned and considered long before the first camera turned', which was itself 'most unconventional in Hollywood', where cinematographers generally have only a few days to prepare to shoot a film. Robert L. Carringer, in his in-depth study of the production, writes that Welles and Toland 'approached the film together in a spirit of revolutionary fervor', and that 'Welles not only

encouraged Toland to experiment and tinker, he positively insisted on it'.

Toland continued to innovate in order to accomplish the particular effects that Welles was after; the long takes from a fixed camera position, with the drama played out on multiple planes of action and in separately lit areas of the massive sets. He used arc lights rather than incandescents to achieve the chiaroscuro effects, and used lens coatings to eliminate glare under difficult lighting conditions. Realizing how unorthodox their conception of the 'look' and the story-telling approach to *Kane* was, Welles and Toland actually passed off the first days of shooting as photographic 'tests'.

While Toland received an Oscar nomination for *Kane*, the association with Welles and the film's aggressively unorthodox visual style led to suggestions that Toland's work was perhaps too eccentric—that, along with Welles, he had upset the delicate balance in commercial cinema between individual artistry and self-effacing professionalism. A subsequent pre-war effort with Wyler on *The Little Foxes* (1941) reasserted that balance, however, further consolidating the Toland style while also displaying its flexibility. (At the film's climactic moment Herbert Marshall's character dies of a heart attack in the background while Bette Davis's character, in the foreground, does nothing to intercede. The composition is a consummate 'Toland shot' with one notable adjustment: Marshall's figure is slightly *out of focus*.)

With the outbreak of the Second World War, Toland accompanied John Ford to the South Pacific for a tour of duty in the navy's Field Photographic Branch. He shot numerous wartime documentaries, including *December 7th*, a collaboration with Ford which received the Oscar for best documentary of 1943. After the war Toland went back to work with Goldwyn, most notably with Wyler on *The Best Years of our Lives* (1946). Wyler also had done documentary work during the war, and that initial post-war collaboration with Toland indicated something of a shift to a more documentary-style realism. Toland had little opportunity to refine his photographic style in post-war Hollywood, however. In September 1948 he died of a heart attack, aged 44.

THOMAS SCHATZ

SELECT FILMOGRAPHY

These Three (1936); Come and Get It (1936); Dead End (1937); Wuthering Heights (1939); Intermezzo (1939); The Westerner (1940); The Grapes of Wrath (1940); The Long Voyage Home (1940); The Little Foxes (1941); Citizen Kane (1941); The Best Years of our Lives (1946)

BIBLIOGRAPHY

Berg, Scott A. (1989), *Goldwyn*.
Carringer, Robert L. (1985), *The Making of Citizen Kane*.
Higham, Charles (1970), *Hollywood Cameramen: Sources of Light*.
Toland, Gregg (1941), 'Realism for "Citizen Kane".'
Turner, George (1991), 'Xanadu in Review: "Citizen Kane" Turns 50'.

Opposite: A scene from *Citizen Kane* (1941), illustrating Gregg Toland's mastery of deep focus and composition in depth

information and which thereby increased the sharpness and resolution of the projected image.

Novel notions of the movie-going experience as a 'montage of attractions' explain, in part, the experimentation with 3-D systems in the 1920s and 1930s. The Plastigram (1921) and Plasticon (1922) processes, as well as MGM's Audioscopiks (1938), all relied on anaglyphic 3-D techniques. Anaglyphic 3-D employed two images—a right-eye and a left-eye perspective—which were photographed through filters of different colours and then projected in the theatre through those same filters. The filters coded the two different views and spectators wore eyeglasses fitted with the same two filters which decoded them, restoring right-eye and left-eye views of the original scene.

THE ZOOM LENS

Sensationalism also governed the usage of the first zoom lenses, which appeared in the transition-to-sound period in films such as *It* (1927) and *The Four Feathers* (1929). The zoom or vari-focal lens possesses the ability to move through a variety of different focal lengths from the wide-angle to the telephoto range. This purely optical movement produces an enlargement or diminution of the contents of the image similar to that achieved by the physical movement of the camera forwards or backwards but does so without any actual movement of the camera itself. Early zoom shots, such as those accomplished with the Cooke Varo lens, which was introduced by the British optical firm Taylor & Hobson in 1932, tend to exploit the technology, rapidly zooming in or out in such a way as to call attention to the sudden transformation of the size of objects within the frame. Thus in *American Madness* (1932) the camera quickly zooms in on a clock as it is struck by a bullet; and in *Thunder Below* (1932) a zoom simulates the point of view (and rapid rate of descent) of a woman as she falls from a cliff to the rocks below.

A modern zoom lens was introduced in the post-war era. In the early zoom lenses, the various optical elements were moved in relation to one another mechanically by means of a series of cams, operated by a crank. In 1946 Dr Frank Back marketed the Zoomar lens for 16 mm. cameras. Unlike the earlier zooms, the Zoomar had no cams or cranks; it was entirely optical in design. And unlike earlier lenses, which necessitated a change in the lens aperture each time there was a change in focal length, the aperture of the Zoomar, which was placed behind all the movable elements of the lens, required no change during shots, thus simplifying the operation of the lens. The Zoomar found immediate use in the television industry and in newsreels where it facilitated the coverage of sporting events. It was not employed extensively in the film industry until the 1960s, when zoom lenses produced in the late 1950s by two French manufacturers, SOM-Berthiot/Pan-

Cinor and Angénieux, enjoyed a more widespread adoption.

With the exception of colour, all of these transition-to-sound technologies disappeared in the 1930s—largely because there was no demand for them from audiences, who had abandoned their penchant for novel spectacularizations of the film medium, in favour of the film message. Fascination with form gave way to concern for content—that is, for the films themselves. In other words, movie-going had become more or less habitual; audiences came to theatres on a regular basis to see their favourite performers in new story situations; it was no longer necessary to lure spectators into the theatres with new forms of motion picture exhibition.

DEEP FOCUS

The chief technological innovation during the 1930s was the development of deep focus cinematography. Deep focus involved the expansion of depth of field, resulting in images that maintained sharp focus from objects in the extreme foreground to those in the distant background. Deep focus was achieved by filming with extremely wide-angled lenses whose apertures had been stopped down. This sort of cinematography was made possible by a variety of developments in related fields of film technology.

Filming in the Technicolor process required greater illumination than did black and white cinematography, leading to the creation of a new, more powerful carbon arc lamp, which was subsequently adopted for filming in black and white. These new lights permitted cameramen to decrease the aperture of existing wide-angle lenses and thus obtain a sharp, deep focus image.

At the same time, improvements in the speed of black and white film stock made it possible to secure adequate exposure with a smaller lens aperture. In competition with German manufacturers, such as Agfa–Ansco, Eastman Kodak increased the speed of its standard, fine-grain, panchromatic Eastman negative from an ASA of 20 (DIN 14) in 1928 to 40 (DIN 17) for Eastman's Super X negative stock in 1935, then to 80 ASA (DIN 20) and 160 ASA (DIN 23) in 1938 for Plus-X and Super XX respectively. The latter possessed a grain comparable to Super X and a speed that was four times as great.

In 1939 the introduction of lens coatings, which permitted 75 per cent more light to pass through the lens to the film inside the camera, enabled cinematographers to decrease the lens aperture an additional stop, facilitating

The coming of widescreen: publicity for *The Robe* (1953), the first film to be released in Twentieth Century–Fox's CinemaScope process

greater image definition. The advent of the Mitchell BNC camera, which was introduced in 1934 but which was not produced in any numbers until 1939, also played a role. This camera dispensed with cumbersome external blimps (i.e. sound-proofing devices) in favour of internal blimping; it thus eliminated the external blimp's glass plate through which the film was shot, further increasing the transmission of light by as much as 10 per cent. The results of these developments can be seen in cameraman Gregg Toland's work for William Wyler (*Dead End*, 1937; *Wuthering Heights*, 1939; *The Best Years of our Lives*, 1946), John Ford (*The Grapes of Wrath* and *The Long Voyage Home*, both 1940), and Orson Welles (*Citizen Kane*, 1941).

As with these other technologies, deep focus traces its origins back to earlier periods. Lumière's actualities of the 1890s possessed tremendous depth of field. These and other films which were shot in exteriors took advantage of relatively short focal-length lenses and abundant sunlight to produce 'deep' images. Jean-Louis Comolli (1980) has connected the demise of early deep focus with the introduction of panchromatic film stock in 1925, which brought with it a different code of photographic realism. According to this new code, the film stock's greater sensitivity to the full range of colours signified a greater realism, while its relative shallow depth of field and softer look (in relation to its predecessor, orthochromatic film stock) duplicated the predominant codes for artistry in contemporary still photography. More importantly, it introduced a lack (of a sense of relief) which supposedly prompted the quest for deep focus in the late 1930s. If the logic of Comolli's argument holds, then deep focus is also an indirect product of technological changes introduced in the transition-to-sound period.

THE 1950S: WIDESCREEN AND STEREO

The creation of a habitual movie-going audience in the 1930s effectively terminated technological experimentation. There was little or no demand on the part of audiences for technological innovation and cost-conscious exhibitors saw no reason to invest in the new projection equipment which 3-D, widescreen, and other exhibition technologies would require. However, the falling off of this habitual audience in the post-war years prompted a search for novel forms of presentation and led to the reintroduction of many of these earlier technologies.

In 1948 the average weekly attendance at motion pictures in the United States stood at 90 million—an all-time high. By 1952 this had dropped to 51 million, largely as a result of the demographic shift of a large percentage of the US population from the cities, where the major movie theatres were located, to the suburbs. At the same time, the return to a forty-hour work week, the institution of one- and two-week paid vacations, and an increase in disposable personal income resulted in the creation of new patterns in leisure-time entertainment. Consumers abandoned passive entertainment, such as film-going, in favour of active participation in forms of recreation such as gardening, hunting, fishing, boating, golfing, and travel. These activities filled greater and greater blocks of the leisure time available to post-war audiences, while television satisfied their need for short-term, passive entertainment.

The American motion picture industry responded to these new patterns by providing more participatory forms of entertainment, which were modelled, in part, on concepts of presence associated with the legitimate theatre. New motion picture technologies involved spectators with the on-screen action in ways which provided them with an enhanced illusion of participation. Thus Cinerama, introduced in September 1952, informed its audiences that 'you won't be gazing at a movie screen—you'll find yourself swept right into the picture, surrounded by sight and sound'.

Advertisements for *Bwana Devil* (1952), which was filmed in 3-D, addressed audiences in similar ways, thrilling them with the promise of 'a lion in your lap' and 'a lover in your arms'. Ads for CinemaScope, which was introduced with the première of *The Robe* in September 1953, told potential spectators that CinemaScope 'puts YOU in the picture'. And ads for Todd–AO's *Oklahoma!* (1955) declared that 'you're in the show with Todd–AO'. They celebrated the sense of presence created by the new, wide film format: 'Suddenly you're there ... in the land that is grand, in the surrey, on the prairie! You live it, you're a part of it ... you're in Oklahoma!'

Cinerama, which was developed outside the film industry by a Long Island inventor, Fred Waller, achieved its remarkable sense of participation by filling the spectator's field of peripheral vision, encompassing an angle of view that was 146 degrees wide and 55 degrees tall. This was accomplished by filming with three interlocked 35 mm. cameras, which were equipped with wide-angle, 27 mm. lenses set at angles of 48 degrees to one another. The Cinerama camera ran at an accelerated speed of 26 frames per second to reduce flicker and exposed 35 mm. negative that was six perforations high rather than the standard four. In the theatre, three interlocked projectors in three different booths were used to project the three separate strips of film on to a huge, deeply curved screen.

Stereo sound was recorded magnetically with from five to six microphones and played back by a sound control engineer through seven speakers in the theatre; five speakers were located behind the screen, while the other two channels were used for surround sound. Magnetic sound recording had been introduced to the film industry via slightly modified German equipment which had been captured during the war. In 1935 the Germans had developed a magnetic recorder called the Magnetophon, which used plastic tape coated with powdered magnetic material. This equipment was brought to the United States in 1946. By 1949 Paramount had used the principles of the Magnetophon to develop equipment which enabled the studio to convert to magnetic sound for purposes of recording and editing, though it, like all the other studios, continued to release films with optical tracks in order to accommodate theatres, which were reluctant to install new sound reproduction equipment.

This Is Cinerama (1952), the first Cinerama feature, grossed over $32 million, though it played in only a handful of theatres, due to the complex requirements of the format's projection system. The first five Cinerama films were all travelogues, and it was not until 1962 that the format was used to film narrative features, such as *How the West Was Won*. Three-strip Cinerama lasted until 1963, when it was replaced by Ultra Panavision, a 70 mm. process which used a slight anamorphic compression to squeeze Cinerama's wide angle of view on to a single strip of film, thus duplicating Cinerama's original 2.77 : 1 aspect ratio (the term 'aspect ratio' refers to the relation of a projected image's width to its height).

The success of 3-D was even more short-lived than Cinerama, lasting for only about eighteen months, from late 1952 to the spring of 1954. In the 1950s 3-D relied upon polaroid filters rather than the anaglyphic format. An inexpensive technology for both producers and exhibitors, it became associated with exploitation genres, such as the horror film (*House of Wax*, 1953; *Creature from the Black Lagoon*, 1954), science-fiction films (*It Came from Outer Space*, 1953), and Westerns (*Hondo*, 1953).

CinemaScope, which was introduced by 20th Century-Fox, attempted to duplicate Cinerama, streamlining it for adoption by the film industry as a whole. The cornerstone of the CinemaScope system was an anamorphic lens, which had been developed back in 1927 by a French scientist, Henri Chrétien. This lens compressed a wide angle of view on to 35 mm. film; a similar anamorphic lens on the projector in the theatre decompressed the image, producing, on a slightly curved, highly reflective screen, a panoramic view that had an aspect ratio of 2.55 : 1 (subsequently reduced to the current standard of 2.35 : 1 when an optical sound-track was added to it in 1954). Unlike Cinerama, which required a separate strip of film to hold the tracks for its stereo magnetic sound, CinemaScope used magnetic oxide striping to place four tracks on the same strip of 35 mm. film which bore the image, thus eliminating the need for additional personnel in the theatre.

Fox engineers crammed all this information on to a single strip of 35 mm. film by redesigning the frame area as well as reducing the size of the perforations along both sides of the film. In doing this, Fox took advantage of the increased durability and stability of safety-based acetate film stock, which had been introduced in 1949 to replace the highly flammable nitrate film stock, which tended to shrink during processing.

CinemaScope also made use of the new Eastman Color film stock, which had been introduced in 1950. The old Technicolor three-strip camera was unable to accommodate a CinemaScope lens so Fox switched to single-strip Eastman Color negative, which could be used in any 35 mm. camera. This tri-pack film drew upon colour research conducted by the German company Agfa in 1939, which was subsequently marketed as Agfacolor. Like Agfacolor, Eastman's film featured three layers of emulsion, each sensitive to a different primary colour. During processing, dyes held within the film were released in response to the degree of exposure of the silver halides in each layer, thus reproducing the original colour. The advent of Eastman Color broke the grip which Technicolor had on production in colour, stimulating a dramatic increase in the number of films made in colour. In 1945, only 8 per cent of all Hollywood films were shot in colour; by 1955, that percentage had climbed to over 50.

CinemaScope quickly became an industry standard; by the end of 1954, every studio except for Paramount, which had developed its own widescreen process known as VistaVision, had adopted the CinemaScope format; and by 1957 85 per cent of all US and Canadian theatres had been equipped to show CinemaScope films. In Europe, the Soviet Union, and Japan, a number of CinemaScope clones emerged, including Dyaliscope and Franscope (France), Sovscope (USSR), and Tohoscope (Japan). In 1958 Panavision developed a high-quality anamorphic lens, which it effectively marketed to the rest of the industry. And by 1967 Fox had retired CinemaScope in favour of Panavision for 35 mm. production and Todd-AO for wide film production.

Not all film-makers, however, were happy with the new widescreen format. Sidney Lumet noted that 'the essence of any dramatic piece is people, and it is symptomatic that Hollywood finds a way of photographing people directly opposite to the way people are built. CinemaScope makes no sense until people are fatter than they are taller.' Fritz Lang joked (in lines which he later repeated in Jean-Luc Godard's Franscope production of *Contempt* (*Le Mépris*, 1963)) that CinemaScope was a format ideally suited for filming snakes and funerals, but not human beings. But by the end of the decade, widescreen had become a new standard. And it gave expression to a new generation of artists—to directors such as Nicholas Ray and Otto Preminger, and to cinematographers such as Joseph LaShelle and Sam Leavitt.

Todd-AO also sought to duplicate the Cinerama experience, using extremely wide-angled lenses, wide 65/70 mm. film, a 30-frames-per-second film speed, a deeply curved screen, and six-track stereo magnetic sound. Todd-AO soon emerged as a premier format, reserved for big-budget blockbusters, which could be shown at top prices on a roadshow basis in the largest, most exclusive theatres. It led the way for other 65/70 mm. processes, such as MGM's Camera 65 (*Ben-Hur*, 1959), Ultra Panavision 70 (*Mutiny on the Bounty*, 1962), and Super Technirama 70 (*Spartacus*, 1960).

Although widescreen became a new standard, stereo magnetic sound quickly disappeared as a new technology. Movie palaces used it as an additional lure for audiences, but independent exhibitors refused to pay the added costs involved in equipping their theatres for stereo. At the same time, audiences accustomed to hearing dialogue emanate from a central theatre speaker resisted multi-track dialogue, which travelled from theatre speaker to theatre speaker. Five- and six-track sound, which accompanied large-format films, provided a more even distribution of dialogue, and continued to satisfy the needs of audiences for spectacle, but three- and four-track sound failed to catch on.

The various production and exhibition technologies introduced during the 1950s constituted a revolution of sorts in the nature of the movie-going experience. Audi-ences were initially overwhelmed by widescreen images in colour, which were projected on large, curved screens and accompanied by multi-track stereo magnetic sound. If the cinema can be said to have begun as a novelty with the peep-show Kinetoscope and with the projection of moving images on a large theatre screen for a mass audi-ence, then the explosion of novel technologies in the 1950s almost amounts to a reinvention of the cinema. For the first time since the transition-to-sound era, movies spec-tacularized the motion picture medium, thrilling audi-ences with displays of its power to move them. The revolution that took place in the 1950s may well represent the last chapter in the cinema's attempt, as a medium, to recapture, through the novelty of its mode of pres-entation, its original ability to excite spectators.

Bibliography
Belton, John (1992), *Widescreen Cinema*.
Comolli, Jean-Louis (1980), 'Machines of the Visible'.
Ogle, Patrick L. (1972), 'Technological and Aesthetic Influences upon the Development of Deep Focus Cinematography in the United States'.
Salt, Barry (1992), *Film Style and Technology: History and Analysis*.

Animation

WILLIAM MORITZ

THE 'GOLDEN AGE' OF AMERICAN CARTOONS

To satisfy the international craze for Mickey Mouse (fuelled by a keen merchandizing campaign patterned after Pat Sullivan's exploitation of Otto Messmer's Felix the Cat), the Disney studios created 100 cartoons starring him in the ten years from 1928 to 1937. In the process they managed to homogenize the character—Ub Iwerks's original Mickey from *Plane Crazy* and *Steamboat Willie* had wiry limbs and a wicked personality that could torture cats and ladies, while the later Mickey became rounder, milder of temperament—and virtually exhausted his possi-bilities. Fortunately the Mickey cartoons spawned sec-ondary characters Pluto, Goofy, and Donald Duck who starred in their own cartoons until the mid-1950s: in fact, the best of the later Mickey Mouse cartoons, such as the 1935 *Band Concert* or the 1937 *Clock Cleaners*, derive as much energy from Donald and Goofy as from Mickey. Equally fortunately, Ub Iwerks initiated a second parallel series of sound cartoons with his 1928 *Skeleton Dance*: the Silly Symphonies, which explored lyrical and whimsical themes in folklore and nature. Free from the gag formula of regular cartoons, Silly Symphonies gave the Disney staff the opportunity to experiment and expand their ani-mation skills, and they won Academy Awards regularly: the full-colour *Flowers and Trees* (1932), *Three Little Pigs* (1933) with its diverse personality characterization for animal protagonists, *The Tortoise and the Hare* (1935), *Country Cousin* (1936), *The Old Mill* (1937) with its atmospheric multiplane depth effects, *Ferdinand the Bull* (1938), and *The Ugly Duckling* (1939).

The technical advances explored in the Silly Sym-phonies partly arose from a rivalry with the Fleischers, who, among all the other animation studios that survived into the sound era, consistently produced excellent car-toons in the early 1930s. Unlike the Disney product, which tended increasingly to an 'illusion of life' live-action imi-tation, the earlier Fleischer cartoons revelled in styl-ization, caricature, unrealistic transformations, elaborate repetitive cycles, direct address to the audience, and illogi-cal developments which seem inherent, distinctive properties or potentials of animation. Disney's Alice seems mundane and leaden beside the Fleischers' Koko, whose surrealistic escapades allow him to intervene in the creative process of *Modelling* (1921), or, with his prison escape in *Koko the Convict* (1926), to bury Manhattan in a cascade of cycling policemen. Dave Fleischer invented the rotoscope process, which he used to allow overtly cartoon figures to mime, uncannily, human actions; Disney used the rotoscope to create realistic-looking human figures. When in 1934 the Fleischers introduced the stereoptical process which gave a sense of realistic depth by using three-dimensional models behind the cel-animated characters, Disney countered by promoting his multi-plane camera which produced similar depth sensations through co-ordinating several layers of moving cels (independent animators such as Lotte Reiniger and Berthold Bartosch had been doing that since the early 1920s).

The Fleischer genius lay not merely in technology, however, but also in their ability to connect the surprising fantastic with a meaningful metaphor that, as in classic fables, exposed an inner truth of human life. While Disney's *Flowers and Trees* irrelevantly superimposes a clichéd melodrama about dirty old man versus young lovers (who eventually triumph in marriage) over images of plants, Shamus Culhane in the Fleischers' 1931 *Cow's Husband* cleverly uses the relationship between human and animal behaviour to debunk the myth of brave bullfighting, culminating in an elegant ballet for the bull.

In *Mysterious Mose* (1930), Willard Bowsky and Ted Sears created a hit starring the new sexy Betty Boop (still with dog ears) falling in love with a seemingly magical Bimbo, who dances to Cab Calloway music but turns out to be an automaton; Bimbo's mysterious charm stems partly from his continuous transformations, which follow a narrative logic, as when his masked heart shoots out to 'steal' Betty's. Bowsky then teamed up with Ralph Sommerville for a sequel, *Minnie the Moocher* (1932), which counts as one of the great animation films; Betty runs away from home because of her authoritarian parents, but encounters in a cave where she hides a 'spook' who brings the title song alive with images that demonstrate the evil wiles of the city and the ungrateful behaviour of children: when kittens suck a mother cat dry, she offers them a bottle, which they transform into a hookah, while ghostly criminals re-enact cycles of crime, walking through prison bars, enjoying electrocution, and scoffing at the authorities as they begin their antics over again. The spook is rotoscoped from Cab Calloway's live-action performance that we see at the beginning of the film, which emphasizes the cartoon qualities of the spook, as do the fine surreal watercolour backgrounds which subtly allow grasping skeleton hands to emerge from the cave walls.

The brilliant success of *Minnie the Moocher* called for another sequel, assigned to Roland 'Doc' Crandall, who had specialized in sing-along cartoons that illustrated popular songs word by word in rebus puns. Crandall's *Snow White* (1933) makes no sense of the fairy-tale, but thrills with a non-stop string of sight gags: no logical reason leads seven dwarfs, Koko, Bimbo, Betty Boop, and

the Witch-Queen into a cave, but Koko's Cab Calloway dance in which he is transformed into the words of 'St James Infirmary Blues' (such as 'shot of booze', and 'gold piece') remains delightful. The cave walls, less subtle than *Minnie*'s, also illustrate phrases, depicting a table of gamblers, or a skeleton with drugs and drink. Later that year Bernie Wolf and Tom Johnson animated yet another Cab Calloway film, *Old Man of the Mountain*, one of the worst Fleischer films. Crude, senseless imitations of earlier skeletons decorate the cave walls, while a tasteless, flimsy story shows Betty Boop visiting a sexy but vicious man who terrorized a town, leaving countless illegitimate babies in his wake.

This weakness reflects not only exhaustion from forced production but also new tighter strictures of the Production Code, which ruined Betty Boop's popularity, demanding her sexiness be hidden and leaving her an insipid woman with a dog and a grandfather. The Fleischers turned their attention to another star, Popeye (the Code had not banned relentless violence), whose more than 100 successful cartoons established a new cartoon mayhem genre that flourished in subsequent imitations including MGM's Tom and Jerry (Bill Hanna/Joe Barbera, 1940-67), and Warners' Tweetie/Sylvester (Bob Clampett/Friz Freleng, 1944-64) and Roadrunner/Coyote (Chuck Jones, 1949, 1952-66) series.

The Warner Bros. cartoon unit blossomed just as the Fleischers began to fade. After two unexceptional beginnings (Bosko, an African-American stereotype by Disney veterans Hugh Harman and Rudy Ising, 1930-3, and Friz Freleng's Buddy, 1933-5, both of whom resembled the Fleischers' Bimbo), the 1936 hiring of anarchic Tex Avery and Frank Tashlin (with his experience in Hal Roach's live-action comedies) boosted Warners' cartoons to original brilliance, using the new character Porky Pig in fast-paced, cinematic burlesques of human behaviour. Bob Clampett joined them in 1937 and Chuck Jones in 1938, helping to create three more memorable characters, Daffy Duck, Elmer Fudd, and Bugs Bunny, who would enjoy careers lasting into the 1960s. The zany gags linked to a consistent plot, the caricature of celebrities, and the overt direct address to the audience that were hallmarks of the Fleischer style continued to be exploited by Warners, and the variety of talents involved seemed to sustain the ideas, as in three clever classics: in the 1938 *Daffy Duck in Hollywood*, Avery lets manic Daffy disturb the shooting of a feature film, then Daffy cuts together an ironic collage of live-action newsreel footage to be shown instead of the feature; in the 1940 *You Ought to Be in Pictures*, Freleng lets Daffy talk Porky into quitting Warners, but (live-action) producer Leon Schlesinger hires Porky back after disastrous adventures on a rival lot; and in the 1941 *Porky's Preview*, Avery lets Porky do his own animation, which resembles children's stick figures.

Bugs Bunny

(c.1940–)

Of all animated characters who enjoyed a vogue as stars—Felix the Cat, Mickey Mouse, Betty Boop, Donald Duck, Porky Pig—Bugs Bunny remains the most beloved to millions of people. He embodies a mythic archetype, the picaresque trickster-survivor, who appears in the medieval Japanese Choju Giga, European Tyl Eulenspiegel, Native American Coyote legends, the African Zomo and his African-American descendant Br'er Rabbit. Bugs has Hemingway's 'grace under pressure', but absolutely no inhibitions. The Hero with a Thousand Faces, he can adopt any disguise instantaneously, be it as Carmen Miranda or a decrepit senior. Bugs always thinks of the witty reply immediately; he copes with every situation, masters every game, be it boxing, baseball, or bull-fighting. He has Chaplin's inventive bravado, and Clark Gable's cool *savoir-faire* to munch a carrot in times of need. Bugs is the suave and capable person we all long to be.

Bugs Bunny was born at Termite Terrace, Leon Schlesinger's animation unit at Warner Bros. Studio. His immediate predecessor, Max Hare in Disney's 1935 Academy Award winning *The Tortoise and the Hare*, had been designed by Canadian animator Charlie Thorson, who subsequently moved to Warners. The first clever bunny at Warners appeared in a small role in Frank Tashlin's 1937 *Porky's Building*. In Ben 'Bugs' Hardaway's 1938 *Porky's Hare Hunt*, the rabbit hardly differed from Daffy Duck in his frenetic, crazy character. Thorson redesigned the hare character to be rather cute for Hardaway's 1939 *Hare-um Scare-um*, which also involves a rabbit hunt, but this time the hare resembles Bugs in cleverness, if not exactly the sleek elegance which Chuck Jones moved toward in the March 1940 *Elmer's Candid Camera*.

The more mature Bugs Bunny first emerged in Tex Avery's July 1940 *A Wild Hare*. His first appearance was actually as a supple arm and hand expressively reaching out of his hole for a carrot, the four fingers wisely discriminating between the vegetable and the hunter's gun. Bugs's opening line, 'What's up, Doc?' delivered (while munching on a carrot) to the armed hunter, became the ultimate symbol of his 'cool' self-confidence—and a byword in the English language. His extravagant death scene, staged to shame the hunter, contains lithe ballet steps, and gently teases Bernhardt's and Garbo's Camille. Here Bugs kisses Elmer Fudd three times partly just to confuse him, but partly to assure that he bears the hunter no malice. Bugs finally marches off as the wounded fifer from the American Revolutionary War icon.

Bugs's début as a capable, witty winner, just at the beginning of the Second World War, contributed to him becoming a hero. Even as a number of hands went into his development, so the more than 160 films he starred in were directed alternately by Friz Freleng, Bob Clampett, Bob McKimson, and Chuck Jones—supported by Mel Blanc's inimitable voice, Carl Stalling's brilliant musical underlining, and the story/gags of writers like Michael Maltese and Tedd Pierce. The talents of animators like Virgil Ross and Bobe Cannon gave Bugs's movements style.

One can hardly find an *auteur* for Bugs, which makes the miracle of his personality more astonishing. Bob Clampett and Frank Tashlin could make Bugs a ballerina for the exquisite 1943 satire of *Fantasia*, *A Corny Concerto*, and Chuck Jones could make Bugs completely fresh as an opera diva in the astonishing 1957 *What's Opera, Doc?*, with its dramatic modern colour and design, and its exceedingly cinematic spatial-time dynamic. Bugs's multiple parentage even leaves one wondering if our beloved rabbit is actually male or female, since Bugs glides effortlessly between manifestations of either sex: in the 1949 Chuck Jones *Long-Haired Hare*, Bugs appears one moment as a giddy teenage girl fan, and the next as a devastating satire of Leopold Stokowski.

Bugs had to wait until 1958 before winning an Academy Award (shared with Friz Freleng and Yosemite Sam) for his performance in *Knighty Knight Bugs*. Even after his last cinema cartoon in 1964, Bugs continued to be seen in television specials and film compilations, and made a guest star appearance in the 1988 Disney feature *Who Framed Roger Rabbit*. Bugs's films still enjoy endless reruns on broadcast television and videotapes. He received his own star on Hollywood Boulevard in 1985.

WILLIAM MORITZ

BIBLIOGRAPHY

Adamson, Joe (1990), *Bugs Bunny: Fifty Years and Only One Grey Hare.*
Jones, Chuck (1989), *Chuck Amuck.*
Schneider, Steve (1988), *That's All Folks*

Bugs in the 1944 Chuck Jones short, *What's Cookin' Doc?*

While a great deal of nostalgia surrounds this period as a 'golden age' of animation—and indeed the demand for new cartoons every week at thousands of cinemas sustained ten animation studios in the USA—the numerical majority of cartoons remained mediocre. Terrytoons continued their silent-era record to produce hundreds of unmemorable cartoons until 1968, perhaps peaking with Mighty Mouse and Heckle and Jeckle in the 1940s and 1950s. Walter Lantz continued to produce Disney's silent-era creation Oswald the Rabbit until 1938; his wimpy Andy Panda and the annoying Woody Woodpecker (modelled after the early zany Daffy Duck) appeared in 1940 and Chilly Willy in the 1950s, but though Lantz continued to produce cartoons until 1972, the level of inspiration, humour, design, and ideation lagged far behind Disney, the Fleischers, and Warners. Van Beuren also flogged its silent-era Aesop's Fables into the mid-1930s, and Columbia continued a lacklustre Krazy Kat until 1939.

DISNEY AND THE ANIMATED FEATURE

Walt Disney began work on a feature-length animation film, *Snow White and the Seven Dwarfs*, in 1934, during his height of success with Mickey Mouse and the Silly Symphonies. Before the feature was finished in December 1937 (barely in time for a Los Angeles Christmas preview), Disney employed more than 300 character animators, designers, background artists, and effects animators. This meant educating many young artists into animation, as well as hiring away the best talents from other studios, so that, for example, Shamus Culhane, Al Eugster, Ted Sears, and Grim Natwick (who had designed Betty Boop) came from Fleischers. Inspirational sketches by European artists Gustaf Tenggren and Albert Hurter were transformed into a lush, charming, and occasionally frightening film by teams which included loner artists like Art Babbitt, John Hubley, and Bill Tytla (all of whom left Disney in the 1941 strike) as well as a tight core of artists who continued to create most subsequent Disney films: Jim Algar, Ken Anderson, Les Clark, Claude Coats, Bill Cottrell, Joe Grant, Wilfred Jackson, Ollie Johnston, Milt Kahl, Ward Kimball, Eric Larson, Ham Luske, Fred Moore, Woolie Reitherman, and Frank Thomas.

Although not the first animated feature (Edera lists eight earlier, including Reiniger's 1926 *Prince Ahmed*, Starewitch's 1930 *The Tale of the Fox*, and Alexander Ptushko's 1935 *The New Gulliver*), *Snow White* enjoyed a phenomenal success (including a special Oscar), with serious impact on industrial animation. Talent was drained from cartoon to feature production everywhere: Paramount insisted the Fleischers begin a rival feature, and encouraged their move from New York to the cheaper Miami, where they made two features, *Gulliver's Travels* (1939) and *Mr. Bug Goes to Town* (1941). *Gulliver*, though an obvious imitation of *Snow White* without all its charm, scored a hit, but *Mr.*

Bug, though artistically superior (in the spirit of Fleischer street-wise New York films), opened in December 1941 (just as the USA entered the Second World War) and flopped. Fleischers had continued to make some shorts, including a dozen Stone Age cartoons (predecessor to the 1960s' *Flintstones*), but enjoyed success only with the nineteen *Superman* cartoons they made from 1941 until the studio closed in 1944.

Disney continued to produce about one animation feature per year into the 1950s, when production slowed. This meant that teams worked on two or three projects at the same time. Disney began preliminary work on *Bambi*, *Pinocchio*, and *Fantasia* in 1937; *Pinocchio* premièred in February 1940, *Fantasia* in December 1940, and *Bambi* (delayed by the war, the strike, and work on the October 1941 *Dumbo*) not until August 1942. Disney's lavish animation reached its pinnacle in *Pinocchio*'s story-book realism and the extravagant classical-music illustration of *Fantasia*. Changing finances due to the war and the 1941 strike required that animation be more economical. Plans for a second 'Fantasia' were modified into two popular-music-based anthology features, *Make Mine Music* (1946) and *Melody Time* (1948), which allowed simpler graphics, partly suggested by inspirational sketches of Mary Blair who favoured a bold stylized design, especially in the 1943 *Saludos amigos*. Disney features like *The Three Caballeros* (1945) and *Fun and Fancy Free* (1947) began to include more live action sequences, and live-action predominated in *Song of the South* (1946) and *So Dear to my Heart* (1949), leading to Disney's all live-action features, beginning with *Treasure Island* (1950). But Disney also continued full animation features on a looser schedule: *Ichabod and Mr. Toad* (1949), *Cinderella* (1950), *Alice in Wonderland* (1951), *Peter Pan* (1953), *The Lady and the Tramp* (1955), and *Sleeping Beauty* (1959).

Unionization and strikes hit animation studios in the late 1930s, with protests against long hours, low salaries, poor working conditions, and the lack of health or pension benefits: the 'golden age' of industrial cartoons was built largely on exploitation of animation artists and craftsmen. The strike against the Fleischers in 1937 lasted six months, and depressed Max Fleischer, who regarded himself as a decent employer and thought of the Fleischer studio as a happy family; family feeling disappeared, and the studio would close half a dozen years later. Walt Disney was similarly depressed by the 1941 strike at his studio, and to a certain degree lost interest in animation because of it, turning his attention to documentaries and the idea for Disneyland. The Terrytoons strike in 1941 lasted nine months. As the Second World War and strikes withdrew many talents from the cartoon industry, slowed production, and encouraged short cuts (including repetition of gags, less complex movements, and simpler designs), most studios experienced a gradual decline in quality.

Tex Avery's sexually provocative *Little Rural Riding Hood* (Warner Bros., 1949)

UPA

A group of animation talents who left Disney after the strike formed United Productions of America. UPA, set up as a co-operative, paid equal attention to all aspects of film-making, including writing, music, graphic design, and the practical tasks of inking and painting. From *Robin Hoodlum* in 1948 to *Jaywalker* in 1956 (both nominated for Academy Awards), this egalitarian attitude led to the creation of an astonishing series of cartoons with modern art styling, non-violent literary scripts, and musical scores by contemporary composers. Bobe Cannon's particularly significant contribution involved designing special movements to express character or ideas, rather than trying to make every motion realistic. Cannon directed UPA's first Oscar-winner, *Gerald McBoing Boing* (1950), using a Dr Seuss story, with design and colour by Hurtz and Engel, animation by Bill Melendez and Cannon, and music by Gail Kubik. In 1952 two further UPA films vied unsuccessfully for the Oscar: *Madeline* and the stylish *Rooty Toot Toot*, which satirizes the American justice system through the old 'Frankie and Johnny' ballad. Further UPA triumphs in 1953 included Hurtz's adaptation of James Thurber's *Unicorn in the Garden* and the Ted Parmelee–Paul Julian adaptation of Edgar Allan Poe's *The Tell-Tale Heart*, which rendered the classic horror story in surrealist graphics, opening theatrical cartoons to serious subject-matter.

At the same time as UPA produced these art films, they also created fresh concepts for advertising films, and pioneered animated titles for feature films with their spectacular contribution to Stanley Kramer's 1952 *The Fourposter*. These commercial ventures became so successful that UPA opened studios in New York and London (George Dunning worked in both) just for title and ad jobs. UPA also made a series of more than fifty cartoons featuring Mr Magoo, who débuted in Hubley's 1949 *Ragtime Bear*, and outlasted UPA itself, since Columbia continued to make them until 1959, after most core talents from UPA had departed.

In a few years, UPA changed commercial animation irrevocably. Other studios tried to imitate their style, and Tex Avery—for whose 1949 MGM classic, *Little Rural Riding Hood*, Bobe Cannon had designed movements that brilliantly differentiate the town and country wolves—openly lifted from UPA's 1949 *The Magic Fluke* for his 1952 *The Magical Maestro* (he also added violence and racist stereotypes). At a memorial screening for Norman McLaren, Grant Munro and Evelyn Lambart reminisced about the whole National Film Board of Canada animation unit standing in line (in the snow) at Ottawa's Elgin Cinema to see the latest UPA cartoon for inspiration. Screenings of UPA cartoons in Yugoslavia and other eastern European countries encouraged animators there to abandon attempts to imitate Disney, and rather adopt modern and folk styling. Meanwhile, Disney also tried to modernize in competition with UPA, and ironically the Disney studio won its first Academy Award in ten years for Ward Kimball's 1953 radically stylized *Toot, Whistle, Plunk and Boom*.

Television also hastened the decline in theatrical cartoons by decreasing cinema audiences until cartoons became an unnecessary luxury, and by stealing away animation talent into more lucrative jobs preparing cartoons for television. UPA had its own television show, *The Gerald McBoing Boing Show*, which broadcast from December 1956 until October 1958 both classic UPA cinema cartoons and freshly made cartoons, including an impressive series on art, from the eighteenth-century Japanese artist Sharaku (*The Day of the Fox*, Sidney Peterson and Alan Zaslove) to current Abstract Expressionism (*The Performing Painter*, John Whitney, Ernie Pintoff, and Fred Crippen). UPA artists Bill Hurtz, Pete Burness, Ted Parmelee, and Lew Keller went to Jay Ward Productions to make the television series *Rocky and Bullwinkle*. Bill Hanna and Joe Barbera left MGM to create their own company to produce several popular TV cartoon series, including *Yogi Bear*, *The Flintstones*, and *The Jetsons*, which not only used an extremely 'limited animation', but also relied on wordy scripts that might as well have been live-action sitcoms. By 1960, studio animation units producing theatrical cartoons were dead.

ANIMATION IN EUROPE

Despite the dazzling splendours of *Fantasia* and the beloved antics of Bugs, the truly great animation of this era was not produced in American studios—though intense merchandising continues to promote older studio products, and television continues to recycle them so that they enjoy familiar nostalgia—but rather in the homes and small studios of independent artists. For these independent animators, sound was no problem, since their art depended not on verbal comedy that could equally well be live action but rather on the magical power of moving graphics and the potential for transformations which lie at the heart of animation. Many of these animators had special musical accompaniments written for their silent-era films, and continued this practice during the sound era. Walter Ruttmann's *Lichtspiel Opus I* ('Light play, opus 1'), a wholly abstract film, painted on glass and

Oskar Fischinger's experimental animation *Allegretto* (1936)

then hand-tinted in multiple colours on the film strip, had its première in April 1921 in a Frankfurt cinema with a specially composed synchronous score for string quintet (Ruttmann himself played cello in the ensemble) by Max Butting. After three more abstract Opus films, Ruttmann would enjoy a great success with his 1927 poetic documentary *Berlin: Symphony of a City* (with a special score by Edmund Meisel) and continued in live-action film, but his friend Oskar Fischinger, who also began abstract animation in the early 1920s, continued to make 'colour music' films into the 1950s. Fischinger's early 'silent' films used live music, including a spectacular abstract multiple-projection piece *R-1, ein Formspiel* ('R-1, a form play', 1927), originally accompanied by the piano music of Alexander Laszlo, but later was performed with a percussion ensemble. In addition to his abstract films, Fischinger also made some representational cartoons to help finance his other work, and created a startling masterpiece of experimental animation in *Seelische Konstruktionen* ('Spiritual constructions', 1927), which shows in fluid silhouette metamorphoses the hallucinations of two drunken men who fight in a bar and stagger home. When the vogue for sound films swept Germany in 1929, Fischinger convinced Electrola Records to allow him to use their discs as soundtracks in exchange for an end title advertising the disc's name and number, so his *Studies* became an ancestor of the MTV video clip. The series of *Studies* were immensely popular internationally, and received prizes at film festivals; Fischinger had completed fourteen of them when the Nazis seized power in 1933, and several more remained unfinished since no censorship permit could be obtained for a 'degenerate' abstract film. He got a permit for his first colour film, *Kreise* ('Circles', 1933), by selling it as a publicity film to the Tolirag advertising agency who inserted an end title, 'Tolirag reaches all circles of society'. Fischinger also scored a huge success with an ad film *Muratti greift ein* ('Muratti gets in the act', 1934) that capitalized on Olympics fever by showing cigarettes parading into an arena and performing sports like ice skating. With the profits from these ad films, he worked secretly on another colour abstract film, *Composition in Blue* (*Komposition in Blau*, 1935), in which brightly coloured cubes and cylinders glide around mirrored spaces. He screened *Composition in Blue* without proper permits, and though it received rave reviews, the Nazi government was displeased. Fortunately, Paramount spirited him off to Hollywood, where he began work on an episode for *The Big Broadcast of 1937*. Fischinger's segment, *Allegretto* (1936), was not used in the black and white feature since he insisted that his work remain in colour; when, with a Guggenheim grant, he bought *Allegretto* back from Paramount and released it as a short, it was acclaimed for its complex cel animation, as a perfectly satisfying piece of visual music, with layers of forms and subtly graduated

colours providing an uncanny complete parallel to Ralph Rainger's symphonic jazz score. MGM distributed Fischinger's 1937 *An Optical Poem* as a short in cinemas. He worked for a year animating for Disney's *Fantasia*, but left in disgust because all his designs got changed. His final masterpieces—*Radio Dynamics* (1941–3, which he shot while employed by Orson Welles on *It's All True*) and *Motion Painting No. 1* (1947)—both probed cinematic possibilities of painting; *Radio Dynamics* uses radical montage of painted images in a silent collage, while the ten-minute *Motion Painting* shows the creation of one specific painting by shooting a single frame each time a brush stroke was made. *Motion Painting* won the Grand Prize at the Brussels Experimental Film Festival in 1949.

Lotte Reiniger employed Walter Ruttmann and Berthold Bartosch as animators on her first feature *The Adventures of Prince Ahmed* (*Die Abenteuer des Prinzen Achmed*, 1926) and during three years' work together they refined a sophisticated multi-layered animation technique. *Prince Ahmed* had a score composed for it by Wolfgang Zeller, and Reiniger's second feature, *Doktor Dolittle und seine Tiere* ('Dr Dolittle and his animals', 1928), had a score by Paul Dessau, Kurt Weill, and Paul Hindemith. Reiniger's sound shorts also used music as counterpoint to her silhouettes, such as the 1933 *Carmen*, for which Bizet's score underlines an ironic feminist retelling of the opera: her gypsy girl, cleverer than both the soldier and bullfighter, ends up dancing on the bull's horns like an ancient Cretan priestess. Reiniger finished thirty-five sound films, mostly based on fairy-tales or operas, as well as special effects for features and advertising films.

Berthold Bartosch made several animated political films before working on Lotte Reiniger's two features, and when he returned to his personal work (after moving to Paris), he moulded motifs from the woodcuts of Frans Masereel into a powerful half-hour film *The Idea* (*L'Idée*, 1932), which follows the naked truth of an 'Idea' (Liberty, Equality, Fraternity—represented by a nude woman, since abstract ideas have feminine gender in European languages), from birth to single martyrdom, to mass social struggle, war, and final apotheosis as an abstract constellation. Bartosch balances the rugged edges of cut-outs based on Masereel with soft luminous appearances created by delicate soap drawing on layers of glass, lit from behind, and 'edits' his imagery (mostly planned into the shooting) in the dynamic style of Eisenstein. Arthur Honegger composed a thrilling score that underlines the magical apparition of Idea with the eerie tones of a new electronic instrument Les Ondes Martinot, parallels the vivid images of the flickering neon streets with jazzy rhythms, and mirrors the escalation in the final battle between strikers and soldiers. Bartosch, over three years, animated the 50,000 frames of this film (many involving up to eighteen layers of superimposition) entirely by himself in the tiny attic where he lived above a Paris cinema. With the financial aid of British film-maker Thorold Dickinson, Bartosch completed a second pacifist film in colour, *St Francis, or Nightmares and Dreams* (*François, ou cauchemars et rêves*, 1939), and an anti-Hitler satire, but when the Nazis occupied Paris, they destroyed the original negative of *The Idea* and all copies of the other two films. Although depressed by losing years of work on *St Francis*, Bartosch began another film, about light and the cosmos, which he left unfinished at his death in 1968. *The Idea*, reconstructed from surviving prints in England and France, remains, in the beauty of its imagery, the grandeur of its social content, and its moving humanity, a supreme achievement of animation.

The book illustrators Alexandre Alexeieff and Claire Parker (a Russian and an American working in Paris) became intrigued with the idea of animating a 'visual music' that would have the subtlety of lithographs and the fluidity of music after seeing a black and white *Study* of Fischinger, Fernand Léger's *Ballet mécanique*, and Bartosch's *The Idea*. They invented a 'Pin Screen'—a white board with 500,000 pins stuck through it so that any pin could be pressed flat against the board to show white or gradually pressed forward from behind the board to show gradations of grey to black. Their 1933 *Une nuit sur le mont chauve* ('A night on the bare mountain') brilliantly depicts Mussorgsky's music with eerie images, such as a fight between a beautiful girl and an ugly hag in which, as they struggle, the girl becomes older and more haggard while the hag regains vitality and beauty—a haunting metaphor for cycles of nature. Parker and Alexeieff also made numerous animated commercials (a few of which they passed on to Bartosch). They fled to America during the war, and built a more complex Pin Screen with a million pins, which they used to create a lovely visualization of a French-Canadian folk song, *En passant* ('Passing by', 1943), for the National Film Board of Canada. After the war, back in Paris, they animated episodes for Orson Welles's 1962 *The Trial*, a wordless version of Gogol's story *The Nose* (1963), and two further Mussorgsky films, *Tableaux d'une exposition* ('Pictures from an exhibition', 1972) and *Trois thèmes* ('Three themes', 1980).

The British painter Anthony Gross, living in Paris, also moved from his graphic art into animated film, bringing an elegant styling to urbane, imaginative episodes, rather like literary short stories. His first two films are lost, but his third, *Joie de vivre* (1934) is a luminous masterpiece that catches the essence of the art deco inter-war decades. The thin thread of plot—two girls trespassing in a power plant are pursued by a guard, who simply wants to return a lost shoe—serves mainly as an excuse for extravagant fancy: the girls somersault from high-tension wires, transform into flowers in order to hide from their pursuer, swim in water represented by modernistic patterns, scramble tracks so express trains weave over and under each other,

and bicycle off into the sky with their new friend, the guard. The magic of the film arises from the perfection of choreography as well as the exquisite graphics: a frog's point of view of the sleeping guard, the funeral procession for a fallen flower, or the satyr statue in the forest. Gross designed and animated the film himself, and painted the 17,000 cels together with a wealthy American artist, Hector Hoppin, and their wives. Tibor Harsanyi composed a musical score that matches the images in elegance and wit. The Museum of Modern Art in New York purchased copies of *Joie de vivre* in 1935, so the film became well known in America and influenced the stylization of later cartoon work in the United States.

After triumphant premières of *Joie de vivre*, Gross returned to London to make a cartoon for Alexander Korda, *The Fox Hunt* (1936), whose brilliant use of colour lends additional levels of absurdity to the spoof of high-society sport, in the spirit of Oscar Wilde's quip, 'the unspeakable in pursuit of the uneatable'. Gross worked on a feature-length version of Jules Verne's *Around the World in Eighty Days*, but it remained unfinished at the beginning of the Second World War, and a surviving episode was only released as a short, *An Indian Fantasy*, in 1955. Surviving sketches for other episodes of the Verne tale, as well as for three other unfinished projects, make one regret that Gross did not find more commercial support for his film-making.

Ironically, three wonderful films resulted from the repression of the Nazi era. When Goebbels could no longer afford to import Disney films into Germany, he ordered all studios capable of producing animation to begin making cartoons to fill cinema programmes in Germany and its conquered territories. Hans Fischerkoesen had begun making animated advertising films in 1921, and devoted himself solely to this genre, creating more than 1,000 before the outbreak of the Second World War. On Goebbels's orders, he turned his small staff to make three cartoons, *Weather-Beaten Melody* (*Verwitterte Melodie*, 1942), *The Snowman* (*Der Schneemann*, 1943), and *The Silly Goose* (*Das dumme Gänslein*, 1944). Fischerkoesen was an anti-Nazi pacifist, and he managed to charge all three films with a subversive message, which, because of the films' technical brilliance, could not be suppressed. Jazz was formally forbidden in Germany as a degenerate Afro-Judaic art form, but *Weather-Beaten Melody* shows a bee discovering a phonograph abandoned in a meadow, and proceeding to play the jazz record with her stinger, to the delight of the forest creatures, who dance sometimes in miscegenated couples. The Snowman is so eager to escape from the grim world of winter that he hides in a refrigerator until summer; even though he melts, it is worth it. The Silly Goose is a non-conformist who refuses to march in line or exercise like her siblings, and while she at first falls for the wily fox, she discovers that he imprisons and tortures animals, and gets other animals to help chase him away, and free his victims. Each of these cartoons uses dazzling depth effects, calibrated on layers of cels to simulate a moving camera, and each contains many joyous, beautiful, funny moments, so they survive the grim context in which they were created. Fischerkoesen went back to advertising films after the war, and won many prizes for his clever commercials.

Many other artists produced fine animation in this period, of whom three may be singled out, though they are only the tip of the iceberg. Hungarian George Pal worked in Germany before the Nazi era, then fled to Holland where he made puppet animation commercials for Philips. When he fled to the USA in 1940, his staff in Holland worked as inbetweeners and ink-and-paint artists for Fischerkoesen. Between 1940 and 1949 Pal produced Puppetoons for Paramount, including a series starring a black minstrel boy Jasper, and the classic *Tubby the Tuba* (1947), which approaches UPA in its non-violent, constructive story and contemporary musical score. Pal turned his animation skills to special effects for fantasy and science-fiction features after 1950.

Paul Grimault began making films in 1936. His 1943 *L' Épouvantail* ('The scarecrow') shares the protest allegory with Fischerkoesen, but lacks the German's charm and finesse. But *Le Petit Soldat* ('The little soldier', 1947), with a script by Jacques Prévert after Hans Christian Andersen, is a classic of sensitive animation for adults as well as children. His feature *La Bergère et le ramoneur* ('The shepherdess and the chimneysweep'), also Prévert–Andersen, was shown in an incomplete hour-long form during the early 1950s to considerable praise; he was only able to finish it and release it under the title *Le Roi et l'oiseau* ('The king and the bird') in 1979.

In Japan, Noburo Ofuji (1900–74) made silent silhouette animation using layers of traditional semi-transparent Japanese paper, not only for delicate effects, as in the 1924 *Haname-zaki* ('Sitting beneath the cherry blossoms'), but also for dynamic action as in the 1927 *Kujira* ('The whale', remade in colour in 1953). His 1955 *Yurei Sen* (*The Phantom Ship*) won a prize at the Venice Film Festival, and his final film was a feature-length *Shaka no Shogai* ('Life of Buddha', 1961).

Bibliography
Beck, Jerry, and Friedwald, Will (1989), *Looney Tunes and Merrie Melodies*.
Bendazzi, Giannalberto (1994), *Cartoons: One Hundred Years of Cinema Animation*.
Canemaker, John (ed.) (1988), *Storytelling in Animation*.
Culhane, Shamus (1986), *Talking Animals and Other People*.
Edera, Bruno (1977), *Full Length Animated Feature Films*.
Thomas, Frank, and Johnston, Ollie (1981), *Disney Animation: The Illusion of Life*.
Vrielynck, Roger (1981), *Le cinéma d'animation avant et après Walt Disney*.

GENRE CINEMA

Cinema and Genre

RICK ALTMAN

GENRE BEFORE FILM

Borrowed from the French word meaning 'kind' or 'type' (and derived from the Latin word *genus*), the notion of genre has played an important role in the categorization and evaluation of literature, especially since the Italian–French Aristotelian revival of the sixteenth and seventeenth centuries. In literary studies, the term 'genre' is used in a variety of ways, to refer to distinctions of different orders between categories of text: type of presentation (epic/lyric/dramatic), relation to reality (fiction/nonfiction), level of style (epic/novel), kind of plot (comedy/tragedy), nature of content (sentimental novel/historical novel/adventure novel), and so forth.

In an attempt to lend order to this confusing situation, nineteenth-century positivism spawned scientific attempts to model the study of literary genres first on Linnaeus' binomial classification of animals and plants (where each separate type is identified by two Latin words indicating genus and species), followed by even more insistent schemes to base the study of genre history on Darwinian notions of the evolution of genus and species. Culminating around the turn of the century, at the very time when cinema was being transformed from a new-fangled curiosity into a lucrative world-wide industry, these appeals to scientific models failed to lend precision to the notion of 'genre', even though generic designators continued to be widely used as broad categories for the sorting and classification of large numbers of texts.

EARLY FILM GENRE

During the earliest years of film production, individual films were most often identified by length and topic, with genre terms applied to films in only the loosest of fashions ('fight pictures' in the late 1890s or 'story films' after 1904). When around 1910 film production finally outstripped demand, genre terms were used increasingly to identify and differentiate films. Whereas literary genre was primarily a response to theoretical questions or to practical large-scale classification needs (such as library organization), early film genre terminology served as shorthand communication between film distributors and exhibitors.

The earliest film genre terminology was commonly borrowed from pre-existing literary or theatrical language ('comedy' and 'romance') or simply described subject-matter ('war pictures'). Subsequent film genre vocabulary was often derived from specifically filmic production practices ('trick film', 'animated picture', 'chase film', 'newsreel', or *'film d'art'*). As cinema production became standardized during and after the First World War, however, genre terminology became increasingly specialized, designating not the broad genres of the literary or theatrical tradition, but diverse subgenres of cinema's two major strains, melodrama and comedy. Before 1910, in the United States, distributors and exhibitors regularly used both a particularizing adjective and a generalizing noun to describe genres ('chase comedy' or 'western melodrama'). During the later silent period, the noun was often dropped, while the adjective took on a substantive role. Thus 'slapstick', 'farce', and 'burlesque' became separate genres rather than simply types of comedy. Similarly, cinema's debt to melodrama was disguised by the use of generic terms like 'Western', 'suspense', 'horror', 'serial', or 'swashbuckler' in the United States, *'Kammerspiel'* in Germany, 'boulevard film' in France, and *'jidaigeki'* (period film) or *'gendaigeki'* (film of modern life) in Japan.

GENRE FILM IN THE STUDIO PERIOD

In dealing with genre terminology, it is important to distinguish among the different functions that the notion of genre may play for the various participants in the cinema process. Three roles in particular must be recognized:

1. Production: the generic concept provides a template for production decisions. As a form of tacit knowledge, it presents a privileged mode of communication among members of the production team.
2. Distribution: the generic concept offers a fundamental method of product differentiation, thus constituting a shorthand mode of communication between producer and distributor or between distributor and exhibitor.
3. Consumption: the generic concept describes standard patterns of spectator involvement. As such, it facilitates communication between the exhibitor and the audience, or among audience members.

By definition, all films belong to some genre(s), at least in terms of distribution categories, but only certain films are self-consciously produced and consumed according to (or against) a specific generic model. When the notion of genre is limited to descriptive uses, as it commonly is when serving distribution or classification purposes, we speak of 'film genre'. However, when the notion of genre takes on a more active role in the production and consumption processes, we appropriately speak instead of 'genre film', thus recognizing the extent to which generic identification becomes a formative component of film viewing.

Nascent and evolving film industries are characterized by weak film genres, while genre films are produced by mature film industries, such as those that developed in the United States, France, Germany, and Japan between the wars, or large industries that produce primarily for a national or regional audience, such as those that exist in China and India today. Though genres are important to the understanding of all national cinema industries, the Hollywood studio system has exercised world-wide hegemony over genre film production since the 1930s. Whereas the US industry has imposed a series of strong genres on audiences around the world for over half a century, genres represented by other national industries have and large generated fewer films and have been less codified, less widely recognized, active only intermittently or restricted to B production, and subject to the influence of US genres.

Growth in genre film production is usually accompanied by a shift from content-based notions of genre to genre definitions based on repeated plot motifs, recurrent image patterns, standardized narrative configurations, and predictable reception conventions. In the United States, the first films that we now think of as 'Westerns' were in fact not so conceived by contemporary audiences. *The Great Train Robbery* (1903), for example, was assimilated to the many other stage melodramas adapted by early film-makers; instead of immediately serving as a model for future Westerns, it first inspired a spate of crime films. Within a decade, however, a growing production of 'western chase films', 'western melodramas', 'western romances', and 'western epics' solidified into a genre called simply the 'Western'. In its early manifestations, as the many possible associations of the adjective clearly suggest, the Western could take on any of a multitude of different plots, characters, or tones. During the 1910s and 1920s, however, the possibilities implied by a simple geographical designator (along with diverse influences from a growing western iconography and literature) were explored, sifted, and codified. Once only a geographical adjective designating a favoured location for films of various types, 'Western' quickly became the name for a loosely defined distribution-oriented film genre capitalizing on public interest in the West. Later a strengthened and conventionalized generic concept would inspire the repeated production of genre films systematically interpreted by spectators according to standards particular to the 'Western'.

In a similar manner, it is commonly alleged that the musical burst on to the Hollywood scene with the coming of sound. In fact, the first films built around entertainers and their music were not identified as 'musicals'. Instead, the presence of music was at first treated simply as a manner of presenting narrative material that already had its own generic affinities. During the early years of sound in Hollywood, we thus find the term 'musical' always used as an adjective, modifying such diverse nouns as comedy, romance, melodrama, entertainment, attraction, dialogue, and revue. Even films currently considered as classics of the early musical were not labelled as musicals when they first appeared. In 1929 *The Broadway Melody* was described in MGM publicity as an 'all talking, all singing, all dancing dramatic sensation', while Warners characterized *The Desert Song* as an 'all talking, all singing operetta'. Not until the end of the year was the term 'musical' promoted to substantive status, with the description of Radio Pictures' *Rio Rita* as a 'screen musical'.

Ironically, the use of 'musical' as a free-standing term designating a specific genre did not achieve general acceptance until the 1930–1 season, when the public's taste for musicals took a nosedive. Only retrospectively, in reference to the production of the preceding years, could films of such differing natures appear to constitute a coherent grouping. While already constituting the type of category that we call film genre, musical films in this early period had not yet become genre films as such, for the conventions characteristic of genre film production and consumption had not yet been established. Not until 1933, with the definitive merger of music-making and romantic comedy, did the term 'musical' abandon its adjectival, descriptive function and become a noun—as when Warners' *42nd Street* was referred to as an 'out-and-out musical'.

As genres gain coherence and win audiences, their influence in all aspects of the cinema experience grows. For production teams, generic norms provide a welcome template facilitating rapid delivery of quality film products. Screen-writers increasingly conceive their efforts in relation to the plot formulas and character types associated with particular genres. Casting agencies are better able to predict the physical types and acting skills required by the film industry. Primary aesthetic personnel (director, cinematographer, sound designer, composer, art director) save time by recycling solutions already worked out in previous genre productions. Other personnel (carpenters, costume masters, make-up artists, location scouts, musicians, editors, mixers, etc.) economize by

Howard Hawks

(1896–1977)

The son of a wealthy paper mill owner, Hawks moved with his family from the Midwest to California at the age of 10. After graduating from Cornell, where he studied mechanical engineering, he returned to Los Angeles to work in the property department of the Famous Players–Lasky studio. During the First World War he served as a flight instructor for the US army in Texas and, after his discharge, he raced cars and built and flew aeroplanes. In 1922 he went to work in Paramount's story department. By 1925 Hawks had moved to Fox, where he was first a screen-writer and was then given a chance to direct (*The Road to Glory*, 1926). He worked, under short-term contracts, for a variety of studios for the remainder of his career, though in the post-war era he took increasing control over his own projects through a series of independent production companies in which he was part owner.

Hawks's social vision was shaped in the 1930s as his films began to examine the dramatic interaction among groups of men engaged in common professions or activities, such as pilots in *The Dawn Patrol* (1930), *Ceiling Zero* (1936), and *Only Angels Have Wings* (1939); gangsters in *The Criminal Code* (1931) and *Scarface* (1932); soldiers in *Today We Live* (1933) and *The Road to Glory* (1936); racing car drivers in *The Crowd Roars* (1932); and fishermen in *Tiger Shark* (1932). These action films glorify male interdependency, collective activity, and the cathartic release of interpersonal tension through action. Though his films celebrate the ethos of action, professionalism, and male stoicism, they also expose the conflict that arises between repressive, professional codes of behaviour and personal desires and feelings. Hawks tends to cast this conflict in terms of a struggle between male and female elements at war within a single (male) psyche. Thus the male stoicism symbolized by the Hawksian hero (e.g. Cary Grant in *Only Angels Have Wings* or John Wayne in *Red River*, 1948) is seen as excessive. These characters need to be humanized by undergoing a feminization of sorts, effected by the influence of women and by the male characters' ultimate recognition not only of their own vulnerability but also of their need for others.

The male characters in Hawks's action films resist change; those in his comedies learn to adapt to it. The comedies involve a similar sexual conflict in which the female characters oversee the 'feminization' of the men, a transformation most brilliantly realized in *Bringing up Baby* (1938), and *I Was a Male War Bride* (1948), when Cary Grant is forced to wear female attire. But in the comedies, Hawks remains more interested in the fluidity of sexual roles and in the unleashing of sexual repression than in resolving any sexual imbalance within a single psyche or between the sexes. Thus the comedies tend to perpetuate sexual antagonism, dramatizing it as a process without closure, while the dramas re-establish sexual harmony, balance, and order.

Hawks's visual style gradually evolved during the 1930s and 1940s to reflect his social vision. His camera remained steadfastly eye-level, engaging with his characters on their own ground; but the space within which they interacted gradually expanded from the relatively shallow depth of field of the early 1930s to the modified deep focus of the 1940s, represented by his work with Gregg Toland (*The Road to Glory*, 1936; *Come and Get it*, 1936; *Ball of Fire*, 1942; *A Song is Born*, 1948), James Wong Howe (*Air Force*, 1943), and Russell Harlan (*Red River*, *The Big Sky*, 1952; *Rio Bravo*, 1959; *Hatari!*, 1962; and *Man's Favorite Sport?*, 1964). In these films, Hawks's characters occupy a well-lit middleground in which they exchange dialogue and gestures with one another in an egalitarian process of give and take. The relationship of the Hawksian individual to a larger group is regularly worked out in spatial terms—through that individual's incorporation into a democratically structured, communal space.

Although his thematic vision was shaped in the 1930s, Hawks remains one of the most 'modern' of Hollywood film-makers. Like Buster Keaton, Hawks is an artist of the machine age. His aviators and race car drivers realize their identity, in part, through their relationship with machines. Though his films are occasionally set in the past, his characters always live in an existential present. Indeed, obsession with the past is viewed as neurotic; psychic health is seen in the ability constantly to revise earlier judgements on the basis of new information and

intuitively to make split-second decisions. Hawks's 'modernity' also informs his representation of women, who enjoy rare independence, autonomy, and power in his films. His women are post-Victorian; neither virgins nor whores, they belong to the post-war (First World War) phenomenon of the 'New Woman'. New Women are women who were 'emancipated' by mass culture (and by the Nineteenth Amendment to the American Constitution). They entered the public sphere, voted, worked, smoked, and engaged in a variety of activities previously reserved for men. The typical Hawks woman, epitomized in Lauren Bacall, has pronounced 'masculine' traits; she is husky-voiced, worldly, tough, insolent, cynical, and sexually aggressive. She lives in a man's world and engages with men on more or less equal footing, yet she also retains her identity as a woman as well as an essential innocence. Though partly a fantasy figure concocted by narcissistic male desire in search of an idealized, female *alter ego*, the Hawksian woman addresses issues of female desire and agency with an openness and directness that are uncommon in American cinema.

Hawks is generally regarded as one of the three greatest American directors, along with Alfred Hitchcock and John Ford. In 1962 the British magazine *Movie* placed Howard Hawks in the 'Great' category, a ranking which he shared with only one other American director, Alfred Hitchcock. (Orson Welles was only 'Brilliant', and John Ford merely 'Very Talented'.) Though Hawks was the subject of a number of full-length studies prior to his death in 1977, relatively little has been written about him since 1982. He has reverted to the state of invisibility in which Andrew Sarris found him back in 1968: 'the least known and least appreciated Hollywood director of any stature.' The problem lies in Hawks's apparent transparency, in a stylistic presence that is relentlessly invisible, self-effacing, difficult to see, and extremely difficult to analyse. The subtlety of Hawks's style is one of the most significant features of his work, but it is also the greatest obstacle to the widespread recognition of his talent as a film-maker.

JOHN BELTON

SELECT FILMOGRAPHY

The Dawn Patrol (1930); Scarface (1932); Twentieth Century (1934); Bringing up Baby (1938); Only Angels Have Wings (1939); His Girl Friday (1940); Sergeant York (1941); Ball of Fire (1942); Air Force (1943); To Have and Have Not (1944); The Big Sleep (1946); Red River (1948); Gentlemen Prefer Blondes (1953); Rio Bravo (1959); Man's Favorite Sport? (1964); El Dorado (1967)

BIBLIOGRAPHY

McBride, Joseph (ed.) (1972), *Focus on Howard Hawks*.
—— (1982), *Hawks on Hawks*.
Mast, Gerald (1982), *Howard Hawks, Storyteller*.
Poague, Leland (1982), *Howard Hawks*.
Wood, Robin (1981), *Howard Hawks*.

Opposite: Humphrey Bogart and Lauren Bacall in a characteristically atmospheric scene from Howard Hawks's *To Have and Have Not* (1944)

recombining previous genre elements (Western sets, period costumes, stock footage, library sound effects, and the like). Each genre film thus benefits from the significant economies associated with assembly-line production.

Distribution and exhibition are also heavily affected by the constitution of generic norms. Instead of considering each spectator as an individual, exhibitors conceptualize spectators in batches thanks to demonstrable audience fidelity to specific genres. Generic identification devices—genre names, imagery, sound bites, plot motifs, or generically identified actors—serve an important publicity function, a sort of mating call to the committed genre viewer. As individual genres gain support and specificity, they increasingly spawn specialized support systems: newspaper columns, fan clubs, commercial products, cartoons and shorts, even art work, magazines, and books.

For audiences, generic norms offer the comfort of a simplified decision-making process. Thanks to generic shorthand, spectators take quite specific expectations to genre film viewing. While the generic audience is often considered rather simple-minded, regularly repeating familiar rituals, it is only through the added level of generic expectations that the most complex viewing patterns can be established, along with the added complication of frustrated generic expectations. This is why many film movements have based their production on implicit generic norms (the French 'Nouvelle Vague', 'New American Cinema' in the USA, and even politically radical Latin American film).

THE GENERIC SPECTATOR

Theoreticians of literary genre never tire of repeating that readers always have some generic concept(s) in mind as they read. Certainly, we must recognize the necessary contribution of genre to all types of comprehension, including the interpretation of films. Yet not all films engage spectators' generic knowledge in the same way and to the same extent. While some films simply borrow devices from established genres, others foreground their generic characteristics to the point where the genre concept itself plays a major role in the film. This is most obviously the case of the many recent films that parody well-known genres, but it is equally true of classic genre films. For a cinema industry based on genre films depends not only on the regular production of recognizably similar films, and on the maintenance of a standardized distribution/exhibition system, but also on the constitution and maintenance of a stable, generically trained audience, sufficiently knowledgeable about genre systems to recognize generic cues, sufficiently familiar with genre plots to exhibit generic expectations, and sufficiently committed to generic values to tolerate and even enjoy in genre films capricious, violent, or licentious behaviour which they might disapprove of in 'real life'.

RKO's 1935 Astaire–Rogers vehicle *Top Hat* offers a particularly clear view of the tensions involved in generic spectatorship. Simultaneously offering dance music, images of dancing feet, and the familiar generically coded names of Fred Astaire and Ginger Rogers, *Top Hat*'s credits provide an obvious cue. 'This is a musical,' they clearly say. 'Don't watch if you don't like musicals, but if you do your musical pleasure is guaranteed.' Now a musical, as the genre's critics regularly remind us, cannot exist without its three constitutive moments: 'Boy meets girl, boy dances with girl, boy gets girl.' But in *Top Hat*, from the very start, this process runs into trouble. When Astaire awakens Rogers with his nocturnal tap dancing, she does what any proper young lady in a posh hotel would do in the 1930s: rather than complaining directly to the offending noise-maker, she complains to the management. According to this scenario, the manager would quieten Astaire, report back to Rogers, and the incident would be closed. And there would be no musical (because there would be no 'boy meets girl'). Already, at this early point in the film, the spectator's allegiances are being tested. Should Rogers obey proper etiquette? Or should she shun society's definition of acceptable behaviour in favour of conduct becoming the musical? The spectator hesitates not a moment: generic pleasure is always preferable to social correctness.

Throughout *Top Hat*, this strategy is repeated. Generic pleasure becomes increasingly distant from and eventually antithetical to society's mores. When Astaire invites Rogers to dance, she believes that he is married to her best friend (though the spectator knows otherwise). Rogers at first hesitates to dance with Fred, once again jeopardizing our generic pleasure ('boy dances with girl'). When Rogers's best friend encourages her not only to dance with Astaire, but to dance closer, the spectator is delighted, for Rogers's sense of participating in a forbidden act only heightens viewing pleasure. So far, we spectators have been successful in keeping clear of any unauthorized desires by projecting them on to Ginger. Shortly, Rogers will 'do the right thing', marrying her employer in order to avoid the temptation of further flings with Astaire, thus jeopardizing our generic pleasure yet again ('boy gets girl'). We are thus delighted when Astaire and the now married Rogers go for a boat ride together. This time we have quite literally had to choose an adulterous liaison in order to guarantee continued generic pleasure.

Earlier, we did not desire the forbidden; we only desired Rogers's desiring the forbidden. Now we find ourselves openly celebrating the emotional consummation of an adulterous love affair. When we are in the world, we follow its rules; when we enter into a genre film, all our decisions are self-consciously modified to support a different kind of satisfaction. In the Western and the gangster film we long for the spectacle of a type of violence that society roundly condemns. In the horror film we actively choose the plot options that assure danger over those that guarantee safety. From one genre to another, the genre spectator always participates in overtly counter-cultural acts.

In the process of generic spectatorship we thus recognize the following elements:

1. Generic audience: sufficiently familiar with the genre to participate in a fully genre-based viewing;
2. Generic rules and conventions: methods of film construction and interpretation consistent with generic norms;
3. Generic contract: implicit agreement between genre producers (to provide advertised generic pleasures) and genre consumers (to expect and prefer specific generic events and pleasures);
4. Generic tension: the tension, built into genre films, between the actualization of generic norms and failure to respect those norms, often in favour of an alternative set of socially sanctioned norms;
5. Generic frustration: the emotion generated by a film's failure to respect generic norms.

As with any signifying system, the generically coded encounter of a genre film with a generic audience remains subject to historical change. What was sensed as generic frustration in the studio era turns into meta-generic pleasure during the recent era of genre parody.

GENRE HISTORY

As Hollywood's size and world-wide influence grew with the transition to sound, generic categories and generic codification took on new importance. Throughout the 1920s, adherence to genre norms was regularly sacrificed to the idiosyncrasies of European directors like Lubitsch, Murnau, and Stroheim; to zany comedians like Chaplin, Keaton, Langdon, Lloyd, and Normand; and to superstar directors like Griffith and DeMille who could follow their own inclinations. By the time the industry had recovered from conversion to sound and its many ramifications, little room was left for idiosyncrasy. With few exceptions, studio financing required that standardized products roll off the production line on a regular, predictable basis. Throughout the studio period, genres were more than just a convenience; they were for all practical purposes a commercial necessity.

Executives of every studio shared the assumption that successful films were the product not of individual genius but of innovative adherence to general formulas. Every successful film might thus potentially generate a new generic model. When Warners produced *Disraeli* as their prestige production for 1929, they were simply choosing a pre-sold script (from the still popular 1911 Louis Napoleon Parker play) and a ready-made leading man (George Arliss, who had played the lead on the stage and in a silent film

A genre of its own? The particular humour of the Marx Brothers (pictured here in a scene from *A Night in Casablanca*, 1946) was one of the many different brands of comedy which flourished in the 1930s and 1940s

version) at a time when every studio was scrambling to locate suitable properties for sound films. Expected to succeed primarily with the up-market audiences usually referred to as the 'carriage trade', *Disraeli* enjoyed a popular triumph exceeding all expectations: six months' stay in New York, a consecutive world-wide run of 1,697 days in over 29,000 separate theatres, and a total audience of over 170 million spectators speaking twenty-four different languages.

As if scientifically assaying the film, Warners produced several series of films during the early 1930s in an attempt to discover *Disraeli*'s formula for success: filmed stage plays, period costume dramas, films about rich statesmen or foreign financiers, and further films directed by Alfred E. Green starring George Arliss. Eventually, a biography of another foreign statesman came close to replicating *Disraeli*'s popular success—*Voltaire* (1933). In fact, it did well enough to convince Darryl Zanuck to take George Arliss

with him as he left Warners to found Twentieth Century Productions. Hollywood's ultimate assayer, Zanuck always recognized gold when he saw it: at his new studio he would feature Arliss in a series of films capitalizing on the biography-of-a-famous-foreigner formula confirmed by *Voltaire*'s success.

Without Arliss, Warners was unable to compete. Not until Paul Muni emerged as a potential leading man for foreign biographies would Warners reap the benefits of their experiments with Arliss. Cheaply produced, Muni's first 'bio-pic', *The Story of Louis Pasteur* (1936), achieved unexpected box-office success, setting off a new assay sequence. When audiences showed little interest in a female medical heroine (Florence Nightingale in *The White Angel*), Warners returned to Muni for *The Life of Emile Zola* (1937). This time, Warners had got it right, so it kept the entire team intact for *Juarez* two years later. This was Muni's third biography of a famous foreigner; director William Dieterle was on

George Cukor

(1899–1983)

Born to a Jewish Hungarian family in New York City, George Cukor began his career in the theatre, stage-managing and directing in summer stock and on Broadway in the early 1920s. With the advent of sound Cukor was able to make the transition to Hollywood, joining Paramount in 1929 as a dialogue coach, and moving quickly to co-directing, then directing. His theatrical background remained evident throughout his career in his penchant for films of plays such as *Dinner at Eight* (1933), *The Women* (1939), and *The Philadelphia Story* (1940), as well as in his loving and sharp-eyed treatment of theatrical settings in films like *What Price Hollywood?* (1932) and *A Star is Born* (1954). These films, along with *Camille* (1936), remain among the best loved of Hollywood films.

Cukor's talents functioned well in a collaborative medium, and his collaborators deeply influenced his films. He valued the work of writers, especially friends Anita Loos, Donald Ogden Stewart, and Zoë Akins, who were often on the set for last-minute script changes. From 1947 to 1954 Cukor made a run of highly successful films with husband-and-wife writing team Garson Kanin and Ruth Gordon: *A Double Life* (1947), *Adam's Rib* (1949), *The Marrying Kind* (1952), *Pat and Mike* (1952), and *It Should Happen to You* (1953). In 1953 Cukor teamed up with his friend photographer George Hoyningen-Huene and Warner Bros. sketch artist Gene Allen to make *A Star is Born* and *Les Girls* (1957). The work of this team brought an added Technicolor visual intensity to Cukor's screen style, proving that he was not just a photographer of stage plays, but that he had strongly developed cinematic as well as dramatic instincts.

Cukor's greatest collaborators were no doubt his stars. Already recognized on Broadway for his work with actresses, Cukor worked effectively and repeatedly with Greta Garbo, Joan Crawford, Katharine Hepburn, and others. Given Cukor's Pygmalion-like efforts, it is not surprising that the theme of a woman's transformation at the hands of a man is a common one in his films. Nor was he a surprising choice to direct *My Fair Lady* (1964), the musical adaptation of George Bernard Shaw's *Pygmalion*.

In many ways, Cukor's collaborative facility made him a perfect company man in the studio system. Although he was not a quick worker, he got on well with studio heads, being willing to do screen tests and fill in for absent directors. Yet despite his compliance, Cukor had several notable disagreements with his bosses. He sued his first employer, Paramount, over his screen credit for *One Hour With You* (1932), which Ernst Lubitsch had supervised. The studio responded by releasing Cukor from his contract, allowing him to move to RKO to work for David O. Selznick, whom Cukor followed to MGM in 1933. When Selznick started his own independent company in 1936, Cukor had contracts with both MGM and Selznick, making him one of the most highly paid directors of the era.

Cukor's most notorious clash with a studio came when Selznick fired him from the set of *Gone with the Wind* (1939), only ten days after the start of production. The expense of his salary, the complications of his two contracts, and disagreements about the script contributed to his dismissal, but reliable accounts also implicate Clark Gable's phobia of Cukor's homosexuality. The incident underlines the difficulties faced by gay men in Hollywood. If Cukor was thought of as a director of 'women's pictures', this merged in many minds with his never-hidden homosexuality: in Joseph L. Mankiewicz's words, Cukor was 'the great female director of Hollywood'. Current critical estimates that Cukor's abilities stemmed from his 'homosexual sensibility' continue to oversimplify his psychological, dramatic, and visual talents.

The breakdown of the studio system did not treat Cukor kindly. He was ill-suited to develop his own projects without the studio machinery, and the production company he had formed with art director Gene Allen in 1963 failed to produce results. His later films did not fare well with either critics or the public. As an artist who had fitted supremely well into Hollywood, Cukor's career declined with the system that had nurtured it.

EDWARD R. O'NEILL

Select Filmography

What Price Hollywood? (1932); Dinner at Eight (1933) ; Sylvia Scarlett (1935); Camille (1936); Holiday (1938); The Women (1939); The Philadelphia Story (1940); Gaslight (1944); Adam's Rib (1949); A Star is Born (1954); Bhowani Junction (1956); Les Girls (1957); My Fair Lady (1964); Travels with my Aunt (1972)

Bibliography

Bernardoni, James (1985), *George Cukor: A Critical Study and Filmography*.
Carey, Gary (1971), *Cukor & Co.: The Films of George Cukor and his Collaborators*.
Clarens, Carlos (1976), *George Cukor*.
Lambert, Gavin (1972), *On Cukor*.
McGilligan, Patrick (1991), *George Cukor: A Double Life*.

Cary Grant and Katharine Hepburn in George Cukor's brilliant comedy *The Philadelphia Story* (1940). The film was remade as the musical *High Society* with Frank Sinatra, Grace Kelly, and Bing Crosby in 1956

his fourth (out of an eventual six); Henry Blanke was producing his third Warners bio-pic; Tony Gaudio was directing photography for his fourth foreign biography. Edward G. Robinson replaced Muni for the last two films in the series. All in all, said Warners' story editor Finlay McDermid in October 1941, 'roughly forty such biographies . . . were contemplated to the point of purchase or partial research development'.

What can we learn about genre from the example of bio-pics? First, while genres are sometimes borrowed fully constituted from literature or theatre, they can be built out of virtually any material. Secondly, every successful film not already identified with a specific filmic genre triggers a process of attempted genre constitution in which the studio tests a series of hypotheses regarding the specific source of success. Thirdly, these attempts at identifying and replicating a successful formula invariably involve organizing the studio's executive, artistic, and technical personnel into semi-permanent mini-units. Fourthly, when a successful formula is discovered, it never escapes other studios, thus leading to the constitution of a full-fledged industry-wide genre. Fifthly, genres 'drift' along with the formulas on which they rely; just as Warners' bio-pic heroes slide from statesmen to medical geniuses, so MGM and Fox shift from European politicians to impresarios, composers, and other musical stars, yet all the while retaining the same basic structure.

It is important to note that film producers are not the only players in the game of genre constitution. While some film genres are recycled from literary or theatrical sources, and others are primarily developed within the cinema industry, still others can be constituted after the fact by critics or audiences. What we today call 'film noir', for example, was named and defined by post-war French critics. Cutting across genres which Hollywood had known by names as various as 'gangster', 'crime', 'detective', 'hard-boiled', or 'psychological thriller', the notion of film noir stressed a different set of traits shared by many wartime and immediately post-war films, transferring attention from similar plot material to a common atmosphere derived from character type, dialogue style, and lighting choices.

This ability to reconfigure generic boundaries depends on strong support mechanisms equivalent to the studio publicity and journalistic criticism institutions traditionally exploited by cinema industries to anchor and perpetuate genre norms. If the notion of film noir gained general acceptance, it is largely because of the growth of cinema studies as an academic and cultural industry.

Today, the fragmentation of both media and audiences, along with the ability to target specific audience segments, makes it far more probable than ever before that new generic configurations will be constituted by contemporary audiences using old genres in new ways. While consumer interests redefine a wide spectrum of films (and television programmes) according to their sartorial splendour, high-tech equipment, or flashy automobiles, counter-culture groups constitute alternative generic grids through attention to feminist, racially oriented, or gay concerns. During the heyday of production-based genre film, from the 1930s to the 1950s, a number of factors militated against audience-based genres: the importance of a shared national public sphere, centralized control of production and distribution, general ideological homogeneity, and the absence of alternative communications systems. As the century closes, to the tune of satellite transmission, electronic mail, facsimile machines, and cellular phones, it seems clear that the generic future will increasingly depend on audience viewing patterns.

A convenient way of configuring the complexities of genre history is to recognize that genres depend on two related but quite different aspects. Minimally, all films of a particular genre share certain separate elements that we may call 'semantic' components. For example, we recognize a film as a Western when we see some combination of horses, rough-and-tumble characters, illegal acts, semi-settled wilderness, natural earth colours, tracking shots, and a general respect for the actual history of the American West (to name but a few of the extremely diverse semantic elements that characterize the Western).

When genres develop from their initial adjective-based breadth to a more focused noun-oriented definition, they develop a certain 'syntactic' consistency by regularly deploying similar methods of making the various semantic components cohere: plot patterns, guiding metaphors, aesthetic hierarchies, and the like. While any film located in the American West might well be characterized as a Western, there are important differences between films that employ western trappings simply to justify a western song, induce a horse laugh, or study Indian customs, and those that systematically oppose expanding civilization to dwindling wilderness, concretize community-supporting laws and divisive individualism in two sets of diametrically opposed characters, and internalize those oppositions in a complex hero combining certain attributes of both sides.

Film genres typically share common semantic features; genre films build common semantic features into a shared syntax. The meanings carried by semantic elements are usually borrowed from pre-existing social codes; syntactic features, on the other hand, more fully express the specific meaning of a particular genre. When genres are said to fulfil a given function within society, it is almost always to the syntax that critics refer. Writing the history of individual film genres (and describing the relationship between genres) is significantly facilitated by an understanding of genre as involving two separable types of

Barbara Stanwyck

(1907–1990)

Barbara Stanwyck's long career includes more than eighty films in over forty years, spread across a variety of genres from romantic comedy to melodrama to Westerns to film noir. By the late 1940s Stanwyck had created such a resilient and commanding image that she was able to continue working thoughout the decline of the studio system and the rise of television, and she remained popular up until her death.

Born Ruby Stevens in 1907, Stanwyck was orphaned young, spending her childhood in a series of foster homes. Beginning her theatrical work as a chorus girl in night-clubs and on Broadway during the early 1920s, Stanwyck made the transition from chorine to successful and serious actress by landing a small part as a chorus girl in a now-forgotten play *The Noose* in 1925. The small part developed into a larger one during out-of-town previews, and Stanwyck's rapid on-the-job training ended in a highly successful Broadway run.

In 1928 Stanwyck moved to Hollywood and after a shaky start had her first success in Frank Capra's *Ladies of Leisure* in 1930. While still an unknown, Stanwyck signed two non-exclusive contracts (with Columbia and Warner Bros.), an arrangement which gave her unusual freedom in choosing films, and allowed her to work with the most prominent directors in Hollywood at the time, including Howard Hawks, Preston Sturges, Billy Wilder, King Vidor, John Ford, and Frank Capra (with whom she made four films, including *Meet John Doe*, 1941). Stanwyck's bold and forthright persona in her films was matched by her professionalism on the set, and she was deeply admired by colleagues as well as audiences.

Stanwyck was not only a virtuoso in the fast-talking comedies of the period, such as Hawks's *Ball of Fire* (1941) and Sturges's *The Lady Eve* (1941), but she was equally powerful in melodramas like King Vidor's *Stella Dallas* (1937) and Mitchell Leisen's *Remember the Night* (1939, based on a Preston Sturges script). Along with Joan Crawford and Bette Davis, Stanwyck dominated the industry in the late 1930s and early 1940s, in 1944 being declared by the Internal Revenue Service to be the highest-paid woman in the USA. Like Crawford, Stanwyck was often cast as a tough working-class woman bent not only on survival but on social advance. In the 1930s films this social climbing could often be crowned with success; but in the noir films of the 1940s, Stanwyck's characters were usually trapped in unhappy marriages, and attempts to escape were often—as, most famously, in *Double Indemnity* (1944)—criminal and usually ill-fated. From her earlier roles as a tough-talking and cynical woman with a heart of gold, Stanwyck's emotional power and directness were refashioned after the Second World War as coldness and even greed.

In the 1950s, her strong image was mobilized in the Western genre. She was drafted into roles as a powerful

Double Indemnity (Billy Wilder, 1944)

and often scheming matriarch (most spectacularly in Sam Fuller's *Forty Guns*, 1957), and made more than twenty films during the decade. Meanwhile television was beginning to co-opt the Western genre, with broadcasts of older films as well as new, inexpensive series, produced on old movie sets. To keep her career alive, Stanwyck crossed to the new medium, playing the family matriarch on *The Big Valley* from 1965 to 1969, and returning to television in the 1980s to play similar roles in the mini-series *The Thorn Birds* (1983), and in ABC's *The Colbys* (1985-6).

Her television work won her three Emmy awards. Although nominated four times, she never won an Oscar until 1982 when she received an honorary award for her entire career. When she died in 1990 at the age of 82, her image as an indomitable star had remained intact, despite the passing of the years, and the passing of the studio system which had produced that image.

EDWARD R. O'NEILL

Select Filmography

Ladies of Leisure (1930); The Bitter Tea of General Yen (1932); Stella Dallas (1937); Remember the Night (1939); The Lady Eve (1941); Ball of Fire (1941); Meet John Doe (1941); Double Indemnity (1944); The Strange Love of Martha Ivers (1946); The Two Mrs. Carrolls (1947); Sorry, Wrong Number (1948); The File on Thelma Jordan (1950); The Furies (1950); The Violent Men (1955); Forty Guns (1957).

Bibliography

DiOrio, Al (1983), *Barbara Stanwyck*.
Smith, Ella (1985), *Starring Miss Barbara Stanwyck*.

coherence, semantic and syntactic, that develop and dissipate at different rates and at different times, but always in close co-ordination, and according to a standardized pattern.

It has often been suggested, following the French anthropologist Claude Lévi-Strauss, that genres serve a ritual purpose, providing a repeated imaginary solution to the questions raised by society's constitutive contradictions. Viewed in this manner, the Western is seen to negotiate the opposing American values of individual freedom and community action, respect for the environment and need for industrial growth, or reverence for the past and desire to build a new future. Thus understood, genre films are produced by the cinema industry only at the behest of a specific audience, which uses films as a mode of cultural 'thinking'.

Other critics have seen genre films as an especially economical form of ideology. Instead of authoring films from afar, spectators are allowed to believe that they are getting what they want, while they are in fact lured into accepting the agenda of an industry, interest group, or government. Viewed in this manner, the Western appears as a complex way to justify seizure of Indian lands, substitution of the rule of law for prior systems of conflict resolution, and institution of a stable regime in the West based on secure settlement, transportation, and communication. In other words, the Western is an apology for the 'Manifest Destiny' doctrine and an excuse for the commercial exploitation of western lands and resources.

Overall, it seems most fruitful to recognize that successful studio film production depends to a certain extent on both functions. The longevity of film genres would be explained by a continued ability to achieve one or the other of these goals, while the special complexity and strength of genre films grows out of their capacity to fulfil both functions simultaneously. The process of establishing a stable generic syntax thus involves discovery of a common ground between the audience's ritual values and the industry's ideological commitments. The development of a specific syntax within a given semantic context thus serves a double function: it binds element to element in a logical order, at the same time accommodating audience desires to studio concerns. The successful genre owes its success not only to its reflection of an audience ideal, nor solely to its status as apology for the Hollywood enterprise, but to its ability to carry out both functions simultaneously. It is this sleight of hand, this strategic overdetermination, that most clearly characterizes successful genre film production.

Just as genres do not simply appear fully formed, so they fade away according to recognizable historical patterns. Typically, genres expose established syntactic solutions to a questioning process that eventually dissolves syntactic bonds, while often leaving semantic patterns in place. Thus certain post-war Westerns, beginning with Delmer Daves's *Broken Arrow* (1950), began to question a number of the conventions constitutive of Western syntax, such as the motives of law-enforcers, the civilizing effect of the cavalry, the warlike nature of the Indians, and the genre's adherence to historical fact. The later Westerns of John Ford, especially *Cheyenne Autumn* (1964), attempt to redress oversimplifications and indeed injustices characteristic of classic Western films, including Ford's own earlier work, while the emerging film-makers of the 1960s, whether Sergio Leone in Italy or Sam Peckinpah in America, systematically subvert all the pieties of the genre. Also in the post-war period, a series of 'reflexive' musicals questioned such assumptions as the association of music with happiness, the relation of music-making to the formation of stable heterosexual couples, and the promise that music-loving couples always live happily ever after their marriage. *Oklahoma!* (1955), *West Side Story* (1961), and *Paint your Wagon* (1969) are examples of film (originally stage) musicals which introduce discomforting elements traditionally excluded from the syntax of the genre. Though such attempts to undermine established syntactic bonds do not always succeed immediately, they eventually reduce a film industry to a new kind of post-generic production, where syntactic genre films give way almost entirely to generic parodies, mixed-genre films, or attempts to forge a new syntax out of familiar semantic material.

When borrowing a literary or theatrical semantics, cinema often imposes an entirely new syntax. The horror novel justifies its horrific effects by a typically nineteenth-century scientific overreaching, while horror films build their syntax around a character's overactive sexual appetite. Since genre systems depend heavily on the faithful viewing of a homogeneous audience, two countries may each develop a different syntax for the same semantic genre (the Hollywood Western and the 'spaghetti' or Italian Western), a single industry may sequentially or even concurrently display multiple different types of syntax for a single semantic genre (the fairy-tale, show, and folk approaches to the Hollywood musical), or one national industry may largely abandon a genre (the Hollywood musical) while other countries continue to exploit a version of that genre (the booming industry of Indian and Egyptian musicals).

Bibliography
Altman, Rick (1987), *The American Film Musical*.
Cawelti, John (1970), *The Six-Gun Mystique*.
Grant, Barry Keith (1986), *Film Genre Reader*.
Neale, Stephen (1980), *Genre*.
Schatz, Thomas (1981), *Hollywood Genres: Formulas, Filmmaking and the Studio System*.

The Western

EDWARD BUSCOMBE

Between 1910 and 1960 the Western was the major genre of the world's dominant national cinema. Its popularity was a vital factor in establishing Hollywood's control of the global film market. But the development of the Western as a distinctive formula within popular culture, with its own conventions and stereotypes, pre-dates the invention of the cinema by a quarter of a century. Two moments in the history of white expansion across the North American continent had a decisive effect. In the aftermath of the Civil War cattle ranchers on the Texas plains were desperate to find a market for their livestock. As the railways spread through Kansas on their way to California, the herds were driven up the thousand-mile-long trail to the new towns of Abilene and Dodge City, strung out along the track. The cowboy, whose accoutrements and life-style derived mainly from the Hispanic culture to the south, quickly sprang to prominence as a mythic figure, a free spirit reliant on nothing but his horse, his gun, and his own manly virtues. Also at this time the smouldering conflict with the Indians burst into a full-scale conflagration, with a series of Indian wars across the plains, culminating in the spectacular and traumatic defeat of General Custer in 1876. As with the cowboy, the Indian, whether in the guise of the noble redman or the screaming savage, was rapidly incorporated into a range of fictional and quasi-documentary discourses, including the novel, the theatre, painting, and other forms of visual and narrative representation.

Though the cowboy and the Indian were to remain the central figures, a motley crew of outlaws, mountain men, soldiers, and lawmen were also pressed into service as Western heroes by the rapidly developing communication and entertainment industries. During the 1880s cheap popular fiction in the form of dime novels featured stories based on real-life personalities such as Jesse James, Billy the Kid, and Wild Bill Hickok, as well as fictional characters like Deadwood Dick. Many of these were also the heroes of stage melodramas. More consciously artistic forms of fiction also began to draw on Western themes. Just after the turn of the century, in 1902, Owen Wister's *The Virginian* provided the definitive portrait of the cowboy hero, a combination of natural gentleman and resolute man of action. Mass circulation magazines such as *Harper's* were also employing the talents of artists such as Frederic Remington to visualize and embroider events out on the plains. Most influential of all, in 1883 Buffalo Bill Cody began touring with his circus-style Wild West entertainment. This included such crypto-narratives as the Battle of Summit Springs, in which Cody rode to the rescue

of white women captured by Indians. The huge popularity of Buffalo Bill, in Europe as well as in America, demonstrated conclusively that the West was an ideal source of raw material for commercial entertainment. By 1900 the West was not only America's national myth, it was a valuable commodity.

The sheer variety of situations, locations, and character types that have attached themselves to the Western has resulted in a form which at times appears fluid, eclectic, and lacking any discernible centre. A generic category such as the Western, however, is more usefully understood not as an internally coherent corpus of texts but as a label employed by the film industry to identify and differentiate its products. The cinema Western, therefore, cannot properly be said to have existed until the industry began to separate out the Western from other films involving lawless acts, and until it had put the term into circulation as a useful description of a novel type of film. But the process was remarkably rapid. Aided no doubt by the fact that the film audience had already encountered Western adventure stories in the theatre and in cheap fiction, the emergent cinema soon developed a recognizable kind of narrative which displayed a distinctive combination of features.

First, the films are set on the frontier, the dividing line between white civilization and its opposite, 'savagery'. On the one side are law and order, community, the values of a settled society. On the other, the outlaw and the savage Indian. Following the landmark essay of Frederick Jackson Turner in 1893, American historians have concurred in fixing 1890 as the year in which the frontier finally disappeared and the continent was deemed pacified. This was also the year of the Battle of Wounded Knee, which ended organized resistance by the Indians. The great majority of Westerns, even those with no very exact historical setting, situate themselves within the period 1865–90, though this limit can extend earlier and later if frontier conditions are deemed to exist. Similarly, the geographical location is usually west of the Mississippi, north of the Rio Grande, but if the film is set in earlier times the location may be further east, and locations in Mexico may also qualify as the 'frontier'. The basic conflict develops from a struggle between the forces of civilization and savagery, and the narrative features lawless acts by those who, because of the frontier location, are beyond the pale of civilization. These acts require forcible retribution before order can be imposed. This combination of a specific time and place, and a transgressive act which these specifics make possible and which because of the nature

Western landscape: James Cruze's *The Covered Wagon* (1923)

of the time and place can only be put right by force, may be said to define the Western genre. Without one or other of these elements a film will not be recognized as a Western either by the industry or by its audience.

THE WESTERN IN THE SILENT PERIOD

The fledgeling film industry, hungry for new sources of ready-made narrative with proven audience appeal, could not long afford to ignore the feast of spectacle and suspense that had been developed from the idea of the frontier. Conventional film history has identified *The Great Train Robbery* (1903) as the first Western fiction film. It certainly contains many elements which we now associate with the Western genre: a train robbery by gunmen, outdoor locations, a chase on horseback, and a final shoot-out. But it is doubtful if contemporary audiences looked upon the film as a Western.

The Great Train Robbery could not boast an authentic frontier location, since it was shot in New Jersey. The first productions shot in western locations were those of the Selig–Polyscope Company in 1907. Titles such as *The Girl from Montana* were advertised in the trade press as set 'in the wildest and most beautiful scenery of the Western country'. Their success encouraged other companies to relocate westwards. In 1909 the appropriately named Bison Company, specialists in Westerns, moved to California. California also saw the rise of the first Western film star. Gilbert M. Anderson had formed a company

named Essanay with George K. Spoor, and in 1910 Anderson appeared in a film named *Broncho Billy's Redemption*. It was a huge success, and Anderson went on to star in nearly 300 more films as Broncho Billy, an amiable cowboy, sometimes an outlaw, who is kind to children and ever ready to rescue damsels in distress.

Broncho Billy's costume, a wide-brimmed hat, neckerchief, leather gauntlets, pistol in a waist-holster, and leather, sometimes sheepskin chaps, was derived ultimately from the garb of the Mexican vaquero, as adapted by Texas cowboys and refined and elaborated by Buck Taylor and other cowboy performers in the Wild West shows. Cowboys were the dominant type in early Westerns, but Indians had a major role as well. In 1911 the Bison Company had amalgamated with the Miller Brothers 101 Ranch Wild West show, and thereby acquired a large troop of genuine Indians together with their tepees and other props. The company, renamed Bison 101, took on a new director, Thomas Ince, who rapidly increased the company's output of Westerns at its Santa Ynez location, popularly known as Inceville. The films frequently centred on stories of the Indian wars and the Indians who appeared were referred to as the Inceville Sioux.

D. W. Griffith was also making Indian stories at this time at the Biograph studio. Some, with titles such as *The Squaw's Love* (1911), were sympathetic tales of Indian life from which white characters were absent, though the roles were rarely played by Indian actors. Others, such as

John Ford

(1894–1973)

Ford's famous definition of himself at a meeting of the Screen Directors Guild ('My name's John Ford. I am a director of Westerns.') was a simplification, and he knew it. His long and continuously successful career went through several distinct phases. Born in Maine, the thirteenth child of Irish immigrants named Feeney, at the age of 20 he followed his older brother Francis to California. Francis already had a flourishing career as actor and director, and he gave the young Jack work as a props man and later as an actor. Ford's first film as director, *The Tornado* (1917) was a Bison Western, distributed by Universal, in which he himself played the lead role. Over the next four years Ford withdrew from acting and made a series of twenty-five films with Harry Carey, one of the leading Western stars of the era, playing the character of 'Cheyenne Harry'.

In 1921 Ford moved to the Fox studio, where he was allowed to extend his range. There were still plenty of Westerns, with Hoot Gibson, Buck Jones, and Tom Mix, but there were also stories of the New York ghetto, rural melodramas, and tales of the sea. In 1924 came *The Iron Horse*, an epic Western about building the trans-continental railway. It was a great success, but when his next Western, *Three Bad Men* (1926), failed, he abandoned the genre for thirteen years. His films for Fox in the late 1920s and early 1930s alternated between Irish comedies like *Riley the Cop* (1928), action pictures such as *The Black Watch* (1929) and *Airmail* (1932), and melodramas such as *Arrowsmith* (1931).

Another change in direction came in 1935. Working from a script by Dudley Nichols, Ford directed *The Informer*, Liam O'Flaherty's novel of Irish republicanism, in a heavily atmospheric style. It won him critical awards and a reputation as a quality director of important literary works. Adaptations of Maxwell Anderson's *Mary of Scotland* and Sean O'Casey's *The Plough and the Stars* followed in 1936.

In 1939 Ford made a triumphant return to the Western with *Stagecoach*. Its success rescued John Wayne's career from the doldrums, and helped revivify a genre which had fallen into decline. Ford described *Stagecoach* as a 'classic' Western, several cuts above his series Westerns of the silent days. By now he was one of the most respected directors in Hollywood, dependent on the studio system to finance his films, but with a measure of choice in his projects. *The Grapes of Wrath* (1940), from John Steinbeck's justly celebrated novel, brilliantly wedded the key Fordian themes of family and home to a bleak vision of the social deprivation of the Depression.

Ford's Hollywood career was interrupted by war service. His lifelong fascination with the military was rewarded with a commission as a lieutenant commander in the navy, and he made a succession of short films for

Henry Fonda as Wyatt Earp in John Ford's classic western *My Darling Clementine* (1946)

the war effort, including *The Battle of Midway* (1942), one of the war's finest documentaries.

After the war Ford produced, in a short burst of four years, a series of great Westerns, including his Wyatt Earp story *My Darling Clementine* (1946), his so-called cavalry trilogy (*Fort Apache*, 1948; *She Wore a Yellow Ribbon*, 1949; and *Rio Grande*, 1950), and one of his own personal favourites, *Wagon Master* (1950).

Ford's films of the 1950s are often intensely personal projects. *The Quiet Man* (1952) was a comedy in which John Wayne played an American in search of his roots in Ireland. *The Rising of the Moon* (1957) also had an Irish setting; one of its three separate stories concerns the IRA. *The Sun Shines Bright* (1953) was based on Irvin S. Cobb's Judge Priest stories, set in the South, which Ford had first filmed in 1934 with Will Rogers.

After a break from the genre which had lasted six years, Ford returned to the Western with *The Searchers* (1956), which many consider to be his masterpiece. John Wayne, in one of his finest performances, plays the Confederate veteran Ethan Edwards, condemned by his own inner turmoil to roam the West for seven years in pursuit of his niece kidnapped by Comanches. In this film Ford brought to perfection his measured and assured shooting style, his command of landscape as realized in his extraordinary vistas of his beloved Monument Valley, and his great skill in humanizing the epic.

Old age and the more protracted schedules of Hollywood production slowed Ford's output in the 1960s. But he still managed to produce a trio of major Westerns, though Ford himself never much cared for *Two Rode Together* (1961), a captivity narrative with a bleak view of human tolerance, in which James Stewart stars as a venal and cynical marshal. *The Man who Shot Liberty Valance* (1962), Ford's last film in black and white, is an elliptically told story about the inseparable mix of fact and myth in the Western, shot in a deliberately archaic style. *Cheyenne Autumn* (1964) is an honourable, if rather pious, attempt to atone for the Western's failure to accord respect to the Indian.

By the time of his death Ford's critical reputation had slipped a little in comparison with other directors of his generation such as Hawks or Hitchcock. The young critics of *Cahiers du cinéma* and *Movie* found him folksy, even sentimental. In the years since, that judgement has been seen as superficial. Ford's sympathies with the underdog have outlasted radical chic, and his unsurpassed instinct for knowing both where to put the camera and what to put in front of it resulted in works of incomparable visual beauty and generosity of spirit.

EDWARD BUSCOMBE

SELECT FILMOGRAPHY

The Tornado (1917); The Iron Horse (1924); Three Bad Men (1926); Arrowsmith (1931); The Lost Patrol (1934); The Informer (1935); The Prisoner of Shark Island (1936); Mary of Scotland (1936); The Hurricane (1938); Stagecoach (1939); Young Mr. Lincoln (1939); Drums along the Mohawk (1939); The Grapes of Wrath (1940); How Green was my Valley (1941); The Battle of Midway (1942); My Darling Clementine (1946); The Fugitive (1947); Fort Apache (1948); She Wore a Yellow Ribbon (1949); Wagon Master (1950); Rio Grande (1950); The Quiet Man (1952); The Sun Shines Bright (1953); The Searchers (1956); Two Rode Together (1961); The Man who Shot Liberty Valance (1962); How the West was Won (1962); Cheyenne Autumn (1964)

BIBLIOGRAPHY

Anderson, Lindsay (1981), *About John Ford*.
Bogdanovich, Peter (1978), *John Ford*.
Ford, Dan (1979), *Pappy: The Life of John Ford*.
Gallagher, Tag (1986), *John Ford: The Man and his Films*.
McBride, Joseph, and Wilmington, Michael (1975), *John Ford*.
Sarris, Andrew (1976), *The John Ford Movie Mystery*.
Sinclair, Andrew (1979), *John Ford: A Biography*.

the ambitious two-reel *The Battle at Elderbush Gulch* (1913), cast the Indians as red devils thirsty for the blood of whites.

One of the performers signed by Ince was a veteran stage actor named William S. Hart, who brought to the emergent genre all the moral fervour of the Victorian melodrama in which he had received his theatrical training. Hart developed the persona of the Good Badman, a figure on the fringe of respectable society who is redeemed by the love of a pure woman, whom he is called upon to rescue from the clutches of villainy. From 1915 Hart was making feature-length films for the Triangle Company, still in association with Ince. In their plots and characterization the films reveal Hart's stage origins; he had appeared in theatrical versions of Owen Wister's *The Virginian* and *The Squaw Man*, a play which became a Cecil B. DeMille film in 1913 and probably the first feature-length Western. But at the same time Hart's films made striking use of the western landscape and their décors managed to give a real feel of the dusty, rather mean little towns that sparsely populated the West.

Hart took both himself and the West very seriously. The cowboy star who was to replace him in the public imagination, Tom Mix, was a very different type. Hart's horsemanship was no more than adequate. Mix seemed to have been born on a horse, though in fact he came from Pennsylvania. He had worked on the very same 101 Ranch which had merged with Bison, and all his life retained links with Wild West shows and circuses. Unlike Hart's, Tom Mix's pictures made no pretence to historical authenticity, being dedicated solely to entertainment. Though not without dramatic values, their appeal was based on a rapid succession of horse-riding stunts, comedy, chases, and fights.

By 1920 there were in fact two distinct kinds of Western film in Hollywood. On the one hand were scores of cheap films, with formulaic plots, often using the same sets and locations, even recycling footage from previous productions. They were made by specialist units within the major studios, such as Universal, Fox, and Paramount, or by smaller independent companies. The films were usually made in series, the same star being contracted for six or eight films at a time. Even within this type of film there were wide variations in budgets and quality. Among the élite stars of Western series in the 1920s were Hoot Gibson, Buck Jones, Fred Thomson, and Tim McCoy. But there were dozens of lesser lights, including such now-forgotten figures as Bob Custer, Buddy Roosevelt, and Jack Perrin, whose pictures were made with the bare minimum of resources necessary to sustain audience belief.

Typically, these films found their chief market in rural areas, especially in the south and west, and among younger audiences. On the other hand there were films conceived not in series but individually, which cast not

John Wayne
(1907–1979)

In his heyday probably the best-known film actor in the world, John Wayne had to wait for success. Born Marion Michael Morrison in Iowa but raised in California, he found work in the props department of the Fox studio while on a football scholarship at the University of Southern California. This led to bit parts in John Ford productions, and eventually to a starring role (appearing for the first time as 'John Wayne') in Raoul Walsh's Western epic *The Big Trail* (1930). The picture's failure at the box-office condemned Wayne to a decade on 'poverty row', in cheap Westerns and other action films for Monogram and Republic.

His second big break came when Ford cast him as the Ringo Kid in *Stagecoach* (1939). This time Wayne did not falter. He followed up with a series of Westerns, and war films such as *The Fighting Seabees* (1944), *Back to Bataan* (1945), and *They Were Expendable* (1945). Though Wayne had been rejected for military service on account of his family of four children, he developed over the next ten years into the very epitome of the American fighting man. As his 6' 4" frame filled out, the authority of his screen presence grew. In Howard Hawks's *Red River* (1947) he revealed unsuspected depths in his playing of the patriarchal rancher Tom Dunson. In the second of John Ford's so-called cavalry trilogy, *She Wore a Yellow Ribbon* (1949), his acting ability was further stretched in the role of an army officer reaching retirement age.

John Ford continued to be a formative influence on Wayne's career, drawing out his gift for comedy in *The Quiet Man* (1952), and eliciting a monumental performance as Ethan Edwards in *The Searchers* (1956). In the final shot Wayne turns away from the camera with his left arm across his body, clutching his elbow. The gesture was a deliberate evocation of Harry Carey, the star of Ford's early silent Westerns. It confirmed Wayne as the legitimate heir to a great tradition. As president of the anti-Communist Motion Picture Alliance for the Preservation of American Ideals Wayne, together with his friend Ward Bond, had been an active supporter of the McCarthyite investigations into Hollywood in the 1940s. In the 1960s Wayne's pronounced right-wing views became more strident. The Vietnam War provoked him into overt propaganda; he both starred in and directed *The Green Berets* (1968), a film which did little either for Wayne's professional standing or for the fortunes of American policy.

It was the Western that best brought out his heroic potential. In Hawks's *Rio Bravo* (1959) and Ford's *The Man who Shot Liberty Valance* (1962) Wayne embodied a relaxed and confident moral authority which disarmed even his liberal critics. But in the later 1960s he increasingly gave the impression of merely going through the motions. In a succession of routine though popular Westerns such as *McLintock!* (1963), *The Sons of Katie Elder* (1965), and *The War Wagon* (1967) his acting ossified into an assembly of mannerisms: the characteristic shambling walk, the grouchy good humour, the laconic delivery of a few catchphrases. As if sensing this, Wayne's performance in *True Grit* (1969) as the reprobate one-eyed Rooster Cogburn was an enjoyable pastiche which earned him his one and only Oscar.

In 1964 Wayne had a cancerous lung removed. For the rest of his life he battled courageously against further attacks of the disease. His last role, one of his finest, came in *The Shootist* (1976), in which he played an elderly gunfighter with cancer of the bowel who resolves to end his life with dignity in the only way he knows, in a final shoot-out.

EDWARD BUSCOMBE

SELECT FILMOGRAPHY

The Big Trail (1930); Stagecoach (1939); The Dark Command (1940); The Fighting Seabees (1944); Back to Bataan (1945); They Were Expendable (1945); Red River (1947); Fort Apache (1948); 3 Godfathers (1949); She Wore a Yellow Ribbon (1949); Rio Grande (1950); The Quiet Man (1952); The Searchers (1956); Rio Bravo (1959); The Man who Shot Liberty Valance (1962); Donovan's Reef (1963); McLintock! (1963); True Grit (1969); The Shootist (1976)

BIBLIOGRAPHY

Eyles, Allen (1979), *John Wayne*.
Levy, Emanuel (1988), *John Wayne: Prophet of the American Way of Life*.
Shepherd, Donald, and Slatzer, Robert (1985), *Duke: The Life and Times of John Wayne*.
Zmijewsky, Steve, Zmijewsky, Boris, and Ricci, Mark (1983), *The Complete Films of John Wayne*.

John Wayne as Captain Nathan Brittles in John Ford's *She Wore a Yellow Ribbon* (1949)

specialist Western actors but mainstream stars from the major studios, and which were most often referred to in the trade press not as 'Westerns' at all but as melodramas or romances. In 1923 Paramount had a great hit with *The Covered Wagon*, a self-consciously epic drama which told the story of westward emigration in the 1840s. Series Westerns, by contrast, were often vague about period and imprecise with their historical references. In some of Tom Mix's films, for example, the action is contemporaneous with the film's date of production.

The next year the Fox studio retaliated by producing another Western epic, *The Iron Horse*, an account of the building of the transcontinental railway in 1869. It entrusted the direction to John Ford, who had begun his career directing Harry Carey in series Westerns. Ford was one of the relatively few film-makers who graduated from the series Western to the big-budget feature. But after one further Western, *Three Bad Men* (1926), he abandoned the genre until 1939.

THE CLASSIC WESTERN

The 1930s saw the series Western flourish once it had adjusted to the introduction of sound, which initially presented problems for location shooting. Around the middle of the decade film exhibitors, attempting to reverse the decline of audiences caused by the Depression, initiated the double bill, which offered two feature films per programme. A ready supply of cheap B features was needed to fill the bill, and 'poverty row' studios such as Monogram rushed to provide them. More prestigious productions were few and far between until the end of the decade, which saw a modest revival. John Ford re-entered the field with *Stagecoach* (1939), produced by Walter Wanger for United Artists after Ford had failed to interest David O. Selznick. The picture revived the career of John Wayne, who had been languishing in 'poverty row' since the failure of Raoul Walsh's epic *The Big Trail* in 1930. *Stagecoach* was a great success, though not so big a hit as a trio of Westerns turned out by major studios in the same year. Cecil B. DeMille's *Union Pacific*, produced for Paramount, was a lavish saga based loosely on the construction of the UP railway. Warners' *Dodge City*, starring Errol Flynn, was a thinly disguised version of the Wyatt Earp story, and in Fox's *Jesse James* Tyrone Power played the notorious outlaw.

The move towards historical subjects, albeit in fanciful versions, was indicative that Hollywood was disposed to take the Western more seriously. In the 1940s the studios saw that the Western could be a vehicle for the exploration of moral issues. In dealing with lynching *The Ox-Bow Incident* (1942) exposed the hypocrisy of respectable society. In 1940 the Western discovered sex, when Howard Hughes began production of *The Outlaw*, starring Jane Russell. Hughes's determination to exploit Russell's sex appeal to

the limit ('What are the two reasons for Jane Russell's rise to stardom?' demanded a poster thrusting her breasts at the public) resulted in a delayed release because of censorship problems. But there was no going back to the innocence of earlier times. *Duel in the Sun* (1946) (known popularly at the time as 'Lust in the Dust') was a lush and operatic melodrama with Jennifer Jones as a half-Indian girl whose open sexuality creates turmoil in the men around her.

The 1950s was the Western's greatest decade. Film-makers found a new confidence in using the Western to explore social and moral conflicts. *Broken Arrow* (1950) dealt deftly with relations between whites and Indians through its story of the marriage of a white scout to an Apache woman. Other pro-Indian Westerns soon followed, such as *Devil's Doorway* (1950), *Across the Wide Missouri* (1950), *The Big Sky* (1952), *The Last Hunt* (1956), *Run of the Arrow* (1957). Another landmark film was Henry King's *The Gun-fighter* (1950), starring Gregory Peck as an ageing gun-fighter who wants to renounce his life of violence but whose past reputation makes him a target for a young killer on the make. *High Noon* (1952) was another film which looked beneath the glamour of a life lived by the gun. Its director, Fred Zinnemann, has always denied that the film was a political parable. But its story of a sheriff who has to stand alone against the bad guys when those who should support him prove cowards was generally read as a commentary on the McCarthyism that was laying waste Hollywood.

John Ford, after his triumphant return to the Western in 1939 with *Stagecoach*, had produced a string of marvellous films after the war, including his version of the Wyatt Earp story, *My Darling Clementine*, in 1946 and his so-called cavalry trilogy *Fort Apache* (1949), *She Wore a Yellow Ribbon* (1949), and *Rio Grande* (1950). Apart from *Wagon Master* (1950), a small-scale but intensely personal film, he was to make only two more Westerns in the 1950s. One was the Civil War film *The Horse Soldiers* (1959). The other was a film little regarded at the time but now widely judged to be not only Ford's finest but perhaps the greatest Western of them all. *The Searchers* (1956) is a profound and troubling examination of the psychopathology of 'the Indian fighter', a pivotal figure in the myth of the West whose origins go back to the beginnings of Western narrative in the eighteenth century. It is also the supreme example of the visual splendour of the western landscape, which has been such an indelible part of the appeal of the genre.

The 1950s were marked not only by an increased seriousness in the thematic content of Westerns. It was also a decade in which aesthetic possibilities were realized with greater verve and flair than ever before. George Stevens's *Shane* (1952) was singled out by André Bazin (1971) as an example of what he called the 'sur-Western', which 'would be ashamed to be just itself, and looks for some additional interest to justify its existence—an aesthetic, sociological, moral, psychological, political or erotic interest, in short some quality extrinsic to the genre and which is supposed to enrich it'. Of course it is in the nature of genre that it seeks constantly to renew itself by adding novel variations. But a definite tendency towards pictorialism is observable in Stevens's careful shots of the Grand Tetons, and the figure of Shane himself, seen through the eyes of the young boy whose hero he becomes, is deliberately mythologized.

Two cycles of films in the 1950s represent not only the Western but Hollywood itself at its best. In 1950 Anthony Mann directed James Stewart in *Winchester '73*, a sparely told but intense story of fratricidal hatred and revenge. The partnership between director and star continued with *Bend of the River* (1951; UK title: *Where the River Bends*), *The Naked Spur* (1952), *The Far Country* (1954), and *The Man from Laramie* (1955). Mann's fluid and confident handling of the camera is put at the service of narratives which focus in tightly on tense and violent emotions, centred round the tormented figure of the James Stewart character.

With the exception of *The Tin Star* (1957), all of Mann's last eight Westerns were in colour, and four of them were in CinemaScope. The Western profited from Hollywood's determination to compete with television through enhanced technology. By the end of the decade colour and widescreen had become the norm. They were nowhere better exploited than in another cycle of films, also based on a close relation between a star and a director, which revived the career of veteran Western star Randolph Scott and established Budd Boetticher as one of the Western's supreme stylists. Their first film together, *Seven Men from Now* (1956), established the character Scott was to play, stoical and implacable beneath his laconic exterior, usually bent upon revenge for some grievous wrong done to him. This partnership, usually in tandem with the script-writer Burt Kennedy, continued through *The Tall T* (1956), *Decision at Sundown* (1957), *Buchanan Rides Alone* (1957), *Westbound* (1958), *Ride Lonesome*, and *Comanche Station* (both 1959).

Randolph Scott was to co-star with another veteran Westerner, Joel McCrea, in *Ride the High Country* (known in the UK as *Guns in the Afternoon*, 1962). This was directed by Sam Peckinpah, a newcomer who had built a successful career in the television Western with shows like *The Rifleman*. Peckinpah's other films in the 1960s included *Major Dundee* (1965), a cavalry Western that owes much to John Ford, and *The Wild Bunch* (1969), a bleak and savage work touched with tragedy which earned Peckinpah notoriety for its scenes of slow-motion violence.

The films of Mann, Boetticher, and Peckinpah were the subject of Jim Kitses's book *Horizons West*, which appeared in 1969. Apart from a couple of typically suggestive essays by André Bazin, little of note had been written on the

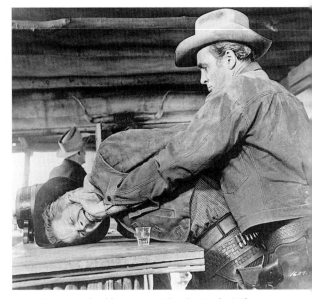

James Stewart getting his revenge on Dan Duryea in Anthony Mann's *Winchester '73* (1950)

genre before that time. Kitses not only attempted to define which *auteurs* were the inheritors and developers of the Fordian legacy, but tried to provide a definition of the Western by adapting Lévi-Strauss's structuralist analysis of myth. Kitses's identification of a central antithesis between wilderness and civilization, from which all other conflicts derive, was persuasive, and was further developed by Will Wright in a more orthodoxly structuralist work, *Sixguns and Society* (1975). Since then, there have been notable works on individual directors, stars, and films, but little of consequence on the genre itself, with the exception of Richard Slotkin's *Gunfighter Nation* (1992), an impressively serious reading of the Western as a commentary on American political ideology.

TRANSFORMATIONS OF THE GENRE

All of Peckinpah's films are in some sense reflections upon the Western itself, and both *Ride the High Country* and *The Wild Bunch* are set at a time when the man on a horse is being superseded by the forces of modern technology. This self-consciousness about the passing of an era is symptomatic of a profound change that was taking place in the genre. In 1950 Hollywood had produced 130 Western features. By 1960 this had sunk to a mere 28. For a time this precipitous decline in output was masked by the remarkable rise of the Italian or 'spaghetti' Western, a phenomenon originally assisted by the migration of a number of Hollywood stars (most notably Clint Eastwood) to Rome. Eastwood's film *Per un pugno di dollari* (*A Fistful of Dollars*, 1964) was directed by Sergio Leone, who had cut his teeth as assistant director on Hollywood biblical epics produced at the Cinecittà studios. By the end of the decade over 300 Italian Westerns had been produced. Though only 20 per cent were ever distributed internationally, many, including Leone's later works such as the two follow-up films with Eastwood, *Per qualche dollaro in più* (*For a Few Dollars More*, 1965) and *Il buono, il brutto, il cattivo* (*The Good, the Bad and the Ugly*, 1966), and his masterpiece *C'era una volta il west* (*Once upon a Time in the West*, 1968), had considerable influence on the future shape of the American Western, most noticeably in the general increase in the level of violence and the obsessive detail with which it was filmed.

The cynicism at the heart of the Italian Western about traditional values of civilization, progress, community, family, and the rule of law doubtless derived from the fashionable Marxism of intellectual Italian film-makers. But this in turn had its effect on Hollywood, accentuating an already discernible drift towards 'exposing' previous pieties. In the 1970s debunking sacred cows became almost obligatory, whether it was Wyatt Earp in *Doc* (1971), General Custer in *Little Big Man* (1970), Billy the Kid in *Dirty Little Billy* (1972), or Buffalo Bill in *Buffalo Bill and the Indians* (1976). A version of the Jesse James story, *The Great Northfield Minnesota Raid* (1971), in the so-called 'mud and rags' mode, rubbed the audience's noses in the squalor of what the West was 'really' like.

The conservative certainties to which the Western had seemed indissolubly wedded were held up for a searching re-examination. The white male protagonist, previously impregnable, now found himself undermined. The distinctly un-macho Jack Crabb (Dustin Hoffman) in *Little Big Man* was one in an increasingly long line of anti-heroes. In *Hannie Caulder* (1971) Raquel Welch played a raped and vengeful woman rampaging against the entire male sex. *Soldier Blue* (1970) managed to be both pro-Indian and pro-feminist at the same time. Even Peckinpah, in *The Ballad of Cable Hogue* (1970), moved beyond the raw and simple machismo of his previous heroes. The 1970s saw hippy Westerns (*Billy Jack*, 1971), black Westerns (Sidney Poitier's *Buck and the Preacher*, 1971), back-to-nature ecological Westerns (*Jeremiah Johnson*, 1972), and the anarchically satirical *Blazing Saddles* (1974), which took aim with a scatter-gun at the entire genre.

After his appearance in John Ford's elegiac *The Man who Shot Liberty Valance* (1962), John Wayne had continued his career as if none of this was happening, getting back to business as usual in a series of routine works enlivened only by Howard Hawks's *El Dorado* (1966). His Oscar-winning *tour de force* in *True Grit* (1969) was a kind of self-parody, seeming to acknowledge that his image was increasingly sclerotic. But his finale was a worthy farewell;

in *The Shootist* (1976) he played an ageing gunfighter dying of cancer, as Wayne himself was at the time.

The 1970s also saw the flowering of Clint Eastwood's career, with *The Beguiled* (1970), a Civil War drama directed by Don Siegel, *High Plains Drifter* (1972), and *The Outlaw Josey Wales* (1976), both directed by Eastwood himself. But by the end of the decade the Western seemed played out. *Bronco Billy* (1980), in which Eastwood played the proprietor of a Wild West show down on its luck, seemed to be the star's appropriately wistful farewell.

DECLINE AND REVIVAL

Many theories have been advanced as to why the Western went into decline. Audiences were growing up, an increasingly urban society could not relate to an agrarian genre, or maybe it was just fashion. But structural changes in box-office demographics probably had their effect. A younger audience was drawn to genres like horror and science fiction which offered more sensational thrills; by contrast, youth in the Western seemed perpetually condemned to be taught a lesson by its elders and betters. What is incontrovertible is that the failure of the elephantine and grossly indulgent *Heaven's Gate* (1980) to recover even a proportion of its huge costs made Hollywood executives wary of further adventures out west. The 1980s was the Western's worst ever decade and production fell away to a trickle. Between 1980 and 1992 even the last great hope, Clint Eastwood, got back in the saddle only once, for *Pale Rider* (1985).

Yet obstinately the Western has refused to die. In the early 1990s a modest revival set in. A successful attempt to remodel the genre for a teenage audience, *Young Guns* (1988), was followed by a sequel, *Young Guns II*, in 1990. In the same year Kevin Costner scored a personal triumph with *Dances with Wolves*, which self-consciously sought to put the record straight on the Indian Question and which was rewarded by the first Oscar for Best Picture received by a Western since *Cimarron* in 1930. Two films in 1992 proved, in different ways, that the genre had not after all exhausted itself. *The Last of the Mohicans* showed that the mythic fictions of the founding father of the Western novel, James Fenimore Cooper, could be updated for modern audiences who would find his prose unreadable. And in *Unforgiven* Clint Eastwood made a film which combined traditional satisfactions (the bad guys are decisively defeated) with a fashionably contemporary *Angst* about the morality of violence.

No one should predict that the Western will ever be restored to the eminence it once enjoyed on the screen. But the richness of the material, both historical and fictional, which remains to be exploited by the movie Western is inexhaustible. Only the indifference of the audience or a failure of nerve by studio executives seem likely to keep the Western off our screens.

Bibliography
Bazin, André (1971), 'The Western, or the American Film *par excellence*' and 'The Evolution of the Western'.
Buscombe, Edward (ed.) (1993), *The BFI Companion to the Western*.
Cawelti, John (1971), *The Six-Gun Mystique*.
Frayling, Christopher (1981), *Spaghetti Westerns*.

Kitses, Jim (1969), *Horizons West*.
Slotkin, Richard (1992), *Gunfighter Nation: The Myth of the Frontier in Twentieth Century America*.
Turner, Frederick Jackson (1962), *The Frontier in American History*.
Tuska, John (1976), *The Filming of the West*.
Wright, Will (1975), *Sixguns and Society*.

The Musical

RICK ALTMAN

The term 'musical' is used in several different senses. In its weakest sense, 'musical' means simply a film with a significant amount of diegetic music (music made by on-screen characters). In this sense, the term designates an extremely diverse international genre, with important examples from every decade since the 1920s and from every continent.

In the 1930s European 'musicals' had little in common. British musical films typically featured music hall stars like Gertrude Lawrence, Evelyn Laye, and Jessie Matthews; German films borrowed their music and plots from the operetta tradition—though also, in the case of *Die 3-Groschenoper* (1931), from the theatre of Bertolt Brecht; in France, René Clair's musical films deployed avant-garde motifs and techniques. From the 1940s to the 1960s, a parade of idiosyncratic European directors created films often referred to as 'musicals', but which had little more in common than the use of diegetic music. British productions included the ballet-oriented films of Michael Powell and Emeric Pressburger, Richard Lester's psychedelic Beatles films, Hollywood imitations such as *Half a Sixpence* (1967) and *Oliver!* (1968), and, more recently, *Absolute Beginners* (1986). France contributed the operatic creations of Jacques Demy, the parodic work of Jean-Luc Godard, and a series of Johnny Hallyday vehicles, while Sweden offered *Abba the Movie* (1977). Outside Europe, Jamaica made *The Harder they Come* and other reggae films and Egypt initiated an entire domestic musical genre. In fact, in recent years the largest producer of musical films has been India, where 'musicals' have long constituted one of the most characteristic Indian genres.

When the term 'musical' is used in its weaker sense, all of these films may be termed 'musicals'; that is, they include a great deal of diegetic music, some produced by principal characters. Such films will be referred to here as 'musical films', while the standalone term 'musical' will be reserved for films featuring not only the presence of music, but also a shared configuration of plot patterns, character types, and social structures associated with that music. In this stricter sense, the musical is not an international genre, but one of the most characteristic creations of the Hollywood film industry. To study the musical is thus primarily to analyse the history of Hollywood's 1,500 or so musical films.

THE EARLY DEVELOPMENT OF MUSICAL FILMS

Born during the heyday of popular melodrama, vaudeville, and song slides, cinema has from its very beginnings made use of various types of music. Even in the silent era, music was not restricted to the role of accompaniment. In the United States, at least as early as the 1907 film version of *The Merry Widow*, films based on operettas offered well-known music to be produced by live musicians in synchronism with on-screen action. In 1911, film versions of popular operas (Pathé's *Il trovatore* and *Faust*, Edison's *Aïda*) were distributed with specially arranged music. In Europe, films like Johan Gildemeijer's *Gloria transita* (1917) and *Gloria fatalis* (1922) employed a similar system, with live musicians singing the operatic arias mouthed by the characters on screen. Throughout the silent era, film producers laced their stories with visible musical sources in order to provide overt opportunities for the use of 'cue' music (i.e. live music synchronized to specific on-screen cues like bugle calls, organ grinders, and national anthems).

Starting in the late 1920s, cinemas around the world exploited new sound technology by building scenarios on a generous dose of diegetic music. In the United States, producers called on every conceivable musical source: opera, operetta, classical music, military marches, Viennese waltzes, folk songs, gospel hymns, Jewish canticles, Tin Pan Alley tunes, night-club numbers, vaudeville routines, jazz riffs, and even burlesque favourites. Ever since, the musical genre has been characterized by its ability to assimilate each new musical style, from swing to rock and from be-bop to heavy metal.

The musical diversity of the late 1920s and early 1930s was matched by the breadth of narrative traditions invoked. Paramount's European directors Ernst Lubitsch and Rouben Mamoulian repeatedly called upon European male music hall stars Jack Buchanan and Maurice Chevalier to partner American opera singer Jeanette MacDonald

'Remember my forgotten man'—choreographed by Busby Berkeley for *Gold Diggers of 1933*, directed by Mervyn LeRoy

in Ruritanian plots borrowed straight from the operetta tradition (*The Love Parade*, 1929; *Monte Carlo*, 1930; *Love Me Tonight*, 1932). In the same period Warners and First National regularly turned to Broadway for proven stage successes (*Gold Diggers of Broadway*, 1929; *The Desert Song*, 1929; *Sally*, 1930). Most studios experimented with the revue format, into which they could easily squeeze pre-constituted musical acts (MGM's *Hollywood Revue of 1929*, Warner's *Show of Shows*, *Paramount on Parade*, Universal's *King of Jazz*). No method of integrating music into film was neglected during the 1928–32 period. Musical films were based on radio shows, stage extravaganzas such as those of Florenz Ziegfeld, or even science-fiction plots (*Just Imagine*, 1930). They served as vehicles for Irish tenor John Mac-Cormack (*Song o' my Heart*, 1930), opera singers (Lawrence Tibbett and Grace Moore were paired together in 1930 in *New Moon*), crooners (Rudy Vallee in *The Vagabond Lover*,

1929), cabaret singers (Fanny Brice, Sophie Tucker, Helen Morgan), or even zany comics (the Marx Brothers in *Cocoa-nuts*, 1929, and *Animal Crackers*, 1930; Eddie Cantor in *Whoopee!*, 1930, and *Palmy Days*, 1931; Buster Keaton in *Free and Easy*, 1930). Throughout the early years of sound, musical films provided a showcase not only for increasingly sophisticated recording technology, but also for a variety of colour processes (often restricted to musical sequences), and even for differing widescreen tech-nologies (*Happy Days*, *Song of the Flame*, both in 1930).

During the early sound years, producers and audiences treated and described music as an independent feature that could be added to films of any type, adopting its function from those films rather than constituting its own generic structures. The term 'musical' thus served as a descriptive adjective rather than as a generic designator. Important groupings of early musical films, each initiated

Fred Astaire
(1899–1987)

Born Frederick Austerlitz, in Omaha, Nebraska, Fred Astaire and his sister Adele were the most esteemed stage dancers of the post-war era (in shows like *Lady, be Good!*, *Funny Face*, *The Band Wagon*). When Adele quit the stage to marry Lord Charles Cavendish, Fred's success in *The Gay Divorce* catapulted him to Hollywood, where, according to legend, his RKO screen test elicited a lukewarm reaction: 'Can't act. Can't sing. Balding. Can dance a little.' After a non-starring role in MGM's *Dancing Lady* (1933), Astaire and new partner Ginger Rogers attracted attention in RKO's *Flying down to Rio* (1933). Elevated to starring status, the couple began a run of successes rarely equalled in the cinema world. All of the next five Astaire–Rogers efforts (*The Gay Divorcee*, 1934; *Roberta* and *Top Hat*, 1935; *Follow the Fleet* and *Swing Time*, 1936) ranked among the year's ten top-grossing films, with five top hit parade songs, and five more that reached second or third. Based on this success, Astaire hosted radio shows throughout the 1935–6 and 1936–7 seasons.

The magic of the Astaire–Rogers films is largely due to Astaire's ability simultaneously to incarnate European suavity and elegance (symbolized by the top hat, white tie, and tails carried over from his stage career) and American informality and looseness (embodied in *Shall We Dance*, 1937, by the taps on the ballet slippers of the great Russian dancer Petrov, who is really the American Pete Peters). A typical 1930s Astaire film thus adds the energy and exuberance of a solo tap dance to the grace and romance of a waltz or fox trot with Rogers. Expanding on the sophisticated irony used with his sister Adele (with whom he never played straight romantic roles), Astaire fostered an overtly competitive on-screen relationship with Rogers. Fed by the evolving conventions of contemporaneous screwball comedy, this approach led to the Astaire–Rogers signature 'challenge dances', where a personality clash is acted out in a competitive dance ('Isn't this a Lovely Day to be Caught in the Rain?', 'Let Yourself Go', 'Pick Yourself up', 'They All Laughed', 'Let's Call the Whole Thing off'), eventually leading to the opponents' recognition of their love, later acted out in a more traditional romantic dance ('Cheek to Cheek', 'Let's Face the Music and Dance', 'Waltz in Swing Time', 'Change Partners'). Using their eyes to infuse the dance with romantic yearning, Astaire and Rogers thus manage to further the plot through the dance.

An eclectic dancer, combining European upper body grace with the lower body energy of American vaudeville and tap traditions, Astaire constantly brings the full body into play. This is why he always insisted that (with the exception of later trick dances) his dances be filmed in full shot with no change of scale, usually with a stationary camera, very few cuts, and no reaction shots, thus guaranteeing the dancers' control over the dance's unity. Throughout his career, Astaire was largely respon-

Fred Astaire with choreographer Hermes Pan at RKO

sible for his own choreography, often with the assistance of Hermes Pan, who usually taught the steps to Astaire's partner. Technically exacting and extremely hard-working (even dubbing his own taps), Astaire nevertheless sought to dissimulate the labour of the dancer(s). Blessed with the best music of the Tin Pan Alley tradition (often written specially for him by Cole Porter, Jerome Kern, Irving Berlin, George Gershwin, Harry Warren, or Harold Arlen), Astaire fashioned a new expressive style. His constant variations in style and tempo (often to different metres in the same number), his apparently effortless delivery, and his eclecticism have influenced not only other dancers, but also contemporary ballet choreographers like George Balanchine and Jerome Robbins.

Throughout the 1940s, Astaire's partners were ever younger, leading to Pygmalionesque plots where the old pro dancer breathes life, love, and dance into a younger woman. From his first retirement in 1946 to his last romantic role in 1957 (excepting the 1949 *Barkleys of Broadway* reunion with Rogers), Astaire's partners averaged twenty-five years his junior, creating vaguely incestuous overtones in his later work. Yet Astaire was ever more innovative as a choreographer. To the purity of his 1930s dance technique he now added speciality numbers, with a drum set (*Easter Parade*, 1948), a pair of flying shoes (*The Barkleys of Broadway*, 1949), a clothes tree (*Royal Wedding*, 1951), and a shoeshine stand (*The Band Wagon*, 1953); in *Royal Wedding* he even dances on the ceiling.

After closing his career as a romantic dancer with *Silk Stockings* (1957), Astaire turned to television, where from 1958 to 1963 he produced and starred in several Emmy-winning specials and series. A number of lacklustre straight acting roles and a final unsuccessful musical were not enough to tarnish the career of one of the world's favourite dancers. Refusing in his later life to dance for the camera, Astaire instead stressed his new career as a songwriter. But his fans continued to concentrate on Astaire's dance achievement: the most varied dance corpus in the history of cinema and perhaps in the history of the world.

RICK ALTMAN

SELECT FILMOGRAPHY

(Musicals with leading lady)
Dancing Lady (1933, Joan Crawford); Flying down to Rio (1933, Ginger Rogers); The Gay Divorcee (1934, Rogers); Roberta (1935, Rogers); Top Hat (1935, Rogers); Follow the Fleet (1936, Rogers); Swing Time (1936, Rogers); Shall We Dance (1937, Rogers); A Damsel in Distress (1937, Joan Fontaine); Carefree (1938, Rogers); The Story of Vernon and Irene Castle (1939, Rogers); Broadway Melody of 1940 (1940, Eleanor Powell); Second Chorus (1941, Paulette Goddard); You'll Never Get Rich (1941, Rita Hayworth); Holiday Inn (1942, Marjorie Reynolds); You Were Never Lovelier (1942, Rita Hayworth); The Sky's the Limit (1943, Joan Leslie); Yolanda and the Thief (1945, Lucille Bremer); Ziegfeld Follies (1946, Lucille Bremer); Blue Skies (1946, Joan Caulfield); Easter Parade (1948, Judy Garland); The Barkleys of Broadway (1949, Ginger Rogers); Three Little Words (1950, Vera-Ellen); Let's Dance (1950, Betty Hutton); Royal Wedding (Wedding Bells) (1951, Jane Powell); The Belle of New York (1952, Vera-Ellen); The Band Wagon (1953, Cyd Charisse); Daddy Long Legs (1955, Leslie Caron); Funny Face (1957, Audrey Hepburn); Silk Stockings (1957, Cyd Charisse); Finian's Rainbow (1968, Petula Clark)
The Towering Inferno (1974, acting role)

BIBLIOGRAPHY

Altman, Rick (1987), *The American Film Musical*.
Astaire, Fred (1959), *Steps in Time*.
Croce, Arlene (1972), *The Fred Astaire and Ginger Rogers Book*.
Green, Stanley, and Goldblatt, Burt (1973), *Starring Fred Astaire*.
Mueller, John (1985), *Astaire Dancing: The Musical Films*.

by a single successful film, all borrow plots and themes from pre-existing genres. RKO's 1929 *Rio Rita* brought music to the Western, while King Vidor's *Hallelujah!* (MGM, 1929) integrated music into a familiar Southern melodrama. Nearly every studio included music in a college comedy, often with a football subplot (for example, MGM in *Good News*, Paramount in *Sweetie*, First National in *Forward Pass*).

The most important influence of the period was exercised by the Al Jolson tear-jerker *The Singing Fool* (Warners, 1928), along with MGM's 1929 backstage love triangle story *The Broadway Melody*. In imitation, every Hollywood studio immediately and repeatedly turned to production of musical melodramas featuring an unlucky-in-love performer, a faithless spouse, a selfish sister, a gangster subplot, a singer on the skids, or a dying child. Often announcing their Broadway connections in the title (*The Broadway Melody*, *Broadway*, *Gold Diggers of Broadway*), these musical backstage dramas showed a predilection for stage shows, but also focused on night-club singers, minstrel shows, vaudeville performers, burlesque routines, or even the circus, ventriloquism, a showboat, or a Hollywood studio itself.

As often happens when a popular film is widely imitated in an effort to capitalize on its success, these early musical films shared surface characteristics: diegetic music, performers as main characters, performance-heavy plots, unhappy love affairs, and an unabashed display of the latest technology. While a stable genre might have been formed around these films' romantic treatment of music as the plaintive expression of the lovelorn, the contemporary press followed Hollywood's own publicity in failing to configure musical films as an independent genre. Not until the public tired of musical films in 1930–1 (from fifty-five musical films in 1929 and seventy-seven in 1930 production fell to eleven musical films in 1931 and ten in 1932—the industry low point until the 1960s), did critics regularly use the term 'musical' as a standalone substantive, usually employed to denigrate the production of the previous years, which in retrospect appeared standardized and limited. While this new recognition of generic coherence might well have led to self-conscious production of melodramatic musicals as genre films, the box-office failings of musical films enforced a *de facto* moratorium on their production, and thus a rupture between the somewhat morose tone of early musical films and the upbeat attitude characteristic of the post-1933 musical.

THE CLASSICAL HOLLYWOOD MUSICAL

The year 1933 constitutes a new beginning in Hollywood's attempts to produce economically viable combinations of music and narrative. Until 1933 there had been a pronounced dichotomy between the operetta and other musical films. Because of the differing traditions from which their plots, characters, and music were derived—and thus the radically divergent casts, sets, musicians, and budgets that they required—these two strains failed to be conceived as a single genre. Early operettas such as *The Love Parade* or *New Moon* maintained a light tone and nearly always concluded with a happy ending, while other musical films often depended on the tear-jerking techniques of popular melodrama.

In 1933 Warners began to produce musicals of a new type. Whereas previous musical films had by and large simply added music to familiar stories, *42nd Street*, *Footlight Parade*, *Gold Diggers of 1933*, and the 1934 *Dames* all equate successful music-making with successful love-making. The opulent song-and-dance spectacles of these films (all choreographed by Busby Berkeley) thus openly celebrate the romance of young stars Ruby Keeler and Dick Powell, without whose talents and emotions the show could never go on. In this new musical world there is no room for dying children, selfish sisters, or intractable foes. Instead, plots are redesigned to further the young couple's romance while celebrating their love through the energy of song and dance.

While this new musical structure first appeared in Warners' backstage films, its popularity eventually facilitated

Ginger Rogers and Fred Astaire in *Swing Time*, directed by George Stevens for RKO in 1936

the genre's spread to every conceivable plot line. No longer grafted to melodramatic stock, but instead mated with romantic comedy, the musical moved into such areas as the bio-pic (*The Great Ziegfeld*, 1936; *The Jolson Story*, 1946; *Night and Day*, *The Glenn Miller Story*, 1953), the troop show (*For Me and my Gal*, 1942), the fashion show (*Cover Girl*, 1944), or even a revivified operetta (especially in MGM's extremely successful pairing of Jeanette MacDonald and Nelson Eddy in *Naughty Marietta* (1935), *Rose-Marie* (1936), and subsequent films).

It was also in 1933 that Fred Astaire and Ginger Rogers first captured the public's imagination. While Astaire had enjoyed a distinguished stage career with his sister Adele (and a film début that year in MGM's Busby Berkeley lookalike *Dancing Lady*) and Rogers had played chorus girl parts (*42nd Street*, *Gold Diggers of 1933*), it was their pairing in *Flying down to Rio* that first introduced them to the public as a couple, thus inaugurating a distinguished series of RKO films which, like the Warners' backstage musicals, consistently use song and dance to celebrate the main couple's romance. What is more, with songs tailored for Astaire and Rogers by the decade's most gifted songwriters (Cole Porter for *The Gay Divorcee* (1934); Jerome Kern for *Roberta* (1934) and *Swing Time* (1936); Irving Berlin for *Top Hat* (1935), *Follow the Fleet* (1936), and *Carefree* (1938); George Gershwin for *Shall We Dance* (1937)), each number of the Astaire–Rogers films plays an active role in the making of the couple. The Astaire–Rogers films had a stabilizing effect on the genre, for they bridged the gap between the fancy costumes and faraway upper-class sets of operetta and the down-to-earth plots and hummable music of the Tin Pan Alley, vaudeville, or folk traditions. Whereas in 1930 there was no single coherent broad-based musical genre, by mid-decade films as diverse as *Gold Diggers of 1935*, *Naughty Marietta*, *Mississippi* (1935), *Broadway Melody of 1936*, *Shipmates Forever* (1935), *Top Hat*, and even *A Night at the Opera* (1935) could all be designated by a single generic term: the musical.

During the mid-1930s, the musical genre developed a durable pattern that may be conveniently defined in terms of a number of semantic and syntactic features:

1. Format: Narrative. Music and dance numbers are linked through a story-line.
2. Characters: Romantic couple in society. Even in Shirley Temple films or animated musicals, a courting couple and the community surrounding them are necessary to the musical's romantic comedy approach.
3. Acting: Combination of rhythmic movement and realism. Both extremes—straight realism and pure rhythm—must be present for the musical to effect its characteristic merging of the two.

4. Sound: Mixture of diegetic music and dialogue. Without diegetic music or dance, there can be no musical. Conversely, films that are all music such as Jacques Demy's *Les Parapluies de Cherbourg* (1964) cannot achieve the musical's constitutive effect of moving from the world of sober speech (in Brecht's phrase) into the musical realm of romance.

These semantic determinants are common to many musical films, but there are also certain syntactic relations evidenced only by those films that constitute the nucleus of the genre:

1. Narrative strategy: Dual-focus. The film alternates between male and female partners (or groups), establishing parallels between the two, identifying each with a specific cultural value, and eventually provoking their confrontation and merger.
2. Couple/plot: Parallelism (and/or causal link) between couple formation and plot resolution. Courtship is thus always closely connected to some other aspect of the film's thematic material.
3. Music/plot: Music and dance as expression of personal and communal joy. As signifiers of romantic triumph over every possible limitation, music and dance serve a celebratory purpose.
4. Narrative/number: Continuity between realism and rhythm, dialogue and diegetic music. The musical's oppositions exist only to be resolved, following the American mythology of marriage as a mystical union of the couple.
5. Image/sound: Classical narrative hierarchy (image over sound) reversed at climactic moments. Through the process of the 'audio dissolve' (realistic sound treatment gives way gradually to a realm of rhythm and rhyme), we enter a world where actions keep time to the music, rather than the more familiar situation where sound is produced by and synchronized with imaged actions.

While not every classical Hollywood musical displays every one of these features (e.g. some musical films aimed at children lack a central romantic couple), the vast majority of Hollywood's musical production during the middle third of this century—the musical's primary genre film era—corresponds to this definition.

Hollywood's self-consciousness about the genre is especially clear in the many post-war attempts to build musicals around overt reflection on the genre. Though such films might easily have led to a serious critique of the genre, instead they reaffirm its implied values. At first expressed in passing, through inversion or foregrounding of familiar motifs (as in the send-up of backstage clichés in the 1941 *Ziegfeld Girl*), the 'reflexive' or 'self-reflexive'

musical appears in its most complete form in MGM films scripted by Betty Comden and Adolph Green such as *The Barkleys of Broadway* (1948), *On the Town* (1949), *Singin' in the Rain* (1951), *The Band Wagon* (1953), or *It's Always Fair Weather* (1955). Even in the many cases where musicals treat alcoholism, gangster attacks, or premature death—as in *A Star is Born* (1954), *Oklahoma!* (1955), *Porgy and Bess* (1959), or *West Side Story* (1961)—clever scripting constantly manages to build a new society around a loving couple (beyond the grave if necessary), with the energy of music and dance celebrating their union.

After a period of rather unimaginative Broadway adaptations (*My Fair Lady*, 1964; *The Sound of Music*, 1965), remakes (*A Star is Born*, 1976) compilations (*That's Entertainment*, 1974), and musical films for children (*Mary Poppins*, 1964), in the late 1970s the musical surprised even its most avid followers with a strong revival. Some of these films were irreverent send-ups of show-business conventions (Robert Altman's 1976 *Nashville* and Bob Fosse's 1980 *All that Jazz*); some were mild remembrances of plots past (Martin Scorsese's 1977 *New York, New York*, Stanley Donen's 1978 *Movie Movie*). But a number of others—including *Saturday Night Fever* (1978), *Hair* (1979, directed by Miloš Forman), and *Dirty Dancing* (1987)—involved a renewed ability to integrate contemporary music and mores into the traditional structures of the musical genre.

CATEGORIES OF THE MUSICAL

Critics of the musical have long differentiated among musical plots, performance traditions, and production methods. Important divisions of the musical into subgenres have been based on the following criteria (and led to the problems enumerated).

Studio

Pinpointing a 'house style' founded on the success of a small group of films, studio distinctions often stress particular stars or production personnel. Paramount is noted for the performances of Maurice Chevalier and Jeanette MacDonald in sophisticated European operettas directed by Ernst Lubitsch or Rouben Mamoulian. Warners is identified with backstage plots in realistic urban locations, where hoofer Ruby Keeler and a chorus of girls carry out Busby Berkeley's choreography, while crooner Dick Powell warbles songs by Al Dubin and Harry Warren. RKO's screwball comedy scripts combine elegant dancers Fred Astaire and Ginger Rogers with offbeat comics Edward Everett Horton and Eric Blore in Van Nest Polglase's classy art deco sets. Fox offers folksy, regional productions featuring blonde stars Alice Faye, Betty Grable, Marilyn Monroe, and Shirley Temple. MGM is touted for its stable of stars (Jeanette MacDonald and Nelson Eddy before the war; Cyd Charisse, Judy Garland, Gene Kelly, Frank Sinatra, Esther

Williams, and an older Fred Astaire in the 1940s and 1950s) in cleverly scripted big-budget spectacles whose high production values and complex choreography are assured by outstanding production personnel (virtuoso editor Slavko Vorkapich; script-writers Betty Comden and Adolph Green; producers Arthur Freed and Joe Pasternak) and dance-sensitive directors (Busby Berkeley, Stanley Donen, Vincente Minnelli, George Sidney, Charles Walters). Useful as an introductory classification, this approach tends to overemphasize a single aspect of each studio's production, while concealing important resemblances and influences among studios.

Director

Auteur critics have concentrated on the efforts of the genre's most innovative directors (Lubitsch, Mamoulian, Minnelli, Donen, Fosse). However, *auteur* criticism of the musical often tends to mask the contributions of non-directorial personnel and of functions other than directing *per se*. More attention deserves to be paid to other sources of innovation and consistency in the musical, notably choreography and performance. Berkeley and Walters both started as choreographers; Fred Astaire and Gene Kelly did their own choreography (and Kelly also directed or co-directed many of the films he stars in), while their role as performers is no less central to their films. Singers too—Chevalier, MacDonald, Crosby, Garland—give a distinct character to films. And no history of the Hollywood musical is possible without recognizing the role of producers such as Arthur Freed at MGM and Joe Pasternak, who produced a string of Deanna Durbin musicals for Universal in the 1930s.

Method of introducing music

While stage conventions fully motivate backstage musical numbers, and the operetta tradition offers only psychological motivation for its musical outbursts (and instant accompaniment), the so-called 'integrated' musical naturalizes its song-and-dance numbers through carefully contrived situations, sets, or character penchants (a convenient piano, an empty stage, a public dance floor, a family singalong, characters who 'just can't stop singing'—or dancing). Usually deployed as part of a historical argument whereby the musical 'improves' by abandoning artificiality in favour of integration, this approach disenfranchises the many musicals that self-consciously seek artificiality or (like *The Band Wagon*) deliberately mix the two elements. It remains useful, however, as a method of concentrating attention on the articulation between narrative and spectacle.

Source

Much has been written about the differences between adaptations from the Broadway stage and original Hollywood musicals. Typically, the Broadway–Hollywood oppo-

sition rests on the assumption that creative energy always flows from New York to California, yet some of Hollywood's most famous borrowings from Broadway involve plays directly inspired by cinematic developments. For example, most of the innovations attributed to the 1943 Broadway version of *Oklahoma!*—usually identified with its composer and lyricist (Richard Rodgers and Oscar Hammerstein)—were actually first introduced by the play's director, Rouben Mamoulian, in his 1937 film *High, Wide and Handsome*.

Audience

As the apparently homogeneous audience of the 1930s succumbed to post-war and then post-modern fragmentation, Hollywood increasingly targeted separate audiences. Depending on such criteria as character age, musical style, and the role of romance, musicals may be distinguished by their implied audience: children, adolescents, or adults. While this distinction is useful for descriptive purposes, it obscures important aspects of the genre's history and structure. Classifying musicals by their intended audience conceals the genre's careful creation of a spectator position requiring a combination of adult and childlike qualities (sexual maturity and innocent optimism). It also fails to recognize Hollywood's systematic attempt to bridge audience sectors with films that provide 'something for everyone' (as when Shirley Temple plays Cupid, Disney's cartoon characters enact adult romances, or *The Barkleys of Broadway* and *Dirty Dancing* mix the music and dance styles preferred by different generations).

SEMANTICS AND SYNTAX

Careful inspection of the genre's basic materials (musical traditions, dance modes, acting styles, costuming fashions, location and set choices, plot motifs, thematic interests) suggests an alternative approach to the musical and a threefold division which is confirmed by analysis of syntactic concerns (especially the set of activities associated with the genre's fundamental action, the making of a couple), yielding the following subgenres:

The fairy-tale musical. Set in distant aristocratic locales (palaces, resorts, fancy hotels, ocean liners) treated in travelogue fashion, the fairy-tale musical makes restoration of order in the romantic coupling process parallel (and often causally related) to the restoration of order in an imaginary kingdom. Guiding metaphor: to marry is to govern.

The show musical. Set in the Manhattan-centred modern middle-class world of theatre and publishing, the show musical associates the constitution of a couple with the creation of a show (vaudeville routine, Broadway play, Hollywood film, fashion magazine, concert). Guiding metaphor: to marry is to create.

The folk musical. Set in the America of yesteryear, from small town to frontier, the folk musical's integration of two disparate individuals into a single couple heralds the entire group's communion with each other and with the land that sustains them. Guiding metaphor: marriage is community.

Each of these subgenres overtly celebrates one particular value associated with the genre as a whole. In the fairy-tale musical (so named for its tendency to predicate the future of a kingdom on the romance of a 'princess' and her suitor), the constitution of an imaginary kingdom stresses the musical's tendency toward transcendence of the real. The show musical (named for the type of production paralleling the couple's success) maximizes the genre's general expression of joy through music and dance. The folk musical (after the characters, music, and general atmosphere) plays up the communitarianism characteristic of the musical's choral tendencies.

While these subgenres develop separately, they may of course be combined in interesting ways. Thus *Rose-Marie* transfers the typical operetta trappings of the fairy-tale musical to a regional location more typical of the folk musical, while *Brigadoon* (1954) combines a folk semantics with a fairy-tale syntax. Similarly, Fred Astaire seems to carry with him the aristocratic underpinnings of the fairy-tale tradition even when he is cast in show musicals like *Easter Parade* (1948), *The Barkleys of Broadway*, or *The Band Wagon*, while Gene Kelly and Judy Garland exude a folk paradigm even in a fairy-tale musical like *The Pirate* (1948).

CULTURAL USES OF THE MUSICAL

For half a century, musical films played a major role in the stabilization of US society (and in representing the USA abroad). As the most expensive of Hollywood products, and the most fully tied to other cultural practices, the musical was regularly exploited for economic, artistic, and social purposes.

Often linked to the development of sound film technology, the history of the musical is actually much better understood through Hollywood's changing relationship to the US music distribution system. In 1929 Warner Bros. began to acquire music publishing companies in an effort to reduce the overall cost of obtaining music for sound films. Other studios soon followed suit, with many going so far as to back Broadway musical plays in order to secure music rights. Never entirely abandoned, this practice reached its height in the 1950s with Columbia's financing of *My Fair Lady*. Through a complex set of subsidiaries and licensing agreements, virtually every studio shared in the profits of one or more music publishers and/or recording companies.

In the early years of sound film, public performance of songs (live, recorded, or broadcast) helped publicize the originating films. During Hollywood's heyday, the musical consistently drove other genres by providing music for which the studio already held rights. Warners used music from their own musicals for their 'Looney Tunes' and 'Merrie Melodies' cartoon series. In the 1940s, Paramount used love songs from early 1930s musicals as dance or atmospheric music in women's films, melodramas, and films noir. In the early 1950s, MGM used the song catalogues of specific songwriters as the basis for innovative musicals (George and Ira Gershwin for *An American in Paris*, Arthur Freed and Nacio Herb Brown for *Singin' in the Rain*, Harold Dietz and Arthur Schwartz for *The Band Wagon*), while other studios raided their song catalogues to make innumerable musical bio-pics.

With the advent of 45 r.p.m. records, top forty lists, and long-playing albums, the direction of influence was reversed. In the 1930s and 1940s, the Hollywood musical had been the prime mover in the American musical system, both generating musical products (live performances, sheet music, records) and profiting from the publicity those products generated. Starting in the 1950s, however, the musical became little more than a publicity resource for the far more profitable recording companies that had once been a Hollywood subsidiary.

Nevertheless, for thirty years Hollywood musicals were inextricably intertwined with the daily lives of a nation of music lovers. With sheet music available in many theatre lobbies and every department store, families regularly gathered around the piano to sing the latest Hollywood hit. Courting couples recreated their favourite Hollywood scene by spooning to a record of the film's music. Every new musical style was instantly turned into a dance craze learnt in Fred Astaire or Arthur Murray Dance Studios and widely practised in ballrooms around the country. Every potential social use of the musical was reinforced by the omnipresence of the genre's music, serving as figure for the broader practices championed by the musical.

Among these practices, none was more important than the American myth of courtship, which the musical consistently embodied throughout its long history. Overtly reinforcing conservative social practices (gender stereotyping, racial separation, sexual prudishness, a preference for heterosexuality bordering on homophobia), the musical offered to every conceivable problem a single solution: courtship and community. While musicals hold out an opportunity to enact transgressive desires for counter-cultural unions (typically involving adultery or disregard of differences in age, religion, ethnicity, or race), it virtually always diverts attention from the underlying cultural problems to the easily resolvable difficulties of the central couple. With popular music as vehicle, the musical rapidly brought this optimistic approach to real-world problem-solving into virtually every household in the western world. Offering both a utopian fantasy and

Vincente Minnelli
(1903–1986)

A prolific director at MGM for over three decades, Vincente Minnelli made important contributions to some of the most celebrated entertainments in history. American critics in the 1940s praised his sophistication and lyrical humanism, and many of the French and Anglo-American auteurists in the 1950s and 1960s regarded him as a sly satirist of bourgeois values. He received an Oscar (for *Gigi*, 1958), and his work profoundly influenced such later directors as Jean-Luc Godard and Martin Scorsese.

Minnelli's first ambition was to paint, but he learnt many of his directorial skills in Chicago's burgeoning consumer economy during the 1920s, working by turns as a window decorator for the Marshall Field department store, an assistant to a portrait photographer, and a designer of stage settings for the Balaban and Katz chain of picture palaces. He subsequently moved to New York, where he created sets and costumes at Radio City Music Hall, and became famous as a designer-director of Broadway revues. After a brief and uneventful stay at Paramount in the late 1930s, he was brought permanently to Hollywood by Arthur Freed, who had assembled a unit of Broadway and Tin Pan Alley artists at MGM. Minnelli remained at that studio until the 1960s, specializing in musicals, domestic comedies, and melodramas. An aesthete who seemed happy in a factory, he frequently made MGM's motto—*Ars Gratia Artis*—sound almost plausible. At the same time, he never forgot his commercial origins. It is no accident that he once filmed a charming comedy entitled *Designing Woman* (1957), and it seems appropriate that one of his melodramas, *The Cobweb* (1955), involves a crisis that breaks out in a mental institution when new curtains are selected for the common room.

Nearly all of Minnelli's work was indebted to the classical Hollywood musical, which might be described as a late, commercialized vehicle for the romantic imagination. Art, show business, and various kinds of dreaming were his favourite subjects. His female characters were reminiscent of Madame Bovary, and his males were often artists, dandies, or sensitive youths. Most of his stories took place in exotic or studio-manufactured worlds, where the boundaries between fantasy and everyday life could easily be transgressed. Even when they were set in provincial America, they burst into remarkable oneiric passages, such as the terrifying Halloween sequence in *Meet Me in St. Louis* (1944), the nightmare in *Father of the*

Bride (1950), the berserk carnival in *Some Came Running* (1958), and the mythic boar hunt in *Home from the Hill* (1960).

Minnelli was strongly influenced by three Parisian artistic formations: the decorative art nouveau of the 1880s, the early modernism of the impressionist painters, and the dream vision of the surrealists. Although he was frequently preoccupied with the kind of psychoanalysis that could be safely adjusted to the Production Code, he was among the least macho of Hollywood directors, and he brought a rarefied sense of camp to musical numbers, making several films that were ahead of popular taste. His pictures were filled with swooping crane shots, voluptuous plays of fabric and colour, and skilfully orchestrated background detail. In the final analysis, however, his musicals were hymns to entertainment, and he never questioned MGM's plush standards of glamour and style.

The paradoxes and contradictions of Minnelli's aestheticism are especially evident in the four melodramas he made with producer John Houseman: *The Bad and the Beautiful* (1952), *The Cobweb* (1955), *Lust for Life* (1956), and *Two Weeks in Another Town* (1962). These all deal with the relation between neurosis and artistic imagination. In each, the artist-hero is a lonely character, who is inhabiting an oppressively patriarchal and capitalist society, and who cannot fully sublimate desire into art. Unlike the musicals, the art melodramas never achieve a utopian integration of daily life with creative energy; as a result they have a distinctly melancholy tone and achieve an impressive atmosphere of stylistic 'excess' or delirium. A fascinating mixture of *Kunst* and kitsch, Minnelli's films challenge the traditional distinction between commerce and artistic legitimacy.

JAMES NAREMORE

SELECT FILMOGRAPHY

Cabin in the Sky (1943); Meet Me in St. Louis (1944); Yolanda and the Thief (1945); The Pirate (1948); Madame Bovary (1949); Father of the Bride (1950); An American in Paris (1951); The Bad and the Beautiful (1952); The Band Wagon (1953); Brigadoon (1954); The Cobweb (1955); Lust for Life (1956); Tea and Sympathy (1956); Gigi (1958); Some Came Running (1958); Home from the Hill (1960); Two Weeks in Another Town (1962); On a Clear Day You Can See Forever (1970)

BIBLIOGRAPHY

Elsaesser, Thomas (1981), 'Vincente Minnelli'.
Harvey, Stephen (1989), *Directed by Vincente Minnelli*.
Naremore, James (1993), *The Films of Vincente Minnelli*.

Opposite: Richard Widmark and Gloria Grahame in Vincente Minnelli's Freudian melodrama *The Cobweb* (1955)

(in Richard Dyer's words) a sample of 'what utopia would feel like', the musical carried this particularly American mythology into every aspect of life, thus defining Americanness abroad and influencing other film genres, the media, musical styles, and dress patterns around the world.

During Hollywood's heyday the musical played a central role in the American public sphere. Its coherence, homogeneity, and ubiquity guaranteed continuity of interpretation and meaning. Now that the musical has given way to the musical film, the genre has lost control over its own fate. Cultural uses of the musical are now controlled by the music industry, the mass media, and even special interest groups for whom musical film offers a unique opportunity for self-expression.

In the late 1960s and 1970s, American Protestant churches regularly built worship services, music programmes, and even sermons around motifs drawn from musical films. With inspirational songs like 'You'll Never Walk Alone' (from *Carousel*, 1956) and 'Climb Every Mountain' (from *The Sound of Music*, 1965) regularly sung at high school graduations and as church anthems, the musical's uplifting nature found a set of new allies. A series of overtly Bible-based musicals were even produced in response to this movement, culminating with *Jesus Christ Superstar* and *Godspell* in 1973.

During the same era, the musical film was turned to entirely different uses by youthful audiences. The films of Elvis Presley, Frankie Avalon, and the Beatles served as rallying points before a spate of rock concert films—*Monterey Pop* (1968), *Woodstock* (1970), *The Last Waltz* (1987)—took over, offering a counter-cultural haven for a generation of Vietnam War protesters. The musical's capacity to be bent into almost any shape has even opened the genre to cult and gay uses, primarily through the influence of the quintessential midnight movie, *The Rocky Horror Picture Show* (1975).

Though the musical may have passed into history, the musical film continues to evolve in new ways, and will doubtless do so as long as ways can be found of putting music and film together. The video revolution of the 1980s has generated one brand-new form, music video, and has given renewed life to one of the oldest, the filmed recording of opera and other musical spectacles. Beyond that the future remains uncertain.

Bibliography
Altman, Rick (ed.) (1981), *Genre: The Musical*.
—— (1987), *The American Film Musical*.
Feuer, Jane (1982), *The Hollywood Musical*.
Hirschhorn, Clive (1981), *The Hollywood Musical*.
Russell Taylor, John, and Jackson, Arthur (1971), *The Hollywood Musical*.

Crime Movies

PHIL HARDY

'New York's Other Side: The Poor', runs the opening intertitle of D. W. Griffith's *The Musketeers of Pig Alley* (1912) over shots of the ghetto that was Manhattan's Lower East Side. The final intertitle is equally revealing. After a shot of a hand passing some banknotes to a cop through a half-opened door, the title 'Links in the Chain' comes up.

Musketeers was an early example of the American crime film, and one, moreover, that deals with crime in a manner that has reverberated throughout the genre down the years. The opening shots and title indicate an underworld that coexists with the world we know, and the last one shows how the two are connected. In between Griffith tells the slight story of an innocent couple almost overcome by poverty but saved through the activities of the Snapper Kid, who has been smitten by Lillian Gish as the innocent wife.

Much has been written about Griffith's borrowings from Charles Dickens in his depiction of poverty, but the narrative of *Musketeers* is more revealing of his borrowings from more simply structured Victorian melodramas and pulp fiction. The central notion behind these is of separate under- and overworlds and the point where the two come into collision is often the attempted seduction of an innocent. The classic literary examples of this are Eugène Sue's *Les Mystères de Paris* (1842–3) and the many pulps written by former police reporter George Lippard in the USA in the 1840s.

The importance of this structure for the crime novel and film lay in its flexibility and adaptability as metaphor of social relations. Consider Marcel Alain and Pierre Souvestre's (and Feuillade's) *Fantômas*: the plot of *Fantômas* is virtually the same as that of *Les Mystères de Paris*. The difference is that the villain is recast as the hero and that Fantômas, though diabolical and a scourge of the bourgeoisie, is not corrupt while the aristocracy from whom he steals Lady Belthan is. It is in short a poetic inversion of Sue's novel in which a prince chooses to live among thieves and expose and correct injustices. Lippard's novels, which were also clearly influenced by Sue, represent a further refinement and simplification. Monk Hall, with its six floors, three above ground, three below, and numerous secret rooms, trapdoors, and secret passages, represents Philadelphia. The central plot concerns the attempted corruption of a young innocent by one who seems a respected member of the overworld but whose wealth comes from the underworld. These simple juxtapositions were seen at their purest in American serials of the 1930s in which villains twitched spider's webs of

intrigue that were as delicate as the Victorian tracery of their pulp forefathers.

Fritz Lang's Dr Mabuse films (*Dr Mabuse der Spieler* ('Dr Mabuse the gambler'), 1922; *Spione* ('Spies'), 1928; *Das Testament des Dr Mabuse* ('Dr Mabuse's will'), 1933; and even *Die tausend Augen des Dr Mabuse* ('The thousand eyes of Dr Mabuse'), 1960) also take as a central notion the contrast between under- and overworlds and the codes that govern them. These films look backward to Victorian notions of conspiracy, but a film title as early as *Underworld* (Joseph von Sternberg, 1927) and as late as *Underworld U.S.A.* (Samuel Fuller, 1961) confirms the durability of the central core of the idea. Further examples of the tenacity of this opposition can be seen in films as different as Lang's *M* (1931), in which the two worlds temporarily unite to seek a killer whose crimes are considered to break the rules of civilized society; Basil Dearden's *The Blue Lamp* (1950), in which the organized criminals themselves choose not to associate with the young tearaways played by Dirk Bogarde and Patrick Doonan because they do not understand about the need for restraint; and Samuel Fuller's *Pickup on South Street* (1953), in which a professional informer will not sell information to an enemy of her country even at the cost of her life.

Seen from this perspective, although *The Musketeers of Pig Alley* may be simply constructed, its articulation of the narrative device of seduction/rape within the structure of a contrast between the over- and underworlds is modern rather than Victorian. Particularly striking is the film's ending, which only offers a moment of respite, a truce between the conflicting forces rather than a victory. Also noteworthy is the fact that the Snapper Kid is both prototype hero and villain. In Victorian melodrama and pulp fiction the theme of seduction/rape and the under-world/overworld contrast are generally held tightly and straightforwardly together. In crime films (and twentieth-century crime novels) the two remain closely connected but are often developed in a variety of different ways. As Ian Cameron (1975) has forcefully pointed out, of all the film genres 'no genre has been more consistently shaped by factors outside the cinema than the crime movie'. To explain the development of the crime movie it is therefore necessary to explore the social reasons that lie behind the changes in the narrative strategies to which the crime movie repeatedly returns.

THE GANGSTER FILM

Nowhere is Cameron's point more visible than in the beginnings of the American gangster film subgenre in

James Cagney in Warner Bros.' trend-setting gangster movie *The Public Enemy* (1931), directed by William Wellman

the late 1920s and early 1930s. The gangster film literally began with stories ripped from the front pages of the nation's newspapers (and often written for the screen by former reporters) about the effects of prohibition. But the genre did not spring to life fully formed. The ground-breaking *Underworld* and *Scarface* (Howard Hawks, 1932), both of which were written by former reporter Ben Hecht, are particularly interesting in this respect. Hecht wrote the first when the genre did not exist as such and the second when the ground rules of the genre had been established. Both foreground the underworld/overworld narrative strand and the rise-and-fall scenario that would be oft repeated and, like so many later films, were clearly grounded in reality (even to the point of restaging particular events, like the St Valentine's Day Massacre, and featuring characters clearly based on real gangsters). Similarly both included many of the iconographic elements that would be featured in later films—the gang, the moll, the newspaper man, the shyster lawyer, the night-club, etc. Yet both, especially if one compares them with the likes of *Little Caesar* (Mervyn Leroy, 1930) or *Public Enemy* (William Wellman, 1931), are far from pure genre films (which in great part is their strength).

Underworld—with its ending in which George Bancroft remains to die in a volley of police bullets to allow Evelyn Brent and Clive Brook, his best friend and his moll now in love and wanting to go straight, to escape via a secret passage—clearly looks backwards to Victorian melodrama. Yet in many ways it is also the more modern of the two films. In the characters of Brent and Brook it solves the problem which the greater realism of the gangster film posed for the seduction/rape scenario aspect of the underpinning narrative. Both characters embody the social aspirations that Bancroft, though possessing crude power (he can bend a silver dollar in half) can only mimic but will never attain. Brook, on the other hand, though down on his luck at the film's opening, is a man of social substance. Thus he is effete, has manners, and is even called Rolls Royce. Brent's Feathers also is the start of a line, the first of many gangster's molls caught in a matrix of conflicting emotions. *Underworld* thus adds to the underworld/overworld contrast a social dimension which fleshed out the robber baron element of gangsterdom and would be consistently picked up by later films.

Scarface is a far more complex film. Essentially a family drama—director Hawks told Hecht he wanted it to be like the story of the Borgias set in Chicago—it has at its core

305

the barely repressed incestuous desire of Paul Muni's Tony Camonte for Ann Dvorak's Cesca and takes for its story an almost infantile celebration of the gaudiness of wealth. The film outlines the motor force behind Camonte's actions with a clarity that was too bold for others to follow; even Brian De Palma's 1983 version of the story can only feebly mimic the central driving thrust of the Hawks film. Its concerns would not be picked up until the late 1940s and film noir. In other words, *Scarface* is as much a Howard Hawks film as a gangster film.

If prohibition and the events of Chicago provided the factual basis of the gangster film genre, its popularity stemmed in no small part from its articulation of the complex network of feelings generated in the USA by the Depression. As Robert Warshaw puts it in his seminal essay 'The Gangster as Tragic Hero' (1948): 'The gangster is the "no" to the great American "yes" which is stamped so large over our official culture.' Warshaw's essay (though occasionally rather too broad in its generalizations) highlights a central truth about 1930s gangster films and their reception. Let down themselves by established official society, audiences during the Depression cheered on the gangsters (often folk heroes in real life as well as on the screen), sharing with them, if only in spirit, the delight of putting on evening dress and mixing with those to whom evening dress was a birthright. In this the appeal of the gangster film was like that of the musical, and particularly the 'show musical' in which the little people put on a show and finally win the approval of those in charge, but only after fierce opposition, with the added bonus of the immediate translation of one of their number from supporting role to star. There is a further similarity between early musicals and gangster films: the central role of energy in both, be it flashing legs, tapping feet, blazing machine-guns, or car chases. (It is no accident that the intensely dynamic James Cagney was a star of both.) It is this energy and social climbing (both features of displaced sexuality) that make the early gangster an optimistic figure and at the same time a tragic one, doomed because his energy can never be enough.

This manic energy can be seen in virtually all early gangster films. Consider *Little Caesar* and *Public Enemy* (both 1931). Each within their rise-and-fall scenario highlights different aspects of the energetic drive to success. In *Little Caesar*, Edward G. Robinson gives Rico an animal physicality and desire for social esteem that verges on the psychotic. In *Public Enemy*, Cagney's drive to gangsterism is briefly explained in terms of family (his father is a policeman), but at the centre is a delight in fast cars and shoot-outs that is almost infantile. These films set the template for the genre throughout the 1930s. Changes would take place: in the wake of the popularity of federal agent Melvin Purvis after the shooting down of Dillinger in 1934 law officers would share the stage with gangsters

(for example *G Men*, 1935); and as the genre became well established twists would be offered to ring the changes resulting in kids' gangster pictures (the Dead End Kids), the gangsters on the range, a common feature of late 1930s Western series, and the comic gangster film (for example John Ford's *The Whole Town's Talking*, 1935, with Edward G. Robinson).

FROM GANGSTERS TO FILM NOIR

By the beginning of the 1940s the gangster as a figure had lost much of his power and was no longer a mirror of the times. The misogyny of a Cagney (in *Public Enemy*) thrusting a grapefruit into the face of Mae Marsh was no longer an acceptable image. Though similar images were to recur later (as when Lee Marvin throws boiling coffee at Gloria Grahame in Fritz Lang's 1953 *The Big Heat*), America's entry into the war in 1942 meant big changes in the position of women which made their portrayal as mere girlfriends problematic. Traditional models for representing sex/gender relations came increasingly into conflict with the realities of a world where women were taking over men's jobs (*and* looking after the home while their husbands were away fighting). Changes in the sexual division of labour did not immediately affect the content of genres such as the crime film. It is more the case, as sociologists Edhol, Harris, and Young (quoted in Denning 1987) suggest, that the emerging contradiction between the sex/gender system and the sexual division of labour 'provided a potential for struggle and questioning, for sexual hostility and antagonism'. Indirectly this contradiction was to work its way into the metaphoric structure of the crime film genre.

While the cultural response to this change in the crime film (let alone cinema at large) cannot be 'read off in advance', once the changed condition is noted it is easy to see how different crime films of the 1940s are from those of the preceding decade. One simple role reversal that follows from this change is that of seducer and seducee (*The Postman Always Rings Twice*, Tay Garnett, 1946). Another feature of the crime films of the 1940s is that women are not only *femmes fatales*, preying on confused males, but often the active party seeking to clear their partner's name (*Phantom Lady*, Robert Siodmak, 1944). It is also worth noting that masculine energy is not a common feature of film noir, surely the most languid of subgenres. In film noir the way a (wo)man held a cigarette was as important as the way (s)he held a gun. In the same way the rise-and-fall narrative, a plot in which energy was essential, is little found in film noir (and when it is it is ironically bookended by flashbacks, as in *Mildred Pierce*, Michael Curtiz, 1946). The rise-and-fall structure is replaced by that of the investigation, often in a present that is seemingly stretched to fill the running time of a

Jean Gabin

(1904–1976)

Arguably the greatest French film star ever, Jean Gabin has a place in the pantheon of cinema as the archetypal proletarian hero in a series of classic films made in France in the 1930s, though his long and prolific career (almost 100 leading parts) offers a much wider range of images and pleasures.

Born Jean Alexis Moncorgé to a family of performers, Gabin started on the Parisian music hall stage as a comic singer, and his early films, including his first, *Chacun sa chance* (1930), bear the marks of this theatrical heritage. Several comedies followed, notably Maurice Tourneur's *Les Gaietés de l'escadron* (1932), but concurrently he began to appear in a melodramatic register as a working-class/criminal figure, for instance in Anatole Litvak's remarkable *Coeur de Lilas* (1931). Julien Duvivier's *La Bandera* (1935), in which he plays a legionnaire, turned him into a star and began to fix his 'myth', a combination of everyday French working-class masculinity with the fatal destiny of a tragic hero, brilliantly described by André Bazin (1983) as 'Oedipus in a cloth cap'. Then followed Gabin's first glorious period, in films directed by the best French directors of the time: Duvivier's *La Belle Équipe* and *Pépé le Moko* (both 1936), Renoir's *Les Bas-fonds* (1936), *La Grande Illusion* (1937), and *La Bête humaine* (1938), Grémillon's *Gueule d'amour* (1937) and *Remorques* (1940), and Carné's *Le Quai des brumes* (1938) and *Le Jour se lève* (1939). Gabin's rugged features and Parisian accent, and his minimalist performance, lent his characters authenticity, while his dreamy eyes, beautifully highlighted by cinematographers like Kurt Courant and Jules Krüger, made him a romantic figure. He was the ideal star of Poetic Realism, epitomizing both the hopes of the Popular Front and the gloom of the approaching war.

Fleeing occupied France, he went to Hollywood, where he made two films, *Moontide* (1942) and *The Imposter* (1943), before joining the Free French forces, for which he was later decorated.

In the immediate post-war period, Gabin seemed to have lost his touch, coming back a visibly older man. Films like *Martin Roumagnac* (1945, with Marlene Dietrich, then his lover) and *Au-delà des grilles* (1948, with Isa Miranda) were less successful than those of the 1930s. But he was rewarded by a dramatic return to pre-war popularity in 1953, in Jacques Becker's ground-breaking thriller *Touchez pas au grisbi* (1953). As Max, the film's hero, he developed a new persona; the world-weary, ageing, though still magnetic, gangster, who would rather have dinner with his tight-knit group of (male) friends than fight gang wars. He triumphed again the following year in Renoir's superb recreation of turn-of-the-century Parisian music hall, *French Cancan*, and thereafter re-established himself as a pillar of French mainstream cinema. Eschewing *auteur* cinema and the New Wave, he produced fine performances in two well-crafted films by Claude Autant-Lara, *La Traversée de Paris* (1956) and *En cas de malheur* (1958, with Brigitte Bardot); in costume dramas, like *Les Misérables* (1957); and in comedies and thrillers, particularly *Razzia sur la chnouf* (1954), *Maigret tend un piège* (1957), and *Mélodie en sous-sol* (1963).

Many have accused Gabin of betraying his earlier proletarian image, as he increasingly embodied *grands bourgeois* and politicians. However, the Gabin of the 1960s and 1970s kept a loyal popular audience, who identified both with the social rise of his characters and with his enduring working-class identity, recognizable through physique and accent. Throughout his long career, he crystallized changing and yet coherent ideals of French masculinity and few stars have had such resonance in their own country. Symbolically enough, he played a very creditable head of state in *Le Président* (1961), and his death was compared to that of General de Gaulle.

GINETTE VINCENDEAU

SELECT FILMOGRAPHY

Chacun sa chance (1930); La Belle Équipe (1936); Pépé le Moko (1936); Les Bas-fonds (1936); La Grande Illusion (1937); La Bête humaine (1938); Gueule d'amour (1937); Remorques (1940); Le Quai des brumes (1938) ; Le Jour se lève (1939); Martin Roumagnac (1945); Au-delà des grilles (1948); Touchez pas au grisbi (1953); French Cancan (1954); L'Air de Paris (1954); La Traversée de Paris (1956); Le Chat (1971)

BIBLIOGRAPHY

Bazin, André (1983), 'The Destiny of Jean Gabin'.
Gauteur, Claude, and Vincendeau, Ginette (1993), *Anatomie d'un mythe: Jean Gabin*.

Jean Gabin as the doomed murderer in Marcel Carné and Jacques Prévert's *Le Jour se lève* (1939)

film, leaving the central character, as it were, trapped in a ceaseless present (*The Big Clock*, John Farrow, 1948) in which time is forever running out.

Just how much the landscape of the crime film changed during the 1940s can be seen in the changing form taken by the contrast between the over- and underworlds. In its straightforward version, as in private-eye films and a number of films noir of the 1940s, corruption ruled and the two worlds sat (often all too easily) side by side with representatives of each world often having a role within the other world as well. Thus the police were expected to be corrupt and the man running the local night-club was expected to be a criminal (*The Big Sleep*, Howard Hawks, 1946; *Murder my Sweet*, Edward Dmytryk, 1944). Increasingly, however, what came to be at issue and under examination was not the group and society but the individual and a divided self. For just as the war brought about a radical change in the cultural pattern of life in America, so the influx of European *émigrés* increased the speed of dissemination in American intellectual life of the ideas associated with Sigmund Freud. As psychology and psychoanalysis found their way to Hollywood in the late

1940s they provided writers and directors with the image of an over- and underworld within a single person (consciousness and the unconscious). Two chapter headings from Parker Tyler's seminal book on the cinema, *Magic and Myth of the Movies* (1947)—'Finding Freudianism Photogenic' and 'Schizophrenia à la Mode'—wittily sum up the impact of Freudian ideas on Hollywood. But notions of doubleness and divided identity also came in via artists steeped in the Romantic tradition or who had worked in the German expressionist cinema in the 1920s. This influence was to surface first in the horror film of the 1930s and then in 1940s film noir.

John Huston's *The Maltese Falcon* (1941), adapted from Dashiel Hammett's novel and one of the earliest films noir, is a convenient starting-point from which to examine changes in the narrative strategies of the crime film and the emergence of noir as the dominant form of the genre throughout the decade. The central plot—the recovery of an obscure object of value—harks back to plots from Victorian times and earlier (Wilkie Collins's *The Moonstone* is an obvious example, and in Sydney Greenstreet's grotesque Gutman there is a character very similar to the

Film noir: Robert Mitchum with Virginia Huston in Jacques Tourneur's evocatively titled *Out of the Past* (1947)

same author's Count Fosco). The film's hero, Sam Spade (played by Humphrey Bogart), is neither a saint nor sinner but a vulnerable and emotional man whose rejection of seductive villainess Mary Astor sums up the battered would-be romantic heroism of the private eye to perfection: 'You'll never understand me, but I'll try to explain . . . When a man's partner is killed he's supposed to do something about it. It doesn't make any difference what you thought of him, he was your partner and you're supposed to do something about it.' The speech marks the transition from the edgy freneticism of the Cagney characters of the 1930s to the crumpled and world-weary charm of the Bogart characters of the 1940s. And then there is Astor herself, a strong, manipulative woman playing at being vulnerable, seen in a mix of gleaming close-ups and a network of shadows that prefigure her journey to gaol. At the centre of this rich mixture are the notions of indulgence, represented by Astor and Greenstreet, against which Bogart guards himself, and doubleness in which the characters can be seen as alternatives of each other.

The one thing that is missing from the film is a flashback. The use of flashbacks was to become a staple item of film noir, where one of its major purposes was to deny the effect of progress. Hence the decline of the rise-and-fall scenario. By suggesting that looking back, as in that marvellously titled film, Jacques Tourneur's *Out of the Past* (1947), was the dominant experience, the hope of the future is forever tarnished. In such a world, where pools of light obscure as much as they reveal, the simpler dramatics that supported the structure of the gangster film, where opposition was countered by a mass of machine-guns, could not survive.

To see how significant a change the arrival of film noir was one only has to look at a minor outing like Robert Siodmak's *Phantom Lady* (1944). The plot is simplicity itself: a man convicted of killing his wife is to be executed in eighteen days. His secretary believes him to be innocent and sets about proving him to be so by finding the missing lady who can supply him with an alibi. She does so and wins his love. What is noteworthy from the outset is that the circumstantial evidence that Alan Curtis is guilty is accompanied by a strong sense that he wanted to kill her, that she deserves to die (she was having an affair), and that her murderer (his 'friend' Franchot Tone), who is described as being a schizophrenic artist, is in a real sense Curtis's double, someone acting out his repressed desires (which of course is the theme of Hitchcock's 1951 *Strangers on a Train*). Having the potential to commit murder or act violently is a common feature of film noir (for example, Nicholas Ray's *In a Lonely Place*, 1950). For most of *Phantom Lady* Curtis is removed from his world, and in the same way Ella Raines spends the whole film discovering another world. Two sequences in particular stand out. In the first she follows a possible witness from her world to his,

through gloomy, narrow streets that bring to mind a Greek rather than criminal underworld. The second is even more extreme. Posing as a prostitute, Raines goes to a late-night jazz session which climaxes with an orgiastic drum solo, highlighted by expressionist lighting and dramatic camera angles, which visually confirms the power of sex (and along the way explains why Tone killed Curtis's wife).

Two films by the veteran director Raoul Walsh highlight how much film noir was grounded in the changes in the patterns of life brought about by the Second World War in America: *The Man I Love* (1946) and *The Revolt of Mamie Stover* (1956). In the first Ida Lupino is the independent woman (a night-club singer) who while on a visit to her sister sorts out her sister's problems, which are mainly caused by the fact that her husband is in a war veterans' hospital suffering from exhaustion. The film touches a number of the generic elements of the crime film but its central focus is on the contrast between a strong woman (Lupino) and a weak man (Bruce Bennett) with a sexual predator (Robert Alda) in the middle. The film is both one of the most optimistic films noir, primarily because Walsh focuses (almost) exclusively on Lupino, and also one of the most mechanistic in its organization of the strong woman versus weak man scenario.

The Revolt of Mamie Stover (in colour and CinemaScope) is not really a film noir. Rather it is a parody of both the gangster film and film noir. Jane Russell is the dance hall girl (i.e. prostitute) who is deported from San Francisco to Honolulu in 1941 and makes a pile of money there through property development (financed by her work in a brothel/night-club) with the US army as her major client. When she discovers love in the form of Richard Egan's rich but weak novelist she reforms to prove her love for him before out of loyalty to others returning to work at the Bungalow (as the brothel is euphemistically called). When Egan discovers this he disowns her; she gives him the chance to forgive her, but when he does not, she sets off for her home in Mississippi. With its rise-and-fall plot, its contrasting worlds, the foregrounding of Russell as a threateningly strong woman, and use of typical genre locations (the Bungalow night-club), *The Revolt of Mamie Stover*, despite its many ragged glories, is an impossible film. It is quite simply out of time, bowdlerized because of the mores of the time in which it was created, and only intelligible in non-generic terms—as the work of its director, Raoul Walsh.

THE 1950S AND BEYOND

In between *The Man I Love* and *The Revolt of Mamie Stover* American society changed and with it the narrative strategies of the crime film. With the return of organized crime on the back of war provision profiteering, the gangster subgenre once more became dominant within the crime film. But the new gangster film had different

Alfred Hitchcock
(1899–1980)

Janet Leigh as Marion Crane hiding the stolen money from the prying eyes of the traffic cop in Hitchcock's *Psycho* (1960)

Alfred Hitchcock is one of the few directors whose image—especially in profile—is famous and whose name has passed into the vernacular in the word 'Hitchcock-ian'. Unanimously recognized as one of the great directors of world cinema, his films gain in stature because of the very tensions and intersections they both embody and conceal. Despite the fact that he worked over a span of fifty years, in both silent and sound cinema, in three countries for numerous studios, as well as independently, his films exhibit an extraordinary unity, a unity which includes the most opposed aesthetic tendencies and which has made these films a critical touchstone for the most diverse interpretations.

Born in 1899 in London's East End, Hitchcock began working for British film studios in 1920 as an artist and set designer, then as a writer, assistant director, and finally director. This context, however, does not by itself reveal the influences of other national cinemas on Hitchcock's work. His first work for the British arm of Paramount already steeped Hitchcock in American studio methods before he even set foot in the USA. He was also heavily influenced both by the montage of Soviet cinema he saw in London and by German expressionist film, having shot some early films in Germany alongside Murnau and Lang.

Hitchcock's name quickly became recognized as a marker of professional polish, as well as thrills. Even in his early films like *The Lodger* (1926), Hitchcock already combined the diverse traits which together make up his 'signature': the pictorial arrangement of light and shadow and complex camera movements reminiscent of German silent cinema; the metaphoric editing of Soviet montage; the tense cross-cutting developed in American cinema. In addition, Hitchcock developed distinctive plots, like the 'wrong man' story, in which a man wrongly accused tries to clear his own name, and a careful control of audience identification through restricted information and point-of-view editing. With the introduction of sound, Hitchcock also explored innovative use of sound and music, as well as silence. The changes he made to accommodate sound in *Blackmail* (1929), which was in production when sound was introduced, demonstrate that he, unlike many of his peers, understood the dramatic potential of the new technology. His most famous English films such as *The 39 Steps* (1935), *The Lady Vanishes* (1938), and *The Man who Knew Too Much* (1934) were complex and effective spy thrillers, but he also filmed popular melodrama, romantic, comic, and historical films.

Arriving in Hollywood in 1939 to film *Rebecca* (1940) for producer David O. Selznick, Hitchcock began a complex relation with the studio system, working not only for Selznick but for Walter Wanger, RKO, Universal, and 20th Century–Fox. Hitchcock depended upon the stu-dios' high degree of organization, but bridled against interference from producers. The greatest interference came from Selznick, who felt personally responsible for all his productions. The resulting conflict both enriched and impeded their films together. Hitchcock had already adapted himself to working within the studio system by his system of 'cutting in the camera', in which he only shot what was absolutely necessary, making it virtually impossible to edit the film other than as he had conceived it.

Nevertheless, Hitchcock did not simply accommodate himself to the studio system but sought independence from it. After a string of films for Selznick, Hitchcock pursued some independent ventures. The first of these, *Rope* (1948), was commercially risky and aesthetically and technically ambitious, involving elaborate, ten-minute long takes. In the end this film brought slim remuneration. After four films for Warner Bros., including *Strangers on a Train* (1951), Hitchcock made five pictures for Paramount. Among these were the popular successes *To Catch a Thief* (1954) and the 1955 remake of *The Man who Knew Too Much*, previously filmed in Britain in 1934, as well as the two films which perhaps most clearly encapsulate the Hitchcock universe, *Rear Window* (1954) and *Vertigo* (1958). To these films Hitchcock wisely retained all rights.

Hitchcock's popularity and identifiability, solidified by his cameo appearances in his own films, afforded the director the opportunity for an unprecedented diversification into television and publishing. Between 1955 and 1965, Hitchcock distantly supervised first *Alfred Hitchcock Presents* and then *The Alfred Hitchcock Hour*, as well as directing over a dozen episodes. He also lent his name to a magazine of horror and mystery stories. These ventures added to his revenue and his mythic status. Hitchcock's signature, soon as recognizable as his profile, functioned like a brand name.

After the spectacular success of *North by Northwest* (1959), made on a lavish scale for MGM, Hitchcock turned in an unlikely direction. Borrowing its shooting schedule and black and white photography from television, and its grisly subject-matter from cheap horror films, *Psycho* (1960) demonstrated the growing influence of the less prestigious end of the industry. But with its mix of brilliant montage and long mobile camera shots, as well as its dramatic shifts in audience identification, *Psycho* also bore the mark of Hitchcock's long-developed techniques. His contract at Paramount by now afforded Hitchcock a profit on the gross box-office over a set amount. This arrangement reportedly repaid $20 million for *Psycho*.

With *Psycho* Hitchcock's films became increasingly unsettling and strange. When at the end of *North by Northwest* the train carrying Mr and Mrs Roger Thornhill vanishes into a tunnel, the marriage has been consummated in a visual joke. But it is virtually the last happy marriage in any Hitchcock film. *Psycho* begins with an illicit lunch-hour affair in a hotel room, and the narrative movement of Hitchcock's earlier romantic adventures gives way to the impossibility of sexual or romantic happiness. In his later films violence towards women increases, and Hitchcock's tendency for narrative and camera to control, investigate, and immobolize his female characters becomes overwhelming. *The Birds* (1963) and *Marnie* (1964) were uneasily received. Later films did even worse, and Hitchcock never regained his popularity with film audiences.

Hitchcock's work has always provided a stepping stone for the development of new theories of film, beginning with his creative use of sound in the early 1930s. His visibility as an *auteur* guaranteed his importance to the French critics of *Cahiers du cinéma*, who argued for the thematic, visual, and structural unity of a director's corpus. Claude Chabrol and Eric Rohmer's book emphasized the relevance of Hitchcock's Catholicism and the proximity of guilt and innocence in the 'wrong man' theme. François Truffaut's book-length interview with the director canonized Hitchcock's own interpretation of his work, and English-language auteurist studies like those of Peter Bogdanovich and Robin Wood helped introduce the perspective into England and America.

Subsequent critical analyses have placed Hitchcock films as a site of contestation for structuralist, psychoanalytic, and, more recently, feminist theories. The amenability of his films to techniques of close analysis, pioneered by Raymond Bellour in his study of a sequence from *The Birds* first published in 1969, has made his work a proving ground for every possible sort of methodology. By contrast, recent historical work on Hitchcock's activities of self-promotion and his interaction with Selznick have helped to place Hitchcock in a historical context, as against the tendency of theorists to see his films as embodying an abstract principle or system, an idea which is already well founded in Hitchcock's films and his commentary on them.

Indeed, the excessive brilliance of Hitchcock's work, which makes it amenable to so many interpretations, seems to lie in the almost mathematical purity of conception in which technique, narrative, and structure are integrated, each aspect self-consciously folding in on the others, in part by a complex reflection on character and audience knowledge. If guilt and innocence are constantly contested in Hitchcock's films, Hitchcock himself leaves us no doubt as to who is the author of the guilty deeds which are his films. These films stand as the perfect crime, not because the author of the crime is hidden, but because he is so clearly exposed in a brilliance at once deeply flawed and absolutely flawless.

EDWARD R. O'NEILL

SELECT FILMOGRAPHY

The Lodger (1926); Blackmail (1929); Murder! (1930); The Man who Knew Too Much (1934); The 39 Steps (1935); The Lady Vanishes (1938); Rebecca (1940); Shadow of a Doubt (1943); Notorious (1946); Rope (1948); Strangers on a Train (1951); Rear Window (1954); The Man who Knew Too Much (1955); Vertigo (1958); North by Northwest (1959); Psycho (1960); The Birds (1963); Marnie (1964); Frenzy (1972)

BIBLIOGRAPHY

Bellour, Raymond (1979), *L'Analyse du film*.
Bogdanovich, Peter (1963), *The Cinema of Alfred Hitchcock*.
Modleski, Tania (1989), *The Women who Knew Too Much : Hitchcock and Feminist Theory*.
Rohmer, Eric, and Chabrol, Claude (1979), *Hitchcock: The First Forty-four Films*.
Spoto, Donald (1983), *The Dark Side of Genius: The Life of Alfred Hitchcock*.
Truffaut, François, with Scott, Helen G. (1984), *Hitchcock*.
Wood, Robin (1989), *Hitchcock's Films Revisited*.
ižek, Slavoj (ed.) (1992), *Everything You Always Wanted to Know about Lacan (but Were Afraid to Ask Hitchcock)*.

Alfred Hitchcock posing on the set of *Frenzy* (1972)

themes and motifs from that of the 1930s. In the 1930s it was the supply of liquor in Chicago's East Side that was at issue. In the 1950s the fate of a nation was under threat externally from the Russians, or internally from the Mafia in films whose stories were taken not from the front pages of the nation's newspapers but from the Kefauver Commission on Crime.

Meanwhile, in the American cinema generally, socially oriented films turned increasingly inwards, to courtship, marriage, the family, and domestic issues. Sexuality, too, in a variety of repressed yet explicit ways (Doris Day and Elizabeth Taylor, Marlon Brando and Rock Hudson) became the centre of attraction of a whole range of films. As a result of these shifts in concerns, the classic narrative strategies perfected by the gangster films of the 1930s and films noir of the 1940s no longer seemed to have an outlet. Instead, the shift to domesticity produced a new focus for the perennial interest in crime and criminality, in the form of films about teenagers and young delinquents and their relationships to authority and to their families. The underworld had found its way into the American home.

Bibliography
Cameron, Ian (1975), *A Pictorial History of Crime Films*.
Cook, Pam, and Johnston, Claire (1974), 'The Place of Women in the Films of Raoul Walsh'.
Denning, Michael (1987), *Mechanic Accents*.
Tyler, Parker (1947), *Magic and Myth of the Movies*.
Warshaw, Robert (1948), 'The Gangster as Tragic Hero'.

The Fantastic

VIVIAN SOBCHACK

DEFINING FANTASY

According to French director François Truffaut, the history of the cinema follows two lines of descent, one deriving from Lumière and basically realistic, and the other deriving from Méliès and involving the creation of fantasy. Though the division is historically dubious, it is nevertheless possible to draw a broad distinction between films (and film genres) which operate generally within the confines of verisimilitude—events which happen according to natural possibilities—and those which defy or extend verisimilitude by portraying events which fall outside natural confines.

The types of film which modern audiences would most readily identify as falling into the second category are, broadly, three: horror, science fiction (SF), and fantasy adventure. These are perceived as distinct genres which have in common the fact that each imaginatively constructs alternative—'fantastic'—worlds and tells stories of impossible experiences that defy rational logic and currently known empirical laws. Furthermore, by exploiting the fantastic elements of their narratives and by utilizing and foregrounding a range of cinematic practices identified as 'special effects', all three genres tend to make these worlds and experiences ostentatiously concrete and visible. All three, quite literally, 'realize' the imagination. 'Horror,' writes Tom Hutchison (1974), 'is the appalling idea given sudden flesh; science fiction is the improbable made possible within the confines of a technological age.' And fantasy adventure and romance is the appealing and impossible personal wish concretely and objectively fulfilled.

More radically, however, it has been argued that most, if not all, films are in some respect fantasies, in that they produce illusions based on the manipulation of an original pro-filmic event by various forms of photographic and montage effect. Fantasy genres, therefore, represent a special case of what is, and always has been, a general characteristic of cinema as a whole. Certainly much early cinema was reflexively fascinated by its own 'fantastic' subversion of the physical laws of space–time and causality to which spectators were subjected. It recognized the medium's inherent illusionism and 'trickality', first in plotless displays of cinematic magic and then in narratives that foregrounded the cinema's ability to realize alternative spatio-temporal frameworks and 'impossible' experiences. A film like Georges Méliès's *A Trip to the Moon* (1902) enacts the transformation of the cinema as an impossible world constituted by special effects into a cinema *about* impossible worlds with special properties. It was only later that the cinema's ontological trickality was displaced into fantastic narratives and commercially exploited in the genres to which the name fantasy is attached. Meanwhile in the more ordinary run of films (which often employ many of the same artificial studio techniques as their fantasy counterparts), the trick element is suppressed and artifice is concealed as nature.

It is worth asking, in this context, why certain other types of film in which non-naturalistic elements are predominant—avant-garde films, animation, musicals, and biblical epics for example—are not generally included in the generic category of fantasy. An answer to this question is quite revealing about the way the cinema operates, and the role of the concept of genre in setting audience expectations.

In the case of avant-garde and experimental film, one reason is institutional. Individual and independently made films stand outside the arena of commercial studio production and so do not fit in with the development of a shorthand of genre conventions shared by producers and consumers. They tend also to belong in a sphere thought of as 'high' rather than popular culture and the points of reference for understanding them are art movements like Expressionism or Surrealism rather than other film genres. The fantastic worlds and events created in his films by French poet and artist Jean Cocteau are therefore assimilated to the fantasy genre only when, as in *La Belle et la Bête* (1946), there are additional cues clearly aligning the film with a pre-existing non-film genre such as the fairy-tale. More significantly, however, avant-garde films tend, much as early film did, to concentrate less on creating fantasy worlds and events *in* the cinema than on reflexively directing spectators back to the all-embracing fantasy attraction that *is* the cinema.

The animated film is also excluded from the genres that constitute fantasy—unless, like *Gulliver's Travels* (1939), it also draws upon material previously associated with those genres. Fantasy adventures such as *King Kong* (1933) and *The 7th Voyage of Sinbad* (1958), and SF films like *The Beast from 20,000 Fathoms* (1953), use and foreground the special effects of model animation, but they do so in the context of a three-dimensional world which is enough like our own or at least constant enough in the rules governing its magic for the figure of a prehistoric beast or an army of skeletons to be perceived by characters and audience alike as 'incredible' and 'special'. In the animated film, anything can defy empirical norms, whereas the fantasy film proper starts from an initial realism which is then violated when the monster emerges or the dead come to life or the space–time traveller enters a different world. Without this realist underpinning, the 'fantastic' aspects of the created world and the 'special' effects which bring them to visibility would have no normative ground upon which their fantastic qualities and their specialness could be figured.

Although there have been extremely popular fantasy musicals such as *The Wizard of Oz* (1939) and *Mary Poppins* (1964), musicals in general are not fantasies. People do not, of course, go about the world breaking into song and dance on a continual basis, nor does an unseen orchestra accompany them when they do. In this respect, however, the world of the musical is an impossible one, but not—in the sense in which the word is used here—a fantastic one. For the spectacular effects of the musical remain grounded in physical law, while the emotions of the characters, although their expressivity is heightened, remain engaged with normal situations. The musical privileges conventional human emotion and extraordinary physical achievement rather than fantastic events and specially marked cinematic 'effects' that transgress the boundaries of quotidian human experience.

The biblical epic also merits a mention, since it is a genre which does often foreground characters who possess empirically impossible, superhuman qualities, and it uses special effects to figure the 'miraculous' event. Samson's superhuman strength brings down the temple in *Samson and Delilah* (1949) and Moses visibly parts the Red Sea in *The Ten Commandments* (1956), and these special events are concretized and figured within the context of an empirically credible (though not always historically accurate) world. None the less, these kinds of films are also not considered fantasies. It is not just their content that marks them as different, since horror films often overtly borrow from religious and spiritual discourse, and fantasy films (however secular their inflection) often figure the Devil or angels among their characters. Dominant tradition in Western culture, however, marks a difference here between the 'fantastic' and the 'miraculous'. Biblical narratives tend to be respectfully ambiguous about the empirical basis for their miracles, and special events and special effects are ambiguously perceived. They are represented and taken up as both historical fact and pure allegory, but almost never as fantasy, which is marked unambiguously as imaginative in nature.

HORROR, SCIENCE FICTION, FANTASY ADVENTURE

In the United States and Great Britain, then, the genres delimited, produced, advertised, and popularly consumed as fantasy films are relatively few: horror, science fiction, and fantasy adventure (which includes fantasy romance). The boundaries between them are extremely permeable, and they often appear in hybrid forms (is, for example, *Frankenstein* a horror or SF film? is *20,000 Leagues under the Sea* an SF or fantasy adventure?). But each of the three genres has a certain distinct 'core' identity relative to the others, and although reductive and open to exception and argument, it is none the less useful to point to their differences.

Thematically, while all three genres are bound by their concern with the limitations of what passes for empirical fact and the possibilities of acquiring knowledge that exceeds the boundaries of what is taken as the factual, the horror film of the studio years generally characterized this desire to move beyond the 'known' as transgressive and in need of punishment. 'There are some things that man is not meant to know' is an apocryphal line which resonates throughout the genre, and whose trespass is the driving force behind its narratives. The SF film, however, even when its narratives are cautionary in relation to such things as alien invasions or monstrous creatures, exceeds the bounds of contemporary empirical knowledge more

Karl Freund

(1890–1969)

Karl Freund was born in Königinhof, Bohemia, and grew up in Berlin. At 15 he was briefly apprenticed to a rubber-stamp maker, but his mechanical bent led him to join a film company as a projectionist. Within two years he had graduated to cinematographer on short films, before becoming a newsreel cameraman for Pathé. Ingenious and resourceful, he worked on an early experiment in synchronized sound, designed a film laboratory for a Belgrade company, and in 1911 was appointed chief camera operator at Union Tempelhof Studios, forerunners of Ufa.

By the end of the war Freund had become the foremost cinematographer in Germany. To him, as much as to any of the directors he worked with, can be credited the great post-war flowering of German cinema. Tirelessly exploring ways to extend the camera's expressive scope, he devised new types of lens and film stock and pioneered a whole host of lighting techniques. His range was far wider than the shadowy, menacing, studio-bound style usually associated with the period. The crisp, luminous exteriors of Murnau's *Die Finanzen des Großherzogs* (1923), shot largely on location, lay equally within his compass.

Freund's credits include several of the masterpieces of the German golden age: Wegener's *The Golem* (1920), Dreyer's *Mikael* (1924), Dupont's *Variete* (1925)—and *Metropolis* (1927), where Freund deployed a whole battery of special effects (especially Eugen Schüfftan's recently devised mirror-process) to create Lang's towering, futuristic cityscape. His most sustained partnership, though, was with Murnau, with whom he made eight films. Their culminating achievement was *The Last Laugh* (*Der letzte*

Mann, 1924), on which Freund worked closely with Murnau and the script-writer Carl Mayer to attain an unprecedented degree of camera mobility. His 'entfesselte' (unchained) camera whirled and staggered in a drunk scene, descended in an elevator and out through a lobby (Freund rode a bicycle with the camera strapped to his chest), and soared up from ground level to a high window (the camera slid down a wire, and the shot was reversed).

On the strength of *The Last Laugh*, which was hugely influential, Freund was appointed production head of Fox Europa. He also made a rare excursion into the avant-garde as producer and co-writer on Walter Ruttmann's experimental *Berlin: die Symphonie der Großstadt* (*Berlin: Symphony of a City*, 1927), for which he devised an ultrasensitized film for shooting with ambient light. An attempt to exploit a new, and ultimately abortive, colour-film process led him to London, New York, and finally Hollywood, where he joined Universal.

The mastery of ominous *chiaroscuro* Freund had developed in Germany stood him in good stead for Tod Browning's *Dracula* (1931), with which Universal inaugurated their classic horror cycle, and for Robert Florey's *Murders in the Rue Morgue* (1932). That same year he made his début as a director with another notable contribution to the cycle, *The Mummy*, which gave Boris Karloff one of his finest roles. Over the next two years Freund devoted himself wholly to directing, making seven more films. Six of them were negligible, but the last, *Mad Love* (UK title: *The Hands of Orlac*, 1935), a macabre study in controlled hysteria with Peter Lorre at his most richly depraved, rivals the best work of Browning or James Whale. On the strength of these two films alone, John Baxter (1968) rated Freund 'one of the best directors of fantasy films in

the Thirties', creator of 'fantasies as beautiful and strange as any ever produced'.

Freund, though, went back to cinematography and never directed another film. Moving to MGM he photographed two of Garbo's most opulent period vehicles (*Camille*, 1936, and *Conquest*, 1937) and won an Oscar for his camera work and intricate special effects on *The Good Earth* (1937). MGM, as if in awe of his professional standing, tended to reserve him for their prestige productions, and consequently his work lost something of its former disturbing edge—though nothing of its quality or subtlety.

Surprisingly, given his key role in the genesis of the noir style, Freund took little part in the noir cycle of the 1940s, leaving it to younger men like John Alton or his own former assistant, Nicholas Musuraca. Only occasionally, as in the anti-Nazi drama *The Seventh Cross* (1944) or Huston's claustrophobic gangster movie *Key Largo* (1948), did a hint of noir colour his work. His film credits tailed off in the late 1940s as he turned his attention to developing exposure meters and other technical devices for his Photo Research Corporation.

Television was the last beneficiary of Freund's inventive genius. As director of photography for Desilu from 1951, he supervised over 400 episodes of *I Love Lucy*, revolutionizing TV lighting and photographic techniques and bringing cinematic production values to a medium hitherto low on visual distinction. That the cinematographer of *Metropolis* and *The Last Laugh* should lavish attention on a television sitcom might seem odd. But Freund, the consummate professional, never discriminated: all his material, serious or trivial, deserved the highest standards he could bring to it.

PHILIP KEMP

SELECT FILMOGRAPHY

As cinematographer
Der Golem, wie er in die Welt kam (The Golem) (1920); Der letzte Mann (The Last Laugh) (1924); Mikael (Michael) (1924); Variete (Variety) (1925); Tartüff (Tartuffe) (1926); Metropolis (1927); Dracula (1931); Murders in the Rue Morgue (1932); Camille (1936); The Good Earth (1937); Conquest (Marie Walewska) (1937); Golden Boy (1939); Pride and Prejudice (1940); The Seventh Cross (1944); Key Largo (1948)
As director
The Mummy (1932); Mad Love (The Hands of Orlac) (1935)
As producer/scriptwriter
Berlin: die Symphonie der Großstadt (Berlin: Symphony of a City) (1927)

BIBLIOGRAPHY

Baxter, John (1968), *Hollywood in the Thirties*.
Eisner, Lotte (1973), *Murnau*.
Maltin, Leonard (1978), *The Art of the Cinematographer*.
Prédal, René (1985), *La Photo de cinéma*.

Opposite: A scene from *Mad Love* (1935), with Peter Lorre. Directed by Karl Freund, it was actually shot by Chester Lyons and Gregg Toland, and is an example of the transmission of German camera and lighting technique to Hollywood in the 30s and 40s

sanguinely; the genre's drive into the 'unknown' is characterized by bold epistemological curiosity and its limited satisfaction, and is fuelled by an 'infinite' and 'progressive' deferral of any final satisfaction. Thus, the slogan of the television series *Star Trek*, 'To boldly go where no man has gone before', resonates with an empirical and technological optimism and openness that ultimately overrides any underlying trepidation. The fantasy adventure exceeds the limits of empirical knowledge with yet another alternative. The genre is less about transgressing the natural or moral boundaries laid down by man's empirical knowledge (as is horror), or about extrapolating and extending those boundaries (as is SF), than it is about superseding them. Fantasy narratives are driven by the act of wishing; magic and the magical event are its fuel, and wish fulfilment both its interim problem and its happy solution.

Distinguishing the genres in their thematic relation to epistemological concerns and their narrative drives, we might say that the horror film contests and complements what is taken to be 'natural' law; the SF film extends it; and the fantasy film suspends it. In releasing and suppressing those monsters who emerge as our doubles and *alter egos*, the horror film recognizes that the congruence of our empirical knowledge and our personal desire is impossible to achieve and that one is always at the mercy of the other. Conversely, the fantasy film not only affirms the possibility of the congruence of empirical knowledge and personal desire, but it also achieves and realizes it. The social world with its 'natural' law is not incompatible with the world of magic and wish. And the SF film, as the most realistic and empirically based of the three genres, sees the congruence of empirical knowledge and personal desire as possible, but recognizes that its achievement is always partial and dependent upon the progressive development of technologies as well as upon the rationality of personal desire.

Horror seems the most organic of the three genres; its focus tends to equate irrationality with the bestial and with the dissolution, decay, and deformation of human bodies (although in its late studio years and after, horror became less overtly about bodily transformation and focused more on psychological transformation). In classic narratives like *Dr. Jekyll and Mr. Hyde* or *The Wolf Man* (1941), protagonists were split in two and the genre foregrounded a reversible preoccupation with the beast in man and man in the beast. With its focus on the dissolution of bodies and psyches, the horror film is about the unmaking of worlds and identities. The SF film is the most technologically focused of the three and it is reversibly preoccupied with the ghost in the machine and the machine in the man. Its manifestations of 'artificial' and 'alien' intelligence such as Robby the Robot in *Forbidden Planet* (1956) or the high-foreheaded Metalunans of *This Island*

Earth (1954) offer us technologized bodies that, during the studio years, glittered with the promise and threat of an appealing yet heartless rationality. Even the genre's awakening and mutation of organic (and often primeval) creatures is linked to and resolved through technology. With its emphasis on the founding of new worlds and the construction of new technologies, the SF film is about world-making. Finally, the fantasy film is the most pre-occupied with the nature of will and the will of nature, this reversibility creating visible correspondences between the physical world and the personal world, and presenting us with classical, idealized human bodies that, nevertheless, can transform and transport themselves at will—whether by magic carpet as in *The Thief of Bagdad* (1924) or tornado as in *The Wizard of Oz* (1939), or through the sheer force of love as in *Portrait of Jennie* (1948) or *Pandora and the Flying Dutchman* (1951). In the ease with which it uses cinematic magic to transport and transform human beings, the fantasy film is about character-making. Indeed, it literalizes the *Bildungsroman* and is often structured around tests of character and action that transcend the division of experience into physical and spiritual.

The three genres also differ in the mode in which they engage the spectator. Each often appeals to a different sort of audience or to a different aspect of each of its audience members. The horror film primarily engages us affectively and viscerally—its aim seems to be to scare and disgust us, to raise the hair on the back of our necks or make us cover our eyes. Fantasy films tend to engage us cognitively and kinetically—that is, to make us aware of human effort and action, to make us feel achievement and the fluidity of motion. And the SF film tends to engage us cognitively and visually—to make us thoughtful and to evoke our wonder. Whatever their differences, however, all three fantasy genres share a common project that was consolidated during Hollywood's studio years and continues to the present day. This project is simultaneously poetic, cultural (or ideological), and industrial (or commercial).

The *poetic* project of horror, SF, and fantasy is to imagine and to make visible to us, within the context of narrative and a certain normative realism, those worlds and beings that escape the constraints of our current empirical knowledge and rational thought, but reside, none the less, in our most fearful nightmares, utopian dreams, and wilful wishes. Horror, SF, and fantasy films are all concerned with the limits of knowledge and with the imaginative making, unmaking, and remaking of worlds and human identities. Thus, all tell stories about and give concrete and visible form to that which is not concrete and visible in our daily existence and under our historical and cultural conditions of knowledge, but which, nevertheless, we feel is there. The horror film of the studio years gives physical shape and concrete presence to metaphysical notions of spirit or moral evil: the created monster in

Frankenstein represents an inchoate and incoherent subjectivity that is visibly realized in the 'crazy quilt' patchwork of his visibly stitched-together body. The SF film concretizes the unseen space and time of the past and future: the prehistoric past, for example, imagined and realized by the supple model animation of dinosaurs in *The Lost World* (1925), and the unknown future by the visible outer space and cracked lunar surface in *Destination Moon* (1950). And the fantasy adventure makes visible to us and tangible to its characters intangible desires and transformations of character: thus, the literalization of the desire for eternal life, love, and power in *She* (1935, 1965), the actual realization of wish and will in *The Man who Could Work Miracles* (1937), the concrete relations between a visible human being and his portrait in *The Picture of Dorian Gray* (1945).

Horror, SF, and fantasy films, then, attempt to imagine and literally to *picture* what escapes personal, social, and institutional knowledge, control, and visibility and, through making the invisible visible, to name, contain, and control it. This containment is their common cultural project, affirming as it does, on the one hand, the recognition of and desire for something potentially limitless and transformative outside the bounds of present existence, and, on the other, the need for social control, personal limits, and institutional protection against that which is limitless and transformative. Thus, while the genres of horror, SF, and fantasy adventure all challenge our complacency with the laws and practices that provide the premises for empirical knowledge and our very notion of reality, they almost all conservatively maintain and promote these laws and practices to assure some measure of personal and social safety, certainty, and stability at their end. Furthermore, in a most paradoxical way, almost all fantasy films promote (even when they challenge) the conservation and maintenance of the ideology of the Enlightenment and the positivist empirical science that developed from its value system. That is, the project of fantasy in the cinema is to transform immaterial and subjective phenomena and qualities into objectively concrete and visible material and, thereby, to 'realize' it. This cultural privileging of objectivity, of the physically concrete, and of vision as a way of knowing the world corresponds closely with the technological nature and commercial goals of cinema as an industry.

During the studio years (as well as after), the common *industrial* project of all fantasy films was, of course, to produce a commercially profitable product. Rick Altman suggests above that the establishment of a successful and relatively stable generic form (or syntax) is dependent upon 'the discovery of some common ground between the audience's ritual values and the industry's ideological commitments', and upon 'accommodating audience desires to studio concerns'. For all three established fantasy genres, the common ground that links audience desire (to see the unseeable) with studio concerns (to sell movies) is their general dependence upon special effects. Through effects that draw upon the latest in new techniques (of make-up, for example) and new technologies (computer imaging, for example) so as to remain 'special', horror, SF, and fantasy genres are able to fulfil the audience's desire that the invisible become visible at the same time they are able to fulfil the industry's ideological commitment to maintain audience desire for the cinema itself. In the fantasy genres, imagination tends to mean literal, concrete, visible *fabrication*.

ORIGINS AND INFLUENCES

Like most other film genres, fantasy films are part of a rich history that extends itself well before and beyond cinema into folk-tale, fairy-tale, myth, legend, chivalric romance, Gothic, Romantic, and utopian literature, as well as into painting and theatre. Furthermore, fantasy genres—as well as their cultural uses—are inflected by historical particularity and national specificity.

Thus, the horror film of the studio years was a crystallization of influences that included east European folk-tales about vampires and werewolves and Caribbean tales about zombies; literary works such as Goethe's *Faust*, Ann Radcliffe's *The Mysteries of Udolpho*, Mary Shelley's *Frankenstein*, Bram Stoker's *Dracula*, Robert Louis Stevenson's *Dr. Jekyll and Mr. Hyde*; and German expressionist painting and theatre design, introduced into the American cinema by the emigration of German film-makers to Hollywood from the mid-1920s onwards.

These influences were absorbed and developed in various ways, depending on the economic opportunities available. On the whole in the 1930s and 1940s the top four Hollywood studios—Paramount, MGM, 20th Century–Fox and Warners—eschewed the horror genre, leaving a market niche for their competitors to exploit. In the 1930s it was Universal who pioneered horror as a low-cost studio genre, with Tod Browning's *Dracula* (1931), starring Bela Lugosi in the title-role, and *Frankenstein* (1931), directed by James Whale, with Boris Karloff as the monster. Whale also made *The Old Dark House* (1933) and *Bride of Frankenstein* (1935). Then in the 1940s it was Val Lewton's unit at RKO which carried the genre forward with *Cat People* (1942), and *I Walked with a Zombie* (1943), both directed by Jacques Tourneur, Mark Robson's *Isle of the Dead* (1945), and others. A similar role was played in Britain by Hammer Films in the late 1950s and early 1960s, drawing upon the talents of Terence Fisher for *The Curse of Frankenstein* (1957), *Horror*

Bela Lugosi in the title role in Tod Browning's *Dracula* (1931), the first of a cycle of horror film's produced by Universal in the 1930s

Val Lewton
(1904–1951)

Val Lewton was born Vladimir Ivan Leventon in Yalta, Russia, in 1904, and migrated to the USA some ten years later, where he was raised by his mother and her sister, stage and screen star Alla Nazimova. Lewton attended Columbia University and enjoyed early success as a writer before going to work in MGM's publicity department. A major break came in 1933, when David O. Selznick signed with MGM as a unit producer and recruited Lewton as his story editor. Lewton quickly learnt the film-making ropes from Selznick, and accompanied him when he left MGM in 1935 to create Selznick International Pictures (SIP). Lewton served as SIP's west coast story editor until 1942, working on such films as *Gone with the Wind* (1939) and *Rebecca* (1940) before striking out on his own in 1942 as a producer with RKO.

Lewton had remarkable autonomy at RKO, developing an in-house production unit which concentrated on low-budget projects. The key figures were director Jacques Tourneur, cinematographer Nicholas Musuraca, art director Albert D'Agostino, set designer Darrell Silvera, composer Roy Webb, and Lewton himself as producer and frequent co-writer, usually under the pseudonym 'Carlos Keith'. This 'little horror unit' (as Lewton referred to it) was central to RKO's efforts to upgrade B-picture production to exploit the over-heated first-run market of the war boom.

Lewton established his credibility and his unit's speciality with his début effort, *Cat People* (1942), a dark, intense thriller about a beautiful Serbian girl (Simone Simon), recently arrived in New York, who apparently becomes a deadly tigress when sexually aroused. A modest critical and commercial hit, *Cat People* was important on several counts. It rejuvenated the declining horror genre by introducing a psycho-sexual dimension, and bringing it 'closer to home' with its New York setting. The film's heavy use of shadow and night scenes established a strong visual style, and served a practical function, disguising and concealing the cheap sets and limited resources with which Lewton had to work. *Cat People* was the first 'monster movie' which never revealed the monster to the audience; a narrative device which proved both economical and dramatically effective.

After *Cat People*, Lewton reworked the 'female Gothic' variation of the horror film with *I Walked with a Zombie* (1943), a veiled remake of *Jane Eyre* (as was *Rebecca*) which many consider Lewton's strongest film. Then in quick succession the unit turned out *The Leopard Man, The Seventh Victim, The Ghost Ship* (all 1943), and *The Curse of the Cat People* (1944). All were low-cost, black and white pictures with running times of sixty to seventy-five minutes, and all evinced the thematic and stylistic qualities of *Cat People*. Despite their B-grade status, they scored with both critics and audiences. As James Agee wrote in *Time* magazine in 1944: 'The hope for great films in Hollywood

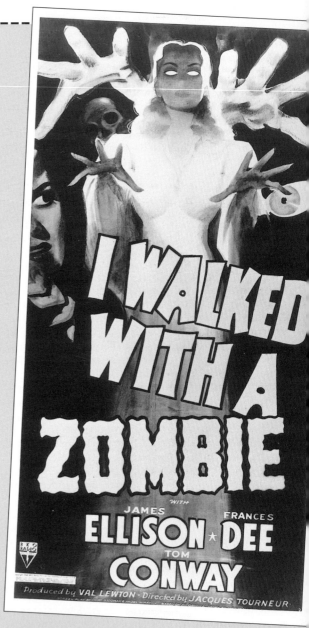

Poster for *I Walked with a Zombie* (1943), produced by Val Lewton for RKO and directed by Jacques Tourneur

seems just now to be shared about evenly by Val Lewton and by Preston Sturges, with the odds perhaps on Lewton . . . His feeling for cinema is quite as deep and spontaneous as that of Sturges, and his feeling for human beings, and how to bring them to life, is deeper.'

After two more conventional efforts in 1944, *Mademoiselle Fifi* and *Youth Runs Wild*, Lewton returned to the horror genre with three successive Boris Karloff vehicles: *The Body Snatcher, Isle of the Dead* (both 1945), and *Bedlam* (1946). All three were period pieces set in foreign locales, and reaffirmed Lewton's ability to attain A-class quality on a B-grade budget. (*Bedlam* was produced for only $265,000 at a time when the average feature cost $665,000, and most A-class features well over $1 million.) But these Karloff vehicles set in the Old World were also throwbacks to the classical horror film and were somewhat at odds with Lewton's earlier pictures. More importantly, they were out of sync with the post-war horrors of the atomic age and the burgeoning Cold War. When *Bedlam* failed to return its production costs, RKO declined to renew Lewton's contract option (which at the time was paying him only $750 per week). Working freelance, Lewton produced three routine features before his untimely death (of a heart attack at age 47) in 1951.

In retrospect, Lewton's horror films occupy a curious, contradictory niche in the genre's development. They ran counter to the science-fiction/horror trend that followed in the 1950s, but, as Robin Wood points out, they 'strikingly anticipate, by at least two decades, some of the features of the modern horror film'. Wood notes that in the earlier RKO films Lewton 'explicitly locates horror at the heart of the family', and directly relates it to sexual repression. Moreover, 'the concept of the monster becomes diffused through the films', to a point where the 'atmosphere' itself is more horrific than any monstrous figure. Lewton's films invariably set up a series of seemingly clear-cut oppositions—between light and dark, American and Europe, Christianity and the occult, human and non-human—which are systematically blurred in the course of the story, to a point where good and evil, the normal and the horrific, become indistinguishable. Thus Val Lewton was a key transitional figure, both as a precursor to the low-budget exploitation filmmakers of the New Hollywood, and also as a harbinger of the modern horror film of the 1960s and beyond.

THOMAS SCHATZ

SELECT FILMOGRAPHY

As producer
Cat People (1942); I Walked with a Zombie (1943) ; The Leopard Man (1943); The Seventh Victim (1943); The Ghost Ship (1943); Mademoiselle Fifi (1944); The Curse of the Cat People (1944); Youth Runs Wild (1944); The Body Snatcher (1945); Isle of the Dead (1945); Bedlam (1946)

BIBLIOGRAPHY

Siegel, Joel E. (1973), *Val Lewton: The Reality of Terror*.
Tudor, Andrew (1989), *Monsters and Mad Scientists*.
Wood, Robin (1985), 'An Introduction to the American Horror Film'.

of Dracula (1958), *The Mummy* (1958) and *Curse of the Werewolf* (1961).

Fantasy adventures drew extensively upon fairy-tales and folk-tales filled with quests, transformations and magic spells, Greek and Nordic myths, legends about spirits, ghosts, and mermaids, epic poems like the *Odyssey* and *Beowulf*, chivalric romances, fantasy adventures of lost worlds like Rider Haggard's *She*, beloved literary classics like Dickens's *A Christmas Carol*, Carroll's *Alice in Wonderland*, and Frank Baum's *The Wizard of Oz*, and theatrical comedies like Coward's *Blithe Spirit*. The talents of such noted model animators as Willis O'Brien (*The Lost World*, 1925; *King Kong*, 1933) and his disciple Ray Harryhausen (*Jason and the Argonauts*, 1963) were exploited and foregrounded most in a genre in which narrative imagination raised dinosaurs and dragons, giant apes, Medusa, and armies of skeletons.

Finally, science fiction, the genre most concerned with our relationship to technology and the most recent in terms of established recognition, drew upon traditions of utopian as well as Gothic and Romantic literature, upon the visionary novels of Jules Verne and H. G. Wells, upon a literature of entrepreneurship and invention best characterized in the popular imagination by the 'real' Thomas Edison and the fictional Tom Swift and expressed in the 1930s by the rise of popular journalism about science and technology and the emergence of monthly magazines solely dedicated to publishing short science fiction. Like horror, SF became a genre privileged at particular studios as a result of a certain class hierarchy among them that determined to some degree the kinds of pictures they aspired or 'stooped' to make and, of course, the particular talents they were able to mobilize. Not known for its prestige films, second-string Universal Pictures specialized in genre films, horror in the 1930s, and then SF in the 1950s. Within this context, SF director Jack Arnold emerged as a leading specialist, creating relatively low-budget, black and white features like *It Came from Outer Space* (1953) and *The Incredible Shrinking Man* (1957) that are now considered genre classics. At the more prestigious Paramount, however, where SF enjoyed less generic privilege, producer George Pal was sufficiently interested in the genre to make big-budget, Technicolor SF films like *When Worlds Collide* (1951) and *War of the Worlds* (1953).

INTERNATIONAL VARIANTS

National identities and histories also inflected the delimitation and popularity of fantasy genres—both in and outside the studio context. Film theorist Siegfried Kracauer (1947) has pointed to the large number of German fantasy and horror films made in the 1920s as symptomatic expressions of the nation's terror of political and economic chaos and, consequently, of national susceptibility to Fascism during the Weimar years. It also seems hardly accidental that a particularly large number of fantasy romances were made in both America and Great Britain immediately before and after the Second World War—many of them like *Here Comes Mr. Jordan* (1941), *A Guy Named Joe* (1943), and *A Matter of Life and Death* (1946; US title: *Stairway to Heaven*) about men who have died getting a second 'fantastic' chance to resolve the moral and emotional dilemmas they left behind them. There is also a clear historical relationship between popular interest in and fear of atomic energy and advanced computer technology in the United States and the emergence of SF as a genre in the early 1950s—as well as between the genre's scenarios of alien invasion and Cold War ideology.

Similarly, the rise of Japanese SF a decade after the end of the Second World War in the guise of *Gojira* (*Godzilla, King of the Monsters*, 1956) stamping on Tokyo marks attempts to figure both the horrors of Hiroshima and Nagasaki and the beginning of normalized relations and increased commerce between the United States and Japan. The subsequent change of the monster Godzilla into a much friendlier (and 'cuter') creature that is more teddy bear than reptile reflects not only normalized US–Japanese relations, but also Japan's transformation from the victim of high technology to high-tech superpower.

In Britain the rise of Hammer Films, beginning with *The Curse of Frankenstein* (1957), and with it the refurbishing of the English Gothic tradition in the mid-1950s, can be attributed to a business decision to capitalize on stories and characters with which the public was already familiar

Jean Marais as the Beast and Josette Day as Beauty in Jean Cocteau's *La Belle et la Bête* (1946)

and which were therefore 'pre-sold'. But the popularity of Hammer's revivals of Frankenstein, Dracula, and werewolves had a lot to do with censorship practices at the time. The containment provided by literary tradition, generic convention, and period costume allowed Hammer's Gothic horror films to exploit eroticism and sadism beyond what was generally acceptable in more realistic genres.

Although fantasy has been an aspect of many national cinemas, it has not always crystallized as a distinct genre, and where it has the reasons involve a mix of cultural and economic factors. The Japanese 'creature' films of the 1950s and 1960s are, on the one hand, indigenous responses to the trauma of Hiroshima and the rebuilding of the nation's economy but they are also, on the other hand, an imitation of American films and were often co-productions made for an American as well as Japanese market. Meanwhile Japanese film-makers tapped into a separate, native tradition of ghost stories for such works as Kenji Mizoguchi's *Ugetsu Monogatari* (1953) or Masaki Kobayashi's *Kwaidan* ('Illusions', 1964). France, too, produced many films with fantastic elements during the silent period, but such films as Gance's *La Folie du Dr. Tube* ('Dr Tube's folly', 1916), Clair's *Paris qui dort* ('Paris asleep', 1923), and Renoir's *The Little Match Girl* (*La Petite Marchande d'allumettes*, 1927) belong less with fantasy as a film genre than with Surrealism and other avant-garde movements. Later a number of 'science-fiction' films were made in the 1960s by distinctive film artists associated with the New Wave, but these—however much they paid homage to genre films produced by the (by then moribund) Hollywood studio system—were on the whole works situated outside and against its traditions. Chris Marker's *La Jetée* (1961), Jean-Luc Godard's *Alphaville* (1965), François Truffaut's *Fahrenheit 451* (1966), Roger Vadim's *Barbarella* (1967), and Alain Resnais's *Je t'aime, je t'aime* ('I love you, I love you', 1968) are all individual works which do not cohere into a commercial constellation or a popularly perceived genre.

Fantasy elements also inform Latin American and Mexican cinemas in a tradition that has only lately crystallized into 'magical realism'—a generic grouping marked by its relationship to contemporary Hispanic literature, its normalization of the fantastic within a realist context, and its philosophical and political subtexts. A contemporary example in Mexican cinema is the popular *Like Water for Hot Chocolate* (*Como agua para chocolate*, 1991), directed by Alonso Arau, but there were earlier works of magical realism such as Roberto Gavaldón's *Macario* (1959) about a poor woodsman who makes a pact with Death, and *The Golden Cock* (*El gallo de oro*, 1964), a critique of both poverty and greed. During Hollywood's declining studio years, however, Mexico (as well as Spain and Italy) primarily afforded cheap labour for American co-productions of horror films meant to appeal to American markets.

It is worth noting that the Soviet Union also has a history of cinematic fantasy—one, however, that brackets that long period between the 1930s and 1970s dominated by Stalinism and its aftermath and aesthetically characterized by a Soviet 'social realism' hardly receptive to the perceived 'escapism' and subversiveness provided by fantastic narratives. None the less, the fantasies made on either side of that period reflect Soviet interest in, on the one hand, science fiction and its mapping of new technological and social relations and, on the other, the selective use of fantastic elements in realist narratives not only for poetic effect, but also for political commentary. Thus, the legacy of the SF narratives *Aelita* (Protazanov, 1924) and *Luch smerti* (*The Death Ray*, Kuleshov, 1924) can be found in Tarkovsky's *Solaris* (1972), and the legacy of Dovzhenko's *Zvenigora* (1928) and *Arsenal* (1929), both of which used fantasy elements to mythic and political purpose, can be found in the political criticism accomplished through the fantasy elements of Abuladze's *Repentance* (1984).

In so far as we think of fantasy films as a general category, it includes a range of films that cross generations and cultures. However, in so far as we think of fantasy genres, we are led back to the regulatory studio system of production, exhibition, and reception that co-constituted and established those recognizable generic structures that we commonly describe as horror, science fiction, and fantasy adventure. It is testimony to the power of these genres, and to their capacity to speak to audiences in a visual poetry that resonates with major philosophical and moral issues, that all have outlived the very studio system in which they were first established.

Bibliography
Brosnan, John (1978), *Future Tense: The Cinema of Science Fiction*.
Coyle, William (ed.) (1981), *Aspects of Fantasy*.
Hutchinson, Tom (1974), *Horror and Fantasy in the Movies*.
Kracauer, Siegfried (1947), *From Caligari to Hitler*.
Pirie, David (1973), *A Heritage of Horror: The English Gothic Cinema, 1946–1972*.
Slusser, George, and Rabkin, Eric S. (eds.) (1985), *Shadows of the Magic Lamp: Fantasy and Science Fiction in Film*.
Sobchack, Vivian (1987), *Screening Space: The American Science Fiction Film*.
Tudor, Andrew (1989), *Monsters and Mad Scientists: A Cultural History of the Horror Movie*.

ENGAGING WITH REALITY

Documentary

CHARLES MUSSER

The Depression and the arrival of synchronized sound had a profound impact on documentary film practices. The modernist aesthetic that had characterized the important documentary work of the 1920s gave way to a new emphasis on social, economic, and political concerns. This shift is symbolized by the career of Joris Ivens, who made short, aesthetically innovative documentaries in the 1920s and then, after a visit to the Soviet Union in 1932, shifted to politically committed works such as *Borinage* (1933), about the oppressive living conditions of miners in Belgium. While documentaries of the 1930s often challenged the policies and politics of established governments, many film-makers in the west and in Japan developed new ties with governments during the decade, often to make films advocating progressive goals. These ties were further developed during the Second World War, as documentary played a crucial propaganda role on both sides of the conflict. During the 1930s and 1940s documentary increasingly became a form that reached and influenced mass audiences for purposes beyond entertainment or art.

The shift from live audio accompaniment to recorded sound came to documentaries later than to fiction film-making, though there were some early and important exceptions. Warner Bros. used the Vitaphone to film vaudeville acts in 1926—short subjects that had documentary value but were soon interpolated into larger fictional frameworks (e.g. *The Jazz Singer*, 1927). Fox Movietone News appeared in 1927, using synchronous recorded sound to film events such as the departure of Charles Lindbergh. As the mainstream industry switched over to synchronous sound, silent cameras flooded the market at little cost and were sometimes acquired by aspiring documentary film-makers. In many instances, the introduction of recorded sound meant that documentary film-makers reapplied the basic format and techniques of the illustrated lecture—narration, music, and sound effects laid over images shot with a silent camera. Recorded sound allowed not only for greater standardization but also for greater precision and complexity in linking image and sound. Innovative film-makers like Alberto Cavalcanti pushed these new possibilities in experimental directions. Moreover, in the 1930s a few film programmes initially presented with live narration and/or music had a synchronized sound-track added, including Luis Buñuel's *Las Hurdes* (*Land without Bread*, 1932).

THE COLONIALIST ADVENTURER AND TRAVELLER

The explorer-adventure-travelogue genre remained highly popular throughout the 1930s. A theme running through many of these was the challenging but triumphant deployment of western technologies in underdeveloped or inaccessible areas. *With Byrd at the South Pole* (1930) traced the plane voyage of Byrd across Antarctica, and *The Mount Everest Flight* (1933), an illustrated lecture by Air Commodore P. F. M. Fellows, depicted 'the official story of man's Conquest by Air of one of the last of the world's explored areas'. Osa and Martin Johnson released *Congorilla* (1932), which included a few scenes among pygmies of the Belgian Congo (Zaïre) shot with synchronized sound. Western arrogance, American racial imagery, and the Johnsons' churlish humour were particularly evident in one sequence: Martin gives a cigar to an unwary pygmy, who smokes it until becoming ill. With African adventure traditionally seen as dangerous and primitive, the presence of the diminutive and attractive Osa added a new twist to the safari film. The heterosocial realm of tourism was added to the homosocial world of male adventure, changing the dynamic. Osa provided a needed element of vulnerability and danger even as the 'dark continent' was being successfully colonized and tamed.

La Croisière jaune ('The yellow cruise', 1934) was a French counterpart to the Johnsons' productions. In effect Léon Poirier (continuity and montage) and André Sauvage (director of the Motion Picture Division of the expedition) were making a promotional film for Citroën car technology; the expedition started off in Beirut and planned to travel to Peking and back. Driving posed few challenges, except that the adventurers decided to take their cars over the Himalayas, which meant disassembling the cars and having native Sherpas carry them through mountain passes. Western technology provided the narrative drive, while native peoples alternately provided exotic spectacle and the labour necessary to execute the rather foolish undertaking. George-Marie Haardt, leader of the expedition, died on the return trip—testimony to the ordeal and self-sacrifice of the adventurers.

Edgar Anstey and Arthur Elton's *Housing Problems* (1935), a sponsored documentary about Britain's slum clearance

Luis Buñuel made a devastating critique of the adventure-travel genre with *Las Hurdes*. He assumes the role of the apparently sophisticated commentator eager to show off his cultural superiority in a documentary about the 'primitive' Hurdanos. His party of travellers feel no responsibility for the people's misfortunes but rather glory in and sometimes add to them. The film's spectator is forced to take an active role in analysing the film and interpreting the images and facts provided, and in the process Buñuel implicitly encourages viewers to assume a more critical stance when seeing other documentaries (like *La Croisière jaune*) in the same genre.

Other documentarians of the time expressed an ethnographic impulse by moving away from the illustrated lecture and looking toward the sync-sound fiction film as a model. *Palos bruderfærd* (*The Wedding of Palo*, 1934), a Danish film made by anthropologist Knud Rasmussen and Frederick Dalsheim, was shot along the coast of eastern Greenland and employed Inuit dialogue. It follows the story of Palo who courts Navarana and finally wins her away from his rival, Samo, and her family, who are reluctant to part with her talents. Robert Flaherty's *Man of Aran* (1934) is a highly romanticized look at the Aran islanders who live off the coast of Ireland. The family is not a real one but Flaherty's fictional creation selected from local 'types'. Once again practising salvage anthropology, Flaherty had the islanders engage in the hunting and harpooning of basking sharks—something they had not done for generations. Since the islanders did not swim, they risked death in their small boats, especially during one sequence when they sought to land their fragile vessels in the midst of a mounting storm.

Flaherty's romanticism ignored the highly exploitative social relations on the Aran Islands: absentee landlords effectively forced many Aran islanders to farm marginal land by turning kelp and earth into patches of soil for agriculture. Likewise Rasmussen and Dalsheim avoided any consideration of the ways that western culture was changing Inuit life. Although the presence of the film-makers was less obvious than in traditional travelogues because they kept themselves and their associates outside the frame, the film-makers continued to shape the representations in profound, often disturbing ways.

GRIERSON, LORENTZ, AND SOCIAL DOCUMENTARY

During the 1930s, Anglo-American documentary increasingly turned to social issues: concerns with the problems facing industrial nations racked by depression and political upheaval. The foremost practitioner of the social issue documentary, one who profoundly shaped non-fiction film-making in Great Britain and eventually throughout much of the world, was John Grierson. Grierson had worked briefly as a film critic in the United States, where he condemned most Hollywood product in vehement terms. Looking for alternatives, he found them in the work of Robert Flaherty, which he applauded for its 'documentary' qualities—thus coining a phrase (or at least popularizing a term which had been used intermittently and with little descriptive force). Grierson returned to England in January 1927 and became Assistant Film Officer for the Empire Marketing Board, a quasi-government bureau. There, using his knowledge of American and Soviet film, he made *Drifters*, a fifty-eight-minute silent documentary about the fishing process.

Drifters was an impressive début; moreover, Grierson used the film to establish the Empire Marketing Board

323

Film Unit in 1930, and hired a group of young, ambitious film-makers such as Basil Wright, John Taylor, Arthur Elton, Edgar Anstey, Paul Rotha, and Harry Watt. He hired Flaherty to make *Industrial Britain* (1931), though he and his staff ultimately had to complete it after the money ran out. As with other Grierson-influenced documentaries of the mid-1930s, its frequent low-angle close-ups heroicize the workers, their patience, and toil. The skills of glass-blowers, machinists, and other craftsmen are, the narration suggests, the bedrock of Britain's industrial might and sustain the British Empire. In his writings, Grierson hailed the British documentaries of the 1930s for their 'continuous and unremitting description of British democratic ideals and work within those ideals'. Yet the Conservative government sponsored these films, and it shows: they fail to acknowledge the efforts of miners and other workers to improve their situation through either union activity or political action. Miners in *Coal Face* (Cavalcanti, 1935) and postal workers in *Night Mail* (Watt, 1936) may be heroicized but they are also shown to be mere cogs in massive, efficient systems of production that ensured British supremacy. These highly polished, aestheticized films ultimately become paeans to British national purpose.

More than anything else, the best British documentaries of the 1930s showed that non-fiction films could be artistically innovative. *Song of Ceylon* (Wright, 1933–4), sponsored by the Ceylon Tea Board through the EMB, looked at a British colony (now Sri Lanka), using an elliptical style that perfectly matched its evocation of an exotic, distant land. In September 1933 the Empire Marketing Board was abolished and the film unit eventually transferred to the General Post Office. There veteran film-maker Alberto Cavalcanti joined the group, adding a new avant-garde impulse to much of their work. Composer Benjamin Britten and poet W. H. Auden contributed to several films, teaming up to provide innovative, modernist sound-tracks for *Coal Face* and *Night Mail*—significant departures from the traditional uses of voice-over narration derived from the illustrated lecture.

Many of Grierson's protégés, feeling their future at the GPO was uncertain and recognizing that it was difficult to make sponsored documentaries through a government organization, either went to work for enlightened commercial patrons like the Shell oil company or formed independent production units after 1935, including the Strand and Realist units. All were loosely affiliated through Grierson-initiated umbrella organizations such as the Associated Realist Film Producers and the Film Centre. Arthur Elton and Edgar Anstey made *Housing Problems* (1935), a film that rejects the use of a modernist aesthetic for a greater faith in the image to document daily life. Sponsored by the British Commercial Gas Association, the documentary is remarkable for its use of

Pare Lorentz's 'New Deal' documentary *The Plow that Broke the Plains* (1936)

synchronous sound interviews which enable working-class people to speak for themselves and detail the decaying, substandard housing in which they live. The film itself offers 'slum clearance' and the building of new government-financed housing projects as the solution to these problems. A government expert provides extensive voice-over narration that assures viewers that a capable and benevolent government is making steady progress. *Housing Problems*, like *Night Mail*, asserts the value of a highly trained bureaucratic élite which will make correct decisions, run the state, and manage society for the general good.

Dozens of other short films were made by the British documentary film movement in the 1930s. *Spare Time* (1939), Humphrey Jennings's first important film, stands out for its sympathetic yet unheroic depiction of working-class leisure activities. And its style, the juxtaposition of only loosely related sounds and images, looks towards his later work.

Grierson had a counterpart in the United States: Pare Lorentz, whose involvement in film also began when he was a reviewer for New York-based newspapers and periodicals. Lorentz called cinema 'the still-born art', railed against censorship, and sought alternatives to mainstream Hollywood film-making. A vocal advocate of President Franklin Roosevelt's New Deal, he was hired in June 1935 by Rexford Tugwell, of the recently created Resettlement Administration, to make *The Plow that Broke the Plains* (1936) and *The River* (1937). Although the United States government had produced numerous documentaries of modest ambition and non-controversial content since the First World War, Lorentz's efforts were different. *The Plow that Broke the Plains* traces the history of farming in the Great Plains, pointing to various environmental abuses. The film culminates with powerful images of the dust storms of Oklahoma and surrounding areas. *The Plow that Broke the Plains* was widely praised for illuminating a problem of national importance, but in that election year politicians and influential citizens from the depicted areas saw the documentary as New Deal propaganda that exaggerated the devastation. A coda, which showed how the government was resettling farmers from marginal land, was ultimately dropped, so the film presented a disaster without any likely solution. *The River* reprised many of the themes of *The Plow that Broke the Plains*. By abusing the land through deforestation and poor farming, Americans had prospered, but were now paying the price, as a generation grew up in the Mississippi Valley 'ill-clad, ill-housed and ill-fed'. Lorentz, with cameramen Willard Van Dyke and Floyd Crosby, filmed the devastating floods of 1937, giving the film a timely and spectacular punch. The government, however, was beginning to put the valley together again through such projects as the dams being built by the Tennessee Valley Authority. Both films lacked

synchronous sound and were cut to music by Virgil Thomson and accompanied by a highly rhetorical, rhythmic narration written by Lorentz. Hollywood saw *The Plow that Broke the Plains* as undesirable government competition and opposed it, though the film was shown in independent theatres. This opposition weakened with the film's success, and Paramount distributed *The River*, which was often paired with Walt Disney's *Snow White and the Seven Dwarfs* (1938).

Late in 1938, after the success of *The River*, Roosevelt established the US Film Service, headed by Lorentz, which was designed to make films for the various departments of the US government. Lorentz started on the never-finished *Ecce Homo* about unemployment, then switched his energies to *The Fight for Life* (1940) about childbirth, infant mortality, and maternity risks associated with unsanitary conditions in poor urban neighbourhoods. This used professional actors in several key roles, though most of the film was shot on location. With Lorentz working on *The Fight for Life*, the Film Service hired Joris Ivens to make *Power and the Land* (1940), about the transforming impact of electrification for farmers who frequently had to rely on the government rather than private utility companies for power. It also hired Robert Flaherty to make *The Land* (1941), a controversial look at man's abuse of the land and the efforts of the Department of Agriculture to manage resources to reduce poverty. The US Film Service lost its authorization in 1940 and Lorentz resigned from the organization.

Despite numerous parallels, there were significant differences between the Grierson group and the one assembled by Lorentz. The Second World War rescued the GPO Film Unit (renamed Crown Film Unit) in Great Britain, even as it assured the end of the US Film Service in the United States. Grierson's organization made many more films, most of which were less ambitious than those that Lorentz produced. Grierson trained a generation of British documentarians while Lorentz consistently hired comparatively experienced film-makers, already well developed in their methods and achievements (Strand, Ivens, Flaherty). Even after 1938, Lorentz continued to be a producer-director-writer, rather than act as a civil servant, while his films dealt with social and economic problems with a forthright, admittedly 'New Deal' stance. Perhaps because Great Britain was often led by a coalition government in the 1930s, the Empire Marketing Board and the GPO made less obviously controversial documentaries: they were public service efforts rather than public advocacy. Yet Grierson's legacy was unquestionably more influential over the longer term. Lorentz ceased to be a presence in American documentary film after 1940, while Grierson not only established the National Film Board of Canada, after his move there in 1939, but became a legendary figure in Anglo-American film-making circles.

Within both Great Britain and the United States, there was a substantial amount of documentary production that addressed economic and social issues from a left-wing standpoint. The Workers' Film and Photo League was active in both countries. In the United States, this group was able to make inexpensive silent newsreels, such as *Unemployment Special* (1931) and *The National Hunger March* (1931), as well as short political documentaries, such as *On the Waterfront* (Leo Seltzer and Leo Hurwitz, 1934). The organization provided a training ground for American film-makers in a similar way to the Empire Marketing Board and the GPO Unit in Britain. Its members left in the mid-1930s to form independent organizations (Nykino, Contemporary Films, Frontier Films). Paul Strand produced *The Wave* (*Redes*, 1935) with a script by Henwar Rodakiewicz and direction by Fred Zinnemann. This film, made in Mexico, tells the story of poor fishermen who struggle to improve their economic situation. Unlike Flaherty's *Man of Aran*, *The Wave* does not present the problem of survival as man against nature, but traces the efforts of the working poor to organize against the local élites.

The City (1939), funded by the American Institute of Planners for exhibition at the New York World's Fair, was directed by Ralph Steiner and Willard Van Dyke from an outline by Pare Lorentz, with a commentary written by city planner Lewis Mumford. Sharing many structural and ideological similarities with *The River* and *Housing Problems*, it contains more humour than the former and greater lyricism than the latter. All three depict a problem, explain how it was created, and offer a solution based on the insights of élite experts of a reformist bent. *The City* paints a grim picture of metropolitan life, both in the industrial city of Pittsburgh and in the 'modern city' of New York. It advocates the development of green-belt villages to mirror the small New England towns of the pre-industrial era; towns, linked by highways which reintegrate man and nature, work and play in a new equilibrium. However, they proved to be little more than disturbing harbingers of post-Second World War suburbanization. Imagining a homogeneous, white, middle-class world with carefully defined gender roles, the film lacks an analysis of the economics and social relations that created the conditions it depicts. Receiving laudatory reviews in the press, this sponsored documentary proved an effective sales pitch for city planning and urban 'renewal'.

PROPAGANDA IN THE SHADOW OF WORLD WAR

The rise of Leni Riefenstahl and the demise of Dziga Vertov reveal much about documentary in continental Europe during the 1930s. The Soviet Union did not produce its first sync-sound documentaries until 1931, when Ilya Kopalin directed *One of Many*, showing everyday activities on a collective farm near Moscow with location sound, and

Vertov produced *Enthusiasm: Symphony of the Donbas*, with its plethora of innovative sound-image techniques. The latter was a modernist ode to industrialization, which functioned within the city symphony genre. While making films for Intourist, Vertov completed his last major film, *Three Songs of Lenin* (1934), a more restrained lyrical detailing of the ways in which Lenin was remembered. But Vertov was an increasingly isolated figure, and Soviet documentary became less and less adventurous as the decade progressed.

Although German film-makers produced hundreds of documentaries which avoided overt Nazi propaganda during the 1930s, Hitler's assumption of power in February 1933 made left-wing film-making impossible. The foremost German film-maker of this period was Leni Riefenstahl, an actress and fiction film director who turned to documentary production after Hitler asked her to film the 1933 Nazi Party rally in Nuremberg (*Sieg des Glaubens* ('Victory of faith')). A year later she returned to Nuremberg and made a similar, but more ambitious, film of the 1934 rally: *Triumph of the Will* (*Triumph des Willens*, 1935), which shares certain methods and concerns with English and American documentaries of the same decade. The building of the autobahns and the state's efforts to put people back to work are referred to in speeches by Nazi Party leaders. Class and regional differences are, Hitler claims, being eliminated. Like many Anglo-American documentaries of this period, *Triumph of the Will* endows the state with a powerful expertise seemingly beyond politics, which the people should unquestioningly accept.

If there are disturbing similarities between *Triumph of the Will* and many Anglo-American documentaries, Riefenstahl's film is ultimately political propaganda of a different order—one calling for obedience not choice, and for racial purification not the (admittedly selective) homogenization of the melting-pot. The past and its problems are meant to function only as an effective counterpoint to the present with its mass of anonymous, sieg-heiling Germans attending the rally. In Walter Benjamin's phrase, Riefenstahl's documentary is the aesthetization of politics, not the politicization of art. Systematically using editing techniques and structures such as the shot/reverse-shot rarely found in previous documentaries, she constructs a cult of personality around Hitler. The editing patterns turn the Führer into an object of desire, one who is looked at adoringly by the crowds that surround him. They complement and realize the speeches of party officials who proclaim, 'Hitler is Germany, the party is Hitler, thus Germany is Hitler and the party is Germany.' The exchanges of looks and salutes create a bond of obedience between these different levels, one in which the identity of self is only found through identifying with the nation and the party. In the process, Hitler and the various troops are eroticized by Riefenstahl's adoring vision. Her omnipresent camera, initially aligned with Hitler as he descends from the clouds and moves through the streets of Nuremberg, looks at the remasculinized nation as led by Hitler and realized by the Nazi Party.

Hitler appointed Riefenstahl to direct a film on the 1936 summer Olympics, resulting in the two-part documentary *Olympia* (1938). This monumental effort was financed by the Propaganda Ministry, headed by Joseph Goebbels, and served the immediate goals of the Reich, then seeking to convince the world that it was interested in furthering international peace and governing Germany in an atmosphere of calm, order, and national purpose.

Political documentary in France followed a very different pattern. After a slow start, the breakthrough came with *La Vie est à nous* ('Life is ours'), an electoral campaign film produced for the French Communist Party in early 1936. Written and directed by a loose collective of film-makers headed by Jean Renoir and including Jean-Paul Le Chanois, Pierre Unik, and Jacques Becker, it combines acted and scripted sequences with stock footage and other non-fiction materials. This syncretic form falls loosely if somewhat uneasily within the parameters of the documentary genre of this period. The making of *La Vie est à nous* led to the formation of Ciné-Liberté, an independent production company affiliated with the Popular Front which won the French election that April. Among its first films was *Grèves d'occupation* ('Strikes and occupations', 1936), which traced the success of labour strikes in the first weeks of the Popular Front government.

When civil war erupted in Spain, the country's film-makers turned to non-fiction film-making in large numbers. Many films were made on the republican side, with Luis Buñuel and Pierre Unik producing *España 1936* (released in 1937 in both Spanish and French versions). The film, made through Ciné-Liberté in Paris, was shaped by Buñuel's surrealist sensibility: brutal and banal images of the war are tied together by a commentary that refuses easy sloganizing and optimistic rhetoric. Meanwhile Helen van Dongen, then in New York with Joris Ivens, was asked to edit footage of the Civil War into a compilation documentary—*Spain in Flames* (1937). Frustrated by the lack of footage from the loyalist side, Ivens found financing that enabled him to travel to Spain and make *Spanish Earth* with the assistance of John Ferno and Ernest Hemingway. It depicts the defence of Madrid and its environs, including a village where an irrigation project is making the land newly productive. *Heart of Spain* (1937) was also shot in Spain, by Hungarian photographer Géza Karpathi and the American journalist Herbert Kline, and then assembled in New York by Kline, Paul Strand, and Leo Hurwitz. Designed to raise money for medical supplies, the film shows the bombing of Madrid, underscoring the bloody devastation caused by German and Italian intervention. It focuses on the role of the hospitals and the donation of blood that saved the lives of combatants and civilian bombing victims. *Spanish ABC* and *Behind the Spanish Line* were produced in England by the Communist-influenced Progressive Film Institute. In the Soviet Union, Esfir Shub collaborated with Vsevolod Vishnevsky to edit news footage, shot by Roman Karmen, into the feature-length film *Ispaniya* ('Spain', 1939). It was completed after the conflict had ended.

The Japanese invasion of Manchuria also attracted the attention of film-makers from many countries. *China Strikes back* (Frontier Films, 1937), showed Mao Zedong in Yan'an after the Long March, and John Ferno and Joris Ivens's *Four Hundred Million* (1939) presented gruesome footage of the Japanese offensive. After filming the Spanish Civil War, Roman Karmen also travelled to China, where he filmed Mao, resulting in the series of short films *China in Battle* (1938–9) and the feature documentary *In China* (1941). Chinese film-makers based in Yan'an with Mao were able to make twenty-one short non-fiction films between 1939 and 1945, most notably *Yenan and the Eighth Route Army* (1939), directed by Yuan Mu-jih. Japanese film-makers also produced documentaries of the war, including Fumio Kamei's *Shanhai* (Shanghai, 1937), a feature made for Toho in which 'talking heads' of Japanese officers describing their victory are intercut with scenes of devastation and Japanese graveyards. According to Kyoko Hirano, Kamei's next film, *Tatakau heitai* ('Soldiers at the front', 1938), which focused on the physical exhaustion of the soldiers rather than their bravery in combat, was nicknamed 'Tsukareta heitai' (soldiers in exhaustion). The film was banned, and Kamei was imprisoned.

THE SECOND WORLD WAR

With World War, documentary assumed a crucial propagandistic role—to instil domestic audiences with the will to persevere and win, and to shape perceptions at home as well as in Allied and neutral countries. Most wartime documentaries were made under the direct control of governments, but in occupied countries such as Denmark and France film-makers engaged in surreptitious filming and screening of non-fiction materials as acts of potent defiance. In Germany, newsreels were filled with footage gathered from the battle fronts, and, in addition, the Reich Propaganda Ministry produced many wartime documentaries. For instance, *Feldzug in Polen* (*Campaign in Poland*, 1940), the first important film of Fritz Hippler, asserts the ongoing abuse of German minorities by the Polish state, and then depicts the rapid collapse of Polish resistance in the face of overwhelming German power. Siegfried Kracauer has remarked that these campaign films were 'intended to impress people rather than instruct them'. They showed off the efficiency of a massive, unstoppable enterprise. Hippler followed *Campaign in Poland* with a similar effort, *Sieg im Westen* (*Victory in the*

Humphrey Jennings
(1907–1950)

Humphrey Jennings was born on 19 August 1907 into a family connected with the Arts and Crafts movement. Before his involvement with John Grierson's GPO film unit he had published verse and dabbled in painting and set design, and was undoubtedly regarded by many of his colleagues as the epitome of the middle-class dilettante. Yet this background brought a unique perspective to the documentary movement.

Jennings was one of the organizers of the International Surrealism Exhibition in 1936 and it is his own interpretation of Surrealism which forms one of the major distinctions of his film-making methods. For Jennings rejected the surrealist dependence upon imagery generated from unconscious processes as too personal and idiosyncratic. His work prefers to focus instead upon an image repertoire that is public, producing a quest for the bizarre in everyday English life through juxtaposition. The other formative influence from the pre-war period was Mass Observation, which Jennings helped found as an attempt to 'make a scientific study of the British Islanders, their habits, customs and social life'.

These two strands come together admirably in his first great film as a director, *Spare Time* (1939). The title alone seems like a challenge to the dominant philosophy of Griersonian documentary, interested in the working classes only when they can be seen to be working. Jennings's film is about the working classes as producers of culture, in times in between shifts in three areas of Britain associated with the steel, cotton, and coal industries. As the sparse commentary suggests, this is the time 'when we can most be ourselves'. Jennings takes images of apparently small significance—eating a pie, window-shopping, rehearsing amateur dramatics—which are given great resonance by their juxtaposition and by the musical sound-track made by the brass ensembles, the male voice choirs, and the kazoo jazz bands of the participants themselves.

But it was the war which provided Jennings with an infrastructure of film production sufficiently adaptable for his methods. Jennings became part of the Crown Film Unit making films for the Ministry of Information. Here he was able, usually in collaboration with the editor Stewart McAllister, to continue explorations in montage cinema at the very moment when the imperatives of wartime propaganda dictated that all aspects of British life should work together against a common foe. Jennings's form had found a worthy content.

His most celebrated film from this period was *Listen to Britain* (1942), which in a mere twenty minutes evokes a day in the life of a nation at war, the sounds and the sights of Britain in the blitz. Throughout the film, images of factory work are juxtaposed with images of dancehall leisure, fighting men with women in machine shops, the popular singers Flanagan and Allen with Dame Myra Hess playing a Mozart concerto. The blitz produces its own images of surreal montage: an office worker walks through rubble carrying his steel helmet; the Old Bailey has become an ambulance station; tanks rumble past the half-timbered tea-room in a postcard English village.

It was also the war that provided Jennings with the op-

portunity to make his first dramatic films. *Fires Were Started* (also known as *I Was a Fireman*) (1943) is about an East End unit of the Auxiliary Fire Service at the height of the blitz and employs the real firefighters as performers. Jennings worked without a dialogue script, improvising speech in a film which culminates in an impressively mounted warehouse fire. Both this film and *The Silent Village* (1944), a restaging of the Lidice massacre in a pit village in south Wales, led Jennings into much closer personal involvement with working people. The war, indeed, was a time in which the hierarchically based, class-bound cultural distinctions were temporarily relaxed. The ruins of the present reveal the possibility of a new, more equitable, and democratic society in the post-war world. This vision provides the thematic core to *Diary for Timothy* (1945), in which the diverse experiences of a farmer, a fighter pilot, and a miner are reviewed for an infant born on the eve of peace. The gentle commentary, written by E. M. Forster, poses a series of questions for the future and epitomizes the nation's aspirations.

Unfortunately, these hopes remained unfulfilled for Jennings as well as for the nation. His legacy from this period remains not a film but *Pandaemonium*, a collection of writings documenting the coming of the machine age: a montage of Science and Literature. His life came to a tragic conclusion on 24 September 1950, when he fell from a cliff during a reconnaissance trip to the Greek islands. Though his entire film work amounts to little more than five hours in length, the depth of his concerns and the mastery of his technique led to Lindsay Anderson's view, expressed in 1954, that Jennings was 'the only real poet the British cinema has yet produced'.

MICHAEL EATON

SELECT FILMOGRAPHY

Post Haste (1934); The Story of the Wheel (1934); Design for Spring (1938); Spare Time (1939); The First Days (1939) (with Harry Watt and Pat Jackson); S.S. Ionian (1939); Spring Offensive (1940); Welfare of the Workers (1940); London can Take it (1940); Heart of Britain (1941); Words for Battle (1941); Listen to Britain (1942) (with Stewart McAllister); Fires Were Started (I Was a Fireman) (1943); The Silent Village (1944); The True Story of Lili Marlene (1944); V 1 (1944); A Diary for Timothy (1945); A Defeated People (1945); The Cumberland Story (1947); Dim Little Island (1949); Family Portrait (1950)

BIBLIOGRAPHY

Hodgkinson, Anthony W., and Sheratsky, Rodney E. (1982), *Humphrey Jennings: More than a Maker of Films.*
Jackson, Kevin (ed.) (1993), *The Humphrey Jennings Film Reader.*
Jennings, Humphrey (1985), *Pandaemonium.*
Jennings, Mary-Lou (ed.) (1982), *Humphrey Jennings: Film-Maker, Painter, Poet.*

Opposite: Fires Were Started (1943)

West, 1941), and in between produced the infamous anti-Semitic documentary *Der ewige Jude* (*The Wandering Jew*, 1940).

In many respects the British documentary movement entered its heroic period with the onset of the war, after Grierson's departure. In a series of magnificent documentaries about wartime England, Humphrey Jennings revealed what was ordinary but quintessentially British in London's determined resistance to the German blitz. The depiction of vulnerability and quiet determination in Jennings's films was the perfect antidote to Nazi campaign films.

None the less, many of Jennings's documentary colleagues criticized his films for not being sufficiently upbeat and aggressive. *Target for Tonight* (1941), which recounts the bombing of a German depot by a Royal Air Force squadron, was more to their taste. This neatly done re-enactment was one of the first pictures to show Britain taking the offensive, and was a huge success. Another combat film, Roy Boulting's *Desert Victory*, won an Oscar for best feature-length documentary of 1943. Using footage taken by sixty-two members of the British Army Film and Photographic Unit as well as captured German film, it offered a dramatic account of the Allied victory over Rommel's forces in North Africa. The achievements of wartime cinematographers, who made such documentaries possible, were celebrated in *Cameramen at War* (1943). For a few moments these anonymous men appear in front of the lens as we ponder the risks they took and the methods they used to capture vivid images of war.

The Soviet Union, with roughly 400 cameramen sending footage back from the front, produced numerous combat newsreels under the supervision of Roman Gregoriev. As had been the case with footage of the Spanish Civil War and Chinese resistance against Japan, much of this material became the basis for longer documentaries, epics of resistance and eventual victory. Ilya Kopalin directed *Stalingrad* (1943), which detailed one of the decisive turning-points of the war, and other documentaries were made by important fiction film directors including Sergei Yutkevich and Alexander Dovzhenko.

After Japan attacked Pearl Harbor (7 December 1941), the US government mobilized rapidly for war and began to produce numerous documentaries through the Army Signal Corps, the Office of War Information (OWI), and other organizations. The military, however, did not turn to left-leaning documentarians who had developed their skills in the 1930s but to directors from Hollywood, who were drafted into the services and given military rank. Frank Capra, director of the populist comedy *Mr. Smith Goes to Washington* (1939), became Major and then Lt.-Col. Capra as he directed *Prelude to War* (1942), an illustrated sermon that celebrated a sanitized version of American history and values and cannibalized enemy propaganda films to create demonic two-dimensional caricatures of Hitler, Mussolini, and Emperor Hirohito. Capra produced six other films in the 'Why We Fight' series, most of them directed or co-directed by Anatole Litvak, including *The Nazi Strike* (1943) and *The Battle of Russia* (1944).

Stuart Heisler, whose Hollywood directing credits included *The Glass Key* (1942), made *The Negro Soldier* (1944), which recognized the presence of African-Americans in the military, without acknowledging that the army was still a segregated institution. John Ford made a thirty-minute army training film on venereal disease (*Sex Hygiene*, 1941), but two of his wartime documentaries won Oscars, including the eighteen-minute *The Battle of Midway*, which Ford shot himself in 16 mm. colour from on top of a power-house being attacked by Japanese aircraft. William Wyler directed *Memphis Belle* (1944) about a bombing raid over Germany, and John Huston made a wartime trilogy: *Report from the Aleutians* (1943), *The Battle of San Pietro* (1945), and *Let There Be Light* (1946). The last film focuses on soldiers suffering from a variety of war-related mental disorders, showing how psychiatric treatment is able to provide seemingly miraculous rehabilitation in many instances. Despite these happy outcomes, the film was banned for thirty-five years, perhaps because it shattered the myth of simple American victory and heroic warfare.

After hostilities ended the US War Department produced such war-related documentaries as *Death Mills* (1946), about the Nazi concentration camps, and *Nuremberg* (1948), about the Nuremberg trials—compiled by Pare Lorentz and Stuart Schulberg. It also provided Henri Cartier Bresson with crucial support for *Le Retour* (1946), which followed French soldiers as they returned home from German POW camps.

POST-WAR DOCUMENTARY

After the war, documentary entered a crisis, which lasted almost fifteen years. The decline transcended region and politics but the general causes were often buttressed by circumstances specific to individual national cinemas. Documentary had become too closely associated with its wartime role as propaganda; its polemical stance was now considered anathema. Documentary, moreover, had traditionally been an alternative practice; in the post-war period television offered employment for those unwilling or unable to work in the feature film industry. (In the United States there were early non-fiction television series such as Edward R. Murrow's *See It Now* and Robert Saudek's *Omnibus*.) Documentarians of the 1930s continued to dominate the field but for a variety of personal and institutional reasons were rarely able to recapture the quality of their pre-war work.

War continued to be a subject for Chinese documentaries, thanks to civil war and then the Korean War. After the revolution, film-makers were more ready to

undertake projects such as *Stand up Sisters* (Shih Hui, 1950), which detailed the oppressive conditions of prostitutes in Peking prior to the liberation. Film-makers from the Soviet Union also collaborated with their Chinese counterparts to make the documentaries *Liberated China* (Sergei Gerasimov, 1950) and *Victory of the Chinese People* (Leonid Varlamov, 1950). The Korean War yielded Hsu Hsiao-ping's *Resist American Aggression and Aid Korea* (1952), shot by twelve different cameramen at the front. Documentaries, however, were increasingly arranged to conform to the requirements of authorities. By 1959, Jay Leyda had concluded that 'the supposedly real films were in a deeper rut than the frankly fictional'. In American-occupied Japan, controversial documentaries often encountered censorship problems. Two were banned: *The Effect of the Atomic Bomb* (1946), about the nuclear bomb dropped on Hiroshima, and Fumio Kamei's *Nihon no higeki* (*The Japanese Tragedy*, 1946), an attack on Hirohito and the emperor system. In 1950s America, the blacklisting of left-wing film-makers effectively excluded many documentarians from fruitful activity (Jay Leyda, for example). The use of synchronous sound equipment on location was increasingly popular, but it was expensive and required ample funding while its bulk limited observational and improvisational techniques. Since commercial cinemas rarely showed non-fiction shorts except newsreels, most documentaries were sponsored by industry, or by state or federal governments. Film-makers wanting to operate outside these constraints turned to low-budget silent or post-synchronous production (typically employing a simple music track). These films often melded documentary and avant-garde impulses. Helen Levitt, Janice Loeb, and James Agee shot their eighteen-minute *In the Streets* (1952) with a hand-held, mobile camera; they presented the street life of a New York neighbourhood without any kind of explicit social commentary. Stan Brakhage's *The Wonder Ring* (1956), Shirley Clarke's *Bridges Go round* (1958), and D. A. Pennebaker's *Day Break Express* (1958) also avoid polemics, while offering a more celebratory vision of the city's potential. In many ways these films returned to the themes of the city film, in which cinematic form played off the dynamism of urban life.

British documentary faced a crisis in the immediate post-war era. The Labour government elected in 1945 seemed to many to be the realization of what they had fought for in the 1930s, and as a result their films lost their polemical edge. Jennings's *Family Portrait* (1951) affirms British identity and purpose by evoking the nation's great men even as it hails the multifaceted qualities of the islands' average, contemporary citizens. Yet *Family Portrait* favours an illustrated lecture approach, as did several other films of the period (e.g. Muir Mathieson's *Instruments of the Orchestra*, 1947, and *Steps of the Ballet*, 1948, which feature the music of Benjamin Britten). *Waverley Steps*

Joris Ivens
(1898–1989)

Joris Ivens, nicknamed 'The Flying Dutchman', had a film life spanning continents and eras. Mainly based in Europe and Asia, he also filmed in Africa (*Demain à Nanguila*, 1960), North America (*Power and the Land*, 1940), South America (*À Valparaiso*, 1962), and Australia (*Indonesia Calling*, 1946).

His early films were studies of the movements generated by the interplay between man and machine (*The Bridge*, 1928), and nature and the city (*Rain*, 1929). *Zuiderzee* (1933), a treatment of the very Dutch theme of land reclamation, was the climax of his experimentalism. Ivens strengthened his montage effects by assigning a camera to each of the protagonists in the final closure of a dyke—the sea, the land, and man in his machine, the crane.

Lifelong support of Communist-led countries and movements made him a politically controversial figure. After the Second World War he spent a decade in eastern Europe, having been deprived of his Dutch passport for his support for Indonesian self-government. The first foreigner to be invited to make a film in the Soviet Union (*Komsomol*, 1931), he went on to make powerful films with a Popular Front politics. *The Spanish Earth* (1937), with a script written and spoken by Ernest Hemingway, focused on the republican defence of Madrid against Franco's army. A year later *The 400 Millions* aimed to alert world opinion to Japanese incursions into China. Neither film gained commercial distribution, and they failed to influence international diplomacy. Despite these limitations, Ivens always defended the role of the political documentary: 'There is a road to freedom for all peoples, and the documentary film should record and assist this progress.'

After his passport was restored he took up residence in France and a 'poetic' Ivens of *Le Mistral* (1965) and other film essays emerged. Yet whatever the subject an absorption with the interconnection of the human and natural world is evident. Nature is both a resource and a strong symbolic element, whether earth, air, water, or fire.

In his war films from *Spanish Earth* to *The Seventeenth Parallel* (1967) the protagonists are farmers, defending their own earth, planting rice or wheat, transforming bomb craters into fish ponds, their peaceful routines disrupted by death's harvest. Fire, the element of war, rarely appears in a heroic light, and where it does—in the blast furnaces of *Komsomol*, the armed struggle of *Le Peuple et ses fusils* ('The people and its guns', 1969)—the films can acquire an unpleasantly didactic tone.

Ivens was criticized by the young film-makers who collaborated on *Le Peuple et ses fusils* for his 'fascination effect', which left the audience thinking, for example, how wonderful the Vietnamese people were rather than how politically astute. Yet his films suffer when designed to serve a political line as distinct from a cause. The most widely debated aspect of his cinema work lay in his use of re-enactment in a search for the 'inner truth' of a political scenario.

In the end Ivens fell back on a bedrock belief in ordinary people and their capacity to transform themselves and their environment. His epic *How Yukong Moved the Mountains* (1976) introduced many to the everyday struggles of the people of China. *Histoire de vent* (1988) is a happy résumé of the themes of a lifetime. Here his quest to film the wind resonates with intimations of death through a dramatic asthma attack and arguments with the local Chinese bureaucracy. The mischievous Chinese Monkey King appears, and fits the description Ivens gave thirty years earlier to the mistral: 'a capricious character who comes and blows as it likes, blows too hard or not at all, blows for a time and then goes away . . .'

Such a long working life as a film-maker, from 1928 to 1988, speaks of immmense energy, a capacity to work with others and to raise the money needed for each venture. His family photographic firm in Amsterdam, CAPI, co-produced many of his films. He worked long term with sound technicians like Helen van Dongen and Marceline Loridan, and on specific projects with Henri Storck, Chris Marker, and the Taviani brothers. His place in cinema history is that of the archetypal 'committed' cineaste.

ROSALIND DELMAR

SELECT FILMOGRAPHY

De brug (The Bridge) (1928); Misère au Borinage (1933, co-director Henri Storck); Zuiderzee (1933); The Spanish Earth (1937); The 400 Millions (1938); Indonesia Calling (1946); À Valparaiso (1962); Le Dix-septième Parallèle (The Seventeenth Parallel) (1967); Comment Yukong déplaça les montagnes (How Yukong Moved the Mountains) (1976); Histoire de vent (1988)

BIBLIOGRAPHY

Delmar, Rosalind (1979), *Joris Ivens*.
Ivens, Joris (1969), *The Camera and I*.

On the boundary between water and earth: *Zuiderzee* (1933)

(1948) returned to the familiar genre of city symphony, but its highly controlled and polished cinematography, and its carefully arranged and acted vignettes, pull it away from the genre's documentary impulse. While distilling themes and methods evident in earlier films of the movement, these efforts were approaching a dead end.

In Britain as elsewhere, documentary practice was most vital at the fringes. Renewal was embodied by the 'Free Cinema', a term coined by young film-maker and critic Lindsay Anderson who subsequently employed it as a programming rubric for innovative documentaries made in England and abroad. British work included Karel Reisz and Tony Richardson's *Momma Don't Allow* (1956), shot in a jazz club, and Anderson's own *Every day except Christmas* (1957), which featured the people who populated the market at Covent Garden over the course of a single, hypothetical day. It looked at the quotidian, distancing itself from—though not entirely abandoning—staging methods developed for fictional film-making. These documentaries refused abstraction and took a more observational style, one more attentive to individual personality and psychology (the film-maker's as well as the subjects').

Among the films admired by Anderson was Georges Franju's *Le Sang des bêtes* ('Blood of animals', 1949), an unblinking look at a Paris slaughterhouse, and *Hôtel des Invalides* (1951), about a French military museum and veterans' home, filled with the relics and living casualties of warfare. As Erik Barnouw (1974) has remarked, these films 'seemed to have the precise beauty of nightmares'. Lionel Rogosin's *On the Bowery* (1956) focuses on a group of alcoholics living in New York City's skid row, sometimes capturing them with a hidden camera. It presents their daily lives without sentiment or moralizing but with a quiet empathy. They are part of, and products of, society; but the social circumstances that produced these desperate men are neither explained nor overtly condemned.

In the post-war period the French government routinely subsidized shorts, particularly documentaries, as a way of rebuilding a national cinema; a law prohibiting the screening of double bills then helped ensure the films a theatrical release. These productions, which served as a training ground for aspiring directors, were often significant in their own right. Alain Resnais started out by making three 35 mm. shorts of modernist painting: *Van Gogh* (1948), which won an Oscar, *Gauguin* (1950), and *Guernica* (1950). *Nuit et brouillard* (*Night and Fog*, 1955) alternates historical material of the Nazi concentration camps with contemporary colour footage of these sites, often shown with long, serene tracking shots. Resnais suggests that the horror has become distant, difficult to recall vividly, and sometimes even covered over. A black and white shot of a gendarme in a control tower at Pithiviers assembly camp, evidence of French col-

laboration in the Holocaust, was censored by the government—and the entire film withdrawn from the Cannes Film Festival. The narration, written by Jean Cayrol, a survivor of the camps, suggests that the horror has not ended but simply moved elsewhere, taking on a different form. The film's implicit reference point was the brutal counter-revolutionary activities of French forces in Algeria.

Jean-Luc Godard began his film career making *Operation Béton* (1954–8), a documentary showing workers constructing the Grande-Dixence Dam in Switzerland. Agnès Varda alternated between fiction and documentary during the 1950s—with films like *L'Opéra-Mouffe* (1958) and *Du côté de la côte* ('On the Riviera', 1959)—and beyond. Chris Marker collaborated with Alan Resnais to make *Les Statues meurent aussi* ('Statues also die', 1953), which examines the destruction of African art by French cultural colonialism.

A new era of ethnographic film-making began to emerge in the post-war period as university-trained anthropologists turned to motion pictures. French anthropologist Jean Rouch began to make ethnographic films in West Africa in the late 1940s and soon emerged as the single most important documentary film-maker in the field. Other important practitioners included Margaret Mead and Gregory Bateson, who produced a series of teaching films, utilizing footage shot in the 1930s. In *Childhood Rivalry in Bali and New Guinea* (1952) they compare the child-rearing methods of two South Pacific cultures. *The Hunters* (1956), made by John Marshall with the assistance of the Peabody Museum at Harvard and anthropology graduate student Robert Gardner, was the story of a giraffe hunt among the Bushmen of the Kalahari Desert in southern Africa, and was constructed, after the fact, out of footage taken over a two-year period. In subsequent decades, Marshall and other film-makers reworked this footage and related materials into additional films. Robert Gardner also went on to have a major career as an ethnographic film-maker in his own right (*Dead Birds*, 1963).

Canada was one country where government support nurtured a rapidly expanding documentary movement. Set up under John Grierson in 1939, the National Film Board of Canada had a staff of 800 by the end of the Second World War, but faced retrenchment, budget cuts, and political criticism. *Royal Journey* (1951), a documentary feature on Princess Elizabeth and Prince Philip touring Canada, helped to rescue the Film Board from a possible demise. Film Board series such as 'Canada Carries on' and 'Faces of Canada' yielded classical documentary short subjects such as *Paul Tomkowicz: Street-Railway Switchman* (Roman Kroitor, 1953) and *Corral* (Colin Low and Wolf Koenig, 1954). The latter, shot in 35 mm. without sync sound, shows a mythic West as a cowboy gallops across the Canadian Rockies. Unit B film-makers at the National Film Board—Kroitor, Koenig, and Terence Macartney-Filgate—were seeking a more direct cinema, one less stilted and more real. They started the television series *The Candid Eye* of half-hour shorts, including *The Days before Christmas* (1958), *Emergency Ward* (William Greaves, 1958), and *The Back-Breaking Leaf* (1959)—the latter about migrant tobacco workers. French-speaking film-makers Michel Brault and Gilles Groulx collaborated on *Les Raquetteurs* (1958), which looks at daily life and everyday language in Quebec. The increased spontaneity of the camera work, which captured activities as they unfolded, often unexpectedly, pointed toward new kinds of documentary which a new generation of lightweight, sync-sound equipment was about to make possible.

Bibliography

Aitken, Ian (1990), *Film and Reform: John Grierson and the Documentary Film Movement.*

Barnouw, Eric (1974), *Documentary.*

Barsam, Richard (1992), *Non-Fiction Film.*

Alexander, William (1981), *Film on the Left: American Documentary Film from 1931 to 1942.*

Buchsbaum, Jonathan (1988), *Cinema Engagé: Film in the Popular Front.*

Graham, Cooper C. (1986), *Leni Riefenstahl and Olympia.*

Grierson, John (1966), *Grierson on Documentary.*

Jacobs, Lewis (ed.) (1979), *The People's Films: A Political History of U.S. Government Motion Pictures.*

Sklar, Robert and Musser, Charles (eds.) (1990), *Resisting Images: Essays on Cinema and History.*

Snyder, Robert L. (1968), *Pare Lorentz and the Documentary Film.*

Sussex, Elizabeth (1975), *The Rise and Fall of British Documentary.*

Socialism, Fascism, and Democracy

GEOFFREY NOWELL-SMITH

The cinema started life as a capitalist industry, and that is what, at most times and in most countries, it has tended to remain. But as a capitalist industry, run for profit on a large scale, it has been the subject of much moral, political, and economic concern on the part of government and society at large. It has been censored (particularly in times of moral panic), regulated (particularly in times of war), and assisted (particularly in times of crisis), by governmental and para-governmental agencies. In most countries, moreover, even in that paradigm of private enterprise the United States of America, it has contained large sectors that were operated not by profit-seeking capital but by artists and activists, or that were sponsored or managed by governments, either for the benefit of the art or for the control of its content. In general the entertainment sector was the most capitalist, with 'art' cinema being state-subsidized, and documentary and educational films the object of more active government intervention. In the Soviet Union and other socialist countries, however, state ownership and control became the norm, not only for documentary and minor genres but for the industry as a whole.

From a conventional western perspective, these various interventions into, and departures from, the working of a mainly capitalist industry can be seen as exceptions to a presumed norm, provoked by exceptional circumstances and for the most part marginal to the main development of the cinema. Such a perspective is broadly valid for the cinemas of pluralist, capitalist countries, in periods of relative normality. But for non-normal times—for nations at war, for societies in the throes of revolution—and for parts of the world where the western capitalist norm does not have the status of normality, its validity is not so self-evident. In particular the idea of a self-contained and mainly self-regulating industry, which fringes upon the world of politics and into which governments are forced to intervene, needs to be put into question. For many situations, a perspective has to be adopted for which politics is not incidental but central, and the tension between social and political systems, cultures and world-views, is seen as a major determinant of the form cinema could take.

In its early years—up to the end of the First World War—the cinema conformed broadly to the 'normal' perspective. It entered the world of reportage as early as the Spanish–American War of 1898; it found its way into the world of moral concern with films such as George Loane Tucker's *Traffic in Souls* (1913); its monopoly practices began to be scrutinized by the courts in the course of the battles waged by Thomas Edison against his competitors throughout the first decade of the century; and, during the World War, governments intervened to regulate news reporting from the front and to encourage patriotic film-making at home. But whereas, by rights, the Armistice of 1918 should have signalled the end of a state of exception and a return to a previously experienced normality, in fact it ushered in a condition of crisis which has affected the cinema ever since. Crisis and conflict became the norm, even if their effects were not always and everywhere apparent.

REVOLUTION

The first sign of the new state of affairs came with the establishment in Hungary in April 1919 of the short-lived

Republic of the Councils (also known as the 'Béla Kun soviet'), one of whose acts was to nationalize the film industry. The film-makers' council, or 'soviet', charged with carrying out this nationalization included among its personnel the perhaps unlikely names of Sándor (later Sir Alexander) Korda and Béla Blaskó (later Bela Lugosi). (Legend also has it that Mihály Kertész, alias Michael Curtiz, the future director of *Casablanca*, returned from Austria, where he was working, to take part in the movement, but this has not been reliably confirmed.) The Béla Kun soviet lasted only four months; it was overthrown in August 1919 and in the repression that followed many of its leaders and supporters—including Kun himself, the philosopher Georg Lukács, Korda, and Lugosi—went into exile. But in the same year, the Russian revolutionary government, concerned at the emigration of film industry personnel and the loss of equipment, also acted to nationalize its film studios and to bring film-making generally under revolutionary control. This was to have consequences which lasted until 1990 and beyond.

The impact of the measures taken in Russia (and soon applied throughout the whole of the new Soviet Union) was in fact far greater than was intended or could have been predicted. The purpose was principally to bring the material side of the industry under control, with a view to its eventual integration into a socialist economy. Meanwhile attempts were made in parallel to harness the activities of artists in the service of the Revolution. It would appear too that the early concerns of Lenin and Lunacharsky (the Bolshevik Commissar for Enlightenment) were above all educational. Lenin's much-quoted statement, 'For us the cinema is the most important of all the arts,' referred principally to its potential for spreading knowledge and socialist ideas to the largely illiterate population of the Soviet Union, rather than to its status within culture.

The new film culture in the Soviet Union was at first markedly internationalist. Films, including American, continued to be imported; Fairbanks and Pickford visited Moscow in 1926, to great acclaim. Foreign styles were imitated. Then, from the mid-1920s a distinctively 'Russian' style developed, based on composition and montage, which, although not conspicuously popular with audiences at home, was very influential abroad. The consolidation of the Stalinist regime at the end of the decade, together with the coming of the dialogue film at about the same time, enforced the abandonment of montage cinema in feature film production and its replacement in the early 1930s by the new model of Socialist Realism. The importing of foreign films dried up to a trickle. But in the mean time networks had been set up in the west, supported by the Communist parties and sympathizing intellectuals, which promoted the original Soviet model in avant-garde circles, from which it spread outwards into documentary and (to a lesser extent) feature film practice. As the Soviet Union withdrew into itself, beleaguered and boycotted by the west and increasingly repressive towards its own people, left-wing intellectuals in western countries promoted an idea of film culture which drew its aesthetic and political inspiration from an idealized notion of Soviet experience and achievement.

Control of the cinema by the Communist Party and by the State (the two were not always easy to distinguish) steadily increased throughout the 1920s and 1930s. In the early years the authorities relied to a large extent on the political commitment and enthusiasm of film-makers to produce films in conformity with revolutionary ideals. As in literature, different schools of thought contended, and produced different results. But with the consolidation of power under Stalin at the end of the 1920s, this changed. The industry became more tightly organized, and deviant ideas began to be suppressed.

What was happening in the Soviet Union was followed with anxiety throughout the west. The American industry was concerned mainly with the loss of a lucrative market for its films. For their part, governments were concerned at the spread of Communist ideas and used various censorship provisions to restrict the public showing of Russian films. As might be expected, these restrictions were only partially effective and were sometimes counterproductive. Eisenstein's *The Battleship Potemkin* was greeted with enormous enthusiasm when it was shown in London by a private organization, the Film Society, in 1929. In the same year Eisenstein and Pudovkin visited London and Eisenstein also attended the conference of avant-garde film-makers held in La Sarraz in Switzerland, and close links were maintained between 'approved' Soviet artists and western sympathizers throughout the 1920s and 1930s.

FASCISM

Not all governments were universally hostile to the Soviet approach. Shortly after the Fascists came to power in Italy in 1922, Mussolini echoed Lenin in proclaiming that 'the cinema is the most powerful weapon'. In 1926 the government nationalized the production of newsreels and documentaries, making them an arm of the State for propaganda purposes. The Russian cinema was also much admired by some of the more committed Fascists among Italian film-makers—for example Alessandro Blasetti, whose *Sole* ('Sun', 1929) shows a clear influence of Pudovkin and other masters of the Russian silent cinema. The ideas of Eisenstein and Pudovkin were taken up by film intellectuals such as Luigi Chiarini and Umberto Barbaro and came, by a roundabout route, to influence the postwar neo-realist generation of film-makers. But, despite their claims to be creating a 'totalitarian' State, the Fascists intervened very little in the entertainment cinema, regarding it (mistakenly) as neither culturally nor politically important. Government intervention was in the first instance economic rather than cultural. It aimed to shore up a crumbling industry and encouraged the making of films which could compete with Hollywood at the box-office. The cultural effects of Fascist intervention were mainly negative, and took the form of censorship and the discouragement of anti-national ideas. Even during the Second World War, when the industry was put on a war footing, few films were unequivocally Fascist (as distinct from nationalistic) in their approach.

An even greater negativity marked the cultural policies of Franco's Spain. Whereas in Italy the government encouraged the film industry and allowed it a great measure of freedom provided it was not overtly critical of the regime, in Spain the alliance of the Francoist government and the Catholic Church was actively hostile to the cinema. After the defeat of the Republic in 1939, all radical voices in the Spanish cinema were silenced. Luis Buñuel, who had made documentaries for the republicans, fled the country along with many other artists. A severe censorship was instituted, in moral and religious matters even more than political, and the Spanish cinema, which during the early 1930s had been a thriving industry with a vigorous export trade with Latin America, entered into a period of inertia from which it did not emerge until the mid-1950s.

Far more dramatic were events in Germany. At the beginning of the 1930s, Germany enjoyed a dominant position in European cinema. It also had a vital left-wing culture, which produced its own films outside the mainstream. The Social Democrats and, in competition with them, the Communists attempted to set up alternative cultural networks during the Weimar Republic, with their own literature, theatre, and leisure and sporting activities. Out of this background came films like Piel Jutzi's 1931 film adaptation of Alfred Döblin's famous novel *Berlin-Alexanderplatz* and Slatan Dudow and Bertolt Brecht's *Kuhle Wampe* (1932). The Nazi seizure of power in 1933 brought a brutal end to this cultural activity. The Nazis set up their own cinema institutions, availing themselves in a debased form of Russian models. Meanwhile left-wing and Jewish film-makers went into exile, fleeing to France, Denmark, Britain, or Switzerland. From there many went on to Hollywood, where they joined an earlier wave of *émigrés*. Of the film industry personnel who remained behind in Germany, several were to die in concentration camps. No Jews were safe, but a number of other anti-Nazi artists and technicians survived, working relatively uncompromised in the entertainment sector of the industry.

It could perhaps be argued that the biggest effect that Nazism, and other Fascisms, had on the cinema did not lie in the films that were produced in Germany and the other Fascist countries so much as in the emigration they

produced, in 1933 and then again in 1940. The silent cinema had been international, but in the early sound years cinema had shown signs of retreating behind national and linguistic borders. By driving so many creative personnel into exile, Germany hurt its own cinema and those of the countries it occupied during the war, but it enriched those of the countries who welcomed the exiles.

The roll-call of exiles includes the distinguished names of directors Max Ophuls, Fritz Lang, Douglas Sirk, Anatole Litvak; actors Peter Lorre and Conrad Veidt; producer Erich Pommer; cinematographer Eugen Schüfftan. Among those who had already left, whether for career reasons or for fear of persecution to come, were Ernst Lubitsch, F. W. Murnau, Billy Wilder, and Alfred Junge from Germany, and Michael Curtiz and Alexander Korda from Hungary. Those who went into temporary or permanent exile from other European countries threatened by Fascism include Luis Buñuel, Emeric Pressburger, Joris Ivens, and, during the war years, Jean Renoir and René Clair. In various ways, these artists fertilized the cinemas of the countries in

Front cover of *Illustrierte Film-Kurier*, showing Ferdinand Marian as Süss in Veit Harlan's 1940 film version of Lion Feuchtwanger's novel *Jew Süss*

Alexander Korda

(1893–1956)

Alexander Korda was born Sándor Kellner in Pusztatúr-pásztó, Hungary, where his father managed the local landowner's estate. While still a student in Budapest he took up journalism, adopting the pen-name Korda, then joined a film distribution company as secretary and general assistant. He directed his first film in 1914 and went on to make some two dozen more, becoming one of Hungary's leading directors before fleeing the country after the fall of Béla Kún's short-lived Communist regime.

Over the next eleven years Korda and his wife, the actress Maria Corda (who preferred the C spelling), settled nowhere for long. He directed four films in Vienna—setting up his own Corda-Film Company for the sub-Griffith *Samson und Delila* (1922), which lost money heavily—and six in Berlin. The last of these, *Eine Dubarry von heute* (*A Modern Dubarry*, 1926), won him an American contract with First National. Korda detested Hollywood—'it was like Siberia'—and of the ten films he made there only one was of much interest. *The Private Life of Helen of Troy* (1927), with Maria Corda in the title-role, was a sardonic debunking of history spiced with sexual innuendo that would furnish the model for his first major hit.

After a row with First National, Korda found himself blacklisted, and retreated to Paris to direct the first (and best) episode of Marcel Pagnol's Marseilles trilogy, *Marius* (1931). Its commercial success led Paramount to invite him to head their British operation, but after one poorly received film the contract was terminated. In an audacious gamble (by no means his last), Korda founded his own outfit, London Films, bringing on board several Hungarian associates—including his brothers Zoltan and Vincent and the script-writer Lajos Biró, a friend from his Budapest days.

The gamble paid off with *The Private Life of Henry VIII* (1933), a shrewdly Anglicized reworking of the *Helen of Troy* formula and a surprise international hit. On the strength of it Korda raised money to start building Britain's largest film studio at Denham, adopting his true vocation of producer-impresario on the grand scale. From now on he directed only six more films himself; the finest of them was *Rembrandt* (1936), a gentle, poignant study with Charles Laughton at his most sensitive in the title-role.

With his cosmopolitan style, grandiose vision, and irresistible Hungarian charm, Korda took the British film industry by storm. Living and spending lavishly, and borrowing heavily, he announced an ambitious slate of films, and imported expensive foreign talent (René Clair, Jacques Feyder, Georges Périnal) to help realize those ambitions. He commissioned scripts from such notables as H. G. Wells and Winston Churchill and nurtured the screen careers of some of Britain's most prestigious actors: Laughton, Olivier, Donat, Leslie Howard, Vivien Leigh, Merle Oberon (who became his second wife).

At their best—as in the Wellsian futurist parable *Things to Come* (1935), the 'Empire trilogy' of *Sanders of the River* (1935), *The Drum* (1938), and *The Four Feathers* (1939), the swashbuckling *Fire over England* (1936) or the soaring fantasy of *The Thief of Bagdad* (1940)—Korda's productions had a vigour and a sweeping ebullience of conception, though often let down by heavy-handed scripting. When the mixture failed to take, the results were flashy and

vapid, cinema without roots, like Feyder's Dietrich-among-the-Bolsheviks confection, *Knight without Armour* (1937).

Underfinanced and overextended, Korda's empire collapsed in 1938 when his backers, the Prudential Assurance Company, took over Denham. Undeterred, he threw himself into the war effort with the brash defiance of *The Lion Has Wings* (1939) and, moving to Hollywood, *That Hamilton Woman* (1941), anti-Nazi propaganda in the flimsiest of period guises. (This, or some undercover work for the British government, earned him a knighthood.) Back in England in 1943 he set up a brief partnership with MGM, which proved expensive for them, and resuscitated London Films.

The post-war Korda was a diminished but still compelling figure. Grand costumed affairs were out of style—both *Anna Karenina* (1947) and *Bonnie Prince Charlie* (1948) flopped badly—but the dark, downbeat romanticism of *The Third Man* (1949) gave him his greatest hit since *Henry VIII*. Not even the worst financial crash of his career, in 1954, could stem his ambition. Finding yet another willing backer, he splashed out on widescreen and Technicolor with Olivier's *Richard III* and *Storm over the Nile* (both 1955, the latter a remake of *The Four Feathers*). At the time of his death he was still planning fresh productions.

A master of the grand gesture, Alexander Korda was perhaps more significant for what he stood for—a glittering, flamboyant, no-holds-barred style of production—than for any of the films he made as director or producer. It was not an act the British film industry could follow. Yet the audacity and enthusiasm of his vision, and the brio of his personality, enriched the lives of all those he came in contact with. For this alone he would qualify as one of the film industry's great producers.

PHILIP KEMP

SELECT FILMOGRAPHY

As director
Eine Dubarry von heute (A Modern Dubarry) (1926); The Private Life of Helen of Troy (1927); Marius (1931)
As producer-director
The Private Life of Henry VIII (1933); Rembrandt (1936); That Hamilton Woman (Lady Hamilton) (1941)
As producer
Sanders of the River (Bosambo) (1935); Things to Come (1935); Fire over England (1936); The Drum (1938); South Riding (1938); The Four Feathers (1939); The Lion Has Wings (1939); The Thief of Bagdad (1940); The Fallen Idol (1948); The Third Man (1949); The Tales of Hoffmann (1951); Richard III (1955);

BIBLIOGRAPHY

Korda, Michael (1980), *Charmed Lives*.
Kulik, Karol (1975), *Alexander Korda: The Man who Could Work Miracles*.
Tabori, Paul (1959), *Alexander Korda*.

Opposite: A scene from *Rembrandt* (1936), produced and directed by Alexander Korda, with sets designed by Vincent Korda

which they took refuge. America gained the most, but Britain, with the Korda family, Pressburger, Junge, and many lesser lights, gained as well, especially in the area of design, where the *émigrés* offered a powerful antidote to the rather platitudinous realism that tended to dog the British cinema.

RESURGENT NATIONALISM AND THE POPULAR FRONTS

The rise of Fascism and the exaggerated nationalism of the 1930s also had economic effects on the cinema. In the 1920s a number of European countries had acted, somewhat belatedly, to stem the tide of Hollywood imports through some form of protectionist legislation. They had also begun to forge economic links among themselves, leading in the early sound period to the making of a number of multilingual productions in which the same script was shot on the same set, often with the same director, but with different actors for different language versions. Multilinguals were made all over Europe, mostly by European companies acting in concert, but also by the Americans, both in Hollywood itself and in Europe. A major incentive to make them disappeared with the introduction of dubbing, which meant that it was no longer necessary for the actors to speak in their own voices. As multilingual production was phased out, national industries retreated again within their own borders. But it was political diffidence that led to a steady decline in co-operation between Germany on the one side and Britain and France on the other. Meanwhile calls for protection against American imports grew stronger and Hollywood was forced to adapt to a steady erosion of its European markets. Germany, which in the 1920s had pioneered the 'contingent' system of limiting imports, closed its market to America in the mid-1930s. In 1938 Italy, rather blunderingly, followed suit: a proposal to nationalize the distribution companies responsible for importing films provoked the withdrawal of the Hollywood majors from the Italian market, and with the outbreak of war all importing of American films came to an end. In France, where the Loi Marchandeau of 1936 had imposed a more or less voluntary limit on imports, German occupation in 1940 brought all trade with America to an end, as well as driving many artists into exile.

Meanwhile a major ideological shift was taking place in Europe, which affected both politics and culture and the relationship between them. The 1920s—the Jazz Age—had been a period of optimism and of a widespread political indifference, but also of extremism of various kinds, in both politics and art. Modernist experiment flourished, and realism was out of favour. A number of avant-garde artists attached themselves to far-left and far-right political movements: the Italian futurists to Fascism, the Russian futurists and constructivists to the Revolution, Dada and Surrealism to Communism and Trotskyism. But

Jean Renoir
(1894–1979)

Jean Renoir was born in Montmartre during the *belle époque* that his father, Auguste Renoir, brought to life so vividly in his Impressionist paintings. During the First World War Renoir suffered a leg injury that left him with a permanent limp. After working as a ceramic artist, he turned to film-making in 1924. His films fall into three periods: the French films from 1924 to 1939; the American films from 1941 to 1950; and the return to European film-making from 1952 to 1969.

La Fille de l'eau (1924), *Nana* (1926), and *The Little Match Girl* (1928), all starring his wife Catherine Hessling, show the influence of both French and German avant-garde film. For *Nana*, an ambitious studio production shot in Paris and Berlin, Renoir's changed view of cinematic realism under the influence of Stroheim and German Expressionism required from Hessling a stylized, anti-naturalistic performance, the opposite of her accustomed style. Nana's power lies in her calculated use of her own artificiality, filmed to emphasize fetishism and sado-masochism. For André Bazin (1974), Hessling combined 'in a disturbing way the mechanical and the living, the fantastic and the sensual, with the result a strange, striking expression of femininity'.

Renoir's films of the 1930s, from *La Chienne* (1931) to *La Règle du jeu* ('Rules of the game', 1939), earned him the reputation of being the master of 'poetic realism' and the most French of the pre-war film-makers. They provide the best cinematic index to French society during those turbulent years, even though many films now considered classics were not understood when they were released. They show a strong social and political sensitivity to the inequities of class structures in France and a sympathy for the working class. They are characterized by Renoir's efforts to offset classical, symmetrical structures with the appearance of spontaneity. To this end, he worked tirelessly on co-ordinating his actors' performances with the creation of an apparently effortless technical framework for their expressions.

The bleak pessimism of *La Chienne* (1931), the strangely hypnotic *La Nuit du carrefour* (1932, starring Renoir's brother Pierre), and the anarchic escape from bourgeois conventions in *Boudu Saved from Drowning* (1932) are partly a response to the economic and social depression of the early 1930s. In *La Chienne* (1931), every significant character deceives someone for personal gain, and a murderer goes free while another man, disadvantaged by class, is condemned in his place. This dark film shows a perfect grasp of the ambiguities inherent in the 'poetic' realism that Renoir was to become known for. *Toni* (1934), filmed on location near Marseilles with Marcel Pagnol's backing, is a tragedy that stems from the poverty and hopelessness of the Italian migrant workers. It was the precursor of Italian neo-realism.

The Crime of M. Lange (1935), set in a publishing house that produces illustrated stories about the cowboy Arizona Jim, was a film made collectively by Renoir with Jacques Prévert and the 'Groupe Octobre' and is the first of his films to convey the utopian optimism of the rise of the Popular Front. In the same spirit, Renoir directed *La Vie est à nous* (1936) for the Communist Party's election campaign and *The Lower Depths* (1936). The theme of unification permeates Renoir's Popular Front films: class bonds transcend nationalism; the unification of France must come through the unification of its working class.

This is expressed with less optimism in *La Grande Illusion* ('The great illusion', 1937), a First World War film against war, in which the successful escape of two prisoners (Jean Gabin and Dalio) must be weighed against the human losses which the film commemorates. This is the film that finally brought Renoir unqualified international recognition.

La Bête humaine (1938), in its unrelenting pessimism, signals the end of the climate of hope and communicates, along with the best films of Carné and Duvivier, the sense of defeat overtaking the country. *Rules of the Game* (1939), Renoir's masterpiece, was released on the eve of the French armistice with Germany and, unlike any of his other 1930s films, portrays French society as class-bound, frivolous, and static. This image of French society, as well as the film's elaborate structure and the absence of conventionally sympathetic and unsympathetic characters, confused critics and provoked hostility in the public. Renoir never recovered from this reaction to the film he had put so much of himself into, including acting as one of the central characters.

In 1940, Renoir was recalled to France from an Italian project (*La Tosca*) and soon obtained an exit visa allowing him to direct a film in Hollywood. During his American career in the 1940s, Renoir was able to make only five

Left: Jean Renoir with Nora Gregor in *La Règle du jeu*. Commercially unsuccessful at the time of its release in 1939, it is now widely regarded as one of the greatest films of all time.

fiction films and one film for the Office of War Information (*Salute to France*, which was edited in a manner unacceptable to him). Although *Swamp Water* (1941) was profitable, Renoir was pre-empted from making key decisions by his producer, Darryl F. Zanuck. In Hollywood Renoir was no longer able to work as a writer-director within a system he understood and could influence effectively. None of his American films is as fully integrated, conceptually and technically, as his works of the 1930s. This is hardly surprising considering how much Renoir counted on working with actors and taking time to achieve the effect he wanted. Although *The Southerner* (1945) comes closest to Renoir's goals, his American films do not express his confident understanding of ordinary people through popular expressions and music, and no longer convey differing perspectives through the subtle observation of detail. As a result, Renoir's films after 1940, including the post-war European films, seem rather distant and abstract. It was for these qualities that André Bazin and the young editors of the *Cahiers du cinéma* appreciated them.

Renoir's discovery of India during the filming of *The River* (1950) provided him with a new acceptance of nature and created a bridge that led him back to Europe. Subsequently, he directed *The Golden Coach* in Italy starring Anna Magnani, a magnificent tribute to the dialectic between theatre and life. *French Cancan* (1954) brought him back to Paris, although he maintained his permanent residence in California. The story of the Moulin Rouge and the primacy of art over life, *French Cancan* was renowned for its use of colour. The films that followed refer to earlier periods of painting or cinema without sentimentality while experimenting with television and the future. Renoir published an important biography of his father as well as his own memoirs, novels, short stories, and plays.   JANET BERGSTROM

SELECT FILMOGRAPHY

La Fille de l'eau (1924); Nana (1926); La Petite marchande d'allumettes (The Little Match Girl) (1928); Tire au flanc (1928); La Chienne (1931); La Nuit du carrefour (1932); Boudu sauvé des eaux (Boudu Saved from Drowning) (1932); Madame Bovary (1933); Toni (1934); Le Crime de M. Lange (The Crime of M. Lange) (1935); La Vie est à nous (1936); Une partie de campagne (1936); Les Bas-Fonds (The Lower Depths) (1936); La Grande Illusion (1937); La Marseillaise (1938); La Bête humaine (1938); La Règle du jeu (Rules of the Game, 1939); Swamp Water (1941); This Land is Mine (1943); The Southerner (1945); The Diary of a Chambermaid (1946); The River (1950); Le carrozza d'oro (The Golden Coach) (1952); French Cancan (1954); Éléna et les hommes (Elena and her Men) (1956); Le Déjeuner sur l'herbe (Picnic on the Grass) (1959); Le Caporal épinglé (The Vanishing Corporal) (1962)

SELECTED BIBLIOGRAPHY

Bazin, André (1973), *Jean Renoir*.
Bertin, Celia (1991), *Jean Renoir: A Life in Pictures*.
Durgnat, Raymond (1974), *Jean Renoir*.
Renoir, Jean (1962), *Renoir, my Father*.
—— (1974), *My Life and my Films*.
Sesonske, Alexander (1980), *Jean Renoir: The French Films, 1924–1939*.

the ideological impact of the avant-garde did not come through its association with political movements (which greeted the artists with caution, to say the least), but through the continuing shock waves that modern art gave to the hallowed certainties of what art was supposed to be. These shock waves were felt more in traditional 'high art' than in new popular forms, such as the cinema, which were also modern, but in a different, less frenetically self-conscious way.

The 1930s brought a dramatic change on a number of fronts. An immediate cause was the Depression which, presaged by the New York stock market crash in 1929, took an increasing toll as the decade wore on in continuing economic stagnation and rising unemployment. But even more significant in its effects was the realignment of the left in response to the rise of Fascism and the consequent formation of the Popular Fronts. In the late 1920s, the international Communist movement, under Soviet leadership, had adopted a hostile position towards the rest of the left, but by 1934 it had begun, belatedly, to repair the breach. Not only were the Communist parties encouraged to seek alliances with the Socialists and other left-wing parties, but Communist artists and intellectuals were persuaded to take up a more conciliatory attitude towards their 'bourgeois' counterparts. The doctrine of Socialist Realism, whose brutal imposition did so much harm to the cinema and other arts in the Soviet Union, was presented to the west in watered-down form as a way of rallying left-wing artists behind the banner of a socially responsible art using relatively conventional aesthetic and expressive means.

'Frontism' offered a formal link between political commitment and a realist aesthetic at a time when the avant-garde was in crisis and many artists (including experimental film-makers) were in headlong retreat from their previous radical positions. It had an additional appeal in the cinema where the triumph of the synchronized dialogue film had undermined the presuppositions of the silent aesthetic.

Not all left-wing artists were seduced by the siren call of frontism, politically or aesthetically. Many liberals were unwilling to throw in their lot with the Communists, while to the left the surrealist group, led by André Breton, maintained their revolutionary intransigence and allied themselves with Trotsky. But the surrealists were few in number (and very few indeed were implanted in the cinema), whereas artists of a more general socialist and leftist persuasion were numerous, including many film-makers, especially in documentary but also in feature-film making.

It was in Spain, where the left was engaged in a desperate struggle to defend the Republic against the invading forces of General Franco, that the ideology and practice of the Popular Front was put to its severest test.

Many artists rallied to the republican cause and joined the International Brigades. Film crews were sent from the Soviet Union and the cameraman Roman Karmen sent back footage to Moscow where it was edited by Esfir Shub into the documentary *Ispaniya* (1939). The Dutch documentary film-maker Joris Ivens enlisted the support of Ernest Hemingway to write and speak the commentary for *Spanish Earth* (1937; the French commentary was by Jean Renoir). French director Jean Grémillon worked with Buñuel on documentaries to alert public opinion in France and abroad. Back in France, André Malraux adapted his eyewitness novel about the war, *L'Espoir*, as a film, which was released in 1939. Although these efforts could not prevent Franco's victory, they contributed to raising a generalized anti-Fascist consciousness in the years preceding the World War.

Meanwhile it was in France that the new frontist alliance had the most effectiveness, culturally as well as politically. A Popular Front government was formed in 1936, under the leadership of the Socialist Léon Blum (later, in 1946, Blum was to lead a delegation to Washington to negotiate various agreements, including one to safeguard the French film industry). The Front polarized French society, exploiting fracture lines which already existed and were to be further deepened under the Occupation of 1940. Whereas in the 1920s the political character of the French cinema had been muted and it made little sense to divide film-makers into left and right, from the mid-1930s film-makers were forced to choose. While some, such as veteran avant-gardists Marcel L'Herbier and Abel Gance, chose the right, many chose the left, joining already committed intellectuals such as Paul Nizan in support of the Front. Nizan himself wrote the script of André Vigneau's documentary *Visages de la France* ('Faces of France', 1937). The career of Jean Renoir is a particularly vivid example, as the anti-bourgeois *Boudu sauvé des eaux* ('Boudu saved from drowning', 1932) gives way to the anti-capitalist *Crime de Monsieur Lange* ('The crime of Monsieur Lange', 1935) and the militant *La Vie est à nous* ('Life is ours', 1936). But Renoir was not alone. Jacques Prévert, Marcel Carné, and Jean Grémillon were all active in the world of the Front, while Julien Duvivier and Marc Allégret, who were not active, were nevertheless claimed for the left by enthusiastic critics.

The Popular Front did not change the industrial structure of the industry, and the most radical films were those made outside the mainstream. But frontism made far deeper inroads into popular entertainment than, for example, in Britain, where the mainstream film industry took very little cognizance of social problems, and where aesthetic innovation was more in the direction of Korda's historical spectaculars than of any serious engagement with social reality. It was left to the reform-minded sponsored documentary pioneered by John Grierson and the more radical and often Communist-inspired workers' film movement to raise social issues and insert 'actuality' into the cinema. But the films of the documentary movement enjoyed only a limited circulation in the pre-war period. They were mostly screened to political and voluntary organizations and were rarely programmed in commercial cinemas. It was not until the war that documentary came into its own as a medium of education and propaganda, and when it did so its goals were subordinated to the war effort.

THE SECOND WORLD WAR

The Second World War began in Europe in September 1939. In cinematic terms, its first immediate effect in Britain was that the government briefly closed all the cinemas and was only reluctantly persuaded to reopen them. Its next effect was that, as the German blitzkrieg progressed, Hollywood lost its lucrative export markets in Europe. National cinemas throve, though in the occupied countries they were subject to strict German censorship and control. As one French historian wryly observed, the Vichy period was a very good one for French cinema, since with a choice of French or German films to go to, the public invariably chose French ones.

In the combatant countries the situation was different. Both Germany and Britain rapidly put their film industries on a war footing, followed in 1941 by the Soviet Union (which was forced to evacuate its Moscow and Leningrad studios and relocate production in central Asia) and, to a lesser extent, the United States (where many film-makers, including John Ford, found themselves drafted for war service). Documentary and newsreels acquired a new importance and, in some cases, popularity. Though many of the obligatory shorts provided by the British Ministry of Information were less than warmly welcomed, Humphrey Jennings and Stewart McAllister's *Listen to Britain* (1942) was rapturously applauded, and Roy Boulting's feature-length *Desert Victory* was a box-office hit the following year.

More interesting was the effect on feature films. Unlike the First World War, the emphasis in most of the combatant countries was much less on whipping up hatred against the enemy, and far more on creating a sense of national unity and solidarity in the face of an external threat. In the Soviet Union this meant abandoning the values of building socialism (and its correlative, the paranoid search for socialism's real or presumed enemies), in favour of those of the united defence of the motherland. In Britain films about men at war emphasized a hard-won solidarity, overcoming differences of rank and class, while an equal place was given to home-front films, with a more feminine bias, in which similar values were expressed in a more domestic vein. In the United States, further removed from the front line, the idea of a home front had less resonance, and the bulk of feature film production re-

Paul Robeson

(1898–1977)

Actor, singer, speaker, civil rights and labour activist, Paul Robeson was intellectually and athletically gifted, an inspiring speaker and a magnetic performer. He enjoyed a unique position at the juncture of popular arts, high culture, and politics. His career difficulties testify to the obstacles which political activism poses to the popular arts.

Born in Princeton, New Jersey, the son of an escaped slave who became a minister, Robeson earned both academic and athletic honours at Rutgers University and graduated from Columbia Law School. Although he passed the bar examination, he never practised law but instead began an adventurous and politicized artistic career. Robeson's theatrical activities ranged from serious modern and classical plays to musical comedy, and whatever role he played became stamped with his name. He became identified with the plays of his friend Eugene O'Neill, appearing in numerous stage productions of *All God's Chillun Got Wings*. He also put his mark on the title-role of *Othello*, played first in 1930 in London, with Peggy Ashcroft as Desdemona, then between 1942 and 1944, touring with Uta Hagen and José Ferrer. Robeson's stage appearances in the Jerome Kern musical *Show Boat*, in both the USA and London, consolidated his popularity.

By contrast, Robeson's participation in film production was fitful and frustrating. Although he acted in films in both Britain and the U.S., he was never under long-term contract to any studio. Despite rewarding work in Oscar Micheaux's *Body and Soul* (1924) and Kenneth McPherson's experimental film *Borderline* (1930) (which also featured poet H.D.), Robeson became frustrated with his limited control of the films in which he appeared. He was so unhappy with the final version of Zoltan Korda's *Sanders of the River* (1935) that he attempted, unsuccessfully, to buy the rights and all the prints to prevent distribution. He came to deplore the depiction of blacks in *Tales of Manhattan* (1942), which proved to be his last film.

It was while acting, singing, and studying African languages in London in the 1930s that Robeson's interest in African culture and politics grew intense, as did his interest in Communism and socialism. In 1934 he made the first of several trips to the Soviet Union at the behest of Sergei Eisenstein, whose plans for a film starring Robeson were never to materialize. Thereafter, Robeson's concerts were imbued with his politics: he developed an eloquent and outspoken speech-making style, and often performed on behalf of favoured causes.

After the Second World War, Robeson's powerful criticism of racial and class oppression in America brought him into conflict with the anti-Communist paranoia of the day. The pinnacle of this conflict came when Robeson's remarks at the 1949 Paris Peace Conference were misquoted by the Associated Press news service to make Robeson appear anti-American and pro-Soviet. Many American blacks grew disenchanted with him as a political spokesman and broke their ties with him. A concert in Peekskill, New York, was disrupted by anti-Communist and racist mob violence. The rioting was chalked up to Communist agitators, and Robeson was blamed and vilified.

Soon after the Peekskill riots, the passports of both Robeson and his wife were revoked by the State Department. Identified by the FBI as 'key figures' in leftist politics, they were subjected to twenty years of almost continual surveillance. Robeson finally retrieved his passport in 1958, permitting him to travel again, but through the 1960s and 1970s suffered from ill-health and severe depression. He lived in seclusion until his death in 1977.

Robeson's film appearances stand as a record of his magnificent bass voice, and the profound personal magnetism that made possible his musical and theatrical careers, and secured his position as spokesman for civil rights and the left. It was his artistic career that made the propagation of his politics possible. That those politics also curtailed his career stands as a testament to the political constraints of the American culture industry.

EDWARD R. O'NEILL

SELECT FILMOGRAPHY

Body and Soul (1924); Borderline (1930); Emperor Jones (1933); Sanders of the River (1935); Show Boat (1936); Song of Freedom (1936); King Solomon's Mines (1937); Jericho / Dark Sands (1937); Big Fella (1937); The Proud Valley (1939); Tales of Manhattan (1942)

BIBLIOGRAPHY

Duberman, Martin (1989), *Paul Robeson: A Biography*.
Foner, Philip S. (ed.) (1978), *Paul Robeson Speaks*.

Paul Robeson in the film version of the Jerome Kern/Oscar Hammerstein II musical *Show Boat* (1936), produced by Carl Laemmle Jr. at Universal and directed by James Whale. Robeson considered his role in both stage and screen versions demeaning to black people and when he sang 'Ole' man river' in concerts he altered the words to make them feistier.

mained unaffected by wartime values (an exception was William Wyler's 1942 tribute to the British in *Mrs. Miniver*). But from Pearl Harbor onwards a number of combat films were made, mostly about the war in the Pacific, adapting stereotypes from earlier Hollywood genre production. A particularly interesting example is Howard Hawks's *Air Force* (1943), in which a bomber crew consisting of men of different backgrounds and ethnicities is forged into a cohesive fighting unit under the pressure of battle. Although one or two other good films were concocted in this new improvised genre, notably Raoul Walsh's *Objective Burma!* and Ford's *They Were Expendable* (both 1945), pride of place among American war films must go to William Wellman's *The Story of G.I. Joe* (also 1945), which definitively eschews any form of élitism or dramatized heroics in favour of a realistic and democratic portrayal of the business of soldiering.

EPILOGUE

The end of the war in 1945, though universally welcomed, had a bitter epilogue in the form of the Cold War. In the Soviet Union and its new satellites, the authoritarian forms of so-called Socialist Realism were imposed, or reimposed, with a vengeance. And in the United States a hysterical wave of anti-Communism overtook a film industry in which ideological tensions, though never absent, had abated in the war years.

During the 1930s there had been many radical voices raised in Hollywood, strengthened by the influx of *émigrés* from Europe. Few feature films were made which expressed these voices. Not that it would have been impossible to make them, but the tightly integrated studio system militated against the release of films which would attract only sectional audiences. Social criticism in Hollywood films of the 1930s took the form of a generic populism (as in Frank Capra's *Mr. Deeds Goes to Town*, 1936, and *Mr. Smith Goes to Washington*, 1939), or expressed itself metaphorically in genre films such as gangsters and Westerns. But a fierce social struggle went on in Hollywood itself, pitting writers and craft unions against a system of power which had developed in the 1920s and fiercely resisted challenges to its control.

Industrial and political concerns overlapped. One reason why film companies had chosen to locate in southern California was that Los Angeles (unlike San Francisco) was a non-union town, and for a long time the studios resisted the formation of labour unions, offering the Academy of Motion Picture Arts and Sciences as an alternative forum for craft and professional issues. Increasingly, however, the system's employees came to resent the power of the studios to fix the conditions under which they worked. Stars began to challenge their contracts and the moulding of their image to studio whims. Literary writers opposed the mechanization of their work

and the absence of any form of author's right over what they had written. (Scott Fitzgerald's Pat Hobby stories, as well as his great unfinished novel *The Last Tycoon*, provide a wonderful, disabused vision of the writer's role in Hollywood.) Even the animators in the Disney studio were driven to form themselves into a guild and to rebel in 1941 against a paternalistic management which granted them no autonomy in their creative work. Industrial struggles continued to smoulder throughout the war, and there was a strike at the Warner Bros. studio in 1945.

The most prominent (if not necessarily the most important) role in these struggles was played by writers, organized into a branch of the Writers Guild, and a major symbolic event occurred in 1936 when screen-writer Dudley Nichols refused to accept an Oscar for his script for John Ford's *The Informer*. Writers in particular became increasingly radicalized politically, and many became associated with the Communist Party (though more often as sympathizers than as members or activists). The wartime alliance of the United States, Britain, and the Soviet Union made this association briefly respectable, but after 1945 Hollywood (and the nation in general) reverted to its pre-war stance. Latent anti-Communism was whipped up into hysteria by the antics of Senator Joe McCarthy and of the previously insignificant Un-American Activities Committee of the House of Representatives (HUAC).

In 1947 HUAC, under the chairmanship of Representative J. Parnell Thomas, turned its attention to Hollywood, and its preliminary enquiries revealed a deeply divided community. A number of artists, including writer (and Russian *émigrée*) Ayn Rand, directors Sam Wood and Leo McCarey, and actors Adolphe Menjou, Robert Taylor, Gary Cooper, and Ronald Reagan, offered to assist the Committee in the fight against Communism (though not necessarily to denounce Communists). Studio bosses Jack Warner and Louis B. Mayer prevaricated, declaring a staunch anti-Communism, but an unwillingness to go along with the idea of a 'blacklist'. With mainly anecdotal evidence to go on, the Committee then decided to interrogate nineteen 'hostile witnesses'—most of them writers. When the witnesses took the stand, they were asked not only the infamous question, 'Are you, or have you ever been, a member of the Communist Party?', but also (in the case of the writers) whether they were members of the Writers Guild. One by one, the first ten witnesses called declined to answer these questions directly, and asserted a constitutional right, under the First Amendment, to answer them in their own way, if at all. The eleventh witness, German dramatist Bertolt Brecht, said that, as a foreigner, he felt he could answer the question, and he was not and had never been a Communist: shortly afterwards he returned to Europe.

The ten witnesses, or 'Hollywood Ten'—John Howard

Lawson, Dalton Trumbo, Albert Maltz, Alvah Bessie, Samuel Ornitz, Herbert Biberman, Adrian Scott, Edward Dmytryk, Ring Lardner, Jr., and Lester Cole—were cited for contempt of Congress and sentenced to a year's imprisonment (Dmytryk later recanted and was released). Trumbo, Dmytryk, Scott (Dmytryk's producer on *Crossfire*), and Cole were fired by their studios. All were blacklisted, and a further 'open blacklist' was instituted. Opposition to the Committee, spearheaded by such luminaries as William Wyler, John Huston, Alexander Knox, Humphrey Bogart, Lauren Bacall, Gene Kelly, and Danny Kaye, fizzled into nothing. The studios blandly turned themselves into the playthings of the Committee. Thus did Hollywood get its revenge for the troubles of the 1930s.

The story did not end there. Blacklisting continued throughout the decade, and reached a new peak in 1951, when a further crop of artists was accused, often by former friends and supporters. For many years they could find work only outside the United States, or using pseudonyms. All in all, it was a shabby episode, which left lasting scars. In a world supposedly made safe for democracy, it offered a grotesque image of the values of the Cold War, and a perverse reflection of what was happening on the other side of the Iron Curtain.

Bibliography
Fitzgerald, F. Scott (1986), *The Collected Short Stories*.
Fofi, Goffredo (1972), 'The Cinema of the Popular Front in France'.
Forgacs, David (ed.) (1987), *Rethinking Italian Fascism*.
Leyda, Jay (1960), *Kino*.

NATIONAL CINEMAS

The Popular Art of French Cinema

GINETTE VINCENDEAU

As in Hollywood, the period 1930 to 1960 constitutes the classical era of French cinema, a period of well-defined genres and industrial structures, and a time when the cinema was the main form of popular entertainment. During these years, many of the great classics of French cinema were produced, films like *Le Million* (1931), *La Grande Illusion* (1937), *Les Enfants du paradis* (1943–5), *Casque d'or* (1951), and *Mon oncle* (1958). At the same time, it was a period marked by recurrent crises in the film industry, serious political unrest, and a World War. If the era opened on the sound revolution, heralding a new film language and the increased popularity of the medium, it ended more ambiguously: the end of the 1950s saw both the exhilarating emergence of the New Wave and the beginning of a decline in cinema attendances.

FROM THE COMING OF SOUND TO THE POPULAR FRONT

The coming of sound took the French film industry by surprise. Though the French cinema was artistically rich in the 1920s, Hollywood was dominant and production had dropped to fifty-five films in 1926. Additionally, though French scientists had invented sound systems as early as 1900, none had been patented, so that American and German systems had to be imported. The first French sound films (*L'Eau du Nil* ('The water of the Nile'), *Le Collier de la Reine* ('The Queen's necklace'), 1929) were little more than silent films with extra sound passages. It took René Clair's *Sous les toits de Paris* ('Under the roofs of Paris', 1930), shot for the German firm Tobis at the Épinay studios, to put French sound film on the map. Initially a flop in France, this populist tale about a street singer (Albert Préjean) became a huge world-wide success. Not only did it use sound and music imaginatively, but it popularized a nostalgic vision of old Paris and its 'little people', which subsequently characterized many French films.

French film-makers quickly adapted to the talkies, and the early 1930s saw a rapid increase in the number of features produced, shooting up to 157 in 1931, settling down eventually at around 130 films per year, a figure which, with the exception of the 1940s, has been kept up until the present day. Apart from two vertically integrated conglomerates, Gaumont-Franco-Film–Aubert (GFFA) and Pathé–Natan, both formed in the late 1920s, pro-

duction was in the hands of a myriad of individual producers, with shaky finances. As in French society at large, scandals and bankruptcies, aggravated by the recession, were common. Both GFFA and Pathé–Natan had effectively collapsed by 1934. Government attempts at putting the French film industry in order came to little, despite repeated demands from the industry, worried also about competition from Hollywood (for every French film shown, there were two to three US ones throughout the 1930s, and distribution was largely in American hands). However, with a few exceptions, top box-office successes of the decade were French.

After their initial weakness, studios around Paris (Épinay, Boulogne-Billancourt, Joinville) and in the south of France (Marseilles, Nice) strengthened their equipment and expertise. The booming film scene was cosmopolitan, occasionally provoking xenophobic attacks from the right, at a time when the political scene was sharply divided and anti-Semitism on the rise. Yet France was, in other ways, welcoming: to the strong Russian community of the 1920s were added layers of German and central European *émigrés*. From 1929 to 1932, many came to make multi-language versions, a method in use before dubbing and subtitling, especially in the Paramount studios in Joinville, nicknamed 'Babel-on-Seine'. Many *émigrés* made lasting contributions to French cinema: Lazare Meerson (a Russian) and the Hungarian Alexandre Trauner dominated set design, creating the famous Parisian décors of the films of Clair, Carné, and others. Star French cameramen like Jules Krüger or Claude Renoir learnt a lot from Ufa-trained Kurt Courant and Eugen Schüfftan, jointly establishing the look of Poetic Realism. Directors like Billy Wilder, Fritz Lang, Anatole Litvak, Max Ophuls, and Robert Siodmak all shot films in Paris on their way to Hollywood; some, like Ophuls, Siodmak, and Kurt Bernhardt, made a substantial number of French films until the war. Ophuls, who eventually took French nationality, came back to Paris in the 1950s.

The coming of sound put an end to the avant-garde, but silent film directors, like Clair, Jean Renoir, Jacques Feyder, Marie Epstein and Jean Benoît-Lévy, Julien Duvivier, Jean Grémillon, Abel Gance, and Marcel L'Herbier, smoothly made the transition and became prominent directors in the 1930s and beyond; they were joined by newcomers like Carné (Feyder's assistant) and the Spanish *émigré* Jean Vigo, who tragically died in 1934, leaving two brilliant features, *Zéro de conduite* ('Nought for behaviour', 1933) and *L'Atalante* (1934). One of the greatest changes brought by sound was the ushering in of a new set of stars, many from the theatre and music hall: Raimu, Harry Baur, Jean Gabin, Arletty, Fernandel, Jules Berry, Louis Jouvet, Michel Simon, Françoise Rosay, to name the most famous. They were supported by many character actors such as Carette, Saturnin Fabre, Pauline Carton, Robert le Vigan, and Bernard Blier; their familiar faces and mannerisms drew popular loyalty just as much as the big stars did, and they became one of the enduring delights of the classical French cinema.

The novelty of sound prompted the two most popular genres of the early 1930s: musicals and filmed theatre. Apart from Clair's *Le Million*, *À nous la liberté* ('Liberty is ours', 1932), and *Quatorze juillet* ('14 July', 1932), in which he bent genre conventions to suit his own auteurist preoccupations, musicals tended to be 'straight' filmed operettas. Some of the most lavish, like *Le Chemin du paradis* ('The road to paradise', 1930), were German films made in Germany in two versions, launching such stars as Henri Garat and Lilian Harvey. Thanks to *Le Million* and *Quatorze juillet*, Annabella became the top female French star. But another, lesser-known type of musical took the French cinema by storm: simple, cheaply made stories built around music hall comic singers, especially Georges Milton, 'Bach', and Fernandel. A very idiosyncratic subset of this genre was the military vaudeville (*comique troupier*), critically scorned but much appreciated by the audience; Fernandel starred in one of its greatest hits, *Ignace* (1937). Many other music hall performers, such as Josephine Baker, Maurice Chevalier, and Mistinguett, appeared, though less frequently, in films, as did, later on in the decade, a new generation of singers and musicians: Tino Rossi, Charles Trenet, and the Ray Ventura band. This was the typical fare of the 'cinema du sam'di soir', when people went regularly to their local flea-pit or to the new picture palaces in big city centres, like the Gaumont-Palace or the Rex in Paris. This popular audience equally loved 'filmed theatre' (straight play adaptations), also frowned upon by critics. Yet filmed theatre, based (directly or indirectly) on satirical boulevard comedies, is now a fascinating testimony to the period; it also gave great actors like Berry or Raimu the opportunity to show off their flamboyant style, and script-writers a chance to sharpen their *bons mots*. Their delight in the French language, shared by the audience, strongly contributed to a specifically *French* cinema, in the face of the Hollywood 'threat'. It also heralded the unique place of script-writers in French cinema. Playwrights like Marcel Achard, and poets like Jacques Prévert, wrote for the screen, and a new generation of script-writers emerged with Henri Jeanson and Charles Spaak. Many directors worked in filmed theatre, such as Yves Mirande and Louis Verneuil, but its two stars were undoubtedly Marcel Pagnol and Sacha Guitry, who both filmed their own plays, with technical help at first. Pagnol celebrated his southern culture, for instance in the *Marius*, *Fanny*, and *César* trilogy (1931, 1932, 1936, providing Raimu with the part of a lifetime, and also starring Orane Demazis and Pierre Fresnay) and *La Femme du boulanger* ('The baker's wife', 1938). Guitry, always starring himself, showcased his urbane and voluble Parisian persona, in such gems as *Faisons un rêve* ('Let's dream') and *Le Roman d'un tricheur* ('The tale of a trickster', both 1936).

But if such light-hearted and comic genres dominated the French box-office, there existed another strong, much darker realist-melodramatic current in French cinema. A few nineteenth-century melodramas were (re)made, such as Raymond Bernard's *Les Misérables* ('The wretched', 1933) and Maurice Tourneur's *Les Deux Orphelines* ('The two little orphan girls', 1932), but new melodramatic genres emerged: the military or navy melodrama (*Double Crime sur la ligne Maginot* ('Double crime on the Maginot line'), 1937; *La Porte du large* ('Gateway to the sea'), 1936), high-society dramas, like Marcel L'Herbier's *Le Bonheur* ('Happiness', 1935) and Abel Gance's *Paradis perdu* ('Paradise lost', 1939), and the 'Slav' melodrama, a type of elaborate costume drama set in a fantasy eastern Europe (*Mayerling*, 1936; *Katia*, 1938), and strongly indebted to the Russian *émigrés*; its romantic stars were Danielle Darrieux, Charles Boyer, Pierre Richard-Willm, Pierre Fresnay, and Pierre Blanchar. But, internationally, the 1930s are especially associated with the more gritty Poetic Realism. Based on realist literature or original scripts and usually set in working-class milieux, Poetic Realist films featured pessimistic narratives and night-time settings, and a dark, contrasted, visual style prefiguring American film noir. Many great *auteurs* of the time chose this idiom: Pierre Chenal (*La Rue sans nom* ('The nameless street'), 1933; *Le Dernier Tournant* ('The last turning'), 1939), Julien Duvivier (*La Bandera*, 1935; *Pépé le Moko*, 1936), Jean Grémillon (*Gueule d'amour* ('The face of love'), 1937; *Remorques* ('Trailers'), 1939–40), Jean Renoir (*La Bête humaine* ('The beast in man'), 1938), Albert Valentin (*L'Entraîneuse* ('The dance hostess'), 1938). Starting with *Jenny* in 1936, Carné and Prévert best represented the tradition with *Le Quai des brumes* ('Misty quay', 1938) and *Le Jour se lève* ('Daybreak', 1939). Though Poetic Realism produced 'mythical' women characters (for instance those played by Michèle Morgan in *Le Quai des brumes* and *L'Entraîneuse*, the Poetic Realist drama was that of the male hero, usually embodied by Jean Gabin.

The doomed universe of Poetic Realist films was said to reflect the gloomy morale of the immediate pre-war years.

Alexandre Trauner
(1906–1993)

Having studied painting at the École des Beaux Arts in Budapest, Trauner arrived in Paris in 1929, where he was engaged as assistant to the designer Lazare Meerson, working at the Épinay-sur-Seine studios. This collaboration would endure up to 1936 over fourteen films including *À nous la liberté* (René Clair, 1931), and *La Kermesse héroïque* (Jacques Feyder, 1935).

Trauner described himself as 'an artisan' and emerged from the background of established design traditions that flourished in the French studio system of the 1930s. Having become chief designer in 1937, Trauner would continue the system of apprenticeships from which he learnt, by taking on Paul Bertrand as assistant for *Jeux interdits* (René Clément, 1952) and *Gervaise* (Clément, 1956). Trauner's reputation was secured by his designs for a series of films made in the 1930s that have become synonymous with the term 'poetic realism'. Alongside director Marcel Carné and script-writer Jacques Prévert, Trauner may legitimately be considered as co-*auteur* of films such as *Quai des brumes* (1938), *Le Jour se lève* (1939), and *Les Enfants du paradis* (1945).

He described the function of set designer as being 'to help the *mise-en-scène* so that the spectator has an immediate grasp on the character's psychology'. His sustained collaboration with Carné and Prévert over eight films from 1937 to 1950 emphasized this function. From the incarceration of François (Jean Gabin) in the top floor of his suburban apartment in *Le Jour se lève* to the teeming streets of Ménilmontant in *Les Enfants du paradis*, Trauner's design allies character with milieu. As Bazin commented on *Le Jour se lève*, the sets have detailed touches which almost give them the feel of the social documentary, and yet are composed as carefully 'as a painter would a canvas'. With stylization applied over a naturalistic base, the décor can take on a dramatic role, as it does in films of German Expressionism.

As a Jew, Trauner was forced into hiding during the war and the Occupation, but it was during this period that he also produced some of his finest work. *Les Enfants du paradis* was shot in the studios in Nice, then under an Italian occupation less harsh than German or Vichy rule. Protected by friends and in hiding nearby, Trauner was able to contribute much to the development of the film's script, as well as designing the spectacular sets of the Boulevard du Crime.

After the war, the gradual decline of the French studios, along with the diminishing budget allocations for set designs, led Trauner to work increasingly with American directors, particularly Billy Wilder, for whom he designed eight films between 1958 and 1978. Trauner's facility for trick perspective was fully employed in the design for the office in *The Apartment* (1960) for which he received an Oscar.

A renewed interest in studio shooting characterized 1980s French cinema, and Trauner's designs returned to favour, visible at both ends of the stylistic spectrum, from the glossy ad-chic of Luc Besson's *Subway* (1985), to the *cinéma de qualité* classicism of Bertrand Tavernier's *Coup de torchon* (1981) and *'Round Midnight* (1986).

CHRIS DARKE

SELECT FILMOGRAPHY

Drôle de drame (1937); Quai des brumes (1938); Entrée des artistes (1938); Le Jour se lève (1939); Remorques (1941); Les Enfants du paradis (1945); Les Portes de la nuit (1946); Othello (1952, for Orson Welles); The Apartment (1960); Subway (1985); 'Round Midnight (1986)

BIBLIOGRAPHY

Barsacq, Léon (1976), *Caligari's Cabinet and Other Grand Illusions*.

'Poetic realism'. A scene from Carné and Prévert's *Le Jour se lève* (1939), designed by Alexandre Trauner

Arletty
(1891–1992)

When the sublime Arletty became world famous as Garance, the romantic heroine of Marcel Carné and Jacques Prévert's wartime classic *Les Enfants du paradis* (1945), she had already had a long career as one of the most popular performers in French film and theatre.

Arletty was born Léonie Bathiat in the Parisian suburb of Courbevoie in a modest family. After a spell working in a factory, she became a model and in 1919 started playing in comic/erotic stage revues and plays (she would subsequently always claim the theatre as her real love). A star of 1920s *tout-Paris*, her beauty was admired, and painted, by artists such as van Dongen. Her ability to combine sex appeal and insolent humour drew filmmakers' attention. From 1929, she appeared in small parts in numerous comedies, as well as in prestigious productions such as Jacques Feyder's *Pension Mimosas* (1934) and Jean de Limur's *La Garçonne* (1935, based on Victor Margueritte's 'scandalous' novel). Arletty's unique voice was high-pitched and scratchy, and, combined with her Parisian working-class accent, extremely funny in both song and dialogue. Carné's *Hôtel du Nord* (1938) launched her film career proper in France; the comic couple she formed with Louis Jouvet completely outshone the film's romantic leads played by Annabella and Jean-Pierre Aumont (not least, it must be admitted, because the script-writer Henri Jeanson gave them the best lines). Her exasperated cry of 'atmosphère! atmosphère! est-ce que j'ai une gueule d'atmosphère?' ('atmosphere! atmosphere! do I look like an atmosphere?') became an instant catch-phrase, forever part of the French vocabulary. In Carné and Prévert's *Le Jour se lève* (1939) she was given a dramatic role; in that film too her charisma was more a match for Jean Gabin than the bland Jacqueline Laurent, who had top billing. Despite her stage experience and glamorous existence, Arletty came across as authentically proletarian, a characteristic which tended to confine women (unlike men such as Gabin) to comedy; she starred in two great comedies of 1939; *Fric-Frac* (with Michel Simon and Fernandel) and *Circonstances atténuantes* (also with Simon).

The war was a mixed blessing for Arletty. It brought her international fame with *Les Visiteurs du soir* (1941) and especially *Les Enfants du paradis*, but also personal misfortune. After *Les Visiteurs du soir*, a medieval tale in which she played the devil's acolyte, Carné and Prévert recreated in *Les Enfants du paradis* the popular Parisian theatre of the 1840s. Whereas the central male characters, played by Jean-Louis Barrault, Pierre Brasseur, and Marcel Herrand, were based on historical figures, Garance, the woman who fascinates them all, was a purely fictional creation, dramatically featuring Arletty's combination of glamour and humour, of the noble and the popular. The film was a triumph, but by the time it came out Arletty had been arrested and imprisoned for her liaison with a German officer (never at a loss for a witticism, her defence was, allegedly: 'my heart is French but my body is international'). She was barred from acting for three years. She eventually resumed work, regaining popular support, but her post-war career was a shadow of its former glory. She made films, including Jacqueline Audry's *Huis-clos* (1954, based on Sartre's play) and Carné's *L'Air de Paris* (1954), in which she was reunited with Gabin. She also worked on the stage, until blindness ended her career in the 1960s. She lived in Paris until her death.

Arletty's charismatic performances, wise-cracks, and indomitable spirit made her one of the great French populist heroines. A female *gavroche*, she personified the mythical Parisian: funny, insolent, and rebellious, and at the same time nonchalantly blasée. In her honour, a new cinema opened in 1984 at the Pompidou Centre, called the Salle Garance. One of her last public gestures was to launch her own perfume, for charity. She called it, naturally, 'Atmosphère'.

GINETTE VINCENDEAU

SELECT FILMOGRAPHY

Pension Mimosas (1934); La Garçonne (1935); Hôtel du Nord (1938); Le Jour se lève (1939); Fric-Frac (1939); Circonstances atténuantes (1939); Les Visiteurs du soir (1941); Les Enfants du paradis (1945); Huis-clos (1954); L'Air de Paris (1954)

BIBLIOGRAPHY

Ariotti, Philippe, and de Comes, Philippe (1978), *Arletty*. Arletty (1971), *La Défense*.

Arletty in Marcel Carné and Jacques Prévert's *Les Enfants du paradis* (1945)

There is some truth in this, though Carné, like many politically conscious directors of the time, had earlier espoused the more hopeful ideology of the Popular Front, the left–centre alliance in power from 1936 to 1938, which spurred a remarkable rallying of intellectuals and artists, including film-makers. Of these, the most prominent director, and undoubtedly the towering artistic figure over the whole decade, was Jean Renoir. His populist comedy *Le Crime de Monsieur Lange* ('Monsieur Lange's crime', 1935), as well as his most directly committed films *La Vie est à nous* ('Life is ours', 1936) and *La Marseillaise* (1937), all engaged with the climate of hope and class solidarity which characterized this brief period. Renoir's achievement was also that he combined a brilliant technique, which both summed up and transcended the practices of the time (such as shooting in depth and using long takes), with popular stars and subjects, as in *La Chienne* ('The bitch', 1931), *Partie de campagne* ('A trip to the country', 1936, a tribute to his father, the painter Auguste Renoir), *La Grande Illusion*, or *La Bête humaine*. His last film of the decade, *La Règle du jeu* ('The rules of the game', 1939, showing the collapse of a corrupt aristocratic society and considered one of the best films ever made), flopped, but with hindsight seems premonitory. *La Règle du jeu* ended a decade of great artistic achievement and vital popular cinema. Film culture was thriving. The Cinémathèque Française was founded in 1936 by Henri Langlois, Georges Franju, and Jean Mitry. Popular magazines like *Pour vous* and *Cinémonde* were read weekly by millions, while the writing of learned film histories had begun, from left-wing (Georges Sadoul) and right-wing (Maurice Bardèche and Robert Brasillach) historians alike. There were exciting plans for the future put forward during the Popular Front—for the reorganization of the whole industry, and for an international film festival at Cannes. The war put a sharp stop to all this.

OCCUPATION AND LIBERATION

Marshal Pétain's capitulation, the German occupation of France, and the division of the country into a 'free' zone (the south) and an occupied one, all had a profound effect on French cinema. Some film-makers and actors—Renoir, Duvivier, Gabin, Morgan—emigrated to the USA, while others, like Alexander Trauner or the composer Joseph Kosma, had to go into hiding because of anti-Semitic laws (some suffered more: for instance Harry Baur was tortured by the Gestapo in 1943). But the majority remained in France and worked relatively smoothly under the new regime. Pétain's Vichy government endeavoured to limit German control over the film industry, creating a new ruling body, the Committee for the Organization of the Cinematographic Industries (COIC), based in Paris. The COIC introduced new regulations which were to have far-

Lino Ventura in Jacques Becker's 1953 thriller *Touchez-pas au grisbi* ('Don't touch the loot')

reaching implications for French cinema until the present day: a sounder financial framework for the industry, box-office control, a boost to short film production, and a new film school (the IDHEC). A number of classics, such as *L'Éternel Retour* ('The eternal return'), *Lumière d'été* ('Summer light'), and *Les Visiteurs du soir* ('The evening visitors'; all 1943), were made in the free zone, but lack of means cut this production short and the majority of films came out of Paris. The Germans set up their own production company there, Continental Films, which, with German capital but French personnel, produced 30 features out of the total 220 made during the war. Despite material hardship, French cinema prospered. Films were scrutinized by German and Vichy censorship, prompting many directors to avoid contemporary or 'difficult' subjects, but on the other hand very few films could be called propaganda. British and American films were banned, leaving French movies to dominate the screens (apart from a few Italian and German films). Cinemas were warm and relatively safe places, and movies a welcome distraction; attendance had never been higher.

The dominant production of these strange years has been called 'escapist': American-style comedies like *L'Honorable Catherine* (1943); thrillers (*Dernier atout* ('Final trump'), *L'Assassin habite ... au 21* ('The murderer lives at no. 21'), both 1942); musicals with Tino Rossi, Charles Trenet, or Edith Piaf; costume dramas, such as *Pontcarral colonel d'Empire* (1942), *La Duchesse de Langeais* (1941), and *Les Enfants du paradis* (1943–5). One third of all wartime production consisted of literary adaptations, and the period saw the rare appearance of a 'fantastic' trend in French cinema, with films like *La Nuit fantastique* ('The fantastic night', 1941), *L'Éternel Retour* (on a script by Jean

Cocteau), and *Les Visiteurs du soir*. Though it has been argued that some of these films, such as *Pontcarral*, contained an oblique critique of the Germans and of Pétain's regime, they were on the whole meant, and received, as entertainment, very much as in the 1930s. This ambiguity is perhaps what characterizes most 'Vichy cinema': Henri-Georges Clouzot's *Le Corbeau* ('The raven', 1943, with Fresnay and Ginette Leclerc), a sombre satire of the provincial bourgeoisie made for Continental, was criticized at the Liberation as anti-French and thus pro-Nazi, yet the Germans at the time found it offensive and refused to distribute it in Germany. Pagnol's *La Fille du puisatier* ('The well-digger's daughter', 1940) has been seen as supporting Pétain's ideology of 'travail, famille, patrie' (work, family, fatherland), yet its story of an abandoned single mother is consistent with Pagnol's earlier work. An interesting generic development of the time was the rise of the 'women's film', with melodramas like Abel Gance's *La Vénus aveugle* ('The blind Venus', 1940), Pagnol's *La Fille du puisatier*, Jean Stelli's *Le Voile bleu* ('The blue veil', 1942), and Jean Grémillon's *Le Ciel est à vous* ('Heaven is yours', 1943). Though, again, these films can be seen as vehicles for the Vichy ideology (exalting sacrificial motherhood and patriotism), they all featured strong women characters, a novelty compared to the pre-war period (and no doubt connected to the larger number of women in the audience); they also gave stars Viviane Romance, Gaby Morlay, and Madeleine Renaud more substantial parts than before. The wacky comedy *L'Honorable Catherine* (with Edwige Feuillère), Albert Valentin's superb melodrama *Marie-Martine* (1943, with Renée Saint-Cyr), and Claude Autant-Lara's trenchant drama *Douce* (1943) are equally remarkable for the narrative centrality of their heroines. The phenomenon was short-lived, and female characters in post-war films tended to resume traditional patterns.

French cinema kept a high profile at the Liberation. A Committee for the Liberation of French Cinema was set up, and a journal, *L'Écran français*, founded. Jewish personnel came back, while, as part of the general *épuration*, Guitry, Arletty, and Chevalier were penalized for fraternizing with Germans (and Clouzot banned from working for two years, on account of *Le Corbeau*), though none had been involved to the extent of actual Fascists like actor Robert Le Vigan (who left France to escape condemnation) or writer Robert Brasillach, shot in 1945. The culmination of the Carné–Prévert Poetic Realist universe, *Les Enfants du paradis*, came out on 9 March 1945. It was a huge popular and critical success, its two central characters, Baptiste (Jean-Louis Barrault) and Garance (Arletty), seen as the embodiment of the indestructible 'spirit of France'.

Post-Liberation French cinema initially dealt with the trauma of the war. Documentaries and fiction films were made, chiefly to the glory of the Resistance, like Jean-Paul Le Chanois's accounts of the Vercors *maquis*. The most famous features were René Clément's 1946 *La Bataille du rail* ('The battle of the railways', a semi-documentary using railway workers who had fought in the resistance) and *Le Père tranquille* ('The quiet father', 1946, with Noël-Noël), while others, such as Christian-Jaque's *Boule de suif* (1945), Autant-Lara's *Le Diable au corps* ('Possessed', 1946), and, later, Clément's *Jeux interdits* ('Forbidden games', 1951), dealt with the topic in a more oblique manner. Soon, however, the subject went more or less under, until the post-de Gaulle era (with the exception of Alain Resnais's *Nuit et brouillard* ('Night and fog'), 1956, and *Hiroshima mon amour*, 1959), though, significantly, it became a favourite subject for comedies for the next three decades.

THE FOURTH REPUBLIC

Like the political regime, the cinema of the Fourth Republic started off on a programme of change. The Centre National de la Cinématographie (CNC), founded in 1946, extending the work of the COIC, laid the modern foundations of French cinema, including the principle of a degree of state control, box-office levy, and help to 'non-commercial' cinema which, in the long run, ensured its livelihood. Substantial efforts were also made to rebuild and modernize France's cinemas. In terms of film culture too, the Liberation sowed the seeds of modern cinema, with the rise of the ciné-club movement, under the aegis of André Bazin, probably the most influential French film critic. Bazin, a Catholic, taught at IDHEC and worked in the Communist Travail et Culture group, which brought film education to working-class people, and he wrote

Gérard Philipe (right) in Christian-Jaque's *Fanfan la Tulipe* (1951)

incisive film criticism in many journals, including *L'Écran français* and *Esprit*. He co-founded *Les Cahiers du cinéma* in 1951; the paper quickly became a forum for François Truffaut, Jacques Rivette, Eric Rohmer, and Jean-Luc Godard, the future New Wave directors (though Bazin did not always share their views). But despite these new beginnings, old structures reasserted themselves, and the French film industry soon faced a number of problems, in particular the reappearance of American films on the French market. To make matters worse, the Blum–Byrnes trade agreements (1946), as part of the settlement of the French war debt to the USA, granted generous import quotas to American films, in exchange for US imports of French luxury goods. In the end, though, the balance of French versus American films was not very different from its pre-war level, and was roughly suited to the production capacity.

French film production in fact went back to its 100–120 films yearly average in the early 1950s, helped by co-productions, especially with Italy. From the late 1940s to the late 1950s, French cinema reached its period of greatest stability and greatest popularity. French audiences peaked in 1957, with 400 million spectators, while they had started declining elsewhere immediately after the war; television was not a significant rival until the 1960s. The industry was better organized, studios better equipped, and they could call on a large reserve of highly skilled professionals, many of whom had worked since the 1920s and 1930s. Alexander Trauner, Jean d'Eaubonne, Léon Barsacq, Max Douy, and Georges Wakhewitch built wonderful décors, baroque constructions like those of Ophuls's *La Ronde* ('Merry-go-round', 1950), or stylized ones, as in Clair's *Les Grandes Manœuvres* (1955). Cinematographers like Henri Alekan, Armand Thirard, or Christian Matras were in high demand, their polished photography one of the hallmarks of what came to be named (often dismissively) the 'tradition of quality'. Scriptwriters kept up the pre-war taste for sparkling repartee; Prévert wrote a few scripts, but this was the era of Jeanson, Jean Aurenche and Pierre Bost, and Michel Audiard. Aurenche and Bost, who specialized in literary adaptations, became especially associated with the tradition of quality. Some pre-war directors—Clair, Duvivier, Renoir, Carné, Ophuls—were back at work, joined by those who had come to prominence during the war, in particular Jacques Becker (*Dernier Atout*, 1942; *Goupi Mains-rouges*, 1943; *Falbalas*, 1945), Autant-Lara, Christian-Jaque, Clouzot, and Clément. It is the slickness and technical virtuosity of this cinema, as well as its literary origins, that the young François Truffaut violently criticized, in his 1954 article in *Les Cahiers du cinéma*, 'A certain tendency of French cinema' (Truffaut 1976). This notorious article had a lasting influence on the way the history of the period has been written, but its conclusions

need re-examining. With hindsight, the fact that French cinema had reached its pinnacle of stability and craftsmanship (as in the Hollywood which Truffaut admired), in short its classicism, is to be celebrated and explored, rather than dismissed.

Truffaut also found the dark moral climate of many of these films objectionable. And indeed, the French noir tradition was much in evidence in the 1940s and 1950s, even though Poetic Realism proper was on the wane. If its final triumph had been *Les Enfants du paradis*, *Les portes de la nuit* ('The gates of night', 1946) was its coda. Carné and Prévert's re-creation of a popular area of Paris, in which the legacy of the German occupation intertwines with 'fate', flopped. Other films, however, took up the gloomy strand of Poetic Realism and extended it, presenting characters who were not only doomed, but lived dismal, often evil, lives, in films that also looked very dark: in particular those of Yves Allégret (*Dédée d'Anvers*, 1948; *Une si jolie petite plage* ('Such a pretty little beach'), 1949; *Manèges* ('Stratagems'), 1950) and Henri-Georges Clouzot (*Quai des Orfèvres*, 1947; *Le Salaire de la peur* (*The Wages of Fear*), 1953; *Les Diaboliques* ('The devilish ones'), 1955; *La Vérité* ('Truth'), 1960), as well as Carné's own *Thérèse Raquin* (1953), starring Simone Signoret. Others focused on a more sociological critique of French *mœurs* (morals and class practices), for example *Les Grandes Familles* ('Grand families', 1958), and adaptations of Georges Simenon's novels such as *La Vérité sur Bébé Donge* ('The truth about Bébé Donge', 1951) and *En cas de malheur* ('In case of misfortune', 1958). But this tradition also fed into the rise of the new French thriller (or *policier*). This renaissance of the genre was also inspired by the enormous success of crime literature, fuelled anew by Marcel Duhamel's publishing imprint Série Noire, as well as the popular Eddie Constantine spoof thrillers like *La Môme Vert-de-gris* (1953). Some 1930s films, such as Renoir's *La Nuit du carrefour* ('The night at the crossroads', 1932) and Chenal's *Le Dernier Tournant*, as well as Clouzot's *L'Assassin habite au 21* and *Quai des Orfèvres*, had prefigured the genre. However, its proper 'birth' belongs to Jacques Becker's 1953 *Touchez pas au grisbi* ('Don't touch the loot'), a distant adaptation of Série Noire writer Albert Simonin, and Jean-Pierre Melville's 1955 *Bob le flambeur* ('Bob the gambler'). Both films codified the genre, in which, typically, ageing gangsters and their 'families' of male friends pursue 'les girls' in Montmartre cabarets, and haunt the cobbled streets of Paris in glistening black Citroëns.

But if, as in the 1930s, the noir tradition and the thriller are the best-known aspects of French cinema abroad, costume dramas and comedies were the mainstay of the popular cinema at home. Sumptuous period reconstructions (some with the novelty of colour), often based on literary classics, demanded studio work and careful planning, as well as big stars: Gérard Philipe, Martine

Jacques Tati

(1908–1982)

Stiff-legged, straight-backed, pipe thrusting up into space, the archetypal Tati character stalked into the cinema with *Les Vacances de M. Hulot* (1953). Determined to enjoy himself at a seaside resort, he doggedly pursues tennis, riding, camping, and country drives. Gravely polite to other vacationers, he is utterly oblivious to the ways he disrupts their placid routines. As M. Hulot, Tati seemed at a stroke to have revived pure pantomimic comedy, finally providing sound cinema with its equivalent of Chaplin or Keaton.

Trained as an athlete, Tati became a music-hall star on the strength of his sporting pantomimes. He also played an unexpectedly dashing ghost in *Sylvie et le fantôme* (Claude Autant-Lara, 1945). His short *L'École des facteurs* (1947; the first film he directed) led to *Jour de fête* (1949), his first feature and a harbinger of what was to come. Tati plays François, a provincial postman who sees a newsreel on US methods of mail delivery and decides to modernize his methods ('Rapidité, rapidité!'). This premiss yields a host of gags in which François's new-found efficiency sows tumult in the village households. There is also a virtuoso sequence in which Tati's inebriated postman tries to bicycle home at night and winds up pedalling frantically astride a fence. Beyond the comedian's turns, however, Tati began to conceive of a film in which the surrounding milieu harbours endless comic possibilities. Unlike Chaplin, he generously gives major gags to minor characters.

From *Jour de fête* it was a short step to *Les Vacances* and the Hulot character. Again, the film centres on the comedian, but Tati's gags are even more 'democratic'—spread across dozens of vacationers and tradespeople. He begins to multiply gags within the frame, so that one will be paying off in the centre foreground while another is being set up in the distance. He also initiates a bold use of pauses and silence, creating a humour of stillness and hiatuses, sharpened by enigmatic looks. Above all, Tati introduces new comic possibilities with his use of sound effects. The flick of a riding crop, the career of a ping-pong ball, the bong of a swinging door, and the glub of a fountain pen dropping into an aquarium gain a new prominence.

Even more successful commercially was *Mon oncle* (1958), which won a special jury prize at Cannes and an Academy Award. M. Hulot lives in a pleasantly run-down quarter of Paris. His sister's family, however, lives in a hideously modern home. The electronic garage, the windows that resemble eyeballs, and the paralysingly inhospitable furniture become obvious targets of Tati's satire. Tati begins to stage entire scenes in long shot, letting the architecture frame the gags and letting the audience search for the action.

Convinced of his popularity, Tati gambled everything on *Play Time* (1967), his boldest experiment. On a vacant lot outside Paris he built a miniature city. The film had virtually no plot—merely the visit of a group of American tourists to Paris. Hulot became less central; Tati asked the viewer to watch strangers drift through a grey landscape of steel and glass. Gags abort; they compete for our attention; some can scarcely be called gags at all, merely oddities or quirks. The climactic sequence in the rapidly disintegrating Royal Garden restaurant—about forty-five minutes of continuous comic mayhem—runs the gamut from centred and obvious gags to quirky bits tucked into the distance or in a corner of the frame. Tati spared no expense, using colour, 70 mm., and stereophonic sound in order to produce a dazzling open field of humour, a 'play time' asking the viewer to pay attention at every instant.

Audiences proved reluctant to do so. *Play Time* proved a failure from which his finances never recovered. He hastily made *Trafic* (1971), a satire on car culture in which Hulot was far more prominent, and followed it with *Parade* (1973), a pseudo-documentary of circus acts for Swedish television. In these, as in the more ambitious works, Tati created a comedy which blended the popular appeal of the slapstick classics with modernist experimentation no less challenging than that of Antonioni or Resnais.

DAVID BORDWELL

SELECT FILMOGRAPHY

L'École des facteurs (1947); Jour de fête (1949); Les Vacances de M. Hulot (Mr Hulot's Holiday) (1953); Mon oncle (1958); Play Time (1967); Trafic (Traffic) (1971); Parade (1973)

BIBLIOGRAPHY

Agel, Geneviève (1955), *Hulot parmi nous*.
Chion, Michel (1987), *Jacques Tati*.
Fischer, Lucy (1983), *Jacques Tati: A Guide to References and Resources*.
Harding, James (1984), *Jacques Tati: Frame by Frame*.
Kermabon, Jacques (1988), *Les Vacances de M. Hulot*.

Jacques Tati as the indefatigable Monsieur Hulot in *Les vacances de M. Hulot* (*Mr Hulot's Holiday*, 1953)

Carol, Michèle Morgan, and Micheline Presle became the main leads in the genre, as Jean Gabin and Lino Ventura were those of the thriller. Costume dramas were so pervasive that not only mainstream directors worked in it, but the great *auteurs* did too. Renoir triumphed with *French Cancan* (1954), Clair with *Les Grandes Manœuvres*, and Ophuls with *La Ronde* and *Le Plaisir* ('Pleasure', 1951). The generic conventions were flexible enough to accommodate individual *auteurs'* thematic or stylistic projects, such as Jacqueline Audry's study of lesbian relationships in *Olivia* (1950, with Edwige Feuillère). Jacques Becker's *Casque d'or*, set in the turn-of-the-century milieu of pimps and prostitutes, was not a popular success, perhaps because of its understated style, but since then Simone Signoret's performance and its heart-breaking romantic narrative have turned it into a classic. Other costume dramas were among the box-office hits of the 1950s: *Fanfan la Tulipe* (1951), *Les Belles de nuit* ('Night-time beauties', 1952), *Le Rouge et le noir* ('Scarlet and black', 1954), and *Potbouille* ('In common', 1957) (all four starring Gérard Philipe as the romantic hero, his delicate handsomeness well served by costumes), as well as *Gervaise* (1955), *Les Misérables* (1958), and *Nana* (1954). The latter film starred Martine Carol, then the biggest female star, who projected smouldering sexuality in other 'risqué' costume films like *Caroline chérie* ('Darling Caroline', 1950), or light-hearted comedies about frivolous Parisian milieux and fashion (*Adorables créatures* ('Adorable creatures'), 1952; *Nathalie*, 1957). In the mid-1950s, Carol was displaced as top French sex goddess by Brigitte Bardot, whose gamine sexuality and insolence had a far greater impact on the culture. 'BB' rose to fame in Roger Vadim's *Et Dieu créa la femme* (*And God Created Woman*, 1956), but the young actress also starred in comedies (*En effeuillant la marguerite* ('Destroying the daisy', 1956); *Une Parisienne* ('A Parisian woman', 1957)). In this, however, she and Carol were exceptions, as the genre was predominantly male. Comic stars included Noël-Noël, Darry Cowl, and Francis Blanche; the 1950s likewise saw the rise of one of the biggest French comics, Bourvil, who imposed his 'country bumpkin' persona in films like *La Traversée de Paris* ('Crossing Paris', 1956) and *La Jument verte* ('The green mare', 1959). It was also the apex of Fernandel's career. Fernandel's humour, like that of many French comics, was largely inexportable because steeped in French social structures and language, but at home he swept the box-office with Henri Verneuil's *La Vache et le prisonnier* ('The cow and the prisoner', 1959), a comedy about a French prisoner of war in Germany who tries, ineffectually, to escape with a cow, and the Franco-Italian *Don Camillo* series (five films directed by Julien Duvivier, starting in 1951), in which he is the priest of a little Italian village, talking to God and fighting with the Communist mayor.

In the comedy stakes, Fernandel did not export well, but Jacques Tati did, for he was an actor-*auteur* in the mould of early silent stars like Max Linder and Charlie Chaplin. Tati's humour was close to slapstick, using his uncoordinated body to hilarious effect, and reducing language to grunts and gibberish, in *Jour de fête* ('Holiday', 1949), *Monsieur Hulot's holiday* (*Les Vacances de Monsieur Hulot*, 1951), and *Mon oncle* (1958). But Tati's originality was also that he was working on the margins of the film industry, using more location shooting than was then customary, working with small teams, and clearly pursuing a personal line. Other such figures began to appear in the post-war period: Agnès Varda (*La Pointe courte*, 1954), Alain Resnais (*Hiroshima mon amour*), Robert Bresson (who had started during the war with *Les Anges du péché* ('The angels of sin'), 1943, and *Les Dames du Bois de Boulogne* ('The ladies of the Bois de Boulogne', 1945), and went on to make *The Diary of a Country Priest* (*Le Journal d'un curé de campagne*, 1951)), Jean-Pierre Melville (*Bob le flambeur*), and Louis Malle (*Ascenseur pour l'échafaud* ('Lift to the scaffold'), 1957; *Les Amants* ('The lovers'), 1958). These directors were extremely disparate aesthetically and ideologically, but they were connected by their difference from, and opposition to, the mainstream industry. Their independence, their emphasis on personal vision, and the relative austerity of their filmic practice marked them as true *auteurs* (in Truffaut's terms), providing counter-models for the young critics at *Cahiers du cinéma* who aspired to direct. It is in this sense that they can all be cited as precursors of (Varda, Resnais, Malle), or models for (Bresson, Melville), the New Wave.

The late 1950s saw the end of the retrograde Fourth Republic, and the new era of General de Gaulle's Fifth Republic, heralding the true modern France. To this political and economic sea-change corresponded the filmic upheaval of the New Wave. The polemical style of its practitioners called for a *tabula rasa* of French cinema, dismissing in its wake most of the previous twenty years as stilted and formulaic, and French film as inferior to Hollywood, with one or two exceptions such as Jean Renoir. If this rejection made sense in terms of these ambitious young men's desire to displace the 'cinéma de papa' (daddy's cinema), it does not historically. Over 3,000 films were made in France between 1930 and 1960, encompassing both the greatest auteurist achievements and enduring popular genres; indeed, one of the characteristics of the period is that great *auteurs* worked for a mainstream audience. The New Wave brought a breath of fresh air and produced memorable, innovative films. It signalled the increased importance of *auteur* cinema in the face of declining audiences. But its own achievements partly stemmed from the strength of the industry, film culture, and film style New Wave directors reacted against. The era of the popular, classical French cinema has gone, but many of its structures, great artists, and popular performers live on.

Bibliography
Armes, Roy (1985), *French Cinema*.
Bandy, Mary Lea (ed.) (1983), *Rediscovering French Film*.
Hayward, Susan (1993), *French National Cinema*.

—— and Vincendeau, Ginette (eds.) (1990), *French Film, Texts and Contexts*.
Truffaut, François (1954), 'A Certain tendency of French cinema'.
Williams, Alan (1992), *Republic of Images: A History of French Film-making*.

Italy from Fascism to Neo-Realism

MORANDO MORANDINI

CINEMA IN THE FASCIST PERIOD

The first sound film made in Italy was *La canzone dell'amore* ('The love song', 1930) by Gennaro Righelli, taken from a short story by Pirandello entitled, ironically enough, 'In silenzio' ('In silence'). Italian cinema in 1930 was in a parlous state. Of the 1,750 films produced between 1919 and 1930, it would be difficult, even with hindsight, to pick out one which achieved even minimal international success. When pushed, cinema historians usually point to a couple of silent films of 1929, by two of the most important directors of the following decade: *Sole* ('Sun'), Alessandro Blasetti's first film; and *Rotaie* ('Rails') by Mario Camerini, which was released in a sound version in 1931.

Mussolini's Fascist movement had come to power in October 1922 and by 1925 had established a totalitarian state. In 1926 it intervened for the first time in the field of cinema, taking over the Istituto Nazionale LUCE—acronym for '*L'Unione Cinematografica Educativa*', the National Institute of the Union of Cinematography and Education—formed in 1924. The regime thus created for itself a monopoly of cinematic information: LUCE produced documentaries and also newsreels, and projection of the latter was made compulsory.

The first Italian sound films were produced at the Itala and Cines studios in Rome, which had been purchased by Stefano Pittaluga, following his acquisition in 1926 of the Turinese company Fert. All the eight films produced in 1930 were the work of Cines–Pittaluga. Pittaluga was an energetic and intelligent entrepreneur, surrounded by peers who were often hasty, incompetent, and amateurish. But he died suddenly in the spring of 1931, at the age of 44, leaving behind him a powerful circuit of interests: a production company, acting studios, technical laboratories, a distribution organization, and a vast chain of outlets all over Italy.

His empire was split into two parts: one for the distribution and exhibition of films, which went into state ownership, forming the basis of ENIC; the other for production and the running of studios. The latter was put into the hands of a banker, Ludovico Toeplitz, who in 1932 appointed the writer and essayist Emilio Cecchi as head of production. In 1935 the Cines studio on Via Vejo in Rome was gutted by a fire and had to be demolished. Cines thus collapsed for the second time, although it was later to be re-formed twice, in 1942 and 1949. With the exception of the official sanctioning of censorship in law in 1923, which was honed and 'perfected' in a series of modifications up to 1929, the Istituto LUCE, and some protectionist measures, the active impact of the Fascist regime on cinema was late in coming, although it perhaps indirectly encouraged the centripetal pull of Rome on the industry. In the first twenty years of silent cinema, the film industry, or rather the film craft, had been spread out between Turin, Milan, Rome, and Naples. Whilst the early history of North American cinema is characterized by the shift from New York to Los Angeles, from east to west, in Italy cinema gravitated towards the centre of political and bureaucratic power.

The first legislative support for the industry came from Law 918 (18 June 1931), which assigned 10 per cent of box-office takings to 'aid all sectors of the film industry and, in particular, to reward those with a proven ability to cater for the tastes of the public'. As in other fields, the Fascist regime and the industry were in full agreement: profit above all.

On a more cultural note, the eighteenth Venice 'Biennale' exhibition of figurative arts began on 6 August 1932, and included the world's first film festival, officially designated as the 'First International Exhibition of Cinematic Art'. The idea was born in Venice, but already in 1934 its organization had been taken over by the authorities in Rome.

In 1933 it became obligatory to show one Italian film for every three foreign films. The year 1934 saw the creation of the Direzione Generale per la Cinematografia, headed by Luigi Freddi, which was given the task of overseeing and co-ordinating production activity. In 1935 the film school Centro Sperimentale di Cinematografia was set up under the aegis of the Ministry of Popular Culture, with Luigi

Ancient Rome as a prescursor of Mussolini's Italy: Carmine Gallone's *Scipione l'Africano* (1937)

Chiarini in control. It moved into its own premises in January 1940. In April 1937 the Cinecittà studios were opened, having inherited the equipment which had been salvaged from the Cines fire of 1935.

Despite Mussolini's slogan, paraphrasing Lenin—'For us cinema is the strongest weapon'—the real question to ask, then, is why the Fascist regime took so long to arrive at these interventionist measures? One can hazard two complementary responses. On the one hand, active intervention followed the example of Nazi Germany, where Hitler and his Minister of Propaganda Goebbels had not hesitated to take control of cinema. On the other hand, Fascist policy in cinema merely reflected the regime's ideological inconsistency, its hasty compromises, and chameleon-like pragmatism ably adapted to any and all necessities. As in other sectors of cultural life, Fascist influence was primarily negative, preventive, and repressive. Rather than forcing artists and intellectuals into prescribed political positions, Fascism merely worked to divert their interest away from present-day reality, which was to be the exclusive preserve of politicians. Hence, after

1930, there were only four films made about the 'Fascist revolution'—its origins in 'squads' and their march on Rome of October 1922, which was in actual fact more of a stroll. These were: *Camicia nera* ('Blackshirt', 1933) by Gioacchino Forzano; *Aurora sul mare* ('Dawn over the sea', 1935) by Giorgio C. Simonelli; *Vecchia guardia* ('Old Guard', 1935) by Alessandro Blasetti; and *Redenzione* ('Redemption', 1942) by Marcello Albani, adapted from a play by Roberto Farinacci, the so-called 'ras di Cremona', a Fascist 'ultra' and one of Mussolini's henchmen.

Only the third of the four merits attention, because of Blasetti's generous and honest commitment to the ideology of the regime. The same good faith was apparent in his other works: in *Sole* (1929) and in *Terra madre* ('Mother Earth', 1930)—rare examples for the period of films set against a realistic social, rural backdrop—and in the militaristic rhetoric of *Aldebaran* (1936) and the nationalist and Francophobe sentiment of *Ettore Fieramosca* (1938).

Fascist propaganda is also evident in around thirty other films (out of 722 produced between 1930 and 1943), and these may be divided into four categories:

1. Patriotic and/or military films: from documentary footage of the First World War to *Scarpe al sole* ('Shoes in the sun', 1935); from *Cavalleria* ('Cavalry', 1936) to *Luciano Serra pilota* (1938) by Goffredo Alessandrini; from films about aviation to films about the navy, including two war films—Commander Francesco De Robertis's semi-documentary *Uomini sul fondo* ('Men in the deep', 1941) and Roberto Rossellini's *La nave bianca* ('The white ship', 1941).
2. Films about Italy's 'African mission': from Roberto San Marzano's documentary about Ethiopia, *A.O. dal Giuba allo Scioa*, to a series of films in the wake of its conquest: *Squadrone bianco* ('White squadron', 1936) by Augusto Genina, *Il grande appello* ('The great appeal', 1936) by Camerini, *Sentinelle di bronzo* ('Bronze sentries', 1937) by Romolo Marcellini, *Abuna Messias* (1939) by Alessandrini.
3. Costume dramas: history rewritten as a parade of precursors of the 'Duce'. The major exemplars are *Scipione l'Africano* ('Scipio the African', 1937) by Carmine Gallone and *Condottieri* ('Soldiers of fortune') by Luis Trenker, who came from near the Austrian border and had previous experience as an actor in German cinema. Both were genuine epics, made in the same year with the backing of ENIC and a total budget of 20 million lire.
4. Anti-Bolshevik and anti-Soviet propaganda films: these include two films on the Spanish Civil War, both from 1939: *L'assedio dell'Alcazar* ('The siege of the Alcazar') by Genina, made with powerful choral elements, and the less polished *Carmen tra i rossi* ('Carmen and the Reds') by Edgar Neville, who went on to direct *Sancta Maria* (1941). Other films in this category are *L'uomo della croce* ('Man of the cross', 1943) by Rossellini, *Odessa in fiamme* ('Odessa in flames', 1942) by Gallone, and *Odissea di sangue* ('Blood odyssey', 1942) by Righelli. Alessandrini's turgid romantic diptych *Noi vivi* / *Addio, Kira* ('We the living' / 'Farewell, Kira', 1942), adapted from novels by Ayn Rand, is a somewhat different case, since it is Stalinism rather than Communism itself which is attacked.

The 'official' cinema of the twenty-year period of Fascist rule aspired to be virile, heroic, revolutionary, and celebratory, but it only represented 5 per cent of national production: superstructure rather than base. The base was bourgeois, or better petty bourgeois, and Janus-faced, divided between family and Empire, between sentimentalism and grandiloquence, between 'dopolavoro' (the 'after-work' workers' clubs set up by the regime) and the military. At the highest level of achievement, these two faces are reflected by the two most important directors of the 1930s: Mario Camerini and Alessandro Blasetti.

Camerini's films appear modest, toned down, marked by a careful attention to detail, a graceful sense of irony, and a European mastery of the techniques of expression. His are shrewd descriptions of the middle and lower middle classes which reveal the customs and habits of the time, to the extent that some have maintained that, had it not been for his collaboration with scriptwriter Cesare Zavattini, De Sica's post-war work would have been but a pale imitation of Camerini.

Two of his comedies—*Gli uomini, che mascalzoni* ... ('Men, what scoundrels! ...', 1932) and *Il signor Max* (1937), both starring De Sica—stand up to comparison with Lubitsch or the Renoir of *La Règle du jeu* (1939), as has been argued recently by Manuel Puig. And at least two of his other films—*Darò un milione* ('I'll give a million', 1935), with screenplay by Cesare Zavattini, and *Una romantica avventura* ('A romantic adventure', 1940)—are works of international class. For *Gli uomini, che mascalzoni* ..., Camerini took the camera out of the studio and on to the streets of Milan, amongst the stands and the people of the commercial fair, thus anticipating a tendency of post-war neo-realism. Location scenes of street life are also a feature of the first film by Raffaello Matarazzo, the little-known *Treno popolare* ('People's train', 1933), which was only rediscovered at the end of the 1970s by a younger generation of critics.

Blasetti's career was less consistently successful and more eclectic than Camerini's. His best films were *1860* (1934), a moving, crisp, and anti-rhetorical reconstruction of the early days of Garibaldi's 'Thousand', and *Un'avventura di Salvator Rosa* ('An adventure for Salvator Rosa', 1940), a witty and perspicacious portrait of the seventeenth-century poet and painter. He also made films of a heroic and grandiloquent kind, most apparent in grand spectacles such as *La corona di ferro* ('The iron crown', 1941) and, after the war, *Fabiola* (1949); and he displayed a more low-key and realistic vein in *La tavola dei poveri* ('The table of the poor', 1932) and, most successfully, in *Quattro passi tra le nuvole* ('A stroll up in the clouds', 1942), written by Zavattini.

Despite the individual talent of figures like Blasetti and Camerini, the driving force behind Italian cinema remained the escapist film, or as Luchino Visconti had it in a 1943 polemic, 'a cinema of corpses'. Its style was much closer than is commonly acknowledged to Hollywood products of the same period: it split into distinct genres; it relied on the cult of stars; and it cultivated, with only occasional success, the image of the director as a professional and author-figure. In this sector, the most significant player by far was Emilio Cecchi's Cines, which was the only production company to resemble a Hollywood-style studio, but which is also noteworthy for its attempt to reconcile experimental innovation with the demands of business, individual creativity with mass production. The principal genres were comedy, melodrama, and costume-cum-historical drama. The comedies were for the most part sentimental, and after 1937 increasingly frivolous and vacuous, based on a rejection of reality in

Totò

(1898–1967)

Antonio de Curtis Gagliardi Griffo Focas Comneno di Bisanzio, alias Totò, first trod the boards in his native Naples in 1917, achieved early success in the 1920s, and became the leader of a review company in 1933. And many of his film performances derive directly from his days in the theatre. Between 1937 and 1967, he made ninety-seven films in all, excluding the eight unfinished films for television, which were broadcast posthumously in 1968. Picking out the best is no easy task: in the words of critic Goffredo Fofi (1977), only an anthology from all his films of the best sketches and scenes would do him justice. Indeed, *Totò a colori* ('Totò in colour', 1952) is already such an anthology.

In the rich panorama of Italian cinema, Totò is a unique phenomenon. In the opinion of script-writer and critic Ennio Flaiano, he did not exist in real life, nor was he a type or a character from the *commedia dell'arte* tradition, even if he mastered its techniques and gags: he only ever played and represented himself. A clown of genius, who drew on both ancient and modern models, and was at times obscene and cruel, at others an intensely humane puppet, an eccentric mannequin, a comic chameleon, an astonishing and inimitable mime, Totò's comedy verges on the metaphysical, according to Flaiano. He does not play characters, but represents imponderables, from the improbable to the grotesque.

His most important influences were undoubtedly Neapolitan, from the tradition of Pulcinella to his great predecessor Scarpetta. In due course, he also played his part in neo-realism—in De Sica and Zavattini's *L'oro di Napoli* ('The gold of Naples', 1954), in Eduardo De Filippo's *Napoli milionaria* ('Millionaire Naples', 1950), and in Steno and Monicelli's *Totò cerca casa* ('Totò goes house-hunting', 1949), and *Guardie e ladri* ('Guards and robbers', 1951). *Totò e Carolina*, made in 1953, was blocked by the censor and released with cuts only in 1955. He worked with Rossellini in *Dov'è la libertà?* ('Where is liberty?', 1952), and, shortly before his death, was cast by Pasolini in two short films and in *Uccellacci e uccellini* ('Hawks and Sparrows', 1966). Totò played a great range of characters, at times of high literary and theatrical origin—from Pirandello, Campanile, Moravia, Martoglio, Marotta, Eduardo De Filippo, and even Machiavelli—but always remained essentially himself, showing up the absurdity of his presence in each of the imaginary worlds he frequented. At the 1970 conference which marked his rediscovery and re-evaluation by a new generation, the director Mario Monicelli confessed that it had been a mistake to play up the humane side of Totò, and thereby to clip his creative wings. The true power and genius of his comedy lay in its dark, inhuman aspect.

Totò's brand of comedy did not travel well. A number of his films were released, dubbed (and losing much of the verbal humour), in Spain and Latin America, but in

The Italian comic Totò in Steno and Monicelli's *Guardie e ladri* (1951)

the English-speaking world he remains unknown, except for his occasional appearances in 'art' films and in Monicelli's *I soliti ignoti* (US: *Big Deal on Madonna Street*). Towards the end of his career, his eyesight began to fail, but once on the set he continued to perform with unfailing professionalism, a sombre, dapper figure, precise in his movements and unpredictable only in the strange intensity he gave to each and every role.

MORANDO MORANDINI

BIBLIOGRAPHY

Fofi, Goffredo (1977), *Totò: l'uomo e la maschera*.

favour of anaemic, dissipated characters who live in an absurd excess of luxury and who talk to each other via the shining 'white telephones' which gave their name to the genre. The direction was minimal, and always secondary to the set and its furnishings, and to the taste for window-shopping.

The era of the 'white telephones' coincided with, and was a direct effect of, the steady increase in the volume of production. In 1937, when Mussolini ordered that 'one hundred films a year' should be the target, only thirty-two feature-length films were made. The following year, when the government suddenly passed a law setting limits on the importing of American films, provoking the pull-out of the Big Four—MGM, Warners, Fox, and Paramount—production leapt to 60 titles, and then to 87 in 1940 and 120 in 1942.

This growth fed the power of the star actors: on top of the group of early 1930s stars—Vittorio De Sica, Assia Noris, Elsa Merlini, Maria Denis, Isa Miranda—came new names such as Amedeo Nazzari and Alida Valli, Osvaldo Valenti and Luisa Ferida, Fosco Giachetti, Clara Calamai, Doris Duranti, and so on.

Around 1940, two new trends in film-making emerged. The first, represented by film-makers such as Mario Soldati, Alberto Lattuada, Renato Castellani, and Luigi Chiarini, returned to the literature of the nineteenth century or to the 'art prose' of contemporary writing. The second attempted to create deep links between film and reality, looking to documentary forms and to the Soviet cinema as with De Robertis's *Uomini sul fondo*, or to the French school as with *La peccatrice* ('The sinner', 1940) and *Fari nella nebbia* ('Lights in the fog', 1942), by Gianni Franciolini.

Ferdinando Maria Poggioli, whom recent critics have tended to set alongside Camerini and Blasetti in importance, belongs to the first trend, but has many affinities with the second also. He was less cultured than Lattuada and Soldati, less refined than Castellani, but he was able to construct stronger narrative lines than others. *Gelosia* ('Jealousy', 1942), *Le sorelle Materassi* ('The Materassi sisters', 1943), and *Il cappello del prete* ('The priest's hat', 1943) are exemplary adaptations of literary texts. *Sissignora* ('Yes, Ma'am', 1941) is a minor but unusual work which combines a sentimental story-line with realist elements and a certain formalist inspiration.

In the war years, reality inevitably loomed large, and the screenwriters, directors, technicians, and actors who were to be the protagonists of the new realist cinema after 1945 were already working. Three films made during the war revealed the hidden face of an Italy in deep crisis—*Quattro passi tra le nuvole*, by Blasetti (1942); *I bambini ci guardano* ('The children are watching us', 1942), by De Sica; and above all *Ossessione* (1943) by Visconti. All three were already works of opposition.

LIBERATION AND NEO-REALISM

With *Rome Open City* (*Roma città aperta*, 1945), shot by Rossellini between 1944 and 1945 in haphazard conditions with economic and practical difficulties of all kinds, Italy returned to the forefront of world cinema. Shortly thereafter, the catch-all term 'neo-realism' became current. It had already been used in the 1930s with reference to literature and the figurative arts. According to Luchino Visconti, the first person to apply it to cinema was the editor Mario Serandrei in 1943, referring to *Ossessione*. Rather than a school—the French labelled it 'l'école italienne de la Libération'—or an artistic current, neo-realism was part of a general turn towards realism in cinema of the time, providing a new way of looking at and representing the reality of war-torn Italy and of the Resistance. It was distinguished not only by its head-on confrontation of the collective problems of the moment, but also by the impulse to suggest a positive solution to those problems and to marry the causes of individuals and of society 'as people wanted it to be'.

At the heart of the implicit ideology of neo-realism lies the positive and generous, if a little generic, desire for a profound renewal of people and society. Hence some have suggested that its base values are humanistic, and that it is therefore inaccurate to talk of a Marxist or revolutionary hegemony behind the films. After all, the renewal of people and things is far from socialist transformation, and fraternity is not the same as class solidarity. Only a few films provided even a latently Marxist vision of reality: *Il sole sorge ancora* ('The sun still rises') by Aldo Vergano, and *La terra trema* ('The earth shakes') by Visconti, both made in 1948. The former, produced by the ANPI—National Association of Italian Partisans—used both propaganda and melodrama to elucidate the class structure of Italy (represented by a Lombard village) under German occupation. The latter was Visconti's free adaptation of Giovanni Verga's famous novel *I Malavoglia* (1881), which narrates the struggles of a family of Sicilian fishermen to free itself from poverty and exploitation.

Most of the directors, screen-writers, and technicians involved in neo-realism had years of experience behind them. De Sica's debt to Camerini is evident, as is Rossellini's to the technical expertise of De Robertis. Another crucial influence was the broadening of cultural horizons carried out by Umberto Barbaro and Luigi Chiarini at the Centro Sperimentale and in the journals *Bianco e nero* (founded in 1937) and *Cinema* (1936), whose contributors included future writers and directors such as Carlo Lizzani, Giuseppe De Santis, Gianni Puccini, and Antonio Pietrangeli. Another group centred on the restless cultural atmosphere of Milan, and included Alberto Lattuada, Luigi Comencini, and Dino Risi. Also foreign influences were far from negligible: French realism (above all Jean

Renoir), Soviet cinema, and American narrative (Elio Vittorini's 1941 anthology *Americana* contributed much to the 'myth of America' current in the unofficial culture of the last years of Fascism).

The most significant figure, and the most original director, of the neo-realist movement was Roberto Rossellini, and his greatest films were *Paisà* (1946) and *Germany Year Zero* (*Germania anno zero*, 1947). He was also the first to distance himself from it to follow a more private, psychological path, more wedded to ethics than to society. Apart from Rossellini's 'war trilogy', a list of the major works of neo-realism would include at least three films by De Sica—*Sciuscià* ('Shoeshine', 1946), *Bicycle Thieves* (*Ladri di biciclette*, 1948), and *Umberto D* (1952)—and two by Visconti (*La terra trema*, 1948, and *Bellissima*, 1951). Rather than setting up a hierarchy of values, one can point to the various forms which neo-realism adopted: Giuseppe De Santis's social polemic with the rhythm of social melodrama in *Bitter Rice* (*Riso amaro*, 1949); Luigi Zampa's moralistic polemic in *Vivere in pace* ('To live in peace', 1946); Renato Castellani's comic proletarian sketches *Sotto il sole di Roma* ('Beneath the Roman sun', 1948) and *Due soldi di speranza* ('Two pennyworth of hope', 1951); Pietro Germi's novelesque naturalism, aping the style of American cinema in *In nome della legge* ('In the name of the law', 1949) and *Il cammino della speranza* ('The way of hope', 1950); the populist fable of De Sica and Zavattini's *Miracolo a Milano* (1950); and the literary eclecticism of Alberto Lattuada in *Il bandito* ('The bandit', 1946) and *Senza pietà* ('Without pity', 1948).

Setting an end point to the development of neo-realist cinema has become a critical convention, as has the use of the term itself. For the writer and critic Franco Fortini, writing in 1953, however, the term is misconceived, and a better term would be 'neo-populism', since neo-realism expressed a 'vision of reality founded on the primacy of the "popular", with its corollaries of regionalism and dialect and its components of Christian and revolutionary socialism, naturalism, positivistic realism and humanitarianism'.

As far as an end point is concerned, if the parabola begins in 1945 with *Rome Open City*, it can be said to end with *Umberto D* in 1952. It very soon went into irreversible crisis for both external and internal reasons. Amongst the internal causes was an inadequate cultural hinterland. Four currents of thought had infiltrated post-war Italian intellectual life: Marxism, existentialism, sociology, and psychoanalysis. In neo-realism, there was some hint of the first and hardly any trace of the other three. Even its most original theorist, Cesare Zavattini, in proposing the rejection of character in favour of the 'true person', immersion in everyday life, and rejection of fantasy, led directors to forget history, and to lose the ability to capture on film the dialectical relations between the various components of reality. The aim to depict everyday life became an excuse for sketchiness, reality turned picturesque, fresh immediacy slipped into local colour (usually Roman or southern), and social commitment was eclipsed by folklore and the powerful but sparse Italian traditions of dialect theatre. Even in the best films, there is an air of the short story or fragment rather than the fully formed novel. In 1953, both the surviving neo-realist films, from ideas by Zavattini, were episode films: *Siamo donne* ('We the women') and *Amore in città* ('Love in the city'). With *Il tetto* ('The roof', 1955), by De Sica and Zavattini, we have entered the Arcadia of the movement.

Meanwhile, with *Francesco giullare di Dio* ('Francis, God's jester', 1950) and *Europa '51* (1951), Rossellini was setting out on the road which would lead him to *Viaggio in Italia* ('Journey to Italy', 1954), whereas Visconti's *Senso* (1954, released in Britain as *The Wanton Countess*) saw him following his vocation for melodrama. Indeed, in retrospect, it may seem untenable to group together under a single denomination directors as diverse as Rossellini, Visconti, De Sica, and others, but it is precisely their marked diversity in the years following neo-realism that proves there was some strong common cause, a cement which held them together for a time. And that cement was, in the last analysis, a product of the political, civic, and existential upheaval of the war and the passage from dictatorship to democracy, and its hopes, projects, and illusions of change.

There were also external causes for the failure of neo-realism. In 1948 the electoral victory of the Christian Democrats provoked the final collapse of the fragile anti-Fascist front which had been one of the ideological sources of the movement. The deep division of the country into two hostile camps was reinforced by the nascent Cold War hostility between the two superpowers. The 1950s brought the transformation of Italy from an agrarian into an industrial nation but also the accentuation of the economic and social imbalance between north and south.

The Christian Democrats' centrist politics used democratic legitimacy as an alibi rather than as a stimulus to civic responsibility. On the cultural level, the 1950s were marked by immobilism, clericalism, and by divisive conflict between two fronts. As a result neo-realist cinema was perceived as an art and culture of opposition, more than it ever was in reality, and, as such, it was targeted by the ruling class. The battle for and against it took on clear political and ideological features, rather than cultural and artistic; and in turn, this made it more difficult for its practitioners to make constructive revisions and developments in their style. Witness, for example, the reluctance of the left to take on board Rossellini's later style, and its distorted overestimation of a number of 'progressive' directors.

THE EASY YEARS

By many criteria, the 1950s were 'Gli anni facili'—the 'easy years', as the ironic title of Zampa's 1953 film had it—for Italian cinema. In 1955, the first year of television in Italy, box-office sales reached a peak of 819 million, never equalled before or since. The 25 films made in 1945 had already become 62 in 1946, 104 in 1950 and, with a high point of 201 in 1954, and a relative slump to 133 in 1955, reached 167 in 1959. With the avalanche of American films, often up to four or five years old, which flooded the market at the end of the war, home products took only a fraction of box-office takings, but nevertheless, the fraction grew from 13 per cent in the immediate post-war years to 34 per cent at the end of the 1950s, reaching 36 per cent in 1954 and edging towards a peak of 50 per cent at the end of the decade.

The era of the 'sex-pot' divas—Gina Lollobrigida, Silvana Mangano, Sophia Loren, Silvana Pampanini—took off. The genre of popular melodrama also scored notable successes through the work of its most important director, Raffaello Matarazzo—*Catene* ('Chains', 1949), *Tormento* (1951), *I figli di nessuno* ('Nobody's children', 1951), and also *Giuseppe Verdi* (1953)—and its most cherished actors, the couple Amedeo Nazzari and Yvonne Sanson. In comedy, there was the extraordinary phenomenon of Totò—the most inspired clown of the second half of the century—whose *Totò a colori* of 1955 was the first Italian film in Ferraniacolor, and the emergence of Alberto Sordi as a genuine archetype of the vices and virtues of the contemporary Italian. In the field of the epic costume drama, or 'supercolossus', Hollywood was challenged at its own game by Camerini's *Ulysses* (*Ulisse*, 1954) with Kirk Douglas, King Vidor's *War and Peace* (1956), Lattuada's *La tempesta* ('The tempest', 1958), and Henry Koster's *La Maja desnuda* (*The Naked Maja*, 1958). These films paved the way for the creation of a new genre, the historical-mythological film, initiated with *Le fatiche di Ercole* ('The labours of Hercules', 1958) by Pietro Francisci. There was also sustained success for the so-called 'neo-realismo rosa' (rose-tinted neo-realism), in the shape of Luigi Comencini's *Bread, Love and Dreams* (*Pane, amore e fantasia*, 1953) and Dino Risi's *Poveri ma belli* ('Poor but beautiful', 1956) among others.

During the 1950s, Cinecittà became known as the 'Hollywood on the Tiber', but the euphoria proved to be fragile and ephemeral. The industry would have to pay the price of a chaotic and excessive production system

Anna Magnani with the little Tina Apicella in Luchino Visconti's *Bellissima* (1951)

Vittorio De Sica

(1901–1974)

Best known outside Italy as the director of *Bicycle Thieves* (*Ladri di biciclette*, 1948), Vittorio De Sica had a long and varied career. Between 1940 and his death in 1973 he directed some thirty films, but he acted in no fewer than 150 between his emergence as a child actor in the early 1910s and his final appearance in Ettore Scola's *C'eravamo tanto amati* ('We all loved each other so much'), released in 1975. The key to understanding him lies in this long career as a professional actor, and in his constant display of amiability and narcissism. In the 1930s, after his success in Camerini's *Gli uomini, che mascalzoni...* ('Men, what scoundrels...', 1932), he became the top star of Italian sentimental comedy cinema, a 'charmeur' as both actor and singer. And he built not only his image as an actor on his sympathetic charm, but also his work as a director, in which, as Franco Pecori (1980) observes, 'the language of narcissism takes over and narrates its own history'.

His career as a director divides into four periods: (1) a preparatory phase (1940–4), with six films, including an important precursor of neo-realism, *I bambini ci guardano* ('The children are watching us', 1943), which also marked the beginning of his collaboration with the writer Cesare Zavattini. (2) A creative phase (1946–52), with four major films: *Sciuscià*, ('Shoeshine', 1946), *Bicycle Thieves*, *Miracolo a Milano* ('Miracle in Milan', 1950), and *Umberto D* (1952). The successes of this period can be put down to the balance between De Sica's careful direction, the use of non-professional actors, and the theoretical input of Zavattini, who championed a poetics of everyday life and of the normal man. (3) A period of compromise (1953–65), with eleven films of which the most critically successful were *L'oro di Napoli* ('The gold of Naples', 1954) and *Two Women* (*La ciociara*, 1960—for which Sophia Loren won an Oscar). (4) Decline (1966–74), with ten films. Of these only *The Garden of the Finzi-Continis* (*Il giardino dei Finzi-Contini*, 1971), whose elegiac beauty won it the Oscar for the Best Foreign Film, is at all memorable.

De Sica's collaboration with Zavattini stretched over twenty-three of his thirty-one films, but it remains unclear who was the brain and who the heart behind their work together. Any assessment of De Sica must acknowledge his undeniable expertise as an actor and as a director of actors. Aside from this talent, he managed to sustain in his films a natural, bourgeois elegance which reined in his at times excessive performing instincts. He also demonstrated an acute sensitivity which made him an unknowing prophet of the human sciences, and, finally, a certain degree of tenderness, which in later years verged on a sense of melancholy and a fear of loneliness.

MORANDO MORANDINI

SELECT FILMOGRAPHY

As actor
L'affare Clemenceau (1918); Gli uomini, che mascalzoni ... (1932); Darò un milione (1935); Il signor Max (1937); Madame de ... (1953); Pane, amore e fantasia (Bread, Love, and Dreams) (1953); Il generale Della Rovere (1959); C'eravamo tanto amati (1975)
As director
Teresa Venerdì (1941); I bambini ci guardano (1943); Sciuscià (Shoeshine) (1946); Ladri di biciclette (Bicycle Thieves / The Bicycle Thief) (1948); Miracolo a Milano (Miracle in Milan) (1950); Umberto D (1952); Stazione Termini (Indiscretion of an American Wife) (1953); L'oro di Napoli (1954); Il tetto (1955); La ciociara (Two Women) (1960); Boccaccio '70 (episode) (1961); Ieri, oggi, domani (Yesterday, Today, and Tomorrow) (1963); Il giardino dei Finzi-Contini (1971)

BIBLIOGRAPHY

Pecori, Franco (1980), *De Sica*.

Vittorio De Sica directing *Bicycle Thieves* (*Ladri di biciclette*, 1948)

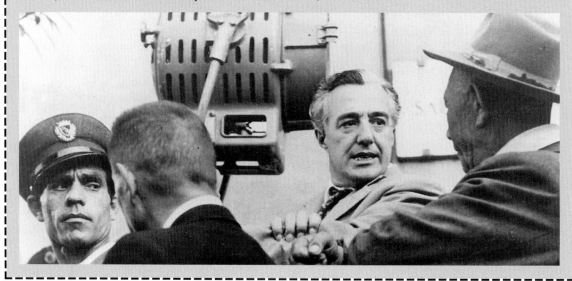

and an imprudent and disorganized administration. A chain of bankrupt production and distribution companies was but one symptom of the problem.

On the 'high' level of art cinema, the trio Visconti–Fellini–Antonioni replaced the 1940s trio Rossellini–De Sica–Visconti. After *La terra trema* (1948), more a sort of enchanting Marxist mystery play than the apotheosis of neo-realism seen in it by many critics (in retrospect, *Bellissima* was probably his most neo-realist film), Visconti moved on to *Senso* (1954), where his penchant for profaned Romanticism and collapse came to the fore. Together with *The Leopard* (*Il gattopardo*, 1962) and *Ludwig* (1972), *Senso* parades more than elsewhere Visconti's qualities as a master of sumptuous *mise-en-scène*, who struggles to reconcile his taste for cultural decadence and his lay, progressive humanism with the scope of the novel and a vocation for melodrama. *Rocco and his Brothers* (*Rocco e i suoi fratelli*, 1960), on the other hand, narrates the destiny of a family when it emigrates from the deep south to the Milan of the boom years and the film represents a return to neo-realism and a sort of ideal continuation of *La terra trema*. It was the 'national-popular' (to use the phrase of Antonio Gramsci) work which Visconti had set his sights on from early in his career.

The two most significant *auteurs* to emerge in the 1950s were Antonioni and Fellini. Michelangelo Antonioni had from his first film, *Cronaca di un amore* ('Chronicle of a love affair', 1950), set himself apart from neo-realism through his lucid and concentrated analysis of bourgeois psychology. From then, with an obstinacy which at times verged on monotony, he confronted the themes and problems, or better the neuroses, of a neo-capitalist society: couples, emotional crises, loneliness, difficulties of communication, existential alienation. His films are 'the blues' of bourgeois crises, in which thinly veiled autobiography serves as a record of the time. Their rejection of traditional plot structures, and insistence on the 'dead time', or stasis, of dramatic action, are designed to restore full causal significance to events and phenomena. His films of the period include *Il grido* ('The cry', 1957) and the trilogy made up of *L'avventura* ('The adventure', 1960), *La notte* ('The night', 1961), and *The Eclipse* (*L'eclisse*, 1962).

If Antonioni seemed, by inspiration and by temperament, European, Federico Fellini seemed conversely intensely provincial, caught between Rome and his native Romagna. After *Lo sceicco bianco* ('The white sheik', 1952) and *I vitelloni* ('The layabouts', 1953), whose grotesque and at times acutely satirical irony—helped by the writer Ennio Flaiano's screenplay—remained rooted in a precise social context, Fellini moved into an inner, visionary dream-world—a first-person cinema—with *La strada* ('The road', 1954). From the spectacle of *La strada* it was then a small step to the self-display which begins with *La dolce vita* ('The good life', 1960), a film which marks a watershed in the history of Italian cinema.

Bibliography
Aprà, Adriano, and Pistagnesi, Patrizia (eds.) (1979), *The Fabulous Thirties*.
Bondanella, Peter (1990), *Italian Cinema: from neorealism to the present*.
Brunetta, Gian Piero, *Cent'anni di cinema italiano*.
——, *Storia del cinema italiano*, Vol I: *1905–1945*.
——, *Storia del cinema italiano*, Vol II: *Dal 1945 agli anni ottanta*.
Faldini, Franca, and Fofi, Goffredo (1979), *L'avventurosa storia del cinema italiano raccontato dai suoi protagonisti, 1935–1959*.
Leprohon, Pierre (1972), *The Italian Cinema*.
Marcus, Millicent (1986), *Italian Film in the Light of Neorealism*.

Britain at the End of Empire

ANTONIA LANT

The commercial exploitation of synchronized sound cinema came about in Britain almost entirely with American technology. Warner Bros.' Vitaphone wax discs, and then Fox's Movietone sound-on-film process, spoke and sang in Britain in the 1930s, with the German Tobis Company jostling for some of the action. This was yet one more sign of the American domination of the British film industry by the 1920s, the outcome of several combined advantages. America had the largest home audience of any national film industry, so producers were able to cover production costs at home, making practically all earnings abroad into profits. American distributors thus had the flexibility to undercut their competitors in foreign markets; even the strongest non-American circuits were unable to overcome the American business practices of price undercutting, block booking, and blind bidding. In 1927 between 80 and 90 per cent of feature films in circulation in Britain were American.

The popularity of American films with audiences made British exhibitors reluctant to book British-made films, further disabling the home industry. The situation became so dire that in November 1924, dubbed 'Black November', film output ceased entirely. As a result the Conservative government passed protectionist measures in its Cinematographic Films Act (or 'Quota Act') of 1927 intended to ban restrictive policies of block booking and blind bidding. The American studios would now have to pay for their dominance by financing the production of a quota of British films while also taking some back for exhibition in the United States. In the event Warner Bros. and Paramount were the only two companies to set up serious production subsidiaries in Britain to fulfil their quota requirements. The rest made 'Quota quickies'—films shot to satisfy the terms of the Act but often financed at a rate per foot and barely intended to be screened. These gained British pictures an even worse name with audiences, though their production provided a useful training ground for future directors, such as Michael Powell.

The 1927 Act also created conditions for the British industry to emulate the American pattern of vertical integration, with the same monopolistic organization producing, distributing, and exhibiting its own films. By the end of 1929, Gaumont-British, an amalgam of companies assembled by Isidore Ostrer and his brothers Mark and Maurice, owned over 300 cinemas, and had under its wing the Gainsborough Company, founded and managed by Michael Balcon. Early in 1928 John Maxwell set up an organization linking the ABC circuit, which was to have eighty-eight cinemas by 1929, with Elstree Studios under Herbert Wilcox (called British International Pictures), and a distribution arm formed from First National and Pathé. For most of the 1930s these two combines would hold sway over British distribution, making it essential that any film have a contract with one of them to attain decent exposure.

The years immediately following the Act witnessed the confused frenzy of the industry's conversion to sound, the impact of which the 1927 Act had not considered. Sound caught some productions in mid-stream. Alfred Hitchcock's *Blackmail* (1929) was reshot in sections to incorporate synchronized sound. Promotional material urged 'See and Hear It. Our Mother Tongue as it Should Be—Spoken!' Multilingual versions of various productions were pushed through. E. A. Dupont's *Atlantic* (1929) about the sinking of the *Titanic* was made at Elstree in three languages, with three casts, for distribution in Germany and France as well as at home. Similarly Michael Balcon scheduled Anglo-German film productions with Erich Pommer at Ufa. British film producers Victor Saville, Herbert Wilcox, and the young Basil Dean visited Hollywood to get the gist of the newly expanded medium. Michael Balcon and Alexander Korda devised Anglo-American co-productions to take advantage of American improvements in camera blimping and microphoning.

CINEMA AND CINEMA-GOING IN THE 1930S

The arrival of talkies dramatically changed the audience's experience of cinema. The expense of conversion caused many independently owned cinemas to go out of business, but the emergence of the combines ABC and Gaumont-British, plus the general popularity of cinema, led to a cinema-building boom, while ticket prices remained low. From late 1928 there arose 'atmospherics', like the Astorias in Streatham, Brixton, and Finsbury Park, and the Granadas, built by Sidney Bernstein at Tooting and Woolwich. Following the American model, these cinemas had large, elaborate interiors, often in a Moorish, oriental, or Gothic cathedral style, designed to supply audiences with 'the romance for which they crave'. Oscar Deutsch's Odeon circuit of cinemas developed in the mid-1930s had a different aura. Unlike the 'atmospherics' they had a uniform, sleek style; they were powerful, cream-tiled buildings with vast curtain walls, streamlined red lettering, and nighttime floodlighting, echoing the designs of the new London underground stations which they frequently neighboured.

The 1930s were a period of general increase in the standard of living, despite the slow-down in industrial production. Unemployment seems to have had little effect upon cinema admissions, even among those who were most affected by it. Audiences were by all accounts poorer, working-class Britons, with urban young people and women (particularly in the afternoon) being the most frequent attenders, and the female population's opinion was carefully monitored by exhibitors as a guide to profits. Contemporary surveys indicate that cinema's appeal lay in its provision of a form of escape, a site for courtship, and a mode of social currency, being able to talk about what you had seen. The main competing entertainment for this audience was variety, in which several of the more popular British film stars of the 1930s initially made their names: Gracie Fields, George Formby, Will Hay, Frank Randle, Sid Field, Tommy Trinder, and the Crazy Gang. The links between the worlds of film and variety were close and some of the exhibition circuits owned halls which still staged variety, while others promoted mixed, 'kine-variety' presentations.

As the decade progressed there was an expansion of cinema-building and cinema-going into middle-class suburbs. 'Super' cinemas constructed in the West End, the suburbs of London, and other major cities of Britain often had cafés, dance halls, and sometimes Palm Court orchestras attached to them, making cinema-going a still more diversionary experience. Attractions often included a Mighty Wurlitzer organ with accompanying lighting sequences and sound effects, or complex lobby entertainment and promotion. The general increase in cinema numbers meant there was more likelihood of a picture house in every neighbourhood, like a local pub or church, serving a wider sector of the population. Cinema attend-

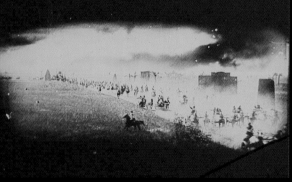

Above: early colour film processes: a still from Percy Smith's experimental *Romance of a Butterfly* (Great Britain, 1912)

Above, left: hand tinted colour: enlargement of a frame from Pathé's 1910 *Life of Christ*. Teams of women workers were used to hand-paint each frame of the film

Left: two frames from Griffith's *Intolerance* (1916). The lower frame is masked top and bottom to create a wide-screen effect. The tinting of scenes for effect was standard practice in the silent period

Below: Nancy Carroll in *Follow Thru*, directed by Lloyd Corrigan and Laurence Schwab for Paramount in 1930. Technicolor's original process, introduced in the late 1920s, used two strips of film bonded together, one red and one green, to create a colour effect

The triumph of three-strip Technicolor: Dorothy (Judy Garland) and the Scarecrow (Ray Bolger) on the yellow brick road. *The Wizard of Oz* (Victor Fleming, 1939) used colour to signify the fantasy world of Oz in contrast to the 'real', black and white Kansas

The 'Sorcerer's apprentice' scene from Walt Disney's Technicolor spectacle *Fantasia* (1940)

Cyd Charisse and Gene Kelly in the extended dance sequence 'Broadway melody' from the classic MGM Technicolor musical *Singin' in the Rain* (Donen, 1951)

John Wayne as Captain Nathan Brittles in *She Wore a Yellow Ribbon* (John Ford, 1949). This picture is an enlargement of a frame still taken from the print of the film recently restored by the UCLA Film and Television Archive

The Masque of the Red Death (Roger Corman, 1964), a tale of medieval decadence and horror photographed by Nicolas Roeg in Panavision and so-called Pathécolor, one of the simplified colour processes introduced in the 1950s

The painter's eye. Derek Jarman echoes the chiaroscuro of the painter's work in the lighting of *Caravaggio* (1986)

Bertil Guve as Alexander in Ingmar Bergman's family drama *Fanny and Alexander* (1982). The subtle and sensitive lighting and Eastmancolor photography represent the culmination of Bergman's long collaboration with the cameraman Sven Nykvist

A Midsummer Night's Sex Comedy (1982): Woody Allen's reworking of Ingmar Bergman's 1955 *Smiles of a Summer Night* showcased the sumptuous cinematography of Gordon Willis

A scene from
Kagemusha (1980),
Akira Kurosawa's 16th-
century *samurai* epic

Ridley Scott's thriller
Black Rain (1989),
filmed in Super 35.
Through impressive sets
and lighting Scott
creates a de-humanizing,
threatening urban
landscape

Week-End (1967) shows Godard's characteristic use of bold, primary colours, here captured by the camera of Raoul Coutard

Michael Keaton in Tim Burton's *Batman* (1989). Saturated, contrasting colours and lots of black give an extra edge to this foray into the world of comic books

The art of the scene-still photographer (G. F. Lelli), art director (Mario Garbuglia), and costume designer (Piero Tosi). *L'innocente* (Visconti, 1976) © G. F. Lelli

ance was divided along class lines, and an observer in 1936 speaks of

the middle and working classes in a small town going to different cinemas as a rule. The middle classes go for the film first and foremost, while the working classes rather as a regular habit, looking on the cinema in their district as a kind of club. The tastes of the two sections of the public differ: the working classes like comedians better than the others, and enjoy horror films almost exclusively. (quoted in Richards 1984)

Working-class audiences generally preferred American-made films over British ones, which they found too posh-talking and slower in pace.

However, there were zones of widespread appeal in British film-making of the 1930s, linked to the possibilities offered by synchronized sound. In the United States sound technology was invigorating old genres and creating new ones: the musical, the gangster film, the screwball comedy. In Britain, sound transformed feature film production in three areas: the suspense cinema of Alfred Hitchcock; musical comedy, especially the popular films of Jessie Matthews, Gracie Fields, Will Hay, and George Formby; and the epic film of empire or historical pageant, accomplished most spectacularly by Alexander Korda's London Films.

Alfred Hitchcock's prolific British period of film-making lasted from 1925 to 1939. He directed twenty-two of his fifty-three films in these years, for Gaumont-British/Gainsborough Films and for British International Pictures. Hitchcock was the foremost, highest-paid British director of the 1930s. His films were successful at the box-office, helping him to attain an unusual degree of artistic control in a climate in which producers usually held sway.

In Hitchcock's British thrillers traits emerge which characterize his mature American cinema: the haunting iconography of significant objects (a knife, a bracelet, a painting of a clown); the recurring characters of the wrongly accused man and the entangled, attractive, young woman; the cunning devices of narrative suspense, in which the audience knows more than the characters and enjoys the role of voyeur; and the use of brilliant visual and sound-editing techniques in which documentary-style footage jars with sudden, unexpected, highly subjective sequences. Anny Ondra in *Blackmail* (1929) plays the first in a long line of tormented and attacked blonde women who will face the horror of witnessing death. The film begins with a documentary chase sequence, and ends with a surreal pursuit using trick effects in a familiar location, the British Museum. The everyday setting harbouring extreme events was to recur, in *The Man who Knew Too Much* (1934), in *The 39 Steps* (1935), in *Sabotage* (1936), in *The Lady Vanishes* (1938), and in others, and is typical of Hitchcock's preference for personal narratives, involving young, innocent couples, set within the troubled European politics of Fascism, espionage, and annexation.

Another strand of production emotionally and dra-matically enhanced by the coming of sound was the imperial film. Set in the historical past or the colonial present, these films celebrated conservative values and institutions—family, matrimony, national pride, central government, monarchy, aristocracy—through clear narratives supported by patriotic musical themes. These 'consensus' films can be seen to reflect the remarkable political stability provided by the National Government through the 1930s. A Conservative-dominated coalition of parties was elected to power in 1931, re-elected in 1935, and ruled for the rest of the decade. Its course was to preserve the peace and maintain the status quo, which required in the late 1930s an appeasement of Hitler and the Nazi government in Germany.

During the 1930s Herbert Wilcox made two hagiographic films about the life of Queen Victoria, *Victoria the Great* (1938) and *Sixty Glorious Years* (1939), and Michael Balcon produced ardent Empire films for Gaumont-British: *Rhodes of Africa* (1936), *The Great Barrier* (1936), and *King Solomon's Mines* (1937). But it was Alexander Korda's London Films which presented the most exuberant myths of a glorious imperial Britain. Korda set up London Films in 1931 after a substantial film career in his native Hungary. With his eye on the American market, Korda hit the jackpot with *The Private Life of Henry VIII* (1933), a costume biography of the notorious monarch directed by himself with Charles Laughton as the King, but also starring the young Merle Oberon and Robert Donat, who was to become a key romantic lead of the 1930s.

A significant marker of his ambition for the picture was Korda's staging of its première at the world's largest cinema, Radio City Music Hall, New York, paving the way for its hugely successful opening in London under the label 'London Film Prestige Production'. The success of *The Private Life of Henry VIII* turned Korda into a major producer with backing from United Artists, promises of American distribution, and British banking and corporate support from the Prudential Assurance Company, which financed new studios at Denham. His acquisition of a half-share in the Odeon circuit in 1936 also guaranteed a much-needed British outlet. The Laughton film heralded a sequence of spectacular Korda-produced releases designed for the international market, emphasizing special effects and colour, in an atmosphere removed as far as possible from the realities of everyday British life.

Korda produced four key Empire films in the second half of the decade: *Sanders of the River* (1935), *Elephant Boy* (1937), *The Drum* (1938), and *The Four Feathers* (1939). They were made with approval and even co-operation from government, suggesting official satisfaction with their vision of the imperial world. Recommendations of the British Board of Film Censors also shaped the films' pro-Empire stance. While the BBFC was not a government body, it had close ties to politics, and consistently rejected

film scripts which 'reflected adversely on imperial institutions'. References to the impact on the Empire of war and independence movements were omitted from the films, as were the tensions and struggles between classes, races, and sexes that Empire entailed. Instead this celluloid empire existed fundamentally undisturbed by change. In the words of Jeffrey Richards (1984), 'The films offer no concrete political, economic, or constitutional justification for the Empire's existence. The Empire is justified in the apparent moral superiority of the British, demonstrated by their adherence to the code of gentlemanly conduct and the maintenance of a disinterested system of law and justice.' In these films British men know how to do the right thing, resulting in the quelling of uprisings and the renewed security of the Empire.

In the colourfully vibrant *The Four Feathers* (directed by Korda's brother Zoltan) Harry Faversham is born to a family of generations of men who have fought for the Empire, but Harry is repulsed by its requirements and refuses to join the forces in Egypt rallying for the reconquest of the Sudan. His wife Ethne now rejects him, explaining that they were both 'born to a code' that they must obey. The film goes on to support Ethne's value system, and Harry, challenged by white feathers of cowardice sent to him by his erstwhile army pals, travels to the desert anyway, infiltrating the dervish army and eventually saving the lives of his comrades and assisting in the defeat of the Khalif. He returns a victor, recognizing the importance of obeying the Empire's codes.

If there is a chink in the imperial narrative armour of these films it is at their domestic edges, where the price to be paid for constructing an Empire through the image of the British gentleman becomes visible. In *Sanders of the River* (again directed by Zoltan Korda) District Commissioner Sanders keeps a local uprising at bay in Nigeria through his alliance with Chief Bosambo, played by Paul Robeson—who uses his fabulous singing to mollify counter-imperial feeling. When Sanders takes a year's leave to marry, disaster threatens, as now Bosambo's people (and above all his wife Lilongo) are vulnerable to the warring King Mofalaba and the corruption of white mercenaries. Sanders's call to conjugal union to propagate the babies of Empire jeopardizes his life's work; his honeymoon must be delayed, perhaps repeatedly, to serve and save the realm. The film ends with Sanders returning to his river, assisting in the rescue of Lilongo and the demise of King Mofalaba and the mercenaries, and creating Bosambo King of the River as he starts his furlough again.

The new possibility of synchronized singing drew the tradition of music hall variety into a more complex relation with cinema, sometimes in self-reflexive form as

Jessie Matthews and Sonnie Hale in Victor Saville's *First a Girl* (1935)

in *Old Bones of the River* (1938), Will Hay's parody of *Sanders of the River*. The most successful films of this genre were those starring Gracie Fields, then at the height of her popularity. Her films contrast with Korda's Empire genre in their rootedness in working life and in the relative complexity with which they present class divisions. *Sally in our Alley* begins with a documentary sequence behind its titles showing children playing in back-to-back terraces accompanied by a barrel organ tune. Most of the events of the film occur in this alley, and air its problems: poverty, poor housing, delinquency, child abuse, absent menfolk. In one section extensive war footage of troop manœuvres and barbed wire imprint on us the grimy, fearful context in which Sally's fiancé is wounded. In *Sing as We Go* (1934), Fields's first film set in her native Lancashire, documentary imagery of mill manufacture situates the story in working people's lives, as does the first narrative event, an announcement of mill closure threatening the livelihood of both boss and employee. Gracie urges the workers to 'Sing as we Go', and when new technology for making artificial silk arrives by the end of the film she leads the workers cheering back to the factory gates, with Union Jacks waving around her. In the interim Gracie has cycled to Blackpool in search of work, providing the opportunity for long location sequences. These serve as background to Gracie's physical comedy but also celebrate the Mecca of working-class seaside holiday resorts, offering cinema audiences tokens of their own lives. However, as the decade progressed Gracie Fields came to be more publicly owned and less strongly tied to the mill town back-to-back. By *Shipyard Sally* (1939) she is singing out for jobs while rearmament is solving the Clyde's unemployment, diffusing the militancy of her acts. Her characters and their worlds increasingly present a more docile, harmonious, consensus view.

The question of cinema's social impact and its role in class relations had become more urgent in the 1930s as the mass unemployed voice became louder, and as sound cinema itself brought the question of class to the fore, given the intensity with which class was coded through spoken accent. A network of film societies and film journals burgeoned, intensively screening and discussing recent Soviet cinema. There was a socialist film movement, organized around independent cinemas and working men's clubs, which made documentaries and distributed Soviet films. In 1933 the British Film Institute was set up with a specifically educational mandate, again distributing documentary work. There was also a flourishing documentary film-making movement, funded by a variety of organizations from the Empire Marketing Board to the gas supply industry, and inspired above all by John Grierson's General Post Office Film Unit. All this activity helped develop a seriousness for film as a social force, a concern which was to spread further into feature film-making and which was to be hastened by the overhaul of the expiring 1927 Quota Act, and by the building ideological pressures of wartime.

In the reconstituted Cinematographic Films Act of 1938, films with a labour cost of under £7,500 would no longer qualify for quota, a statute designed to improve quality. The old clause that 75 per cent of the wages paid on any film must go to British citizens was relaxed, and the rule that the scenario had to be written by a Briton was omitted. Both changes allowed greater use of American stars and technicians and encouraged American majors to invest in film-making in Britain more extensively, a trend that was to pave the way for Korda's MGM–London Films deal whose first release was *Perfect Strangers* (1945). The increased presence of American film-making helped boost the currency of the social problem film, a narrative genre well established in the USA which provided an outlet for the desire for a socially conscious cinema. MGM's first British production under the new agreements was King Vidor's *The Citadel* (1938), based on A. J. Cronin's novel, a story condemning the practice of private medicine in a Welsh mining community. Two more miners' films quickly followed: Carol Reed's direction of Cronin's *The Stars Look Down* (1939) and Michael Balcon's production of *The Proud Valley* (1939) at Ealing, starring Paul Robeson and directed by Pen Tennyson. At the same time Victor Saville shot a highly successful version of Winifred Holtby's *South Riding* (1938), about corruption on a district planning board which jeopardizes new housing projects and school facilities for working people.

THE SECOND WORLD WAR

With the outbreak of war, scrutiny of the social role of cinema intensified. Recognizing the profound influence of film-going on psychological mood and opinion, Parliament issued official guidelines to studios advocating certain subject-matters and forbidding others. Recommended themes were 'what Britain is fighting for', 'how Britain fights', and 'the need for sacrifice if the fight is to be won'. Films were to be submitted for security censorship at the Ministry of Information Films Division, and cinemas were warned that they were liable for prosecution if they showed films containing material that might be useful to the enemy. The government's effects on film-making took an even more material form as it requisitioned studio space for storage, factory use, and the making of official films, and eventually drafted two-thirds of film technicians, though some for its own film-making. Ultimately only nine studios were left in operation, and home feature production fell from 108 films in 1940 to an average of 60 per year until the end of the war, with a nadir of 46 in 1942.

However, Britons were going to the pictures more than ever; in canteens, Army and Navy Camp Film Societies,

Gracie Fields

(1898–1979)

'Our Gracie' dominated British musical film comedies in the 1930s, sang on stage, made sound recordings, had her own radio programmes, and eventually acted for television before being made a Dame of the British Empire in 1979. In the course of her career she developed a bewilderingly wide singing range, encompassing operetta, blues, ditties, and homespun crooning. *Sally in our Alley* (1931), her first film, came after more than a decade of music hall experience in her native Rochdale and the West End. She completed eleven films in the 1930s, to become Britain's highest-paid screen star, holding the number one British box-office ranking in 1936 and 1937.

Throughout her career she never shed her distinctive Lancashire accent nor her association with the urban poverty into which she had been born. As Grace Stansfield, she had left school aged 12 to work in the local mills. In her early films she played working-class parts, set in their home milieu; she later played variety singers, or (as in *Queen of Hearts*, 1936) working-class characters who become singers. In several films her role name echoes her own, as if to certify the continuity between real and reel life: Grace Milroy in *This Week of Grace* (1933), Grace Platt in *Sing as We Go!* (1934), Grace Pearson in *Look*

up and Laugh (1935), Grace Perkins in *Queen of Hearts* (1936), and Gracie Gray in *Keep Smiling* (1938). Her physical appearance on screen was usually down to earth, tough-bodied in cotton print dresses and aprons, and slightly aged (she was 33 when she began screen work), her voice abrading customers and lovers with its rasping tones and vernacular turn of phrase. She was typically shown as inspired to sing by the bar or café crowd. Often referred to as 'Our Sal' or 'Our Gracie' on screen, she played a character known by everyone in the community, one who symbolized the neighbourhood through her singing, determination, and zest for life.

Her powerful appeal, which crossed class lines, lay in the combination of her personal success story with her specific regional and class identity on screen; her career and filmic performances merged different strands of class allegiance. But there was tension in this combination, detectable in Fields's numerous screen jokes at the expense of the film fan, and her sneers at, and facetious imitations of, Hollywood's culture (this despite her later deal with 20th Century–Fox which signed her up for four films for £200,000 in 1938). This tension is lessened as the 1930s progressed; while still rooted in working life, and still acknowledging class structure, her characters gradually shift to inhabit a more docile, less strident register. As Jeffrey Richards (1984) has argued, Gracie Fields, the spokesperson for industrial Britain, was transformed

during the decade from a potentially disruptive working-class heroine in *Sally in our Alley* into 'a symbol of national consensus'. In 1931 the class barrier was unbreachable and intolerable: Gracie is awkward in the strappy black evening gown lent by the hostess for her singing display in *Sally in our Alley*; she is humiliated and ignored at the snooty party where she is out earning a penny and drowning her sorrows. Eight years later in *Shipyard Sally* (1939), Fields' character ably and elegantly adopts ballgown attire to enter Lord Randall's society, and at the end of the film is content with losing her boss—the 'only man [she] has ever loved'—to a more beautiful woman of his own class, making do in exchange for a job as his Welfare Officer. Where she was angry at being used and discarded by the upper classes in *Sally in our Alley*, by *Shipyard Sally* she accepts not having her man, promoting an ethos of going without; the powerful message of so many wartime films around the corner.

The determined cheerfulness of Gracie Fields's grin-and-bear-it characters combined with the emotional power of her community singing style made her ideally suited to patriotic, troop-entertaining concerts at the outbreak of the Second World War. She made successful fund-raising tours to Canada, the United States, North Africa, the Pacific Theatre, and France, where on one trip she represented 'Britannia' alongside Maurice Chevalier's 'France'. Her rapport with her public was eroded when, at the outbreak of war, she immediately left for the States with her Italian-born husband. Questions were then asked in Parliament about the exceptionally large quantity of money she had obtained permission to take with her—far in excess of the legal allowance. However, her 1943 song 'Wish Me Luck as You Wave Me Goodbye' galvanized the nation in the crisis as much as her theme tune for unemployment, 'Sing as We Go', had in the 1930s.

After the war, she made her home in Capri, where she died in 1979.

ANTONIA LANT

SELECT FILMOGRAPHY

Sally in our Alley (1931); Looking on the Bright Side (1932); This Week of Grace (1933); Love, Life and Laughter (1933); Sing as We Go! (1934); Look up and Laugh (1935); Queen of Hearts (1936); The Show Goes on (1937); We're Going to be Rich (1938); Keep Smiling (US: Smiling Along) (1938); Shipyard Sally (1939); Stage Door Canteen (cameo role) (1943); Molly and Me (1945); Paris Underground (Madame Pimpernel) (1945)

BIBLIOGRAPHY
Burgess, Muriel, and Keen, Tommy (1980), *Gracie Fields*.
Fields, Gracie (1960), *Sing as We Go*.
Pollitt, Elizabeth (1978), *Our Gracie*.
Richards, Jeffrey (1979), 'Gracie Fields: The Lancashire Britannia'.
Richards, Jeffrey (1984), *The Age of the Dream Palace*.

Opposite: Gracie Fields in a characteristic pose in Basil Dean's *Sing as We Go!* (1934)

factory halls, and mobile vans as well as in cinemas, enduring air raid sirens and evacuations during shows. Cinema has never been as popular in Britain as it was by the end of the Second World War; audiences seemed to thrive on the visual luxury and seeming daring of luminous screen display which contrasted so powerfully with the black-out conditions outside.

The main beneficiary of the wartime film industry was J. Arthur Rank, who by 1943 had amassed assets equivalent to those of an American major: he bought distribution rights to Gaumont-British/Gainsborough in 1937; took over Korda's Denham studio in 1938; acquired Elstree–Amalgamated Studios in 1939; and bought the Odeon chain and Gaumont-British in 1941 when prices were low over the uncertainty of war's effect on screenings. Fifty-six per cent of studio space in Britain was now owned by Rank, and a booking with one of the major exhibition circuits, of which the most important were Rank-owned Gaumont/Odeon and ABC, was essential for the successful exploitation of any feature in the United Kingdom. Rank opted to divert some of his profits to independent film-makers linked to his organization through an umbrella group, Independent Producers Ltd. Here he supported four important director/producer units: the Archers (Michael Powell and Emeric Pressburger); Individual Pictures (Frank Launder and Sidney Gilliat); Cineguild (David Lean, Anthony Havelock-Allan, and Ronald Neame); and Wessex (Ian Dalrymple). By this arrangement Rank contributed to the diversity of film output during and after the war, funding and distributing Powell and Pressburger's *The Life and Death of Colonel Blimp* (1943) and *A Matter of Life and Death* (1946), David Lean and Noël Coward's *Brief Encounter* (1945), and Launder and Gilliat's *I See a Dark Stranger* (1946).

Others who benefited from the crisis were newsreel and documentary teams, needed to provide official instructional and informational pictures. After two years of war they were busier than ever, showing their wares in touring vans, service camps, and public libraries as well as cinemas. War blurred the distinction between documentary and feature film-making. There was a freer exchange of personnel between the two limbs of the industry because of general staff shortages, and new demands on the medium to represent the realities of fighting Britain. Many feature films incorporated documentary footage of fleets, flypasts, parades, and explosions, pulling narratives away from stagy interiors and theatricality.

War produced an acute demand for coherent representations of the nation that showed its divisions—of region, of class, of sex, of age—as underpinning the ultimate identity, character, and above all unity of the country. One response to this need was to adopt documentary strategies for rooting a fiction in the country's present crisis, and pursuing a narrative in which a diverse group of citizens from different regions or different

Michael Powell and Emeric Pressburger

(1905–1990) (1902–1988)

The collaboration of Michael Powell and Emeric Pressburger is the most remarkable in the history of cinema. The two men met while working for Korda's London Films at the end of the 1930s. Powell, who had been directing low-budget 'Quota quickies', had attracted Korda's attention with his work on *The Edge of the World* (1938). Pressburger, a Hungarian refugee, had worked as a screen-writer at Ufa in Germany, and in Austria. Their first collaboration was *The Spy in Black* (1939).

In 1942 they established their own production company, The Archers. Beginning with their first film under this banner, *The Life and Death of Colonel Blimp* (1943), they signed all of their films together under the joint credit: 'Produced, Written and Directed by Michael Powell and Emeric Pressburger.'

This credit did more than allow them to insist on the collaborative nature of their working relationship. In its singularity it established their maverick-like status apart from the realm of assembly-line studio production methods. It also blurred the careful division of labour considered crucial by the large studios in the production of feature-length films. While using all the resources that major studio talent and technology could offer, and often casting their films with prominent British stage and screen stars, The Archers operated as independent film-makers, albeit on a lavish scale. The films themselves also went against the grain of British cinema of the period, which was dominated by a realist approach to form and content. The films of Powell and Pressburger resist comfortable categorizing and draw on a rich and complex range of stylistic modes and traditions.

Powell–Pressburger films repeatedly address issues which strike at the heart of the nature of cinema itself: What is the relation between realism and artifice? What are the cinema's ties to theatre, painting, and music? What connections are there between this most contemporary and technological of art forms and the oldest forms of narrative? What role does the individual artist have to play in shaping these issues? Is it possible to create a work which simultaneously addresses a popular audience and an élite one?

In spite of their formal and visual sophistication, the Powell–Pressburger films often refer to or explicitly evoke narrative at its origins: the myth, the fable, the fairy-tale. They are able to create a world which is immediately accessible to a popular audience (most especially a British audience) raised on such myths and methods of story-telling: Chaucer (*A Canterbury Tale*, 1944), Hans Christian Andersen (*The Red Shoes*, 1948), E. T. A. Hoffmann (*The Tales of Hoffmann*, 1952). But Powell and Pressburger are also concerned with documenting anxieties about the highly industrialized post-war British culture

in which connections to the mythical and mystical British past are suppressed or denied. These concerns emerge in the contemporary setting of *I Know where I'm Going!* (1945), in which the heroine, Joan Webster (Wendy Hiller), is forced to abandon her materialistic desires, and her marriage to a middle-aged wealthy man who embodies those desires, in favour of Torquil MacNeil (Roger Livesey) and the world he inhabits, dominated by centuries-old legends, curses, and myths.

Fascination with the mythical and the fantastic does not end at the narrative or social level for Powell and Pressburger. Their work is profoundly Romantic in its impulses, dominated by its love of the mystical and of the 'natural world' and by its lack of decorum and 'good taste'. There is a tension in many of their films between the desire to document aspects of contemporary British culture and the desire to retreat from it entirely, into a world of inner experience, and art for art's sake. A sense of 'dying for art' permeates their most famous and financially successful film, *The Red Shoes*, as well as *The Tales of Hoffmann*, which overflow with emotional excess, stylized and hysterical behaviour, and highly eroticized masochism. The narrative space is often fragmented and fantastic, defying any classical sense of balance, order, and homogeneity, and, in its extreme stylization, often aspires to the condition of animated cinema. (Powell was a great admirer of Walt Disney.) Myth and legend become vehicles through which the cinema is instilled with a magical and transcendent quality, and in which the relationship between image and music is closely

linked. This has resulted in adaptations of operas and op-erettas (*Oh... Rosalinda!!* (1955), *The Tales of Hoffmann*) and in what Powell has called 'the composed film', in which editing, dialogue, and all forms of cinematic movement, from camera movement to the movements of the actors, take on a strongly predetermined rhythmic and choreo-graphed dimension. *A Matter of Life and Death* is perhaps the richest example of the tendency in Powell–Press-burger to create a film which is at once a highly stylized fantasy, an analysis of post-war British culture, and a meditation on the meaning and construction of cine-matic images.

Powell was to take this meditation on the cinema sev-eral steps further in the notoriously vilified *Peeping Tom* (1960), his most important film without Pressburger. The film's reputation has steadily risen since its making, as has much of the Powell–Pressburger body of work. Often attacked by mainstream critics of the time, heavily cut and altered for overseas distribution, and not always connecting with general audiences, the films of Pow-ell–Pressburger have since assumed the singular status that they deserve, influencing a new generation of film-makers from Francis Coppola, John Boorman and Martin Scorsese (who did much to revitalize Powell's reputation in the USA), to Derek Jarman, Sally Potter, and Aki Kau-rismäki.

JOE MCELHANEY

SELECT FILMOGRAPHY

Powell (without Pressburger)
The Edge of the World (1938); The Thief of Bagdad (1940); Peeping Tom (1960); Age of Consent (1969)
Pressburger (without Powell)
Twice upon a Time (1952)
Powell and Pressburger
The Spy in Black (1939); Contraband (1940); 49th Parallel (1941); The Life and Death of Colonel Blimp (1943); A Canterbury Tale (1944); I Know where I'm Going! (1945); A Matter of Life and Death (1946); Black Narcissus (1947); The Red Shoes (1948); Gone to Earth (1950); The Elusive Pimpernel (1950); The Tales of Hoffmann (1952); Oh... Rosalinda!! (1955); The Battle of the River Plate (1956); Ill Met by Moonlight (1956)

BIBLIOGRAPHY

Christie, Ian (1994), *Arrows of Desire*.
Macdonald, Kevin (1994), *Emeric Pressburger*.
Powell, Michael (1986), *A Life in Movies*.
Powell, Michael (1992), *Million Dollar Movie*.

Opposite: The 'stairway to heaven' in Michael Powell and Emeric Pressburger's *A Matter of Life and Death* (1946)

classes are shown pulling together for the common good. Documentary strategies (and existing documentary footage) were adapted for films of the period, including in 1943 Leslie Howard's *The Gentle Sex* about seven women training and fighting in the Auxiliary Territorial Service; Anthony Asquith's *We Dive at Dawn* describing the pursuit and sinking of an enemy ship by a British submarine; and Charles Frend's *San Demetrio, London*, based on actual events surrounding a merchant ship bringing oil cargo across the Atlantic to the Clyde.

All these films required Forces and government co-oper-ation during production. Their plots follow several charac-ters with equal interest rather than singling out a central romantic hero or couple, and often pursue several parallel narrative strands. The films thus appear to have a rather spontaneous structure, lurching from one round of wartime duties and crises to the next, in the conversion of ordinary citizens into tenacious, patriotic fighters. If their plots are not shaped by the vicissitudes of het-erosexual romance, they are nevertheless highly ordered, through the organizational structure of the military unit or ship's company, and ultimately through belonging to the urgency of the wider, wartime moment.

EALING, GAINSBOROUGH, AND HAMMER

The loudest and most influential of the many wartime voices calling for a new school of realist cinema in Britain had been that of Michael Balcon. He had taken charge of the small Ealing Studios in 1938 from Basil Dean, and although continuing to make the popular musical com-edies that had been the studio's mainstay through the 1930s, he wanted a cinema more in touch with the issues of contemporary British life, in both appearance and story. For this he recruited two key figures from the docu-mentary sector: Harry Watt, who had written and directed *Target for Tonight* (1941) for the Crown Film Unit; and Brazilian-born Alberto Cavalcanti, who had been a member of the Parisian avant-garde in the 1920s and had come to England in 1934 to work for John Grierson at the GPO.

Balcon also recruited Charles Frend, Charles Crichton, and Robert Hamer, and these three, together with Watt and Basil Dearden, remained at the studio well into the 1950s, directing the majority of its output. This continuity of personnel, who had lowish but regular wages, together with continuity in the script-writing department (including above all T. E. B. Clarke and Angus McPhail), and in art direction (Michael Relph was chief art director at the studio from 1942, before becoming Dearden's pro-ducer and an occasional director) allowed Ealing to develop a distinct studio style which emphasized, in Bal-con's terminology, 'realism' over 'tinsel'.

After the war, Ealing experimented with a number of film genres ranging from a solitary but highly successful attempt at horror with *Dead of Night* (1945), to *Pink String and Sealing Wax* (1945), a stage melodrama set in Victorian London. However, comedy returned as the studio's dominant product. While Ealing's Will Hay and George Formby films had been popular in the war years, comedy had then taken a back seat until *Hue and Cry* (directed by Charles Crichton) in 1947. The film adopts realist, documentary-inspired camera work to create a familiar background of post-war London life, and then develops a fantastic, contrasting plot in that setting to produce humour. This provided the model for the famous comedies that followed: *Passport to Pimlico* (1949), *Whisky Galore!* (1949), *The Man in the White Suit* (1951), *The Lavender Hill Mob* (1951), *Kind Hearts and Coronets* (1949), and *The Ladykillers* (1955), the last four starring the inimitable Alec Guinness. In *Passport* treasure found in an unexploded bomb crater proves that Pimlico is actually part of French Burgundy, and not England at all; the local community experiments with the idea of secession, a joke which would have been in very poor taste just a few years before in wartime.

Balcon had been a fierce spokesman during the war for the role of the independent film producer, serving on the government's Palache Committee in 1943 to investigate monopoly in the film industry. However, after the war he had signed a very attractive distribution deal with Rank which provided 50 per cent financing on all Ealing films, ensuring Balcon a degree of freedom from international pressures. This proved short-lived, and although the post-war Ealing comedies tended to be very successful in the United States, as was Frend's war film *The Cruel Sea* (1953), it was not enough to sustain the studio. Despite loans from the newly established National Film Finance Corporation in the early 1950s, Ealing Studios were forced to close in 1955.

The end of the 1940s had seen a crisis in the British cinema, which had affected even the largest studios, and from which many never recovered. In June 1947 the Labour government slapped a 75 per cent 'Dalton Tax' (named after the then Chancellor of the Exchequer) on all earnings in Britain of foreign films, intended to aid the ailing British economy. Hollywood responded with a six-month boycott of the British market. Stocks of American films in Britain were sufficient for six months, so there was no immediate gap to be filled, and reissues of old films were exempt from the tax. However, the American embargo renewed temptation among British producers to beat Hollywood at its own game: Rank's reaction was to step up production in the absence of US films. In March 1948 Hollywood lifted its ban after the signing of a new four-year pact favouring American interests, and lifting the 75 per cent tax. The market was flooded and all British films lost heavily, particularly because many of them had been rushed through production and were of poor quality. By mid-1948 Korda's new company, British Lion, was on

the verge of bankruptcy, and the Rank Organization was also suffering. In July the government announced approval of the National Film Finance Corporation to provide loans for British film-making. This rescued Korda and helped through such productions as Carol Reed's *The Third Man* (1949), but by February 1949 only seven of the twenty-six British film studios were in operation and only seven films were actually being made.

Cinema attendance was falling, as a result of audiences' changed social and economic circumstances, the arrival of television, and new suburban patterns of living. In response the government introduced the 'Eady Plan', an adjustment to the rate of Entertainment Tax on cinema tickets to enable a proportion of box-office revenue to find its way back to producers. Permanent government subsidy through taxation and loans enabled the failing film industry to see out the 1950s.

During the war Gainsborough Studios had made a wide range of films, from military adventures like *We Dive at Dawn* (1943) to women's pictures, such as *Love Story* (1944). After the war the studio increased its range to include problem pictures about pregnancy, bigamy, and the underworld, and noirish thrillers. However, it was the costume melodrama that brought them most profit and notoriety. This cycle began during the war with *The Man in Grey* (1943), starring James Mason and Margaret Lockwood, a successful pairing soon to be repeated in *The Wicked Lady*, the most successful film of 1946.

Gainsborough had been founded by Michael Balcon in 1924, and had studios in London, first in Islington and later in Shepherd's Bush. After 1936 it was run by Ted Black, who led the company through its most successful years, starting in 1937 with Carol Reed's *Bank Holiday*, Hitchcock's *Young and Innocent*, and Will Hay's *Oh Mr. Porter!*. In 1941 J. Arthur Rank acquired Gaumont-British and with it Gainsborough. This was a valuable alliance as it ensured a large distribution network for the films produced. Despite changes in leadership, the studio maintained a consistent policy, looking to box-office profit above critical approval, and a consistent output, developing a powerful stable of stars to support this pursuit: Margaret Lockwood, Stewart Granger, James Mason, Patricia Roc, Phyllis Calvert.

Gainsborough's costume melodramas were disapproved of by critics for straying too far from the realist base of British cinema, matured in the stresses of war. The costumes, sets, and emotions of *The Wicked Lady* were criticized for their excesses, thought particularly frivolous and tasteless in a time of rationing. Lady Barbara Skelton (Margaret Lockwood) is a noblewoman by day, but by night is a masked, armed highway robber who kills for the excitement. The popularity of the film with audiences suggests that the character of a murdering sexy woman gave form to fantasies kept at bay in a society shaped by

Alexander Mackendrick

(1912–1993)

Born in Boston to Scottish parents and raised in Glasgow, Alexander Mackendrick studied at Glasgow School of Art before working for ten years in advertising. During the war he served with the Psychological Warfare Branch, an oddball Anglo-American outfit which involved him in (among other things) making documentaries in Italy. In 1946 he joined Ealing Studios as a script-writer and 'sketch artist', drawing pre-production set-ups to guide cast and crew. His first assignment was Ealing's most expensive flop, the elaborate costume drama *Saraband for Dead Lovers* (1948).

Mackendrick got his chance to direct with *Whisky Galore!* (1949). A comedy set—and largely filmed—in the Outer Hebrides, it pitted islanders bent on plundering a shipwrecked cargo of whisky against the repressive forces of Customs officials and the blustering English laird. While adopting the basic small-is-beautiful pattern of Ealing comedies, the film countered the risk of cosiness with an underlying ruthlessness and sharp dramatic intelligence.

Mackendrick's skill at subverting Ealing conventions found further scope in *The Man in the White Suit* (1951), a lethally funny satire about a man whose invention of an indestructible cloth opens up—in Charles Barr's view (1977)—'a vision of the logic of capitalism as extreme as anything in Buñuel or Godard'. An equally mordant view of England's hidebound, class-ridden society informed *Mandy* (1952), a moving study of a deaf-mute child and Mackendrick's only non-comedy at Ealing.

A second Scottish-based comedy, *The Maggie* (1954), suffered from uncertainty of tone, but Mackendrick's final film for Ealing, *The Ladykillers* (1955), found him back on top form. A macabre Gothic fantasy scripted (like *The Maggie*) by the American expatriate William Rose, this was the last of the great Ealing comedies—at once an apotheosis and a parody, mocking the studio's (and England's) fixation on age and tradition. The film's gleeful mayhem, with a daffy old lady in a rickety Victorian house unwittingly destroying a whole gang of seedy crooks, gave full play to Mackendrick's black humour and his recurrent theme of innocence versus experience.

The same theme, in a very different register, resurfaced in his first American film, *Sweet Smell of Success* (1957), a gleamingly rancid study of blackmail, corruption, and twisted sexuality set in the paranoid night world of Manhattan showbiz journalism. Tony Curtis, playing a sleazily ambitious publicity agent, gave the performance of a lifetime, with Burt Lancaster's monstrous columnist not far behind. Aided by James Wong Howe's glistening cinematography, Clifford Odets's gutter-baroque dialogue, and Elmer Bernstein's raunchy, jazzy score, Mackendrick created a masterpiece of late noir, the darkest expression of his corrosive vision.

At this point, his career ran into trouble. Fired from a Shaw adaptation, *The Devil's Disciple* (1959), and then from Carl Foreman's ambitious production of *The Guns of Navarone* (1961), he did not make another film until 1963, after his return to Britain. *Sammy Going South* (1963) was the picaresque saga of a young boy trekking the length of Africa.

In 1965 Mackendrick finally achieved his long-held ambition of filming Richard Hughes's classic novel *A High Wind in Jamaica*, whose story—naïve pirates destroyed by the unthinking callousness of the children they capture—exactly matched his preoccupations. Although mutilated by the studio, the film managed to preserve much of the novel's hallucinatory power, turning it into Mackendrick's most complex and poignant exploration of the lethal nature of innocence.

Disillusioned by the failure of his *Don't Make Waves* (1967), and by the collapse of two long-cherished projects (*Rhinoceros* and *Mary Queen of Scots*), Mackendrick withdrew to take up a teaching career at the newly-founded California Institute of the Arts. He gained a formidable reputation as a teacher, but that was small consolation to audiences—or to fellow film-makers—for the loss of such a subtle and witty director.

PHILIP KEMP

SELECT FILMOGRAPHY

Whisky Galore! (Tight Little Island) (1949); The Man in the White Suit (1951); Mandy (The Crash of Silence) (1952); The Maggie (High and Dry) (1954); The Ladykillers (1955); Sweet Smell of Success (1957); Sammy Going South (A Boy Ten Feet Tall) (1963); A High Wind in Jamaica (1965); Don't Make Waves (1967)

BIBLIOGRAPHY

Armes, Roy (1978), *A Critical History of British Cinema*.
Barr, Charles (1977), *Ealing Studios*.
Kemp, Philip (1991), *Lethal Innocence: The Cinema of Alexander Mackendrick*.
Perry, George (1981), *Forever Ealing*.

Ealing Studios present another comedy:

ALEC GUINNESS
JOAN GREENWOOD
CECIL PARKER in

THE MAN IN THE WHITE SUIT

A MICHAEL BALCON PRODUCTION   DIRECTED BY ALEXANDER MACKENDRICK

Ealing Studios poster for Alexander Mackendrick's *The Man in the White Suit* (1951), starring Alec Guinness

austerity measures, and in which women, though conscripted, never gained access to the trigger of a gun.

The Gainsborough costume formula was repeated late into the 1940s, and partly imitated in Cineguild's extraordinary *Blanche Fury*, produced by Anthony Havelock-Allan in 1948, a film set in Victorian England about the vengeance of an illegitimate heir (Stewart Granger), as seen through the eyes of a woman giving birth to another bastard, his child. The film ends with a fade-to-black from the mother's subjective point of view. This is one of the most florid of all costume melodramas, leaving the audience to identify with a dead woman.

Gainsborough did not survive the vicissitudes of the late 1940s film industry, and ceased production at the end of the decade, but its output was a vigorous, successful, and vibrant counterpoint to the prevailing realist ethos.

The only studio that truly weathered these difficult years was Hammer Films. It focused on the international market from the beginning, enabling it to ride out the rocky years of the late 1940s. The studio had its origins in a distribution company, Exclusive Films, started in 1935 by Enrique Carreras and Will Hinds, whose stage name was Will Hammer. In 1947 the company was reorganized to move into production and renamed Hammer Films, with Carreras's son James as managing director. Carreras prudently insisted on tight financial controls, with NFFC loans paid back on time, and production costs ruthlessly controlled. One technique was to make all films in one rented location rather than renting a studio for each production and having to transport equipment, sets, and personnel. Hammer experimented with two or three sites before settling at Down Place, Bray, converting the house to Bray Studios, which it used until 1966.

A stable working base facilitated continuity of crews and set designers who acquired great expertise in making films inexpensively but without making them look cheap. Hammer made about six films a year, most being completed within a year with shooting schedules of about a month; one film was worked on at a time, a policy which helped focus and unify the staff. Costs were also controlled by the extensive pre-planning of scripts and even of poster artwork and other promotional design that went on in advance. Scripts tended to draw on familiar stories: Dick Barton (from the radio show of that name), Robin Hood, Dracula, Frankenstein, and *The Quatermass Experiment* (a horror film developed from a television show). The public could anticipate content, enabling the studio to predict popularity and minimize financial risk.

The success of *The Quatermass Experiment* (1955) prompted Carreras to pursue the horror theme, assigning Terence Fisher (who had started at Gainsborough and had edited *The Wicked Lady*) to direct *The Curse of Frankenstein* (1957). This was highly profitable on both sides of the Atlantic, leading to an agreement with Universal to make

Dracula (1958), and deals with Columbia, United Artists, and other American companies for pre-production financing and marketing in the United States, the lucrative audience Carreras most desired. Although they expanded into other genres, such as science fiction and psychological thrillers, horror became and remained Hammer's staple. Like Gainsborough's, Hammer's films were scorned by critics but loved at the box-office. They revived the gamut of movie history's horror favourites; mummies and werewolves, vampires and monsters. Fisher's *The Curse of Frankenstein* was followed by *The Revenge of Frankenstein* (1958) and *The Evil of Frankenstein* (1963); his *Dracula* (1958) was succeeded by *The Brides of Dracula* (1960), and so on. These mythical fantasies were usually set in Victorian Britain, inviting a plush and cloying Technicolor *mise-en-scène* of velvet chairs and curtaining, and gigantic castle fireplaces, contrasted with dank, haunted beechwoods entered by fiercely driven carriages, and frightened fainting maidens. In their plots the repressive Victorian sexual code is endlessly placed in tension with the designs of male marauders and the erupting sexuality of their young, curvaceous female victims.

This lush, baroque *mise-en-scène*, and the displacement to a remoter historical moment or culture, provided an outlet for the emotional expression of sexual intensity and physical violence. Meanwhile, however, a similar quality was also emerging in the more realist products of the 1950s, as the patriotic strictures of wartime community (with its shelving of individual desire and fear) broke down. This ranges from Dirk Bogarde's compelling performance as the small-time murderer-on-the-run in *The Blue Lamp* (1949) with his impulsive lust for danger and sex, to Carl Boehm's chilling role in Michael Powell's *Peeping Tom* (1960) as the tormented son of a neurologist who murders women while filming them, forcing them to view their own deaths in a mirror attached to his tripod equipped with a deadly protruding blade and then arousing himself by projecting the films in the intimacy of his own darkroom. In both films the intensity of the drives of violence and desire are in stark contrast to the impoverished background of derelict bomb sites, humdrum London streets, and confined flats.

With some historical distance from the war it became possible for cinema to question the conventions of masculinity required by patriotism and conventional gender roles. Charles Frend's *The Cruel Sea* represents this through the sea captain's depression over killing in 'the war, the

(Top) Margaret Lockwood in the immensely successful Gainsborough melodrama *The Wicked Lady* (1945), directed by Leslie Arliss. A number of scenes had to be reshot for American release because of the low necklines

(Bottom) Christopher Lee in the Hammer production *Dracula Prince of Darkness* (1965), directed by Terence Fisher

whole bloody war', through its empathy for his tears and drinking, and through its discussion of the nature of the relationship between himself (played by Jack Hawkins) and his first lieutenant (Donald Sinden), which, it suggests, may range from military duty to eroticized love. Anthony Asquith's *The Browning Version* (1951), based on the Terence Rattigan play, indicts any version of manhood which sets store by stoicism, silence, and repression of feeling. A classics master (Michael Redgrave) is shown to have become a wizened, embittered husk through years of mute tolerance of his wife's unfaithfulness, and because of a failure to show his own emotional life, either to her, or to his pupils. In *Victim* (1961) Dirk Bogarde plays a lawyer who is forced publicly to defend his identity as a homosexual and expose a blackmailing ring after his lover hangs himself, even though this may end his career and shatter his marriage. The pressures to hide this part of his manhood have become intolerable.

Traditional values of masculinity had been disturbed by the war, and these uncertainties, combined with relaxation in BBFC rulings, permitted the emergence of a realist cinema which tested out new versions of the male, paving the way for the British 'New Wave', and the cinema of the so-called Angry Young Men. In many respects this gave new life to the British cinema, but not in all; and for a British cinema of angry women, we have to turn back to the early films of Gracie Fields, the 1940s Gainsborough costume cycle, and some home-front films, or forward to the feminist movement of the 1970s and beyond.

Bibliography
Armes, Roy (1978), *A Critical History of British Cinema*.
Atwell, David (1980), *Cathedrals of the Movies*.
Barr, Charles (1977), *Ealing Studios* (repr. 1993).
Curran, James, and Porter, Vincent (eds.) (1983), *British Cinema History*.
Dickinson, Margaret, and Street, Sarah (1985), *Cinema and State*.
Lant, Antonia (1991), *Blackout: Reinventing Women for Wartime British Cinema*.
Perry, George (1985), *The Great British Picture Show*.
Richards, Jeffrey (1984), *The Age of the Dream Palace: Cinema and Society in Britain, 1930–1939*.
Ryall, Tom (1986), *Alfred Hitchcock and the British Cinema*.
Stead, Peter (1989), *Film and the Working Class: The Feature Film in British and American Society*.
Taylor, Philip M. (ed.) (1988), *Britain and the Cinema in the Second World War*.

Germany: Nazism and After

ERIC RENTSCHLER

THE NAZI PERIOD

Audio-visual machinery played a crucial role in National Socialist designs for living, in radical attempts to monitor human activity and dominate the physical world. Adolf Hitler and his Minister of Propaganda, Joseph Goebbels, were keenly aware of film's ability to mobilize emotions and immobilize minds, to create powerful illusions and captive audiences. Calculating *metteurs-en-scène*, they employed state-of-the-art technology to implement a society of spectacles, a profusion of celebrations, light shows, and mass extravaganzas. Hitler's regime involved a sustained cinematic event, as Hans Jürgen Syberberg would later put it, 'a film from Germany'. If the Nazis were movie mad, then the Third Reich was movie made, a fantasy construction that in equal parts functioned as a dream machine and a death factory.

German cinema of the Third Reich, even half a century after Hitler's demise, still prompts extreme reactions and hyperbolic formulations. Given the atrocities of National Socialism, the movies, newsreels, and documentaries made under its aegis represent for many commentators film history's darkest hour. The corpus of 1,100 narrative features produced between 1933 and 1945, German critic Wilhelm Roth once observed, catalyses visions of a cinematic hell, where one's torments alternate between hideous propaganda, formal bombast, and unbearable kitsch. To this day Nazi cinema in many minds resembles Mabuse's 1,000 eyes or *1984*'s panoptic state apparatus.

Immediately after assuming power, the National Socialists purged a once internationally recognized industry of its artistic vanguard and the greater portion of its professional craft and technical expertise. More than 1,500 film-makers—many of whom were Jews as well as progressives and independents—would flee Germany, replaced in many instances by politically subservient hacks and second-rate opportunists. In the minds of its most severe detractors, Nazi cinema represents the antithesis of Weimar's revered 'haunted screen' (Lotte Eisner). An infamous entity, its most memorable achievement is the systematic abuse of film's formative powers in the name of mass manipulation, state terror, and world-wide destruction.

Goebbels set out to 'reform German film from the ground up'. The new film must renounce the sins of the Weimar *Systemzeit*, its art-for-art's-sake dalliance, intellectual liberalism, and commercial pandering. It should emanate from political life and find its way to the deepest recesses of German spirit. In his early programmatic declarations, he mixed natural and martial metaphors, speaking of film as a body and a territorial surface, declaring himself the physician whose surgery would exorcize an afflicted organism of harmful alien elements. 'It takes imagination', he proclaimed, 'to grant life to the innermost purpose and innermost constitution of a new world.' Repeatedly, Goebbels stressed how film should exercise a discernible effect (*Wirkung*), how it must act on hearts and minds. Its calling should be that of a popular art (*Volkskunst*), an art that simultaneously serves state purposes and fulfils personal needs. Political ideas were to assume aesthetic and affective force. That did not mean, however, simply re-enacting party parades, documenting stormtroopers, and fetishizing flags and emblems. Authentic film art must transcend the everyday; indeed, it should 'intensify life'.

The primary task as the NSDAP assumed power in 1933 was to reshape public imagination in accordance with its own persuasions, that is, to present an appealing and compelling *Weltanschauung*. That is not to say that National Socialism had a systematic programme or a coherent world-view. It was a function of effects enacted in stirring spectacles and constant demonstrations. Film provided the special effects with which the Third Reich created itself in its own image. Leni Riefenstahl's pseudo-documentary of the 1934 Nuremberg party rally, *Triumph of the Will* (*Triumph des Willens*, 1935), is a heroic epic about the new order, a monumental act of hagiography, and a modern media event staged for an army of cameras. The film shrouds the Reichs Chancellor in mythic garb, as a saviour descending from the clouds to animate his loyal followers, who, gathered as imposing mass ornaments, swear him unconditional allegiance. In Riefenstahl's chronicle of the 1936 Berlin Olympics (*Olympia*, 1938), the Führer literally becomes a classical deity and an omnipotent gaze. The prologue begins in Greece at the Temple of Zeus and ends in Berlin with an image of Hitler's profile. The leader stands as an unrivalled master of ceremonies, the Supreme Being who grants shape to a nation and its people. In decisive ways, show business and National Socialism were of a piece. The flow of images and the movement of a party afforded non-stop excitement and ever-shifting perspectives. Each employed elaborate choreographies and dramatic displays in the name of making fictional worlds become real.

Nazi cinema took form as a site of transformation, an art and technology implemented to engineer emotion, to create a new man—and to recreate woman in the service of the new order and the new man. The first Ufa feature with substantial NSDAP support, Hans Steinhoff's *Hitler Youth Quex* (*Hitlerjunge Quex*, 1933), metamorphosed a

young boy into a selfless servant and a political medium. Murdered by Communist agitators, Heini Völker's body dissolves into a waving flag that becomes a staging ground for soldiers marching into the off-screen future. There was to be a long procession of Teutonic martyrs, larger-than-life heroes typically played by Emil Jannings, Werner Krauss, or Heinrich George, portraits of great politicians (*Fridericus*, 1937; *Bismarck*, 1940; *Carl Peters*, 1941), artists (*Friedrich Schiller*, 1940; *Andreas Schlüter*, 1942), and scientists (*Robert Koch*, 1939; *Diesel*, 1942; *Paracelsus*, 1943). Only rarely do women assume an active role, except as a challenge and a hindrance. (There is a veritable subgenre of Nazi moral tales focusing on the taming of shrews and the re-education of wilful wives and lovers.) Female presence is mainly reduced to ever-understanding accommodators and domestic companions. The wartime blockbusters Eduard von Borsody's *Request Concert* (*Wunschkonzert*, 1940) and Rolf Hansen's *Die große Liebe* ('The great love', 1942) are films about women who wait and learn to suffer patiently while their loved ones serve a greater German cause.

Nazi fantasy production left little room for independent movement, seeking to occupy and control all territory, both physical and psychic, in an effort to eradicate alterity. The Tyrolean hero of *The Prodigal Son* (*Der verlorene Sohn*, 1934), played by the indefatigable Austrian original, Luis Trenker (who also directed), wants to partake of different sights and sounds, to visit exotic places he has only seen on a map. The athletic champion travels to New York and becomes a homeless vagrant. The narrative ultimately brings the protagonist to curse the New World, but more importantly to renounce all fascination for a life beyond his native horizon. *The Prodigal Son* grants a wish in order to vanquish wishful thinking, just as *Liebe, Tod und Teufel* ('Love, death, and the devil', 1934) and *Die unheimlichen Wünsche* ('The uncanny wishes', 1939) show how indulged fantasies yield disastrous results. An exercise in negative *flânerie*, Trenker's film subjects a mountain boy to a bad trip, a nightmarish thrashing by a soulless modernity, a traumatic humiliation on foreign terrain. Individuals who step off the beaten track such as the itinerant musician in *Friedemann Bach* (1940) or the nomadic woman of the theatre in *Komödianten* ('Theatre people', 1942) come to a bad end. Being abroad in Nazi cinema means potential attraction to the foreign, distance from the homeland and all sources of well-being and stability. Africa appears as the breeding ground of sickness and death in *Germanin* (1943) and Puerto Rico harbours an insidious fever in *La Habanera* (1937).

Travellers are thus problematic figures in Nazi films—unless, of course, they are explorers or colonizers out to extend the German Empire. We see many refugees in films of the 1930s, but rather than political fugitives fleeing the Reich, they are Germans headed back to the homeland. Johannes Meyer's *Der Flüchtling aus Chikago* ('The fugitive

from Chicago', 1934) featured an enterprising German emigrant who returns from the American Midwest to run an automobile factory in Munich. Once there he confronts the malaise of Weimar Germany: economic uncertainty, mass unemployment, incompetent leadership. Surmounting a host of difficulties, the re-emigrant soon has the business back on its feet and the workers on his side. Paul Wegener's *Ein Mann will nach Deutschland* ('A man must go to Germany', 1934) portrayed a German engineer living in South America who hears in 1914 of war across the ocean. Realizing his obligation, he heads for Europe, joined by a German comrade. The road back involves physical hardships, treacherous terrains, and hostile seas, obstacles faced by patriots who have, as Oskar Kalbus put it, 'only one thought: home to Germany, to help protect a fatherland under attack'.

Hallowing German soul also meant protecting German soil from its adversaries and assailants. Nazi cinema's gallery of enemies is equally extensive: vicious Communists who oppress German minorities living abroad, in *Flüchtlinge* ('Fugitives', 1933), *Friesennot* ('Friesian peril', 1935), or *Heimkehr* ('Homecoming', 1937); Frenchmen who embody foppish, idle, and self-indulgent manners, in *The Old and the Young King* (*Der alte und der junge König*, 1935); mercenary and war-mongering British imperialists in *Ohm Krüger* (1941); foreign saboteurs and spies who threaten the Reich from within in *Traitors* (*Verräter*, 1936) and *Achtung! Feind hört mit!* ('Careful! the enemy is listening', 1940). The era's most egregious hate pamphlets, however, both released in 1940, were Veit Harlan's feature *Jew Süss* (*Jud Süss*) and Fritz Hippler's documentary *The Wandering Jew* (*Der ewige Jude*), cinematic rehearsals of the Final Solution meant to intensify anti-Semitic sentiment and to legitimize a state-sponsored Holocaust. A year later, Wolfgang Liebeneiner's melodramatic apologia for euthanasia, *Ich klage an!* ('I accuse!'), showed a husband's mercy killing of his afflicted spouse as a noble deed, lending support to the merciless extermination of 'inferior human material'. An eleventh-hour attempt to rouse shattered German spirits, Harlan's *Kolberg* (1945) has soldier males join with patriotic citizens in a suicidal last-ditch battle against foreign invaders. With the Reich collapsing around him, Goebbels spent over 8 million marks on what he envisioned as the greatest film of all time, 'a spectacular epic outrivalling the most sumptuous American super-productions'. From *Hitler Youth Quex* to *Kolberg*: one might describe Nazi cinema as an elaborate dance of death, a prolonged exercise in violence and devastation.

Nazi cinema, though, was not just the product of a Ministry of Fear. It was, more than anything, a Ministry of Cheer and Emotion. The customary tropes of the uncanny

and horrendous do not accurately characterize the vast majority of the epoch's films, light and frothy entertainments set in urbane surroundings and cosy circles, places where one never sees a swastika or hears a 'Sieg Heil'. Paul Martin's *Glückskinder* (1936—released as *Lucky Kids*), the Ufa remake of *It Happened One Night* starring Lilian Harvey and Willy Fritsch, for instance, unfolds in a realm that knows nothing of Riefenstahl's demonstrations of brute strength or Steinhoff's paeans to self-sacrifice. We encounter neither steeled bodies nor iron wills, no racist slurs, state slogans, or party emblems. Martin's characters dance about with zest, singing of joyful lives without responsibility, making merry, and consuming great amounts of liquor.

The vast majority of films made under Goebbels, many revisionist historians now insist, bear few signs of ideological resolve or official intervention. *Hitler Youth Quex*, *Jew Süss*, *Bismarck*, *Ohm Krüger*, *Kolberg*, and other state-sponsored productions may well warrant the appellation Nazi propaganda. None the less, such 'state films' constitute a very small portion of the era's films, posing exceptions and not the rule. So-called 'unpolitical' features in fact provided the overwhelming majority; besides a plethora of melodramas, crime stories, and bio-pics, almost 50 per cent of the epoch's films were comedies and musicals, light fare directed by ever-active industry pros like E. W. Emo, Carl Boese, Georg Jacoby, Hans H. Zerlett, and Carl Lamac, peopled with widely revered stars like Hans Albers, Willi Birgel, Marika Rökk, and Zarah Leander, as well as character actors such as Heinz Rühmann, Paul Kemp, Fita Benkhoff, Theo Lingen, Grete Weiser, Paul Hörbiger, and Hans Moser. Many of these films receive recognition as noteworthy achievements, as unblemished classics of German cinema, in some cases even as bearers of subversive energies. Such works seem to demonstrate that the Nazi regime created space for innocent diversions; they reflect a public sphere not completely lorded over by state institutions and reveal an everyday with a much less sinister countenance.

It is in any case clear that National Socialism governed less by external compulsion than by an appeal to the imaginary. If Hitler's State expected sacrifice and devotion, it also offered amenities in the forms of consumer goods and creature comforts. Films of the Third Reich recall the 'feelies' of Huxley's *Brave New World*, innocuous and agreeable packages of diversion. Goebbels sought to imbue mass culture with cultic values, to aestheticize the political in order to anaesthetize the populace. All films, he was fond of saying, are political, most especially those which claim not to be. His diaries espouse a popular cinema free of overt intellectualism, political heavy-handedness, artistic and technical incompetence. Contrary to *völkisch* cohorts like Alfred Rosenberg, Goebbels believed German films could learn from their ideological enemy,

The body beautiful: Leni Riefenstahl's *Olympia* (1938)

especially regarding cinema's ability to intoxicate mass audiences. The strength of Hollywood lay above all in its visceral appeal, its grand power to enchant and enrapture, its capacity for fostering viewer identification with sights and sounds made by someone else. It could sustain interest, gripping and engrossing spectators while granting them the illusion of comfort and freedom. American film offered escape from the everyday in the form of compelling fantasies and worlds larger than life.

In his essay of 1926, 'Cult of Distraction', Siegfried Kracauer had described a new urban mass public desperately hungry for experience, seeking in the dark of cinemas the stimulation and excitement which the everyday withheld. Goebbels knew well that an enthralled and spellbound subject would prove much more malleable than a viewer harangued by audio-visual terror. The Minister no doubt sponsored a fair number of official state productions with a distinct political slant and worked hard so that newsreels might yield tendentious effects. None the less, he clearly favoured subtle persuasion over the obvious touch. For this reason he lauded the imagistic strength and visual seduction of Trenker and Riefenstahl and actively cultivated stylists like Willy Forst, Detlef Sierck (soon to emigrate and become Douglas Sirk), and Victor Tourjansky, even occasionally tolerating less reliable non-conformists like Reinhold Schünzel, Helmut Käutner, and Wolfgang Staudte. German films would become a crucial means of dominating people from within, a vehicle to occupy psychic space, a medium of emotional remote control. And in the endeavour to create the definitive dominant cinema, Goebbels and his minions in crucial regards let Hollywood be their guide.

When speaking of American cinema, reviewers in the Third Reich often saw the popular German film in terms of the Propaganda Ministry's dreams. Among the Hollywood successes, nobody's films figured as strongly as those of Walt Disney. 'I present the Führer with thirty of the best films from the last four years and eighteen Mickey Mouse films for Christmas,' Goebbels noted in his diary on 20 December 1937. 'He is very pleased.' Disney cartoons raised pure immanence and artistic illusion to transcendent heights. 'Mickey Mouse films', claimed a critic assessing the German film crisis late in 1934, 'are the best films without political content, sublime embodiments of films which could not be more different from *Potemkin*.' Observers mused about Hollywood delights while lamenting that the Reich's domestic cinema rarely elicited such favourable responses. Although light films and musicals constituted roughly half (and sometimes more) of annual feature production through 1937, only *Glückskinder*, Sierck's *April, April!*, Reinhold Schünzel's *Amphitryon*, Willi Forst's *Allotria*, Carl Froelich's *Wenn wir alle Engel wären* ('If we were all angels'), and Wolfgang Liebeneiner's *Der Mustergatte* ('An ideal husband') stood out as truly resonant comedies. Taking stock in 1937, Goebbels tried to sound confident and upbeat, but none the less had to admit: 'Art is no light matter. It is inordinately hard and sometimes even brutal.' The art of entertainment was neither simple nor straightforward; it was, if anything, a serious political business.

Lilian Harvey in *Der Kongress tanzt* ('The congress dances', 1931), directed by Erik Charell

The NSDAP 'co-ordinated' institutions and organizations. The Ministry of Propaganda monitored film scripts, oversaw studio productions, and orchestrated press responses. Despite all these measures, one could not simply mandate that German audiences like German films. Cultivating Hollywood above all meant a more effective means of disciplining distraction, a German popular cinema that could provide the ultimate application of power, a power that works discreetly, by signs and representations. *Glückskinder* emulated American film in an attempt to incorporate it in a native dream factory. Martin's film propagated a Never Never Land created in a studio and made for the cinema, a site of irresponsibility, reverie, and good cheer. This realm would serve as both a compromise and a consolation. People more readily accepted National Socialism because it offered them a collective identity as well as the illusion of a private life. Films crafted along classical American lines, engaging mass entertainments seemingly devoid of politics, provided a respite from the hard work increasingly demanded of Germans, the constant sacrifice, the atmosphere of threat. Cinema, rather than espousing party mythologies, would become the site of grand illusions. And the grandest illusion created in German studios increasingly under state control was the illusion that within this State certain spaces remained beyond control—especially the space of cinema and fantasy production.

German studios created realms of illusion which, on the surface, reflected little of everyday realities. By and large sound-stage productions with little location shooting, these films preferred a seemingly timeless present or stylized period settings. Weimar's galvanizing mix of fantastic reverie and realist exploration vanished in great measure in a cinema that privileged space over time, composition over editing, design over movement, and sets over human shapes. And yet there existed undeniable continuities between Weimar and Nazi cinema, be it the remakes of *The Student of Prague* (1935), *Schloss Vogelöd* (1936), and *The Indian Tomb* (1938), be it the rereleases of Lang's *Nibelungen* and Fanck/Pabst's *The White Hell of Piz Palü* (*Die weisse Hölle vom Piz Palü*), be it the uninterrupted cycles of Prussia films, mountain epics, costume extravaganzas, be it musicals with Willy Fritsch and Lilian Harvey, the rough-and-tumble exploits of Harry Piel, or Ufa culture films that traversed the world's landscapes and fathomed nature's smallest secrets. What changed above all was the structure of the public sphere and the way in which state agencies managed the making and partaking of domestic and imported images.

The Nazi public sphere operated along the lines of what Goebbels called an 'orchestral principle'. Not every instrument plays the same thing when we hear a concert; still the result is a symphony. Hardly monolithic or monotone, Nazi culture energized a division of labour between light

touches and heavy hands. Films worked together with other forms of diversion (radio programmes, mass rallies, tourist offerings) to organize work and leisure time in an effort to militate against alternative experience and independent thought. State productions and escapist entertainments functioned in tandem so that similarly 'extreme perspectives of extreme uniformity' could be, for instance, found in the party document *Triumph of the Will* and the Tobis musical of 1939, *We're Dancing around the World* (*Wir tanzen um die Welt*). Generic pleasure and ideological indoctrination became of a piece. Nazi escapist fare offered no escape from the Nazi status quo.

With the onset of war, Nazi film truly came into its own. It brought in unparalleled profits and conquered wide foreign markets. Eliminating American competition altogether in 1940 and occupying most of Europe, Goebbels had his longed-for captive audiences. Josef von Baky's *Münchhausen*, the lavish Ufa colour production premièred at the studio's state-sponsored twenty-fifth anniversary on 5 March 1943, at once demonstrated the grotesque gap between wartime realities and screen illusions as well as their confluence. Things had taken a disastrous turn at Stalingrad and a few weeks earlier the Minister had called for 'total war'. *Münchhausen* pleased audiences with its episodic tale of the engaging famous raconteur, a painted figure who winks in the film's opening shot in an animated special effect, establishing a relationship between a hero who fabricates tales and a medium that trades in illusions. Rarely did Nazi Germany so graphically display its awareness of the captivating potential of film technology. The famous image of Hans Albers seated on a cannonball flying through the sky provides the film's ultimate icon, essentializing a connection between cinema's power over human imaginations and war's tools of aggression.

National Socialism recognized that war involved both material territories and immaterial fields of perception. Film ultimately became a weapon, an explosive arsenal of surprises and effects which made minds reel and emotions surrender under a constant barrage of stimulation. (It was no coincidence, Paul Virilio has noted, that colour production expanded during the Second World War and that the ultimate German war films, *Münchhausen* and *Kolberg*, appeared in Agfacolor.) What is interesting about *Münchhausen*—and this holds for Nazi cinema in general—is the limits of its self-knowledge, the moments where cynical sophistication yields to a troubled subjectivity and a decided self-blindness. *Münchhausen* enacts a peripatetic soldier's fantasy of control and likewise exhibits the fearful psyche that wants, needs, and produces this fantasy. It shows us a Nazi hero created for an official celebration; it also grants us glimpses of the pathology that shaped this hero and this occasion. Film provided a mighty weapon, but, in the end, filmic illusions could not

Alfred Junge

(1886–1964)

Born in the Prussian town of Görlitz, Junge entered films in 1920 as an art director at Ufa, at that time the most creatively stimulating film studio in the world, where he worked with Dupont, Leni, and Holger-Madsen. When Dupont was invited to London by British International Pictures he took Junge with him to design two elaborate prestige productions, *Moulin Rouge* (1928) and *Piccadilly* (1928)—both far more impressive for their staging than for their scripts. Rachael Low (1971) dismissed the plot of *Moulin Rouge* as 'tripey nonsense', but added that it was 'perhaps the first film in Britain . . . to have been designed with any distinction'.

Returning to Germany, Junge worked on a few more Dupont films before moving to Paris to design the first of Pagnol's Marseilles trilogy, *Marius* (1931). His sets pungently evoked the waterfront tang of the Vieux Port, making the occasional location shot seem pallid by comparison and revealing his knack for creating a stylized atmosphere more real than reality. *Marius* was directed by Alexander Korda, and Junge followed him to London for Korda's first British film, *Service for Ladies* (1932). There he was spotted by Michael Balcon, always on the look-out for German-trained talent, who appointed him head of the art department at Gaumont-British.

At Gaumont, Junge found scope for his managerial no less than his creative skills. Disciplined and stunningly proficient, he co-ordinated the studio's whole staff of designers and draughtsmen, and every Gaumont production of this period—whether credited to him or not—bears the stamp of his influence. It was an influence that could extend even to the camerawork: Junge sketched each set-up in charcoal with a free, bold line, and often as not the final composition, lighting, and camera angle derived from his original sketch. Under his tutelage there grew up a whole generation of future British art directors such as Michael Relph and Peter Proud.

His theatrical flair, already displayed in *Moulin Rouge*, came to the fore in the Jessie Matthews musicals *Evergreen* (1934) and *It's Love Again* (1936). But he also tackled Hitchcock thrillers (*The Man who Knew Too Much*, 1934), costume dramas like *Jew Süss* (1934), action adventures (*King Solomon's Mines*, 1937), Aldwych farces, Jack Hulbert comedies, and George Arliss vehicles. For each he found the appropriate look and atmosphere, from near-realism to total stylization.

When Gaumont cut back production Junge moved to MGM, taking over from Lazare Meerson on *The Citadel* (1938) and creating the nostalgia-soaked school-world of *Goodbye, Mr Chips* (1939). Briefly interned when war broke out, he was released into the crowning period of his career: his six-film partnership with Powell and Press-

burger. Within the family ethos of the Archers (where he was known as 'Uncle Alfred')—and especially in the three great Technicolor productions, *The Life and Death of Colonel Blimp* (1942), *A Matter of Life and Death* (1946), and *Black Narcissus* (1947)—Junge's artistic personality reached its finest fruition. By combining exactitude of detail with a heroic grandeur of conception, he lent credibility to the Archers' most extravagant fantasies. Junge's scrupulous sense of style underpins and anchors the expressionist First World War trenches of *Blimp*, the soaring Stairway to Heaven of *Life and Death*, the hothouse studio-built India of *Narcissus*. In his autobiography (1986), Powell paid fulsome tribute: 'He was a professional among amateurs . . . a Prussian, and fought his pictures through as if they were campaigns. . . . He was probably the greatest art director that films have ever known.'

PHILIP KEMP

SELECT FILMOGRAPHY

Das Wachsfigurenkabinett (Waxworks) (1925); Moulin Rouge (1928); Piccadilly (1928); Marius (1931); I Was a Spy (1933); Evergreen (1934); Jew Süss (1934); The Man who Knew Too Much (1934); Young and Innocent (1937); The Citadel (1938); Goodbye, Mr Chips (1939) ; The Life and Death of Colonel Blimp (1942); A Canterbury Tale (1944); I Know Where I'm Going! (1945); A Matter of Life and Death (1946); Black Narcissus (1947); Ivanhoe (1952); Invitation to the Dance (1954); A Farewell to Arms (1957)

BIBLIOGRAPHY

Carrick, Edward (1948), *Art and Design in the British Film*.
Low, Rachael (1971), *The History of the British Film* iv, *1918-1929*.
Powell, Michael (1986), *A Life in Movies*.
Surowiec, Catherine A. (1992), *Accent on Design: Four European Art Directors*.

Opposite: A scene from Victor Saville's *Evergreen*, starring Jessie Matthews and Sonnie Hale, and designed by Alfred Junge, with *(below)* an original sketch by Junge for the scene

win the war, even if Goebbels held out the desperate hope that *Kolberg* might catalyse a last-minute turn of Germany's fortune.

For a fleeting moment, Goebbels had seemed close to his longed-for film empire. Writing in his diary on 19 May 1942, he reflected:

> We must take a similar course in our film policy as pursued by the Americans on the North American and South American continents. We must become the dominant film power in Europe. Films produced by other states should only be allowed to have local and limited character.

THE POST-WAR YEARS

After the Nazi surrender in May 1945, foreign troops occupied a decimated Reich and American films swiftly went about re-establishing their dominance on the European market. Goebbels's policies and Allied interventions in equal measure would bear responsibility for the sorry state of post-war German film culture, its undeniably 'local and limited character'.

On three separate occasions in the post-war period, German film-makers declared their intention to create a new German film. In 1946, Hans Abich and Rolf Thiele issued a 'Memorandum Regarding a New German Film' and established a studio in the British sector, the Filmaufbau Göttingen. They spoke of making 'films against the film of National Socialism', anti-Ufa productions with a constructive resolve. Their first project, however, *Liebe 47* (1949), touted as its director former Ufa production head Wolfgang Liebeneiner. After a promising series of neo-realistic and critical 'rubble films' like Wolfgang Staudte's *The Murderers Are among Us* (*Die Mörder sind unter uns*, 1946), there would be no decisive break and no novel impetus during the so-called Adenauer era (1949–62). German films of the epoch have a poor reputation, a consequence of American hegemony over the country's film economy and the short-sighted media policies of the ruling Christian Democratic Party.

The result was a provincial cottage industry, one-fifth of whose entire production consisted of sentimental 'homeland films' like *Grün ist die Heide* ('Green is the heather', 1951) and *Der Förster vom Silberwald* ('The game warden from the Silver Forest', 1954), compensatory images of fields, forests, and villages untouched by devastation. There were remakes of Weimar classics (*The Last Laugh* and *The Congress Dances* in 1955, *Mädchen in Uniform* in 1958) and of Nazi standards: *Bel Ami* in 1954, *Kitty und die große Welt* ('Kitty and the big world') in 1956, while Liebeneiner recast Ritter's *Urlaub auf Ehrenwort* ('Leave on parole') in 1955 and Käutner's *Auf Wiedersehen, Franziska* ('Goodbye, Franziska') in 1957. And there was a crop of moribund literary adaptations and strained attempts to emulate Hollywood's blockbusters with reduced means.

There were few memorable titles, no noteworthy discoveries or dramatic breakthroughs. The faces remained familiar, the formulas well known: in 1957 about 70 per cent of all West German feature films employed either a director or script-writer who had been active under Goebbels.

A second initiative came at the end of the 1950s from the group DOC 59, a gathering of documentary film-makers, cinematographers, composers, and the film critic Enno Patalas, and urged closer connections with the international art scene. They wished to merge documentary and fiction, to commingle authenticity and script narrative. Despite a poignant awareness of the dead-end state of German film culture, DOC 59 did not succeed in reviving an arid and provincial state of affairs dominated by worn-out genre fare, mindless escapism, and paint-by-number production schemes, a national cinema with no international presence, distinctive stylistic emphases, alternative strategies, or up-and-coming talents. Returning émigrés like Fritz Lang and Robert Siodmak received no cordial welcome and found only limited success. West German films of the 1950s offered few examples of critical will, of a desire to confront and comprehend the Third Reich. The most striking rare instances of an often called-for but rarely pursued project of *Vergangenheitsbewältigung*, or coming to terms with the past, included Helmut Käutner's *Des Teufels General* ('The Devil's general', 1954), Kurt Hoffmann's *Aren't We Wonderful?* (*Wir Wunderkinder*, 1958), and Bernhard Wicki's *The Bridge* (*Die Brücke*, 1959). With their humanistic rhetoric, the films consoled rather than asked hard questions, focusing on victims of circumstance (a jovial *Luftwaffe* general, a well-meaning political intellectual, a group of boys drafted into the army at the war's end), innocent sufferers held captive by situations they neither control nor fathom. National Socialism was equated with unceasing fear and misery, especially for the average German citizen. At its best, West German film of the 1950s pursued a displaced dialogue with the past; at its most typical, it took an extended vacation from history.

The dire situation, recognized almost universally, reached its nadir when the government awarded no state prize for the best film of 1961, and Ufa suffered financial collapse. During the same year, publicist Joe Hembus's famous polemic, *Der deutsche Film kann gar nicht besser sein* ('German film can in no way be better'), analysed the disastrous situation: '"German film". Every newspaper reader in the Federal Republic habitually responds to this phrase with negative associations, thinking of it in terms like "provincial, mediocre, uninteresting".' In this setting, a third attempt at renewing German film transpired, resulting in the Oberhausen Manifesto of February 1962, a document lamenting the bankrupt state of German film as an art and an industry and promising, brashly and arrogantly, a collective desire to 'create the new German feature film'.

Films of the Adenauer era remain ephemeral items, all but unknown abroad and remembered at best in Germany today as quaint artefacts from the early years of the Federal Republic. Nazi productions have had a much more durable and dynamic effective life. Films of the Third Reich play regularly on German television (often in the guise of old standards and reprises), in matinees for senior citizens, and in festival retrospectives. The few remaining Ufa stars appear regularly on talk shows and reminisce about the 'golden age of German cinema'. More than 200 features from the era are available today as video cassettes. Far from simply being banished to the dustbin of history as aberrations and atrocities, the sights and sounds of National Socialism play a prominent role in contemporary mass culture. SS uniforms and party regalia have become the stuff of popular imagination and trends in fashion. Nazi phantasms have engendered television series and movies of the week. Ritualistic scenes of leather-clad taskmasters and supine victims provide the chic sadomasochistic flair for art-house reflections of the Third Reich like Luchino Visconti's *La caduta degli dei* (*The Damned*) or Liliana Cavani's *The Night Porter*. George Lucas restaged the final scene from *Triumph of the Will* to conclude his blockbuster *Star Wars*. Nazi horrors repulse; Fascism also fascinates. Hitler 'was on again last night,' says a character in Don DeLillo's novel *White Noise*. 'He's always on. We couldn't have television without him.'

Bibliography

Berger, Jürgen, *et al.* (eds.) (1989), *Zwischen gestern und morgen: Westdeutscher Nachkriegsfilm, 1946–1962*.

Bessen, Ursula (ed.) (1989), *Trümmer und Träume*.

Bock, Hans-Michael, and Töteberg, Michael (eds.) (1992), *Das Ufa-Buch*.

Courtade, Francis, and Cadars, Pierre (1972), *Le Cinéma nazi*.

Friedländer, Saul (1989), *Reflections of Nazism*.

Hembus, Joe (1961), *Der deutsche Film kann gar nicht besser sein*.

Jacobsen, Wolfgang, Kaes, Anton, and Prinzler, Hans Helmut (eds.) (1993), *Geschichte des deutschen Films*.

Kreimeier, Klaus (1992), *Die Ufa-Story: Geschichte eines Filmkonzerns*.

Petley, Julian (1979), *Capital and Culture: German Cinema 1933–45*.

Virilio, Paul (1984), *Guerre et cinéma, i: Logistique de la perception*.

East Central Europe Before the Second World War

MAŁGORZATA HENDRYKOWSKA

EARLY DAYS

The beginnings and subsequent development of cinematography in the countries of east central Europe share a number of common features. In what are now the Czech Republic, Slovakia, Hungary, Serbia, Croatia, and Poland (then partitioned between Austria, Prussia, and Russia) the first Lumière film shows took place in 1896, in keen competition with entrepreneurs using the apparatus of Thomas Alva Edison. 'Edison's men' arrived in Prague five days before Eugène Dupont, the representative of the Lumière brothers. The Lumière Cinématographe was first exhibited in Belgrade in May 1896, and in the Austrian sector of Poland in November of that year, though other Polish cities such as Poznań, Warsaw, and Lvov were already familiar with the idea of animated photographs thanks to displays of Edison's Vitascope.

There were many pioneers working on the idea of animated photography in east central Europe, the most important being the Czech Jan Krizenecký, and the Poles Jan Lebiedziński, Kazimierz Prószyński, and Jan Szczepanik. This initial period of film development also saw the first theoretical works of Bolesław Matuszewski, the Polish photographer and film operator resident in Paris: 'Une nouvelle source de l'histoire (création d'un dépôt de cinématographie historique)', and 'La photographie animée, ce qu'elle est et ce qu'elle doit être', published in March and August 1898 respectively. Emphasizing the significance of motion picture photography, its historical value and vast cognitive potential, Matuszewski was the first to postulate the need to create a comprehensive film archive, comprising every kind of film documentation.

In the countries of east central Europe, the first generation of people who worked with film were mainly stage actors, theatrical directors, journalists, professional photographers, and authors of popular literature. Pioneers of film production in Hungary included Mihály Kertész, an actor at the National Theatre, and the journalist Sándor Korda. After a decade and a half of film-making in Hungary (their film output between 1912 and 1919 comprised thirty-nine and twenty-four items respectively), they went on to work with distinction in film industries abroad; Kertész in America, under the name Michael Curtiz, and Korda in England, as Alexander Korda.

The first full-length feature films in east central Europe were created after 1910, at the same time as in Italy and France. In 1911, with the participation of artists from the Variety Theatre in Warsaw (then in the Russian sector) where he was both actor and director, Antoni Bednarczyk made the first Polish feature film entitled *The History of Sin*, based on the scandalous and highly popular novel by Stefan Żeromski. A further ten feature films were made in the same year, including three in Yiddish. By the outbreak of the First World War, over 50 full-length feature films, and some 350 shorts (fiction, news films, documentaries) had been produced by the three sectors of partitioned Poland.

In Hungary, the first 'artistic film drama' was directed in 1912 by Mihály Kertész from a screenplay by Ivan Siklosi and Imre Roboz, and entitled *Ma es holnap* ('Today and tomorrow'). The main roles were played by Artur Somlay and Ilona Aczel, actors from the National Theatre, and Mihály Kertész himself (from the Hungarian Theatre). The film's première, on 14 October 1912, is generally considered to be the birth of Hungarian cinema. The greatest success of Czech feature production was the screening of Bedřich Smetana's opera *The Bartered Bride*, directed by Oldrich Kminak (1913). In Belgrade, the first feature film involving the participation of actors was produced in 1910. Entitled *Karadjordje*, it was directed by a Serb, I. Stojadinović, the camera operator being Jules Berrie, a Frenchman from the firm of Pathé.

The period before the First World War also saw the founding of the first indigenous film production companies, most notably Antonin Pech's Kinofa (1907–12) and Max Urban's Fotokinema (later ASUM) in Prague, and Aleksander Hertz's Sfinks in Warsaw. A cinema network was well developed, especially in the big cities, where films were the most popular and accessible form of entertainment. Before 1914, over 300 permanent cinemas were in operation on Polish territory. One hundred and fourteen cinemas were opened in Budapest in 1913 alone. Film magazines soon began to appear: *A kinematograf* (1907), *Mozgofenykep hirado* (1908), and the film periodicals published by Korda, *Pesti mozi* (1912), *Mozi* (1913), and *Mozihet* (1915–19) in Hungary; the Polish *Kino-teatr i sport* ('Cinema-theatre and sport', 1914) and *Scena i ekran* ('Stage and screen', 1913). Like the films of the time, they show the mutual penetration of élite and mass culture.

THE FIRST WORLD WAR

The advent of the First World War influenced the development of these national cinemas to an uneven extent. Both Serbia and Croatia (then part of the Austro-Hungarian Empire) mainly produced films reporting on military operations, and shorts and middle-length propaganda films. Between 1915 and 1918 Hungary produced a total of 100 films. On Czech and Slovak soil the war similarly favoured the intensive development of a self-sufficient film industry. Historians often trace to this period the beginnings of the trend known as 'cinema of small realism', among whose precursors was Antonin Frencel's *Zlate srdecko* ('Little heart of gold', 1916).

As most of the fighting on the eastern front took place on Polish territory, the young Polish film industry found itself in a far more difficult position. The first mobilization destroyed film production companies in the Austrian sector, and when evacuating Warsaw, the Russian army deported many of the actors who had hitherto supplied the basic film casts. In practical terms, the only film company still operating on Polish territory during the war years was Aleksander Hertz's Sfinks, where Pola Negri made her film début in *Slave of her Senses* (*Niewolnica zmysłów*, 1914). Between 1915 and 1917 Pola Negri played in seven other films produced by Sfinks, which in spite of considerable difficulties succeeded in completing twenty-four full-length feature films over that period.

During the First World War, many Polish actors, producers, and operators made their débuts beyond the frontiers of Poland, with mixed success. Soava Gallone (born Stanisława Winawerówna) and Helena Makowska gained great popularity in Italy. In 1917 Pola Negri (born Apolonia Chałupiec) left Warsaw for Berlin, as did Hella Moja (Helena Mojezewska) and Mia Mara (Maria Gudowicz, later known as Lya Mara). Władysław Starewicz (later Ladislas Starewitch), who produced his first animated films in Polish Lithuania in 1910, achieved an important position as a producer in Moscow. Ryszard Bolesławski also made his début as an actor in Russia, emigrating later (after a brief return to Poland) to western Europe and then the United States. Of all the expatriate Polish actors on Russian soil, however, it was Antoni Fertner who attained the greatest popularity.

THE POST-WAR YEARS

The end of the war and the collapse of the multi-national empires brought independence to the peoples of east central Europe and the creation of nation states in Poland, Hungary, Czechoslovakia, and Yugoslavia, influencing both the evolution of local film production and the thetics of the movies themselves. The dominant trend in most of these countries was towards screen adaptations of national classical literature and of popular best sellers.

Yugoslavia

After the war, film production activity was, relatively speaking, least dynamic in the newly created Kingdom of Serbs, Croats, and Slovenes. As from 1918, film production was concentrated mainly in two centres, Zagreb in Croatia

and Belgrade in Serbia. At the beginning of the 1920s the production company Yugoslavia Film operated in Zagreb, and turned out several feature films, documentaries, and news films, before folding a few years later. The Italian director and actor Tito Strozzi formed his own production company, Strozzi Film, and produced a full-length feature entitled *Deserted Palaces* (1925) which is considered to be one of the best Yugoslav silent films. In the 1920s several silent films were also produced in Belgrade, notably the film grotesque *King of Charleston* (1926, directed by K. Novaković) and the patriotic drama *With Faith in God* (1932, directed by M. A. Popović). In Slovenia several films were made to popularize tourism. When sound was introduced, domestic production virtually ground to a halt, and the first Yugoslav sound films were produced by American and German firms (for instance *Love and Passion*, 1932; *The Vampire from the Mountain of Durmitor*, 1932). After 1933, Yugoslav production was limited mainly to documentaries and reportage.

Czechoslovakia

From the very beginning, Czech cinema drew inspiration from national literature and theatre. In the independent State of Czechoslovakia the A–B Company had by 1921 launched a studio with modern equipment in Vinohrady. That same year saw the screening of the fairy-tale *Zlaty klicek* ('The gold key', 1921), based on an original screenplay by Karel Čapek, and of Bozena Nemcowa's popular novel *Babicka* ('Grandmother', 1921), produced by František Čáp. In 1925 another popular work was adapted for the screen, Alois Jirásek's play *Lucerna* ('Street lamp', 1925), and a first attempt was made to film Jaroslav Hašek's novel *The Good Soldier Schweik*. The era of the silent film witnessed the production of three episodes from Hašek's book: *Švejk v ruském zajétí* ('Schweik in Russian captivity', dir. Svatopluk Inneman, 1926), *Švejk na fronte* ('Schweik at the front', dir. Karel Lamač, 1926) and *Švejk v civilu* ('Schweik in mufti', dir. Gustav Machatý, 1927).

After 1925, Gustav Machatý was to play an important role in Czech cinema, and his enormously successful film *Erotikon* (1929) is generally considered to be a pioneering work in the history of erotic cinema. Four years later, he harked back to the poetic conception of *Erotikon* in *Ecstasy* (*Extase*, 1933), engaging foreign actors in the leading roles as he had in the earlier film. The shocking scene of a girl bathing naked in a pond was performed by the Viennese actress Hedy Kiesler (later Hedy Lamarr). She was partnered by Aribert Mog in the German, and Pierre Nay in the French version, while the part of her husband was played by the Yugoslav Zvonimir Rogoz. Enriched with sound effects, *Ecstasy* was a world-wide sensation, causing the moral censor to intervene, and incurring the disapproval of the Catholic Church. But it was greeted enthusiastically by independent-minded viewers, and the

American writer Henry Miller wrote an extensive analytical study of the film.

In the heyday of the silent cinema, the Czech film industry was producing between thirty and thirty-five feature films annually. The first Czech sound film was released in February 1930, and thereafter the number of sound films increased steadily. In Czechoslovakia as elsewhere, audiences were hungry for sound films in their native tongue, and the Czech film industry, unlike the Yugoslav, was able to equip itself to supply them.

Hungary

Dramatic political events in the immediate post-war years meant that Hungarian cinema followed a different course from its neighbours. During the brief period of the Hungarian Republic of Councils (April–August 1919), the film industry was nationalized; this was the first time this had happened anywhere, preceding the Soviet Union by several months. A programme for the future development of national cinema was elaborated, but following the collapse of the Republic, it was never implemented. After 1919 Hungarian film production was checked, and output fell dramatically. During the regime of Admiral Horthy, many talented film-makers and actors of European renown emigrated abroad, among them Mihály Kertész, Paul Fejos, Sándor Korda, the actors Peter Lorre, Marta Eggerth, Paul Lucas, Bela Lugosi, Mischa Auer, and the theoretician of the cinema, Balázs. The decline in production was partially compensated by the development of a Hungarian school of theoretical writing about the cinema. Forced into emigration, Balázs published one of the seminal works of early film theory, *Der sichtbare mensch* (*The Visible Man*), in Germany in 1924. The following year, in Budapest, Ivan Hevesy brought out his study *A filmjatek osztetikaja es dramturgaja* ('Aesthetics and Structure of Film Drama'), which, however, remained largely unread outside his native Hungary. It was some years before Hungarian film production revived following the world-wide expansion of sound cinema.

Poland

In Poland there were many obstacles to the creation of a film industry and market. Although the newly independent Polish State had a central administration, there were still colossal administrative, legal, economic, social, and national differences between the former Russian, Prussian, and Austrian sectors. In the circumstances the State evinced no interest in the development of a nationwide film industry. In the immediate post-war years up to 1922, the main emphasis was on the purchase of foreign films, and domestic production accounted for only a small percentage of films shown on screen—twenty titles in 1922. The number of cinemas in this period is estimated at 700 to 750, but only 400 were active seven days a week.

Of the numerous production companies that came to life in this period only Sfinks (collaborating with Ufa) survived and strengthened its position. This was where the greatest star of Poland's inter-war cinema, Jadwiga Smosarska, made her début in 1920. Between 1923 and 1926 the crisis in Polish cinema deepened, hitting a record low in 1925 when only four films were produced, the main reason being that the State imposed exceptionally harsh financial conditions on potential film producers and cinema owners, including 75 per cent taxation.

Despite this unpromising situation, most of the top-ranking west European and American titles reached the Polish market, and Polish artists and intellectuals began to take a serious and systematic interest in film, seeing in it not only a form of popular entertainment, but a new form of artistic expression. Foremost among critics and writers about cinema in the 1920s were the poet and columnist Antoni Słonimski, Leon Trystan, and the art historian Stefania Zahorska. The literary critic and novelist Karol Irzykowski wrote *The Tenth Muse: Aesthetic Problems of the Cinema* (1924), a pioneering work on the theory of cinema that is still insufficiently known in Europe.

Over a dozen film directors were active in this period in Poland, only three of whom—Franciszek Zyndram-Mucha, Wiktor Biegański, and Henryk Szaro—could boast genuine artistic achievements. After the May coup of 1926, the screening of national literary masterpieces became the order of the day—notably *Pan Tadeusz* (directed by Ryszard Ordyński and based on the epic poem by Adam Mickiewicz), *Promised Land* (*Ziemia obiecana*, based on the novel by Władysław Reymont and directed by M. Krawicz and M. Galewski), and *Early Spring* (*Przedwiośnie*, based on the novel by Stefan Żeromski and directed by Henryk Szaro). In the second half of the decade some of the future big names such as Leonard Buczkowski, Aleksander Ford, Józef Lejtes, and Michał Waszyński, made their débuts as directors.

SOUND AND DOMESTIC FILM PRODUCTION

Hungary

The first sound film to be shown in Budapest was Warner Bros.' *The Singing Fool* with Al Jolson, in September 1929. Hungarian sound films began to be made in the early 1930s. Between 1934 and 1944 the repertory predominantly consisted of run-of-the-mill comedies, and melodramas that were artistically and technically primitive, generally being produced in little more than a fortnight. However, two productions of this period enjoy a permanent position in the history of Hungarian film. The first artistically significant film was *Hortobagy*, a fictionalized documentary about the life of the inhabitants of Puszty Hortobagy directed by Georg Höllering in 1935. The second was István Szöts's drama *Emberek a havason* (*The*

Martin Frič's *Janošík* (1936)

Mountain People, 1942). Dealing with the life of woodcutters in Transylvania, and filmed within a realistic convention and in natural scenery with the participation of many eminent actors, it received the main prize at the Venice Biennale in 1942.

The Second World War had major effects on the Hungarian film industry, first positive and then negative. With the outbreak of war the industry found itself in a new situation as the influx of west European and American films was halted, and it began to produce some fifty films annually (forty-five feature films in 1942, fifty-three in 1943). But this halcyon period (in terms of quantity if not quality) was followed by disaster as the German army on the Eastern Front collapsed before the Red Army onslaught. The technical base of Hungarian cinema was totally devastated. The retreating German troops evacuated most of the production equipment, film studios had been bombed into ruins during military operations, and only 280 cinemas in the entire country were still functioning.

Czechoslovakia

The first Czech sound films were an adaptation of Erwin Egon Kisch's novella *Tonka Šibenice* (*Whence there is no Return*, 1929), directed by Karel Anton with the Yugoslav actress Ita Rina in the main role, and *Když struny Lkají* (*Her Boy*, 1930), directed by Fryderyk Feher. Major success came with Karel Lamac's film *C. a K. polni marsalek* (*The False Marshal*, 1930), with the participation of the distinguished comic actor Vlasta Burian. Screenings of particularly outstanding literary works soon began to appear. Martin Frič adapted Hašek's novel *The Good Soldier Schweik* (*Dobry vojak Švejk*, 1931) and Nikolai Gogol's *The Government Inspector*.

In the 1930s the Czechoslovak film industry underwent considerable expansion, with new studios and laboratories created. In 1933 a modern production company was launched in Barrandow. Despite strong tendencies towards commercialization, film-makers such as Josef Rovenský, Gustav Machatý, Martin Frič, and, later, Otakar Vávra and Hugo Haas, created works of original and innovative artistic merit that earned Czech cinema a foremost position among the other countries of east central Europe. International recognition was not slow in coming. A group of films enjoyed international acclaim at the Venice Film Festival in 1934; Josef Rovenský's film *Reka* ('The river', 1933), a subtle tale about the tragic love of two teenagers; a documentary about the Slovak countryside called *Zem spieva* ('The earth sings', 1933) by Karel Plicki; together with Machatý's *Ecstasy*, and the short *Boure nad Tatrami* ('Storm on the Tatras', 1932) by Tomas Trnka. They were awarded the Cup of the City of Venice, the prize for the best set of films of high artistic merit, for direction and skill in presenting an original picture of nature. In 1936 Rovenský enjoyed another triumph in Venice with *Marysa* (1935), a suggestive folk drama from southern Moravia based on the play by Alois and Vilem Mrstik. The folk ballad *Janošik* (1936), directed by Martin Frič, was also awarded a medal at this same festival, and two years later Otakar Vávra's *Cech panien kutnohorskich* ('Guild of the girls of Kutna Hora', 1938) was likewise honoured in Venice.

The mid-1930s saw a substantial increase in the number of films produced in Czechoslovakia—thirty-four in 1934, forty-nine in 1936, forty-one in 1938. By 1938 the Republic could boast 1,824 cinemas with 600,000 seats overall. After the signing of the Munich Pact a number of film people, including Voskovec and Haas, emigrated abroad. However, far from being reduced during the war, the technical production base of Czech cinema, like the Hungarian, underwent considerable expansion, and many artistic and auxiliary workers continued on in the industry throughout the war. The German occupation regime in Czechoslovakia was less brutal than in Poland or Russia, and this protected the production potential of the film industry. More than 100 feature films were produced by Czech studios during this period, with the Germans further expanding the modern production base in Barrandow in Prague. After the end of the war in 1945, Czechoslovak cinema was able to go into production without delay.

Poland

In Warsaw, as in Budapest, the first sound film to be shown was Warner Bros.' *The Singing Fool* in September 1929. The first Polish sound film was shown there six months later, in March 1930, and was *Moralność Pani Dulskiej* ('The morality of Mrs Dulska'), based on the well-known drama by Gabriela Zapolska. The Warsaw firm Syrena Record was commissioned to create a sound-track using gramophone records. In its early days the sound film in Poland frequently drew on existing cabaret forms, exploiting its songs, sketches, and specific brand of humour. Pre-war Polish cabaret was on a par with the best revues in western Europe, so the sound film benefited from this symbiosis. Theatre and cabaret actors played an essential part in raising the standards of Polish film in the 1930s. Among the Polish film-makers Michał Waszyński beat all records

for dynamism, producing (also as co-author) forty-one feature films between 1929 and 1939. Juliusz Gardan, Ryszard Ordyński, and Józef Lejtes (the most highly individualistic artist among them), all enjoyed the reputation of ambitious and dedicated film talents, with Lejtes's films particularly noteworthy among the artistic achievements of Polish cinema in the inter-war period.

In the first half of the 1930s the bulk of Polish film production consisted of comedies, of which the majority did not reach above the level of banal farce. There was, however, no lack of first-rate comic actors, including the ever-popular Antoni Fertner, of young romantic leads, or of distinguished theatrical actors who turned in first-rate performances in often relatively mediocre films.

After 1935 the predominance of comedy gave way to adaptations of novels with a social accent or message. In 1937 Józef Lejtes made *Dziewczęta z Nowolipek* ('The girls from Nowolipki Street'), adapted from the novel by Pola Gojawiczyńska, following it in 1938 with *Granica* ('The frontier'), from the novel by Zofia Nalkowska. Also in 1938, Eugeniusz Cekalski and Karol Szolowski together directed *Strachy* ('Ghosts'), based on the novel by Maria Ukniewska. All three combined sound craftsmanship with an in-depth study of controversial aspects of contemporary manners and morals. Historical films were also well represented, with Lejtes again making two major contributions to the genre: *Barbara Radziwillowna* (1936), and *Kosciuszko pod Raclawicami* ('Kosciuszko at the Battle of Raclawice', 1938). Adaptations of popular literature included Gardan's *Tredowata* ('The leper woman', 1936) and Szaro's *Ordynat Michorowski* ('Count Michorowski', 1937), from novels by Helena Mniszek; and *Znachor* ('The witch-doctor', 1937), *Profesor Wilczur* (1938), and *Trzy serca* ('Three Hearts', 1939), based on the novels by Tadeusz Dolega-Mostowicz and directed by Michał Waszyński. A noteworthy feature of many of these Polish films was the music specially written for them by such composers as Henryk Wars, Jerzy Peterburski, Władysław Szpilman, Jan Maklakiewicz and Roman Palester.

Although not much exported, Polish films of the 1930s enjoyed considerable international esteem and films by Lejtes and other Polish directors won prizes at Venice. Production levels rose slowly throughout the decade, from fourteen films per year in 1932–4 to between twenty-three and twenty-six in 1936–8. Artistic standards rose too, but production was hampered by the lack of an adequate technical base and the reluctance of producers, dependent as they were on exhibitors, to take artistic risks. Meanwhile, outside the commercial sector, film culture throve. Important works were written by Zofia Lissa on film music, by Boleslaw W. Lewicki on the influence of film upon young people, and by Leopold Blaustein on the psychology of the film spectator. There was a lively culture of ciné-clubs, where people met to watch and discuss films of all

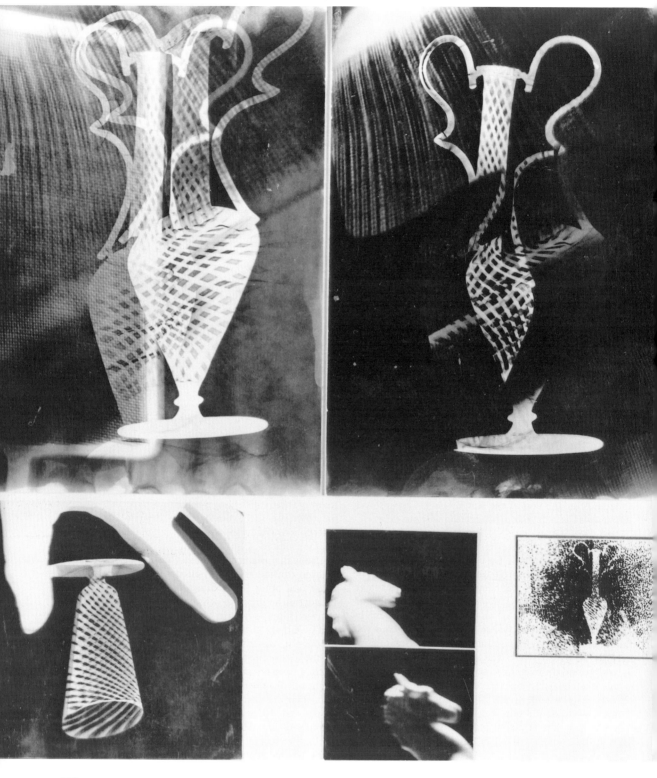

types, the most important being START in Warsaw and Awangarda in Lvov. Mention should also be made of the experimental film work of Franciszka and Stefan Themerson, who carried on the traditions of the European avant-garde in films such as *Apteka* ('The pharmacy', 1930), *Europa* (1932), and *Przygoda czlowieka poczciwego* ('The adventures of a good citizen', 1937).

The outbreak of war in September 1939 put a definitive end to this period of artistic ferment and conflictual evolution. Over the next six years many actors, directors, script-writers, and composers lost their lives at the hands of the Nazi invaders. Others, including Józef Lejtes, Michał Waszyński, Henryk Wars, Franciszka and Stefan Themerson, Ryszard Ordyński, and Stanisław Sielański, ended up in foreign countries, where they carried on working in their profession. After 1945 only a few of the wartime *émigrés* chose to return to a homeland devastated by war and now under Communist domination.

Images from Franciszka and Stefan Themerson's *Moments musicaux* (*Drobiazg melodyjny*). Made in Poland in 1934, the film itself is now lost, but surviving materials were collaged together by Stefan Themerson in London in the 1940s.

Bibliography

Balázs, Béla (1952), *Theory of the Film*.

Bartošek, Luboš (1986), *Naš film: kapitoly z dějin, 1896–1945* ('Our [Czechoslovak] film; chapters in its history').

Hendrykowska, Małgorzata (1993a), '*Śladami tamtych cieni: film w kulturze polskiej przelomu stułci, 1895–1914* ('In search of distant shadows: film in Polish turn-of-the-century culture').

—— (1993b). *Sladami tamtych cieni: film w Kulturze polskiej pr prezełomu stuleci, 1895–1914*.

Kosanović, Dejan (1986), *Poceci kinematografija na tlu Jugoslawije, 1896–1918* ('The beginnings of cinema in Yugoslavia').

Ozimek, Stanisław (1974), *Film polski w wojennej potrzebie* ('Polish film under the stress of war').

Rittaud–Hutinet, Jacques (1985), *Le Cinéma des origines: les frères Lumière et leurs opérateurs*.

Toeplitz, Jerzy (1970), *Historia sztuki filmowej* ('History of film art'), vol. v.

Soviet Film Under Stalin

PETER KENEZ

THE 1930S AND SOCIALIST REALISM

At the end of the 1920s Soviet film enjoyed a well-deserved world-wide reputation, but within a short time the fame and influence of the great directors was lost; the golden age was brief and the eclipse sudden and long lasting. The coming of the sound film made the famous 'Russian montage' outdated, and therefore was a factor in the decline. But far more important in destroying the reputation of the Soviet cinema were the political changes that took place in the early 1930s.

From 1928 to 1932 the Soviet Union experienced a massive transformation, touching on all aspects of life. The changes introduced in the cultural sphere were part and parcel of wider changes that included forcibly collectivizing the countryside, liquidating the kulaks, and attempting to build an industrial civilization in the shortest possible time. The destruction of the moderate pluralism that had existed in the 1920s came to be called by the Stalinists, perversely, 'Cultural Revolution'. Artists were cajoled and coerced to come up with principles and methods that would be suitable in the new order. Some were passive victims, but all too often they collaborated.

Although in its golden age Soviet film was widely admired, the Stalinist leadership was dissatisfied. The Bolsheviks considered film to be an excellent instrument for bringing their message to the people, and they aimed to use it, more than any other artistic medium, for creating the 'new socialist man'. These excessively high expectations were bound to lead to disappointment: films that were artistically successful and made in a Communist spirit did not attract a large enough audience. The government wanted artistically worthwhile, commercially successful, and politically correct films. It turned out that these requirements pointed in different directions and no film-maker could possibly satisfy them all.

The Cultural Revolution aimed to remedy what seemed a fault to the Bolshevik leaders: the most interesting and experimental works from an artistic point of view remained inaccessible to simple people. In order to make an impact on workers and peasants, audiences had to be attracted. Bolshevik policies brought about some of the desired results, and in the course of the 1930s film-going for the first time became part of the life of the average citizen. In the 1920s cinema was basically an urban entertainment, but the bulk of the people lived in villages. Now the peasantry was coerced to join collective farms and the collectives were pressured to buy projectors. Between 1928 and 1940 the number of installations quadrupled and the number of tickets sold tripled.

Soviet industry was finally successful in producing its own raw film, projectors, and other equipment. Although the technical quality of Soviet production remained far behind the west, this was still a considerable achievement. The coming of sound was attractive to the propagandists, for simple ideas could, it was thought, be better conveyed with sound than with images. On the other hand, the technological burden of reorganizing the industry was great. Even as late as the Second World War the Soviet Union was forced to make silent versions of most films, because much of the country lacked sound projection equipment.

The choice available to film-goers greatly diminished. The import of foreign films, which had been very popular in the previous decade, dried to a trickle. The number of domestically produced films also declined. Whereas in the late 1920s the industry had been producing between 120 and 140 films yearly, by 1933 output dropped to 35 and remained stationary for the rest of the 1930s.

Numerical decline went hand in hand with a reduction in stylistic variety, as the heavy hand of the Party made itself felt in the control of film production. This process began in the late 1920s and steadily intensified. Socialist Realism was declared to be the USSR's official artistic practice in 1934, but it derived from the politics of Cultural Revolution of 1928–32. Militant cultural organizations, notably RAPP (the Russian Association of Proletarian Writers), called for the suppression of all works by non-Communist or non-proletarian artists. These views won Party support during much of the Cultural Revolution, but the Central Committee consolidated all literary organizations in 1932, thus effectively suppressing the more militant factions like RAPP, and looked to a long-range artistic policy that promised to support Soviet development while remaining accessible and legible to the masses. In so doing it promoted certain works which both conformed to conventions of mimetic fiction and provided clear social messages strengthening the Soviet system. This was soon codified as Socialist Realism.

Socialist Realism derived in part from nineteenth-century realism. Its 'transparent' style was considered an appropriate vessel for topical themes concerning socialism and Soviet development. Its tenets held that artists should infuse works with precise ideological formulations such as so-called *partiinost* (party spirit), the idea that the Party's leadership in social affairs should be affirmed at all times.

By the time Socialist Realism was formally adopted at the First All-Union Writers' Conference in 1934, it had been made doctrinal practice in all the arts. Its application to cinema coincided with the process of bringing the films under central planning in line with other industries during the First Five Year Plan. Soviet film studios were incorporated into a single state bureaucracy (in contrast to the semi-market system of the 1920s), assuring increased control over creative affairs.

Socialist Realist novels and films followed a master plot: the hero, under the tutelage of a positive character, a Party leader with well-developed Communist class-consciousness, overcomes obstacles, unmasks the villain, a person with unreasoned hatred for decent socialist society, and in the process himself acquires superior consciousness—that is, becomes a better person.

Although Socialist Realism as applied in the Soviet Union made appeal to models of literary and artistic realism, and purported to represent Soviet life in accordance with the reality of socialist development, it was a very suspect form of realism. It can therefore also be seen in negative terms—not just for what it did, but for what it did not do. By replacing genuine realism with an appearance of realism, it impeded the contemplation of the human condition and the investigation of social issues: people were portrayed as they were supposed to be, and Soviet society was portrayed as successfully on the road to socialism. To put across this simplistic view, Socialist Realist art had to be given an absolute monopoly, for it had to convince the audience that it alone depicted the world as it really was. It therefore required a political context in which it could be imposed forcibly. Socialist Realism is middlebrow, formulaic art, which excludes irony, ambiguity, and experimentation. Such qualities would impede immediate comprehension by the half-educated and therefore lessen the didactic value of the product.

Between 1933 and 1940 inclusive, Soviet studios made 308 films. Of these 54 were made for children, including some of the best films of the decade, such as Mark Donskoi's Gorky trilogy. These films were didactic and aimed to educate children in the Communist spirit by showing, for example, the difficult life of children in capitalist countries, their heroic struggle, and, most importantly and frequently, the importance of the collective.

Historical spectacles became especially frequent in the second half of the decade, as the regime paid increasing attention to rekindling patriotism by old-fashioned appeals to national glory. These films were made about heroes such as Alexander Nevsky, Peter the Great, or Marshal Suvorov, and were often shamelessly anachronistic: Pugachev and Stenka Razin, for example, two Cossack rebels, were shown analysing class relations in Marxist terms and before their executions consoling their followers by predicting the coming of a great and glorious revolution.

Sixty-one films dealt with the Revolution and Civil War. These included such well-known films as *Chapayev* (1934), directed by Sergei and Georgi Vasiliev, the most popular and perhaps best film of the decade; Kozintsev and Trauberg's Maxim trilogy (1938–40); and Alexander Zarkhi and Iosif Kheifits's *The Baltic Deputy* (*Deputat Baltiki*, 1936). Each national republic that had a studio made at least one film on the establishment of Soviet power.

The rest of the films were set in the contemporary world. Of these only twelve took place in a factory—a remarkably small number when one considers the significance of economic propaganda in the Soviet agenda. Film-makers seem to have found it difficult to make interesting films about workers and tended to avoid them. By contrast seventeen took place on a collective farm, many of them musical comedies—giving rise to the impression that life in the countryside was a never-ending round of dancing and singing. Film-makers, and presumably audiences, liked exotic locales and many films were made about the exploits of explorers, geologists, and pilots; between 1938 and 1940 alone, eight films had pilots as heroes.

A recurrent theme in films dealing with contemporary life was the struggle against saboteurs and traitors. This was an age of denunciations, phoney trials, and uncovering unbelievable plots. In the films, as in the confessions at the show trials, the enemy carried out the most dastardly acts out of an unreasoned hatred for socialism. In more than half the films about contemporary life (fifty-two out of eighty-five), the hero unmasked hidden enemies who had committed criminal acts. The enemy turned out to be sometimes his best friend, sometimes his wife, and sometimes his father.

In 1940 a curious phenomenon occurred. Of the thirty films in that year with contemporary subjects, not one focused on traitors. The internal enemy disappeared and his place was taken by foreigners or their agents. The country was preparing to face a foreign foe: instead of ferreting out the presumed internal enemy, films now preached how the nations making up the Soviet Union must work together for the common good.

All through the 1930s the films depicted the outside world as undifferentiated, threatening, and uniformly

High jinks on the collective farm: Grigori Alexandrov's *Volga—Volga* (1937)

„ВОЛГА – ВОЛГА"
РОИЗ-ВО МОСКОВСКОЙ ОРДЕНА ЛЕНИНА
к/т МОСФИЛЬМ укрж № 110   9

Boris Babochkin (right) as a Red Army commander in a scene from the popular and much-imitated Civil War drama *Chapayev* (1934), directed by Sergei and Georgi Vasiliev

miserable. In this world people were starving to death, brutal police were repressing the Communist movement, and the ultimate concern of workers was the defence of the Soviet Union, the workers' fatherland. A recurring theme was foreigners coming to the USSR and finding there a rich and happy life. Twenty films were set outside the Soviet Union, the choice of locales varying with the twists and turns of Soviet foreign policy. Before 1935 an unnamed foreign country was usually portrayed. Ivan Pyriev's *Konveyor smerti* ('Conveyor of death'), for example, took place in a generic west, in which street signs are in English, French, and German. Pudovkin's *Deserter* (*Dezertir*, 1933), where Germany was specified, not only did not comment on Fascism, but (in accordance with the line then taken by the Comintern) depicted the Social Democrats as the main enemies of the Communist workers. Between 1935, when the Comintern line shifted, and 1939, six anti-Nazi films were made, the best and most prominent of which were *Professor Mamlok* and *Semia Oppenheim* ('The Oppenheim family'). In 1939 audiences could see how the Red Army brought a better life to Ukrainians and Belorussians, just liberated from supposed Polish oppression.

The fundamental cause of the decline in the number of films made and exhibited in the Soviet Union was censorship. The authorities set ever more stringent requirements that made film-making cumbersome and time-consuming (particularly if the Party line changed during the making of the film). Making a film in the Soviet Union took much longer than in the west, or than it had done in the 1920s.

Censorship aggravated the script famine, a problem that had plagued Soviet Russian film from the earliest days. According to official doctrine, it was the script-writer, rather than the director, who was the crucial figure and ultimately responsible. Stalin thought that the director was merely a technician whose only task was to position the camera, following instructions already in the script. Publicists of the time insisted on the 'iron scenario', strictly limiting the independence of the director, and denounced the idea of directorial freedom as a remnant of formalism. It obviously made no sense to examine the script carefully at many levels of censorship and then allow the director to make changes as he saw fit. A by-product of this situation was that, while only a few directors lost their lives during the terror, a far larger number of script-writers suffered this fate.

From the late 1930s until his death in 1953, Stalin became the supreme censor, who personally saw and approved every film released. Like Goebbels in Nazi Germany, he micro-managed the cinema, suggesting changes in titles, supporting favoured directors and actors, and reviewing scripts. In some politically sensitive films, such as Friedrich Ermler's *The Great Citizen* (*Veliky grazhdanin*, 1939), the changes were substantial and Stalin could be regarded almost as a co-author. On one occasion he countermanded the censors and not only allowed a comedy by Alexandrov to be shown but went to the trouble of thinking up twelve different titles for the film, eventually choosing 'Shining Path' in preference to 'Cinderella'.

Through its insistence on making every film accessible even to the least literate, the obstacles put in the way of artistic experiment, and the denunciation of every trace of individual style as 'formalist', the regime destroyed the talent of great artists. It was often the most 'revolutionary', the most 'leftist' artists who suffered the most. The wonderful originality of Vertov's, Dovzhenko's, and Pudovkin's talent gradually disappeared. The formerly innovative team of Grigory Kozintsev and Leonid Trauberg became increasingly conservative. Kuleshov stopped making films. Even Eisenstein, whose individuality was indestructible, was forced to restrain his 'formalist' tendencies. When finally he was allowed to complete a film, *Alexander Nevsky*, in 1938, his style had undergone significant changes, though his personality remained clearly visible.

Film-makers contributed to the climate of denunciation by justifying it. In this respect, no prominent director with the exception of Kuleshov, who stopped making films after 1933, has a very good record. Eisenstein made his film *Bezhin Meadow* (*Bezhin lug*, 1935–7) on the basis of a story by Pavel Morozov, its purpose being to justify the son's betrayal of his father. In Dovzhenko's *Aerograd* (1935) a man shoots his friend because he turned out to be a traitor. In Pyriev's *Partiinyi bilet* ('Party card'), perhaps the single most distasteful film of the decade, the wife shoots her husband, who was the hidden enemy. Ermler's *Vstrechny* ('Counterplan', 1932–co-directed by Sergei Yutkevich) was about the necessity of fighting saboteurs, while *The Great Citizen* related the Stalinist version of the murder of Kirov and the great purge trials. (During the making of *The Great Citizen* four people associated with it were arrested.) In a period of terror and confusion none of these directors seems to have actively tried to avoid involvement in making these films. Everyone was under threat if they failed to conform and many were at least partially convinced of the rightness of what they were doing.

THE GREAT PATRIOTIC WAR

The wartime Soviet cinema presents an irony. In every country cinema became more controlled by the State, and more heavily propagandistic. In the Soviet Union too, cinema was mobilized for the war effort, and the films

produced were obviously propaganda films. Nevertheless, given the immediate past and future of Soviet cinema, the period of the war appears now as an oasis of freedom. The regime allowed a measure of artistic experiment. During the war film-makers engaged with subjects about which they cared deeply and expressed genuinely felt emotions.

In June 1941 Hitler invaded the Soviet Union and German troops advanced rapidly towards Moscow. The leaders of the Soviet film industry dealt with the difficult situation to the best of their abilities and mobilized the industry with astonishing speed. They devoted most of their scarce resources to making documentaries and prevailed on leading directors to take on the task of editing newsreels. Studios changed the scenarios of those features that were already in production by adding war themes. *Mashenka*, directed by Iuli Raizman, for example, which was almost ready before the invasion, had to be remade. Originally planned as a light comedy showing the happy lives of Soviet youth, its plot was changed so that in the new version, released in 1942, the hero gets his girl by exhibiting heroism in volunteering for the front. Some recently made films in circulation with anti-British or anti-Polish themes were withdrawn, and Mikhail Romm's *Mechta* ('Dream'), which showed the cruelty of the Polish ruling class, was held up for two years. Since the public needed feature films, pre-war movies with patriotic themes such as *Peter the Great* (*Piotr pervy*, 1937) and Dovzhenko's *Shchors* (1939) were revived. Particularly important was Eisenstein's *Alexander Nevsky*, since it was a bitterly anti-German film which had been taken out of circulation for the duration of the Molotov–Ribbentrop pact.

Necessity became the mother of invention. Since it was impossible to make feature films with powerful propaganda content quickly, studios made short films and compiled them into collections. Anti-Nazi shorts were put into production straightaway, and the first collection appeared in cinemas on 2 August 1941, with two more following later that month. Each consisted of a group of shorts, as few as two or as many as six. Numbers 1–5 made up a series entitled *Victory Will Be ours*. Seven collections appeared in 1941 and five more in 1942, the last of them in August, by which time the practice could be discontinued as the relocated and reorganized industry could now produce full-length features. The content of the collections, known as *kinosborniki*, was extremely heterogeneous. They included Allied documentaries such as one on the British navy and another on the air war over London, and excerpts from previously successful features such as Lyubov Orlova's singing mail carrier from *Volga–Volga* (1937).

People craved movies: they wanted to be taken away from their everyday miseries; they wanted hope; they wanted their faith in ultimate victory to be confirmed. Film-going was one of the few remaining forms of entertainment. But in wartime conditions both making and

Alexander Dovzhenko

(1894–1956)

Alexander Dovzhenko is best remembered as cinema's great chronicler of the Ukrainian experience. In the course of his thirty-year film career, he traced the economic and political development of his native Ukraine, and its accommodation to the modernization policies of the larger Soviet Union.

Born into a peasant family in north-eastern Ukraine, he was reared during a period of tsarist repression of Ukrainian native culture, an experience which embittered him toward the imperial order. He came of age during the revolutionary events of 1917 and aligned himself with the radical political movements then proliferating in Ukraine, eventually joining the Ukrainian Bolshevik Party, which fought against Russian colonialism while advocating an alliance with Russian Bolsheviks to establish a modern socialist system. During his brief career as a painter and political cartoonist, Dovzhenko associated with the VAPLITE literary organization, centre of a circle of Ukrainian intellectuals committed to socialist development under Soviet rule and the preservation of a native cultural heritage.

Dovzhenko entered Kiev's main film studio as an aspiring director in 1926. His apprenticeship was as screenwriter on a slapstick comic short *Vasia-reformator* ('Vasia the reformer', 1926), and he stayed with comedy in his first directing effort, *Yagodka liubvi* ('Love's berry', 1926), a satire on social and sexual mores. His first feature-length effort was *Sumka dipkurera* ('Diplomatic bag', 1928), a political thriller based on a true incident in which a Soviet courier was murdered by anti-Bolshevik agents. Dovzhenko turned this into a tale of international intrigue and working-class solidarity by implicating the British secret police in the killing, and having British workers deliver the Soviet diplomatic papers to the USSR.

Dovzhenko later dismissed these initial efforts as a failed period of apprenticeship, and certainly none of them enabled him to pursue his interests in Ukrainian themes. He considered his first serious project to be *Zvenigora* (1927), an elaborate allegory on Ukrainian historical development involving a rich mixture of ancient Ukrainian folklore and ideologies supporting modern development under Soviet rule. Its highly elliptical editing defined Dovzhenko's contribution to the Soviet montage style.

Dovzhenko carried these qualities over to his next major assignment, *Arsenal* (1929). This historical drama recounts events from the Civil War when Ukrainian Bolsheviks barricaded themselves in Kiev's 'Arsenal' munitions factory and battled the troops of anti-Bolshevik Ukrainian nationalists. Again, however, Dovzhenko enriches the ideology of the film with allusions to the Ukrainian past. The final scene in which the Bolshevik hero repels bullets, for example, derives from an eighteenth-century folk-tale.

With *Earth* (*Zemlya*, 1930), Dovzhenko dealt more specifically with Ukrainian modernization under the Soviets. The film treats the topical issue of collectivization of Ukrainian peasant farms in line with the USSR's agricultural policy. It consolidates this issue into a tale of a rift within one family, as a resistant older generation is challenged by a younger generation enthusiastic about political change. When the young hero is murdered by kulaks trying to sabotage collectivization, his hitherto recalcitrant father joins village Komsomols in celebrating the collective.

With his first sound film, *Ivan* (1932), Dovzhenko took up the subject of industrialization under the first Five-Year Plan, setting his story at the construction site of the massive Dneprostroi hydroelectric complex in central Ukraine. Dneprostroi was built to be a showcase project of the Soviet industrialization campaign, and Dovzhenko used this backdrop to study the place of the individual worker in the new industrial system. The title character is a Ukrainian peasant recruited to work at the construction site, and his difficult adjustment to an industrial routine offers a microcosm of his generation's response to change.

Dovzhenko's own career did not escape the consequences of political changes then taking place. The consolidation of Party control of Soviet artistic practice was accompanied by particular scrutiny of any signs of 'nationalist deviation' by artists in the non-Russian republics. Both *Earth* and *Ivan* were severely criticized by Party critics for 'formalism' and 'nationalism'. As a result, Dovzhenko moved away from Ukrainian affairs with *Aerograd* (1935), a film set in Russia's far east. This adventure story concerns sabotage of Soviet developmental efforts near the Siberian frontier, and it shows traces of the anti-subversive fears perpetrated under Stalin.

At Stalin's own suggestion, Dovzhenko returned to the Ukrainian experience with the historical biography *Shchors* (1939). The film concerns the Civil War exploits of Ukrainian Red Army commander Nikolai Shchors, and is part of a line of biographical films—most notably the popular *Chapayev* (1934)—which were officially sanctioned under Socialist Realism and which contributed to the Stalinist 'cult of personality'.

As was common among Soviet film-makers, Dovzhenko's productivity declined as the Soviet film industry became more bureaucratic and as Party censorship tightened. During the Second World War, Dovzhenko supervised propaganda documentaries, and he completed only one feature during the post-war period. This was *Michurin* (1948), a biography of the Russian scientist Ivan Michurin, who was officially credited with developing a 'materialist science'.

Dovzhenko hoped to return to his abiding interest in Ukrainian development in 1956 with *Poem of the Sea* (*Poema o more*) but died while the project was still under way. His wife and long-time artistic collaborator Julia Solntseva (1901–89) completed the film in 1958 and went on to direct other features from Dovzhenko's unrealized scripts and stories, including *Journal of the Flaming Years* (*Povest plamennykh let*, 1961), and *Enchanted Desna* (*Zacharobannaia Desna*, 1965). Her career helped sustain Dovzhenko's project of documenting Ukraine's modern development.

VANCE KEPLEY

SELECT FILMOGRAPHY

Yagodka liubvi (1926); Sumka dipkurera (1928); Zvenigora (1927); Arsenal (1929); Earth (Zemlya) (1930); Ivan (1932); Aerograd (1935); Shchors (1939); Osvobozhdenie (Liberation) (1940) (documentary); Bitva za nashu Sovetskuiu Ukrainu (The Battle for our Soviet Ukraine) (1943) (documentary), Pobeda na Pravoberezhnoi Ukrainu (Victory in Right-Bank Ukraine) (1945) (documentary); Michurin (1948)

BIBLIOGRAPHY

Dovzhenko, Alexander (1973), *Alexander Dovzhenko: The Poet as Filmmaker*.
Kepley, Vance (1986), *In the Service of the State: The Cinema of Alexander Dovzhenko*.
Oms, Marcel (1968), *Alexandre Dovjenko*.
Schnitzer, Luda, and Schnitzer, Jean (1966), *Alexandre Dovjenko*.

Opposite: Zvenigora (1927)

exhibiting films had become extremely difficult. Theatres were destroyed, and the number of available projectors in the first years of the war was halved. Making films in distant central Asia was fraught with problems. One of the most successful films of the period was Mark Donskoi's *Raduga* ('Rainbow', 1944). Set in wintertime Ukraine, it was shot in Ashkhabad in the summer of 1943 in temperatures of over 40°C; the 'snow' was made of cotton, salt, and mothballs, and the actors had to play their scenes in heavy overcoats, with a doctor on hand in case they collapsed.

Between 1942 and 1945 Soviet studios turned out seventy films (not counting children's films and filmed concerts), of which twenty-one were historical dramas. Films dealing with the experience of soldiers at the front were surprisingly few and, with the exception of Georgi Vasiliev's *Front* (1943), mostly undistinguished. As long as the fighting continued, there was little desire to romanticize it. Instead of depicting the war as a series of heroic exploits, film-makers preferred to show the barbaric behaviour of the Germans and the quiet heroism and loyalty of ordinary simple people in extraordinary circumstances. The most memorable films of the period, therefore, dealt with the home front and with partisan warfare in German-occupied territories.

Three particularly memorable films were made about partisan warfare. The first of these, Ermler's *Ona zashchishchaet rodinu* ('She defends the fatherland'), appeared in theatres in May 1943. It was artistically primitive, endowing its heroine with few individual characteristics and carrying the simplest political message: the necessity of vengeance. *Raduga*, which came out in January 1944, was more complex. It is about a woman partisan, Olena, who returns to her village to give birth. She is captured and subjected to dreadful torture, but does not betray her comrades. Finally *Zoya*, directed by Lev Arnshtam, which appeared on the screens only in September 1944, was based on the martyr death of the 18-year-old partisan Zoya Kosmodemyanskaya. She, like Olena in *Raduga*, endures torture and prefers death to betraying her comrades. In all three films women are the protagonists. By showing the courage and suffering of women, they aim both to arouse hatred for the cruel enemy and to instil the idea that men should do no less than these women did.

The films show an interesting evolution. At the end of *Ona zashchishchaet* the partisans liberate the village and save the heroine from execution. In *Raduga* the heroine is killed, but her death is avenged when the partisans liberate her village. *Zoya*, by contrast, ends with our witnessing a martyr death. The explanation for the differences is simple. In 1942, when the script of *Ona zashchishchaet* was written, Soviet audiences would have found it too disheartening to witness an execution. But by the summer of 1944, the people were confident of ultimate victory and did not need the consolation of an imaginary rescue.

Films dealing with the home front also usually had women as protagonists, and extolled the same virtues of loyalty, endurance, and self-sacrifice. Sergei Gerasimov's *Bolshaya zemlya* ('The great land') is typical in this respect, showing a woman who, after her husband's departure for the front, makes her contribution to victory by becoming an excellent worker in an evacuated factory.

As in the case of other combatant countries, vigilance was an important theme. Spy mania was obsessive. In the early war films everyone, including children and old women, unmasked spies. In the short film *V storozhevoi budke* ('In the sentry box'), which came out in November 1941, Red Army soldiers uncover a German spy who speaks flawless Russian and is dressed in Soviet uniform. He gives himself away by not recognizing on the wall a baby picture of Stalin. The story is based on a realistic premiss: no one who lived in the Soviet Union in the 1930s could possibly fail such a test. But it is the subtext which is important: Stalin protects his people, even in the form of an icon on the wall.

Especially in the early films, the Nazis were not only bestially brutal, but also silly and cowardly. The portrayal of decent Germans was vetoed. In 1942 Pudovkin made a film called *Ubiytsy vykhodiat na dorugu* ('Murderers go out on the road'), based on stories by Brecht, which attempted to show German victims of Hitler's regime and fear among ordinary citizens, but it was not allowed to be distributed.

The war against Germany was referred to as the 'Great Patriotic War' and soldiers of the Red Army went into battle 'for motherland, for honour, for freedom, and for Stalin'—not for socialism or Communism. But what did patriotism mean in a multi-national empire? Latent hostilities within the very heterogeneous population of the Soviet Union clearly presented a danger—which, particularly during the latter part of the war, Nazi propagandists did their best to exploit. In response, film studios turned out films showing the 'friendship of peoples', so that, for example, a Georgian and a Russian soldier would go on a dangerous mission whose success depended on their co-operation; at the end the Russian would save the Georgian or vice versa.

The turn from Marxist internationalism to old-fashioned patriotism had begun before the outbreak of war, with a spate of films about national heroes in the late 1930s. But during hostilities the process accelerated and films were regularly made to show how a single, great individual (sc. Stalin) could influence history. A typical film was Vladimir Petrov's *Kutuzov* (1944), about the general who had saved Russia from the Napoleonic invasion over a century earlier. In the film Kutuzov is shown as a brilliant strategist—reversing the conception of the character in Tolstoy's *War and Peace* where Kutuzov

is victorious because he allowed his armies to lead him. A less typical film was Eisenstein's masterly *Ivan the Terrible* (*Ivan grozny*, 1944), which succeeded in depicting Ivan not only as a great national hero but as a troubled and complex character.

Minority nationalism was a difficult issue. Each major nationality was encouraged to make one great epic about national heroes: *Bogdan Khmelnitsky* in the Ukraine, *Georgii Saakadze* in Georgia, *David Bek* in Armenia, *Alshin-Mal-Alan* in Azerbaijan. Needless to say, these national heroes could never struggle against Russian oppressors; on the contrary, the 'friendship of peoples' had to be projected into the past.

On the other hand too much nationalist feeling threatened to undermine the system that was based on the 'leading role' of the Russians. The Ukraine presented a particular problem, since the Germans were actively trying to turn the Ukrainians against the Soviet regime. It was felt important not to give Ukrainian nationalism too much space, and Stalin personally banned a scenario by Dovzhenko which he considered too nationalistic. As a consequence the great Ukrainian director made no feature films during the war.

Almost all historical films made anywhere or at any time are presentist, and aim to appeal to modern audiences by dealing with modern issues. It would be naïve to expect Soviet cinema in the midst of a bitter war to have depicted past events dispassionately and for their own sake. Even so it is extraordinary how brazenly some Soviet films distorted the past. An entire series of films, for example, dealt with the German invasion of the Ukraine in 1918. In these films the Germans are always vicious, the Red Army always manages to defeat them, and Stalin always provides wise leadership. In reality the Red Army in 1918 had not engaged the Germans, except for some minor skirmishes, let alone defeated them; nor was Stalin its leader. Reality however did not deter the film-makers. Leonid Lukov's *Alexander Parkhomenko* (1942) and the Vasilievs' *Oberona Tsaritsyna* ('The defence of Tsaritsyn', 1942) depict battles that never occurred, and had they occurred would have resulted in resounding defeat for the Reds.

THE LAST YEARS OF STALIN

The end of the war did not lead to more freedom for film-makers. On the contrary, in the autumn of 1946 the Stalinist leadership took steps to re-establish ideological control that had been loosened during the war. The capricious demands of the authorities and their constant intervention in film-making became so oppressive that the film industry almost ground to a halt. During the worst years of the period—often referred to as the time of film hunger—Soviet studios produced fewer than ten films a year, and some of the films made, such as Eisenstein's

Ivan the Terrible Part II (1946), were not shown until after Stalin's death. Studios stood idle and young directors had no opportunity to develop their talents. Of necessity, theatres were forced to reshow pre-war and wartime films. These were not only Soviet works but also the so-called 'trophy films'—war booty taken from Germany by the Red Army. Between 1947 and 1949 approximately fifty of these were distributed. By an absurd irony, while Soviet film-makers were finding it impossible to live up to stringent political demands, recut and retitled Nazi and American films were able to circulate. These films were extremely popular, though they were never reviewed.

Between 1946 and 1953 Soviet studios produced 124 feature films. Apart from a few children's films, they are almost all unwatchable today. They fall into three categories: 'artistic documentaries', propaganda films, and film biographies.

The most famous example of the first genre was Mikhail Chiaureli's *The Fall of Berlin* (*Padeniye Berlina*, two parts, 1949–50). This represented the apogee of the Stalin cult. Chiaureli depicted the Soviet leader as a supernatural figure, one who could see into the hearts of simple human beings, whose very appearance was accompanied by the singing of angels. He was also a military genius who not only defeated Hitler practically single-handed, but also held off the Americans, who secretly sympathized with and helped the Nazis. Films in the propaganda genre were made to support some immediate goal of Soviet domestic or foreign policy. Abram Room's *Court of Honour* (1948) takes up the theme of the necessity for struggle against 'rootless cosmopolitans'. Two Soviet scientists, on the verge of a major discovery, are seduced by the 'false notion of internationalism in science' and the promise of fame, and decide to publish their research in an American journal. American scientists—who turn out to be spies—come to the Soviet laboratory and are amazed at how well equipped it is. The two Soviet scientists are punished: one is willing to acknowledge his mistakes and is pardoned, but the other is given over to Soviet justice.

A number of well-known directors and script-writers themselves became victims of the anti-cosmopolitan campaign. Leonid Trauberg, Dziga Vertov, and Sergei Yutkevich, all of them Jewish, were bitterly attacked and could make no more films so long as Stalin was alive. Meanwhile the film biography genre continued unabated, with seventeen biographies being made, based on the lives of military and civil heroes—including the composers Glinka, Mussorgsky, and Rimsky-Korsakov. These films were so similar to one another that even contemporary journals noted that dialogue could safely be lifted from one and added to another without anyone noticing.

During these desperate years, the cinema suffered more than ever from bureaucratic interference, one-dimen-sional political messages, the suppression of individual style, and the primacy of the word (the 'iron scenario') over the image. Just before Stalin's death, however, Party leaders were beginning to recognize how barren Soviet culture had become. They were concerned that novels, plays, and films no longer served the agitational needs of the Party, and tentatively took a few hesitant steps away from orthodoxy. G. M. Malenkov devoted some of his speech at the Nineteenth Party Congress in October 1952 to the problems of Soviet culture, calling, among other things, for more films to be made and implicitly repudiating the previous position of the leadership that insisted on making only 'masterpieces'. As Mikhail Romm observed: 'To make a few films turned out to be by no means easier than to make many. The idea that we must concentrate our attention on a few works (as if in this way it would be possible to produce only excellent quality) turned out to be utopian.'

The decision to produce more films had far-reaching consequences. Republican studios that had been neglected could be revived; perspectives would open to young talents; studios would be able to stop concentrating on spectaculars and make more films; genres that had almost disappeared could be resurrected. Malenkov expressed special concern for the lack of Soviet comedies. As he put it: 'We need Soviet Gogols and Shchedrins, who with the fire of satire would eliminate everything negative, unpleasant, and dead, everything that slows down our movement forward.' Conflict also needed to be reintroduced into films, which were widely recognized as stereotyped, schematic, and boring. It had, however, to be the 'right' type of conflict (e.g. between the remnants of the old and the new) leading to the right resolution (the victory of the new). What no critic could dare to say was that more courageous films could not be made so long as film-makers lived under a bloody tyranny.

The changes of 1952–3 did not immediately affect film production. In the Soviet Union it took a considerable amount of time to see a film project through from its conception to its release, and the films that came out in 1953 were as dreary as before. Another essential precondition for change was the death of Stalin himself. This took place in March 1953, and was followed by profound changes in the political order. The revival of Soviet film then came quickly, as the effects of the thaw spread to every part of Soviet culture. In the mid-1950s many of the old restrictions were lifted. Output grew impressively. Directors who had done interesting work in the distant past took advantage of the new opportunity and returned to experimentation. New and talented directors were able to emerge. Artists turned to genuine issues and expressed themselves with passion. Cinema became heterogeneous. In a system which politicized all aspects of life, any film which depicted the world more or less realistically and thereby pointed to problems had inherently subversive potential. Although Soviet cinema never regained the world-wide prestige it had enjoyed in the late 1920s, films once again became worth watching and a positive contribution to cultural life.

Bibliography
Kenez, Peter (1992), *Cinema and Soviet Society, 1917–1953*.
Leyda, Jay (1960), *Kino: A History of Russian and Soviet Film*.
Stites, Richard (1992), *Soviet Popular Culture: Entertainment and Society in Russia since 1900*.

Indian Cinema: Origins to Independence

ASHISH RAJADHYAKSHA

India is one of the largest and most culturally varied countries in the world. It is second only to China in population, and second only to the United States in the scale and importance of its film industry. Indian films are popular not only in India itself, but in large parts of Asia and Africa and in many other countries where there are communities of Indian descent. The roots of a distinctive Indian cinema stretch back a long way and encompass a variety of cultural traditions. While Bombay was, and is, the main centre of Indian film production, film industries grew up early in the century throughout the subcontinent—in Calcutta, Madras, Lahore, and other major centres—basing their activity on theatrical and artistic modes which combined western and indigenous models. Out of this fusion sprang a number of genres such as the 'mythological' (based on Hindu myths and legends) which are unique to India.

THEATRE TO FILM: THE COLONIAL ENTERPRISE

Bombay and the Parsee theatre
History in India, as the historian D. D. Kosambi liked to show, often expresses itself geographically. In Bombay, even today, an arc in the heart of the city swings from the textile mills of Parel and Lalbaug to the famous dockyards adjoining Reay Road, the giant seconds market Chor Bazaar, the red-light area of Falkland Road, and towards the industrial wholesale trade up to Lohar Chawl and Crawford Market. This area, not over 10 square miles, saw the rise of the first (and then the richest) industrial working class in India, and was the base of the country's colonial economy on the west coast. It was also the place where the Indian film industry was born. The Kohinoor Film Company in Dadar, the Ranjit Movietone in Parel, and the Imperial Film Company adjoining today's Nana Chowk, the three largest studios India ever saw, flourished by the late 1920s within a few miles of each other.

The country's trader-capitalists, the kind who invested in the nascent entertainment industries of theatre and then film, emerged as a powerful economic class mainly through coastal trading with the west, Middle East, and China. Many of the first shipping enterprises of Surat and Bombay were set up by Parsees, later the founders of the nationally famed genre of the Parsee theatre.

The Parsee theatre, often considered the direct ancestor to the song-dance-action stereotype of the Hindi cinema, established itself as an industry when Sir Jamsedjee Jeejeebhoy bought the Bombay Theatre in 1835. Jeejeebhoy was one of India's biggest trader-industrialists, with a flourishing export business with China and Europe in silk, yarn, cotton, and handicrafts, and later the founder of the influential art academy, the J.J. School (1857), while the Bombay Theatre had begun in 1776, built as a straight copy of London's Drury Lane theatre and known, until then, mainly for performances of plays like Sheridan's *School for Scandal* and for its colonial British clientele. The combination established both a genre and an industry: the Bombay Theatre was followed by the even more famous Grant Road Theatre (1846), adapting local themes to the Elizabethan stage idiom. The romance drama, the 'mythological', the 'historical', and the adventure saga taken from popular Indian legendary tales such as Firdausi's tenth-century *Shah Nama* were accompanied by the first big adaptations of Shakespeare into Gujarati and Urdu. The music they used was inspired by the opera to transform the popular 'light-classical' north Indian musical, and thus to invent one of the ancestors of the early Hindi film song.

In Bombay, Calcutta, Madras, and Lahore, but also in other cities, this brand of theatre was exhibited in a series of theatre palaces, usually ringed around the 'native' parts of town, in such a way as to be available to its richer clientele but also to keep its cultural distance from them. In Bombay the Edward, the oldest surviving theatre in India, was built in 1860, and was followed by the Empire, the Gaiety (now Capitol), and the Royal Opera House.

Exhibition
In its earliest days film exhibition was restricted to travelling tent theatres using the Edison and after 1907 the Pathé projection systems. From 1910, however, the first cinemas began to be built while the famous theatre

palaces in major cities were converted en masse into 'bioscope' projection houses. When the Lumière shorts were unveiled as the 'marvel of the century, the wonder of the world', on 7 July 1896, it was at Bombay's élite Watson's Hotel; but film then moved to the 'native' Novelty Theatre and the former premises of the city's most famous Parsee stage repertory, the Victoria Theatre Company. The Novelty was, even then, known for its double-pricing strategy to accommodate a 'lower-class' audience in the stalls (Rupees 1.50) and pit (4 annas).

In 1899 a Professor Stevenson exhibited *A Panorama of Indian Scenes and Procession* alongside the Calcutta stage hit *The Flower of Persia* at the Star Theatres, generating what for the next decade remained the dominant mode of exhibition in that city. Hiralal Sen (1866–1917), India's 'first' film director, started the Royal Bioscope Company and filmed several plays from the foremost commercial theatre groups in Calcutta, Star Theatres and Classic: he did *Alibaba and the Forty Thieves* in 1903 starring Classic's major attraction Kusum Kumari, who thus became India's first movie star. Most of his films were screened after the plays themselves, as part of the evening's entertainment.

In Maharashtra the Shahu Maharaja of Kolhapur, who already had extensive theatrical interests, financed the first movie studio in the region, the Maharashtra Film Company (1917–32). Started by a low-caste painter of stage props, Baburao Painter (1890–1954), the studio took part in the renaissance in popular Marathi stage music, the *natyasangeet*. Under Painter's auspices, key composers in the genre, such as Govindrao Tembe and Master Krishnarao, gradually moved into film, as did many popular stage stars.

This trend is repeated in region after region. In Andhra Pradesh it was the Surabhi Theatres troupes which featured in the first big movies in Telugu. In Madras leading roles were taken by playwright Pammal Sambandam Mudaliar, who did much to establish a 'respectable' cinema in Tamil, and by the stage company (and later producer of Tamil sound films) TKS Brothers. In Karnataka, the Gubbi Veeranna Company and other theatre groups proliferated in the vicinity of Mysore, seat of the Wodeyar royalty, and later controlled the Kannada cinema well into the 1960s. They provided all its key directors, like H. L. N. Simha, B. R. Panthulu, and G. V. Iyer, its stars led by Rajkumar and Leelavathi, and most of its early commercial hits: *Bedara Kannappa* (1953), for instance, the first big success in the Kannada cinema, adapted a Gubbi Company stage play written by G. V. Iyer to introduce the mythological adventure movie into that language. Much later, with *Hamsa Geethe* (*The Swan Song*, 1975), Iyer, now an 'art film' director,

D. G. Phalke's *Raja Harishchandra* (1913), generally credited as the first Indian feature-length film

returned to the genre as exemplifying a classical—and not merely an urban popular—legacy.

The Punjab

In Lahore, the cultural and economic capital of the Punjab (now in Pakistan), 1901 saw two developments that were to transform the Indian entertainment industry. The Gandharva Mahavidyalaya was set up that year: a music school that for the first time made classical musical training available outside the feudal system of the guru and the *shishya* (disciple), causing a major revolution by publishing musical texts till now jealously guarded by various *gharanas*. It led to a major spread of the music school system, throwing up most of the major stage musicians, and then singing stars like the Prabhat Studios' Shanta Apte, and, still more influentially, composers like Rafique Ghaznavi and Master Krishnarao. Meanwhile, a Land Act that year curtailing urban investment in agriculture led to large-scale investment in the entertainment business. Initially this took the form of theatre-building, first for the stage and then for film. Throughout the silent period local film-making enterprise was limited to sponsored documentaries and 'educational' films for government agencies, particularly the railways. But a deal struck with RKO Pictures by Rewashankar Pancholi's Empire Film Distributors, which also gave them rights to RCA–Photophone equipment with the coming of sound, created a well-established distribution infrastructure, albeit one restricted almost solely to American imports. The first Punjab-based features, by B. R. Oberai's Pioneer or A. R. Kardar's Playart Phototone, were adventure quickies merging Arabian Nights fantasies with RKO dramas—for example *Husn Ka Daku* (*Mysterious Eagle*, 1929) or *Sarfarosh* (*Brave Hearts*, 1930). A mass-entertainment formula thus developed whose initial audience was the displaced peasantry turned industrial working class in towns like Ludhiana and Amritsar, creating virtually archetypal conditions for the formula to be adopted by the Hindi cinema after the Second World War. The Hindi 'masala' movie in its current sense can trace its origins to Pancholi's musical successes *Khazanchi* (1941) and *Zamindar* (1942), followed by Kardar's Hindi films, followed in turn by one of the biggest producers of the 1960s–1970s, B. R. Chopra.

Madan Theatres

The cultural transition of India's nineteenth-century mercantile élite is best demonstrated by the spectacular career of the controversial Madan Theatres, founded in Calcutta by Jamsedjee Framjee Madan (1856–1923). A former actor in the Bombay Parsee theatre, Madan caused a business revolution when he acquired the two front-ranking Bombay companies Khatau-Alfred and Elphinstone, including their theatre premises, rights to all their productions, their repertory of actors, and their writers. Shift-ing his base to Calcutta, where he started J. F. Madan & Co. in 1902, he initially ran the Elphinstone Theatrical Co., and his flagship theatre, the Corinthian. Much of his stage work of this time is exemplified by his key in-house playwright Aga Hashr Kashmiri (1879–1935), best known for his adaptations of Shakespeare into an indigenous version of orientalism: dramas of feudal blood-ties, battles for honour, sacrifice and destiny. Kashmiri's influence persisted in Indian theatre and cinema well into the 1940s, emerging in the work of film-makers like Sohrab Modi (*Jailor*, 1938) and Mehboob Khan (*Humayun*, 1945).

Madan saw the cinematic 'crossover' potential of his own theatrical property relatively late in his spectacular career as an entrepreneur. He first moved into film when he bought agency rights for Pathé, converting his own theatres into projection houses. He then went on acquiring theatres, until at its peak the Madan distribution empire ran 172 theatres throughout the subcontinent and earned half the national box-office. As an importer, Madan bought films before the First World War mainly from British sources such as the London Film Company, but then in the 1920s got the prize contracts of Metro Pictures and United Artists. Madan was explicit in his marketing plan of catering to the Anglicized urban élite and for several years distributed hardly any Indian films.

This marketing strategy had several cultural resonances not perhaps evident on its surface. During the war, Madan had taken advantage of wartime subsidies to build theatres for the entertainment of British troops. Earlier, the Parsee theatre's ideal of a self-respecting indigenous capitalist culture, evoking its own version of Victorian grandeur, had pioneered a whole industry of bazaar art, including still photography and painting, aimed at a local 'westernized' audience. The famous 'Company school' of painting was an influential, often highly innovative form of bazaar art catering specifically to the British and Indian colonial bureaucracy, painting colonial architecture, portraits, and street scenes. Oil painters commissioned by India's nobility to paint scenes of court splendour were gradually replaced first by still photographers and graphic artists, and then by film crews hired from photographic companies like Clifton & Co. in Bombay or Bourne & Shepherd, Calcutta, to shoot durbars, royal visits, festivals and tea parties, and events of state. Much of the first locally made Indian cinema comes directly out of the 'Company-school' aesthetic on commissions from the Pathé Exchange, the International Newsreel Corporation, or Fox Films Co., who bought news footage at $2 per foot and 'review' films like F. B. Thanawala's *Splendid New Views of Bombay* (1900) for between 10 cents and $1 per foot.

By the time Madan Theatres moved into film production around 1917, the group's idea of updating the Parsee theatre's classicist aspirations came to mean very different things politically from in the group's heyday a decade or

The Hindi mythological *Lav Kush*, directed in 1951 by Nirupa Roy

two earlier. In its first years, the Madan brand of orientalism was crucially determined by its key *auteur*, Aga Hashr Kashmiri, with star Patience Cooper playing an early version of Nargis: the woman exemplifying kin honour, the site over which men fought their battles for domination. In 1923 the company co-produced the sexually explicit *Savitri* with Cines of Rome. Directed by Giorgio Mannini and featuring Italian stars Angelo Ferrari and Rina De Liguoro, this adaptation of the Mahabharata legend was advertised as a 'charming Hindu story . . . taken amid the world-renowned Cascades of Tivoli in Rome'. The company then hired Rina and her husband Giuseppe, and Italian cameraman (and later director) T. Marconi, emphasizing the Italian connection as a way of boosting the classical ancestry of the operatic Parsee theatre and its film variations. Then in 1932 Madan produced *Indira Sabha*, one of India's biggest sound films to date, featuring sixty-nine songs, and adapted from a play originally written in 1852 in Wajid Ali Shah's Avadh court, but now filmed in a manner inspired by Broadway and Hollywood musicals.

Political resonances

By the 1920s, the idea of an indigenously manufactured popular culture, 'on a par with' the west—which was to be the dominant refrain of the 1927–8 Indian Cinematograph Committee headed by Dewan Bahadur T. Rangachariar—had opened out into a new political era, that of 'Swadeshi'. In 1918 the Montagu–Chelmsford Reforms, which allowed for the first time a limited Indian participation in government while calling for a revitalized post-war Indian industry, also brought about the first legislation on the Indian cinema. The 1918 Cinematograph Act instituted censorship and a licensing policy for film theatres. Municipal and police rules followed in 1920, stipulating that films be shown only in built-up premises, and asserting the need for greater financial accountability on the part of distributors.

In 1926 came the proposal for an Empire Films Corporation, a British initiative meant to revive the British film industry by reserving compulsory screen time for films made inside the 'Empire'. There was wide disagreement amongst Indian producers over this proposal: some felt that, as the pre-eminent film industry in the British Empire, the Indian cinema should legitimately claim its share of the compulsory screen time and thus export to other countries in the Empire, while others argued that similar proposals in other industries had never worked in the past. It was only one set of the numerous arguments and dissensions, as the process of nationalist hegemony finally came of age in the cinema industry and cinema started to be acknowledged as the most influential of India's popular arts.

The influential Bengali director Dhiren Ganguly (1893–1978) was a leading supporter of Empire Films. Himself a product of the colonial academic art discipline, a portrait painter and photographer, Ganguly's photographic self-portraits and his first big film *Bilet Pherat* (*England Returned*, 1921), along with his studios British Dominion and Indo-British Film, translated into film a well-established idiom of satirical literature, theatre, and popular painting that reflected the colonial world-view as seen through the eyes of the city's *bhadralok* (bureaucratic upper middle class). In its self-reflexivity, its ability simultaneously to view the outsider's stereotypes of an Indian middle class, as well as translate into film the well-established production sectors of Bengali painting and theatre, Ganguly's work opened up the richest vein yet in the establishment of a culturally valid and economically successful cinema industry.

Ganguly's successor was P. C. Barua (1903–51), one of the most famous directors in the pre-Independence period. Barua joined films as a shareholder in Ganguly's British Dominion, before both Barua and Ganguly found employment in the biggest Indian studio of the 1930s, the New Theatres. There Barua's melancholy love stories, set amid a nihilistic aristocracy and evoking feudal romance literature, used a static, mask-like actorial countenance counterposed by the most mobile subjective camera of his time in Indian film. In his most famous melodramas, *Devdas* (1935) and *Mukti* (*The Liberation of the Soul*, 1937), the effect was devastating. The story of a love-crazed hero drowning his sorrows in liquor before he dies at his beloved's door (*Devdas*), and that of the infantile artist who leaves his wife to keep company with a wild elephant in the forest (*Mukti*), were not only among the biggest hits of their time in Indian film, but opened up the richest avenue yet for assimilating into the mainstream the realism promoted by the Communist Party-affiliated Indian Peoples' Theatre Association (IPTA).

Barua's cameraman for both these films was Bimal Roy, who was later to direct the landmark *Do Bigha Zameen* (*Two Acres of Land*, 1953) with IPTA actor Balraj Sahni and

composer Salil Choudhury. The story of a peasant forced to migrate to the city to repay a debt and reclaim his ancestral 2 acres was a musical melodrama but also the Indian cinema's first concentrated assimilation of a new western influence—the realism of Vittorio De Sica's *Bicycle Thieves*, shown in India's first international film festival in 1951. Barua's colleague Nitin Bose and disciple Hrishikesh Mukherjee were among those to create the generic context for the work of the country's greatest post-Independence *auteurs*: Satyajit Ray, Mrinal Sen, and Ritwik Ghatak.

SWADESHI TO MELODRAMA: THE REFORM FILM

In 1895 the long social reform movement in India entered a new phase when, in protest against the discriminatory cotton tariffs imposed by the British government, the Swadeshi movement was launched. Literally *Swa-deshi* ('own-country'), it became in 1905 the major plank of the nascent Congress Party, as a nationalist call to boycott all foreign manufactured goods. On the one side this was a straightforward assertion that India had a developed indigenous industry, but the movement also claimed linguistic and cultural justification in terms of indigenous traditions and unifying collective memories. The two sides did not always mesh together, and from the outset the capitalist ambitions of the traders and investors ran counter to Gandhi's view that Swadeshi industry had to see itself in radically different terms from colonial industry and concentrate, for instance, on rural uplift. These conflicts at the heart of the Swadeshi movement found a powerful focus in the development of indigenous Indian cinema.

'My films are Swadeshi in the sense that the capital, ownership, employees and stories are Swadeshi,' wrote Dhundiraj Govind (Dadasaheb) Phalke (1870–1944). Phalke's first feature *Raja Harishchandra* (1913) is in all official history books seen as the birth of the Indian cinema industry (Phalke himself made the claim later), not only because it is the first full-length feature made in the country, but because of the inflection it gave to the idea of an 'Indian' film industry. Like Dhiren Ganguly, Phalke was a product of the colonial academic-art discipline, and indeed of Jamsedjee Jeejeebhoy's J.J. School of Art, and he went on to become a professional still photographer, set designer, and printer. Then in 1910 came the much-quoted revelation: 'While the *Life of Christ* was rolling fast before my eyes I was mentally visualizing the gods, Shri Krishna, Shri Ramchandra, their Gokul and Ayodhya ... Could we, the sons of India, ever be able to see Indian images on the screen?' Phalke, who started the Phalke Films Co. as a cottage industry by converting his kitchen into a makeshift laboratory, later became a partner in the Hindustan Cinema financed by industrialist Mayashankar Bhatt. But he never got the sort of mainstream financial support that the Kohinoor or Imperial Studios did, remaining marginal to the Bombay film industry. His work however, like that of Baburao Painter and the Maharashtra/Prabhat Studios in Kolhapur, remained a crucial cultural standard exemplifying the Swadeshi ideal and a measure for all the other claims to cultural and economic authenticity that followed.

All the big studios in Bombay, established in the 1920s, felt the rumbles. The Kohinoor, the Imperial, the Ranjit Movietone, and, slightly later, the Sagar Film Company were all started through the expansion of the film-exhibition sector; all four had been established along the lines of the Hollywood studios, committed to building an in-house star system and a production assembly line; and all were initially influenced largely by the colonial/orientalist stereotypes of Company-school painting and the Parsee theatre.

Imperial

The Imperial was established in 1926 by former exhibitor Ardeshir Irani. Renowned for having produced the country's first sound feature *Alam Ara* (1931), it had created several major in-house stars in the silent era, of which the most famous was Sulochana. Playing Theda Bara-style roles in films like *Wildcat of Bombay* (1927) and in costumed period movies like *Anarkali* (1928), Sulochana was also cast in 'realistic' films like *The Telephone Girl* and *Typist Girl* (both 1926), and the modernization melodrama *Indira B.A.* (1929) with its story of a retired judge, drunken suitor, and liberated 'westernized' woman. As extended further in the 'searing exposés' of Bombay's mercantile capital class in Manilal Joshi's *Mojili Mumbai* (*The Slaves of Luxury*, 1925), this realism translated its orientalist origins into a new kind of primitive frontier where the colonial-versus-nationalist conflict could itself become a quasi-period fantasy. This is most evident in the films of the Wadia Movietone (an offshoot of Imperial established in 1933), starring Fearless Nadia, an actress of Australian origin, who appeared in the Fairbanks/Niblo *Zorro*-type series (*Hunterwali*, 1935; *Miss Frontier Mail*, 1936) as well as in Hindu mythologicals and melodramas with Shakespearian actor Jal Khambatta (for example *Lal-e-Yaman*, 1933, reputedly inspired by *King Lear*).

Indeed realism, at this time, developed via Phalke some of its most influential reference points. Inflected in the direction of indigenism in a combative cultural struggle around the Swadeshi debate, its two major extensions remained until the late 1940s in the mythological and in the orientalist drama (including in this the Kashmiri-type costumed historical). The Kohinoor studio's début *Bhakta Vidur* (1921), starring its producer Dwarkadas Sampat, was on the surface a straightforward mythological, adapting the story of a Mahabharata legend. But it provoked a major dispute when it was banned by the censors, on the

grounds that the character Vidur was portrayed as a 'thinly-clad version of Mr Gandhi'.

Baburao Painter also made mythologicals, and when he hired novelist Apte to adapt his own novel for a film version of the reform classic *Savkari Pash* (1925; remade 1936), he had already established a wide range of political, technological, and cultural references for his brand of Swadeshi traditionalism. A former painter of stage backdrops, Painter went further than Phalke in actually physically assembling his own movie camera, cannibalized from Williamson and Bell & Howell spares from Bombay's second-hand flea market. His early work for the Maharashtra Film Company was in the mythological genre and his films *Seeta Swayamvar* (1918) and *Surekha Haran* (1921) were much admired by nationalist leader B. G. Tilak, who apparently dubbed him 'Cinema Kesari'. But he extended the genre first into the historical, using legends featuring the Maratha royalty (*Sinhagad*, 1923; *Baji Prabhu Deshpande*, 1929), and then into the reform novel genre, to show, for the first time, the possibility of shifting literary stereotypes through the process of equating the 'recognizable' in narrative traditions with a generic context that designated them as specifically 'Indian'. *Savkari Pash* (1936), the first substantial 'social', scripted by a novelist with all the reform credentials Painter needed, told the story of a peasant who is forced by a greedy money-lender to surrender his property and migrate to the city, where he becomes a mill-worker.

The social reform novel

By the late 1920s the social reform novel had replaced the stereotypes of the Company school with a different brand of authenticity. Through the late nineteenth century the reform novel had established itself in several Indian languages, notably Bengali, Marathi, Telugu, Malayalam, Kannada, Urdu, and Gujarati, effectively launching the first modernist movements in those regions and narrativizing a series of mutations of 'tradition' into a reformist discourse of middle-class neo-traditionalism. By the 1920s it had established itself in the popular literary mainstream, with the rise of literary journals, the short story, and serialized fiction, establishing a range of literary stereotypes virtually waiting to be transformed into a theatrical and cinematic language.

The prototypical social reform writer was the Bengali Saratchandra Chatterjee, whose novel *Devdas*, written in 1917, was the subject of several film versions, including that of Barua in 1935. Chatterjee dealt in more than half his writing with the condition of the widow. This was in line with the reform programme call for widow remarriage, and several other programmes addressing the condition of women. But it also created potent symbols of neo-traditionalism, generating revenge sagas and family dramas incorporating a mother symbol, relations between

Nargis

(1929–1981)

Nargis is a major Hindi star associated principally with Raj Kapoor, with whom she acted in some of the most enduring melodramas of the Indian cinema in the 1950s. Born in Allahabad as Fatima A. Rashid, she was the daughter of Jaddanbai, an actress, singer, and one of the earliest female film-makers in India. Nargis began appearing in her mother's productions at the age of 5, under the name Baby Rani.

Her first adult roles were with Mehboob Khan, who in the 1940s was the Indian cinema's foremost maker of costume dramas. She played the dancing girl in his lightweight comedy *Taqdeer* (1943), but really made her mark in Mehboob's next film, the historical *Humayun* (1945), in which she plays the commoner Hamida Bano with whom the Mughal emperor Humayun (played by Ashok Kumar) falls in love. In this film she was cast for the first time in what was to become her best-known screen image; a classic stereotype from Islamic literature and music, the innocent heroine who is doomed to cause destruction and conflict by her beauty. In 1947 she produced and starred in *Romeo and Juliet*, scripted by the Urdu playwright Aga Hashr Kashmiri, who had used the *femme fatale* stereotype to combat the orientalization of India. In this film Nargis brought a degree of authenticity to the Arabian Nights-type fantasy that was unprecedented in the Indian cinema of the time.

In another key Independence melodrama, *Andaz* (1949), she was pivotal to Mehboob's attempt to merge the symbols of feudal patriarchy into those of capitalism. She played Neeta, the westernized daughter of an industrialist, who is in love with an infantile playboy (played by Raj Kapoor). However she is also friendly with a young man who is technically her employee, being the manager of her father's company (Dilip Kumar). He loves her, and believes she reciprocates his feelings, but this leads to a major conflict that only ends when Neeta shoots the manager dead and, at the murder trial, reveals her father's views on the evils of modernity.

Nargis achieved superstardom with her second film with Raj Kapoor, the epic *Awara* (1951). If Mehboob located her screen image at the crux between 'traditional' authenticity and capitalist modernity, Kapoor brought a whole range of associations into his predominantly Oedipal melodramas. In *Awara* Nargis plays a lawyer who defends her childhood sweetheart in court after he kills his surrogate father. The intensity of the melodrama spills over into a kind of hallucinatory pictorialism, evident in the ecstatic, soft-focus song duets the lead couple sing. *Awara* built on the success of *Barsaat* (1949), Nargis's first film under the direction of Kapoor, and was followed by other hugely successful collaborations between the two, including *Shri 420* (1955). In these Kapoor fantasies a love story was mapped onto the class divisions of independent India, becoming the major dramatic pivot for the whole question of 'belonging', social legitimization, and the twin opposites of acceptance and renunciation. They were major successes, in the USSR and Arab countries as well as India.

Many of the Nargis 1950s melodramas were tragedies; S. U. Sunny's *Babul* (1950), Kidar Sharma's *Jogan* (1950), and above all Nitin Bose's *Deedar* (1951), in which she plays the hero's childhood sweetheart, separated from him by class inequalities. The hero (played by Dilip Kumar) goes blind and becomes an itinerant singer, but meets a benevolent eye surgeon who brings his sight back. When he discovers that his benefactor is married to his sweetheart he puts his eyes out again.

Nargis's last major film, and the pinnacle of her career, was Mehboob's *Mother India* (1957), an epic potpourri of psychoanalytic, historic, and technological symbols condensing the dominant iconography of the post-war 'All India film'. Shortly after *Mother India* she married the Hindi star Sunil Dutt and retired from acting, although for many years she remained an important public figure. She became a Congress (I) Member of Parliament, from which platform she mounted a scathing attack on Satyajit Ray, accusing him of peddling India's poverty abroad.

ASHISH RAJADHYAKSHA

SELECT FILMOGRAPHY

Pardanasheen (1942); Taqdeer (1943); Humayun (1945); Nargis (1946); Romeo and Juliet (1947); Andaz (1949); Barsaat (1949); Babul (1950); Jogan (1950); Awara (1951); Deedar (1951); Amber (1952); Shri 420 (1955); Mother India (1957)

BIBLIOGRAPHY

Abbas, Khwaja Ahmed (1977), *I Am not an Island*.
Vasudev, Aruna, and Lenglet, Philippe (ed.) (1983), *Indian Cinema Superbazaar*.
Willemen, Paul (1993), 'Andaz'

Nargis in *Barsaat* (Rain, 1949), a tale of love and identity directed by Raj Kapoor.

an elder sister-in-law and a younger brother-in-law, and so on, that were to become the very stuff of the Indian melodrama in the years to come. (In the neo-traditional mainstream Indian cinema, widows have never been allowed to remarry, and this unstated law becomes the reason why Amitabh Bachchan is killed off at the end of the mega-hit *Sholay* (1975). In a sense the entire establishment of cinematic genre as a language of industrialized mass culture in India lay in the effort to translate the neo-traditional idiom of feudalism, kinship, family, and patriarchy into current discourses of statehood, democracy, and law.)

Indian star Mehtab as the heroic Rain of Jhansi, in S. M. Modi's *Jhansi-ki-Rani*, the first Indian film to be shot in Technicolor.

Ranjit and Sagar

The two studios which best succeeded in translating reform literature into the genre of filmic melodrama were the Ranjit Movietone and the Sagar Film Company. Ranjit, established in 1929 as an offshoot of Kohinoor, supported simultaneously by the Jamnagar royalty and by the Motor & General Finance Company, employed a new generation of scenarists to write scripts for its famous in-house female lead, the 'Glorious' Gohar. The best-known of these was one of India's leading pre-war playwrights, Pandit Narayan Prasad Betaab. Betaab's Hindu mythologicals for Gohar such as *Devi Devayani* (1931) established her as an example of the virtues of Indian womanhood, paving the way for her best-known screen role as *Gunsundari* (1934), the suffering but dutiful housewife ready to sacrifice all for a wayward husband and a large joint family.

The Sagar Film Company, established in 1930 as a subsidiary of the Imperial studio, also started off making reform socials, and hired the politician, playwright, and novelist K. M. Munshi to do scripts for Sarvottam Badami. Badami's *Vengeance Is Mine* (1935) accompanied other melodramas like *Dr. Madhurika* (also 1935), in which Sabita Devi plays a man-hating feminist tamed at the end into accepting traditional values.

Sagar's main claim to fame, however, was that it introduced into the cinema the team of scenarist-directors Zia Sarhadi and Ramchandra Thakur, and their celebrated colleague Mehboob Khan. The careers of this trio, Marxist fellow-travellers of the Indian Peoples' Theatre Association, were in the mid-1940s to take them to two other studios: Prabhat, with its major in-house star film-maker V. Shantaram; and the Bombay Talkies, then engaged in a transition to a new generation of script-writers such as K. A. Abbas and directors such as Gyan Mukherjee. These various strands came together around the making of N. R. Acharya's *Naya Sansar* (1941), a story of a fearless radical journalist, at Bombay Talkies; Mehboob Khan's *Aurat* (1940), in which a good mother fights feudal oppression (an original version of his classic *Mother India*, 1957); and Shantaram's *Dr Kotnis Ki Amar Kahani* (*The Immortal Story of Dr. Kotnis*, 1946). These, along with the Barua and Bimal Roy films mentioned earlier, were to be influential in the re-establishment of the star system in the years after the war and Independence, the continuation of the studio infrastructure into the new economy that the S. K. Patil Film Enquiry Committee (1951) characterized as 'entrepreneurs ... prepared to gamble for high stakes, often at the cost of the public and the prosperity of the industry'. Films of this school, especially those scripted by K. A. Abbas for Raj Kapoor, were to be the site where Nehru's post-Independence Congress Party vision of a sovereign and industrialized nation was to find expression in the cinema.

M.G. Ramachandran

(1917–1987)

Maradur Gopalamenon Ramachandran, known popularly as MGR, was one of the biggest movie stars in the Indian cinema, and a politician who after his death was deified with at least one temple in his native Madras. Born in Kandy, Sri Lanka, his family moved to Madras and apparently lived in poverty after his father's death. At the age of 6 he joined the Madurai Original Boys, a uniquely Tamilian popular costume theatre featuring children.

He made his screen début in 1936 with *Sati Leelavati* (1936), a Tamil mythological, and worked for over a decade before he received his first lead role, in A. S. A. Sami's *Rajakumari* (1947). Ostensibly an Arabian Nights-type adventure movie in which a humble villager marries a princess, it allowed Ramachandran to exploit his fascination with Douglas Fairbanks's stunts. The success of this film coincided with events that were to influence his entire career. In 1949 the Dravida Munnetra Kazhagam (DMK), a political party in defence of the Dravidians (or the indigenous peoples of south India), was formed by the playwright and script-writer C. N. Annadurai on an anti-north, anti-Brahmin, and atheist platform. It concentrated its propaganda on a series of commercial film hits.

Ramachandran, who had already established his credentials in the stunt sequences of *Rajakumari* wearing a black shirt, the uniform of the Dravida Kazhagam, became a star of the Tamil cinema with the major DMK film *Manthiri Kumari* (1950). Written by future Chief Minister M. Karunanidhi, the film adapted an eighth-century Tamil text into an adventure saga in which the good prince defeats the evil son of a corrupt priest. Its success led on to a series of further adventure movies, including an *Alibaba and the Forty Thieves* (1956), before his next big DMK movies *Madurai Veeran* (1956) and *Nadodi Mannan* (1958) made him the icon of the DMK, and its biggest crowd-puller. These films were quasi-historicals about 'ancient times'. Madurai Veeran is a popular Tamil Nadu village deity and the subject of numerous ballads and plays; the film was set in the sixteenth century, where the infant prince Veeran, abandoned in the forest, is protected by an elephant and a snake, and raised by a cobbler. He falls in love with a princess who is also the king's (his real father's) mistress. He is sentenced to death and killed, just before the king realizes that Veeran is his son. Veeran, his wife, and his lover all ascend to heaven, thus allowing the star to be a tragic lover, a prince, and a god all at once.

Manthiri Kumari and *Madurai Veeran* both continued a DMK-inspired revisionist rewriting of Tamil history, and a political appropriation of icons of the agrarian lower castes. *Nadodi Mannan*, Ramachandran's directorial

début, differed from this pattern, being a directly political adventure fantasy addressing a wholly fictional past. He played a double role, which he was to do many times subsequently; the good king who is replaced with a look-alike commoner by the corrupt high priest. The priest was a barely disguised reference to the ruling Congress Party, and colour sequences in the otherwise black and white film showed the red and black DMK flag being hoisted as well as shots of the rising sun, the party's symbol. The 100th day of its commercial run became an occasion for a massive DMK political rally, in which Ramachandran sat on a chariot drawn by four horses.

Through the 1960s, Ramachandran consolidated his political and cultural position with films that became increasingly realistic, while maintaining his invincible screen persona. A series of screen references underscored his credentials as a representative of the poor. In *Thozhilali* (1964) he plays a manual labourer who educates himself, and leads an uprising against a tyrannical employer whom he eventually reforms. He played a peasant, a boatman, a quarry worker, and a shoeblack, and, in P. Neelakantan's *Mattukkara Velan* (1969), a cowherd who helps to solve a murder case that has baffled a lawyer. Later, even more effectively, he plays a rickshaw-puller (*Rickshawkaran*, 1971).

He was briefly a member of the State Legislative Assembly in 1967, the year the DMK came to power in Tamil Nadu. That year, when fellow actor M. R. Radha shot at and injured him, affecting his speech, he achieved virtually demi-god status as numerous fans immolated themselves in order to propitiate the gods and hasten his recovery. Within three years he fell out with the party leaders, and used the DMK film style to critique the party itself in an extraordinary fantasy, *Nam Naadu* (1969), where the nationalist hero masquerades as a smuggler in order to record on film the confessions of the real villains of society, a doctor, a builder, and a merchant. He set up a rival party, the Anna-DMK, eventually leading it to power in 1977. He remained the Chief Minister of Tamil Nadu until his death, winning three consecutive elections, despite a despotic, totalitarian, and highly populist rule. The power base of his party was the All-World MGR Fans' Association which continues to have 10,000 branches across the state.

ASHISH RAJADHYAKSHA

SELECT FILMOGRAPHY

Sati Leelavati (1936); Rajakumari (1947); Velaikkari (1949); Nallathambi (1949); Manthiri Kumari (1950); Alibaba and the Forty Thieves (1956); Madurai Veeran (1956); Nadodi Mannan (1958); Thozhilali (1964); Mattukkara Velan (1969); Nam Naadu (1969); Rickshawkaran (1971)

BIBLIOGRAPHY

Pandian, M. S. S. (1992), *The Image Trap: M. G. Ramachandran in Film and Politics*.

Opposite: Enga Veetu Pillai (1965)

Shantaram and Prabhat

Shantaram started as Baburao Painter's most prized disciple, and his lead actor in *Savkari Pash*, but in 1929 he broke away along with several of Painter's key associates, sound technician A. V. Damle and set designer S. Fattelal, to start the Prabhat Film Company. Lacking aristocratic or influential backers like Tanibai Kagalkar, this was a more modest and middle-class concern than its predecessor, Maharashtra Film, especially when in 1933 the studio shifted premises to Pune. In 1931 Shantaram made *Ayodhyecha Raja*, a Mahabharata fable addressing the issue of Untouchability which was shot in starkly realist-expressionist style, notably in the sequences where the former king, now employed in a cremation ground, faces his wife with the order to execute her. His later 'saint film' on Sant Eknath (*Dharmatma*, 1935) was also a nationalist parable, promoting Gandhian arguments on caste.

In 1933 when Prabhat moved to Kolhapur, cutting thereby their final umbilical cord with feudal resources, Shantaram's modernist aspirations also came to the fore. That year the Marathi theatre had seen its first major avant-garde experiment, the naturalist play *Andhalyanchi Shala*, set to original music by Keshavrao Bhole, and featuring Keshavrao Date, the actor who transformed theatre performance in the direction of British stage naturalism. The influence on the performance was that of Bernard Shaw, rather than Ibsen or Stanislavsky, and Shantaram initially wanted to adapt the entire play to film. This project failed, but he did manage to hire both Bhole and Date, and with them made his baroque drama *Amritmanthan* (1934), and the even more spectacular *Kunku* ('The Unexpected', 1937). Both films were influenced by the German expressionist cinema, and *Kunku* adapted a *Kammerspiel* strategy into a story about the rebellion of a young woman (singing star Shanta Apte) forced into marrying an old man (Keshavrao Date), to produce India's most successful melodrama ever.

Shantaram's daring experiments with lighting and performance should be seen in the context of the extremely strong generic undertow of a nationalist, popular, industrially established, cultural neo-traditionalism that flourished in literature, theatre, and painting as well as in cinema. Shortly before *Kunku*, indeed, the Prabhat studio had converted the unpromising material of a miracle-laden saint film biography of *Sant Tukaram* (1936) into what has remained one of the Indian cinema's most famous classics of all time. Integrating the still mesmeric power of the proletarian saint's poetry and dance, performed by Vishnupant Pagnis, into a starkly realist narrative about social exploitation, the film performed what critic and film-maker Kumar Shahani refers to as the rarest of filmic phenomena, the apparently unmediated translation of belief into action: and Shahani places this film on a par with Chaplin or the early Rossellini.

407

Tamil and Telugu cinema

The intersection of pervasive neo-traditional popular art, politics, and cultural authorship is particularly evident in the best-known cinema of the third (after Bombay and Calcutta) production centre in the country: Madras. Cinema effectively began here with R. Natartaja Mudaliar, whose six mythologicals between 1916 and 1923 inaugurated what K. Sivathamby suggests was a remarkable function of the cinema: to provide for virtually the first time in modern Tamil history an egalitarian audience space, violating the class/caste biases traditionally segregating audiences. Traditional Tamil élitism, continued into film by the Congress Party, was strongly opposed by producer-director K. Subrahmanyam (1904–71). Subrahmanyam, credited with the first local production infrastructures in Madras and with the setting up of state bodies like the South Indian Film Chamber of Commerce, moved away from mythologicals to make his best-known film, the politically strident *Thyagabhoomi* (1939). This story about a temple priest who joins the freedom struggle, and his daughter who abandons her unhappy marriage and her wealth to do the same, was to have a major cultural impact on Tamil cinema, spawning two contradictory but definitive movements. On the one side his financier S. S. Vasan, who took over Subrahmanyam's studio to start Gemini Pictures, launched with *Chandralekha* (1948) a new aesthetic of mass entertainment that he himself dubbed 'pageants for our peasants'. On the other, the influential separatist grouping Dravida Munnetra Kazhagam (DMK), a political party that won state power through using film as its major medium of propaganda, also traced many of its devastatingly effective uses of melodramatic convention to Subrahmanyam's films. DMK activists like C. N. Annadurai and M. Karunanidhi, stars like M. G. Ramachandran and Sivaji Ganesan, and directors including Krishnan-Panju, P. Neelakantan, and A. S. A. Sami collaborated with several Madras, Salem, and Coimbatore-based studios to make epic fables of grief and chastity to promote the party's anti-north, anti-Brahmin, and anti-religion ideals. *Parasakthi* (1952), the best known of the early films, included sensational sequences where the epitome of chaste womanhood is molested by a villainous temple priest inside a temple, forcing the hero to murder the priest in front of the deity, and eventually propound his (and his party's) ideals in a courtroom. Numerous films have followed the same pattern ever since, especially in Tamil.

Although the DMK was using not a national but a more specific Tamil subnational allegory for its family dramas, it also brought an intense degree of political awareness to the genre that most characterizes the post-Independence Indian cinema: the epic melodrama. Likewise in neighbouring Andhra Pradesh, the work of B. N. Reddi's Vauhini Pictures, which pioneered a local Telugu cinema with films like *Sumangali* (1940), *Devatha* (1941), and *Swargaseema* (1945), we find melodrama exploited on a large scale. In these films the woman, as the 'keeper' of the tradition (and the nation), is attacked, ravaged, but survives and transforms the world with her principles and her chastity intact. In several films, the melodrama borrows not only from the reform novel genre, but also more directly from the mythological, and in Tamil and Telugu it assimilated yet another genre: the costumed adventure movie. In both languages, the two major stars associated with the quasi-mythological adventure action movie, M. G. Ramachandran and N. T. Rama Rao, converted themselves into mythological mega-heroes eventually to become politicians and have a messianic hold over their regions.

Bombay Talkies and the epic melodrama

By the mid-1930s, prefiguring the 'all-India' cinema aesthetic inaugurated by the success, notably, of *Chandralekha*, a series of economic shifts had already established the pre-conditions of greater market integration through the country. The volume of film imports had levelled off, and even declined (from 440 films in 1933–4 to 395 in 1937–8). Paralleling the boom in indigenous trading during the war years, more and more financiers representing the 'managing-agency' system had begun investing in film. Several studios, including Ranjit and New Theatres, benefited (but also suffered) from this new area of high-interest finance. Bombay Talkies, which was established in 1934, originated in orientalist international co-productions set up in the silent period: *Prem Sanyas* ('The light of Asia', 1926), *Shiraz* (1929), and *Prapancha Pash* ('A throw of the dice', 1929) were all funded by European finance, and directed for Himansu Rai by the German Franz Osten, who later made most of the big Devika Rani movies for the Bombay Talkies. Rai imported, with Osten, his German and British crew, and with them established a studio that included in its board of directors three of the 'dozen individuals [who] by their control over banks, insurance companies and investment trusts, occupy commanding positions in the industrial life of Bombay' (Ashoka Mehta, quoted in Desai 1948). Bombay Talkies was mainly funded by the Kapurchands, a Kathiawar family that made its fortune in textiles in Bangalore, and provided its shareholders with regular dividends three years after it was established. The studio's ruralist melodramas in the 1930s reflect their sponsors' vision of a manifestly artificial rural utopia counterpointing their own industrial programme, much as the Parsee theatre had earlier reflected the aspirations of its trader-sponsors.

In 1942 a breakaway group set up the spectacularly successful Filmistan studio and Bombay Talkies went into decline, losing the services of all the big stars of the Hindi film industry. But by 1947, through the initiative of Bombay Talkies and its successors, the film melodrama had acquired the status of the privileged form of representation of an industrialized, modernizing nation-state, and the means by which the key hegemonies informing the post-war and post-Swadeshi idea of a 'national' culture were expressed. The triumphant mercantile class of investors who replaced the studio system soon after the war also symbolized for directors like Raj Kapoor or Guru Dutt the state of a nation that specifically excluded their utopia. The conditions of the industry itself proved paradigmatic for the state of a nation reduced to a smash-and-grab fly-by-night cultural adventurism; but it also allowed, for the first time, a sense of Indian nationhood for which the epic melodrama acted as a cultural vanguard.

Bibliography

Choudhury, Ashim (1975), *Private Economic Power in India*.

Desai, A. R. (1948), *Social Background of Indian Nationalism*.

Report of the Indian Cinematograph Committee, 1927–8 (1928).

Rajadhyaksha, Ashish, and Willemen, Paul (eds.) (1994), *The Encyclopaedia of Indian Cinema*.

Sivathamby, K. (1981), *The Tamil Film as a Medium of Political Communication*.

China Before 1949

CHRIS BERRY

Chinese cinema before the establishment of the People's Republic in 1949 was not only pre-revolutionary but also post-colonial. Primary source histories, written with the constraints of either Chinese Communist Party or Kuomintang Nationalist orthodoxy, and later works derived from them, have stressed the former and downplayed the latter. Yet it was precisely this paradox that animated the celebrated canon of resistant films from the two 'golden ages' of the 1930s and 1940s, which are claimed as heritage by both the mainland and Taiwan-based governments.

Shanghai was the Chinese cinema capital throughout this period. The first film screening in China occurred there on 11 August 1896 as an 'act' on a variety show bill. A great cosmopolitan entrepôt at the mouth of the Yangtze, Shanghai's growth and development was entirely the outcome of China's reluctant encounter with the west and the 'modern'. It was at once on the outermost margins of east and west, and also the central nexus of exchange between them; the point where they met, clashed, intermingled, hybridized, and, above all else, traded.

From Shanghai, the foreign cameramen-showmen fanned out along the trade tributaries, bringing the cinema to the other major littoral cities and the imperial capital, Beijing, in 1902. Right up until 1949, the cinema flourished where foreign penetration was most complete, and foreign films and foreign distribution and exhibition networks dominated the industry. Initially, the Japanese (in Manchuria) and the Germans showed greater skill in penetrating the interior, but by the 1930s 90 per cent of product shown was foreign and 90 per cent of that American.

This utterly foreign pedigree positioned cinema as an exotic, rather expensive form of entertainment. Within the exhibition hierarchy, foreigners and cosmopolitan Chinese paid the most to see the latest foreign films and less well-off Chinese paid less to see older releases. It was in this lower echelon of marginal profitability that local production inserted itself in the 1910s and 1920s and planted the seeds for the remarkable hybrid that was to develop soon afterwards.

The Fengtai Photography Shop in Beijing became the unlikely home of China's first films, when its owners started to record local opera in 1905. However, they soon realized greater opportunity lay in Shanghai and moved there in 1909. Most Shanghai production companies in this initial period were joint ventures with foreigners, and it was only in 1916 that the Hui Xi Company became the first wholly Chinese concern.

Hui Xi's first effort, *Wronged Ghosts in an Opium Den*, does not survive, but the film was a notable success, still playing seven years later. An examination of its plot and the earliest surviving film, *Romance of a Fruit Pedlar* (1922), indicates affinity between the cinema and the 'mandarin duck and butterfly' vernacular literature that also boomed in the cities at this time. These melodramatic and sentimental tales dramatized the disjunctures and contradictions of life in the modern, westernized city. If they were tragedies, decline and misfortune were inexorable, but if they were comedies, the wondrous device of coincidence would intervene. The scion of a rich Confucian family would fall in love with a poor mill girl, incurring the wrath of his parents, but then a long-lost relative would die, bequeathing her a fortune.

In the case of *Wronged Ghosts*, a family is ruined by the quintessential symbol of western imperialism in China: opium. *Romance of a Fruit Pedlar* is a gentler comedy, presenting the efforts of a greengrocer to woo a doctor's daughter in the rough and tumble of an urban streetscape full of conmen and gambling dens. The film mimics Hollywood silent comedy with much mugging for the camera

Shirley [Yoshiko] Yamaguchi
(1920–)

Yamaguchi was born in 1920, in Fushun, Manchuria, to expatriate Japanese parents. She grew up in the multicultural cities of the region, acquiring fluency in Chinese, Japanese, and Russian. She studied classical western singing, and started giving song recitals in her youth. Later, she attended a mission school for Chinese girls in Beijing, where she learnt English, but otherwise lived in a totally Chinese environment.

When the Japanese started transmitting radio programmes in Chinese for the 'edification and entertainment' of the Chinese population in Manchuria, they sought her services as a singer. Still a schoolgirl, she sang Chinese songs under a Chinese pseudonym. In 1938, when Man-Ei, the Japanese-run Manchurian Film Company, was established, the Japanese military authorities approached her again to star in their first musical. She adopted the name of her godfather, General Li, a close friend of her father, and a collaborator with the Japanese. She was known as Li Hsiang Lan in Manchuria and China, and as Ri Ko Ran (the Japanese reading of her Chinese pseudonym) in Japan, always dressing in Chinese dress for public appearances and maintaining the masquerade of the seductive Chinese songstress.

She was paired with Japanese matinée idols in a series of 'interracial' romances, set in various 'exotic' locations, in which she played the Chinese lover of a Japanese officer or engineer. These co-productions between Toho and Man-Ei were big hits in wartime Japan, as were her visiting concert performances and recordings. Between her other engagements, she managed to fit in performances for the troops at the front.

Her biggest hit in Japan was *Shina no Yoru* (*China Night*, Toho, 1940). In it she plays a dirty and defiant Chinese war orphan, who is picked up on the streets of Shanghai, cleaned, and tamed by a Japanese naval officer (Hasegawa Kazuo), whose adoring slave she becomes. Japanese audiences welcomed its Hollywoodish romantic excesses, as a respite from the repressive wartime ideology of asceticism, and as a fantasy that transformed Japanese aggression against China into a love story.

In occupied China, Chinese audiences resisted the paternalistic propaganda of Japanese productions, preferring Chinese films even when made under the watchful eyes of the Japanese authorities. *Wanshi Liufang* (1942–3) commemorated the anniversary of the first Opium War, and featured three Chinese heroines resisting the western imperialist plot to turn the Chinese into opium addicts. As one of the heroines, Li Hsiang Lan serenaded the patrons of a bar with a song about the evils of opium and inspired her addict lover to fight his addiction. The western villains were played by Chinese actors wearing false noses and fancy wigs and speaking bad Chinese. She also starred in an (unreleased) Man-Ei musical, shot in Harbin with Russian dialogue, directed by veteran Japanese director Yasuliro Shimazu, and known as *My Nightingale* or *The Sing-Song Girl of Harbin*, in which she played the part of the adopted daughter of a white Russian family.

After the war, her birth certificate saved her from execution as a traitor—the fate of many who collaborated with the Japanese—and she was sent 'home' to Japan. She resumed work as a film actress with Toho, under her Japanese name (Yamaguchi Yoshiko), but never regained her wartime popularity. In 1950 she went to the United States, starring in King Vidor's *Japanese War Bride* and appearing in the Broadway musical *Shangri-La*. She was briefly married to Japanese-American sculptor Isamu Noguchi, but returned to Japan soon after. She provided the romantic interest in another Hollywood film, Sam Fuller's *House of Bamboo*, 1955—this time as the 'kimono girl' for the GI, rather than the Chinese urchin for the Japanese officer.

She retired from film in 1958, when she married a Japanese diplomat named Hiroshi Otaka, but went on to enjoy a successful career, first as a television presenter and journalist, and, since 1974, as a Liberal Democratic Party member of the Upper House of the Japanese Diet.

FREDA FREIBERG

SELECT FILMOGRAPHY

Song of the White Orchid (1939); China Night (1940); Vow in the Desert (1941); Sayon's Bell (1943); Eternal Fame (Wanshi Liufang) (1942–3); The Brightest Day of my Life (1948); Desertion at Dawn (1950); Scandal (1950); Japanese War Bride (1952); House of Bamboo (1955); The Bewitching Love of Madame Bai (1956)

BIBLIOGRAPHY

Anderson, Joseph, and Richie, Donald (1982), *The Japanese Film: Art and Industry*.
Freiberg, Freda (1992), 'Genre and Gender in the Wartime Japanese Cinema'.
Yamaguchi, Yoshiko, and Fujiwara, Sakuya (1987), *Ri Ko Ran: Watashi no Hansei*.

Below: Robert Stack with Shirley Yamaguchi in Sam Fuller's drama set in Tokyo, *House of Bamboo* (1955)

and slapstick tumbling, but in its very mimicry asserts agency and represents scenes and events recognizable to its audience as their own.

Romance of a Fruit Pedlar was made by the Mingxing Company, which was to become one of the major production houses in Shanghai. However, the fate of Hui Xi was more typical of the chaotic and difficult economic conditions endured by early Chinese film-makers. While its first film was still playing seven years later, the company itself was long gone. It distinguished itself only by its ability to produce a film before going bankrupt, whereas many other film companies folded before shooting anything. Of the 120 companies established in 1921, only twelve were still operating a year later.

The incredible plots and sentimentality of the films of the 1920s have since been much disparaged by historians as vulgar indulgences that did little to encourage either nationalism or revolution or elevate audiences' tastes. The beginnings of the nationalistic May Fourth Movement in 1919 had seen the appearance of new approved literary works, and from this perspective, the cinema seemed backward. This dismissal of pre-1930s cinema manifests the established Confucian preference for art as education and dislike of popular culture that integrated well with the 'modern' projects of both the Kuomintang nationalists and the Communists. They preferred the 'progressive' or 'left-wing' films that began to emerge in the 1930s.

However, holding up these leftist films in contrast to earlier productions erects a false barrier between them. Although the earlier films may not have directly encouraged political engagement, they did give agency to Chinese film-makers and represent recognizable contemporary conditions to Chinese audiences. The leftist films did not replace populist entertainments, but supplemented them, although this is often forgotten because the entertainment films have been written out of retrospectives of the period. Finally, the leftist films themselves shared more in common with pure entertainment films than is usually acknowledged, and they demonstrate that agitation and popular culture can be one and the same thing.

The impetus for the leftist cinema lay in the Japanese invasion of China. Beginning with the seizure of Manchuria in 1931, within a year the Japanese had bombed Shanghai and come near to taking the city. These events stimulated nationalism amongst audiences and film-makers alike. The Communist Party's front organization, the League of Left-Wing Writers, set up a film group in 1932, and this body infiltrated two of the best-established studios of the period, the Mingxing and the Lianhua. The Kuomintang government's appeasement policy limited direct expression of anti-Japanese sentiment. However, the leftist film-makers were aided in their efforts by the progressive political sentiments of at least some of the studio owners, and their coincident realization that the mood of the times made such productions profitable.

One of the earliest results of the leftist infiltration of the industry was Mingxing's adaptation of a Mao Dun short story, *Spring Silkworms*, released in 1933. The plot shows the inexorable destruction of a silk-farming family by fluctuations in international market prices and other machinations completely beyond their control. An almost documentary detailing of the back-breaking labour entailed in silk production makes the final tragedy all the more moving.

Sun Yu's *Big Road* (also known as *The Highway*), which came out at the beginning of 1935, is an excellent example of the merger of the pre-revolutionary and the post-colonial in one film. The plot involves a group of six unemployed workers who decide to join a road-gang building a strategic highway for the army. Censorship reasons made it impossible directly to name the Japanese as the enemy being fought, but the reference could hardly have been lost on any contemporary viewer. To this patriotism, the film adds class politics, with the inclusion of an evil landlord who sells out to the Japanese. What makes this film effective, however, is its adoption and deployment of the very vulgar entertainment elements so disliked by later critics. Two of the workers form a comedic pairing that is at once modelled on Laurel and Hardy and the cross-talk, stand-up comedy teams of Chinese variety shows. The film has sound effects and music but no dialogue. In scenes where the pair indulge in slapstick, percussion enlivens their performance, and in another scene where the landlord's agent gets whirled around on one of the workmen's shoulders, a little animated aeroplane and dizziness stars buzz around his head. The workmen also encounter two women, one of whom sings for them in the little roadside restaurant they repair to when the day's work is done. Perched on a table, and given the soft-focus treatment employed for the alluring starlets of the period, she attracts the men's attention, but the song she sings is of the woes of China, beset by flood, famine, and war. Their desiring gaze upon her is not answered by shots of her, but by documentary footage of tanks, explosions, and refugees.

Other leftist films of the period also deployed comedy, song, and other elements of populist entertainment to similar ends. Notable titles include *The Goddess*, *Plunder of Peach and Plum*, *Crossroads*, *Street Angel*, *Little Toys*, *A Bible for Women*, *March of Youth*, *The Lianhua Symphony*, *Song of the Fishermen*, and many others. Made in 1937 just before the outbreak of full-scale war with Japan which brought this brief period of remarkable production to a close, *Street Angel* even adds references to Eisenstein to its post-colonial pastiche.

In the face of the Japanese take-over of all of Shanghai except for the foreign concessions, the Chinese film

The popular melodrama *A Spring River Flows East* (1947), directed by Zheng Junli and Cai Chushen, followed the sufferings of one family under Japanese occupation

industry and its personnel fragmented. Some remained on the 'orphan island' of the concessions until they too were taken over in 1941. Others fled to Hong Kong, adding Mandarin-language film-making to the established Cantonese industry, until the Japanese take-over in late 1941 brought film production to an end there too. Still others fled with the Kuomintang into the interior, first to Wuhan and then further inland to Chongqing. Shortages of film stock in the war diverted most of them into other activities, such as the patriotic drama troupes that toured during the war years.

Other more leftist artists made an effort to join the Communist Party in its wartime base at Yen'an in Shaanxi province. Among them was the ex-starlet Lan Ping, soon to enjoy a come-back as Mao's third wife, Jiang Qing. Also among them were the director Yuan Muzhi and his actress wife Chen Bo'er, who became Communist China's first Film Bureau head and Minister of Culture respectively in 1949. Film production only commenced at Yen'an in 1939 when Joris Ivens brought the gift of a camera, but even then, shortages of film stock limited production to a small number of documentaries.

While free Chinese film-making came to a halt during the war, a thriving local industry continued under the Japanese occupation. For whatever reasons, the Japanese had encouraged local film production from their invasion of Manchuria, and after 1937 they added a Shanghai-based industry to their propaganda machine. Unsurprisingly, Chinese historians have preferred to draw a veil over this period, but recent studies indicate that the Japanese in Shanghai ruled the film industry with less brutality than they used elsewhere, and that films with patriotic subtexts, such as the 1939 *Huang Mulan Joins the Army*, based on a traditional legend, still got through the Japanese censors.

The Mingxing Company had collapsed with the coming of the Japanese, but the Lianhua Company re-established itself in Shanghai at the end of the war and once again became the base for the activities of leftist and progressive film-makers. The films of this period document the corruption and spiralling inflation that characterized the period of the civil war with the Communists that broke out immediately. Proclaimed as 'social realist' films as opposed to the Socialist Realism that soon took over with the establishment of the People's Republic in 1949, the productions of these three short years are considered the second 'golden age' of Chinese film production.

Where the films of the first 'golden age' were exuberantly disjunctive and hybrid mixes of entertainment and exhortation, the films of the later 1940s were smoother melodramas with more seamless plots and unity of tone. Perhaps the best-known example is *A Spring River Flows East*, a two-part epic, made by Lianhua in association with the Kunlun studio, and released in 1947 and 1948. Known as China's *Gone with the Wind*, the film can still provoke floods of tears from older Chinese audiences when shown today. The film opens with an ideal couple and their son. However, they are separated by the war when the husband retreats with the Kuomintang to the interior. There he is gradually corrupted and becomes the lover of a rich society woman. His faithful wife suffers through the war in Shanghai, waiting patiently for his return, but he comes back as a Kuomintang carpet-bagger, and the film climaxes when his wife discovers that he is the husband of the woman for whom she is working as a maid. He disowns her and she drowns herself in the Yangtze.

Disillusion with the Kuomintang and their hangers-on is even more pronounced in the films that depict post-war conditions. Films like *Myriads of Lights*, *Crows and Sparrows*, and *San Mao* (adapted from a newspaper cartoon about an orphan) were all enjoyable and humorous, but none attempted to hide the appalling social contradictions of these years and the resentment those who had suffered in Shanghai felt towards their compatriots who had managed to profit from the war. Stylistically, these films featured more subtle ensemble playing from actors seasoned by many years of stage work. Although less obviously pastiched than the films of the 1930s, they too represent post-colonial appropriation for pre-revolutionary ends, but this time drawing on the western spoken stage drama and its cinematic equivalents, rather than popular culture.

The second 'golden age' ended China's pre-1949 cinematic history on a fitting high note. In retrospect, it is remarkable that five years of film-making in the 1930s (1932–7) and three years in the 1940s (1946–9) should stand out so strongly in a total film-making history of forty years (1909–49). However, it would be wrong to suggest that these two 'golden ages' appeared out of the blue. Rather, they represented windows of opportunity when talent that had been long developing was able to make itself visible. Some would argue that such an opportunity was not to present itself again for another forty-five years, until *One and Eight* and *Yellow Earth* (both 1984) heralded the arrival of another golden age of Chinese cinema.

Bibliography

Bergeron, Régis (1977), *Le Cinéma chinois, i: 1905–1949*.

Berry, Chris (ed.) (1991), *Perspectives on Chinese Cinema*.

Cheng Jihua *et al.* (1963), *Zhongguo dianying fazhanshi* ('History of the development of Chinese cinema').

Clark, Paul (1987), *Chinese Cinema: Culture and Politics since 1949*.

Du Yunzhi (1972), *Zhongguo Dianyingshi* ('History of Chinese cinema').

Leyda, Jay (1972), *Dianying: Electric Shadows*.

Quiquemelle, Marie-Claire, and Passek, Jean-Loup (eds.) (1985), *Le Cinéma chinois*.

Toroptsev, Sergei (1979), *Ocherk istorii kitaiskogo kino 1896–1966* ('Essays on the history of Chinese cinema').

The Classical Cinema in Japan

HIROSHI KOMATSU

The Great Kanto Earthquake of the first of September 1923 destroyed Tokyo and the culture it had supported. The Japanese chose not to rebuild the city as it had been and abandoned its old forms for a new appearance. The destruction caused by the earthquake also gave the decisive impetus for the development of new kinds of Japanese film. From 1924 to the early 1930s a number of classics of Japanese cinema were made at Nikkatsu, Shochiku, Teikine, Makino, and some small independent studios. Production and invention were stimulated as archaic forms were abandoned and film-makers embraced new European art cinemas.

Although the destruction caused by the earthquake was the decisive catalyst for these changes, they had been underway for several years before. As early as 1922, such films as *Reiko no wakare* ('On the verge of spiritual light', Kokkatsu/Kiyomatsu Hosoyama) and *Yōjo no mai* ('Dance of a sorceress', Shochiku/Yoshinobu Ikeda) had appeared in the New School genre. These were influenced by German Expressionism, partially employing the contorted stage settings featured in *The Cabinet of Dr Caligari* (1919) and *From Morn to Midnight* (*Von Morgens bis Mitternacht*, 1920). Formula rather than story had been the important factor in Japanese film-making since its inception, and so the German expressionist style could be incorporated very swiftly. Film-makers took the German imports as a 'film art' template; a new formula to reproduce. Kenji Mizoguchi imitated the form in his *Chi to rei* ('Blood and Spirit', Nikkatsu, 1923) completed just before the earthquake and one of the last to be made in Nikkatsu's famous Mukojima studio.

The earthquake did not destroy the Mukojima studio, but it made film-making in Tokyo very difficult. Nikkatsu closed the studio and moved its entire production section to Kyoto, where it would remain for the next ten years. Kyoto, the ancient capital, was traditionally the production centre of period drama (*jidaigeki*), and the surroundings of old houses and streets would seem to provide a perfect backdrop for this form. Modern dramas (*gendaigeki*) were always set in Tokyo, but now Nikkatsu had to shoot them in the Kyoto studio with set reproductions of the city. The Kyoto production base allowed for the development of artificial styles, particularly Expressionism, in the sets of Nikkatsu *gendaigeki*. The other major company, Shochiku, also moved the work of its Tokyo studio to Kyoto in the aftermath of the earthquake, but they found it difficult to create the right atmosphere for *gendaigeki* there and returned to Tokyo two months later.

The studio-based *gendaigeki* produced by Nikkatsu in Kyoto were clearly distinguishable from those made in Tokyo by Shochiku and other companies. The Tokyo films emphasized the place of human relationships in modern society by representing the daily lives of ordinary people. Nikkatsu, on the other hand, produced films in its Kyoto studio which depicted a clearly fictive world detached from daily life, similar to that represented in literary and theatrical works or foreign films.

Two directors, Minoru Murata and Yutaka Abe, were instrumental in establishing the characteristics of Nikkatsu *gendaigeki* although they had very different influences and styles. European cultural influences had been felt in Japan since the Meiji period, and it was from

these sources that Murata took his inspiration. His film *Rojo no reikon* ('Soul on the road', Shochiku, 1921) represented the imaginative world and lacked typical Japanese realism. He studied German film and theatre and the impact of Expressionism can be seen in his film for Nikkatsu, *Untenshu Eikichi* ('Eikichi the chauffeur', 1924), in which he partially employed expressionist settings. In utilizing chiaroscuro, added quite artificially on to the theme of the drama, Murata presaged future Japanese films, notably the works of Teinosuke Kinugasa. A scene from *Seisaku no tsuma* ('Seisaku's wife', Nikkatsu, 1924), in which the heroine in fetters, played by Kumeko Urabe, stands in despair on the street, is similar to the last scene in Kinugasa's *Jujiro* ('Crossroads', 1928), but was in fact borrowed directly from the snowy night scene in the German expressionist film *From Morn to Midnight*. *Osumi to haha* ('Osumi and mother', 1924) and especially *Machi no tejinashi* ('The conjuror in the town', 1925), with which he visited France and Germany, showed Murata's penchant for European art cinema.

Yutaka Abe, the other major director of Nikkatsu *gendaigeki*, had been working as an actor in Los Angeles, and brought Hollywood-style modernism to Japanese film. Abe particularly admired the sophisticated comedy of Lubitsch, and was inspired to put erotic elements into his works. His films can be seen as a reaction to the New School melodrama. Abe's films *Ashi ni sawatta onna* ('The

Minoru Murata's German Expressionist-influenced *Osumi to haha* ('Osumi and Mother', 1924)

woman who touched the legs', 1926), *Riku no ningyo* ('The mermaid on the land', 1926), and *Kare wo meguru gonin no onna* ('Five women around him', 1927) were welcomed by film-goers, and their popularity led to a fundamental change in the form of *gendaigeki*.

The trend towards modernism can also be seen in the films produced by Shochiku, the company that had imitated the methods of American cinema from its earliest days. At Shochiku the producer Shiro Kido encouraged directors to make films which dealt with the lives of the middle classes, who composed the majority of the cinema audience at that time. Traditionally, Japanese cinema had been based on established plot formulas, the worlds created on screen being detached from the reality of the lives of the audiences. By focusing on the daily life of the middle classes, Shochiku films of this period manifested an awareness of class without overt political implications. However, this deviation from traditional cinematic formula and subject-matter was not wholly revolutionary. The description of ordinary people's daily lives existed in Japanese literature of the Edo period. American films, particularly those of the Bluebird Company, were popular in Japan in the 1910s and so audiences had seen that the daily life of ordinary people could be an entertaining and attractive cinematic spectacle. Shochiku's middle-class films were characterized by a message of class-consciousness seen through the scenes of daily life that attracted the middle-class audiences; themes like the problems of a white-collar worker.

Gendaigeki was not the only form to change fundamentally after the earthquake. Even the Kyuha (Old School) genre, the most traditional costume drama, changed in this period. While very traditional films continued to be made, a new form developed from its roots and became known as period drama or *jidaigeki*. This genre too moved away from the repetition of formulas based on familiar and traditional stories. The more modern form of *jidaigeki* was established around 1923–4, and after the death in 1926 of Matsunosuke Onoe, the superstar actor who had virtually symbolized the Old School style, the new form completely detached itself from the archaism of the traditional costume drama.

Since 1909, when he directed his first film at the Yokota Company, Shozo Makino had made many Matsunosuke Onoe films as a specialist Old School director. However, in 1921 he founded his own independent company, Makino, and began to make period dramas that differed in form and style from the formula Matsunosuke Onoe films. Not only did he direct, but he acted as a producer, discovering and nurturing talented directors, script-writers, and actors. Among the directors, Koroku Numata, Bansho Kanamori, and Buntaro Futagawa made *jidaigeki* for the Makino Company. The writer Rokuhei Susukita developed scripts that had nihilistic and sometimes anarchistic

content, injecting a current of leftist ideology into the *jidaigeki*.

Despite the death of their star Matsunosuke Onoe, the Nikkatsu studio continued to make orthodox *jidaigeki*. Tomiyasu Ikeda, the main *jidaigeki* director at the studio, borrowed his themes from well-known and traditional historical stories, and so his films lacked the boldness of Makino's period films in which the heroes were always heading towards ruin. Ikeda directed large-scale static *jidaigeki* such as *Sonno joi* ('Revere the Emperor, expel the barbarians', Nikkatsu, 1927) and *Jiraika gumi* ('Jiraika group', Nikkatsu, 1927–8), and he became the undisputed master of the most traditional *jidaigeki* from the late 1920s into the 1930s. However, not all of Nikkatsu's *jidaigeki* directors were content with making orthodox period drama. For example, Kichiro Tsuji conducted unique experiments with the form. His film *Jigoku ni ochita Mitsuhide* ('Mitsuhide gone to hell', Nikkatsu, 1926) was a *mélange* of *jidaigeki*, comedy, revue, Expressionism, and *gendaigeki*. He was sensitive to the influences of film art and introduced them into his own work. In the late 1920s he even approached the proletarian cinema, making the masterpiece *Kasahari kenpo* ('The mending umbrella swordsmanship', Nikkatsu, 1929), but as the Japanese socialist movement was suppressed by state and police he returned to orthodox *jidaigeki*, building a world that evoked a period feel.

However, it was Daisuke Ito who raised *jidaigeki* of the late 1920s to the heights of what was seen in retrospect to be avant-garde. His films, like the trilogy of *Chuji tabi nikki* ('A diary of Chuji's travels', Nikkatsu, 1927), have extremely pessimistic themes, but were technically advanced and critically acclaimed for their moving camera, rapid cutting, and refined, plastic beauty.

Although famous for avant-garde films like *Kurutta ippeiji* (*A Page of Madness*, 1926), Teinosuke Kinugasa also opened a new horizon for *jidaigeki* by his effective direction. He originally acted as an *oyama* (the male actor who always played women's roles) in the New School films made at Nikkatsu's Mukojima studio, before joining the Makino Company as director. He became acquainted with the contemporary young novelists with whom he made *Nichirin* ('The sun', 1925), a film dealing with Japanese mythology. The influence of European art cinema can be seen in his films *Kurutta ippeiji* and *Jujiro* (1928). These films were exhibited in Tokyo in a theatre normally reserved for foreign films and attracted a different audience from the usual for Japanese films.

The *jidaigeki* form, then, was continuously refined in the late 1920s, through the innovation of many directors in different production companies. The films' contents were constituted not only from the traditional sword plays, but also from the ideas inspired by new ideologies. Daisuke Ito's *jidaigeki* of this period described the oppression of townspeople and peasants, and riots against the ruling classes became an important theme in some *jidaigeki*. Rebellion by the people was too controversial a subject to be dealt with directly in the cinema, but the *jidaigeki* were set in a period over 100 years previously and so some ideological content was tolerated. Thus out of traditional period drama a new form of leftist cinema, the tendency film, developed.

In 1929 Tomu Uchida's *Ikeru ningyo* ('A living doll') was released from Nikkatsu's Kyoto studio. This *gendaigeki* dealt with the themes of evil and the contradictions of capitalist society, and was one of the first true tendency films. Following this model, Nikkatsu made *Tokai kokyogaku* ('Metropolitan symphony', 1929, directed by Kenji Mizoguchi) and *Kono haha wo miyo* ('Look at this mother', 1930, by Tomotake Tasaka), employing realist forms influenced by Soviet and German cinema. The success of Nikkatsu's tendency films caused a wave of imitators. Even Teikine, the film company that specialized in entertainment films, followed the trend by making *Nani ga kanojo wo so saseta ka* ('What made her do it?', 1930, directed by Shigeyoshi Suzuki), depicting the life of a poverty-stricken female arsonist. This achieved particular box-office success, largely because it lightened its social criticism with vulgar elements to amuse the audience.

The censor interfered with all tendency films, particularly cutting parts that represented the destruction of social order. It was impossible for films to admire revolution or to suggest the legitimacy of Communism, and even the representation of the bare reality of poor people was prohibited. This meant that the degree of realism in these tendency films was weaker than that of their Soviet and German counterparts. Furthermore, to attract audiences the tendency films had to depend on sensationalist subject-matter, which limited the possibility of the ideological development of the film. However, they opened the eyes of Japanese film-makers and audiences to the reality of society, at the same time as influencing the development of the film industry by incorporating the methods of European realist cinema.

The production of tendency film indicated the difference in the characters of the two main film companies in Japan: Nikkatsu was a liberal company boldly producing this kind of film in its Kyoto studio, but Shochiku, which was founded on the conformist ideology of American cinema, remained wary of the 'dangerous' ideology of the tendency film. However, after the tremendous success of *Nani ga kanojo wo so saseta ka*, even Shochiku had to make concessions to the new form. Yasujiro Shimazu directed *Seikatsu sen ABC* ('Life line ABC', 1931) for Shochiku, containing scenes of striking workers. The tendency film continued to be immensely popular up to 1931, when the censor began to interfere more severely than ever, until such films became impossible to release.

As tendency films disappeared, propaganda of a different kind took its place. In 1932 Shochiku and some small companies began to make films that glorified war and nationalistic ideology, particularly supporting Japan's Manchurian policy.

THE MOVE TO SOUND

Sound and silent film coexisted in Japan for many years, with silent films being made up until 1938. There were several reasons for this, both financial and cultural. First, Japanese film companies of the early 1930s tended to be insufficiently financially developed to equip their studios with the machinery for sound film production. Even if the studio was so equipped, it took time and money to install the necessary sound film projectors and amplifiers in all the cinemas. As long as some could only show silent films, these had to be made in parallel with sound films. The second reason for the slow transition to sound was the resistance of the *benshi* (who explained the filmic image to the audience). They fought the transfer to sound film production in order to protect their jobs and positions. Indeed in Japan some of the audience went to the movies for the pleasure of hearing the skill of the *benshi*. Japanese audiences had been used to the role of the *benshi*, which had given films a vocal commentary from their earliest days, and sound film was therefore not experienced as so revolutionary in Japan as it was in Europe and the USA.

Despite these obstacles, sound films were produced in Japan from a relatively early date. In 1925 Yoshizo Minagawa acquired the rights to Lee De Forest's Phonofilm and renamed it Mina Talkie (Mina Tôkii), and several sound films were produced by this system from 1927 to 1930, including Kenji Mizoguchi's first sound feature *Furusato* ('Hometown', Nikkatsu, 1930). In 1928 Masao Tojo invented the Eastphone (Iisuto Fon) system that reproduced sound on discs, in a similar manner to Vitaphone. Using this system, sound films began to be made at the Nikkatsu and Teikine studios. These two methods of sound production were dropped when superior systems were invented. One of these, the Tsuchihashi sound system developed by Takeo Tsuchihashi, came to be widely used, notably on one of the first complete sound films made in Japan, Heinosuke Gosho's *Madamu to nyobo* ('The neighbour's wife and mine', Shochiku, 1931). However, the production of sound films was not realized systematically, and even at Shochiku it took four months to produce *Madamu to nyobo*'s successor: Gosho's *Waka ki hi no kangeki* ('The deep emotion in one's youth', Shochiku, 1931).

Shochiku and Shinko Kinema adopted the Tsuchihashi process. Nikkatsu, however, forced to abandon the primitive Mina Talkie system and lagging behind its rivals in sound film production, adopted the Western Electric system, but did not produce a film with it until Daisuke Ito's *Tange sazen* in 1933. PCL developed a system and

A scene from Heinosuke Gosho's comedy *Madamu to nyobo* ('My neighbour's wife and mine', 1931), one of the first Japanese films with synchronized sound

recorded sound for news films and the features of Nikkatsu. This proved successful and the company launched its own sound film production section in 1933. By the middle of the decade there was effectively a two-tier system, with the small companies continuing to make silent films, while all the films made by PCL and most of the output of the big studios Shochiku and Nikkatsu were shot with dialogue. By 1937 PCL was reorganized as Toho and had the best equipped sound studio in Tokyo.

Many important Japanese directors did not make sound films until well into the 1930s. Yasujiro Ozu's *Mata au hi made* ('Until the day we meet again', Shochiku, 1932) had music and sound effects but was still structured as a silent film with intertitles. During the 1930s his films became tinged with a kind of gloomy social consciousness, and this culminated in his first sound film *Hitori musuko* (*The Only Son*, Shochiku, 1936). However, unlike the tendency films of the previous decade, Ozu portrayed this gloom not as the result of the social structure, but rather as the loneliness of the human condition. This outlook, characteristic of Ozu's films, emerged from Shochiku's Kamata studio and its petty bourgeois tradition of films lacking an overt political ideology. However, Ozu's films reached beyond the standard studio fare and attained a unique view of the depths of human loneliness.

There was another director at Shochiku's Kamata studio who found new and original expression through the medium of the sound film. Working as a director since 1924, Hiroshi Shimizu had established himself as one of the most original stylists in the Japanese cinema of the time. His famous silent film *Fue no shiratama* ('Diamond', Shochiku, 1929) displayed avant-garde techniques with rapidly changing and unexpected camera angles, and the use of dream-like settings. The most remarkable of his sound films were the 'Road Movies' series, such as *Arigato-san* ('Mr Thank-You', Shochiku, 1936) and *Hanagata senshu* ('A star athlete', Shochiku, 1937), in which the camera becomes the eyes of the characters with the passing landscape shown through subjective shots. Shimizu refined this technique into a kind of abstraction.

Mikio Naruse had been directing silent films for five years in Shochiku. His films were characterized by unique frame composition and character movement, which, with his relatively static direction, created the illusion of deep space, and films of great pictorial beauty. Shochiku was the starting-point of Naruse's career, but even after he moved to Toho in 1935, his films carried echoes of the Shochiku style.

These directors absorbed contemporary modernism from western cinema and in adapting it uncovered a modernist impulse in Japanese culture and cinema.

Despite this shift to new film forms by many filmmakers, there were more orthodox directors working at Shochiku; notably Yasujiro Shimazu and Heinosuke

Kenji Mizoguchi

(1898–1956)

Mizoguchi became internationally famous only in the last years of his life. Outside his native Japan his reputation still rests almost entirely on his films of the 1950s—mainly on the lyrical dramas with medieval settings such as *Ugetsu monogatari* (1953), *Sansho dayu* ('Sansho the bailiff', 1954), or *Shin-heike monogatari* ('New tales of the Taira clan', 1955), but also (to a lesser extent) on sensationalist modern dramas such as his very last film *Street of Shame* (*Akasen chitai*, 1956). But his career stretches back as far as 1920, when he first entered the Nikkatsu Mukojima studio as an assistant to New School (Shinpa) directors such as Eizo Tanaka, and it is to his roots in the New School of the 1920s that one must look for an understanding of his art.

New School films were melodramas in the western sense. Derived from the urban drama that emerged in the Meiji period (particularly in the 1890s), they used male actors (*oyama*) to play female roles, and their stories typically focus on the sacrifice of women for the sake of the family. Mizoguchi began to direct his own New School dramas, employing *oyama*, at Mukojima in 1923, and the formula at the heart of the genre was to form the basis of his art throughout his career.

During his early years, Mizoguchi worked in a wide variety of genres and styles. Outside the New School melodrama, he made detective films, expressionist films, war films, comedies, ghost stories, and proletarian films. During this period he also borrowed boldly from the expressive repertoire of American and European art cinema. In the scenario of *Nihonbashi* (1929), for example, he specifically called for a scene to be directed like a scene from Murnau's *Sunrise* (1927). Using the formula of the New School as a foundation, he practised a variety of expressive techniques, which changed from film to film with each new-found enthusiasm. Throughout this early period he was a director with a multitude of faces, who cannot be easily grasped under the western notion of an *auteur*. It was with *Kaminingyo haru no sasayaki* ('A paper doll's whisper of spring', 1926), from a script by Eizo Tanaka, that he first revealed his own accomplished Japanese style, inheriting the spirit of Tanaka's own masterpiece *Kyoya erimise* ('Kyoya, the collar shop', 1922). But he also made a number of mediocre films, both then and later; even in the post-war period he continued to work outside his favoured mode (as in the American-influenced *Wara koi wa moenu*—'My love has been burning', 1949), with somewhat uneven results.

In spite of this diversity of output, his concern for persecuted women inherent in the New School tradition is consistent to the end. This is particularly evident in the trilogy of films adapted from the novels of Kyoka Izumi: *Nihonbashi*, *Taki no shiraito* ('The water magician', 1933) and *Orizuru Osen* ('The downfall of Osen', 1935). But the influence of New School schemas can also be seen in his

'tendency' films (realist, political dramas), such as *Tokai kokyogaku* ('Metropolitan symphony', 1929) or *Shikamo karera wa yuku* ('And yet they go on', 1931). Involvement in the tendency film seems to have changed Mizoguchi's attitude towards women. In New School films, women end up destroyed victims of male society. But in Mizoguchi's work from the 1930s onwards the women characters are vital enough to fight for their own survival against the social system, as in *Naniwa erejii* ('Osaka elegy', 1936). His later films are often centred on women who are resilient and even powerful.

In the early period Mizoguchi absorbed many stylistic influences from foreign cinema, beginning with the expressionist *Chi to rei* ('Body and soul', 1923). In the late 20s he experimented with bold devices like rapidly changing scenes, frequent dissolves, and (in the trilogy of Izumi adaptations) a unique use of flashback. These traits are the opposite of what was to become his mature style, characterized by long takes and unobtrusive direction, as it emerges in *Zangiku monogatari* (The Story of the Last Chrysanthemums, 1939) and *Genroku chusingura* (The Loyal Forty-seven Ronin, 1941).

If one sees the New School film form as at the heart of Mizoguchi's work, his most famous post-war films can be more richly interpreted. The suffering women of *Ugetsu monogatari* and *Sansho dayu*, and the vital women of *The Life of Oharu* (Saikaku ichidai onna, 1952) and *Music of Gion* (Gion bayashi, 1953), may seem different, but they share the same roots. The static and yet lyrical images in his post-war works were only created after passing through the diverse film forms of the foreign avant-garde and the New School films of the Mukojima studio.

HIROSHI KOMATSU

SELECT FILMOGRAPHY

Kaminingyo haru no sasayaki (1926); Tokai kokyogaku (1929); Nihonbashi (1929); Taki no shiraito (1933); Orizuru Osen (1935); Naniwa erejii (1936); Zangiku monogatari (1939); Genroku chusingura (1941); The Life of Oharu (1952); Music of the Gion (1953); Ugetsu monogatari (1953); Sansho dayu (1954); Shin-heike monogatari (1955); Street of Shame (1956)

BIBLIOGRAPHY

Freiberg, Freda (1981), *Women in Mizoguchi Films*.
Kirihara, Donald (1992), *Patterns of Time: Mizoguchi and the 1930s*.
McDonald, Keiko (1984), *Mizoguchi*.

Opposite: The Story of the Last Chrysanthemums (Zangiku Monogatari, 1939)

Gosho. Although Shimazu did not develop such a personal style as some of his contemporaries, he made many large-scale star-vehicles within the Shochiku studio system. He was often conservative in his direction, but he came to be considered one of the most trustworthy directors at Shochiku by making sensitive films such as *Tonari no yae-chan* ('The girl next door', 1934). Heinosuke Gosho was another of the more orthodox directors at Shochiku, and he was entrusted with the company's first two sound pictures. His personal cinematic style developed after the war, when his films began to display a tendency towards literary idealism, while his contemporary Naruse's post-war films were still very much in the Shochiku studio style.

From the mid-1920s onwards makers of *jidaigeki* were at the forefront of developing innovative forms of Japanese cinema. In the 1930s, two directors particularly became renowned for creating a new age of *jidaigeki*. Mansaku Itami directed nihilistic *jidaigeki*, making such films as *Kokushi muso* (1932) and *Yamiuchi tosei* ('The life of a foul murderer', 1932). Sadao Yamanaka introduced elements of the *gendaigeki* (modern drama genre) into the *jidaigeki*. In addition to these two, Nikkatsu's director Tomu Uchida brought modern elements from his previous work to the sword film *Adauchi senshu* ('The revenge champion', Nikkatsu, 1931). The high-quality *jidaigeki* of the early 1930s incorporated the ironical content and style of contemporary European cinema. For example, Sadao Yamanaka's *jidaigeki*, *Hyakuman-ryo no tsubo* ('The pot worth a million ryo', Nikkatsu, 1935) was directly inspired by René Clair's *Le Million* (1931).

Kenji Mizoguchi, who had developed many different themes in the course of his career, deployed his mastery of *mise-en-scène* in a series of films that took the Meiji period as their setting. In the mid-1930s his film-making methods in *Naniwa erejii* ('Osaka elegy', Daiichi Eiga, 1936), *Gion no kyodai* ('Sisters of the Gion', Daiichi Eiga, 1936), and *Aienkyo* ('The gorge between love and hate', Shinko Kinema, 1937) heightened his fame as *the* maker of realist *gendaigeki*. This realism attained the highest stylistic beauty in *Zangiku monogatari* (The Story of the Last Chrysanthemums, Shochiku, 1939). In an uneasy atmosphere of nationalism and war, Mizoguchi escaped into the world of traditional Japanese beauty, a direction he would successfully pursue for most of the rest of his career.

THE WAR AND AFTER

The war cast a dark shadow over the whole Japanese film industry. A law was passed in 1939 which laid virtually all Japanese cinema under the control of state power. It became difficult to make films which did not praise the war or actively promote Fascist ideology. Yasujiro Ozu confined himself to a world unrelated to that of contemporary politics by making *Chichi ariki* (There was a Father,

Yasujiro Ozu

(1903–1963)

At first an assistant cameraman, Yasujiro Ozu began directing for Shochiku Films, one of Japan's largest studios, in 1927. When he died in 1963 at age 60, he had made fifty-three films, nearly all for Shochiku. By common consent, he had become Japan's greatest director.

During the late 1920s, Japanese cinema was in the process of 'modernizing'. Studio heads had built a vertically integrated oligopoly comparable in many ways to America's. Directors adapted many stylistic and narrative conventions of Hollywood cinema in an effort to compete with the slick, smooth films that attracted Japanese audiences.

The young Ozu flourished in this milieu. Confessing himself bored by most Japanese films, he absorbed the lessons of Chaplin, Lloyd, and Lubitsch in order to create comedies that combined physical humour with social observation (*I Was Born, but...*, 1932). He made films about college life, street thugs (*Dragnet Girl*, 1933), and domestic tensions (*Woman of Tokyo*, 1933). In all of them he displayed a mastery of close-ups, editing, and shot design. His distinctive style was based on placing the camera at a low height and intricately intercutting objects with facial reactions. Ozu also displayed a quirky humour which could create *nansensu* ('nonsense') gags around the circulation of a pair of mittens (*Days of Youth*, 1929) or an empty coin purse (*Passing Fancy*, 1933). He could also turn modern Tokyo into a landscape of mysterious poignancy. A shot may dwell on a scrap of paper fluttering down from an office building, a secretary's compact on a window sill, an empty sidewalk. All of these tendencies came to focus in his first talking film, *The Only Son* (1936), about a country woman who comes to Tokyo and finds that her son has failed to make a career. By this time Ozu was already considered one of Japan's top directors.

His output slowed during the war period as a result of military service, but he did make such 'home-front' films as *Brothers and Sisters of the Toda Family* (1941) and *There Was a Father* (1942). His first post-war film was a 'neighbourhood' movie reminiscent of his 1930s work, *Diary of a Tenement Gentleman* (1947), but his most famous films would be elaborations of *Brothers and Sisters*—patient studies of an extended family undergoing a quiet crisis that brings out contrasts across generations.

The most famous of these extended-family films is *Tokyo Story* (1953). Like the mother in *The Only Son*, an elderly couple journey to Tokyo. Their children, preoccupied with their jobs and families, treat them coldly; only their daughter-in-law Noriko, widow of their son lost in war, shows them affection. On the trip back, the grandmother falls ill; she dies at home. The grandfather gives

Yasujiro Ozu

Noriko his wife's watch and resigns himself to a life alone. This bare anecdote becomes, in Ozu's hands, an incomparable revelation of the varied ways in which humans express love, devotion, and responsibility.

A child grows up and leaves the family; friends must separate; a son or daughter must marry; a widow or widower is left alone; an aged parent dies. In film after film, Ozu and his script-writer Noda played a set of variations on these elemental motifs. Each film, however, reworks the material in fresh ways. *Late Spring* (1949) is a largely sombre study of the necessity for father and daughter to part; Ozu's last film, *An Autumn Afternoon* (1962), integrates the theme with a satire on consumerism and a nostalgia for pre-war values. *Early Summer* (1951) also centres on the daughter marrying, but here the action is embedded in a network of domestic comedy and lyrical evocation of suburban life. *Ohayo* (1959), in some ways a remake of the children's comedy *I Was Born, but...*, treats domestic conflict in a more vulgar key, giving us a boys' farting contest which Ozu and Noda compare to the aimless pleasantries of adult conversation.

Throughout these works, Ozu's style remained crisp, rigorous, and capable of great modulation of emphasis. His static shot/reverse-shots, often frontally positioned, match characters within the frame across the cut, so that the screen becomes a field of minutely changing masses and contours. His camera movements, often virtuosic in the 1930s work, are eliminated completely in the colour films—a decision which only throws into relief the vibrant hues of tiny props arranged carefully in the sets. Above all, his famous low camera height remains obstinately there, as if he aimed to show that across nearly forty years a single, simple stylistic choice could yield infinite gradations of composition and depth. The subtleties which Ozu found in apparently simple technique have their counterpart in the emotional richness of dramas which seem as close to everyday life as any the cinema has given us.

DAVID BORDWELL

SELECT FILMOGRAPHY

Tokyo no gassho (Tokyo Chorus) (1931); Umarete wa mita keredo (I Was Born, but...) (1932); Tokyo no onna (Woman of Tokyo) (1933); Hijosen no onna (Dragnet Girl) (1933); Degigokoro (Passing Fancy) (1933); Hitori musuko (The Only Son) (1936); Todake no kyodai (Brothers and Sisters of the Toda Family) (1941); Chichi ariki (There Was a Father) (1942); Nagaya shinshiroku (Diary of a Tenement Gentleman) (1947); Banshun (Late Spring) (1949); Bakushu (Early Summer) (1951); Tokyo monogatari (Tokyo Story) (1953); Higanbana (Equinox Flower) (1958); Ohayo (Good Morning) (1959); Samma no aji (An Autumn Afternoon) (1962)

BIBLIOGRAPHY

Bordwell, David (1988), *Ozu and the Poetics of Cinema*.
Burch, Noël (1979), *To the Distant Observer: Forms and Meaning in the Japanese Cinema*.
Hasumi, Shiguehiko (1983), *Kantoku Ozu Yasujiro* ('Director Yasujiro Ozu').
Richie, Donald (1974), *Ozu*

Shochiku, 1942), and Mizoguchi's *Genroku chusingura* (*The Loyal Forty-seven Ronin of the Genroku Era*, Shochiku, 1941–2) was also a refuge from the war. But lesser directors could not avoid producing films that supported national policy. The Japanese cinema suffered in other ways in the war years; the number of productions decreased because of the lack of film stock, and by August 1945 40 per cent of all the cinemas in Japan had been destroyed by fire bombs.

Problems continued after the war. In December 1945, four months after the Japanese surrender, the film law of 1939 was revoked, and in 1946, at the demand of the occupying forces, war criminals in the film world were expelled. The occupation army also prohibited the production of nationalistic films and ordered the burning of 225 films from the pre-war era. In this situation it became difficult to make *jidaigeki*, as they were based on traditional Japanese forms and took place in the past, and often appeared to promote fidelity to the feudalist system. Thus the studios produced films for democratic education and films attacking past nationalistic tendencies. Despite such externally imposed requirements on the content of films, the film industry enjoyed a freedom that had not existed in the war years.

In the period just after the war hedonistic films of a kind never permitted before were produced. Mizoguchi was one of the directors who took advantage of this new freedom to express sensuality. Shochiku's veteran directors reflected these developments in their own ways: Ozu's films developed in the direction of static formalism, taking the daily world as their subject; Shimizu became interested in depicting the lives of children; Naruse, who had been working at Toho since 1935, continued to make melodramas from a realistic viewpoint; Gosho became an idealist director who made films that adopted the current ideology—existentialism for example—in a schematic and predictable way.

The most important of the new directors of the post-war period was Akira Kurosawa. His films adopted a western style of construction to examine dramatically the subject of human nature. His *mise-en-scène* was accessible to a foreign audience, and drew world-wide attention to Japanese cinema.

Tadashi Imai's films were concerned with the problems of Japanese society, although he sometimes presented them in a naïve or simplistic manner. From the post-war period of democracy and enlightenment his films began to take on the ideology of the labour movement and left-wing politics. Keisuke Kinoshita continued to make traditional melodramas in the Shochiku style, but he opened audiences' eyes to the possibility of new forms of art cinema in the 1950s. He also made the first Japanese colour feature *Karumen kokyo ni kaeru* ('Carmen comes home', Shochiku, 1951). Kaneto Shindo wrote many scripts for the major studios while he established an independent production company to direct his own films. After the release of his most famous film *Hadaka no shima* ('The naked island', 1960) he tried, often unsuccessfully, to bring some experimental elements to his work.

Television broadcasting began in Japan in 1953, and to cope with this new competition Japanese film companies moved towards the adoption of colour and the widescreen format. Nikkatsu made its first colour film in 1955, and Toei made the first widescreen film in 1957. By the late 1950s colour and widescreen were prerequisites for a film's commercial success.

In the Japanese cinema of the 1930s the coexistence of sound and silent film had continued for many years due to insufficient capital and special cultural circumstances. The 1940s cinema can be divided into two completely opposing periods; the Fascist ideology films of the war years and the films of democracy from the second half of the decade. The ideological changes established by the occupation did not add anything fundamentally new to the form of Japanese cinema, as the assimilation of the American cinema style had already been achieved by the 1930s. The majority of film art in post-war Japan was created by directors with an occidental vision, like Kurosawa. However, at the same time Mizoguchi and Ozu, two important, if very different, directors from the pre-war period, could carry on developing their Japanese aesthetic in the post-war era. The war and liberation gave Japanese cinema the opportunity to foster both occidental and Japanese sensibilities.

Bibliography

Anderson, Joseph L., and Richie, Donald (1982), *The Japanese Film: Art and Industry.*

Hirano, Kyoko (1992), *Mr. Smith Goes to Tokyo.*

Nolletti, Arthur, Jr., and Desser, David (eds.) (1992), *Reframing Japanese Cinema: Authorship, Genre and History.*

Sato, Tadao, *et al.* (eds.) (1986), *Koza Nihon Eiga*, vols. iii–v.

Tanaka, Junichiro (1976), *Nihon Eiga Hattatsu Shi*, vol. iii.

The Emergence of Australian Film

BILL ROUTT

PIONEERS AND EARLY FEATURES

Projected films were first commercially exhibited in Australia on 22 August 1896 by an American magician, Carl Hertz, using British films and apparatus obtained from (R. W.) Paul's Animatograph Works, Ltd. If this event may be considered the 'birth' of Australian cinema, the infant's parentage is both unquestioned and significant. Like other parents, the United States and Britain came to be simultaneously loved and hated by the film industry they fostered, and to serve their progeny as models of patronage and exploitation, to be imitated and overcome.

The film business in Australia was at first chiefly a business of exhibition. Many of the 'pioneer' Australian exhibitors T. J. West, Cozzens Spencer, and J. D. Williams (all of whom branched into production in some way) were British or American. For the first thirteen years the most successful and influential exhibitor and producer, however, was the Salvation Army, whose Limelight Division toured the country with shows featuring non-fiction and fiction films, slides, lectures, and live music. Birmingham-born Joseph Perry conceived, produced, and organized these elevating evenings of entertainment, becoming in the process Australia's premier, if not absolutely its first, film-maker.

Perry's evening-long programmes sometimes contained more than one hour of footage on a single non-fiction topic—what today would be called 'feature-length documentaries'—and in 1904 he made a short fiction film about Australian bushranging, almost undoubtedly the earliest example of 'an Australian cinema *par excellence*', blending movement, landscape, and mythology in a kind of counterpart to the American Western. Within two years William Gibson, Millard Johnson, and John and Nevin Tait had combined Perry's multi-reel documentaries and the bushranging legend into *The Story of the Kelly Gang*, a show featuring four reels of film tableaux glorifying the bandit rebel Ned Kelly along with a lecture commentary, musical accompaniment, and sound effects.

The critical and commercial success of the Salvation Army and *The Story of the Kelly Gang* provided the impetus for six years of local multi-reel production before such lengthy films were common in most of the rest of the world, and set the pattern for the peculiarly Australian genre of bushranging films, which flourished until such films were banned by the state government of New South Wales in 1912 for their supposed pernicious (social and political) influence. Bushranging films have continued to be produced sporadically, at times secretly, to the present day.

The vogue for bushranging films seems to have contributed to a short-lived boom in early Australian production. Between the release of John Gavin's bushranging melodrama *Thunderbolt* in November 1910 and July 1912 some seventy-nine titles were released, at least nineteen of them four reels or more (and twelve about bushranging). The precise causes of the boom—or bubble—are not clear, but its abrupt deflation by the middle of 1912 suggests such a level of production was not sustainable in the local market. By 1913 the principal exhibition/distribution/production firms had merged to form Australasian Films, known to its competitors and many enemies as 'the combine'. Distribution interests seem to have dominated the decisions of the combine. At any rate, Australasian called a halt to multi-reel production and apparently acted clandestinely and forcefully for many years to ensure that most Australian-made features would find only limited distribution and exhibition in Australia.

THE FIRST WORLD WAR AND ITS AFTERMATH

The First World War represents a watershed for Australian cinema as it does for the rest of the world. The war actually stimulated local feature production (Australasian broke its own house rule and made three features during 1914–15), but its aftermath saw what had been the (French) world film market become Hollywood's film market, to the detriment of stable national film production and ultimately even to the combine's distribution and exhibition business. Culturally, however, this familiar situation was complicated by Australia's relation to Britain. Independent by 1901, Australia had none the less fought on England's behalf during the war as part of the British Empire. The resulting carnage and glory provided the foundation for filmic responses to the motherland as ambivalent and conflicting as those provoked by Hollywood's hegemonic crassness and commercialism.

For half a century Australian films remained resolutely, not to say obsessively, populist. Nothing like an 'art cinema' existed in Australia during these years. Nor was there a serious Australian cinema of contemporary social issues until after the Second World War. At the same time, graphic or intense depictions of sex and violence, those flagrant markers of the 'liberty' of anti-establishment art as well as of the irredeemable commercialism of Hollywood, were absent in above-ground productions. Instead, Australia tended to image itself in a disarmingly tentative way as a rough and ready society of innocence in which conventional class hierarchies were questioned, if not overthrown, and as a place in which good people were sometimes able to survive the rigours of a hostile nature.

These twin thematics were deployed with the greatest box-office success in another home-grown genre, the backblocks farce. Like bushranging melodramas, these broad comedies of stereotyped rural families 'making a go' of farming enjoyed considerable popularity on stage before their first cinematic simulation by Beaumont Smith (*Our Friends, the Hayseeds*, 1917). Smith—'That'll Do Beau' to the trade—became something of a backblocks specialist, and his cheap, quick productions contributed to the genre's vulgar reputation. The popularity of backblocks films had waned by the mid-1920s, but the genre was to gain a new lease of life after the introduction of sound.

The high-point of Australian cinema for more than half a century, and one of the most worthy films made anywhere before 1920, is Raymond Longford's *The Sentimental Bloke* (1919). Centred on an extraordinarily appealing performance by Arthur Tauchert as its lumpen protagonist, the film—which survives more or less intact today—is an adaptation of a popular series of poems and exclusively employs their versified modification of urban slang as intertitles. If this were not remarkable enough, *The Sentimental Bloke* is narrated in the first person, certainly the most successful, if not the only, example of such narration in silent cinema.

Longford, who made films in close collaboration with his partner, Lotte Lyell, until she died in 1925, directed three sequels to *The Sentimental Bloke* and also contributed to the backblocks genre with two films based on stories by Steele Rudd which are apparently the original sources of the genre. Longford's aims were avowedly more serious and 'realistic' than those of most of his contemporaries, but it is difficult to judge whether these ambitions were matched by achievement on the level of *The Sentimental Bloke*, for of a lifetime's output of at least twenty-one features only four survive in anything like a complete state.

Many Australian films of the 1910s and 1920s, like most of Longford's and the backblocks farces, capitalized on their Australianness, attempting to attract local audiences with recognizable local landscapes, character types, Australian literature and theatre. But others traded on the regional exoticism of the South Pacific or played down their locale in favour of a species of occidental upper-class melodrama. Significantly, examples of these productions have found their way into some histories of British film.

Some film-makers, like the stars Snowy Baker and Louise Lovely and the directors Charles Chauvel and Paulette McDonagh, attempted to translate successful Hollywood formulas to Australian settings (Fairbanks films, 'women's pictures', Westerns, and high-society melodramas). Americans themselves used Australia as a place in which to try out for, or escape from, Hollywood. The most notorious of these was Norman Dawn, a retake and glass shot specialist, who milked Australasian of a considerable sum to make *For the Term of his Natural Life*, the country's first 'super-production', in 1927, an inadequate and antiquated film even for its own day. Dawn's association with the combine extended beyond the resounding flop of this venture, to a remake (or perhaps a reissue) of a 1920 South Pacific feature he had directed for Universal, and culminated in his acquisition and botched employment of out-of-date disc equipment in 1930–1 for Australasian's first sound feature, a truly awful musical.

From 1919 to 1928 Australian production averaged nine features a year. Although real Hollywood movies were gaining ever greater shares of the Australian market, Australasian, the one viable vertically integrated company, only determined to commit itself to regular feature production after 1925. In 1927 the Australian government convened a Royal Commission to inquire into the state of the local film industry at the same time that the British government was considering legislation to ameliorate a similar situation in the United Kingdom. When finally passed, the British legislation defined 'British' in such a way that Australian productions were included in the United Kingdom's quota protection. This looked like providing the larger market that Australia required for a stable production industry, pre-empting the Australian Commission, most of whose fifty recommendations were not enacted. No Australian features were released at all in 1929, but in spite of impending economic depression and

drastic technological change, the 'Empire quota' gave some producers reason to hope that good times were just around the corner.

THE COMING OF SOUND

The Jazz Singer premièred in Sydney on 29 December 1928. By 1936 only four countries in the world were entirely 'wired for sound': the United States, the United Kingdom, New Zealand, and Australia. As in years before, Australia found itself most strongly affected by what was going on in Hollywood and in Great Britain; for if the commercial and popular pressure for sound in cinemas was strongest because of Hollywood, another kind of pressure had its sources in Britain. It seemed that the sound of related patterns of speech, coupled with the quota provisions of the 1927 British Cinematographic Films Act, might make a viable market of the entire British Empire. 'British-only' sound cinemas were opened during the early 1930s in Sydney and Melbourne. Australasian reorganized itself

Arthur Tauchert (centre) as the hero of Raymond Longford's 1919 film *The Sentimental Bloke*, which was based on a book of Australian cockney verse

and dubbed its distribution arm 'British Empire Films', indicating both the expected source of the films it was to supply to its own Greater Union Theatres and the expected overseas market for its Cinesound feature productions.

The foundation of Cinesound's production was its newsreel arm, which made use of locally produced sound technology. Cinesound and its most prominent newsreel rival, Fox Movietone (which had shown the first Australian-made sound newsreel items in 1929), produced Australian news until television effectively shanghaied their market in the 1950s. From 1932, Cinesound also released at least two features a year until after the outbreak of the Second World War, all but one of them directed by Ken G. Hall, who guided the company's feature production.

Cinesound's films were popular and populist, like others which had been made in Australia since the beginning of the century: economically produced entertainment designed to please ordinary Australian and British audiences. The company announced itself by reviving the rural 'backblocks' genre which had proved so successful in the previous decade, bringing to the screen for the first time a popular theatrical version of *On our Selection*, written and played for broad farce and melodrama by Bert Bailey, who had become synonymous with the character of Dad Rudd. Bailey continued to write and play Dad in the Dad and Dave series of backblocks farces for Cinesound until 1940. Cecil Kellaway began his international career in Australia with performances in the same vein.

The Dad and Dave films were modestly successful in the United Kingdom. This seems to have been generally true for other Cinesound productions, which were melodramas and comedies often featuring minor English and American stars as well as Australian characters and settings. Until 1934 Cinesound's strongest local competition came from a company named Efftee, after the initials of its founder, Frank Thring. Thring imported RCA sound equipment and aimed to provide a full evening's programme (feature and supporting shorts) of 'quality' films, exploiting the resources of Australian theatre and music hall. Efftee then, like Cinesound, attempted to identify itself as an alternative to what was commonly available, playing on Hollywood's presumed vulgarity and the shoddiness of many of the earliest sound films from the United States. Ironically, perhaps, Efftee's most astute move was to star the 'vulgar' music hall comedian George Wallace in three films. After Efftee's demise, Wallace continued his film career at Cinesound, where his direct, sometimes balletic, physical humour and sunnily simple characterization graced two more films, to the greatest sustained effect in *Let George Do it* (1938).

Efftee finally went under in the wake of the failure of the other states of Australia to follow the lead of New South Wales in imposing quotas on 'foreign', including British, films. The introduction of sound and an expanded market had promised to bring stability to Australian production, but, after a decade averaging five features a year, this hope was obliterated by the combined effects of the Depression and the expense of cinema construction and rewiring. When, in 1938, Great Britain repudiated the 'Empire quota', there did not seem to be much future for a secure Australian feature production industry.

POST-1940

The World War changed things, just as it had twenty-five years before. Charles Chauvel, who had been making features independently since 1926, released his most popular work, *Forty Thousand Horsemen*, in 1940. This film, an optimistic adventure based on the exploits of Australian Light Horsemen in the First World War, is still shown in the halls of the Returned and Services League around Australia. Chauvel's work, always aggressively nationalist and somewhat naïve and quirky, seemed to find a new confidence with the Second World War. With his wife Elsa as an often uncredited script-writer, he made four propaganda shorts and another, rather bleak, war feature before 1945. The Chauvels went on to put their unmistakable signatures on *The Sons of Matthew* (1949), one of the most accomplished Australian post-war films; *Jedda* (1956), a passionate and excessive racial melodrama which was the country's first colour feature; and an idiosyncratic travel series for the BBC about Australia's Northern Territory, called *Australian Walkabout* (1957).

The war also brought newsreels back into prominence. Cinesound shut down its feature operation after 1940, and only five features were made during the war. However in Damien Parer, a daring and accomplished camera operator, Australian wartime films happened upon a figure of near mythological proportions. Parer's news footage was exciting and sometimes brutal. *Kokoda Front Line*, which he shot and narrated in 1942, won Australia its first Oscar, sharing the American Academy's first documentary awards with Ford's *Battle of Midway*, Capra's *Prelude to War*, and Varmalov and Kopalin's *Moscow Strikes back*. Parer was killed on the front line in 1944, working for Paramount News, and became something of a hero of Australian realist film in the years thereafter.

The Second World War also definitively destroyed what institutional stability Australian production had achieved in the 1930s with Cinesound. Cinesound produced one post-war feature before its parent company arranged to allow Britain's Ealing Studios to establish a production arm in Australia. Ealing made a series of identifiably 'Australian' films in Australia, the best known of which was the first, *The Overlanders* (1946). Perhaps most important to the future of Australian film-making was the socially committed attitude of the Australian Ealing films and certain of the studio's British personnel, especially the director, Harry Watt. Australian fiction features had not really engaged with issues of social justice before the Ealing sojourn, and it seems that the example of the Ealing film-makers and of Joris Ivens, who put together a controversial documentary, *Indonesia Calling*, in 1946 with support from the Sydney Waterside Workers Union, may have helped to create the climate for a number of the post-war period's most interesting films: *Mike and Stefani* (1952), *Three in One* (1957), *The Back of Beyond* (1954), and the afore-mentioned *Jedda*.

From 1946 to 1969 an average of just over two films a year were made in Australia—and none at all in 1948 and 1963–4. More than a third of these were 'foreign' productions. Increasingly 'Australian films' came to mean films made in Australia—by Britain (Rank and Korda, among others), by Hollywood (including *On the Beach* and *The Sundowners*), by France, and even, briefly, by Japan.

Lee Robinson may have been the last of the early Australian film-makers. The six features he directed between 1953 and 1969 were intended strictly as entertainment adventures and were produced with dispatch and economy, involving the extensive deployment of outdoor locations and of easily recognizable populist 'Australian' characters, particularly those played by Chips Rafferty, his partner until 1958. Although the Robinson–Rafferty partnership was engaged in co-productions with France in the mid-1950s, their films were always aimed at 'Saturday night' audiences: the very backbone of any nation's cinema.

In 1965 a post-war Italian immigrant named Giorgio Mangiamele completed a film called *Clay*, the first example of feature-length 'art cinema' with a claim to be considered 'Australian'. *Clay* was shown at Cannes that year, but did not impress Australian critics, who were uninterested and unmoved by its historical significance. Coincidentally, the British Michael Powell was in production that same year with *They're a Weird Mob*, the first 'Australian' feature to focus exclusively on the life of (Italian) migrants in their new country, and a populist comedy differing perhaps only in subject-matter from many earlier Australian films.

Charles Chauvel's racial melodrama *Jedda* (1955), which starred Ngarla Kunuth as an Aborigine girl adopted by a white family

Michael Powell directed another comedy in Australia, *Age of Consent* (1969), but Mangiamele did not get the opportunity to make another feature. Yet what he had begun, others took up. *The Pudding Thieves* (1967), *Time in Summer* (1968), and, especially, *Two Thousand Weeks* (1969) drew, as *Clay* had, on European models of art cinema and, in so doing, established a new understanding of what film in Australia might become—not British, not American—and laid the foundation for the important films of the next decades.

Bibliography

Bertrand, Ina (ed.) (1989), *Cinema in Australia: A Documentary History*.

Cunningham, Stuart (1991), *Featuring Australia: The Cinema of Charles Chauvel*.

Long, Chris (1994), *Australia's First Films*.

Pike, Andrew, and Cooper, Ross (1980), *Australian Film, 1900–1977: A Guide to Feature Film Production*.

Shirley, Graham, and Adams, Brian (1989), *Australian Cinema: The First Eighty Years*.

Tulloch, John (1981), *Legends on the Screen: The Narrative Film in Australia 1919–1929*.

Cinema in Latin America

MICHAEL CHANAN

COLONIAL BEGINNINGS

Moving pictures first reached Latin America with representatives of the Lumière brothers, who sent out teams around the world on planned itineraries designed to capitalize on the fascination which the new invention created everywhere; two teams went to Latin America, one to Rio de Janeiro, Montevideo, and Buenos Aires, the other to Mexico and Havana. The Lumière Cinématographe served as both projector and camera and men like Gabriel Veyre, who arrived in Mexico in the middle of 1896 and Cuba the following January, were also briefed to bring back scenes from the countries they visited. Hard on their heels came the Biograph men from New York and other adventurers, from both the United States and Europe. The North Americans tended not to penetrate very far south, where European immigration was at its height, and in Argentina and Brazil the pioneers were French and Belgian, Austrian and Italian. The earliest moving images of Latin America were thus mostly taken by European immigrants or residents, possessing both the minimum expertise needed to set up a film business and the contacts in the Old World to ensure a supply of films for exhibition. The varying dates of these first films—1896 in Mexico, 1897 in Cuba, Argentina, and Venezuela, 1898 in Brazil and Uruguay, 1902 in Chile, 1905 in Colombia, 1906 in Bolivia, 1911 in Peru—bespeak the steady penetration of film across the continent, for they usually follow the dates of first exhibition fairly quickly.

The scenes that were shot follow the expected trends: they picture official ceremonies and presidents, with their families and entourages; military parades and naval manœuvres; traditional festivities and tourist scenes, including views of city architecture, picturesque landscapes, and pre-Columbian ruins. The Brazilian film historian Salles Gomes (1980) reckoned that the work of the first Latin American *cineastas* was roughly divided between depicting 'the splendid cradle of nature' and 'the ritual of power'. A good proportion consisted in the kind of exotic scenes popularized by nineteenth-century photographers; in the words of Susan Sontag, 'the view of reality as an exotic prize . . . tracked down and captured by the diligent hunter-with-a-camera'. Adopting the point of view of the outsider, who gazes on other people's reality with curiosity, detachment, and professionalism, the photographer behaves as if the captured view transcended class interests, 'as if its perspective is universal' (Sontag 1977). In the condition of dependency which characterizes an underdeveloped continent like Latin America, this not only served to gratify the audience—which in Latin America was initially the upper and middle classes—with flattering images, but also to secure finance—by advancing the cause of publicity. And if in Mexico newspapers sponsored free film shows which they financed by including colour slides carrying advertisements, in Havana in 1906 an entertainment park commissioned the Cuban film pioneer Enrique Díaz Quesada to make a film for its publicity campaign in the United States. Early attempts at narrative often followed in the same ideological mould by taking up safe patriotic subjects, like the Argentinian film *El fusilamiento de Dorrego* ('The shooting of Dorrego') of 1908.

There is no necessary connection, however, between these early endeavours and subsequent developments. Cuba, Venezuela, Uruguay, Chile, Colombia, and Bolivia saw no significant film production for several decades, only a few sporadic attempts. In the smallest countries, like Uruguay, Paraguay, Ecuador, and those of Central America, there is still no significant production of feature-length fiction today, though documentary and video production are now in evidence. A continuous history of production with significant contributions in successive periods can only be found in the larger countries—Mexico,

Argentina, and Brazil—for only these had internal markets to provide an audience large enough for production costs, if low enough, to be covered at home. But if rock-bottom production costs are one of the constants of Latin American cinema, until the coming of sound this was no great disadvantage, and a modest level of film production was able to develop in several countries.

The early audience was essentially an urban one, limited to cities connected by the railways. Even in Mexico, where film spread rapidly to rural districts with the itinerant showmen known as *cómicos de la legua*, they only reached a little beyond the railway network. In this too film is associated with economic colonialism: in *One Hundred Years of Solitude*, the novel by Gabriel García Márquez, film arrives in the town of Macondo with the same trains that bring the United Fruit Company.

However, local conditions and national histories varied, with assorted results. In Cuba the War of Independence arrived at its final stages with the intervention of the USA against Spain in 1898. Cameramen from North America arrived with the troops (as they were also to do in Southern Africa the following year with the Second Boer War). When they failed to bring back any real battle scenes among their footage, they had no compunction in faking them, relying, as one of them wrote in his autobiography, on the imperfection of early film and lenses to conceal the crudity of their efforts. These films Albert E. Smith later claimed in *Two Reels and a Crank* (1952) as 'the forerunner of the elaborate "special effects" techniques of modern picturemaking'.

The same ready dissimulation occurred during the Mexican Revolution, which served as a school for film-making equivalent to the First World War in Europe. Indeed, the Mexican film historian Aurelio de los Reyes (1983) reckons that around 1910–13 the skill of Mexican film-makers in structuring a documentary narrative was in advance of the North Americans. North of the border the films inspired by Mexican events went from tales of arms smuggling (like *Mexican Filibusters* of 1911) to simplistic stories (like *The Aztec Treasure* of 1914) which generally extolled the superiority of white-skinned heroes among the violent, irresponsible, and treacherous Latin, whether bandit, revolutionary, or greaser. Such developments betray the patriotic populism, the thrall of the American Dream and its doctrine of 'manifest destiny', in which North American cinema was gripped from the very start—an ideological servility which inevitably distorted their lensing of the Latin south. The assassination of Madero and the threat of US intervention not only prompted a number of North American films clearly designed to justify US action, on the grounds that Mexicans alone were incapable of bringing peace, order, justice, and progress to their country, but also drew more North American cameras across the Rio Grande. Pancho Villa became a

film star when he signed an exclusive contract with the Mutual Film Corporation. For a fee of $25,000 he agreed to keep other film companies from the scene of his battles, to fight in daylight whenever possible, and to reconstruct the battle scenes if satisfactory pictures were not obtained in the heat of conflict. In fact the best battle scenes in Mutual's *The Life of General Villa* (1914), on which Raoul Walsh cut his teeth, were studio reconstructions, but the dawn executions were real: Walsh, future director of more than a hundred Hollywood movies, himself—he tells us—asked Villa to delay his summary administration of justice, which used to occur at four in the morning, until there was enough light to film with.

It is no accident that Mexicans became the first to protest the misrepresentation of their reality by Hollywood. A declaration to the newspapers by two film-makers in 1917 condemned 'that savagery, that backwardness which is used to depict us in false movies'. Five years later, provoked to fury by a Gloria Swanson movie, *Her Husband's Trademark*, in which the heroine is all but raped by a gang of desperadoes while her husband is doing business with the Mexican oil industry, the Mexican government imposed a (temporary) embargo on all films of the Famous Players–Lasky Corporation (Paramount). But the problem persisted. Despite the 'Good Neighbour' policy of the 1930s, when Washington was trying to defuse the revolutionary nationalism abroad in Latin America from Cuba to Chile, and advised the studios to tone things down, Hollywood seemed incapable of not offending Latin American sensibilities. The founder of university film studies in Cuba in the 1940s, J. M. Valdés Rodríguez, wrote of a film of the time, *Under the Texas Moon*, as 'openly offensive to Mexican women, the projection of which in a movie-house in the Latin section of New York City provoked a terrible tumult' caused by the enraged protests of some Mexican and Cuban students, in which one of them was killed.

INDIGENOUS FILM-MAKING

In Brazil, according to Salles Gomes (1980), if cinema did not take root for about a decade after its introduction, 'it was due to our underdevelopment in electricity. Once energy was industrialized in Rio de Janeiro, exhibition halls proliferated like mushrooms'—and production soon reached a hundred films a year. A foretaste of things to come was the success in 1910 of a satirical musical review called *Paz de amor* ('Peace and love', Alberto Botelho), perhaps the first film to engage the Brazilian vocation for the carnivalesque. But films like this, projected in theatres with appropriate musical accompaniment, were limited to audiences of the better-off. By the time cinema reached the popular classes, North American distributors had begun to move in, turning the growing Brazilian market into a tropical appendage of Hollywood. Indeed, cashing in on the decline in European production due to the war, and following a general shift in US trade, from the end of 1915 onwards American firms adopted a new strategy of direct dealing by opening more subsidiaries outside Europe (and not only in Latin America). By 1919, Fox, Paramount, the distribution arm of Famous Players–Lasky, and Samuel Goldwyn were operating between them in virtually every Latin American country, displacing local distributors and local films. By the 1920s, Argentina and Brazil had become Hollywood's third and fourth largest export markets after Britain and Australia; in Brazil they had an 80 per cent market share—while Brazilian production itself could only manage 4 per cent.

Given that these were indeed growing markets and that film-making was still artisanal and cheap, Brazil's peculiarity was that, while the vast size of the country prevented the national organization of film distribution, it allowed a number of regional centres of production to develop. There were 'regional cycles' in half a dozen provincial capitals, prominent among them Recife, where thirteen films were made in the course of eight years by a community of some thirty film technicians. Here, in films like Tancredo Seabra's *Filho sem mãe* ('Motherless son', 1925), emerged one of the first indigenous fictional genres of Latin America, where landscape plays a preponderant role and the central protagonists are rural characters and *cangaçeiros*, the 'bandits' of the *sertão*.

The *cangaçeiro* is cousin to the Argentine gaucho film, which first appeared around 1915 with *Nobleza gaucha* ('Cowboy nobility'). Based on an episode from the popular nineteenth-century epic *Martin Fierro* by José Hernández, in which a peasant girl is raped, taken to Buenos Aires by force as the landowner's mistress, and rescued by a gaucho from the estate whom the *patrón* falsely accuses of cattle rustling, the story, says the Argentine film historian J. A. Mahieu (1966), may be simple and ingenuous but the filmic rhythm is effective and its scenes of almost feudal exploitation make it the first film to portray the oppression of the rural classes in Argentina. At just the moment when new European films were scarce and the North Americans had not yet captured the market, this film, which cost 20,000 pesos to make and earned more than 600,000, was a major box-office hit showing simultaneously in twenty theatres. As striking a demonstration as one could wish that Latin America could not only command its own narratives, but they had an import which gave the lie to the sanitized representations preferred by commercial and state interests. There was even, a year later, a film shot in the province of Santa Fe by an anthropologist called Alcides Greca, *El último malón* ('The last Indian uprising'), which Mahieu describes as a kind of documentary reconstruction of an uprising that took place at the beginning of the century, filmed in the authentic locations with the Indians as protagonists of their own story.

It is almost as if a pattern is at work in which the most original of films are always made in the most marginal of circumstances, where film-making is at its most basic but there is room for maverick initiatives outside the generic themes of the commercial industry. There are also examples in Mexico, like *El hombre sin patria* ('The man without a country', Miguel Conteras Torres, 1922), the first film to address the theme of Mexican workers in the USA; and even in Bolivia, where two films of the 1920s, *Corazón aymara* and *La profecía del lago* ('Aymara heart' and 'The prophecy of the lake') dealt with indigenous themes (though they ran into censorship problems). A film of 1929, Mario Peixoto's *Limite* ('The boundary'), is a landmark of the Brazilian avant-garde, an experiment in multiple narration—Eisenstein, no less, remarked on its 'genius' when he saw it in London in 1932.

But if these are isolated examples, they belong to an unknown history. It is a history recently evoked by the Venezuelan director Alfredo J. Anzola in his feature documentary *El misterio de los ojos escarlata* ('The mystery of the scarlet eyes', 1993), which provides a rare glimpse of previously unseen images of Venezuela in the 1920s and 1930s. The footage is that of his father, Edgar Anzola, who made documentaries and two silent feature films, now lost, in the 1920s, and then acquired a 16 mm. camera and filmed mostly documentary footage throughout the 1930s and 1940s. His efforts of the 1920s had not led him to a career in film, and these 16 mm. films were not made for public viewing; they were the work of an *aficionado*. Anzola earned his living as right-hand man to a local North American entrepreneur, who, among other things, opened Venezuela's first radio station, Radio Caracas, in 1930, of which Anzola became the director; a radio serial written and produced by Anzola *père* provides the title of his son's film about him. How many others among the all-but-nameless Latin American film-makers of the early years had similar careers? And may have left undiscovered archives? And how many of these *aficionados* have not even left their names behind? And one other thing: Anzola, as portrayed by his son, was clearly no intellectual, but he was a keen cineaste who took his camera with him to events where he had entry as a radio producer. The point of view is uncritical and marked by his social class. But *aficionados* of the same class in succeeding decades were the very people whose first film-making efforts represent the initial stirrings of the powerful new movement in Latin American cinema which emerged in the late 1950s.

THE SOUND PERIOD

The coming of the talkies at the end of the 1920s was both a boon and a disaster for Latin American production. Sound offered the promise of films featuring popular

Gabriel Figueroa

(1907–)

Although towards the end of his fifty-five-year career he shot a number of films in colour, Gabriel Figueroa will always be remembered as one of the world's greatest masters of black and white cinematography. 'Black and white films', he once said, 'are like engravings. Their force as an artistic medium is unrivalled by colour, in films or any other artistic medium. . . In colour films it is very difficult to capture the dramatic force that is almost inherent in black and white.'

Born in Mexico City, he was orphaned at an early age. He enrolled in the Music Conservatory and Art Academy of San Carlos, but turned to still photography out of economic necessity. In 1932 he took a job as a stillman and later camera assistant to cinematographer Alex Phillips. In 1935 he won a scholarship to study in Hollywood, and, by luck, the teacher who took a liking to him was the master innovator Gregg Toland. In 1936 he shot his first film as a director of photography: Fernando de Fuentes's *Allá en el Rancho Grande*, a film that became a cornerstone of Mexico's fledgeling film industry and its first major international hit.

In 1943 Figueroa and director Emilio Fernández began one of world cinema's legendary partnerships with the making of *Flor Silvestre*, which also celebrated the return to Mexico of actress Dolores del Rio after nearly twenty years in Hollywood. Figueroa went on to shoot all but one of Fernández's films between 1943 and 1953, including *María Candelaria* (1943—winner of the Palme d'Or at Cannes in 1946), *The Pearl* (*La perla*, 1945), *Enamorada* (1946), *Rio Escondido* (1947), *Maclovia* (1948), *Pueblerina* (1949), and *Salón México* (1949). Together they took Mexican cinema to a new level. Fernández allowed Figueroa almost complete freedom of lighting, composition, and camera placement, leaving himself free to concentrate on acting and story.

Over the years Figueroa created many of the beautiful and indelible images we now associate with Mexico and its people. Margarita de Orellana, a noted essayist of the Mexican Revolution, wrote: 'Not only have these images changed the way Mexicans look at the cinema, but even, perhaps, the way they view their lives.'

In 1946 Samuel Goldwyn refused to release Toland to shoot John Ford's *The Fugitive*, an adaptation of Graham Greene's novel *The Power and the Glory*. Toland recommended Figueroa, and, after a few days on the set, Ford responded to Figueroa much the way Fernández had, allowing him almost complete freedom to create his images. The success of *The Fugitive* led to a lucrative offer of a contract from Goldwyn, but, after careful deliberation, Figueroa refused, preferring to remain in Mexico with his family and circle of artistic friends.

His versatility enabled him to work with a diversity of directorial styles: the ornate settings, picturesque skies, and dramatic angles of the Fernández films; the lean, even primitive non-style sought by Luis Buñuel in *Los olvidados* (1950), *Él* (1952), *Nazarín* (1958), *The Exterminating Angel* (1962) and *Simon of the Desert* (1965); the action pyrotechnics required by Don Siegel for *Two Mules for Sister Sara* (1969); the actor-driven personal dramas of John Huston in *Night of the Iguana* (1964) and *Under the Volcano*

(1984); and the enormously difficult night-time battle sequences in Brian Hutton's *Kelly's Heroes* (1970).

In his work on lenses, filters, laboratory innovations, and formulas of composition, Figueroa often drew upon painting and on classical principles of aesthetics. Dissatisfied with the rushes of *Allá en el Rancho Grande*, he turned to a passage on atmospheric colour in Leonardo's *Treatise on Painting*, which led him to experiment with black and white filters to counteract the layer of air which he felt was getting between the camera and the landscape. From then on 'Figueroa's skies' became a feature of his work, earning him universal recognition and several prizes.

He was close friends with the great Mexican painters of the period. Diego Rivera influenced his ideas of colour and composition, and they shared a passion for pre-Hispanic figures; with José Clemente Orozco and Leopoldo Méndez he traded ideas of the power of black and white and its relation to popular art in engravings and photography; and with Doctor Atl he shared concepts of curvilinear space; but most importantly it was David Alfaro Siqueiros whose theories of *escorzo* or foreshortening helped him attain unique effects of depth.

Figueroa's work is marked by stunning contrasts of light and shadow, rich textures, and a frequent use of dark foregrounds and bright backgrounds; torches, candles, flames, and fireworks are often in evidence; sharp angles set subjects against atmospheres of intense blacks and whites, or bright colours depicting the decorative visual splendour and folklore of Mexico; deep focus captures extensive action in one shot despite foregrounds which fill the screen.

Throughout his long career, Figueroa worked almost exclusively in his native Mexico. A nationalist and an internationalist, he took position against Franco's Spain, opened his Mexico City home to blacklisted writers run out of Hollywood by McCarthy's witch hunts, and fought to establish fair unions for his domestic industry.

Asked what a cinematographer does, Figueroa replied that a director describes the shot and the general camera placement, then the cinematographer goes to work. 'Lighting creates an atmosphere in which the story will develop. . . Lighting is the privilege of the cinematographer. He is the owner of the light.'

MICHAEL DONNELLY

SELECT FILMOGRAPHY

Allá en el Rancho Grande (1936); María Candelaria (1943); La perla (1945); Enamorada (1946); The Fugitive (1947); Rio Escondido (1947); Los olvidados (1950); Él (1952); Nazarín (1958); Night of the Iguana (1964); Two Mules for Sister Sara (1969); Kelly's Heroes (1970)

BIBLIOGRAPHY

Paranaguá, P. A. (1995), Mexican Cinema
Ramírez Berg, Charles (1994), 'The Cinematic Invention of Mexico'.

Opposite: A scene from *Pueblerina:* one of the celebrated collaborations between Figueroa and director Emilio Fernández.

singers and comedians, singing and performing adaptations and fusions of the musical genres of popular culture: the *tanguera* in Argentina, the *chanchada* in Brazil, the *ranchera* in Mexico. But the dependent state of distribution and the increased costs of production took their toll, and film production remained a risky business which barely kept its head above water.

To force the conversion of Latin American cinemas to sound, at a time before the technical development of either dubbing or subtitling (which is not much use for a largely illiterate audience anyway), Hollywood began producing factory-made Spanish-language versions of selected productions in California, on which many apprentice film-makers from south of the Rio Grande learnt their trade. Meanwhile, it was in the studio complex in the Paris suburb of Joinville set up by Paramount for foreign-language versioning and low-budget production that the great Argentine tango singer Carlos Gardel made a number of films in 1931–2, together with other Argentine touring artists. Hugely successful throughout Latin America, Gardel made four more films for Paramount out of New York before he was killed in an air crash in Colombia in 1935. He was the first international Latin American musical film star, and the influence in Argentina and elsewhere of his urbane macho image was enormous.

The Brazilian *chanchada* was partially modelled on North American musicals but with roots also in Brazilian comic theatre and Carnival, of which Salles Gomes wrote that, while the universe constructed by North American films was distant and abstract, the derisive fragments of Brazil in these films at least described a world lived in by the spectators. Hollywood cinema prompted superficial identification with the behaviour and fashions of an occupying culture; in contrast, popular enthusiasm for the rascals, scoundrels, and loafers of the *chanchada* suggested the polemic of the occupied against the occupier.

The most significant single film-maker of this period was Humberto Mauro, later cited by Glauber Rocha as a precursor of Cinema Novo. Mauro's originality is a prime example of what Salles Gomes called the Brazilian's 'creative incapacity for copying'. A product of Brazil's regional film movements, his first films, made in Minas Gerais before he migrated to Rio de Janeiro, 'creatively copied' models ranging from Thomas Ince Westerns to Ruttmann's *Berlin: Symphony of a City*. Best known for *Ganga bruta* ('Brutal gang', 1933), he later teamed up with the leading Brazilian cinematographer Edgar Brasil; the French film historian Sadoul (1972) praises his 'remarkable feeling for images and backgrounds, a highly original conception of filmic space, and an impassioned feeling for people and the landscapes of his country'.

In Mexico, where Eisenstein filmed his abortive portrait of Mexican culture *Que viva México!* in 1931, his artistic example was followed in 1935 by the group who made

431

Luis Buñuel
(1900–1983)

One of the oddities of Buñuel's late flowering career is that it almost did not happen. Often regarded as Spain's greatest director, Luis Buñuel spent most of his life in exile and made almost all of his films in either Mexico or France. Had he not escaped from Spain during the Civil War, he remarked, he would probably have been remembered only as 'a Spanish film-maker who died before his time, director of *Un chien andalou*, *L'Âge d'or* and *Las Hurdes*. Shot by Franco's forces just as he began a promising career.'

Un Chien andalou, made in France in 1928, in collaboration with Salvador Dalí, earned Buñuel entry into the surrealist group. *L'Âge d'or* (1930) confirmed his originality and caused one of the great surrealist scandals, when ultra-rightists attacked the cinema where it was showing and the authorities responded by banning it. Both films brought the surrealist credo to the screen in a blazing series of oneiric images and a blistering attack on the tyranny of a social system which repressed imagination and sexuality alike. As Jean Vigo wrote of *Un Chien andalou*: 'Beware of the Andalusian dog. It bites.'

Returning to Spain, in 1932 he made the documentary *Las Hurdes* (also known as *Tierra sin pan* / *Land without Bread*), which in turn was banned by the Spanish authorities. (A similar fate was also to befall *Viridiana*, which in 1961 was the first film Buñuel had shot in Spain in almost thirty years.)

In the mid-1930s Buñuel found work as a dubbing director for Paramount and Warner Bros. in Paris and Madrid, then as an executive producer of popular Spanish commercial movies. When the Civil War broke out in 1936, he was sent to Paris to produce a documentary about the war using newsreel material shot by the Russian cameraman Roman Karmen and others. He went to Hollywood as official adviser on films about the war, but the US government placed an embargo on his projects and when the Spanish Republic fell to Franco's forces he found himself stranded. He got a job at the Museum of Modern Art, New York, preparing propaganda films for distribution in Latin America, but was forced to resign when the mercurial Salvador Dalí, with whom he had fallen out just before shooting *L'Âge d'or*, accused him of atheism and Communism. After four years odd-jobbing in the United States, chance brought him an invitation to direct a film in Mexico, where he settled until his death in 1983.

Los olvidados ('The Young and the Damned', 1950), Buñuel's third Mexican film, was a caustic portrayal of delinquency among children of the shanty towns, combining carefully researched realism with powerful dream sequences which deepened the portrayal of its characters. Criticized by many Mexicans for blackening Mexico's name, its international success resuscitated Buñuel's reputation. The years which followed were Buñuel's most prolific period—another sixteen films in ten years, including *Él* (1952), a disturbing study of a respectable man consumed by a paranoid jealousy which destroys his wife; the quietly ironic adaptation of *Robinson Crusoe* (1952), shot in English as a Mexican–American co-production; and *Nazarín* (1958), a deceptive portrayal of quixotic religiosity against brutish reality, and the first of two adaptations of novels by the Spanish writer Galdós, whom Buñuel had known in his youth.

Buñuel's Mexican years have often been seen as a middle period, harbinger of the late maturity which followed his return to Europe to make *Viridiana*, but there are strong continuities between the two periods and indeed the whole of Buñuel's work is informed by the same preoccupations: his Jesuit education and Surrealism, he said, marked him for life. Thus the saintly defrocked priest of *Nazarín* becomes a nun in its companion piece, *Viridiana*, with its famous beggars' orgy, a burlesque on the Last Supper to the strains of Handel's 'Hallelujah Chorus', and one of Buñuel's most mordant pieces of religious parody. At the same time, the films which foreground the irrationality of religious belief—which also include *Simon of the Desert* (*Simon del desierto*, 1965) and *The Milky Way* (*La Voie lactée*, 1968)—are matched by those which deal with the consequences of repressed sexuality. Thus *Él* finds a counterpart in *Tristana* (1970), the second of Buñuel's Galdós adaptations, as well as *Belle de jour* (1967) and *Cet obscur objet du désir* (*That Obscure Object of Desire*, 1977). In none of these films, it should be said, does Buñuel fall into a simple Manichaean opposition between male and female, but rather male concupiscence is confounded by female will in forms which ridicule the pretensions of machismo.

Buñuel returns to full-blown Surrealism with his last two Mexican films, *The Exterminating Angel* (*El ángel exterminador*, 1962) and *Simon del desierto*. With the highly comic irrationality of the former, a biting critique of the pretensions of the Mexican ruling class, and the illusion-

Silvia Pinal in Luis Buñuel's *Viridiana* (1961)

ism of the latter, a satire against the delusions of religious faith, Buñuel begins a process in which he completely dismembers the premises of the rational illusion on which not just realism but all narrative cinema depends.

The basis of the surrealist method employed by Buñuel is the dream, gateway to the unconscious. Dream images were the origin of *Un chien andalou* and dream sequences occur in many of Buñuel's films from *Los olvidados* on—though Buñuel himself makes a careful distinction between such different mental states as dream, fantasy and delirium. At the same time, in *L'Âge d'or* the narrative form itself is taken from dream language, with its irrational displacements, or what Buñuel himself called 'discontinuous continuity', and this is the technique he explores to its furthest point in his last films, above all *The Discreet Charm of the Bourgeoisie* (*Le Charme discret de la bourgeoisie*, 1972) and *The Phantom of Liberty* (*Le Fantôme de la liberté*, 1974). In these two films, which represent the summit of Buñuel's art, the plot is both nonsensical and logically impossible, the mere semblance of narrative, but the fact that it would be absurd to try and explain the symbols and metaphors is not to say that the films are meaningless. On the contrary, their elusive deconstruction of narrative conventions insinuates a lucid commentary on social and ideological pretensions, in which Buñuel remains ever faithful to Surrealism's revolutionary convictions.

MICHAEL CHANAN

SELECT FILMOGRAPHY

Un Chien andalou (1928); L'Âge d'or (1930); Los olvidados (1950); Él (1952); Las aventuras de Robinson Crusoe (1952); Ensayo de un crimen (The Criminal Life of Arcibaldo de la Cruz, 1955); Nazarín (1958); La joven (The Young One) (1960); Viridiana (1961); El ángel exterminador (1962); Simon del desierto (1965); Belle de jour (1967); Tristana (1970); Le Charme discret de la bourgeoisie (1972); Le Fantôme de la liberté (1974); Cet obscur objet du désir (1977)

BIBLIOGRAPHY

Buñuel, Luis (1983), *My Last Sigh*.
Pérez Turrent, Tomás, and de la Colina, José (1992), *Objects of Desire*.

Redes (*The Wave*) at the invitation of radical Mexican government officials: the New York photographer Paul Strand and the young Austrian director Fred Zinnemann, assisted by the Mexican Emilio Gómez Muriel, with Mexico's most original composer Silvestre Revueltas providing a wonderful orchestral score. The first of an uncompleted series of films on Mexican life, *Redes* portrays the struggle of Vera Cruz fishermen against exploitation and explicitly argues for collectivization—a rare early instance of what will later (in the 1960s) become a major tendency of politically committed film-making in every corner of Latin America. A rare example, too, of co-operation between North and South as a collaboration between equals, it was also (as Sadoul observed) one of the first successes of the New York school of the 1930s.

For the most part, however, Mexican cinema consisted in numerous *rancheras*, and the varieties of melodrama—tragic, sentimental, and costume. Tragic melodrama in Mexican cinema goes back to *Santa* (Luis G. Peredo) of 1919, about an innocent girl from the provinces forced into prostitution in the big city and finding redemption only in death, first of a long line of Mexican films romanticizing the prostitute, down to the *cabaretera* or brothel films of the 1950s. *La sangre manda* ('Blood dictates', José Bohr, 1933) initiated a cycle of sentimental middle-class melodramas, which later mutated into the costume melodrama, such as *En tiempos de Don Porfirio* ('In the days of Don Porfirio') of 1939, nostalgic and reactionary evocations of a world before revolution. The *ranchera* was born in 1936 with a singing cowboy film, *Allá en el Rancho Grande* ('Over there on the Rancho Grande') by Fernando de Fuentes, a comedy which added a pastoral fantasy to the Gene Autry/Roy Rogers formula, says the Mexican cultural critic Carlos Monsivais, whose success both in Mexico and the rest of Latin America was so extraordinary that it changed the direction of Mexican cinema. This rural idyll was very different from the reality of the years of Agrarian Reform, and this cinema is fundamentally escapist.

The expansion of Mexican cinema began in the mid-1930s, when the leftist President Lázaro Cárdenas provided funds for new studios. This was not quite the first government intervention on behalf of cinema in Latin America: that honour goes to the Brazilian President Getulia Vargas with a fairly innocuous decree of 1932 imposing minimal exhibition quotas for Brazilian films. But the Mexican industry was stronger, and saw the formation of the first film union in Latin America in 1934. By 1937, with fewer films coming from Spain as a result of the Civil War, Mexican production reached thirty-eight films and growing in one year, and overtook that of Argentina. It was boosted again in 1943 when the United States, angered by Argentina's neutrality in the war and suspicious of its links with Fascism, took measures which included cutting off its supplies of virgin film stock in

Leopoldo Torre Nilsson's Argentinian classic *La casa del angel* (1957)

favour of Mexico. Hollywood, moreover, angled much of its wartime output towards propaganda genres, leaving space in Latin America for Mexican producers to fill the gap with new variations of established genres by a new generation of film-makers. The 'golden age' of Mexican cinema is the period of the actor-turned-director Emilio ('El Indio') Fernández, once described as Mexico's John Ford; the cinematographer Gabriel Figueroa; and of stars like Maria Felix, Dolores del Rio, the comedian Cantinflas, and several more. Some of these films are individually pleasing, like Fernández and Figueroa's exemplary *María Candelaria* (1943), which gives the theme of the fallen woman an Indianist treatment. But by the 1950s, there is nothing of any lasting value in Mexican cinema except the work of Buñuel (including several of his most distinguished films as well as some of the least successful).

The gradual recovery of Argentinian cinema after the war coincided with the rise of Juan Perón, who both before

and after becoming president in 1946 sponsored various measures to support the film industry, like quotas and state bank production loans funded by a tax on admissions, as well as restrictions on the repatriation of profits by foreign distributors. On the other hand, Perón, who carefully cultivated his Carlos Gardel film-star looks, and his minor film-star wife Evita were both intensely conscious of the power of imagery, and maintained a subsecretariat to keep a close eye on the content of the movies, with predictable results. Nor was government support a great success economically, being either weakened in response to bullying by Washington, or else ineffectively policed. If these conditions produced films largely angled to safe urban bourgeois sensibilities, the period boasted its one distinguished stream of work in the films of Leopoldo Torre Nilsson, a staunch anti-Peronist, who stylishly dissected the social psychology of the Argentine ruling classes in a mode that was readily recognized, at home and abroad, as a national version of *auteur* cinema; the International Press Prize at Cannes in 1961 went to his *La mano en la trampa* ('The hand in the trap').

Brazil had come up with another Cannes prize-winner a few years earlier. Lima Barreto's *O cangaçeiro* (1953), which revived the old theme of the bandits of the *sertão* in the guise of a Western—but shot in São Paulo, where the landscape was hardly authentic—was a world-wide success distributed in some twenty-two countries, though not exactly Brazilian cinema at its most original. The production company responsible for this film was the short-lived Vera Cruz film company, set up in 1949 with backing by São Paulo's industrial bourgeoisie in 1949 and bankrupted in 1954. São Paulo attempted, says Salles Gomes, to create a more ambitious cinema both industrially and artistically; the *paulistas* dismissed the popular virtues of *carioca* cinema (that of Rio) and tried to give their films the look of Old World movies, usually with a European *mise-en-scène*. When they finally rediscovered the *cangaçeiro* genre, or turned for inspiration to radio comedies, it was already too late. The project was a disaster not only culturally but also economically. While the company invested huge sums in production, it overlooked the question of distribution. Thus, in handing over distribution of *O cangaçeiro* to Columbia Pictures in order to reach the international market, the millions earned by the first world-wide success in the history of Brazilian cinema went to fill the coffers of Hollywood. Nothing demonstrates more clearly the ramifications of a cinema of underdevelopment in the years before it awoke to a new vocation.

Bibliography

Chanan, Michael (1985), *The Cuban Image*.

De los Reyes, Aurelio (1983), *Cine y sociedad en México, 1896–1930*.

Johnson, Randal, and Stam, Robert (eds.) (1982), *Brazilian Cinema*.

King, John (1990), *Magical Reels: A History of Cinema in Latin America*.

Mahieu, José Agustín (1966), *Breve historia del cine argentino*.

Sadoul, Georges (1992a), *Dictionary of Filmmakers*.

—— (1992b), *Dictionary of Films*.

Salles Gomes, Paulo Emilio (1980), *Cinema: trajetória no sub-desenvolvimento*.

Schumann, Peter B. (1987), *Historia del cine latinoamericano*.

Smith, Albert E. (1952), *Two Reels and a Crank*.

Sontag, Susan (1977), *On Photography*.

Thompson, Kristin (1985), *Exporting Entertainment*.

THE POST-WAR WORLD

After the War

GEOFFREY NOWELL-SMITH

The Allied troops landed in Normandy in June 1944. Behind the troops came the para-military personnel of the American Psychological Warfare Branch (PWB), bearing films, mostly documentaries but also a selection of features. Apart from a few smuggled in from Spain and other neutral countries, these were the first recent American films to be seen in occupied Europe for four years. After these first films came the negotiators, Hollywood executives, some with military rank, preparing the way for a resumption of the film trade between America and Europe, or rather from America to Europe. Political and economic objectives were inextricable. In their dealings with the former Axis powers, Germany, Italy, and Japan, the western Allies were concerned to eradicate traces of Fascism from their cultures, and to ensure that any resurgent film industries in those countries did not perpetuate the ideologies that had brought the world to destruction. But the Americans were also keen to ensure that when trade was resumed it would be on free-market lines, without a return to the protectionism that had marked the European response to Hollywood penetration in the 1930s.

The task of reconstructing the devastated film industries in the defeated countries was entrusted to specialist commissions, part military and part civilian. In Germany, Erich Pommer played a prominent role, while in Italy Alexander Mackendrick, then with the PWB, and Stephen Pallos, a colleague of Alexander Korda, were brought on to the film commission. But reconstruction was not the only item on the agenda. At a meeting in Rome in 1944, the chairman of the Allied Film Board, the American Admiral Stone, roundly declared that Italy, as a rural and former Fascist country, did not need a film industry and should not be allowed to have one. His fellow Americans concurred, but the British did not, seeing it as a transparent move to restore, not so much democracy, as Hollywood hegemony. And, with a five-year backlog of films (including *Gone with the Wind* and *Citizen Kane*) waiting to be unloaded on the European market, this was indeed what the Americans had in mind.

It was not only the American companies, but European audiences as well, who wanted Hollywood films back on the screen. A conflict soon emerged in many European countries between the exhibitors, sensitive to public demand, and film-makers and producers, eager to establish a new cinema in the climate of cultural renewal after the war and the fall of Fascism. Governments for their part were anxious to limit imports and protect the balance of payments. But the Americans were adamant. The Motion Picture Export Association was supported by its government. As far as possible, films were to be freely traded commodities like any other and free trade in films was written into the GATT agreement and the preparations for the Marshall Plan. The Europeans, who needed American aid more than the marginal improvement to the balance of payments obtained from import restrictions, were forced to capitulate, securing only modest concessions to protect the rebirth of their industries. The scene was set for a long, long struggle.

The situation in the west was mirrored in the east. With the onset of the Cold War, the Soviet Union took steps to assert its control over the countries it had liberated in 1944–5. In the 'People's Democracies' east of the Elbe, film industries were nationalized and the Soviet-dominated regimes imposed as a model the Socialist Realist aesthetic that had been mandatory in the Soviet Union since 1934. The cinemas of eastern and central Europe entered into a phase of development distinct from their western counterparts. Cultural relations with the west were restricted, but eastern-bloc film-makers did at least get to see some of the new cinema coming out of western Europe. The 'cinema of reconstruction' in east and central Europe was thus able to avail itself of the parallel experience of Italian neo-realism as well as of Soviet models.

Western European cinemas differed considerably in their response to the changed post-war situation. In Britain, Michael Balcon at Ealing Studios pursued a policy of making films 'projecting Britain and the British character' that can be seen as a continuation of Ealing's wartime patriotism. Although traditionalist in their values, the Ealing films of the 1940s and early 1950s, particularly the comedies, reflected the political mood that had brought the Labour government to power in 1945 and—without contradiction—the rebellion against austerity that brought Churchill back in 1951. For the industry as a whole, however, it was business as usual, and a return to the dubious certainties of the pre-war years. There is barely a trace, for example, in Michael Powell and Emeric Pressburger's wonderful *Black Narcissus* (1947), set in India and made on the eve of Indian independence, or even in Harry Watt's *Where no Vultures Fly* (1951), in Africa, of the convulsions that were tearing the Empire apart.

In Italy, however, a more original cinema emerged, in the form of neo-realism. With the main studios at Cinecittà temporarily in use as a refugee camp, film-makers took to the streets and made films reflecting post-war conditions and the will for change generated by liberation. The neo-realist cinema had to compete in the market with the flood of American films that entered the country from 1946, and with other home-grown genres—especially comedies and sentimental melodramas—which were often more entertaining to audiences. Box-office results were patchy, and the generally leftish stance of the films (and the public pronouncements of their makers) did not find favour with the right-of-centre government that came to power in 1948. But even as neo-realism began to falter in Italy, its ideas began to be picked up elsewhere, not only in Europe but also, and especially, in Latin America and India, where its directness of expression and simplicity of means had more relevant application, probably, than in Italy itself.

Neo-realism was conceived very much within a national—or 'national-popular'—perspective. But the economic and political reality of Europe demanded a broader approach. The first steps in this direction were taken with the signature of a Franco–Italian agreement on co-production of films, which came into effect in 1952. Other bilateral agreements, opening up the market to Europe-wide co-production, followed later in the decade. At first these agreements were treated as little more than expedients, giving easier access to foreign markets to films which in content were far less international than, for example, the multilinguals of the early sound period. But ambitious producers, particularly in France and Italy, soon realized that a market could be created for big-budget productions for international release. These films were also dubbed into, and occasionally shot in, English, in the hope (not often realized) of breaking into the more inward-looking American and British markets, and American stars were imported to increase their box-office appeal. Italian producers in particular began to look across the Atlantic for markets and sources of investment. For their part, American companies, frustrated by the difficulty of repatriating distribution revenues and attracted by lower labour costs and the pool of talent existing in Europe, began to invest in European production.

A pioneering role in the new internationalism was played by Roberto Rossellini. In 1947, before the first European agreements were signed, he had made *Germany Year Zero* (*Germania anno zero*), set in war-devastated Berlin but mainly shot in Italy, as a tripartite Italian–French–German co-production. Then in 1949 he persuaded RKO to invest in *Stromboli*, a film set on the volcanic island of that name off the coast of Sicily. *Stromboli* starred Ingrid Bergman, then a major box-office attraction in both America and Europe, and was shot in English (with the aid of the dubious expedient of imagining that many of the island's inhabitants had been short-term emigrants to America and so spoke the language). But the film was not a success. Bergman's off-screen affair with Rossellini during the making of the film, coupled with the fact that on screen she was represented as leaving her husband, meant that it fell foul of American moralism and the Production Code. The studio cut the film to pieces, and released it without fanfares. Rossellini made four more films with Bergman, now his wife, exploring themes of cultural difference between northern and southern Europe. These films, in particular *Viaggio in Italia* ('Journey to Italy', 1954), were notable for their spontaneity and freedom of expression and were to have a great influence on the French New Wave of the early 1960s, but they did badly at the box-office, and Rossellini's precocious experiment of making films for the English-speaking market proved a failure.

Other examples of international film-making were more successful. With *Senso* (1954, released in Britain as *The Wanton Countess*), Luchino Visconti showed that it was possible to make a film for international audiences which nevertheless had a distinct national content. At one level a sumptuous melodrama, *Senso* was politically radical and, in Marxist terms, realist in its denunciation of the opportunism and compromise underlying the myth of Italian national unity. In France, Jean Renoir profited from Italian co-production finance for his most spectacular films of the 1950s, *The Golden Coach* (*La carrozza d'oro* 1953), *French Cancan* (1955), and *Éléna et les hommes* ('Éléna and men', 1956). And Max Ophuls made *Madame de . . .* (1953) in Paris as a Franco–Italian co-production, and then went to Munich to make the spectacular *Lola Montès* (1955), in colour and CinemaScope, with an international cast, as a German–French co-production.

The new pattern of international co-production was mainly confined to Italy, France, West Germany, and (from the late 1950s) Spain. While all countries outside the Soviet bloc shared the problem of competing with American imports, most did so on their own home market alone. France and Italy were the most successful exporting countries. Italy had a thriving export trade with the eastern Mediterranean, while in the Far East Hong Kong increasingly became the film-producing centre for the Chinese diaspora. Britain and Scandinavia remained aloof from European developments. Neither Denmark nor Sweden ever regained the international role they enjoyed in the silent period. Heavily protected by the government, however, Swedish cinema maintained a strong production

Roberto Rossellini
(1906–1977)

After the liberation of Rome in 1944, Roberto Rossellini got together with script-writer Sergio Amidei and a small group of colleagues, including a young journalist called Federico Fellini, to prepare a film that would capture the desperate atmosphere of the city under German occupation. Shot in improvised conditions, the film was finished and released in 1945, under the title *Roma città aperta* (*Rome Open City*). Occasionally (and inevitably) melodramatic, its extraordinary immediacy and raw realism made it an instant success, not only in Italy (where it topped the box-office charts for 1945-6) but elsewhere in Europe and in the United States.

Encouraged by this unprecedented success, Rossellini went on to make *Paisà* (1946), a film in six episodes tracing the encounters of the Allied troops with the native population as they fought their way up the Italian peninsula in 1943-5, and *Germany Year Zero* (*Germania anno zero*, 1947), set in Berlin. Both these films were aimed at international audiences as well as Italian ones, and their bleakness (particularly in the final episode of *Paisà*) is tempered by a spirit of faint hope that understanding will prevail between the victors and the vanquished.

Unlike most of his neo-realist colleagues, whose horizons were limited by their national-popular aspirations, Rossellini continued to think internationally. A Catholic, with connections to the Christian Democrat Party, Rossellini adopted a firm Atlanticist political orientation. From *Paisà* onwards, his films have as a recurrent theme communication (or the lack of it) between north and south and between Anglo-Saxon and Latin cultures. In *Stromboli* (*Stromboli, terra di Dio*, 1949), *Europa '51* (1952), and *Viaggio in Italia* (1954), the 'northern' character is embodied in the character played by Ingrid Bergman, then his wife. The films also show a preoccupation with the moment of grace, when a character is momentarily touched with a God-given sense of shared humanity.

Rossellini's political and spiritual orientation made him an isolated figure in the mainly left-wing culture of post-war Italy, while his much-publicized desertion of the popular actress (and star of *Roma città aperta*) Anna Magnani in favour of Ingrid Bergman lost him support in Catholic circles. As well as betraying Magnani, he was also regarded as having betrayed neo-realism. But he found defenders in France, particularly among the critics of *Cahiers du cinéma*. André Bazin argued that the attentive, observational style displayed in *Viaggio in Italia* was in fact the true neo-realism, and in a famous metaphor described him as someone who crossed rivers on stepping stones provided by nature rather than by constructing an artificial bridge of bricks.

In the 1960s Rossellini further refined his observational style by his creative use of the Pancinor zoom lens, which permits continuous variation of the camera's visual field. His new technique proved particularly applicable to the television screen, and from the mid-1960s onwards almost all his work was made for television. After *The Rise to Power of Louis XIV* (*La Prise de pouvoir par Louis XIV*), made for French television in 1966, he embarked on a series of independent productions covering major events in the development of world civilization, from prehistoric times to the present. He returned to the cinema and to the problems of post-war Italy with *Anno uno* (1974), a film about the Christian Democrat leader Alcide De Gasperi; but the most successful works of his later years are probably the tele-films *Blaise Pascal* (1971) and *Cartesio* (*Descartes*, 1974).

Overall, Rossellini's work is characterized by a mixture of observation and didacticism and of simplicity and occasional grandiosity. Usually he is content to show, but sometimes (particularly in the tele-films) he insists on demonstrating. Sometimes his vision is amazingly naïve, sometimes it is pretentious; but at his best he attains a poignant truthfulness that has few parallels in the cinema. He once described his credo as 'the facts are there, why manipulate them?'—though he often did manipulate them, with very uneven results. Intuitive rather than intellectual, he had a unique ability to catch reality on the wing. Recent critics have tended to disparage this gift, but his fellow film-makers, from Fellini to Godard to Scorsese, have justly admired and appreciated it.

GEOFFREY NOWELL-SMITH

SELECT FILMOGRAPHY

L'uomo dalla croce (1942); Desiderio (1943–44); Roma città aperta (1945); Paisà (1946); Germania anno zero (1947); Stromboli, terra di Dio (1949); Francesco giullare di Dio (1950); Europa '51 (1952); Viaggio in Italia (1954); Angst (La paura / Fear) (1954); India (1958); Il Generale Della Rovere (1959); Viva l'Italia (1960); La Prise de pouvoir par Louis XIV (1966); Atti degli apostoli (The Acts of the Apostles) (1969); Socrate (1970); Blaise Pascal (1971); Cartesius (1974); Anno uno (1974); Il Messia (The Messiah) (1975)

BIBLIOGRAPHY

Brunette, Peter (1987), *Roberto Rossellini*.
Guarner, José Luis (1970), *Rossellini*.

Paisà (1946). A black GI discovers the appalling conditions in post-war Italy

Innocents abroad: Alida Valli and Joseph Cotten in Carol Reed's atmospheric thriller *The Third Man* (1949), set in post-war Vienna

infrastructure, with directors like Gustav Molander and Alf Sjöberg continuing to produce distinctly Swedish films for a mainly domestic audience. Export success (though limited to the 'art-house' market) was achieved by Ingmar Bergman in the 1950s; then, from the 1960s onwards, 'sexually liberated' Swedish and Danish cinema found a wider niche in export markets, sometimes for interesting films (such as Vilgot Sjöman's 1967 *I Am Curious, Yellow*), but increasingly at a level of soft-core exploitation.

Bemused by the 'special relationship' and a common language, Britain concentrated its export efforts on the American market, in the hope (vain, as it turned out) of replicating Alexander Korda's pre-war triumphs in getting major distribution for prestige pictures. J. Arthur Rank was a prime mover in these attempts, but Korda himself scored an isolated success with *The Third Man* in 1949. The polished look of British films was much appreciated in America (*Great Expectations*, *Black Narcissus*, and *The Third* Man all won Oscars for their photography), but production levels in Britain were too low to sustain an all-out assault on the market and it was only a handful of prestigious films that succeeded in making an impact. Financially Rank's efforts were a failure. When a later wave of British films hit American screens in the 1960s it was the result of American investment in British production, not the entrepreneurial efforts of British producers.

FILM CULTURE

In general the 1950s were a good period for European cinema. The impact of television and of changing patterns of leisure was slow to make itself felt. Audiences in most countries continued to rise until the middle of the decade (except in Britain, where they peaked in 1946), and domestic industries recaptured much of the share of box-office they had lost to Hollywood in the 1940s. It was a period of

Luchino Visconti
(1906–1976)

Born in Milan to a family that was both aristocratic (on his father's side) and very rich (on his mother's), Luchino Visconti was drawn to the cinema and to an involvement with left-wing politics when fashion designer Coco Chanel introduced him to Jean Renoir in 1935. After a short while working with Renoir in the France of the Popular Front, he returned to Fascist Italy and made an extraordinary first film, *Ossessione* (1942), which was a direct challenge to the official culture of the period and was widely hailed, on its release after the war, as a precursor of neo-realism. In 1948 he made the mammoth *La terra trema*, an epic about a Sicilian fishing family, loosely inspired by Giovanni Verga's classic novel *I Malavoglia*.

If *Ossessione* was a precocious forerunner of neo-realism, *La terra trema* equally surely outran it. Shot on location, with non-professional actors speaking their own lines in incomprehensible dialect, *La terra trema* emerged, paradoxically, as closer in style to grand opera than to the documentary realism it originally aspired to. With *Senso* (1954), his first film in Technicolor, Visconti was given the brief of making a film that would be 'a spectacle, but [*sic*] of high artistic value'. Set in the Risorgimento, *Senso* tells a complex story of betrayal and counter-betrayal, in which personal and political are closely but ambiguously intertwined.

The historical process recounted in *Senso* is one of passive revolution and of muted change achieved by accommodations and compromise. The same process also figures in *The Leopard* (*Il gattopardo*, 1962), an adaptation of Giuseppe Tomasi di Lampedusa's novel. In both these Risorgimento films the mechanism of the plot works through betrayal, whether sexual or political, while the underlying thematic concern is with the survival or otherwise of class and family groupings in the context of historical change. In *Rocco and his Brothers* (*Rocco e i suoi fratelli*, 1960) the same mechanisms are returned to a modern setting—the life of a family of southern immigrants in Milan during the 'economic miracle'. The peasant family is torn apart under the pressure of urban life and its destruction is seen as the tragic but necessary price to be paid if the individuals composing it are to survive. In *Vaghe stelle dell'Orsa* (US: *Sandra*, 1964) a family is also destroyed, but the forces motivating its collapse are more internal. The story of *Vaghe stelle* is that of the *Oresteia*, and in particular of Electra, the daughter dedicated to avenging her father's death at the hands of her mother and step-father. Daughter Sandra suspects her mother of having betrayed her father, a Jewish scientist, to the Nazis, resulting in his death in Auschwitz. Sandra in turns plays on her brother's (incestuous) love for her and betrays him, leading to his suicide. Sandra however survives and there is a sense at the end of the film that a future exists not only for her but for other survivors as

well. History continues despite or even because of the family's destruction.

In his later films, however, Visconti shows himself more and more sceptical about history as a progressive development. In *The Damned* (*La caduta degli Dei*, 1969), the story of a German capitalist family destroyed by Nazism, there are no survivors. Nor are there in *Ludwig* (1972), where the mad king is incarcerated by his ministers, leaving nothing behind him. Both these films are set in a recognizable history, whose development is cataclysmically blocked. In *Death in Venice* (*Morte a Venezia*, 1971) and *The Intruder* (*L'innocente*, 1976), on the other hand, there is no history at all. The films are set in their own present, which is our past. They have neither a future of their own nor any connection forward, even implicit, to our present. This cutting off of the past from the present goes along with an increasing interest in deviant sexuality. The protagonists of these late films are painfully aware of being the last of their line. Significantly, few children are procreated, and none survive. This contrasts sharply with the world of *Rocco* or *La terra trema*, where the breakup of the family leaves behind children who are free to grow and develop. As Laurence Schifano (1990) has noted, this involution of Visconti's concerns connects with ambivalent feelings about his own homosexuality and with fears of his approaching death (during the making of *Ludwig* he had a severe stroke from which he never fully recovered). He died in 1976. In spite of his increasing pessimism and his fascination with decadence, he never abandoned the Marxist convictions he had formed in his youth.

Deeply immersed in all aspects of European culture, Visconti was also an accomplished musician and a renowned stage director. He directed operas in Paris and London as well as at La Scala in Milan and in other Italian opera houses. Among his finest productions were Verdi's *La Traviata* and *Don Carlo* for Covent Garden. For the theatre he directed Shakespeare, Goldoni, Beaumarchais and Chekhov as well as contemporary plays. He had a great sense of scenic design and was a superb director of actors for both stage and screen.

GEOFFREY NOWELL-SMITH

SELECT FILMOGRAPHY

Ossessione (1942); La terra trema (1948); Bellissima (1951); Senso (1954); Le notti bianche (White Nights) (1957); Rocco e i suoi fratelli (Rocco and his Brothers) (1960); Il gattopardo (The Leopard) (1962); Vaghe stelle dell'Orsa (Of a Thousand Delights / Sandra) (1964); Lo straniero / L'Étranger (1967); La caduta degli Dei (The Damned) (1969); Morte a Venezia (Death in Venice) (1971); Ludwig (1972); Gruppo di famiglia in un interno (Conversation Piece) (1974); L'innocente (The Intruder) (1976)

BIBLIOGRAPHY

Nowell-Smith, Geoffrey (1973), Visconti.
Schifano, Laurence (1990), Luchino Visconti: The Flames of Passion.

Opposite: Farley Granger and Alida Valli in Luchino Visconti's *Senso* (1954)

both mass-circulation (such as, in Britain, *Photoplay*) and specialist film magazines. In Italy *Cinema* and *Bianco e nero* (both founded before the war) had an important role in the development of neo-realism. In France *Cahiers du cinéma* (founded in 1951 by André Bazin, Lo Duca, and Jacques Doniol-Valcroze) was to be equally important in preparing the way for the New Wave, while in Britain *Sequence* (founded by Lindsay Anderson and Peter Ericsson in 1947) played a similar role for its short-lived British equivalent.

Cahiers du cinéma and *Sequence* in particular were militant magazines, expressing the ambitions of their writers (François Truffaut, Jean-Luc Godard, Jacques Rivette, and others on *Cahiers*; Anderson, Karel Reisz, and Tony Richardson on *Sequence*) to become film-makers themselves. They shared with other magazines (*Positif* in France, *Filmkritik* in Germany) a hostility to the run-of-the-mill commercial cinema of their own countries, but were by no means so hostile to Hollywood. Indeed *Cahiers du cinéma* is best remembered for its pantheon of Hollywood *auteurs*—with Hitchcock and Hawks at the top, followed by Orson Welles, Otto Preminger, Anthony Mann, Nicholas Ray, Sam Fuller, and many others not always highly rated either by the intellectuals or by the general public. What the *Cahiers* critics mostly prized was individuality, but they were prepared to find it in genre films and even in B pictures, as well as in the work of more obvious artists like Welles or Ford. They also admired Rossellini, Ingmar Bergman, and Kenji Mizoguchi, and, among French directors, Jacques Becker, Renoir, and Ophuls.

Without question the most original thinker among the *Cahiers* critics was André Bazin. A left-wing Catholic, much influenced by phenomenology, Bazin expounded a theory of cinematic realism explicitly opposed to the Marxist notions that had wide currency elsewhere in the culture. He saw in the long take and the use of depth of field to permit multiple action to take place in front of the camera an opportunity for reality to express itself without the need for montage or other distorting techniques. He praised the sober classicism of directors such as John Ford and William Wyler, but also, and especially, the attempts by the Italian neo-realists (notably Rossellini and Vittorio De Sica) to simplify film technique to the point where *mise-en-scène* hardly existed and the reality of events spoke directly to the spectator.

Even before his death in 1958 at the age of 40, Bazin had lost his steadying influence over *Cahiers du cinéma*. From the late 1950s onwards, the dominating tendency on the magazine became that of the *politique des auteurs* associated with the name of François Truffaut. It was the ideas of the *politique* (which in its crudest form stated that only good directors could make good films and good directors only made good films) that were to be influential in film criticism outside France when taken up by the

441

British magazine *Movie* and by American critic Andrew Sarris in the early 1960s.

CINEMATHEQUES, FESTIVALS, FILM SOCIETIES

While much of the film culture of the 1950s had been formed by the influx of American films after 1945 and the contemporary experience of Italian neo-realism, a wider experience of cinema was provided for specialist audiences by the activities of festivals and cinematheques. A particularly important role was played in France by the Cinémathèque Française, started by the collector Henri Langlois in 1936. The Cinémathèque was not the world's first film archive (that honour should probably go to Britain's National Film Archive, founded in 1935). But it, along with New York's Museum of Modern Art, whose regular programme of film screenings began in 1939, was the first to pursue a vigorous policy of showing films of all types to a public of enthusiasts. MOMA and the Cinémathèque Française were followed, after the war, by the London Telekinema (later to become the National Film Theatre), which opened in 1951, the year of the Festival of Britain, and by cinematheques in Belgium, Germany, and other European countries, whose programming stretched both backwards into the history of cinema and outwards to developments throughout the world.

Festivals were also important in the shaping of an international film culture after the war. The Cannes Film Festival was founded in 1946, mainly as a showcase for French films. But for a long while Venice was more significant internationally. Founded in the early 1930s, the Venice Festival had been discredited at the end of the decade by its association with the Italian–German 'axis'. Revived after the war, it not only promoted Italian cinema (Visconti's *La terra trema* ('The earth shakes') was shown there in its complete form in 1948, to great acclaim), but provided European audiences with their first opportunity to see films by Kurosawa (*Rashomon*, winner of the 'Golden Lion' in 1951) and Mizoguchi (*Ugetsu monogatari*, shown in 1953). Satyajit Ray's *Pather Panchali* had its European première in Cannes in 1956, though only after a successful run in the United States, where it had won an Oscar for best foreign film earlier that year. Conversely it was at the Indian Film Festival in Calcutta in 1951 that Indian audiences first saw *Bicycle Thieves* and other neo-realist films—and also *Rashomon*.

Showcasing of films at festivals often led to their being taken up by small distributors for circulation through 'art et essai' cinemas (generally in 35 mm.) or film societies (generally in 16 mm.). The situation varied from country to country, but in general foreign films were released with subtitles (the distributors could not afford, and audiences often did not like, dubbed sound-tracks). In the larger countries mainstream American films were usually dubbed, as had been the case since the early 1930s, and

specialist dubbers took on the task of reproducing the distinct vocal timbre of actors such as James Stewart, Humphrey Bogart, or Bette Davis. But in the smaller European countries (and in Japan), even mainstream films were subtitled. The number of European films dubbed for general release in other European countries was never very great, but French films were often dubbed into Italian and vice versa, a practice that was given a fresh impetus by the emergence of the new pattern of co-production from the early 1950s onwards. In Paris (though on the whole not elsewhere) major films were released in both dubbed and subtitled versions.

The result of these various procedures was a differentiation of film culture both horizontally and vertically. Smaller countries often enjoyed the most varied cultures. Domestic production would account for only 15 or 20 per cent of the market, the rest being taken up by films from other European countries and America. At the other extreme, in Britain almost all box-office was taken up by British or American films, with few European films receiving commercial release (and even that quite restricted), while a wider experience of cinema was confined to small, self-selected groups. (In the United States itself the situation was even more extreme, but the existence of ethnic markets meant that there was room for some imports from Europe and the Far East.) In between stood countries like France, which retained a strong industry competing with Hollywood for mainstream audiences, but also imported films widely for different types of release.

ECONOMIC PROTECTION AND CULTURAL IDENTITY

The struggles over free trade in films in the immediate post-war years produced a stand-off. All European countries enacted protectionist measures of one kind or another, few of which acted as more than an irritant to their major competitors. The main motivation behind protection was economic. What was being protected was an industry and opportunities for profit and employment, and, of course (particularly in the crisis years of the late 1940s), the balance of payments. But behind the economic lurked another motivation, which was cultural. Negatively this took the form of a thinly disguised anti-Americanism, exacerbated by the presence in Europe of the United States as a (benevolent) occupying power. Hollywood movies were seen as the spearhead of a generalized Americanization of culture ('colonizing our subconscious', as Wim Wenders was to put it). More positively, however, it was felt that cinema was an important expression of national and other forms of identity. National cinemas embodied national traditions and spoke for national concerns; potentially, too, revitalized national cinemas could speak for social groups and interests under-represented either in Hollywood or in the mainstream of European cinema itself.

Three sorts of argument therefore came to be deployed in the defence of national cinemas against Hollywood domination: the straightforwardly economic; the national-cultural; and the 'new cinema' argument, whose national rhetoric masked a more urgent concern for change. Economic arguments tended to be the most persuasive—though it was well known that wholesale protection for an industry in the form of tariffs and quotas ran the risk of retaliation from the Americans, as well as encouraging poor-quality domestic production. Cultural arguments began to make headway at the end of the 1950s, when it was realized that a more limited form of support for 'art' and 'quality' could satisfy cultural aspirations without negative economic effects. When De Gaulle returned to power in 1958, with André Malraux as his Minister for Culture, the French government instituted a new system of support for the cinema, designed to encourage quality films which had at least a reasonable chance of box-office returns. Although intended to shore up the mainstream quality tradition and reaffirm French national values in the cinema, the new system proved particularly beneficial to producers willing to back the young and iconoclastic film-makers of the emerging New Wave.

Selective forms of government support were also to play a role in the development of new cinemas in Italy and Germany—and indeed in countries throughout the world where the cinema was regarded as a national cultural asset. Of the main film-producing nations, Britain alone persisted in a completely non-selective support policy, mechanically redistributing a proportion of exhibitors' revenue from all films to 'British' producers on the sole criterion of box-office success. When first introduced in the late 1940s, the 'Eady levy', as it was called, had seemed a quite ingenious and painless way of supporting the sort of British cinema that existed at the time. By the end of the 1950s, however, that cinema was crumbling. By persisting with the levy, and rejecting culturally based calls for selective support for new enterprise, the government discouraged the growth of a new British cinema and helped turn Britain into Hollywood's bargain basement.

Bibliography
Hillier, Jim (ed.) (1985), *Cahiers du cinéma: The 1950s*.
Jarvie, Ian (1992), *Hollywood's Overseas Campaign*.
Jeancolas, Jean-Pierre (1988), *D'un cinéma à l'autre*.
Quaglietti, Lorenzo (1980), *Storia economico-politica del cinema italiano, 1945–80*.

Transformation of the Hollywood System

DOUGLAS GOMERY

In the years after the Second World War, the Hollywood film industry underwent a major transformation. Increased competition from foreign films, the decline of cinema audiences, and attacks on the studio structure by government agencies led to a loss of revenue which crippled the American industry, and forced it into rapid and profound change. Perhaps the most important shift began in the late 1940s, when audiences at US movie houses began to fall. By the early 1960s they were half what they had been during the glory days, and thousands of formerly flourishing theatres had closed forever.

This decline cannot simply be blamed on the rise of television, as it began five years before television existed as a viable alternative to movie-going. After the Second World War there was a demographic and cultural shift in urban America that profoundly altered the leisure patterns of US society. People were cashing in the savings bonds accumulated during the war and buying houses in the suburbs, accelerating a trend which had begun at the turn of the century. This took away the demographic heart of the film-going audience. Suburbanization also raised

the cost of going out to the movies; upon relocation it became inconvenient and expensive to travel to the centre of town simply to see a film.

The Hollywood studios were not oblivious to these trends. They saw the need to provide new suburban theatres, and, once the necessary building materials became available, began the process of constructing 4,000 drive-ins throughout the USA. The drive-in theatre offered a pleasant, open space where movie fans in parked cars could watch double features on a massive screen. By June 1956, at the very height of suburbanization and the baby-boom, for the first time more people in the USA went to the drive-ins than to traditional 'hard-top' theatres.

A more permanent solution arrived with the shopping centre theatre. As new malls opened in record numbers during the 1960s, the locus of movie attendance permanently shifted. With acres of free parking and ideal access for the car, shopping centres generally included a multiplex with five or more screens.

The shift of movie houses out of town centres and into the suburbs where the audience was now located did

Marlon Brando

(1924–)

Marlon Brando was born in Omaha, Nebraska, where his father was a prosperous farm supplies salesman. His mother, a leading light of the Omaha Community Playhouse, encouraged him to act, but his father hated the idea of a stage career and sent him to military academy. Getting himself expelled, Brando headed for New York, where he studied with Stella Adler and Erwin Piscator and joined the Actors' Studio. In 1947 he erupted on to Broadway as Stanley Kowalski in *A Streetcar Named Desire*, under Elia Kazan's direction. His sweaty, bellowing, brutish performance won him acclaim as a stage actor of overwhelming talent; but despite professed contempt for film acting he promptly quit the stage for good in favour of the cinema.

The best-known graduate of the Stanislavskian school of Method acting, Brando trained for his screen début as a paraplegic in Zinnemann's *The Men* (1950) by spending weeks in a wheelchair among wounded war veterans. It paid off in a performance of tormented sensitivity concealed under surface truculence. Next he recreated his *Streetcar tour de force*, again for Kazan (1951), marking the role as his for keeps. In *Viva Zapata!* (1952), also for Kazan, his clenched intensity as the revolutionary leader redeemed the banalities of Steinbeck's script. To prove his range, and counter gibes about 'the scratch-and-mumble school', he turned to Shakespeare, and as Mark Antony in Mankiewicz's *Julius Caesar* (1953) earned the admiration of Gielgud.

The Wild One (1954) was a low-budget exploiter about motorcycle gangs. Brando gave it class, his brooding, leather-clad biker achieving iconic status and defining a generation: 'What are you rebelling against, Johnny?' 'Whaddya got?' His third, and last, film for Kazan, *On the Waterfront* (1954), featured the first of the great Brando masochistic displays, as his beaten, bloody docker who 'coulda been a contender' lurches blindly back to work, defying the power of the racketeers.

Six films, all shrewdly chosen; four Academy nominations, crowned by an Oscar for *On the Waterfront*. Brando was now the hottest property in Hollywood, despite—or maybe because of—his studied nonconformism, slobbing it in T-shirt and jeans, insulting columnists, and scorning the studio publicity machine. Stunningly handsome (his Roman profile rescued from prettiness by a broken nose), magnetic, dangerous, and witty, he was hailed as the supreme post-war screen actor, against whom every ambitious newcomer must measure himself. According to Robert Ryan, Brando 'ruined a whole generation of actors'; certainly for years afterwards a succession of players—Dean, Newman, Pacino, De Niro—would have to fight their way out of his shadow.

With *Désirée* (1954), an inane costume drama forced on him by Fox in which he played Napoleon, the glowing career showed its first trace of tarnish. There followed

Brando in the role that made him famous: Stanley Kowalski in *A Streetcar Named Desire* (1951).

some odd choices: *Guys and Dolls* (1955), where singing and dancing opposite the suavity of Frank Sinatra did him no favours; and *Teahouse of the August Moon* (1956), where he failed to achieve the requisite comic touch. *The Young Lions* (1958) was an improvement, though Brando insisted on turning his blond *Übermensch* into a virtuous anti-Nazi. He clashed with Magnani over *The Fugitive Kind* (1960) and saw off two directors (Kubrick and Peckinpah) on his first Western, *One-Eyed Jacks* (1961), before taking over the reins himself—with more than creditable results.

Mutiny on the Bounty (1962) repeated the pattern. Carol Reed quit; Lewis Milestone, though keeping screen credit, sat back and let Brando do as he liked. What he did was masterly—a languidly insolent Fletcher Christian with an effete British accent. His best film in the remainder of the decade was Huston's *Reflections in a Golden Eye* (1967), potentially overheated melodrama kept faultlessly in check, with Brando giving a portrayal of emotional repression so intense it hurt to watch.

He made his come-back as *The Godfather* (1972), framing offers no one could refuse in a throaty whisper. A performance of immense, if slightly hammy, authority, it earned him his second Oscar, which he refused on political grounds. *Last Tango in Paris* (1973), practising loveless sex with Maria Schneider in a bare rented room, was deliberate risk-taking that almost came off; at once brutal and helpless, touchingly exposing his vulnerability. As a sadistic 'regulator' in Penn's off-beat Western *The Missouri Breaks* (1976) he was outrageously mannered, but the film could take it—whereas his bravura turn as Kurtz in *Apocalypse Now* (1979) threatened seriously to unbalance Coppola's powerful epic.

Brando has never disguised his opinion of film-making ('dull, boring, childish work') and has repeatedly announced his retirement, but he still returns for the occasional cameo, most of them best forgotten. Yet just on the strength of that devastating run of early performances, bursting with an energy, power, and sheer physical presence rarely equalled on screen, he still ranks as one of the greatest actors of the cinema.

PHILIP KEMP

SELECT FILMOGRAPHY

A Streetcar Named Desire (1951); Viva Zapata! (1952); Julius Caesar (1953); The Wild One (1954); On the Waterfront (1954); Guys and Dolls (1955); The Young Lions (1958); The Fugitive Kind (1960); One-Eyed Jacks (1961—also director); Mutiny on the Bounty (1962); The Ugly American (1963); Reflections in a Golden Eye (1967); Queimada! (Burn!) (1970); The Godfather (1972); L'ultimo tango a Parigi (Last Tango in Paris) (1973); The Missouri Breaks (1976); Superman (1978); Apocalypse Now (1979)

BIBLIOGRAPHY

Brando, Marlon (1994), *Songs My Mother Taught Me.*
Higham, Charles (1987), *Brando: The Unauthorized Biography.*
McCann, Graham (1991), *Rebel Males: Clift, Brando and Dean.*
Ryan, Paul (1991), *Marlon Brando: A Portrait.*
Schickel, Richard (1991), *Brando: A Life in our Times.*

not, however, immediately halt the decline in attendance. Meanwhile, the shift itself created another problem for the Hollywood studios. The disappearance of the division between 'first-run' houses in town centres showing prestige pictures, and local neighbourhood cinemas, changed the pattern of film demand, necessitating a major change in the organization of film production.

A further blow to the stability of the studio system was delivered by the government. The years immediately after the war saw the culmination of federal anti-trust action against the Hollywood studios; a campaign that had started in the 1930s, but had been temporarily halted by the war. The studios had fought hard against attempts to break up their vertically integrated systems of production, distribution, and exhibition. They appealed the case all the way to the Supreme Court; but 1948 proved to be the end of the road, and, in what became known as the 'Paramount decision', the court ruled for the divorce of production and exhibition, and the elimination of unfair booking practices. During Hollywood's 'golden age' the major studios had directly controlled their own destinies by owning the most important theatres. Now they were forced to sell these off, and split their companies in two; one division handling production and distribution, the other grappling with the decline and change of the theatre business. The 'golden age' was over, and a new era loomed.

The Hollywood studios still retained a significant measure of direct control through international distribution. The 'Paramount decision' wounded Hollywood, but did not break it. Although the major companies would have adjusted far better to the new conditions had they retained their theatres, they still held sway as long as they produced what exhibitors wanted.

CHANGES IN PRODUCTION

Hollywood looked to innovation and new technology to tempt patrons back to the theatres. Films were designed on a spectacular scale, clearly superior to the black and white video images broadcast into the home. The first of the 'new' film technologies, colour, had long been available to the movie industry. In 1939 Technicolor had lit up the screen in *Gone with the Wind*, but throughout its early years had only been employed for a select group of features, principally historical epics and lavish musicals. In 1950 Technicolor lost its market monopoly as a result of anti-trust laws, and the giant Eastman Kodak soon surged into the market, introducing Eastman Color, which required only one, not three separate negatives. The studios brought out Eastman Color under a variety of names, and by the early 1960s virtually all Hollywood movies were being made in colour.

In 1952 the Hollywood studios went one step further, and made their movies bigger. Cinerama offered spectacular widescreen effects by melding images from three synchronized projectors on a vast curved screen. To add to the sense of overwhelming reality, it also included multi-track stereo sound. However, theatres which contracted for the new process were required to employ three full-time projectionists and invest thousands of dollars in new equipment, and this financial outlay proved too much for most.

The process for creating 3-D effects had been around since the 1920s. In 1952 Milton Gunzburg and Arch Oboler launched *Bwana Devil*, a crude African adventure story starring Robert Stack. The narrative and stars may not have been top drawer, but the 3-D effects, advertised as 'A lion in your lap', caused a stir. During 1953 and into 1954, 3-D was hailed as the saviour of the Hollywood film industry, and the studios rapidly produced their own versions to ensure that they were not left behind. Warners issued what was to be the most successful of these efforts, *House of Wax* (1953), and classic genre fare followed: MGM's musical *Kiss me Kate* (1953), Columbia's crime tale *Man in the Dark* (1953), and Universal's science-fiction feature *The Creature from the Black Lagoon* (1954). However, the complication of special 3-D attachments to projectors, and the inconvenience of the glasses which had to be issued to patrons, meant extra expense that was never fully matched by the extra take at the box-office.

What the Hollywood studios needed was a widescreen process without the added complications of 3-D, or the prohibitive investment of Cinerama. Fox's CinemaScope seemed the answer; a widescreen process which used an anamorphic lens to expand the size of the image. The first CinemaScope film, *The Robe* (1953), an overblown biblical tale, starring Richard Burton and Jean Simmons, dazzled audiences and a rosy future seemed in sight.

By the end of 1953 every major studio, except for Paramount with its rival VistaVision process, had jumped on the CinemaScope bandwagon. Within a year, half the theatres in the USA were showing CinemaScope, but again equipping theatres proved more expensive than had been anticipated and profits were difficult to maintain.

Other processes were tried, and rejected, including Todd-AO for *Oklahoma!* (1955) and *Around the World in Eighty Days* (1956). The long-term solution to widescreen images eventually came from the Panavision Company. Robert Gottshalk perfected anamorphic projection attachments that permitted flexible filming and little additional expense for the theatre owner. One could summon up a variety of anamorphic power with a simple turn of a knob. By the late 1960s Panavision had become the industry standard.

THE PACT WITH TELEVISION

Throughout this period of transition in Hollywood, the major studios had stonewalled the television industry, refusing to sell or rent feature films to the small screen. However, minor movie companies, always looking for easy profits, did offer their wares. In 1951, for example, Columbia Pictures established Screen Gems as a wholly owned subsidiary to proffer filmed material to TV. The smaller Hollywood studios also rented their back lots to fledgeling TV producers, and unemployed film actors and craftspeople took up television work.

The first feature films shown on US television came from abroad, the bulk from struggling British film studios, like Ealing, Rank, and Korda. Unable to break into theatrical exhibition in the USA, and unwilling to release their product for TV screening at home, the British capitalized on American television's eagerness to show any available filmed entertainment.

It was eccentric billionaire Howard Hughes, owner of RKO, who broke the log jam and sold RKO's film library to TV in 1954. Millions of dollars were made in this deal, and this impressed even the most recalcitrant movie mogul. In the next two years, all the remaining major Hollywood companies released their pre-1948 titles to television. (These titles did not require the payment of residuals to performer and craft unions.) For the first time, a national audience was able to view, at its leisure, a broad cross-section of the best and worst of Hollywood talkies.

From this point on, black and white films functioned as the mainstay of innumerable 'Early Shows', 'Late Shows', and 'Late, Late Shows'. A decade later more than 100 different films were aired each week on New York television stations.

In 1955 the majors plunged ahead into producing specifically for television. Warner Bros. led the way with *Cheyenne*, *77 Sunset Strip*, and *Maverick*, all series based on scripts and films the studio already owned. Almost overnight, Hollywood replaced New York as the centre of television production, and by 1960 film companies supplied the majority of prime-time fare, from TV series to feature films shown every night of the week.

THE FIGHT FOR SURVIVAL

The new economic conditions in the 1950s could not be faced simply by moving into television production; major changes in the structure of the studios were also inevitable.

The studios also readjusted by shedding their in-house production lines. The talent that had been kept on the books during the classical era now proved too expensive, and independent producers were contracted in to make features. Foreign markets also became increasingly important as the domestic market contracted, and the studios concentrated more on distributing their films around the world. These changes ensured the survival of all the major Hollywood studios, except RKO. However, in the ups and downs of the transformation, the studios' rankings changed, and the grand leaders, like MGM, struggled to fight on equal terms with formerly minor theatreless companies, like Columbia or Universal.

MGM faced the greatest threat to survival. Long-standing head Nicholas Schenck clung to 'his' theatres long after all the other majors had sold out, and it was 1959 before the company split into two, with MGM making movies and Loew's exhibiting them. This period saw the departure of many of the bosses of the 'golden age': Louis B. Mayer, Dore Schary, Arthur Loew; and violent corporate struggles for power racked the studio through the late 1950s.

By 1965 the once-mighty MGM was a shell of its former self, and in 1969 investor Kirk Kerkorian bought MGM solely for its 'Leo the Lion' symbol for his new Las Vegas hotel. Senior executive James T. Aubrey, Jr., formerly with CBS, cancelled the films that were about to enter production, sold off the back lot, and began churning out low-budget movies. Some, like the black exploitation film *Shaft* (1971), made money; most did not. In October 1973, just before he resigned, Aubrey ended MGM's role as distributor; the once-mighty Leo the Lion was out of the movie business and would remain so for almost a decade.

MGM was not the only great Hollywood studio to encounter troubles in the 1950s; Warner Bros. was also

Farley Granger and Cathy O'Donnell on the run in *They Live by Night*, Nicholas Ray's first feature, made for RKO in 1948

John Huston
(1906–1987)

John Huston was born in Nevada, Missouri, son of the actor Walter Huston and the journalist Rhea Gore. After his parents separated he spent a peripatetic childhood shuttling between them, and a picaresque youth which took in boxing, journalism, and a brief spell with the Mexican cavalry. He finally settled to more-or-less steady employment in 1937 as a script-writer at Warner Bros., where his credits included such prestige hits as *Jezebel* (1937), *Juarez* (1939), *Sergeant York* (1941), and *High Sierra* (1941). But he longed to direct, and the studio, pleased with his work, decided to indulge him with 'a small picture'.

The Maltese Falcon (1941), adapted from Dashiell Hammett's thriller and filmed in clean, uncluttered style with a flawless cast, was hailed as an instant classic—scrupulously faithful to Hammett while exploring Huston's fascination with character under stress. (It also, along with *High Sierra*, helped to crystallize the definitive Bogart screen persona.) In 1942 Huston joined the Signal Corps and made three documentaries, all stark, direct, and free from patriotic bombast: *Report from the Aleutians* (1943), *The Battle of San Pietro* (1944)—and *Let there Be Light* (1945), about soldiers disabled by psychological battle-scars, which so alarmed the War Department that it suppressed the film for thirty-five years.

Huston's first post-war film, *The Treasure of the Sierra Madre* (1948), mapped out his favourite theme—a quest, obsessively pursued to a disastrous end. James Agee, his most consistent champion, called it 'one of the most visually alive and beautiful movies I have ever seen; there is a wonderful flow of fresh air, light, vigor, and liberty through every shot'. *Key Largo* (1948), by contrast, was claustrophobic and fog-bound. Another study of relationships under pressure, it suffered from the staginess of its origins (a Maxwell Anderson verse drama), though redeemed by fine performances from Bogart, Bacall, and Edward G. Robinson.

With *The Asphalt Jungle* (1950), Huston laid down the template for every heist movie that followed. Presenting crime as an occupation like any other, 'a left-handed form of human endeavor', he watched his bunch of doomed, small-time hoods with dispassionate sympathy. The genial upside of his habitual pessimism was indulged in *The African Queen* (1951) where the overreachers for once succeed in their quest. Both films revealed Huston's flair for casting: the shrewdly chosen character actors, not a star player among them, as the crooks of *The Asphalt Jungle*, and the inspired pitting of Bogart against Katharine Hepburn in *The African Queen*.

After this, Huston's career lurched badly off the rails. He was always an uneven director, interspersing committed films with throwaway assignments—not to mention sardonic private jokes like *Beat the Devil* (1953) or *The List of Adrian Messenger* (1963). But at this period

overblown seriousness blighted his most deeply felt projects, such as the ambitious attempts to film the unfilmable in *Moby Dick* (1956) and *Freud* (1962). His love of the visual arts prompted him to seek aesthetic correlatives in the look of his films—Toulouse-Lautrec's paintings in *Moulin Rouge* (1952), or Japanese prints in *The Barbarian and the Geisha* (1958)—but they seemed merely attempts to compensate for the shortcomings of the scripts.

Matters improved in the 1960s. *The Unforgiven* (1960), his first Western, and *The Misfits* (1961), a latter-day Western whose modern cowboys catch wild mustangs for dogfood, wore their allegories a little too consciously, but were lifted by Huston's wry tolerance and instinct for spatial dynamics. His knack of defusing potentially melodramatic material served him well in Tennessee Williams's *Night of the Iguana* (1964), and even better in *Reflections in a Golden Eye* (1967), an expertly controlled version of Carson McCullers's hothouse Southern Gothic.

Post-Agee, Huston's critical reputation had plummeted. Andrew Sarris (1968) summed up for the prosecution, accusing him of 'middle-brow banality' and 'evasive technique', of 'displaying his material without project-

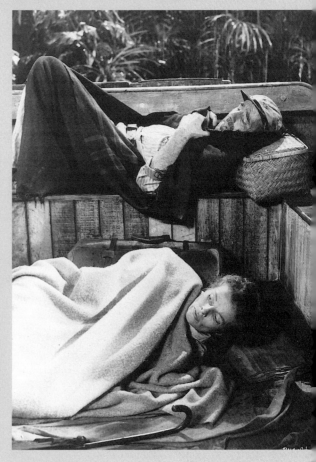

ing his personality'. The pendulum began to swing back with *Fat City* (1972), a study of small-time, dead-end boxers, filmed with laconic sympathy and unmistakable, seemingly effortless authority.

Huston's run of assured late masterpieces continued with *The Man who Would Be King* (1975), a sweeping, resonant expansion of Kipling's fable of the delusions of adventure and empire. Self-delusion also fuelled *Wise Blood* (1979), a blackly comic parable of sin and salvation set in Bible Belt Georgia and filmed with ironic relish for its characters' absurdities. By now, even Sarris (1980, in Studlar and Desser's anthology) was moved to recant: 'What I have always underestimated in Huston was how deep in his guts he could feel the universal experience of pointlessness and failure.' Not that Huston ever renounced his what-the-hell, gambler's-luck attitude to film-making: *Wise Blood* was followed by the offhand rubbish of *Phobia* and *Escape to Victory* (both 1981).

His final two films, though, found him at his best. The ruthless farce of *Prizzi's Honor* (1985) gleefully sent up Mafia movies (and propelled Huston's daughter Anjelica to stardom). And *The Dead* (1987), the last and perhaps most perfect of his many literary adaptations, treated Joyce's short story with love, joy, and quiet regret—an achingly poignant valediction, glowing with the beauty and transience of life.

PHILIP KEMP

SELECT FILMOGRAPHY

The Maltese Falcon (1941); The Battle of San Pietro (1944); The Treasure of the Sierra Madre (1948); Key Largo (1948); The Asphalt Jungle (1950); The African Queen (1951); Moby Dick (1956); The Unforgiven (1960); The Misfits (1961); Freud (Freud: The Secret Passion) (1962); Reflections in a Golden Eye (1967); Fat City (1972); The Man who Would Be King (1975); Wise Blood (1979); Prizzi's Honor (1985); The Dead (1987)

BIBLIOGRAPHY

Agee, James (1963), *Agee on Film.*
Grobel, Lawrence (1989), *The Hustons.*
Sarris, Andrew (1968), *The American Cinema: Directors and Directions, 1929-1968.*
Studlar, Gaylyn, and Desser, David (eds.) (1993), *Reflections in a Male Eye: John Huston and the American Experience.*

Opposite: Humphrey Bogart and Katharine Hepburn in John Huston's *The African Queen* (1951)

forced to struggle for survival. In July 1956 founding brothers Harry and Abe Warner sold their shares, and Jack only stayed on to help the new owners move quickly into the TV production business. With the development of the pioneering series *77 Sunset Strip* and *Maverick*, the languishing Warner lot hummed once again. But Warner the movie company was unable to attract hits from independent producers. For every success like *Camelot* (1967) or *The Great Race* (1965) they backed dozens of failures. Warners' balance sheet moved deeply into the red, and Seven Arts Productions Ltd. of Canada took over.

In July 1969 Kinney National Services Inc., a New York conglomerate dealing in parking lots and funeral homes, purchased Warners. In his rush for new acquisitions, Steven J. Ross moved to fashion the ultimate media conglomerate, Warner Communication. From John Wayne's independent company, Batjac, and a string of successes from other quarters including *Deliverance* (1972), *What's up Doc?* (1972), and *The Exorcist* (1973), Warner Bros., now a mere division of the mighty Warner Communication, settled into a period of consistent earnings.

Paramount had been Hollywood's most profitable studio, with the largest theatre chain in film history. This had ended in 1949, when Barney Balaban, the long-time president, seeing no reason to fight the Supreme Court's rulings, split his empire in half. Paramount Pictures retained ownership of the production and distribution arms, and throughout the 1950s followed a fiscally conservative strategy. When 20th Century–Fox successfully developed CinemaScope, Balaban countered with Paramount's less expensive VistaVision, a process which could be used on traditional projectors and thus required a smaller investment on the part of the exhibitor.

However, the hits stopped coming, and in 1963 Paramount made a loss for the first time; Balaban retired a year later and take-over attempts commenced. In autumn 1966 a giant conglomerate, Charles Bluhdorn's Gulf + Western Industries, bought Paramount. Bluhdorn installed himself as president and hired former press agent Martin S. Davis to run things in New York and former actor Robert Evans to revitalize the studio. By 1972, and Francis Ford Coppola's *The Godfather*, the new Paramount was once again churning out profits, but now for its parent company, Gulf + Western.

20th Century–Fox also faced financial problems despite its innovation of CinemaScope, used to particular effect in the Marilyn Monroe films of the 1950s. The company was still robust in 1956 when long-time studio boss Darryl F. Zanuck resigned to enter independent production. In 1963 Zanuck was called back to try and rescue the company after the financial disaster of *Cleopatra*. But the management techniques that Zanuck had employed so successfully in the 1930s and 1940s did not measure up in the 1960s. *The Sound of Music* (1965) proved only a temporary saviour; the multi-million dollar failures of *Doctor Dolittle* (1967), *Star!* (1968), *Hello, Dolly!* (1969), and *Tora! Tora! Tora!* (1970) best characterize this era of corporate misery. In 1970 20th Century–Fox lost a record $77 million, and Zanuck was fired. During the early 1970s, the new MBA managers, led by Dennis Stanfill, regained Fox's profits and position in the studio hierarchy, through a policy of producing star-studded, high-action blockbusters, such as *The French Connection* (1971), *The Poseidon Adventure* (1972), and *The Towering Inferno* (1974).

Columbia, like Universal and United Artists, did not own a string of theatres, and so was less affected by the changes of the 1950s. As a smaller-scale company, it was also more flexible, and adapted to the move to an independent producer system with relative ease. From independent movie-makers Fred Zinnemann, Elia Kazan, Otto Preminger, Sam Spiegel, and David Lean, Columbia produced hits like *From Here to Eternity* (1953), *On the Waterfront* (1954), *The Caine Mutiny* (1954), and *The Bridge on the River Kwai* (1957). This success continued into the 1960s. Abe Schneider and Leo Jaffe succeeded Harry and Jack Cohn, and acquired *Lawrence of Arabia* (1962), *A Man for All Seasons* (1966), *Guess who's Coming to Dinner* (1967), *To Sir, with Love* (1967), *In Cold Blood* (1967), *Oliver!* (1968), and *Funny Girl* (1968). As well as working with established film-makers, Columbia found hits in unexpected places. In 1969 it released *Easy Rider*, which cost less than half a million dollars, and made stars of Jack Nicholson, Dennis Hopper, and Peter Fonda. The lack of a large, rigid, vertically integrated studio structure had been disadvantageous to Columbia in the 1930s, but proved to be the way to make millions in the new Hollywood system.

This was confirmed by Universal, which had been only marginally profitable during the golden age of the 1930s and 1940s. When the company was sold in 1952 to Decca Records, Edward Muhl looked for independent deals to match those made by Columbia. He signed James Stewart and Anthony Mann for *Winchester '73* (1950) and *Bend of the River* (1951), as well as making deals with Tyrone Power, Gregory Peck, and Alan Ladd. Universal did so well that the MCA talent agency, under super-agent Lew Wasserman, bought it and created a Hollywood power-house of television production. Wasserman also attracted such film-making talents as Alfred Hitchcock, Clint Eastwood, Robert Wise, and Steven Spielberg. Indeed, by the time Universal released Spielberg's blockbuster *Jaws* in 1975, it had reached the top of the studio pile.

United Artists entered the 1950s in the worst shape of any major movie company. Awash in red ink, founders Charlie Chaplin and Mary Pickford sold out to a syndicate headed by two New York entertainment lawyers, Arthur Krim and Robert Benjamin. Timing could not have been better for the New York wunderkinds, who wooed independents Stanley Kramer, John Huston, Burt Lancaster,

Billy Wilder, John Sturges, and Otto Preminger. Benjamin and Krim handled the financing, distribution, and publicity, freeing these creative talents to make movies. Krim and Benjamin ultimately cashed in on the conglomerate boom of the 1960s, and made millions selling out to Transamerica Company, although they stayed on to run the United Artists division.

The one new major Hollywood player to emerge during this period was the Walt Disney Corporation. This studio had existed on the fringes of the film industry since the 1920s, specializing in animation, but in 1953 formed its own distribution arm, Buena Vista. To feed this new channel, Disney commissioned family films, like *20,000 Leagues under the Sea* (1954) and *Mary Poppins* (1964), as well as regularly releasing (and rereleasing) such classics as *Snow White and the Seven Dwarfs* (1938) and *Pinocchio* (1940).

THE PRODUCT

Young people, the baby-boomers, came to dominate the theatrical audience during this era; and consequently, their expectations and desires increasingly influenced the types of films released. To broaden its audience base, Hollywood loosened and reorganized its censorship standards; in November 1968 the United States became the last major western nation to institute some kind of systematic age classification of motion pictures, with the 'G', 'PG', 'R', and 'X' ratings.

The new economic order in Hollywood did not mean that the classical Hollywood narrative style was jettisoned. Genres changed, new film-makers entered the system, and Hollywood moved from studio to independent production, but the story-telling form of the films remained much the same. Hollywood took on more daring themes, but crafted them in the classical style. The director was now touted as an artist, identified and praised as the centre of the creative process, and, in general, film-makers and stars gained more control over the films with which they were involved. However, the economic basis of the Hollywood industry remained the regular production of genre films, those most easily sold on a mass scale around the world.

Television did alter the way Hollywood made movies, in aesthetic, as well as institutional terms. In the 1960s, after it became clear that television was a major market for features, film-making was forced to become visually simpler. The centre of the frame (for both widescreen and standard ratio) became the focus of all but the least important narrative actions, so that it could be seen on a television rebroadcast. The classical Hollywood cinema, which had been created to offer a narrative flow without interruption, had to learn to accommodate an audience's casual use of TV, and the breaks demanded by advertisers.

Many directors formed their own companies, producing films to be distributed through the majors. New models of production from Europe added another dimension to Hollywood film-making, at least on the margin; Hollywood learnt, absorbed, and adapted European art cinemas, and so altered the look of American narrative cinema. There was a looser, more tenuous linkage of narrative events for which absolute closure was not necessary. Stories were located in real settings and dealt with the contemporary (often psychological) problems of confused, ambivalent, and alienated characters. Whereas characters in the classical Hollywood cinema had to be well rounded, operating with clear-cut motives and characteristics, the European influence allowed for the possibility of confused characters, without obvious goals. At the same time strict rules on continuity editing were relaxed and jump cuts gave a new look to comedies and sequences of violence.

However, the Hollywood institutional structure would not permit film-makers to fashion a style totally removed from the tenets of the classic Hollywood text. Continuity of time and space remained in force, with any radical departures encompassed within genre conventions, primarily of comedy. The European cinema may have provided alternatives which gave Hollywood a new façade, but it never seriously shook the foundations of the classical Hollywood form.

The television age proved to be an era of transition; the old studio system was supplanted by a more flexible means of independent production, and the last of the veterans from the silent era were replaced. The old-style studio moguls, who had guided the great Hollywood companies for decades, proved unable to adapt to the necessities of the new era. However, a number of great film-making talents, with long experience in the industry, led Hollywood through the changes. Indeed, John Ford, Howard Hawks, and Alfred Hitchcock, among others, produced some of their best work during the early years of the television era.

Bibliography
Bordwell, David, Staiger, Janet, and Thompson, Kristin (1985), *The Classical Hollywood Cinema*.
Gomery, Douglas (1986), *The Hollywood Studio System*.
—— (1992), *Shared Pleasures*.
Schary, Dore (1979), *Heyday*.
Schatz, Thomas (1988), *The Genius of the System*.

Independents and Mavericks

GEOFFREY NOWELL-SMITH

The Hollywood studio system in its heyday was much admired abroad both for efficiency and quality of product and for its ability to match supply and demand. Other national industries did their best to copy it, hoping to gain strength and competitiveness from its tight industrial organization and forms of market control. From the late 1940s onwards, however, the complex structure developed in the 1920s and 1930s was beginning to fall apart. This was a world-wide phenomenon, though the causes were not everywhere the same. In Germany and Italy, for example, it was an effect of the dismantling of the state-controlled structures of the Fascist period. In India it came about as one of the many consequences of Independence and the arrival of a new entrepreneurial class. In America itself the causes were complex. One pillar of the system, the vertical integration of production, distribution, and exhibition, which provided a crucial linkage between supply and demand, had been knocked out by anti-trust legislation confirmed by the Paramount case in 1948. On the demand side, audiences were falling, while on the supply side the smooth mechanisms for harnessing creative talent to audience-oriented production were showing severe signs of strain as artists at all levels rebelled against being made cogs in the studio machine.

Even if the causes were different, the results were the same: a change in the pattern of production and a greater independence of film-makers from, or within, the system which both nurtured and confined them. This was apparent not only in much quoted cases like Italy, with the pullulation of neo-realism and its offshoots, but even in Britain, where J. Arthur Rank had taken the bold step of devolving production to independent units, and in Hollywood itself.

Contested and much derided though it was, the classic Hollywood production system, with its minute division of labour, had in the 1930s produced impressive results on the creative as well as the industrial side. Individual creativity sometimes appeared to be suppressed, but it could also be fostered, as the careers of many great artists showed. Comedy flourished especially well under the studio system—and indeed not only in Hollywood but in other countries as well.

It was always recognized by the studios that comedy could not be produced to order. But comedy also thrives on formula, and finding and sustaining a successful formula was exactly what the studios were best at. In the early sound years Paramount in particular had a whole stable of comedy stars brought in from theatre and vaudeville,

Burt Lancaster

(1913–1994)

Born in what was then the Irish quarter of East Harlem, Lancaster showed an early aptitude for sport and athletics. He enrolled at New York University, but dropped out to form an acrobatic duo with a boyhood friend, Nick Cravat, billed as 'Lang and Cravat'. They played several circus troupes before injury forced Lancaster to quit. During the war he served in the army entertainments section, and on his discharge decided to take up acting. His first role, as juvenile lead in a Broadway play, brought him a stack of Hollywood offers (he signed with Hal Wallis) and a partnership with agent Harold Hecht.

Lancaster's inexperience and the narrowness of his range, evident in such early roles as the fall-guy in Siodmak's *The Killers* (1946) and the victimized con in Dassin's taut prison drama *Brute Force* (1947), were more than offset by the intensity of his screen presence—a brooding, feral power that even in supposedly weak characters, such as Stanwyck's scheming husband in *Sorry, Wrong Number* (1948), conveyed a sense of barely suppressed violence. It was a quality new in Hollywood leading men, as Lancaster himself acknowledged: 'I was part of a new kind of furniture—tougher, less polished, grainier.'

This dangerous edge fitted him perfectly for the noir films of the period. Its upside, played with an infectious air of self-mockery, was a swashbuckling zest that made him one of the most exhilarating of action heroes. In *The Flame and the Arrow* (1950) and *The Crimson Pirate* (1952)

Lancaster, reteamed with his old partner Nick Cravat, swung, soared, and tumbled with balletic grace and evident delight in the sheer physicality of his performance. By comparison, even Flynn and Fairbanks seem earthbound.

Some critics, seeing no further than the superb physique and the toothy grin, derided him as beefcake, missing the fierce intelligence he brought to every role. Lancaster, well aware of his own limitations, was constantly pushing to extend his range and reveal the vulnerability beneath the brawn—as with his weary, ex-alcoholic doctor in *Come Back, Little Sheba*, cannily underplaying to Shirley Booth's *tour de force* as his wife.

Lancaster was too shrewd to sell himself into the contractual slavery that had trapped most pre-war stars. His box-office appeal, allied to Hecht's financial acumen, created the first of the actor–agent partnerships that would break the power of the Hollywood studios. Later joined by the script-writer James Hill, Hecht–Hill–Lancaster became the most successful independent production company of the 1950s, always willing to take on risky projects. Some of them paid off—such as *Apache* (1954), a pro-Indian Western that appealed to Lancaster's staunchly liberal politics. But Mackendrick's late-noir masterpiece *Sweet Smell of Success* (1957) failed at the box-office, despite one of Lancaster's most chilling performances as the monstrous showbiz columnist, king of a predatory night-world.

Westerns suited his rangy physique and relaxed athleticism. He turned the grin to fine villainous account opposite Gary Cooper's principled loner in *Vera Cruz* (1954),

Burt Lancaster, with Kirk Douglas behind, in John Frankenheimer's political thriller *Seven Days in May* (1964)

then swapped roles to play a staid, controlled Wyatt Earp to Kirk Douglas's maverick Doc Holliday in *Gunfight at the OK Corral* (1957). And few actors were better equipped to play con-men, cold-eyed and ruthless beneath purring charm: he was good in *The Rainmaker* (1956) but overwhelming as *Elmer Gantry* (1960), drunk on the flow of his own swaggering oratory.

Hecht–Hill–Lancaster broke up around 1960, and Lancaster turned to quieter, more reflective roles, though never losing the sense of contained menace: in *Birdman of Alcatraz* (1962) his condemned killer handles tiny fragile creatures with infinite gentleness, and his megalomaniac general of *Seven Days in May* (1964) is all the scarier for an air of glassy-eyed calm. But his portrayal of the Sicilian prince in *Il Gattopardo* (*The Leopard*, 1963) came as a revelation. Few people—including initially Visconti himself—had thought him capable of such poised aristocratic melancholy. The film revealed unexpected depths in him; Visconti called him 'the most perfectly mysterious man I have ever met'. This mysterious quality was exploited again by Visconti in *Conversation Piece* (1974), where Lancaster plays the lonely professor enticed out of his isolation by the decadent 'family' which moves in next to his book-strewn apartment.

Lancaster's later films were variable, but they include some of his finest roles as age relaxed and mellowed him. In *Ulzana's Raid* (1972) he exuded innate authority as the grizzled, fatalistic scout, dying stoically for the stupidity of others. He good-humouredly guyed his own dynamic image for Bill Forsyth's quirky comedy *Local Hero* (1983), and contributed a touchingly wistful cameo to *Field of Dreams* (1989). But he was at his best, blending pathos with bravado, in Malle's *Atlantic City USA* (1980) as the ageing two-bit gangster granted the chance to live out his own absurd fantasies. 'I think I may have a respectful following, but not an affectionate one', Lancaster once observed, but time has proved him wrong. Not only did his range broaden and deepen with age; he also—against all expectations—became lovable as well.

PHILIP KEMP

SELECT FILMOGRAPHY

The Killers (1946); Brute Force (1947); The Flame and the Arrow (1950); The Crimson Pirate (1952); From Here to Eternity (1953); Apache (1954); Vera Cruz (1954); Gunfight at the OK Corral (1957); Sweet Smell of Success (1957); Elmer Gantry (1960); Birdman of Alcatraz (1962); Il Gattopardo (The Leopard, 1963); Seven Days in May (1964); The Train (1964); Ulzana's Raid (1972); Gruppo di famiglia in un interno (Conversation Piece, 1974); Novecento (1900, 1976); Atlantic City USA (1980); Local Hero (1983); Field of Dreams (1989)

BIBLIOGRAPHY

Clinch, Minty (1984), *Burt Lancaster*.
Crowther, Bruce (1991), *Burt Lancaster: A Life in Films*.
Parish, James Robert (1976), *The Tough Guys*.
Windeler, Robert (1984), *Burt Lancaster*.

including the Marx Brothers, Mae West, and W. C. Fields, and carefully nurtured and developed their different talents. It was at Paramount that the Marx Brothers made what are generally agreed to be their best and most anarchic films, culminating in *Duck Soup* (1933, directed by Leo McCarey); enticed to MGM by Irving Thalberg, they scored a great hit with *A Night at the Opera* (Sam Wood, 1935) but thereafter their comedy became tamer. It was also at Paramount, a decade later, that playwright and script-writer Preston Sturges was enabled to make the switch to directing his own screenplays, beginning with *The Great McGinty* (1940), and following it with (among others) such idiosyncratic classics as *The Lady Eve* (1941), *The Palm Beach Story* (1942), and *Hail the Conquering Hero* (1944). It was when he let himself be seduced away from the studio, to become his own producer under the aegis of aircraft industry millionaire Howard Hughes, that Sturges's career went into decline.

The studio system also provided a favourable environment for the growth of other formula-dependent genres, such as the Western and horror film. But it was suspicious of films which sought to get away from formula and were therefore regarded as a market risk, and its strict division of labour militated against films for which either the writer or the director insisted (for whatever reason) on a high degree of creative control crossing the boundaries between specialities. Writers and directors with clout could get round the restrictions, sometimes by becoming their own producers. Howard Hawks, for example, directed a few films for independent producers like Samuel Goldwyn or David O. Selznick but otherwise produced most of his films himself from *Tiger Shark* (1932) onwards, and consequently enjoyed a degree of creative control denied to the majority of contract directors.

LOOSENING THE BONDS OF THE SYSTEM

In the 1940s there was a general loosening of the bonds that tied the system together. Producers, directors, writers, and actors found working in the studio context increasingly irksome. The studio managements for their part found it harder to exercise the smooth control that had characterized the system in its heyday. Gaps grew up in the interstices of the system. While the studios struggled to find new formulas with which to retain an audience which was dwindling year by year, the American cinema subtly began to change. Well-crafted, machine-produced films, though numerically still the majority, came to seem less important as new directors emerged with rawer, more distinctive styles.

The 1950s is often seen as a great decade of *auteur* cinema. French critics in particular saw in the work of directors such as Orson Welles, Otto Preminger, Nicholas Ray, Sam Fuller, Douglas Sirk, and others who emerged or re-emerged in that decade qualities of authorial presence

Orson Welles

(1915–1985)

Orson Welles was born in Kenosha, Wisconsin. His mother, a pianist, died in 1923, and his father four years later. Young Orson quickly affirmed his theatrical talent, staging and acting in plays, especially Shakespeare, at the Todd School in Illinois. Often seen as a self-created prodigy, Welles's culture was formed first by his home background, and then by the diverse cultural institutions with which he interacted in both the United States and Europe. Having left school at 16, he became an actor with the Gate Theatre in Dublin and, on his return to the USA, became involved in the radical theatre movement in New York, whose experiments with making highbrow culture, both literary and theatrical, accessible to popular audiences (particularly via the radio) played a formative role in his precocious development.

In New York he joined forces with John Houseman to direct a number of productions first for the short-lived New York Federal Theater and then for the Mercury Theatre, which he and Houseman founded in 1937. He also directed and acted in weekly broadcasts of adaptations of literary classics, notably Dickens and Shakespeare. These broadcasts displayed some of the features which were to distinguish Welles's films—a dependence upon voice-over narration, and complex narrative structures involving embedded narratives. His most famous broadcast, however, was his 1938 Hallowe'en adaptation of H. G. Wells's *The War of the Worlds*, which simulated a special news broadcast interrupting a normal evening of radio programming. Although clearly marked as fiction, the broadcast deceived thousands of listeners, creating a panic on the east coast. Welles's velvety baritone had already become so well known that Welles remarked after the panic, 'Couldn't they tell it was my voice?'

For all its baroque stylization and exploitation of the medium—deep focus, a fake newsreel replete with phoney historical footage, multiple narrators, and complex narrative structure—Welles's first feature film, *Citizen Kane* (1941), would also strike too close to reality, just as the *War of the Worlds* broadcast had done. Newspaper tycoon William Randolph Hearst saw in Charles Foster Kane an intentional portrait of his own megalomaniac personality. Hearst threatened legal action against the film and blocked publicity in his own newspapers, successfully delaying release of the film and muting the impact of its numerous rave reviews.

Fifty years on, *Kane* remains contentious. French critic André Bazin, who saw it in 1946 at the same time as Italian neo-realism, argued that its extensive use of deep focus promoted the reality of the phenomenal world of the film, but subsqunt critics have noted that the film is also highly self-conscious, artificial, and even baroque. The use of deep focus was not unique, and director of photography Gregg Toland had already experimented with it on other productions. Welles's role as 'author' of the film has also been hotly contested, notably by Pauline Kael (1974), who argued, probably incorrectly, that the script was solely the work of Herman J. Mankiewicz. But even if *Kane* was not completely novel in its structures or techniques, it remains the fact that these techniques are masterfully integrated in the film's complex texture. When Welles arrived at RKO, he compared the studio to the biggest toy train set in the world, and there is no doubt that he enjoyed manipulating the studio technology just as he had the radio.

Welles's first studio film, *Citizen Kane* also marked the beginning of his problems with the studio system. These problems were to mar his subsequent films within the system and eventually force him to leave Hollywood for European independent production. His next completed film was *The Magnificent Ambersons* (1942), which further developed the use of complex camera movements and long takes, as well as deep focus, this time with director of photography Stanley Cortez. But when Welles left Hollywood early in 1942 to film the abortive *It's All True* in Brazil, *Ambersons* was drastically edited by the studio in order to make the film fit into a double bill. Welles then attempted to make three films on time and under budget for various studios in order to demonstrate his ability to work within the system, but *The Lady from Shanghai* (1948), starring Welles himself and his then wife Rita Hayworth, met with anger and incomprehension from Columbia studio boss Harry Cohn; and neither *The Stranger* (1946), filmed according to an editor's pre-set shooting plan, nor *Macbeth* (1948), made for the low-budget studio Republic, had any box-office success.

During the 1940s Welles continued his career as a film actor (including a bravura performance as Rochester in *Jane Eyre* in 1943). In 1947 he moved to Europe, hoping to earn enough money as an actor to produce his own films. For most of the rest of his career (apart from a brief return to Hollywood to make *Touch of Evil* in 1958), Welles filmed on location with post-sync sound, with borrowed costumes or with none, taking several years to complete each film due to the necessity of constantly stopping to raise money. *Othello* (1952), *Mr. Arkadin* (also known as *Confidential Report*, 1955), *The Trial* (1962), and *Chimes at Midnight* (1966) were filmed under such trying circumstances, much of *The Trial* being shot in the Gare d'Orsay, then an abandoned railway station, after funding had collapsed. If Welles's Hollywood work relied heavily for its technical brilliance upon studio technicians, in his European films Welles relied upon his own talent for assembling disparate footage filmed miles and months apart into an ingenious puzzle. During this period Welles retained his reliance on literature, but his style took on a greater simplicity. *Chimes at Midnight*, based on the Falstaff scenes from *Henry IV* and *The Merry Wives of Windsor*, is generally recognized as the culmination of his Shakespearian career.

At the time of his death, he left numerous unfinished projects, ranging from scripts to scraps of film to partially edited works. His film *Don Quixote*, which he had never finished, was recently completed by other hands. Welles's films often centre on a powerful figure and an outsider, the latter being caught up in the former's search for a lost past, the narrative that emerges itself caught between truth and fiction. He enjoyed creating (and playing) figures who were braggarts and liars, or were surrounded by a web of mystery and deceit, never fully uncovered. When Welles died in 1985 at the age of 70, he had for nearly forty years been both the powerful man and the outsider, the master trickster and the roving vagabond. Two years after his death, when Welles's ashes were buried in Spain, the grave bore no name.

EDWARD R. O'NEILL

SELECTED FILMOGRAPHY

Citizen Kane (1941) ; The Magnificent Ambersons (1942); Journey into Fear (not credited, 1943); The Stranger (1946); The Lady from Shanghai (1948); Macbeth (1948); Othello (1952); Mr. Arkadin / Confidential Report (1955); Touch of Evil (1958); The Trial (1962); Chimes at Midnight (1966); The Immortal Story (1968); F for Fake (1973)

BIBLIOGRAPHY

Bazin, André (1978), *Orson Welles: A Critical View*.
Carringer, Robert (1985), *The Making of Citizen Kane*.
France, Richard (1977), *The Theatre of Orson Welles*.
Kael, Pauline (1974), *The Citizen Kane Book*.
Leaming, Barbara (1985), *Orson Welles: A Biography*.
Welles, Orson with Bogdanovich, Peter (1992), *This Is Orson Welles*.

Opposite: Orson Welles as Falstaff in his late masterpiece *Chimes at Midnight* (1966)

that had been less easy to locate in any but a handful of the directors of the previous generation. It was not just the John Fords and Howard Hawkses who seemed to be in a full sense authors of the films they directed, but directors lower down the Hollywood scale who previously would have had less chance of self-expression. In fact the new directors did not enjoy huge amounts of creative freedom, and when they tried to exercise more freedom than was granted them they often ran foul of the system. But the fact that they were able to run these risks, with whatever result, was a clear sign that times were changing.

Not all the directors now hailed as *auteurs* had the same relation to the system. Some, like Welles, were uncontainable and after a number of brushes with the system ended up working outside it entirely. Others, like Preminger, followed the traditional route of carving out a niche as producer-director. Joseph Losey, now best known for his later collaboration with playwright Harold Pinter, made most of his early Hollywood films as a lowly contract director; his brushes with the system had to do with his politics, rather than his artistic aspirations. Fuller flourished as a maker of low-budget action films, which he wrote, directed, and generally produced himself, exploiting the freedom that came with not being held responsible for too much studio money to spend.

Increasing variety in the production system was signalled by the emergence of independent production companies in which creative artists held a great degree of control. A number of such companies had come into being in the mid-1940s, and though their rise was temporarily checked in 1947 by unfavourable tax legislation, the momentum proved unstoppable. The great independent producers of the 1930s and 1940s, Samuel Goldwyn and David O. Selznick, gave way in the 1950s to less ambitious operations. There were changes inside the studios, too, as producers negotiated themselves positions as 'in-house independents', with more freedom of manœuvre than they would have enjoyed under previous forms of contract.

As well as directors, many leading actors of the period set up production companies in association with career producers outside the studio. While they often did this to increase their bargaining power with the studio, the actor-producers were also instrumental in assisting directors and writers, both new and established. The most famous of these actor-producer companies was probably that formed by Burt Lancaster and producer Harold Hecht (later joined by James Hill). Although partly devoted to creating starring roles for Lancaster himself, the Hecht–Hill–Lancaster company helped to bring in new directors from theatre and television to the Hollywood cinema.

Perhaps the most distinguished figure in the field of independent production in the 1950s, however, was John Houseman. Co-founder with Welles of the Mercury Theatre, he played an important role in the production of

455

Citizen Kane. Returning to Hollywood after war service, he produced films of Max Ophuls (*Letter from an Unknown Woman*, 1948), Nicholas Ray (*They Live by Night*, 1948; *On Dangerous Ground*, 1952), Fritz Lang (*Moonfleet*, 1955), and John Frankenheimer (*All Fall down*, 1962). During a spell working in-house for MGM in the 1950s he was also responsible for redirecting the career of Vincente Minnelli, best known as a director of musicals. Although Minnelli continued to make musicals for Arthur Freed's unit at the studio in the early 1950s, Houseman's tutelage enabled him to break new ground with two reflexive films about the film industry, *The Bad and the Beautiful* (1952) and *Two Weeks in Another Town* (1962), the sophisticated Freudian drama *The Cobweb* (1955), and the remarkable film biography of Van Gogh, *Lust for Life* (1956).

THREE AUTEURS

The story of *They Live by Night* is an interesting example of how the system began to be opened up in the post-war period. Its director Nicholas Ray, like Welles and Losey, had a background in New York's radical theatre and had worked with Houseman in both theatre and radio before and during the war. *They Live by Night* was produced by Houseman for RKO in 1948. But it was not properly released for over a year, and then more because of the critical interest it had generated on both sides of the Atlantic than because the studio had any confidence in it. During the 1950s Ray went on to make a number of unorthodox and off-beat genre films—mainly crime films but also Westerns—notable not only for their visual fluidity but for the edgy intensity of their character portrayal and their rejection of the prevailing conformist ethos. He reached a peak of success (or notoriety) with his direction of James Dean as the tormented teenager in *Rebel without a Cause* (1955), but two films on either side of it, the Western *Johnny Guitar* (1954) and the family melodrama *Bigger than Life* (1956), were in many ways more typical of his harsh approach to the dilemmas of masculinity and the omnipresence of violence in American life. Ray showed a particular mastery of the wide screen, adapting it to domestic drama as well as to films on a larger scale. But when, on the strength of his skills at *mise-en-scène*, he was offered the opportunity to direct a biblical epic, *King of Kings* (1961), and a historical spectacular, *55 Days at Peking* (1962), his distinctive talent was—perhaps inevitably—diluted. Though his more fervent admirers (for example on the British magazine *Movie*) continued to see signs of individuality in his work, Ray himself suffered a deep crisis of confidence, and gave up feature film-making entirely, resurfacing as an actor when invited to take part in Wim Wenders's *The American Friend* in 1976.

Perhaps the most striking feature of Ray's films, whether produced within the system or on its fringes, was

the intensity of their criticism of American life, all the greater for not being expressed as a propagandistic 'message'. Although films critical of aspects of American society had been made in the 1930s, they mostly exuded a general air of long-term optimism and a sense that wrongs were superficial and could be righted. Radical scripts were easily toned down and, with the possible exceptions of Fritz Lang and Erich von Stroheim, few directors were able to impose an overall vision deeply at odds with the prevailing ethos.

Douglas Sirk was another director with a deeply pessimistic view of American society. As Detlef Sierck he had enjoyed a successful career in Germany, first in the theatre and then in the cinema, before emigrating in 1937. In Hollywood he at first found little outlet for either his political radicalism or his sense of stylistic refinement. But he found a niche at Universal, making low-budget films of various kinds. In the 1950s he came under the control of producer Ross Hunter, who specialized in cranking out sentimental melodramas. In these unfavourable conditions he learnt to exploit the basic implausibility of the genre with an irony that laid the films open to conflicting readings. His best films of the period, however, were those in which he did not have to use irony as a subterfuge to undercut the pieties of the genre: *The Tarnished Angels* (1958), and *Written on the Wind* (1959). Significantly, both these films were produced not by Ross Hunter but by Albert Zugsmith, who had earlier overseen Orson Welles's only studio film of the 1950s, *Touch of Evil*.

At first sight, the Westerns of Budd Boetticher look like the most classical products of the studio era, inexpensively made formula pictures recycling well-worn themes of solitude and revenge. But their consistency is far from mechanical or merely formulaic and stems in large measure from the imagination of their director and the collaborative conditions under which he was able to work. The first of Boetticher's late-1950s cycle of Westerns starring Randolph Scott was *Seven Men from Now* (1956), and was actually made by John Wayne's company, Batjac, for Warners. All the rest were made for Columbia by a company formed by Scott and producer Harry Joe Brown, known first as Scott–Brown productions and then as Ranown. With this structure in place, and with the regular use of either Burt Kennedy or Charles Lang as script-writer, Boetticher was able to devote himself single-mindedly to the making of films which exploited the potential of Scott's craggy physique and measured performing style to explore themes central to the Western genre. Elegant in their *mise-en-scène*, the films of Boetticher's 'Ranown cycle' are also the profoundest commentary, alongside the work

Jane Wyman as a lonely widow who falls in love with her gardener in *All That Heaven Allows* (1955), one of a series of 1950s melodramas directed by Douglas Sirk and produced by Ross Hunter

Stanley Kubrick

(1928–)

Son of a doctor in the Bronx, New York, Stanley Kubrick left school early to indulge his passion for chess, photography, and cinema. After four years working as photographer/reporter for *Look* magazine and devoting his leisure hours to watching films at the Museum of Modern Art, he made a short documentary about a boxer, *Day of the Fight* (1951), whose 'film noir' lighting and interest in isolation, obsession, and violence already prefigured his later work. *Day of the Fight* was sold to RKO-Pathé who commissioned another short, *Flying Padre* (1951). A third short, *The Seafarers* (1953), this time in colour, was followed by an attempt at a feature film, *Fear and Desire*, which Kubrick shot and edited himself, on a shoestring budget borrowed from a relative. Dissatisfied with *Fear and Desire*, he nevertheless persevered and in 1955 made *Killer's Kiss*, an extraordinary film noir set in the world of boxing.

Killer's Kiss was bought by United Artists who also distributed Kubrick's next two films. *The Killing* (1956) pushes noir conventions to the limit with a story told from different points of view and a complex time structure. *Paths of Glory* (1957) was an anti-war film which starred Kirk Douglas and was distinguished by the rigorous geometry of its camera movements and *mise-en-scène*. It was Douglas who, as executive producer, took on Kubrick to replace Anthony Mann as director of *Spartacus* (1960). Kubrick, who had himself just yielded the direction of *One-Eyed Jacks* to Marlon Brando, thus found himself in charge of the most expensive film made in the United States to date, and the only one over which he did not have full creative control. He was nevertheless able to develop some of the stylistic and thematic elements of *Paths of Glory* and above all to master the techniques of large-scale production and demonstrate his ability to tailor his intellectual ambitions to the needs of the industry.

Kubrick's next project was for an adaptation of Vladimir Nabokov's *Lolita*, the tragic tale of a middle-aged professor's erotic obsession with a young girl. Censorship problems at home led the director to transfer his base of operations to Borehamwood studios in England, where he has been based ever since. The resulting film was widely criticized for its 'betrayal' of Nabokov's novel (if only because of the need to make Lolita into a fully-fledged teenager rather than the pubescent 'nymphet' of the original). But it shares with his next film *Dr. Strangelove, or How I Learned to Stop Worrying and Love the Bomb* (1963) an uncanny ability to mix drama and the grotesque, as well as a sharp satire on the pathology of sexual frustration.

Increasingly reclusive in his habits and secretive about his plans, Kubrick then spent four years preparing *2001: A Space Odyssey*, a science fiction of great technical accomplishment and a visionary quality without precedent in the history of cinema. With its mixture of grand spectacle and reflections of space, time, possible worlds, and the nightmare of intelligence, *2001* became a cult classic. It also brought to the fore what was to become the hallmark of Kubrick's method—the precise deployment of information expressed through control, strategy, and project, as in a game of chess. This method received a further twist in *A Clockwork Orange* (1971), where the choreography of violence acts as a grotesque mask for a deep

pessimism towards utopian beliefs in the rational management of social tension and conflict.

In *Barry Lyndon* (1975) Kubrick took his pessimism a stage further, turning Thackeray's novel into a chilling theorem on the illusions of the Enlightenment and the ontological limits of the human condition. *The Shining* (1980)—ostensibly a horror movie but one which transcends the normal conventions of the genre—uses the story of a writer imprisoned in self-isolation and demonically possessed by his own previous and parallel existence to create a vertiginous odyssey of inner space analogous in its metaphysical concerns to the science-fiction narrative of *2001*. But in its development of the theme of the defeat of reason it stands alongside *Barry Lyndon* as one of the key expressions of the author's system of thought.

With *Full Metal Jacket* (1987) Kubrick returned to the war film genre. Although nominally set in Vietnam, its characters seem dominated by timeless, ahistorical drives, while the author himself seems more anguished than ever in the face of the senselessness of human affairs. Kubrick's formidable synthesis of art, scientific knowledge, political and social interests, and moral and metaphysical preoccupations (though regarded with scepticism by some critics as pretentiously formalist) resembles that aspired to by Goethe in the last century. In this respect, Kubrick can be seen as a paradigmatic figure in the art of the twentieth century, a symbol of the irreconcilable conflict between reason and passion, of the ambition for global knowledge, accompanied by the hubris of a will to control and determine the course of events and the devastating illusion of being able thereby to achieve an sort of immortality of the intelligence, the only possible response to the cruel non-sense of physical existence.

PAOLO CHERCHI USAI

FILMOGRAPHY

Day of the Fight (1951); Flying Padre (1951); The Seafarers (1953); Fear and Desire (1953); Killer's Kiss (1955); The Killing (1956); Paths of Glory (1957); Spartacus (1960); Lolita (1961); Dr. Strangelove, or How I Learned to Stop Worrying and Love the Bomb (1963); 2001: A Space Odyssey (1968); A Clockwork Orange (1971); Barry Lyndon (1975); The Shining (1980); Full Metal Jacket (1987).

BIBLIOGRAPHY

Ciment, Michel (1980), *Kubrick*.
Coyle, Wallace (1980), *Stanley Kubrick: A Guide to References and Resources*.
Kagan, Norman (1972), *The Cinema of Stanley Kubrick*.
Nelson, Thomas Allen (1982), *Kubrick: Inside a Film Artist's Maze*.

Opposite: Sue Lyon, a slightly over-age 'nymphet' in Stanley Kubrick's 1961 adaptation of Vladimir Nabokov's *Lolita*, with James Mason

of John Ford, on the values represented by the Western and the mythic 'American West'.

Different though they are, the films of Ray, Sirk, and Boetticher, together with those of other *auteurs* of the period, have one thing in common. They all represent responses to changes in a production system which had become less powerful, more flexible, and less confidently geared to formula. And they all display an individuality which is that of the director, but which would not have flourished if the production system had not opened up to make room for its expression.

INTO THE 1960S

After 1960 (as is explained in more detail in Part III of this book) the production system opened up still further, and the generation of directors who entered the cinema around this time enjoyed a greater freedom than in past periods (while conversely enjoying less job security than the old-style contract directors had done). Lacking confidence that old formulas were paying off with the smaller and more segmented audiences that still chose to come to the cinema in preference to other forms of entertainment, producers and studios were necessarily open to experiment.

The 1960s saw a loosening of the categories of the genre film and a tendency towards self-reflexivity and a play with genre conventions. If the typical Westerns of the 1950s were those of Boetticher or of Anthony Mann (*Bend of the River*, 1951; *The Man from Laramie*, 1955), the 1960s were marked by the arrival on the scene of Sam Peckinpah (*The Deadly Companions*, 1961) and the first 'spaghetti' Westerns of Sergio Leone (*A Fistful of Dollars*, 1964). Both Peckinpah and Leone are highly form-conscious directors and their films derive their power as much from the way they reshape the conventions of the genre as from their content. Even the old masters were affected by the new trend. John Ford's *The Man Who Shot Liberty Valance* (1962) is an elegiac reflection on the old West and on the Western itself.

Another director remarkable for his ability to turn genre conventions to his own idiosyncratic advantage was Don Siegel, who worked in and around a variety of genres in the 1950s and 1960s without attracting much attention before finding his niche with a series of films which converted the image of Clint Eastwood from that of Leone's lonely gunfighter to the rogue cop of *Dirty Harry* (1971). But perhaps the director who best typifies the new cinema of the 1960s was Arthur Penn. Trained (like many of his generation) in the theatre, and with professional experience in television, Penn made his name in the cinema with an unusual Western, *The Left Handed Gun*, in 1957. More admired in Europe (particularly in France) than in his native country, he had difficulty in establishing a

A scene from *Night Moves* (1975) directed by Arthur Penn and edited by Dede Allen

steady career in Hollywood until *Bonnie and Clyde* (1967). Loosely and often episodically constructed, and held in shape more by the heroic efforts of his favoured editor, Dede Allen, than by conformity with the conventional Hollywood rules of dramaturgy, Penn's films do not so much play with genre conventions as strain against them, extracting significance from the constant pressure of content upon form.

In other respects, however, the 1960s in America were a period of transition between 'classic' Hollywood and the new world inaugurated by the success of Francis Coppola's *The Godfather* in 1972. The distance between those two worlds can be measured by the difference between the comedy of Frank Tashlin and Jerry Lewis in the 1950s and that of Woody Allen in the 1970s and 1980s. Tashlin, a former animator, directed Lewis (and Dean Martin, and Jayne Mansfield, and other popular entertainers) in a number of brashly hilarious films, released by Paramount or 20th Century-Fox but often produced by Lewis himself, in the 1950s and early 1960s. (From 1960 onwards Lewis increasingly became his own director.) His style is that of popular broad comedy, distinguished by an animator's flair for parodic gesture. Though highly sophisticated (again like the best Hollywood animation), it wears its sophistication lightly. Tashlin's films can be seen as the last fling of a popular culture formed by Hollywood in its heyday.

Bibliography
Eisenschitz, Bernard (1993), *Nicholas Ray: An American Journey*.
Garcia, Roger (ed.) (1994), *Frank Tashlin*.
Halliday, Jon (1971), *Sirk on Sirk*.
Houseman, John (1979), *Front and Center*.
Kitses, Jim (1969), *Horizons West*.

③

The Modern Cinema

1960–1995

Introduction

GEOFFREY NOWELL-SMITH

The changes that have taken place in world cinema since 1945 have been for the most part gradual. There is no single event comparable to the rapid transition to sound that took the world by storm around 1930. Nevertheless the years around 1960 can be seen as a watershed, with developments across the world concurring to make the modern cinema different in many respects from that of previous periods.

The most significant change—though also the most gradual—was that produced by the breakdown of the Hollywood studio system and of its competitors and imitators elsewhere. By the early 1960s the Hollywood system was in severe disarray. Declining audiences and a series of costly flops left the major studios on the verge of bankruptcy or open to hostile take-over. While the studios floundered, new companies such as American International Pictures stepped in, making low-budget movies for the new youth and drive-in markets. These movies tended to be formulaic almost by definition, but the formulas were flexible and new genres and sub-genres came into being, such as the road movie, which were to prove influential not only on more mainstream American films but throughout the world. The mainstream itself was forced to innovate, drawing inspiration both from the down-market competition and from the new cinemas emerging in Europe.

The crisis facing the studios did not mean the end of their power, since the companies were able to transform themselves and indeed to consolidate their grip on worldwide distribution. But by the 1960s the traditional fully integrated system, with the same company controlling all aspects of a film's progress, from conception to production to distribution to exhibition, had definitely become obsolete. This was the case not only in the United States but also in other countries which had followed the American model and which were beginning to face similar problems of declining audiences and unstable markets.

In Europe the most important single event was the sudden explosion on to the scene of the French New Wave—the Nouvelle Vague—with first features by Claude Chabrol, François Truffaut, Jean-Luc Godard, and Alain Resnais following each other in quick succession in 1958 and 1959. The New Wave had been briefly preceded in Britain by the 'Free Cinema' movement, and was followed by the 'Young German Cinema' which announced its exist-

Jitka Čerhová and Ivana Karbanová as the subversive Marie I and Marie II in Věra Chytilová's Czech new wave comedy *Daisies* (*Sedmikrásky*, 1966)

ence in the Oberhausen Manifesto of 1962 and went on to renovate the lacklustre West German cinema later in the decade. In Italy the change was less sudden but none the less significant, with the release of Federico Fellini's *La dolce vita* and Michelangelo Antonioni's *L'avventura* in 1960 signalling both the definitive demise of neo-realism and the arrival of a new art cinema.

Eastern European cinema also experienced a renaissance in the 1960s. It began slowly, as the 'Thaw' initiated after the death of Stalin in 1953 spread its effects throughout the Communist world. Always tentative, it was extinguished with the Soviet invasion of Czechoslovakia in 1968—the very year in which the wave of student rebellion saw a brief politicization of the cinema in the west, particularly in France and Germany.

Changes in the 1960s were not confined to Europe. The Cuban Revolution in 1959 gave an impetus to the growth of new cinemas throughout Latin America, notably in Brazil. In Japan the studio system which had nurtured the work of the great masters such as Mizoguchi and Ozu was also in crisis, and in the changed situation allowed for the entry on to the world stage of directors like Nagisa Oshima, who was to play a role in Japanese cinema similar to that of Godard in France.

The new cinemas greatly extended the boundaries of film art. They brought new audiences into the cinema, for whom films assumed an unprecedented cultural importance. Throughout the 1960s and into the 1970s the cinema spoke more directly to these mainly young audiences than did any of the more traditional art forms. But outside Italy and France the new cinema was not a mass-market phenomenon. Because of the limits on the size of the audience, the new cinema had to be low-budget or propped up by subsidy (sometimes both) in order to survive. By the late 1970s the effervescence of the new cinema had begun to subside; it either became marginal or was absorbed into the mainstream. In the process, however, the mainstream was renovated, not only in Europe but in the United States where a new ciné-literate generation of film-makers emerged whose first industrial experience may have been in the 'grindhouse' of cheap exploitation pictures but whose cultural horizons were formed by watching a mixture of old American movies on TV and European films in art-houses and on the campus circuit. From Coppola to Spielberg to Scorsese to Woody Allen to Quentin Tarantino, most of the major American film-makers who have come to the fore since the 1970s owe a great debt to European cinema.

But this European cinema is now in crisis in its turn.

Meanwhile the American studios, after the convulsions experienced in the 1960s, have reasserted their power. Not only have they held off the challenge of independent producers and distributors in the domestic market. They have also acquired, or reacquired, the global dominance that they came close to enjoying in the 1920s before being thwarted by a combination of factors between 1930 and 1970. In cinema terms, the 'new world order' following the collapse of Communism threatens to be not just the triumph of West over East or North over South, but a specifically American victory over all competition.

Another development whose origins go back a long way but which has assumed increasing importance in the decades since 1960 has been the growth of competing forms of mass media, and especially television. The modern cinema exists in a very different environment from that which prevailed in the silent and early sound periods and both its present form and its potential for future development are shaped by the way this environment has changed and continues to change. The first challenge to cinema's monopoly (together with attendant possibilities of 'crossover') came from radio. This was followed, and intensified, by television, which has in turn been followed by video. This part of the book therefore opens with a section 'Cinema in the Age of Television', which starts by looking at the steady growth—at first unnoticed, then regarded with hostility, and now the object of an uneasy coexistence—of the rival media which have come to form cinema's environment in the modern period. The impact of television and related media was felt first in the United States and it was there that strategies first began to be devised to cope with it. Television and the challenge it posed to cinema as traditionally understood was a major factor in the way the film industry, and Hollywood in particular, reorganized itself in the 1960s and 1970s. It also promoted technological change as the cinema came to affirm its difference from its small-screen rival through CinemaScope and stereo sound while also borrowing from it, notably in the adaptation of lightweight equipment for documentary and experimental film-making.

One of the many results of the weakening of the old Hollywood system was the collapse of the tight system of regulation and censorship—the famous Production Code. As a further way of differentiating itself from the wholesome family fare being served up on television (and also as a way of facing up to competition from the less heavily censored films being imported from Europe and elsewhere), Hollywood revised and liberalized its censorship categories. The cinema acquired a new freedom of expression—but also a new form of market-oriented regulation as films became classified according to the amount of sex and violence regarded as necessary to attract different audiences and age groups into the cinema.

The liberalization of censorship can also be seen as part and parcel of a wider process of social change that swept through western society generally in the 1960s. In the United States the single most important element in the process was the shift in the balance of majority and minority cultures initiated by the civil rights movement in the 1960s. Appropriately, the section 'American Movies' begins by examining the presence of black people in American cinema and the changes that have taken place since the days when white people first peered into a Kinetoscope to watch *The Pickaninnies Doing a Dance* and similar titles. The growing presence of blacks (and other minorities) in the cinema has not, however, seriously challenged the mainstream, middle-American orientation of Hollywood cinema. From top to bottom, from multimillion-dollar blockbuster to cheap and cheerful grindhouse quickie, the Hollywood movie remains a machine in which social conflict is managed—and massaged—for the comfort of the supposed majority audience. Racial, sexual, and generational conflicts are resolved in favour of an imaginary and idealized centre from which only modest deviations are permitted. It tends only to be movies which are prepared to split the audience—by being addressed mainly to gays, or to blacks, or to the youth market—that operate outside the broad framework of consensus values. A main thread of this section, therefore, is the way the new Hollywood since the 1970s has absorbed and to a great extent neutralized the pressures on it from non-mainstream cinema on the one hand and from an increasingly fissiparous society on the other.

Both artistically and politically, the most exciting developments in world cinema since 1960 have taken place outside the mainstream. The questioning political climate of the 1960s combined with the introduction of new lightweight technology to produce a revolution in documentary, symbolized by the idea of *cinéma-vérité*. The film avant-garde, quiescent since the 1930s, revived in the same climate, symbolized in the 'Underground'. The quasi-disappearance of animated films from mainstream exhibition was compensated by an extraordinary vitality among independent animators—whose work remains sadly too little known except when programmed on TV. Meanwhile within the mainstream itself it is often the sound-track and the musical score in particular that carry the burden of innovation. Every variety of modern music, from serial minimalism to rock 'n' roll, can be encountered on the sound-track of films since 1960. In this respect at least, Hollywood films can be as artistically daring as the more openly modernist 'art films' emerging from Europe and Japan. The section 'Extending the Boundaries' surveys all these areas, concluding with a look at the rise and fall of the (mainly European) art film as a rival focus of attention to mainstream popular cinema.

More than anything else, however, the period since 1960 is noteworthy for the affirmation, often against the odds, of a complex of world cinema cultures. From New Zealand to Senegal, from Taiwan to Quebec, national and regional cinemas often have an importance that cannot be measured in terms of pure box-office. In some parts of the world, such as sub-Saharan Africa, indigenous film production is a recent development. In others, such as the Indian subcontinent, it has a long and distinguished history. But throughout the world, and for similar reasons—notably the collapse of European colonialism since 1945—cinema has been a crucial element in national and local self-affirmation and it retains this role in the context of American neo-imperialism and Hollywood hegemony. Whether conservative or radical, traditional or modernist, the world's regional cinemas often define themselves against the metropolis and the centres of political and cultural power. Even at their apparent blandest they affirm a right to difference—the right of Czechs to be Czech and not just satellites of Soviet power, the right of the people of Quebec to be Québécois rather than Canadian or American, the right of Africans to see their own culture reflected in the face of westernization.

The panorama presented here includes countries with highly commercial cinemas, such as Hong Kong; countries whose cinemas are (or have been until very recently) state subsidized and controlled, like those of the Soviet bloc; and countries in which the cinema has often been politically oppositional, as in much of Latin America. It includes countries such as India where indigenous cinema has a strong local audience base and a thriving export trade, and countries (too numerous to mention) whose cinema reaches only a minority audience, even at home. It also includes countries whose cinemas show a mixture of different trends—for example where 'popular' and 'art' cinemas coexist but occupy separate spaces (Germany) or where the boundaries between them are fluid (Italy). The diversity of national and regional cinemas is in fact too great for any neat categorization to be applied to it and the essays in the 'Cinemas of the World' section have been allowed to speak in their own way, addressing the issues specific to the country or region in question.

The book ends with two very different essays. The first is about the new concepts of film that have arisen over the past thirty years and the effects these have had both on the way cinema is thought and talked about and also (to a lesser but none the less significant extent) on the kind of films that have been made, whether in the margins or in the mainstream. One place that the former type of effect is felt, of course, is this book itself, since the writing of film history has been the chief beneficiary of the long revolution in thinking about the cinema that has taken place since the mid-1960s.

The second and concluding essay takes leave of history in the strict sense to look at the state of cinema today and the shifting balance between Hollywood and other cinemas and between cinema and other audio-visual media. Contrary to the often-expressed opinion that the cinema is in a state of irreversible decline, it argues that the cinema is very much alive—both in the form of new films being made and in that of a history which (thanks to television and video) is now more available than ever to audiences across the globe.

CINEMA IN THE AGE OF TELEVISION

Television and the Film Industry

MICHÈLE HILMES

Cinema and television are generally thought of as distinct, whether as industrial practices or as viewing experiences. In fact the two have been quite closely interwoven, ever since television first emerged as a possible rival to cinema on an industrial scale. This was particularly true in the United States, where crossover between radio and cinema interests began in the 1920s, extending to television with the start of commercial television broadcasting in 1939. In European countries, where broadcasting was in the hands of state monopolies, they remained separate for longer, but since the 1950s there has been a growing convergence at all levels. By the 1980s, with the advent of large-screen television on the one hand and home video on the other, all the distinctions had become blurred. Electronic formats are increasingly used for cinema presentation; the same companies produce material for both cinema and television; and films made for the cinema are more often viewed on the television screen (whether broadcast or on video) than in theatres.

BEFORE TELEVISION

In the United States, broadcasting developed as a system of privately owned, commercial stations tied together by two great networks and ineffectively regulated by the federal government. Hollywood studios first proposed an alternative programming structure which would have supported broadcasting from box-office profits. Paramount and MGM attempted to initiate their own film-based radio networks in the late 1920s, using film talent under contract to provide entertainment with publicity value in promoting films. However, a combination of exhibitors' objections and inability to obtain the necessary connecting land lines from AT&T blocked these efforts, and the studios turned to station ownership and the provision of talent to the advertising agencies and sponsors who produced the bulk of radio programming in the 1930s and 1940s. Hollywood stars and properties figured large in radio's golden age. Paramount purchased an interest in CBS in 1928, which it was forced to surrender under financial pressure in 1932; Paramount, MGM, and Warner Bros. all operated radio stations in the 1920s and 1930s. By the same token,

in 1929 the Radio Corporation of America, operator of the NBC network, formed its own film company, RKO, in part to market its sound-on-film system, but also as a source of radio programming.

Thus US broadcasting and film interests, though providing differentiated product, were already highly integrated in the years prior to the introduction of television. Within the highly commodified competitive environment of US mass media, there was struggle over the form and audiences appropriate to broadcasting and film. Although broadcasting, with its need to accommodate commercial advertising messages, developed a shorter, segmented, frequently disrupted discursive structure built around such broadcasting-specific forms as the situation comedy, the daytime serial, and the quiz programme, Hollywood's influence showed up particularly in movie-adaptation programmes such as the *Lux Radio Theater*, hour-long drama, and the musical variety show.

In return, radio stars and properties formed a significant part of Hollywood's film output in the 1930s and 1940s. Stars such as Amos and Andy (Freeman Gosden and Charles Correll), Rudy Vallee, Bing Crosby, and many other lesser lights made films based on their radio personalities. Following AT&T's federally mandated restructuring of land line rates in 1936, radio production moved to the west coast, where each of the major networks built their main studios. Despite federal regulation which consistently favoured the interests of the large radio corporations over those of the film companies—already considered too powerful in their own field and subject to frequent anti-trust complaints—Hollywood took a lively interest in and received considerable economic benefit from broadcasting activities, and had every reason to expect to play a role in the emerging television industry.

In contrast, European radio generally followed a public service model with broadcasting facilities and programming owned and/or controlled by the State, from which cinema interests were not only economically removed but conceptually distinct. Though the British film industry, for example, had benefited from protective legislation since the 1920s, it was a commercial industry opera-

466

ting outside the public service sphere, with a different and conflicting set of cultural obligations and allegiances. From the beginning the BBC had found amicable relations with the cinema difficult to establish; most cinema representatives could perceive no benefit to their industry in diluting the box-office appeal of films in order to assist a state-supported entertainment competitor.

Without the competitive demands to increase audiences on which advertising-supported broadcasting was constructed, a more deliberate approach to programming was possible. The early BBC concentrated on 'serious' music and drama, 'talks' and discussion, educational broadcasts, and children's programmes, with more popular variety-based formats developing slowly. The serial comedy/drama form did not emerge on the BBC until the mid-1930s, inspired by US programmes as heard on Radio Luxembourg. Few opportunities for co-operation or mutual benefit between cinema and broadcasting could develop under these circumstances. As the BBC under John Reith developed its mission of programming for cultural edification and education, the cinema retained its association with the vulgar taste of the masses, catered to by the kind of commercial interests to be avoided in broadcasting. This model predominated in broadcasting/cinema relations throughout Europe and also in Japan. Where cinema interests could not actively benefit, through ownership control or commercial sponsorship, from a connection with state-run monopoly broadcasting, the two industries remained distinct or even hostile. They were united only by a concern to resist invasive US competition in both radio—via Radio Luxembourg and its ilk—and film exported to European theatres by the Hollywood majors.

TELEVISION: THE AMERICAN MODEL

Foreshadowings of television's imminent arrival occurred in the United States, Great Britain, France, Germany, and Russia as early as the mid-1930s. Though the war temporarily diverted production and planning away from domestic television, in the USA both networks and studios prepared to hit the ground running as wartime restrictions eased. However, warned in 1945 by the Federal Communications Commission (FCC) that a significant ownership stake in television broadcasting would be badly received due to pending anti-trust investigation, Hollywood studios turned to alternative schemes for a profitable film-based television service. These included theatre television, the broadcasting of special-appeal events such as sports, theatre, or opera on cinema screens, and subscription television, an early version of pay-per-view movies to be viewed in the home. Though unfavourable FCC policy reviews and decisions restricted growth of these competitive uses of the medium, Hollywood repeated its performance with radio by moving decisively into other avenues for marketing its products.

By the mid-1950s, resolution of the Paramount anti-trust case had caused US studios to sell off their exhibition arms, effectively removing their most pressing and vocal opposition to television involvement. While one of the major spun-off exhibition divisions, United Paramount Theatres, did merge with a broadcaster (ABC), most activity took place on the studio side and production for the emerging medium started up in earnest. By 1965, almost 70 per cent of prime-time filmed programming emanated from the newly converted television facilities of the major and minor studios. The divestiture agreement also accelerated the breakup of the classic Hollywood integrated studio, and, as independent producers formed companies around two or three key broadcast or film properties, the former majors assumed a vital role in distribution. Any space on the back lots not used directly for studio production was rented out to the many small 'indie prods' (in *Variety*'s classic prose) such as Frederick Ziv, 'Desilu' (Desi Arnaz and Lucille Ball), Jerry Fairbanks, and Hal Roach. In the 1960s the networks began scheduling regular showings of theatrical films. This was made possible because residual payment problems with musicians' and actors' unions had been settled, and network advertising revenues had climbed to a level that allowed sufficient compensation for the films. The success of such theatrical 'packages' on the networks led to the creation of a new form: the 'made-for-TV' movie, leading the networks into their own form of film production.

Hollywood also actively entered the syndication business, providing an alternative to network programming by selling direct to stations across the country. In 1971 the so-called 'fin/syn' laws (financial interest and syndication) required the television networks to reduce their interest in production. This allowed the Hollywood studios to consolidate their already strong position in production and syndication for network television. American television became, *de facto* if not *de jure*, a joint endeavour between broadcasting powers and Hollywood image factories. By the same token, while feature film production would remain the dominant factor in Hollywood's image, by the 1970s the studios' sound stages and back lots were largely television production centres.

The studios largely eliminated the production of B films, reflecting changed exhibition conditions as well as the shift of low-budget production to television. Newsreel production and exhibition—a thriving component of 1940s cinema—came to an abrupt halt, as news and documentaries shifted to television and newsreel theatres closed their doors. The Hollywood 'women's picture'—low-budget melodramas of special appeal to the female audience—disappeared from the theatres, in favour of both daytime and prime-time television material. The 'blockbuster' phenomenon, with its roots in the vertical disintegration of the Hollywood system, reflected the 'Make

Lucille Ball and Desi Arnaz ham it up in an episode of *I Love Lucy*

them Big; Show them Big; and Sell them Big' philosophy of Hollywood during the transition years. An economy of excess resulted, as competition for major stars and properties bid up production values and costs. 'Big' theatres, however, were quickly being left behind by populations expanding out of the inner cities to the suburbs, where shopping-mall multiplexes and drive-ins began to replace the long-standing system of first-run palaces/second-run neighbourhood theatres so long a feature of urban life.

EUROPE AND JAPAN

In contrast to the United States, the integration of European film and television industries faced significant barriers, made more difficult throughout by the problem of US media exports and investments. In Great Britain, co-operation between the film and television industries was hampered by several factors also common to European experience in general. Characterized by an official Board of Trade Committee Report as 'among the businesses least appropriate for state ownership and operation' in 1949, the post-war film industry again found linkages with the emerging BBC television service difficult to establish. Three factors seem to have influenced this inter-industry stand-off: the close identification of film industry interests with those of the powerful and vocal cinema exhibitors, who

stood only to lose in a closer relationship of film production with television; the association of the major British film organizations (notably Rank and ABPC) with commercial uses of television, via proposals for theatre television and the much-debated creation of commercially sponsored TV channels; and the heavy involvement of American studios in British film production, which lent an unwanted 'foreign' element to discussions of closer co-operation.

While debates raged, the BBC proceeded with its own in-house television experimentation and production, attempting to preserve the kind of public service programme standards which it had established in radio. Even the introduction of ITV in 1955 and BBC2 in 1964 did little to resolve the cinema question, except to heighten demand for film product through increased competition. Exhibitors intensified their resistance efforts with the formation of the Film Industry Defence Organization (FIDO) in 1958, which extracted a per-ticket levy on theatres to create a film purchasing fund designed to 'rescue' British films from sale to television and to impose restrictions on television sales and scheduling. Already suffering from the 'Eady levy' on admissions imposed in 1950 and an additional Entertainments Tax in 1956, British theatres shut down at an alarming rate while exhibitors sounded an increasingly desperate note. Dennis Walls, past president of the Cinema Exhibitors Association (CEA), declared flatly in *Kine Weekly* in 1953: 'We should not be a part of giving the public free entertainment. It is a bad principle.'

Ironically, it could be argued that the efforts of exhibitors (and government) to save the film industry only exacerbated the downward spiral of profits and production by preventing British film producers from diversifying into television—a more reliable source of potential funds for film financing, given shifting population patterns and entertainment habits of the post-war public. Also, by resisting sale of films and more direct co-operation with television, British film-makers may have encouraged the BBC to expand into areas of film production that it might have avoided had outside product been available, particularly the newsreel. Exhibition suffered too, as taxes placed on cinema exhibition discouraged the building of new theatres in the growing suburbs and 'new towns' across the country. Cinema's 'lost audience' turned increasingly to television.

Complicating matters for both British exhibitors and producers, an ample supply of American film product remained available for sale to emerging commercial services, and was actively marketed across Europe by the MPEA, the export arm of the Motion Pictures Producers Association. By 1964 MCA, United Artists, Goldwyn, and Selznick had sold film packages to British television; the exhibitors' dam had burst. In that year 13 per cent of the programming on British networks consisted of feature films, British and foreign. Meanwhile, the BBC continued to produce 85 per cent of its programming in-house. But, as in the USA, the major British cinema companies soon found ways of diversifying into television: the Rank organization purchased an interest in Southern Television, one of the ITV companies, in conjunction with Associated News-papers Group and D. C. Thomson; Lew Grade's ABPC became the integrated regional company ATV, serving the Midlands area; and Sidney Bernstein's Granada received the first franchise for the North of England.

A similar pattern emerged in the major film-producing European countries of France, Germany, and Italy, though more slowly. In each case, the post-war broadcasting indus-try remained under greater or lesser degrees of direct government ownership or control, perceived as an instru-ment of national culture and public service; the film indus-try, on the other hand, though subsidized and protected to some extent by government-imposed quota systems, remained essentially a private commercial enterprise. Tele-vision was slower to develop in Europe than in the USA, allowing cinema admissions to continue to grow through the 1950s. Indeed, Italy enjoyed a cinematic renaissance during the post-war years, with production, number of theatres, and ticket sales at a higher level than ever before (or since). In France theatre admissions began to decline even before television had reached significant penetration levels, indicating that post-war population shifts and changes in consumer habits may have contributed to the world-wide drop in cinema-going even more than com-petition from television.

However, by the 1960s decline in theatre revenues and competition for audiences with American film exports was having a similar effect on all European film industries. In those countries such as Italy and Canada, where govern-ment-owned networks were at least partially funded through advertising, US-produced television pro-gramming competed with national product for space on the television schedule. Most countries responded by estab-lishing quotas to restrict imports of American film and tele-vision, both as a proportion of films exhibited per month and as a percentage of total television time. One result was an increase of joint US–European film production, as well as inter-European joint ventures. Various systems of government subsidization of the film industry also helped to maintain the cinema's role in national culture, though problems in correlating funding with film quality and appeal sometimes worked against long-term benefits. In Germany, for example, film production rose to new heights in the 1950s, under a subsidy system again based on ticket sales that encouraged a form of low-budget, critically deplored 'package' (or series) production much resembling the situation comedy form developed in the USA for tele-vision. Yet, until the 1970s, little cross-financing or true co-operation existed between the stubbornly self-contained cinema and broadcasting institutions.

Simultaneously with divestiture, changing US tax laws freed studios from their attachment to domestic locations and moved much American production abroad in the 1960s. Combined with efforts to circumvent strict import quotas in most European countries, this led to an increase in American investment in European productions as well as joint productions. However, national film industries found independence harder than ever to maintain. Television continued to nibble at the edges of the industry; by 1973 British documentarist John Grierson could write, 'You must see the BBC in Britain as taking over the documentary film movement which I directed in the thirties.' However, the growing television industry was seen to benefit most from enforced merging of interests; the mostly non-profit or heavily regulated commercial networks, limited in the amount of advertising time they were allowed to sell, could

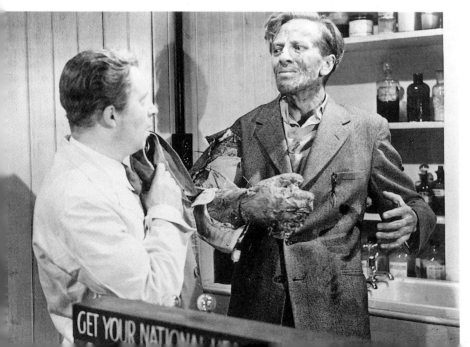

Toke Townley and Richard Wordsworth in the film version of the highly successful BBC television serial *The Quatermass Experiment* (1955)

Robert Altman
(1925–)

Born in Kansas City, Missouri, in 1925, Robert Altman was raised Roman Catholic and attended Jesuit schools. After serving in the military as a bomber pilot, he studied mathematics and engineering, but left these behind to move to Hollywood to sell scripts. Finding little success, Altman returned to Kansas City for six years, where he made industrial films as well as a low-budget feature *The Delinquents* (1957), produced on local funding. United Artists bought the rights to this social problem melodrama about troubled youth, and on the strength of this success, Altman was able to return to Hollywood, where he made a documentary *The James Dean Story* (1957) and worked extensively in television, making episodes of *Alfred Hitchcock Presents*, *Bonanza*, *Bus Stop*, *Kraft Mystery Theater*, and *Kraft Suspense Theater*.

In 1963 he started a film company, Lion's Gate Films, to develop his own projects, but studios expressed little interest in having Altman direct. When Altman did persuade Warner Bros. to let him direct *Countdown* in 1966, the studio found the overlapping dialogue incomprehensible, and recut the film. After working with little recognition, Altman directed the phenomenally successful *MASH* (1970), which brought him notoriety and greater liberty in realizing his own projects. A long run of movies in the early 1970s attracted much critical acclaim, reaching a climax with *Nashville* (1975), Altman's signature multi-character, multi-story portrait of a few days in the life of the South's country music capital.

Subsequent films were less successful, culminating, in 1980, with *Popeye*, which failed to live up to the studio's blockbuster expectations. Altman sold his company Lion's Gate, and his Hollywood career languished. During this period of Hollywood rejection, Altman directed a series of movies based on successful plays, as well as shooting plays for television and staging operas, often working outside Hollywood and on small budgets. Among this work, his 1988 series for HBO, *Tanner '88* (1988), is particularly noteworthy for mixing Altman's penchant for semi-documentary portraits of places with fictional characters. *Vincent and Theo* (1990), his film based on the life of Vincent Van Gogh and his brother, again earned Altman more critical attention, and he was eventually hired to direct *The Player* (1992), a wicked satire of Hollywood, based on Michael Tolkin's novel. *The Player* was highly successful, both critically and at the box-office, and Altman once again became Hollywood's darling as he had been twenty years earlier—despite the fact that *The Player* criticized Hollywood movies in its form as well as its content.

The success of *The Player* allowed Altman to film his long-time dream project *Short Cuts* (1993), based on several stories and a poem by Raymond Carver. The project became a three-hour-plus film which used Altman's characteristic multiple story-lines, testifying to his continued desire to rework Hollywood narrative structures. His influence in Hollywood continues to be seen in the work of his friends and former assistants such as Alan Rudolph and Michael Ritchie.

Altman's films are distinguished by innovations of technique as well as structure. Early on he developed techniques for recording live sound with actors' voices on separate tracks, thus expanding the aural space and

complexity of film sound, as well as capturing the haphazard rhythms of his actors performances. Whether diegetic or extradiegetic, music and voice-overs often function in Altman's films to tie together seemingly disparate narratives and images, as do Leonard Cohen's songs in *McCabe & Mrs. Miller* (1971), the music of *Nashville*, and the singing of Annie Ross in *Short Cuts*.

The visuals of Altman's films are equally inventive. His use of a telephoto lens flattens the visual space of his films, giving the images a pictorial quality not unlike pointillism. His camera floats freely, the camera operator improvising new compositions as the actors explore their roles. The films that result are often a collage of ever-changing angles and drifting camera movement.

Altman has also challenged the form of traditional Hollywood genres. He has made Westerns like *McCabe & Mrs. Miller* and *Buffalo Bill and the Indians* (1976), and crime films like *Thieves Like Us* (1974), *The Long Goodbye* (1973), and *The Player*. But in each of these films, the conventions of the genre are turned inside out: in *McCabe & Mrs. Miller*, the hero is neither a gunslinger nor a lawman but a pimp and entrepreneur; in *The Player*, the criminal is never caught, and the Hollywood happy ending discussed by the characters becomes the ending of the film we are watching.

Altman repeatedly examines communities through the fragmentation of the disparate and irreconcilable lives of their individuals, giving a prismatic portrait of an individualistic society. He has refused to create heroes and has consistently poked holes in the way such heroes are manufactured, whether by politics, the press, or cinema itself. Altman's portraits of particular places thus turn back on themselves and become self-portraits of the culture industry, documentary films about themselves as fiction. Altman's upending of Hollywood cinematic form seems to be his way of staying in exile from Hollywood even while it embraces him.

EDWARD R. O'NEILL

SELECT FILMOGRAPHY

That Cold Day in the Park (1969); MASH (1970); McCabe & Mrs. Miller (1971); The Long Goodbye (1973); Thieves Like Us (1974); Nashville (1975); 3 Women (1977); Popeye (1980); Come back to the 5 and Dime, Jimmy Dean, Jimmy Dean (1982); Secret Honor (1984); Fool for Love (1986); Tanner '88 (1988, for TV); Vincent and Theo (1990); The Player (1992); Short Cuts (1993); Pret-a-Porter (1994)

BIBLIOGRAPHY

Bourget, Jean-Loup (1980), *Robert Altman*.
Kagan, Norman (1982), *American Skeptic: Robert Altman's Genre-Commentary Films*.
Keyssar, Helene (1991), *Robert Altman's America*.
McGilligan, Patrick (1989), *Robert Altman : Jumping off the Cliff*.
Wexman, Virginia Wright, and Bisplinghoff, Gretchen (1984), *Robert Altman: A Guide to References and Resources*.

Opposite: Sissy Spacek and Shelley Duvall in Robert Altman's *3 Women* (1977)

not or would not pay sufficient sums to film producers to compensate for loss of theatre revenues.

Japan provides a similar experience to Europe, with interesting variations. Direct US control of broadcasting after the war did not allow television development to expand until the late 1950s—by which time a heavy presence of American films on broadcast channels had become standard. However, Japan adopted a mixed commercial/public system by which NHK, the state organization, ran two networks while privately owned stations were allowed to operate commercially. This system encouraged both Japanese production for television and closer links with the film industry, to the benefit of both media. Quota barriers, used in Europe to prevent the domination of American product, never took hold in Japan. In 1969 over thirty US films were aired on NHK, compared to seven Japanese and twenty from all other countries; the weekly schedule regularly included US-produced television programmes such as *The Doris Day Show*, *Green Acres*, and *Cowboy in Africa*. The Japanese developed sophisticated dubbing techniques which made the conversion of English-language programmes so convincingly natural that one historian reports the common audience impression that 'these foreigners speak excellent Japanese'.

It was not until the 1970s that more widespread co-operation began between European television and cinema industries, spurred by the increased commercialization of avenues of broadcasting, and further motivated by developing distribution technologies. In 1974 Italy allowed private local broadcasting stations and cable systems to go commercial. This initially resulted in an upsurge in the market for American TV and films, but the Italian film industry began to benefit from the demand for product built up by competitive pressure. Both RAI, the large government-owned broadcasting company, and Silvio Berlusconi's Fininvest networks began to invest heavily in film production.

In Germany, the decentralized *Länder* system of regional broadcasting companies led to more flexible relations between TV and cinema. By 1974 a formalized 'Film/Television Agreement' encouraged film–TV co-productions, structured the allotment of production subsidies in exchange for broadcast rights, and created a government-funded grants pool for independent productions. The acclaimed *Arbeiterfilm* of the 1970s, developed by WDR Cologne, included the efforts of such directors as Rainer Werner Fassbinder and drew on television family drama structures to provide a realistic and politically informed depiction of the lives of German working-class families. The 'New German Cinema' of the 1970s also owes much of its success to such television-based financial support; by the late 1980s, both of Germany's largest film studios were at least partially owned by broadcasting interests. In France, too, intra-industry co-operation helps to support a vital film industry, a process made smoother by the traditional

Clint Eastwood

(1930–)

Though a native Californian, born in San Francisco, nothing in Eastwood's early life prepared him for Hollywood. But after a succession of dead-end jobs, he was invited to apply for a screen test while working as a petrol station attendant. A series of tiny parts followed, beginning with the horror film *Revenge of the Creature* (1955). Eastwood's career seemed destined for obscurity when he landed the part of Rowdy Yates in the television Western *Rawhide*. The series was a great success, running for 217 episodes between 1958 and 1965.

One episode happened to be seen by the Italian director Sergio Leone, who was looking for an inexpensive American actor to play in a Western he was developing. He cast Eastwood as the cool, taciturn Man With No Name in *A Fistful of Dollars* (*Per un pugno di dollari*, 1964). Loosely based on Kurosawa's *samurai* epic *Yojimbo*, the film was a hit, and Eastwood appeared in two further 'dollar' films, *For a Few Dollars More* (*Per qualche dollaro in più*) and *The Good, the Bad and the Ugly* (*Il buono, il brutto, il cattivo*).

The combination of Eastwood's pared-down acting style and Leone's Italian cynicism about the pieties of community and duty gave new life to the virtually moribund Western genre. Over the next five years Eastwood moved easily between the Western and the crime film, initially under the tutelage of his mentor, Don Siegel. Eastwood's first film with Siegel was *Coogan's Bluff* (1968), virtually a mix of the two genres in which an Arizona sheriff journeys to New York on the trail of an escaped prisoner. Siegel was to direct him in another Western, *Two Mules for Sister Sara* (1969), in *The Beguiled* (1970)—a bizarrely Gothic Civil War melodrama—and, most memorably, in *Dirty Harry* (1971). This was Eastwood's first appearance as Harry Callahan, a maverick cop engaged in a one-man struggle against the rising tide of street crime and the bunglings of well-meaning liberals. Four more Dirty Harry films followed over the next seventeen years, ending with *The Dead Pool* in 1988.

By 1971 Eastwood felt he had learnt enough to try directing himself. *Play Misty for Me* was a deftly handled thriller about a disc jockey menaced by a disturbed woman. It instituted the pattern later developed more fully, in which the ostensibly macho Eastwood persona is put under pressure by the unsuspected strength of women. With self-deprecating wit he has come, almost single-handedly, to personify the battered psyche of the macho white male under siege by feminism. In *The Gauntlet* (1977) he finds Sondra Locke (Eastwood's long-time companion) a more than worthy adversary. In *Tightrope* (1984) Eastwood as a tough cop investigating a serial killer of prostitutes is forced to confront his own dark impulses by Geneviève Bujold.

His first film back in the States after his Italian escapade, *Hang 'em High*, had been partly produced by Eastwood's own company, Malpaso. As his position in the industry grew more secure following box-office success, Eastwood moved towards a more direct involvement in the production side. His later films have all been made for Warner Bros. under an arrangement which gives Malpaso control of the logistics of production as well as the creative side. By all accounts, the set of a Clint Eastwood

movie is as lean and spare as the man himself. Eastwood likes short shooting schedules and is usually surrounded by technicians who have proved their worth over many years of involvement with the star.

In Eastwood's later career obviously commercial properties such as the Dirty Harry sequence or the two comedies (*Every which Way but Loose*, 1978, and *Any which Way You Can*, 1980) in which Eastwood co-starred with an orang-utan have been astutely alternated with more personal projects. In *Honkytonk Man* (1982) Eastwood plays an ailing country singer in the 1930s, trying to make the Grand Ole Opry before tuberculosis strikes him down. *Bird* (1988) was Eastwood's version of the life of the jazz great Charlie Parker, while *White Hunter, Black Heart* (1990) is a thinly disguised account of John Huston in Africa preparing to make *The African Queen*. None of these films performed well at the box-office, but there is no doubt that Eastwood is proud of them.

However, it is the Western that Eastwood has made uniquely his own in the past twenty years. While virtually every other film-maker has abandoned the genre, Eastwood's stature has grown with every venture out West. *High Plains Drifter* (1972) was a tale of apocalyptic revenge, in which Eastwood returns and burns to the ground the town in which he has been whipped to death. The supernatural dimension surfaced again in *Pale Rider* (1985), a virtual remake of *Shane*, with Eastwood as a black-clad champion of poor miners against a powerful corporation. *The Outlaw Josey Wales* (1976) had also cast Eastwood as an outsider, a Confederate whose family are murdered by northern guerrillas and who eventually gathers a multi-ethnic substitute family around him in the West. The summit of his achievement in the Western so far is *Unforgiven* (1992), in which Eastwood turns his increasing age to advantage in the tale of a retired gunfighter persuaded to take up arms once more in the cause of the poor and oppressed.

EDWARD BUSCOMBE

SELECT FILMOGRAPHY

Rawhide (TV) (1958-65); Per un pugno di dollari (A Fistful of Dollars) (1964); Per qualche dollaro in più (For a Few Dollars More) (1965); Il buono, il brutto, il cattivo (The Good, the Bad and the Ugly) (1966); Hang 'em High (1967); Coogan's Bluff (1968); Two Mules for Sister Sara (1969); The Beguiled (1970); *Play Misty for Me (1971); Dirty Harry (1971); *High Plains Drifter (1972); Magnum Force (1973); *The Outlaw Josey Wales (1976); The Gauntlet (1977); Every which Way but Loose (1978); Escape from Alcatraz (1979); *Bronco Billy (1980); Tightrope (1984); *Pale Rider (1985); *White Hunter, Black Heart (1990); *Unforgiven (1992); *The Bridges of Madison County (1995)
*also director

BIBLIOGRAPHY

Frayling, Christopher (1992), *Clint Eastwood*.
Smith, Paul (1993), *Clint Eastwood: A Cultural Production*.

Opposite: Clint Eastwood preparing for a shoot-out in the film which created his star persona, Sergio Leone's *A Fistful of Dollars* (1964)

status of French film as an important outlet for national culture.

In Great Britain, on the other hand, it took the advent of the long-awaited Channel 4 to revive meaningful co-operation between Britain's still-struggling cinema and the television industry. Formed in 1981, Channel 4 does not provide in-house programmes but instead finances independent productions mostly of a less commercial, more innovative nature. The timing of this new network was fortunate in that by 1980 several developments had occurred that expanded greatly the world-wide market for film product: the rise of satellite-distributed services, either by direct broadcast satellite (DBS) or by cable; the introduction and rapid spread of home video recorders; and sweeping deregulation of European television systems.

THE NEW ENTERTAINMENT ORDER

In the USA, the first significant crumbling of the three-network television system came in the late 1970s as cable spread rapidly across the country, spurred by the potential of satellite distribution and relaxed FCC regulations on cable programming, including release of feature films. From 1972 to 1982, the number of households subscribing to cable jumped from 6.5 million to 29 million. With the success of satellite-distributed pay-TV services providing uninterrupted feature films to cable systems—notably Time Inc.'s Home Box Office (HBO) and its competitor Showtime, owned by Viacom—Hollywood perceived both a new threat and a new opportunity. A type of vertical integration had begun to develop in the major cable television MSOs (multiple systems operators), with such companies as Time Inc. and Viacom investing in film production, obtaining exclusive pay-TV rights, and exhibiting films on their wholly owned cable TV franchises nation-wide. To combat the domination of these two firms over cable, four studios (Columbia, Paramount, 20th Century–Fox, and Universal) proposed their own joint pay-TV service in 1978, called Premiere. Once again, anti-trust regulations enforced by the Justice Department stopped this service before it had a chance to enter the market, and studios were forced to accommodate the dominant pay-TV services by signing exclusive contracts in the late 1980s. However, new opportunities for film studios to profit from the distribution explosion of the 1980s soon developed, including direct investment in cable television channels and broadcasting stations, the emerging videocassette market, and continued production of both network and syndicated programming.

Of these, the most significant for the cinema may be videocassette distribution, the revenue from which grew to exceed box-office income in the later half of the 1980s. In the light of this revolution, a new pattern of release for theatrical films has developed, with theatrical exhibition rapidly succeeded by release on video and pay per view, usually during the first year of a film's life, followed by cable TV, network showing, and finally syndication. As British film-maker David Puttnam (later to enjoy a brief stint as head of Columbia Pictures Corporation) predicted as early as 1982, exhibition in theatres, while profitable for the biggest box-office hits, now functions primarily as a promotional device for subsequent avenues of release, somewhat ironically supporting a renaissance in theatre investment and building.

Videocassette distribution may benefit from this phenomenon as well: in March of 1993 Blockbuster Video, the USA's largest chain of video retail stores, bought a controlling interest in Spelling Entertainment, a leading independent television and film production company. By spring 1994 Blockbuster was powerful enough to be a player in the take-over of Paramount Pictures Corporation. A successful theatrical opening, with attendant publicity, promotion, and critical reviews, can be the single largest factor affecting a film's marketability in international and ancillary sales. Though video discs proved disappointing in their first appearance in the distribution chain, new applications combining laser recording with computer accessibility may open up new possibilities in the 1990s.

These changing technologies and conditions of distribution both stemmed from, and intensified, corporate integration between former film and television entities. The Hollywood studios have become one arm of huge media conglomerates that operate both production and distribution chains in film, television, video, and often music and publishing as well.

The situation is, if anything, more volatile in European markets, where deregulation of state broadcasting systems combined with the rise of satellite-distributed pan-European services has stimulated the film-production industry. France began a new subscription service, Canal +, in 1984, consisting primarily of feature films, added two private television networks in 1985, and privatized one of the previously state-owned channels in 1987. Canal + now figures as the French film industry's largest investor, both through direct investment and in sale of broadcast rights. However, despite Canal +s 'cinematheque' function, an agreement not to schedule films on Friday nights had to be devised as a gesture to mollify the film industry's fears of increased competition. Germany introduced four new commercial channels in 1984; in Italy, besides the commercialization of local broadcasting, media magnate Silvio Berlusconi acquired three national networks in the 1980s, and set up new film-production facilities to support his investments. (Berlusconi's elevation to Italian Prime Minister in 1994 is the ultimate demonstration of the power of the new media magnates.) In Great Britain, the success of Channel 4's film venture led other ITV companies to establish 'film arms' to diversify into direct film production for television. In 1988 the BBC announced its intention to produce at least six films a year under the supervision of a newly appointed editor for independent drama productions with ties to the film industry.

In addition to national services, the unification of the European economy has contributed to the sudden explosion in DBS services. This includes the five channels initially assigned to British Satellite Broadcasting (BSB) and Rupert Murdoch's Sky Channel; now 'merged' as BSkyB, and based in Luxembourg to serve all of Europe. Though fairly severe quotas were originally established to restrict the number of American films and television programmes on these services, it seems clear that the demand created by this channel proliferation must eventually be filled with imported material. Just as satellite distribution creates 'television without frontiers', with broadcasting systems no longer confined to one country, so film and television production must adapt for the multi-cultural market. By 1992 this process had begun in earnest, typified by a production such as Gaumont Television's international series *The Highlander*. Financed jointly by Rysher Entertainment (USA), TF1 (France), RTL Plus (Germany), Reteitalia (Italy), and Amuse Video (Japan), this hour-long action-adventure series was produced co-operatively and marketed internationally for syndication on national broadcasting systems. Gaumont Television, a subsidiary of one of France's oldest film studios, Gaumont SA, is the copyright holder and co-ordinated a production process that carefully encouraged creative input and approval from its national partners. Another example of such international co-production activity is the same company's agreement with Warner Bros. Television to produce a series based on the Gaumont film *Nikita* (1990), for which Warner also purchased the rights for a theatrical remake, *Point of no Return* (UK: *The Assassin*, 1993). Cross-licensing and co-production arrangements such as these blur both film/television and national distinctions. These processes seem likely to increase, despite concerns over the protection of national cultures and media industries, and renewed calls for import quotas and internal regulation.

DIFFUSION

Hollywood has frequently been characterized as a kind of aesthetic vacuum, producing films devoid of any true national character but, by virtue of its huge home market, sucking in talent from around the world. Certainly a common pattern has developed whereby talented directors from many different countries, once they have achieved a level of success, export their talents to Hollywood. British directors such as Ridley Scott, Adrian Lyne, and Alan Parker work almost exclusively in the USA; Gérard Depardieu seemed for a while to spend as much time in American productions as in French. However, European films are finding new ways to tap into that American market. US cable channels are looking to diversify into new products and video makes possible a kind of long-term distribution never before available. Though the balance of power between Hollywood and other national industries may not be easily redressed, the loosening of avenues of distribution and changing circumstances of exhibition at least provide more possibilities than ever before.

The boundaries set between television and the cinema, shaped as they were in the very specific conditions of the 1950s and 1960s, can now be seen as far more arbitrary, and far less necessary, than the discourses inherited from these earlier periods would have us believe. Definitions set as long ago as the 1920s enforced distinctions and erected barriers that impeded a freer adaptation of old forms to new, and restricted potential audiences and uses of developing media. It was the introduction of new technology that, in most cases, finally broke down these now transparent and largely obsolete distinctions. However, new technology does not develop by itself, but serves to open avenues for competing sets of institutional interests to intervene forcefully in established arrangements. Though technology may provide the opportunity for change, it is shifting political and economic alliances that either spur or slow technological growth, and determine how such technology will be used.

Thus, television did not develop—as popular myth would have it—as a new and potent interloper which conquered cinema by capturing its audience. It developed as an adjustment of a complex set of interests already arranged along mutually contested and shifting lines. In this relationship broadcasters, cinema producers, distributors and exhibitors, and the regulatory apparatus of the State play the major roles. It is in the balance of power between these forces established in the 1950s and 1960s that our everyday understanding of the basic meaning of 'film' and 'television' was formed, and which the advent of new technologies of distribution in the 1980s and 1990s begins to overturn.

Bibliography

Balio, Tino (ed.) (1990), *Hollywood in the Age of Television*.

Briggs, Asa (1979), *The History of Broadcasting in the United Kingdom*, vol. iv: *Sound and Vision*.

Caughie, John (1986), 'Broadcasting and Cinema 1: Converging Histories'.

Dickinson, Margaret, and Street, Sarah (1985), *Cinema and State*.

Emery, Walter B. (1969), *National and International Systems of Broadcasting*.

Gorham, Maurice (1949), *Television: Medium of the Future*.

Hilmes, Michèle (1990), *Hollywood and Broadcasting: From Radio to Cable*.

Nippon Hoso Kyokai (1967), *The History of Broadcasting in Japan*.

Noam, Eli (1991), *Television in Europe*.

Nowell-Smith, Geoffrey (1989), *The European Experience*.

Sandford, John (1980), *The New German Cinema*.

Scannell, Paddy, and Cardiff, David (1991), *A Social History of British Broadcasting*.

Sorlin, Pierre (1991), *European Cinemas, European Societies, 1939–1990*.

The New Hollywood

DOUGLAS GOMERY

The Hollywood film industry entered a new age in June 1975, with the release of Steven Spielberg's *Jaws*. Two years later, George Lucas's *Star Wars* spectacularly confirmed that a single film could earn its studio hundreds of millions of dollars in profits, and convert a poor year into a triumph. The place of movies within the Hollywood production system changed; increasingly the focus was on high-cost, potentially highly lucrative 'special attractions'—leaving the studio mogul-managers to look for regular, predictable cash flows from the 'ancillary' markets of television series production and, from the mid-1980s, videocassette sales.

IN THE HOME AND AT THE MULTIPLEX

Although important changes occurred in Hollywood movie-making, the major transformation in this period was in where fans watched Hollywood's offerings. The rise of the made-for-TV movie, the introduction of cable (and satellite) film channels, and particularly the home video revolution, transformed film viewing in the 1970s and 1980s.

This began in the mid-1970s as the TV movie expanded into the mini-series, and millions of Americans viewed critically acclaimed series like *War and Remembrance* and *Lonesome Dove*. The average made-for-TV drama, however, is a successor to Hollywood's B movies of the past, and mini-series like *Hollywood Wives* or *The Thorn Birds* are regularly produced and give a big boost to ratings. Since the turnaround time from production to presentation is so short, made-for-TV films can deal with topical issues, as in 1983 when *The Day After* provoked a national discussion about the possibility of nuclear disaster.

At around the same time, the world of cable television in the United States was transformed by Time Inc.'s innovative Home Box Office (HBO). For a monthly fee of about $10, cable television subscribers could see recent Hollywood motion pictures—uncut, uninterrupted by commercials, and not sanitized to please network censors. For the first time, Hollywood had found a way to make TV viewers pay for what they watched in their living rooms. HBO drew back the older movie fan who did not want to go out to a cinema, but loved watching second-run films on television at home.

Once it became clear that this market existed, other companies were eager to emulate HBO's success. In 1986 Ted Turner purchased an ailing MGM, not for its current productions, but for access to and control of its film library. Turner's SuperStation and TNT (as well as American Movie Classics and Bravo) fill the cable day with the best and the worst of old Hollywood films, and movie fans have a rich repertory cinema at home.

This movie viewing revolution reached its apex with the home video. Sony introduced its Betamax half-inch home videocassette recorder in 1975. Originally priced at more than $1,500, the cost of the Beta machines and their newer rivals, VHS, dropped to just over $300 by the mid-1980s, and an enthusiastic American public (plus millions in other nations) snapped up so many machines that by 1989 two-thirds of households were equipped to tape off the air or run pre-recorded tapes. To satisfy this new demand, the number of available cassettes of new and old films soared into the millions. New video releases were regularly reviewed in major newspapers, and achieved equal status to network and cable television.

At first, ironically, the Hollywood moguls loathed the new home video machine. Jack Valenti, president of the Motion Picture Association of America, declared that the VCR was a parasitical instrument robbing Hollywood's take at the box-office. Valenti's major studio clients underestimated the public demand for films in the home. Change only came about when outside entrepreneurs throughout the United States began to buy multiple copies of pre-recorded movies and to rent them to the public. Soon stores renting video popped up on every street corner, and the Hollywood majors, seeing the huge profit potential of the medium, began to capitalize on this apparently insatiable demand. By 1986 'ancillary' video sales passed box-office take from theatres in the USA, and by the 1990s the VCR was generating more than $10 billion in rentals and sales in the USA alone. The Hollywood studios found a new market for their product; blockbusters were given a second lease of life when distributed on video, and certain films, like Brian De Palma's *Scarface* (1983), which were only modestly successful at the theatres, found their audience through home video rentals. More people were watching more Hollywood films than ever before—at home.

Despite the dramatic changes ushered in by the video revolution, and the fears of the studio bosses, audience attendance at movie theatres did not collapse. In fact, by the beginning of the 1990s an average of nearly 20 million fans each week were visiting multiplex cinemas in the

Al Pacino as the mafia godfather Michael Corleone taking advice from his lawyer, in the trial scene of one of the most commercially and critically successful sequels of all times: Francis Ford Coppola's *Godfather Part II* (1974)

United States. In 1990 there were more available movie screens in the United States than at any time since the late 1920s.

In the blockbuster seasons (summer, Christmas and spring holidays) Hollywood sponsored multiplexes so as to have room to release more potential blockbusters in more locations, simultaneously. Films like *Batman* (1989) and *Batman Returns* (1992) thus opened on nearly 3,000 screens across the United States. This meant that, during the 'low' seasons of autumn and spring, screens were available for lower-budget films, with smaller potential audiences. As a consequence, black film-maker Spike Lee was able to distribute *She's Gotta Have It* (1986) and *Do the Right Thing* (1989) through Hollywood companies to thousands of screens; David Lynch's cultish, violent *Blue Velvet* (1986) found an audience during the autumn months; *Platoon* (1986), a serious look at the Vietnam War, reached the status of a hit; and Warner Bros. was willing to release *Blade Runner* (1982) in a 'director's cut' version for two weeks in late September 1991, following it with a widespread rerelease in 1993.

IN THE BOARDROOM

The Hollywood majors sought to take full advantage of all the new markets for their product, in the home and at the multiplex. For all the technological transformations in movie viewing, the major movie corporations lost none of their power. In the new climate, they not only survived, they prospered. A handful of companies, formed more than half a century previously, continued to monopolize the creation of movies, and their distribution throughout the world. In the 1980s, the profits of these companies attracted buyers from abroad, and many gained new owners, but they showed no signs of weakening. Indeed, if anything, they seemed to be getting ever stronger, eliminating all serious competition.

The $20 billion consolidation of Time and Warner in 1989 created renewed interest in the concentration of power and profit in the Hollywood studios. Matsushita's take-over of MCA (and its Universal Studios) a year later proved the huge prices that rich foreign corporations were willing to pay for a place in Hollywood. Many film fans look back to the 1930s and 1940s as the 'golden age' of the movie business, but in fact the 1990s stood as the era when Hollywood achieved an international influence, a mass-entertainment market-place superiority, and millions in profits unparalleled in its history.

Many independent film-makers have established their own production companies as a legal means to make their pictures, such as Spike Lee's corporate umbrella 40 Acres and a Mule or Ray Stark's Rastar. However, they are still almost wholly dependent on the distribution arms of the vertically integrated majors: in the 1990s—Paramount, Warner Bros., Matsushita's Universal Pictures, 20th

Century–Fox, Disney, and Sony's Columbia Pictures. Independent distributors still have very little share of the market, and triumphs like *The Crying Game* (1992), distributed in the USA by Miramax, only serve to underline the extent of the Hollywood domination. Not all Hollywood-based operations deserve the name major studio, nor achieved equal success in this period. Orion Pictures, run by Arthur Krim, who a generation earlier had revitalized United Artists, went bankrupt. This, despite millions made from *RoboCop* (1987) and *Dances with Wolves* (1990), and despite the regular release of Woody Allen's films.

Paramount Pictures took a new direction in the early 1980s, when president Charles Bluhdorn died and long-time assistant Martin S. Davis took his place and began to sell off the non-entertainment-related businesses. By 1989 what remained, now titled Paramount Communications, encompassed television and film properties including a share of the US cable network (in partnership with MCA/Universal), an active television production unit, a home video division, and the publishers Simon & Schuster. Paramount also retained its movie studio on Melrose Avenue (the last lot actually situated in Hollywood), from which it produced a regular supply of films, from the *Star Trek* series (1979 to 1994) to *The Hunt for Red October* (1990).

Warner Communication, formed at the start of the 1970s, grew to include divisions handling popular music, publishing, and cable television, as well as the core Hollywood movie-making and movie distribution operations. When Warner Bros. merged with Time in 1989, they created Time Warner, the largest media company in the world and the quintessential media conglomerate. Cable properties, magazines, and television production provided consistent profits, and the Warner Bros. studio produced a number of the top grossing films of the early 1990s including *Batman* and *Batman Returns*, both of which had started as 'properties' in Warner's DC Comics unit.

MCA/Universal has long provided a formidable rival to Paramount and Warner, particularly through its film-production operation, Universal Studios. In 1959 talent agency MCA bought Universal. Faced with a governmental suit, because it then both employed and represented talent, MCA shed the original agency business and began a process of development and acquisition, evolving into a media conglomerate with theme parks, a chain of gift shops, book publishing, and a popular music division. MCA's diversified success attracted Japan's giant Matsushita Corporation, and in December 1990 it bought MCA for an estimated $7 billion.

In 1985 20th Century–Fox was bought by the Australian (now naturalized American) media tycoon Rupert Murdoch. From the base of his world-wide media conglomerate, News Incorporated, Murdoch transformed the ailing film studio into a media empire with formidable film and television operations. Fox's television division,

Jodie Foster

(1962–)

Jodie Foster began appearing in television commercials at the age of 3, and by the time of her movie début in *Napoleon and Samantha* (1972) seven years later she was a seasoned television performer. In 1976 she appeared in two films that confirmed her as perhaps the most talented and versatile child star that Hollywood has ever produced. Her performance as the painfully precocious child prostitute in Martin Scorsese's *Taxi Driver* (1976) played on the youth and frailty under her veneer of adult sexuality, and in *Bugsy Malone* (1976) she stood out in the all-child cast for the strength and maturity of her performance as the gangster's moll. She rarely played traditional 'little girl' roles; in *The Little Girl who Lived down the Lane* (1976) she was a murderer, and in the Disney children's film *Freaky Friday* (1976), a daughter who 'swaps' bodies with her mother. The power of her performances, and the hint of (disturbing) adult sexuality often associated with them, should have made her move to adult roles easier, but in the late 1970s her career went into decline, and it looked as if she was destined for the adulthood obscurity that is the traditional fate of child stars.

Foster had a strong academic background. She had attended Los Angeles' bilingual Lycée Français (and later made several films in France, including *Le Sang des autres*, 1984, for Claude Chabrol) and, when her acting career faltered, she took up a place at Yale. While she was there, John Hinckley, Jr., shot President Reagan, blaming his actions on an obsession with Foster and her role in *Taxi Driver*. She was thrown into the media spotlight and presented as an image both of the power of the screen star, and, in a bizarre inflection of the role she had played, as victim.

The Hinckley incident threatened to overshadow Foster's acting career. The early 1980s saw her appear in a series of films which failed at the box-office even while her performances were praised—notably Tony Richardson's *Hotel New Hampshire* (1984), where she plays a young *femme fatale* caught up in destruction and incest. *The Accused* (1988) proved to be the turning-point. It was her first truly adult part, and one in which she could shake off the taint of sexual victim, by embracing the role and then fighting back. Sarah Tobias, gang-raped in a bar, takes her attackers to court, and demands the opportunity to take the stand and bear witness herself—to take control and tell her story. The film was hugely popular and immensely controversial, and Foster won an Oscar for her performance, placing herself on the A list of Hollywood actresses, and so firmly in the mainstream.

Despite the success of *The Accused*, Foster had to fight hard for what would be her second Oscar-winning role, that of Clarice Starling in *The Silence of the Lambs* (1991). (It was originally earmarked for Michelle Pfeiffer.) In some ways a development of the Tobias character, Starling is a gritty working-class young woman, an FBI recruit who

must put herself at risk in order to pursue a killer and rescue his latest victim. Unusually for Hollywood, this risk is specifically not a sexual one, but involves both physical and psychological danger, as Starling becomes emotionally involved with one serial killer in order to catch another. *The Silence of the Lambs* was also the centre of controversy, being criticized by gay groups for its portrayal of the transsexual killer. Ironically, given the de-sexualized nature of the role she played, criticism was focused personally on Foster, and she became the centre of a fierce 'outing' campaign, which threatened to over-shadow the strength of her performance.

In the year of the release of *The Silence of the Lambs*, Foster made her directorial début with *Little Man Tate* (1991). Acting in the film as well as directing it, she plays the mother of a child prodigy who finds herself locked into conflict with the woman who runs a special school for gifted children to which the boy has been sent to develop his talents, only to find them possessively exploited. An intelligent and personal film, *Little Man Tate* was nearly aborted when its backers, Orion, collapsed before its completion. Foster then had to shoulder some of the tasks of producer, campaigning hard to ensure her film's release, and eventual success. This interest in the business side of the industry led her to establish her own company in 1991. Financed independently with $100 million from Polygram, Egg Pictures gave Foster total creative freedom to act, direct, or produce her own projects; a unique position for a female star in Hollywood. Meanwhile, she proved her ability in more traditional roles for a Hollywood leading lady—as the heroine of a romantic costume drama, *Sommersby* (1993), and, more surprisingly, as a Southern belle in *Maverick* (1994), a comedy-Western, with Mel Gibson.

Foster is not a conventional Hollywood beauty. She is, as B. Ruby Rich (1991) said, 'someone whose guts showed on her face'. In the 1990s she seemed to find a balance between strength and fragility, and more importantly has managed to avoid being defined solely in terms of sexuality. In an era of manufactured heroines, Jodie Foster is one of the few women in Hollywood who has managed, at least in part, to carve out her own destiny.

KATE BEETHAM

SELECT FILMOGRAPHY

Alice Doesn't Live Here Anymore (1974); Taxi Driver (1976); Bugsy Malone (1976); Freaky Friday (1976); The Little Girl who Lived down the Lane (1976); Candleshoe (1977); Carny (1980); The Hotel New Hampshire (1984); Five Corners (1987); Stealing Home (1988); The Accused (1988); The Silence of the Lambs (1991); Little Man Tate (also director, 1991); Sommersby (1993); Maverick (1994); Home from the Holidays (as director, 1995)

BIBLIOGRAPHY

Rich, B. Ruby (1991), 'Nobody's Handmaid'.

Opposite: Jodie Foster behind the camera in her first feature as director, *Little Man Tate* (1991)

running both network and cable channels, rapidly became one of the most important in the USA. Fox also produced television programmes like *LA Law* and feature films like *Home Alone* (1990) which pushed millions of dollars into News Incorporated's coffers.

Disney, which had achieved the status of a major with the establishment of its distribution arm, Buena Vista, in 1953, also underwent a radical expansion in the 1980s. A new management team, led by Michael Eisner and Jeffrey Katzenberg, both from Paramount, fashioned a fresh role for Disney. The company took bold steps, making 'R'-rated adult films through new releasing subsidiaries Touchstone and Hollywood Pictures, and opening theme parks in Japan and France. The Disney cable channel consistently made money targeting its youthful audiences and their parents; it made *Golden Girls* for NBC-TV, and syndicated *Siskel & Ebert* to television stations around the USA. By the late 1980s, Disney could even lay claim to being the top studio operation in Hollywood by signing off-beat talents to exclusive deals, and producing *Three Men and a Baby* (1987) and *Dead Poets Society*.

During the 1980s the fortunes of Columbia Pictures suffered, even as its owner, mighty Coca-Cola, tried to bring research-oriented, marketing philosophies to bear on the movie business. Despite skilful attempts at cross-promotional advertisements (e.g. Diet Coke and the 1987 film *Roxanne*), Coke was unable to produce a regular supply of blockbusters, and in October 1989 the Sony Corporation paid more than $3 billion for Columbia. A massive multinational experiment was on; could Sony use Columbia films to sell its new 8 mm. VAR?

New viewing venues and ownership questions aside, the majors' power continued to derive from their unique ability to distribute films internationally. At considerable expense, they maintained offices in nearly 100 cities around the world where their representatives were in constant contact with the heads of the dominant theatre chains. Only Hollywood regularly offered a 'hit parade' at the box-office; producers of other nations continued to struggle to match the regularity of blockbuster production of Hollywood. Indeed, in the early 1990s, Hollywood grew more dominant as foreign nations abandoned their ailing film industries and turned to assisting their television production.

ON THE SCREEN

Ironically, in this age of Hollywood hegemony, its films were increasingly treated as art. The influential *New York Times* reviewed movies with a seriousness once reserved for dance and theatre, and specialist magazines heralded a new age of American cinema.

The 'new' Hollywood dates from the 1975 release of Steven Spielberg's *Jaws*, which marked the entry of a new, younger generation of Hollywood directors. Born in the

1940s, they had grown up with cinema, and had a passion for the films of classical Hollywood, but also had studied and were influenced by the masters of foreign cinema. For example, both Spielberg (on *Jaws*) and Lucas (on *Star Wars*) consciously modelled the pace and look of their blockbusters on Kurosawa's classic *The Seven Samurai*. Francis Ford Coppola proved with *The Godfather* (1972) that remaking Hollywood genres from the past, with the influence of art cinema, could also mean millions and millions of dollars. George Lucas and Steven Spielberg followed Coppola's lead, making blockbusters, and in the process virtually taking over Hollywood. *Jaws* and *Star Wars* correctly anticipated a return to classic principles. Indeed the very basis of the success of 'New' Hollywood was the regular production of genre films; those that could be most easily packaged, and sold on a mass scale to audiences around the world.

The return to genre production in Hollywood can partly be seen as a response by producers to the increase in budget sizes, and the related risk involved with blockbuster production. Elements of a film that have already been market tested, or on which a film can be marketed, become crucial in this climate (this is also why certain stars commanded such enormous fees). Central to this trend was the sequel. By 1990 there had been five *Rocky*s, four *Superman*s, five *Halloween*s, and eight *Friday the 13th*s. Indeed, *Superman* was originally conceived as two films— an original (1978) plus a sequel (1980). Successful films also generated whole genre cycles. The gangster film (from *The Godfather*) and the horror film (from *The Exorcist*, 1973) produced dozens of spin-offs. In the late 1970s monsters arose in every possible form: werewolves in Joe Dante's *The Howling* (1980) and John Landis's *An American Werewolf in London* (1981); vampires in John Badham's *Dracula* (1979) and Tony Scott's *The Hunger* (1983); and zombies in George Romero's *Dawn of the Dead* (1979) and in John Carpenter's *The Fog* (1979). Hollywood sought a follow-up that matched the box-office power of the original.

Aimed directly at teenage audiences, who made up an increasing share of box-office revenue, were an ever-growing number of 'coming-of-age' filmic parables. Over and over Hollywood movies portrayed teenagers trying to convince a sceptical adult world to take them seriously. It was Lucas's *American Graffiti* (1973) that spawned this new set of films. Reformulated from the comic books and Hollywood serials of his youth, Lucas's portrait of the day and night before the hero goes off to college was a winner at the box-office. Produced by Coppola, with its sound-track of rock'n'roll songs from a decade earlier, *American Graffiti* boosted the careers of Harrison Ford, Ron Howard, and Richard Dreyfuss. It made Universal a great deal of money and made Lucas a force in contemporary Hollywood.

Myths could come from the distant past as well.

Through the mid-1980s, every summer brought a new sword-and-sorcery blockbuster, from John Boorman's *Excalibur* (1981) to John Milius's *Conan the Barbarian* (1981) and its follow-up, *Conan the Destroyer* (1982). George Lucas and Steven Spielberg teamed up to create the mythic adventures of a twentieth-century archaeologist battling evil forces from the past in the phenomenally successful *Raiders of the Lost Ark* series.

Comedy was also transformed and recrafted for the teenage audience, often combined with a 'coming-of-age' narrative. For every comic romance with a light touch, such as John Hughes's *Pretty in Pink* (1986) or Paul Brickman's *Risky Business* (1983), there have been many more based on the broadest possible humour, such as *Rock 'n' Roll High School* (1979), *Fast Times at Ridgemont High* (1982), and *The Breakfast Club* (1985). Inspired by the antics of NBC-TV's *Saturday Night Live*'s 'Not Ready for Prime Time Players' (including John Belushi, Dan Aykroyd, and Bill Murray), nothing was too obvious to become the source of a 'new' comedy. The movie that revitalized this genre, John Landis's *National Lampoon's Animal House* (1978), offered an irreverent anti-intellectual look at university life with Belushi as Bluto and his Delta 'frat' buddies deciding to disrupt the homecoming parade in one final 'really futile, stupid gesture'. In the final credits (which also serve to update the lives of the characters), we learn that Bluto became a United States Senator. That one credit seemed to sum up the new Hollywood comedy's ever hip, ever cynical attitude toward the official adult world.

These films with slapstick humour share traits with the science-fiction and adventure films noted above. Both demand that we suspend our belief about the 'real' world; any physical and social act seems possible, and the world, past and present, becomes a playground for fun. At times this reaches surrealistic heights as in *Cheech & Chong's Next Movie* (1980), *The Blues Brothers* (1980), *Bill and Ted's Excellent Adventure* (1989), and *Wayne's World* (1992).

AMERICAN AUTEURS

If George Lucas and (to a degree) Steven Spielberg are now best known for their successes as movie producers, there have been many contemporary directors who have stuck to directing. Probably the most famous *auteur* film-maker in the 1980s, at least to the general public, has been Woody Allen. Allen achieved film-making distinction first as a star, then as director. Audiences loved his neurotic humour in *Love and Death* (1975), the Oscar-winning *Annie Hall* (1977), the black and white *Manhattan* (1979), and as the 'human chameleon' in *Zelig* (1983). Allen has also made more self-consciously serious films, such as *Interiors* (1978) and *Stardust Memories* (1980), loosely based on Ingmar Bergman's *Cries and Whispers* (1972) and Federico Fellini's $8\frac{1}{2}$ (1963) respectively.

Critics have cited *Annie Hall*, released the same year as

Diane Keaton and Woody Allen in *Manhattan* (1979)

Star Wars, as the first major Woody Allen-as-*auteur* film. Collaborating with screen-writer Marshall Brickman and cinematographer Gordon Willis, Allen created an autobiographical work which, through its meta-narrative filmic devices, stands apart from his earlier comic efforts. Subtitles reveal what is really going on; a superimposed Annie watches herself and Alvie (the Woody Allen character) make love; and a split screen shows Gentile and Jewish family dinner scenes. Since then, Woody Allen and his collaborators have tried many ways to express intellectual concerns to a mass audience. *Interiors*, in which Allen does not appear, is a serious study of human psychology, family life, the influence of one's mother, and the attempt to deal with the real world. *Manhattan* marked Allen's return to the New York Jewish milieu with which he is most associated, and, as *Bullets over Broadway* (1994) proved, there continued to be a large international audience for his work in the 1990s.

Martin Scorsese, a graduate of New York University's School of Cinema, seemed to offer the flip side of Woody Allen's nostalgic rendering of life in New York City. Scorsese established his critical reputation with *Mean Streets* (1973), an autobiographical work concerned with four Italian-American youths coming of age in modern cities in the United States, struggling with traditional values and modern economics. He went on to make the critically acclaimed (if not always financially successful) *Taxi Driver* (1976), *Raging Bull* (1980), and *King of Comedy* (1982).

While Allen has enjoyed a unique relationship with a major Hollywood studio—total creative control over his productions (first at United Artists, and then at Orion)—Scorsese has had a much more uneven (and more typical) time. He suffered several box-office disasters, notably his ambitious musical *New York, New York* (1977), and despite his high critical reputation had to fight hard to get his projects funded. In the contemporary Hollywood system, talented directors cannot simply rest on past laurels. *Star Wars* is an ever-growing memory, while duds like *Howard the Duck* (1986) remind Hollywood's chieftains that even George Lucas can make very expensive mistakes. Spielberg's amazing 1993 successes, *Jurassic Park* and *Schindler's List*, have given him an aura of infallibility, but even he has had his failures; *1941* (1979) proved a financial disaster for Universal, and his television series *Amazing Stories* proved a flop.

With no film-maker or star ever able to guarantee a film's success, Hollywood continues to play it conservatively. The studios look to formula for the future, whether in the form of sequels or, increasingly, remakes—of old Hollywood films (*Always*, 1989), French mainstream dramas (*Sommersby*, 1993; *Three Men and a Baby*, 1987), or popular television series (*The Fugitive*, 1992; *The Addams Family*, 1991; *The Flintstones*, 1994).

HOLLYWOOD ABROAD

The international market is central to the profits of the studios in 'New' Hollywood. Blockbusters, such as *Fatal Attraction* (1987), *Rain Man* (1988), and *Cocktail* (1988), all grossed more money overseas than in theatres in the United States, and stars such as Arnold Schwarzenegger, Sylvester Stallone, and Eddie Murphy are able to command multimillion-dollar salaries, in part because of their international appeal. Hollywood moguls are concerned about the possible volatility of international film markets, and this has led, in recent years, to joint deals between Hollywood and foreign companies to build theatres in Great Britain, Australia, Germany, Spain, and France, even in major cities across the former Soviet Union. In Britain alone, Hollywood companies (led by MCA's Cineplex Odeon) helped sponsor the construction of more movie screens than had been seen in a generation. This move back towards total vertical integration is seen as an ideal way for studios to protect their interests abroad and maximize their profits.

Some nations have been able to deal with the influx of Hollywood product by offering their own, culturally identifiable, genre films. In India, for example, a remarkable 250 film-making companies, using more than 60 studios, continued to produce 700 feature films a year throughout the 1980s. The central government encouraged the making of Indian films by requiring all commercial cinemas to screen at least one Indian film per show. The government also offered grants, loans, and a system of prizes to reward the 'best' films. A star system, much like Hollywood's of the 1930s and 1940s, continued to be strong. Indeed Indian stars work on several productions at the same time and can become enormously wealthy.

Other Asian countries have also been strong producers of film. Hong Kong, a country of only 5 million people, produces more films than Hollywood. Into the 1990s Hong Kong's citizens watched Hollywood and native productions in about equal numbers, and in the 1980s Hong Kong martial arts films were distributed world-wide in large numbers (often straight on to video).

Given the rise of cable and satellite broadcasting, Hollywood's ability to penetrate even these markets seems inevitable, and its future limitless. Throughout most of the world, Hollywood film-makers and stars, such as Steven Spielberg and Arnold Schwarzenegger, have become the cultural idols of a generation. With the economic stranglehold of Hollywood corporations and the return to classical principles of film-making and genres, the 'New' Hollywood looks (and functions) remarkably like the 'old' Hollywood.

Bibliography
Bart, Peter (1990), *Fade Out*.
Gomery, Douglas (1992), *Shared Pleasures*.
Lees, David, and Berkowitz, Stan (1981), *The Movie Business*.
Pye, Michael, and Myles, Lynda (1979), *The Movie Brats*.
Squire, Jason E. (ed.) (1992), *The Movie Business Book*.

E.T. prepares to return home in Steven Spielberg's simple tale of a cute alien. It became the biggest grossing film of all time, not to be surpassed until *Jurassic Park* more than a decade later

New Technologies

JOHN BELTON

CINEMA AND TELEVISION

In January 1950 the Society of Motion Picture Engineers, an organization which had been founded in 1916 and which was dedicated to 'the advancement in the theory and practice of motion picture engineering', changed its name to the Society of Motion Picture and Television Engineers. In doing so, the Society both acknowledged and anticipated the changes that were taking (and would take) place in post-war entertainment technology.

Television would, of course, become an increasingly powerful presence in leisure-time activities. As the number of home receivers skyrocketed in the early 1950s (from 4 million in 1950 to 32 million in 1954 in the United States alone), more and more people traded their movie-going habit in for a home-viewing habit. However, 'television' means more than the familiar broadcasting of TV signals and reception on home TV sets. It also encompasses a broad array of other electronic recording, transmission, and playback technologies. Broadly understood, television includes any technology involving electronic signal encoding. If not in name, the SMPE had been the SMPTE in fact since the mid-1920s, when it helped to engineer the transition to sound, expanding its interests to include radio, electrical recording, signal amplification, and other electronic technologies.

In a sense, stereo magnetic sound, in which electronic signals are recorded on magnetic tape, is a television technology. More properly, television is a *sound* technology, evolving out of radio, electronic transmission, and other sound-related technologies. It is clear that the two technologies are closely interrelated. It is no accident that film sound expert Ray Dolby, an American physics student at Cambridge who founded Dolby Laboratories in London in 1965, was, as an undergraduate at Stanford, a central figure in the development of the Ampex videotape recorder (1956). At Dolby Labs in London, Dolby developed a crucial noise reduction system for sound recording (c.1966). Later, at Dolby Labs in San Francisco, he introduced a four-track, optical stereo sound-on-film system (Dolby SVA, 1975); a six-track, 70 mm. magnetic format; a spectral recording system (Dolby SR, 1986), as well as a digital sound technology in 1991.

In short, motion picture technology is necessarily bound up with television technology, especially in the present era. The major technological events that have occurred in the aftermath of the widescreen revolution of the 1950s have been the so-called 'second coming' of sound ushered in by Dolby in the mid-1970s and the influence of video on film production (High Definition Tele-

vision, editing on video), distribution (cable, videotape, and disc), and exhibition (home video).

SOUND

The attempts by 20th Century–Fox to innovate and diffuse stereo magnetic sound in the 1950s failed, largely because small and independent exhibitors refused to install the necessary equipment. However, large urban theatres continued to run CinemaScope films in four-track, magnetic stereo, as well as 70 mm. films, made in Todd-AO, Super Panavision 70, Ultra Panavision 70, and other wide film processes which featured six-track, stereo magnetic sound. The 70 mm. blockbuster dominated the market-place in the 1960s. It included films such as *Ben-Hur* (MGM Camera 65, 1959), *Spartacus* (Super Technirama 70, 1960), *West Side Story* (Super Panavision 70, 1961), *Lawrence of Arabia* (Super Panavision 70, 1962), *Cleopatra* (Todd-AO, 1963), *The Sound of Music* (Todd-AO, 1965), and *2001: A Space Odyssey* (Super Panavision 70/Super Cinerama, 1968).

The multi-track stereo sound in 70 mm. houses was dramatically better than that in the average movie theatre and better than that which most audiences could hear at home on their FM radios and record players, which, for most consumers, were monaural. But home sound systems gradually began to improve. In 1948 Columbia Records had started to release high-fidelity $33\frac{1}{3}$ r.p.m. longplaying records. By the mid-1950s, a number of audiophiles owned high-end, reel-to-reel stereo tape players.

But home stereo did not begin to secure a foothold in the market-place until 1957, when the American record industry began to release (two-track) stereo records. Within a few years, stereo recordings (of largely classical music) were being produced for home listeners in the United States and Europe. By 1961 a handful of American FM stations began to broadcast radio programmes in stereo. The allocation of space to potential broadcasters on the FM bandwidth was initially limited; the American Federal Communications Commission did not open up the FM spectrum until 1964. Even so, FM and FM stereo remained limited phenomena until the 1970s. By 1969, all music, both classical and popular, had gone from mono to stereo; and improvements in home stereo systems had filtered down from the audiophile to the average consumer. As Steve Handzo notes (1985), 'by the early 1970s there was a better sound system in the average American teen-ager's bedroom than there was in the neighborhood theatre.'

Dolby Stereo brought high-fidelity, four-track stereo sound within the financial reach of the average neighbourhood theatre and rapidly developed trade-name rec-ognition among general audiences. Dolby's involvement with motion picture sound began in 1971, when a Dolby noise reduction system designed to reduce tape hiss was used in the recording and rerecording of Stanley Kubrick's *A Clockwork Orange*. Between 1975, when Dolby's four-track optical stereo format was introduced, and 1988 over 11,000 theatres world-wide were equipped for Dolby Stereo.

In 1975 Dolby's stereo optical system was introduced with the release of *Tommy*. For the first time since Cinema-Scope, four-track stereo accompanied a 35 mm. film. But unlike CinemaScope, Dolby's stereo tracks could be optically printed at the same time that the film itself was printed, avoiding the costly process of magnetic striping and of transferring the sound to the various magnetic tracks. Dolby's optical stereo also enjoyed the advantage of being compatible with non-stereo projection equipment, which could play the prints monaurally.

But it was the success of *Star Wars* in 1977, which fea-tured an elaborate and spectacular sound design, that made Dolby a household name. Dolby SVA (Stereo Variable Area) sound upgraded the low end of the exhibition market-place. At the high end, Dolby perfected a six-track 70 mm. system that incorporated an extended bass response that transformed 70 mm. showings of *Star Wars* into multi-sensory events.

Star Wars was filmed in 35 mm. Panavision and blown up to 70 mm. for roadshow exhibition. The practice of 70 mm. blow-ups from 35 mm. began in 1963 with the release of Otto Preminger's *The Cardinal* and effectively ended the original filming of motion pictures in more costly, wide film (65 mm.) formats. Original photography in 65/70 mm. effectively ceased in 1970 with the release of *Ryan's Daugh-ter*, which was filmed in Super Panavision 70. However, Soviet film-makers continued to use 70 mm. (Sovscope 70), as did the makers of films for Imax and Omnimax theatres. In addition to *Tron* (1982) and *Brainstorm* (1983), *Far and Away* (1992) was filmed in 65 mm. Blow-ups permitted producers to film on less expensive 35 mm. stock and to decide during post-production whether or not to blow the film up for roadshow release. Unfortunately, blow-ups to 70 mm. fail to duplicate the aspect ratio of the original 35 mm. negative, cropping the sides of 2.35 : 1 anamorphic images down to 2.21 : 1.

The success of *Star Wars* in Dolby Stereo (in 35 mm. and in 70 mm.) led hundreds of exhibitors to convert to Dolby. In 1977, there were only 100 Dolby-equipped theatres; a year later, there were 450; by 1981, there were 2,000, and by 1990 over 16,000 world-wide (with 10,000 in North America alone). When magnetic tape was challenged by compact discs using digital recording in the mid-1980s, Dolby engineered a dramatic improvement in the circuit functions used in magnetic recording technology to increase signal purity and to reduce noise and distortion.

Dolby dubbed the process spectral recording (Dolby SR) and successfully introduced it into the film industry in 1986, effectively forestalling for several years the seem-ingly inevitable shift to digital sound recording. By 1990, over 43,000 recording studios and broadcast facilities around the world had installed the Dolby SR system.

Digital sound in motion pictures remains at the exper-imental stage. In the late-1980s Eastman Kodak, together with Optical Radiation Corp., pioneered a short-lived optical digital sound system, called Cinema Digital Sound, that was unveiled with the release of *Edward Scissorhands* (1990) and *Dick Tracy* (1990). Digital technology enabled engineers to put six discrete channels of sound on a 35 mm. print, potentially enabling exhibitors who lacked 70 mm. equipment to provide a six-track stereo sound that could be comparable to that in 70 mm. houses. Unfor-tunately, Cinema Digital Sound necessitated the costly establishment of two release print inventories—one for analog optical and another for digital. And if the digital equipment malfunctioned, exhibitors would be unable to play the film.

In 1991, Dolby solved that problem by introducing an optical digital sound system, Dolby SR * D, which com-bined an analog optical track with a digital sound-track. More recently, Universal released *Jurassic Park* (1993) in 35 mm. in analog (optical) Dolby Stereo as well as in the studio's own new process, DTS (Digital Theatre Sound) Digital Stereo. All prints carried an optical stereo sound-track as well as an optical time code which enabled the film to be synced up to a separate CD player with compact discs carrying a digital stereo sound-track. If, for some reason, the separate six-track digital sound-track failed, the system would instantaneously switch to the analog four-track Dolby Stereo sound-track on the print.

ELECTRONICS AND SPECIAL EFFECTS

In the wake of *Star Wars* (1977), *Close Encounters of the Third Kind* (1977), *Star Trek: The Motion Picture* (1979), and other high-tech. science-fiction films, the art of special effects entered the space age. Special-effects work generally requires the exact matching of two or more separate film strips. In the 1950s and 1960s, this was accomplished by relying on precision matte work. Matte work involves the successful combination of two or more images by means of a masking device, which eliminates part of one image and substitutes part of another. However, the matching of the various motions of objects and characters in these multiple strips of film required painstaking and time-consuming labour. Even the most successful matte work often revealed matte lines, was difficult to light, and, as a result, seemed somewhat fake.

Computer technology dramatically improved the illusion of reality in motion picture special effects. A com-

Technicians at the Dolby laboratories mixing the stereo sound-track for *Apocolypse Now* (1979)

puter-operated motion control camera enabled film-makers to secure special effects footage in two 'passes', that is, in two shots. The first shot would contain the actor or central action and the second would have the same framing and camera movement as the first shot but would lack the actor or action. The computer records the camera's framing and movement and can exactly reproduce it in successive shots.

More recently, computers have been used to generate graphics or to provide the equivalent of matte shots without matte lines or other visible signs of artifice. The use of digital technology enables effects experts to transform a 35 mm. image into pixels, to replace certain pixels with those from another image, and to recompose the image. This technology was used extensively to animate the metamorphoses of the T-1000, liquid-metal man (Robert Patrick) in *Terminator 2: Judgment Day* (1991).

In 1983 the first machines designed for electronic post-production were introduced. The 35 mm. film to be edited would be printed with an SMPTE time code and transferred to videotape. Using a computer-driven Editdroid (or other brand-name electronic editing system), an editor could rapidly select shots, cut, and splice, assembling and rearranging the shots at will. The results could be instantly previewed and the various arrangements stored, along with original time code information, for subsequent review and selection. The SMPTE time code enabled editors to locate exact frames on the film and the video

copies; a central computer stored the precise time code information, which would be used in editing a 35 mm. film negative. Today, virtually all television programming originally shot on film is electronically edited. An increasing number of theatrical features rely upon this new technology. State-of-the-art 35 mm. motion picture cameras now feature SMPTE time code generators which place an optical time code on the negative during filming.

The development of High Definition Television has encouraged a handful of film-makers to experiment with the format, using it for original cinematography and post-production then transferring it to 35 mm. film for theatrical exhibition. More commonly, HDTV is used for filming and making special effects, largely because of the creative options it offers to film-makers in those areas. Internationally acclaimed animator Zbigniew Rybczynski, for example, relied on HDTV in the filming of *Kafka* (1992) in order to generate multiple images and to achieve virtually limitless camera movements. The majority of cinematographers, however, are reluctant to film in HDTV, insisting that it lacks the 'look' of 35 mm. motion picture film.

FORMATS

Satellite transmission, cable, and video have demonstrably transformed the distribution and exhibition of motion pictures, with an increasing number of viewers seeing films in the home. In 1975 Home Box Office began transmitting recent motion pictures and other entertainment programmes via satellite to cable subscribers, introducing a 'premium' service that augmented the 'basic' cable service (which consisted of the rebroadcast of network and local stations to subscribers in regions with poor reception) that had been in existence for several decades.

In 1977 Ted Turner turned to satellite transmission for his 'superstation', TBS, which broadcast old movies, sporting events, and other programmes. Shortly thereafter, Showtime (1978) and The Movie Channel (1979) entered the home movie channel market-place, joining forces in 1983. Similar developments took place in the late 1980s in Britain and Europe where Rupert Murdoch's BSkyB and a number of European competitors introduced satellite-delivered channels running movies, music videos, sports, and other entertainment programming.

The distribution of movies on videotape and disc, together with cable broadcast and pay-per-view, has changed the nature of the movie-going experience for most audiences, who now watch films in the comfort of their own homes. Home video technology has effectively eliminated second-run theatres, repertory cinemas, and porno houses. In certain markets, such as the United Kingdom, it has had a disastrous effect on first-run movie-going, with admissions falling from 143 million in 1974 to 53 million in 1984—though they have since recovered somewhat. It has also had an impact on the making of widescreen films, which, when seen on television screens, are routinely cropped or panned and scanned. Film-makers have, since 1961, learnt to protect their films from mutilation in the panning and scanning process by composing them for the television screen. They do this by keeping all narrative information in what cinematographers call the 'safe action' area, that is, that portion of the image that could fit on the average television screen. The advent (and limited popular acceptance) of letterboxing, which involves the use of masking above and below the image to preserve its original widescreen ratio, in the late 1980s and 1990s has tended to encourage film-makers to return to the notion that widescreen films should fully exploit the widescreen format.

Large format film-making continued after the demise of three-strip Cinerama (1963), one-strip Super Cinerama (1970), and 65 mm./70 mm. productions (c.1970) in the form of special presentation formats, such as Showscan, Imax, Omnimax, and other 70 mm. systems. Developed by special-effects artist Douglas Trumbull, Showscan (c.1984) is a 70 mm. system in which images are photographed and projected at 60 frames per second (the standard rate is 24 frames per second). The high speed results in an extremely steady, sharp, and detailed image. Several dozen shorts have been made in the process for exhibition at special theatres located at tourist destinations around the world.

The Imax and Omnimax systems, launched at various expos, world fairs, and theme parks, also employ 65 mm./70 mm. film. The Imax process, introduced at Expo '70 in Osaka, Japan, relies on a 65 mm. camera in which the film moves at 24 frames per second *horizontally* (as in the VistaVision camera), exposing a frame that is fifteen perforations in length. This results in an image area that is roughly three times that of conventional 65 mm. camera systems. The projected Imax image, unlike standard wide-screen images (which range from 1.66 : 1 to 2.77 : 1), is taller than it is wide, possessing an aspect ratio of 1 : 1.43.

Omnimax, which was introduced at a planetarium in San Diego in 1973, is a related system (using the same camera and frame size) which employs an extremely wide-angled (a 180-degree fish-eye) lens in photography and which projects these images upon a concave dome-screen in the ceiling of the theatre. Subsequent developments of Imax technology resulted in Omnimax 3D (1985), Imax 3D (1986), Imax Solido (1990), and Imax Magic Carpet (1990).

Imax Solido is a 3-D system that projects a 70 mm. image on to an umbrella-shaped screen that is roughly 79 feet in diameter. Spectators wear battery-powered goggles filled with liquid-crystal diodes; the left and right lenses of the goggles open and close in synchronization with a pair of Imax projectors which show first the left-eye view and then the right-eye view of each frame.

Imax Magic Carpet relies on two Imax projectors and two large Imax screens, projecting one image on a screen in front of the audiences and another on a screen below the audience but visible through a transparent floor. Promotional copy suggested that it 'will make people feel as if they are floating in space—like the magic flying carpet of Arabian Nights'.

PORTABILITY

During the post-war era professional motion picture production equipment underwent a transformation. The 35 mm. cameras became lighter, more compact, and more portable. The lightweight Arriflex, which was developed in Germany in 1936, found its way into Hollywood production as early as 1945 (*Dark Passage*), though it did not enjoy widespread use until the 1960s. The Arriflex camera introduced an innovative reflex viewing system in which a mirrored shutter, which was set at a forty-five-degree angle to the plane of the lens, reflected the image as seen through the lens to the viewfinder. Today, virtually all motion picture cameras employ an Arriflex-style, reflex viewing system. Éclair's 35 mm. Cameflex camera, developed in France in 1947, was used extensively by French film-makers during the New Wave, perhaps most influentially by Jean-Luc Godard and Raoul Coutard on À bout de souffle (1959).

Lightweight cameras ultimately permitted greater mobility and flexibility in 35 mm. film-making. By the

Raoul Coutard

(1924–)

'No more confectionery. We're going to shoot in real light.' Jean-Luc Godard's injunction to Raoul Coutard, the cinematographer on his début film *À bout de souffle* (1959), signalled the arrival of the Nouvelle Vague, with a *cinéma-vérité* style consciously opposed to the aesthetic of the traditional French *cinéma de qualité*.

Coutard and Godard were brought together by Georges de Beauregard. He had produced the three Pierre Schoendoerffer documentaries which featured Coutard as chief camera operator, and would later produce many of Godard's films. As Godard's *opérateur-fétiche*, Coutard collaborated with the director on thirteen films up to 1967, and contributed to their influential aesthetic style.

Coutard's background was in photojournalism, having worked as a correspondent for *Paris-Match* and *Life* magazines in Indo-China between 1945 and 1950. His early work as an assistant camera operator was in documentary films for the French Ministry of Information. He carried a documentary aesthetic over into his feature work. His use of hand-held cameras, natural light, and film stocks normally reserved for photojournalism ideally suited the Nouvelle Vague location-based shooting practices. Coutard worked on films across the *nouvelle vague* canon, from the marginal but highly influential *Chronique d'un été* (Jean Rouch and Edgar Morin, 1961) to Jacques Demy's *Lola* (1961) and four Truffaut films including *Tirez sur le pianiste* (1960) and *Jules et Jim* (1961).

In the 1970s Coutard proved adept at producing a more conventional style for a series of mainstream French films, which he alternated with shooting television commercials and directing his own features. *Hoa-Binh* (1970), filmed in Vietnam, won the Prix Jean Vigo, although the film was criticized for its political ambiguity, and Coutard lambasted for his claim that war might be considered as aesthetically 'beautiful'. He returned to his documentary origins with *La Légion saute sur Kolwezi* (1979), a chronicle of a military operation in Africa, and was re-united with Godard in the mid-1980s for two films, *Prénom Carmen* (1983) and *Passion* (1985).

CHRIS DARKE

SELECT FILMOGRAPHY

As cinematographer
À bout de souffle (Godard, 1959); Tirez sur le pianiste (Truffaut, 1960); Lola (Demy, 1961); Jules et Jim (Truffaut, 1961); Une femme est une femme (Godard, 1961); Chronique d'un été (Rouch, 1961); Vivre sa vie (Godard, 1962); Le Mépris (Godard, 1963); La Peau douce (Truffaut, 1964); Une femme mariée (Godard, 1964); Alphaville (Godard, 1965); Pierrot le fou (Godard, 1965); Made in USA (Godard, 1966); Weekend (Godard, 1967); The Confession (Costa-Gavras, 1969); Hoa-Binh (script and director, 1970); Prénom Carmen (Godard, 1983); Passion (Godard, 1985)

BIBLIOGRAPHY

Coutard, Raoul (1966), 'Light of Day'.
Russell, Sharon A. (1981), *Semiotics and Lighting: A Study of Six Modern French Cameramen*.

Raoul Coutard with Anouk Aimée on the set of Jacques Demy's *Lola* (1961)

Setting up the famous penultimate shot of Antonioni's *The Passenger* (*Professione: Reporter*, 1974) in which the camera is transferred on to an exterior crane after passing through the narrow bars of a window

1970s, more and more professional cameras were light enough to be carried by a single operator, but hand-held camerawork remained somewhat intrusive in Hollywood films because it was less steady than traditional camera supports. However, in European and other non-Hollywood films, such as Mikhail Kalatozov's *Ya ... Cuba* (*I am Cuba!*, 1963), hand-held cameras served to foreground authorial presence.

In 1976 camera operator Garrett Brown perfected the Steadicam, a camera-stabilizing system. The Steadicam was a rig which was worn by operators and which enabled them to move the camera fluidly through space without shakes, jiggles, or jitters. The Steadicam, which was first used to film certain sequences in *Rocky* (1976), freed the motion picture camera from traditional camera supports, such as cranes, dollies, tracks, and platforms, which restricted its movement. At the same time it reduced production cost by eliminating the need for extra camera crew members to move dollies and for the time-consuming laying of tracks. The Steadicam was used extensively in the filming of Stanley Kubrick's *The Shining* (1980), where it effectively simulated the movement of a child's tricycle as it raced down empty hotel corridors.

Both Arriflex and Éclair (as well as Auricon) also manu-

factured lightweight 16 mm. cameras, which played a major role in the development of documentary film-making in the 1960s and later. (16 mm. film had been introduced by Eastman Kodak in 1923 for amateur, home movie-making; it was used by combat photographers in the Second World War and by documentary and avant-garde film-makers after the war; however, it was not until the development of these new lightweight cameras in the late 1950s and early 1960s that 16 mm. achieved major significance as a format for professional film-making.) This new technology served as the basis for a new school of film-making. The Éclair NPR, which weighed only 19 lb., became a staple of *cinéma-vérité* film-makers, such as Jean Rouch and Edgar Morin (*Chronique d'un été* ('Chronicle of a summer'), 1961) and Chris Marker (*Le Joli Mai* ('Lovely May'), 1963). In the United States, 16 mm. Auricon cameras served as the basis of the 'direct cinema' movement, which was centred around the work of Richard Leacock, D. A. Pennebaker, and Albert Maysles. Together they made *Primary* (1960), a documentary about the 1960 Democratic presidential primary in Wisconsin. Leacock and Pennebaker also shot *Happy Mother's Day* (1963–4) with an Auricon, while Albert Maysles, working with his brother David, made *Showman* (1962) using the same equipment.

Other crucial elements of this new motion picture technology included the portable Nagra tape recorder, which permitted sync-sound recording, and the zoom lens. Developed by the Swiss inventor Stefan Kudelski in 1959, the Nagra recorded sync sound monaurally on to Quarter-inch magnetic tape and was fully portable, weighing only 14 lb. Previous magnetic sound systems recorded sound on 17.5 mm. and 35 mm. sprocketed film or on Quarter-inch tape but were not portable, weighing from fifty to several hundred pounds. Though most commercial productions, especially films made on the sound stages of elaborately equipped studios, continued to use the heavier equipment, documentary film-makers immediately adopted this new equipment, which enabled them to make sync-sound films inexpensively on location.

THE ZOOM

A primitive zoom lens had been developed in England and the United States in the late 1920s; it was used for individual, 'special effects' shots in a handful of films (for example, in *Love Me Tonight* (1932) the camera zooms in on a Parisian window in the film's opening 'city symphony' sequence). The first modern zoom lens was perfected in 1946 by Dr Frank Back, who marketed it as the Zoomar lens. Unlike traditional lenses which possess only one focal length, the zoom lens was a varifocal lens, which meant that it had a variety of different focal lengths ranging from wide angle to normal to telephoto. This enabled it to cover events in ways that were difficult, if not impossible, for a fixed focal length lens. Events (such as baseball games) that previously required several cameras outfitted with different focal length lenses to ensure continuous coverage of action taking place at different distances from a central point (or multi-camera set-up) could now be filmed with a single camera equipped with a zoom lens that could zoom in to a close up or zoom out to a wide shot.

In 1963 the French company Angénieux marketed a zoom lens that could move through a range of focal lengths from 12 mm. to 120 mm., dramatically improving on the narrower zoom ratios (17.5 mm. to 70 mm.) of earlier zoom lenses. Zoom lenses, which could be used for zooming or as 'fixed' focal-length lenses, became the primary (or only) lenses for many *cinéma-vérité* and direct cinema film-makers, as well as for certain 'fiction' film-makers such as Roberto Rossellini (*The Rise to Power of Louis XIV* (*La Prise de pouvoir par Louis XIV*), 1966; *L'età di Cosimo de'Medici* ('The age of Cosimo de'Medici'), 1972). In the 1960s zoom lenses were routinely the only lenses mounted on Super 8, home movie-making cameras. And today, most video cameras, from studio cameras to camcorders, come with zoom lenses. By the 1970s the zoom lens, which was primarily used either in conjunction with conventional camera movement or as a 'fixed' focal-length lens, had

become a staple of commercial film-making throughout the world. During the early 1970s film-makers experimented with rapid zooms from one extreme focal length to another (*The Strawberry Statement*, 1970), shots which awkwardly called attention to the new technology. By the late 1970s and early 1980s, film-makers had abandoned 'extreme' zoom shots for more moderate zooms, which often functioned in conjunction with actual camera movements to extend them by a few feet.

AMATEUR AND EXPERIMENTAL FILM-MAKING

In many ways, amateur film-making serves as a site of intersection for the development of new film technology and of new film-making practices. Documentary and avant-garde film-making, for example, not only depend upon but are empowered by this new technology. A majority of film-makers in the post-war era relied on relatively inexpensive 16 mm. equipment to make and exhibit films. Although the 8 mm. format, which was introduced in 1932, was primarily used by amateurs in the making of home movies, one or two film-makers appropriated this technology to make avant-garde or documentary films. Stan Brakhage, for example, began as a 16 mm. film-maker (*Anticipation of the Night*, 1958; *Window Water Baby Moving*, 1959), but then made a series of experimental films in 8 mm. (*Songs 1–30*, 1964–9), as did Saul Levine (*Breaking Time, Parts 1–4*, 1978–83) and Marjorie Keller (*By Twos and Threes: Women*, 1974). Among the most famous images in the world is the documentary footage of John F. Kennedy's assassination in Dallas in 1963, shot on 8 mm. by an amateur photographer named Abe Zapruder.

The great majority of avant-garde and experimental film-makers, however, worked in 16 mm., which continued, following Maya Deren's pioneering work in the 1940s (*Meshes of the Afternoon*, 1943; *Ritual in Transfigured Time*, 1946), to serve as the dominant exhibition standard for film artists well into the 1970s. Major 16 mm. film-makers included Brakhage (*Mothlight*, 1963; *Dog Star Man*, 1961–4), Peter Kubelka (*Unsere Afrikareise* ('Our trip to Africa'), 1966), Jonas Mekas (*Reminiscences of a Journey to Lithuania*, 1972), Michael Snow (*Wavelength*, 1967), Andy Warhol (*Sleep*, 1963), Hollis Frampton (*Zorns Lemma*, 1970), Kenneth Anger (*Scorpio Rising*, 1964), and others. Midway between the mainstream and the underground, John Cassavetes filmed both *Shadows* (1960) and *Faces* (1968) in 16 mm., blowing them up to 35 mm. for commercial distribution.

In 1965 a new amateur format called Super 8 was introduced. By reducing the size of the perforations and increasing the height of the frame, Super 8 was able to provide 50 per cent more image area than standard 8, thus producing a larger, brighter, and sharper image when projected. (A related development took place in regard to 16 mm. formats when Super 16 mm., which had 40 per

cent more image area than standard 16 mm., was introduced in 1970–1, offering film-makers a relatively inexpensive format that facilitated blow-ups to 35 mm.) In
some instances, Super 8 was used as a simple recording
device by performance artists, such as Vito Acconci, who
captured a number of his 'acts' on Super 8 (e.g. *See Through*,
1970). Manuel DeLanda used Super 8 to compose a portrait
of New York City street life (*Harmful or Fatal if Swallowed*,
1975–80) and to document his own spray-painted graffiti
(*Ismism*, 1977–9).

When Super 8 sound cameras were introduced in 1974,
several former 8 mm. artists, such as Saul Levine (*Notes of
an Early Fall*, 1976; *Bopping the Great Wall of China Blue*, 1979),
switched to Super 8 sound. But the format also spawned
a new generation of artists, such as the Filipino film-maker
Raymond Red (*Pelikula*, 1985), punk feminist Vivienne Dick
(*Guerillere Talks*, 1978; *Beauty Becomes the Beast*, 1979), Ericka
Beckman (*We Imitate: We Break-up*, 1978; *Out of Hand*, 1980),
and Beth B and Scott B, whose *The Offenders* (1978–9)
achieved the status of an underground punk classic.

Though a number of film-makers, like the Bs (*Vortex*,
1982), moved up from Super 8 to 16 mm., many film-
makers continue to work in Super 8, ultimately transferring their films to video for distribution and exhibition.
Taking advantage of the cheapness and flexibility of
amateur equipment, British director Derek Jarman (*The
Tempest*, 1979; *The Last of England*, 1987) often shot his orig-

inal cinematography on Super 8. The image quality was
good enough to enable him to transfer this footage to 1"
video, to transfer it to 35 mm. where it was intercut with
footage originally shot in 35 mm., and to release his films
theatrically in 35 mm.

Video technology continues to become increasingly
important in the production of commercial motion pictures. Within the next few years, more and more films are
likely to be shot on HDTV. And, in the area of exhibition, an
increasing number of films will undoubtedly be released
simultaneously to theatres and to home viewers via pay-
per-view cable transmission. But, despite all these
changes, for the immediate future, the 35 mm. motion
picture format introduced more than 100 years ago by
Thomas Edison (and his assistant W. K. L. Dickson) remains
the medium of record.

Bibliography
Belton, John (1992), *Widescreen Cinema*.
Handzo, Stephen (1985), 'A Narrative Glossary of Film Sound Tech-
nology'.
Issari, Mohammad Ali, and Paul, Doris A. (1979), *What Is Cinema
Verite?*
Lipton, Lenny (1975), *The Super 8 Book*.
Salt, Barry (1992), *Film Style and Technology: History and Analysis*.
Souto, H. Mario Raimondo (1977), *The Technique of the Motion Picture
Camera*.

Sex and Sensation

LINDA WILLIAMS

In American movies before the 1960s, Hollywood's notorious Production Code dictated that characters got shot
without bleeding, argued without swearing, and had
babies without copulating. Censorship especially wreaked
havoc with plot and motivation in films which either
elided or occluded sexuality as an event in human life.
This is not to say that sexual desire did not circulate in
American films, but it was displaced: the objects of this
desire tended to be exotic, often European, *femmes fatales*—
unattainable, glamorous, female ideals like Garbo and
Dietrich whose bodies were always somehow distanced
from the desires they animated.

In Europe, and particularly Scandinavia, on the other
hand, sexual representations had always been comparatively less censored. French and Italian cinemas were
more open to the representation of adulterous, or otherwise 'illicit', liaisons which, if not explicitly shown, were
at least fully there in the narrative. Sexual desires were, for
example, fully ensconced as theme and motive in French

silent and sound films from Renoir's *Nana* (1926) to Max
Ophuls's grand French films of the 1950s, *La Ronde* ('Merry-
go-round', 1950), *Le Plaisir* ('Pleasure', 1952), and *Madame
de ...* (English title *The Earrings of Madame de ...*, 1953). In
Italy, where a certain earthiness had always prevailed,
motives had often been sexual. A telling example is Visconti's *Ossessione* ('Obsession', 1942), adapted from James
Cain's hard-boiled novel *The Postman Always Rings Twice*,
which portrayed the physical and material hungers of
provincial characters in a visceral way that the 1946 American film of the novel could not. In Italy, the return to
contemporary reality called for by neo-realism meant that
films as diverse as Rossellini's *Il miracolo* ('The miracle',
1948), De Santis's *Bitter Rice* (*Riso amaro*, 1948), and later
post-neorealist films such as De Sica's *Two Women* (1960)
and Fellini's *La dolce vita* (1960) would explore sexual
themes across a wide range of settings, from Anna Magnani's 'innocent' immaculate conception to Marcello Mastroianni's decline into decadent sexual play.

Despite these national differences, around 1960 many cinemas experienced, in the various renaissances and New Waves, a marked relaxation of whatever formal or informal censorships had previously been in place. Along with new styles and more independent modes of production, many national cinemas moved towards a new level of sexual explicitness, even a new sensationalism. In Europe this liberalization was less remarkable than in the USA. For example, Roger Vadim's *And God Created Woman* (*Et Dieu créa ... la femme*, 1956) caused a sensation with Brigitte Bardot's portrayal of a sexually experimenting lost soul on the French Riviera. Though not radically different from earlier French films about romantic liaisons, the film's youthful context, relatively large number of extended sex scenes, vivid colour, and widescreen format gave it a new urgency and impact—an impact that was not lost on the New Wave to come. One of the most important aspects of this New Wave was the prevalence of love stories in which what took place in the bedroom was as important as what took place everywhere else. Louis Malle's *Les Amants* (*The Lovers*, 1958) explored the tensions of a love affair between a younger man and a married woman; Alain Resnais's *Hiroshima mon amour* (1959) linked sexual desire, death, and the bomb; Truffaut's *Jules et Jim* (1961) explored the pitfalls of a triangular affair with the eternal feminine as its apex; Jean-Luc Godard's *Vivre sa vie* (*My Life to Live*, 1962) was a contemporary update on Zola's *Nana* that cast a clinical, analytical eye on the exchanges of money and sex.

In eastern Europe the relaxing of censorship coincided with the rise of alternative models of socialism and the end of Stalinism, eventually even the end of Communism. Not surprisingly the New Waves of these countries combined sexual expression with social critique. Films were sometimes banned—as was the Yugoslavian *The City* (*Grad*, 1963) for its reduction of life to what critics derided as senseless lust. But by the mid-1960s Serbian director Dušan Makaveyev had cleverly woven lust into a series of brilliant satires of sexual and social life, in his films *Switchboard Operator* (1967) and *W.R.: Mysteries of the Organism* (1968). In Czechoslovakia, a country of well-established film tradition and the place of origin of the famous *Extase* (*Ecstasy*, 1932), the early 1960s saw the arrival of an anti-Stalinist, anti-Socialist-Realist, sexual playfulness and anarchy, most notably in the films of Věra Chytilová, especially her surreal, exuberant study of two anarchistic women, *Sedmikrásky* (*Daisies*, 1966).

In Sweden a more Lutheran guilt seemed to dictate that sexuality would be used for somewhat bleaker purposes. Ingmar Bergman regularly used sexual representations to dramatize existential *angst* as, for example, in the famous rape scene in *The Virgin Spring* (*Jungfrukällen*, 1959), the masturbation scene in *The Silence* (*Tystnaden*, 1963), and the orgy description in *Persona* (1966).

In Hollywood, by contrast, the long history of a smooth functioning, self-censoring Production Code had so effectively banished the direct representation of sexual motive from narrative that, when such motives began to appear, they did so with all the vehemence of the return of the repressed. Challenge to the code had begun as early as Otto Preminger's *The Moon Is Blue* (1953), whose sexual language (even the tame words 'virgin' and 'mistress') prevented code approval. Further challenges continued with Preminger's *Advise and Consent* (1962), with a plot turning on the homosexuality of a member of Congress, and later with Mike Nichols's *Who's Afraid of Virginia Woolf* (1966), with a non-stop marital fight whose *coup de théâtre* was the revelation of a hysterical pregnancy.

Gerald Mast (1986) has argued that what was most distinctive about the post-Production Code New Hollywood was its particular use of sex and violence to cast a 'cynical look back on the genre films of old Hollywood'. To Mast it was the revision of the gangster genre, for example in *Bonnie and Clyde* (1967), or the Western, in *The Wild Bunch* (1969), *Butch Cassidy and the Sundance Kid* (1969), and *McCabe & Mrs. Miller* (1971), that best revealed the 'sensualization of a previously more externalized, active genre'. *Bonnie and Clyde* was perhaps most representative of the particularly American reintegration of sexual motives with its mix of both sex (a plot turning on male impotence and sexual release occasioned by bank robbery) and violence (the dramatic climax in an epoch-making slow-motion shoot-out of balletic beauty and spilled guts) in an elegiac revision of the gangster film.

Looking back today, however, on the changes wrought on Hollywood in the 1960s the film that seems most prescient is Alfred Hitchcock's *Psycho* (1960). It was derided in its time by critics for excesses of both sex and violence—as was its British companion, Michael Powell's less influential but perhaps equally symptomatic *Peeping Tom* (1960). In both these films sex functioned as the dirty secret, finally let out of the closet. Indeed, it might be possible to argue that Hitchcock's commercial success at exploiting this 'secret' despite initial critical disfavour was a crucial factor in determining the future sensationalism of sex and violence in American cinema, just as much as Powell's commercial failure closed off a similar avenue of representation in Britain. If today the excesses of *Psycho* seem tame, even predictable, it is because its mix of sex and violence became paradigmatic not only of a whole cycle of low-budget 'psycho-horror' but also of the high-budget erotic thriller: films like Brian De Palma's *Dressed to Kill* (1980), and more recent blockbusters like *Fatal Attraction* (1987) and *Basic Instinct* (1992).

Psycho represents an important turning-point in American film history: the moment when the experience of going to a mainstream film began to be constituted as a sexualized thrill; a sort of sado-masochistic roller-coaster

Brigitte Bardot
(1934–)

Brigitte Bardot is more than a French film star; she is a cultural phenomenon. From magazine covers, postcards, documentaries, and even songs, her image, as well as her nickname 'B.B.', are familiar to millions of people who have not seen a single one of her films. And yet, Bardot's impact comes from her embodiment of a certain idea of French womanhood in a few films in the late 1950s and early 1960s.

Bardot was born in the Parisian *haute bourgeoisie*. Her ballet training gave her a graceful posture which, combined with her sensational looks, led to a promising début in modelling. She married the photographer (later film-maker) Roger Vadim in 1952, and began her film career with small parts in comedies like *Le Trou normand* (1952) and costume dramas such as Clair's *Les Grandes Manoeuvres* (1955). Her sexual impact was still contained within these genres (as it was in the British *Doctor at Sea*, 1955), meshing with that of other 'starlets' such as Mylène Demongeot and Pascale Petit. It took the melodramatic *And God Created Woman* (*Et Dieu créa . . . la femme*, 1956), directed by Vadim, to turn her into a star. It has sometimes been claimed that this film presaged the New Wave, but beyond the location shooting (in Saint-Tropez, henceforth a major tourist attraction), it was a conventional story, traditionally shot. However, from the first image of her sunbathing naked, Bardot was launched as *the* female sexual myth of 1950s France, and a valuable export when international markets, especially Hollywood, craved the 'natural' sexuality of European actresses.

The dominant Bardot image popularized by *And God Created Woman* was that of the sex kitten, combining powerful, unruly sexuality with childish attributes: a lithe, youthful body with full breasts, long 'wild' hair—now and forever bleached—offset by a girlish fringe and often done up in a pony-tail. Her mature sexual power created havoc, yet she pouted, sulked, and giggled like a little girl. Her untrained, naturalistic acting (often much criticized), added authenticity to this potent mix. But after her spectacular breakthrough, she starred in unremarkable vehicles, professing a lack of interest in acting. Nevertheless, Autant-Lara's *En cas de malheur* ('My Love is my Profession', 1958), and Clouzot's courtroom drama *La Vérité* (1960), are fascinating testimonies to her cultural status in modern France; in both films her sexuality as well as her generation are simultaneously the object of fascination, and on trial. Malle's semi-biographical *Vie privée* (1962), and Godard's *Le Mépris* (1963), which in their different ways comment on, rather than feature, her image, signalled the end of her brief period of true filmic stardom. Her iconic status, however, endured.

Bardot was idolized. Her clothes (especially her gingham wedding dress for her second marriage, to Jacques Charrier in 1959) and hairstyle were copied by millions of women then, as they are by today's 'supermodels'; she modelled for Marianne, the effigy of the French Republic. But she was also viciously abused and attacked. The key to Bardot's impact is that she was both the archetypal object of male fantasies ('the impossible dream of married men', as Vadim put it), and a sort of female James Dean. Her guiltless pleasure in her own sexuality and assertive show of desire led Simone de Beauvoir to term her 'as much hunter as she is prey'. As such, she was an obvious, if unrealistic, figure of identification for young women in repressive 1950s France.

The limited 'shelf-life' of the purely sexual star is evident in the rapid decline of her career in the late 1960s and early 1970s. Apart from Malle's *Viva Maria!* (1965) and the funny pastiche Western *Les Pétroleuses* (*The Legend of Frenchy King*, 1971, directed by Christian-Jaque), her late films tend to degenerate into self-conscious soft pornography.

However, unlike her contemporary Monroe, and despite suicide attempts, Bardot had both stamina and business sense. She retired from acting and 'men' in 1973, a rich woman, going on to live in her various properties with numerous animals (although she did marry again, for the fourth time, in 1992). In the 1980s and 1990s she has been a committed campaigner for animal rights.

GINETTE VINCENDEAU

SELECT FILMOGRAPHY

Le Trou normand (Crazy for Love) (1952); Les Grandes Manoeuvres (1955); Helen of Troy (1956); La Mariée est trop belle (The Bride is Too Beautiful) (1956); Et Dieu créa . . . la femme (God Created Woman) (1956); Une Parisienne (1957); En cas de malheur (Love is my Profession) (1958); La Femme et le pantin (The Female, 1959); Babette s'en va-t-en guerre (Babette Goes to War) (1959); La Vérité (The Truth) (1960); Les Amours célèbres (1961); Le Repos du guerrier (Love on the Pillow) (1962); Le Mépris (1963); Viva Maria! (1965); Shalako (1968); Les Pétroleuses (The Legend of Frenchy King) (1971); Si Don Juan était une femme (Ms. Don Juan) (1973)

BIBLIOGRAPHY

De Beauvoir, Simone (1961), *Brigitte Bardot and the Lolita Syndrome*.
Rihoit, Catherine (1986), *Brigitte Bardot: un mythe français.*

Brigitte Bardot on the set of *And God Created Woman* (1956)

ride whose pleasure lay in the refusal completely to re-establish equilibrium. Only in retrospect can we put the generic label 'horror' on *Psycho*; the label is legitimate because the film makes us feel horror, but in its time what we felt was a particularly rich mix of eroticized pleasure and fear which could not be reduced to or explained by genre formula.

Another measure of the vehemence with which sexuality emerged in American cinema as the secret that could finally be told was in the new prevalence of method acting. Its well-known verbal inarticulateness was integrated with a bodily eloquence rooted in sexuality, especially in conflicting masculine–feminine, masochistic–sadistic motivations. Stars like Marlon Brando, James Dean, and Montgomery Clift set the stage for a whole new generation of male stars whose masculinity was, unlike a John Wayne or a Cary Grant, both complicated and conflicted—Robert De Niro, Al Pacino, Warren Beatty. It was, of course, a different story for actresses, whose bodies had always been more 'sexually saturated' and whose emotions had always been more visible. Increased sexual motivations seemed to have a narrowing effect on the expressive range of women on the screen, supplanting the intelligence and toughness of Bette Davis with the all-round softness of Marilyn Monroe, or the one-dimensional brittleness of Jane Fonda.

Sex and violence—once the two great off-scene forces of popular American cinema—thus began to become in the 1960s the very *raison d'être* for a whole new cinematic tradition. Mainstream Hollywood became unashamedly 'exploitative' not only with *Psycho*, but with former exploitation directors—Scorsese, De Palma, Coppola—becoming legitimate, bringing their hard-earned genre lessons to bear on a now visceral, sensational mainstream. Hard-core pornography, on the other hand, moved from the position of illegal underground to the position of the former exploitation films. *Deep Throat* (1972), for example, while a decidedly indifferent pornographic product, was enormously important as the first one to be seen by mainstream audiences.

Meanwhile the American avant-garde underground, following in the tradition of Surrealism and Dada, enjoyed a heady moment in the 1960s as a place of a freewheeling, transgressive sexual display—whether in the beat-oriented *Queen of Sheba Meets the Atom Man* (Ron Rice, 1965–7), in the camp of *Flaming Creatures* (Jack Smith, 1963), in a ritual gay mythologizing of *Scorpio Rising* (Kenneth Anger, 1964) and *Lucifer Rising* (1966–80), in the ironic dead-pan of Andy Warhol's *Blow Job* (1964) and *Nude Restaurant* (1967), or in the superimposed ecstasies of Carolee Schneeman's sexually explicit *Fuses* (1964–7).

This avant-garde would eventually die a slow death,

Sex and violence: Faye Dunaway and Warren Beatty in Arthur Penn's highly influential *Bonnie and Clyde* (1967)

Pier Paolo Pasolini
(1922–1975)

Pier Paolo Pasolini was a poet, novelist, film-maker, essayist, and controversialist. Born in Bologna, where he later went to university, he spent most of his childhood in Friuli in the far north-east of Italy. His early years were marred by the death of his brother, killed in internecine fighting between the Partisans in 1945, and by the frequent rows between his mother and his increasingly drunken ex-Fascist father. As a young man he joined the Communist Party, but was expelled from it in 1949 because of a scandal involving alleged sexual activities with adolescent boys. He seems to have regretted, rather than resented, his expulsion from the Communist Party, and proudly regarded himself as a Communist to the end of his life, in spite of his many public disagreements with the Party and with the rest of the left.

In 1950, Pier Paolo set out for Rome, taking his mother with him. There he soon established a reputation with two volumes of poetry, *Le ceneri di Gramsci* (1957) and *La religione del mio tempo* (1961), and two novels making creative use of Roman dialect and slang, *Ragazzi di vita* (1955) and *Una vita violenta* (1959). His skill with vernacular dialogue brought him work in the film industry, notably on the script of Fellini's *Le notti di Cabiria* (1957).

His first two films as director—*Accattone* (1961) and *Mamma Roma* (1962)—had Roman low-life themes, but were distinguished by a strong utopian current, enhanced by the use of music by Bach and Vivaldi on the sound-track. A short film, *La ricotta* ('Curd-cheese'—episode of the 1962 compilation film *RoGoPaG*) featured Orson Welles acting as a (dubbed) mouthpiece for Pasolini, and a parody of the Deposition from the Cross which led to charges of blasphemy. By contrast *Il vangelo secondo Matteo* (1964) was a stark and sober retelling of the Gospel according to Matthew, which earned him the inaccurate label of Catholic-Marxist.

Pasolini's attitude to religion was in fact highly ambivalent. He was interested in all aspects of what he called 'the sacred' (*sacrale*), but increasingly he came to locate this quality in primitive religion and myth. In *Oedipus Rex* (*Edipo re*, 1967), *Porcile* ('Pigsty', 1969), and *Medea* (1970), he explored mythic notions of the transition from primitivism to civilization—to the implied disadvantage of the latter. In general he placed his own utopias as far away as possible from the modern, capitalist, bourgeois world of which he felt himself a member and a victim, moving downwards (to the peasantry and sub-proletariat), outwards (to southern Italy and then to Africa, the Arab world, and India), and backwards in time (to the Middle Ages and pre-classical Greece), in his desperate search for a mythic home.

In the 1960s his long-standing interest in language drew him in the direction of semiotics, and he attempted to theorize his approach to cinema in two essays, 'The Written Language of Reality' and 'A Cinema of Poetry'

(reprinted in *Heretical Empiricism*, 1988). Here he argued for a natural basis of film language in reality itself, which is endowed with meaning when the film-maker turns it into signs. His own film work is far from naturalistic. Eschewing narrative continuity, Pasolini concentrates on the production of single, powerful images whose expressivity seems at first sight independent of any relationship to 'reality' as ordinarily conceived. What underlies them, however, is an almost desperate search for a kind of pre-symbolic truth, an emotional reality which modern man can no longer grasp.

After his brutal dissection of the bourgeois family in *Theorem* (*Teorema*, 1968) and in the 'modern' section of *Porcile*, Pasolini set all his films in the historic or pre-historic past. In 1970 he embarked on a series of films based on medieval collections of tales—*The Decameron* (1970), *The Canterbury Tales* (1971), and *The Arabian Nights* (*Il fior delle mille e una notte*, 1974). Though all three have their darker side, these films—the so-called 'trilogy of life'—were seen as a celebration of a lost world of joyful and innocent sexuality. But if this had been Pasolini's intention, he promptly repudiated it. Increasingly convinced that 'sexual liberation' (including gay liberation) was a sham, he turned in his journalism to a fierce denunciation of contemporary sexual mores. Having courted unpopularity on the left for his criticisms of the radical students of 1968, he compounded it with his opposition to the liberalization of Italy's archaic abortion law, and was forced to beat a muddled and hasty retreat. Then in 1975 he made *Salò* (*Salò o le centoventi giornate di Sodoma*), setting De Sade's novel in the last years of the Fascist regime in Italy, and explicitly linking Fascism and sadism, and sexual licence and oppression. Apart from the unfinished novel *Petrolio*, posthumously published in 1992, this terrifying document was to be his last work. On the morning of 2 November 1975, his battered body was discovered on a piece of waste ground near the seaside resort of Ostia, outside Rome.

GEOFFREY NOWELL-SMITH

FILMOGRAPHY

(feature films)
Accattone (1961); Mamma Roma (1962); Il vangelo secondo Matteo (The Gospel According to St Matthew) (1964); Uccellacci e uccellini ('The hawks and the sparrows') (1966); Edipo re (Oedipus Rex) (1967); Teorema (Theorem) (1968); Porcile ('Pigsty') (1969); Medea (1970); Il decamerone (The Decameron) (1970); I racconti di Canterbury (The Canterbury Tales) (1971); Il fior delle mille e una notte (The Arabian Nights) (1974); Salò o le centoventi giornate di Sodoma (Salò) (1975).

BIBLIOGRAPHY

Pasolini, Pier Paolo (1988), *Heretical Empiricism*.
Rohdie, Sam (1995), *The Passion of Pier Paolo Pasolini*.
Viano, Maurizio (1993), *A Certain Realism*.
Willemen, Paul (1976), *Pasolini*.

Opposite: Maria Callas in *Medea* (1970)

challenged by both the more inexpensive medium of video and the increasing perversion of the mainstream. In effect, the hallowed avant-garde belief that sex was the privileged means of cutting through artificial civilization to arrive at a supposedly primitive (but just as often uncritically phallic and misogynistic) bedrock of human existence had become the newly discovered 'truth' of the mainstream. Sensational, 'transgressive' sexual representations were now *de rigueur*. The avant-garde no longer held the franchise.

Thus, although the lifting of external or internalized censorship meant different things in different national contexts, there is no question that something that might be called both 'liberalization' and a greater 'realism' of sexual representation did occur. Histories of the period tend to cite social and technical advances as enabling this new 'realism', as if cinema simply extended its already significant powers of realism at a time of more liberal attitudes towards sex. This newly realistic attitude towards those aspects of life that were once censored is explained as coinciding with the advent of *cinéma-vérité* techniques, more realistic colour stock, the shift to wide-screen formats, and wrap-around sound. However, this technologically deterministic explanation always reaches a point at which the realism seems to go 'too far', exceeding newly drawn limits of good taste or community standards. The significant point is that the post-1960s game became that of perpetually challenging whatever limits were currently in effect. The notoriety of films such as Pasolini's *Salò* (1975), an excruciating version of the Marquis de Sade's *120 Days of Sodom* which transforms Sade's libertines into leaders of Mussolini's Italy, or of Nagisa Oshima's *Ai no corrida* (*In the Realm of the Senses*, 1976), a film whose transgressive love affair between a female servant and master climaxed in an act of sado-masochistic strangulation and castration, or of Peter Greenaway's highly schematized degradations in *The Cook, the Thief, his Wife and her Lover* (1989), all depends upon their ability to offend large numbers of their audiences.

In the USA an entire genre of hard-core pornography depends upon its ability to exceed the limits of mainstream standards of representation. Frequently cited as the place where sexual representations reveal the fundamental misogyny of all representation, it turns out to be one of the few places where sexual representation functions for purposes of pure arousal, and one of the few places in all cinema where women could be seen seeking sexual pleasure without being punished for it.

The similarities of all these works are more striking than their differences. Whether art or exploitation, whether mainstream or margin, there is a new prevalence of sexualized sensation across the board in world cinema. To understand fully the proliferation of sex and sensationalism in post-1960s cinema, we need to place cinema within the intellectual framework suggested by Michel Foucault and see it as part of various productive discourses of sexuality—sexology, psychoanalysis, advertising—which are themselves part of a larger matrix of power–pleasure relations. To begin to do this we need to see, as David James has pointed out, 'how inflation in explicitness took place in cinemas of widely different social positions' and how 'whatever personal freedoms were won ... they were coextensive with an unprecedented invasion of the private sphere by the industrialization of the entire field of sexuality' (James 1989).

James suggests that liberalization is an inadequate explanation for the greater sexual 'freedom' of American—or indeed any other—cinema. A good case in point is what happened following the final demise of the Hollywood Production Code and its replacement in 1968 by the MPAA ratings system. This system, designed to label works according to degrees of sexual representations, language, or violence, had the effect of becoming a crucial marketing tool. Although 'G' (general audience) films were supposedly appropriate for all audiences, in effect 'G' came to mean bland entertainment appropriate for children and other people not conversant with the facts of life. In contrast, the categories of 'PG' (parental guidance suggested for children under 17), 'PG-13' (inappropriate for children under 13), and 'R' (restricted—persons under 17 must be accompanied by an adult) became an ascending order of often truly gratuitous sex, language, or violence in films seeking more 'adult' level ratings. As for the 'adult' category itself—'X' (prohibited to all persons under 17, known as 'NC-17' since 1990)—it has become the repository of the thriving low-budget high-profit realm of pornography.

The ratings system, designed as a labelling device, to *contain* sexual and sensational representations to age-appropriate spheres, became the inadvertent cause of the incitement of sexual representations. Directors worked hard to get the desirable 'R' rating but fall just short of being the pornographic 'X'. Adolescents aspired to see the category just beyond their reach. American cinema had embarked on a quest to bring larger spectacles and more 'adult' sensations to audiences in specifically labelled, predictable packages. Since sex was the one sensation children were not supposed to feel or were too vulnerable to be exposed to, television (before the advent of cable) became the place for general audience entertainment, and movies began to do 'it' with a vengeance.

With the ratings system, as with the American obscenity law, sex was officially acknowledged as the new 'motive force' of the film industry. Just as increased efforts to define the hard core of sexual representation by Supreme Court Justice William Brennan are widely viewed as having opened the door to the legalization of hard-core pornography, so the new ratings system functioned to control a sexuality increasingly necessary to the marketing of films. It is true that under the Production Code graphic instances of sex and sensation had been kept off screen, and that under the new ratings system such representations forcefully came on screen. However, the rigidly policed and stratified ways in which they did so gives evidence of not just labelling, but productive shaping and incitement by the industry.

If cinema, since the 1960s, has become an increasingly obscene arena of representation—in the literal sense of the word as bringing on-scene what was once off-scene— it is not simply because a liberalization of censorship has permitted the emergence of erotic and violent contents that were once suppressed. Rather, it is because the very censorship that had kept such contents off-scene from a mass-market audience also had the effect of making them rare, desirable, and hence marketable. Once marketable the very notion of obscene effectively disappears. Everything comes on-scene; the only question is how and for whom.

Bibliography

Clover, Carol J. (1992), *Men, Women and Chain Saws: Gender in the Modern Horror Film*.

Foucault, Michel (1978), *History of Sexuality*.

James, David (1989), *Allegories of Cinema: American Film in the Sixties*.

Mast, Gerald (1986), *A Short History of the Movies*.

Mulvey, Laura (1975), 'Visual Pleasure and Narrative Cinema'.

Williams, Linda (1989), *Hard Core: Power, Pleasure and the Frenzy of the Visible*.

AMERICAN MOVIES

The Black Presence in American Cinema

JIM PINES

EARLY CINEMA

Images of black people have featured prominently throughout the history of American cinema. They go back to the earliest days of the filmic process itself, when Thomas A. Edison utilized black subjects in a number of his peep-show Kinetoscope movies, including *The Pickaninnies Doing a Dance* (1894), *Three Man Dance* (*c*.1894), *Negro Dancers* (1895), which W. K. L. Dickson, Edison's associate, made for the Edison Company, and *A West Indian Woman Bathing a Baby* (*c*.1895). This pseudo-ethnographic imagery continued through the embryonic years of American cinema, as movie presentation evolved from the peep-show format to the large screen, with such characteristic titles as *Dancing Darkey Boy* (Edison, 1897), *Dancing Darkies* (American Mutoscope Company, 1897), *West Indian Girls in Native Dance* (Edison, 1903), and *Jamaica Negroes Doing a Two-Step* (Edison, 1907).

Although these early movies were technically crude and lacked the iconic power of later, more developed modes of cinematic representation, they were none the less instrumental in setting the cultural tone of black racial representation in the newly emerging mass-entertainment medium of motion pictures. The racial (and racist) thrust of this cinematic cultural imagery was especially pronounced in comic motifs, which tended to stress grotesque stereotypes of blacks based on Southern plantation lore. The repertoire of black-related characters and situations was therefore extremely narrow and centred mainly on 'plantation' spectacles, such as watermelon-eating contests and fish fries, buck-dancing and cake-walking, and so on.

Edison's *Chicken Thieves* (1897), *Watermelon Contest* (1899), and *The Pickaninnies* (1905) were among the first of the so-called ethnic comedy shorts which helped to establish the cinematic image of blacks as figures of comic relief. Many of the themes and conventions employed in these early film comedies were, in fact, carried over from the theatrical black-face minstrelsy and vaudeville traditions. Hence the common practice during the silent film period of using white actors with burnt cork or black-face to play 'black' or 'Negro' parts. Needless to say, the story situations in which these pseudo-blacks appeared were often ludicrous, if not downright condescending.

In *The Gator and the Pickaninny* (Edison, 1903), for example, a black man (white actor in black-face) chops open an alligator with an axe and rescues a black child who has been swallowed by the alligator. This story is indicative of the way black children were invariably depicted as hapless imps, in the 'Little Black Sambo' vein, in early movies. *The Wooing and Wedding of a Coon* (1905) was promoted as 'a genuine Ethiopian comedy' though, in fact, it was a typical minstrel farce which caricatured the courtship of a 'Negro' couple. *Interrupted Crap Game* (Selig, 1905), another seemingly innocuous example in this early cycle of racial comedies, crudely mixed racist metaphors with its depiction of a group of black-face minstrel characters abandoning a dice game in order to chase a chicken!

Sigmund Lubin, another early film pioneer of considerable note, also made a fairly successful career out of exploiting racial comic motifs, notably with his popular 'Rastus' comedy shorts—*How Rastus Got his Pork Chop* (1905), *How Rastus Got his Turkey* (1910), and *Rastus in Zululand* (1910)—and his 'ethnic' satire *Coon Town Suffragettes* (1914), which ridiculed the contemporary women's movement with a story about a group of black charwomen who organize themselves in order to control their wayward husbands.

These early racial motifs were usually set in socially and racially segregated situations, in which the black-face characters played out a variety of exaggerated comic set pieces for white audiences' amusement. There was no dramatic interaction of any significance between black and white characters in the story situations; indeed, the emphasis was on self-contained 'ethnic' vignettes which were designed to work in their own right as visual novelties. Sometimes a film was promoted with a lot of hype about it being ethnically authentic, as in the case of *The Wooing and Wedding of a Coon* mentioned above. Production companies employed this tactic presumably to distinguish their product from other similar minstrel farces which were being made at the time and which were undoubtedly popular with fascinated white audiences.

Another strand of film comedy which was popular

during this period centred on quasi-sexual encounters between black and white characters. Many of these pseudo-interracial comedies relied on the black-face visual gag to achieve their effect, however, with the black-face characters appearing predictably as stooges to the films' white (usually male) protagonists. *The Colored Stenographer* (Edison, 1909) is typical of the genre—a mischievous white husband hides his blonde secretary from his wife by substituting a black charwoman in her place. The black-face gag was also a key element in the cycle of nuptial comedies—such as *The Masher* (1907), *The Dark Romance of a Tobacco Can* (1911), and *Seven Chances* (1925)—in which a hapless wooer, who has to marry quickly in order to claim his inheritance, is seen nearly wedding a black woman accidentally before being 'saved' by a lucky escape. These comedy shorts were not concerned with the controversial theme of miscegenation as such, however, but were driven mainly by the exigencies of the black-face visual gag and the sexual misadventures of the films' white protagonists.

The Fights of Nations (Biograph, 1907) was rather more pernicious in its intentions and is perhaps more indicative of early cinema's tendency toward pejorative images of blacks. This pastiche of racial stereotypes depicts a series of ethnic pairs—including Jews, Mexicans, Irish, and blacks—fighting each other and generally playing out their respective stereotypical roles. However, the film's tableau ending includes a reconciliation of all the ethnic combatants except the blacks. In other words, the emblematic blacks are categorically excluded or disenfranchised in the film's utopian (and racist) vision of civil society and universal harmony.

It was not uncommon for silent films to disparage blacks in such extreme terms, though there was probably a stronger tendency toward paternalistic constructions which stressed relatively gentler, if no less racist, notions of black servility and comic relief. Southern plantation mythology played a key role in anchoring this racist imagery within a readily identifiable cultural framework. It constituted an established body of quintessentially white American cultural and literary motifs which could easily be recast in cinematic terms.

The plantation genre was thus established very early on in the repertoire of American cinema. Its literary prototype was Harriet Beecher Stowe's classic anti-slavery novel *Uncle Tom's Cabin* (first published in 1852). This enormously popular book provided early movie-makers with the archetypal plantation narrative, replete with melodramatic familial setting, recognizable characters (including stereotypical blacks), dramatic chase scenes, quaint imagery of pseudo-aristocratic *ante bellum* life, and so on. By 1928 there were at least seventeen film versions of Stowe's book, including Edwin S. Porter's landmark production for the Edison Company in 1903, which was one of the longest and most expensive movies up until that time.

Film versions of *Uncle Tom's Cabin* tended to follow the approach already established by numerous theatrical presentations: they celebrated the submissiveness of the Uncle Tom character and made the Topsy figure into a grotesque minstrel ragamuffin. The book's ethical subtext tended not to figure strongly in the film adaptations, although, interestingly, the 1927 production (directed by Harry Pollard for Universal) was marked by controversy when Charles Gilpin, the outstanding black stage actor chosen to play the title role (thus making him one of the few veritable blacks to do so during the silent film period), quit the production in protest against the unsympathetic development of his character. The part subsequently went to another black actor, James B. Lowe, but Gilpin's 'political' point had been registered.

The plantation genre, along with its associated racial imagery, reached a pinnacle during the silent film era with D. W. Griffith's cinematic masterpiece *The Birth of a Nation* (1915). This film has been rightly venerated for its artistic achievements and, at the same time, justly condemned for its deeply racist content. It deals with the prickly subject of the American Civil War and the period of Reconstruction in the South—a national trauma from which many Americans were still recovering when Griffith made the film. Griffith himself was a Southerner, raised on the conservative values and traditions of the Old South. But his epic portrayal of that parochial experience succeeded in blurring sectional interests and antipathies in the interest of broader ideological objectives. He achieved this by interweaving the lives of two families representing North and South respectively, whose contrasting lives are eventually reconciled in the common interest of white supremacy or, as one of the film's intertitles puts it, 'in defence of their Aryan birthright'.

The Birth of a Nation continued the pattern of grotesque racial stereotyping which was indicative of earlier films, such as *The Fights of Nations*, but it did so with much greater intensity, within a more sharply defined ideological framework, and with stronger emphasis on the image of blacks as villains. It was also one of the few films which blatantly exploited the sexual stereotype of the black male, in order to articulate white supremacist values. This sexual racism plays a pivotal role in the film's thematic development and culminates in the last-minute rescue finale which justifies the actions of the Ku Klux Klan—captioned by Griffith as 'the saviour of white civilization'.

Race feeling ran high wherever the film was shown, which resulted in rioting in several major cities across the United States. While the publicity that this generated undoubtedly increased box-office receipts, Griffith himself was strongly attacked in the liberal and black press for his blatant racism and romanticization of the notorious Ku Klux Klan (whose membership trebled within months of the film's release). Cinemas were pick-

Oscar Micheaux
(1884–1951)

Oscar Micheaux was the first African-American film-maker to produce feature-length films and establish a distribution and exhibition circuit to ensure that his films reached an audience. In 1918 he established the Micheaux film and Book Company, with his brother Swan Micheaux as secretary treasurer. Charles Benson, the general booking manager, assisted Swan in Chicago-based distribution, and Micheaux also had a south-western distribution office in Roanoke, Virginia. Micheaux's films were designed for a primarily black audience, and several factors contributed to the establishment of this cultural market in the 1910s and 1920s. The Harlem Renaissance of the 1920s gave voice to the imaginative reflections of a proud, aggressive New Negro who condoned retaliatory action against white racist aggressions. New cultural objects, such as Micheaux's films, were created for this group of urbanized, race-conscious blacks, some of whom had fought in Cuba, in Mexico, or in Europe and were now ready to fight racism in America. The cultural impetus of the Harlem Renaissance, although essentially New York based, fanned out to other major cities with significant black populations, and thus helped establish definable links between African-American communities across the country. Around the same time there emerged the so-called race records; black music produced for a black market, which, like the Harlem Renaissance Movement, consolidated the notion of a definable African-American cultural market.

In northern urban areas like New York and Chicago, Micheaux's films were usually presented along with a musical vaudeville act. The vaudeville circuits—which comprised both white- and black-owned theatres—provided a relatively secure system through which black-oriented entertainments could be exhibited. In the South, where racial segregation was strictly enforced, seating was segregated, or there were specific nights for black audiences to be admitted.

Micheaux's productions attracted audiences by dramatizing subjects that other black films avoided. They introduced the themes of interracial intimacy, of black people 'passing' for white, lynching, and controversial subjects, such as urban graft, wife beating, gambling, rape, and prostitution. Perhaps the clearest example of Micheaux's treatment of these themes appears in *Within our Gates* (1920), his second feature, and the earliest surviving black-directed feature film. *Within our Gates* presents a horrifying enactment of the lynching of an African-American couple as well as the attempted rape of their stepdaughter by a white man who is later revealed to be her biological father. Micheaux so graphically depicted the lynching and attempted rape that the racially mixed Chicago censorship board fought against its Chicago screening, when it was released only months after the city had experienced its most violent race riot.

Although Micheaux's films attempted to address sensitive or controversial themes which other black and Hollywood films avoided, many of them were none the less entertainment led—in other words, whatever 'message' they evoked or suggested would happen within the overall context of an entertainment framework. A good example of this is the 'innocent victim of the city' story-line in *Ten Minutes to Live* (1932), in which the drama is framed by an attractive night-club setting, replete with variety acts including an extraordinary minstrel skit performed by two blacks in black-face. The suspense drama which roughly forms the story-line—a broken-hearted girl arrives at the club with the intention of murdering the deceitful city slick who seduced and abandoned her—is almost incidental to the array of activities which Micheaux builds around the film's loose plot.

Micheaux was successful, then, not only in raising finance and organizing distribution, but in producing films which his audiences wanted to see, and which tackled issues that Hollywood would not touch until after the Second World War.

MARK A. REID

SELECT FILMOGRAPHY

The Homesteader (1919); Within our Gates (1920); The Symbol of the Unconquered (1921); The Gunsaulus Mystery (1921); Body and Soul (1924); The Conjure Woman (1926); The House behind the Cedars (1927); The Girl from Chicago (1932); Veiled Aristocrat (1932); God's Step Children (1937); Underworld (1938); Lying Lips (1939); The Notorious Elinor Lee (1940); The Betrayal (1948).

BIBLIOGRAPHY

Cripps, Thomas R. (1977), *Slow Fade to Black: The Negro in American Film, 1900–1942*.
Peterson, Jr., Bernard L. (1979), 'The films of Oscar Micheaux: America's first Fabulous Black filmmaker'.
Reid, Mark A. (1993), *Redefining Black Film*.
Sampson, Henry T. (1977), *Blacks in Black and White: A Source Book on Black Films*.

Edna Mae Harris in Micheaux's 1939 film *Lying Lips* (Courtesy of the Edward Mapp Collection)

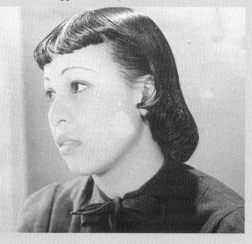

eted, and the newly formed National Association for the Advancement of Colored Peoples (NAACP) succeeded in getting the film banned in several states. The NAACP also opened negotiations with Carl Laemmle of Universal, with the idea of making an alternative film entitled *Lincoln's Dream*, a celebration of African-American progress, but the project never materialized. In a parallel initiative, African-American Emmett J. Scott, a personal secretary to black rights leader Booker T. Washington, set out to produce his own epic-length counter-irritant film to Griffith's racist masterpiece. Despite organizational and financial difficulties which nearly killed the project, a shortened version of the film was eventually released in 1919, entitled *The Birth of a Race*.

These protests against *The Birth of a Nation* and efforts to produce a counter-irritant film were important in terms of signalling the need for some form of oppositional cinema practice *vis-à-vis* racist representation. However, this activity also highlighted the weak position of independents—especially of African-American independents who were just beginning to establish a presence in film production—in relation to the emerging studio system. In other words, alternative or oppositional initiatives simply could not dislodge dominant modes of (racial) representation.

SOUND AND 1930S 'OLD SOUTH' REVIVALISM

The advent of sound in the late 1920s hastened the institutional development of (American) cinema. It also made an impact on racial representation, in so far as it enabled a degree of refinement to enter into otherwise traditional forms. It was in the context of corporate battles within the motion picture industry that Warner Bros., one of the larger independent producing companies, gained the initiative with the first commercially successful mass-oriented synchronous sound film—*The Jazz Singer* (1927), followed by *The Singing Fool* (1928). The commercial success of both these films was largely due to their star, however—the popular white stage actor-singer Al Jolson, who was famous for his so-called black-face 'Negro imitations'.

Jolson's 'artistic' use of black-face in these films is an interesting variation on a traditional theme. While it is obviously based to some extent on racial caricature, it does not fall strictly into the same category of grotesque 'Negro imitations' as early cinema's use of the convention. Jolson's black-face *alter ego* usually appears at a crucial moment in the film's plot development, but it functions more like a clown in the circus sense, than a caricatural 'Negro' in the traditional minstrelsy sense. Thus, his black-faced rendition of 'Mammy' at the end of *The Jazz Singer* (which, incidentally, is a Jewish story) is motivated more by the desire to exploit for melodramatic purposes the emotive content or pathos which the minstrel image is intended to convey, than by the need to imitate a 'Negro' as such.

By 1929, several major studios were planning all-Negro productions which would utilize the new sound technology. Fox were still experimenting with their Movietone sound system when they released *Hearts in Dixie* (1929). Hailed at the time as Hollywood's first 'all-Negro talkie', this film was a typical song-and-dance plantation spectacle replete with traditional racial stereotypes. MGM, utilizing their own Vitaphone system, produced King Vidor's *Hallelujah!* (1929), which was a superior film artistically, even though it was also essentially a plantation spectacle.

Hallelujah! brought a new dimension to cinematic black representation, in the way that it articulated racial imagery within the formal dynamic of the film. Vidor's remark that he was 'primarily interested in showing the Southern Negro as he is' smacks of old-fashioned paternalism; but it can also be read as a 'liberal' reaction to the stereotypical images of blacks which were prevalent in American films at the time. Indeed, there are close similarities between Vidor's stylistic preoccupations in *Hallelujah!* and the Southern realist literary movement of the 1920s and 1930s, in that they both sought to counteract Southern conservative orthodoxy through the use of (literary) 'naturalism'. Thus, Vidor's creative use of sound and image not only emphasizes the naturalistic iconography of the rural South but it also evokes a style of racial imagery which was unprecedented in dominant cinema.

The strident paternalism which underpinned *Hallelujah!* had very little impact on subsequent images of blacks in films, however. Even Vidor had completely abandoned his paternalistic realism by the time he made *So Red the Rose* (1936). This typical Civil War drama espoused the same romanticized notions of the *ante bellum* South, replete with reactionary racial content, as the numerous other pro-South Civil War films made during the 1930s.

A more critical image of the American South was provided in the series of 1930s social realist films—including *I Am a Fugitive from a Chain Gang* (1933), *Fury* (1936), *They Won't Forget* (1937), *The Black Legion* (1937), and *Legion of Terror* (1937)—which focused on controversial contemporary themes, such as the region's notorious penal codes, mob violence, and lynchings. Audiences were evidently horrified by this 'realistic' image of the region, with its emphasis on endemic social injustice and sense of isolation. However, the films themselves failed to undermine completely the more popular image of the romanticized South which Hollywood continued to propagate.

The *ante bellum* genre culminated in the epic blockbuster *Gone with the Wind* (1939), which was based on Margaret Mitchell's expansive novel (first published in 1936). The producers of the film were evidently conscious of the controversial tone of *The Birth of a Nation* and concluded that adopting a similar approach for *Gone with the Wind* might have an adverse effect on the film's box-office prospects. The film thus kept clear of the genre's more excessive uses of racial caricature and concentrated instead on the melodramatic romance between Scarlett O'Hara and Rhett Butler. Indeed, Hattie McDaniel's exuberant performance as the bolshie 'Mammy'—for which she won an Academy Award (the first black person to do so) as best supporting actress—provided a superficially 'humanized' inflection of black servility which enabled the film's racial constructions to avoid controversy.

Gone with the Wind brought to a close Hollywood's infatuation with the *ante bellum* genre. Yet it still managed to inspire and perpetuate a curious nostalgia for the *ante bellum* past and way of life. This nostalgia played an important part in uplifting a nation coming out of the Great Depression and on the verge of entering another World War.

POST-SECOND WORLD WAR LIBERALISM

The years following the Second World War saw major changes in the representation of blacks in American films.

A new social conscience emerged in Hollywood which began to consider the dynamics of black–white interracial relations within a liberal-humanist framework. There was now a conscious effort to project 'positive' images of blacks, to stress humanistic (as opposed to caricatured) qualities, and to focus more sharply on the social and inter-personal dynamics of race relations in contemporary American society. Much of this imagery was constructed around 'race problem' motifs, however, and today it comes across as rather narrow and simplistic in approach. But at the time it represented a radical break with earlier forms of racial imagery. Four films—all released in 1949—marked the arrival of this new trend: *Intruder in the Dust*, *Home of the Brave*, *Pinky*, and *Lost Boundaries*.

Intruder in the Dust, based on the William Faulkner novel, centred on a proud and noble black man (Juano Hernandez) whose stoicism forces a Southern white community to confront its own bigotry. This image was new, particularly in relation to representations of the American South, though it was integral to Faulkner's idealist notion of 'the Negro' as ['keeper] of white America's conscience'. *Home of the Brave* problematized race quite differently,

Hattie McDaniel, the first black person to win an Oscar, accepting the award for her performance in David O. Selznick's lavish southern epic, *Gone with the Wind* (1939)

501

focusing instead on a traumatized black GI (James Edwards) whose 'illness' (paralysis hysteria), we discover, is rooted in his psychological insecurity with the white world! The use of a 'pathologized' central black character who lacks a coherent sense of self-identity was, in fact, untypical of liberal film representation and did not reappear in subsequent liberal-assimilationist films.

While the image of blacks as powerless victims of bigotry was prominent in the two other transitional liberal conscience films of the period—*Pinky* and *Lost Boundaries*, both of which were 'tragic mulatto' or 'passing for white' melodramas—this tendency gave way to more proactive characters designed to play a more consequential role in race problem narratives. Initially, these liberal-oriented black 'heroes' were stereotypical 'good guys' on the side of moral right; but this narrow construction became less prominent by the late 1950s, as more rounded (i.e. less emblematic) black characterization began to be developed.

Black–white interracial confrontation was none the less a recurring motif in social conscience films during this period. This motif usually involved pairing a 'good' black protagonist with an unsympathetic white antagonist—the conflict symbolized a kind of moral struggle which would eventually be resolved through mutual respect and understanding. *No Way out* (1950)—Sidney Poitier's feature film début as an actor—is a typical example of this motif, where the Poitier 'hero' not only emerges as the moral victor over his white racist tormentor but also shows an enormous capacity for forgiveness.

The black 'hero' in liberal films characteristically eschewed violence as a mode of (re)action—violence was the domain of racially intolerant characters, both white and black, who were sometimes 'killed off' by the end of the story (e.g. the doomed angry black man in *No Way out*). But a number of films explored the racial intolerance theme in terms of mutually hostile black and white characters, whose antagonisms verged on mutual self-destruction. *The Defiant Ones* (1958) is undoubtedly the classic example of this motif, where two hard-nosed escaped convicts (played by Poitier and Tony Curtis) from a Southern penitentiary are forced to resolve their mutual animosity while shackled together.

An interesting variation on the racial intolerance theme was explored in *Odds against Tomorrow* (1959), where the interracial conflict between the Harry Belafonte and Robert Ryan characters was finally resolved through their mutual annihilation. What is particularly interesting about this construction is the way the film worked within the conventions of the gangster/robbery genre, using racial tension as the primary destructive force that ultimately wrecks group cohesion and prevents the success of the robbery. This anti-racist narrative can also be read as a metaphor for society at large, in which racial intolerance

poses a threat to social cohesion and the pursuit of common goals.

1960s CIVIL RIGHTS THEMES AND IMAGES

The black civil rights movement of the 1960s marked a critical turning-point for race relations in the United States. African-Americans reassessed their position in society and began to articulate new self-images based on stridently 'positive' notions of 'blackness' (e.g. Black is Beautiful, Black Power, and so on). These social, political, and cultural developments inevitably impacted on dominant media representation, not so much in terms of radicalizing black imagery, but more in terms of broadening the range of black-related themes and images which continued to be articulated within the framework of ethical liberalism.

The simplistic race problem motifs which had predominated in the previous decade gave way to relatively more complex constructions during the 1960s. Blacks were no longer portrayed simply as emblematic figures or as the embodiment of liberal-integrationist ideals; they could now be seen as *individuals* struggling against society at large, or against their own conscience. Black actors and actresses also began to appear in a diversity of story situations and genres, including roles which were not specifically motivated by black- or race-related themes. Racial understatement shifted the emphasis from race as a principal theme to the personal or human qualities of the black character(s) in the narratives. In other words, race was no longer automatically privileged in story situations involving black characters.

Indeed, the appearance of black characters in mainstream genres and story situations not only conveyed a more plausible image of plural society but it also 'naturalized' the presence of blacks in both everyday and extraordinary human circumstances. Examples of this new orientation included the James Edwards character in *The Manchurian Candidate* (1962), Woody Strode in *The Professionals* (1966), Sidney Poitier in *The Bedford Incident* (1965), and Jim Brown in numerous films made during this period, including *Rio Conchos* (1964), *The Dirty Dozen* (1967), *Ice Station Zebra* (1968), *100 Rifles* (1968), *Riot* (1968), and *El Condor* (1970).

A number of films working within popular genres, such as the Western, incorporated social conscience themes during this period as well. John Ford's *Sergeant Rutledge* (1960), for example, recast the Western/cavalry film in black-related terms, partly to highlight the black contribution to the expansion of the American frontier and partly to articulate a pro-black theme of racial equality. The film's eponymous black 'hero' (Woody Strode) is portrayed as the helpless victim of bigotry but he emerges in the end as an archetypal noble figure. Sam Peckinpah's *Major Dundee* (1964), on the other hand, was a more

One of the first black actors to become a mainstream Hollywood star, Dorothy Dandridge dances in the title role in *Carmen Jones* (1954), Otto Preminger's adaptation of Bizet's opera, featuring an all-black cast

complex reworking of the Western genre and placed less emphasis on ennobling the racially victimized black character in the story (Brock Peters) or overstating liberal-integrationist themes.

The 1960s also saw a series of low-budget, independently produced films which were notable for their intense realism and sensitive handling of racial subjects, though they were also noted for their cynicism. For example, John Cassavetes's *Shadows* (1960) explored the theme of 'passing for white' not in conventional terms of the 'tragic mulatto' but, rather, against the backdrop of white racism. Shirley Clarke's *The Cool World* (1963) explored the underworld of urban black youth and the criminal street hero. Larry Peerce's emotive drama about a mixed marriage, *One Potato, Two Potato* (1964), highlighted the problem of racial prejudice in relation to both interpersonal and insti-

tutional relations. Michael Roemer's *Nothing but a Man* (1964) was one of the few films which focused on black male–female relationships. Robert Downey's *Putney Swope* (1969), a satire set in an advertising agency which has been taken over by blacks, articulated the white independent genre's cynicism most sharply.

The 1960s Hollywood social conscience genre reached a pinnacle with Norman Jewison's *In the Heat of the Night* (1967), a classic race relations drama which, echoing the confrontational narrative in *The Defiant Ones*, pits a sophisticated black detective (Poitier) against a bigoted Southern white policeman (Rod Steiger). The film works within the traditional conventions of the crime/detective thriller genre, but the expectations of the genre—such as the resolution of the murder mystery—are undermined by having a black detective as the central protagonist

503

Sidney Poitier

(1927–)

Born to poor Bahamian parents in Miami, Florida in 1927, Sidney Poitier rose to become one of the most famous black actors in the history of Hollywood cinema. He entered the acting profession soon after the Second World War, joining the renowned American Negro Theatre in Harlem, New York, where he became part of the new generation of post-war black actors that included Harry Belafonte, Ossie Davis, and Ruby Dee. He appeared in a number of Negro stage productions and was an understudy in the Broadway and touring productions of *Anna Lucasta* (1946–49), before making his Hollywood screen début in Joseph L. Mankiewicz's *No Way Out* (1950). This powerful drama about racial bigotry was part of the cycle of post-war social conscience films which centred on black–white interracial relations in contemporary American society. Poitier's striking performance as the young 'Negro' intern in a white hospital, who becomes embroiled in a tense racial situation, not only won him critical acclaim but also established him as American cinema's first (and only) emblematic integrationist black screen hero. It set the tone for all his subsequent roles which, in one way or another, reiterated and consolidated the image of the noble black hero overcoming the machinations of racial intolerance.

This theme was especially poignant in the classic interracial drama *The Defiant Ones* (Stanley Kramer, 1958), in which Poitier played a tough-minded convict who manages to escape from a Southern penitentiary with a raging white bigot shackled to him. Characteristically, the two men's mutual antagonism gradually evolves into a grudging friendship, then finally mutual respect. Poitier and co-star Tony Curtis both received Academy Award nominations for their performances; and Poitier himself won the award for best actor at the 1958 Berlin film Festival.

Poitier won the Academy Award for Best Actor in 1964 for his performance in *Lilies of the Field* (Ralph Nelson, 1963), a low-budget production in which he played what some critics have described as the definitive 'good-guy'— a footloose handyman who reluctantly agrees to help a group of German nuns build a chapel in the Arizona desert. Poitier's 'Ebony saint' image was now firmly established and reached a pinnacle in the 1960s, notably with Norman Jewison's classic interracial drama *In the Heat of the Night* (1967), in which he played the sophisticated detective Virgil Tibbs who inadvertently gets caught up in the machinations of a hostile Southern town. This was followed in the same year with *To Sir, with Love*, and Stanley Kramer's then controversial romantic comedy *Guess Who's Coming to Dinner*, in which he plays a socially sophisticated doctor who woos the daughter of a white suburban couple. These were three of the biggest grossing films of 1967.

Poitier's rise to Hollywood stardom coincided with the American civil rights movement which was itself prodding the consciousness of (white) America during the 1950s and 1960s. However, by the end of the 1960s, his screen image seemed to drift out of sync with social and political developments. Paradoxically, he became typecast in quite narrow terms, as a saint-like figure and paragon of (black) middle-class values and expectations. He attempted to shift his image by playing untypical roles—for example, a 'gambler and bon vivant' who falls in love with a black domestic in *For Love of Ivy* (1968), a black militant who commits a robbery to help 'the struggle' in *The Lost Man* (1969)—but these attempts were not particularly successful.

Poitier's career underwent yet another phenomenal upturn, however, when he took over the direction of *Buck and the Preacher* (1971), a Western comedy-drama which dealt with the little-known aspect of post-Civil War American history during which freed slaves were tracked down by bounty hunters and forced to return to unofficial slavery in the South. Poitier was the film's executive producer, director, and star—suggesting that he had decided to exercise greater control over his own screen image. *Buck and the Preacher* was a particularly impressive directorial début, in the sense that the film attempted to re-

work the generic conventions of the Western from an African-American perspective, while at the same time avoiding the more exploitative aspects of blaxploitation films which predominated in the early 1970s.

The 1970s saw Poitier finally succeeding in shaking off his 'Ebony saint' image and developing his characters beyond the narrow definitions of liberal integrationism. This change in emphasis was signalled in *Buck and the Preacher* but it was firmly established in his 1974 comedy *Uptown Saturday Night*, in which he cast himself against type doing slapstick. Interestingly, Poitier seems to have taken comedy as his particular directorial forte since the mid-1970s. However, while his comedies have contributed greatly to establishing non-stereotypical modes of black comic representation in Hollywood, there is none the less a sense in which Sidney Poitier will always be remembered for his serious dramatic roles in such ground-breaking films as *No Way Out, Blackboard Jungle* (1955), *Edge of the City* (*A Man is Ten Feet Tall*, 1957), *The Defiant Ones, A Raisin in the Sun* (1961), and *In the Heat of the Night*.

JIM PINES

SELECT FILMOGRAPHY

No Way Out (1950); Cry, the Beloved Country / African Fury (1952); Blackboard Jungle (1955); Something of Value (1957); Edge of the City / A Man is Ten Feet Tall (1957); The Defiant Ones (1958); Porgy and Bess (1959); A Raisin in the Sun (1961); Lilies of the Field (1963); To Sir, with Love (1967); In the Heat of the Night (1967); Guess Who's Coming to Dinner (1967); For Love of Ivy (1968); Buck and the Preacher (1971, also directed); Uptown Saturday Night (1974, also directed); Let's Do It Again (1975, also directed); A Piece of the Action (also directed); Stir Crazy (1980, directed); Hanky Panky (1982, directed); Ghost Dad (1990, directed).

BIBLIOGRAPHY

Poitier, Sidney (1980), This Life.

Opposite: Sidney Poitier as Inspector Tibbs in Norman Jewison's *In the Heat of the NIght* (1967)

operating in a hostile Southern white milieu. Yet the most striking feature of the film is the way that it constructs a relatively complex and dramatically interesting dimension around the familiar 'ebony saint' image of the Poitier hero. Typically, however, the central tension of racial conflict is resolved in the film in terms of the personal and the individual rather than the possibility of social change.

HOLLYWOOD 'BLAXPLOITATION' FILMS OF THE 1970s

The first half of the 1970s saw the proliferation of black exploitation, or so-called blaxploitation films. These films were designed to appeal primarily to black audiences in terms of their subject-matter, characters, and milieu. They were mainly preoccupied with projecting stridently black superheroes. This marked a major shift away from the social conscience imagery of the 1950s and 1960s. This shift in imagery coincided to some extent with the new militancy and black pride which had come to the fore during this period; though there was also an undertone of cynicism, especially following the assassination of Martin Luther King in 1969, which had come to define this post-civil rights representation. But while blaxploitation effectively overturned liberal-integrationist motifs, it was none the less essentially concerned with commercially exploiting the new black-oriented market. Many people felt at the time that this was a price worth paying, given the chequered history of black representation in mainstream American cinema.

Ossie Davis's *Cotton Comes to Harlem* (1970), based on black crime writer Chester Himes's popular novel, was the first in the blaxploitation cycle. Despite its rough edges and sometimes over-exaggerated caricatures, the film none the less evoked the whole tone of the genre to wonderful effect. Gordon Parks's *Shaft* (1971) articulated the marriage between blaxploitation and commercialism to even greater effect, however, with its typical Hollywood look and seductive evocation of the black urban milieu, its attractive male lead, and Isaac Hayes's Oscar-winning music score. The commercial success of this film was also helped by the way that it worked within the familiar private detective genre; this enabled the film to appeal to both black and white audiences. *Shaft* helped establish within mainstream commercial cinema the notion of the sophisticated black superhero.

However, Melvin Van Peebles's independently produced, iconoclastic film *Sweet Sweetback's Baadasssss Song* (1971) is widely credited with having initiated the real breakthrough in black-oriented films and the establishment of the black hero within popular (American) cinema. Though lacking the polish of Hollywood blaxploitation productions, *Sweetback* nevertheless had a sharp political and cultural edge which identified it explicitly as a stridently political black film. Van Peebles's film was also a huge commercial success, which led many critics to conclude that Hollywood blaxploitation merely cashed in on *Sweetback*'s marketing breakthrough but stressed instead a diluted form of black cultural imagery and political radicalism. Significantly, the profits earned from blaxploitation films helped stabilize the financially troubled Hollywood motion picture industry as well.

The detective/gangster film was undoubtedly the most popular of the blaxploitation genres. These films were set in the contemporary urban milieu, they romanticized the iconography of the black ghetto—its subcultural styles in dress, speech, behaviour, and attitudes—and glorified the ghetto as a kind of noble jungle. The films often contained a lot of sex and violence, and their heroes were invariably shown coming out on top in confrontations with the white establishment. With the possible exception of *Across 110th Street* (1973), the majority of blaxploitation crime films were more preoccupied with mythologizing black-specific themes and images than with formally reworking the conventions of the detective/crime genre.

Similarly, blaxploitation Westerns set out to recast the genre in black terms, though the majority of films were driven primarily by popular entertainment concerns. One of the most interesting black-oriented Westerns during the period was undoubtedly Sidney Poitier's directorial début film *Buck and the Preacher* (1972). This film not only highlighted the historical presence of African-Americans in the expansion of the American frontier but it also adhered fairly closely to the conventions of the Western/wagon-train genre. However, the series of blaxploitation Western action-adventures which featured ex-football star Fred Williamson—including *The Legend of Nigger Charley* (1972), *The Soul of Nigger Charley* (1973), and *Black Bounty Killer* (1974)—were more popular with audiences largely because of Williamson's cultivated machismo, which conformed perfectly to blaxploitation's notion of the black superhero.

Blaxploitation films were widely criticized by black rights organizations and professional bodies as having a corrupting influence on young blacks in particular, who made up the bulk of the audience for such films. The NAACP and the Congress for Racial Equality (CORE), for example, formed an alliance in 1972 to attack the blaxploitation trend, while local organizations across the country formed committees to 'vet' film scripts and to provide production companies with 'permission' to film in black neighbourhoods. A number of black-owned production companies were also established to try and meet growing demands for a more responsible approach to black-oriented films.

Certain films were celebrated on the other hand as meaningful or positive representations of black life. Among these were Gordon Parks's *The Learning Tree* (1969), based on his autobiographical novel about growing up in Kansas during the 1930s; Martin Ritt's *Sounder* (1972), another 1930s story about a young boy's experiences in the South; Ossie Davis's *Black Girl* (1972); and John Korty's *The Autobiography of Miss Jane Pittman* (1974), an ambitious television film in which Cicely Tyson portrays a 110-year-old black woman recounting her life from slavery to the civil rights years. These films, it was argued, reinstated a sense of humanity in the screen image of African-Americans—which many people felt had been badly damaged in the post-civil rights 1970s.

The demise of the blaxploitation cycle in 1975–6 saw a complete reversal of the Hollywood black-oriented trend. For the remainder of the decade, there was virtually a total absence of prominent black characters or images in popular mainstream films, exploitative or otherwise. Black characters still appeared fairly regularly in Hollywood films, of course, but they were now marginal figures—indeed, often stereotypical villains seen being

The blaxploitation heroine: Tamara Dobson as a CIA agent who destroys a ring of drug pushers in Warner Bros.' *Cleopatra Jones* (1973)

knocked into place by the decade's new white super-heroes, such as Dirty Harry. There was also a shift in industry thinking regarding the market, as Hollywood 'discovered' that black audiences constituted a significant proportion of the general movie-going public. This made it no longer necessary or important to target black audiences specially; in other words, blaxploitation could be abandoned without it having an adverse effect on the industry's improved financial position.

'CROSSING OVER' INTO THE 1980S AND 1990S

By the early 1980s the emphasis had shifted again, but this time towards the notion of 'crossing over'—that is, having black characters or dramatic situations which would appeal to a wider (i.e. predominantly white) mass audience, while retaining expressions of black identity (however this might be defined). Louis Gossett, Jr.'s Oscar-winning role as the demanding drill sergeant in *An Officer and a Gentleman* (1981) exemplified this shift in black representation quite aptly, both in the way that it articulated the black 'antagonist' figure as a kind of deracialized bogeyman (for the predominantly white recruits at the military academy) and in terms of the racially understated tension between his character and the film's central white protagonist (Richard Gere). This confrontational inter-racial relationship was devoid of any ethical or moral underpinning; it functioned instead as a conduit for a particularly intense form of myopic individualism.

Three Hollywood black stars in particular epitomized the impulse towards crossing over during the period—Richard Pryor, Eddie Murphy, and Whoopi Goldberg. Interestingly, all of them had made their names as raunchy comics, but what they brought to the screen was an expression of (often manic) black comedy which broke completely with traditional racist motifs. However, the commercial success of these new black stars in Hollywood depended a great deal on their potentially destabilizing presence being 'sanitized' or 'domesticated' for the mass market. Thus, in a perverse sort of way, they had come to symbolize complete racial integration in popular American cinema.

The incorporation of black themes and images into mainstream popular cinema during this period was also highlighted in the cycle of big-budget productions made by leading white directors—which included notably Miloš Forman's *Ragtime* (1981), Francis Coppola's *The Cotton Club* (1984), Norman Jewison's *A Soldier's Story* (1984), Steven Spielberg's *The Color Purple* (1985), and Clint Eastwood's *Bird* (1988). As an indication of just how far things had moved on, none of these films articulated the sense of liberal-humanist idealism which had been so pivotal for an earlier generation of Hollywood liberals. Thus, in the 1980s, black situations either stood on their own terms, or they functioned as an inflated but exotic backdrop to essentially white-oriented story-lines.

The Color Purple was a notable exception, not so much in terms of its ethical stance as in terms of its handling of the subject-matter. Based on black author Alice Walker's best-selling, Pulitzer prize-winning novel, the film centred on the gradual awakening of a poor rural Southern black woman (Whoopi Goldberg) who has suffered mental and sexual abuse by men all her life. This was the first time that Hollywood had focused on such a theme (black male–female relationships) so sharply; it was obviously a far cry from the traditional 'mammy' stereotype; but it also proved highly controversial, especially in the hands of Spielberg, who characteristically manipulated the emotive content of the drama to full effect.

The most significant turning-point during the decade was undoubtedly African-American director Spike Lee's low-budget commercial hit *She's Gotta Have It* (1986). This film about a young black woman's sexuality and relations with men avoided the *angst*-ridden melodrama of *The Color Purple* and stressed instead a kind of humorous Brechtian exploration of sexual desire and intrigue. But, more importantly, Lee's film effectively set the tone for a new wave of African-American popular cinema which not only explored a range of themes from within a black perspective but did so within the terms of mainstream commercial cinema.

This development is clearly seen in Lee's own subsequent films which focus on colour caste and social class relations in the context of an all-black college (*School Daze*, 1988), interracial relations in a mixed New York urban neighbourhood (*Do the Right Thing*, 1989), interracial sexual relations (*Jungle Fever*, 1991), black jazz/music culture (*Mo' Better Blues*, 1992), follwed by the expansive bio-pic of the late African-American political leader Malcolm X. Lee achieved the kind of market breakthrough which only Melvin Van Peebles had succeeded in doing fifteen years before him, with the cult hit *Sweet Sweetback's Baadasssss Song*. And, like the earlier film, Lee's films, along with a number of those made by other African-American directors from the late 1980s onwards (such as Robert Townsend, Mario Van Peebles, Bill Duke, John Singleton, and Reginald and Warrington Hudlin), succeeded in appealing to wider audiences without necessarily adopting all the values of 'crossing over'.

By the 1990s, the preoccupation with African-American experience began to address the controversial but highly pertinent theme of inwards-directed urban violence and 'gun culture'. John Singleton's *Boyz N the Hood* (1991), which was set in the now mythologized South Central district of Los Angeles, dramatized the sense of despair and hopelessness which seemed an integral feature of social fragmentation and political cynicism within urban African-American experience from the mid-1980s

Spike Lee

(1958–)

Spike [Shelton Jackson] Lee was born into an artistic family in Atlanta, Georgia (USA), in 1958. He grew up in New York City, where his father Bill Lee, the renowned folk/jazz bassist (who later scored the music for many of Lee's films), had moved the family in 1960. Lee attended Morehouse College in Atlanta, one of the leading all-black colleges in the United States, graduating in 1979 with a BA in Communications Studies. He later graduated from the New York University's Graduate Film School. His thesis film *Joe's Bed-Stuy Barbershop: We Cut Heads* (1982), about a Brooklyn barber who gets embroiled in the numbers racket, won an Academy of Motion Picture Arts and Sciences Student Award in 1983, and quickly established him as one of the most dynamic talents to emerge in the new wave of contemporary African-American film directors.

Spike Lee as Mookie in *Do the Right Thing* (1989)

Lee's first feature film *She's Gotta Have It* (1986), about a young, sexually liberated black woman's relationship with her three male lovers, was a phenomenal box-office success and won wide acclaim for its witty handling of what many people regarded as a potentially explosive subject. The film won the Prix du Film Jeunesse at the Cannes Film Festival in 1986, and helped launch Lee's international reputation, making him one of the few African-American directors to enjoy such status.

Lee's penchant for provocative subjects was demonstrated again in his next film, *School Daze* (1988), a semi-musical set in a southern all-black college campus which explored the theme of colour caste and class in the context of warring factions of black students. The film in particular revealed Lee's willingness to explicate sensitive black-specific themes within the context of mainstream entertainment cinema. Lee's subsequent films have tended to delineate black–white interracial relations much more sharply, however, revealing his own political (and cultural) orientation in the post-civil rights 1980s.

In *Do the Right Thing* (1989), for example, Lee draws the audience's attention particularly to the contemporary African-American dilemma represented by the contrasting political philosophies of Malcolm X and Dr Martin Luther King. His preoccupation with cultural identity and political activism is explored further in *Jungle Fever* (1991), a film which was partly motivated by the racial killing of a black teenager in an Italian-American neighbourhood in New York in 1989. However, some critics have attacked Lee for apparently veering towards cultural nationalism, particularly in relation to *Jungle Fever*, in which the central ill-fated romance seems to point towards a separatist cultural and political message for African-Americans.

Nevertheless, Lee has been extraordinarily successful in articulating major African-American cultural and political themes within the context of mainstream commercial cinema. In that respect, he has almost single-handedly de-marginalized one strand of African-American cinema. Indeed, his controversial bio-pic of the late radical African-American political leader Malcolm X not only shows Lee at his best trying to merge significant historical themes with present-day political experience, but also represents the culmination of his cinematic technique. In *Malcolm X* (1993), Lee utilizes relatively complex camera movements, multiple story-lines, and music as counterpoint to characters' dialogue with much more fluidity than in any of his previous films, including *School Daze* where these techniques were first deployed in a coherent style.

Spike Lee has undoubtedly played a pivotal role in popularizing radically new images of African-Americans in Hollywood films in the 1980s and 1990s. This shift must be seen as especially important during a period which also saw the alarming increase in black-on-black violence and 'gun culture' within black urban conurbations. But whilst Lee's films consciously set out to address these sort of issues squarely, they nevertheless are equally and strongly identified as quintessentially (cinematic and) commercial products. In that respect Lee has brilliantly achieved what no other African-American has been able to do up to now; to merge a form of black political-cultural nationalism with efficient cultural capitalism on a large scale.

JIM PINES

FILMOGRAPHY

Joe's Bed-Stuy Barbershop: We Cut Heads (1982); She's Gotta Have It (1986); School Daze (1988); Do The Right Thing (1989); Mo' Better Blues (1990); Jungle Fever (1991); Malcolm X (1993); Crooklyn (1994); Clockers (1995).

BIBLIOGRAPHY

Lee, Spike, *et al.* (1991), *Five for Five: The Films of Spike Lee.*

onwards. This film especially captured the haunting sense of a culturally and politically marginalized urban milieu which is under constant surveillance by the state.

The impossibility of escape, the fragile nature of intra-black community relations, were also prominent themes in Mario Van Peebles's violent urban crime drama *New Jack City* (1991) and Matty Rich's *Straight out of Brooklyn* (1991), which was particularly about the desire to escape. The ironic point about these contemporary African-American urban dramas, however, is that they suggest the total collapse of liberal integrationism, in which the black cinematic subject has been reinvented and reenslaved within the segregated confines of a strange, exotic, sometimes dangerous 'otherness'. After 100 years of American cinema, black representation remains an acutely unresolved problem.

Bibliography

Bogle, Donald (1989), *Blacks in American Films and Television*.
Cripps, Thomas (1977), *Slow Fade to Black: The Negro in American Film, 1900–1942*.
Klotman, Phyllis Rauch (1979), *Frame by Frame: A Black Filmography*.
Leab, Daniel J. (1975), *From Sambo to Superspade: The Black Experience in Motion Pictures*.
Nesteby, James R. (1982), *Black Images in American Films, 1896–1954*.
Pines, Jim (1975), *Blacks in Films*.
Sampson, Henry T. (1977), *Blacks in Black and White: A Source Book on Black Films*.

Exploitation and the Mainstream

KIM NEWMAN

Post-1980 time travel films like *The Philadelphia Experiment* (1984) and *Back to the Future* (1985) are obliged to feature the gag in which a disbelieving inhabitant of a naïve past discovers that Ronald Reagan is in the White House. 'And who's Secretary of the Treasury,' Christopher Lloyd asks Michael J. Fox, 'Jack Benny?' The joke, persisting well after the Reagan presidency in *Late for Dinner* (1990), comes from an awareness that a film-goer of the 1940s or 1950s would be unable to conceive of a future in which a second-string movie star is President. Though the New Hollywood is increasingly self-aware, as witness the inside approaches of *The Player* (1992) or *Last Action Hero* (1993), no time travel film dares suggest that a 1940s film-goer warped into any year after 1977 would find it ridiculous that *Star Wars* (1977, derived from *Flash Gordon*), *Superman* (1978), *Raiders of the Lost Ark* (1981), or *Dick Tracy* (1990) were big-budget, A-ticket movies. The originals of these properties were despised, marginalized efforts, creeping out of 'poverty row', playing to children at Saturday matinées. As a new generation of baby-boom executives take control of the product, time-travellers from the 1960s would now face the spectacle of a future in which the throwaway media of their own time has been reincarnated in major studio reruns of *Batman* (1989), *The Addams Family* (1991), *The Fugitive* (1992), and *Maverick* (1994). In the 1950s and 1960s, changes were made which radically affected the shape of mainstream American cinema.

David O. Selznick and Louis B. Mayer would never have considered making the films which constitute *Variety*'s current box-office top ten, though they would have understood *Gandhi* (1982) if Paul Muni had been available. Even if *Beverly Hills Cop* (1984) or *Ghostbusters* (1983) had been green-lighted in the golden age of Hollywood, they would have been double-bill fillers with Abbott and Costello or the Bowery Boys. Old-style studio heads recognized this sort of product as necessary, but never dreamt it merited the big stars, lavish productions, major effects, or mammoth promotional budgets afforded 'important' motion pictures like *Marie Antoinette* (1938) or *The Best Years of Our Lives* (1946). The attitude was universal; in the last years of her life, actress Gale Sondegaard was staggered that her Oscar-winning work on *Anthony Adverse* (1936) was less remembered than her villainy in the Sherlock Holmes quickie *The Spider Woman* (1944). In the 1930s and 1940s, there were few A-feature Westerns, horror films, urban crime stories, or sex melodramas; these genres throve at the mini-majors or the 'poverty row' independents. Beyond Hollywood were such murky fringes as the all-black 'race' film industry (*Son of Ingagi*, 1938), or supposedly 'educational' films shown on the carnival circuit (*Reefer Madness*, 1936), which produced a flow of films shown outside the majors' distribution channels.

In the 1950s, as the industrial structure of Hollywood changed, so did the cinema itself. The studios were forced to divest themselves of their theatre chains, vastly increasing the risk involved in any given production. The establishment of alternative systems of distributing foreign, art, or pornographic movies made available a wider range of cinema, especially to an impressionable college generation who would become film-makers themselves. The peak audiences of the war years subsided as television became the primary entertainment medium, and the New York-based TV industry began to create its own stars, genres, and monopolies. The family pattern of cinema

Jack Nicholson

(1937–)

Jack Nicholson's entry into films came through Roger Corman, whom he met while attending acting classes in Los Angeles. Corman had set up as a poverty-row producer and offered Nicholson the lead in a teen-delinquent movie, *Cry Baby Killer* (1958). For ten years Nicholson remained within the orbit of Corman's ramshackle, shoestring outfit, not only acting but scripting, producing, and even directing, often uncredited and unpaid. One or two roles hinted at the manic Nicholson to come: a joyously masochistic dental patient in *Little Shop of Horrors* (1960), and, in *The Raven* (1963), a man bewitched by Boris Karloff's magic and driving madly to the abyss.

His acting career stagnating in the mid-1960s, Nicholson formed a company, Proteus films, with the director Monte Hellman. They produced two spare, existential Westerns, *The Shooting* and *Ride in the Whirlwind* (both 1965), which Nicholson took to Cannes. They became cult hits in France, but were ignored in the USA. Nicholson was over 30 when he struck lucky with his nineteenth film. Cast at the last minute (to replace Rip Torn) in the counter-culture's surprise hit *Easy Rider* (1969), Nicholson—as the Southern laywer seduced by the hippiedom of Dennis Hopper and Peter Fonda—walked off with the film. Suddenly his star quality, overlooked for a decade, seemed unmissable.

With his snake eyes, lopsided killer grin, and lack of superficial vanity—already balding when stardom hit, he never troubled to disguise it—Nicholson looked like an icon for the disaffected, rebellious 1970s. At the same time he harked back to the era of larger-than-life idols; there were echoes of Cagney's pugnacity and Bogart's soiled integrity, of the 'misfit' stars like Garfield and Brando. This double lineage paid off in Bob Rafelson's *Five Easy Pieces* (1970) in which Nicholson convincingly played an oil-rigger escaped from a high-culture, classical-music background. The film featured the first of his trademark 'explosions'—a cathartic outburst of fury at an obstructive waitress in a diner.

Nicholson's sexual charm, a teasing mix of danger and irreverence, allowed him to play unpleasant or even psychotic characters without forfeiting audience sympathy. The compulsive womanizer of *Carnal Knowledge* (1971) callously humiliates his conquests, yet Nicholson invites pity for the emotional void that prompts such behaviour. The more outrageous his roles, the more the audience sided with him, rooting happily for his crude, loudmouthed petty officer in *The Last Detail* (1973) and his gleefully disruptive mental patient in *One flew over the Cuckoo's Nest* (1975). Mostly he played outsiders, though not always flamboyant ones: in *The King of Marvin Gardens* (1972) he was twitchy and reclusive, leaving the extrovert fireworks to Bruce Dern.

Intelligent and discriminating, Nicholson spurned conventional star roles, and often waived his full fee to

help out a friend—such as Rafelson on both *Marvin Gardens* and *Man Trouble* (1992)—or to work with a director he admired, as with Antonioni on *The Passenger* 1975). His taste for European directors also led to one of his finest roles, as the cynical private eye Jake Gittes in Polański's *Chinatown* (1974). Indifferent as ever to glamour, he nonchalantly played much of the film with a huge bandage on his nose.

Throughout the 1970s, Nicholson's performances remained bold, incisive, and powerful, even holding his own against a shamelessly mannered Brando in *The Missouri Breaks* (1976). The turning-point came with *The Shining* (1980), where Kubrick allowed, or encouraged, him to go ludicrously over the top as the would-be writer turned axe murderer. Since then, Nicholson has been increasingly prone to wheel out the same 'Mad Jack' party turn. His acting in *The Witches of Eastwick* (1987) and *Batman* (1989), though never less than hugely entertaining and compulsively watchable, was a shallow, cartoon reduction of his real talents.

Given a role that challenges his imagination, Nicholson can still rise to the occasion; his booze-embittered Eugene O'Neill was the best thing in Warren Beatty's ponderous *Reds* (1981). His reprise of Jake Gittes in *The Two Jakes* (1990), which he also directed, was well up to the original; and the film itself, like his other directorial outings, *Drive, He Said* (1970) and *Goin' South* (1978), was offbeat, accomplished, and undeservedly neglected. But the wistful recluse of *Marvin Gardens* may now be beyond his range, and as *Hoffa* (1992) proved, when he plays stolid even Jack Nicholson can be dull.

PHILIP KEMP

SELECT FILMOGRAPHY

The Shooting (1965); Easy Rider (1969); Five Easy Pieces (1970); The King of Marvin Gardens (1972); The Last Detail (1973); Chinatown (1974); Professione: Reporter (The Passenger) (1975); One flew over the Cuckoo's Nest (1975); The Missouri Breaks (1976); The Shining (1980); The Postman Always Rings Twice (1981); Terms of Endearment (1983); Prizzi's Honor (1985); Batman (1989); The Two Jakes (1990); Hoffa (1992); Wolf (1994)

BIBLIOGRAPHY

Brode, Douglas (1990), *The Films of Jack Nicholson*.
Crane, Robert David, and Fryer, Christopher (1975), *Jack Nicholson Face to Face*.
Parker, John (1991), *The Joker's Wild: The Biography of Jack Nicholson*.

Opposite: Jack Nicholson in *One Flew Over the Cuckoo's Nest*, adapted from Ken Kesey's novel by émigré Czech director Miloš Forman

attendance was broken, along with long-held stereotypes about family behaviour, as parents stayed in to watch *Dragnet* and *I Love Lucy* while children and teenagers, eager to be away from direct supervision, thronged to movie houses and drive-ins. Hollywood's short-term reaction to these crises was to come up with gimmicks like 3-D or innovations like CinemaScope, and to switch over more extensively to colour films. Sheer spectacle was supposed to lure back the lost audiences, but the idea fundamentally misunderstood that times, and audiences, had changed.

Typical of the faint air of desperation that surrounds major studio product of the 1950s are Curtis Bernhardt's remake of *The Merry Widow* (1952) with Lana Turner, Michael Curtiz's solemn spectacle *The Egyptian* (1954), Selznick's troubled super-production of *A Farewell to Arms* (1957), or such all-star oddities as *The Story of Mankind* (1957). The studios thought these were the films that would recapture the glory days of the 1930s, but the truly important and outstanding movies of the period tended to arise from the involvement of major talents with formerly low-esteem genre material. Robert Aldrich's *Kiss Me Deadly* (1954), Anthony Mann's *The Man from Laramie* (1955), John Ford's *The Searchers* (1956), or Alexander Mackendrick's *The Sweet Smell of Success* (1959) were released without much fuss and taken for granted, but now stand as far more resonant and rewarding than, say, best picture Oscar winners *Around the World … in 80 Days* (1956) or *Ben-Hur* (1959). A symbiotic relationship existed between the majors and the independents, with any given success inspiring no-frills follow-ups, so that serious, adult pictures like *Blackboard Jungle* (1955), which expects its audience to side with Glenn Ford rather than Vic Morrow, would lead to the likes of *High School Caesar* (1960), in which teachers and parents are marginalized background figures and troubled kids carry the weight of the drama. Even *Rebel without a Cause* (1955) was located in a grown-up genre of psychological problem picture, though Nicholas Ray and James Dean skewed it away from mediating authority figures in order directly to address a teenage audience. It was in this climate that the fringe areas of the motion picture industry began to thrive commercially and that exciting film-making began to exist outside the umbrella of the major studios.

At American International Pictures, a low-budget 'grindhouse' independent, mini-moguls Samuel Z. Arkoff and James H. Nicholson employed freshman producers Herman Cohen, Roger Corman, Bert I. Gordon, and Alex Gordon to make sixty- to seventy-minute black and white movies geared to a teenage audience that had made stars of James Dean and Elvis Presley and were contributing to the 1950s booms in rock 'n' roll and comic books. AIP did not strictly make B movies: the plan was to issue double bills and haul in all the rental fees rather than get stuck with the thin slice left if their quickie went out with a major's A feature. In the mid-1950s, AIP turned its hand to traditional 'poverty row' formats, assigning Corman and Alex Gordon to odd Westerns (Corman's *Gunslinger*, 1956; Gordon's *Flesh and the Spur*, 1956), and followed up the majors' flirtation with science fiction by producing the likes of Corman's *The Day the World Ended* (1956) and Edward L. Cahn's *The She-Creature* (1956), which also coasted on tabloid interest in nuclear war and reincarnation.

Realizing that *The Merry Widow* or *The Egyptian*, which boasted production values AIP could never aspire to, were fossils with no appeal whatsoever to a high-school constituency, Nicholson and Arkoff encouraged their stable to make films about monsters, rock 'n' roll, teenage rebellion, sex and violence, and fast cars. Between 1956 and 1959, the leads of AIP films got younger. Westerns gave way to post-*Rebel without a Cause* teen cut-ups: *Dragstrip Girl* (1957), *High School Hellcats* (1958). Typical of the strange relationship exploitation has with the mainstream is Corman's remarkable *Sorority Girl* (1957), an instant sex-change remake of Jack Garfein's *The Strange One* (1957), with sorority tyrant Susan Cabot replacing military school tyrant Ben Gazzara.

The archetypal AIP title is the Cohen-produced *I Was a Teenage Werewolf* (1957), which came out just as Hammer Films in Great Britain were taking another tack in reviving the Universal horror cycle of the 1930s and 1940s. While Hammer added a spirited and mainly serious period style, along with colour and quality performances (producing horror films George Cukor might have admired), AIP went with monochrome, contemporary settings, dodgy teenage performers, and a technique best described as functional. While Hammer rejected the grey science fiction predominant in American monster movies in favour of colourful supernatural themes, AIP stuck with radiation-plagued mutant movies, reviving the werewolf, Frankenstein, and vampire subgenres with pseudo-scientific nonsense. Herman Cohen's high-school werewolf (Michael Landon) and his teenage vampire (Sandra Harrison) are created by mad scientists who somehow feel these Gothic creatures are best fitted to survive atomic warfare. There are moments in AIP's late 1950s repertoire, mainly in Corman films (*The Undead*, 1958), where directorial intelligence is clearly involved, but the woodenness of Bert I. Gordon or Alex Gordon is more characteristic.

Major studios dabbled in science fiction in the 1950s, but films like Paramount's *War of the Worlds* (1953) and Fox's *The Fly* (1958) are tame and professionally dull by comparison with Allied Artists' *Invasion of the Body Snatchers* (1955) or William Castle's *The Tingler* (1959, released through Columbia). As with the Western—probably at its peak during the 1950s as Budd Boetticher and Anthony Mann rode in to replace Hoppy and Gene Autry—this area of cinema was thriving when it was least valued. MGM

Peter Lorre and Vincent Price in Roger Corman's horror-comedy *The Raven* (1963), made for AIP. It also featured Boris Karloff, who had starred in a film of the same name made by Universal in 1935

had to dignify *Forbidden Planet* (1956), their contribution to the science-fiction cycle, by basing it on Shakespeare's *The Tempest* and structuring it around a Freudian notion ('monsters from the id'). At A-A (formerly the despised Monogram) Don Siegel was free to make *Invasion of the Body Snatchers* as a film whose lack of a *specific* meaning makes it universally powerful and open to any one of a dozen valid and potent readings. The subtexts of *Forbidden Planet* are as carefully layered as cake filling, but those of *Invasion of the Body Snatchers* splurge neurotically all over the screen. The majors had better special effects, but, characteristically, George Pal's sober Universal production *Destination: Moon* (1950) is far less enjoyable (and dramatically worthwhile or thematically interesting) than Lippert's lurid quickie imitation *Rocketship XM* (1950).

By the late 1950s, even Universal (the studio most at home with monsters and Abbott and Costello) was cooling off its science fiction/horror/teenage output, leaving the field almost clear for AIP, Hammer, and their few competitors. This was the period of peak production for flamboyant outsiders like William Castle and Albert Zugsmith (Sirk's *Written on the Wind*, 1957; Welles's *Touch of Evil*, 1958; Arnold's *High School Confidential*, 1958), who emerged from the conventional studio mills but refused to make unobtrusive B pictures for the rest of their careers. The majors were losing not only their grip on the audience, but also their monopoly on the rising talent. When studios had their own B units, there was a place to train and test the big names of tomorrow. With B production hived off to independents, directors of the future no longer had a career structure to aspire to. The film-happy kids of the 1950s were as likely to wish to model themselves on Bergman or Corman as on Vincente Minnelli or John Ford.

Anthony Mann, Nicholas Ray, Robert Aldrich, and Don Siegel (but notably not Sam Fuller) graduated from promising, cheap, exciting, and important early 1950s work to variously fallow, expensive, disastrous, and non-existent late 1950s and early 1960s spectacles (a period Aldrich and Siegel would recover from). Their position with audiences, and a growing number of critics, was taken by Roger Corman and his numerous protégés, associates, followers, imitators, and collaborators. Mann, Ray, Aldrich, Siegel, and Fuller (five of nature's independents) were schooled and nurtured by the faltering studio system, and Sam Peckinpah and Robert Altman came to the movies through working for the majors' television divisions. The next generation of film-makers got their breaks in exploitation, graduating from student or underground films (Francis Ford Coppola even started out shooting nudie movies) to horror or biker pictures. It is a rare Hollywood name of the 1970s and 1980s who did not make his first commercial pictures under the aegis of Roger Corman. Once, directors emerged through the ranks by serving apprenticeships, like Siegel's in Warner Bros.' montage department or Mann's on Bs like *Dr Broadway* (1942); since the 1960s a system of patronage has come into force, with successful producer-director-writers acting like Renaissance princes.

Corman was a key figure in the emergent post-studio system, persuading Arkoff and Nicholson to take a new tack with *The Fall of the House of Usher* (1960). Reputedly convincing his bosses that Poe's story was basically a monster movie ('only the house is the monster'), Corman overcame their resistance to a respectable (if out of copyright) literary source and stumped up the extra budget for a name actor (Vincent Price), colour and widescreen, and the services of a reputable writer (Richard Matheson). Influenced by the production values of Terence Fisher at Hammer, the delirious American Gothic of *Usher* superseded the pulpy horror-comic feel of *I Was a Teenage Werewolf* and initiated a run of Corman–Poe–Price movies: *The Pit and the Pendulum* (1961), *Tales of Terror* (1962), *The*

Haunted Palace (1963). After spoofing the cycle in *The Raven* (1963), Corman switched the base of production to England and borrowed a few Hammer personnel for *The Masque of the Red Death* (1964), a Bergman-influenced baroque, and *Tomb of Ligeia* (1965), an early Robert Towne script. Corman also found time to inaugurate trends for horror comedy (*A Bucket of Blood*, 1959; *The Little Shop of Horrors*, 1960), visionary science fiction (*The Man with X-Ray Eyes*, 1963), cynical war epics (*The Secret Invasion*, 1964), biker movies (*The Wild Angels*, 1967), period gangster films (*The St Valentine's Day Massacre*, 1967), and drug pictures (*The Trip*, 1967), meanwhile dashing off a rare 'serious' work in the racial drama *The Intruder* (1962), reputedly his only financial loser.

Corman broke free of AIP, became his own mogul, and gave chances to Francis Coppola, Monte Hellman, Robert Towne, Jack Nicholson, Dennis Hopper, Peter Bogdanovich, Martin Scorsese, Robert De Niro, Sylvester Stallone, Joe Dante, Jonathan Demme, Barry Levinson, Gale Anne Hurd, and James Cameron. This generation, who would gain prominence in the 1970s and beyond, would eventually become the Hollywood establishment as the Movie Brats became mini-moguls.

Corman founded the companies Filmgroup in 1960 and New World in 1970, and through them Hellman directed the 1964 Western masterpieces *The Shooting* and *Ride in the Whirlwind*; Coppola made *Dementia 13* (1963); Bogdanovich supervised the re-editing of a Soviet science-fiction film into *Voyage to the Planet of Prehistoric Women* (1968) and then directed the remarkable *Targets* (1969); Scorsese got his first break directing *Boxcar Bertha* (1972); and Jonathan Demme made *Caged Heat* (1974) and *Crazy Mama* (1975). AIP, not to be left out, hired John Milius to direct *Dillinger* (1973) and Brian De Palma for *Sisters* (1973). As a group, these movies are remarkable (it could be argued that Hellman, Bogdanovich, and De Palma have never been better) as much for their absorption of off-Hollywood influences as anything else. *Targets*, as befits a film made by a critic, is as bound up with celebrating and rejecting Hollywood conventions and icons (the reliable Karloff) as anything by the French Nouvelle Vague. There was mainstream American input—*Boxcar Bertha*, *Dillinger*, and *Crazy Mama* all take off from Arthur Penn's *Bonnie and Clyde* (1967)—but these were films which seemed open to world cinema to such an extent that it was seriously possible to discern the influence of Jean Renoir *and* Jean-Luc Godard in the nurse movies of Stephanie Rothman (*The Student Nurses*, 1970).

Even further out of Hollywood were the directors who pushed back the frontiers of censorship in the early 1960s: Russ Meyer, who specialized in sex farces, and Herschell Gordon Lewis, who inaugurated the hard-core gore horror movie with *Blood Feast* (1962). Meyer, a genuine if one-track talent whose *Faster Pussycat, Kill, KILL!* (1964) is some sort of masterpiece, eventually flirted with Hollywood by making *Beyond the Valley of the Dolls* (1970) for 20th Century–Fox, but Lewis, whose productions are primitive, had to be content with a place in the reference books and a run of near unwatchable movies. The importance of Meyer and Lewis, who were rediscovered by cult fans in the 1970s and 1980s, has less to do with their individual movies than with the precedents they set for off-Hollywood film-makers. The creation of distribution systems (drive-ins, college theatres, independent repertory houses, grind-houses) capable of playing Meyer's and Lewis's products made screen-space for one-offs like Herk Harvey's Kansas-made horror-art item *Carnival of Souls* (1964) and, later, the ground-breaking movies of George A. Romero (*Night of the Living Dead*, 1968), John Waters (*Pink Flamingos*, 1971), Wes Craven (*The Last House on the Left*, 1972), Tobe Hooper (*The Texas Chain Saw Massacre*, 1973), David Cronenberg (*Shivers*, 1976), and David Lynch (*Eraserhead*, 1977).

The cult film or 'midnight movie' phenomenon made major successes out of *The Rocky Horror Picture Show* (1975)—a Fox flop on its regular release—and *El Topo* (1971), while the relative openness of the small, down-market circuits allowed foreign product (Italian Westerns and horror movies, Chinese martial arts pictures, German soft-core sex) to feed the gene pool of the predominantly American exploitation industry. There was a revival of the race movie in the blaxploitation boom of the 1970s. Inaug-

Killings at the summer camp—a scene from the exploitation shocker *Friday 13th* (1980) which was extremely successful at the box-office and spawned a host of sequels

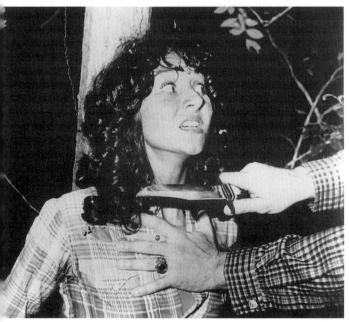

urated by major studios' movies like MGM's *Shaft* (1971) and Warners' *Superfly* (1971), blaxploitation soon passed to the likes of AIP for hybrids like *Blacula* (1972) before going into a hibernation from which the form arose, with rap replacing soul, in *Def by Temptation* (1990). By this time, the matter of major studio vs. independent production had come to mean a lot less: Spike Lee's small, personal, and irreverent *Do the Right Thing* (1989), made for UIP, was officially a major studio product, while James Cameron's machine-made box-office blockbuster star vehicle *Terminator 2: Judgment Day* (1991), made for Carolco, was an independent. The old Hollywood studios function more and more as releasing houses, and are as likely to be found pushing a horror movie or a youth musical as a literary adaptation or a big budget bio-pic.

The last gasp of old Hollywood was the misleading but monumental success of *The Sound of Music* (1965), which prompted the majors to sink enormous budgets into star-studded, stodgily expensive musicals which died at the box-office, just as audiences reared on AIP were flocking to Dennis Hopper's *Easy Rider* (1969), itself an offshoot of Corman's *The Wild Angels* and *The Trip*. With a determination to repeat the disasters of history, Hollywood reacted by taking the money they were wasting on imitations of *The Sound of Music* and wasting it on imitations of *Easy Rider*, resulting in such misconceived mini-genres as the campus protest cycle or interesting but commercially doomed ventures like Michelangelo Antonioni's *Zabriskie Point* (1969) and Hopper's *The Last Movie* (1972). Nevertheless, lessons percolated to the mainstream, with George Roy Hill's *Butch Cassidy and the Sundance Kid* (1967) demonstrating a grasp of the superficialities of the counterculture with its pop poster stars and self-conscious irony, while Peckinpah's *The Wild Bunch* (1969) took aboard the energy, immediacy, and stylized violence of Romero, Hellman, and Leone and wed them to the grand tradition of Ford and Hawks. Only in this environment could MGM give Stanley Kubrick the licence to make *2001: A Space Odyssey* (1968), fortuitously tapping into hippie trippiness, though the Academy Awards were still so set in old ways that the 1968 best film Oscar went to *Oliver!*

In the early 1970s, catalysed by a wave of American introspection in the wake of Vietnam and Watergate, Robert Altman, Robert Aldrich, Sam Peckinpah, Bob Rafelson, Clint Eastwood, Don Siegel, Arthur Penn, Terrence Malick, and Francis Coppola made outstanding films despite the directionless floundering of the film industry. Often, these talents were backed by major studios and rewarded by commercial success. Later in the decade and into the 1980s, directors emerged from the underground (David Lynch, David Cronenberg) or exploitation (John Carpenter, Oliver Stone, Wes Craven, George Miller) and turned out a different stamp of state-of-the-nation film, filtered through both the avant-garde and the traditional genre movie. When the Corman-trained generation came to the fore, they often returned to the material of AIP with a new, penetrating intelligence: Coppola and Lucas made *American Graffiti* (1973), which owes a debt to AIP's beach party musicals. Coppola's *The Godfather* (1972) and its sequels owe much to Corman's gangsters, but the director imports their intelligence and enthusiasm to a sumptuous Paramount production and produces a movie which is also heir to the tradition of Selznick (and Visconti).

Hollywood regained its financial footing in the mid-1970s by abandoning the concerns that had made the best American movies important. Spielberg's *Jaws* (1975), the first of the Movie Brat mega-hits, is a reduction of the liveliness of the best monster movies into an efficient thrill machine. The films that have subsequently scaled the box-office heights have been exploitation movies with multimillion budgets. While it is obvious that the *Star Wars* or Indiana Jones films are emptily expensive, if sometimes pleasing, retreads of old-fashioned kiddie genres, it is less remarked that Ridley Scott's *Thelma & Louise* (1991) is essentially a better-packaged rerun of Michael Miller's *Jackson County Jail* (1975). In smoothing the technical rough edges that make most exploitation movies unacceptable to a mainstream multiplex audience, blockbusters have almost always taken out the thematic concerns or unusual attitudes that make them interesting to their by-no-means unsophisticated audiences. This led to the retaking of the commercial high ground by the majors, and to a cinema characterized by the mechanical assemblies of *Home Alone* (1990) and *Basic Instinct* (1991).

Exploitation cinema continues, but after *Friday the 13th* (1980)—significantly, a Paramount release—has been less likely to encourage the unusual, and increasingly dominated by worthless, self-hating product like Troma's *The Toxic Avenger* (1985). The repetition of slasher conventions in the literally hundreds of horror films that have poured forth to feed the direct-to-video market has led to a self-awareness that sometimes bears fruit, as in Wes Craven's original *A Nightmare on Elm Street* (1984), but more often encourages a flip, joky knowingness that muzzles any attempts at being seriously unsettling. The strangest thing about the Troma product ('a film packed full of unnecessary sex and violence') is that it is so inoffensive. Traditional exploitation distribution circuits have been superseded by home video, whose voracious need for mid-list product has encouraged gluts of slicker, emptier films. It is now possible for a film to turn a healthy profit and have a run of sequels even if it proves a theatrical flop or is never seen on anything but a television screen. While this means a useful afterlife for some fine movies which would otherwise be written off, the take-over of the video rental market by conservative chains (along with the passage in the UK of the Video Recording Act) has ordered the interesting chaos of the early days of the industry and encouraged the production of genre films that are actually generic. Exploitation, especially as practised by companies like New Line, has become a matter of franchises, with sequels hitting video racks as if films were McDonald's meals, each instalment in the *Elm Street* or *Child's Play* series required to deliver *exactly* the same qualities as the last.

The 1980s and 1990s successors to Scorsese, Romero, and Altman come from a tradition that stands as much in opposition to grindhouse formulas as it is set against the gloss of the majors, siding with oddballs like Larry Cohen or David Lynch rather than the pop promo or TV 'ad grads' who are assigned to direct *Elm Street* sequels before signing up to do big star action movies for Joel Silver. Oddities like Abel Ferrara's *King of New York* (1989), John McNaughton's *Henry: Portrait of a Serial Killer* (1989), and Quentin Tarantino's *Reservoir Dogs* (1992) are influenced by the 1970s horror tradition but alienated from the 1980s and 1990s horror industry. As comfortably assessed as art films as exploitation, these are post-modern exploitation movies which deconstruct traditional plots or themes while delivering the sort of state-of-the-nation addresses last seen in the cutting edge of early 1970s cinema. These are extreme movies and often find themselves at the centre of a censorship uproar which rarely troubles less daring luridity, but which at least serves to make the films literally visible. No studio picture would go as far as Ferrara's *Bad Lieutenant* (1992) does, with the utmost unexploitative seriousness, in violence, drugs, sleaze, male nudity, religious imagery, or emotional agony. Ideas are as dangerous as images and obsession is more rewarding than prurience. The seam of vital, irreverent bizarre movie-making persists in America, but, with the mainstream *and* the independents ossified into mirror-images, has had to break away from established set-ups and seek new outlets.

Bibliography
Corman, Roger (1992), *How I Made a Hundred Movies in Hollywood and Never Lost a Dime*.
Hillier, Jim, and Lipstadt, Aaron (1981), *Roger Corman's New World*.
McCarthy, Todd, and Flynn, Charles (1975), *Kings of the 'B's*.
Newman, Kim (1988), *Nightmare Movies*.
Weldon, Michael (1983), *The Psychotronic Encyclopedia of Film*.

Dreams and Nightmares in the Hollywood Blockbuster

JOSEPH SARTELLE

The blockbuster hit of 1991 was James Cameron's *Terminator 2*, which offered audiences some of the most spectacular special effects since the *Star Wars* era of the late 1970s and early 1980s. Formally, *Terminator 2* also resembled the blockbusters of that period in its extremely fast pace and its emphasis on plot over character. Ideologically, like those earlier movies its motivating anxieties were rooted firmly in the Cold War. Although the film made a passing reference to the fact that the Russians were now 'our friends', the story concerned the chilliest fear of the previous forty years, the destruction of humanity in a nuclear holocaust (spectacularly simulated in a dream sequence within the film). Finally, *Terminator 2* recalled the *Star Wars* era blockbusters in its faith in the capacity of human beings to control their destinies on a grand scale, since its team of heroes succeed in altering future history and preventing nuclear obliteration.

However, considered in relation to its blockbuster predecessors, *Terminator 2* also showed how much had changed. Like many other popular movies of the late 1980s and early 1990s, the film was dark, brutally and routinely violent, and preoccupied with issues of sheer survival. Just whose survival was in question was suggested by the fact that the two adult white male stars of the film (Arnold Schwarzenegger and Robert Patrick) both played killing machines that only superficially resemble human beings. The sequel added a twist to the original film (1984's *The Terminator*) by having Schwarzenegger's Terminator work on the side of the good guys this time around, and the film played for both comic and sentimental effect the subplot in which the white male killing machine is re-educated to be a responsible, protective caretaker. But just when the Terminator has been reformed enough to understand why people cry, he insists that he must be destroyed if the world is to be saved. The film thus suggested that his identity was too closely tied to his origins as a killer, something which even sensitivity training could not overcome. In short, like so many films of its time, *Terminator 2* was a meditation on the problem of the white man.

The period of which *Terminator 2* is representative is often called the era of the modern blockbuster, and stretches from George Lucas's 1977 state-of-the-art space opera *Star Wars* up to and beyond Steven Spielberg's 1993 state-of-the-art dinosaur epic *Jurassic Park*. As many critics have observed, the period is 'post-generic' in the sense that, while films belonging to the traditional Hollywood genres were still being made, they coexisted with an explosion of emerging new categories which made use of the older elements by recombining them in various ways. One example of such a 'hybrid' genre is, of course, the special-effects oriented blockbuster. It is also a period marked by an unusually strong and self-conscious convergence between American popular culture, especially Hollywood movies, and American political culture. The era was defined by the presidency of Ronald Reagan, a former minor Hollywood star who used lines from blockbusters to promote his national policy initiatives (including *Back to the Future*'s 'Where we're going, we don't need roads'; *Star Wars*'s 'The Force is with us'; and *Sudden Impact*'s 'Go ahead, make my day!').

The most highly successful and broadly popular movies of this era are best understood as ideological fantasies about the relationship of the American nation to the realities and implications of its own recent history, which included the assassinations and social upheaval of the 1960s and the political scandal and corruption of Watergate in the early 1970s. But even more important for the purposes of this discussion, that history included on the one hand America's traumatic experience of defeat in Vietnam, and on the other the emergence of newly militant demands by women and 'minorities' (racial, ethnic, and sexual) for greater representation and equality at all levels of American society and culture.

THE TRIUMPHAL MODE

The big blockbusters of the late 1970s and early 1980s responded to these historical developments by denying them, in fantasies which sought to escape or otherwise transcend present realities altogether. In the case of the *Star Wars* trilogy, the story was set 'a long time ago, in a galaxy far, far away'. *Raiders of the Lost Ark* (1981) offered the nostalgic moral certainties of 1930s Nazi villainy, while *Back to the Future* (1985) found nostalgic refuge in the simpler world of 1950s American suburbia. A different group of movies, most notably Steven Spielberg's *Close Encounters of the Third Kind* (1977) and *E.T.* (1982), held out the hope of extraterrestrial intervention to redeem and rescue us from our everyday lives (as did the mid-1980s films *Cocoon* and *2001*). Such films were significant in their straightforward confessions of the wish to escape from present-day realities. However, in their reliance upon rescuers from outer space, they displayed their doubts about whether the American nation was capable of escaping, on its own, the implications of its recent history.

The shaky confidence of the ET-intervention films coexisted with a much more 'triumphal' sensibility in most of the period's blockbusters. In one way or another,

Arnold Schwarzenegger

(1947–)

During the 1980s, the films of Arnold Schwarzenegger reportedly grossed $1 billion world-wide. His path from Mr Universe to major Hollywood star was made possible by changes in the film industry itself; the rise of fantasy, science-fiction, and action-adventure genres after *Star Wars*, the return of heroism on a grand scale after a series of counter-cultural anti-heroes in the 1970s, and the importance of physical culture in the 1980s. Like Madonna, Schwarzenegger embodies the fantasy of success. This self-made man has literally crafted his own body to fit the appetites of the culture industry and a health-conscious American society, fearful of morbidity while fascinated with the spectacle of mortality. Like Madonna, Schwarzenegger's charm derives in part from a self-mocking humour which in no way detracts from the appeal of his exaggerated masquerade of gender.

Born in Graz, Austria, in 1947, Schwarzenegger grew up idolizing such muscular athletes-turned-stars as Johnny Weissmuller, Steve Reeves, and Mickey Hargitay, whom he would later play in a TV movie *The Jayne Mansfield Story*. In 1968, Schwarzenegger moved to Los Angeles and was groomed by body-building promoter Joe Weider, from whom he borrowed the money for his first of many real estate investments. While making $14,000 a year working as a bricklayer, Schwarzenegger won a string of body-building titles, including multiple crownings as Mr Universe and Mr Olympia.

Schwarzenegger's early endeavours in film were inauspicious. His first lead was the title role in a comedy called *Hercules in New York* (1969), and throughout the 1970s he had small television roles and walk-ons in Hollywood: he can be glimpsed in Robert Altman's *The Long Goodbye* (1973), eagerly disrobing and flexing his pectoral muscles. He garnered more attention in the documentary *Pumping Iron* (1977), which chronicled his canny drive for the Mr Olympia title, and in Bob Rafelson's *Stay Hungry* (1976), a fiction film about the private life of a body-builder and a promoter.

With the boom of post-*Star Wars* science-fiction and fantasy films, Schwarzenegger's 'ideal' body gave him an entrée into mainstream film-making with starring roles in the violent sword-and-sorcery dramas *Conan the Barbarian* (1982) and *Conan the Destroyer* (1984). During the same period, the action-adventure genre was established, emerging from the rogue cop *policiers* of Clint Eastwood and Charles Bronson and the Reagan–Bush era *Rambo* cycle which glorified the power of the individual to solve political problems through a combination of extensive firearms and musculature. The spectacular surprise success of the science-fiction action film *Terminator* (1984) helped put Schwarzenegger on the map, and he capitalized on his new-found success with a spate of action films: *Commando* (1985), *Raw Deal* (1986), *The Running Man* (1987), *Predator* (1987), *Red Heat* (1988). Though not as high-profile as Sylvester Stallone's Rambo series, these films nevertheless consolidated Schwarzenegger's box-office power in an expensive but remunerative genre.

Schwarzenegger attempted to broaden his range by appearing in two comedies, *Twins* (1988) and *Kindergarten Cop* (1990), but his roles in the mega-hits *Total Recall* (1990) and *Terminator 2: Judgment Day* (1991) cemented his stranglehold on the expensive, special-effects-crammed, action genre. Budgets for such epics increased dramatically during the late 1980s, and sequels and stars became necessary to assure box-office draw. *Terminator 2* reportedly cost over $80 million, a budget that included $14 million for Schwarzenegger—twice the entire budget of the original *Terminator*.

After playing the killing-machine-villain in *Terminator*, Schwarzenegger's subsequent move to the role of hero necessitated changes in his image. In contrast to his former roles as an ultra-violent hero, *Terminator 2* presented a killing machine who befriends the young boy-hero of the future and learns to become kinder and gentler (he no longer kills, only shoots people in the leg), helpfully destroying himself at the film's end in order to save the world. This shift was consolidated in *Last Action Hero* (1993), which was marketed at a younger audience, and in which comedy and self-parody were as important as the violence. Despite its $70 million price-tag the film failed to live up to its expectations, in part because Columbia insisted on releasing it opposite Spielberg's *Jurassic Park*, which attracted a greater share of media and box-office attention. The film's failure shook Hollywood's confidence in Schwarzenegger, once considered box-office insurance for expensive action films.

EDWARD R. O'NEILL

SELECT FILMOGRAPHY

Stay Hungry (1976); Pumping Iron (1977); The Terminator (1984); Red Sonja (1985); Commando (1985); Raw Deal (1986); The Running Man (1987); Predator (1987); Red Heat (1988); Total Recall (1990); Terminator 2: Judgment Day (1991); Last Action Hero (1993); True Lies (1994); Junior (1994).

BIBLIOGRAPHY

Butler, George (1990), *Arnold Schwarzenegger: A Portrait*.

Arnold Schwarzenegger in *Conan the Barbarian* (1982), directed by John Milius

these films addressed the problem of America's performance anxieties in the wake of more than a decade of what was now perceived as domestic and international failure and humiliation. What they had in common was a commitment to reviving American self-confidence through reimagining the strong white male hero. The *Star Wars* and Indiana Jones movies, for example, were allegories of international relations: they sought to restore faith in the American ability to compete and perform successfully in a global political economy. In *Raiders of the Lost Ark* (1981), archaeologist and model entrepreneur Indiana Jones moved freely through both the First and Third Worlds, and always found friendly non-white natives happy to help him appropriate their historical treasures (i.e. their material resources). The *Star Wars* trilogy imagined the Cold War as a battle in which the Rebel Alliance, composed of white heroes and their differently speciesed helpers in a pastiche of American liberal pluralism, prevails over the evil Galactic Empire, whose military men wore uniforms that looked suspiciously like those of the Soviets. Even *Close Encounters* and *E.T.*, which had their doubts about American society, eased anxieties about foreign affairs by comfortingly projecting a universe in which the aliens were perhaps a little scary at first but ultimately friendly and well intentioned.

In all these movies, we were meant to understand that the success of the white male hero lies in his capacity to have faith in his own abilities. In a scene in *The Empire Strikes Back* (1980), old and tiny Jedi Master Yoda used the Force to raise Luke Skywalker's fighter from the swamp. 'I don't believe it,' Luke says, having been unable to accomplish this himself. 'That is why you fail,' Yoda responds, succinctly expressing these films' wish to believe that overcoming history was simply a matter of having the confidence to believe that you could. In this manner, the movies mirrored the Reagan administration's political rhetoric and its use of public spectacles (such as the inaugurations and the Los Angeles Olympics), just as Reagan himself often seemed to think that he was acting out a Hollywood blockbuster—the most notorious example being his eagerness to embrace the label 'Star Wars' for his massively expensive Strategic Defense Initiative. Both Hollywood and Reagan offered images which sought to convince the American people of what Reagan's favourite economist George Gilder called 'the necessity for faith' in his 1981 bestseller, *Wealth and Poverty* (copies of which Reagan distributed to the members of his first cabinet). The special effects-oriented blockbusters and the Reagan presidency converged in their exhortations to the American people to share in this triumphal attitude, which also characterized films of the period such as *Rocky* (1976), *Superman* (1978), *Fame* (1980), *Risky Business* (1983), and *The Karate Kid* (1984), as well as the blockbuster hits already mentioned.

The defining features of the triumphal period were summed up in a remarkably literal form in 1985's *Back to the Future*. In the original film and its sequels, a direct connection was established between the 1950s and the 1980s; they dealt with the trauma of the intervening decades of American history by acting as if they did not exist, effectively eliminating them altogether. Teenager Marty McFly is accidentally sent back to 1955 when his friend, the inventor of a time machine, is attacked in a shopping mall parking lot by the Libyan terrorists who provided him with plutonium (the film thus connected itself to Reagan-era anxieties about international politics and US imperialism). Once in the past Marty must see to it that his parents meet and fall in love as they were meant to, or he will cease to exist. Marty teaches his shy and nerdy father how to stand up to a bully and win the favour of Marty's mother, thus assuring his own future birth. But Marty does not just preserve the present, he remakes it for the better. Because he taught his father to 'stand tall' (to invoke the Reagan rhetoric), when Marty returns to 1985, his formerly strange and embarrassing parents and siblings are now smart and hip, the family has more money as well as good taste, and Marty has been given the truck of his dreams.

MULTI-CULTURALISM

By the middle of the 1980s, however, the triumphal periods of both Hollywood blockbusters and the Reagan presidency were coming to an end. A variety of factors were forcing a redefinition of 'American' identity, including the beginning of the end of the Cold War and the increasingly apparent damage caused by the administration's neglect of domestic problems, particularly the desperate situation of urban African-Americans. The celebratory can-do mood of the country had begun to break down. The Reagan era unravelled in the Iran-Contra and Oliver North scandals, and the triumphal attitude of Hollywood's big action films was replaced by a more grim, violent, and survivalist sensibility—as though the American experience in Vietnam was now being replayed in internal and domestic terms.

This shift can be seen in *Top Gun* and *Aliens*, two of the biggest-grossing films of 1986. *Top Gun* was the apotheosis of the triumphal sense of renewed American confidence and power, in which present-day American military life was depicted with all the action and excitement of a *Star Wars* instalment. Tom Cruise's Maverick was a combination of Luke Skywalker and Han Solo (i.e. Oedipal conflict and roguish masculine posturing); the breathtaking special effects sequences were between high-tech. fighter aircraft rather than spaceships. The film's Cold War anxieties were explicit in the Russians' jets which the hero battles and defeats, and Vietnam performance anxiety was implicitly invoked and overcome, as the film's military prove that the Force is once again with them. The film was widely received as a kind of two-hour advertisement for military service and nationalist pride (director Tony Scott had in fact come from a background making television commercials), and the navy reported a significant increase in recruitment after the movie was released.

James Cameron's *Aliens* initially gave us a version of *Top Gun*'s military bravado and can-do faith, in its team of 'Colonial Marines', who are sent with Lt. Ripley (Sigourney Weaver) to cleanse a human colony of the murderous alien monsters first encountered in Ridley Scott's 1979 film *Alien*. However, by the film's end all of the marines are killed except for one, a handsome white male. In a more typical action film (such as 1987's *Predator*, starring Arnold Schwarzenegger), this character would go on to be the triumphant hero, but in *Aliens* he is badly wounded and removed from the story before the concluding and most important battles begin. The final victory over the giant alien queen is won by a woman (Lt. Ripley), with the help of a girl child and a male android—in other words, a team of symbolic 'minorities'. The movie celebrates the military but also shows it to be ineffective, and while the protagonists finally win their battle, the concluding mood of the film is not at all triumphal. The heroes survive rather than succeed, since all but one of the marines and all but one of the colonists (the little girl) are dead, and the survivors are left drifting in space, uncertain of rescue.

Aliens rendered the surviving white man unconscious and gave the heroic victory to a woman. It was an early instance of a trend in American popular culture that would become stronger: the commitment to multi-cultural consciousness, what both proponents and critics soon came to refer to as 'political correctness'. Commentators on the late 1980s have discussed multi-culturalism (also sometimes known as the politics of identity) as the mainstreaming of a new sense of racial and ethnic pride, which arose as a compensatory response to the inability of minorities, especially African-Americans, to achieve the social and economic equality that the integrationist civil rights movement had promised. What has been specific to the multi-cultural agenda is its emphasis on the politics of cultural representations, such as school textbooks or Hollywood movies. In Hollywood, a multi-cultural sensibility first manifested itself in an increasing number of movies designed to appeal to both white and minority (especially black) audiences, including, for example, films starring Eddie Murphy and Whoopi Goldberg, or the genre of bi-racial 'buddy movies' such as the very popular *Lethal Weapon* series.

However, even if Hollywood was making more movies with black performers, they were still being made almost exclusively by white men. Steven Spielberg's 1985 film *The Color Purple*, a white man's adaptation of a black woman's novel about a black woman's life and experiences, became the focus of an intense debate about the politics of Hollywood's representation of non-white peoples and cultures. Hollywood's solution to this controversy was to give a small but growing number of independent minority film-makers the opportunity to make movies for mass audiences; for example Spike Lee, who became the most famous, important, and influential black director in Hollywood history. The critical and popular success of *Do the Right Thing*, Lee's 1989 study of explosive racial tensions in a small inner-city neighbourhood, gave rise in the early 1990s to a series of movies made by black directors with largely black casts. These were most often stories about the violence afflicting urban black families and communities, and included *Boyz N the Hood*, *Straight out of Brooklyn*, *New Jack City*, and *Menace II Society*. Initially restricted to movies by, for, and about African-Americans, Hollywood's multi-culturalism showed signs of opening up to other minorities such as Asian-Americans. For example, the lavish, big-budget film version of Amy Tan's novel *The Joy Luck Club* (1993) was directed by Wayne Wang, who, like Spike Lee, began his career making low-budget, independent films.

Women also benefited from the multi-cultural climate in Hollywood. There were gains at the level of representation, beginning with the middle-class empowerment fantasy *Nine to Five* (1980), all the way up to the outlaw tragicomedy of 1991's *Thelma & Louise*. As a modest concession to protests against the stereotypical roles assigned to women, a number of Hollywood movies included a strong female character in what traditionally had been all-male groups; for example, *Lethal Weapon 3* (1992) added a tough female martial-arts expert to the series' buddie-team formula. A more complicated response to feminism was seen in a genre of what might be called 'women-with-guns' movies, such as *Aliens* and the early 1990s films *Terminator 2*, *Blue Steel*, and *The Silence of the Lambs* (as well as *Thelma & Louise*). While some critics charged that these films merely portrayed women in a kind of masculine drag, they were meditations on the unstable nature of gender roles and identification in American culture during this period. Additionally, by the late 1980s, Hollywood had rediscovered the profitability of movies targeted specifically to female audiences, resulting in films like *Steel Magnolias* (1989), *Beaches* (1988), and *Fried Green Tomatoes* (1991).

At the level of production, there were advances especially for women directors, whose small but growing number included Barbra Streisand, Martha Coolidge, Susan Seidelman, Kathryn Bigelow, and Lili Fini Zanuck. Perhaps the most notable success story was Penny Marshall, a former TV sitcom actress who went on to direct several critically well received and financially successful movies, including *Big* (1987), *Awakenings* (1989), and *A League of their Own* (1992).

Steven Spielberg

(1947–)

In less than twenty years, Steven Spielberg went from being a talented young director of television programmes to a producer-director whose personal wealth of over $200 million made him among the richest individuals in the USA, alongside such entertainment industry figures as Roy Disney, Mark Goodson, Lew Wasserman, and Merv Griffin. This trajectory reveals as much about the prevailing conditions of the film industry during this period as it does about Spielberg's talents. Unlike George Lucas and Martin Scorsese who graduated from film school, Spielberg started directing for television at 22, never having finished college. From 1969 to 1973 he directed episodes of *Columbo*, *Marcus Welby, M.D.*, *Night Gallery*, and *The Name of the Game*, as well as an excellent segment of the movie-length episode of *Night Gallery* (1969).

Spielberg's rapid rise to industrial dominance was conditioned by the match between his own directorial aptitude for suspense and his talent for both anticipating and following changes in the profitability of Hollywood genres. With the return to economic dominance of the fantasy, horror, and action genres during the 1970s and 1980s, Spielberg was able to find a profitable outlet

for his talents. He rode the crest of the post-*Star Wars* science-fiction–fantasy wave with *Close Encounters of the Third Kind* (1977) and *E.T. the Extraterrestrial* (1982), capitalized on the post-*Exorcist* terror boom with *Jaws* (1975), and gave the action-adventure genre a comic-book twist with his *Raiders of the Lost Ark* series (1981, 1984, and 1989; created with friend and *Star Wars* director George Lucas). With *The Color Purple* (1985) and *Empire of the Sun* (1987) Spielberg attempted to gain greater recognition as a serious artist, although these attempts were marred by the heavy hand with which he deployed his considerable skill at evoking emotions. From 1989 to 1991 Spielberg suffered two notable commercial and critical failures, *Always* (1989) and *Hook* (1991), which threatened his position as a major commercial director, but his return to directing with *Jurassic Park* and *Schindler's List* (both 1993) simultaneously landed him box-office success and heightened critical recognition.

Spielberg's role in contemporary Hollywood goes further than that of director. Not only did he usually produce the films he directed, often with Kathleen Kennedy and Frank Marshall, but he has served as producer or executive producer, often in tandem with Universal as distributor, on a diverse list of films, including some of the largest financial successes of the 1980s. A long-time supporter of Robert Zemeckis, Spielberg had a hand in *Back to the Future* (1985) and its sequels, as well as *Who Framed*

Roger Rabbit (1988). In addition, he played a role in producing Tobe Hooper's *Poltergeist* (1982), Joe Dante's *Gremlins* (1984), and Akira Kurosawa's *Dream* (1990).

Although his own films have been consistent in their technical expertise and the brilliance of their suspense construction, Spielberg's preoccupations have shifted notably since his early work. In his gripping thrillers *Duel* and *Jaws*, Spielberg created a nihilistic vision of a world in which senseless violence could erupt at any time, taking ordinary individuals prisoner. But with *Close Encounters*, Spielberg shifted to creating daydreams, in which movie magic is marshalled to reproduce, in public, Spielberg's own childlike wonder at the emotional power of film. It is hardly surprising that one of Spielberg's enduring themes is the reconciliation between generations, between adult and child, as in the ill-fated *Hook*, where the now-adult Peter Pan must recapture his sense of childish fancy. The darker edge of his earlier films having largely faded, Spielberg's concern with violence has become simplified into a Manichean opposition between good and bad.

The bitter horror of Spielberg's early work still survives in the ferocity of *Jurassic Park*, which sits uneasily alongside the film's tidy moral lessons. *Schindler's List* also provided a darker moral fable in which an impresario-like capitalist entrepreneur finds his moral conscience during the Holocaust. At the film's end, the real-life survivors saved by Oskar Schindler and their children accompany the actors who played them to place stones on the real Schindler's grave, thus reconciling not only Hollywood and historical reality, but parents and children, and Spielberg and his Jewish heritage.

Schindler's List finally earned Spielberg a long-awaited Oscar for best director. The same year that *Jurassic Park* displaced *E.T.* as the biggest world-wide money-maker of all time, *Schindler's List* brought recognition for the serious endeavours of Hollywood's most consistently profitable producer-director. In Hollywood's long-time struggle between its artistic and moral aspirations and the hard realities of the box-office, Steven Spielberg has managed to find some reconciliation.

EDWARD R. O'NEILL

SELECT FILMOGRAPHY

Duel (1972); Sugarland Express (1974); Jaws (1975); Close Encounters of the Third Kind (1977); 1941 (1979); Raiders of the Lost Ark (1981); E.T. the Extraterrestrial (1982); Indiana Jones and the Temple of Doom (1984) ; The Color Purple (1985); Empire of the Sun (1987); Indiana Jones and the Last Crusade (1989); Always (1989); Jurassic Park (1993); Schindler's List (1993).

BIBLIOGRAPHY

Sinyard, Neil (1987), *The Films of Steven Spielberg*.
Pye, Michael, and Myles, Lynda (1979), *The Movie Brats*.

Opposite: Dennis Weaver as the travelling salesman terrorized by a truck in one of Spielberg's earliest and most effective thrillers, *Duel* (1972).

The rise of a multi-cultural sensibility promised to give new power to everyone except white males. However, while Hollywood began to produce more movies which offered the view from the margins of the dominant culture, most films continued (of course) to express the dominant culture's point of view—which was increasingly nervous about the implications of multi-culturalism for the position of the white male in both American and global society. For example, in *Back to the Future Part II* (1989), Marty McFly's entrepreneurial spirit, which allowed him in the first film to rewrite history and improve the present, this time ends up changing things for the worse. In a complicated series of plot twists, Marty's plan to get rich with a book of sports scores from the future (suggesting Wall Street insider-trading scams) results in a version of 1985 in which his middle-class white family's suburban neighbourhood becomes a ghetto hell of drive-by shootings and bombed-out cars. Marty's house is occupied by a black family, and Marty is mistaken for a rapist when he enters through his bedroom window and finds a black teenage girl in his place. What was repressed in the original returns in the sequel. The 'alternative' 1985 of *Back to the Future Part II* is actually, as the black people in Marty's house suggest, the violent urban reality of the 1980s which both the Reagan administration and blockbuster fantasies had tried so hard to forget. The film thus represented two different experiences of life in the 1980s not as the differing points of view of whites and non-whites, but as two contradictory and incompatible alternatives. The film confessed its anxieties about multi-culturalism by associating multiple perspectives and versions of history—basic principles of multi-cultural awareness—with disorientation, loss of individual agency and control, and even the possible end of the world.

The dominant culture's fears about the politics of identity were also visible in Tim Burton's hugely successful blockbusters *Batman* (1989) and *Batman Returns* (1992). Multi-culturalism took the allegorical form here of struggles between the vigilante-hero Batman, who is really rich white male Bruce Wayne, and his various criminal foes, each of whom has a distinctive 'marginal' identity, in the sense that they exist outside of Gotham City's 'normal' society (significantly, some critics attacked the portrayal of the Penguin in *Batman Returns* as anti-Semitic). Their freakish identities are clearly figures for the underclass of urban minorities: they are associated with crime, they are organized like gangs, and they seek political power (as in the Penguin's effort to become mayor). The films offered a straightforwardly fascistic solution to the social decay and disruption which they attributed to people with deviant or marginal identities. But the films also showed a deep ambivalence about the embodiment of that solution, namely Batman himself. As the Penguin tells Batman in *Batman Returns*, 'You're just jealous because I'm a real freak, and you have to wear a costume.' If the criminals in the *Batman* films were cartoon minorities (including Catwoman and her equally cartoonish 'feminism'), then Batman's costumed identity was a kind of minority drag, a way of identifying with or occupying the position of the margins while still preserving his privilege as a wealthy white male. In other words, the Batman fantasy was an example of the mixed response of the white male hero to the threat posed by the new multi-cultural sensibility: it is as if he envies and wishes to identify himself with the very same marginal and outcast people he must oppose as threats to social order.

As the *Batman* movies indicate, Hollywood's block-busters, which offered fantasies of white male triumph and transcendence in the late 1970s and early 1980s, had become more and more self-conscious that the white male identity was now unavoidably a problem. This development is related to what at first may seem to be a very different Hollywood genre of the period: star-performance vehicles. These showcased amazing acting performances of the sort associated with Robert De Niro, Al Pacino, and Dustin Hoffman, who are famous for roles in which the impressiveness of the acting is a function of how successfully the actor transforms his own persona in the performance. It is significant that these roles involved performing the identities of almost anybody but the average white male, whose normative status marked him as in some sense having no *particular* identity. Such films represented a response to a question posed by the rise of multi-cultural power: how does the white man get an identity? The star-performance movies provided an answer in the white actor's simulation of non-normative identities, as in De Niro's transformation into white working-class boxer Jake LaMotta in *Raging Bull* (1980), Hoffman's simulation of a woman in *Tootsie* (1982), and Tom Cruise's histrionic portrayal of Ron Kovic, a paraplegic Vietnam War veteran and political activist, in Oliver Stone's *Born on the Fourth of July* (1989).

As the last example suggests, films which showcase acting technique and performance developed in the late 1980s into a genre which we might call 'disability films', in which the actor portrays white men who are victims of disabilities of one sort or another. In *Rain Man* (1988), Dustin Hoffman played an autistic man; Pacino was blind in *Scent of a Woman* (1992); De Niro played a man who is temporarily revived from the coma-like state he had been in for years in *Awakenings* (1989); and Harrison Ford became a kinder, gentler white man after taking a bullet in the head in *Regarding Henry* (1991). These movies and roles suggested a kind of envious fascination with and desire to inhabit a victim's position (a desire expressed much more literally in the tremendously popular genre of 'slasher' movies). They were the closest that white actors could come, after the advent of identity politics, to per-

forming racial and ethnic identities (homophobia made playing gay men too risky an option for major male stars, at least until Tom Hanks's Oscar-winning performance as a man with AIDS in Jonathan Demme's 1993 film *Philadelphia*, which portrayed gay identity as a kind of disability). Whatever particular story each of these movies told, they were all fantasies of identity transformation, both in the sheer spectacle of the actors' performances and very often in the thematics of the films themselves, which were frequently self-reflexive stories *about* individual performance and transformation. Their emergence as an identifiable category was a rather literal symptom of a cultural wish to see the normative (heterosexual and middle-class) white male turn himself into somebody else, and specifically somebody with a claim to minority status.

THE WHITE MAN AS VICTIM

By the end of the 1980s, a number of critics were arguing that American culture in general had become characterized by a fetishization of the victim (for example, in books like Robert Hughes's *Culture of Complaint* and Charles J. Sykes's *A Nation of Victims*). Since white males could not credibly claim victim status by virtue of race, ethnicity, or gender (the categories privileged by the multi-cultural sensibility), disability films offered one way in which white males could be imagined as a victimized group. The appropriation of others' identities shown in the acting performance-oriented movies were relatively benign versions of a group of films which might collectively be called 'white male paranoia fantasies'. In addition to the two *Batman* films and *Back to the Future Part II*, discussed above, examples include the series of back-to-Vietnam movies from the mid-1980s like *Rambo*, *Missing in Action*, and *Uncommon Valor*, as well as films as diverse as *RoboCop* (1987), *Die Hard* (1988), *Falling Down* (1993), and *Jurassic Park* (1993). Whereas the disability film showed white men performing the identities of individuals struggling against real affliction and victimization, these other movies—which were tremendously popular and successful—sought in various ways to present the normative white male as *himself* a victim. Like the blockbusters of the triumphal period, these films featured a white male hero who overcomes terrible villains and circumstances. But unlike earlier heroes, the protagonist of the white male paranoia fantasy must spend most of the movie enduring horrible physical and psychological punishment. Even in movies like *RoboCop* and its sequels, or *Universal Soldier* (1992) or the two *Terminator* films, in which the bodies of the male action heroes are fused with hard metal machinery, the narrative emphasizes the hero's capacity for suffering: he is shot, stabbed, crushed, dismembered, burned, or otherwise tortured. The hypermasculine bodies of these films' heroes do not protect them from brutalization so much as they make possible an intensification of the spectacle of their punishment.

The blockbuster hit *Die Hard*, starring Bruce Willis as tough New York cop John McClane, displayed the various ways in which white men understood both themselves and the American nation as victims of various historical developments. The film takes place almost entirely within the symbolically laden space of a corporate office building in Los Angeles owned by the Japanese company which employs McClane's estranged wife. In case we do not get the point, in one of the movie's opening scenes the wife's Yale-educated Japanese boss responds to McClane's grudging admiration of the new building by joking, 'Hey, Pearl Harbor didn't work out, so we got you with tape decks.' Anxieties about global competition and multi-culturalism are also seen in the Euro-dominated but multinational and multiracial team of élite criminals who, claiming to be terrorists, seize the building and hold its employees hostage (including McClane's wife) while they attempt to access the building's high-tech. vault. In addition to foreign competition, McClane is also afflicted by federal government bureaucracy, in the form of bumbling FBI agents who refuse to listen to or support him in his solitary battle within the building, considering him a nuisance and obstacle to their own incompetent but by-the-book efforts.

However, *Die Hard* also suggested that the real problem for the white male hero in this movie was his relationship with his wife. Offered a promotion that required her to move to Los Angeles, she chose separation from McClane over sacrificing her own career. A parallel is drawn in the film between anxiety about American performance in the global economy and anxiety about masculine performance in the domestic economy: international competition has taken McClane's wife and family from him. His victimization by these forces is made most clear in a scene in which he must walk barefoot across an office floor covered with broken glass in order to save himself and thus survive to rescue his wife; we must then watch as he digs the pieces out of the soles of his feet. The threat posed to McClane's masculinity by his wife's career targets feminism as one of the forces victimizing the American white male. *Die Hard* and other white male paranoia fantasies were in this way related to another important group of films from the same period; 'backlash' movies in which strong and independent women were, in various ways, punished and put in their proper (subordinate) place. The most notorious of these was *Fatal Attraction* (1987), but the group also includes such diverse films as *Baby Boom* (1987), *Misery* (1990), and *Pretty Woman* (1990).

The white male paranoia movies expressed the white male's sense of resentment and anger in reaction to a perceived loss of privilege; they told us that the normative American white male *felt* like a victim even if the rest of society told him he was the oppressor. But as the global and economic dimensions of *Die Hard* indicate, they also had a larger political agenda. They brought together into a single basic narrative a whole range of anxieties about the erosion of American power and privilege in the face of increasingly successful competition from non-white peoples, coupled with a simultaneous decline in American performance. As responses to the rise of both multiculturalism and feminism, these films presented heroes who now stood for all white men in relation to women and other minority groups, but also continued to represent a fantasy 'America', threatened by Third World and other non-white nations which could both claim the moral high ground and in some cases outperform the United States.

Retrospectively, it would be difficult to underestimate how important the American experience in Vietnam was for virtually all of Hollywood's most successful movies from the middle of the 1970s up to the white male paranoia movies of the late 1980s and early 1990s. For example, as Peter Biskind has observed, even the *Star Wars* saga 'couldn't help evoking Vietnam with its conflict between the weak rebels and the powerful Empire'. Thus Luke Skywalker and the rest of the Alliance stood in for the Vietcong, especially in the climactic battle on the moon of Endor in *Return of the Jedi* (1983), in which the clearly non-white and underdeveloped Ewoks use guerrilla warfare tactics, in a jungle-like forest setting, and prevail against the technologically superior forces of the Empire. Even if the allegory was not that specific, the *Star Wars* movies portrayed their white male heroes as the sympathetic underdogs fighting on the side of the Empire's victims. The Empire is an entirely white male organization, literalized in the all-white body armour of the faceless Imperial Stormtroopers. Luke Skywalker and Han Solo, in contrast, are allied with a variety of 'minorities' (Chewbacca, R2-D2 and C-3PO, and the trilogy's only featured black character, Lando Calrissian). In other words, Americans were recast as members of Third World resistance movements, freedom fighters struggling against totalitarian imperialists with more advanced technology and weapons (which made the Empire a condensation of both the United States and the Soviet Union). The *Star Wars* trilogy can therefore be seen as a fantasy in which America got to win the Vietnam War after all, by siding with the Vietcong.

In Lucas and Spielberg's *Indiana Jones and the Temple of Doom* (1984), the opening chase scene leaves Indy and his companions deep in the forests of India, where he becomes entangled in a local power struggle: the evil Thuggees of the cult of Kali (associated with the local ruling class) have stolen the sacred stone of a small village along with all its children, destroying its livelihood. The American white male comes to the rescue of the unfortunate Third World peasants, but only because Indy sees the possibility for

The white male hero: Harrison Ford as Dr Indiana Jones in Steven Spielberg's *Raiders of the Lost Ark* (1981),
saving natives, beating Nazis, and making money

'fortune and glory' in the sacred stone, which he believes to be a priceless archaeological treasure. Indy's double motive for helping the villagers recalls America's role in Vietnam, which concealed material economic interests behind a rhetoric of heroic altruism. The film's narrative is consistent with the operations of wartime propaganda, since the natives are divided into either helpless pacifists or satanic murderers. Once inside enemy territory, Indy is captured by the Thuggees, whereupon he is drugged, enslaved, tortured, and made to participate in rituals of human sacrifice—stopping just short of sending his female companion Willie to her death. The cruel and excessive abuse Indy suffers at the hands of the Thuggees works to legitimize his intervention in the local conflict as well as the destruction of an entire ancient culture.

The Vietnam subtext that was still implicit and disguised in the *Star Wars* and Indiana Jones movies was made explicit and literal in the first two films starring Sylvester Stallone as Vietnam veteran John Rambo; the character whose name became globally synonymous with the renewed imperialist rhetoric of the Reagan presidency. Early instances of the white male paranoia fantasy, the films are most interesting for the ways in which they

sought to position Rambo as both a white male hero *and* a victimized 'minority'. In the original *First Blood* (1982), Rambo was established as a victim both of the Vietnamese, who tortured him while he was their prisoner, and also of his own fellow Americans, who have no respect for and abuse veterans like himself. In *Rambo* (1985), the blockbuster sequel, Rambo gets to fight the war all over again (but this time 'we' win) when he is sent back to Vietnam to search for evidence of surviving American prisoners of war, whom he successfully rescues. As in the *Star Wars* movies, *Rambo* wished to identify the white male American hero with the very enemy he had fought against, the Vietcong. First of all, Rambo fights and kills Soviet soldiers, the imperialist forces occupying Vietnam. This positions Rambo, who was once a part of American imperialist occupation of Vietnam, as a Vietcong-like resistance fighter. Second, like the Ewoks of *Return of the Jedi*, Rambo fights with guerrilla warfare techniques and primitive weapons (knives, rocks, bows and arrows) against technologically better-equipped adversaries. Third and most important, he even becomes figuratively Vietnamese. When his Vietnamese contact, a woman named Co Baa, is killed, Rambo puts her necklace around his own neck, appropriating her identity. When Rambo begins his killing spree at the end of the movie, he is meant to be seen as a heroic freedom fighter liberating the victimized prisoners of war.

As a fantasy response to America's defeat in Vietnam, *Rambo* showed how, at least as Hollywood made use of it, Vietnam was something like the perfect basic narrative for articulating the anxieties of the dominant (white male) group about competition from non-white peoples: it allowed foreign relations and domestic multi-culturalism to be collapsed together. With their depictions of white men as victims of forces both internal and external to the American nation, these films expressed deep frustration and fear at the erosion of the dominant group's privilege and power, along with a desire to somehow 'make things right' again (for example, by going back to Vietnam and 'winning'). Once the white man is established as a victim, he is able to lay claim to the moral entitlement that goes along with victim status. In other words, the white male paranoia fantasy, which emphasizes both the suffering *and* the retribution of the hero, allows the white man to engage in the same violently aggressive behaviour that earned him his reputation as the world's chief oppressor, while freeing him from guilt by recoding that behaviour as justifiable acts of vengeance.

THE END OF THE ROAD?

However, in two movies released in 1993, *Falling Down* and *Jurassic Park*, the fantasy seemed to be reaching a dead end. *Falling Down* tells the story of Bill Foster, referred to throughout the film as 'D-Fens', a name taken from the custom licence plates on the car he abandons in the middle of a Los Angeles motorway traffic jam in the film's opening scene. The rest of the film is a series of encounters between an increasingly unstable and violent D-Fens and the multi-cultural realities and identities of Los Angeles' social geography. As in other white male paranoia fantasies, D-Fens is multiply victimized by the usual combination of social forces: the global political economy (he has been laid off from his job in the defence industry because of the end of the Cold War); feminism (his wife divorced him because of his violent temper, and has secured a restraining order to prevent him from seeing their daughter); and multi-culturalism (Chicano gang members hassle him for infringing on their turf—he does not recognize the cultural significance of their graffiti tags).

But *Falling Down* was ambivalent at best about seeing the white man as a victim; the film represents something like a confession of the pathetic reality for which *Batman*'s vigilante hero was the paranoid fantasy solution. By having D-Fens wander through a multi-cultural urban landscape filled with victimized identities, and specifically by linking him in several ways to a similarly dressed black man protesting a bank's refusal to lend him money, the film makes D-Fens look increasingly like just one more victimized identity among others. The white man is 'normative' here precisely because he is understood as a victim, not because he represents the American success story, the privilege and security that others wish to achieve. *Falling Down* was thus a kind of critical commentary on the white male paranoia of which it was also an example. Movies like *Die Hard* or *Rambo* were fantasies of having it both ways: the white male hero retained his privilege while identifying with and appropriating a

Michael Douglas as 'D-Fens' 'just trying to get home' in *Falling Down* (1993)

victim's position. Whereas the white man was triumphant at the conclusion of these films, in *Falling Down* he is dead—or, alternatively, he is on the verge of retirement, as in the case of the detective Prendergast, who shoots D-Fens at the end and functions throughout as his sympathetic double (he is the only one who understands him).

The paranoia reached another dead end in *Jurassic Park*, Spielberg's special effects extravaganza about genetically engineered dinosaurs, which surpassed the earnings of *E.T.* to become the biggest-grossing movie of all time. Anxieties about global multi-culturalism (as opposed to *Falling Down*'s domestic focus) were reflected in the combination of the film's setting on an island off Costa Rica, and the fact that the island's 'primitive' dinosaur population is divided up in exactly the same way as were the natives in *Temple of Doom*: they are either peaceful and friendly (the plant-eating 'vegi-saurs') or utterly murderous and terrifying (the velociraptors and the T-Rex). In what amounts to a straightforward allegorical confession of white fears about the eroding power of the white man, once the park's advanced computer-driven restraining systems break down, the exclusively female dinosaur 'natives' are set loose, and the white man finds himself at a distinct disadvantage. Unlike so many earlier special effects-oriented blockbusters, there is no triumph at the end. In the film's climactic scene, just when the characters are cornered by the viciously intelligent raptors and apparently doomed, the T-Rex shows up and attacks the raptors. The white people escape death not through their own actions but because the predatory dinosaur identities are fighting among themselves. *Jurassic Park*, like *Falling Down*, worried that the white man would not survive in a multi-cultural world.

Of course, outside the world of Hollywood fantasies the American white male was not an endangered species, only an identity in need of reconsideration in light of specific historical developments. As *Falling Down* and *Jurassic Park* suggested, the problem for American society was to reimagine the role of the white man in a diverse and violent world which was constantly trying to escape his control. Hence the re-emergence of the Western as a popular Hollywood genre at the same time that the white male paranoia fantasy seemed to be reaching its peak and sliding toward its logical dead end. *Back to the Future Part III*, released in 1990, sent Marty McFly on yet another rescue mission, this time all the way back to the overtly mythical American frontier of 1885, where Doc Brown has been stranded due to a freak accident involving the time machine. The first film of the *Back to the Future* trilogy

offered a fantasy of the white male's triumph over historical conditions, and the second was a paranoid nightmare of the multiplication of identities and histories associated with multi-cultural sensibility. The trilogy's conclusion suggested that the answer to the confusion and disruption caused by this multiplicity is to be found in a return to America's basic fantasy narrative about its own origins, namely the Western. Marty's excursion through this particular generic landscape allowed him finally to bring back the new and improved 1985 that he had come home to at the end of the first film and had lost in the course of the second. The Western's mythic power restores the white man's control over history.

But while *Back to the Future Part III* used the Western in a Reaganesque manner, as a fantasy that enabled the white male hero to 'stand tall' once again, the actual Westerns that Hollywood began to turn out in steadily increasing numbers going into the 1990s were, as a group, much more confused and ambivalent about the genre's meaning and utility as a national myth. The new Westerns seemed to be of two basic types. On the one hand there were multi-cultural Westerns, which sought to represent the actual cultural (racial and ethnic) diversity of the American West that the traditional Hollywood Western had ideologically erased from view; particularly the culture and perspective of the Indians. Examples include *Dances with Wolves* (1990), *The Last of the Mohicans* (1992), *Geronimo* (1993), Mario Van Peebles's film about a band of black cowboys, *Posse* (1993), and perhaps the inevitable 'women-with-guns' variation on the genre, *Bad Girls* (1994). On the other hand there was a series of Westerns that considered the white man's historical double role as both killer and protector, such as Clint Eastwood's *Unforgiven* (1992), and two adaptations of the often-told story of Wyatt Earp, *Tombstone* (1993) and *Wyatt Earp* (1994). Unlike *Back to the Future Part III*, these revisionist Westerns understood the white male hero as a problem even if they still proposed him as an answer. The films made use of the genre's elements in an effort to reimagine an American white male identity that might be able to hold together (or at least survive within) the multi-cultural diversity which, in the paranoid imaginings of *Falling Down*, threatened to tear American society apart.

Bibliography
Biskind, Peter (1990), 'The Last Crusade'.
Clover, Carol J. (1992), *Men, Women and Chain Saws*.
Gilder, George (1981), *Wealth and Poverty*.
Hughes, Robert (1993), *Culture of Complaint*.
Sykes, Charles J. (1992), *A Nation of Victims*.

EXTENDING THE BOUNDARIES

Cinéma-Vérité and the New Documentary

CHARLES MUSSER

The introduction of portable, synchronous sound equipment around 1960 provided a decisive leap forward in documentary film-making. This was followed in the 1980s by the increasing availability of inexpensive video equipment, and, more than fiction film-making, documentary practice came to embrace video for purposes of production. Television came to provide the key exhibition outlet, usurping the non-theatrical networks that had developed in the post-war period. Television provided unprecedented levels of funding, but tended (though with a handful of creditable exceptions) to impose strict controls over approach, style, and ideological content.

Since 1960, documentary film has increasingly become an international phenomenon; and in the developed nations film-makers have emerged from more diverse backgrounds in terms of race, gender, and sexual orientation. Documentary practitioners have also become theoretically more self-conscious; the perceived technological shortcomings of earlier equipment have been overcome, inviting greater reflection and speculation about the nature and potential of documentary forms.

THE EMERGENCE OF CINÉMA-VÉRITÉ

Film-makers in France, Canada, and the United States led the way in the adoption of portable, synchronous sound 16 mm. motion picture equipment, complemented by faster film stocks for indoor and night-time shooting. In the hands of innovative practitioners, this new technology resulted in a departure from and transformation of previous documentary practice, and was given the labels 'direct cinema', 'cinéma direct', and 'cinéma-vérité'. These terms have taken on different emphases, with direct cinema/cinéma direct suggesting observational methods, and cinéma-vérité a more confrontational approach. In practice, however, it has generally proved more useful to think of the cinéma-vérité film-maker operating as participant observer. An emphasis on the film-maker who intrudes into the pro-filmic space and provokes the subject has been most characteristic of French cinéma-vérité. A more observational method, in contrast, has been most often championed by the Americans, particularly by a group of film-makers who worked at Drew Associates in the early 1960s: Robert Drew, Richard Leacock, D. A. Pennebaker, Albert and David Maysles, Hope Ryden, Joyce Chopra, and James Lipscomb.

The breakthrough film at Drew Associates and for American cinéma-vérité was Primary (1960), shot during the Wisconsin state presidential primary. The film-makers followed the two principal Democratic candidates, John F. Kennedy and Hubert Humphrey, and their wives as they presented themselves and their viewpoints to potential voters. The film juxtaposes two quite different kinds of personalities—the self-confident, charming, urban sophistication of Kennedy with the folksy, anti-establishment, rural populism of Humphrey. Viewers are given a 'behind the scenes' glimpse of the candidates, with the cameraman (Leacock) unobtrusively present. At other points we see the candidates posing or being posed for the media. One implication is that we have access to the 'real' Kennedys while others are seeing a carefully constructed image. However, the film-makers themselves seemed well aware that their subjects were performers who were constantly shaping their own self-presentations for others, whether for long-standing friends or for the newly portable sync-sound camera.

American cinéma-vérité came out of a journalistic impulse and has generally been fiercely anti-psychological. The camera does not seek to penetrate the subject's outer, public shell to reveal an inner or secret self, but to capture a range of self-presentations, from which the film-maker and the spectator can form an opinion of the subject. The Drew film-makers often chose public performers as their subject—racing car driver Eddie Sachs in On the Pole (1960); actress Jane Fonda in Jane (1962); and the Kennedys again in Crisis: Behind a Presidential Commitment (1963). They also sought to film moments of crisis, situations which could produce stories with a climax, resolution, and ending. The crises put these people under pressure, revealing something about their judgement and ability to cope with stress, and gave the subjects something more important with which to concern themselves than the camera. By following individuals for lengthy periods of time, the film-makers become part of their subjects' daily existence.

In contrast to prior practice, cinéma-vérité film-makers in America refrained from telling the subjects what to do or how to act; they refused to 'direct' the film. Subjects would occasionally acknowledge the camera or even talk to the film-makers, but it was considered preferable for the subject to interact directly with the outside world on his or her own terms. If the subject sought direction, then that wish for guidance becomes a proper and revealing moment worth including in a film. The film-maker's goal was to respond to these presentations of self rather than to re-present, and therefore construct, the subject according to his own preconceptions. Many *cinéma-vérité* films thus credited the producer, camera crew, and editor but refused to name a director—in fact the cameraman was typically seen as the film's 'author'.

American *cinéma-vérité* can be contrasted with the French approach championed by Jean Rouch and Edgar Morin (the sociologist who coined the phrase *cinéma-vérité*). In an article written in the January 1960 issue of *France observateur* Morin declared that 'a new cinéma vérité was possible', one in which the documentary captured 'the authenticity of life as it is lived'. In this approach, the film-maker becomes an active participant and helps to create a sociodrama for the camera. The subject is given the chance to play out his life before the film-maker, a game 'which has the value of psychoanalytic truth, that is to say precisely that which is hidden or repressed comes to the surface'. The emphasis on psychology and the film-maker's active participation in the *mise-en-scène* distinguishes this approach from the observational style of the Americans.

Morin and Rouch collaborated on *Chronique d'un été* (*Chronicle of a Summer*, 1961), a film that elaborated on the methods they had advocated, turning ethnographic insights towards the metropolitan centre. Shot in Paris and the south of France during the summer of 1960, the film employed the still emerging technology of portable cameras. For *Chronique d'un été*, Morin and Rouch filmed a gradually widening circle of people, asking them if they were happy and how they lived. They set up scenes (Marceline walking through the Place de la Concorde and talking to herself, her dead father, and the microphone) and arranged meetings among the principals (Angelo, a factory worker, talks with Landry, a student from West Africa). Not only do the film-makers routinely challenge their subjects with questions and frequently appear in front of the camera, they sometimes turn their subjects into film-makers: Marceline, for example, does a series of man-in-the-street interviews and also carries the tape recorder during her monologue. At the end, those associated with the film view the edited footage and comment on what they have seen. The documentary concludes with the two film-makers, the participant observers, walking through the Musée de l'Homme and discussing the sometimes unexpected responses of their participant subjects. Edgar Morin remarks, 'to see now that people that I like

very much, like Marilou and Marceline, are criticized, that upsets me. I believed the viewer would like the characters that I liked.' As he concludes, 'That's the difficulty of communicating something. We are too implicated.'

Morin and Rouch made choices that differed substantially from those of Drew and his associates. Both groups favoured a mobile camera and long takes, but the Americans tended to focus on celebrities who were in some ways skilled at presenting themselves to a spectator, to a public (and often even to a camera). Drew sought to 'cover a story' within the conventions of mainstream journalism, with a clear demarcation between the film-maker reporters and those people appearing in the documentary. The French operated more within an anthropological framework, which had little interest in a story-line: the film unfolds in loose chronological fashion. The film-makers embrace their subjects but end up questioning the very process of documentary film-making, recognizing its possibilities for exploitation and perhaps celebrating its unpredictability.

Primary was the first of twenty *cinéma-vérité* documentaries funded by Time-Life (an investment of roughly $2 million) and made by the Drew group between 1960 and 1963. When Time-Life failed to sell most of these films to television in the United States, the demise of this ambitious undertaking was inevitable. Although the Drew group broke up in 1962–3, the different film-makers went on to make an array of films that elaborated and refined many of the *cinéma-vérité* principles. D. A. Pennebaker's *Don't Look back* (1966) chronicles Bob Dylan's 1965 tour of England. Dylan fends off reporters trying to 'understand' and pigeon-hole his music, politics, and personality while Pennebaker, a tour insider, quietly films those situations that animate the singer as he flirts with fame. In Dylan's low-tech. music (he sings solo, playing an acoustic guitar and harmonica) Pennebaker sees a counterpart to his own film-making (with its images derived from a 'home-made', one-man camera). Pennebaker went on to make *Monterey Pop* (1968), an early and successful concert film (or 'rockumentary'), in which his camera-work responds to, and complements, the performer and his music—particularly in the sequence featuring Jimi Hendrix.

The Maysles' post-Drew contributions moved away from the 'crisis' style of early *cinéma-vérité* films to focus on the mundane. They continued, however, to feature prominent personalities such as Joseph E. Levine (*Showman*, 1962) and Marlon Brando (*Meet Marlon Brando*, 1965). *Salesman* (1969) was notable for its look at a group of 'ordinary Americans', men making a marginal living by selling bibles door to door. Once again the subjects were performers, but here the film-makers were indeed seeking to penetrate an individual's public persona; the camera plays the role of psychoanalyst as we watch Paul Brennan go through a personal crisis. Brennan has lost his ability to sell, to

Jean Rouch

(1917–)

Among the totemic ancestors of the factual film three figures, all of whom may be labelled 'Jean Rouch', can be discerned. These figures have certain characteristics in common—a background in the French administrative and intellectual class, an education at the Haute École des Ponts et Chaussées, and a subsequent career in anthropology primarily working with the Songhay people of West Africa.

The first Rouch is an ethnographer with a particular interest in possession cults. Rouch extended participation-observation techniques to embrace a willingness to join, rather than just observe, the activities of his informants. It is, then, reasonable that this ethnographer of possession should come to describe such major works as *Les Magiciens de Wanzerbe* ('The magicians of Wanzerbe', 1948–9) and *Les Mâitres fous* ('The mad masters', 1953–4) as *ciné-transe*.

Rouch is more generally important because he is one of the few leading anthropologists to use film as his primary ethnographic tool. Indeed since the completion of his Doctorat d'État on Songhay religion and magic in 1960 he has produced no long texts or monographs, only the occasional article; but he has filmed more than seventy-five titles.

Despite his enormous empathy for traditional life, Rouch has been accused (by Sembene Ousmane, among others) of observing Africans 'like insects'. *Les Mâitres fous*, in particular, has been controversial, and for much of his career Rouch has been embroiled in such seemingly inevitable anthropological rows.

The second Rouch is a cineaste and documentarist, one of the Cinématheque Française circle in Paris during the Second World War and a film-maker intimately involved in the revival, since the 1960s, of the 1920s Russian debate as to the nature of documentary film authenticity. Rouch, by using the term *cinéma-vérité*, brought back into vogue Vertov's reflexive documentary practice (as in *The Man with a Movie Camera*, 1929). For instance, Rouch forced French and African teenagers at an Ivory Coast high school to interact with each other—and showed his audience that he was doing this—for *La Pyramide humaine* ('The human pyramid', 1958-9). Returning to France to film 'the strange tribe that lives in Paris' the following year, Rouch and the sociologist Edgar Morin elaborated a similar 'sort of cinema truth' in the seminal *Chronique d'un été* (1960). Here the subject of the documentary becomes the making of the documentary itself, with Rouch and Morin prominent among the filmed participants. This sort of reflexivity then began to influence Rouch's more traditional ethnographic films, such as *La Chasse au lion à l'arc* ('Lion hunt with bow and arrow', 1957-64), where even the telegrams summoning the crew to the hunt are featured. While this honesty is attractive it has been criticized for being both glib and limiting.

Rouch's ethnography owes much to a French tradition which, for instance, concentrates on cosmologies rather than kinship patterns, and his documentary practice comes from a French style of personal film (as in the work of Chris Marker). Nevertheless Rouch is an original. This can be seen most clearly in the work of a more elusive third Rouch, the creator of 'ethno-fictions'. Already in *Jaguar* (1954-67), a reconstructed film about the traditional migration of young Songhay men to the Guinea coast to find work, Rouch was ready to allow his informants to suggest the very idea for the film. Rouch went a step beyond reconstructing what had or could happen, as Flaherty had done, and moved to reconstructing what could not be filmed—namely the interior life of his informants. This can be seen in *Moi, un noir* ('I, a black man', 1957), in which a group of urban Africans are invited to live out their weekend fantasies, in Rouch's words: 'a sort of mythic Eldorado, based on boxing, the cinema, love, and money.'

Rouch has said that 'fiction is the only way to penetrate reality'. In the long term, given the problematic status of the documentary image as evidence in a world of post-modern theory and digital manipulation, this willingness to abandon the strait-jacket of objectivity could be his most important legacy for documentary practice.

BRIAN WINSTON

SELECT FILMOGRAPHY

Les Mâitres fous (1953–4); Moi, un noir (1957); La Pyramide humaine (1958–9); Chronique d'un été (1960); La Chasse au lion à l'arc (1964); Jaguar (1954-67); Cocorico Monsieur Poulet (1977)

BIBLIOGRAPHY

Eaton, Michael (ed.) (1979), *Anthropology—Reality—Cinema: The Films of Jean Rouch*.

Les Mâitres fous (1953-4), Jean Rouch's ethnographic study of a possession cult.

Chris Marker
(1929–)

'I am writing to you from a distant land.' With its emphases on travel and on writing, the opening of the commentary from his film *Letter from Siberia* (*Lettre de Sibérie*, 1958) indicates the twin features and enduring preoccupations of the work of Chris Marker (real name Christian François Bouche-Villeneuve).

A polyglot and *engagé* intellectual, Marker came under the influence of the twin post-war figures of André Malraux and André Bazin. He worked with Bazin (reputedly after a spell in the Resistance) in the theatre section of 'Travail et Culture' (then under the ideological aegis of the French Communist Party), and was a contributor to early issues of *Cahiers du cinéma*. Spells as an itinerant photographer and journalist followed. His literary career includes a novel (*Le Coeur net*, 1950), a book of criticism on Jean Giraudoux, and an association during the 1950s with the Paris publisher Éditions du Seuil that yielded a series of photographic essays entitled *Coréennes* and the editorship of the travelogue series 'Petite Planète'. The format of these travelogue books, a juxtaposition of photographs with allusive, poetic commentaries, was—Gilles Jacob has suggested—to influence the style of his early films.

In the 1950s and early 1960s Marker established a reputation with a highly distinctive series of documentary film essays shot in locations that ranged across the globe, taking in Finland (*Olympia 52*, 1952), China (*Dimanche à Pékin*, 1956), Siberia (*Letter from Siberia*, 1958), Israel (*Description d'un combat*, 1960), Cuba (*Cuba, si!*, 1961), and Japan (*Le Mystère Koumiko*, 1965). Partly documentary films, partly travelogues, but never completely one or the other, these films often addressed specifically political issues and events and were distinguished by their quizzical, sceptical, and sometimes lyrical commentaries explicitly foregrounding the role of the film-maker and his access to the 'truth' of the events portrayed. Most notable in this respect are the sequences in *Letter from Siberia* showing Soviet labourers building a road. Marker employs the same footage accompanied by three slightly differing commentaries to undermine traditional notions of documentary 'objectivity': depending on the commentary the images are shown to represent the workers as, alternately, 'happy', 'unhappy', or, simply, 'Soviet'.

Associated with the so-called 'left bank' group of the French New Wave, Marker also co-directed *Les Statues meurent aussi* (1950) with Alain Resnais and provided the narration for Resnais's *Le Mystère de l'atelier quinze* (1957), Joris Ivens's *À Valparaiso* (1962), and François Reichenbach's *La Sixième face du pentagon* (1968).

Throughout this period, Marker's work was identified with the highly personalized film-essay whose playful sense of literary digression was enhanced by the prosaic nature of the reality from which it departed. *La Jetée* (1962) stands apart from the other films of this period. A short science-fiction narrative of some twenty minutes, and, once again, a travelogue of sorts—only this time the travel being through time rather than through space—*La Jetée* is composed almost entirely of a montage of still images. The momentary instant of the image's *movement*, of the photographic becoming filmic, that of a woman opening her eyes, is one of the most truly breathtaking in modern cinema.

As with many other French film-makers of his generation, the period around May 1968 was a turning point in Marker's activities. In keeping with the idea of effacing

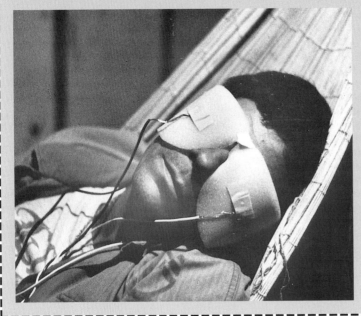

Seeing into the future: the virtual reality machine in Marker's 1962 montage short, *La jetée*.

the director's authorship of a film, Marker abandoned his individual approach to organize a co-operative group of militant film-makers under the name SLON (Société pour le Lancement des Oeuvres Nouvelles). Along with a number of anonymous *ciné-tracts*, SLON made *Le Train en marche* (1973), both as a dialectical reassessment of Marker's earlier *Letter from Siberia* and as an examination of the radical historical example of the Soviet agit-trains and the work of revolutionary film-maker Alexander Medvedkin, a figure who was to prove an enduring presence throughout Marker's career.

One could divide Marker's work into three distinct periods of before, during and after 1968. *Le Fond de l'air est rouge* (1977), his two-part assessment of the May 'events', was a straightforward settling of accounts with the memories and images of the period. But, as such, it proved to be an incomplete reckoning. The same concerns were to return as part of *Sans soleil* (1982), where issues of political commitment and 'guerrilla film-making' were linked with haunting images from Tokyo and Guinea Bissau, the 'twin poles of survival', and were framed (echoes of *La Jetée* here) by a narrative concerning time-travel. For the eloquence of its melancholic take on the perishable ideological certainties of the 1960s, as much as for its astute and humorous examination of the status of the image in multi-media societies, *Sans soleil* deserves to be recognized as one of the major films of the 1980s.

The 1980s and 1990s have seen Marker expand his interest in new audio-visual technologies into multi-media installation work (*Zapping Zone* for 'Passages de l'Image' at the Centre Pompidou, 1992) and music video (for Electronic's *Getting Away With It*, 1990), as well as television. Particularly notable are his thirteen part series on history *L'Héritage de la chouette* (1989) and his last assessment of Medvedkin, taking the form of a post-perestroika obituary for the Soviet film-maker, *Le Tombeau d'Alexandre* (*The Last Bolshevik*, 1992).

CHRIS DARKE

SELECT FILMOGRAPHY

Les Statues meurent aussi (co-directed with Alain Resnais, 1950); Lettre de Sibérie (1958); Le Joli Mai (1962); La Jetée (1962); Le Fond de l'air est rouge (1977); Sans soleil (1982); Le Tombeau d'Alexandre (1992).

BIBLIOGRAPHY

Bensaia, Reda (1990), 'From the Photogram to the Pictogram: On Chris Marker's *La Jetée*'.
Jacob, Gilles (1966), 'Chris Marker and the Mutants'.
Marker, Chris (1961), Commentaires.

manipulate customers, to perform. His cynicism gives way to a new sincerity—perhaps prodded by the camera—and he no longer believes his own routine. The exploration of a subject's inner, psychological world is pushed further in *Grey Gardens* (1975), which looks at Edith and Eddie Beale, a mother and daughter who live in a rundown house in exclusive Easthampton, Long Island. Their superficially supportive, though mutually destructive, relationship is a study in family pathology. The film-makers move away from an observational approach and act as catalysts in this film, actively interacting with their subjects. The Maysles' growing affinity with Rouch's *cinéma-vérité* techniques was already evident in *Gimme Shelter* (1969), a look at the Rolling Stones' US tour, which ended with a free concert at Altamont, California, and the death of a gun-toting fan who was butchered by the Hell's Angels. Mick Jagger, unaware of the killing until later, was brought into the editing room to view footage of the murder, enabling the Maysles to exploit the violence even as they offer a self-reflexive critique.

Richard Leacock became a controversial teacher at the Massachusetts Institute of Technology and an advocate for Super 8 , one-person film-making. Such equipment, he felt, was less intrusive and a further rejection of commercial technologies. Leacock and several of his students (Marisa Silver, Jeff Kreines, and Joel DeMott) returned to the documentary mainstream when working on Peter Davis's documentary series 'Middletown' (1982). Leacock (camera) and Silver (sound) made *Community of Praise*, examining one family's desperate search for faith and religious meaning in Muncie, Indiana. Kreines and DeMott followed a group of high-school seniors, focusing on a white woman engaged in an interracial romance with a black student. This controversial film was ultimately banned from commercial airways. Robert Drew himself returned to independent production for public television with *For Auction: An American Hero* (1986) which examined the farm crisis of the 1980s, at a time when family farms were going bankrupt: the programme's protagonist, an auctioneer, was doing booming business.

Many other film-makers contributed to the *cinéma-vérité* 'revolution' in the United States, including Michael Roemer and Robert Young (*Cortile Cascino*, 1961), Jack Willis (*Lay my Burden down*, 1965), Arthur Barron (*Sixteen at Webster Groves*, 1966), and William C. Jersey, Jr. (*A Time for Burning*, 1966). Jonas Mekas's *The Brig* (1964) is a *cinéma-vérité* record of the Living Theater's rigorous stage re-enactment of life in a Marine stockade; Mekas went on to make a series of diary films such as *Diaries, Notes and Sketches (Walden)* (1968) and *Reminiscences of a Journey to Lithuania* (1972).

In France, as well, the new documentary was gaining practitioners. Mario Ruspoli took an observational approach with *Les Inconnus de la terre* ('The unknowns of the world', 1961) and *Regard sur la folie* ('A look at madness',

1961). Chris Marker also produced two *cinéma-vérité* works, *Cuba, sí* (1961) and *Le Joli Mai* (*The Lovely Month of May*, 1963). The latter, shot in 16 mm. and then blown up to 35 mm. for theatrical release, relies heavily on interview techniques to yield a broad sociological study of Paris in May 1962, as the Algerian War had finally concluded.

Canadians, funded by the National Film Board of Canada, provided significant contributions to the *cinéma-vérité œuvre*. As in France and the United States, their documentaries were often made by a team of producer-directors. *Lonely Boy* (1961), directed by Wolf Koenig and Roman Kroitor, a breezy portrait of singer and teen idol Paul Anka, anticipated later, more in-depth treatments of pop music stars. Claude Jutra, Michel Brault, Claude Fournier, and Marcel Carrière of L'Équipe Française made *La Lutte* ('The contest', 1961), about commercial wrestling, its phoniness, and the fans that it attracted. Brault, Carrière, and Pierre Perrault produced Quebec's first feature-length documentary, *Pour la suite du monde* (*For Posterity*, 1963), which follows a group of geographically isolated French Canadians who revive the almost forgotten practice of whale hunting. Allan King's *Warrendale* (1967), which looked at children in a treatment centre for emotionally disturbed youth, was barred from broadcast by the CBC.

Not all countries or film-makers embraced the technology and techniques of *cinéma-vérité* so enthusiastically. In eastern Europe and the Soviet Union prestige documentaries were still shot in 35 mm. However, in general, during the 1960s, documentary enjoyed a prestige and popularity that were unprecedented, at least in peacetime. Fiction films such as Stanley Kubrick's *Dr Strangelove* (1963), Jacques Rozier's *Adieu Philippine* (1962), and Richard Lester's *A Hard Day's Night* (1964) recognized the achievements of *cinéma-vérité* by appropriating its techniques in order to provide a greater sense of realism.

1968 AND AFTER

The year 1968 was the year of the Tet offensive in Vietnam, of student revolts and factory occupations in France and across the world, of the Prague Spring and its repression by Soviet tanks. Among students and those concerned with media representations, the notion of objectivity in non-fiction film was greeted with increasing levels of scepticism. Documentary was seen more and more as a vehicle for expressing ideological positions. In opposition to the point of view put forward in official propaganda and on television, documentary film-makers in America and elsewhere set out to present an alternative understanding of the Vietnam War. The veteran Joris Ivens was invited to Vietnam to make *Le Dix-septième parallèle* (*17th Parallel*, 1967); the North Vietnamese released *Vai Toibac Cua de Quoc My* (*Some Evidence*, 1969), which detailed the impact of American bombs and weaponry on people, animals, veg-

etation, and buildings; and in America established documentarian Emile De Antonio offered a critical view of his government's policy in *In the Year of the Pig* (1969).

In 1968 and the years following, new film-making collectives sprang up world-wide to offer radical perspectives on the global crisis. In France Jean-Luc Godard and Jean-Pierre Gorin formed themselves into the Dziga-Vertov group, while Chris Marker joined with some younger film-makers to form SLON. In Japan, Group Vision made *Shisha yo kitarite waga tairo o tate* ('Dead come and cut off my retreat', 1969), about the struggle of workers in smaller industries, while Britain saw the formation of Cinema Action and the Berwick Street Collective.

Newsreel was the leading radical film-making organization in the United States, with chapters in most major cities. Started in late 1967 and in active production by 1968, the group was closely connected to SDS (Students for a Democratic Society), which took increasingly radical positions in the late 1960s. Working in a collective, if somewhat male-dominated fashion, the members of Newsreel sought to supply the movement with films for informational and organizational purposes. A particularly striking example of Newsreel's work, *Black Panther* (1968–9), presented interviews with Panther leaders Huey Newton and Eldridge Cleaver, displays of Panther strength, and a recitation of the Panthers' ten-point programme by Bobby Seale. Newsreel relied on a syncretic style that combined re-filmed photographs, material shot by members, out-takes of news footage 'liberated' by sympathetic workers inside the media industry, narration, and sync interviews. All the films were in black and white, and the dirty images were organized by disjunctive editing strategies indebted to the theories of Eisenstein and Vertov.

Newsreel's style, however, was most directly indebted to the documentaries then coming out of Latin America and Cuba in particular. The polemical montage juxtapositions of Cuban documentarist Santiago Alvarez were a major influence, but other Cuban shorts, such as Octavio Cortázar's enchanting *Por primera vez* ('For the first time', 1967), recording the reactions of country people seeing the cinema for the first time, also had their effect on American and European film-makers.

Latin American documentary really came of age with the epic three-part *Hour of the Furnaces* (*La hora de los hornos*), made by the Argentinians Fernando Solanas and Octavio Getino between 1966 and 1968, a film counterpart to their powerful manifesto 'Towards a Third Cinema', published in 1969. In the manifesto they call for films of decolonization, which actively oppose the System. Such films are part of a battle 'against the ideas and models of the enemy to be found inside each one of us':

The man of the third cinema, be it *guerrilla cinema* or *a film act*, with the infinite categories that they contain (film letter, film poem, film essay, film pamphlet, film report, etc.), above all counters the film industry of a cinema of characters with one of themes, that of individuals with that of masses, that of the author with that of the operative group, one of neo-colonial misinformation with one of information, one of escape with one that recaptures the truth, that of passivity with that of aggression.

The film portrays Argentina as a tragic and somewhat bizarre example of economic and cultural neo-colonialism. The country's natural resources are exported to pay for consumer goods imported from the United States and Europe. Despite its anger at cultural as well as economic imperialism, *Hour of the Furnaces* is rich with references to cinema's own history: the butchering of cattle in Eisenstein's *Strike* and the cemetery scene in Vigo's *À propos de Nice*. *Hour of the Furnaces*, both as a work in progress and a completed film, was often shown clandestinely, and screenings were meant to provoke discussion. Participating in the exhibition thus became a politicizing activity.

The new documentary also flourished in Africa. Before the late 1960s most 'African' documentaries had been made by white film-makers (with a few notable exceptions such as Timité Bassori, who made several shorts for Senegal in 1963), but from 1967 onwards a new generation of film-makers began to emerge in francophone Africa, chronicling changing patterns of life in the newly independent states. In the Ivory Coast Timité and Henri Duparc made numerous documentaries between 1967 and 1972, while in Senegal Mahama Johnson Traoré and Safi Faye made films on migration from the countryside to the cities and on urban life. Trained by Jean Rouch, Niger's Mariama Hima made 'Babu Banza' (1985–90), a series of shorts on the recycling of materials (tyres, cars). Many of the leading African film-makers such as Idrissa Ouedraogo, Souleymane Cissé, and Gaston Kabore began their careers as documentarians.

The extension of documentary film-making around the world was paralleled in the late 1960s by a new diversity among documentary film-makers in the west, first with the affirmation of the civil rights movement in the United States, and then with emergence of feminist and gay movements in both America and Europe. Under pressure from the Kerner Report on Civil Disorders, television stations in the USA felt compelled to undertake a number of initiatives to improve the representation of the country's black and minority population. Public television agreed to show *Still a Brother: Inside the Negro Middle Class* (1968), a documentary made by African-American film-makers William Greaves and William Branch. Greaves, who had received documentary training at the Natonal Film Board of Canada, became executive producer of the magazine-format television programme *Black Journal* (1968–70) and subsequently made a wide range of documentaries about the African-American experience, including *Ali, the Fighter*

A still from Latin American documentarist Santiago Alvarez's *LBJ* (1968), an indictment of the presidency of Lyndon Johnson and the history of American imperialism, created through a montage of found footage and filmed photographs

(1970), about the politically controversial heavyweight boxing champion Mohammed Ali. *Black Journal* and similar programmes gave opportunities to a new generation of black documentarians such as St Claire Bourne (*In Motion: Amiri Baraka*, 1985) and Caroll Parrott Blue (*Two Women*, 1977).

Latin Americans in the USA—particularly Chicanos and Puerto Ricans—were soon demanding similar access to television and production opportunities. Public television's *Realidades* presented a series of controversial documentaries during its three-year run (1972–5). Film-maker José Garcia had made a pilot for the show, *La carreta* ('The oxcart', 1970), a free 'translation/adaptation' of the melodramatic play written by Puerto Rico's renowned author René Marqués. The film began with an interview of the director, then offered some excerpts of the play, before dissolving the story-line back into a urban documentary.

Newsreel also came under pressure to respond to the need for racial and gender diversity. After a period of turmoil (during which it was singled out by the magazine *Rat* as a bastion of 'male-left supremacy'), it developed an increasingly Third World emphasis. Many of the original members left, and in the end a handful of predominantly Third World members remained and renamed the organization 'Third World Newsreel'.

Asian-American Chris Choy and African-American Susan Robeson made *Teach our Children* (1972) as Newsreel was falling apart. Their next works were made possible by state and national arts funding, including *In the Event*

Anyone Disappears (1974), about oppressive living conditions in women's prisons. It was only with *From Spikes to Spindles* (1976), which focused on the immigrant Chinese experience and a growing political activism in New York's Chinatown, that Choy began to address issues within her own ethnic community. Henceforth these would figure prominently in much of her work—*Mississippi Triangle* (1984) and *Who Killed Vincent Chin?* (1989, with Renee Tajima). Choy subsequently made *Homes Apart: Korea* (1991) with J. T. Takagi, a Korean-American who returned to her homeland and a family that had been separated for more than forty years by the country's division into North and South.

With the resurgence of feminism in the early 1970s, many women were drawn to documentary film-making, seeing in it a useful and accessible vehicle for campaign films and for more personal explorations of women's issues, often linked under the slogan 'the personal is political'. Barbara Kopple's *Harlan County U.S.A* (1976) chronicled the struggle for unionization in the coalfields, in which women played a crucial role. Joyce Chopra looked at the tensions between work and having children in *Joyce at 34* (with Claudia Weill, 1972), and in *Nana, Mom, and Me* (1974) Amalia Rothschild probed the relationships among three generations of women, including herself. In Canada, Anne Claire Poirier made *Les Filles du Roy* (1974), which traced the historical struggles of Québécoise women, and Anne Wheeler produced *Great Grand Mother* (Canada, 1975), about women who settle in the prairie. German feminists produced many documentaries during the 1970s, the

A scene from Connie Field's *The Life and Times of Rosie the Riveter* (1980) which uses interviews to examine the lives of women working on the home front during the Second World War

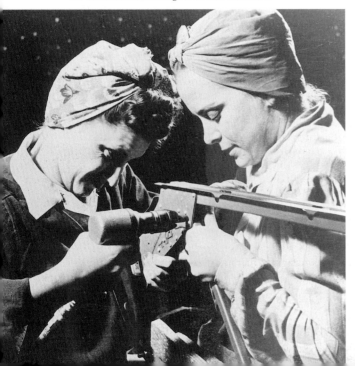

most prominent being Helke Sander, who foregrounded women's issues in documentaries of the 1970s such as *Macht die Pille frei?* ('Does the pill liberate?', 1972) and continues to do so with her historical epic *Befreier und Befreite* (*Liberators Take Liberties*, 1992), about German women who were raped by Soviet soldiers at the end of the Second World War. In Britain a number of feminist documentaries were produced, including a pioneering exploration of women's history in *Women of the Rhondda* (1971), but on the whole the movement fought shy of traditional documentary forms and focused on film-making practices that put both documentary and fictional images of women in question. This tendency spread beyond the bounds of feminist film-making proper, as in the Berwick Street Collective's deconstructive *Night-cleaners* (1975).

Third World women generally found greater opportunities a decade after their counterparts in North America and western Europe. The Colombian collective Cine Mujer produced several documentaries in the 1980s, often with fictional elements, and in Brazil short documentary videos were made by Lilith Video, a women's video collective, including Silvana Afram's *Mulheres negras* ('Black women', 1985), about racial identity and racism in Brazil, and Jacira Melo's *Beijo na boca* ('Kiss on the mouth', 1987), composed of interviews with prostitutes.

Women in India likewise found new opportunities. Before turning to feature film-making, Mira Nair made *So Far from India* (1982), which looks at an immigrant's life in New York City, and *India Cabaret* (1985), about the travails of women cabaret dancers. The women's collective Media Storm made videos about the ongoing subjugation of women: *In Secular India* (1986) protested the infamous Muslim Women's Bill while *From the Burning Embers* (1988) exposed and condemned the resurgent practice of *suttee* after an 18-year-old woman was burned alive on her husband's funeral pyre.

Gay and lesbian film-makers began to make documentaries as part of the gay rights movement in the mid-1970s: *Word Is out*, made by Peter Adair and the Mariposa Film Group in 1976, and *Gay U.S.A.*, shot on Gay Freedom Day in 1977 by Arthur Bressan, Jr., and Artists United for Gay Rights. Historical figures were featured in such films as Liz Stevens's and Estelle Freedman's *She Even Chewed Tobacco* (1983), about lesbians in nineteenth-century California, and Robert Epstein's and Richard Schmiechen's *The Times of Harvey Milk* (1984), about the gay activist who was assassinated after becoming mayor of San Francisco. By the late 1980s, the focus turned to the issue of AIDS, which was devastating the gay community.

CINÉMA-VÉRITÉ AND ITS DISCONTENTS

Although *cinéma-vérité* continued after 1968, it also developed in new directions. In the United States this trend was evidenced in the rise of Frederick Wiseman, whose substantial and still growing body of work has focused on important institutions in American life. His first documentary, *Titicut Follies* (1967), looked at the Massachusetts Correctional Institution–Bridgewater, a mental health facility outside Boston. Although the film is apparently objective in its observational methods, use of long takes (averaging 32 seconds per shot), and avoidance of narration, it provides little contextualizing information for its disturbing images, and the mental health workers appear incompetent, callous, and sometimes sadistic toward their wards. It can be read as supporting a mental health agenda of de-institutionalization, but also as an allegory for a more general relationship between the state and its citizens. The state of Massachusetts promptly sought injunctions to block screenings of the film and ultimately succeeded in restricting the documentary's exhibition to selected professionals.

Wiseman continued to use (and to refine) his observational approach, filming, among others, a Philadelphia high school (*High School*, 1968) and a New York City hospital (*Hospital*, 1970). Appearing at the rate of roughly one per year, Wiseman's documentaries have become longer as they seek to immerse audiences in his chosen milieu: *Near Death* (1989), shot in an intensive care unit, is 358 minutes; *Central Park* (1990), about New York City's prize public space, is a more modest 176 minutes.

Two other leading figures in this second generation of *cinéma-vérité* film-makers are Roger Graef and Marcel Ophuls. Graef has been intent on exploring institutions at work, particularly the processes of decision-making at the upper levels of management. This approach matured in the early 1970s with the BBC series 'The Space between the Words'. In *Steel* (1975), Graef looked at the state-owned British Steel Corporation as it considered investing $50 million in a new plant. Though never stating it in such crass terms, management hints that such a facility would help keep labour in line and, since the plant would require comparatively few employees to operate, would prove particularly valuable if steel workers were to strike. Like Wiseman, Graef tends to focus on politically sensitive issues, but he insists on the difference of his approach. Wiseman, he declared at one point, has had an adversarial relationship with the institution he examines, tries to 'rip the place open', and ultimately produces a much more personal and 'artistic' statement. Graef, in contrast, has been seeking 'to develop a highly specialized observational technique' which captures the vital essence of the institution so that 'the people in the institutions say: "Yes, that's exactly what happened"'. Like Wiseman, however, Graef seeks to immerse his spectators in an unfamiliar world and so force them to take an active role in understanding and evaluating what they are seeing: 'Suddenly we open the door and you're in the boardroom of British Steel and you don't know who anybody is. You don't know what the rules are … And your brain races along to figure it out.'

Marcel Ophuls has likewise immersed audiences in his chosen subject-matter, using approximately four and a half hours for *Le Chagrin et la pitié* (*The Sorrow and the pity*, 1970), which examines French collaboration and resistance during the Second World War, focusing on the town of Clermont-Ferrand, part of Vichy France until the Germans occupied it in 1942. Ophuls often appears on camera as he gently but insistently questions his subjects. These scenes of 'talking heads' are intercut with newsreels and other stock footage scenes to provide a moving account that is remarkable in its historical specificity. The topic of collaboration was still a highly explosive one in France, where television stations avoided showing the film

Randall Adams (Adam Goldfine) is interrogated by a Dallas investigator in a typically stylized scene from Errol Morris's *The Thin Blue Line* (1990), courtesy J&M Entertainment Limited/Miramax Film Corp.

until 1981, despite its success in theatres. Ophuls is an even more active presence in *The Memory of Justice*, which examines German war crimes and the Nuremberg trials. Here Ophuls compares and contrasts the Holocaust to French actions in Algiers and American atrocities in Vietnam. The film applies the standards of humanity and justice articulated at Nuremberg to other situations where those responsible have rarely been held accountable.

Ophuls's work points toward the resurgence of a long-standing documentary genre which had been relatively neglected in the face of *cinéma-vérité*'s seemingly endless possibilities—the historical documentary. Intelligently handled, this form has proved particularly suitable for mainstream television, as is shown by the case of the twenty-six-part series *The World at War* (1974–5), produced by Jeremy Isaacs for ITV in Britain, which provided a compelling history of the Second World War, mixing stock footage of the war with interviews with diverse participants.

Left-wing film-makers of the 1970s and early 1980s tried to reclaim labour history, by interviewing surviving participants. Connie Field used interviews for *The Life and Times of Rosie the Riveter* (1980), which demythologized the situation of working women on the home front, during and immediately after the Second World War. *The Wobblies* (Stuart Bird and Deborah Shaffer, 1979) looked at the industrial workers of the world in the 1910s and 1920s, relying heavily on oral history. Despite its value as a moving reclamation of an important lost cause, the film unfortunately reveals the limitations of oral history in documentaries.

In the late 1970s and early 1980s, it was often theoretically fashionable to minimize or erase the distinctions between fiction and non-fiction film-making. Quoted somewhat out of context, Christian Metz's assertion that 'every film is a fiction film', along with the theoretical writings of Hayden White and Michel Foucault, fostered such an outlook. This breakdown between fiction and non-fiction modes is evident in such films as Michelle Citron's *Daughter Rite* (1978), and Trinh Min-ha's *Surname Viet, Given Name Nam* (1989), which appear to be employing traditional interviews but in fact have actors delivering lines derived from or suggested by earlier research. Although the combining of fictive and non-staged methods has frequently produced provocative films, the tendency of the promoters of 'reality as discourse' to dismiss documentary's evidentiary function is reductive and potentially dangerous. Although documentary film-making is dependent on the film-maker's subjectivity, and the camera's presence does typically affect the responses of the subject, these realities do not necessarily undermine the distinctive potential of non-fiction film-making.

During the 1970s and early 1980s, the contributions of ethnographic film-makers stand out as they sought to explore documentary's many possibilities and to reflect on, expand, and refine its techniques. In this regard, Jean Rouch with his emphasis on self-reflexivity emerged as a central figure—his eminence matched by an outpouring of films of different lengths, ambitions, and purposes.

One of the most influential essays in the *cinéma-vérité* and post-*vérité* period has been David MacDougall's 1975 article 'Beyond Observational Cinema'. MacDougall endorsed Rouch's methods, evident in *Chronicle of a Summer*: 'The value of a society lies as much in its dreams as in the reality it has built. Often it is only by introducing new stimuli that the investigator can peel back the layers of a culture and reveal its fundamental assumptions,' MacDougall suggested. He was surprised by 'how few of the ideas of this extraordinary film managed to penetrate the thinking of the ethnographic film-makers in the decade after it was made'. But he wanted more than just active intervention by the film-makers: 'a film-maker putting himself at the disposal of his subjects and, with them, inventing the film.' Such a project was largely realized with *Two Laws* (1981) about Aboriginal land rights in Australia. The film was produced by Alessandro Cavadini and Caroline Strachan, but the Borooloola Aboriginal community collectively decided what to film and how to film it.

The participatory potential of documentary has been exploited in the late 1980s and early 1990s, as the peoples who have been the traditional subjects of ethnographic film-making have begun to make films about their own lives and cultures. (Sol Worth and Jon Adair did this on an experimental basis in 1966 with *The Spirit of the Navajos*, by Maxine and Mary J. Tsosie.) Such films include the ongoing assemblage film of Filipino Kidlat Tahimik, *I am Furious Yellow* (1981–93), which follows the growth of his three sons, and Aboriginal film-maker Frances Peters's hour-long documentary *Tent City* (1992) about Aboriginal land rights. Several members of the Kayopó tribe in Brazil began using video in 1985; they recorded local ceremonies and the elders telling their village's history. They also used video to document the destructive activities of illegal miners and smugglers.

In the First World, documentaries have also become increasingly personal in tone. In *Sherman's March* (1986), Ross McElwee records his daily life as he tries to find his perfect mate. He meets one blind date with a running camera on his shoulder. Throughout much of *Roger & Me* (1989), director Michael Moore is on screen as he seeks an interview with Roger Smith, the highly paid president of General Motors, the car manufacturer. Unable to interview Smith, Moore documents the impact of GM's plant closings and of 'deindustrialization' in Flint, Michigan. British film-maker Nick Broomfield often places himself in problematic situations and keeps his cameras rolling to see what will unfold. *Chicken Ranch* (1982) is about life in a house of prostitution: the film conveniently reaches a climax when the camera crew is finally thrown out of the door. In *Aileen Wuornos: The Selling of a Serial Killer* (1993) Broomfield participates in the media circus surrounding Wuornos, a prostitute who was convicted of killing seven of her customers and was billed as the first female serial killer. Broomfield records his financial negotiations with her lawyer and adopted mother—both of whom are primarily interested in the large fees they will receive. In the end Broomfield exposes the ways in which justice has been corrupted and Wuornos's case exploited by law enforcement officials eager to make money selling their stories to producers for potential TV movies.

Although Errol Morris does not appear in *The Thin Blue Line* (1988), the film-maker's presence is strongly felt throughout the film due to distinctive choices in lighting, editing, and music, and the introduction of scenes staged in a highly stylized fashion. This powerful documentary proves that an innocent man was wrongly convicted of killing a Dallas police officer, and eventually reveals the ways in which the state allowed itself to be easily fooled by the real killer, an appealing young teenager who went on to kill again. Morris invested much of the considerable cultural capital he gained from this film to revive and reframe the concept of film truth that had fallen in disrepute over the previous fifteen years: that truth is not guaranteed, but it is essential to seek. Likewise in Susana Muñoz's and Lourdes Portillo's *Mothers of the Plaza de Mayo* (1985), the Argentine military claims that it is not responsible for the 'disappearance' of young students and political leftists; against such pretences, the army's participation in these murders emerges as a damning truth.

In this period, documentaries have developed in two divergent directions. While independent documentaries have flourished on the festival circuit and enjoyed critical attention, the vast majority are commissioned and underwritten by television stations which have tended to see them as programming units that must conform to their needs. In many cases the resulting series are international co-productions which have to satisfy the underlying ideological assumptions of several different government-funded/sponsored/controlled corporations, including their somewhat divergent articulated standards for objectivity. This was true, for example, with the twelve-episode *Vietnam: A Television History* (series producers: Richard Ellision and Stanley Karnow, 1983), which was done as an international co-production with WGBH in the USA, Central Independent Television in Great Britain, and Antenne-2 in France. Perceptions of the war tended to be quite different in these three nations. More generally, television executives want to build audience loyalty to specific programming slots by maintaining a consistent tone or look from programme to programme and season to season. Documentary has always had to accommodate to the demands of its sponsors. More and more its survival as a valid form depends on finding sponsors who respect its right, and duty, to seek truth first and make accommodations second.

Bibliography

Barnouw, Erik (1974), *Documentary: A History of the Nonfiction Film*.

Ellis, Jack (1989), *The Documentary Idea: A Critical History of English-Language Documentary Film and Video*.

Hockings, Paul (ed.) (1975), *Principles of Visual Anthropology*.

Mamber, Stephen (1974), *Cinema Verite in America*.

Nichols, Bill (1980), *Newsreel: Documentary Filmmaking on the American Left*.

Rosenthal, Alan (1980), *The New Documentary in Action*.

Solanas, Fernando, and Getino, Octavio (1969), 'Towards a Third Cinema'.

Stoller, Paul (1992), *The Cinematic Griot: The Ethnography of Jean Rouch*.

Avant-Garde Film: The Second Wave

A. L. REES

European avant-garde film was reborn surprisingly soon after the war, from the 1950s, with the provocative neo-Dada of Fluxus, Lettrisme, and Action-Art. As in the original *Cabaret Voltaire*, and for similar reasons, mockery and excess were weapons of social and cultural protest. But film as an aspect of 'bomb culture' was often defiantly marginal, even after the aptly named Underground surfaced to public view in the 1960s. Only one film by the Situationist Guy Debord has been shown in Britain, for example, at the Institute for Contemporary Arts in 1952.

Even by then, the lead had passed to the USA, as it had with painting when New York replaced Paris as the cultural capital of modernism. As Abstract Expressionism triumphed in the 1940s, new waves of experimental film-makers began to explore film as a fine art. More positive than the Europeans about their shared Dada-Surrealist heritage, the Americans wanted to make art, not abolish it. Their hallmark was personal vision, the basis both of

A signed still from the classic avant-garde film *Meshes of the Afternoon* (1943) by Maya Deren and Alexander Hammid, featuring Deren as the entrapped protagonist

the California-based abstract film and of the short film-poems made in the artists' colonies of Los Angeles, San Francisco, and New York.

This personal stance was as much material as ideological. Portable 16 mm. cameras with variable lenses and shooting speeds could be found on the war surplus and amateur film markets. Cheap and flexible technology literally put the means of production in the film-maker's hands. As 16 mm. became the regular projection format in colleges, ciné-clubs, and arts groups, new circuits opened for the avant-garde. Like the live poetry readings which grew in this decade, film-makers often presented

and discussed the films in person. At a time when *auteur* theory was controversially being applied to the mainstream, the avant-garde here underlined personal and direct authorship, and audience response, to challenge the regime of commercial cinema, from production to reception.

On the west coast, Oskar Fischinger presided over the revival of abstract 'Motion Painting', the title of his 1947 film. Like his fellow exile Len Lye, his work became more pure and absolute as his commercial career foundered (Fischinger's watershed crisis was seemingly Disney's rejection of his abstract designs for *Fantasia*). A handful of native pioneers also explored abstract animation, including Mary Ellen Bute, the pioneer of electronic visual art, Harry Smith, who hand-painted his early films, and the brothers John and James Whitney who turned to technology and light-play experiment to explore Duchampian 'chance operations'.

PSYCHODRAMA AND BEYOND

Along with the revival of synaesthetic abstraction, American film-makers reinvented the narrative film-poem. The 'psychodrama' (or 'trance-film') was modelled on dream, lyric verse, and contemporary dance. Typically, it enacts the personal conflicts of a central subject or protagonist. A scenario of desire and loss, seen from the point of view of a single guiding consciousness, ends either in redemption or death. Against the grain of realism, montage editing evokes swift transitions in space and time. The subjective, fluid camera is more often a participant in the action than its neutral recording agent.

This new narrative avant-garde was symbolized in the now-classic *Meshes of the Afternoon* (1943) by Maya Deren and Alexander Hammid. Its Chinese-box narrative form entraps the young protagonist (played by Deren) as much as the disjointed domestic space around her. An emblematic knife and key elude her grasp. Actions are interrupted; a record plays in an empty room, a phone is off the hook. A fantasized pursuit of a glimpsed figure ends in violence, perhaps suicide. Erotic, and irredeemably Freudian (despite Deren's protestation at the label), the film combines its spiral structure with pictorialist camera work and intricately crafted matte shots (as when the sleeping woman faces her other 'selves' who replicate within successive dreams). Both protagonist and spectator search for connecting threads, as the quest theme resonates equally in the film's subject-matter and its style.

The 1940s renaissance of film, for which Deren tirelessly campaigned, was part of a wider revolution in American culture. It included the rise of 'American-type' painting (in Clement Greenberg's phrase), competing schools of post-Poundian poets and post-Joycean writers, and the innovations of Merce Cunningham in dance and John Cage (a close associate of the film avant-garde) in music. The mixture of the arts at this point was promiscuous rather than programmatic. If some Europeans were exploring the melt-down factor in mixed-media assemblage, the Americans wished less to blur the edges between the arts than freely to discover their limits. In this light, the reappearance of film drama in a cultural milieu led by purely abstract art, music, and dance is less aberrant than it looks. It rehearsed the old argument between film-as-painting and as camera-eye vision, each claiming to express film's unique property as a plastic art form.

Some film-makers (such as Harry Smith) moved between both modes, but many held to absolute non-figuration (like the Whitney brothers) which yet others saw as denying the camera's ability to depict 'the way things are' (Deren). For Deren, film had an objective aspect which the other arts innately lacked. At the same time, the manipulation of time and space was equally a property of film form, so that editing could undermine the surface realism of cinematography to create a new language that was film's alone.

This period of experimentation included the first films of Kenneth Anger, Curtis Harrington, and Sidney Peterson. Their keynote was black humour and Oedipal crisis. The fleeing son of Harrington's *On the Edge* (1949) is literally hauled back to mother by her knitting yarn, while in James Broughton's *Mother's Day* (1948) the roles of children are played by adults. Peterson's *The Lead Shoes* (1949), made with San Francisco art students who were also war veterans and survivors, features a distorting anamorphic lens, a Californian Kali of a mother, her diver-suited son, and a raucous 'scratch' rendition of old ballads ('What's that blood on your knife, Edward?', chants a dissonant chorus).

By contrast, the fantasy sailors of Anger's *Fireworks* (1947) who savagely beat the hero are culled from Eisensteinian montage rather than the US Navy, to both of which the film pays homage along with 'American Christmas and being seventeen'. Burning illumination leads the dreaming protagonist to trauma and death, from which he is redeemed by the seminal pouring of milk over his body and the showering of light from a phallic firework. The dreamer awakes to a new consciousness, still in bed but 'no longer alone'.

Marie Menken had already taken a crucial step to free the camera from the centralized human eye assumed by all narrative film, even the most radical psychodramas. In *Visual Variations on Noguchi* (1945)—originally planned to accompany the Cage–Cunningham ballet *The Seasons*—her hand-held camera pans round an abstract sculpture to create an improvised dance in film space. Fluently bridging the abstract and the figurative, it seeks lyric form without narrative mediation. Her later experiments in the transformation of 'dailiness' by camera, light, and pixillation are compiled in *Notebook* (1963). Menken's liberation from film drama—unlike most of the avant-garde she was a painter, not a writer—inspired the young Stan Brakhage to adopt the free camera work of his transitional *Anticipation of the Night* (1958).

Deren and Anger also moved away from psychodrama in the 1950s. Their films became more gestural and abstract. Both were drawn to magic and became experts on their founding myths, Haitian Voudoun for Deren and Aleister Crowley for Anger. However, their films were also rooted in a tradition which gave primacy to photogenic sight and montage structure. Anger stressed the first of these, most elaborately in his *Inauguration of the Pleasure Dome* (1954–66), which occupied him for most of the 1950s and which he issued in different versions—including triple screen projection—over twenty years. Dissolves and super-impositions of the Magus's sparkling rings and regalia lead to an orgiastic initiation rite, in which masks, body-paint, and ham-acting serve to deflate and ironize the film's high mannerist style.

Myth and dance were central to both Anger and Deren. In Deren this took classical form, as in the final film of her psychodrama trilogy, *Ritual in Transfigured Time* (1949), in which Anaïs Nin also appears. Here, a cocktail party becomes a children's game (by freeze-frame rhythms), statues come alive (by stop-motion), and the two female protagonists—played by Deren and the black actress Rita Christiani—change identities in an underwater closing scene, 'the passage from widow to bride', shown in nega-tive.

Her final films no longer psychologize the trance state. In *Meditation on Violence* (1953), trance is embodied in the balletic ritual gestures of a Chinese ritual boxer. His slow-building solo performance displays the sinuous geometry of unarmed combat, to flute music. The pace quickens with drumbeats until a sudden montage cut from interior to rooftop shows the whirling boxer now with robes and sword. The first sequence is repeated, this time in almost imperceptible reverse-motion. Overshadowed by her early brilliance, the formal minimalism of Deren's later films anticipates the structural film a decade later, while they look even further ahead in their hybrid mixture of cul-tures and in Deren's explicit articulation of 'a woman's voice'.

Anger's work was also to prove prophetic, though in a different way. After spending the 1950s in Europe where he made the strangely baroque *Eaux d'artifice* (1953) and started work on other projects, he returned to America where he made a surprising (and for him unique) turn to contemporary life—vividly mythologized—in *Scorpio Rising* (1964), a response to the new rock and youth culture he found there after his fifteen-year absence. This heralded for Anger an imminent Luciferian age, whose symbols were encoded in the narcissistic rites of the 'bike boy' cult. The film opens with a cool, documentary invocation of these demonic brothers, later seen donning Nazi-style gear and posing in hieratic shots. Slowly, the montage becomes subjective; a glue-sniffing biker 'sees red', scenes of Brando (*The Wild One*, on TV) and Christ (from a silent religious film) are intercut with comic-strips and flash-frames (Fascism and sex). After clan initiation and church desecration, the film ends in a rapid montage of racing bikes and death, sirens, and police lights.

Scorpio became an Underground cult classic, partly due to its transgressive theme of 'doomed youth'. Unusually open-textured for Anger, but in the now preferred style of the Underground, it incorporates found footage, stylized portraits, improvisation, and documentary (within a formal structure that moves from inside to outside, opening and closing with artificial light). Above all, and preceded only by Bruce Conner's *Cosmic Ray* (1961), the sound-track is made up of contemporary rock music (including 'Blue Velvet', later the title for a film by David Lynch). Partly through the mediation of Anger's British admirer Derek Jarman, *Scorpio* was to have a major effect on the development of sophisticated forms of music video, at the same time celebratory and ironic towards its subject, in the 1980s.

UNDERGROUND

The 1950s institutionalization of modern art under its newly acquired name ('modernism') bred a reaction from disestablished or oppositional artists. Aiming to keep art outside the museum and its rules, they looked back to earlier times (especially to Dada) when its 'negative moment'—art as a critique of reality—was most heigh-tened. This movement later became the 'counter-culture' or more popularly 'the Underground'. The shift of empha-sis is telling; one military term—an 'advanced guard' scouting ahead of the pack—is replaced by another which reflects clandestine resistance, tunnelling rather than charging, to echo a post-war identification with partisans and prisoners.

The Underground was made up of loosely affiliated groups and individuals who mixed humour, iconoclasm, and intransigence. Its manifestations ranged from Beat Poetry, to aggressive performance art, to the automatic painting of Pino-Gallizio, the experiments of the Fluxus group, and the 'random music' of John Cage. Its culture was fuelled by a burgeoning 'underground press' of pamphlets and magazines, which spread the new *Zeitgeist* as far afield as Japan and even (where it was truly underground) the USSR.

The roots of the Underground which flowered in the 1960s lay in the aftermath of world war. During the early 1950s films were again made in France by fringe dis-sidents, hostile to the 'culture industry'. The assault on culture began with the Lettriste group in Paris, led by Isidore Isou from 1947. Its attacks on meaning and value look back to Rimbaud, Nietzsche, and Dada, and antici-pate William Burroughs. Among their tactics of 'détour-nement' or subversion, Isou and Maurice Lemaître cut commercial found footage literally to pieces, scratching and painting the film surface and frame, adding texts and sound-tracks to dislocate its original meaning further. These often very long works joined a Lettriste armoury of collage-poems, manifestos, and provocations.

Art as a form of social 'intervention' was taken further (at least theoretically) by the Situationists, an inter-national grouping which included disaffected Lettristes who followed Debord after his 1952 schism with Isou. Their journal *Internationale situationniste* (1958–69) influenced Godard by its unique attack on the 'society of the spectacle' with a mixture of collage, invective, and urbanist theory. For the Situationists, however, Godard was 'just another Beatle'. Debord's own six films (1952–78) are rigorously collaged from found footage, with added voice-overs largely made up of quotations. Rarely screened, they were withdrawn altogether by Debord in 1984, in protest against the unsolved murder of left-wing publisher Gerard Lebovici, and so they remained until Debord's suicide ten years later.

In Vienna, radical artists in the immediate post-war period were similarly hostile to the 'commodification' of art but did not reject artistic activity (as the Situationists did). One Viennese group included the artists and filmmakers Felix Radax, Peter Kubelka, and Arnulf Rainer. Their experiments with formal and mathematical systems drew on Webern and the pre-war Vienna School, as in Kubelka's sound and kinetic montage for *Mosaik im Vertrauen* ('Mosaic in confidence', 1954–5). His abstract film *Arnulf Rainer* (1958–60) used a graphic score to predetermine its alternating patterns of black and white frames, while *Adebar* (1957) and *Schwechater* (1958) employ cyclic repetition of small human movements and fluid colours. Several of Kubelka's films were commissioned, in spite of their purist ambitions: *Adebar*, with its strobe-flattened dancers, was an advert for a café of that name.

Another group, which included Kurt Kren, was attracted to the idea of confrontational 'live-art' performance, as practised by Hermann Nitsch and Otto Muehl under the banner of 'Material-Action'. Kren recorded Muehl's transgressive events in films which simultaneously explore perception and film-time. He also made over thirty short films which permutate shots in a strict series (*TV*, 1967), or use rapid motion and cutting (*48 Faces from the Szondi Test*, 1960). Yet others take a new look at the everyday, as in the witty and self-explanatory *Eating, Drinking, Pissing and Shitting Film* (1967), or view nature through time-lapse and multiple exposure, as in *Trees in Autumn* (1960) or *Asyl* (1975).

Underground film in the USA at first encompassed a range of non-, anti-, or semi-commercial activities, including documentary and narrative fiction, and extending far beyond the bounds of the artistic avant-garde in the narrow sense. Spontaneity and improvisation were the keynote, with frequent recourse to *cinéma-vérité* techniques, as in the early work of John Cassavetes and that of Shirley Clarke, a former dancer who turned from dance films to making features such as *The Connection* (1960—with the Living Theatre) and *The Cool World* (1962). In 1960, the New York artists' avant-garde joined with these other independents to form the New American Cinema Group: 'We don't want false, polished, slick films—we prefer them

rough, unpolished, but alive,' ran their manifesto. 'We don't want rosy films—we want them the colour of blood.' The mood of the epoch is ironically cued in Cassavetes's *Shadows* (1957), where street-wise toughs confront an exhibition of modern art.

Similarly semi-improvised was Robert Frank and Alfred Leslie's *Pull my Daisy* (1958), which stars the Beat poets Allan Ginsberg and Gregory Corso (and, sheltering under a pseudonym, the young Delphine Seyrig), with voice-over commentary by Jack Kerouac. Equally playful and anecdotal is Ron Rice's quasi-narrative Beat film *The Flower Thief* (1960), starring Taylor Mead. But even these looser narratives were soon abandoned. Rice's *Chumlum* (1964) and Jack Smith's *Flaming Creatures* (1963) visually celebrate the orgy as *opéra bouffe*, shot in delirious dissolved colour (by Rice) or on grainily pallid outdated stock (by Smith).

The magazine *Film Culture* was founded by Jonas Mekas in 1955 to support the new documentary and fiction film, along with the smaller group of experimental film artists. In the end, these routes parted; the documentary and narrative branches of New American Cinema were committed to forms of realism which the artists' avant-garde rejected. By 1962 the balance of forces had swung the other way for Mekas, and his magazine was thereafter devoted mainly (but not exclusively) to the experimental film, post-Deren and Brakhage, as was his influential column in the *Village Voice*. Mekas, a Lithuanian war refugee, made the beat-era narrative *Guns of the Trees* (1961) before turning to more personal film-making. In *Diaries, Notes and Sketches* (1964–9) fragments of New York life are glimpsed with a hand-held Bolex camera. As with Andrew Noren, David Brooks, and Warren Sonbert, the 'diary film' maintains the quotidian spirit of the NAC; films shaped by daily life rather than scripts.

'Action painting' also impelled film to an involvement with process and with gestural, mixed-media live art, pioneered by Jacobs, Smith, and (later) Warhol. An important link was made by the neo-Dada Fluxus movement. Fluxus films (1962–6) are typically tongue-in-cheek explorations of extreme close-up (Chieko Shiomi's *Disappearing Music for Face*—a slow-motion smile), permutation (Yoko Ono's 'Bottoms' film), repetition (John Cale's *Police Light*), cameraless films (George Maciunas), single-frame films (Paul Sharits), and banalized humour (George Landow's *The Evil Faerie*).

In similar vein, Bruce Conner made films from archive footage. His milestone work is *A Movie* (1958), which moves from the hilarious (crazy races, a chase scene with cars and cowboys) to the disturbing (shivering refugees, an execution, air crashes). The act of viewing is questioned by the film's montage just as it plays on 'a movie' as both kinetic event and emotional affect. Conner maintains his scepticism in *America Is Waiting* (1982), which lampoons

John Cassavetes

(1929–1989)

John Cassavetes called himself a 'professional' actor and an 'amateur' director, and it was his success as a commercial actor that permitted him the financial liberty to make his own films at various degrees of distance from Hollywood's studios.

Born in New York City in 1929, the son of Greek immigrants, Cassavetes studied acting at the American Academy of Dramatic Art in New York City. Graduating in 1953, Cassavetes worked on the stage, in television (this was the so-called 'golden age' of realist TV drama), and in films during the 1950s. In the 1960s he worked with Don Siegel, Martin Ritt, and Robert Aldrich, and was nominated for an Oscar for his performance in *The Dirty Dozen* (1967).

His first film, *Shadows*, released in 1960, was made for a mere $40,000. Based on improvisations which originated in Cassavetes's acting workshop, *Shadows* won the Critics' Award at the 1960 Venice Film Festival and caused French critics to hail Cassavetes as the American cousin of the French New Wave. This critical enthusiasm provided him the opportunity to direct in Hollywood. *Too Late Blues* (1961) with Bobby Darin as a jazz musician, and *A Child is Waiting* (1961) with Judy Garland as a woman working with retarded children, are touching films which display great technical facility and stylishness, but they bear little resemblance to *Shadows* or his later work. Cassavetes vowed never to direct another studio film, explaining, 'People cannot be paid to care.'

The rest of the films Cassavetes directed received various degrees of Hollywood support and critical acceptance. His second independent feature, *Faces* (1968), told the story of a dissolving marriage and the lovers to whom the couple turn for solace. Shot in black and white on 16 mm. for a budget of $200,000, *Faces* took six months to shoot, and almost four years to edit, in part because of Cassavetes' painstaking methods: he printed every take, and the screening of daily rushes lasted two to three hours instead of the usual thirty minutes. *Faces* won five awards in the 1968 Venice Film Festival, and three Oscar nominations. The powerful acting and dialogue made audiences assume the film was improvised like *Shadows*, but in fact it was entirely scripted, as were all of Cassavetes's subsequent films. One reviewer summarized both the positive and the negative view of Cassavetes by calling *Faces* the 'longest, most ambitious, most brilliant home movie ever made'.

During the 1970s Cassavetes continued to act in Hollywood, while making a series of remarkable, singular films. After *Faces*, he was able to find Hollywood distribution for *Husbands* (1970) and *Minnie and Moskowitz* (1971), while he himself distributed *A Woman under the Influence* (1974), *The Killing of a Chinese Bookie* (1976), and *Opening Night* (1977). Later, Cassavetes achieved another *rapprochement* with Hollywood, getting distribution for *Gloria* and *Love Streams* (both 1980), the latter being produced by Cannon.

Sometimes exasperating, often exhilarating, always remarkable, Cassavetes's films have had a mixed critical reception and their unwieldiness has made them hard for the current critical vocabulary to come to terms with.

But the titles of his films give a good impression not only of his themes but of his innovations. *Faces* points to his interest in the expressiveness of the human face in cinema; *Opening Night* to the theatricality of his chosen actors, their endless public demands for love; *Love Streams* to the unwieldy aspect of emotions. So much attention has been given to the extraordinary acting in Cassavetes's films that critics have often failed to see the originality of his narrative structures and visual style. After *Shadows* his use of improvisation shifted from the actors to the camera and the editing room: his camera takes on a great liberty in interrogating its subjects, and each successive cutting of a film was likely to vary wildly from the previous one.

Cassavetes strayed further from the mainstream in his relentless examinations of gender: in *Husbands* three middle-aged men try to break free from their homes on the occasion of a friend's death. Cassavetes criticized Hollywood for representing women as 'either high- or low-class concubines, and the only question is when or where they will go to bed and with whom or how many. There's nothing to do with the dreams of women . . . nothing to do with the quirky part of her, the wonder of her.' In films like *A Woman under the Influence* and *Love Streams*, Cassavetes gives unprecedented scope to women who are misunderstood and ill-adapted to their world. Even in *Gloria*, ostensibly his most commercial vehicle, Cassavetes twists the era's violent rogue cop films by casting Gena Rowlands as a gun-wielding former mob moll who is a strange combination of toughness and sensitivity.

If friends and families, husbands and wives, are his consistent themes, this is hardly separable from Cassavetes's own dependence on a devoted group of actors and friends like Peter Falk, Ben Gazzara, Seymour Cassel, and above all his wife and muse Gena Rowlands, who gives astounding performances, most notably in *A Woman under the Influence*.

EDWARD R. O'NEILL

SELECT FILMOGRAPHY

Shadows (1960); Too Late Blues (1961); A Child is Waiting (1961); Faces (1968); Husbands (1970); Minnie and Moskowitz (1971); A Woman under the Influence (1974); The Killing of a Chinese Bookie (1976); Opening Night (1977); Gloria (1980); Love Streams (1980); Big Trouble (1986)

BIBLIOGRAPHY

Carney, Raymond (1985), *American Dreaming: The Films of John Cassavetes and the American Experience*.
Jousse, Thierry (1989), *John Cassavetes*.

Opposite: John Cassavetes shooting *A Woman Under the Influence* (1974)

the military machine to a rock sound-track by Brian Eno and David Byrne.

Self-expression, in psychodrama's sense, was also no longer a goal for Jacobs when he chose junk footage for *Blond Cobra* (1963)—which also calls for live radio sound-track when screened—nor in Peter Kubelka's savage montage of 'safari' footage commissioned from him by Austrian tourists. His *Unsere Afrikareise* ('Our trip to Africa', 1966) documents and subverts the voracious eye. Its complex editing system is quasi-musical, linking shots by duration, shape, and analogy. But the film is far from purely formal (the aspect stressed by Kubelka himself). Scraps of folk-song and banal conversation are cut to images of hunted or dead animals, and universal myth (evoked by tourists admiring the moon) is undercut by neo-colonial reality. Its final sardonic line—'I hope to visit your country one day, man'—is spoken (in English) by an African, as another is seen walking off naked into the distance.

A pair of shots from Peter Kubelka's ironic *Unsere Afrikareise* (1966)

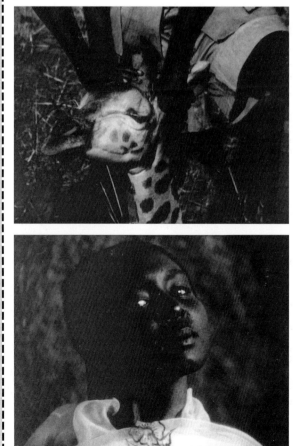

543

Andy Warhol

(1927–1987)

Born Andrew Warhola in Cleveland, Ohio, in 1927, Andy Warhol studied art at the Carnegie Institute of Technology in Pittsburgh, then moved to New York in 1949 where he worked as a graphic artist and window display decorator. Warhol became the central figure in pop art, his work representing a joyful camp rejection of a modernist aesthetic of high moral seriousness. Against Abstract Expressionism's still-romantic idealization of the freedom and expressivity of a strong and lonely heroic subjectivity, Warhol celebrated the mass-produced objects and images of modern culture.

Warhol's art was already deeply influenced by Hollywood as an industry and a social phenomenon when he started making films. His references to mass-produced commodities went beyond his mock Brillo boxes and paintings of Campbell's soup cans to include comic-book heroes like Superman and Batman, and stars like Elizabeth Taylor and Marilyn Monroe. His portraits of celebrities not only reproduced Hollywood glamour shots, they often included a serial repetition which reproduced the effect of a strip of motion picture film. In underlining the fantasmatic aspects of film and mass-media imagery, Warhol reappropriated reproducible images under his own signature in order both to borrow and to point up their auratic, shimmering beauty. In dubbing his own

workshop 'The Factory', Warhol admitted its resemblance to Hollywood as a film factory. He even created a sort of star system gone haywire, manufacturing and glorifying such instant stars as Viva, Ultra Violet, Mario Montez, Candy Darling, Edie Sedgwick and Joe Dallesandro.

Warhol's films can be periodized into early, middle, and late. The early films, dating from 1963 and 1964, are silent and bear a family resemblance to the Lumières' films, but with a minimalist inflection by way of Duchamp. *Empire* (1964) is a static long shot of the Empire State Building lasting eight hours; *Sleep* (1963) depicts a sleeping male figure for six hours; *Blowjob* (1963) is a 45-minute close-up showing the face of a man being fellated. In such works Warhol drastically reconceived cinematic time and the relation of the spectator to the film: he saw film as a kind of furniture which one could take or leave; watching would be distracted, not fascinated. These films have no editing as such, and Warhol even changed the speed of projection to make up for missing time taken in loading the camera.

In his middle period, from 1965 to 1967, Warhol used sound more frequently, recording scenes improvised within a minimal situation. These films, such as *My Hustler* (1965), *Chelsea Girls* (1966), and *Lonesome Cowboys* (1968), were influenced by the New York film world of Shirley Clarke and John Cassavetes, and also by the art world's emerging performance art and 'happenings', and by the campy theatre art of Jack Smith. In *Chelsea*

Girls, colour and black and white reels were projected side by side on the screen in no particular order. Unlike Warhol's earlier more art-world-oriented ventures, films like *Lonesome Cowboys* were exhibited in theatres, and, given their minimal costs, could actually make money.

As Warhol moved closer to commercial exhibition, however, the sexuality, homosexuality, and transvestism of his films confronted the legal limitations imposed on the market. Although his films contained plentiful nudity and various kinds of sexual by-play, Warhol's aesthetic of distraction and boredom is the opposite of pornography. Warhol's sex is a sex without excitement, a sex which is more talk than action, a sex undone by camp. Nevertheless, the gay overtones of *Lonesome Cowboys* were enough to pique the wrath of the FBI, who investigated Warhol for interstate transportation of obscene material. In 1969 the film was seized in Atlanta, cut, and returned to screening, although the FBI recommended local authorities prosecute for obscenity. Later, *Blue Movie / Fuck* (1968) was declared hard-core pornography in New York City; a decision upheld all the way to the Supreme Court.

In Warhol's last phase of film production, he lent his name to a series of films made with Paul Morrissey. The precise nature of Warhol's involvement with these later films is not clear, but it seems that Morrissey was responsible for what is generally called direction, while Warhol presided over the events as a sort of omnivoyant catalyst. In films like *Flesh* (1968), *Trash* (1970), and *Heat* (1972), a minimal narrative permits a series of improvised scenes to be strung together into something resembling a story, usually involving sexual and economic exchanges and misfires. When George Cukor saw *Flesh*, he called the film 'an authentic whiff from the gutter'—a phrase which pleased Warhol so much that the quote was used in advertising for the film. These films remained far from Hollywood standards of narrative and decorum, but nevertheless represented Warhol's penetration into the industry he mocked, adored, and idolized.

EDWARD R. O'NEILL

SELECT FILMOGRAPHY

Tarzan and Jane Regained... Sort of (1963); Kiss (1963); Sleep (1963); Blow Job (1963); Empire (1964); Couch (1964); The Thirteen Most Beautiful Women (1964); Restaurant (1965); Kitchen (1965); My Hustler (1965); The Chelsea Girls (1966); **** / Four Stars (1966); Lonesome Cowboys (1968); Blue Movie / Fuck (1968); Flesh (1968); Trash (1970); Heat (1972); Bad (1976).

BIBLIOGRAPHY

Finkelstein, Nat (1989), *Andy Warhol: The Factory Years*.
Hackett, Pat (1989), *The Andy Warhol Diaries*.
Koch, Stephen (1973), *Stargazer: Andy Warhol's World and his Films*.
O'Pray, Michael (1989), *Andy Warhol Film Factory*.
Warhol, Andy (1975), *The Philosophy of Andy Warhol: From A to B and Back Again*.

Opposite: Andy Warhol shooting his 'Western' *Lonesome Cowboys* (1968).

The romantic strain in film-making was most strongly maintained by the prolific and influential Stan Brakhage. In his early psychodramas, his typically abrupt editing style is used to elicit quasi-symbolist metaphor. In *Reflections on Black* (1955), a blind man 'sees' events behind closed tenement doors, an illicit kiss is intercut with a coffee pot boiling over, and a final hand-scratched image makes light appear to stream from the blind man's eyes. Similarly, *The Way to Shadow Garden* (1955) ends with the inner vision of an Oedipally self-blinded hero, shown in the unfamiliar reverse form of negative film stock. Sight is restored but transfigured.

In *Anticipation of the Night* (1958), this concern for poetic myth and illumination was displaced on to the formal plane of light and colour, away from fictional diegetic space and the singular narrative subject. The break was not final; *Anticipation* evokes the suicidal state of an unseen protagonist. But the camera treats this genre theme with a fresh and painterly eye, hovering freely over the surface of domestic, daily objects. At times, diffused light and focus draw attention to the physicality of the film medium. Elsewhere, the imagined dreams of sleeping children are elicited by direct shots of 'the real'—a fairground, landscape, animals—and subjective point of view replaces even the vestigial reverse-field editing of the earlier films. Yet immediate empathy is punctuated by repetition, cluster-shots, darkness, and erratic movement. These devices, which both construct and distanciate, draw on Gertrude Stein's prose and on Menken's camera style.

Brakhage's films challenge film conventions even by their varied length, from nine seconds in *Eyemyth* (1972) to five hours in *The Art of Vision* (1965). They include intimate portraits of friends and family, film-poems, landscape films, autobiography, and more recent collaborations with composers and writers. His personal creation myth centred on the act of shooting and editing. Equally, the objective side of his films—their rhythms, metrics, camera style, subject-matter—make uncompromising demands on the viewer to elicit and construct meaning, thus shifting attention from the author's voice to the spectator's eye. Viewing avant-garde film is here very close to the process of viewing modern painting.

Brakhage's prodigious output included his 'birth-film' *Window Water Baby Moving* (1959)—Anthony Balch told Burroughs it made him faint—to films about the seasons (*Sirius Remembered*, 1959), childhood (*The Weir-Falcon Saga*, 1970), and light (*Riddle of Lumen*, 1972). By contrast, *Mothlight* (1963) is a bravura collage of moth-wings, pollen, and leaves, while *The Act of Seeing with One's Own Eyes* (1971) unflinchingly documents the work of a Pittsburgh morgue—the title is a literal translation of 'autopsy'.

Lyric films—short, poetic, and visual—flourished in this decade, particularly on the west coast, where Bruce Baillie matted and superimposed the stately freight trains of

Castro Street (1966). But for some newer film-makers, in the run-up to 'post-painterly abstraction' and minimal art, both the lyric mode and Brakhage's visibly hand-held camera (index or trace of the artist's response to experience) were too uncritically subjective. The main mentor of the anti-subjective approach (and of the shortly to emerge structural film) was Andy Warhol, whose brief film-making career dated from 1963 and whose urban, disengaged, and impersonal art challenged Brakhage's romanticism. Warhol's tactics—static camera, long take, no editing—opposed current avant-garde styles and were a direct attack on film as dream and metaphor. In *Sleep* (1964), for example, Warhol parodies the trance-film: we see a man sleeping for six hours, but not his dreams. In contrast to most of the avant-garde, Warhol's films parody the pursuit of authenticity and selfhood. Improvisation and confession, often hallmarks of realism, here undermine the certainty of seeing and knowing.

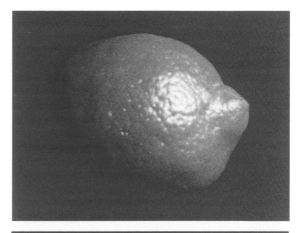

Warhol's objective camera-eye inspired a turn towards the material aspect of film. With loop-printing, repetition, and blank footage—devices unique to the film medium—Warhol made works of extreme duration. He also subtly manipulated time, questioning the seeming simplicity of the long take. *Empire* (1965), filmed in near-darkness, provokes the eye to scan the screen for nuances of change, leading persistent viewers to examine their own experience of viewing the film.

STRUCTURAL FILM

Structural film led the avant-garde to the high ground, seeking to explore visual ideas of structure, process, and chance then appearing in the other arts (Cage, Rauschenberg, and Johns). It turned away from visual sensation and towards self-reflexiveness. In structural film, form became content. A cinema of vision was replaced by one which posited viewing as an act of reading (literally so in films by Michael Snow, Hollis Frampton, and George Landow), shifting the experimental film into a new philosophical territory.

Canadian artist Michael Snow was an early exponent of this new approach. His best-known film, *Wavelength* (1967), explores the illusion of deep space. For forty-five minutes, a camera slowly and irregularly zooms into the far wall and windows of a loft, accompanied by a rising sine wave. The zoom is interrupted by colour changes induced by filters and film stock, and also by some minimal sub-drama (a conversation, a hammed death, a phone call) which the lens literally passes over in a casually anti-narrative gesture. The film ends in extreme close-up—a photograph of sea waves. A decade later, Snow issued its short counterpart, *Breakfast* (1972–6), where the camera pushes slowly across a breakfast table and observation turns into intervention as it snags the tablecloth and gradually smashes all before it.

Still lemon: in Hollis Frampton's seven-minute *Lemon* (1969) neither the camera nor the object moves and the effect of change is produced by the movement of the off-screen light

Snow continued his perceptual and time-based experiments with *La Région centrale* (1971), in which a remote control camera pans and pivots endlessly over a mountain landscape. In the labyrinthine *Rameau's Nephew* (1974) he takes another tack, exploring different literal structures of mapping film, drama, and fiction; in one sequence, actors speak their lines backwards to imitate a tape played in reverse, in another they all use different languages. This semiotic side of Snow's work continues in *Presents* (1981), where the apparent realism of the stage-set is literally taken apart (by fork-lift trucks) and in *So Is This* (1982), which is wholly made up of words and phrases interrogating the act of watching the film.

Like Snow, Frampton was drawn to systems, numbers, and linguistics. *Zorns Lemma* (1970)—the mathematical title alludes to an 'axiom of disorder'—is based on the number 24, linking film speed to the letters of the Roman alphabet (without 'j' and 'v'). An early American ABC—a moral as well as linguistic 'primer'—is read over a blank screen. The film then permutates one-second shots of the alphabet with images which gradually replace each repeated letter. Some images are static or repetitious (a tree, a shop-sign) while in others a continuous action is completed at the end of the cycle (a wall painted, a tyre changed, an egg cooked). Finally, women's voices read a medieval text on light, to a metronome-beat, while two small human figures and a dog are seen walking across a wintry landscape until they 'white-out' in snow and film-flare.

Also like Snow, Frampton was attracted to the idea of making films on a grand scale, mirroring in duration the spatial extensiveness of the 'land art' of the period. In the late 1970s he embarked on a project, unfinished by his death in 1984, for an epic cycle of films, one for each day of the year, entitled *The Straits of Magellan*. A late example of the American sublime, its grand scale ironically incorporates the ideas on serial minimalism Frampton discussed in the early 1960s with the young sculptor with Carl Andre, when both artists were seeking to undermine pop art.

Not all film-makers associated with the structural film movement came from a visual arts background or were so rigorously interested in the spatio-temporal aspects of the medium. Yvonne Rainer, for example, came (like Shirley Clarke) from a dance background. Her early films, beginning with *Lives of Performers* (1972), start from a perspective which is non- (rather than anti-) narrative, but as time went by she increasingly came to incorporate narrative and psychological elements into her work.

Few film-makers approved of the term 'structural film', introduced in the early 1970s by the critic P. Adams Sitney to describe post-Warholian film-making in which 'the film insists on its shape, and what content it has is minimal and subsidiary to its outline'. Perhaps fearing an onrush

of academic theory over artistic practice (later justified), they were unwilling to see the parallel rise of 'structuralism' in the human sciences as more than coincidence (or bad news), even as Frampton, Snow, and George Landow were forging links to it by their semiotic or linguistic turn.

Structural film proposed that the shaping of film's material—light, time, and process—could create a new form of aesthetic pleasure, free of symbolism or narrative. It typically combined predetermination (of camera position, number of frames or exposures, repetitions) with chance (the unpredictable events that occur at the moment of shooting). The phrase printed over a shot of a running man in Landow's *Remedial Reading Comprehension* (1970)—'This is a film about you, not about its maker'—alludes to the goal of eliminating personal expression and eliciting the active participation of the viewer in the film. The running man in this case is played by Landow, so the statement equally applies to him (as another image, or 'you'). Landow parodies trance-film to suggest that viewing is more like reading or thinking than dreaming.

Up to then, the avant-garde film tradition from the cubists to Deren and Brakhage had been essentially pictorial and often silent. This made it both cheap and (so Brakhage affirmed) 'pure', an alternative to naturalistic sound film and 'filmed drama'. A more demotic visuality came with the 1960s, at the Underground's height, when it broke taboos on sexual imagery, as in the much banned *Flaming Creatures*, dubbed by Mekas 'Baudelairean Cinema'. Warhol (*Couch*, 1966), Carolee Schneeman (*Fuses*, 1968), and Barbara Rubin famously explored erotic vision. At the same time, the west coast avant-garde (Jordan Belson, Bruce Baillie, Pat O'Neill, Scott Bartlett) were celebrating Tantric symbolism and desert landscapes. Their richly pictorial colour-music was highly romantic and yet commercially adaptable, influencing mass culture from adverts (a growing genre) to mainstream film (often in 'psychedelic' sequences, notably Kubrick's *2001*). The rise of structural film interrupted this florid romanticism, but did not destroy it, and aspects of it were to re-emerge in the 1980s.

BRITAIN AND EUROPE

Experimental film-making in Europe from the late 1960s followed a parallel but not identical course to America. The London Film Makers' Cooperative grew from partly American roots between 1965 and 1969, as the Co-op principle spread from New York into Europe, and attracted artists like Steve Dwoskin and Peter Gidal who had been part of Warhol's 'Factory'. But English film-makers quickly found their own direction. With the aid of a (home-made) printing machine, the London Co-op took up direct film-making in the craft ethos of the art schools from which most of its film-makers came. Many films reflected the abstract, minimalist concerns of the day. The printing machine became the focus of experiment with film as material, as in Annabel Nicolson's *Slides* (1971), where 35 mm. slides, light-leaked film, and sewn film were dragged through the contact printer to produce a result which was a record of the process by which the film was made.

Structural film in Europe generally showed more concern for film's 'material substrate'—its physical qualities—than for the image or shot, the province of the North Americans. For example, *Rohfilm* ('Raw film', 1968) by Wilhelm and Birgit Hein uses collage, wandering frame-lines, and sprocket holes to affirm the film's substance and its physical presence in the projector. Early structural film in Europe shared the Underground's libertarian and anarchic credo, seen in Steve Dwoskin's 1975 book *Film Is* (subtitled 'the international free cinema'), where praise of the 'wild' Ron Rice and Jack Smith sits alongside close analysis of structural films by Kurt Kren and Peter Gidal.

Such unions were short-lived, as schism grew between the American and the European avant-gardes. Links were never severed, but were often strained. Film-makers like Jeff Keen, David Larcher, and Dwoskin himself—who kept up the anarchic Underground tradition—were for a time marginalized by the Co-op structuralists. For much of the decade their extensive bodies of work, often incorporating the tropes of structural film, were more appreciated in France, Germany, and Holland than at home.

Experimentation with film's raw substance was combined with the English landscape tradition. In *Whitchurch Down (Duration)* (1972), Malcolm Le Grice alternates three views, each in different tones and colours. Gidal's *Clouds* (1969) loops a shot of the sky in which a glimpse of an aircraft wing sets the scale. Chris Welsby's *Park Film* (1972) uses time-lapse to compress three days on a busy walkway into six minutes of film time. Such films sought film equivalents for natural light and motion. They aimed to renew perception by using the whole register of film language, underlining its normally invisible aspects (frame, surface, print stock) and its 'mistakes' (flare, slippage, double exposure). For Le Grice, this constituted a 'politics of perception' (he hopefully titled a series of films in the early 1970s *How to Screw the CIA*). The 'pure' landscape films of Raban and Mike Leggett (*The Sheepman and the Sheared*, 1970–5) also allude to the passage of historical time, later explored by Raban in the neo-documentary *Thames Film* (1986) and in colour-field studies of Docklands (*Sundial*, 1992). Welsby, an 'unrepentant dualist', followed a more philosophical concern for eye and mind, while Gidal sought to align critical theory and formal film through 'structural-materialism'.

Such films had no fictional narrative content; they seem to leap over the history of film, and back to the experiments of Demenÿ, Muybridge, and the Lumières. Here, a line of descent traced from the earliest cinema, with narrative as a grand detour. Bypassing the industrial norms of production and division of labour, the primitive or artisanal mode also led to 'expanded cinema' (or 'making films with projectors'). Le Grice's *Horror Film I* (1970) is a 'live shadow performance' in which a naked figure in front of the screen plays with coloured light. In Guy Sherwin's *Man with Mirror* (1976), live action duplicates multi-screen illusion, while in Annabel Nicolson's *Reel Time* (1973) a looped image (the film-maker sewing) is slowly destroyed by passing the film through a sewing-machine. All of these films wittily expand film (a fixed medium) into the realms of chance; they underline transience and challenge the illusion that 'real time' is ever suspended in the act of viewing.

The Co-op movement led to strong links across Europe, with film-makers gathering at festivals in Knokke (Belgium), Berlin, and London's National Film Theatre. Structural film flourished particularly in Germany, with the work of Werner Nekes, Klaus Wyborny, and Wilhelm and Birgit Hein. Wim Wenders began his career in Munich with such post-Warholian long-take films as *Same Player Shoots Again* (1967). Numerous groups (or factions) were formed in France, and important outposts spread to Yugoslavia, Holland, Italy, and Japan. In France, however, and elsewhere in continental Europe, the powerful political cultures emerging from May 1968, and the opportunities opened up for independent film-making closer to the narrative mainstream, gave a different thrust to formal experiment. The work of Jean-Luc Godard in France, and that of Jean-Marie Straub and Danièle Huillet (French-born, but working mainly in Germany), showed a questioning approach to the image which had affinities with that of the structural avant-garde, but came from a different tradition and pursued different objectives.

PRIMITIVES AND POST-STRUCTURALISTS

In both the USA and Europe, the avant-garde's interest in early film form coincided with a revisionist history of the primitive era. Historians as well as film-makers saw primitive cinema as an alternative to the mainstream, not just an ancestor. These interests coincided between 1977 and 1984, as a 'new film history' emerged alongside coverage of the avant-garde film in journals from *Screen* and *Afterimage* to *Studio International* and *Art Forum*. These conjunctions are heralded in Ken Jacobs's deconstructionist *Tom, Tom, the Piper's Son* (1969–71), which scrutinizes texture and motion in a 1905 Billy Bitzer film; re-shooting from the screen expands it from four minutes to two hours. Equally ambitious, Klaus Wyborny's *Birth of a Nation* (1973) explores pre-Griffith film space, here reduced to a few actors in a bare landscape. The viewer is kept at a distance by long shot and ellipsis. In Brakhage's *Murder Psalm* (1981), an instructional film is re-cut and tinted to evoke an eerie childhood dream. The austere and magisterial *Eureka* (1974) by Ernie Gehr simply slows down an early one-shot film, in the 'Hales Tours' genre, to eight frames per second. The frontal 'view' is taken from a street-car heading down a busy San Francisco Street until it reaches the terminus. Extreme slow-motion sharpens perception, just as the film distils complex metaphor (journey, history, movement, closure) from seemingly chance images.

By scanning early films, Jacobs and Gehr sought to unlock their meanings by a process of self-revelation. European film-makers showed less respect for the authority of early footage. Le Grice's *Berlin Horse* (1970) alternates two brief shots, one of a horse running in a circle, the other a fragment from Hepworth's 1900 film *The Burning Barn*. With colour added in the printer, the two shots merge in blended rhythm, to a Brian Eno sound-track. The film can be shown on one, two, or four screens. In *Kali Film* (1988), Birgit Hein collages early porn with war films and sexploitation movies, finding resistance as well as oppression in films made at the anarchic fringes of 'official' culture.

Structural film had begun as strongly anti-narrative, as were most contemporary arts at this time. Le Grice's first film, *Castle One (The Light Bulb Film)* (1966), was basic cinema. Here, a real light bulb flashes next to the projected film (showing another flashing bulb and a collage of TV documentary shots, mainly industrial or political). But a decade later, his trilogy (*Blackbird Descending*, 1977; *Emily—Third Party Speculation*, 1979; *Finnegans Chin*, 1983) elaborated on point-of-view and narrative space. The environment is domestic, the tone personal and allusive, the style more baroque in colour and vision. Le Grice has made no films since this long statement, with its implication that 'the spectre of narrative' (Frampton) always haunts the film medium. He has since returned to electronic and computer-based art, with its more open form and its

underlying systems for the manipulation of source material.

The political roots of the international Co-op movement (and hence of the structural film which dominated it) lay in the campaign against the—heavily televised—Vietnam War. The 'politics of perception' were a weapon of politicized art to 'demystify' media power. In Britain, the avant-garde was vocal from 1974 in campaigns for public access film workshops and innovative TV. Channel 4 (from 1983) was partly shaped by these debates, but by then the context had changed. The renewal of a youth-oriented mass cinema by the 'Movie Brats'—including such late-Underground progeny as Cronenberg, Scorsese, and Lynch—was followed by a 'New Spirit' in painting, largely atavistic and expressionist, in the shape of Beuys, Clemente, and Baselitz. With a combination of a powerfully boosted 'commodity culture', suspicion of new media in the arts, and a now fractious political left, the epoch ended with the avant-garde in retreat.

A tentative return to narrative signalled the avant-garde's unease with its own reputation for obscurity. Non-narrative styles (poetic, lyrical, abstract, or structural) were never a popular genre, and groups from Cinema 16 to the Co-ops consequently sought new audiences outside the mainstream. But the tensions of this period produced some remarkable new artists, who combined the avant-garde's formal tradition with the autobiographical twist which Le Grice's trilogy also touched on but which was most successfully explored in Lis Rhodes's *Light Reading* (1979).

In the USA, Sue Friedrich (*Gently down the Stream*, 1981) and Leslie Thornton (*Adynata*, 1983) combined elements from the trance-film (dream as source), structural film (hand-made process), direct performance (via Yvonne Rainer), and feminist theory. In Britain, structural rigour was inflected by personal vision and memory. John Smith rivals George Landow in humour and style, as in the finely crafted *Slow Glass* (1988–91), where an engaging personal narrative is slowly revealed as both a filmic construction and a metaphor of urban history. Jayne Parker, by contrast, uses elliptical metaphor and photogenic clarity to convey emotional states directly, although her long videotape *Almost Out* (1986) is an analytic exploration of speech, confession, nakedness, and duplicity. Like Smith's, her most recent films have TV backing (e.g. *Cold Jazz*, 1993), and a prospective audience outside the avant-garde 'ghetto'.

Although the origins of structural film lay well outside the academy (in Kren, Warhol, and Fluxus), by the 1970s it was largely based in the colleges where many practitioners taught—from Buffalo and San Francisco to London, Hamburg, and Łódź. Initially a strength, as education expanded, by the end of the decade structural film was charged with pedantry and élitism. The context too was altering. The conceptual base of structural film stressed

Malcolm Le Grice's *After Lumière* involves a re-enactment of the Lumière brothers' *Watering the Gardener*, with fellow film-makers William Raban as the gardener and Marilyn Halford as the boy

non-identity (sound and image; word and object; screen and viewer). This message was out of favour by 1979, with mainstream cinema poised for the consumer revolution and younger film-makers urged by post-punk aesthetics to break free of the structural grid.

Their rebellion came in the early 1980s, with a wave of low-tech. 8 mm. and fast-cut video. 'Scratch' (i.e. improvised) video-makers in Britain (George Barber, the Duvet Brothers, Guerilla Tapes) re-edited TV footage with Reagan, Thatcher, and the 'military-industrial complex' as main targets, using montage to create parody in the style of Ivor Montagu's *Peace and Plenty* and the films of Bruce Conner. Politically astute and sharply cut (often to rock sound-tracks), its devices were swallowed up by TV advertising and promos with alarming speed. So were the more rigorous montage stylistics of the Polish film-maker Zbigniew Rybczynski (*Tango*, *Steps*), imitated by a now-famous 'flicker-edit' ad for Ariston washing-machines.

In Britain the 'New Romanticism' revived interest in Kenneth Anger, Jean Cocteau, and Jean Genet, as film-makers outside the structural canon. Genet's *Chant d'amour* (1950) became an emblem of the radical gay film culture. Clandestine love between warder and prisoner is evoked in high symbolism (hands pass a rose between barred windows) and grainy realism (men in cells). It inspired a new 'cinema of transgression', promoted by the charismatic Derek Jarman and seen notably in the early films of John Maybury and Cerith Wyn Evans. Tellingly, an early compilation film from this milieu was titled *The Dream Machine* (1984).

The turn to 'low-tech.' and often to super 8 coincided with the rise of a commercial fringe, pioneering the eclectic rise of rock videos and promos in which this group took part. By the end of the 1980s, the margins had spread to the core of the new commercial rock culture. Sophie Muller's *Savage* (1987), for the Eurythmics, blends avant-garde elliptical editing with comic pastiche (from Americana to Julie Andrews) and 1980s urban paranoia. This new subcultural style drew heavily on the aesthetics of experimental film. Paradoxically, the residues of structural form (repetition, duration, flicker, and blur), never eradicated from New Romantic films, finally seeped into industrial film and video.

The breakup of the structural mould coincided with the growth of militant minority cultures which succeeded the collapse of the broad political left in the USA and Europe. As well as 'gay' film-making, black and feminist artists also turned to forms of contestational cinema which both rebelled against 'formalist' structural film and (as with the pop promo) continued its iconoclasm. The early films of Spike Lee (USA) and Isaac Julien and John Akomfrah (UK) shared this cultural milieu of the post-avant-garde, exploring fragmentation and sound montage to evoke black urban experience.

By turning away from structural 'purism', the retro-garde of the 1980s paradoxically helped to spread the audio-visual language of experiment into a wider culture eager for self-renewal. In reaction to the consumerist aspects of this phenomenon, some artists turned to the video medium, linking to the new wave of installation and site-specific work within fine art, a move pioneered in the 1960s and 1970s by Wolf Vostell in Germany, Nam June Paik in the USA, and David Hall in Britain. Current work by Bill Viola and Gary Hill (USA), Maria Veder (Germany), or Judith Goddard (UK) exemplifies this turn, now drawing on elements of the baroque and the surreal which the western visual arts have lately revalidated.

The current state of experimental film (and now video) defies summary. While it lacks the clear profile which the classic avant-gardes attained in their various heydays, from cubism to structural film, those privileged moments are themselves the products of historical hindsight as well as of unique conjunctions between artists' film and wider cultural tendencies. Commercial media culture—rarely able to generate new ideas—still draws from the reservoir of experimental art. Consequently, the hybrid and voracious nature of the mass media impels reactions that range from 'ultra' rejection (Gidal) through calls for intervention (Hall) to almost full participation (Greenaway).

While the avant-garde is often declared dead, most of the living artists mentioned here—and many more unlisted—continue to make films regardless, as do large numbers of younger film-makers. The European scene is scattered (most avant-gardes anywhere are loose collections of individuals), but the USA sustains such important journals as *Millenium*, *Cinematograph*, *Motion Picture*, and *October*, often devoted to the contemporary 'iconology of the body' pioneered by film-makers from Menken to Dwoskin. Even *Film Culture*, long dormant, has reappeared, as eccentric as ever. As the electronic media fill the gap between the mega-budget feature film and the low-budget experimental film, it may be that these two extremes of cinema will be the sole survivors of the film era. If so, they will continue to confront each other in newly heightened ways, across the cultural divisions which the next century of film will necessarily inherit from its past.

Bibliography
Curtis, David (1971), *Experimental Cinema*.
Drummond, Phillip, Dusinberre, Deke, and Rees, A. L. (1979), *Film as Film*.
Dwoskin, Stephen (1975), *Film Is*.
Hein, Birgit (1971), *Film im Underground*.
James, David (ed.) (1991), *To Free the Cinema*.
Le Grice, Malcolm (1977), *Abstract Film and Beyond*.
MacDonald, Scott (1993), *Avant-Garde Film*.
Renan, Sheldon (1967), *An Introduction to the American Underground Film*.
Sitney, P. Adams (1974), *Visionary Film*.

Animation in the Post-Industrial Era

WILLIAM MORITZ

By 1960 cartoon shorts were no longer screened as part of the regular programme in cinemas, and studio animation units were closed or producing exclusively for television. For independent animators the major distribution focus became the film festival, which could make films known to an international audience of entrepreneurs and connoisseurs who in turn might arrange for them to be screened on television, or in cinemas as part of package programmes. At first animation had to vie with live-action features at general film festivals like Cannes or Venice, but after the creation of ASIFA (the International Association for Animated Film) in 1960, festivals specializing in animation began in Annecy, Zagreb, Ottawa, Hiroshima, and a number of other locations, allowing independent animators from around the world to meet yearly and share their films.

EXPERIMENTAL ANIMATORS

A small number of experimental animators had already enjoyed an alternative community for some decades, as a part of experimental art film. The presence of Oskar Fischinger in Los Angeles encouraged the brothers John and James Whitney to turn from music and painting to the creation of abstract animation, with hard-edged geometric imagery synchronized to astonishing 'electronic' music drawn directly on the film strip by a series of finely calibrated pendulums (*Five Film Exercises*, 1943–4). In 1946 the San Francisco Museum of Art held the first of some dozen Art in Cinema festivals which screened classic avant-garde films of the 1920s (Buñuel, Man Ray, Cocteau) beside new works by Maya Deren, Fischinger, and the Whitneys. This encouraged two other young painters, Jordan Belson and Harry Smith, to take up abstract animation; Belson favoured dynamic polymorphous colour manifestations (*Allures*, 1961; *Samadhi*, 1967; *Light*, 1973) while Smith tended toward geometric forms, at first hand-painted on the film strip (*Film No. 1 and 2*, 1947–9) then later composed by the superimposition of pre-animated melodic units in a live, multiple-projector performance which was then refilmed from the screen (*Film No. 7*, 1951).

Fischinger, James Whitney, Belson, and Smith were all devoted to mystical, spiritual ideals. Smith combined his abstract imagery with sacred representational figures cut out from nineteenth-century lithographs and animated in intricate synchronization to the music of Thelonius Monk and Dizzy Gillespie (*Film No. 10 and No. 11*, 1955). While these four artists formed the core of a 'California School of Color Music', by 1957 Art in Cinema festivals had shown abstract films by seventeen other west coast

and nine east coast artists. The 1949 Experimental Film Festival in Brussels not only awarded Fischinger the Grand Prize, but also recognized the Whitney brothers' *Film Exercises* as best use of sound. After the Second World War, John Whitney turned more to technological experimentation and became a pioneer of computer graphics, while James Whitney (like Jordan Belson) continued producing hand-made animations of great beauty and spiritual grandeur (*Yantra*, 1955; *Lapis*, 1963; *Wu Ming*, 1976; *Kang Jing Xiang*, 1982).

Other abstract animation artists flourished in various locations. The New Zealander Len Lye created the 1928 *Tusalava* (drawings and cut-outs) in London and the 1958 *Free Radicals* (scratched directly on black film) in New York. He made ten other abstract films in between, while working for the British GPO unit (*A Colour Box* painted on film in 1935, and *Trade Tattoo*, optically printed live action and abstraction together, 1937) or supporting himself with painting, sculpture, and commercials. In Ohio and New York, painter Dwinell Grant made nine abstract films (including *Themis*, 1940; *Stereoscopic Composition*, 1945; *Composition 6 'Dream Fantasies'*, 1985) while supporting himself by designing for the theatre and animating medical films. Hy Hirsh lived off still photography while making clever oscilloscope patterns synchronize with infectious Caribbean and African music (the 3-D *Come Closer*, 1952). He then turned to spectacular optical printing of live-action and animated footage (as Lye had done in *Trade Tattoo*), for *Gyromorphosis* and *Autumn Spectrum* (1958), *Scratch Pad* (1960), and *La Couleur de la forme* (1961).

This tradition of abstract animation continues unbroken to the present, with artists like Jules Engel who (in addition to commercial work at Disney, UPA, and an Academy Award nomination for the 1963 *Icarus Montgolfier Wright*) has created some thirty abstract animations. These range from refined computer graphics (*Silence*, 1968) to dynamic studies in kineticism (*Rumble*, 1975) and hand-drawn parallels to his canvas paintings (*Villa Rospigliosi*, 1988), and are all infused with a fine conceptual wit. Computer artists Larry Cuba (*Two Space*, 1978) and David Brody (*Beethoven Machinery*, 1989) control the complex potential of their technology to produce a subtle visual music, while artists like Sara Petty (*Preludes in Magical Time*, 1987) and Dennis Pies (*Luma Nocturna*, 1974) continue to render thousands of delicate drawings for each film.

The British artist Robert Darroll (now resident in Germany) created, by intricate layers of hand-painted images, a trilogy of films *Lung* ('Dragon', 1985), *Feng Huang* ('Phoenix', 1987), and *Stone Lion* (1990), based on his experience with Korean Buddhism, and subsequently made *Memb* (1992), which uses the computer's warping facility to give an intense impression of an abstract cosmos in a time–space flux. In a 1988 statement, Darroll spoke for many of these abstract animators:

I am not interested in Film as visual literature, or trying to communicate other information that could better be expressed in words. I am interested in Film as a visual process which can evoke, via physical awareness, also a metaphysical awareness. During concentrated perception, each pictorial area becomes a closed system which indicates the possibilities of seeing, experiencing, understanding the way in which things exist—to understand what is experienced, rather than merely experiencing what is already understood.

Norman McLaren enjoyed the greatest career of any of these experimental animators. In 1933, as an art student, he drew an abstraction directly on the film-strip. John Grierson hired him to work at the GPO film unit in London, and there he did such diverse things as shooting a documentary film about the Spanish Civil War and drawing directly on film a surrealist ad for airmail, *Love on the Wing* (1939). A pacifist, he fled to America in 1939, first to New York (where he animated a film for Mary Ellen Bute, *Spook Sport*, 1940), then to Canada, where he would spend the rest of his life at the National Film Board of Canada. He made forty-two films for the NFB, ranging from the educational to the political, from the representational to the abstract.

Only eight of these films are specific 'propaganda' films—and one of these, the charming 1942 drawn-on-film *Hen Hop*, still screens as entertainment, long after the 'buy war bonds' message became obsolete. Six other 'educational' films include a documentary about Parker and Alexeieff's Pinscreen, and *Rythmetic* (1956) and *Canon* (1964), two films of such wit that they also continue to entertain, while teaching subliminally about mathematics and musical structure. Five illustrate Canadian folk-songs (the 1944 *C'est l'aviron*, with its dynamic canoe 'zooming' through the landscape, is particularly impressive); and five others, like the surrealist *Phantasy* (1952), are representational art films. Three films depict ballet from different perspectives: the 1967 *Pas de deux* analysing movement, by optically printing the many stages of a gesture together in the same image, the 1972 *Ballet Adagio* slowing down the movement, and the 1983 *Narcissus* creating a magical filmic world to express the mythic dance. Four of McLaren's NFB films might be categorized as 'political': the Oscar-winning *Neighbors* (1952) showing the absurdity of 'pixillated' (live actors shot single-frame) neighbours' escalating warfare; the scratched-on-black film *Blinkity Blank* (1955) celebrating diversity; and *A Chairy Tale* (1957), recommending equality for servants.

The largest group of McLaren's NFB films is his eleven abstract films, which include the folksy drawn-on-film *Fiddle-de-dee* (1947), the superb Abstract Expressionism with Oscar Peterson's jazz *Begone Dull Care* (1949), sensuous oscilloscope patterns of the 3-D *Around is Around* (1951), the structural trilogy *Lines Vertical*, *Lines Horizontal*, and *Mosaic*, and his summation *Synchromy* (1971), for which he composed a drawn sound-track and used the actual sound elements logically deployed across the screen as the picture. McLaren's masterful achievements were made possible by the security of steady financial support from the NFB over forty-five years, and also the continuing collaboration of his co-workers—including Guy Glover, Evelyn Lambart, and Grant Munro.

ANIMATION IN EASTERN EUROPE

Government support systems like Canada's NFB also sustained flourishing animation studios in many of the new socialist republics of eastern Europe. In Czechoslovakia after the Second World War, Karel Zeman and Jiří Trnka distinguished themselves as puppet and cartoon animators. Zeman advanced from conventional puppets to a new level of artistry with his 1948 *Inspirace* ('Inspiration'), in which he follows the reverie of a (live-action) glassblower who imagines his glass creations coming to life. The film gathers a great deal of its magic from the careful conceptual balance in the imagery, between the fluid rain on the window and the mirror water in 'glass-land', between the fragile rigidity of crystal and the astonishing flexibility of the dozens of moving glass figures, including a racing chariot pulled by a team of horses. Zeman made ten features, including four children's stories (*Poklad ptačiho ostrova*, 'The treasure of Bird Island', 1952), and six which combine live actors with animated models and drawings, often in the style of old engraved book illustrations, which allowed live actors to perform the 'science fantasy' of dinosaur hunting (*Cesta do pravěku*, 'Prehistoric journey', 1954).

Jiří Trnka worked as puppeteer and book illustrator before 1945 when he began making animated films with five sophisticated cartoons. His sixteen subsequent puppet films show increasing subtlety and brilliance: from the hilarious spoof of Westerns *Árie prérie* ('Song of the prairie', 1949), to the feature-length version of the popular Czech satirical novel *The Good Soldier Schweik* (*Osudy dobrého vojáka Švejka*, 1954); from the lovely feature-length textless version of Shakespeare's *Midsummer Night's Dream* (*Sen noci svatojánské*, 1959), to the bitter satire of Boccaccio's *Archanděl Gabriel a Paní Husa* ('The Archangel Gabriel and Mrs Goose', 1964); and his final masterpiece, *Ruka* ('The hand', 1965) which protests against all forms of totalitarianism through the conceptual allegory of a giant (live-action) Hand that tries to force a puppet potter to make only images of Hands instead of flower pots.

Czech animation flourished with dozens of artists producing hundreds of films; including Hermína Týrlová's children's puppet fables, Eduard Hofman's feature Stvořeni světa ('The creation of the world', 1957), and Břetislav Pojar (who began as Trnka's assistant, won the Grand Prix at the first Annecy Festival in 1960 for his Lev a písnička ('The lion and the song'), and later worked in Canada at the NFB). Many of the lesser-known Czech films are superb, e.g. Jana Marglová's chilling 1966 Genesis (in which dolls are manufactured only to be beheaded), or Lubomír Beneš's beautiful 1980 Král a skřítek ('The king and the gnome'), which updates the fable of Midas' golden touch into an environmental parable. The animator Vlasta Pospíšilová collaborated on two fine films in 1982: Jiři Barta's Zaniklý svět rukavic ('The extinct world of gloves', which nods ironically to Trnka's Ruka in its excavation of a era in which elegant gloved hands rule lush décor), and Jan Švankmajer's Možnosti dialogu ('Dimensions of dialogue', which won grand prizes at both Berlin and Annecy).

Švankmajer, a graphic artist as well as puppeteer, belongs to a living Czech surrealist tradition, and each of his twenty-eight films (including several MTV video clips) balances a dream-like absurdity, menace, and eroticism in the true spirit of Surrealism. His experience with the famous Laterna Magika theatre in Prague (where live actors perform with puppets, projected animation, and other 'special effects') inspired him to employ mixtures of live action with all sorts of animation from drawn and puppet to clay and pixillated objects. Beginning with his first film in 1964, almost every one of his animations won major festival prizes. The 1971 Jabberwocky consists primarily of genuine Victorian toys interacting in combinations that suggest the cruelty and sexuality inherent in Lewis Carroll's classic tales. He elaborated this in the eerie feature-length 1988 Alice, which follows a live-action

Czech animator Jiří Trnka's allegory of totalitarianism, *Ruka* (The Hand, 1965)

Alice through an animated land of wonders rather starker than Carroll may have intended. The breathtaking masterpiece *Možnosti dialogu* presents three episodes: a confrontation between two heads composed alternately of food, tools, weapons, and other contrasting objects which can devour and absorb each other; a romantic encounter between two clay figures who melt into one another; and an ironic dysfunction between two officials who offer proposals and challenges as objects on their tongues—and effect such excruciating misunderstandings as sticking a tongue in a pencil sharpener. His 1994 feature *Faust* updates Goethe to post-Cold-War Europe, again mixing a live-action hero with animated marvels.

Švankmajer's Surrealism has had a profound influence on other animators, especially the American twins Stephen and Timothy Quay, who attended the Royal College of Art in London, and have done most of their animation in Britain, supported by Keith Griffiths at the British Film Institute and by Channel Four Television. Their 1984 *The Cabinet of Jan Švankmajer* preceded their moody masterpiece *Street of Crocodiles*, which takes motifs from the memoirs of Polish artist Bruno Schulz (killed by the Nazis in 1942), such as the eroticism of tailor's dummies or the sinister decay of buildings in the old quarters of town, weaving them into an atmospheric, mysterious pageant of seamstresses sewing meat and screws releasing themselves from bondage.

Other eastern European countries maintained a tradition parallel to (if not as rich as) the Czech: Ion Popescu-Gopo in Romania (*Scurta istorie*, 'Brief history', 1957); Marcell Jankovics (*Sisyphus*, 1974) and Ferenc Rófusz (*A bogar*, 'The bug', 1980) in Hungary; the 'Zagreb School' of cartoonists in Croatia—Dušan Vukotić's 1961 *Surogat* becoming the first foreign cartoon to win an Oscar—and busy studios in Bulgaria. Only Poland, however, has left a legacy as original and complete as the Czech, with three geniuses, Walerian Borowczyk and Jan Lenica (who fled to France and Germany after their brilliant collaboration *Dom* ('Home', 1957) won a grand prize at Brussels), and Witold Giersz.

Dom depicts the fantasies of a woman waiting at home in a series of episodes composed with different techniques: a pixillated wig roams a kitchen devouring food, a live-action woman makes love to a male mannequin which disintegrates beneath her passion, old postcards and scientific diagrams are collaged in cut-outs, and live-action gestures repeat (through optical printing) until they reach a pitch of absurdity. Borowczyk showed similar virtuosity in the eight films he made in France, with pixillated objects (*Renaissance*, 1963) and cut-out graphics (the haunting *Jeux des anges*, 'Games of angels', 1965, an elegy for the victims of Auschwitz), before turning to live-action features. Lenica used cut-outs in his own ten films, including the classics *Labyrinth* (1962), *Rhinoceros* (after Ionesco,

1963), and *A* (1964), as well as two features, *Adam II* (1969) and *Ubu Roi* (1977).

After five conventional films, Witold Giersz turned to painting on glass as his primary animation medium—beginning with the 1960 *Maly Western* ('Little Western'). He continued this technique with *Czerwone i czarne* ('Red and black', 1963), in which the painted characters in a bullfight take over the animation process by turning the camera on the film-makers, and his two masterpieces *Kon* ('Horse', 1967) and *Pozar* ('Fire', 1975), in which the textures of brushstrokes become an integral part of nature's processes.

THE OLYMPIAD: ANIMATION AROUND THE WORLD

At the time of the 1984 Olympic Games in Los Angeles, a large international jury was convened for an Animation Olympiad. The jury chose Yuri Norstein's *Tale of Tales* (*Skazka skazok*, 1979) as the greatest animation film of all time—a well-deserved and probably enduring distinction. The film's protagonist, a little wolf of Russian folklore and also the animator's *alter ego*, accepts the burden of memory—in sequences recalling the Romantic era of Pushkin, the World Wars, and childhood loss of innocence—and so asserts the role of the artist in keeping the past alive. Norstein's wife Francesca created the cut-out characters, which Yuri animates with grace, expressive nuance, and vigour. Another prize-winning animation (Grand Prix, Zagreb, 1988), the Estonian Priit Pärn's *Eine murul* ('Déjeuner sur l'herbe' or 'Lunch on the grass', made in 1983 but suppressed until 1986), also focuses on the fate of the artist in society. It tells the tale of a Picasso character who is hounded by bureaucrats until a tank runs over his arm, transforming it into a wing. His story is interwoven with the lives of four people who suffer severe trials and humiliations in order to experience a peaceful picnic, which coalesces for an instant into the Manet painting of a century before. Pärn's stylized figures drawn with thin uneven lines evoke expressionistic grotesqueries—particularly emphasized not only by the contrast with Manet, but also, for a moment in which one of the protagonists dreams of being a world-class playboy, with a lush air-brushed scene of almost photographic realism.

Pärn's contorted graphic style influenced the Russian Igor Kovalyov in his films *Ego zhena kurica* ('His wife the hen', 1990) and *Andrei Svislotsky* (1992), but, though Kovalyov also protests against the bureaucratic nightmare, his weird Surrealism contrasts sharply with Pärn's ultimately poetic Realism. Ironically, Kovalyov has ended up in the United States making realist television series cartoons like *Rugrats*. The gentle nuances of Norstein's cut-outs and the sharp stylization of Pärn and Kovalyov both contrast with the romantic films of Alexander Petrov—*Korova* ('The cow',

1989) and *Dream of a Ridiculous Man* (1992)—which are painted on glass with great skill and detail.

Caroline Leaf's *The Street* (1976), also painted on glass, took second place in the Olympiad of Animation, as well as an Oscar nomination and the Grand Prix at Ottawa. Its sensitive illustration of a story by Canadian author Mordecai Richler shows a boy's viewpoint of the death of his grandmother. Other Canadian animators also produced superb work. Jacques Drouin's *Le Paysagiste* (*Mindscape*, 1977), made on the Parker–Alexeieff pinscreen, and Clorinda Warny's *Premiers Jours* ('Beginnings', 1980), both NFB productions (as was *The Street*), also got high placings in the Olympiad, while the animation colleges were the source of Wendy Tilby's 1987 *Tables of Content* and Jon Minnis's Oscar-winning 1983 *Charade*. Remarkable animations have also been produced for commercial sources: the Canadian Broadcast Co. supported the remarkable animator Frédéric Back, who emigrated to Canada in 1948 at the age of 24. In six early films (1970–8) Back refined and developed his technique before creating the 1981 masterpiece *Crac*, which encapsulates Québécois culture by following a rocking chair through generations of family and festivities until it is discarded, then 'recycled' by a museum guard. Back avoids sentimentality but remains truly moving—as in *Crac!*'s closing sequence when paintings come to life and dance—partly because his fluid graphics, drawn on frosted cels with coloured pencils, allow perfect control of delicate nuance or bold strength of design. *Crac* was placed sixth in the Olympiad, and won an Oscar, as did Back's 1987 half-hour *The Man who Planted Trees*, illustrating Jean Giono's ecological parable.

Independent animation flourishes in almost every country of the world, with so many memorable films that only an encyclopedic work like Bendazzi's 500-page *Cartoons* can hope to give an adequate overview. Each country boasts masters—from Belgium, Raoul Servais, who produced the unforgettable mythological *Harpya*, with its subtle mixture of live actors and animated models (Palme d'Or, Cannes, 1979); from Denmark, the solitary genius Lejf Marcussen whose *Tonespor* ('Soundtrack', 1983) provides one of the most compelling visualizations of music, and whose magnificent *Den offentlige røst* ('The public voice', 1989) zooms for ten minutes into the hidden depths of a surrealist painting; from Italy, the delightful stylish opera renditions of Luzzati and Gianini; from Germany, the austere conceptual line drawing of Raimund Krumme's *Seiltänzer* ('Rope dance', 1986), Solveig von Kleist's dramatic scratch-on-film *Criminal Tango* (1985), and the Oscar-winning puppet film *Balance* (1989) by the twins Christoph and Wolfgang Lauenstein; from Britain Nick Park's witty *Creature Comforts* (1989), with its juxtaposition of immigrant voices with caged zoo animals, and also Barry Purves's dazzling Shakespearian pageant *Next* (1989)

and his serene, elegant Japanese *Screen Play* (1992); from Japan the wild, wicked Yoji Kuri, the delicate puppeteer Kihachiro Kawamoto, and the prolific Osamu Tesuka, who has made on the one hand comic-book (limited-animation) action films like *Astro Boy* (1963) and *Kimba, Emperor of the Jungle* (1965), and on the other hand experimental films like the spectacular *Jumping* (1984), with its flying landscapes, and *Broken down Film* (1985), which spoofs traditional cartoons by applying true laws of gravity and tensile strength to standard gags.

Experimental animation flourishes, including Jane Aaron (*Traveling Light*, 1985) and Al Jarnow (*Incidence of the Northern Moon*, 1981), with their fascination for time-lapse; Christine Panushka (*Sum of Them*, 1984), Maureen Selwood (*Odalisque*, 1981), and Susan Pitt (*Asparagus*, 1979), who explore women's dreams and visions; while Ruth Hayes (*Reign of the Dog*, 1994), George Griffin (*Lineage*, 1979), and Gary Schwartz (*Animus*, 1981) practise flip-book work as well as film-making.

A number of film artists produce personal animations as well as pursuing a career in commercial animation: thus the Belgian animator Paul Demeyer has made the highly individual *Papiers animés* (1977) but also, in a very different vein, the children's film *The Goose Girl* (1989, for Channel Four Television); Joyce Borenstein is author of the personal *Traveller's Palm* (1976) while mainly working with the NFBC; and Joan Gratz, a modeller for Claymation, won an Oscar for her individual *Mona Lisa Descending a Staircase* (1992). Such independent artists also collaborate on 'Anijams' (reminiscent of the surrealist 'exquisite corpses'), in which several animators each privately do a brief segment, linked by a medium (*Candy Jam*, 1987) or a sound-track (*Pink Komkommer*, 1990).

FEATURES

Other than television production (including sit-com series like *The Simpsons*, commercials, and MTV rock videos), features are the only area in which industrial animation still flourishes, because cinemas can accommodate them. Hundreds have been produced, from most countries of the world, but few of these enjoyed success, perhaps because animation needs special qualities, mood, and development to maintain audience interest for more than an hour. Experimental features, like Borowczyk's 1967 *Théâtre de M. et Mme Kabal*, with its endless domestic violence and grotesque graphics, are often too bizarre and demanding for the prolonged concentration of all but a few. However, many 'mainstream' animated features have also proved to have a limited audience; numerous Disney-imitation fairy-tale/animal features have had too little charm or intricacy to sustain interest (some shipwreck on the Disney convention of musical numbers)—and even Disney itself suffered from recherché banality in its 1970s features (*Robin Hood* might just as well have been live-action),

A still from the Sibelius 'Valse Triste' section of Bruno Bozzetto's Italian feature *Allegro non troppo* (1976), a parody of Disney's *Fantasia*

before a new crew of younger talents began making the highly successful updated features *The Little Mermaid* (1989), *Beauty and the Beast* (1991), *Aladdin* (1992), *Nightmare before Christmas* (1993), and *The Lion King* (1994). Serious subjects, such as the 1954 Halas–Batchelor *Animal Farm* based on Orwell's political satire, constantly teeter on the expectation of cuteness that Disney films engendered. On the other hand, certain serious features—Masaki Mori's *Hadashi no Gen* ('Barefoot Gen', 1985), Isao Takahata's *Hotaru no haka* ('Tombstone for fireflies', 1989), and Jimmy Murakami's *When the Wind Blows* (1986), all of which deal with effects of radiation from nuclear blasts—gain precisely a sympathetic perspective and access to young audiences by their use of animation.

A number of excellent animated features have triumphed over these obstacles. René Laloux's 1973 *La Planète sauvage* ('Fantastic planet') and Jean-François Laguionie's 1985 *Le Livre de sable* (*The Book of Sand*, or *Gwen*) both employ elaborate hallucinatory cut-outs to tell ecological science-fiction parables for adults. *Yellow Submarine* (1968) remains a stunning document of the psychedelic revolution of the late 1960s, with its Beatles music and colourful mod graphic style. Director George Dunning brought decades of experience with experimental animation (at the NFB in the 1940s and UPA in the 1950s) to the design of the imaginative musical numbers, which also employed the talents of other distinguished animators including the

Dutchman Paul Driessen (*Cat's Cradle*, *Spotting the Cow*) and the Irish-American Bob Mitchell (*Further Adventures of Uncle Sam*, *K-9000, a Space Oddity*). The great beauty of Dunning's 1971 *Damon the Mower* (with pencil-drawn images on small pieces of paper that move following the action), and surviving fragments of a proposed feature-length animation of Shakespeare's *Tempest*, make us regret that this feature was left incomplete at his death in 1979.

Bruno Bozzetto's 1976 *Allegro non troppo* offers a brilliant satire on Disney's *Fantasia*, with a live-action frame that mocks Disney's high-serious treatment of Stokowski's orchestra by making pretension and labour relations key issues, and six animated musical numbers that parody Disney's episodes: Ravel's *Bolero* is presented as a plodding evolution of dinosaurs and humans into monsters (re 'Rite of Spring'), and Debussy's *Afternoon of a Faun* as the pathetic attempts of an ageing satyr to seduce pretty young nymphs (re the perverse sexuality of 'Pastoral' Symphony nipple-less colour-coded centaurettes). Bozzetto's vivid graphics and wit triumph in these musical numbers, but also, in the Sibelius *Valse triste*, he ingeniously manages to transform a big-eyed cat that might have drifted in from a kitsch greeting-card (or a Disney film) into an object of genuine sentiment when we understand its loneliness as it wanders through the ruins of a demolished apartment building where it once lived. Similarly, Bozzetto manages a chilling sequence showing live-action animator Maurizio Nichetti drop a piece of paper on which he has drawn a cartoon character; the paper catches fire and slowly burns, as the animated character vainly struggles to preserve himself from the encroaching flames. This scene as well as dozens of other gags Bozzetto devised for a 'false ending' climax to *Allegro* have been continuously plagiarized by other independent animators.

NEW TECHNOLOGIES

New technology and contemporary art trends have altered animation radically in recent decades. The rise of 'Performance Art' found its echo in the animation world in the work of artists such as Kathy Rose and Dennis Pies, who danced live with film material they had specially animated for performance. Video technology improved enough for animators to shoot frame-by-frame directly on to video (Ruth Hayes's *Wanda*, 1989), and many animations shot on film are now seen exclusively on video (Henry Selick's 1989 *Slow Bob in the Lower Dimensions*, contracted to MTV). The distinction between 'film' and 'video' seems more tenuous—and all festivals now screen video beside film. Pat O'Neill, for example, had done superior, complex matting and optical printing on such films as *Saugus Series*

(1974) which had not been accepted as animation, but when Zbigniew Rybczynski won both the Grand Prix at Annecy and the Oscar for animation with his 1980 *Tango*, an optically printed live-action film, the barriers against expanded-definition, new-technology animation were definitively broken.

Early experimental computer graphics were costly and time-consuming, and produced awkward and simplistic imagery. Although useful for abstract patterns, only a rare gifted artist, like Peter Foldes, could realize how to exploit this for representational figures—as seen in his biting 1974 film *Hunger*. By the mid-1980s, improvements in imaging technology allowed artists to simulate three-dimensional shapes, but tended to provide only glossy textures in limited colours. Again, a particular artist—John Lasseter, who had studied traditional character animation at California Institute of the Arts—had the artistic imagination to couple these potentials with a story that suited them: two desk-lamps, mother and son, disagree about playing ball. The film, *Luxo Jr.* (1986), won prizes at Annecy, Berlin, and Hiroshima as well as gaining an Oscar nomination.

Only a few years later, scanners would allow a photographic image to be altered by computers, and suddenly

New technology and performance art: Kathy Rose dances live with her own animations, *Primitive Movers*, (1983)

the field of animated special effects took on new significance. Many special effects had been animated since the silent film days. Willis O'Brien animated models of prehistoric animals for *The Lost World* (1925), *King Kong* (1933), and *Mighty Joe Young* (1947); Warren Newcombe painted mattes (for hundreds of films, including *The Wizard of Oz*, 1939) that allowed actors to appear in imaginary surroundings; Linwood Dunn optically printed actors together with models, paintings, or other film strips (*Citizen Kane*, 1941; *The Birds*, 1963). In many films these effects are compiled together in scene after scene—in the Ray Harryhausen mythological *Jason and the Argonauts* (1963), a live-actor Neptune rises up out of the sea in slow motion to push apart two cliffs (one a matte painting, one a model) so that a model ship can sail through, narrowly missed by falling boulders (a real-time live-action film strip). The success of Kubrick's *2001* (1968) depended heavily on the brilliance of its special effects including intricate models and slit-scan motion-control camera work, and a staff of more than twenty-five technicians.

George Lucas's Industrial Light and Magic company integrated all forms of animation, from models and make-up to computer effects, to provide comprehensive service not just for the *Star Wars* films, but also for an increasing number of science-fiction, horror, fantasy, and action films dependent on dazzling visual magic to sustain them. The introduction of computer scan and morphing modification allowed frames of film to be altered (including combining two or more image elements from different sources) on computer-video, then transferred back in the enhanced form to a final film negative. This process can be used for individual special effects in pure live-action features, like *Terminator 2*, and as a continuous live-action/animation meld (as in the 1988 Disney feature *Who Framed Roger Rabbit*, for which the animated characters were shaded to correspond with their equivalent live-action movements while being printed together with the actors), or as an integral part of the creation of all-animated features, like *Aladdin* (for which, for example, the magic carpet was designed as a flat object, and the computer 'animated' all the curves and ripples in its pattern as it flew). Today, through the wonders of Industrial Light and Magic's computer animation, Tom Hanks's Forrest Gump can walk and talk with John Kennedy and John Lennon; soon Tom Hanks will be able to star in a new film of Chekhov's *Three Sisters* with Greta Garbo, Marlene Dietrich, Marilyn Monroe, Tyrone Power, and Laurence Olivier . . .

Bibliography

Bendazzi, Giannalberto (1994), *Cartoons: One Hundred Years of Cinema Animation*.

Edera, Bruno (1977), *Full Length Animated Feature Films*.

Halas, John (1987), *Masters of Animation*.

Noake, Roger (1988), *Animation: A Guide to Animated Film Techniques*.

Pilling, Jayne, (ed.) (1992), *Women and Animation: A Compendium*.

Russet, Robert and Starr, Cecile (ed.) (1981), *Experimental Animation: Origins of a New Art*.

Modern Film Music

ROYAL BROWN

Early in the sound era, film-makers established a norm for musical scoring which, by 1960, had changed very little. That norm dictated the use of musical cues kept outside the narrative universe (the diegesis) and specifically tailored to the action of a particular film. It also dictated that the musical styles derive from those of 'classical' music, which might be simply defined as music, generally intended for the concert hall, that stands in opposition to the more popular forms of the art, whether songs, dance tunes, or jazz.

Film composer Miklós Rózsa (1983) has described 'the accepted Hollywood style' as being in a 'Broadway-cum-Rachmaninoff idiom'. However, numerous different classical styles and idioms, some of them quite modern, had begun to manifest themselves as early as the silent era. By 1960 most 'classical' music sounds, from the Romantic period onward, were showing up in some film score or another. Perhaps more significantly, other musical idioms, in particular jazz and pop, formerly used almost exclusively either as diegetic ('source') music or in musicals, played a larger and larger role in background scoring. New ways of envisaging film/music interactions also began to emerge in commercial cinema, due to (1) changes and evolutions in audience taste and profile, (2) greater commercial tie-ins between the cinema and other areas of marketing, such as sound recordings, and (3) a greater aesthetic influence on the part of non-Hollywood film-making, particularly from Europe.

ROMANTICISM

In 'classical' idioms, a number of the styles and film/music interactions that prevailed up to 1960 continued to manifest themselves for at least two more decades, albeit with interesting shifts in aesthetic motivation. Lush, Romantic scores had been popular for decades; some with big themes, such as Max Steiner's 1939 *Gone with the Wind*, some without, such as Erich Korngold's 1938 *The Adventures of Robin Hood*. But with the need to compete with television, Hollywood embarked on a major upgrading in the technologies of sound recording and, in some theatres, playback. This can be seen as one of the major stimuli for the very tonal orchestral bombast and big themes Maurice Jarre scored for David Lean's *Lawrence of Arabia* (1962) and *Doctor Zhivago* (1965). An emerging politics of nostalgia in the United States also played a major role in the self-conscious return to the romantic/heroic style of Erich Korngold in John Williams's score for *Star Wars* (1977), which established a trend that has still not played itself out. More subtle forms of Romanticism and more creative uses of tonality in large instrumental settings also appeared, frequently for films of literary inspiration and in scores that also featured more modernistic writing in other cues. Examples here would include the lush, pastoral music composed by Richard Rodney Bennett for *Far from the Madding Crowd* (John Schlesinger, 1967) and *Lady Caroline Lamb* (Robert Bolt, 1972), or the more autumnal, bittersweet score by veteran Franz Waxman for *Hemingway's Adventures of a Young Man* (Martin Ritt, 1962).

In France, the action-specific cue often gave way to broader musical canvases whose lyricism served more as an emotional counterbalance than as a complement to the filmic action: for instance, Georges Delerue's heavily tragic scores for such 'New Wave' melodramas as Jean-Luc Godard's *Contempt* (*Le Mépris*, 1963) and François Truffaut's *La Peau douce* ('Silken skin', 1964). A more dramatic contrast between score and action was found in Italy, where the prolific Ennio Morricone began a series of 'spaghetti Western' scores that usually include extended, *bel canto* melodic lines, often intoned by a vocalizing soprano. Two of the more notable of these themes, in Sergio Leone's *C'era una volta il west* (*Once upon a Time in the West*, 1968) and *Giù la testa* (*Duck, You Sucker*; also known as *A Fistful of Dynamite*, 1972), stand in stark contrast to the brutality of the films' action.

MODERNISM

More modern musical styles had been used in early Hollywood and elsewhere to back darker dramatic action: whether in Max Steiner's often primitivistic music for *King Kong* (1933), or in Miklós Rózsa's stark, morbid dissonances for *Double Indemnity* (1945). This tendency continued into the 1960s and beyond: in the non-resolving dissonances in barely tonal harmonic contexts of Bernard Herrmann's athematic score for *Psycho* (1960), or in the brittle orchestrations and acidic harmonic style composed by Dmitri Shostakovich for Grigory Kozintsev's *Hamlet*

(1964). However, by the 1960s, modern musical styles had become more of the norm, as the models provided by late-Romantic, middle-European composers were giving way to more characteristically twentieth-century sounds, and not just for films with sombre narratives. One thing that raised Stanley Kubrick's 1960 *Spartacus* above William Wyler's biblical epic *Ben-Hur*, which preceded it by a year, was its score by Alex North, with its harmonically violent brass and wind configurations, and its jarring and rhythmically inventive percussion figures. Aaron Copland definitely influenced much of the Americana heroism evoked by Elmer Bernstein's *The Magnificent Seven* (John Sturges, 1960), while there is more than a hint of Benjamin Britten in the string writing for Jerry Goldsmith's *The Blue Max* (John Guillermin, 1966). Stravinsky shows up in many of the orchestral concoctions and the choral chanting of Goldsmith's influential score for the satanistic thriller *The Omen* (Richard Donner, 1976). Stravinsky's presence can be felt in numerous post-1960 scores, including such homages as Jerry Fielding's *Straw Dogs* (Sam Peckinpah, 1971) and Pierre Jansen's *Juste avant la nuit* (Claude Chabrol, 1971), while Bartók's influence informs parts of several scores by Fielding. A more light-hearted style, recalling Prokofiev, shows up in Goldsmith's *The Great Train Robbery* (Michael Crichton, 1979). More recent composers have also continued to work in a modernistic, big orchestra idiom; including Patrick Doyle on *Henry V* (Kenneth Branagh, 1989) and *Dead Again* (Branagh, 1991), and George Fenton on *Dangerous Liaisons* (Stephen Frears, 1988) and *We're No Angels* (Neil Jordan, 1989).

From 1960 onwards, composers writing in a modern, 'classical' style also discovered that ensembles smaller than the standard forty- or fifty-piece orchestra could be used to provide effective backing for certain films. For instance, in the same year that Maurice Jarre overwhelmed film-goers with big-theme orchestral bombast in *Lawrence of Arabia*, Elmer Bernstein highlighted the poignancy and nostalgia of Robert Mulligan's *To Kill a Mockingbird* by featuring simple themes played by small groupings of instruments, such as solo piano, vibraphone, and celeste. In France, Pierre Jansen wrote a mostly non-tonal set of cues for piano, violin, and cello that not only mirror the love triangle of Claude Chabrol's *La Femme infidèle* ('The unfaithful woman', 1968) but also communicate the austerity of the murderous husband's lifestyle. For the villain in Chabrol's flamboyant melodrama *La Rupture* ('The break', 1970), Jansen devised a choppy, dissonant theme played by a string quartet. This style was employed into the 1980s, for instance in Per Nørgaard's quiet score for Gabriel Axel's *Babette's Feast* (1987), with its close, acerbic harmonies and its long *sostenuti*, using a violin–viola–cello–piano quartet.

Single instruments underscore the psychological and existential solitude of the main characters in certain films:

Jacques Loussier's solo piano in Alain Jessua's *La Vie à l'envers* 'Life upside down', 1964), or David Shire's moody, bluesy solo piano in Francis Ford Coppola's *The Conversation* (1974). Brian Easdale's solo piano music for Michael Powell's masterpiece of self-reflective perversity *Peeping Tom* (1960) modernistically evokes silent-film music.

ADVANCED MODERNISM

More advanced 'classical' techniques also began to be used more widely in film scoring around 1960, almost invariably for films dealing with grim and sombre subjects. Indeed, film scores, which most audiences listened to with only half an ear, gave certain composers a chance to experiment; a chance they would not have had were they composing strictly for the concert hall. In 1955 Leonard Rosenman provided mainstream cinema's first atonal score based around a Schoenbergian tone row, for Vincente Minnelli's Freudian drama *The Cobweb*. He did

not exactly open the floodgates for this practice, although there are elements of atonality in Pierre Barbaud's score for the grim *Les Abysses*, and in Schoenberg-pupil Roberto Gerhard's music for Lindsay Anderson's *This Sporting Life* (both 1963). Johnny Mandel opened his music for John Boorman's off-beat, bleak, 1960s film noir *Point Blank* (1967) with a tone row presented in a sparsely scored setting, highlighting the alto flute.

On the other hand, post-Schoenbergian techniques and other advanced forms of modernism fared somewhat better. In post-1960 films with darker narrative bases, one often finds examples of musical pointillism, in which short, athematic fragments set in discontinuous instrumental contexts replace the more developed themes and more fluid orchestrations of traditional scoring. For example, the music by David Amram that appears shortly into the Korean War action of the pre-title sequence for *The Manchurian Candidate* (1962) creates its military aura

Stéphane Audran, as the young schoolteacher, is confronted by the butcher, Jean Yanne, in Claude Chabrol's tense and atmospheric thriller *Le Boucher* ('The butcher', 1969)

only with a snare-drum tattoo, over which non-tonal motivic shards jump quickly across such instruments as the timpani, pizzicato strings, bowed strings, xylophone, solo clarinet, a pair of oboes, brass choir, flute, and piccolo.

One of the most elaborate uses of a non-tonal musical pointillism can be found in another score by Pierre Jansen—for Claude Chabrol's *Le Boucher* ('The butcher', 1969), which deals with a serial killer in a provincial French town. Scored for a small group of particularly resonant instruments—electric organ, piano (with the strings sometimes plucked from within), guitar, vibraphone, harpsichord, chimes, harp, and percussion—the music for *Le Boucher* never establishes anything resembling a theme. Instead, the score offers non-tonal interplays of timbres that generally define themselves in short phrases, with the plucked piano strings producing some unsettling microtones. The entire effect is both ultra-modern and ultra-primitive, as in the cave paintings at Lascaux seen at one point in the film, and as in the mind of *Le Boucher*'s serial killer.

For Franklin J. Schaffner's 1968 *Planet of the Apes*, Jerry Goldsmith deployed such 'instruments' and instrumental effects as tuned, aluminium mixing bowls, a bass slide-whistle, a triangle stick scraped over a gong, a ram's horn, air blown through brass instruments with inverted mouthpieces, all to produce musical moods that simultaneously evoke both the modern and the primitive. One of the most important deployments of modernistic devices can be found in John Williams's music for Robert Altman's 1972 *Images*, a film that examines the schizophrenic breakdown of a married woman. Williams's music mirrors the split between the heroine's creative and sexual sides, although in ways more subtle than one might expect. On the one hand, the composer offers a tonal, very minor-mode, almost dirge-like theme heard on a solo piano backed principally by strings. On the other hand, Williams engaged Japanese percussionist Stomu Yamashta to perform in various non-tonal, all but arhythmic cues that burst violently on to the music track throughout the film. Among the 'instruments' struck by mallets and rubbed with the fingers by Yamashta are metal sculptures by Baschet. Further, Williams's score mobilizes such non-western timbres as those of the Inca flute, kabuki wooden percussion instruments, and wood chimes, while also putting 'normal' instruments, including the human voice, through unusual manœuvres.

Other modernistic devices, again often deployed for films with a grimmer aspect, contributed to the originality of a number of scores since 1960. For Terence Young's *Wait until Dark* (1967), a thriller about a blind woman terrorized by a psychotic hood and his accomplices, Henry Mancini created unsettling harmonic colorations by using two pianos tuned a quarter-tone

apart. The extremely subtle narrative/music interaction from this movie has been described by Irwin Bazelon, himself a film composer: '... actor Alan Arkin, who plays a psychopathic killer, enters a room where Audrey Hepburn is alone. She is blind but capable of detecting the presence of an uninvited stranger. Henry Mancini's music track at this point contains one isolated note played on a piano, immediately followed by the same note produced out of tune. The tonal distortion convincingly delineates Arkin's disturbed psychoneurotic personality, (Bazelon 1975). The 'out of tune' note Bazelon refers to is played at the interval of a quarter-tone, which is not found in traditional western music, whose smallest interval is the half-tone. Mancini used quarter-tones even more elaborately in Laslo Benedek's *The Night Visitor* (1970), about a mental-institution escapee out on a mission of revenge. The cold sound obtained by the composer came from a seventeen-piece wind and keyboard ensemble with two pianos and two harpsichords tuned at a quarter-tone to each other.

ELECTRONIC MUSIC

A major avant-garde mode of 'classical' composition that developed after the Second World War was electronic music. Although certain primitive electronic instruments, in particular the Theremin and the Ondes Martenot, had already made their way into film composing, a style grew up in the early 1950s that involved the use of oscillators, filters, and other sound generators. Sounds obtained in this manner, combined with sounds recorded both from musical instruments and a large variety of other sources (*musique concrète*), often electronically modified, were painstakingly edited on to magnetic tape into musical compositions. By far the best-known film score created in this manner was made by Louis and Bebe Barron for *Forbidden Planet* (1956). This method of composing had little future outside avant-garde film-making. However, the electronic pioneer Vladimir Ussachevsky did score one narrative film, although hardly a mainstream one: the 1962 version of Sartre's bleak, existential parable *No Exit*, directed by Tad Danielewski, in which, along with various electronically generated timbres, Ussachevsky introduces such 'concrete' sounds as a tape-loop of wind, a crackling fire, a ticking clock, hogs grunting, and rifle fire.

Also interesting for their use of electronic music are the collaborations between director–writer Alain Robbe-Grillet and composer Michel Fano. In the director's various attempts to redefine the cinematic language, they merged sound- and music tracks into a kind of ongoing *musique concrète* that helped free both the sound- and music tracks from what Robbe-Grillet refers to as the 'ideology of realism'. In *The Man who Lies* (*L'Homme qui ment*, 1968), Fano's sparsely used, avant-garde music is only one part of the overall *partition sonore* (sound score), which also includes such 'concrete' sounds as a woodpecker pecking (electronically generated), breaking glass, creaking doors, vibrating blades, and an axe chopping a tree.

The 1960s saw the arrival of various synthesizers— Prophet, Arp, and Moog, among others—which, in a self-contained unit, offered many of the sounds and timbre manipulations previously obtainable only through trial and error in the laboratory. In certain cases, these instruments were used to replace earlier electronic instruments. Moog pioneer Walter (later Wendy) Carlos composed some purely synthesized cues for Stanley Kubrick's *A Clockwork Orange* (1971), also using synthesizer to create mod renderings of some of the film's classical music. To suggest the tortured interactions of mental energies in David Cronenberg's *Scanners* (1981), composer Howard Shore transferred twelve hours of improvisation at the synthesizer on to a twenty-four-track tape recorder, building up complex layers of sound that he later added to and recorded with some written-down cues for acoustic orchestra.

The arrival of synthesizers has had a great impact on film music. Since synthesizers have often replaced entire symphony orchestras on some music tracks, their financial implications have been considerable. Requiring technical expertise and a trained ear, more than traditional musical training, synthesizers have also opened the way for certain amateurs to score films. Director John Carpenter scored or co-scored many of his works, notably his 1978 film *Halloween*, where the simplistic but devastatingly gripping suspense-thriller narrative was complemented by an equally simplistic—and equally gripping— electronic score.

In the early 1980s, even more sophisticated electronics based on modern computer technologies came to play a major role in film scoring. Digital sampling made it possible to produce flute timbres, for instance, on guitar-like instruments, while pre-programming allowed for the creation of complex rhythmic patterns. Electronic wind instruments (EWIs), electronic drums, and all sorts of keyboards have become commonplace in film-studio ensembles, and rare is the contemporary film score, even when written mostly for a full symphony orchestra, into which electronic timbres do not merge at some point. The composer Maurice Jarre, formerly a proponent of the big orchestral sound, turned almost exclusively to electronics in his most recent film scores (such as the hallucinatory *Jacob's Ladder*, directed by Adrian Lyne in 1990), in which he often used an ensemble of six or seven electronic instruments as a kind of chamber group. Jerry Goldsmith's more sophisticated, more modernistic harmonic language has worked particularly well in electronic scores such as the moody music for *Criminal Law* (Martin Campbell, 1989) and the more violent strains for Michael Crichton's *Runaway* (1984), which Goldsmith performed on Yamaha digital keyboards programmed by his son, Joel Goldsmith. In a more popular vein, Henry Mancini, for Blake Edwards's *Switch* (1991), used two synthesizers, two EWIs, electronic drums, electronic guitar, and only one 'acoustic' instrument.

Electronic timbres have become an almost *de rigueur* part of so-called 'New Age' music, which presents simple, non-dissonant, but also non-melodic patterns evolving minimally, often within sustained expanses of sound. Scores in this style include the Synclavier portions of Michael Convertino's *Children of a Lesser God* (Randa Haines, 1986), which suggest the inner universe of the deaf woman on whom the film focuses; and Christopher Young's *The Haunted Summer* (Ivan Passer, 1988), which musically evokes the ethers inhabited by Lord Byron, Percy Bysshe Shelley, Mary Godwin Shelley, and John Polidori during their various attempts at mind expansion one summer.

MINIMALISM

Although non-melodic in the traditional sense and using compositional cells that are basically fragments, minimalism stands against avant-garde techniques by using tonal harmonies and by deploying these fragments in hypnotically repeated loops. These redefine musical time not by pointillistically breaking it down but by expanding it to such a point that it seems to dissolve the linear confines of physical space and chronological time. This style is used by Philip Glass in his non-stop musical backings for Godfrey Reggio's trilogy of non-narrative examinations of landscapes and people-scapes, *Koyaanisqatsi* (1983), *Powaqqatsi* (1988), and *Anima mundi* (1992). Glass scores also appear on the music tracks of Paul Schrader's stylized portrayal of Yukio Mishima in *Mishima* (1985), and Errol Morris's 1988 documentary *The Thin Blue Line*, in which the music complements an almost childlike visual style.

A different kind of style that might be referred to as 'baroque minimalism' shows up in the work of Michael Nyman. He frequently incorporates figures that might be found in a baroque- or classical-period composition into cues raucously performed by a small ensemble that inevitably includes the decidedly un-baroque saxophone. For Peter Greenaway's savagely anti-romantic *The Draughtsman's Contract* (1982), Nyman imitated certain 'repetitive harmonic schemes' found in the music of Henry Purcell and resited them in the 'infinitely repeatable/ variable/recyclable/layerable harmonic structures' that form the backbone of his 'minimalist' style and that mirror similar structures in Greenaway's film. Greenaway's partnership with Nyman remains one of the most important director–composer collaborations in current cinema.

JAZZ

Around 1960, film music also began to turn towards non-classical idioms, and it looked for a while as if jazz, both swing and bebop, would make major inroads into the cinema. The 1950s saw jazz appear in scores, almost all of them tied in with crime narratives. This music was written both by established film composers such as Alex North (*A Streetcar Named Desire*; Elia Kazan, 1951), Elmer Bernstein (*The Man with the Golden Arm*; Otto Preminger, 1955), David Raksin (*The Big Combo*; Joseph H. Lewis, 1955), and Henry Mancini (*Touch of Evil*; Orson Welles, 1958), and by major jazz musicians, including Miles Davis (*Lift to the Scaffold* (*L'Ascenseur pour l'échafaud*); Louis Malle, 1957), Duke Ellington (*Anatomy of a Murder*; Otto Preminger, 1959), and John Lewis (*Odds against Tomorrow*; Robert Wise, 1959).

However, 1960 marked the virtual end of big-name jazz musicians as film composers. Duke Ellington's only other major score, for Martin Ritt's *Paris Blues* (1961), is more a part of the narrative action than a film score in the traditional sense. Miles Davis appeared as an instrumentalist in other film scores and was partial co-composer with Marcus Miller in the music for Mary Lambert's disturbing and somewhat surreal *Siesta* (1987). Established jazz musicians appeared in film music mostly in recyclings, more often than not used as source music, of compositions they had already recorded. This tendency climaxed in two films from the 1980s, Bertrand Tavernier's *'Round Midnight* (1986), a fictionalized, quasi-biography inspired by the lives of Bud Powell and Lester Young, with tenor-saxophonist Dexter Gordon playing—in all senses of the word—the lead role, and Clint Eastwood's more literal film-biography of Charlie Parker in *Bird* (1988).

The fate of jazz as film music strongly resembles that of classical music: it was taken over by established film composers like Henry Mancini, Lalo Schifrin, Dave Grusin, John Barry, and Michel Legrand, who took elements of its basic language and integrated them into a 'mod' style tailored to the flow of the film. A perfect example of this is Lalo Schifrin's score for Don Siegel's police thriller *Dirty*

Dexter Gordon portrays Dale Turner, a famous jazz musician in 1950s Paris, in a scene from Bertrand Tavernier's *'Round Midnight* (1986), which was scored by Herbie Hancock

Harry (1971). Although the cue for the pre-title murder is strongly dissonant and features some unusual timbres, including some electronics and a female voice, the music plays over a jazzy tattoo on the snare drum and pedal cymbal, with occasional punctuation from a guiro. Elsewhere in the score, a jivey bass line contributes to the score's jazz profile, while other sounds, such as a flute blown while the player is also humming, could just as easily be considered bebop as avant-garde classical. In this score and others, Schifrin creates a fusion of jazz and classical idioms; film scoring has provided him with the opportunity and the liberty to create this style. John Barry contributed a bouncy score for Richard Lester's comedy *The Knack … and How to Get It* (1965) and some haunting night jazz for Lester's disturbing *Petulia* (1968). Barry's jazz and pop training also shows up in the often brassy cues for his numerous James Bond scores, including the orchestration of the famous 'James Bond Theme', but many of his 007 cues also move into a more purely modern/classical style. David Shire's score for *Farewell, my Lovely* (1975) has a Gershwin-influenced classical-jazz elegance, while Shire's darker music for the 1974 thriller *The Taking of Pelham One Two Three* (Joseph Sargent) audaciously offers atonal figures played over traditional jazz, Latin-flavoured accompaniment figures. On the other hand, many of Henry Mancini's jazz-based scores, such as *The Pink Panther* (Blake Edwards, 1964), step back from bebop into a kind of big-band swing style appropriate for the lighter filmic genres in which he worked. Typical of Mancini are elaborate bass lines—almost melodies in themselves—over which suave, well-developed melodies take shape, as in *A Shot in the Dark* (Blake Edwards, 1964) and *The Thief who Came to Dinner* (Bud Yorkin, 1973).

NEW FILM/MUSIC INTERACTIONS

One of the most important developments in film scoring after 1960 took place, not in the type of scores appearing, but in the relationship between the music and the film. By 1960, the quality of recorded sound, both in the movies and in the various audio formats, had caught up with the visual qualities of the cinema. Furthermore, formal changes were occurring in areas like the 'New Wave' in France that accelerated the release of other elements of the film-making process from subordination to the narrative; the visual image, the sound, and the music became significant elements in their own right. For *Pierrot le fou* (1965), for instance, Jean-Luc Godard instructed composer Antoine Duhamel to write four separate, complete musical 'themes', which the director then used not as action-specific cues but as a form of imaged material just as subject to cutting and editing as the visual images.

One of the results of these tendencies was the elevation, in certain films, of the music track to the status of another type of image, interacting on an equal footing with the visually and narratively generated images. Two prominent examples of this are the 1967 Swedish film *Elvira Madigan*, directed by Bo Widerberg, and Stanley Kubrick's pioneering *2001: A Space Odyssey* (1968). To complement the often pastoral photography and the love-tragedy narrative of *Elvira Madigan*, Widerberg turned to excerpts from the second movement of Mozart's twenty-first Piano Concerto, which he used not as traditional musical cues, as had been done with pre-existing classical music from the outset of the cinema, but as a musical image running parallel to, and expressing, what was being expressed elsewhere in the visual and narrative images. For *2001*, Kubrick deployed an even more elaborate set of musical images, which he apparently had in mind as he was shooting the film. These are taken from music that progresses from late Romantic (Richard Strauss) through early modern (Aram Khachaturyan) to avant-garde modern (György Ligeti). Jean-Luc Godard frequently turned to the classics, particularly in his 1962 short *Le Nouveau Monde* and his 1964 feature *Une Femme mariée*, both of whose music tracks continually and obsessively bring back brief fragments from five different Beethoven string quartets.

A new twist in film scoring has been the intrusion into the narrative universe of music previously restricted to the non-diegetic music track. This reflects back to the film audience music's movie-like status as a major cultural provider of images. It is within this perspective, for instance, that one can best appreciate the hoodlum's addiction, in Kubrick's *A Clockwork Orange*, to 'Ludwig van' and other classical composers whose music wanders in and out of the film's diegesis. Jean-Jacques Beineix's *Diva* (1982), which gave world-wide recognition to an aria from *La Wally*, a previously obscure opera by Alberto Catalani, has as its central point of inquiry the very status of music as image. The appearance in Tony Scott's *The Hunger* (1983) of the aria 'Viens, Malika' from Léo Delibes's opera *Lakmé* not only helped to get the work back on the boards in New York, but turned the aria, like the aria from *La Wally*, into something of a music-track staple, both for TV commercials and for other films—in this case Ridley Scott's *Someone to Watch over Me* (1987), Tony Scott's *True Romance* (1993), and Brian De Palma's *Carlito's Way* (1993). Music, and its quasi-addictive powers as an escapist image, also play a major role in several of the black comedies directed by Bertrand Blier, most notably *Préparez vos mouchoirs* (*Get out your Handkerchiefs*, 1978), in which the Mozart favoured by the film's two male protagonists ultimately loses out to the Schubert favoured by their teenage rival.

POPULAR MUSIC

A very similar aesthetics was responsible for allowing popular music, in its various manifestations, to play a much more significant role in narrative cinema after 1960. Previously relegated almost exclusively either to film

Paul, George, Ringo, and John run to escape from their fans in Richard Lester's supremely successful film *A Hard Day's Night* (1964), with music by the Beatles, arranged by George Martin

musicals or to be used as 'source' (diegetic) music, popular songs, whether already written or composed specially for a given film, began to interact in deeper ways with the visual and narrative content of certain films. Elaborate title sequences often became the venue for pop songs, such as John Barry's title song, belted out by Shirley Bassey, for *Goldfinger* (1964) or Michel Legrand's 'The Windmills of your Mind' for Norman Jewison's *The Thomas Crown Affair* (1968). Harry Nilsson's previously composed and recorded 'Everybody's Talkin'' became the theme song for John Schlesinger's *Midnight Cowboy* (1969). Pop songs also appeared on non-diegetic music tracks to back significant—often romantic—moments. Examples of this would include Burt Bacharach's 'Raindrops Keep Fallin' on my Head' in *Butch Cassidy and the Sundance Kid* (1969) and Barry's 'We Have All the Time in the World' (sung by Louis Armstrong) for *On Her Majesty's Secret Service* (1969). Pop music also expanded substantially beyond the confines of the pop tune. In order to create a musical parallel for the autobiographical dramas of certain films by Federico Fellini, such as $8\frac{1}{2}$ (1963), *Juliet of the Spirits* (*Giulietta degli spiriti*, 1965), and *Amarcord* (1974), Nino Rota devised a unique musical style incorporating foxtrots, marches,

and light classics that became an integral part of the director's vision.

Rock groups became such a major cultural phenomenon that their members were able to become a part of their own cinematic fiction, with their songs more often than not functioning as a part of the action rather than commenting on it. Obvious examples include the three Beatles films—*A Hard Day's Night* (Richard Lester, 1964), *Help!* (Richard Lester, 1965), and the animated *Yellow Submarine* (George Dunning, 1968)—and the Monkees' *Head* (Bob Rafelson, 1968). Significantly, the anti-establishment status of these groups pushed the writers and directors of their films towards a free-form, occasionally psychedelic (particularly in *Yellow Submarine* and *Head*) visual and narrative style. Jean-Luc Godard, forever exploring the nature of the cinematic image, built a large portion of *Sympathy for the Devil* (1970) around the Rolling Stones' recording session of that hit. More subtly, Alan Price and his band move in and out of the action of Lindsay Anderson's picaresque *O Lucky Man!* (1973), commenting, like modern troubadours, on the narrative via their songs. The entire narrative of Robert Altman's *Nashville* (1975) is a collage of mostly second-rate country-and-western songs, many of them composed by the film's actors and actresses, that ultimately centre the viewer/listener's focus on the very politics of image-making.

More off-beat rock groups have likewise become the 'composers' of various film scores. For Barbet Schroeder's 1969 *More*, Pink Floyd wrote and performed a series of dreamy songs that established an effective atmosphere for the film's drug-tragedy narrative. Having also scored Schroeder's *La Vallée* ('The valley', 1972), Pink Floyd later had their entire album *The Wall* turned into a partially animated, feature-length rock video, directed by Alan Parker, entitled *Pink Floyd: The Wall* (1982). Tangerine Dream, a generally non-vocal group featuring electronically generated sounds set in hypnotic patterns, came into constant demand following their score for William Friedkin's *Sorcerer* (1977). One of their most successful efforts was for *Thief* (1981), directed by Michael Mann, who has built his career around crime narratives, very stylized visuals, and electronic pop on the music track (see also the *Miami Vice* TV series, conceived by Mann, and the 1986 *Manhunter*). Perhaps the most sophisticated avant-garde/pop-group sounds to make it to film have come from a German group called Popol Vuh, founded in 1969 by Florian Fricke. Popol Vuh has had a particularly fruitful collaboration with New German Cinema director Werner Herzog, starting in 1972 with *Aguirre, Wrath of God*, which features quasi-eastern-religion chanting from a large chorus over instrumental and electronic drones set to a slow beat. The collaboration peaked with *Nosferatu the Vampyre* (1979), whose morbidity is complemented from the outset by Popol Vuh's eerie evocation of a Gregorian chant over wind and percussion.

The new types of interactions between film and pop music that arose in the 1960s spelled the demise of the film musical by 1970. The only survivors were the Disney animated features of the late 1980s and early 1990s, such as *Beauty and the Beast* (1991), with music and songs by Alan Menken and lyrics by Howard Ashman.

By the 1980s, cine-pop-music strategies often involved slipping as many already recorded songs as possible on to a given film's music track, generally as source music, in order to attract younger audiences and to generate audio recordings that recycled these songs on to albums billed as 'original sound-tracks'. The most common venue for original songs, generally performed by popular recording stars and often totally out of sync with the mood of the film, has become the long, end-credit sequences that are now a permanent fixture in the cinema. But the heigh-tened prominence in the cinema of music as an independent image medium has led to an intensification of the commercial viability of film-related music, whether classical, jazz, pop, or various combinations. Many more classically oriented film scores than in the past have become the object of audio recordings. Even discarded scores such as Herrmann's *Torn Curtain* (Alfred Hitchcock, 1966) and North's *2001* have been recorded. Indeed, entire recording companies such as Entr'acte (now Southern Cross) and Varèse Sarabande devote their energies almost exclusively to classical film-music releases. Films such as *2001* and *Platoon* (Oliver Stone, 1986) have greatly increased the commercial visibility of the classical works incorporated on to their music tracks.

Coming full circle, Henryk Górecki's 1977 Third Symphony, one of the most popular works of recorded classical music over the last decade and a half, has made it to the music track of Peter Weir's *Fearless* (1993). Various genres of pop music, particularly rap, have acquired such importance in current cine-marketing that they have become a part of pre-marketing strategies, with TV spots occasionally listing the stars and songs that will be heard on the music track of a forthcoming film. And where pre-1960 films usually maintained a certain purity and consistency in their cine-musical profile, recent films offer all sorts of post-modern melanges. No fewer than three audio recordings followed the 1990 release of Warren Beatty's *Dick Tracy*. One contained the large-orchestra, heroic-classical background score penned by Danny Elfman, a former rock-group performer. A second contained 1930s-style pieces composed for the film's source music by Andy Paley. And the third—but the first to appear—was a Madonna album featuring three songs written by Broadway composer Stephen Sondheim and performed by the rock superstar in the film.

Bibliography

Bazelon, Irwin (1975), *Knowing the Score: Notes on Film Music*.
Brown, Royal S. (1994), *Overtones and Undertones: Reading Film Music*.
Karlin, Fred (1994), *Listening to Movies: The Film Lover's Guide to Film Music*.
— and Wright, Rayburn (1990), *On the Track: A Guide to Contemporary Film Scoring*.
Mancini, Henry, with Lees, Gene (1989), *Did They Mention the Music?*
Meeker, David (1981), *Jazz in the Movies: A Guide to Jazz Musicians, 1917–1977*.
Prendergast, Roy M. (1992), *Film Music, a Neglected Art: A Critical Study of Music in Films*.
Rózsa, Miklós (1983), *Double Life: The Autobiography of Miklós Rózsa*.

Art Cinema

GEOFFREY NOWELL-SMITH

At the beginning of the 1960s the prospects for European cinema looked good. Although audiences were declining, types of cinema were emerging which took account of the new realities. Co-productions reached a broader international market, while the French New Wave showed the way in low-budget film-making which did not need large audiences to cover its costs. By the 1980s, however, the picture was distinctly less rosy. The new cinemas of the 1960s and early 1970s ran out of steam. Cinema audiences declined still further, often vertiginously. Hollywood tightened its grip over the major film markets, and seized an increasing share of dwindling box-office revenues. In many European countries, particularly the smaller ones, the making of home-grown popular films—comedies, crime films, and other traditional bread-and-butter genres—dwindled to a trickle, and production became sporadic, sustained by subsidy and the occasional international success. National cinemas in either the economic or the cultural sense—that is to say, cinemas capable of producing a regular crop of films for the national market addressing national cultural concerns—now exist in only a handful of European countries, west or (since the fall of Communism) east.

As a result, European cinema is increasingly characterized (at the low- and mid-budget levels) as 'art cinema' and (at the upper end) as 'international film'. These categories fairly accurately reflect the situation that has come into being since the 1980s, but the notion of art cinema in particular can be quite misleading when applied retrospectively to European films of earlier periods. Many of the films marketed in Britain and America under the 'art cinema' label, and imagined to be somehow different from 'commercial' films, were in fact (and sometimes still are) mainstream products in their country of origin, enjoying popular success at home before being sold abroad for more restricted 'art-house' release, and the same is true of Japanese and Indian films.

THE NEW ART CINEMA

The idea of an 'art film' (or *film d'art*) occupying an different economic and cultural space from run-of-the-mill commercial production is almost as old as cinema itself. Making films with superior (or at any rate distinctive) artistic qualities could be an industrial strategy for producers and entrepreneurs as well as an aesthetic aim for directors—though both sides often discovered, to their cost, that the two objectives were not necessarily compatible. After 1945, government policy in many countries

specifically favoured the making of films that would serve as vehicles of national cultural expression. Though these policies were often ambiguous, both in intention and in effect, they opened up spaces in which non-mainstream film-making could be financially viable, if not a reliable source of profit.

The new art cinema which took shape in Europe in the 1960s was not a homogeneous phenomenon. It comprised the cheaply made and often playful films of the French New Wave and solemn super-productions such as Visconti's *The Leopard*, made in Italy but financed by 20th Century–Fox. Within the New Wave itself, different tendencies emerged. Some directors, such as Jean-Luc Godard, retained a commitment to radical experiment, while others, such as Claude Chabrol, moved increasingly towards the genre film (in Chabrol's case, the Hitchcock-inspired thriller). Whichever route directors chose, however, they could find producers to back them, secure in the knowledge that the market was flexible enough to support many different types of film, for both domestic and international release. In Britain market conditions were less favourable. The directors from the 'Free Cinema' stable were more dependent on mainstream releasing; although they enjoyed some international prestige, their main road to success was via America rather than Europe.

The turning-point for European art cinema came in 1959–60, with the release of Truffaut's *Les Quatre cents coups*, Alain Resnais's *Hiroshima mon amour*, Godard's *À bout de souffle*, Michelangelo Antonioni's *L'avventura*, and Fellini's *La dolce vita*. The cultural conditions for the success of this new cinema had been laid in the 1950s, initially through the work of film societies and small-circulation magazines, and harbingers of the explosion to come could be found in the enthusiastic reception given to films like Ingmar Bergman's *The Seventh Seal* in 1957. But the popular appeal of the New Wave and associated cinemas was wider, and based less on their properties as 'Art' than on features such as their openness to a variety of experiences and (compared with mainstream British and American cinema, still mired in restrictive censorship codes) their sexual frankness. This appealed in particular to the young, educated audiences which were becoming proportionally more important with demographic and cultural change. Throughout the 1960s it was so-called art cinema which presented rough-hewn narratives, with a real-life inconclusiveness to them, while the mainstream, whether in the product of the major Hollywood studios or the survivors of the French 'quality tradition', offered a well-crafted, artistic product, confectioned for a middle-

Michelangelo Antonioni

(1912–)

In May 1960 Michelangelo Antonioni's *L'avventura* was premièred at Cannes. Greeted with catcalls from sections of the audience, it was passionately defended by a handful of critics and went on to run for several months in Paris, when it opened there in September. Shot entirely on location, beset by constant logistical and financial problems, *L'avventura* was its 46-year-old director's sixth feature film.

The star of *L'avventura* was the hitherto unknown actress Monica Vitti. She reappears (in a black wig) in his next film, *La notte* (1961), and is the star (blonde again, opposite Alain Delon) in *The Eclipse* (1962) and (hair dyed red) in *Red Desert* (1964). The Vitti character, intelligent, vital, on the edge of (and, in *Red Desert*, tipping over into) neurosis, defines this group of films from the early 1960s, with their intensely pictorial values and their concern with moral disorientation in a modern world which has lost its traditional bearings.

The themes of the Vitti films, though more sharply focused, were not new in Antonioni's work. Existential disorientation is a feature not only of the characters in his previous fiction films from *Cronaca di un amore* ('Story of a love affair', 1950) but of the real-life figures from his early documentaries, especially the failed suicides interviewed for the episode film *L'amore in città* in 1953. And his placement of characters in a landscape which absorbs them and (especially in *Red Desert*) makes them seem vulnerable and even incidental likewise has clear precedents in earlier films. It was only in the 1960s, however, that Antonioni's bold modernism struck a chord with the new young audience for art cinema.

The success of *L'avventura* gave Antonioni access to larger budgets and the opportunity to work with international stars: a languid Marcello Mastroianni and morose Jeanne Moreau in *La notte*, a wonderfully dynamic Delon in *The Eclipse*, and a rather doltish Richard Harris in *Red Desert*. He was then engaged by producer Carlo Ponti to make a series of international co-productions, the first of which was *Blowup* (1966), a perceptive foreigner's eye-view of 'Swinging London' starring David Hemmings and with a guest appearance by Jeff Beck and the Yardbirds. A similar recipe applied to the world of American campus revolt in *Zabriskie Point* (1969) was ruthlessly and crassly panned by the American critics, and it was another five years before Antonioni was able to complete his commitment to Ponti with *The Passenger* (*Professione: reporter*, 1975).

In 1972, at the invitation of the Chinese government, and during the height of the Cultural Revolution, Antonioni made a 220-minute documentary in China for Italian television. His hosts were bitterly disappointed and the film was fiercely denounced in the Chinese press for seeing the 'wrong' China (just as *Zabriskie Point* had been denounced for seeing the wrong America). Antonioni's film, *Chung Kuo Cina*, is in fact a tender (but very much off-the-record) picture of a society in transformation and shyly opening itself up to a foreigner's curious gaze.

At the end of *The Passenger*, Antonioni and his crew planned and executed what is perhaps the most remarkable shot in the history of cinema—a long slow travelling shot which begins in a room, passes through the iron grille covering the window, circles around a courtyard, and returns to look back into the building where the character with whose point of view the shot began is now dead, murdered by mysterious gunmen fleetingly seen during the camera's wandering around the yard. With

his next film, *Il mistero di Oberwald* (1980), Antonioni attempted another technical *tour de force*, shooting the entire film on video with electronically generated colour effects and then transferring it to 35 mm. film. Unfortunately the technology was not really up to the effects that Antonioni wanted, and the film's failure was compounded by his uncharacteristic choice of a melodramatic story (Jean Cocteau's *L'Aigle à deux têtes*).

In a tribute in 1980, the French critic Roland Barthes described Antonioni as the quintessential modern artist, whose watchwords were 'wisdom' (*sagesse*), 'vigilance', and 'fragility'. Barthes admirably pinpoints the qualities of a work in which meaningfulness in the ordinary sense is suspended and the attentiveness of the director is devoted to capturing the fleeting moment of self-definition in the midst of uncertainty and flux. Nowhere are these qualities more in evidence than in *Identification of a Woman* (1982), a story about a film director whose search for the heroine of his new film becomes inextricably linked with that for a new woman in his life. The director does not find his heroine (nor his woman) but his explorations give him some sense of how his dilemma is to be resolved. Throughout Antonioni's work, the journey counts for more than the destination. Conclusions are open-ended and the attainment of a precarious moral enlightenment takes the place of narrative closure. *Il grido* (1957) and *The Passenger* end with deaths, *La notte* with a couple locked into a loveless marriage, but more often the films end with a sense that hero or heroine will move on. The extraordinary quasi-abstract montage that concludes *The Eclipse* suggests strongly that Piero and Vittoria's affair is over, but equally strongly that each will love again.

A severe stroke in 1985 which left him half-paralysed seemed to have put paid to his film-making career, but amazingly in 1995 he directed *Beyond the Clouds* (*Par-delà les nuages*) based on some of his own short stories. Meanwhile retrospectives of his work across the world have confirmed his reputation as a director whose work is still vibrant and contemporary.

GEOFFREY NOWELL-SMITH

SELECT FILMOGRAPHY

(feature films)
Cronaca di un amore (1950); I vinti (1952); La signora senza camelie (1953); Le amiche (1955); Il grido (1957); L'avventura (1960); La notte (1961); L'eclisse (1962); Il deserto rosso (1964); Blowup (1966); Zabriskie Point (1969); Chung Kuo Cina (1972); Professione: reporter (The Passenger) (1975); Il mistero di Oberwald (1980); Identificazione di una donna (1982); Par-delà les nuages (Beyond the Clouds) (1995)

BIBLIOGRAPHY

Barthes, Roland (1980), 'Cher Antonioni'.
Chatman, Seymour (1985), *Antonioni*.
Nowell-Smith, Geoffrey (1993), 'Beyond the Po Valley Blues'.
Rohdie, Sam (1990), *Antonioni*.

Opposite: Monica Vitti in *The Eclipse* (1962)

of-the-road audience which was steadily deserting the cinema.

The 1960s was also the period of authorship, or the *film d'auteur*. Hollywood films were increasingly recognized (and advertised) as the work of their directors, although the concept of the director as author had no legal status within the Hollywood production system. In Europe, where they had long enjoyed greater control of their work and more legal protection, directors took advantage of the new audience to present films which were intellectually challenging as well as shocking.

In Italy the novelist and essayist Pier Paolo Pasolini turning to film-making as an alternative mode for the expression of his ideas on myth and contemporary politics and culture. In France two protagonists of the *nouveau roman*, Marguerite Duras and Alain Robbe-Grillet, both of whom had written scripts for Resnais (Duras for *Hiroshima mon amour* in 1959 and Robbe-Grillet for *Last Year in Marienbad* in 1961), went on to explore the potential of film narrative as directors in their own right. With his return to Europe from Mexico in the early 1960s, the exiled Spanish director Luis Buñuel embarked on a series of films which, in line with his long-standing commitment to Surrealism, defied and undermined conventional morality and narrative logic alike.

Common to many films of the 1960s and 1970s was a freedom to bend or neglect the rules of narrative construction, traditionally subordinated to the demands of action and plot, and to tell stories disjointedly (Godard, Buñuel) or with an equal emphasis on action and on the 'dead time' in which nothing appeared to be happening (Antonioni, Eric Rohmer, Wim Wenders). In the words of French philosopher Gilles Deleuze, the movement-image gave way to the time-image. Experience of space and time was allowed to prevail over the pressure of narrative development expressed through conventional procedures of continuity editing. A number of directors—notably Theodoros Angelopoulos in Greece (*The Travelling Players*, 1975), Miklós Jancsó in Hungary (*The Confrontation*, 1968), and the Brazilian Glauber Rocha (*Antonio das Mortes*, 1969)—based their narratives around a systematic use of the panoramic long take in which the atmosphere built up steadily over a period of time and was broken only occasionally by a cut or, even more rarely, a move into close-up. By contrast (though sometimes in conjunction) with the image-based approach, other directors used voice-over and various forms of verbal interpolation to undercut and comment on the evidence of the image. The laid-back, observational style of Antonioni is in sharp opposition to the interventionist approach of Godard, while some directors, such as Truffaut or Fellini, moved between one approach and the other.

The heterogeneity of art cinema in the period makes a mockery of the attempts that have occasionally been made

A typical scene from Theodoros Angelopoulos's *The Travelling Players* (*O thiassos*, 1975), which uses a flashback structure to uncover the personal histories of a troupe of travelling actors, and the political history of Greece

to treat it as a distinct genre analogous to those that flourished in Hollywood and other mainstream commercial cinemas. It is true that were many films which had in common a defiance of the rules of genre-film construction and even shared a number of positive characteristics—open narratives, prevalence of dead time, 'alienated' heroes or anti-heroes, etc. But the difference from the mainstream was exploited in many contrasting directions, not easy to assimilate into a single category. There were also considerable differences in the degree of deviation from the mainstream. Alongside the radical iconoclasts like Godard, there were sophisticated genre directors like Chabrol, and others, like Truffaut, occupying a position in between; against directors like Jacques Rivette whose every film was a new departure, there were those like Rohmer who very deliberately ploughed a single furrow, almost to the extent of creating a subgenre of their own.

A more substantial common ground can be found at the level of the market. Films made outside the mainstream were dependent for international success on showcasing at festivals—preferably Cannes, Venice, or Berlin, but failing that Locarno, San Sebastian, Karlovy Vary, or one of the lesser ones that sprang up in the period. They were then dependent on the efforts of critics and distributors, and above all on the existence of a public that was eager for novelty and tolerant of occasional moments of boredom. Prior even to that they needed the commitment of producers like Anatole Dauman or Pierre Braunberger in France or Franco Cristaldi in Italy who were prepared to back original work, moderate the sometimes extreme demands of directors, and exploit the possibilities of the system. These possibilities were greatly enhanced by the introduction in the 1960s of new forms of state aid, such as the French system of *avance sur recettes*, and in the 1970s by support for the cinema from television, notably ZDF in Germany and RAI in Italy. With these mechanisms in place, films could be placed on the market which might or might not find an audience, and audiences could be found for films outside the narrow world of the specialized 'art et essai' circuits. Heterogeneous as they were, the new European cinemas of the

Anatole Dauman

(1925–)

Anatole Dauman was born to a family of Russian-Polish Jewish *émigrés*, and received a summary education at the Lycée Pasteur in Neuilly, Paris (where Sartre taught and Alain Resnais and Chris Marker were students), interrupted by distinguished service in the Resistance movement. With his friend Philippe Lifchitz, the young Dauman launched himself into what he was to describe as 'the roulette game that post-war producers are playing' by founding Argos Films in 1949.

Dauman ensured that the stakes were not too high, partly through the initial modesty of his ambitions for Argos to be a production, rental, and distribution house for short films, for which there existed a reliable market as supports for main features. Argos prospered, and established its own identity by taking advantage of factors that were transforming French cinema. At the institutional level, the state had created an 'aide automatique' to film-makers in 1948, supplemented by the 'aide sélective' in 1953 and, in 1959, the interest-free loans of the 'avances sur recettes' system, all conceived to promote production. As an independent producer, Dauman was eligible for such assistance. He also benefited from technological innovations—portable cameras, faster film stock—that reduced crew size and costs and enabled directors to step out of the studios to shoot on location. Whilst the production of early shorts by Marker, Resnais, and Varda was in part facilitated by these innovations, Argos's singularity rested with Dauman's conceptualization of its purpose.

Although he is often considered as one of a trio of French producers, alongside Georges de Beauregard and Pierre Braunberger, attached almost exclusively to the films of New Wave directors, Dauman alone took on the conceptual baggage of the *auteur* well before the wave crested. This was to endow Argos's production with a distinct and enduring identity. Alexandre Astruc's seminal essay 'A New Avant-Garde: The Caméra-Stylo' (1948) and the release of Bresson's *The Diary of a Country Priest* (*Le Journal d'un curé de campagne*, 1951) were the decisive influences in the Argos commitment to the new concept of a literary cinema; one which Dauman defined as being 'not of literary adaptations but of *cinéastes* who invent an exceptional relation between the text and the images. Argos's authors . . . succeed in this because they borrow literature from no-one but themselves: they are writers.' In keeping with this self-imposed remit Argos's first feature was *Les Crimes de l'amour* (1953), a 'package' of two medium-length films (Astruc's *Le Rideau cramoisi* and Clavel and Barry's *Minade Vaughel*) made financially possible by a series of prize-winning, commercially successful shorts that included documentary and animated work.

Dauman's commitment to *auteur* cinema was rewarded in 1959 by the collaboration of Marguerite Duras with Alain Resnais on the landmark *Hiroshima mon amour*, and continued throughout the 1960s with Argos picking up projects that others had refused, notably *Au hasard, Balthazar* (Robert Bresson, 1967) and *2 ou 3 choses que je sais d'elle* (Godard, 1966).

The late 1970s and early 1980s saw Argos assist in a number of films that proved to be international breakthroughs for their directors. This, notoriously, was the case with the *succès de scandale* of Oshima's *Ai no corrida* (*In the Realm of the Senses*, 1976). More conventionally lauded were Volker Schlöndorff's *Tin Drum* (1979), and Wim Wenders's *Paris, Texas* (1984), both Cannes Palme d'Or winners. Dauman's co-production partnership with Wenders continued throughout the 1980s with *Wings of Desire* (1987) and *Until the End of the World* (1991). Argos were also to produce Tarkovsky's last film, *Sacrifice* (1986). Since the late 1980s Dauman has been involved in the protracted production of *Beyond the Aegean*, a new film by Elia Kazan.

In October 1989 the Centre Georges Pompidou in Paris organized a complete retrospective of films produced by Argos in tribute to Dauman's forty years of single-minded *auteur* production.

CHRIS DARKE

SELECT FILMOGRAPHY

As producer
Les Crimes de l'amour (1953); Nuit et brouillard (Resnais, 1955); Lettre de Sibérie (Marker, 1958); Hiroshima mon amour (Resnais, 1959); L'Année dernière à Marienbad (Resnais, 1961); 2 ou 3 choses que je sais d'elle (Godard, 1966); Au hasard, Balthazar (Bresson, 1967); Ai no corrida (Oshima, 1976); The Tin Drum (Schlöndorff, 1979); Paris, Texas (Wenders, 1984); Wings of Desire (Wenders, 1987)

BIBLIOGRAPHY

Gerber, Jacques (1992), *Anatole Dauman*.

Giorgio Albertazzi and Delphine Seyrig in a scene from *Last Year at Marienbad* (1961), directed by Alain Resnais and co-produced by Dauman

Ingmar Bergman
(1918–)

Bergman was born in Uppsala, Sweden, the son of a Lutheran pastor. A highly strung child, he developed an early aptitude for the performing arts, mounting shows in a puppet theatre and showing films of his own devising before he was in his teens. Rebelling against his parents' strict morality, he left home at 19 to become a stage director. His incisive productions soon gained attention and in 1944 he was appointed director of the Helsingborg City Theatre. There were subsequent appointments in Malmö, Gothenburg, and Stockholm; even at the height of his cinematic career stage work still occupied much of his time, feeding into and colouring his films. Theatre, he once remarked, 'is like a loyal wife, film is the great adventure, the costly and demanding mistress'.

He also wrote plays of his own, and it was as a writer that he made his film début. In *Frenzy* (1944), scripted for Alf Sjöberg, a young man overcomes the domination of a sadistic schoolteacher. The theme of young people oppressed by malevolent father-figures recurs throughout his early work as a director, whether scripted by him or by others. Often clumsy and laboured, these prentice films suggest an intense personal vision struggling through the half-digested influences of pre-war Carné and Italian neo-realism.

With his tenth film Bergman found his own voice. *Summer Interlude* (1951) is an elegiac account of a doomed teenage love affair, all the more poignant for its freshness, charm, and lyrical feeling for landscape. He brought similar qualities to *Summer with Monika* (1953), drawing from Harriet Andersson—the first of many players whose careers he would foster—a performance of ripe carnality. But there was little charm, and less consolation, in *The Naked Night* (1953), in which a tawdry travelling circus frames a vision of the humiliation and loneliness of the individual.

Bergman came to international fame with *Smiles of a Summer Night* (1955), a poised, Mozartian comedy whose elegant ironies temper its sense of the transience of love and happiness. There followed three films that, for the post-war generation, came to epitomize not just the Scandinavian cinema but the European art movie in general. In *The Seventh Seal* (1957), a metaphysical allegory set in plague-torn medieval Europe, a knight returned from the Crusades plays chess with Death. In *Wild Strawberries* (1957), Bergman's most Ibsenesque film, an ageing professor (played by the veteran director Victor Sjöström) delves back through his memories to confront the emotional failure of his life. Another medieval drama, *The Virgin Spring* (1960), retells a legend of murder and expiation. Underlying all three films is the search for meaning in the face of suffering and despair.

The austere beauty of Bergman's images seemed to match his high seriousness of purpose—qualities for which, when fashions changed, he would be mocked and parodied as the prime purveyor of 'Nordic gloom'. It may be that he never took himself quite so seriously as did his admirers: he liked to call himself 'an illusionist . . . a mountebank', ridiculing the pretensions of his critics in sardonic comedies such as *The Face* (1958—a gleeful Gothic parable of the artist as charlatan), and *Now about These Women* (1964). But at the same time the main thrust of his work was heading, as Peter Cowie (1992) put it, 'inward rather than outward, to the cellar of the subconscious'. Shedding the period trappings, slimming down his cast and locations to chamber-music proportions, Bergman created a trilogy of bleakly desolate films. The characters of *Through a Glass Darkly* (1961), *Winter Light* (1963), and *The Silence* (1963) torment themselves and each other, seeking guidance and comfort in a world from which God is absent.

Persona (1966), in which two women, a traumatized actress and her nurse, psychologically devour each other, marked a new departure—away from metaphysics into the killing-fields of personal relationships. Close-ups, always a key element in Bergman's cinema, here exerted a hypnotic intensity. Not until *Cries and Whispers* (1973), another claustrophobic study of mutually lacerating female relationships, did he regain the same level, fiercely

concentrated gaze. In between came a series of agonized reflections on the ineffectuality—social, political, emotional—of the artist: *Hour of the Wolf* (1968), *The Shame* (1968), and Bergman's first film made for both television and cinema, *The Rite* (1969).

In the 1970s Bergman's film career faltered as he ventured outside his national base and the close-knit family of actors and crew who, in theatre as in cinema, formed his personal rep company. *The Touch* (1971), his only film in English, felt tentative and slight, while two films made in Germany (for tax reasons) succumbed to hysterical over-emphasis. *Cries and Whispers* apart, his most powerful work of the decade was *Scenes from a Marriage* (1973), a scrutiny of a splintering relationship all the more harrowing in its five-hour television version.

He made a triumphant return to form—and to his roots—with *Fanny and Alexander* (1982), a colourful, expansive family saga set in turn-of-the-century Uppsala. Its warmth and generosity surprised many, though Bergman had given a foretaste in his joyous treatment of *The Magic Flute* (1975). After it he announced his retirement from film-making, and to date—barring a couple of minor pieces for television—has kept his word.

It seems unlikely Bergman will ever regain his towering reputation of the early 1960s. Few would now endorse Woody Allen's awestruck assessment ('probably the greatest film artist . . . since the invention of the motion picture camera'). Even so, no other director has dominated a national cinema the way Bergman did—and to some extent still does. And few have created such an uncompromisingly personal and coherent body of work. From the early 1950s onwards all his films, good or bad, have explored his individual preoccupations with a wholly distinctive style and tone of voice. He can claim to be the first film-maker to use the cinema as an instrument of sustained philosophical meditation—and so far, he has no successor.   PHILIP KEMP

SELECT FILMOGRAPHY

Sommarlek (Summer Interlude) (1951); Sommaren med Monika (Summer with Monika) (1953); Gycklarnas afton (The Naked Night / Sawdust and Tinsel) (1953); Sommarnattens leende (Smiles of a Summer Night) (1955); Det sjunde inseglet (The Seventh Seal) (1957); Smultronstället (Wild Strawberries) (1957); Ansiktet (The Face / The Magician) (1958); Jungfrukällan (The Virgin Spring) (1960); Såsom i en spegel (Through a Glass Darkly) (1961); Nattvardsgästerna (Winter Light) (1963); Tystnaden (The Silence) (1963); Persona (1966); Vargtimmen (Hour of the Wolf) (1968); Skammen (The Shame) (1968); En passion (The Passion of Anna / A Passion) (1969); Viskningar och rop (Cries and Whispers) (1973); Scener ur ett äktenskap (Scenes from a Marriage) (1973); Trollflöjten (The Magic Flute) (1975); Fanny och Alexander (Fanny and Alexander) (1982)

BIBLIOGRAPHY

Bergman, Ingmar (1973), *Bergman on Bergman*.
—— (1988), *The Magic Lantern: An Autobiography*.
Cowie, Peter (1992), *Ingmar Bergman: A Critical Biography*.
Wood, Robin (1969), *Ingmar Bergman*.

Opposite: Bibi Andersson and Liv Ullmann in *Persona*

1960s and 1970s were thus assured of support at home and shared outlets with other new cinemas emerging in Latin America, India, Japan, and elsewhere.

AN INTERLUDE: MAY 1968 AND POLITICAL CINEMA

Even before the climactic moment of May 1968 a new radical climate was making itself felt in the cinema, sharpened by opposition to the American war in Vietnam. A foretaste of what was to come was the compilation film *Far from Vietnam* (*Loin du Viêt-Nam*, 1967) which brought together veteran documentarist Joris Ivens, American independent William Klein, and representatives from the full spectrum of the French New Wave—Godard, Resnais, Agnès Varda, and, unlikeliest of all, the highly commercial Claude Lelouch—to launch a combined protest against the conduct of the war. Already before that, Godard, whose sympathies had seemed until then to lie with the political right, had begun working references to the Vietnam War into the disjointed texture of his films, beginning with *Pierrot le fou* in 1965. Godard went on, with *La Chinoise* in 1967, to devote his attention to the burgeoning world of the Maoist and other far-left groups which were to burst on the scene dramatically a year later.

In the heady political climate of May 1968, a number of French film-makers—directors, technicians, and others—formed themselves into the Estates General of the Cinema and put forward various sets of proposals, all somewhat utopian, for the democratic restructuring of the French cinema. The restoration of order by the government of President De Gaulle put a rapid end to this grand design, but there was a brief flowering of political film-making and the movement in France influenced independent film-makers throughout Europe and encouraged the building of networks for the showing of political films to radicalized audiences. Almost all the major film-makers were in some way caught up in May 1968 and its aftermath. Even the generally apolitical Chabrol took part in the Estates General and later explored the world of the 'groupuscules' in *Nada* (1974).

There were, however, sharp divisions within political film-making, basically opposing those who sought to inject a political content into films with a more or less conventional narrative form which would appeal to mass audiences and those who set out to find alternative forms to express political ideas, even if this meant narrowing audience appeal. In the former category belonged Gillo Pontecorvo, who followed up the success of *The Battle of Algiers* (1965) with *Queimada!* (*Burn!*, 1968), starring Marlon Brando, and Marin Karmitz with the militant *Camarades* ('Comrades', 1969). On the other side stood Godard, whose films of the late 1960s both explored film language (*Le Gai Savoir*, 1968) and adopted an aggressive political stance (most notably *British Sounds*, 1969).

Godard's slogan of 'making films politically' and his

attacks on mainstream cinema ('Hollywood-Mosfilm') picked up on ideas which had their origin not in Europe but in Latin America, where the Cuban film-maker Julio García Espinosa had put forward the notion of 'imperfect cinema' in 1966 and the Argentinians Fernando Solanas and Octavio Getino had issued their manifesto 'Towards a Third Cinema' in 1969. In the long run, it was Solanas and Getino's idea of a Third Cinema equally opposed to Hollywood and to European art cinema (and its offshoots elsewhere) that proved the most influential. By the mid-1970s most European film-makers who were in a position to do so returned to the making of feature films, inflected to varying degrees by the political and aesthetic radicalism of the late 1960s. But the idea of Third Cinema has continued to reverberate long after the heady period of sixty-eightism was over, and has been a particular inspiration to Third World film-makers and the black diaspora in Europe and North America.

THE INTERNATIONAL FILM

The runaway popular success of *Last Tango in Paris* in 1972 drew attention to the increasing internationalization of cinema that had been taking place since the 1950s. Directed by Bernardo Bertolucci, with a cast including Marlon Brando, Maria Schneider, and Jean-Pierre Léaud, *Last Tango* was an Italian–French co-production for United Artists release. This was by no means the first time that a European film by an 'art-cinema' director had crossed the line into production for the world market. In the 1960s the Italian producer Carlo Ponti had reached agreement with MGM for a series of three films directed by Antonioni, which began with *Blowup* (1966) and *Zabriskie Point* (1969) and was to be completed with *The Passenger* (1975). And there had been the dubious experience of Visconti's *The Leopard* in 1962, again with an international cast (Burt Lancaster, Alain Delon, Claudia Cardinale) but released by Fox in Britain and America only in a severely cut and visually diminished version.

Generally, however, the practice of European film-makers was to make films principally for the domestic market, albeit one enlarged by the practice of co-production to include two or more countries, and then to seek wider release elsewhere. Film-makers in the smaller European countries were at a particular disadvantage, since they needed partners from at least one of the larger countries—France, Italy, or West Germany—to make a film viable. The Belgian director André Delvaux, for example, made most of his films from *Un soir, un train* in 1968 as Franco–Belgian co-productions, with Germany as a third partner for *Rendezvous à Bray* (1971). Other directors were less fortunate: with only a minuscule (and not necessarily sympathetic) home market behind them, they were crucially dependent on festivals and art-market distributors abroad. (This was most dramatically the case with films

like Angelopoulos's *The Travelling Players*, made in Greece in more or less clandestine conditions under the dictatorship.) While co-production undoubtedly helped to find adequate markets for more modestly budgeted productions, more expensive films needed a larger market if costs were to be recouped.

The key to obtaining this larger market was seen to lie in American participation. Involvement of a major American distributor not only opened up the American market, but could provide better distribution in Europe itself. But the market in America was more for productions with a European 'quality' cachet than for films with the nebulous characteristics of art cinema. Only a small number of films have been able to reach the American market in this way. They include most of the recent work of Bertolucci, Jane Campion's *The Piano* (a Franco–Australian co-production), and Ridley Scott's ill-fated *1492: The Conquest of Paradise*. British productions have on the whole been more successful in breaking into the American market, thanks to a common language and the long-standing links between the two industries. But even here a price has to be paid in the form of an insipid mid-Atlanticism and the marketing of Britain and Europe generally as a site of 'heritage'. The values of Art, which the New Wave seemed to have dismissed, have returned with a vengeance, and for American audiences European art cinema is once again identified with films like Ismail Merchant and James Ivory's 1987 adaptation of E. M. Forster's *A Room with a View*.

Films made for mainly European audiences have also suffered from a certain degree of homogenization and the faking of a generically European subject-matter. There is, however, no such thing as a generic European audience on which such films can rely, and the most successful 'heritage' films tend to be those which retain a degree of national specificity, to be experienced either as agreeably familiar or as charmingly exotic. While in the 1970s many films were made about the recent past (Fascism, colonialism, the Second World War), the tendency in the 1980s has been to turn to a past cut off from the present and remote from contemporary experience. This sense of remoteness is accentuated by a recourse to nineteenth- and early twentieth-century literary sources, which imposes on the film the secondary filter of 'classic' art. Only occasionally, as in Sally Potter's imaginative adaptation of Virginia Woolf's *Orlando* (1992), does the past erupt creatively into the present.

In these circumstances, the nationality of a film now has less and less importance, except as a matter of locacal colour. Small countries still produce occasional successes, such as Gabriel Axel's *Babette's Feast* (*Babettes gæstebud*, Denmark 1987), Bille August's *Pelle the Conqueror* (*Pelle erobreren*, Sweden/Denmark, 1987), or Aki Kaurismäki's *I Hired a Contract Killer* (Finland/Sweden, 1990). Kaurismäki is par-

ticularly interesting because his work stands in a oppositional relationship to conventional art cinema rather as
the French New Wave did to the 'quality tradition' in the
1960s. It is in fact arguable that there are now two forms
of international art cinema. On the one hand there is the
official kind, very close to the mainstream both in its
cinematic values and in its distribution. Under this head
one would need to include not just European art films but
films such as those from the Chinese 'fifth-generation'
film-makers such as Zhaug Yimou and Chen Kaige which
receive international acclaim for their artistic qualities.
And on the other hand there are low-budget independent
films coming from a variety of countries, including the
United States, which offer a different sort of experience.
Film-makers such as Jim Jarmusch (*Mystery Train*, 1989) or
David Lynch (*Blue Velvet*, 1986) have at least as much a
claim to belong in this category as do their European
counterparts such as Wenders or Kaurismäki. Some directors, including the Spanish Pedro Almodóvar, with his

bold explorations of sexual politics, and even Wenders
himself, occupy positions midway between the two categories, making films which are artistically original but
also reach a mainstream audience. There is also an overlap
between directors like Lynch, working imaginatively with
classic film (and television) genres, and the more exotic
fringe of Hollywood exploitation pictures.

More than ever, therefore, art cinema has become a
portmanteau term, embracing different ideas of what
cinema can be like, both inside and outside the mainstream. What it reflects, above all, is the fact that there is
still room for difference, even in a world of reconsolidated
monopoly power.

Bibliography
Browne, Nick (1990), *Cahiers du cinéma*, vol iii.
Harvey, Sylvia (1977), *May '68 and Film Culture*.
Hillier, Jim (ed.) (1983, 1984). *Cahiers du cinéma*, vols. i and ii.
Solanas, Fernando, and Getino, Octavio (1969). 'Towards a Third
    Cinema'.

CINEMAS OF THE WORLD

New Directions in French Cinema

PETER GRAHAM

From 1960 to 1993 France was Europe's leading film-making country, both quantitatively and qualitatively. Although attendances fell over the period, they held up much better than in other countries, even after the home video market took off in the late 1980s. In 1991, for example, France made more feature films (156), had more screens in operation (4,531), and sold more tickets (117.5 m.) than any other western country except the USA. There are three main, and interrelated, reasons for the French cinema's good health: a state-inspired industrial structure that assists film production at every stage, from project to distribution, through its governing body the Centre National de la Cinématographie (CNC); a large reservoir of talent in every department of film-making; and a very receptive public and a lively film culture.

The period falls naturally into three broad phases, each beginning with a major politico-cultural event: the New Wave; May 1968; and the arrival of the Socialist government in 1981.

INDUSTRIAL STRUCTURES

Several mechanisms helped to bring in the New Wave, which took the industry by surprise in 1959 (the term had been coined a year earlier by Françoise Giroud in the weekly *L'Express*). The political context was favourable: the newly installed Gaullist regime, keen to promote a home-grown industry to counter what it saw as the cultural menace of Hollywood and its large slice of box-office revenues, introduced the *avance sur recettes* system. This film subsidy, funded by a levy on ticket sales and repayable by a percentage of the film's takings, enabled many unknowns to get their first directing chance. That chance was eagerly seized on by a group of dynamic critics centred on the magazine *Cahiers du cinéma*, who carried many other new directors in their wake. Technical developments such as faster film stock and lighter cameras and sound recording equipment facilitated the location shooting, improvisation, and experimentation that were the hallmark of the New Wave directors. Another factor was the attitude of producers: the box-office success of *And God Created Woman* (*Et Dieu créa ... la femme*, 1956), directed by 28-year-old Roger Vadim, had helped convince them of the viability of young film-makers.

In the aftermath of the May 1968 'events' the production system changed considerably. The *avance sur recettes* subsidy was reformed so that not only producers but directors could apply for it; membership of the eligibility committee was broadened to include industry representatives and prominent cultural figures instead of civil servants alone. A special fund was set up for first-time directors, and exhibitors got tax-breaks if they showed 'quality' French films.

Beginning in the early 1980s, even more comprehensive changes aimed at helping French film production were introduced by the Socialist Minister of Culture, Jack Lang, as part of his campaign against American 'cultural imperialism'. He appreciably increased the *avance sur recettes* fund, helped distributors to modernize theatres, and in 1985 implemented a tax-shelter system which enabled individuals or companies to invest indirectly in film productions through financial vehicles called *soficas*. *Sofica* money went to about a third of all films produced in 1991. Television was encouraged to produce or co-produce films, and by the beginning of the 1990s the film branch of the television channel Canal Plus was investing more in the film industry even than the CNC. A new tax-break aid system was introduced for films with budgets over FF50m., and the number of expensive films being made increased. Changes of government during the 1980s and the election of a right-wing government in 1993 made little difference to the general drift of film policy. In 1993 the CNC's aid fund was further boosted by a 2 per cent tax on the sales of videocassettes; even more dramatically, the new French government fought hard during the 1993 GATT negotiations to secure a better share of the market for French (and other European) films in the struggle against Hollywood domination.

THE NEW WAVE

Although the traditional genres of French cinema—*policiers*, comedies, social dramas, costume films, etc.—continued to thrive throughout the period, and have held up on the whole much better than their equivalents in other European cinemas, the most striking development in French cinema has been the proliferation of *auteur* films, particularly in the years of the New Wave.

The New Wave, spearheaded by the outspoken François Truffaut and his colleagues on *Cahiers du cinéma*, was a reaction against the mainstream 'quality tradition' of the 1950s, condemned for being formulaic and studio-bound. The first two *Cahiers* critics to attract media attention and trigger off the New Wave when their first features were released early in 1959 were Claude Chabrol, with *Le Beau Serge* ('Handsome Serge', 1958) and *Les Cousins* (*The Cousins*, 1959), and Truffaut himself, with *Les Quatre cents coups* (*The 400 Blows*, 1959). They were followed by fellow *Cahiers* critics—Eric Rohmer with *Le Signe du lion* ('The sign of the lion', 1959), Jacques Rivette with *Paris nous appartient* ('Paris belongs to us', 1960), Jacques Doniol-Valcroze with *L'Eau à la bouche* (À game for six lovers', 1959), and Jean-Luc Godard with *À bout de souffle* (*Breathless*, 1959). These early films by *Cahiers* directors had in common a casual approach to the 'rules' of mainstream cinema, a freer editing style, and loosely constructed scenarios. The years 1959 and 1960 also saw the release of first or second features by other new directors not from the *Cahiers* stable, notably Alain Resnais's *Hiroshima, mon amour* (1959), and the term 'New

Wave' was used indiscriminately to cover them as well, although many were quite conventional or (as with *Hiroshima*) very composed and deliberate in their introduction of formal innovation.

After the inventiveness of *Les Quatre cents coups* and, even more strikingly, *Tirez sur le pianiste* (*Shoot the Pianist*, 1960), Truffaut opted for a more classical mould in *Jules et Jim* (1961) and *La Peau douce* ('Silken skin', 1964). Subsequently he explored a quasi-autobiographical vein with the Antoine Doinel series (with Jean-Pierre Léaud mirroring Truffaut) and tried his hand at several genres, from the *policier* to literary adaptation and period reconstruction. Detached understatement (often with a musical counterpoint by the versatile composer Georges Delerue) emerged as his preferred way of expressing emotion (*Deux Anglaises et le continent* (*Anne and Muriel*), 1971), passion (*Le Dernier Métro* (*The Last Metro*), 1979), and even obsession (*La Chambre verte* ('The green room'), 1978). In two of his most rewarding films, *L'Enfant sauvage* (*Wild Child*, 1965) and *La Nuit américaine* (*Day for Night*, 1972)— he himself acts in both—he explores, indirectly and

Jeanne Moreau, Henri Serre, and Oskar Werner form a *ménage à trois* in François Truffaut's third feature, *Jules et Jim* (1961)

directly, the relationship between director and film, reality and fiction.

Claude Chabrol was by far the most prolific of the New Wave directors and also the first to move into mainstream cinema, with a succession of skilful films, many in the psychological thriller genre. Leavened with flashes of acidic wit, Chabrol's genre films reflect his cynical disgust with the petty bourgeoisie (*La Femme infidèle* (*Unfaithful Wife*), 1968; *Les Noces rouges* (*Red Wedding*), 1972) and a rather jaundiced view of women, whether as schemers (*Violette Nozière*, 1977) or victims (*Le Boucher* (*The Butcher*) 1969).

Jacques Rivette, by contrast, proved the least prolific of the *Cahiers* group. Very long and largely experimental, his films mix fiction and documentary, rely on improvisation, and explore the relationship between director and actor or artist and model, inviting us, as does Godard, to reflect on film as a system of signs rather than a narrative process. While films like the massive *Out One: Spectre* (1973) proved altogether too daunting for mass audiences, and even for the distributors, he scored a modest success with *Céline et Julie vont en bateau* (*Céline and Julie go Boating*, 1974) and a definitive one with *La Belle Noiseuse* (1990), a study of a painter's obsession with his model/muse, released in both a two-hour and a four-hour-long version.

The oldest of the *Cahiers* group, Eric Rohmer, has steadily built up a recognizable personal universe in his films. With deceptive simplicity and the 'elegant sobriety' and 'art of economy' that he admired in the American cinema, he convincingly describes the emotions, sexual urges, hesitations, and moral dilemmas of his characters, in particular the women, as they move between town and country, work and holidays, family and personal commitments. Most of his films are grouped together in series—six 'moral tales', each with a first person narrator, including his first success, *Ma nuit chez Maud* ('My night with Maud', 1969), six 'comedies and proverbs', and four seasonal tales. His films build up detailed depictions of specific environments, particularly the suburban spaces of the modern city, although he has made a few period pieces, notably a brilliant adaptation from Kleist, *Die Marquise von O ...* (1976). While often dominated by conversation, his films remain eminently cinematic.

The predominance of former *Cahiers* critics among the New Wave directors has tended to obscure the role played by that magazine's inveterate rival, *Positif*. The latter's militancy and anticlerical stance contrasted with the avowedly apolitical but in fact right-of-centre sympathies of the Catholic-tinged *Cahiers*. While *Positif* critics could be as scathing in their use of language as Truffaut (particularly when attacking Godard or when referring to the montage of Robert Bresson's *Le Procès de Jeanne d'Arc* as 'a kind of spastic ping-pong'), they could also muster invaluable enthusiasm for major film-makers like Alain Cavalier, Claude Sautet, and Maurice Pialat, whom *Cahiers*

virtually ignored in the early part of their careers. In addition, from the outset *Positif* backed various directors whose talents had begun to emerge before the New Wave. These included Georges Franju and the so-called 'Left Bank' group of Alain Resnais, Chris Marker, and Agnès Varda.

Co-founder of the Cinémathèque Française with Henri Langlois in 1937, Georges Franju had made several remarkable documentaries before directing his first feature *La Tête contre les murs* (1959), at the age of 46. He made a handful of other features in the 1960s and early 1970s, including *Judex* (1963), a tribute to Louis Feuillade. Features and documentaries alike, his films create a grim, crepuscular world with strong surrealistic overtones, but it is probably for the documentaries that he will be remembered.

Like Franju, Alain Resnais started as a maker of documentary films. The relationship between past and present, memory and imagination, which had already been the theme of some of his remarkable short films of the 1950s, provided the backbone of his first features, *Hiroshima mon amour*, which intercuts contemporary Hiroshima with wartime France, and *Last Year in Marienbad* (*L'Année dernière à Marienbad*, 1961). The theme of traumatic memory is pursued further in connection with the Algerian War in *Muriel, ou le temps d'un retour* (1963) and the Spanish Civil War in *La Guerre est finie* ('The war is over', 1966). His subsequent films vary widely in subject and tone, from the period reconstruction of *Stavisky* (1974) and the hypnotic 'filmed theatre' of *Mélo* (1985) to the cogently discursive *Mon oncle d'Amérique* (1979), the satirical *La Vie est un roman* ('Life is a novel', 1982), and *Providence* (1976), a magisterial and deeply moving incursion into the fantasies of a dying man. What his films have in common is an extreme formal rigour in a self-avowed attempt to explore the film-maker's, and the spectator's, unconscious.

Agnès Varda had divided her directing activities between some highly individual documentaries, and features: *Cléo de 5 à 7* (1961), shot in 'real time', and the tragic *Sans toit ni loi* (*Vagabonde*, 1985), both of which address feminist issues in a curiously oblique way. Their starkness contrasts with the glossy *Le Bonheur* ('Happiness', 1964) and *L'Une chante, l'autre pas* (*One Sings, the Other Doesn't*, 1976). *Jacquot de Nantes* (1990) is a moving investigation into the boyhood of her late husband, Jacques Demy.

Louis Malle is often associated with the New Wave, despite having little to do with the *Cahiers* group. He started his Protean career with a stylish *policier*, *L'Ascenseur pour l'échafaud* (*Lift to the Scaffold*, 1957), which also launched the career of Jeanne Moreau. His second film, *Les Amants* (*The Lovers*, 1958), again starring Moreau, dealt with the cynical unfaithfulness of a young mother, and caused a scandal by its explicit (for the period) sexual description. Like *And God Created Woman*, *Les Amants* helped to pave the

Alain Delon

(1935–)

One of the most mercurial leading men of post-war French cinema, Alain Delon's career has both benefited and suffered from a desire to be all things to all cinema-goers; popular French 'vedette' and international idol; commercial attraction and 'serious' actor; director and producer.

After serving as a parachutist in Indo-China, Delon came to the cinema through his friendship with actor Jean-Claude Brialy. His early career comprised of light-weight romantic comedies like *Quand la femme s'en mêle* (Yves Allégret, 1957), his first film, and *Christine* (Pierre Gaspard-Huit, 1958), his first of five screen pairings with Romy Schneider, to whom he was engaged and with whom he appeared on the Parisian stage in 1961 in *'Tis Pity She's a Whore*, directed by Visconti.

The death of Gérard Philipe in 1959 had left French cinema lacking a leading man of equal charisma, and Delon, up to a point, fitted the bill, particularly after *Plein Soleil* (René Clément, 1960) caught for the first time the 'devilish presence beneath the angelic surface', as the Larousse *Dictionnaire du cinéma* aptly put it. It was this ambiguity that other major directors saw and exploited, leading Delon to the most prestigious and fruitful period of his career. This included roles in Visconti's *Rocco and his Brothers* (1960) and *The Leopard* (1963), and Antonioni's *The Eclipse* (1962), where his petulant dynamism is at odds with the usual atrophied masculinity of Antonioni's male characters.

Delon's films with Jean-Paul Belmondo and Jean Gabin emphasized a continuity in the tradition of French screen acting, personified by Gabin's laconic and unaffected style. These films were also instrumental in fixing Delon's screen persona as the elegant tough guy. The paradigmatic films in this latter respect were the period gangster piece *Borsalino* (Jacques Deray, 1970), in which Delon and Belmondo co-starred, and the string of 'le flic' ('cop') films that Delon starred in across the late 1970s and early and mid-1980s, acting sporadically as director and producer (*Pour la peau d'un flic*, 1981, and *Le Battant*, 1982).

Jean-Pierre Melville's *Le Samouraï* (1967) employed Delon's screen persona in an intelligent fashion, abstracting all but the essence of his glacial menace, in the characterization of a killer with an overridingly powerful death drive. It was this aspect of the persona, allied with his undeniable glamour quotient, that had led Delon to assert that he, unlike Belmondo, was 'equipped for an international career'. Delon moved to Hollywood in the mid-1960s, but his American film career was short and unspectacular, never really breaking into the international market,

Delon also found it increasingly difficult to vary his popular persona at home. This was compounded by a drugs scandal in 1969, and his admission of former involvement with the Marseilles 'mafia'. Delon's career hit a fallow patch in the 1980s and, despite a 'César' for his role in *Notre histoire* (Bertrand Blier, 1984), he was reduced to third billing behind Jeremy Irons and Ornella Muti in *Swann in Love* (Volker Schlöndorff, 1984). His production company, Adel, founded in 1964, became an important adjunct to his performing career. A recent attempt at a major 'come-back' mirrors the basic division of his entire career—that between art-cinema prestige and commercial popular spectacle—with Godard in *Nouvelle Vague* (1990) and in *Le Retour de Casanova* (Eduard Niermans, 1992), a film that failed to draw an audience on the attraction of the Delon name alone. 1996 saw a career-length retrospective at the Cinémathèque Français.

CHRIS DARKE

SELECT FILMOGRAPHY

Plein Soleil (1960); Rocco and his Brothers (1962); The Eclipse (1962); The Leopard (1963); Le Samouraï (1967); Borsalino (1970); Mr Klein (1976); Notre histoire (1984); Swann in Love (1984); Nouvelle Vague (1990)

BIBLIOGRAPHY

Dazat, Oliver (1988), *Alain Delon*.
'Delon/Borsalino' (1973).

way for the New Wave films, proving that a controversial and innovative low-budget film made by a young director could be successful at the box-office. Malle has always had a penchant for taboo subjects, going on to cover issues from incest, in *Le souffle au cœur* ('Murmur of the heart', 1971), to child prostitution, in his first American film, *Pretty Baby* (1978). He also broached the silence around French collaboration with the Nazis during the war, using the period as the background for a film that showed collaborators as human beings, *Lacombe Lucien* (1974). Malle also made exuberant comedies (*Zazie dans le métro*, 1960), and a fictionalized examination of the Bardot myth, with Bardot as herself (*Vie privée*, 1961).

Of the ninety-seven directors who got a chance to embark on their first feature between 1958 and 1962, many made no mark and vanished without a trace. Others are chiefly remembered for one or two films, such as Jean-Gabriel Albicocco (*La Fille aux yeux d'or* ('The girl with golden eyes'), 1960), Jacques Rozier (*Adieu Philippine*, 1962), Alain Jessua (*La Vie à l'envers* ('Life upside down'), 1964), and Henri Colpi (*Une aussi longue absence*, 1961).

Among the directors who had more substantial careers, Jacques Demy and Alain Cavalier were perhaps the most original. Demy's admiration for Max Ophuls shows in his attention to set design and the musicality of his *mise-en-scène*: his début feature, *Lola* (1961), was dedicated to Ophuls. In *Les Parapluies de Cherbourg* (*The Umbrellas of Cherbourg*, 1964) and *Les Demoiselles de Rochefort* (*The Young Girls of Rochefort*, 1967), music takes over completely; both are musicals in which not only the numbers but the dialogue are entirely sung. The other quality of his very coherent world, a kind of nostalgic melancholy, shows through in his last film, *Trois places pour le 26* ('Three seats for the 26th', 1988), in which the actor-singer Yves Montand plays himself.

Cavalier's uneven career began with two powerful films set against the then unfashionable backdrop of the Algerian War, *Le Combat dans l'île* ('Combat on the island', 1961), and *L'Insoumis* ('The absentee', 1964), which were notable for their economical, almost elliptical, use of cinematic language and subtle suggestion of character. After several standard assignments, he demonstrated the same qualities again in *Martin et Léa* (1978), *Un étrange voyage* (1980), and the hieratic *Thérèse* (1986).

The strength of French film culture in these years was demonstrated by the involvement of famous contemporary novelists, not only as script-writers but as directors as well. Alain Robbe-Grillet, exponent of the *nouveau roman* and scriptwriter of *Last Year in Marienbad*, turned to direction with *L'Immortelle* (1962), whose rather stilted eroticism was to become the leitmotif of his career as a film-maker. With *La Musica* (1966), Marguerite Duras, the novelist who had scripted *Hiroshima mon amour*, began a cinematic œuvre distinguished by its modernity and exper-

imentation, in particular with sound. Her frequent use of non-naturalistic, repetitive voice-over perhaps reflects her declared belief in the superiority of the novel over the cinema as a medium.

TOWARDS THE MAINSTREAM?

Jean-Pierre Mocky, a prolific but erratic director, began his career in the late 1950s, and was at his best indulging his taste for caustic and often coarse satire, directed at anything from the Church (*Un drôle de paroissien*, 1963), the education system (*La Grande Frousse*, 1964), and television (*La Grande Lessive*, 1968)—all starring the popular comic Bourvil—to the bourgeoisie (*Snobs*, 1961), and football supporters (*À mort l'arbitre!*, 1983). Philippe de Broca was another prolific director who started directing features around the same time. He had begun as an assistant to Truffaut and Chabrol, but for his own features he moved away from the influence of the New Wave and specialized in light and amiable comedies, often with fast-moving action and a dash of exoticism. He achieved international success with *L'Homme de Rio* ('The man from Rio', 1964), written by his preferred scriptwriter Daniel Boulanger and starring Jean-Paul Belmondo, but his inspiration, like Mocky's, seemed to flag in the 1970s and 1980s.

Michel Deville started his career with a succession of stylish *marivaudages* scripted by Nina Companeez—frothy, largely verbal comedies centred on young women's love lives, including *Adorable Menteuse* ('Adorable liar', 1962) and *L'Ours et la poupée* ('The bear and the doll', 1969). In his later, equally polished films he broadened his palette with *policiers* (*Le Dossier 51*, 1978) and social comedies (*La Lectrice*, 1987). In 1962, director-actor Pierre Étaix was revealed as the most original new comic talent to emerge since Tati (with whom he had worked). His films (particularly *Le Soupirant* ('The suitor', 1962), *Yoyo* (1964), and *Tant qu'on a la santé* ('As long as health lasts', 1965)) are burlesque in their own right, while referring constantly to American silent comedies of the 1920s (especially Keaton). He has since worked mainly in the circus.

Other directors were able to explore personal visions within the action genre. Pierre Schoendoerffer vividly recreated his experience of war in Vietnam in *La 317ème Section* (1964) and *Dien Bien Phu* (1992). Colonial France was also the subject of his *Le Crabe-Tambour* (1976) and *L'Honneur d'un capitaine* (1980). Claude Sautet began his career in similar vein with *Classe tous risques* ('All risks', 1959) and *L'Arme à gauche* (1965), but he then revealed himself to be one of the most sensitive directors working in mainstream cinema. His later films, from *Les Choses de la vie* (1969) to *Un cœur en hiver* (1991), focus on couples and/or groups of friends, their relationships, and their emotions, with a deceptive simplicity in the tradition of Jacques Becker. Costa-Gavras made a spectacular début with a *policier*, *Compartiment tueurs* (1964), before successfully specializing in

Claude Leydu as the lonely
and suffering young priest in
Robert Bresson's *Le Journal
d'un curé de campagne* (*The
Diary of a Country Priest*, 1950)

films about political repression in various countries: *Z* (1967) in Greece, *L'Aveu* (1969) in Czechoslovakia, *State of Siege* (*État de siège*, 1973) in Uruguay, *Section spéciale* (1974) in occupied France, and *Missing* (1982) in Chile.

Several other prolific directors working in popular genres began their careers during the post-New Wave period. Gérard Oury specialized in rather unsubtle comedy, and made the two biggest post-war hits to that date, *Le Corniaud* (1964) and *La Grande Vadrouille* (1966), both starring Bourvil and Louis de Funès. This was the genre also favoured by Édouard Molinaro, director of *Oscar* (1966), *Hibernatus* (1968)—both with de Funès—and *La Cage aux folles* (1978). Actor-director Yves Robert made a series of films, several of them huge box-office successes (*La Guerre des boutons* (1961), and *La Gloire de mon père* (1988)), in which he combined, through deceptively skilful direction, hilarious comedy with genuine affection for his characters. The *policier* genre was exploited by several directors, notably Jacques Deray (*Borsalino*, 1970) and Pierre Granier-Deferre (*Une étrange affaire*, 1981). Claude Lelouch enjoyed a respectable career after his highly successful *Un homme et une femme* (1965), but all too often his popular films, while technically polished, have been overloaded with trite sentimentality (*Si c'était à refaire*, 1976), or naïvely pretentious messages (*La Belle Histoire*, 1990).

Many directors both inside and outside the mainstream whose careers were already well established by the time of the New Wave continued to make worthwhile films in the 1960s and 1970s. They included some who found favour with the *Cahiers* critics. Robert Bresson occupies a unique place, neither with the established mainstream cinema nor attached to the New Wave. He pursued his relentless exploration of the theme of redemption in his increasingly idiosyncratic yet compelling manner (flat, austere images, scant psychological description, lack of conventional story-line, unrealistic dialogue emphasized by the use of non-professional actors) in *Le Procès de Jeanne d'Arc* ('The trial of Joan of Arc', 1961), *Au hasard Balthazar* (1965), *Mouchette* (1966), *Une femme douce* (1968), and *Le Diable probablement* (1976).

Jean Renoir was still active during this period, but he turned increasingly towards television and book-writing. He did look back on the world of *La Grande Illusion* in *Le Caporal épinglé* (*The Vanishing Corporal*, 1961). Jean-Pierre Melville continued to affirm his *auteur* status within a single genre, the *policier*, creating a dark and predominantly male universe with a strong and almost ritualistic flavour of the American film noir he so loved (*Le Deuxième Souffle*, 1966; *Le Samouraï*, 1967; and *Un flic*, 1972).

Other well-established pre-New Wave directors continued to turn out polished films of the kind that had earned them their reputations: they included René Clément (*Plein Soleil*, 1959; *Le Passager de la pluie*, 1969), Henri-Georges Clouzot (*La Vérité*, 1960), and Henri Verneuil, who pitted Jean Gabin against Belmondo in *Un singe en hiver* (1961), and against Alain Delon in *Mélodie en sous-sol* (1962) and *Le Clan des Siciliens* (1968).

Of the directors of the old guard sneered at by *Cahiers*, some (Jean Delannoy, Henri Decoin, Julien Duvivier, and Marcel Carné) made only a few films in the 1960s, most of them unremarkable. Despite ever-increasing financial difficulties, Jacques Tati continued to satirize modern civilization through his *alter ego* Monsieur Hulot. In *Playtime* (1961) and *Trafic* (1969) his meticulously thought-out gags are perhaps less poetic than in his earlier work; but they can be extraordinarily subtle, sometimes to the point of being almost imperceptible.

MAY 1968 AND AFTER

The May 1968 'events' affected not just production structure but film content. With film-makers themselves having a greater say in the attribution of the *avance- sur-recettes* from 1969 on, a wider spectrum of directors (including many women) got a chance to make their first features in the early 1970s. A handful of militant films that focused on the 'events' themselves and their repercussions were made: Godard and Jean-Pierre Gorin's *Tout va bien* (1971), Marin Karmitz's *Coup pour coup* (1971), and René Vautier and Nicole Le Garrec's *Quand tu disais Valéry* (1975). René Allio, who had already directed a touching comedy about a 'merry widow', *La Vieille Dame indigne* (1964), looked at history through the prism of May 1968 in *Les Camisards* (1970) and *Moi, Pierre Rivière* (1975), before concentrating on more specifically regional issues in *Retour à Marseille* (1978).

More generally, May 1968 created a climate of greater freedom in which the censorship of hard-core pornography was lifted (though it was heavily taxed) and certain historical and political taboos were swept away. Marcel Ophuls's documentary *The Sorrow and the Pity* (*Le Chagrin et la pitié*, 1971) was the first to examine in detail the long-occluded question of French collaboration with the Germans during the last war.

The way May 1968 affected social attitudes can be sensed most directly in two films by *auteur* directors, Jean Eustache's *La Maman et la putain* ('The mother and the whore', 1972) and Jacques Doillon's *Les Doigts dans la tête* (1974), both of which explore personal relationships in a searingly intense way. Doillon went on to make a series of increasingly claustrophobic, psychodramatic films, including *La Femme qui pleure* (1978) and *La Vengeance d'une femme* (1989). Like Doillon, Maurice Pialat sometimes appears in his own films, often relies on improvisation, and demands considerable commitment from his actors

(through confrontation rather than empathy in Pialat's case). Emotional violence is never far below the surface of Pialat's films, coming across more convincingly in his earlier work, which centres on the problems of young people (*Passe ton bac d'abord*, 1976) or the couple (*Loulou*, 1979). A similar 'intimist' flavour pervades the uneven if elegant œuvre of André Téchiné (*Souvenirs d'en France*, 1974; *Hôtel des Amériques*, 1981; *Ma saison préférée*, 1993; and the acclaimed *Les Roseaux sauvages*, 1994).

Yves Boisset and Bertrand Tavernier, both former film critics whose love of American cinema and culture is reflected in their directing styles, excel at denouncing political and police abuses in the best radical humanist tradition. When he has a good script, Boisset is as good at understatement in his moving portraits of a woman cop (*La Femme flic*, 1979) or a spy (*Espion lève-toi*, 1980), as he is at hyperbole when lambasting racism (*Dupont Lajoie*, 1975) or the abuses of television (*Le Prix du danger*, 1979). Although sometimes verging on the gently sentimental, Tavernier is a sinewy director whose meticulous attention to psychological and historical detail serves him well. He has tackled a very wide range of subjects: the world of Simenon (*L'Horloger de Saint-Paul*, 1973), death (*La Vie et rien d'autre*, 1988), the police (*L.627*, 1991), and various episodes from French history, from the Middle Ages (*La Passion Béatrice*, 1986) and the Régence (*Que la fête commence*, 1974), to life in a pre-war French African colony (the hilarious *Coup de torchon*, 1981).

Whereas Tavernier could be said to have turned his back on the New Wave ethos (he has more than once used the services of Truffaut's *bête noire*, veteran script-writer Jean Aurenche), Bertrand Blier's misogyny, rejection of realism, fetishistic use of actors, and love of paradox—though not his sense of humour—are strongly reminiscent of Godard. Delon plays a drunken cuckold in *Notre histoire* (1983), and Gérard Depardieu a homosexual in *Tenue de soirée* (1985) and a husband who falls in love with a less attractive woman than his wife in *Trop belle pour toi* (1988). Many of Blier's films, including *Les Valseuses* (1973), which shot Depardieu to stardom, are adaptations of his own novels; hence the coherence of his comic-absurd universe.

FILM PRODUCTION IN THE 1980S AND 1990S

The 1980s saw the emergence of three new directors of considerable personality: Jean-Jacques Beineix, Luc Besson, and Leos Carax. Their cinema, sometimes described as post-modern, or the 'cinema du look' (roughly speaking the image is the message), had greater success with spectators, particularly young ones, than with critics. Beineix began with two visually inventive thrillers, *Diva* (1979), and *La Lune dans le caniveau* (The Moon in the Gutter, 1982), before making *37.2° au matin* (Betty Blue, 1985), a meandering study of *amour fou* (in the literal sense) which launched the career of Béatrice Dalle and gained cult status both inside and outside France. The influence of—some would say contamination by—the aesthetics of commercials and rock videos is evident in his films, as it is the work of Luc Besson. After making the dazzling, heavily cross-referential *Subway* (1984), Besson hit the box-office jackpot with *Le Grand Bleu* (*The Big Blue*, 1987), a simple tale of people and dolphins. He returned to the more classical thriller form and confirmed his mastery of cinematic technique and designer violence with *Nikita* ('Nikita', 1990).

Carax, as obsessive in his film work as he is reclusive in real life, is the odd one out of the three directors, in terms of both his influences and the work he produces. After two convoluted works, deeply indebted to Godard, the low-budget black-and-white *Boy Meets Girl* (1983), and *Mauvais Sang* (*The Night Is Young*, 1985), constructed in primary colours, Carax embarked on *Les Amants du Pont-*

Neuf (1990). Its production was a three-year saga of disasters, mismanagements, and escalating costs (and involved the reconstruction of the bridges and banks of the Seine in a reservoir outside Montpellier), and the finished film was an exercise in jazzed up poetic realism, with moments of great power.

Other directors who were showing freshness, originality, and promise at the beginning of the 1990s included Étienne Chatiliez (*La Vie est une longue fleuve tranquille* ('Life is a long quiet river'), 1987), Eric Rochant (*Un monde sans pitié* ('A world without pity'), 1988), and Cyril Collard, who directed *Les Nuits fauves* ('Savage nights', 1991), which attracted acclaim and controversy for its depiction of the relationships of a bisexual man who is HIV positive. Thanks to very tight direction, Jean-Marie Poiré achieved a comic pace worthy of the Marx brothers in *Papy fait de la Résistance* (1983) and *Les Visiteurs* (1992),

Designer violence: Anne Parillaud as the cop-killer turned government assassin in Luc Besson's thriller
Nikita (1990)

which became the most successful film ever at the French box office.

The 1980s also saw the emergence of a new phenomenon, *cinéma beur*; films made by, and focusing on, the lives of young, second-generation North Africans ('beur' is back-slang for 'Arabe'). Consisting of both popular mainstream features and low-budget 8 mm. films shown outside normal distribution channels, *beur* films eschew the subject of racism and instead employ a mix of genres, including comedy, to draw a naturalistic picture of life in the working-class suburbs of Paris. Although there have been relatively few *beur* films made, the best, such as Mehdi Charef's *Le Thé au harem d'Archimède* (1986) and Rachid Bouchareb's *Cheb* (1990), have had great impact, due to their originality and their success in bringing a new section of French society realistically on to film.

As well as new film-makers, established directors continued to make an impact—particularly at the box-office. Jean-Jaques Annaud, an excellent technician who came to feature films after directing over 400 commercials, made several big-budget, high-profile films in the 1980s and 1990s. They ranged from the story of a bear cub, *L'Ours* (*The Bear*, 1989), to an explicit adaptation of Marguerite Duras's autobiographical novel *L'Amant* ('The lover', 1992).

A major feature of the period since the mid-1970s has been the emergence of an increasing number of women directors. Up to this point Varda and Duras had been virtually on their own. The phenomenon can be explained by the rise of the women's movement since May 1968, and the fact that the *avance sur recettes* system now supports independent film-makers. Women directors have often addressed feminist concerns, but, with the ebb of feminism in France from the late 1970s on, they have mostly worked in isolation and shunned the notion of a structured 'woman's cinema'. Nelly Kaplan, who had been Abel Gance's assistant in the 1950s, started the feminist breakthrough with her corrosive *La Fiancée du pirate* (UK: *The Pirate's Fiancee*; US: *Dirty Mary*, 1969), a film about an abused woman who gains control over a village by becoming a prostitute. Like some of her later films (for instance *Plaisir d'amour*, 1990), it cleverly uses surrealist humour to deflate the male ego. Yannick Bellon, who, after a distinguished career as a maker of shorts, directed her first feature in 1972 at the age of 48, has tackled large social issues in a sensitive and often moving way, in *L'Amour violé* (1977), *L'Amour nu* (1981), *La Triche* (1983), and *Les Enfants du désordre* (1988). Coline Serreau scored a huge box-office hit with her comedy *3 hommes et un couffin* ('Three men and a cradle', 1985—remade in the USA as *Three Men and a Baby*). All her films are social parables which gently satirize sexual stereotypes (*Pourquoi pas?*, 1977), racism (*Romuald et Juliette*, 1988), and hypocrisy (*La Crise*, 1992).

In this period, many women directors made films that were largely or partly autobiographical. This is true of Diane Kurys's best work, *Coup de foudre* (1979) and *Diabolo Menthe* (1977), in which she remembers her childhood and adolescence with engaging freshness. Véra Belmont's *Rouge Baiser* (1984) looks back at the Saint-Germain-des-Prés of the 1950s, and Euzhan Palcy investigated the history and mythology of her native Martinique in *Rue Cases-Nègres* (1983) and *Siméon* (1990).

Personal memories of what life was like for white settlers in the French colonies are skilfully handled by Marie-France Pisier in *le Bal du gouverneur* (1989), Brigitte Roüan in *Outremer* (1987), and Claire Denis in her successful *Chocolat* (1987). Virginie Thévenet's *La Nuit porte jarretelles* (1986), Arielle Dombasle's *Les Pyramides bleues* (1988), Claire Devers's way-out *Noir et blanc* (1986), and Juliet Berto's *Cap Canaille* (1981) have more in common with the 'cinéma du look'. Aline Issermann is a powerful director whose second feature, the post-modern *L'Amant magnifique* (1984), disconcerted those who had admired the cogency of her social comment in *Le Destin de Juliette* (1982). Josiane Balasko recreated the exuberant atmosphere of *café-théâtre* in *Les Keufs* (1987).

Like several of the women film-makers mentioned above—as well as Anna Karina, Jeanne Moreau, and Nicole Garcia, who have also directed films—Balasko is better known as an actress than as a director. She started in *café-théâtre*, a subversive cross between shoestring theatre and cabaret that came into its own after May 1968. It provided the cinema with a wealth of excellent performers whose naturalness, no-holds-barred sense of humour and lack of narcissism suited the mood of the 1970s. In addition to Balasko, they included Depardieu, Miou-Miou, Thierry Lhermitte, Coluche, Patrick Dewaere, Michel Blanc, Dominique Lavanant, Gérard Jugnot, and Christian Clavier. All of them (apart from the late Dewaere and Coluche) continue to make a dynamic contribution to French cinema, and Depardieu has become an international star.

The 1960–93 period in general was notable for its wealth of acting talent. In the 1960s, already established stars like Fernandel and Jean Marais pursued their careers successfully, but the biggest crowd-pullers were the knockabout comedians de Funès and Bourvil. Jean Gabin maintained his star status until his death in 1976, playing increasingly patriarchal roles, sometimes set off against popular actors of the younger generation like Delon and Belmondo. The latter two stars' respective fortes (the internalization and externalization of emotion) were mirrored, to a certain extent, by two leading young actresses, the inscrutably beautiful Catherine Deneuve and, from the mid-1970s on, the explosive Isabelle Adjani. By the end of the 1980s, Juliette Binoche and Béatrice Dalle had shown that, given the right material and director, they possessed an iconic screen presence. Curiously, however, no actress since 1960, with the possible exception of

Gérard Depardieu

(1948–)

Gérard Depardieu has in the early 1990s reached global stardom on a scale unprecedented for a French film actor. Already a star in France from the mid-1970s (and top at the box-office since 1985), he has become familiar outside his own country as the proletarian hero of *auteur* films such as Bertolucci's *1900* (1976) and Maurice Pialat's *Loulou* (1980), and the eponymous lead of the very popular *Jean de Florette* (Claude Berri, 1986). The Hollywood-style comedy *Green Card* (Peter Weir, 1990) turned him into a somewhat clichéd icon of 'Frenchness': a connoisseur of wines and red meat who seduces women and smokes Gauloises. His fame has percolated to all corners of popular culture, from film journals to gossip magazines. His extra-filmic activities include the wide range of media interventions now required of major film stars: producing films, mounting stage productions, and buying classic films for distribution; he was president of the jury of the 1992 Cannes festival.

Beyond charisma, talent, and stupefying energy (over seventy films to date), Depardieu's popularity relates to the deep resonances of his persona within French culture. His adolescence in working-class Châteauroux, marked by delinquency (later coming back to haunt him in the USA when he was nominated for an Oscar for *Green Card*), gave a seal of authenticity to his performance of proletarian characters. In addition, his training in the theatre of the late 1960s, strongly marked by the libertarian *café-théâtre*, contributed to his rebellious image and naturalistic acting. After a dozen minor film parts, including in Marguerite Duras's *Nathalie Granger* (1973), his co-starring role in Bertrand Blier's *Les Valseuses* (1973)—an iconoclastic film strongly influenced by *café-théâtre* themes and aesthetics—turned him into France's young male sensation. Since then, his star has not stopped rising.

Depardieu's screen persona, emerging in the post-1968 era, was an updated version of the familiar criminal/working-class hero of French populist cinema. Another key to his success was his ability to channel this persona into two strands: the comic, as in *Les Valseuses*, and the (melo)dramatic, epitomized by *Loulou*. Consequently, Depardieu has been both a star of mainstream French comedy (*Inspecteur La Bavure*, 1980; *La Chèvre*, 1981; *Les Compères*, 1983; *Les Fugitifs*, 1986), and the tormented, 'suffering macho' of *auteur* films such as those of Marco Ferreri (*The Last Woman*, 1976, in which he castrates himself), Pialat (after *Loulou*: *Police*, 1985), Alain Resnais (*Mon oncle d'Amérique*, 1980), and François Truffaut (*Le Dernier Métro*, 1980). The two strands are united by his intense physicality (Depardieu's body, bulky in youth, is now massive), combined with surprising gentleness, leading to his own exaggerated claims of 'femininity'. Blier's films have made the best use of this dichotomy, especially *Tenue de soirée* (1986), in which Depardieu plays a 'gay' character who ends up in drag, while retaining his virile heterosexual image.

Depardieu's acting versatility has encompassed other genres including the increasingly popular heritage film, both for indigenous consumption (*Fort Saganne*, 1984, a colonial drama) and for international release. *Jean de Florette* was a breakthrough in this respect, the film's nostalgic evocation of rural Provence matching Depardieu's off-screen claims of affinity for the *terroir* ('wine-grower' is the profession listed on his passport). Like Jean Gabin before him, Depardieu sums up an idealized French masculinity which merges working-class virility, populist 'authentic' roots, and romanticism. He has adapted this to good effect in portrayals of historical figures in heritage movies such as *Cyrano de Bergerac* (1990), to the great benefit of French film exports. In the process of exporting himself, the complexities of his persona may be lost—as in *Green Card*, or Ridley Scott's *1492* (1992), in which he plays Columbus. But he has undoubtedly been instrumental in helping French cinema maintain its place in the globalized media of the 1990s.

GINETTE VINCENDEAU

SELECT FILMOGRAPHY

Les Valseuses (1973); 1900 (1976); La Dernière Femme (The Last Woman) (1976); Le Camion (1977); Loulou (1980); Mon oncle d'Amérique (1980); Le Dernier Métro (The Last Metro) (1980); Le Retour de Martin Guerre (The Return of Martin Guerre) (1981); Danton (1982); Jean de Florette (1986); Tenue de soirée (1986); Les Fugitifs (1986); Camille Claudel (1988); Drôle d'endroit pour une rencontre (A Strange Place to Meet) (1988); Trop belle pour toi (1989); Cyrano de Bergerac (1990); Green Card (1990); 1492 (1992); Germinal (1993); Le Colonel Chabert (1994)

BIBLIOGRAPHY

Gray, Marianne (1992), *Depardieu: A Biography*.

Gérard Depardieu in Andrzej Wajda's *Danton* (1982)

Deneuve, has really been a box-office draw in her own right.

The high quality of French cinema in the last three decades could not have been sustained without strong back-up from the other contributors to the film-making process: set designers Alexandre Trauner and Bernard Évein, cinematographers Henri Alekan, Raoul Coutard, Nestor Almendros, and Sacha Vierny, composers Georges Delerue and Philippe Sarde, script-writers Jean-Claude Carrière, Gérard Brach, and Jean-Pierre Rappeneau (also the director of two stylish films, *La Vie de château*, 1966, and *Cyrano de Bergerac*, 1987), and producers Anatole Dauman, Pierre Braunberger, Georges de Beauregard, Serge Silberman, Claude Berri (who also directed several well-crafted films, including *Jean de Florette* and *Manon des sources* (1986), from the Pagnol novel, which, in their nostalgic depiction of life in Provence, struck a chord with audiences, and launched a vogue for nostalgia). This favourable creative environment, combined with the attractions of state aid and a liberal attitude to political exiles, prompted many major non-French directors to make films in France. They included Luis Buñuel, Walerian Borowczyk, Andrzej Wajda, Roman Polanski, Chantal Akerman, Agnieszka Holland, and Raul Ruiz, among others.

France's lively film culture is reflected in the existence of many film magazines. At the 'serious' end of the market, *Positif* has remained true to its old principles, though it is now less militant, and attracts the same sort of readership as its bigger-selling rival *Cahiers du cinéma*. The more popular *Première* and *Studio Magazine* have large circulations. The cinema is given wide coverage in other printed media and on radio and television. Paris offers a choice of films unparalleled anywhere in the world. Several commercial cinemas pursue a programming policy of one-off showings not very different from that of subsidized film theatres, of which there are three: the Cinémathèque Française, the Pompidou Centre (Salle Garance), and the Vidéothèque de Paris. As a result, over 350 different films are shown in any given week in Paris. France hosts over a dozen film festivals each year in addition to Cannes. The favourable cultural environment partly explains why attendances and the number of screens have decreased very slowly compared with the rest of Europe.

Since the momentum of interest in film will no doubt continue to be self-sustaining for some time, and since state subsidies and incentives have not been significantly eroded as a result of the change of government in 1993, the French cinema can expect to remain in relatively good health for the foreseeable future.

Bibliography

Armes, Roy (1985), *French Cinema*.

Browne, Nick (ed.) (1990), *Cahiers du Cinéma: 1969–1972: The Politics of Representation*.

Forbes, Jill (1992), *The Cinema in France after the New Wave*.

Graham, Peter (ed.) (1968), *The New Wave: Critical Landmarks*.

Hayward, Susan (1993), *French National Cinema*.

—— and Vincendeau, Ginette (eds.) (1990), *French Film: Texts and Contexts*.

Hillier, Jim (ed.) (1985), *Cahiers du Cinéma: The 1960s*.

Jeancolas, Jean-Pierre (1979), *Le Cinéma des Française Le Vème République (1958–1978)*.

Italy: Auteurs and After

MORANDO MORANDINI

The year 1960 was a remarkable one for Italian cinema. For the first (and only) time since 1946 Italian films not only overtook Hollywood films in popularity in the domestic market but captured over 50 per cent of total box-office. Three films released that year—Luchino Visconti's *Rocco and his Brothers* (*Rocco e i suoi fratelli*), Federico Fellini's *La dolce vita* ('The good life'), and Michelangelo Antonioni's *L'avventura* ('The adventure')—also went on to be major successes abroad.

The triumphs of 1960 had been prefigured in 1959, which was also a year of commercial revival and in which two Italian films—Roberto Rossellini's *Il Generale Della Rovere* and Mario Monicelli's *La grande guerra* ('The Great War')—shared the Golden Lion at the Venice festival. But there is no doubt that 1960 was the watershed, ushering in a period of generalized renewal of modes of expression in the cinema. While *Rocco* (and another great box-office success of that year, Luigi Comencini's *Tutti a casa* ('Everybody go home')), might be seen as throwbacks to earlier modes, *L'avventura* and *La dolce vita* definitively turned their backs on the past and prefigured the surge of developments to come.

Although *L'avventura* was perhaps the more aesthetically innovative of the two, *La dolce vita* was historically the more important. It provided proof, if proof were needed, of the demise of neo-realism, and it was a crucial turning-

Federico Fellini

(1920–93)

Orson Welles once dismissed the work of Fellini as a country boy's dreams of the big city. When Fellini's *Roma* came out in 1972, it was greeted as the last part, after *La dolce vita* (1960) and *Satyricon* (1969), of a trilogy on the Eternal City—Alma Mater and Great Whore—upon which Fellini had descended from his provincial home town of Rimini, and with which he had developed an ever less affectionate and more hostile rapport. Rome and his native Romagna are the two poles of Fellini's cinema, as they are of his origins: his father Urbano, a travelling salesman, was from Romagna; his mother Ida Barbiani was Roman. Twenty years after *I vitelloni* (1953), Fellini went back with *Amarcord* (1973) to the Rimini he had already revisited in *I clowns* (1970). Even the film which first brought him international fame, *La strada* (1954), set in the bleak uplands of central Italy, can be seen as an ideal journey between Rome and Romagna. On only two occasions—*Casanova* (1976) and *E la nave va* ('And the ship sails on', 1983)—did he venture outside Italy, and even then not very far. In all he made twenty-four films and three shorts over a period of forty years, from *Luci del varietà* ('Variety lights', 1950), co-directed with Alberto Lattuada, to *La voce della luna* ('The voice of the moon', 1990), the only one of his films to draw on a contemporary literary source (Ermanno Cavazzini's 1987 novel *Il poema dei lunatici*).

Even in his early films, made when neo-realism was still the reigning orthodoxy, Fellini preferred to draw on the subjective resources of memory and fantasy for his inspiration. From $8^{1}/_{2}$ (1963) onwards, with its portrait of a film director unable to complete a film until he could make sense of his memories, this subjectivist and autobiographical tendency became more accentuated. He is generally considered, for good or ill, the most autobiographical of the major Italian directors, from the way in which he has quite literally made a spectacle of himself, in a parade of oneiric and solipsistic visions that border on the obsessive. His autobiography rarely takes the form of a deep soul-searching, but expresses itself rather in a carnivalesque splurge of imagery drawn from collective as well as individual sources. Because of this ability to tap other people's memories and fantasies, as well as his own, it is likely that, in the future, Fellini's work will be seen as offering a rare insight into the history of twentieth-century Italy, from the 'ordinary fascism' of the 1930s retrospectively evoked in *Amarcord* to the cosmopolitan Rome of the 1960s, 1970s, and 1980s. Undoubtedly a special place belongs here to the widescreen panorama of Roman high-life in *La dolce vita*, but a firm critical consensus, in Italy and abroad, regards $8^{1}/_{2}$, with its mixture of modernity and recollection, as Fellini's most representative film.

More than a director of individual films, however, Fellini was the author of an oeuvre which holds together

Giulietta Masina as Gelsomina in Federico Fellini's *La strada* (1954)

as an unit. The modes and tones changed with the years, as he changed, as society and the world changed, but his films continued and developed the same essential themes and ideas.

MORANDO MORANDINI

SELECT FILMOGRAPHY

Luci del varietà (1950) (co-directed with Alberto Lattuada); Lo sceicco bianco (The White Sheik) (1951); I vitelloni (1953); La strada (1954); Il bidone (1955); Le notti di Cabiria (1956); La dolce vita (1960); Boccaccio '70 (1961) (episode); $8^{1}/_{2}$ (1963); Giulietta degli spiriti (Juliet of the Spirits) (1965); Histoires extraordinaires (1968) (episode); Fellini Satyricon (1969); I clowns (1970); Roma (1972); Amarcord (1973); Il Casanova di Federico Fellini (Casanova) (1976); Prova d'orchestra (1978); La città delle donne (City of Women) (1980); E la nave va (1983); Ginger e Fred (1985); Intervista (1988); La voce della luna (1990).

BIBLIOGRAPHY

Bondanella, Peter (1992), *The Cinema of Federico Fellini*.

point in the battle against censorship and for freedom of expression, thereby liberating the Italian cinema from the shibboleths of left and right alike.

NEW DIRECTORS OF THE 1960S AND 1970S

The years 1961 and 1962 saw a remarkable series of first films from new directors, which can only be compared to the explosion of the French 'Nouvelle Vague' which just preceded it: Pasolini's *Accattone*, Vittorio De Seta's *Banditi a Orgosolo* ('Bandits of Orgosolo'), Ermanno Olmi's *Il posto* ('The job'), and Elio Petri's *L'assassino* ('The assassin'), all from 1961; *La commare secca* ('The grim reaper') by Bernardo Bertolucci and *Un uomo da bruciare* ('A man for the killing'), by the Taviani brothers and Valentino Orsini, both in 1962; not to mention films by Tinto Brass, Ugo Gregoretti, Giuliano Montaldo, Alfredo Giannetti, and others, all in 1962.

The two most heterodox film-makers of this generation were Pier Paolo Pasolini and Marco Ferreri. For Pasolini, cinema was the continuation of a literary and political discourse already elaborated in poetry, novels, criticism, theatre, and journalism, carried out with an irrepressible need for self-promotion, combined with a fierce will to create scandal and to risk his own person, which his tragic death near the beach at Ostia only served to reaffirm. His cinema began in a style of spirited dilettantism, which contrasted strikingly with the traditional conventions of film, and his early films—*Accattone*, *Mamma Roma* (1962), *La ricotta* ('Curd-cheese', 1962), *The Gospel According to St. Matthew* (1964), and *Uccellacci e uccellini* ('The hawks and the sparrows', 1966)—have an iconoclastic freshness which his later work never recaptured.

In a survey of twenty Italian critics for the 'Premio Bolaffi', awarded to the best film of the decade 1966–75, the winner was *Dillinger è morto* ('Dillinger is dead', 1969) by Marco Ferreri, followed by Antonioni's *Blowup* (1966), *Uccellacci e uccellini*, and *La Grande Bouffe* (*La grande abbuffata*, 1973), also by Ferreri. A fierce moralist and tender misanthrope, Ferreri, known as the 'Spanish Milanese', undertook in collaboration with the Spanish writer Rafael Azcona a sustained analysis of relations between the sexes, founded on a mixture of cruelty and suffering, ridicule and emotion, sarcasm and a sense of tragedy, with a taste for the repulsive and the abnormal which derived from an aspect of the Spanish temperament and culture which formed him.

His career began with *L'ape regina* ('The queen bee', 1963), and he went on to make a number of films whose titles alone are sufficient to give a sense of the themes explored in them—*La donna scimmia* ('The ape-woman', 1964), *L'harem* ('The harem', 1967), *La cagna* ('The bitch', 1970), and *L'ultima donna* ('The last woman', 1977). *Dillinger è morto*, a nocturnal 'happening' about alienation and the horror of the everyday, was followed by *Il seme dell'uomo* ('Man's seed', 1969), an apocalyptic fable of the end of the world. His films alternate between realism and metaphor, concentrating on themes such as destruction, negation, and death, but they are often, as in *La Grande Bouffe*, tempered by a vitality and a sense of gallows humour. There are also more optimistic metaphors in his work, such as in *L'udienza* ('The hearing', a variation on Kafka's *The Castle*, 1972), and in *Chiedo asilo* ('I request asylum', 1979). In the 1980s, along with many of his peers, Ferreri entered a period of crisis, unable to keep up with the transformation of Italian society, and his films have become more unfocused, more uncertain, and less inventive.

Lino Ventura as the police chief investigating the murders of local magistrates, in Francesco Rosi's Italian–French co-production, *Cadaveri eccellenti* (*Illustrious Corpses*, 1975)

Two of the most representative films of the new, young cinema of the 1960s were Bernardo Bertolucci's *Before the Revolution* (*Prima della rivoluzione*, 1964), and *Fists in the Pocket* (*I pugni in tasca*, 1965) by Marco Bellocchio. In the first phase of his career, up until *The Spider's Stratagem* (*Strategia del ragno*, 1970), Bertolucci was part of the general 1960s trend towards a renewal of narrative forms, whilst his second phase, from *The Conformist* (*Il conformista*, 1970) to *The Tragedy of a Ridiculous Man* (*La tragedia di un uomo ridicolo*, 1981), was marked by a search for a new space within the more traditional forms of cinema, without ever aban-

doning the sense of 'authorship'. *1900* (1976) was a risky compromise between an intensely regional subject-matter and costly international production values, made possible by the extraordinary success of *Last Tango in Paris* (1973).

I pugni in tasca was talked of as a case of 'cinema of cruelty', very much in the spirit of Antonin Artaud's 'theatre of cruelty'. The force of Bellocchio's style lay in its direct, savage, and occasionally grotesque critique of institutions; from the family, in his first film, to the politics of the centre left in *China is Near* (*La Cina è vicina*, 1967), Catholic education in *In the Name of the Father* (*Nel nome del padre*, 1971), journalism in *Sbatti il mostro in prima pagina* ('Splash the monster on the front page'), the army in *Marcia trionfale* ('Triumphal march', 1976), and psychiatric hospitals in *Nessuno o tutti* ('No one or everyone', 1974—a two-part inquiry produced by a collective including Silvano Agosti, Sandro Petraglia, and Stefano Rulli).

The three directors who each in their own way recovered and injected new, original energy into the legacy of neo-realism in this period were the Neapolitan Francesco Rosi, the Lombard Ermanno Olmi, and the Sardinian Vittorio De Seta. Rosi was formed by the rationalist tradition of the Enlightenment, as his masterpiece, and the best film ever made on the south of Italy and all its problems, *Salvatore Giuliano* (1960), indicated. The character of the infamous bandit Giuliano is here set to one side, over-shadowed by the links between mafia, banditry, political power, and economic power. No one intermingles as smoothly as Rosi documentary reconstruction and fiction, opening up new perspectives and asking probing dia-lectical questions in films like *Hands over the City* (*Le mani sulla città*, 1963), *The Mattei Affair* (*Il caso Mattei*, 1972), and *Lucky Luciano* (1973). The investigation of power and its perverters continued in *Illustrious Corpses* (*Cadaveri eccel-lenti*, 1976), from a novel by Leonardo Sciascia, but a certain abstract, metaphysical tone and a formalistic, decorative texture which were hinted at there came to the fore in the films that followed—*Three Brothers* (*Tre fratelli*, 1981), *Carmen* (1984), and *Chronicle of a Death Foretold* (*Cronaca di una morte annunciata*, 1987, from the novel by Gabriel García Márquez).

The critical and surprise popular success of Olmi's *Tree of the Wooden Clogs* (*L'albero degli zoccoli*, 1978), a solemn and harmonious poem on the memory of peasant ways, work in the fields, its joys and hardships, crowned a career of admirable artistic and moral consistency. Isolated from the Roman film industry and faithful to an artisanal, low-cost filmcraft, yet stylistically rigorous and of a refined clarity even in his only literary adaptation and only high-budget film, *The Legend of the Holy Drinker* (*La leggenda del santo bevitore*, 1988), Olmi tells the ordinary stories of ordi-nary people in their ordinary, but never-before narrated, worlds. Over the years, he has toned down his poetic vein and turned an ever-harsher critical gaze on his subjects, as in *Camminacammina* ('On and on', 1983), in which he reinvented with high fantasy the story of the Three Wise Men, and in the harsh documentary *Milano '83*. Since the deaths of Rossellini and Pasolini, Olmi is the only living Italian director with a profound sense of the sacred.

Vittorio De Seta can be related to Olmi through the solitary and marginal nature of his work, and through his origin as a documentarist. He is almost unknown outside Italy, and unfortunately abandoned cinema in the 1970s. His first film *Banditi a Orgosolo* (1961) was a dramatic and lyrical tale on the backwardness of Sardinia, and won him

critical acclaim, but his next film, *Un uomo a metà* ('Half a man', 1966), a Jungian story of neurosis, had a more mixed reception. His most important film was *Diario di un maestro* ('Diary of a schoolteacher', 1973), a TV mini-series in four episodes in which the neo-realist ethic was filtered through the techniques of live filming. It was also the only film to follow up the issues raised by Don Lorenzo Milani's controversial and innovatory book on schooling, *Letter to a Teacher*, published five years earlier.

The Tuscan brothers Vittorio and Paolo Taviani won the Palme d'Or at the 30th Cannes festival in 1977 with their seventh film *Padre padrone*. From 1954 onwards, first along-side Vittorio Orsini and after 1964 on their own, they have developed a partnership which for its longevity and its success can be compared to the case of Merchant–Ivory, and is certainly unprecedented in Italian cinema. From *I sovversivi* ('The subversives', 1967) until *Il prato* ('The meadow', 1979), via *St Michael Had a Rooster* (*San Michele aveva un gallo*, 1971)—perhaps their best—their cinema has been a committed reflection from the left on lost cer-tainties, on illusions and historic compromises, on methods, risks, generational conflicts, conflicts between utopians and pragmatists, between revolutionary haste and patient work for long-term change. With *The Night of the Shooting Stars* (*La notte di San Lorenzo*, 1982), on the 1943–5 civil war seen through the eyes of a child, ideological commitment gave way to the joy of story-telling and of the recall of our earliest feelings, and this tone continued, somewhat unevenly, in *Kaos* (1984), inspired by Pir-andello's short stories, and in *Good Morning Babylon* (1987), the saga of two Italian emigrants who end up working in D. W. Griffith's crew during the making of *Intolerance*.

While the above-named count as the major *auteur* direc-tors who emerged in the 1960s and 1970s, they were flanked on the one side by the actor and theatre director Carmelo Bene, who crossed over into cinema with five experimental films in the 1960s, and on the other side by a number of directors who continued to produce dis-tinguished work in the traditional cinema. These include the comedy writer Franco Brusati, best known for *Pane e cioccolata* ('Bread and chocolate', 1974); Mauro Bolognini, a refined illustrator of literary texts such as *Il bell'Antonio* (1960); Franco Rossi, with the delicate *Odissea nuda* ('Naked odyssey', 1961); Sergio Citti, the only Italian director of working-class origin, who began as a collaborator of Paso-lini and went on to direct *Ostia* (1970) and *Casotto* (1977); and Valerio Zurlini. With films like *Estate violenta* ('Violent summer', 1959) and *La ragazza con la valigia* ('The girl with the suitcase', 1960), Zurlini achieved a reputation as one of Italian cinema's few love poets, but apart from *Cronaca familiare* ('Family chronicle'), which shared the Golden Lion at Venice with Tarkovsky's *Ivan's Childhood* in 1962, his work is little known abroad. His style was uncluttered by ideological trends or fashions of any kind. He tended instead towards sensitive dissection of emotions, together with an unspoken vocation for historical narrative which was most fully expressed in *Il deserto dei Tartari* ('The desert of the Tartars', 1976).

ITALIAN COMEDY

Comedy had flourished in Italy in the 1930s and had been revitalized in the 1950s by the effects of neo-realism, so that, come the 1960s, it became the genre which propped up the entire national film industry. More or less consciously, the makers of comedy films aimed to record, year after year, the changing face of society's behaviour, values, and customs, to hold up a critical but light-hearted mirror to the nation's foibles. A historian of the twenty-first century could well trace through the development of film comedy a sort of anthropological-cum-cultural history of the period 1960–79. However, two factors detract from the representative value of the comedy genre in those years: first, directors, writers, and actors (in ascending order of importance for the ideology and structure of these films) were all themselves products of values which provided their own perspective on their subject-matter; and secondly, over the years, the narrative structures found in the genre became crystallized into schemata and rules, which restricted the potential for analysis of the events and characters presented.

The five dominant personalities and showmen ('mattatori') in this field for twenty-five years were: Alberto Sordi, whose screen character was an idle opportunist, a hypocritical Catholic and 'mamma's boy'; Nino Manfredi, whose humour was patient and slow; Vittorio Gassman, with his particular taste for excess; Ugo Tognazzi, the most flexible of the five (and the only one to offer his services to an *auteur*-director, Ferreri); and, set apart somewhat, Marcello Mastroianni, the most accessible and malleable, and the only one not to be imprisoned in the comedy genre, and to achieve real international fame.

With rare exceptions, such as some of the films of Antonio Pietrangeli, Italian comedy has been a male genre, and very often a chauvinist one. Monica Vitti was the only actress who managed in the 1970s, after her work with Antonioni, to challenge the dominance of the five

Marcello Mastroianni and Sophia Loren in De Sica's three-part comedy *Yesterday, Today and Tomorrow* (1963)

male stars, and the four of the younger generation—Lando Buzzanca, Adriano Celentano, Johnny Dorelli, and Giancarlo Giannini. Other actresses—Claudia Cardinale, Catherine Spaak, Laura Antonelli, Stefania Sandrelli— were either short-lived successes, or restricted to supporting roles.

The themes treated by comedies were broadly the following five: (1) the family: bachelors, bigamists, holiday separations, adultery, divorce, and hence male/female relations in general; (2) the provinces, often southern, with their rituals, prejudices, and matriarchs—most notably in Pietro Germi's work, from *Divorce Italian Style* (*Divorzio all'italiana*, 1961) to *L'immorale* ('The immoral man', 1967); (3) the professions and careers which showed the failures of Italian democracy; (4) the Italian abroad, portrayed with all his prejudices and his garish unruliness; (5) the Catholic Church, seen almost exclusively through various priestly scandals. The focus was largely on the lower middle and middle classes, but there were examples of upper-middle-class settings and even working-class or underclass worlds, as in Ettore Scola's *Brutti, sporchi e cattivi* ('The filthy, the bad, and the ugly', 1974).

The important directors were Dino Risi, Mario Monicelli, Pietro Germi, Luigi Comencini, followed by Alberto Lattuada, Nanni Loy, Franco Giraldi, Lina Wertmüller and others. But the screen-writers were even more important than the directors: they included Age and Scarpelli, Rodolfo Sonego, Metz and Marchesi, Ruggero Maccari (initially together with Ettore Scola, before the latter moved into direction), Benvenuti and De Bernardi, Ennio de Concini, Bernardino Zapponi, and Ugo Pirro.

POLITICAL CINEMA

Ever since 1945, Italy has had a long and intense tradition of political cinema. In the 1950s, this was borne out by the notable success of the Don Camillo series, from the books by Giovanni Guareschi, in which the eponymous hero (played by the French actor Fernandel) and his rival Peppone (Gino Cervi) embodied the Catholic–Communist feud in their rural, backward community. For convenience, political cinema after 1960 can be divided into four categories.

1. The south: the southern question was and is the most intractable political and social problem produced by Italian Unification. From *La sfida* ('The challenge', 1959) to *Dimenticare Palermo* ('Forget Palermo', 1990) and *Diario napoletano* ('Neapolitan diary', 1992), with their passionate involvement with the south, and their robust story-lines, Francesco Rosi's work was the standard-bearer in this area. Sicily, as a land of beauty and of Mafia, has also been treated by Germi, Lattuada (*Mafioso*, 1962), Pasquale Squitieri (*Il prefetto di ferro* (*The Iron Prefect*, 1977), Damiano Damiani, and Giuseppe Ferrara.

2. War, Fascism, anti-Fascism, and the Resistance: this current began with Rossellini's *Rome Open City* in 1945 and reached a quantitative peak between 1960 and 1963, when over forty films on these topics were released. Some of the most significant were *Estate violenta* by Valerio Zurlini, *La longa notte del '43* ('The long night of 1943', 1960) by Florestano Vancini, *Tutti a casa* by Luigi Comencini, *Una vita difficile* ('A difficult life', 1961) by Dino Risi, *La villeggiatura* ('Holidays', 1973) by Marco Leto, and *Il sospetto* ('The suspect', 1975) by Francesco Maselli.

3. Justice: a number of films deal with the dysfunctional state of the police and the magistracy, and with the connivance between the political-economic classes and organized crime. Perhaps the most typical example of this category was *Indagine su un cittadino al di sopra di ogni sospetto* ('The investigation of a citizen above suspicion', 1970), by Elio Petri, written with Ugo Pirro and starring a magnificent Gian Maria Volonté, the best actor in Italian cinema and the protagonist of two other political grotesques by Petri, *La classe operaia va in Paradiso* ('The working class goes to Heaven', 1971) and *Todo modo* (1976), from the novel by Leonardo Sciascia.

4. History: films in this category reconstruct historical events and characters as a way of making indirect political comment on the present. Liliana Cavani began with a TV film of this kind, *Francesco di Assisi* ('Francis of Assisi', 1966), and *Galileo* (1968), before achieving international fame with her investigation of the sado-masochistic aspects of Nazism in *The Night Porter* (*Il portiere di notte*, 1974). She returned to Francis of Assisi in 1989 with a film starring Mickey Rourke. Also worthy of note are *Sacco e Vanzetti* (1971) and *Giordano Bruno* (1973), by Giuliano Montaldo; *Bronte—cronaca di un massacro* ('Bronte—the story of a massacre', 1970) by Florestano Vancini, based on an episode of the Risorgimento played down by historians; and (by an Italian director, but not set in Italy) Gillo Pontecorvo's *The Battle of Algiers* (*La battaglia di Algeri*, 1965) and *Burn!* (*Queimada!*, 1969). The costume comedies of Luigi Magni— *Nell'anno del Signore* ('In the year of our Lord', 1969), *In nome del papa re* ('In the name of the Pope and King', 1977)— occupy a slightly eccentric position in this category, with their sharp anti-clerical satire and their revision of the history of Papal Rome.

'PEPLUMS', HORROR, AND 'SPAGHETTI WESTERNS'

The history of Italian cinema is littered with the corpses of new genres which were born, flourished briefly, and were then destroyed by the repetition *ad nauseam* of formulas which had brought their initial success. In the 1950s, for example, there was a short-lived vogue for exotic 'documentaries', which in the 1960s degenerated into trivial (and often racially insensitive) cocktails of sex and violence, as in Gualtiero Jacopetti's *Mondo cane* ('A dog's world', 1962) and *Africa addio* ('Africa, goodbye', 1966).

Bernardo Bertolucci

(1941–)

With *The Last Emperor* (1987), Bernardo Bertolucci, son of Attilio, one of the greatest Italian poets of the century, and brother of Giuseppe, another respected film director, reached a peak of success, winning praise from both a world-wide audience and the vast majority of critics, as well as the 4,747 members of the Academy, who awarded the film nine nominations and then nine Oscars.

This apotheosis was a far cry from his start in 1962, when the 21-year-old from Parma, who had published a slim volume of poetry (*In cerca del mistero*), which won the Viareggio Prize for a first work, and who had been Pasolini's assistant on *Accattone* (1961), directed his almost unnoticed first film, *La commare secca* ('The grim reaper'). He attracted more attention with his next film, *Before the Revolution* (*Prima della rivoluzione*, 1964), an autobiographical *Bildung* caught between passion and ideology. Several years of enforced inactivity followed, interrupted only by a long television documentary, *La via del petrolio*; a short film *Agonia* ('Agony') with Julian Beck and the Living Theatre; and a strange, experimental, Godardesque film, inspired by Dostoevsky, *Partner* (1968).

In 1970 came two films which were to put him on the path to international critical and popular success, *The Spider's Stratagem* (*Strategia del ragno*) and *The Conformist* (*Il conformista*—from the novel by Moravia). Set in Fascist Italy, both films explored the bourgeois roots of Fascism and centred on the theme of the father. Both also inaugurated important collaborations: *The Spider's Stratagem* that with director of photography Vittorio Storaro, and *The Conformist* the equally valuable ones with art director Ferdinando Scarfiotti and editor Kim Arcalli. With these films Bertolucci's films begin to acquire their characteristic pacing and 'look', with diffuse lighting, warm colours, and a relaxed rhythm interrupted by explosions of violent intensity.

His international status was consolidated by the *succès de scandale* of *Last Tango in Paris* (1973). Aided by an extraordinary performance by Marlon Brando, *Last Tango* earned $16 million in America, and the highest ever box-office in the history of Italian cinema, despite a magistrate's order for its seizure and destruction.

The film *1900* (1976) followed the parallel lives of two characters, a peasant and a landowner, born on the same day in 1900 on a central Italian farm estate. Its two parts, lasting 320 minutes (later cut to 240), make it a work of scope and ambition, built around a dialectic of opposites: a film on the class struggle in Italy, it was nevertheless funded by American dollars, had an international cast, and attempted to merge Hollywood melodrama of the *Gone with the Wind* variety with socialist realism, and with a final scene worthy of Chinese ballet-film. It emerges as a political melodrama, half Marx and half Freud, with a nod in the direction of Verdi.

Like *Last Tango*, *1900* was an international co-production. Technically European, its making and release were heavily constrained by the marketing needs of the American companies who had backed it and acquired world-wide distribution rights. Difficulties with the distributors (not dissimilar to those experienced by Visconti on *The Leopard* in the early 1960s) led Bertolucci to seek production arrangements which would be less constricting. His next two films were Italian productions, while for his return to international production with *The Last Emperor* he teamed up with British-based producer Jeremy Thomas, who remained his producer for *The Sheltering Sky* (*Il tè nel deserto*, 1990) and *Little Buddha* (1993).

La luna ('The moon', 1979) was, like *1900*, at heart a melodrama, on a mother–son relationship and on the incestuous impulse which lies, more or less imagined, at its centre. With *The Tragedy of a Ridiculous Man* (*La tragedia di un uomo ridicolo*, 1981), Bertolucci attempted to come to terms with the difficult, confused, and violent state of Italy in the 1970s, narrated for the first time from the point of view of the father. *The Sheltering Sky* (from the novel by Paul Bowles) escapes the world of Oedipal narrative (except for a sub-plot involving a mother–son relationship) and is a love story, but one in which love is entwined with pain, death, and self-destruction. *Little Buddha*, by contrast, is an unexpectedly serene film, from which class struggle and tortured sexuality have been (at least temporarily) banished.   MORANDO MORANDINI

FILMOGRAPHY

La commare secca (1962); Prima della rivoluzione (Before the Revolution) (1964); Partner (1968); Agonia (episode of Amore e rabbia) (1969); Il conformista (1970); Strategia del ragno (The Spider's Stratagem) (1970); L'ultimo tango a Parigi (Last Tango in Paris) (1973); 1900 (1976); La luna (1979); Tragedia di un uomo ridicolo (Tragedy of a Ridiculous Man) (1981); The Last Emperor (L'ultimo imperatore) (1987); The sheltering Sky / Il tè nel deserto (1990); Little Buddha (1993)

BIBLIOGRAPHY

Casetti, Francesco (1975), *Bernardo Bertolucci*.
Kolker, Robert Phillip (1985), *Bernardo Bertolucci*.

Dominique Sanda confronts an inscrutable Jean-Louis Trintignant in *The Conformist* (1970)

There were also cycles of derivative genres of all kinds, such as spy films, cop films, erotic-pornographic films, and macabre mystery films, each trying to cash in on the latest fad, but with only ephemeral results.

Three genres, however, enjoyed a degree of longevity and commercial and even critical success. Heir to a tradition stretching back to *Cabiria* (1914), the so-called 'historical-mythological' (or 'peplum') film was inaugurated in its modern guise by Pietro Francisci's *The Labours of Hercules* (*Le fatiche di Ercole*) in 1958 and flourished until 1964. The genre featured strong-man heroes, usually called Hercules or Maciste and often played by American actor and former Mr Universe Steve Reeves, and achieved a certain distinction, aided by a tone of wit and detachment in films like Vittorio Cottafavi's *Hercules Conquers Atlantis* (*Ercole alla conquista di Atlantide*, 1961), and lurching into cheerful self-parody in Duccio Tessari's *The Titans* (*Arrivano i Titani*, 1961).

Around the same time Riccardo Freda, with *I vampiri* ('The vampires', 1956), and Mario Bava, with *La maschera del demonio* ('The mask of the demon', 1960), set in motion a new genre of Italian horror cinema, which was to enjoy a remarkable growth in the following two decades. In Dario Argento the horror film found its most savage practitioner. His delirious formalistic excess made him a cult director both for the public and for many of the younger generation of critics.

An equally important role, in terms of both quality and duration, was played by the 'Western all'italiana', or 'spaghetti Western'. Between 1964 and 1975, 398 were made, often with Spanish, French, or German input. At the height of this boom, in 1968, 72 were made in one year. The most striking feature of the genre was its recourse to an extreme sado-masochistic violence which spilled over into caricature and parody. Sergio Leone was by far the most talented director of spaghetti Westerns, but his best film was probably not a Western but the gangster epic *Once upon a Time in America* (*C'era una volta in America*, 1984), one of the few great Italian films of the 1980s.

GENERAL DECLINE AND PARTIAL RECOVERY

'Everyone for themselves, disaster for everyone' was the title given to a survey of the European film industry published in 1979 by the French newspaper *Le Monde*. It noted a general, growing, and irreversible drop in attendances all over Europe; but in Italy the situation was little short of catastrophic—a collapse in tickets sold from 514 million in 1976 to 276 million in 1979. The following few years brought similar falls, to 165 million in 1983, 120 million in 1986, and only 90 million in 1992. Beyond the factors which Italy shared with other European countries, including those in eastern Europe, the failure of the Italian market was also due to particular local conditions. Most important of these was the neglect of the film industry by

the State, or by the ruling political class, and the rapid proliferation after 1976 of private television stations whose schedules were built around the transmission of films—up to 1,500 per week. Such uncontrolled proliferation led inexorably to the powerful monopoly of Silvio Berlusconi's Fininvest group, with its three television networks, and many others under its indirect control, in open competition with the three state 'RAI' networks. The effect on freedom of cinematographic production was swift and serious. Since 1988, 80 per cent of all Italian fiction films have been financed to some degree by one or other of these groups.

In the second half of the 1970s, reflecting the general deterioration in the social and political climate of the country (terrorism, organized crime, drugs, crises of political institutions), Italian comedy underwent a profound transformation. The heritage of the old 'masters'—Comencini, Monicelli, Risi, Scola—was turned more towards a harsh, dramatically intense, even grotesque style. A new generation of actor-directors emerged in the 1980s to pick up this trend, the most prominent being Massimo Troisi, Maurizio Nichetti, Carlo Verdone, Francesco Nuti, and Roberto Benigni. The way was opened for these new comics by Nanni Moretti with *Io sono un autarchico* ('I am an autarchist', 1976), filmed in Super 8 and enlarged to 16 mm., followed by *Ecce Bombo* (1978), *Sogni d'oro* ('Sweet dreams', 1981), *Bianca* (1984), *La messa è finita* ('Mass is over', 1985), and *Palombella rossa* ('Red wood-dove', 1989). Moretti is more of a humorist than a comic, and has more affinities with the young directors of the 1960s than with his peers. His films are marked by ironic and affectionate attention to the detail of young urban life, by the problem of new narrative modes, a neurotic melancholy, and the search for new values, or a return to old values, in reaction to a present reality which is ever more dispersed, degraded, and nasty. *Sembra morto . . . ma è solo svenuto* ('He looks dead . . . but he's only fainted', 1986) is the title of a film by Felice Farina, but it could just as well stand as a motto for Italian cinema in the 1990s. Others have spoken of it as an iceberg, with only a small part of it reaching the surface.

In the 1980s, production of feature films was reduced to an average of eighty to ninety titles a year, of which less than half were afforded full distribution and display in cinemas. Hollywood products dominated the market, taking up to 70–75 per cent of box-office receipts, leaving only 20 per cent for home-grown films. In the rather comatose state of Italian cinema in this period, few of the new (if not always young) talents which emerged were able to make much impact either at home or abroad.

Although Oscars for best foreign film were won by Giuseppe Tornatore with his second film *Cinema Paradiso* (*Nuovo cinema paradiso*, 1989), and by Gabriele Salvatores with *Mediterraneo* (1991), his fifth work, it is Gianni Amelio

Franco Cristaldi
(1924–1992)

Much of the strength (and weakness) of the Italian cinema after 1945 can be traced to the entrepreneurial activities of its producers—whether household names, like Carlo Ponti and Dino De Laurentiis, or less well known but equally important, like Riccardo Gualino at Lux and Goffredo Lombardo at Titanus. The most successful of all, however, in terms of consistency, quality, and intelligent and scrupulous business practice, was undoubtedly Franco Cristaldi.

Slightly younger than Ponti or De Laurentiis, Cristaldi came to Rome from his native Turin in 1953. He brought with him the tastes and interests of a highly cultured man together with the practical lucidity of a businessman, a forceful character, and the courage and intuition of an entrepreneur passionately devoted to his chosen activity. He could read a screenplay or assess a screen test as well as he could read or assess a balance sheet.

Of the hundred or so films produced by his company Vides from 1953 on, alone or in collaboration with other companies, there are first or second films by Francesco Rosi, Marco Bellocchio, Gillo Pontecorvo, Elio Petri, Francesco Maselli, and, last but not least, Giuseppe Tornatore, whose *Cinema Paradiso* (*Nuovo cinema paradiso*, 1988) was creatively reshaped by Cristaldi himself before going on to win a second prize at Cannes and an Oscar as the best foreign film.

Alongside his role as promoter of new talent, he also worked with Fellini—*Amarcord* (1973), *E la nave va* ('And the ship sails on', 1983)—and Visconti (*White Nights* (*Le notti bianche*, 1957) and *Vaghe stelle dell'Orsa* (US: *Sandra*, 1964)—and other established directors, and branched into production for television with Giuseppe Montaldo's *Marco Polo* in 1981. The list of his international successes includes Mario Monicelli's *I soliti ignoti* ('Persons unknown', 1958), Pietro Germi's *Divorce Italian Style* (*Divorzio all'italiana*, 1961), Louis Malle's *Lacombe Lucien* (1973), and Jean-Jacques Annaud's *The Name of the Rose* (1986). His films won three Oscars, four Palmes d'Or at Cannes, three Golden Lions at Venice, and a host of lesser prizes. He attempted to plan a collective future for a new Italian cinema in the image of the French New Wave and to set up a series of initiatives and investments for the medium term: he built his own studios, he began a school for young, unknown actors whom he then placed under contract (including Claudia Cardinale, later his wife), he systematized the writing of scripts using the best screen-writers he could find. Vides also organized the first Italo–Soviet co-production—*La tenda rossa* ('The red curtain', 1969), by Mikhail Kalatozov. He followed each film closely through pre-production, filming, and post-production. Without Cristaldi, the panorama of modern Italian cinema would have been markedly poorer. When he died, one newspaper headed his obituary 'A producer and a gentleman'.

MORANDO MORANDINI

SELECT FILMOGRAPHY

As producer (with director)
Le notti bianche (Visconti, 1957); I soliti ignoti (Monicelli, 1958); Arrivano i titani (Tessari, 1961); L'assassino (Petri, 1961); Divorzio all'italiana (Germi, 1961); Salvatore Giuliano (Rosi, 1962); La ragazza di Bube (Comencini, 1963); I compagni (Monicelli, 1963); Sedotta e abbandonata (Germi, 1963); Vaghe stelle dell'Orsa (Visconti, 1964); Ruba al prossimo tuo (Maselli, 1968); La tenda rossa (Krasnaya palatka) (Kalatozov, 1969); Nel nome del padre (Bellocchio, 1971); Il caso Mattei (Rosi, 1972); Amarcord (Fellini, 1973); Lacombe Lucien (Malle, 1973); The Name of the Rose (Annaud, 1986); Nuovo cinema paradiso (Tornatore, 1988)

Claudia Cardinale with Renato Salvatori in Mario Monicelli's *I soliti ignoti* (*Persons Unknown*, 1958). Protégée and later wife of producer Franco Cristaldi, Cardinale went on to become a major star of the Italian cinema in the 1960s. After her divorce from Cristaldi her career stagnated for a while, but she recovered to give accomplished performances in Marco Bellocchio's *Enrico IV* (1983–from Pirandello) and Luigi Comencini's *La storia* (1984).

who most deserves consideration in the generally depressing panorama of Italian cinema of the late 1980s and early 1990s. Born in 1945, Amelio began his career working for RAI television in the 1970s. As a feature film director he came to public attention with *Colpire al cuore* ('To strike at the heart', 1982), one of the few and one of the best Italian films on the theme of terrorism. *Porte aperte* ('Open doors', 1990) dealt with the problems of justice in Sicily, but it was with *Il ladro di bambini* ('Child snatcher', 1992) that Amelio managed to adjust his refined and almost aristocratic idea of cinema to the needs of an emotional and painful story poised between sentiment and social concern and thereby to score a significant popular success.

At the end of 1992, at the instigation of the Turin International Youth Festival of Cinema, a survey of critics, journalists, and scholars was set up to identify 'five young directors for the year 2000'. Of the five winners to emerge, two—Bruno Bigoni and Silvio Soldini—live and work in Milan; a third, Daniel Segre, is based in Turin; and a

fourth, the highly rated young theatre director Mario Martone whose first film was *Morte di un matematico napoletano* ('Death of a Neapolitan mathematician', 1992), works in Naples. Only the Venetian Carlo Mazzacurati, who has directed three films, lives in Rome, the traditional home of the greater part of the film world. It may be that the rebirth of Italian cinema will come from precisely such a shift away from Rome and towards the decentralized variety with which it began.

Bibliography

Bondanella, Peter (1990), *Italian Cinema: from neorealism to the present*.

Brunetta, Gian Piero (1982), *Storia del cinema italiano. Vol II. Dal 1945 agli anni ottanta*.

—— (1991), *Cent'anni di cinema italiano*.

Faldini, Franca, and Fofi, Goffredo (1981), *L'avventurosa storia del cinema italiano raccontato dai suoi protagonisti, 1960–1969*.

—— (1984), *Il cinema italiano di oggi, 1970–1984: raccontato dai suoi protagonisti*.

Spain After Franco

MARSHA KINDER

Just as the Spanish Civil War of 1936–9 has frequently been called a rehearsal for the Second World War, so Spain's surprisingly rapid transition from Francoism to democracy can be seen as prefiguring the sudden collapse of the Cold War paradigm which followed in 1945. Spanish cinema played an important role in figuring Spain's move to democracy, not only after Franco's death in 1975, but in the years preceding it. From the 1950s onwards a hermetically sealed Spain began to be opened to foreign influence and a new Spanish cinema emerged on the world scene.

LOOSENING THE BONDS OF DICTATORSHIP

According to historian Stanley Payne (1987–8), Spain underwent a three-stage process of defascistization, which began when Franco realized that Hitler and Mussolini would lose the Second World War; was accelerated at the height of the Cold War (1945–57) when Spain began moving toward the new European democracies whose resurgence was partially financed by the US Marshall Plan; and was formalized in the 1960s through a policy of *aperturismo* ('opening up') that was actively promoted by Franco's new Minister of Information and Tourism, Manuel Fraga Iribarne. This drive toward liberalization contained a double irony. First, despite its overtures to foreign investors, the Francoist regime continued to impose a monolithic culture at home. This contradiction provided a focal point for film-makers who wanted to create a cinema of

opposition that could project a different image of Spain both at home and abroad. Yet equally ironically, these film-makers helped accomplish Franco's goals, especially when their films won prestigious awards at international festivals, demonstrating that a modernized Spain was now capable of generating (and tolerating) an articulate oppositional culture.

These contradictions were dramatized in *Bienvenido, Mr Marshall!* ('Welcome, Mr Marshall!', 1952), which was Spain's official entry at the Cannes Film Festival. This clever satire (co-written by Luis Berlanga and Juan Antonio Bardem) shows inhabitants of a small Castilian village competing with other Spaniards for their share of the Marshall Plan by dressing up as gypsies and matadors, complete with fake movie sets. This illusion evokes the *españolada*, a popular genre that promoted regional images of an exotic Andalusia as a cultural stereotype for all of Spain. The film exposes the dual address of every so-called 'national' cinema—a fictional unity imposed at home at the cost of cultural and regional difference in order to be successfully promoted abroad as a distinctive 'national' commodity. The villagers do have 'real' needs, the kind that were then being depicted in Italian neorealist films; yet they turn to Hollywood fantasies which get them only deeper in debt. In a series of humorous dreams, we see how they refigure their needs through foreign movie images they have internalized. The mayor dreams he is a sheriff in a saloon doing what cowboys typically do in Hollywood Westerns, but when the saloon's star singer reverts back to the *españolada*, he is left clinging to the old stereotype. A peasant dreams of a tractor being dropped from heaven by a plane. Although both vehicles carry a USA label, the style in which they are represented clearly comes from Soviet Socialist Realism. The film demonstrates how foreign conventions can be reinscribed through hybridization to forge a new filmic language that is capable of challenging the monolithic Francoist culture.

The opposition's critique of Francoist cinema was formalized in May 1955 at a four-day national congress in the university town of Salamanca. Like the meetings in Oberhausen that led to the Young German Cinema of the 1960s, these 'Salamanca Conversaciones' generated a harsh diatribe against the current state of cinema: 'After 60 years of films, Spanish cinema is politically ineffective, socially false, intellectually worthless, aesthetically non-existent, and industrially crippled.' Although written by Bardem (a member of the Spanish Communist Party), this judgement was widely shared by participants at the congress of all political persuasions, including José María García Escudero, the government's former undersecretary for cinema. Escudero had been forced to resign in 1952 for having denied the 'national interest' category to *Alba de América* (1951), a big-budget historical drama personally backed by Franco, while granting it to Spain's first neo-realist film *Surcos* ('Furrows', 1951), which was directed by former Falangist José Nieves Conde.

At Salamanca film-makers from both the left and the right looked to Italian neo-realism as a model, setting it in opposition to Hollywood conventions and using this dialectic to structure many of the key films of the period. In 1971 this dialectic was evoked by Basilio Martín Patino (one of the organizers of the Salamanca congress) in his subversive compilation film on popular memory, *Canciones para después de una guerra* ('Songs for after a war'). Patino includes a resonant image from De Sica's *Bicycle Thieves*, one of the neo-realist films shown in Madrid in 1951 during an Italian film week that deeply influenced Bardem and Berlanga. It shows the working-class protagonist hanging a movie poster featuring Rita Hayworth in *Gilda*, a glamorous image that distracts both him and the spectator away from the street where his bicycle is soon to be stolen. This image was emblematic of the choice facing Spanish film-makers in the 1950s: whether to emulate the neo-realist documentation of pressing socio-economic problems or to follow Hollywood's escape into spectacle, melodrama, and stardom.

Bardem's *Muerte de un ciclista* ('Death of a cyclist', 1955), one of the first Spanish films to win a major prize at an international festival, uses this dialectic between Italian neo-realism and Hollywood melodrama to express a political discourse that was otherwise repressed from representation. The film adopts the language of the classical Hollywood melodrama—its editing syntax, its strategies of binding the spectator to the text, its glossy surface, and its emphasis on glamorous close-ups to privilege the star. Yet it exaggerates these conventions to expose their ideological implications, especially their privileging of the bourgeoisie. Then it ruptures that style with neo-realist sequences whose deep-focus long shots reduce the size of the protagonist and reposition him within a broader context of class conflict.

The film opens with an off-screen collision between a car carrying an adulterous bourgeois couple and a bicycle ridden by a worker. It takes place on a desolate road that was formerly a battlefield in the Civil War, enabling both the present and past violence of this terrain to function as a structuring absence. Yet as soon as the film cuts to a close-up of the lovers in the car, the spectator is firmly positioned within the narrative vehicle of bourgeois melodrama and drawn into identification with the individualized killers rather than with their anonymous victim whose face and corpse we never see and who is left to die in the road. We see only the wheel of his broken bicycle spinning in the foreground, an image that evokes *Bicycle Thieves*.

This dialectic opposition between the two foreign aesthetics helped to forge the subtle, indirect language of the New Spanish Cinema, a term that García Escudero introduced in the 1960s when he was reappointed by Fraga as the new general director of cinema and when he would officially promote this art cinema abroad, claiming, 'a film is a flag.... We must have that flag unfurled.... If you can't beat Hollywood on its own ground [a commercial cinema], you can...on Europe's home ground: intelligence.' Yet to the film-makers of the opposition, the primary enemy was still the Francoist regime, which continued imposing censorship at home.

The film-maker who pushed hardest against the official censorship in the 1960s was Basque-born producer Elías Querejeta, who assembled a collaborative team which created a distinctive style of indirection that could subtly address political issues. His team included the brilliant cinematographer Luis Cuadrado, who was known for cultivating the 'blackness' of the great seventeenth-century Spanish masters like Murillo, Ribera, Zurbarán, and Velázquez; editor Pablo G. Del Amo, who developed an elliptical style that served a wide range of narrative functions; and composer Luis de Pablo, whose expressive, minimalist scores frequently suggested musically what could not be verbalized.

Querejeta's best-known works in the 1960s were directed by Carlos Saura, who soon became Spain's most respected international *auteur*. Adopting Buñuel as his model, Saura expanded the language of cinematic violence, which had been censored during the Francoist era along with politics, sex, and sacrilege. In *La caza* ('The

Drawing on traditional forms of Spanish culture, Carlos Saura's *Blood Wedding* (*Bodas de Sangre*, 1981) follows the rehearsals of a dance version of the Lorca play

hunt', 1965), the ritualized violence of the hunt substitutes for the Civil War and its reciprocal savagery. Although the hunt is a common trope in many cultures for narrativizing violence allegorically, it had special meaning in Spain, where it was a favourite pastime for Franco and his cohorts. Everything in *La caza*—its claustrophobic narrative, its spare landscapes, its emotional rhythms in dialogue and *mise-en-scène*, its percussive music and montage, its oppressive silences and ellipses, its interplay between extreme close-ups and long shots, and its blatant specularization of the violent gaze—moves inexorably toward the final explosive shoot-out and heightens its intensity once it comes. This powerful orchestration of violence had a major impact on American director Sam Peckinpah, who reportedly told Saura that seeing *La caza* changed his life; and in films like *The Wild Bunch* and *Straw Dogs*, Spanish modes of representing violence were culturally reinscribed.

In *Peppermint frappé* (1967), a psychological thriller dedicated to Buñuel, Saura exposes the legacy of brutality that lay hidden beneath the surface beauty of the Fascist and neo-Catholic aesthetics. We see little violence on screen. Instead we see how objects are fetishized in the dual con-

texts of orthodox Catholicism and post-modern consumer capitalism with their clashing discourses of repression and liberation—a combination that drives both Spain and its repressed protagonist Julian to psychopathic excesses. Like the poisonous drink named in the title and the modern image of Spain then being promoted by Franco's technocrats, the surface of this lushly coloured melodrama is pleasurable to the gaze but its deep structure proves deadly.

The early 1970s were known as the *dictablanda*, those five or six years of soft dictatorship that immediately preceded Franco's death, a period when Spanish artists were making new inroads against government censorship and when the New Spanish Cinema enjoyed some of its biggest successes world-wide.

Victor Erice's *The Spirit of the Beehive* (*El espíritu de la colmena*, 1973) is structured around a child's reinscription of images she has seen in James Whale's 1931 version of *Frankenstein*. She uses them to deal with the painful experiences in her own Spanish context (a small rural village in Castile shortly after the end of the Civil War), especially her interactions with a republican fugitive who is captured and murdered by local authorities and with

Lola Gaos as the devouring mother Martina finally rejected by her son in José Borau's *Poachers* (*Furtivos*, 1975)

her father who is suffering from a state of inner exile. The film implies that the children of Franco would turn out to be the children of Frankenstein—precocious yet emotionally stunted by historical traumas that could still not be directly represented on screen. The opening sequence details, with an almost ethnographic interest, the cultural specificity of the distribution and exhibition of a Hollywood import—revealing the evocative power of the foreign cinematic image for a culture that had been forced into hermetic isolation. In Erice's film it is the *process* of cultural reinscription that is emphasized more than the particular conventions being reinscribed—a process that relies heavily on elliptical editing, sound–image relations, and cultural and historical reverberations.

A different approach to reinscription was pursued by director-producer José Luis Borau in *Furtivos* ('Poachers', 1975), which he co-wrote with Manuel Gutiérrez Aragón. Opening in Madrid two months before the death of Franco, it was the first film to be exhibited in Spain without a licence from the censors, which helped it become one of the top-grossing Spanish films up to that time.

Furtivos exposes the harsh reality that lay beneath Franco's false description of Spain as 'a peaceful forest'. In depicting extreme acts of treachery, incest, and murder, the film dramatizes the chain of brutalization that passes from authority to subject, hunter to prey, and parent to child. All the main characters are both emotionally stunted adults and victimized children, including the civil governor evoking Franco (who is played by Borau himself) and the infantilized protagonist Ángel who is trying to break an incestuous bond with his mother. Borau claims the germinal idea for the film was the actress Lola Gaos, who played Saturna in Buñuel's *Tristana*: 'Like Saturn devouring his son in the painting by Goya ... Saturna is devouring her son in a forest. That was the origin.'

Despite the deeply Spanish specificity of the film's sources and thematics, Borau adopts the stylistic conventions of the Hollywood action film—its transparency, linearity, pacing, and economical editing. This combination is especially effective in the powerful sequence where Ángel literally throws his mother out of her bed so that he can sleep with his new bride. There is a direct cut from the young lovers in bed to the displaced mother Martina, seated at a table drinking and crying and then restlessly pacing the room as if seeking some way to vent her rage. The sound-track combines the wind with the cries of a she-wolf chained outside. These cries express Martina's pain and also reveal the target on whom it will be displaced. When the film cuts to a long shot of Martina entering the cave-like site where the wolf is restlessly pacing, we know what is going to happen. Yet we are still shocked by the brutality of the beating and by the matched close-ups of the dying beast and of Martina's face. This matching helps us foresee that the she-wolf functions as a surrogate not only for Ángel's bride (whom Martina will later murder) but also for Martina herself (who will share a similar fate at the hands of her son). From the extreme brutality of this wordless action sequence, the film cuts directly to a long shot of a beautiful pastel landscape, the false image of Franco's 'peaceful forest' whose deceptiveness has been exposed through purely cinematic means.

FREEDOM, CRISIS, AND TRANSGRESSION

In 1978 (only three years after Franco's death) Spain had a parliamentary democracy which restructured the nation into seventeen Autonomous Communities (*Comunidades Autonómicas*). This dramatic decentralization was more effectively refigured on television than in cinema, partly because of the immediacy and dailiness of the broadcast medium and partly because of changing economic con-

Pedro Almodóvar directs Victoria Abril in *High Heels* (*Tacones lejanos*, 1991), one of his parodic melodramas that helped make her an international star

ditions. At the same time that Spanish film production was sharply declining, there was an equally dramatic growth in Spanish television which occurred both at the microregional level (with seven new regional networks broadcasting in regional languages and being run by provincial governments) and at the macroregional level (with three new private networks at least partially controlled and financed by outside European interests). As multinational corporations strove to enter this market, advertising sales for Spanish television during the 1980s increased sevenfold, a faster rate of growth than for any other nation during that period. This increase contributed to a sharp decline in cinema-going (from 331 million spectators in 1970 to 101 million in 1985) as well as to an alarming decrease in the number of cinemas. To make matters worse, foreign films were gaining a greater share of the shrinking market. By 1985 Spanish films held only 17.5 per cent of the home market as opposed to 30 per cent in 1970, and by the end of the decade that figure was down to 10 per cent. Film-makers from all regions in Spain had to cope with this dire financial crisis, which now seemed more threatening to Catalan and Basque directors than Castilian domination, especially since expression of their regional language and culture was no longer legally banned. As Berlanga observed in 1983, 'Instead of the political and ideological censorship that we used to have we are now feeling the effects of what one might call economic censorship.'

In 1982 the incoming Socialist government under Felipe González appointed film-maker Pilar Miró general director of cinema, as if to signal the beginning of a new socialist era of total artistic freedom, and she immediately set out to solve the crisis. Despite the 1977 law ending censorship, in 1980 her controversial film *El crimen de Cuenca* had been confiscated by the police because of its negative depiction of the Guardia Civil. When the film was finally released in 1981, like *Furtivos* it broke Spanish box-office records. By 1983 she realized that few Spanish films could expect to survive in the home market, so she introduced a new law that protected Spanish films against foreign imports and substantially increased government subsidy. Yet Spanish film production continued to plummet (reaching a new all-time low of forty-seven films in 1989); the only increases were in production costs and government expenditures. Miró's critics attacked her for encouraging 'self-indulgent' artists to ignore the realities of the market-place and the changing tastes of Spanish audiences.

It was time for a change, and this was provided by Pedro Almodóvar, who claimed:

My films represent ... the new mentality that appears in Spain after Franco dies—especially after 1977. ... Everybody has heard that now everything is different in Spain ... but it is not so easy to find this change in the Spanish cinema. . . . In my films they see how Spain has changed … because now it is possible to do … a film like *Law of Desire*.

When *Law of Desire* (*La ley del deseo*, 1986) received critical raves at the 1987 Berlin festival and did well commercially in foreign markets, the Socialist government used it to promote Spain's culture industry—a strategy that was similar to Franco's earlier use of oppositional figures like Saura and Querejeta. Despite the film's homo-erotic sex scenes and its backstory of homosexual incest, *Fotogramas y video* (Spain's oldest and largest circulation film journal) heralded it as a model for Spain's cinema of the future, one that could arouse interest abroad 'not only at the level of … cultural curiosity but as an exportable and commercially valid product'. Yet Almodóvar's success was based on risk-taking. By watching his erotic cinematic hybrids, spectators risk having their own future refigured and their sexuality destabilized and reinscribed, which is precisely what happens to the Antonio Banderas character after watching the inset homo-erotic porn at the opening of *Law of Desire*. Almodóvar soon succeeded in establishing an outrageous protean sexuality (in place of the *españolada*) as the new cultural stereotype for a super-liberated post-Franco Spain. Thus he subverted the centre by redefining it as the marginal, and ironically this inversion helped to demarginalize Spanish cinema in the world market. In fact, in 1991 *Variety* reported that six of Spain's all-time top thirteen exports to the USA were directed by Almodóvar.

This global success was to become even more crucial in the 1990s as Spain moved toward convergence with other members of the European Community. In contrast to 1983, when González was eager to demonstrate Spain's ideological transformation and therefore supported the Miró decree, in 1992 he was more interested in demonstrating fiscal responsibility to his European peers so that Spain could meet the economic criteria established at Maastricht in December 1991. Given the increasing pressure to stop subsidizing industries that were losing money, the crucial question was whether the film and television industries should be exempt since they manufacture unique cultural products that construct images of national identity for world consumption.

In June 1992 Spanish film-makers held a three-day conference in Madrid called Audiovisual Español 93. Participants urged the government to pass a new law to protect Spanish cinema from Hollywood domination and from the 'Euro-pudding' co-productions of the EC that threatened to erase the cultural specificity of Spain and its autonomous regions. Like the Salamanca congress, it ended with a dire pronouncement, this time by conference president Román Gubern, who warned that, without government protection, 'in 1995, instead of celebrating the centennial of Spanish cinema, we will celebrate its funeral'. The exclusion of film and television from the 1993 General Agreement on Tariffs and Trade (GATT) made such protection possible by acknowledging the unique status of these industries.

Despite Gubern's dire prophecy, in the early 1990s Spain has already had three major triumphs in the North American market that were not directed by Almodóvar, even though he helped pave the way for their success: Vicente Aranda's *Amantes* ('Lovers', 1990), Bigas Luna's *Jamón Jamón* ('Ham, ham', 1991), and Fernando Trueba's *Belle Époque* (1992). All three were directed by film-makers who are highly regarded in Spain but hardly known abroad. All three attempt to associate the post-Franco stereotype of a super-liberated Spain with the oppositional culture of an earlier era. All three mine the subversive potential of melodramatic excess, a tradition that can be traced back to Buñuel's surrealistic classic *Un chien andalou* in the 1920s and was mainstreamed by Almodóvar in the 1980s. While remaining within a predominantly heterosexual discourse, all three are driven by female desire.

Amantes exposes the subversive power of female sexuality that lies at the core of film noir, a post-Second World War genre with a strong international heritage. Based on an actual murder which took place in Spain during the repressive 1950s, *Amantes* demonstrates that *cine negro español* can make an important contribution to the genre. As played by Victoria Abril (who, despite her long collaboration with Aranda, first became an international star in Almodóvar's *Tie Me up! Tie Me down!* (*Átame!*, 1989)), Luisa is a *femme fatale* who not only seduces the young hero and actively pursues her own desire but who also controls every aspect of their love-making. The extraordinary explicitness of the sex scenes helps reveal why the fear of female sexuality is the structuring absence of the genre.

Jamón Jamón seems to question whether the effects of Spain's historic shift to democracy and post-modern consumerism is really as liberating as advertised. The substitution of erotic images for the Andalusian stereotype is overseen by a businessman played by Juan Diego, the actor who first represented Franco on screen in a fictional film (Jaime Camino's *Dragón Rapide*, 1986). In the opening shot we see a desolate Spanish plain through the silhouette of one of those gigantic black bulls advertising Osborn brandy, a composition dominated by the beast's huge testicles which are cracked and creaking. This traditional sign of Spanish machismo is later rivalled by an equally giant post-Franco billboard with a crotch shot of Samson-brand briefs, which Manuel's family firm has manufactured for three generations. Yet this parodic fast-paced melodrama and its hyperplotted narrative are driven by female desire, a gender reversal that is introduced in the comical scene where Manuel's wife literally selects the *cojones* for the jockey-shorts billboard from a line-up of desirable young studs. In a culturally over-determined

Manoel de Oliveira
(1908–)

Manoel Candido Pinto de Oliveira was born in Oporto, the second city in Portugal, to a well-off bourgeois family. The eldest son, he was educated by the Jesuits who, chased from Portugal by the republican, anti-clerical revolution, had opened a school at La Guardia across the border in Spain.

As a youth Oliveira excelled at sports, was a fanatic for 'flying machines', and was a motor racing champion in Portugal and abroad. The cinema fascinated him as a sign of a new age; André Deed, the Italian divas, Max Linder, American serials, and Chaplin all captivated him. He was inspired to make films himself after seeing Walter Ruttmann's *Berlin: Symphony of a City* (1927). He took drama lessons from the Italian Rino Lupo, acted in one of his films, *Fatima Miraculosa* (1927), and posed, back naked, for cinema magazines. His career thus developed along a very different path from the other Portuguese film-makers of his generation who caused the first 'revolution' in Portuguese cinema (in the late 1920s and early 1930s), and who came from theatre and journalism.

Despite this erratic start, Oliveira stunned European critics in 1931 with his first film, the city symphony *Douro, faina fluvial* ('Douro, work on the river'), a remarkable exercise in montage, similar to avant-garde works of the period of which he was unaware. He acted in *A canção de Lisboa* ('Lisbon song', Cottinelli Telmo, 1933), the first sound film completely shot in Portugal, and during the 1930s he continued to write scripts, but without backing only made commissioned works (now all lost). Mean-

while Oliviera developed links with Portuguese intellectuals who had liked *Douro*, and when he finally came to make his first full-length film, *Aniki Bóbó* (1942), it expressed a metaphysical and aesthetic concern strikingly different from the populist and conventional Portuguese cinema of the time. After the war, *Aniki Bóbó* was shown in Europe and critics were surprised by its similarities to Italian neo-realism (particularly in its use of natural settings and untrained child actors).

Oliveira's ambitions seemed to end there, and he considered abandoning the cinema for good to take over his father's textile factories. But artistic worries gnawed at him constantly and he returned to the cinema in 1956 with the short film *O pintor e a cidade* ('The painter and the city'). By now, however, it was no longer editing that interested Oliveira but the links between cinema and theatre, and the ability of film to present 'all of the real'. He started to use long takes, and give careful attention to theatrical texts and actors' words. *Acto da primavera* ('Act of spring', 1960) and *A Caça* ('The hunt'), released in 1963, anticipate what Pasolini later defined as 'cinema-poetry'. If his documentaries of the late 1930s, 1940s, and 1950s were fictions, they were fictions which became documentaries.

However, it was only when Oliveira was in his sixties that he began an unbroken film career, with his 'tetralogy of unrequited love' between 1971 and 1981. 'The cinema,' he claimed, 'does not exist. Theatre exists. Cinema is a way of capturing it.' He adapted Claudel's *Le Soulier de satin* in a seven-hour film that won the Golden Lion at the Venice film Festival in 1985. He questioned the role of the creative artist and of cinema in *Mon Cas* (1986). In *A divina comédia* ('The Divine Comedy', 1991) he attacked the cen-

tral mysteries of the human condition. In *Não, ou a vã gloria de mandar* ('No, or the commander's vainglory', 1990) he gave his own view of the history of Portugal. He reinterpreted bovaryism in *Val Abraham* (1992), and he analysed human microcosms in *A caixa* ('The box', 1994).

Oliveira has become the public image of Portuguese cinema, showered with honours in Europe, Japan, and America. But in Portugal he is a lonely figure, spurned by a public which finds his films too difficult. Indifferent to popular acclaim, he defends the aristocracy of the art of cinema in the age of the 'audio-visual'.

The amazing paradox of his career, which started with silent films and culminated after his eightieth birthday, comes from the way he re-thought cinema. He has never strayed from the experimental side which was already obvious in *Douro*, but his pursuits have outstripped formal research, to become questions about the very nature of cinematic art or about art itself. Sometimes he makes films with ten-minute takes (*Le Soulier de satin*) and sometimes he cuts by the millimetre (*The Divine Comedy*). There are sweeping shots such as only appear in the classics (the opening of *Não*, the end of *Val Abraham*), then he inserts the most minimal, the most stripped of experiences (*O dia do desespero* ('Day of despair', 1992), *A caixa*). Some works echo great themes (History, Love, Death), in others the scenario is reduced to a few essential lines. Sometimes he appears a profound metaphysician, at others he appears to mock totalizing visions.

A film-maker of profound intellect, he is both the last of the great early film-makers (he can be compared to Dreyer and Ford) and one of the paradigmatic representatives of modern cinema. For him, the world which represents itself is the world which presents itself, a world haunted by the dream of an initial and ultimate unity. And, if he has built an unmistakable style (an Oliveira film is recognizable in every shot), he has not become fixed in one theory or theme. Each film seems to question everything we thought we knew about him.

JOÃO BÉNARD DA COSTA

SELECT FILMOGRAPHY

Douro, faina fluvial (1931); Aniki Bóbó (1942); O pintor e a cidade (1956); Acto da primavera (1960); A caça (1963); O passado e o presente (1971): Benilde ou a virgem mãe (1975); Francisca (1981); Le Soulier de satin (1985); Mon Cas (1986); Os canibais (1988); Não ou a vã gloria de mandar (1990); A divina comédia (1991); Val Abraham (1992); A caixa (1994).

BIBLIOGRAPHY

Bénard da Costa, João (ed.) (1981), *Manoel de Oliveira*.
—— (1988), *Manoel de Oliveira: Alguns projectos não realizados e outros textos* (Manoel de Oliveira: some unrealized projects and other texts).
Lardeau, Yann, Tancelin, Philippe, and Parsi, Jacques (1988), *Manoel de Oliveira*.
Wakeman, John (1987), 'Manoel de Oliveira' in *World Film Directors, i (1890–1945)*.

Opposite: A scene from Oliveira's first feature, the internationally acclaimed *Aniki Bóbó* (1942), shot in the slums of Oporto.

choice, she picks those that belong to a young would-be bullfighter named González who delivers salamis for the Hernán Cortés 'Los Conquistadores' meat company. Like the billboards, this film's sexy images are clearly addressed to the erotic tastes of both genders. Bigas Luna's films are as excessive as Almodóvar's, yet they are usually populated not by emancipated lovers but (as in Saura's *Peppermint frappé*) by emotionally stunted characters whose sexuality turns pathological in a consumerist context. His films suggest that the post-Franco images of a super-liberated Spain may be as bogus as the Francoist *españoladas*.

In contrast, Fernando Trueba's *Belle Époque* shows that this so-called 'new liberated mentality' has historic roots in Spain's pre-Civil War era, a period he recovers as a utopian fantasy for the same global audience that made Almodóvar a star. The film is bracketed by two suicides that are committed by figures whose culturally specific meanings will probably be understood only by Spanish spectators (a Guardia Civil with anarchistic tendencies and a Catholic priest devoted to the philosophy of Unamuno), yet the transgressive comedy at its centre helped it beat China's *Farewell my Concubine* for best foreign film at the 1994 Academy Awards. However, the film is not so transgressive as it appears, for in its most carnivalesque scene (where the beautiful lesbian sister in military drag seduces the hero who is convincingly dressed as a maid), cross-dressing is repositioned within heterosexual bounds. When Trueba accepted his Oscar, his humorous speech reaffirmed this radical posture. After apologizing for being an atheist who was incapable of thanking God, he thanked Billy Wilder instead, the very film-maker whom Almodóvar always acknowledges as his most important influence. Like Almodóvar, Wilder is another European who made good in Hollywood both in gender-bending comedies like *Some Like It Hot* and in classic reflexive noirs like *Double Indemnity* and *Sunset Boulevard*. This is precisely the terrain now being explored by a super-liberated Spanish cinema which is ardently pursuing that obscure object of global desire.

Bibliography

D'Lugo, Marvin (1991), *Carlos Saura: The Practice of Seeing*.
Hopewell, John (1986), *Out of the Past: Spanish Cinema after Franco*.
Kinder, Marsha (1987), 'Pleasure and the New Spanish Mentality: A Conversation with Pedro Almodóvar'.
—— (1993), *Blood Cinema: The Reconstruction of National Identity in Spain*.
Kovács, Katherine S. (1983), 'Berlanga Life Size: An Interview with Luis García Berlanga'.
Maxwell, Richard (1994), *The Spectacle of Democracy: Spanish Television, Nationalism and Political Transition*.
Payne, Stanley (1987–8), 'Spanish Fascism'.
Smith, Paul Julian (1992), *Laws of Desire: Questions of Homosexuality in Spanish Writing and Film, 1960–1990*.

British Cinema: The Search for Identity

DUNCAN PETRIE

The history of British cinema has always been at best an uneven one, marked by cycles of confidence and expansion followed by decline and stagnation. The period from 1960 saw similar fluctuations but with one crucial difference: by the early 1990s it was possible to argue that the British cinema, as an entity rooted in a particular industrial infrastructure producing a certain critical mass of audio-visual fictions for exhibition in cinemas, no longer existed. Films continued to be made but most were primarily for a television audience, with perhaps a brief theatrical 'window' as a kind of showcase, and the films that were most self-consciously 'English' were predominantly made with American money and for the American market. This period, then, marks a process of fundamental transition or terminal decline, depending on your view of what cinema is or ought to be. It begins in the middle of a boom, but one which already marked a shift on the part of certain British producers to establish a degree of independence from the dominant structures of the industry. Such 'independence' would achieve even greater significance in the 1980s, but by then the industry itself had changed irrevocably.

FROM FREE CINEMA TO 'NEW WAVE'

The dawning of the 1960s coincided with a period of invigoration in the British cinema after what many had regarded as the inert complacency of the previous decade. The British 'New Wave', with its focus on contemporary working-class experience, grew out of 'Free Cinema', a movement of oppositional film-makers and critics like Lindsay Anderson, Karel Reisz, and Tony Richardson, committed to shaking up moribund British film culture. These film-makers had produced influential documentaries in the late 1950s, such as *Momma Don't Allow* (Richardson, 1956), *Every Day except Christmas* (Anderson, 1957), and *We Are the Lambeth Boys* (Reisz, 1959), on subjects such as the emerging youth culture and more traditional aspects of working-class life. Their ambitions to graduate into features required both appropriate subjects and sources of finance.

As so often in British cinema history, the inspiration for these film-makers was provided by literature and the theatre. This came in the shape of the works of the 'Angry Young Men': frank and uncompromising slices of 'real life' served up by young writers John Braine, Alan Sillitoe, John Osborne, and others. Their collective disenchantment with the smugness and false promises of post-war British society struck an ideological chord with the proponents of Free Cinema. In 1959 Tony Richardson and John Osborne

came together to form Woodfall Films with American impresario Harry Saltzman, which led to screen versions of Osborne's plays; *Look back in Anger* (1959), with Richard Burton, and *The Entertainer* (1960), with Laurence Olivier, both of which Richardson had previously directed at the Royal Court.

Woodfall was supported by another independent, Bryanston Films, chaired by industry stalwart Michael Balcon, which enabled them to release their films through British Lion. The bridgehead established, Richardson's Free Cinema colleagues followed him into features, often with the collaboration of the authors and playwrights whose works inspired them. Karel Reisz made his highly successful adaptation of Alan Sillitoe's *Saturday Night and Sunday Morning* (1960), perhaps the most accomplished of the northern working-class 'young man on the make' scenarios due largely to the central performance of Albert Finney. Lindsay Anderson contributed the raw and brutal *This Sporting Life* (1963), adapted by David Storey from his own novel. However, Richardson continued to be the most prolific of the group, collaborating with Shelagh Delaney (the only woman in the 'Angry' coterie) on *A Taste of Honey* (1961) and with Sillitoe on *The Loneliness of the Long Distance Runner* (1962).

Allied Film Makers, a new independent company formed by Bryan Forbes and Richard Attenborough, also emerged under the British Lion umbrella. The company produced several films including *Whistle down the Wind* (Forbes, 1961) and *The L-Shaped Room* (Forbes, 1964), a rare example in the genre of a contemporary subject featuring a young woman's experiences in London's bedsit land. Outside the aegis of Woodfall and British Lion other notable contributors to the British 'New Wave' included John Schlesinger, another former documentarist, who directed *A Kind of Loving* (1962) and *Billy Liar* (1963). The latter shared the working-class, urban milieu of the genre, but deflected its characteristic anger and desperation into comedy, centred around an undertaker's clerk who lives in a world of fantasy.

Collectively these films constituted the latest manifestation of a progressive realist aesthetic in British cinema, dating back to Grierson's 'documentary ideal' which involved a gradual extension of the cinematic franchise to include realistic representations of the lower orders in society. And while many can be criticized for their overt sexism and machismo, the New Wave films did mark a certain aesthetic evolution in British cinema, from the initial largely studio-based productions of *Room at the Top* and *Look back in Anger*, to the freer *cinéma-vérité* style of

Rita Tushingham, Robert Stephens, Murray Melvin, and Dora Bryan in Tony Richardson's *A Taste of Honey* (1961)

A Taste of Honey and *The Loneliness of the Long Distance Runner*. Aided by technical developments such as lightweight portable cameras and faster film stock Richardson and his cinematographer Walter Lassally were able to make extensive use of real urban locations—northern industrial landscapes in Manchester and Salford—integrating them as a central feature in the drama as the film-makers of the French 'Nouvelle Vague' had begun to do with the streets of Paris.

These films also marked the emergence of a new breed of British actor: a tough, street-wise, and instinctive performer, whose acting style owed more to Brando and Dean than to Olivier and Guinness. The 'authenticity' of the likes of Albert Finney, Tom Courtenay, and Rita Tushingham also helped to give the New Wave films a class-conscious edge which had previously been lacking.

COMMERCIAL SUCCESS AND AMERICAN FINANCE

The New Wave represented an extremely dynamic, but short-lived, period of film-making. By 1963 it was eclipsed by the phenomenon of 'Swinging London', and an upsurge in international interest in British culture. In that year Richardson directed his first colour film: an adaptation of Henry Fielding's eighteenth-century picaresque novel *Tom Jones*, with Albert Finney as the bawdy fun-loving hero. Despite its period setting the production was thoroughly modern in style, with Lassally's freewheeling cinematography matched by Richardson's formal trickery: the varying speeds, jump cutting, and direct address to camera, inspired by the early work of Godard. Corresponding to the prevailing *Zeitgeist* with devastating accuracy, *Tom Jones* was a huge commercial success, helping to establish a new phase of 1960s British cinema which shifted the focus away from provincial life and back to the metropolis, and was fuelled less by anger and frustration than by a celebration of new freedoms and social possibilities. The excitement surrounding this new ethos, establishing London as the international focus of fashion and the new youth culture, attracted a surge of American finance into British cinema which was to under-

Joseph Losey
(1909–1984)

Joseph Losey was born in La Crosse, Wisconsin, and grew up in the poorer branch of a wealthy and cultured family, comprised mostly of lawyers. After taking a Master's degree at Harvard's theatre programme, he moved to New York City in the early 1930s and supported himself with work as a freelance critic.

A trip in 1935 to the Soviet Union brought Losey into contact with Soviet theatre, which would profoundly influence his own work for the stage and screen. During the Depression in New York, he created a series of political and pedagogical theatrical projects, including an anti-Fascist cabaret, and the 'Living Newspaper', which explained topical political issues to workers. Losey also organized elaborate spectacles that combined mime and voice-over to benefit war relief organizations, as well as producing and directing ninety politically-oriented shows for the radio.

Losey's first films were produced for various foundations and government agencies, and he also made training films during his brief military service. In 1945 Losey moved to Hollywood. Under contract to MGM but inactive, he returned to theatre, and, with Brecht's aid, directed an acclaimed production of *Life of Galileo* starring Charles Laughton.

Eventually released from his MGM contract without ever having made a feature film, Losey moved to RKO, where he made *The Boy with Green Hair* (1948), a powerful anti-McCarthy allegory about the irrational fear of a boy whose hair has suddenly turned green. Losey went on to make a series of low-budget black and white quickies (*The Lawless*, 1950, and *The Prowler*, *M*, *The Big Night*, all 1951), in which he first developed the stylistic traits which would mark his subsequent films. Visual stylization, long takes, and complex camera movements make these films rich and intensely dramatic.

In 1952 while in Italy filming *Imbarco a mezzanotte* (*Stranger on the Prowl*, 1952), Losey found he had been named as a Communist and subpoenaed to testify before the House Un-American Activities Committee. Rather than return to a likely gaol sentence and subsequent blacklisting, he moved to England. There he continued to make films on low budgets for little pay, at first working under pseudonyms due to the long arm of Hollywood's blacklisting. Winning a professional alliance and friendship with the highly successful actor Dirk Bogarde permitted Losey to make *The Sleeping Tiger* (1954), and that film plus *The Intimate Stranger* (1956) were successful enough to win Losey continued work in the commercial industry. His crime films of the late 1950s—*Time without Pity* (1957), *Blind Date* (1959), and *The Criminal* (1960)—were acclaimed in France, but not on the whole in Britain until the magazine *Movie* took up the cudgels on his behalf in 1962.

In 1963 Losey began a collaboration with British playwright Harold Pinter which produced three films—*The Servant* (1963), *Accident* (1967), and *The Go-Between* (1971). These films, which combine his trenchant and stylized social critique with Pinter's feeling for subtle power struggles, finally established Losey's critical reputation, and remain among his best works. Losey's leftist political sensibilities led him to a deep and abiding interest in the workings of the British class system, and it was a subject he turned to repeatedly up until his death in 1984.

Throughout his career Losey worked against budgetary and institutional constraints, but made films which retained a political and pedagogical character: *The Boy with Green Hair*, *The Damned* (1962), and *King & Country* (1964) speak out against war; *The Lawless* against

racism; *Time without Pity* and *Blind Date* against the judicial system and the death penalty. More generally, Losey's films present acute analyses of the destructiveness of institutions, whether prisons, bourgeois marriage, or social class. In films like *Eve* (1962) and *The Servant*, self-deluded characters in a position of social superiority find themselves manipulated and victimized by social inferiors with a greater understanding of the intricacies of rank and power.

Losey's films display an intense visual stylization, where architecture expresses the power relations between the characters. Losey shot almost exclusively on location, whether in pre-existing buildings like the villas of Palladio in *Don Giovanni* (1979) or in sets constructed on location. He was aided by a close collaboration first with John Hubley and later with Richard MacDonald. With these artists, Losey worked out all the visual details of the film, from architecture to set dressing and props, before shooting started. The style of each film was often organized around a key visual influence: *The Lawless* was patterned after the photographs of Paul Strand and Walker Evans, *The Gypsy and the Gentleman* (1958) after Rowlandson prints, *Time without Pity* after Goya, *Modesty Blaise* (1966) after pop art, *Accident* after pointillism. This 'pre-designing' assured visual consistency while allowing the actors and the camera operator great latitude in their work, thus combining aspects of constriction and liberty which were also thematically central for Losey.

In his later films, where he functioned with less studio interference, the visual density of his films seems to blunt Losey's didactic and pedagogical tendencies, producing images that are rich but enigmatic. This visual ambiguity is heightened by use of apparently autonomous insert shots which can be interpreted either as flashbacks or as flashforwards, as in *Accident*, *The Go-Between* (1970), and *Mr. Klein* (1976).

The formal orderliness of Losey's films mirrors the oppressiveness of the social order he depicts. The tension between social constriction and dangerous emotional freedom represented in Losey's films is closely linked with his own experience as an outsider; an independent film-maker struggling against the limitations of commercial cinema to express his political conscience and his social analysis in images of immense beauty.

EDWARD R. O'NEILL

SELECT FILMOGRAPHY

The Boy with Green Hair (1948); The Prowler (1951); M (1951); Time without Pity (1957); Blind Date (1959); Eve (1962); The Servant (1963); King & Country (1964); Modesty Blaise (1966); Accident (1967); Boom! (1968); Secret Ceremony (1968); The Go-Between (1971); Mr. Klein (1976); Don Giovanni (1979).

BIBLIOGRAPHY

Ciment, Michael (1985), *Conversations with Losey*.
Milne, Tom (ed.) (1968), *Losey on Losey*.

Opposite: James Fox with Dirk Bogarde as the sinister manservant in Joseph Losey's *The Servant* (1963)

pin the bulk of production during the rest of the decade.

Tom Jones was backed by United Artists, and following its success a host of American studios began investing in British cinema, ensuring a buoyancy of production. This interest was on such a scale that, as Dickinson and Street (1985) put it: 'after 1961 it became increasingly difficult to define any part of the industry as British rather than Anglo-American.' At around the same time UA also financed two other films whose success heralded a new era in British cinema. *A Hard Day's Night* (1963), directed by the American Richard Lester, was a semi-fictional vehicle starring the new British pop sensation, the Beatles, whose irrepressible energy and youthful irreverence leapt off the screen in what today is clearly a feature-length prototype for the ubiquitous pop promo. Meanwhile, Harry Saltzman (who had quit Woodfall in 1961) and his new partner Albert 'Cubby' Broccoli secured backing from UA for a modestly budgeted adaptation of Ian Fleming's thriller *Dr No* (Terence Young, 1962). The subsequent popularity of this film—due in no small way to the unlikely, but inspired, decision to cast a relatively unknown Scottish actor, Sean Connery, as Fleming's suave English agent James Bond—inaugurated one of the most commercially successful series in British cinema history. Connery repeated his role in *From Russia with Love* (1963), *Goldfinger* (1964), *Thunderball* (1965), *You only Live Twice* (1967), and *Diamonds are Forever* (1971). However, by the early 1970s he was keen to develop his career in other directions and abandoned the part. After an unsuccessful attempt to replace him with George Lazenby in *On Her Majesty's Secret Service* (1969), Roger Moore assumed the role of Bond in 1973 with *Live and Let Die*, retaining it for the next fourteen years before handing it over to Timothy Dalton. After two James Bond films (including *The Living Daylights*, 1987) Dalton also relinquished the role in turn, handing over in 1994 to Hollywood-based Irish actor, Pierce Brosnan.

Alongside the early Bond movies other cinematic series continued to thrive. Screen comedy in the 1960s was dominated by the 'Carry On' cycle of films (produced by Peter Rogers and directed by Gerald Thomas), which had been sparked off by the unexpected success of *Carry on Sergeant* (1958), an affectionate send-up of National Service. The early 'Carry Ons' tended to revolve around British institutions such as hospitals (*Carry on Nurse*, 1959); schools (*Carry on Teacher*, 1959); and the police (*Carry on Constable*, 1960), but as the series developed it began to favour the generic parody of *Carry on Spying* (1964), *Carry on Cleo* (1964), *Carry on Cowboy* (1966), and *Carry on ... up the Khyber* (1968). All shared a comforting, and hugely popular, familiarity and owed a great deal to liberal doses of slapstick, farce, and innuendo. The series ran until 1978 by which time a total of twenty-nine films had been made. (A thirtieth, *Carry on Columbus*, was made in 1992, as a nostalgic revival.)

The British horror genre was similarly healthy, dominated by Hammer Films, whose output earned the studio a Queen's Award for Industry in 1967. The bulk of their films continued to be directed by either Terence Fisher or Freddie Francis although subsequent directors such as John Gilling (*Plague of the Zombies*, 1965) and Peter Sasdy (*Taste the Blood of Dracula*, 1970) did attempt to modify the Hammer formula. The genre also produced one of British cinema's most promising young talents, Michael Reeves. He died tragically of a drug overdose after directing just three films, including the impressive *Witchfinder General* (1968), starring the ubiquitous Vincent Price.

The trend towards youthful exuberance continued through the mid-1960s. Lester followed *A Hard Day's Night* with *Help!* (1965), also starring the Beatles, this time within the semblance of a fictional narrative, while John Boorman made his début with *Catch us If You Can* (1965), featuring the Dave Clark 5. Many of the 'Swinging London' films appeared to function loosely as sequels to the New Wave cycle—their protagonists representing reincarnations of characters who had been desperate to escape the boredom of provincial life and were now sampling the delights and excitements of modern metropolitan life. This was compounded by the fact that they often featured the same performers: Rita Tushingham in *The Knack* (Richard Lester, 1965), Julie Christie who had appeared as an ambitious teenager in *Billy Liar* was John Schlesinger's *Darling* (1965), while in *Charlie Bubbles* (1966) Albert Finney played a successful metropolitan writer returning to his roots in Manchester. Meanwhile, new talent emerged on the British screens, more appropriate to the slick city feel of the 'Swinging London' era. *Alfie* (Lewis Gilbert, 1966) introduced Michael Caine as a working-class cockney Lothario, and Caine went on to consolidate his popularity with three appearances as secret agent Harry Palmer, a rather dowdy bespectacled anti-Bond character, in adaptations of Len Deighton's novels: *The Ipcress File* (Sidney Furie, 1965), *Funeral in Berlin* (Guy Hamilton, 1967), and *Billion Dollar Brain* (Ken Russell, 1967).

Alongside the newcomers, certain more established figures made their contributions to the life of 1960s British cinema. Funded by an American studio (Columbia), David Lean directed the international epics *Lawrence of Arabia* (1962) and *Doctor Zhivago* (1965), while Carol Reed enjoyed a swan-song with the Oscar-winning musical *Oliver!* (1968). Meanwhile, many foreign directors of stature were also choosing to work in Britain for a variety of reasons, not least the availability of American finance. Roger Corman made several of the films in his Poe cycle in Britain. Stanley Kubrick arrived after the creative battles over *Spartacus* and enjoyed full creative control over an eclectic bunch of projects including *Lolita* (1962) and *Dr Strangelove* (1964). His countryman Sidney Lumet made *The Hill* (1965), set in a British prison camp in North Africa, which remains one of the rawest and most brutally powerful films of the decade. Fred Zinnemann, on the other hand, directed a lush version of Robert Bolt's *A Man for All Seasons* (1966), with Paul Scofield as the tormented figure of Sir Thomas More.

European directors also gravitated towards 'Hollywood, England'. After establishing his critical reputation with *Knife in the Water* (1962), the young Polish director Roman Polanski moved to London to make *Repulsion* (1965), an unnerving study of mental breakdown with Catherine Deneuve, which he followed with the similarly tense *Cul-de-Sac* (1966). Established *auteurs* also passed through with varying success: François Truffaut made his much-maligned adaptation of science-fiction writer Ray Bradbury's *Fahrenheit 451* (1966) and, in the same year, Michelangelo Antonioni directed *Blowup*, with David Hemmings and Vanessa Redgrave, a seminal modernist film concerned with issues of perception which is also an interesting critique on the rather fickle nature of trendy London.

The American Joseph Losey had come to Britain in the early 1950s to escape the McCarthyite black list. He subsequently began to establish himself as a director of gritty thrillers but it was the three films he made in collaboration with playwright Harold Pinter that established his reputation. These films addressed a uniquely English subject: each explores the power relationships and game-playing at the heart of the class system. *The Servant* (1962) featured Dirk Bogarde as the manservant who turns the tables on his young aristocratic employer James Fox. *Accident* (1967) focuses on the mid-life crises and infidelities of two Oxford dons (Stanley Baker and Dirk Bogarde), while *The Go-Between* (1970) is about a young boy unwittingly manipulated by Julie Christie and Alan Bates, whose affair transgresses the class divide.

The late 1960s boom in production also benefited several British directors who had established themselves in television and were now able to make the breakthrough into features. Amongst their number were Ken Loach, who along with Tony Garnett had been at the forefront of the most innovative social drama with single television plays like *Up the Junction* (1965) and *Cathy Come Home* (1966). His first cinema film was *Kes* (1969), a deeply moving account of a working-class childhood, filmed on location in Barnsley with a partially non-professional cast. Ken Russell, a graduate from the BBC television arts series *Monitor*, began a career which established his reputation as the *enfant terrible* of British cinema. He began quietly enough with *French Dressing* (1963) and *Billion Dollar Brain* before catching attention with his adaptation of D. H. Lawrence's *Women in Love* (1969), perhaps best remembered for the nude wrestling match between Alan Bates and Oliver Reed. But Russell's notoriety stems from his next two films, *The Music Lovers* (1970), a lurid bio-pic of Tchaikovsky, and *The Devils* (1971), perhaps his most extreme work, dealing with possession in a seventeenth-century convent, which had several sequences cut by the censor. His output remained prolific and, after a spell in America, he returned to Britain in the mid-1980s to make a series of uneven low-budget shockers, which displayed energy, occasionally wit, and a continuing controversial edge.

Another iconoclastic film-maker who emerged at the same time as Russell was Nicolas Roeg. Previously an established cinematographer, Roeg made his directorial début (sharing the credit with Donald Cammell) with *Performance* (made 1968), which successfully combined the world of 1960s psychedelia with the brutality of the London gangland, represented by Mick Jagger's reclusive rock musician and James Fox's hitman on the run. The film spun a web of intrigue, mixing dream and reality in a work which Roy Armes (1978) described as having a 'visual complexity and ambiguity that one associates with such modernist directors as Bergman and Antonioni'. The results were so disturbing that it was kept under wraps by its distributors, Warners, until 1970.

As the hopes and promises of the decade began to look a little tarnished, so elements of British cinema took on a darker edge. Social criticism returned as a popular subject, as film took on a radical flavour against a backdrop of discontent, student politics, and protest against the war in Vietnam. This was most visible in Lindsay Anderson's *If...* (1968), a vitriolic attack on the British public schools and the deeply divided society which they continued to underpin, and Tony Richardson's epic anti-war polemic *The Charge of the Light Brigade* (1968), which was as much a response to Vietnam as a savage condemnation of Britain's 'glorious' imperial past.

THE 1970S: THE BUBBLE BURSTS

In 1969 90 per cent of the investment in British cinema came from America. Then almost overnight the bubble burst. Having increasingly succumbed to blockbuster mentality, the American majors found that they had overspent on a series of big-budget films, including British productions like *The Battle of Britain* (Guy Hamilton, 1969), *Cromwell* (Ken Hughes, 1970), *Goodbye, Mr Chips* (Herbert Ross, 1969), and *Half a Sixpence* (George Sidney, 1967), which all failed dismally at the box-office. Moreover, US audiences were turning towards more modest indigenous films like *The Graduate* (1967), *Bonnie and Clyde* (1967), and *Easy Rider* (1969), which were providing the excitement and freshness which British films were no longer delivering. The result was that the Americans pulled out in their droves leaving the British industry bereft of a major part of its production finance.

During the 1970s, certain corporate giants emerged to fill the gap created by this collapse. EMI, which had begun life in the music industry, bought the Associated British

Picture Corporation in 1969 and established Bryan Forbes as the production chief at Elstree Studios. In 1976 EMI acquired the British Lion Company and with it Barry Spikings and Michael Deeley—two particularly ambitious film producers. At British Lion they had produced Roeg's *The Man who Fell to Earth*, made entirely in America. This gave them the idea to make American films for primarily American audiences, and with the financial muscle of EMI behind them this is what they set out to do. Thus within a decade a bizarre reversal had taken place; instead of American companies investing in the production of British films, the largest British company was investing exclusively in American films. EMI had a successful start with Michael Cimino's *The Deer Hunter* (1977), but Deeley subsequently left and Spikings embarked on a series of expensive flops including *The Jazz Singer* (1980), *Can't Stop the Music* (1980), and *Honky Tonk Freeway* (1981), the last film alone losing £25 million. Spikings's policy, which included rejecting British ideas in addition to concentrating on American subjects, proved to be a total failure and it was left to the giant Thorn Company to step in to keep EMI afloat.

Capturing the lucrative American market had been the dream of British film financiers since before the days of Alexander Korda, and was a motivating factor behind Lew Grade's venture into international film-making. Grade, whose ITC company had built its international reputation on the back of popular television series, was essentially a salesman and his technique was to pre-sell films around the world, using the advances and guarantees to finance production. He also embarked on a series of big-budget films aimed at the American market, using well-known actors and 'safe' subjects such as adaptations of best-selling novels and remakes of old classics. The results were generally bland and unpopular with audiences, culminating in the débâcle of the $35 million *Raise the Titanic* (1980) which, like the famous liner, sank without trace, taking Grade with it.

An alternative production strategy to the corporate manœuvrings of EMI and Lew Grade was for an energetic lone producer to sell individual projects to a North American distributor. One successful exponent of this technique was David Puttnam, who during the 1970s produced *That'll Be the Day* (Claude Whatham, 1973), *Stardust* (Michael Apted, 1974), and *Bugsy Malone* (Alan Parker, 1976). While directors like Apted and Parker subsequently joined the drain of talent to Hollywood, Puttnam was to be a leading player in the next upturn in the fortunes of the British cinema.

1980S: ON THE MARGINS

Just as the situation looked particularly bleak for British cinema, an unexpected revival in indigenous product was sparked. This was first recognized on Oscar night 1982 when a modest British production, *Chariots of Fire* (1981), directed by Hugh Hudson and produced by Puttnam, unexpectedly picked up several awards including best film. This prompted writer Colin Welland to pronounce the legendary words 'the British are coming', in his acceptance speech. The following year seemed to confirm his optimism when Richard Attenborough's epic *Gandhi* (1982) topped *Chariots* by winning a total of eight awards, prompting speculation of a renaissance in British cinema. At the forefront of the new British cinema was Goldcrest, a production company headed by Canadian Jake Eberts which had provided development for *Chariots* and, after Eberts had raised a substantial portfolio of investment,

had backed Attenborough's film. Goldcrest consolidated their position with a programme of films, mainly produced by Puttnam, which earned both critical and box-office plaudits. This included *Local Hero* (Bill Forsyth, 1983), *The Killing Fields* (Roland Joffé, 1984), and *Another Country* (Marek Kanievska, 1984).

Of these film-makers Forsyth stood out as the most imaginative and idiosyncratic. His view of lower-class Scottish life, displayed in films like *That Sinking Feeling* (1979) and *Gregory's Girl* (1980), made on minuscule budgets, attracted the attention of David Puttnam. Although related to the tradition of Ealing comedy, Forsyth's wry observations and generosity of spirit betray a wide range of cinematic influ-

Mick Jagger in Donald Cammell and Nicolas Roeg's *Performance*, made in 1968, but not released until 1970

ences including Frank Capra, Jacques Tati, and Ermanno Olmi. He made two more films in Britain, *Local Hero* and *Comfort and Joy* (1984), before being tempted to North America where he made the rather underrated *Housekeeping* (1988). The financiers were Columbia Pictures under their new production chief, David Puttnam.

Alongside Goldcrest, a handful of other new companies seemingly committed to a more dynamic concept of British cinema began to emerge. They included HandMade films, formed in 1978 by ex-Beatle George Harrison to rescue *Monty Python's Life of Brian* which had been disowned by EMI. The company tended to concentrate on comedy subjects, often involving members of the Monty Python comedy team: Terry Gilliam's *Time Bandits* (1981), a huge success which grossed $45 million in North America, *Privates on Parade* (1982), *The Missionary* (1983), and *A Private Function* (1984). HandMade were joined by Virgin Vision, an offshoot of Richard Branson's music empire whose productions included *Nineteen Eighty-Four* (1984), Michael Radford's atmospheric rendering of Orwell's classic. Palace Productions, set up by Nik Powell and Stephen Woolley, was also an offshoot of a video and film distribution company and made its production début in 1984

with Neil Jordan's impressive cinematic telling of Angela Carter's Red Riding Hood story, *The Company of Wolves*.

The mini-'renaissance' driven by Goldcrest did not last many years. In 1986 the company collapsed in the wake of the failure of an over-ambitious production roster which included three big-budget films: *Absolute Beginners* (Julien Temple, 1986), *Revolution* (Hugh Hudson, 1986), and *The Mission* (Roland Joffé, 1986). The first two films went substantially over budget, and none of them made the necessary impact at the box-office. Goldcrest was reduced to little more than a sales agency. Meanwhile Virgin, which also had an investment in *Absolute Beginners*, was forced to withdraw from film production after only four years. The continuing precarious nature of the business was again demonstrated in 1992 when Palace, despite a continually high profile, was forced to close its production and distribution activities.

Despite the international prestige attached to a healthy film industry, the British government did little either incentive to assist revival or prevent collapse. Indeed their actions during the 1980s were almost entirely negative: they phased out tax breaks which had provided an important incentive to investors; discontinued the Eady levy,

Anthony Higgins as the young draughtsman in Peter Greenaway's stylized first feature *The Draughtsman's Contract* (1982)

which had been one of the major attractions for American studios during the 1950s and 1960s; and scrapped the National Film Finance Corporation. The corporation was replaced in 1986 by British Screen, a semi-privatized body, funded partly by government, partly by the industry. Essentially a lending organization rather than a source of subsidy, British Screen quickly became a major provider of finance for a whole array of British film-makers.

At the same time, developments at the low-budget end of the production spectrum appeared to provide the industry with a lifeline. In 1982 the fourth British terrestrial television channel was launched, marking the dawn of a new relationship between the cinema and television industries in Britain. The chief executive of Channel 4, Jeremy Isaacs, announced that the company would invest directly in production by commissioning films which could be given a theatrical 'window' before being shown on television. Previously the TV companies had bought films only after they had been shown in cinemas and often for ridiculously low prices. Channel 4's decision proved to be the transfusion the industry required, particularly in the area of innovative low-budget production; the company financed around 150 films in their first ten years, including *My Beautiful Laundrette* (Stephen Frears, 1985), *A Letter to Brezhnev* (Chris Bernard, 1985), *Comrades* (Bill Douglas, 1987), and *High Hopes* (Mike Leigh, 1988).

In addition to its own commissioning programme, Channel 4 also made significant financial contributions to the sustenance of British cinema through British Screen and the British Film Institute Production Board, helping to sustain their small but innovative film-making programme. In the late 1970s the BFI changed their film-making policy away from a concentration on experimental avant-garde production towards more accessible cinematic forms, in particular narrative features. The first film to be made under the new policy was Chris Petit's *Radio on* (1980) and subsequent works have included *The Draughtsman's Contract* (Peter Greenaway, 1982), *Caravaggio* (Derek Jarman, 1986), and *Distant Voices, Still Lives* (Terence Davies, 1988).

Channel 4 and the BFI were also able to broaden the base of British film culture through the workshop sector, giving access to the means of production to under-represented groups including ethnic minorities. The work produced also embraced a variety of forms including documentary and animation. For example, the articulation of the black and Asian experience through film and video engendered fresh aesthetic approaches developed to represent what were effectively unrepresented cultural experiences. While the Black Audio collective tended to work through the poetics of documentary, with productions like *Handsworth Songs* (1986), *Who Needs a Heart* (1991), and *Seven Songs for Malcolm X* (1992), the group Sankofa utilized fiction to articulate a politics of identity

which not only embraced race and ethnicity but also questions of sexuality in works such as *The Passion of Remembrance* (1986). Although the workshop initiative diminished in the 1990s some film-makers who trained in the sector went on to make independent features, including Isaac Julien, formerly of Sankofa, whose feature début *Young Soul Rebels* (1991) was produced by the BFI.

The wider impact of Channel 4 and its partnerships with British Screen and the BFI has been this opening up of a debate about British culture, identity, and history, precisely by allowing such a diversity of voices to be heard, many for the first time. But the channel has also attracted criticism for destroying cinema, by encouraging a hybrid tele-movie which owes more to the traditions and aesthetics of small-screen drama than to the cinema. This is a charge which could also be laid at the door of the other television companies which have followed Channel 4's example in investing in feature 'films': Thames, through their subsidiary Euston Films; London Weekend; Granada (although they have contributed substantially to a revival of cinema with *My Left Foot* and *The Field*); and Zenith, set up by Central TV in the mid-1980s.

The BBC has also dipped a toe in the water but it too has tended to concentrate on single dramas intended primarily for television slots with very few being given any significant big screen exposure (Mike Newell's *Enchanted April* (1991) and Stephen Frears's *The Snapper* being among the few exceptions). This would seem to confirm the view that if the British cinema exists anywhere it is on television.

There does remain a rump of something which can be called 'cinema', of material which either has a respectable life at the box-office, or which demonstrates a cinematic imagination, or occasionally both. One popular British genre which has proved extremely successful at home and abroad is the 'heritage film': a particular kind of 'tasteful' and opulent upper-class period drama, based on the work of writers like Evelyn Waugh and E. M. Forster. Ironically, the genre had its roots firmly in television—the BBC literary drama—and was initially inspired by the success of the television adaptation of Waugh's *Brideshead Revisited* (first screened in 1981). Epitomized by the films of the producing and directing team of Ismail Merchant and James Ivory (ironically, neither of them British), this genre was still proving to have great box-office draw in the 1990s with *Howards End* (1992) and *Remains of the Day* (1993). Their popularity was partly due to their ability to package the pleasures of a certain nostalgic and comforting image of Englishness which gelled with the prevailing political climate of the 1980s. Although marketed on their 'Englishness', and the quality of the performances by their British casts, these films tend to be internationally financed and produced, and often can only be considered as British films in the most tenuous way.

However, this is not the only product which has kept the last vestiges of British cinema afloat. An array of striking images continue to be created under the auspices of, for the want of a better term, 'art cinema', in films such as *The Crying Game* (Neil Jordan, 1992), *Orlando* (Sally Potter, 1992), and *The Long Day Closes* (Terence Davies, 1992). Indeed, in a cinema devoid of an orthodox mainstream, the margins have effectively moved to the centre with the result that the foremost British film-makers of the period are highly idiosyncratic individuals—Peter Greenaway and Derek Jarman.

Greenaway's lush, enigmatic images in films like *Belly of an Architect* (1987) and *Drowning by Numbers* (1988) have won him many admirers. His interests are in intellectual game-playing shot through with a welter of artistic and cultural references and highly stylized performances. His visual imagination is undoubtedly impressive but he has been criticized for an anti-humanistic approach to his characters, which frequently renders them hollow ciphers, pawns in an elaborate game.

Derek Jarman was one of the most constantly innovative British film-makers, from his début, *Sebastiane* (1975), up to his death in 1994. Like Greenaway his background was in painting, giving him a refreshing approach to the potential of the image. This was perhaps most strikingly explored in *The Last of England* (1987) and *The Garden* (1990) which utilized the poetic freedom of Super 8, a medium hitherto associated with amateur production. Jarman's explorations of homosexual identity, working contemporary concerns through historical subjects such as *Caravaggio* (1986) and *Edward II* (1992), gave his work an interesting relationship to the past which took it out of the museum and into the realm of active communication. As a film-maker who demanded the active participation of his audience, his last film, *Blue* (1993), about his life with AIDS, took this to the ultimate degree, eschewing images altogether in favour of a blue screen, a canvas upon which viewers must create their own interpretation.

Jarman's career, like so many others in British cinema, was an uphill struggle. Talent apparently exists but while there is no viable mainstream in British cinema, film-makers must either remain on the underfunded margins or move to Hollywood (as did Karel Reisz, John Boorman,

Ridley Scott, Bill Forsyth, etc.). In the mid-1990s, funding remains as difficult to come by as ever. British cinema may have been saved by television, but with production levels at an alarmingly low level it is difficult to predict a future for British cinema outside extremely restricted terms of reference. Interest in the domestic product may have been rekindled by the spectacular success of *Four Weddings and a Funeral* (Mike Newell, 1994), a modest (£3 million) romantic comedy which grossed more than $240 million worldwide. But despite the temporary ego-boost to British cinema we should all be wary of proclaiming a new 'renaissance'. The enthusiastic reports of a rejuvenated production sector are based on the fact that the Americans are, for the moment, choosing to make films at Shepperton and Pinewood. Similarly, despite the directorial hand of Neil Jordan, *Interview With the Vampire* (1994)—instigated by David Geffen, bankrolled by Warner Brothers—is no more 'British' than *Star Wars* or *Superman* were. Beyond the scale of *Film on Four* there is no British cinema, there is only a British input into international (American) cinema. In the late 1950s the formation of independents like Woodfall Films was forced by a certain conservatism on the part of the major industry players, but in the 1990s there is little that could be identified as an industry that film-makers can rebel against. The boom of the 1960s seems as far away as the golden years of Alexander Korda and J. Arthur Rank.

Bibliography
Armes, Roy (1978), *A Critical History of British Cinema*.
Auty, Martin, and Roddick, Nick (eds.) (1985), *British Cinema Now*.
Dickinson, Margaret, and Street, Sarah (1985), *Cinema and State*.
Eberts, Jack, and Ilott, Terry (1990), *My Indecision is Final: The Rise and Fall of Goldcrest Films*.
Hill, John (1986), *Sex, Class and Realism*.
Murphy, Robert (1992), *Sixties British Cinema*.
Park, James (1990), *British Cinema: The Lights that Failed*.
Perry, George (1985), *The Great British Picture Show*.
Petrie, Duncan (1991), *Creativity and Constraint in the British Film Industry*.
—— (ed.) (1992), *New Questions of British Cinema*.
Pirie, David (1973), *A Heritage of Horror*.
Walker, Alexander (1985), *National Heroes: British Cinema in the Seventies and Eighties*.
—— (1986), *Hollywood, England: The British Film Industry in the Sixties*.

The New German Cinema

ANTON KAES

The slow but steady rise of German post-war cinema from provincial obscurity to international fame is often told as a story with a bold beginning (the Oberhausen Manifesto on 28 February 1962), a climax (*Time* calling it 'the liveliest cinema in Europe' in 1978), and an abrupt ending (Fassbinder's death on 10 June 1982). This story also has a trajectory—a national cinema involved in coming to terms with the blemished identity of the country it represents. Many German films of that period also react to the troubled history of the medium itself as the prime Nazi propaganda tool. 'Never before and in no other country have images and language been abused so unscrupulously as here,' said Wim Wenders in 1977. 'Nowhere else have people suffered such a loss of confidence in images of their own, their own stories and myths, as we have.' The legacy of the National Socialist film—an instinctive distrust of images and sounds that deal with Germany—has deeply preoccupied the younger generation of German film-makers for the past quarter-century. How were they to find and create images of their country that deviated from those of the highly popular National Socialist film industry? A programmatic rejection of the Nazi film tradition has become a cornerstone of the identity and unity of German film since the 1960s.

CREATING A 'NEW' CINEMA

The years 1961–2 were years of crisis in Germany: the Berlin Wall, erected in August 1961, seemed to cement the division of Germany into two alternative social systems (West/East; capitalist/Communist); the Eichmann trials in Jerusalem (concluded in December 1961) threw glaring light on the unprecedented crimes committed by the Nazi regime; and Chancellor Adenauer's attempt to quell the freedom of the press in the so-called *Spiegel* Affair was met with an unexpected storm of protest. It was also a critical juncture for German cinema. The commercial film industry that during the 1950s mass-produced highly popular, profitable, and unabashedly provincial films had to cope with a sudden collapse of its market. Within a few years, German cinema had lost more than three-quarters of its audience to television. While the number of television sets jumped from 700,000 to 7.2 million between 1956 and 1962, the number of movie-goers plummeted from 800 million to 180 million per year. For young film-makers in Germany the spectacular crash of the commercial cinema offered a chance and an incentive to experiment with alternative visions. They began to direct their own short films, several of which were awarded prizes at international festivals. Encouraged by the success of the British

Free Cinema movement (1956–9) and the French Nouvelle Vague (the début films by Godard, Chabrol, and Truffaut appeared in 1959–60), a group of twenty-six German film directors and film critics, all between 20 and 30 years old, demanded a new cinema for Germany, a cinema that would link up with the emerging European modernist art cinema. Their brief but powerful manifesto, published on the occasion of the 8th West German Short Film Festival at Oberhausen on 28 February 1962, proudly proclaimed:

The collapse of the conventional German film finally removes the economic basis for a mode of film-making whose attitude and practice we reject. With it the new film has a chance to come to life. We declare our intention to create the new German feature film.

This new film needs new freedoms. Freedom from the conventions of the established industry. Freedom from the outside influence of commercial partners. Freedom from the control of special interest groups. We have concrete intellectual, formal, and economic conceptions about the production of the new German film. We are as a collective prepared to take economic risks.

The old film is dead. We believe in the new film.

The very claim to create a new film *ex nihilo*, in negation of history and tradition, recalls not only the futurist and other avant-garde manifestos in the early part of the century; its stance of pure creation also points to a Romantic notion of authorship not bound by economics or the expectations of an audience. Furthermore, the sharp line drawn between the 'old film' and the young foreclosed any productive co-operation between the industry and its enthusiastic challengers. In contrast to the French New Wave that was soon integrated into the mainstream, rejuvenating it in the process, hardly an attempt was made by the established German producers to finance the rebel film-makers, nor was there any desire on the part of the old guard to reform the industry from the inside. This lack of co-operation between the old and the new, the commercial and the experimental, the popular and the avant-garde has plagued the German cinema to this day.

Even though the manifesto failed to address the question of subsidies, it was tacitly understood that state support was needed to allow film-makers to be *auteurs*. Realizing the cultural benefits of a strong national cinema, the government installed a central funding agency, the 'Kuratorium Junger Deutscher Film', which with 5 million marks supported the production of twenty

Hannelore Hoger in *Artisten in der Zirkuskuppel Ratlos* (*Artists at the Top of the Big Top, Disorientated*, 1968). Alexander Kluge weaves stills, newsreel, and found film into the story of Leni Peickert who tries to develop a new kind of circus

films between 1966 and 1968. But in 1967, under pressure from the industry, a so-called Film Subsidy Bill (*Filmförderungsgesetz*) was passed, the first of several that gave subsidies only to those films that were certain to bring in at least half a million marks—an unmistakable disincentive for the young film-makers and a shot in the arm for the industry. Over the years an extraordinarily intricate and interlocking system of loans, grants, subsidies, advances, prizes, and awards by government agencies as well as state and city governments has developed, making independent film-making very much dependent on committee decisions and bureaucratic checks and balances. After the mid-1970s, German television has increasingly involved itself as a co-producer of films that could not be made otherwise. Because most of the films did not generate enough capital to pay for new productions, the number of films the New German Cinema produced was determined by the amount of subsidy available. In 1981 the German states (*Länder*) and the federal government made a full 80 million marks available for native film production. Although the government subsidies for opera, music, and theatre are still significantly higher, a sum of this magnitude carried obligations, particularly since the film audience in Germany showed shockingly little interest in the New German Cinema. The state-subsidized, 'artistically ambitious' German film had, more than in any other country, accepted a secret cultural task: to present a new Germany to the rest of the world through the mirror of its films.

Neither the Young German Film of the 1960s nor its successor, the New German Cinema of the 1970s, was ever a school or unified movement, but rather a loose alliance of autonomous *auteurs* who had little in common except their status as outsiders. Most of them were inexperienced, often self-taught film-makers who valued documentary authenticity or essayist openness in their films higher than conventional story-telling and dramatic closure. They agreed in their criticism of German society, of its capitalism, conformity, and complacency; they wanted to serve as a critical voice in the life of the Federal Republic. This desire corresponded to a new interest in questions rarely broached in the cinema of the Adenauer era, questions about the stigmatized German past and its persistence in the present. Not surprisingly, the first two feature-length films of the 'Young German Film' thematized this troubled relationship of Germans to their past.

1960S: DEALING WITH THE PAST

The title of Alexander Kluge's 1966 début film, *Abschied von gestern* (released as *Yesterday Girl* but literally meaning 'Farewell to yesterday'), is meant to be ironic. The film demonstrates that there can be no escape from the past. Set in the mid-1950s, its subject is a young Jewish woman from the German Democratic Republic who, after fleeing

to the west, is unable to find a home in the Federal Republic. Her past catches up with her again and again. Like many later films of the New German Cinema, it emphasizes more the continuities than the ruptures in German history. Volker Schlöndorff's *Der junge Törless* ('Young Törless', 1966), based on Robert Musil's 1906 novella of boarding school life, looks to the prehistory of the Third Reich. The film tells the story of a student who watches, half fascinated and half repelled, as two other students torment a fellow student of Jewish descent. The film's subtext resonates with the history of the many intellectual conformists during National Socialism who stood by silently as atrocities were committed.

The films of Kluge and Schlöndorff are radically different in the formal treatment of their subject-matter—the causes and consequences of National Socialism. Schlöndorff translated Musil's text into a well-made film, highly expressive, with stark black and white photography, while Kluge experimented with a more open and playful form that allowed voice-over commentary, intertitles, and associative montage sequences that juxtapose still photos, found film, and written text.

In 1962 Jean-Marie Straub and Danièle Huillet, both born in France but living in Germany since 1958, had provoked enraged attacks not only for their treatment of German history but also for their relentless avant-garde aesthetics that used Brechtian distancing devices in film. *Machorka-Muff* (1962), a short film based on a story by Heinrich Böll, satirizes the continuing power of the German military in the West Germany of the 1950s. 'Germany missed out on its revolution and did not free itself from Fascism,' remarked Straub. 'For me it is a country that moves in a circle and cannot free itself from its past.' Straub and Huillet's filmic adaptation of Böll's novel *Billiard um halbzehn*, with the revealing title *Nicht versöhnt oder Es hilft nur Gewalt, wo Gewalt herrscht* (*Not Reconciled, or Only Violence Helps Where Violence Rules*, 1965), is even more directly political. Unmarked flashbacks intertwine the presentation of the Fascist past with the 1950s in the Federal Republic. The youngest son is 'not reconciled' with his present, which exists without thought of the guilty past. In strict opposition to the opulent images of the Nazi films, Straub and Huillet maintain an almost ascetic relation to images. The camera is usually static, while the dramatic structure is limited to the bare essentials, resulting in disconcerting gaps, leaps, and ellipses. Straub prefers to use non-professionals as actors who follow Brecht's method by not identifying with the fictional figure but 'quoting' it. In order to document the act of filming in the film itself, Straub uses original sound. A film for Straub was political only to that extent that it revolutionized representation, i.e. broke every convention that Hollywood had established. His Brecht-inspired critique of representation and his radical politics had a lasting impact on the Young German Film, especially on Alexander Kluge and the early Rainer Werner Fassbinder.

The Young German Film was a cinema of resistance—against the mass-produced entertainment industry of the Nazi period and the 1950s, against the visual pleasure of lavish productions, and against the ideology of conformism that flourished in the decade of the economic miracle. Nothing was more insidious to the young directors than the archetypal German genre, the provincial *Heimat* film with its unbroken tradition from the 1930s to the early 1960s. Its slick, richly coloured images of German woods, landscapes, and customs, of happiness and security, seemed to them deceitful movie kitsch; they also took offence at the continuity of themes and forms from the 1930s to the 1960s. Still, despite all its negative connotations—blood and soil, provinciality and kitsch—this archetypal German film genre challenged the young German film-makers again and again. Peter Fleischmann's *Jagdszenen aus Niederbayern* ('Hunting scenes from Lower Bavaria', 1968), Volker Schlöndorff's *Der plötzliche Reichtum der armen Leute von Kombach* ('The sudden wealth of the poor people of Kombach', 1971), and Reinhard Hauff's *Mathias Kneissl* (1971) deconstructed the genre conventions to create a 'critical Heimat film', while Edgar Reitz both quoted and subverted the genre's ideology as well as visual form in his sixteen-hour television serial *Heimat* (1984). *Heimat* films in the 1970s and 1980s allowed the film-makers to reflect on German identity and trace those traditional (patriarchal, authoritarian) family and social structures that a few decades earlier made Fascism possible, even inevitable.

IMAGES OF GERMANY

In autumn 1977, the kidnapping and murder of a German industrialist and former Nazi Party official and the mysterious deaths of three imprisoned members of the Baader–Meinhof terrorist gang as well as the severe counter-measures of the government (such as the news black-out and the witchhunt of leftist sympathizers) caused the Federal Republic's most severe political crisis since its inception. The desire for a deeper historical understanding of West Germany's repressed past became overwhelming since all these events resonated with memories of the psychological terrorism of the Hitler regime—memories which suddenly ruptured the collective amnesia. West German film-makers considered it their mission to look for the roots of this crisis in the German past. At the suggestion of the *Spiegel* magazine, nine film-makers associated with the New German Cinema, among them Kluge, Schlöndorff, Reitz, and Fassbinder, collaborated to produce a film that would be both chronicle and commentary of the German autumn. The collective project, entitled *Deutschland im Herbst* (*Germany in Autumn*, 1978), was also a means of countering the government's news black-out and an attempt to answer the 'official' version of events with an unofficial version. The fifteen- to thirty-minute contributions by individual film-makers are not individually identified, even though the final 'look' of the film clearly carries the signatures of Alexander Kluge and his editor, Beate Mainka-Jellinghaus. On its surface, the film imitates the structure of a television programme, with its mixture of documentary shots, interviews, and fictional scenes. But it shows images, tells stories, and provides perspectives that would not have been possible on German television. It was here in this film, made co-operatively and without governmental subsidies, that the New German Cinema could articulate itself as a group, unified not by style but by an oppositional political stance.

Framed by two public ceremonies of mourning, the state funeral of the industrialist and the burial of the terrorists, the film shows images of violence in German history ranging from Rosa Luxemburg to Field Marshal Rommel. The nexus of inextricable relations between the present and the past suddenly becomes clear when Rommel's son Manfred, the mayor of Stuttgart, demands in an interview that the terrorists be buried with dignity. In discussing the goals of their undertaking in 1978, the film-makers emphasized that they had not tried to present a unified theory to account for terrorism. That would be a 'film without images'. 'Something seemingly more simple roused us: the general German amnesia . . . For two hours of film, we try to retain memory.' And they voiced their specific determination: 'We want to deal with the images of our country.'

It is no accident that a collective work such as *Deutschland im Herbst* inspired several projects dealing with 'the images of our country'. Alexander Kluge elaborated on his short episode showing Gabi Teichert, the history teacher who digs with her spade for the roots of German history, in his film *Die Patriotin* (1979). Fassbinder's contribution, a staged conversation between him and his mother about democracy, Fascism, and the need for an authoritarian leader, motivated him to look further into the history of the parent generation in his so-called 'Federal Republic of Germany Trilogy'—*Die Ehe der Maria Braun* (*The Marriage of Maria Braun*, 1979), *Lola* (1981), and *Die Sehnsucht der Veronika Voss* (*Veronika Voss*, 1982). Volker Schlöndorff filmed Günter Grass's novel *Die Blechtrommel* (*The Tin Drum*) in 1979, which earned him the Oscar for the best foreign film in 1980.

Deutschland im Herbst could have served as a model of how to exhibit German history and identity on film in a critical way. But its public impact was limited because both its politics and its experimental montage form run counter to most viewers' expectations for a movie. A year after *Deutschland im Herbst*, these expectations were fulfilled by the American television series *Holocaust*, the first

Rainer Werner Fassbinder
(1945–1982)

With Rainer Werner Fassbinder's untimely death at the age of 37, New German Cinema itself seemed to have come to a premature end. The sheer quantity of his creative output—more than forty films and television productions within fifteen years—had won him an undisputed reputation as the 'heart' of New German Cinema; moreover his relentlessly critical perspective on West Germany made him appear as the 'conscience of his nation'. For *Le Monde* Fassbinder represented 'the rage of a young generation that opened its eyes in the 1960s and learned what his elders had left behind: the destruction of German identity through National Socialism'.

Fassbinder embodied a generation that, born at the end of the war, rebelled against 'the system'; the capitalist economy, conservative state, and an authoritarian older generation associated with the Nazis. The generational discontent exploded in 1967 when simultaneous protests against the Vietnam War, against the new state emergency laws, and against a right-wing mass-circulation press erupted with a force previously unknown in the Federal Republic. Fassbinder, whose career began in the mid-1960s, never departed from the radical utopian-anarchic ideals of this period. They form the horizon against which the reality (and integrity) of his heroes and heroines is measured. It is no accident that all his films thematize the failure of these uncompromising ideals and the final shattering of illusions. They explore oppressive power relations and dependencies, melodramatic emotions, hapless compromises, double binds, and inescapable situations which more often than not end in suicide.

Born in Bavaria into a middle-class family, he dropped out of high school and took acting lessons, joining the action theatre group in 1967 and starting his own theatre company, the Antiteater, in Munich in 1968. In 1969 he embarked on a ten-year uninterrupted production of 35 mm. feature films that yielded between two and six films and TV productions per year in addition to theatre productions and occasional appearances as actor. In the last three years of his life the pace was even more frantic with the production of *Berlin Alexanderplatz* (1979–80), a fifteen-hour TV film in thirteen parts and an epilogue, and four major international co-productions. The boundless energy and speed (in his later years drug-induced) with which Fassbinder was able to work also had to do with the way he produced films: keeping a circle of collaborators around him, including Peer Raben, who wrote the scores to virtually all of Fassbinder's films; Harry Bär, his production assistant; a small number of cameramen (Dietrich Lohmann, Michael Ballhaus, Franz Xaver Schwarzenberger); and actresses and actors (among them Hanna Schygulla, Irm Hermann, Kurt Raab), with whom he worked in the style of a small repertory theatre. This arrangement also accounts for the unmistakable 'look' of Fassbinder's films despite their wide generic and stylistic range.

From the beginning, Fassbinder experimented with radically different modes of film-making. He appropri-

ated genre conventions of the American gangster film into a Munich underground milieu in *Liebe ist kälter als der Tod* (1969) and in *Der amerikanische Soldat* (1970). Stylistically on the other extreme, he used Brechtian distanciation effects and theatrical stylization in *Katzelmacher* (1969), his film about a Greek immigrant worker who exposes the exploitative and racist environment that the first generation of foreign workers encountered in Germany. The minimalist, self-reflexive filmic language in *Katzelmacher* (with Fassbinder playing the main part of the Greek worker) is indebted to Jean-Marie Straub, who briefly worked as guest director at Fassbinder's theatre.

In 1971 Fassbinder saw films by Douglas Sirk, the Hamburg-born Hollywood director, for the first time, and was deeply impressed by Sirk's ability to make popular films without compromising a subversive, 'European' sensibility and an inimitable style; he 'adopted' the exiled German as his spiritual father, secretly hoping to be able one day to make a German Hollywood film. Fassbinder's *Händler der vier Jahreszeiten* (*The Merchant of Four Seasons*, 1971) and *Angst essen Seele auf* (1973) consciously have recourse to Sirk's style, making use of melodramatic plots, unrealistic lighting, obtrusive camera movements, an artificial, highly stylized decor, and a highly intricate interplay of glances, gazes, and looks, expressing desire, recognition, and estrangement. Overly melodramatic music breaks the illusion, and a theatrical gestural language keeps the viewer at a critical distance despite the open display of unbridled emotions.

Fassbinder's historical films appeared in rapid succession after 1977: *Despair* (1977), *Die Ehe der Maria Braun* (1978), *Berlin Alexanderplatz* (1979/1980), *Lili Marleen* (1980), *Lola* (1981), and *Die Sehnsucht der Veronika Voss* (1981). Against the backdrop of German history from the cynical 1920s to the garish 1950s, these films deal with the unfulfilled desires of individuals, the exploitation and exploitability of their emotions, and the destruction they bring down on themselves. In his adaptation of Alfred Döblin's 1928 novel *Berlin Alexanderplatz* as a TV series, he shows a country slowly undergoing a change of identity. Berlin here represents the treacherous and inhospitable social space that determines the life and times of the reformed criminal Franz Biberkopf. Fassbinder's subsequent film *Lili Marleen* (1980) tightens the fit between the private and public realm: a cabaret singer, who hits big time with her home front song about Lili Marleen, becomes entangled in the cynical political machinations of both the Nazis and the organized Resistance. Fassbinder adopts the Nazi Ufa style in lighting, sets, costumes, and camera; exaggerating the glamour to the point of parody.

The period that fascinated Fassbinder most was the period of his own lifetime, i.e. the post-war era after the rupture of 1945, the time in which a new beginning seemed possible, even necessary. The Federal Republic was not yet firmly established, and in Fassbinder's view utopian hopes could be nurtured. The films of his Federal-Republic-of-Germany Trilogy (BRD-Trilogie) provide increasingly despondent pictures of West German misery as Fassbinder understood and felt it from the perspective of the 1970s: the subjugation of emotions to mercenary material greed in the reconstruction years (*The Marriage of Maria Braun*); the ubiquitous corruption one had to accept in the years of opportunistic conformity (*Lola*); and the haunting memories of a traumatic past that had to be exorcized (*Veronika Voss*). The films show the inevitable conflicts that arose from a collective denial of the past; they end with annihilation (*The Marriage of Maria Braun*), cynicism (*Lola*), or utter resignation (*Veronika Voss*).

Fassbinder's late films on Germany operate within the 'micro-politics of desire' (Guattari), showing how the hopes, aspirations, and frustrations of everyday people interrelate with concrete historical situations. Fassbinder's female protagonists shape their epoch as much as they are shaped by it. Their wishes contribute to, and implicitly criticize, the dominant mentality of their time. Fassbinder's films thus supplement official historiography with a psychological and utopian dimension. By the late 1970s, however, he had become convinced that the hopes he had for Germany were delusions, and his later films are expressions of that overriding despair. To the extent that Fassbinder's films are about human values and visions, they transcend his obsession with German history and identity. Ultimately, all of his films are about dreams and longings for an 'undamaged life' (Theodor W. Adorno).

ANTON KAES

SELECT FILMOGRAPHY

Liebe ist kälter als der Tod (Love is Colder than Death) (1969); Katzelmacher (1969); Warum läuft der Herr R. Amok? (Why Does Herr R. Run Amuck) (1969–70); Der amerikanische Soldat (The American Soldier) (1970); Warnung vor einer heiligen Nutte (Beware of a Holy Whore) (1970); Die bitteren Tränen der Petra von Kant (The Bitter Tears of Petra von Kant) (1972); Acht Stunden sind kein Tag (Eight Hours Don't Make a Day) (1972); Angst essen Seele auf (Fear Eats the Soul: Ali) (1973); Fontane Effi Briest (Effi Briest) (1972–74); Faustrecht der Freiheit (Fox and his Friends) (1974); Mutter Küsters Fahrt zum Himmel (Mother Küsters Goes to Heaven) (1975); Die Ehe der Maria Braun (The Marriage of Maria Braun) (1978); Berlin Alexanderplatz (13 parts, 1979–80); Die Sehnsucht der Veronika Voss (Veronika Voss) (1981); Querelle (1982).

BIBLIOGRAPHY

Fassbinder, Rainer Werner (1992), *The Anarchy of the Imagination. Interviews, Essays, Notes*, ed. Michael Töteberg and Leo A. Lensing.
Katz, Robert (1987), *Love Is Colder than Death: The Life and Times of Rainer Werner Fassbinder*.
Rayns, Tony (ed.) (1976), *Fassbinder*. 2nd edn.

Opposite: Margit Carstensen and Hanna Schygulla in *The Bitter Tears of Petra von Kant* (1972).

619

Werner Herzog

(1942–)

Often called the romantic visionary of German cinema, Werner Herzog has become a symbol of the film-maker as adventurer, vagabond, and daredevil. Documentaries about Herzog, the most famous of which is Les Blank's *Burden of Dreams* (1982), invariably portray him as an obsessed, half-crazed *auteur* willing to risk his life for a film. His protagonists—rebellious dreamers and heretics, fanatics and maniacs—serve as doubles for the independent film-maker who seeks to realize his vision against all odds. All of his films explore and validate otherness; most take place in exotic settings—from the South American jungle (*Aguirre, Wrath of God*, 1972) to Africa (*Cobra Verde*, 1987). Even his native Bavaria in *Herz aus Glas* (1976) appears as a pre-modern far-away country. Herzog's embrace of the traditions of exoticism and primitivism implies a radical, often apocalyptic critique of western civilization and instrumental rationality.

Born Werner Stipetic in Munich in 1942, Herzog (his fictional name) wrote his first film script at 15, and, after a few years of studying at the university, became a self-taught film-maker using (allegedly) a stolen 35 mm. camera. His powerful début, *Lebenszeichen* ('Signs of life', 1967), translates alienation, madness, and aggression into stark black and white images. The story follows a wounded young German soldier who is left on a Greek island to guard a useless ammunition dump. The barren landscape and the unrelenting sun trigger a nervous breakdown that expresses itself as rebellion first against his military superiors, but soon against the sun and the universe itself. The camera objectively records the buildup of the crisis and the explosion into madness in the style of a documentary, sparingly commenting on it with extreme wide-angle shots, jump cuts, and destabilizing hand-held camera movements.

Aguirre, der Zorn Gottes (*Aguirre, Wrath of God*, 1972), depicting the life of the sixteenth-century colonialist adventurer Don Lope de Aguirre, has a similar trajectory. In open and irrational defiance of nature and God, Aguirre (played by the inimitable Klaus Kinski, a Herzog regular) is determined to conquer the mythical kingdom of El Dorado. With its incongruous adherence to courtly grandeur in the midst of the Amazon jungle, the film is both a parody and criticism of colonialism. By means of extreme camera angles and long shots, Herzog visualizes primordial nature as an antagonistic and terrifying force that dwarfs and eventually destroys the colonizer.

In 1982, after four extremely difficult years in production, Herzog released *Fitzcarraldo* as another, even more darkly ironic version of the colonialist story. It chronicles the grotesque aspiration of a rich adventurer to bring Italian opera to the natives in the Peruvian jungle. Herzog critiques the colonizers' preposterous arrogance, *naïveté*, and simple lack of respect for otherness. Ironically, his own project came under fire for precisely re-enacting what the film meant to criticize. His crew's invasion of Indian territory and the exploitation of the native population made news after his camp was burned down in protest by native Indians.

Only a year later, Herzog explored the colonialist dream in economic terms. In *Wo die grünen Ameisen träumen* (*Where the Green Ants Dream*, 1984), modern-day *conquistadores*—the engineers of a mining company in search for uranium—destroy a site held sacred by the Australian aborigines. The natives lose the fight against industrial 'progress' and unscrupulous profiteering. Nature, denuded and depressingly barren, is here no longer romantically set against man; myth and modernity stare each other in the eye.

Herzog's unique blend of ethnographic and narrative film challenges all traditional genre divisions, particularly distinctions between documentary and feature film. *Fata Morgana* (1970) is an early example of Herzog's numerous documentaries that deconstruct the genre with their contradictory mix of filmic enunciations. Images of the litter-strewn desert are juxtaposed on the sound-track with Lotte Eisner's recitation of the creation myth, and intermittent off-screen comments by Herzog rupture any sense of objective truth. The film's perspective is that of *post-histoire* or the end of history, a mythical realm after progress and modernity have destroyed the planet.

Herzog's pessimistic view of civilization and social constrictions is also repeatedly played out in his narrative films. *Jeder für sich und Gott gegen alle* (*The Mystery of Kaspar Hauser*, 1974) employs a lay actor, Bruno S., an illiterate and slightly deranged-looking Berlin street per-

son, to illustrate the painful and unsuccessful integration of the wild child Kaspar Hauser into an early nineteenth-century German community. The film critiques the unctuous pomposity and ridiculous pedantry of the villagers from the perspective of the natural man unspoiled by the phoney rites of 'civilized' society. In *Stroszek* (1977) three outcasts—a man released from gaol, a prostitute, and an whimsical old neighbour—try to start a new life in the American Midwest, which Herzog portrays as no less impenetrable and exotic than the Peruvian jungle.

Maladjusted citizens or outsiders in a fatal clash with society also appear in *Nosferatu, Phantom der Nacht* (*Nosferatu, the Vampire*, 1978), a remake of F. W. Murnau's celebrated silent vampire film of 1922. Similar to Murnau's style, Herzog's film language oscillates between documentary and dream-like passages, between ethnographic authenticity and surrealistic vision. A strong tension between picture and story is typical of all of Herzog's films: the rich imagery and the operatic staging tend to exceed the economy of a tight narrative. His recent, more straightforward documentations on nomads in the Sahara (*Wodaabe: die Hirten der Sonne*, 1989) or on Kuwait (*Lektionen in Finsternis*, 1992) let the powerful images carry the message, unencumbered by fictional characters and a story-line.

ANTON KAES

SELECT FILMOGRAPHY

Lebenszeichen (1967); Fata Morgana (1970); Aguirre, der Zorn Gottes (1972); Jeder für sich und Gott gegen alle (The Mystery of Kaspar Hauser) (1974); Herz aus Glas (Heart of Glass) (1976); Stroszek (1977); Nosferatu, Phantom der Nacht (1978); Fitzcarraldo (1980–81); Wo die grünen Ameisen träumen (1984); Cobra Verde (1987); Wodaabe: die Hirten der Sonne (Wodaabe: Shepherds of the Sun) (1988–89); Lektionen in Finsternis (Lessons of Darkness) (1991–92); Glocken aus der Tiefe (Bells from the Deep) (1993)

BIBLIOGRAPHY

Blank, Les, and Bogan, James (eds.) (1984), *Burden of Dreams: Screenplay, Journals, Reviews*.
Carrère, Emmanuel (1982), *Werner Herzog*.
Corrigan, Timothy (ed.) (1986), *The Films of Werner Herzog*.
Herzog, Werner (1980), *Screenplays*.
Jansen, Peter W., and Schütte, Wolfram (eds.) (1979), *Werner Herzog*.

Opposite: Klaus Kinski in Werner Herzog's *Aguirre, Wrath of God* (1972)

major commercial attempt to exploit the persecution and systematic slaughter of millions of European Jews in a fictional film. As such, it was bound to evoke an especially strong response in the Federal Republic, where it was shown in January 1979. *Holocaust* not only triggered an unprecedented flurry of emotional reactions and probings into a past which had been taboo for so long, it also came to stand as document for the supposed failure of German film-makers to grasp images and stories from recent German history in a way that engages the emotions of the audience.

Soon afterwards, Edgar Reitz began working on his sixteen-hour TV series *Heimat* (shot in 35 mm.) as a programmatic response to the American *Holocaust*. A chronicle of over sixty years of family life in the fictitious German village of Schabbach in the Rhineland, the epic *Heimat* begins in 1919 and ends in 1982. It was screened as a film in two parts in European film festivals and all major German cities in summer 1984 and then released as an eleven-part TV series in September and October of that year. It became the most widely known—over 20 million viewers saw it on German TV—and also critically acclaimed history film of the New German Cinema. *Heimat* depicts German political history of the twentieth century through its impact on private lives in a rural village. According to Reitz, the attention to detail in the reconstruction of the various historical periods distinguishes his film from previous historical films, including the American *Holocaust* film, which, says Reitz, showed no sensibility for 'German images'. The original title of *Heimat*, 'Made in Germany', a polemical title directed against *Holocaust*, which presented German history 'made in Hollywood', is still visible in the first image of the film, engraved in a milestone. By pursuing history in terms of personal stories, Reitz seeks to restore a sense of continuity to the discontinuous and fragmented history of Germany. 'We Germans', he said in an interview, 'have had a hard time with our stories. Even now, 40 years after the war, we are still afraid that our little personal stories could recall our Nazi past and remind us of our mass participation in the Third Reich.' Reitz historicizes the Hitler regime and integrates it into the lived experiences of simple, unpolitical German folk who consequently appear more as victims than agents of history.

If Reitz is the naïve story-teller, Kluge is the cerebral and ironic essayist. In his film *Die Patriotin* (1980) the very practice of representing the past in a self-contained story has become problematic; history is no longer conceived as a sequential series of events, but as a disparate number of unique contacts between past and present which have to be constituted and constructed by the historian. Kluge's misgivings about progress in history have led him also to reject the narrative mode of history-writing which believes in the idea of historical continuity and linear development. His critical historiography is based instead on the principle of juxtaposition and montage. The gaps and breaks between the shots as well as the heterogeneity of forms are intended to demonstrate the impossibility of a narrative totality and closure in history. His radical departure from the traditional narrative form of historiography has led him to a nomadic approach which ranges freely over 2,000 years of German history. By suspending the time–space continuum he also suspends causality; the spectator is forced to be active in combining the various fragments and thereby to co-produce, rather than simply consume, the meaning of the film.

Kluge's subsequent films—*Die Macht der Gefühle* ('The power of feelings', 1983), *Der Angriff der Gegenwart auf die übrige Zeit* (*The Blind Director*, 1985), and *Vermischte Nachrichten* (*Odds and Ends*, 1987)—use the essay film format to prod viewers to reflect on filmic representation and the danger to the public sphere from global advertising and media corporations. Kluge himself has been indefatigably involved over the last decade in producing a weekly half-hour cable television programme that provides a minuscule sphere of alternative viewing in the midst of crass commercialism.

CINEMA AS MYTH-MAKER

Holding on to notions of high culture, experimentalism, and self-reflection, Kluge is surpassed only by Hans Jürgen Syberberg, whose ambitious films have found a more enthusiastic following in France than in Germany. His grand opus, the six-hour myth-laden jeremiad *Hitler, ein Film aus Deutschland*, is ultimately about the impossibility of historical representation in film altogether. Since no access to the past exists, only self-conscious simulation and re-creation are possible. Syberberg does not even attempt to reconstruct the past; the film has virtually no visual documentary footage, no interviews, no location shots, no story. The entire film takes place in a studio on a sound stage, using the artificiality of the setting and the theatricality of the presentation as devices to counter any verisimilitude with conventional Nazi imagery. It does not represent Hitler but presents representations of Hitler—as house painter, as Napoleon, and, most revealingly, as a pedantic petty bourgeois who continually fusses about his socks and underwear. Most of the visual clichés about Hitler and the Nazi period still used in regular Hollywood movies are quoted in Syberberg's film and defused by irony and exaggerated pathos.

For Syberberg, film itself functions as a myth-making medium, a kind of compensation for the progress of technological and economic rationality in this century. The demythologization by science, he says, finds an answer in 'a remythologization that only film can accomplish in the sensory immediacy of its images and sound'. His earlier films *Ludwig: Requiem für einen jungfräulichen König* (*Ludwig:*

Requiem for a Virgin King, 1972) and *Karl May* (1974) are 'positive mythologizings of history through the devices of cinema'. Syberberg believes that Ludwig, the naïve late nineteenth-century King of Bavaria, who built fairy-tale castles and supported Richard Wagner, as well as Karl May, the popular writer who, without ever leaving Saxony, brought fantasies of artificial paradises to millions of Germans, are symbols of the German search for a lost paradise. *Ludwig* and *Karl May* both embrace archaic myths and utopias as a compensation for the increasingly hostile world of industry and commerce. Despite ironic exaggeration, kitsch, and camp, both films are serious attempts to come to grips with the mythological dimension of German history. Even more than *Ludwig*, *Karl May* deals with the soil in which the Third Reich grew and took shape, a soil saturated with trivial literary myths. The telos of both *Karl May* and *Ludwig* is the Hitler film; the unspoken goal of this trilogy is to discover the unchanging mythic structures behind the historical figures and events. Syberberg seeks to fathom the characteristic, unalterable nature of the romantic German soul that yearns for artificial paradises and falls victim to fantastic delusions in its search for the grail.

Syberberg radicalized his nonconformist stance by directing such idiosyncratic filmic performance pieces as an adaptation of Richard Wagner's *Parsifal* (1981) as well as the six-hour oratorio *Die Nacht* (*The Night*, 1984–5), which fantasizes about the decline and imminent end of the western world. The film consists of nothing but Edith Clever reciting fragments from Shakespeare, Hölderlin, Nietzsche, Novalis, Goethe, Richard Wagner, and others—a highly eclectic pastiche of quotations from 2,000 years of poetry and prose centred around the motif of the night; the camera is fixated on her face and her gestures; no extraneous material enters this concentrated world of myth. The post-modern panoply of the literary sources stands in striking contrast to the radical barrenness of the staging. Wanting to preserve classical literary culture on film, Syberberg pushes the limits of the medium's own language to extremes.

Werner Schroeter, too, has consistently used high culture in his films—from his experimental shorts about Maria Callas (1968) to his recent filmic adaptation of Ingeborg Bachmann's experimental novel *Malina* (1990; script by Elfriede Jelinek). *Der Tod der Maria Malibran* (1971) centres on a nineteenth-century opera singer who allegedly sang herself to death—a perfect metaphor for Schroeter's radical belief in the consummate power of art, visualized by lavish sets and grand gestures that often border on camp. In his *Palermo oder Wolfsburg* (1979–80), he uses the life of a young Italian immigrant worker from Palermo who comes to work in the Volkswagen plant in Wolfsburg to visualize the contrast between the warm life in Sicily and the cold, isolated living conditions in

Germany. His documentaries explore Third World countries: the Philippines in *Der lachende Stern* ('The laughing star', 1983) and *De l'Argentine* (1983–4). Not unlike Herzog in his ethnographic interests, Schroeter has been seeking alternative visions and images that force him to see Germany through the eyes of a stranger.

THE CINEMA OF OUTSIDERS: WOMEN AND GERMAN HISTORY

Outsiders and misfits abound in German cinema. Influenced by the American independent film, a sizeable underground film community has emerged in Berlin since the 1970s. Rosa von Praunheim, Robert von Ackeren, Elfie Mikesch, Lothar Lambert, Monika Treut have produced films that glorify sexual difference in ever new formal ways—from the comedy of *Bettwurst* (1970) to the three-part documentary *Die AIDS-Trilogie* (1989–90), both by Rosa von Praunheim; from the stylish thrillers *Die flambierte Frau* (1982) and *Die Venusfalle* (1988) by Robert von Ackeren to the sado-masochistic Surrealism of Monika Treut in *Die grausame Frau* (1986). It is no coincidence that most of these films eschew geographical and national identities; they are more often than not filmed in New York or San Francisco and open to full houses in lesbian and gay film festivals around the world.

Genuinely fascinated with otherness, Ulrike Ottinger has moved from radical experimental and feminist films to ethnographic film-making, often blurring the lines between them (as in *Johanna d'Arc of Mongolia*, 1988–9). *Madame X—eine absolute Herrscherin* (1977) and *Bildnis einer Trinkerin* (1979) subvert the conventional portrayal of women as the passive object of the male gaze; Ottinger's female protagonists return the look and position the viewer in new ways. Her recent turn to filmic travelogues, *China: die Künste—der Alltag* (1985) and the ethnographic epic of more than eight hours' duration, *Taiga* (1991–2), seeks the exotic but in an unobtrusive way. In long sequences and steady long-to-medium shots she quietly and compassionately observes the alien world and implies that this world will ever remain impenetrable to western eyes.

The politically engaged feminist cinema at the end of the 1960s originated in the context of the extra-parliamentary opposition movement. A group of women film-makers set out to educate audiences about women-specific issues of discrimination and oppression (equal rights, equal pay, abortion) and to create female solidarity. These early, mostly documentary feminist films consciously defined themselves against the melodramas of the so-called women's film mostly made by men. By the mid-1970s, influenced by French theory, German feminists developed more radical theories centred around the filmic construction of the female subject and narrative conventions in general. New ways of story-telling and expression were demanded in opposition to the classic narrative cinema of Hollywood. Feminist films must become 'counter-cinema': 'Where women are true, they break things,' wrote Helke Sander, who in 1974 was also a founding editor of the feminist film journal *Frauen und Film*, the first of its kind in Europe. This project of the 'deconstruction' of dominant cinema's reigning codes created affinities between the feminist film and the experimental and avant-garde cinema.

Helke Sander's own best-known film, *Die allseitig reduzierte Persönlichkeit: REDUPERS* ('All-round reduced personality', 1977), explores the life of a single mother and feminist in the divided city of Berlin, using the barren urban landscape as a metaphor for the 'reduced personalities' living there. Long travelling shots from her car and an unglamorous, gritty black and white photography make the film into a semidocumentary about the harried life of Edda who tries to do justice to her conflicting roles as mother, professional photographer, lover, and member of a women's group. Sander's voice-over commentary vacillates between sardonic quips (reminiscent of Kluge) and autobiographical comments about the character that the film-maker plays in the film. The film's narrative structure is as erratic and fragmented as her life that splinters into too many different roles. The emphasis is on her everyday experiences, on her desire to make sense of the ordinary. Sander's *Der subjektive Faktor* (1980), a highly ironic and self-reflexive examination of the radical student movement that failed to include women, again employs a mixture of filmic enunciations—fictional story, voice-over, photographs, and documentary passages, including a videotaped speech that Sander herself gave at a women's political rally in 1968.

Helma Sanders-Brahms's *Deutschland, bleiche Mutter* (*Germany, Pale Mother*, 1979) adopts formal elements of the feminist film (the presence of an authorial speaking and listening voice, the unorthodox narrative economy in the extensive fairy-tale sequence, the avoidance of the 'male gaze'), but places traditional women-specific interests (the relation between the sexes, the mother–daughter relationship, the critique of patriarchy) in the context of German history. *Deutschland, bleiche Mutter* tells the story of the film-maker's mother from 1939 to 1955 from the perspective of the daughter. Autobiographical, fictional, and historical elements blend into each other. Women's experiences of German history, particularly of the Hitler regime and the war, are for Sanders-Brahms the point of reference for portraying the past. Her feminist perspective challenges the very notion of history as the collective memory of the past. Sanders-Brahms records life experiences which are gender-specific and typically absent from the male version of history; in particular, she portrays the experience of many German women who discovered their own strength during the war and then suffered the devaluation of those

Wim Wenders

(1945–)

One of the first graduates of the Munich Academy of Film and Television, Wenders has concerned himself overtly with the theoretical issues involved in cinematic representation. His extensive essayistic writings stand in a symbiotic relationship with his films: they all revolve around the power of the image, the difficulties of storytelling, and the vicissitudes of perception. Wenders believes in film's ability to explore, rediscover, and thus redeem the physical world.

His early shorts *Schauplätze* (1967) and *Same Player Shoots Again* (1967) are formal experiments involving stasis and movement as if he wanted to discover for himself the medium-specific properties of the motion picture. Wenders always had a sceptical relationship to strong narratives—maybe out of fear that they might overpower the delicate imagery. Indeed, a highly self-conscious tension between story and picture runs through all of Wenders's work from his first feature, *Summer in the City* (1971), to *In weiter Ferne, so nah* (*Far Away, so Close*, 1993).

Summer in the City (1971), dedicated to the Kinks, uses an alienated young man's search for his friends as a pretext to explore physical space in relation to music and movement. Similarly, *Alice in den Städten* (*Alice in the Cities*, 1974) examines the nexus between perception, experience, and estrangement. A journalist is unable to write about America because he finds the innumerable polaroid pictures he has shot and collected more powerful and truthful than words. He ends up by accident with an abandoned 9-year-old girl, and his passive non-involvement as observer finally breaks down when the two return to Germany to look for the house of the girl's grandmother, of which they have only a photograph. In a wider sense, this road movie suggests a quest for the site of one's lost childhood, and of identity.

Falsche Bewegung (*The Wrong Move*, 1974), based on Handke's screenplay, which itself follows Goethe's *Bildungsroman Wilhelm Meisters Apprenticeship*, also invites the viewer to examine German landscapes and cityscapes. Wilhelm, a writer, undertakes an educational journey from northern to southern Germany and admits at the end that he made a 'wrong move' by not listening to the story of one of his travel companions, Laertes, a former member of the Nazi Party, who embodies Germany's recent past. The Federal Republic appears in this film as a country of lost souls because of its history.

'The only thing, I was secure with from the beginning and felt had nothing to do with fascism was rock music,' Wenders said in a 1976 interview. In nearly all his films and writings, Wenders thematized the inexorable influence that America (through its popular culture) held over the German post-war generation. His position, however, was ambivalent. While he was drawn to America to the point of living for several years in New York and Los Angeles, a character in his road movie *Im Lauf der Zeit* (*Kings of the Road*, 1976) also claimed that 'the Yanks have colonized our subconscious'. A tangible shift from adulation to scepticism occurred during the ill-fated production of *Hammett* (1982), for which he was hired as director by Francis Ford Coppola. In production for almost four years between 1979 and 1982, the film had to be reshot and recut before it was deemed releasable for an American audience.

Both before and after *Hammett*, Wenders had made films either set in the United States or which explored the tension between Europe and America. The psychological thriller *Der amerikanische Freund* (*The American Friend*, 1977) deals with a shady American con artist (played by Dennis Hopper) who befriends and betrays an honest German craftsman. Wenders's experiences with the production of *Hammett* were the incentive for the semi-autobiographical black and white film *Der Stand der Dinge* (*The State of Things*, 1981), which reflects on the rift

Alice (Yella Rottländer) takes a polaroid of Philip (Rüdiger Vogler) in Wim Wenders's road movie *Alice in the Cities* (1974).

between American and European cinema. The film ends with the protagonist, an independent German film-maker, killed on a Hollywood street.

Paris, Texas (1984), written by Sam Shepard, carries the tension between the old and the new world in its title. The film's first part belongs to Wenders's favourite genre, the road movie, with characters aimlessly driving in search of the past and the future. In the second part, the camera comes to rest in a peepshow, as the protagonist attempts to win back his wife through a window which doubles as a one-way mirror. Robby Müller (Wenders's cinematographer for the majority of his films) uses this set-up for highly evocative and self-referential camera work.

By the mid-1980s, as questions of national identity seemed to climax, Wenders returned to Germany to work on *Wings of Desire* (*Himmel über Berlin*, 1986–87), a film about Berlin and Germany, its past and present. The narrative perspective is that of two angels who invisibly traverse the various urban spaces of modern Berlin (strikingly photographed in classical black and white by Henri Alekan). The film has often been cited as a post-modern text in its deconstruction of the time-space nexus (the angels exist outside time and place) and in its discontinuous and fragmentary narrative that incorporates de-personalized utterances. But *Wings of Desire* only radicalizes tensions present in Wenders's other films, between space and time, image and narration, aesthetics and ethics, history and identity, desire and action.

Until the End of the World (1991), a $23 million, romantic, high-tech. science-fiction road movie, spans fifteen cities and four continents. It addresses the crisis of communication and memory in a technological environment in which video images besiege us from all sides; it also highlights a striking reversal in Wenders's old struggle to combine story and image. 'I've turned from an image maker into a storyteller. Only a story can give meaning and a moral to an image.'

ANTON KAES

SELECT FILMOGRAPHY

Summer in the City (1967–71); Die Angst des Tormanns beim Elfmeter (The Goalkeeper's Fear of the Penalty) (1971–2); Alice im den Städten (Alice in the Cities) (1973–4); Falsche Bewegung (Wrong Move) (1974); Im Lauf der Zeit (Kings of the Road) (1976); Der amerikanische Freund (The American Friend) (1977); Nick's Film: Lightning over Water (1981); Der Stand der Dinge (The State of Things) (1981); Paris, Texas (1984); Der Himmel über Berlin (Wings of Desire) (1986–7); Bis ans Ende der Welt (Until the End of the World) (1991); In weiter Ferne, so nah (Faraway, so Close) (1993); Lisbon Story (1995)

BIBLIOGRAPHY

Dawson, Jan (1976), *Wim Wenders*.
Geist, Käthe (1988), *The Cinema of Wim Wenders*.
Grob, Norbert (1991), *Wenders*.
Kolker, Robert Phillip, and Beicken, Peter (1993), *The Films of Wim Wenders*.
Wenders, Wim (1989), *Emotion Pictures: Reflections on the Cinema*.
—— (1991), *The Logic of Images: Essays and Conversations*.

strengths and their achievements when the men returned after the war. She made the film, she told an interviewer, to show her daughter that the history of her country consisted of more than just Hitler, concentration camps, and war. 'This is the positive history of Germany under fascism, during the Second World War and afterwards. The history of the women who kept life going while the men were being sent to kill.'

Sanders-Brahms's film best illustrates the shift in German attitudes in regard to Germany's stigmatized history, from the question of guilt and atonement to an emphasis on personal memory and a yearning for a less problematic national identity. All these films, including Syberberg's Hitler film, Kluge's *Die Patriotin*, and Edgar Reitz's *Heimat*, prefigure the debates that were soon afterwards hotly discussed among historians in the so-called 'Historikerstreit'. The search for female identity, the separation from the mother, the settling of accounts with the father, the gender-specific historiography, and the perspective of memory: these motifs also recur in Jutta Brückner's autobiographical *Hungerjahre* (1980), which deals, in a more open, essayistic form, with the numbing domestic atmosphere in Germany during the economic miracle and the Cold War. The film's perspective is that of a 13-year-old girl, whose gradual alienation from her parents, her environment, and even her own body is recounted by means of voice-over, literary quotations, and against a background of ascetic black and white images. The story, which ends in the girl's suicide attempt, is told nostalgically and at the same time despairingly from the viewpoint of the remembering retrospective subject. Brückner's film mirrors the hypocritical, repressive family structures of the Adenauer era, but, unlike *Deutschland, bleiche Mutter*, there is no allegorical reference to Germany as a fateful whole. The title alludes to the hunger of those years for life, love, experience, and meaning. The result of this impoverished period is the terrorism of the 1960s and 1970s. Margarethe Von Trotta's celebrated film *Die bleierne Zeit* (*The German Sisters*, 1981) explores the personal and feminist dimension of the suicidal mission of the terrorist Baader–Meinhof group in the maximum security prison in Stammheim. Both in its realistic filmic style and investigative mode, *Die bleierne Zeit* is clearly more political than personal.

AFTER FASSBINDER

The year 1982, with Fassbinder's death, for some marked the end of the New German Cinema. The year was a turning-point on other fronts as well: a more conservative political climate helped Helmut Kohl and his Christian Democratic Party win the elections and the new Minister of the Interior caused a stir when he showed himself unwilling to continue to finance what he deemed 'élitist', 'critical', and 'immoral' films. Herbert Achternbusch's

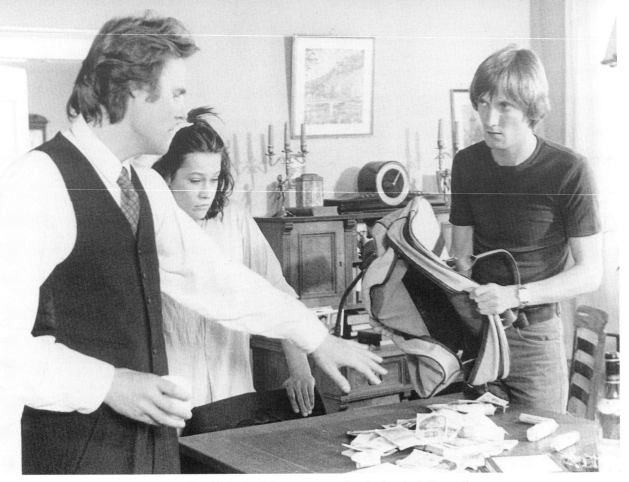

Tina Engel as the schoolteacher who robs a bank to help save a nursery from bankruptcy in Margarethe von Trotta's *Das zweite Erwachen der Christa Klages* (*The Second Awakening of Christa Klages*, 1977)

film travesty *Das Gespenst*, in which Christ, played by the director, walks with a nun through today's Bavaria, was accused of blasphemy and set off an inquiry into the use of public funds for uncensored film production. Moreover, several of the best-known film-makers, such as Wim Wenders, Volker Schlöndorff, and Werner Herzog, began to work outside Germany on international co-productions, using script-writers and actors from Paris or Hollywood. After highly popular and commercially successful filmic adaptations from German novels, like *Die verlorene Ehe der Katharina Blum* (after Heinrich Böll, 1975), Volker Schlöndorff turned to French–American financed films of works by Marcel Proust (*Un amour de Swann*, 1983) and Arthur Miller (*Death of a Salesman*, 1985). Percy Adlon, who had made *Fünf letzte Tage* (1982), a highly stylized film about the German resistance group Weisse Rose, has found wide acceptance in Hollywood with his commercial films *Sugar Baby* (1984) and *Bagdad Cafe* (1987, with Marianne Sägebrecht). After his phenomenal international success with the revisionist war film *Das Boot* (1980–1), Wolfgang Petersen moved to Los Angeles, making such Hollywood action movies as *Enemy Mine* (1985) and *In the Line of Fire* (1993). A growing number of German directors,

actors and actresses, and even producers are currently relocating to Hollywood, while Germany still provides a haven for alternative film-makers, including American ones.

By the mid-1980s German cinema became once again a national 'minor cinema', having to define itself more than ever against the domination of Hollywood, whose German market share reached as high as 82.9 per cent in 1993. German film production dropped to 10 per cent the same year (in comparison to France where indigenous production was still 35 per cent). There are still many fascinating films made that explore 'German topics' or deliberately challenge the codes of traditional film-making, but, without a strong native film industry or film culture, their impact is often limited to late-night television and the art-cinema circuit. Germany's reunification in 1989 seems to have had minimal effect on German film production; the DEFA studios were bought by a French corporation. A series of light comedies and heavy melodramas followed the fall of the Wall but no major film has emerged about the manifold implications of this event for a 'new Germany'.

If the films about Germany of the 1960s and 1970s

searched for a national identity, those of the 1980s began to emphasize the multi-cultural experience within Germany's own borders. In the tradition of Fassbinder's pioneering films about guest workers—*Katzelmacher* (1969) and *Angst essen Seele auf* (*Fear Eats the Soul*, 1973)—a host of films have recently tried to call into question facile oppositions between insider and outsider, domestic and foreign, dominant and marginal. Feature films like Jeanine Meerapfel's *Die Kümmeltürkin geht* (1984), Hark Bohm's *Yasemin* (1987), and Doris Dörrie's *Happy Birthday, Türke!* (1991) confront Germans with different, invariably uncomfortable perspectives on their own country. In particular, films by foreign-born film-makers—Sohrab Shahid Saless (*In der Fremde*, 1975) and Tevfik Baser (*Abschied vom falschen Paradies*, 1988)—present Germany as a multi-cultural society in which ethnic minorities have their own internal conflicts, such as the patriarchal treatment of women in a Turkish family living in Berlin, which Baser critically examines in *40 Quadratmeter Deutschland* (1986).

Contemporary German cinema of the 1990s is not moribund. What it lacks is a centre that has the magnetic pull and impact of a Fassbinder; it also lacks the sense of solidarity, common purpose, and identity that was evident in *Deutschland im Herbst*. What current German cinema boasts, instead, is an astounding variety of political agendas, styles, and aesthetic sensibilities, ranging from revisionist *Heimat* and war pictures, to 30-year-old Christoph Schlingensief's violently aggressive anti-German satires about reunification, *Das deutsche Kettensägenmassaker* (1990) and *Terror 2000: Intensivstation Deutschland* (1992); from highly intellectual, political essay films (Harun Farocki's *Videogramme einer Revolution*, 1993) to low-brow comedies (*Wir können auch anders*, 1993); from the vibrant underground film culture of Berlin to a new ethnographic cinema fascinated with otherness (Schroeter, Ottinger, Herzog). As the memory of the Nazi period fades—a memory that defined much of the German cinema from the 1960s to the 1980s—a new cinema emerges: one that valorizes difference over identity.

Bibliography
Corrigan, Timothy (1983), *New German Film: The Displaced Image*.
Elsaesser, Thomas (1989), *New German Cinema: A History*.
Kaes, Anton (1989), *From Hitler to Heimat: The Return of History as Film*.
Knight, Julia (1992), *Women and the New German Cinema*.
Rentschler, Eric (ed.) (1988), *West German Filmmakers on Film: Visions and Voices*.

East Germany: The DEFA Story

HANS-MICHAEL BOCK

The post-war division of Germany began with the establishment of the four occupied zones in 1945—American, British, and French to the west, and Soviet to the east—and was formalized by the consolidation of the three western zones into the Federal Republic of Germany and the conversion of the Soviet zone into the German Democratic Republic (GDR) in 1949.

DEFA (Deutsche Film AG), which sounds like the name of a capitalist production company and is a direct echo of Ufa, the biggest and most powerful film organization Germany ever saw, was in fact set up on the orders of the Soviet Military Government in Germany and for nearly forty-five years was the only film-producing entity in East Germany. Its original core was formed by a group of film-makers who had spent the Nazi years either in exile or working as technicians in the film industry and who came together in 1945 to plan the rebuilding of the German cinema. DEFA itself was officially founded (as a Soviet company) the following year and passed into German control in 1949. On 1 October 1950 the 'DEFA-Studio für Spielfilme' was formed for the production of feature films. Simultaneously studios were set up for newsreels and documentary films and for animation films. In 1953 they were officially designated as VEB (Volkseigener Betrieb), companies owned by 'the people'.

STRUCTURE

DEFA used the traditional studio structure modelled on Ufa or the Hollywood of the 1930s, but with one crucial difference: in Hollywood, and even in Nazi Germany, there were other, competing production companies to turn to; in the GDR there was only the one, controlled by state (and Party) authorities.

In January 1954 a department known as the Hauptverwaltung (or HV) Film was set up in the Ministry for Culture. Headed by a deputy minister for cultural affairs, HV Film controlled all aspects of the film industry: production, import and export of films, distribution, cinemas, even the film archive. Through the HV all income from the cinemas and from film export was collected as part of the state budget. At the same time all funds for production officially came from the state through HV Film, creating the illusion that the state cared and paid for film as an art and propaganda medium.

Officially there was no censorship but all films had to pass a 'Zulassung' by HV Film.

The DEFA (ex-Ufa) studio at Potsdam-Babelsberg followed the tradition of big studios by having virtually all film-making personnel on its payroll: writers, directors, set designers, cinematographers, technicians, and even some actors. This led to high standards of craftsmanship (particularly in set design, where the old German tradition of masters and apprentices was kept alive). But it severely restricted artistic risk-taking: ideas and scripts were subjected to a long series of checks by studio and party officials and reworkings by the 'Dramaturgen' (story editors), some of whom also served as secret informants of the state police.

It was difficult to become a director without following a strictly preordained path which included attendance at the Film School at Babelsberg. DEFA, however, was able to attract many of the country's leading writers as occasional or regular script-writers. By a curious irony some important literary works such as Jurek Becker's *Jakob der Lügner* ('Jakob the liar') or Ulrich Plenzdorf's *Die neuen Leiden des jungen W.* ('The new sorrows of young W.') started life as banned film scripts and were only later made into films after their success as books or plays.

Relying on a broad reservoir of stage actors, DEFA developed some first-class screen performers, some (in particular Manfred Krug and Jutta Hoffmann) becoming popular stars and remaining so even after they had left the GDR for the west. Erwin Geschonneck (who had worked with Brecht) became the biggest East German star and sometimes used his influence to get banned films (including his own) released. In 1951 *Das Beil von Wandsbek* ('The hatchet of Wandsbek'), directed by Falk Harnack, was banned becamse Geschonneck's portrayal of a butcher turned Nazi executioner did not conform to the official black and white clichés.

EARLY CLASSICS

The suppression of *Das Beil von Wandsbek* marked the end of a period which in five years had already resulted in some lasting classics, beginning with Wolfgang Staudte's anti-Nazi film *The Murderers Are Among Us* (*Dir Mörder sind unter uns*), shooting for which started on 16 March 1946, before DEFA was even officially founded.

Stylistically, *The Murderers Are Among Us* goes back to pre-Nazi traditions of expressionist lighting and one big dilemma of the early DEFA was how to react to the 'Ufa tradition' of Nazi films and how to produce anti-Fascist stories with technicians and artists who had worked in the Nazi film industry for an audience which was used to the slick escapist style of Nazi cinema. The official policy was not to employ directors or writers who had blackened their names with propaganda films, while on the other hand accepting all others who were 'merely' technicians.

In his first feature film *Ehe im Schatten* ('Marriage in the shadows', 1947) Kurt Maetzig told the story of a married couple of actors who are driven to suicide by the Nazis because the woman is Jewish. The film, shown in all four parts of Germany, was the most successful of the period with an attendance of more than 10 million in the first three years. When the film was shown in Hamburg, Nazi director Veit Harlan was expelled from the cinema. (Ironically, the music of *Ehe im Schatten* was composed by Wolfgang Zeller, who had written the score for Harlan's *Jud Süß* in 1940.)

The most important films were those that used history to tackle contemporary problems. Erich Engel's excellent *Affaire Blum* (1948) dealt with a real crime from the early 1930s when the state authorities covered up a murder by blaming an innocent Jew. Both Maetzig and writer Friedrich Wolf showed the close ties between chemicals giant IG Farben and the Nazis. Staudte's *Der Untertan* (1951), from the novel by Heinrich Mann, was a biting satire on the German petty bourgeoisie and was for years banned in West Germany.

This era of DEFA ended around 1950 when, after the foundation of the GDR, the educated and rather liberal Soviet supervisors and film officers left and handed DEFA over to such German Stalinists as Generaldirektor Sepp Schwab.

SOCIALIST REALISM TO THE THAW

With the Cold War, the Communist authorities' grip on 'their' film intensified. DEFA's production reached an absolute low in 1952 and 1953, when only five films per year were finished. In July 1952 at a party conference of the ruling Socialist Unity Party or SED (the Communist Party) and then in September 1952 at a conference of film-makers, a new doctrine in film-making was proclaimed: to intensify the 'methods of socialist realism', using 'positive heroes', and dealing more with 'problems of the German working-class movement'.

The most famous film in response to this was Kurt Maetzig's two-part *Thälmann—Sohn seiner Klasse / Führer seiner Klasse* ('Thälmann, son of his class / leader of his class', 1953–5), a biased portrait of the German Communist leader in the 1920s and 1930s. Films of this type, however, were in the minority, as DEFA pursued a policy of trying to present the GDR as the inheritor of the German cultural tradition by adapting famous fairy-tales and classic dramas such as Schiller's *Kabale und Liebe* ('Intrigue and love', 1959, directed by Martin Hellberg) and Lessing's *Minna von Barnhelm* (1962, also Hellberg).

In order to enhance its international reputation DEFA also engaged in a series of co-productions, mainly with France (including *Les Aventures de Til l'Espiègle*, directed by Gérard Philipe in 1956), but also with Sweden and with West Germany. An East–West German co-production of

Thomas Mann's *Buddenbrooks*, supported by the writer, was prohibited by the West German government.

Following Khrushchev's speech at the 20th party congress in 1956 denouncing Stalinism, and the release of Soviet 'Thaw' films such as *The Cranes Are Flying* and *Ballad of a Soldier*, new talented German directors who had studied at the film schools in Moscow and Prague or had worked as assistants at Babelsberg started to find their own less dogmatic way of dealing both with the anti-Fascist tradition and with contemporary topics. The most important representative of this generation was Konrad Wolf, son of the Communist writer Friedrich Wolf. Raised in exile in Moscow, Konrad Wolf returned to Germany as an officer of the Red Army in 1945—a story he was to tell later in his film *Ich war neunzehn* ('I was nineteen', 1967). After his studies at VGIK in Moscow, he started directing for DEFA. In 1965 he was made president of the Academy of Arts, a most important position, which he used to influence cultural policy and to help other artists who came into conflict with the authorities.

Wolf's fourth film *Sonnensucher* ('Sun-seeker', 1958), a bleak, detailed portrayal of German and Russian uranium miners in the late 1940s, was withdrawn shortly before its première and released officially only in 1972. *Sterne / Zwedzy* ('Stars', 1959) was—after intervention by the West Germans—presented at the Cannes Festival as a Bulgarian film and awarded a special jury prize.

Some of the most interesting stylistic approaches were to be found in films that dealt with the Fascist past, a field that was politically correct. Heiner Carow in *Sie nannten ihn Amigo* ('They called him Amigo', 1958) told the story of a boy in Berlin who hides a fugitive from a concentration camp. Prague-trained Frank Beyer took the Spanish Civil War as the background for *Fünf Patronenhülsen* ('Five cartridge cases', 1960). The influence of the new Czech and Polish cinemas was even more in evidence in Beyer's *Königskinder* ('Royal children', 1962) and in *Der Fall Gleiwitz* ('The Gleiwitz case', 1961), directed by Gerhard Klein from a script by Günter Rücker and Wolfgang Kohlhasse. (Klein and Kohlhasse had previously collaborated on *Berlin—Ecke Schönhauser* ('Berlin—Schönhauser corner', 1957) and a number of other films with stories taken from everyday life in Berlin, told in a neo-realistic style.)

CRACK-DOWN

On 13 August 1961 the East German police and army closed off the border to West Berlin and started building the Wall. Before the year was out DEFA started shooting *... und deine Liebe auch* ('... and your love too', Frank Vogel, 1962), about two brothers torn between west and east. Konrad Wolf's *Der geteilte Himmel* ('Divided sky', 1964), from the novel by Christa Wolf (no relation), offered a highly artistic treatment of the topic and provoked an intense discussion as to whether DEFA films should be

A return to the aesthetics of pre-Nazi cinema? Ernst Borchert and Hildegard Knef in Wolfgang Staudte's *Die Mörder sind unter uns* (*The Murderers Are Among Us*, 1946)

'volksverbunden' (popular, i.e. conservative) or try to tell their stories with modern means, sometimes condemned as 'formalist'.

After the 'bleeding wound' of the open border was sealed off, intellectuals and artists—especially those favourable to socialist ideas—hoped for more freedom to criticize the many internal social and political problems. Frank Beyer hinted at economic difficulties in *Karbid und Sauerampfer* ('Carbide and sorrel', 1963), one of the best German film comedies. Günter Rücker in his directorial début *Die besten Jahre* ('The best years', 1965) compared the hopes of the early post-war years with reality. Other leading DEFA directors were also working on new critical films when, in November 1965, the crack-down came. At a party conference—the '11th Plenum'—originally scheduled to deal with economic reform, party hardliners (Walter Ulbricht, Erich Honecker) started attacking the development of literature (Christa Wolf, Heiner Müller, Wolf Biermann) and film, especially Kurt Maetzig's *Das Kaninchen bin ich* ('I am the rabbit'). This adaptation of an unpublished novel which criticized an opportunistic judge was accused of 'scepticism' and 'subjectivism'. Nearly the whole of DEFA's production was indicted, including Klein's *Berlin um die Ecke*, Egon Günther's satire *Wenn du groß bist, lieber Adam* ('When you're grown up, dear Adam'), Herrmann Zschoche's *Karla*, Frank Vogel's *Denk bloss nicht, ich heule* ('Just don't think, I'm howling'), Günter Stahnke's *Der Frühling braucht Zeit* ('Spring needs time'), and Jürgen Böttcher's *Jahrgang 45* ('Born in 45'). A few months later even Frank Beyer's *Spur der Steine* ('Trail of the stones') with Manfred Krug—which had a successful première and was set to represent the GDR at the film festival in Karlovy Vary—was 'withdrawn from circulation' after Party-organized protests in an East Berlin cinema.

The top executives of DEFA were removed and the careers of some film-makers were destroyed. Stahnke never again made an interesting film, Beyer retreated to the theatre in the provinces and made TV series before returning to the cinema nearly ten years later, Jürgen Böttcher never again directed a feature film but became an important documentary film-maker and painter. Konrad Wolf formulated the following notes for discussion: 'We are facing the greatest catastrophe in our film production. What now? ... If all our films dealing with contemporary topics are wrong—then something must be wrong with the ideology—clear logic!' DEFA fell back on making 'Indianerfilme' ('Red Indian films'), their own special brand of Western, showing how the native Indians were suppressed by greedy white Americans—some even containing allusions to the Vietnam War.

REVIVAL

The first interesting film to come out of Babelsberg after the débâcle was Konrad Wolf's *Ich war neunzehn* (1967),

which also marked the beginning of a lasting partnership between Wolf and writer Wolfgang Kohlhaase. Meanwhile a new generation of film-makers was preparing to leave the film academy at Potsdam-Babelsberg and to enter the DEFA studio, bringing with them new ideas. Going back to neo-realism, they started to work under the banner of 'dokumentarischer Spielfilm' ('documentary fiction film', a term coined by Lothar Warneke), mixing fictional and documentary elements in telling stories from everyday life. They abandoned the concept of the 'positive hero' and 'typical characters', turning instead to the depiction of individuals with specific problems. These new trends were underpinned by a theoretical treatise entitled 'Subjektiver Faktor und Filmkunst' ('The subjective factor and film art') edited by the Party Academy of the SED and written by a former student of the film school, Dr Rudolf Jürschik. He later became 'Chef-Dramaturg' (artistic head) of the DEFA studio.

The model for this group was Jürgen Böttscher's suppressed *Jahrgang 45*, shot in the streets of Berlin by cameraman Roland Gräf. In 1968 Gräf was behind the camera for Vogel's *Das siebente Jahr* ('The seventh year'), in 1969 for Zschoche's road movie *Weite Straßen—stille Liebe* ('Long roads, silent love') and for Lothar Warneke's *Dr med. Sommer II*, before himself turning to directing with *Mein lieber Robinson* ('My dear Robinson', 1970). All those films told contemporary stories without wider political implications.

In 1971 Erich Honecker took over from Walter Ulbricht as head of the Communist Party, renewing hope for more liberal cultural policies. One of the first films to come out after this was Egon Günther's *Der Dritte* ('The third'), which won prizes for its director and for its star Jutta Hoffmann at Karlovy Vary and Venice, as well as the 'Nationalpreise', the highest award for an artist in the GDR. It was also a huge success with audiences. From a script by Günter Rücker, it told the unspectacular, humorous tale of a young woman in search of her third partner. With his next film, *Die Schlüssel* ('The keys', 1972), co-written with Helga Schütz, Günther ran into trouble again and he stopped filming contemporary topics.

The biggest success of those years was Heiner Carow's *Die Legende von Paul und Paula* ('The legend of Paul and Paula', 1972), a bitter-sweet love story of a young woman who tries to fulfil her love against all obstacles. The script was written by Ulrich Plenzdorf, whose banned screenplay 'Die Leiden des jungen W.' had become popular as a book and a play. Another banned screenplay which had become a successful book, Jurek Becker's *Jakob der Lügner*, finally made it to the screen in 1974. Directed by Frank Beyer, and his first feature film after *Spur der Steine*, it broke with the traditions of the anti-Fascist genre by treating the story of Jews in a Nazi ghetto as a sentimental fairy-tale. It was successfully shown at the Berlin Film Festival and was nominated for an Oscar.

A TIME OF CAUTION

After all the leading directors—including Konrad Wolf with *Der nackte Mann auf dem Sportplatz* ('The naked man in the sports ground', 1973)—had run into problems with contemporary topics, they reacted by turning to the 'safe' genre of anti-Fascism or to 'camouflage' films which employed literary classics or the biographies of artists as a means of exploring the conflict between individual and society.

Goethe was a special favourite. Siegfried Kühn adapted his novel *The Elective Affinities* (*Die Wahlverwandtschaften*, 1974); Egon Günther tried to reach the international market with a version of Thomas Mann's story about Goethe, *Lotte in Weimar* (1975), and followed that with *Die Leiden des jungen Werthers* ('The sorrows of young Werther', 1976) before moving to the west. Lothar Warneke in *Addio, piccola mia* (1978)—his only historical picture—gave his view of the students' rebellion in the west through a portrayal of the life of Georg Büchner.

When film-makers tried to deal openly and critically with contemporary issues, as did Carow in *Bis daß der Tod euch scheidet* ('Till death you do part', 1978), and Wolf and Kohlhasse in *Solo Sunny* (1979), the Party immediately reacted with a 'discussion' in the official press demanding a more positive view of the 'advantages of socialist society'. In 1981 Rainer Simon's *Jadup und Boel*—only completed after a considerable tug of war between the studio and the Party—was banned. Film-makers resorted once more to camouflaging their critique by filming stories about women in society (Warneke's *Die Beunruhigung* ('The disturbance'), 1981); using successful books as subject-matter (Gräf with the excellent *Märkische Forschungen* ('Researches in the Brandenburg Marches'), 1982); or exploring anti-Fascist themes (Beyer with *Der Aufenthalt*, (1982), Kühn with *Die Schauspielerin* ('The actress'), 1988).

The style of these films was cautious and professional, heavily dependent on dialogue supported by good cinematography, and taking few risks with the precarious power of the image. Creative imagination could, however, be given freer rein in the safe genre of the children's film, as in *Gritta von Rattenzuhausbeiuns* ('Gritta of Rats-in-our-house', 1984) by director and cinematographer Jürgen Brauer.

The greatest talent to emerge from the Babelsberg film school in the 1970s was Ulrich Weiss. After starting with documentaries and children's films, he made two adult features, *Dein unbekannter Bruder* ('Your unknown brother', 1981) and *Olle Henry* ('Ole Henry', 1983), whose unusual combination of bleak pictures and hopeless situations met with furious criticisms from the authorities. Throughout the rest of the 1980s all his projects were shelved, and he returned to film-making only after the collapse of the GDR.

The years 1984–5 saw the presentation of two films by relatively recent Babelsberg graduates, Karl Heinz Lotz's *Junge Leute in der Stadt* ('Young people in the city'), set in the immediate pre-Nazi years, and Peter Kahane's *Ete und Ali*. Kahane's film was a success with young audiences, who responded favourably to its light touch and youth-oriented critique of everyday life. But his more radical project, *Die Architekten*, which openly criticized the circumstances leading to the creation of sterile suburbs, encountered many obstacles, and it was only finished in 1990, on the eve of reunification.

SELL OUT

In the 1980s growing numbers of entertainment films were imported from the west by the centralized distribution service, thereby pushing DEFA's own films even more into the ghetto of art houses and youth clubs. The production heads of DEFA thus faced a new dilemma, and one which mirrored the situation of the East German economy as a whole. To continue to reach their audience, they needed to keep up with western film technology, for which there was very little hard currency available. To keep the public interested they also needed to take a more critical stance towards the social situation, which the party leaders were reluctant to allow. One of the last attempts in this direction was Warneke's *Einer trage des anderen Last...* ('Let one take up the other's burden', 1987), a mild plea for tolerance between Church and state and a big success with audiences, which took it as a starting-point for more in-depth debate. Meanwhile DEFA intensified its contacts with the west by entering into co-productions with Austria and pre-selling films to West German television, and using the money thus raised to buy colour film stock from the west (the East German ORWO stock was slow and lacked brilliance) or the rights to popular music. Ties with West Germany became closer. DEFA offered its services to western film companies and television stations, arranging for the shooting of West German films in East Germany (*Frühlingssinfonie* ('Spring symphony', 1982), with Nastassja Kinski) or producing films commissioned by West German television. In 1988 they finally made a film openly aimed at the West German market. *Der Bruch* ('The break') was directed by Frank Beyer, who had recently been working mainly in the west, from a script by Wolfgang Kohlhasse, returning here to his favourite genre of realistic comedy set in Berlin in the immediate post-war years, and used an ensemble of popular actors from both sides of the Wall.

In 1988 the long-standing head of DEFA, Hans-Dieter Mäde, a member of the Central Committee of the Communist Party, resigned and was replaced by former technical director Gert Golde. Rudolf Jürschik, who as Chef-Dramaturg had fought hard, though mostly in vain, to widen the artistic and critical perspectives of the studio, was made artistic director. Old projects were resurrected and new ones developed in contravention of long-standing taboos. The Film Ministry even agreed late in 1989 to the formation of an independent film-production group outside DEFA—the DaDaeR group, which took its name from its first completed film, Jörg Foth's *Letztes aus der DaDaeR* ('Latest news from the GeeDeeaR').

So, when at the end of 1989 the old Communist leadership was ousted and the Wall came down, DEFA had ready for release some critical films which mirrored the new political realities. But the audience was gone: they had either driven away to the west in their Trabis, or had simply lost interest in anything concerning the old regime.

Bibliography

Behn, Manfred, and Bock, Hans-Michael (eds.) (1988–9), *Film und Gesellschaft in der DDR.*

Jacobsen, Wolfgang (ed.) (1992), *Babelsberg: ein Filmstudio.*

Rülicke-Weiler, Käthe (ed.) (1979), *Film- und Fernsehkunst der DDR: Traditionen, Beispiele, Tendenzen.*

Schenk, Rolf (ed.) (1994), *Das zweite Leben der Filmstadt Babelsberg.*

Changing States in East Central Europe

MAREK HENDRYKOWSKI

The post-war cinema in east central Europe follows a chronology quite different from that of its western counterparts. Its main stages are signposted by a series of caesuras: 1945, 1948–9, 1956, 1968, 1970, 1980–1, 1989, each of which is connected with crucial political events in the eastern bloc and points to the major influence of politics and ideology on its development.

While 1945 itself marks the liberation of eastern and central Europe from German occupation, 1948–9 marks the negative side of that liberation. For it was then, with 'satellite' regimes established throughout the region (with the partial exception of Yugoslavia), that the Socialist Realist doctrine imported from the USSR was forcibly imposed on the cinemas of Poland, Czechoslovakia, Hungary, and other countries under Communist rule. The year 1956 is then a major landmark for Poland and Hungary in particular, signalling the beginning of the slow but irreversible process of de-Stalinization; 1968 brought the 'Prague Spring', followed in August of that year by the Soviet invasion of Czechoslovakia which cruelly wrote off the achievements of the Czech and Slovak 'New Wave'. In Poland (though not in other eastern bloc countries) 1970 in turn proved to be a political turning-point, as did August 1980, with the birth of the Solidarity movement, and December 1981, with the introduction of martial law. Finally, in 1989 the fall of the Communist system was of paramount importance everywhere, though in Yugoslavia it signified the pending collapse of the federal state and the subsequent catastrophe of civil war.

This periodization, and the political factors that determined it, is a specific feature of post-war east central European cinema, and it is hardly surprising that for several decades cinema critics and historians were chiefly interested in the 'political' (i.e. 'anti-regime') film, and aesthetic criteria often took second place to political. Now that the old political contexts have lost their immediacy and relevance, artistic criteria can once again reassert themselves, making it possible to re-evaluate such masterpieces as Andrzej Wajda's war tetralogy *A Generation, Canal, Ashes and Diamonds,* and *Lotna* in the 1950s, Miloš Forman's triptych *Peter and Pavla, A Blonde in Love,* and *The Firemen's Ball* in the 1960s, and Márta Mészáros's three-part 'Diary'—*Diary for my Children, Diary for my Loves,* and *Diary for my Father and my Mother* in the 1980s.

EVASIVE STRATEGIES

Political circumstances, and film-makers' responses to them, led east central European cinemas in the post-war period to adopt a number of distinct strategies, which can be summarized as follows:

Historicism

In the Hungarian and Polish cinema, and to a lesser extent the Czech, there is often an obsessive interest in national history seen through the prism of an evil fate and the notion of an irreversible catastrophe by which both individuals and entire communities are foredoomed. Over the years strategies have evolved for overcoming this fatalism through ironic distance and black humour, often highly suggestive, as in the films of Andrzej Munk (*Eroica,* 1957; *Bad Luck,* 1959), Vojtěch Jasný (*September Nights,* 1957; *All my Good Countrymen,* 1968), Jiří Menzel (*Closely Observed Trains,* 1966; *Cutting It Short,* 1981), and Péter Bacsó (*The Witness,* 1968; *Oh, Bloody Life,* 1983). In these films history remains crucial, but it is framed in the categories of tragicomedy, which triggers off a process of collective therapy in the form of often bitter, cathartic laughter.

Documentarism

In east central Europe the cinema of fiction in particular is characterized by its documentary quality and attachment to concrete reality, on the basis of which it can then be used as an instrument of social diagnosis. There is in fact no conflict or contradiction in terms between fiction and documentary, from which feature films constantly draw inspiration; and it is no accident that many of the eminent directors of east central Europe—Miklós Jancsó, Andrzej Munk, Miloš Forman, Krzysztof Kieślowski, Károly Makk, to name but a few—made their débuts as directors of documentaries. In their hands the original 'document' is refashioned into a more or less conventionalized world, which however remains firmly rooted in the minutiae of the reality represented.

A subtle mixture of fiction and documentarism is particularly characteristic of the development of the Czech school of the 1960s, whose socio-political diagnoses were of increasing concern to the Communist authorities, even in films as seemingly innocent as Forman's *The Firemen's Ball*, Menzel's *Capricious Summer* (1968), Jan Němec's *The Party and the Guests* (1966), or the lesser-known work of Evald Schorm (*Everyday Courage*, 1964; *Martyrs of Love*, 1966; *End of a Priest*, 1969). The Czech model for analysing a selected segment of society as a sample of the system at large soon caught on both in Yugoslavia—in the work of Aleksandar Petrović, Živojin Pavlović, and Boro Drašković—and in Poland, where it had a marked influence on Krzysztof Zanussi (*Structure of Crystals*, 1969; *Illumination*, 1973) and Marek Piwowski (*The Cruise*, 1969). A decade later Agnieszka Holland, a graduate of FAMU in Prague and the author of *Provincial Actors* (1978), succeeded in further refining the Czech formula and adapting it along creative lines.

Literary affinities

East central European cinema has frequent recourse to literature as a major source for theme, style, and philosophical outlook on life, and a considerable number of eminent Czech, Polish, and Hungarian films are adaptations of classical and contemporary literary works. Writers working in films have made a substantial contribution to the development of film art in Poland, Czechoslovakia, and Hungary—for instance Tadeusz Konwicki, the author of *The Last Day of Summer* (1958), a foremost novelist and film director whose authorial films reflect and develop the themes of his novels, and Jerzy Stefan Stawiński, who has written some of the Polish school's most significant screenplays. Since the 1960s the Czech cinema has enjoyed the patronage of Bohumil Hrabal, Josef Škvorecký, and Milan Kundera. Without Tibor Déry, Károly Makk would never have created the masterpiece of Hungarian cinematography that is *Love* (1977). This literary connection, a quasi-symbiosis of literature and film, enabled Polish and Czech cinema in the 1950s to evolve a unique formula for transposing a literary work freely and creatively to the screen.

Aesopic film language

This stems from the harsh rigours of censorship imposed on art and cinematography in the eastern bloc countries. For several decades a subtle use of metaphors, symbols, allusions, subtexts, and understatements effectively enabled film-makers to communicate with their public above the head of the censor, though at the same time it created a hermetic cultural code which made the deeper intricacies of films by Wajda, Jancsó, Konwicki, or Jerzy Skolimowski less readily accessible to foreign audiences. Faced with the impossibility of depicting anything directly, film-makers perfected this method of communication, resorting in the process to a rich variety of semantic tropes and stylistic devices whenever they needed to circumvent the censor's taboos. On occasions it yielded magnificent artistic results, as with *Ashes and Diamonds* (1958), *Ashes* (1965, based on the novel by Stefan Zeromski), and *The Wedding* (1972, based on Stanislaw Wyspianski's political symbolist drama), all directed by Andrzej Wajda; *The Red and the White* (1967) and *Red Psalm* (1972), by Miklós Jancsó; *The Stud Farm* (1978) by András Kovács; and Károly Makk's *Another Way* (1982). Other, less unequivocally successful examples include István Szabó's *Father* (1966) and András Kovács's *Labyrinth*, and Krzysztof Kieślowski's *No End*, filmed after martial law in 1984. Aesopic language continued to be practised in Polish cinema well into the 1980s.

Artistic values

Throughout east central Europe the cinema has consistently been treated as a full-fledged art in its own right, on a par with literature, theatre, painting, and music—an equality inspired by the Romantic notion of *correspondance des arts*. Since the foundation of the Polish film school in 1956, the notion of artistic cinema has played a prominent role in the countries of east central Europe and cinema enjoys high artistic prestige. The authorial film is not a commodity but a contemporary art form, directed to a mass audience. This approach is closely linked with the notion of the mission of art and the responsible position of the artist characteristic of the Romantic cultural tradition in Poland and Hungary in particular and renewed in the period of Communist rule. Accordingly, the filmmaker is an artist called upon to stir the conscience of society and tackle the most vital issues of the nation. This is how Wajda, Munk, Zoltán Fábri, and Jancsó have seen their role, and the same could be said of Mészáros, Jerzy Kawalerowicz, Konwicki, Juraj Jakubisko, Lordan Zafranović, and others, who are similarly fascinated by the heritage of national history and culture, and dedicated to perpetuating its memory.

Andrzej Wajda

(1926–)

The son of a cavalry officer, Andrzej Wajda was barely 13 years old when the Germans invaded Poland in 1939, and 16 when he joined the Resistance. After liberation, he studied painting at the Academy of Fine Arts in Cracow for three years, but in 1949 decided to become a film-maker and went to the Film School in Łódź, where he made a number of short films before graduating in 1952. In 1954 he directed his first feature, the resistance drama *A Generation* (*Pokolenie*), which had Tadeusz Łomnicki in the main role and Roman Polański and Zbigniew Cybulski in minor roles. He then made *Kanał* (1957), set in the Warsaw sewers during the 1944 Uprising, and on the strength of its success was appointed head of the so-called Polish Film School. The relative liberalization introduced in Poland after 1956 enabled him to complete his 'Warsaw trilogy' (as it came to be called) with the even more remarkable *Ashes and Diamonds* (*Popiół i diament*, 1958), in which Cybulski plays the starring role as the hero Maciek Chełmicki. With his dark glasses and diffident tough-guy look, Cybulski was to become a national icon and a hero of the generation growing up under Communism after the war. His life and his tragic death in a train accident in 1967 were to form the theme of Wajda's *Everything for Sale* (*Wszystko na sprzedaż*, 1968).

He was to return to the theme of Poland's Second World War experience in *Landscape after the Battle* (*Krajobraz po bitwie*, 1970), but he also delved further back into history, as in *Ashes* (*Popioły*, 1965), set in the Napoleonic Wars, and the British-made *Gates to Paradise* (1967), about the Children's Crusade. During the Thaw in the 1960s he was also able to make charming contemporary films such as *Innocent Sorcerers* (*Niewinni czarodzieje*, 1960) and the 'Warsaw' episode of the compilation *L'Amour à vingt ans* (1962). But it was with the repression that returned in 1970 and the subsequent emergence of the Solidarity movement that he reacquired a role as a national figure and focus of resistance through his leadership of the 'X' film ensemble and his own films *Man of Marble* (*Człowiek z marmuru*, 1976), *Without Anaesthetic* (*Bez znieczulenia*, 1977—also known as *Rough Treatment*), and *Man of Iron* (*Człowiek z żelaza*, 1981), in which he probed Poland's Stalinist past and neo-Stalinist present in a manner that was both uncompromising and uncomfortable to the authorities—and which owed a lot to his formal experiment with *Everything for Sale*. In 1982 he made the remarkable *Danton*, with Gérard Depardieu. During the mid-1980s he spent much of his time in quasi-emigration in the west. In 1989, with the coming to power of the Solidarity-led government he became a member of the Polish Senate, a just reward for the proud role he had played in national political and artistic life over four decades.

GEOFFREY NOWELL-SMITH
MAREK HENDRYKOWSKI

FILMOGRAPHY

A Generation (Pokolenie) (1954); Kanał (1957); Ashes and Diamonds (Popiół i diament) (1958); Lotna (1959); Innocent Sorcerers (Niewinni czarodzieje) (1960); Samson (1961); Lady Macbeth of Mtensk (Sibirska ledi Magbet) (1962); Warsaw (1962); Ashes (Popioły) (1965); Gates to Paradise (1967); Everything for Sale (Wszystko na sprzedaż) (1968); Hunting Flies (Polowanie na muchy) (1969); Landscape after the Battle (Krajobraz po bitwie) (1970); The Birch Wood (Brzezina) (1970); Pilatus und andere (1972); The Wedding (Wesele) (1972); Promised Land (Ziemia obiecana) (1974); The Shadow Line (Smuga cienia) (1976); Man of Marble (Człowiek z marmuru) (1976), Without Anaesthetic (Bez znieczulenia) (1977); The Maids of Wilko (Panny z Wilka) (1979); Dyrygent (The Conductor) (1980); Man of Iron (Człowiek z żelaza) (1981); Danton (1982); A Love in Germany (Eine Liebe in Deutschland) (1983); Chronicle of a Love Affair (Kronika wypadków milosnych) (1986); Les Possédés (1987); Korczak (1990); The Girl with a Crowned Eagle (1992); Nastassja (1994).

BIBLIOGRAPHY

Michałek, Bolesław (1973), *The Cinema of Andrzej Wajda*.

Zbigniew Cybulski as the Polish resistance fighter at the end of the war, in Wajda's violent tale of political conflicts, *Ashes and Diamonds* (1958).

Even unambiguously political films were artistically far more important than was often appreciated at the time, when their artistic merit tended to be overshadowed by the 'hot' political context out of which they emerged. Wajda's *Man of Marble* (1976), for example, is mainly famous for having broken the censor's taboo that had shrouded the Stalinist era in silence for two decades in Poland and other eastern bloc countries, and on that basis it attracted millions of spectators in Poland and earned considerable fame abroad. But its artistic originality will undoubtedly outlast its immediate context, and if *Man of Marble* is often repeated in cinemas and on television, this is as much on account of its artistic qualities, which will ensure it a permanent place in Polish cinema, as for its political relevance.

For some Polish, Czech, and Hungarian film-makers artistry has become an autonomous value, as borne out by the aesthetically refined works of Karel Zeman (*An Invention for Destruction*, 1958), Wojciech Jerzy Has (*The Saragossa Manuscript*, 1964—based on the novel by Jan Potocki), Zoltán Huszárik (*Sinbad*, 1971), and the animations of Jan Švankmajer (*The Flat*, 1968; *The Garden*, 1968; *Dimensions of Dialogue*, 1982; and *Alice*, 1988). The cult of artistry provided an escape from the conflicting pressures of having to make films to satisfy, elude, or challenge the censoring authorities.

CHRONOLOGY

Cinema in the countries of east central Europe falls into four basic stages of development:

1945–1956

The nationalization of the film industry according to the Soviet model in Poland, Hungary, and Yugoslavia in 1945, and in Czechoslovakia in 1948, brought with it certain advantages but also imposed a heavy, and sometimes unsupportable, burden on the cinema. The obvious advantages of state investment and permanent subsidies were bought at the heavy cost of extreme centralization and the administrative-ideological dictate of the Party. The fact that the cinema of 'real socialism' is not governed by money and the laws of the free market did not mean that film-makers enjoyed total freedom for their artistic creation: they were allowed only so much as lay in the interests of state patronage. Every project was controlled and analysed *ab ovo* by the official party apparatus until the screenplay was finally approved for production. Prior to release the film was again subjected to a terminal inspection. This was particularly true during the Stalinist period. But in Poland even as late as 1982 the tempestuous viewing of Ryszard Bugajski's *Interrogation* during martial law very nearly resulted in the destruction of the film's photographic materials by neo-Stalinist forces, and was possibly the most notorious instance of

its kind in the entire history of east central European cinema.

In view of the high degree of ideologization to which Eastern bloc cinema was subjected in the 1940s and 1950s, one may well wonder why films enjoyed such popularity among mass audiences. The answer reveals another basic cultural difference between east central Europe and the west in those years. Paradoxically, education of the masses awakened the cultural needs of a collectivity living behind a hermetically sealed Iron Curtain and denied access to the so-called bourgeois imperialistic culture of the west. The spontaneous demand for cultural goods far exceeded their strictly limited supply. In a time of ideological deprivation people flocked to the cinema in their millions regardless of what film was being shown. Comedies, war films or films about the partisans, thrillers, spy or detective stories, adventures, dramas, even a film about factories might prove attractive, independently of its ideological message. In this manner the cinema of east central Europe survived the first decade after the war, giving birth on occasion to such quality films as Géza Radványi's *Somewhere in Europe* (1947), Wanda Jakubowska's *The Last Stage* (1948), Jiří Trnka's version of *The Good Soldier Schweik* (1955), Károly Makk's *Liliomfi* (1954), and, perhaps most famously, Andrzej Wajda's *A Generation* (1954).

1956–1968

The beginnings of the Thaw in 1953–6 and the decisive social and political events of 1956 resulted in a flowering of the Polish cinema in the second half of the 1950s, followed by a renaissance of Czech, Hungarian, and Yugoslav cinema. First the Polish film school (between 1956 and 1960), and then in the 1960s the new waves in Czechoslovakia and Yugoslavia and the new Hungarian cinema, brought to the fore a crop of talented young film-makers. These included Andrzej Wajda, Andrzej Munk, Wojciech Jerzy Has, Jerzy Kawalerowicz, Roman Polański, Jerzy Skolimowski in Poland; Miklós Jancsó and Károly Makk in Hungary; Věra Chytilová, Miloš Forman, and Jiří Menzel in Czechoslovakia; and Aleksandar Petrović and Dušan Makavejev in Yugoslavia. The fact that these film-makers and others like them were able to make films of world standing was a direct result of the de-Stalinization process and the abandonment of the Socialist Realist doctrine in art. From 1956 onwards, though with a number of ups and downs, film-makers steadily gained a wide margin of creative freedom. The changes initiated by the reform of Polish cinematography in June 1955 resulted in the creation of Film-Makers' Ensembles, a unique form of self-governing film-production body that gave a significant degree of autonomy in decision-making to the artists concerned. The best-known film ensemble was 'Kadr' which flourished from 1955 to 1968, and with which Wajda,

College students face the police in Miklós Jansó's *The Confrontation* (1968), which combines an allegorical treatment of Hungarian history after 1945 and an original, almost manneristic, cinematic style

Munk, Kawalerowicz, Has, Kutz, and Konwicki were all connected. The tradition of 'Kadr' was then carried on by the film ensemble 'X', under Wajda's direction, in the years 1972 to 1983, and similar practices spread to other countries, the film ensemble 'Objektiv' in Budapest, directed by Peter Bacsó, enjoying particular prestige.

Increasing freedom led rapidly to international success at festivals and on the art-cinema circuits in the west. Wajda's *Kanal* (1957) and *Ashes and Diamonds* (1958) were followed by Kawalerowicz's *The Devil and the Nun* (1961), and Roman Polański's début feature *Knife in the Water* (1962). The years preceding the 'Prague Spring' brought Forman's *Peter and Pavla* (1963), *A Blonde in Love* (1965), and *The Firemen's Ball* (1967), Chytilová's *Daisies* (1966), and Menzel's *Closely Observed Trains* (1966), all films based on observation of the everyday and enlivened by a wry humour and subtle eroticism. A very different course was followed by Miklós Jansó in Hungary, whose *The Round-up* (1965), *The Red and the White* (1967), and *The Confrontation* (1968) inaugurated a series of national allegories marked by epic scale, singing, and sweeping camera movements.

The world-wide interest aroused by these 'eastern bloc'

films was taken in the west as evidence of the gradual democratization taking place behind the Iron Curtain, and while this was obviously in the interests of the Communist authorities (or at least the more liberal sections of them), it also encouraged the film-makers further to exploit the freedom which success had brought them. But the spurious nature of this freedom became only too apparent in June 1960, when the Polish school of 1956–60 was attacked by the Party authorities and closed down by order of the Politburo. The harsh administrative and ideological rigours to which Polish cinema was subsequently subjected resulted in stagnation. Although this did not prevent the sporadic appearance of such eminent works as Polański's *Knife in the Water*, Jerzy Skolimowski's *Walkover* (1965), Has's *The Saragossa Manuscript*, Kawalerowicz's *Pharaoh* (1965), and Wajda's *Ashes* (1965) and *Everything for Sale* (1968), conditions remained tense throughout the period. *Knife in the Water* was denounced as an 'anti-socialist film', and shortly afterwards Polański emigrated to the west, followed somewhat later by Skolimowski.

Events in Czechoslovakia were even more dramatic. In

the spring of 1968 the Czech cinema enjoyed an unprecedented freedom in circumstances which suggested that de-Stalinization was already a reality. Few of the films made were overtly anti-regime. Many, however, were quietly critical of the state of Czech society, while others celebrated the freedom of the Prague Spring by avoiding political topics entirely. Following the Soviet invasion, all this varied production, in Slovakia as well as in the Czech part of the country, was wiped out. Some film-makers stayed behind, to make whatever films they were permitted to; others, including Ivan Passer and Miloš Forman, emigrated and tried to continue their career abroad—in Forman's case with some success.

The Czech experience also brought to the fore the peculiar feature of cinema life in eastern bloc countries known as the 'shelf film'. This is the term given to completed films which are then banned (often in perpetuity) by the authorities and 'shelved' for reasons of political censorship. This practice was fairly widespread throughout the eastern bloc, particularly at times when a partial liberalization was followed by a clamp-down, as happened in East Germany around 1965–6. In the Czech case the shelving of the progressive films produced before August 1968, and tightened censorship thereafter, led to the obliteration of an entire artistic trend, which was never able to resurface.

In multinational Yugoslavia, which had escaped some of the worst rigours of Stalinism, the 1960s saw the cinema attain a new artistic maturity. In Zagreb (Croatia), from the 1950s onwards, Dušan Vukotić and his colleagues pioneered a new freewheeling graphic style of animation, which offered a welcome alternative to conventional 'Disney' styles, while Belgrade (Serbia) became a centre of documentary production. The prestige of Yugoslav cinema both at home and abroad was further enhanced by the increasingly confident output of features. Aleksandar Petrović—with *Days* (1963), *Three* (1965), *I Even Met Some Happy Gipsies* (1967), and *It Rains in my Village* (1968)—and Živojin Pavlović—notably with *When I'll Be Dead and White* (1967)—were the main beneficiaries. But what particularly captured public attention was the meteoric career of Dušan Makavejev, whose *Man Is Not a Bird* (1965), *The Switchboard Operator* (1967), and *Innocence Unprotected* (1968) mounted a flamboyant attack on the sexual repressiveness enshrined in official socialist values.

The 1970s and 1980s

The cinema of east central Europe continued to perform an important social role throughout the 1970s and 1980s. Even in post-1968 Czechoslovakia a number of quality films were produced, including *Seclusion near Forest* (1977) and *Cutting It Short* (1980) by Jiří Menzel, *Jara Cimrman, Lying Asleep* (1983) by Ladislav Smoljak, *Dimensions of Dialogue* (1982) and *Down to the Cellar* (1983) by Jan Švankmajer,

and *Prefab Story* (1979) and *The Very Late Afternoon of a Faun* (1983) by Věra Chytilová. But it was Slovak rather than Czech cinema that came to the fore from the mid-1970s onwards. Slovak cinema had little distinct identity in the 'New Wave' years and after 1968 film censorship was less rigorous in Slovakia than in the Czech capital. As a result film-makers such as Štefan Uher, Dušan Hanák, and Juraj Jakubisko were able to pursue their careers relatively unimpeded (though Hanák's 1969 film *399*, winner of an award at Mannheim, was banned in Czechoslovakia itself).

Of the many distinguished films produced in Slovakia between 1975 and 1985 (generally modest in scale, but none the worse for that), Jakubisko's magnificent poetic fresco *The Millennial Bee* (1983) is in a class apart. This film saga about the Pichand family from Liptow displays a bewitchingly sensuous beauty of images and supernatural screen events—a falling star, green rain, a spherical shaft of lightning. Through its contact with nature and its feeling of participating in something indestructible and more durable than the life of the individual bee, Jakubisko's epic film invests the fate dogging the industrious Slovak with a historical and philosophical dimension that makes it possible to look into the future with hope.

Meanwhile in Poland in the mid-1970s, in the face of sundry censorial sanctions and stringencies, a new artistic trend called Cinema of Moral Concern came into being, characterized by sensitivity to ethical problems and a special focus on the relation of the individual to society and the state. Foremost titles include Wajda's *Man of Marble* (1976) and *Rough Treatment* (1977), Marcel Łoziński's *How Are We to Live* (1977), Zanussi's satire *Camouflage* (1976) and *The Constant Factor* (1980), Kieślowski's *The Scar* (1976) and *Camera Buff* (1979), Agnieszka Holland's *Provincial Actors* (1979), and Feliks Falk's *Top Dog* (1977).

The rise of the Solidarity movement refocused attention on politics. The chronicle of the strike in the Gdansk shipyard in August 1980 was recorded live by a team of documentarists ('Workers 80'). Many leading Polish film-makers, including Kieślowski and Holland, were involved with the Solidarity movement and their films contributed to the political ferment of the time. Pride of place, however, must go to Wajda's *Man of Iron* (1981), winner of the Palme d'Or at Cannes, and to Ryszard Bugajski's *Interrogation* (1982), which chronicled the nightmare of terror applied by the Stalinist security apparatus.

After martial law was lifted, Polish cinema became increasingly commercialized. This did not, however, prevent the making of films such as Zanussi's *The Year of Quiet Sun* (1983), Wiesław Saniewski's *Surveillance* (1984), and Kieślowski's *No End* (1984). Relatively unknown until then outside Poland, Kieślowski sprang into prominence with his 'Decalogue' (1988–90), a series of films about the Ten Commandments made for television, two of which in particular—*A Short Film about Killing* and *A Short Film about Love*—enjoyed a successful international cinematic release.

Events in Hungary pursued a calmer course, with the authorities pursuing a reformist policy which was to lead to a relatively smooth transition to liberalism and a market economy at the end of the 1980s. Meanwhile in the early 1970s Jancsó continued his series of allegorical films with *Red Psalm* (1972) and *Elektreia* (1974). Briefly tempted westwards to make the bizarre *Private Vices, Public Virtues* as an Italian–Yugoslav co-production, he returned to Hungary to make *Allegro Barbaro* and *Hungarian Rhapsody* (both 1978). By this time, however, he was by no means the only Hungarian film-maker to enjoy a world-wide reputation. Besides the established Károly Makk and Peter Bacsó, new talents had also emerged including Pál Gábor (*Angi Vera*, 1978) and András Kovács (*The Stud Farm*, 1978). More important still were István Szabó, whose films of the 1980s were to include the Oscar-winning *Mephisto* (1981) and *Colonel Redl* (1984), and Márta Mészáros.

Trained in Moscow, Mészáros's career as a film-maker had begun in the 1960s, but it was with *Adoption* (1975) that she first came to world attention. Although she always rejected the feminist label given to her by her admirers in the west, she was (with the possible exception of Chytilová) the first woman director in east central European cinema to explore from a woman's point of view the relations between political and personal life. Precariously combining realist and romantic aspects, her films of the 1970s sympathetically explore the day-to-day tribulations of mainly female characters. More recently, particularly in her three-part 'Diary' (1982–90)—*Diary for my Children*, *Diary for my Loves*, and *Diary for my Father and my Mother*—these concerns have been enriched by an autobiographical and emotionally charged element, enabling her not only to confront personal traumas but to address and come to terms with historical themes, including the suppressed revolution of 1956.

Aleksandar Petrović, for long a leading light of Yugoslav cinema, made his last film in his home country, *The Master and Margarita*, in 1972. The year before Dušan Makavejev had taken his sexual-liberationist ethic to the limits of the permissible with *W. R.: Mysteries of the Organism* (loosely inspired by Wilhelm Reich's *The Function of the Orgasm*), before departing for the United States. The loss of these film-makers opened the way for the emergence of a new generation. Among these, Lordan Zafranović, creator of the magnificent *Occupation in 26 Scenes* (1978) and *Evening Bells* (1986), is probably the most exceptional talent, followed by Srdjan Karanović (*The Scent of Wild Flowers*, 1978; *Petrija's Wreath*, 1980; *A Throatful of Strawberries*, 1985). In terms of international success, however, pride of place goes to the Bosnian Emir Kusturica, whose *Do You Remember Dolly Bell?* won the Golden Lion at Venice in 1981 and *When Father Was away on Business* the Palme d'Or at Cannes in 1985. With *Time of the Gypsies* (1989) Kusturica further affirmed his reputation as a world-class European director.

Catherine Deneuve in Roman Polański's first British film, *Repulsion* (1965)

Part of his ten-film series the Decalogue, *A Short Film about Killing* (1989) launched Krzysztof Kieślowski's international directing career

Émigrés

Considering the amount of political repression exercised in the Soviet bloc countries throughout the post-war period, it is remarkable how few film-makers chose the route of emigration during those years. Those who did emigrate, moreover, rarely encountered the sort of success abroad that they had enjoyed in their home countries— or, for that matter, the success of some of their predecessors from the waves of *émigrés* who escaped from Russia in the 1920s or Germany in the 1930s. Among those who emigrated, however, on a permanent or more or less permanent basis, were at least four film-makers of exceptional talent: Roman Polański and Jerzy Skolimowski from Poland, Miloš Forman from Czechoslovakia, and Dušan Makavejev from Yugoslavia. Of these only Polański and Forman were able to carve out distinctive careers for themselves in the west.

For a time in the 1960s Skolimowski attempted to pursue a film-making career on both sides of the Iron Curtain, but the banning in Poland of his anti-Stalinist *Barrier* (1967) effectively persuaded him that he had no future in his own country. His subsequent career took him to the United States as well as Belgium, France, Germany, and Britain. He had great difficulty establishing a base for himself, but his sharp eye for nuances of behaviour enabled him to make at least two very good films set in Britain, *Deep End* (1970) and *Moonlighting* (1982).

Roman Polański also made Britain a port of call after leaving Poland, directing two quasi-surrealist horror films, *Repulsion* (1965, with Catherine Deneuve) and *Cul-de-Sac* (1966), before settling in the United States. The foreigner's eye-view evident in the use of London locations in *Repulsion* was deployed to even greater effect in *Chinatown* (1974), which must count as one of the best films ever made about Los Angeles. But Polański's most distinctive feature remains the cruelty of his vision and the voyeuristic and sadistic approach to characters (particularly women) under the stress of sexual terror. These were not characteristics which he would have found easy to exploit in the repressive Polish context.

By contrast with Polański, Forman is by temperament a gentle director. His first film in the United States, *Taking off* (1971), attempted to study American family life and teenage rebellion with the same delicacy of observation he had shown in his Czech films. Thereafter he was to tackle an assortment of themes and subjects. An interest in the fragile borderline between sanity and madness sustains both *One Flew over the Cuckoo's Nest* (1975) and *Amadeus* (1984), but otherwise he found it difficult to recover the consistency of style that had marked his early work.

THE POST-COMMUNIST ORDER

Following the political changes of 1989, the cinemas of Poland, Hungary, the Czech and Slovak republics, and the fast disintegrating Yugoslavia entered an entirely new phase. Political censorship was done away with, but the shift to a market economy led to drastic cuts in state subsidy for the cinema, particularly in the Czech Republic and Hungary, and a massive drop in indigenous film production. In the component parts of the former Yugoslavia (with the exception of Slovenia) production underwent a catastrophic decline as the country was plunged into civil war.

Polish cinema is relatively speaking in the best shape, being still partly subsidized by the state. Over thirty feature films were made in Poland in 1992, and this level of output was sustained through 1993. In Hungary and the Czech and Slovak republics, however, the decline in subsidized production left massive facilities lying idle and collapse was averted only by renting out studio space and services to film and television companies from the west.

The cinemas of all the post-Communist countries have come to depend increasingly on co-production for their survival. Co-production with both east and west was not uncommon in the past, but it always left space for a core of production which was national at heart. Now it has become a necessity and, as such, a mixed blessing. While providing a lifeline for struggling industries, it brings with it the risk of standardization and homogenization of film production, and a consequent threat both to individual creativity and to national specificity. The internationalization of film production is changing the character of the films produced and threatening their cultural identity in a world where the commercial-entertainment cinema genres prevail.

Films of eminent artistic quality still continue to be produced on a national basis or as international co-productions by the leading directors of central and eastern Europe. One might mention here *The Double Life of Veronica* (1991) by Krzysztof Kieślowski, *Virginia* (1991) by Srdjan Karanović, *Europe, Europe* (1991) by Agnieszka Holland, *Meeting Venus* (1991) by István Szabó, *The Silent Touch* (1992) by Krzysztof Zanussi, and *Arizona Dream* (1991), made with French money by Emir Kusturica. Paradoxically, the Bosnian *émigré* Kusturica made his film abroad at the very time the French documentarists Thierry Ravalet and Alain Ferrari were making their disturbing documentary *Un jour dans la mort de Sarajevo* in Bosnia. Will the future spare the cinemas of central and east Europe such paradoxes? Knowing the range of talent of which these countries dispose, and the strong national traditions developed, some sort of revival can be predicted. But, as the smaller countries of western Europe have already learnt, film production without protection or subsidy is hard to maintain when serving only a small domestic market and exposed to the blast of foreign competition.

Bibliography

Goulding, Daniel J. (ed.) (1989), *Post New Wave Cinema in the Soviet Union and Eastern Europe*.

Liehm, Mira, and Liehm, Antonin J. (1977), *The Most Important Art: Eastern European Film after 1945*.

Michałek, Bolesław, and Turaj, Frank (1988), *The Modern Cinema of Poland*.

Russia After the Thaw

VIDA JOHNSON

STALIN'S LEGACY

Although the Communist Party's and Stalin's personal control over cinema clearly had a highly deleterious effect on cinema as an art form from the 1930s to the mid-1950s, Soviet cinema developed into a large-scale industry in the 1930s primarily because of the serious attention paid to it by the government and the resources which were chan-nelled to the major studios. Cinema became not only a political and ideological tool for mass indoctrination, but also a medium of mass entertainment modelled on Hollywood. Some of the most popular films ever made in the Soviet Union are classics from the 1930s such as the Vasilievs' *Chapayev* (1934) and Grigory Alexandrov's *Volga–Volga* (1938). During the era of 'few films' in the last years of Stalin's rule, these, along with Western 'trophy' films, entertained the audiences as the few, monumental, bombastic, and ultimately dull epics produced in that period could not. Paradoxically, thanks to Stalin, a big movie fan himself, Russians had became avid movie-goers in the 1930s, particularly in the big cities. The popularity of the movies among the masses, pent-up demand for new films, large production capacity, numerous talented directors, script-writers, and cameramen (educated at the state's expense at VGIK, the All-Union State Institute of Film-Making) itching to get back to work or to make their first films—all helps to explain the rapid resurgence of cinema after Stalin's death.

From 1956 to the early 1960s, Soviet films annually won major awards at international film festivals, often causing a popular sensation as well. In contrast, the recent dismantling of the government-run cinema industry, especially of the big studios such as Mosfilm, and the privatization of film-making on the road to capitalism has had a disastrous effect on the ex-Soviet film industry, in many ways even more serious than Stalin's control in the period of few films.

Some film-makers and film critics (even those of a liberal political bent) are re-evaluating the role of Goskino, the government organization which ran the whole Soviet cinema industry. One side is well known: the officious character of the cinema leadership which controlled creativity from above; coercion of artists; irrational distribution of resources; local censorship and the punishment of original thinking; paternalism; and bureaucracy. But there was another side: the creation of a multinational cinema power-house ranked in the top five in the world; generous subsidy of film production and distribution which allowed film-makers to experiment and create artistic films; the encouragement of film education in other Soviet republics (for example, Georgia, Latvia) and socialist countries (Poland, Hungary, Czechoslovakia); the education of creative cadres; the freeing of the artist from material concerns; and the co-ordination of different branches of the industry. During the Stalin period the former side of Goskino prevailed, but during the Thaw which followed Stalin's death the latter, positive side was mainly in evidence.

THE THAW

The Thaw received its name from a 1954 work by the writer Ilya Ehrenburg, but it applied in equal measure to all the arts. Writers began calling for 'truth' and 'sincerity' in art and a renewed focus on individual human beings. They were not rejecting Socialist Realism, but giving it a gentler, more individualized human face. Artists and the public alike were tired of literature and cinema with stereotyped heroes in simplistic, monumental epics that rewrote history. After Khrushchev's denunciation of Stalin's 'cult of personality' at the 20th Communist Party Congress in 1956, the Thaw was in full force in all spheres of political and cultural life. The first major Thaw films appeared in 1956 and film critics consider the decade that followed—1957–67—as the time in which the liberal 'generation of the sixties' (*shestidesyatniki*) held sway in cinema.

This group's designation identified a new film style and thematics rather than the age of the film-makers themselves. In fact the group included established directors who began filming in the 1920s and 1930s such as Mikhail Kalatozov and Mikhail Romm, war veterans whose studies and film débuts were delayed by the war and the era of few films like Grigory Chukhrai, and a large talented pool of young film-makers who finished at VGIK in the late 1950s to early 1960s and whose début films made a splash, such as Andrei Tarkovsky and Andrei Konchalovsky. As these directors' projects were quickly approved by a cinema administration bent on changing the Stalinist system, film production increased with dizzying speed from fewer than ten films a year in the early 1950s to forty in 1954, and to a hundred feature films by the end of the decade.

The Soviet film industry would continue to increase output to 140–50 features per year in the 1970s and 1980s, the vast majority produced in the studios of the Russian republic, particularly in Moscow and Leningrad. However, the 1960s also saw the reopening of regional studios and the revival of national film traditions which had been suppressed under Stalin. This was particularly evident in Lithuania, where the talented director Vitautas Zhalakevichius worked, and the Ukraine, where the tradition of Dovzhenko was carried on by Sergei Paradjanov and his cameraman turned director Yuri Ilienko, who directed the beautiful *White Bird with a Black Spot* (*Belaya ptitsa s chernoy otmetinoy*, 1971).

Western sources on the cinema of the Thaw generally tend to focus on the 'serious' films which garnered the most international attention, yet an extremely popular hit of 1956 was *Carnival Night* (*Karnavalnaya noch*), the debut of Eldar Ryazanov, one of the most prolific and successful comedy directors of the last forty years. Comedies had disappeared after the war, and the hunger for the genre was so acute in the mid-1950s that even Party leaders were calling for a revival. *Carnival Night* pits a young enthusiastic group of Komsomol youth, who are planning a fun-filled New Year's Eve celebration in the House of Culture, against a middle-aged, portly, self-satisfied bureaucrat who, afraid of what the higher-ups might say, wants to make the occasion serious, educational, and uplifting by inserting Communist slogans which are ludicrously out of place. Igor Ilinsky, a famous comedy actor from the silent period, reprised the role of the obnoxious bureaucrat from the ever-popular 1938 Alexandrov musical comedy *Volga–Volga*. *Carnival Night* remained popular for decades.

The Thaw: Grigory Chukhrai's second feature, *The Ballad of a Soldier* (*Ballada o soldate*, 1959), deals with the suffering and loss inflicted on ordinary Russians during the Second World War

Comedies allowed directors and the audience to poke fun at the highly bureaucratic Communist system, even if, until *glasnost*, they never questioned its foundation. They were not only extremely entertaining and therapeutic, but also mirrored the absurdities of Soviet life and changing social and political concerns. Ryazanov followed *Carnival Night* with more hits, many of which were hailed by critics, the masses, and the educated élite alike, and remain some of the most watched films of the last forty years: *Beware of Automobiles* (*Beregis' avtomobila*, 1965), *An Office Romance* (*Sluzhebny roman*, 1978), *Train Station for Two* (*Vokzal na dvoikh*, 1983), *Forgotten Melody for Flute* (*Zabytaya melodiya dlya fleyty*, 1987), and most recently *The Promised Heavens* (*Nebesa obetovannye*, 1992).

Ryazanov was not the only successful director of comedies in this era. Leonid Gaidai (totally unknown outside the Soviet Union) made numerous lighter, often slapstick, comedies which entertained audiences through the 1960s and 1970s. *The Diamond Arm* (*Brilliantovaya ruka*), for example, starred the well-known comedian Lev Nikulin as a bumbling overworked economist whose wife sends him on what is meant to be a restful cruise. He becomes embroiled in a diamond theft when, due to mistaken identity, the diamonds are encased in a cast on his arm. The police then use him as bait to catch the thieves, and a riotously funny chase ensues, poking fun along the way at the foibles of simple Russians and bureaucrats alike.

The films that brought Soviet cinema back on to the world stage (first and foremost the festival stage at Cannes) were those which reconsidered Soviet history, focusing on human beings and downplaying the virtues of the monolithic Communist system. After a decade of Cold War politics, the earnest and emotional lyricism of the films coming out of the Soviet Union stunned the West. The first film to be recognized both at home and abroad was Grigory Chukhrai's début, *The Forty First* (*Sorok pervy*), a 1956 remake of a silent film. Set in the civil war, this love story of two stranded enemies, a Red commissar and her White prisoner, which ends tragically when she carries out her duty by killing her forty-first enemy, focuses on the complexities of the characters' emotions rather than the inevitable conflict of love versus duty. Lev Anninsky (1991), a well-known cultural and film historian who has written widely on the Thaw, calls the film a 'celebration of the human body ... a hymn of love', full of 'spirituality', running in parallel to the revolutionary theme.

In 1956 there were at least two other films which paved the way for new trends in Soviet cinema: Alexander Alov and Vladimir Naumov's *Pavel Korchagin*, a starkly romantic reinterpretation of Nikolai Ostrovsky's canonical Communist text *How the Steel Was Tempered*, and Marlen Khutsiev's and Felix Mironer's début *Spring on Zarechna Street* (*Vesna na Zarechnoy ulitse*), the first of a number of films by Khutsiev on the lives and loves of young adults. This is a story of a young, naïve teacher and her adult student who resists her attempts to tame and educate him. One of the film's innovations is the open ending which only hints at the further development of the love story. It opens up the world of emotions on the screen, while grounding the protagonists through a wealth of physical details in a specific, mostly urban Soviet environment. This film has given rise to two different trends, one leading to numerous sentimental youth films but, more importantly, one pointing towards the expression of psychological states and a poetry of the spirit.

Khutsiev's best and most controversial later film, *The Lenin Gate* (*Zastava Ilyicha*), cut, re-edited, renamed, and finally released as *I Am Twenty* (*Mne dvadtsat let*, 1962–5), is a much more complex story of the lives of three young friends making their way in the revitalized capital, Moscow. In this film the city is as much a star, and as full of promise, as the young men themselves. The first sign perhaps that the Thaw was to be short-lived was the attack on this film and its censoring and mutilation by the studio.

Two major themes were to predominate and overlap in the films of the Thaw period: youth coming of age and revisionist views of the war, focusing not on its glory but on its human cost. *I Am Twenty* was a subtle exploration of these themes, which had been poignantly and dramatically raised in the late 1950s by an internationally recognized triptych of war films: Kalatozov's *The Cranes are Flying* (*Letyat zhuravli*, 1957); Chukhrai's second feature, *The Ballad of a Soldier* (*Ballada o soldate*, 1959); and Sergei Bondarchuk's début based on a short story by Mikhail Sholokhov, *Destiny of a Man* (*Sudba cheloveka*, 1959).

These films allowed their audience the cathartic experience of sharing the pain, loss, and suffering of the Second World War which touched the life of every family in the Soviet Union. While rejecting the artificial heroism of the

war epics made in the last years of Stalin's rule, they do reach back to some of the highly emotional wartime films such as *The Rainbow* (*Raduga*, 1944). But while then the Russian soldiers, dressed in white camouflage, fought the Germans and won in a symbolically pristine white winter landscape, the soldiers in the war films of the Thaw period are literally mired in mud as they slog their way to battle. Bleak, burnt-out, muddy landscapes predominate and signal a new, unglorified view of war. The focus shifts from a common struggle and victory that unites 'the people' to the toll the war takes on individual human beings and their relationships.

In *The Cranes are Flying*, the winner of the Palme d'Or at Cannes in 1957, Boris, the hero, is felled by an unseen enemy's bullet as he trudges through a swampy landscape. In his final thoughts, visualized on the screen, he imagines his wedding, that will now never take place, to Veronika, the young woman he left behind. The 'war' film then becomes the story of Veronika's suffering, her transformation from a bright, lively, innocent girl to an emotionally dead 'fallen' woman who finally is redeemed by helping the war wounded and sharing their pain and grief, and by rescuing a little boy, also named Boris, from certain death.

Though the plot is pure melodrama, unusual casting and the excellent acting by Alexei Batalov and Tatiana Samoilova (as Boris and Veronika) combined with revitalized cinematography made this film the most highly acclaimed of all Soviet films of the 1950s. In international reputation it would only be surpassed by *Ivan's Childhood* (*Ivanovo detstvo*, 1962), Andrei Tarkovsky's first feature, which continued the youth in war theme, but presented it in a dramatic new way.

Tarkovsky takes a sparse, detached, realistic war story of a young scout's exploits and eventual death, and intersperses it with the boy's dreams of a happy, but tentative, childhood and of the mother and sister he lost in the war. As with other revisionist war films of the period, there is remarkably little action with only hints of fighting indicated by off-screen sounds, and a hallucinatory, burnt-out landscape that suggests a mental rather than a physical reality. What distinguishes *Ivan's Childhood*, however, is Tarkovsky's visual and aural presentation, his stylized, often expressionistic camera work and sound, all used to present the sharp contrasts between Ivan's two worlds: the shadowless dream world is bright, clean, full of sounds and images of the living beauty of nature; his real world is dirty, dark, deeply shadowed, distorted, with a silent, decimated landscape. Ivan is a man-child whose normal childhood is destroyed by the war and his psyche warped by the desire to avenge his dead family. While Tarkovsky was highly original in his style and presentation of his young hero, films focusing on children's experiences were quite popular, particularly in diploma or début works.

(Anninsky invents the term 'paedomania' to describe the times.) Partially under the influence of Albert Lamorisse's *The Red Balloon*, directors sought the fresh perspective of children not burdened by life's experience, politics, or ideology: Marlen Khutsiev's *Two Fedors* (*Dva Fedora*, 1959), Georgy Danelia and Igor Talankin's *Seriozha* (1962), and, probably the best in this genre, Mikhail Kalik's *Man Follows the Sun* (*Chelovek idyot za solntsem*, 1962), a boy's lyrical, fable-like journey through the city to face a number of separate vignettes both good and evil.

In a widely attended conference on 'The Language of Cinema' held in March 1962 at the Film-Makers' Union, Tarkovsky's teacher the director Mikhail Romm touted *Ivan's Childhood* as an example of a new, truly contemporary cinematic language. When the film won the Golden Lion at the Venice Film Festival in August, the instant international recognition was to make Tarkovsky (along with Sergei Paradjanov) into the leading figure of Soviet cinema in the west, but also was in the future to exacerbate his problems with the cinema bureaucracy and the censors at home.

While Kalatozov, Kalik, and Tarkovsky, among others, may have stylistically challenged the realism in the Socialist Realist formula, other directors, both younger and older, were seeking a new realism through a spare, more understated style. In the Thaw, a variety of filmic styles was once again possible, and the poetic lyricism of *Ivan's Childhood* could exist side by side with the narrative prose cinema of, for example, Yuli Raizman's *And what if It's Love?* (*A esli eto lyubov?*, 1962).

Raizman's film is a Romeo and Juliet story—a highschool romance which is destroyed by town gossip and the suspicious meddling of parents and teachers who do not believe in the possibility of innocent love. A shrewd observer of changing social mores, Raizman grounded his film in the physical reality of everyday life, and pointed to a need for a different way of treating the young in these new times. The oldest living Russian director (91 in 1994), Raizman made films from the 1920s to the late 1980s— for almost the whole history of Soviet cinema—but has received little recognition abroad, perhaps because he managed to survive all the political changes unscathed, and western critics are suspicious that those who were allowed to make films under Stalin must have done so by compromising themselves. Raizman's films reflect much that is universal in human nature, always presenting memorable and real human beings, and this perhaps is the best explanation of his ability to persevere.

The Thaw period was remarkable in the variety of individual styles and the number of different generations of directors all producing films; film-makers flourished, many producing the best work of their careers. Of the older generation, besides Raizman and Kalatozov, the most striking new beginning was made by Mikhail Romm,

who was known, particularly abroad, as a rather conservative director of films such as *Lenin in October* (1937). A highly erudite man and a well-respected teacher of the new generation (Tarkovsky, Konchalovsky, Shukshin, and many others), Romm underwent a transformation to produce one of the most striking films of 1962. In *Nine Days of One Year* (*Devyat dnei odnogo goda*) Romm raised contemporary issues and problems, capturing the mood of the 1960s through the philosophical discussions and actions of the protagonists—two scientists, rivals for the same woman, one of whom is living under sentence of death because he has, for the benefit of humanity, knowingly exposed himself to harmful radiation.

Romm followed up with a documentary masterpiece, *Ordinary Fascism* (*Obyknovenny fashizm*), providing the voiceover narration for selected German archival footage which recorded the ordinary lives of German soldiers under the rise of Fascism. While attempting to answer the question of what led to Fascism, the film makes a clear though unstated parallel with Stalinism.

A child of the Thaw period, the Moscow International Film Festival was founded in 1959 in order to provide a showcase for Soviet films, and re-establish the contact with western cinema which had been severed under Stalinism. For film-makers, film students, and particularly the intelligentsia, the Thaw was an exciting time of cultural exchanges with the west in all the arts. The Italian neo-realists, the French New Wave, Bergman, and Kurosawa joined the Soviet film-makers of the 1920s as role models for directors in a search for a new, more truthful realism.

Andrei Konchalovsky's first two feature films represented a new development toward a poetic yet gritty neo-realism. *The First Teacher* (*Pervy uchitel*, 1965) was shot on location in the stark mountains of Kirghizia where a naïve young Communist teacher tries to enlighten and rescue a local girl, who falls victim to the merciless patriarchal traditions of the area. *The Story of Asya Klyachina* (*Istoriya Asi Klyachinoy*, 1966, also known as *Asya's Happiness* (*Asino shchastie*)) documents the hard life of a typical Soviet collective farm (shot on location with the farmers playing all but the major roles) while telling the story of a handicapped young woman, an unmarried mother, who flouts convention for love and independence. It was banned outright in 1967 for demonstrating so clearly the economic failures of Communism. With the banning of *Asya*, along with Tarkovsky's second film, *Andrei Roublev*, and Alexander Askoldov's classic *The Commissar* (*Kommissar*, 1967), the Thaw came to an end in 1967.

Askoldov's film was considered so unsuitable that not only was it banned, but he was officially stripped of his profession and was never allowed to make a film again. Not even Paradjanov, who was goaled (on trumped-up charges of homosexuality and inciting nationalism), was prevented from making films upon his release. *The Commissar* was shelved not only because it offered an uncomfortably ruthless portrait of a female commissar during the Revolution, who leaves her baby with a Jewish family to go back and fight, but it also presented the Jews more sympathetically than the Communist heroine. Jews were simply a taboo subject in cinema and remained so until *glasnost*.

Not only was the wider public denied access to major new films, but within the industry itself the shelving of these films had a stifling effect on new movements and experimentation. The Party and industry bureaucracy reasserted their control over the artists, and censorship increased with the banning of more than a hundred feature films in the so-called period of stagnation from the late 1960s to the early 1980s. The critical brand of neo-realism developed by film-makers under the Thaw was not to survive, and instead a kind of 'pedagogical realism' was to prevail throughout the 1970s.

STAGNATION

Although the best of the Thaw films broke new ground in both stylistics and thematics, many established directors sought the relative safety of non-political, non-contemporary subjects by filming recognized literary classics during the Thaw and stagnation periods. The best of these, such as Grigory Kozintsev's *Don Quixote* (1957), *Hamlet*

(1964), and *King Lear* (*Korol Lir*, 1971), offered original interpretations of literary classics *and* critical reflections upon Soviet reality. With increasing censorship, film-makers used a kind of Aesopian language, the language of allegory and parable, to say what could not be said openly. Russian audiences were very good at interpreting such coded messages.

Literary adaptations of Chekhov provided particularly fertile comparisons between the bored, decaying society of the Brezhnev era and its precursor at the turn of the century. The best were Konchalovsky's *Uncle Vanya* (*Dyadya Vanya*, 1970) and his brother Nikita Mikhalkov's *Unfinished Piece for the Player Piano* (*Nezakonchennaya pyesa dlya mekhanicheskogo pianino*, 1977). Both directors excelled in lush, beautiful cinematography, and recreating period pieces with outstanding acting ensembles. An excellent actor himself, Mikhalkov already had a popular hit with his 1976 film *Slave of Love* (*Raba lyubvi*), a backward-looking, at times comic, melodrama about a silent film star whose political consciousness is raised during the Civil War. Konchalovsky's and Mikhalkov's films stood out as technically accomplished in a period that in general was marked by increasing professionalism. In the 1970s the Soviet film industry had an eye to commercial success, and the best of Hollywood once again became a role model.

The literary adaptation was increasingly popular among directors in the period of stagnation. Sergei

Grigory Kozintsev's *King Lear* (*Korol Lir*, 1971), based on Boris Pasternak's translation of the Shakespeare play

Andrei Tarkovsky

(1932–86)

Andrei Tarkovsky was born in the Russian countryside near the town of Yuryevets. His father, the poet Arseny Tarkovsky, whose works are frequently quoted in his son's films, separated from his mother when Andrei was 4; the largely autobiographical *Mirror* (1975) reflects this childhood trauma, and the themes of an absent father and a close but tense relationship with a mother who is loved but resented are particularly prominent in Tarkovsky's early films.

Tarkovsky achieved international recognition with his first feature film, *Ivan's Childhood* (1962), the tragic story of a young war scout, which won the Golden Lion at the 1962 Venice Film Festival. *Andrei Roublev*, loosely based on the life of a famous medieval Russian icon painter, was completed in 1966, but not released in the Soviet Union till 1971—largely because of its portrayal of the conflict between the artist and the political power structure. Despite increasing tensions with the cultural bureaucracy, Tarkovsky was allowed to continue working, producing *Solaris* (1972), based on a science-fiction novel by Stanislaw Lem; *Mirror*; and another ostensibly futuristic work, *Stalker* (1979), from a novella by Boris and Arkady Strugatsky. During this period, his problems with the authorities derived less from political unorthodoxy—he constantly refused to label himself as a 'dissident'—than from the intensely personal nature of his films, their intellectual 'difficulty', and their total disregard of the still surviving canons of Socialist Realism in both theme and style. His refusal to compromise with anything that he felt might damage the artistic integrity of his work both harmed and benefited him, causing hostility and opposition but also gaining him grudging respect even from his opponents (supported by his growing international reputation).

After being allowed to film the Soviet–Italian co-production *Nostalghia* (1983) in Italy, Tarkovsky announced in July 1984 that he intended to continue living abroad, citing personal harassment by the Soviet authorities and their frustration of many of his most cherished film projects. After completing *The Sacrifice* (1986) in Sweden, he was diagnosed as suffering from lung cancer and died in Paris in December 1986.

Tarkovsky's films are distinguished by an intense moral seriousness matched by only a handful of other film-makers—most notably two of his own favourites, Robert Bresson and Ingmar Bergman. As his book *Sculpting in Time* makes clear, he wanted film to be an art, not of entertainment, but of moral and spiritual examination, and he was prepared to make extreme demands, both of himself and of his audience, to achieve this. Despite the move from Russia to the west, his films display a continuity and development of theme and style that transcend differing political systems. They explore what he saw as eternal themes of faith, love, responsibility, loyalty, and personal and artistic integrity. In his last three films in particular this is combined with an increasingly strident attack on the soulless materialism of both 'east' and 'west', their reliance on technology as a solution to

human problems, and the dehumanization and destruction of the natural environment that result. These themes are expressed through a complex system of imagery and a challenging narrative structure that remain essentially constant and yet develop throughout his career. Tarkovsky always insisted that audiences should 'experience' his films before attempting to 'understand' them, and he objected to criticism that attempted to explain his work in terms of its supposed symbolism. Beginning on a relatively simple scale with *Ivan's Childhood*, his narratives block and frustrate conventional methods of analysis, forcing an essentially personal reaction to their meaning; an understanding created through response to patterns of sound and imagery, to rhythm, movement, and the handling of space and time, rather than through dialogue and accepted notions of character conflict and analysis. His increasing reliance on the long take, with several shots lasting six minutes and longer in his last three films, is intended to fuse the experience of both character and spectator and to 'free' the spectator from the predetermined and manipulated control associated with the editing techniques of directors such as Eisenstein.

The most characteristic element of Tarkovsky's films, however, is the creation of a filmic world that has the power, mystery, ambiguity, and essential reality of a dream. In *Ivan's Childhood* the dreams, though vivid and moving, are clearly distinguished from the everyday world. In *Solaris* and *Mirror*, however, certain scenes take on a hallucinatory quality that speaks directly to the subconscious of the viewer, and by *Stalker*, *Nostalghia*, and, especially *The Sacrifice*, this aspect has permeated the structure of the whole film, eliminating the possibility of one single interpretation of its meaning or even of what actually 'happens' within it. In this way Tarkovsky bypasses the rational, scientific analysis that he so much distrusted, and is able to speak directly to the receptive viewer by means of images whose beauty and suggestive power resonate with a forcefulness unmatched by almost any other film-maker.

GRAHAM PETRIE

SELECT FILMOGRAPHY

The Steamroller and the Violin (Katok i skripka) (1960) ; Ivan's Childhood / My Name is Ivan (Ivanovo detstvo) (1962); Andrei Roublev (1966, released 1971); Solaris (1972); Mirror (Zerkalo) (1975); Stalker (1979); Nostalghia (1983); The Sacrifice (1986).

BIBLIOGRAPHY

Johnson, Vida T. and Petrie, Graham (1994), *Tarkovsky: A Visual Fugue*.
Le Fanu, Mark (1987), *The Cinema of Andrei Tarkovsky*.
Tarkovsky, Andrei (1986), *Sculpting in Time: Reflections on the Cinema*.
—— (1991), *Time within Time: The Diaries 1970-1986*.
Turovskaya, Maya (1989), *Tarkovsky: Cinema as Poetry*.

Opposite: Futurist fantasy and political allegory; Tarkovsky's *Stalker* (1979).

Bondarchuk, a great actor and established director, filmed a safe and rather pompous version of Tolstoy's *War and Peace* (released in four parts from 1965 to 1967), and it was submitted by Goskino to Cannes instead of Tarkovsky's *Andrei Roublev*. However, it is wrong to see only political expediency in the return to literature and the past; directors began to abandon contemporary urban themes and the idyll and tragedy of the individual, in order to search for common roots in history, in a national tradition and a shared memory. This links the great yet disparate epics of the late 1960s, *Andrei Roublev* and *War and Peace*, the first banned and the second officially approved.

The return to the subject of the Russian land itself (heralded by *Andrei Roublev*, and much of the so-called village prose of the period) explains the phenomenal popularity of the prose and films of the writer, actor, and director Vasily Shukshin. Basically ignoring Communist ideology, Shukshin turned away from the corruption of modern urban life to the vitality and moral purity of the countryside, without glossing over its material and at times spiritual poverty. His country-bumpkin heroes are unintentionally comical, lively, honest, and ultimately very real and likeable. His masterpiece, *The Red Snowball Bush* (*Kalina krasnaya*, 1974), is the story of an ex-convict (played by Shukshin) who comes back to his village to start a new life, only to be killed by his old gang. The sheer popularity of this hard-hitting film probably kept it from being banned.

Audience attendance and the commercial potential of films became a major concern of Goskino in the 1970s, and this led to a predominance of realistic, narrative cinema and light genres which often presented ideology as entertainment. Television provided stiff competition, and, despite a few big hits, cinema attendances dropped from close to 5 billion tickets per year in the 1960s to 4.2 in 1977, with a (still high) average per capita attendance of 16.4. As in Hollywood, a few films—some 15 per cent—accounted for 80 per cent of ticket sales. As far as foreign films were concerned, Russian audiences were fed a steady diet of third-rate Indian and other little-known Third World films.

There was a new focus on genre films—comedy, melodrama, science fiction, detective stories, musicals. One of the most popular films of this period was Vladimir Motyl's *The White Sun of the Desert* (*Beloe solnce pustyny*, 1970), a commercial 'Western' self-consciously based on Italian 'spaghetti' Westerns. A lone hero of the Revolution, who looks and acts like a larger than life fairy-tale hero of the past, is on his way home through the desert of central Asia, and inherits a cluster of wives abandoned by a local Muslim renegade leader. He tries not only to protect them, but also to instruct them in the new ways of modern women liberated by the Revolution, with some predictably funny results. Against amazing odds and with much exciting action, the hero destroys the evil leader and his band, and again sets off for home.

Two other films of the 1970s stand out as popular Hollywood-style blockbusters: Vladimir Menshov's *Moscow Does not Believe in Tears* (*Moskva slezam ne verit*, 1979), which won an Oscar for best foreign film, and Andrei Konchalovsky's epic *Siberiade* (*Sibiriada*, 1979). Some 70–80 million viewers saw each film. Despite the fact that intellectuals scorned the Soviet Cinderella story of *Moscow . . .*, and the glorification of the Revolution in *Siberiade*, both films were appealing, with excellent acting and good story-lines. *Siberiade* is a vast saga of two families, one rich, one poor, and their intertwined lives from the beginning of the century through the Revolution, the Second World War, and to the new industrialization of the 1960s—all shot on the background of the magnificent, mythic Siberian landscape. The special effects of the fire scenes alone are equal to Hollywood's best.

Moscow . . . is a story of three friends, small-town working-class girls who come to Moscow in the late 1950s. The simple and sweet Tonya marries a fellow-worker and quickly settles down to raise a family. The 'bad' girl Lyuda spurns work and, seeing Moscow as a lottery, wants to marry a rich man but ends up divorced and alone. However, she is endearing in her ability to survive, her devotion to her friends, and her unswerving faith in life. The main story-line belongs to Katya, who is beautiful but also serious, hard-working, and determined to succeed. Even her early 'mistake', an out-of-wedlock baby, does not deter her in following the well-trodden path of socialist heroes—from a simple factory worker to, twenty years later, a factory director. Although the film reads as good Socialist Realist propaganda, albeit with some acknowledgements of real problems in Soviet society, it offers likeable and believable characters, especially in Katya, superbly acted by Valentina Alentova. In contrast to Stalinist films, where meeting the production quotas overshadowed the private life of the hero, here the successful but lonely Katya finally finds true love in an eccentric worker played by Aleksei Batalov, the sensitive leading man of the period.

Such 'slice-of-life' (*bytovye*) films dealing with contemporary social issues and ranging from comedies to melodramas dominated the screen in the 1970s and early 1980s. *Moscow . . .*, like many of these films, appealed primarily to a female audience with its consideration of the many roles women are called upon to play in Soviet society and the tension between their public and private life. The best women directors such as Larissa Shepitko (*Wings* (*Krylya*), 1966), Kira Muratova (*Brief Encounters* (*Korotkie vstrechi*), 1968; *Dolgie Provody* (*The Long Farewells*), 1971), and the Georgian Lana Gogoberidze (*Some Interviews on Personal Matters* (*Neskolko intervyu po lichnym voprosam*), 1979) have presented much more complex female protagonists in whose lives that conflict between career and family, or duty and love, remains more realistically unresolved.

Although the number of women directors making feature films was small, their contribution was disproportionate to their numbers as they tended to make honest, hard-hitting, and controversial films. Muratova's *Brief Encounters* was quickly buried, and *The Long Farewells* was banned outright. Both films presented complex, mostly unhappy family relationships in contemporary Soviet society, with women carrying the major burden. They subtly yet disturbingly questioned the value and the results of the much-touted Communist emancipation of women.

It was not only as directors that women contributed to the cinema of the period. Inna Churikova, arguably the greatest actress in contemporary Russian cinema, profoundly influenced the depiction of women on screen. Directed almost solely by her husband Gleb Panfilov in a collaboration that began in 1968, Churikova has created a number of memorable female protagonists from the simple worker who plays Joan of Arc in a movie and exhibits the same courage in real life (in *The Beginning* (*Nachalo*), 1970), to the determined mayor of a small town in *May I Have the Floor* (*Proshu slovo*, 1977); and in a remake of Vsevolod Pudovkin's silent film *Mother* (*Mat*, 1926) she played the famous peasant woman turned revolutionary. Churikova combines physical vulnerability with inner strength and has an unusual, luminous beauty, her face often blending sad and comical expressions with an excruciating honesty.

Despite the censorship, the increase in bureaucratic red tape, and the pressures put on directors to conform, the sheer number of banned films testifies to the artists' continued pushing of the boundaries of the permissible, and perhaps even to some willingness on the part of the studios to back problem films. Nikolai Sizov, in the 1970s the director of Mosfilm, the largest of all the Soviet studios, was very adept at balancing the demands of overseeing body Goskino and the creative endeavours of his directors. Tarkovsky shot all of his films at Mosfilm, and they were all released, even the extremely experimental *Mirror*, with relatively minor cuts, albeit in a small number of prints which assured rather poor distribution. Andrei Konchalovsky's recent complaint on how Columbia buried his film on Stalin, *The Inner Circle* (1992), with poor advertising and distribution shows that the commercial tyranny of the big Hollywood studios and companies has often produced the same results as the political control of the Communist system. The compromises the film directors are asked to make for financial reasons in the west can legitimately be compared to the compromises and cuts directors were forced to make in the Soviet Union by their ideological watchdogs.

THE 1980S: GLASNOST AND PERESTROIKA

It is possible to identify three somewhat overlapping periods in the decade of film-making since the beginning of *glasnost*: *glasnost* proper (1986–8), marked by openness, and the exciting release of banned films; *perestroika* (1988–91), the restructuring phase; and post-*perestroika* (1991–4).

However, even before the onset of *glasnost*, the best of the films that dealt with contemporary social issues had understated the socialist message and concentrated on the realism aspect of the Socialist Realist formula. The early 1980s also witnessed a number of attempts to produce films fundamentally critical of the corruption of Soviet society and the loss of Communist ideals in the period of stagnation. Rolan Bykov's *The Scarecrow* (*Chuchelo*, 1984) raised a public outcry for its depiction of the brutality and sadism of provincial schoolchildren who torment a newcomer wrongfully accused of telling tales on them to the teacher. The team of Vadim Abdrashitov and script-writer Alexander Mindadze produced a number of films which exposed the absurd nature of Soviet society through a complex narrative strategy and a web of fantastic, even surreal occurrences often steeped in allegory. In *The Train Stopped* (*Poezd ostanovilsya*, 1982), for example, the police investigation of a train wreck produces multiple versions of the story as townspeople shield themselves behind lies, a fitting commentary on a society for too long buried in hypocrisy. Film-makers were ready for *glasnost*, and the cinema industry was among the first to respond to it. *Repentance* (*Pokoyanie*, 1984–6) a surreal, tragicomic denunciation of Stalinism by the Georgian film-maker Tengiz Abuladze, was the first major *glasnost* film, released after a brief stay on the shelf, at the beginning of 1986. Finally not only the social decay of Soviet society, but its political bankruptcy and its Stalinist heritage, were to be exposed on the screen.

In the film industry the era of stagnation officially ended and *glasnost* was inaugurated at the 5th Congress of the Union of Film-Makers in May 1986 with the election of a new, liberal leadership under the 1960s director Elem

Inna Churikova as the worker whose role of Joan of Arc in a movie affects and reflects on her life, in Gleb Panfilov's *The Beginning* (*Nachalo*, 1970)

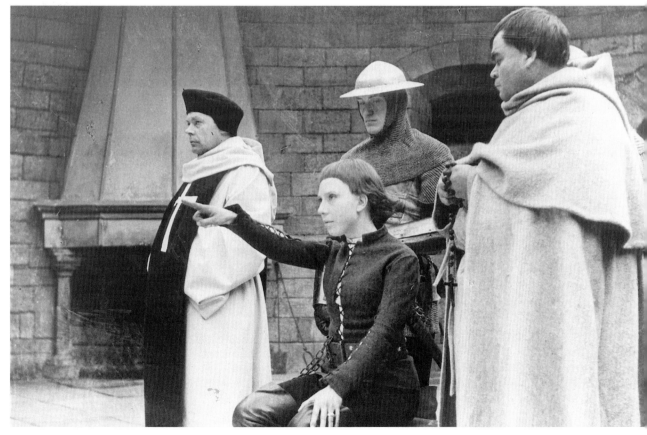

Klimov, and the establishment of the Conflict Commission to reconsider banned films. By 1987 most of these films were released, among them Askoldov's controversial *The Commissar*, Kira Muratova's *Brief Encounters* and *Long Farewells*, Gleb Panfilov's *The Theme* (banned for treating the subject of Jewish emigration), Elem Klimov's *Agony* (*Agoniya*, 1976—shelved for a sympathetic portrayal of the last tsar), and two outstanding films by Alexei German, *Trial by the Road* (*Proverka na dorogax*, 1971—not released because of a sympathetic portrayal of a Second World War POW) and *My Friend Ivan Lapshin* (*Moy drug Ivan Lapshin*, 1983—a gritty, realistic story of a police investigator in the Stalinist 1930s). The *glasnost* period was marked by the rediscovery of lost cinematic treasures, attesting to the richness of artistic talent even in the period of stagnation. Andrei Tarkovsky, who had decided to stay in the west in 1984 after filming *Nostalghia* and thus had become a non-person, was now not only reclaimed by the cinema establishment, but even canonized after his death at the end of 1986.

One contemporary film-maker in the Tarkovskian tradition of 'difficult', non-commercial, *auteur* cinema was Alexander Sokurov, whose increasingly silent films refocused the viewer's attention on the essential visual nature of film—something that had almost been lost in Socialist Realist cinema (most of which could have been listened to on the radio), and something that Tarkovsky had kept alive in his own work. Freed of censorship and miraculously able to keep financing his films, Sokurov produced marvellous visual elegies, including almost silent documentaries on Tarkovsky, Yeltsin, and Landsbergis.

By 1988 Soviet cinema had entered the restructuring, or *perestroika*, stage, and changes occurred with dizzying speed. By 1990 Goskino had lost most of its power to control and censor films, and a new hybrid structure of partly private and partly government-subsidized production was in effect, with most directors having to find private sponsors for their films. New money, much of it from the grey market or illegally gained, was laundered through films. In 1991 an astounding 400 or so feature films were made, but almost none released, as the state-run distribution system collapsed. As the Soviet Union disappeared, so did the country-wide cinema organizations, and by 1992 young directors, particularly from non-Russian former republics, were calling for the re-establishment of governmental subsidies for the whole of the CIS.

The International Film Festival in Moscow is rapidly being outmanœuvred by a private festival, the Cinetaur (Kinotavr) held in Sochi and sponsored by Mark Rudinshtein, one of the new businessmen-patrons of the arts. The 1994 Cinetaur festival found critics and film-makers alike bemoaning the death of the movie theatres: with average audiences of seven to ten people, many are closing their doors, and those that are still open screen primarily American movies, which are cheaper to buy than Russian movies are to make. Cinema tickets are expensive and there is much competition from a video boom (fuelled by pirated films), cable TV, and even first-run films on TV. New laws to control copyrights, production, and distribution are lacking, and there is general agreement that unrestrained capitalism is running the once great cinema industry into the ground. However, 137 feature films were produced in 1993 and some will surely find their way into movie theatres, given the continuing demand for home-grown fare, now called *otechestvennye filmy* (literally, 'films of the native land').

These films, of the *perestroika* phase, explored the legacy of Stalinism, exposed the depths of degradation of Soviet society, and broke every taboo of Socialist Realism with a vengeance (especially the prohibition against nudity and sex: one critic noted that every film had to have Stalin and a naked woman in it). They also ended up depressing or confusing their audiences and driving them out of the movie theatres. Some film-makers tried to examine the heritage of Stalinism directly, and documentaries once again become important. Realistic feature films on Stalinism were often meant to look like docu-dramas, shot in gritty black and white to recreate the atmosphere of the times: the best of these were *Coma* (*Koma*, 1989), the first depiction of women's prison camps, by Nijole Adomenaite, and *Defense Counsel Sedov* (*Zashchitnik Sedov*, 1989), the story of a lawyer who clears men falsely accused in the hysteria of 1949, only to discover that all the witnesses he called have in turn been arrested. Seeking new stylistic devices to reflect the insanity and absurdity of Stalinism, some film-makers abandoned realistic narrative and opted for a grotesque Surrealism instead. The most notable of the latter films were Valery Ogorodnikov's *Prishvin's Paper Eyes* (*Bumazhnye glaza Prishvina*, 1989) and Sergei Soloviev's *Black Rose Stands for Sorrow, Red Rose Stands for Love* (*Chernaya roza emblema pechali, krasnaya roza emblema lyubvi*, 1989), which begins with a lunatic listening repeatedly to a medical report of Stalin's death and treats the viewer to everything from newsreel footage of the battleship *Aurora* (an icon of the Russian Revolution) to images of contemporary youth cults.

In this period, cinema acted as a barometer of social and political change, offering a steady diet of dark, claustrophobic, communal apartments, broken families, familial as well as random, meaningless violence, rape, drugs, prostitution, crime, the total alienation of youth, and the embarrassing helplessness of their parents. As during the Thaw, films about the problems of youth predominated, at times with a strong dose of rock and roll as in Valery Ogorodnikov's *The Burglar* (*Vzlomshchik*, 1987). One of the most watched films of 1988 and perhaps the best of the new youth films was Vasily Pichul's *Little Vera* (*Malenkaya*

Vera), a hard-hitting, realistic exposé of working-class life in the Soviet Union and the failed promises of Communism for its youth. Vera herself, a tough, wise-cracking, yet touchingly vulnerable teenager, outstandingly played by the newcomer Natalia Negoda, is the most memorable and strongest female character in all of recent cinema. (The film was scripted by Pichul's wife Maria Khmelik.) Fifty million Soviets saw the film, most of them lured by the first sex scene in Soviet cinema.

However, many of these contemporary social melodramas did not abandon Socialist Realism, but simply turned it on its head. They were still formulaic 'message' films trying to tell people how or how not to live, and are full of new clichés: dirty, communal apartments instead of shiny, clean ones, social outcasts instead of heroes of labour, and a requisite unhappy ending instead of a happy one.

Since 1991, film-makers have moved into a post-*perestroika* phase. After much self-exploration, and stylistic and thematic experimentation in film, directors are attempting to make more commercially viable films. Light comedies and modest, feelgood films are making a comeback, after a flood of depressing dark films, pejoratively labelled *chernukha* (black), *bytovukha* (grungy, everyday life), and *pornukha* (porno). Vyacheslav Krishtofovich's *Adam's Rib* (*Rebro Adama*, 1991) typifies this new type of film. It is a warm story, both humorous and touching, of how three generations of women cope and survive in these difficult times. The director relies on excellent acting (the film stars the incomparable Inna Churikova) to help create real characters the audience can identify with. Yuri Mamin's *A Window to Paris* (*Okno v Parizh*, 1993) is a slapstick tale of the improbable adventures of some simple Russians who find a miraculous window to Paris in their run-down apartment house in St Petersburg.

The mostly young 'new wave' film-makers reject all vestiges of Socialist Realism, or of socially redeeming cinema with an educational or ideological message. They are a diverse group: some embrace western cinema, the classics of Hollywood as well as of Europe, the French New Wave,

for example, and the newer post-modern cinema of Peter Greenaway and David Lynch. The guiding force of this group is Sergei Soloviev, an established film-maker, teacher, the director of his own studio (first at Mosfilm, now independent). He is the mentor of the talented Rashid Nugmanov, whose 1988 film *The Needle* (*Igla*) began the Kazakh 'new wave' and will surely become a post-modern cult classic, along with Soloviev's own *Assa* (1988). Other directors are creating their own 'retro' films, ironic and often nostalgic remakes of films from the Thaw or even earlier Stalinist periods. Still others are trying to abandon dialogue altogether in their rediscovery of silent, black and white film.

It is impossible to describe in brief the variety and vitality of the cinema since the beginning of *glasnost*, despite regular complaints from critics that there are no any good films. The abolition of censorship was clearly beneficial, although at first it did confound older directors who were used to fighting for their ideas. While financing and production are shaky in this period of transition to capitalism, films are being made and film-makers are slowly adapting to a new western cost-consciousness. The unsolved problem remains distribution—how to get at least a few of the best films to the screen. In the mean time there is not a little nostalgia for the days of Goskino and the state-subsidized, state-run film industry.

Bibliography
Anninsky, Lev (1991), *Shestidesyatniki i my* ('The generation of the sixties and me').
Horton, Andrew, and Brashinsky, Michael (1992), *The Zero Hour: Glasnost and Soviet Cinema in Transition.*
Lawton, Anna (1992), *Kinoglasnost: Soviet Cinema in our Time.*
Liehm, Mira, and Liehm, Antonin J. (1977), *The Most Important Art: Soviet and Eastern European Film after 1945.*
Shlapentokh, Dmitry, and Shlapentokh, Vladimir (1993), *Soviet Cinematography 1918–1991.*
Zorkaya, Neya (1991), *The Illustrated History of Soviet Cinema.*
— (1993), *Konets stoletiya: predvaritelnye itogi* ('The end of the century: tentative conclusions').

Cinema in the Soviet Republics

JEAN RADVANYI

For the studios of the southern republics, as in the rest of the USSR, the Thaw that followed Stalin's death signified a double rebirth. First, there was a noticeable return to film-making after the 'era of few films' when only Stalinist masterpieces could be produced. It had been a particularly dark period for these small studios: of just less than 290

full-length films produced in the USSR between 1945 and 1955, the five central Asian republics only produced nineteen and the three Trans-Caucasian republics only produced twenty-two, twelve of which were from the relatively favoured republic of Georgia. This renewal of production assumed particular importance in two republics:

in Turkmenistan the decision was taken in 1953 to rebuild the Ashkhabad studios, which had been completely destroyed by an earthquake in 1948, and the first film was produced at the new studios in 1954. In 1955 the first Kirghizian film was made; Vasily Pronin's *Saltanat* was produced in Moscow but filmed on location, and the studios built in Kirghizia during the war had, until then, only produced documentaries. In general, the end of the 1950s was a period of investment: in the capitals of several republics new studios were built and fitted with the most modern Soviet equipment.

Secondly, on the creative side, the rebirth in production was marked by the arrival of a new generation of directors whose stylistic break with the past was comparable to the storm in Russia over Chukhrai's first films. There were the débuts of the Georgians Tengiz Abuladze and Rezo Chkheidze with *Magdana's Donkey* (1955), in Armenia that of Grigory Melik-Avakian (*The Singing Heart*, 1956), in Azerbaijan that of Tofik Tagi-Zade (*Meeting*, 1956). This renaissance occurred slightly later in central Asia, with Shukhrat Abbasov's first films, *All Makhallia is Talking about It* (1960), and *You're not an Orphan* (1962) in Uzbekistan, and Bulat Mansurov's *The Competition* (1963) in Turkmenistan. These short, simple films were radically opposed to Stalinist academicism. Their heroes were ordinary people in concrete surroundings described in a quasi-sociological or ethnic way. This break with the past was not easily achieved. Abuladze has spoken of his intense struggle with the directors of the Tbilisi studios who tried to halt the filming of *Magdana's Donkey* and change its directors. To complete the project it was necessary to enlist the help of intellectuals and, in particular, writers. However, the rupture brought about by the Thaw was such that directors of previous generations who were still active, like Amo Bek-Nazarov or Mikhail Chiaureli, were now unable to create convincing works.

THE PARADOXICAL ROLE OF MOSCOW

In the years that followed, the role of Moscow proved to be eminently paradoxical. On one hand, the authorities created exceptional circumstances in which the national cinema of small and economically weak republics could blossom. On the other hand, they made every effort to restrict productions with a yoke of finicky ideology. This production system had two major peculiarities: a lack of any direct link between the decision to make a film and the decision to distribute it, and the insistence from the centre on minimum production quotas for each republic. However, this resulted in the emergence (albeit at the price of tiring struggles for the directors) of authentic works anchored in national realities, far removed from the level represented by Socialist Realism.

The role of the Moscow film training institutes (VGIK, the All-Union State Institute of Cinematography, and,

from 1960 for scriptwriters and from 1963 for directors, the Two-Year Further Diploma) was crucial to the development of the national cinemas. These institutions trained all the future directors in an incredible melting-pot of nationalities around prestigious masters: Eisenstein, Pudovkin, Trauberg, Dovzhenko, and their successors Savchenko, Raizman, Romm, Gerasimov. Bearing in mind the largely positive effects of 'goodwill' selection (there was a quota of places set aside for students from the small republics), the particularly fertile cultural atmosphere in Moscow in the period between 1955 and 1965 had a profound effect on these young creative artists, and the network of friendships developed here would last for decades.

In central Asia the lack of sets and experienced technicians led to a remarkable experiment born from the spirit formed in Moscow. Several of the more gifted directors from the republics were invited to make their first films in central Asia, one of the objectives being to attract and build up sets on location. This is how Eldar Shengelaya (*Legend of the Icy Heart*, 1958), Larissa Shepitko (*Torrid Heat*, 1963), Vladimir Motyl (*The Children of Pamir*, 1963), and Andrei Konchalovsky (*The First Teacher*, 1965) made their débuts. The impact of these Moscow-trained film-makers inspired many in the republics: Tolomush Okeyev was the sound engineer and Bolot Shamshiev the sound assistant and actor for Larissa Shepitko. Konchalovsky was the co-script-writer of several Kazakh, Kirghiz, and Uzbek films of the period.

THE GEORGIAN AND ARMENIAN SCHOOLS

The 1960s and 1970s witnessed the arrival of a group of young directors, trained in Moscow, who, in their various ways, surged into the breach opened up by Abuladze and Chkheidze. There was a great diversity of themes and styles, but the influence of Italian neo-realism and the French New Wave on many directors was apparent—in the first films of Lana Gogoberidze, Otar Yosseliani, and Frunze Dovlatian, for example. At the same time, dominant traits of national cinema became stronger, reviving the traditions pioneered in the great films of the silent era. In Georgia and Armenia, particularly, the works of the major studios managed to develop a new cinematic language that was rooted so firmly in the centuries-old traditions of these two peoples that it was possible to distinguish an actual national cinematic school. Rezo Chkheidze immersed himself in the realist tradition to describe the daily heroism of the ordinary people (*The Father of the Soldier*, 1964). Tengiz Abuladze used the past to reveal great moral questions, in a vision which mixed naturalism and symbolism in the style of the great poet from the end of the nineteenth century, Vaja Pshavela (*The Incarnation*, 1967; *The Wishing Tree*, 1976). While Georgy Shengelaya showed the dramatic intensity of historical

The 'baroque aestheticism' of Sergei Paradjanov's Armenian masterpiece *Saiat Nova* (*The Colour of Pomegranates*, 1968)

situations through a remarkable study of the social universe (old Tiflis in *Pirosmani*, 1969; the rural crisis at the end of the nineteenth century in *Journey of the Young Composer*, 1984), his brother Eldar preferred to manipulate a biting humour (*The Amazing Exhibition*, 1968; *Stepmother Samanishvili*, 1978).

Frequent recourse to symbolic and metaphorical distancing and poetico-humoristic language are the hallmarks of Georgian films—at their best in Mikhail Kobakhidze's miniature masterpieces (*The Marriage*, 1964; *The Parasol*, 1967), or in other examples of short films from the Georgian school (Irakli Kvirikadze's *The Jar*, 1971), and above all in the work of Otar Yosseliani. *Fall of Leaves* (1966) and *There Was a Singing Blackbird* (1970) struck a whole generation with their poetically sad, lucid vision of the world—so profoundly different from the Socialist Realism which was still in force. The uncertain future of a society in the grip of modernization but refusing to break with its roots was, moreover, at the heart of many films (*The Large Green Valley* by Merab Kokochashvili, 1967; *Limits* by Lana Gogoberidze, 1968), and made the best productions from Tbilisi universally appealing.

The situation in Armenia, where the studios also had a strong underlying tradition, was fairly similar, even though the number of productions and directors was smaller than that of Gruziafilm at Tbilisi. From a New Wave of creative artists such as Armand Manarian (*Tejvejik*, 1961), Dmitri Keussaian (*Master and Servant*, 1962; and *Avdo's Motorcar*, 1966), and Bagrat Hovhanessian (*The Green Grape*, 1973; and *Autumn Sun*, 1977), three figures stand out: Frunze Dovlatian, Henrik Malian, and Artavazd Pelechian.

In the realist vein, using a cinematic language without surprises, to which he remained faithful, Dovlatian was first noticed with *Hello, It's Me* (1965) and *Chronicle of Erevan Days* (1972). He stood out for his way of tackling difficult themes, such as the moral evolution of Armenians, with brave allusions to religion and genocide, which were still taboo subjects. Narrower in scope, Malian's work (*The Triangle*, 1967; *We Are Mountains*, 1969; *The Father*, 1972; and *Nahapet*, 1977) was more creatively inscribed in Armenian culture and history. Without excluding the use of humour, he marked his films with a tragic seriousness, clearly linked to the recent history of his people. This is what sharply distinguishes the majority of Armenian films from Georgian films which are otherwise similar in many ways. Malian's best films speak, even if metaphorically, of an essential loss, a broken harmony, the loss of integrity in a country that remains at heart Armenian. More marginal in relation to the Erevan studios, Malian shot his films on location but edited them in Moscow and with sound-tracks in Russian, contrary to almost all the New Wave directors in the Caucasus who used their national language.

Artavazd Pelechian (*Beginning*, 1967; *Us*, 1969; *Seasons*, 1972) was without doubt, however, the most innovative of the Armenian directors. He was known for his theory of 'editing at a distance'. By forging new links between image and sound, his documentaries represented a remarkable visualization of structures symbolic to Armenian culture: from mountainous scenery (based on his research into the verticality of settings) to the place of religion, making reference to the value of the land and the people who live on it.

Maintaining a distance from the national school was Sergei Paradjanov, an Armenian from Tiflis who, as an inspired *provocateur*, seemed to flout all attempts at classification. After a promising start to his career in the Ukraine, he returned to his birthplace in the Caucasus, as clouds of trouble gathered over his head. In three full-length films (*Sayat Nova*—also known as *The Colour of Pomegranates*—Armenfilm, 1968; *The Legend of the Surami Fortress*, Gruziafilm, 1984; and *Kerib the Minstrel*, Gruziafilm, 1988), shot over twenty years and interspersed with several stays in prisons or camps, he transgressed all ethnic and aesthetic boundaries by reworking the intermingled cultural heritage of the Caucasus. This essentially transcultural work, with its baroque aestheticism frequently spilling over into eclecticism, has influenced several generations of directors throughout the USSR, without ever really having a following in either Georgia or Armenia.

CENTRAL ASIA: THE PERIOD OF THE 'NEW WAVE'

Without overlooking the contribution of pioneers such as Kamil Yarmatov or Nabi Ganiev, it would be true to see the 1960s and 1970s, with the New Wave which arose in all central Asian republics, as the moment of birth for the cinemas of central Asia. Having broken with the tradition of using oriental imagery, the young Moscow-trained directors set about anchoring the art of the cinema in their national heritage, which, despite its ancient lineage, hardly seemed to favour the development of the seventh art. The role of VGIK, and of the Russian and Caucasian directors who came out to central Asia to make their first films, has already been mentioned. Also important was the role of theatre, from which several young film-makers and even more national writers emerged. Mukhtar Auezov, Chingiz Aitmatov, Olyas Suleimenov—all prominent writers—played an active role in the cinema of their republics. Aitmatov became the secretary of the Kirghiz Union of Film-Makers; Suleimenov was his counterpart in Kazakhstan; and by exerting their authority as writers, they often defended the more 'delicate' film projects, both in Moscow and in the republics themselves.

The subjects tackled appeared to fit well into the Soviets' ideological constraints: the civil war (*Shots in the Karach Pass* by Bolot Shamshiev, 1968; *Tashkent, City of Bread* by Shukhrat Abbasov, 1968), the Second World War (*You're not an Orphan* by Abbasov, 1962; *The Daughter-in-Law* by Khodjakuli Narliev, 1972), the transformation of the countryside (*White, White Swans* by Ali Khamrayev, 1966; *The Sky of our Childhood* by Tolomush Okeyev, 1967). However, the approach and the cinematic language had been completely renewed. The visual style, often similar to that of documentaries, allowed much space for the traditions of these nomadic or recently settled peoples, even if Islam remained a taboo subject. The influence of the French and Italian New Waves was also clear, as in Elior Ishukhamedov's early films. In *Tenderness* (1967) he adopted a poetic approach in order to examine urban society, and the film caused a sensation. There were also explicit references to the great Japanese and Indian masters (Kurosawa, Ray), and Toshiro Mifune would not look out of place in certain sequences of Okeyev's *The Sky of our Childhood* or *Without Fear* by Ali Khamrayev. The latter is one of the most individual of creators. He could tackle any style: musical (*Dilorom*, 1967), oriental Western (*The Seventh Bullet*, 1972), as well as commissioned films (*Hot Summer in Kabul*, 1982), and the moral and aesthetic heritage of these societies is magnificently integrated into his best films (*Man Follows the Birds*, 1975; *Triptych*, 1978).

The best works from the five republics spring from both an indisputable kinship and a true diversity. A kinship of themes, rhythm (often slow), and approach (the frequent recourse to fantasy sequences, to earth symbolism, to epic tragedy as well as melodrama) indicates as much a shared historical and cultural tradition as the Soviet mould. However, there is also real diversity in the outstanding films, expressing the profound differences which separate these peoples: the mountain nomadism of the Kirghizs, the great open spaces of the steppes for the Kazakhs, the desert civilization of the Turkmens, the ancient urban civilization of the Uzbeks and Tadjiks, with the latter also greatly influenced by the Persians.

THE CINEMA AND ITS PUBLIC

From the mid-1970s, these republics reached their optimum output, producing four feature-length films a year and a large number of shorts. However, by the end of the decade a certain lack of vitality was beginning to make itself felt. The new, young talents, like Suren Babaian in Armenia (*The Eighth Day of Creation*), 1980 and Davlat Khudonazarov in Tadjikistan (*The First Morning of Youth*,

1979), had difficulties making their names. In Georgia they were more numerous—Alexander Rekhviachvili (*Chronicle of Georgia in the Nineteenth Century*, 1979), Rezo Esadze (*The Windmill by the Town*, 1981), Nana Djordjadze (*Journey to Sopot*, 1980), and Temur Babluani (*Migrating Sparrows*, 1980)—but this was largely because Georgia had decided to establish its own cinema school at Tbilisi, thus breaking the Moscow monopoly.

The weight of the Moscow yoke was increasingly felt, both in the teaching (which had lost its openness) and on the level of production. Goskino, as the supervising authority, tightened its control on both scripts and the financing of films, as well as their circulation. Films whose authors had strayed from the prescribed track often had their distribution reduced to a minimum. Official critics accused them of transgressing the borders of sacrosanct Socialist Realism and lapsing into nationalist tendencies. Directors were banned from presenting their films at international festivals. At the same time, by using the bias of state-commissioned productions, either for television or cinema, Goskino favoured the rise of a commercial cinema closer, in its opinion, to what the Soviet public wanted. A kind of specialization became apparent in the different studios: comedy in Georgia, detective films and ridiculous comedies in Azerbaijan, Westerns, oriental epics, and musical melodramas in central Asia, all this as well as films linked to the ideological interests of the moment which were put at the top of the production lists. A cultural and ideological over-determination was prevalent at the 'Asian, African and Latin American Film Festival' at Tashkent, set up in 1968, which, after some

initial surprises, quickly sank back into conformity. These ideological manœuvres did not please the majority of the Soviet public who subsequently stayed away from national productions. They preferred films from the west which were occasionally distributed in the USSR, and in central Asia and Azerbaijan there was an incredible infatuation with Egyptian and Indian films, in which most viewers found the sentimentality they liked. The struggles necessary to bring an original film to completion had become exhausting. Otar Yoseliani and Ali Khamrayev have recounted their conflicts with the various levels of censorship (local, and emanating from Moscow), forcing them sometimes to shoot a sequence in two different ways, one for the censor and the other for the final version! But it was only with backing at the highest level that the more ambitious projects could be realized. Such a film was *Repentance* (1984) by Tengiz Abuladze, the first film openly to criticize the Stalinist terror; it was supported from start to finish by the then secretary of the Georgian Communist Party, Edvard Shevardnadze.

THE UPHEAVALS OF THE 1980S

After Gorbachev had come to power, film-makers from the southern republics took a more active part in denouncing the harmful role played by the central administration which they felt had disadvantaged them. Several of them were present in May 1986 at the 6th Congress of the Union of Film-Makers which led to a re-evaluation of the prerogatives at Goskino concerning choice of production. Some of them went on to a political career in the new assemblies and the Tadjik film-maker Davlat

The culture of Central Asia: a scene from Ali Khamrayev's *Triptych* (1978)

Khudonazarov became the first secretary of the Union of Soviet Film-Makers in 1990. These years of political disturbances were marked by intense upheavals in the cinema of all the republics. Until 1991, the situation seemed to favour national productions. Federal censorship had all but disappeared while state budgets allotted to the cinema by Moscow had been renewed and added to by the first private backing. In many studios, the number of films made beat all previous records and there was also an emergence of independent producers, either co-operatives or private, and often headed by renowned film-makers: Kelechek (Tolomush Okeyev), Salamalekfilm (Bolot Shamchiev), + 1 (Rezo Esadze), Samarkandfilm (Ali Khamrayev), etc.

The loosening of censorship and the lifting of taboos encouraged the rise of a new generation of directors who broadened approaches in the different studios. One of the first genres to benefit from this opening was the documentary, which could at last tackle subjects that had for a long time been banned. One of the best examples is the Armenian documentary school led by Ruben Gevorkiants at the Haik studios (*Islands*, 1984; *Requiem*, 1989) and by Harutiun Khachatrian (*Kond*, 1987; *The White Town*, 1988). Notable young film-makers from this generation are the Georgian Zaza Khalvashi (*There, with Us*, 1990), the Uzbeks Djakhongir Faiziev (*Kiadia*, 1988; *Who Are You?*, 1989) and Zulfikar Musakov (*History of a Soldier*, 1989), or the Tadjik Bako Sadykov (*Blest Bukhara*, 1992). In Kazakhstan the arrival of a group of young film-makers was a definite new wave, imposing a stylistic break with noir films influenced by the new German and American film-makers Fassbinder, Wenders, and Jarmusch: Rashid Nugmanov (*The Needle*, 1988), Serik Aprymov (*Terminus*, 1989), A. Baranov and B. Kilibaev (*Trio*, 1989), and others.

But alongside these innovations, increasing commercial pressures on the cinema led to a pursuit of fashionable themes. Each republic produced its own films about the gulags, the Mafia, drugs, and delinquency. For the few films of interest such as *The Stain* by the Georgian A. Tsabadze (1985) and *The Bastard* by the Azerbaijani Vagif Mustafayev (1989) there are numerous worthless films which have contributed to the public's growing disillusionment with national cinema.

Since 1991, independence for the republics has created a completely new situation full of uncertainty. While western films and videos of all kinds, usually pirated, flood across the screens, national productions are in a period of crisis: national authorities baulk at the prospect of renewing financial backing to studios they believe ought to be self-funding. The film-makers hit back by showing that this would be the death of all creative national films. Certain states (Georgia, Armenia, Kazakhstan, Turkmenistan) have agreed to finance some films, but the emphasis has been put on co-productions in the hope that this will finance the re-equipping of studios. However, the increase in armed conflicts and the economic crisis have reinforced instability and it is to be feared that, in the republics, the blossoming of national cinema may shortly be no more than a memory, one that is, paradoxically, linked to the Soviet experiment.

Bibliography
Passek, Jean-Loup (ed.) (1981), *Le Cinéma russe et soviétique.*
Radvanyi, Jean (ed.) (1988), *Le Cinéma géorgien.*
—— (1991), *Le Cinéma d'Asie centrale soviétique.*
—— (1993), *Le Cinéma arménien.*

Turkish Cinema

YUSUF KAPLAN

Cinema arrived in Ottoman Turkey almost the same year as in the west. Pathé Frères' representative in Turkey, the Romanian Sigmund Weinberg, conducted the first film screening in early 1897 at the Restaurant Sponeck in Beyoglu, the cosmopolitan district of Istanbul. Within a few years, film screenings had spread to all the major cities of the Ottoman Empire.

The first film productions in Ottoman Turkey were documentaries made by foreign cameramen. It was not until 1914 that a film made by a Turk was completed: *The Demolition of the Russian Monument at St. Stephan*, a documentary made by Fuat Uzkinay, an officer in the Ottoman army.

Early productions by Turkish film-makers followed this pattern, being documentaries produced for the Army Film Centre (AFC), which had been formed in 1915 by Enver Pasha, the General Commander of the Ottoman Army and the Minister of War. The first Turkish feature film was not produced until almost twenty years after the first film screening. Weinberg began to shoot *The Marriage of Himmet Ağa* in 1916, again for the AFC, but it was not completed until after the First World War. The first feature films to be completed were produced by the National Defence Association; *The Claw* (1917) and *The Spy* (1917), both directed by a young journalist, Sedat Simavi.

The first feature production company, Kemal Film, was established by the Seded brothers in 1922. Although the company only lasted two years, their approach to film production was more professional than anything that had gone before, and resulted in four features, *A Love Tragedy in Istanbul* (1922), *The Mystery on the Bosphorus* (1922), *The Shirt of Fire* (1923), and *The Tragedy at Kizkulesi* (1923), all directed by a young stage actor and director, Muhsin Ertuğrul. Ertuğrul was to dominate film production in the next two decades, steering the Turkish cinema in what was to prove a misleading direction. In this early period, five features out of six were adapted from stage works, and three directors out of four were stage directors. This phenomenon determined the future shape of the Turkish cinema.

ONE-PARTY STATE, ONE-DIRECTOR CINEMA

The new secular Turkish Republic, established in 1923, gave enthusiastic support to the western-oriented Turkish music, theatre, and opera, but did not show any interest in the cinema. Within the first five years of the republican period, the Turkish cinema was completely inactive. In 1928, a new production company, Ipek film, was set up by the Ipekçi brothers, who also owned several movie theatres. This company monopolized film production in Turkey for the next thirteen years; rising budgets caused by the move to sound production in this period helped prevent the growth of any competition.

Ertuğrul directed some twenty films in the period up to 1941, including *The Streets of Istanbul* (1931), *A Nation Awakens* (1932), *The Million Hunters* (1934), *Victims of Lust* (1940). The only film director of the period, Ertuğrul worked with friends at the Municipal Theatre in Istanbul, making films only when the theatre season was over. At that time the Turkish theatre was heavily under the influence of western theatre. This was in line with official ideology that directed all Turkish writers and intellectuals to create an 'imagined community' which mirrored the cultural, social, and political structures of western society. Film productions of this period used all the elements of western-style theatre. French and German vaudeville, operettas, and highly exaggerated German melodrama were simply recreated for the camera, with only the names of characters changed. It is fitting that the films made by the only director of the period reflected the pre-occupations and concerns of the one-party state. This tendency prevented the creation of a truly national cinema in Turkey, which had rich and unique musical, visual, and theatrical traditions of its own, on which the foundations of a national Turkish cinema could have been built. The development of Turkish cinema was also stifled by the introduction of a brutal censorship law, inspired by Italian Fascist models. Its destructive and limiting effect has had a profound impact on Turkish film production.

THE TRANSITION PERIOD: 1939–1950

After the end of the one-party system, a second film production company, Ha-Ka Film, was set up to rival Ipek Film. The company gave two young movie technicians, Faruk Kenç and Sçadan Kamil, the opportunity to make their own films, and they directed several features for the company. This development was important, as Kenç and Kamil broke the directing monopoly of Ertuğrul, and opened the way for other young directors, including Baha Gelenbevi and Aydin Arakon, to emerge and set up their own film companies. Although still to an extent under the influence of theatre, these film-makers contributed to breaking the stranglehold of the old theatricians on the Turkish cinema, in terms of both artistic and industrial concerns, and so encouraged other young people to enter film-making, as actors, directors, producers, and technicians.

One of the most important developments of the period was the reduction of government taxes on local film production, which in 1948 were set at 20 per cent, as against 70 per cent on foreign films. This ensured that the film industry was considered an interesting and potentially profitable business, and a new generation of enthusiastic film-makers emerged.

1950–1960: THE FORMATIVE YEARS

The coming of the multi-party system under the premiership of Adnan Menderes witnessed tremendous transformations in the political, economic, cultural, and social structures of Turkey. An open economic system replaced the existing one, with the help of the industrialization programme supported by Marshall Aid. A great number of Anatolian small businessmen moved into Green Pine Street in Istanbul, and established film production companies. From this base the film industry witnessed an explosion in production that would lead the Turkish cinema to be labelled Green Pine Cinema. Between 1917 and 1947 fifty-eight films had been made, whereas by 1956 the total number of Turkish films produced had increased to 359. After 1957, annual film production rose steadily from 100 to 150, and then 200. This quantitative increase also led to an increase in quality.

When Ömer Lütfi Akad directed his first feature film, *Death to the Whore*, in 1949, it was clear that a promising new talent had emerged. His second feature, *In the Name of the Law* (1952), heralded a new era in Turkish film history by achieving a truly cinematic style of narration, composition, and editing. Akad was the Griffith of the Turkish cinema, emerging almost forty years later, but having a similar impact on the film-making style of his own nation. Akad's other important films of the period were *Killer City* (1954), which had a sensibility of poetic realism, and the village saga *The White Handkerchief* (1955), which showed

Akad's mastery of depicting the realities of village life and its problems.

Following Akad's example, several young and talented film directors made their first films during this period, including Metin Erksan, Atif Yilmaz, and Osman Seden. Atif Yilmaz began his career by adapting popular fiction and directing 'naïve' melodramas and comedies. In 1957, he directed his first major feature, *The Bride's Murat*, a small-town comic drama, which saw him develop his own style. In 1959 he made two important films, *Alageyik* and *The Passion of Karacaoglan*, successfully incorporating elements of Turkish folklore.

The most typical director of the period was Memduh Ün. After directing numberless 'cheap' melodramas, Ün made his contribution to the development of the language of Turkish cinema with *Three Friends* (1958). Osman Seden made various formal experiments, bringing eroticism and violence into the Turkish cinema with films like *The Enemy*

Cut down the Ways (1959), a film about the war of independence, and *For the Sake of Honour* (1960).

The directors of this period oversaw the emergence of Turkish film genres; melodramas, village sagas, city films. Linked to this was the development of a Turkish star system, with Osman Seden, particularly, playing a crucial role as 'star maker'. Among the most popular Turkish stars of the era were Ayhan Işik as a typical Turkish male character, Belgin Doruk, the 'little lady' of high-society films, Muhterem Nur, the victimized, innocent heroine, and Göskel Arsoy, the romantic hero.

THE SEARCH FOR A NATIONAL CINEMA: 1960–1970

After the 1960 military coup, the cultural, political, and social map of Turkey changed considerably. Due to the misleading westernization programmes initiated by the nineteenth-century Ottoman ruling class and accelerated during the secular republican period, the repressed

The conflict between the cultures of the east and the west in Halit Refiğ's *I Lost my Heart to a Turk* (1969)

Yilmaz Güney
(1937–1984)

Yilmaz Güney was born in 1937 in Adana, a southern city of Turkey, to a Kurdish family of seven children. He began his movie career as an actor, appearing in over sixty popular action films, twenty of which he scripted himself. He created the legendary hero the 'ugly king', who had an amazing appeal for the audience which identified with his search for justice in the name of the exploited, the repressed, and the hopeless.

In the mid-1960s Güney moved to the other side of the camera, working as assistant to the great Turkish director Ömer Lütfi Akad on *The Law of the Border* (1966), and collaborating as scriptwriter on several films with Atif Yilmaz. He successfully used this experience when he made his directorial début in 1968 with *Seyyit Han*, an epic film with touches of realism and poetry. In 1970 Güney directed *The Hope*, an autobiographical film about poverty and oppression in rural Anatolia. It was unanimously acclaimed as the best Turkish film ever made. With its epic style, tender camera work, and successful narrative organization, it contributed enormously to the development of Turkish film language. However, the film's subject matter was controversial, and Güney's approach was criticized in many quarters.

In 1971 Güney made four films. *The Elegy* and *The Sorrow* were based on the themes of rural oppression and revolt against the authorities. *The Desperate Ones* and *The Father* were centred on urban capitalism, and were less successful, partly due to their appeal to rather heavy melodramatic solutions.

In 1971 the Turkish military staged a coup, and soon after Güney was imprisoned for his political views. The film he had been in the process of making, *The Poor Ones*, was later completed by Atif Yilmaz. In 1974 Güney was released, and returned immediately to film-making, directing *The Friend*, a film about urban corruption, which was his best since *The Hope*.

Güney was imprisoned again the same year, and sentenced to nineteen years for murder, but in spite of these difficult conditions, he did not give up his movie career. He continued writing scripts, and began directing from prison 'by proxy'. He completed *The Herd* (1979), and *The Enemy* (1980), both directed for him by Zeki Ökten, and *Yol* (1982), directed by Serif Gören. Güney was able to edit *Yol* himself in France, where he was now in exile. *Yol* was awarded the First Prize at Cannes in 1983, alongside Costa-Gavras's *Missing* (1982). Güney shot his last film, *The Wall* (1983) in France, where he died in 1984.

Güney was the most innovative, talented, influential, and internationally acclaimed directors Turkey has ever produced. He became a source of inspiration for a generation of young directors. He heralded the development of the New/Young Cinema movement, and, in doing so, determined the future direction of Turkish film-making.

YUSUF KAPLAN

SELECT FILMOGRAPHY

Seyyit Han (1968); The Hope (1970); The Elegy (1971); The Sorrow (1971); The Desperate Ones (1971); The Father (1971); The Friend (1974); The Herd (1979—dir: Zeki Ökten); The Enemy (1980—dir: Zeki Ökten); Yol / The Way (1982—dir: Serif Gören); The Wall (1983).

A scene from *The Wall* (1983), the last film of Turkish director Yilmaz Güney

feeling and collective unconscious of the Turkish people imploded. During the 1960s Turkish society witnessed unprecedented cultural and political conflicts, leading to a civil war that lasted into the late 1970s.

This intensely affected Turkish film practices. Film-makers who felt the need of a new and genuine national film culture began to debate the formal and narrational principles of a cinema inspired by the visual, literary, theatrical, and musical traditions of Turkey. These debates continue to this day, but several short-lived film movements emerged in the 1960s which aimed to establish the cultural foundations and aesthetic principles of a national Turkish cinema. The first was social realism, initiated by Metin Erksan and others. The exemplary films of the movement were Seden's *For the Sake of Honour*, Atif Yilmaz's *The Criminal* (1960), and two Erksan films, *The Revenge of the Serpents* (1962), a story of one man's fight against rural and traditional authorities, and *Dry Summer* (1963), which won the Golden Bear at the Berlin Film Festival in 1964. Despite their conventional narrative organization, these films went beyond the dramatic conventions employed in popular Turkish cinema, and used semi-realist forms to narrate stories of conflict in rural Turkey.

A young and talented film director and critic, Halit Refiğ, was inspired by the ideas and works of the great Turkish novelist and thinker Kemal Tahir. Refiğ, together with his colleagues Metin Erksan, Atif Yilmaz, and Ö. Lütfi Akad, founded an important, but relatively short-lived, film movement; the national cinema movement (Ulusa Sinema Hareketi). Following his début film *Forbidden Love* (1960) Refiğ directed a series of films in which he developed his notions of a Turkish national cinema: *The Stranger in Town* (1963), a film about the conflict between western and eastern (i.e. Islamic-Turkish) values, *Four Women in the Harem* (1965), *I Lost my Heart to a Turk* (1969), and *Mother Fatma* (1973). Other exemplary films of the movement were Metin Erksan's *A Time to Love*, a masterpiece using the symbols of, and inspired by the ideas of, Islamic mysticism; Akad's *The Law of the Border* (1966), *Red River, Black Sheep* (1967), *The River* (1972), *The Bride* trilogy (1967), *The Wedding* (1974), and *The Retaliation* (1975); Atif Yilmaz's *Kozanoğlu* (1967) and *Koroğlu* (1968).

Another, conflicting, national film movement developed at this time, directly opposed to the ideas of Refiğ. Milli Sinema, based on Islamic ideas, was started by director and critic Yücel Çakmakli and colleagues Salih Diriklik and Mesut Ucakan, who had come together within the National Association of Turkish Students. This movement produced several important films during the early 1970s, including *The Converging Paths* and *My Country*.

These directors, advocating different versions of a national film movement, produced a number of important films and contributed to a vibrant film culture. However, this did not last, due to fierce political and ideo-logical conflicts, and the lack of any vigorous film industry or state support. Towards the end of the 1960s, annual film production dropped dramatically, due largely to the advent of television and, later, the expansion of video across the country. In order to survive this crisis, the Turkish film companies produced a wave of pornographic films, which caused the loss of family audiences and the closure of considerable numbers of movie theatres.

THE NEW TURKISH CINEMA: 1970-1994

In 1970 the Turkish film industry looked in danger of collapse; there was no base for consistent domestic film production, no dependable foreign markets, the technical quality of most Turkish film was poor, and almost half the existing movie theatres had closed down in the face of competition from television. However, the Turkish film industry survived, thanks largely to a new generation of innovative, talented directors who entered the field, creating a New Wave of Turkish cinema. The way was led by Yilmaz Güney.

In the 1960s, while debates about the creation of a national Turkish cinema were intensifying, Güney began his movie career as a player in 'cheap' Green Pine films. He directed his first feature in 1968, but it was his second film, *The Hope* (1970), which ushered in a new era in Turkish cinema. Inspired by Italian neo-realism, Güney developed his own personal style of epic and poetic realism, and attempted to create a new, distinctive film language suitable for Turkish subjects.

One of the most promising directors to follow Güney was Zeki Ökten. In 1975 he directed *Return of the Soldier*, a film employing psychological elements which, up to this point, had been lacking in the Turkish cinema. He went on to direct *The Herd* (1978), and *The Enemy* (1980), both of which were conceived and scripted by Güney, who was in prison and unable to direct. With *Strike the Interests* (1982), *The Wrestler* (1984), and *The Voice* (1986), he developed his own distinctive style, with epic narration, rich characterization, and successfully organized rhythm and tempo. These films introduced new elements into the nation's cinema; notably a richness of detail and a sensitive and elaborate sense of irony.

Other directors who made major contributions to the development of New Turkish Cinema included Serif Gören, Erdin Kiral, and Ömer Kavur. Serif Goren, inspired by Güney, produced several commercial melodramas with a realistic and poetic touch. He directed a number of innovative films, including *The Earthquake* (1976), *The River* (1977), *Station* (1977), *The Remedy* (1983), *Blood* (1985), and *You Sing your Songs* (1986), which displayed a mastery of the depiction of nature, but which had weak narrative structures. Erdin Kiral was one of the most talented of the directors of the movement. His feature *A Season in Hakkari* (1979) won the second prize at the Berlin Film Festival in

1983, and *The Blue Exile* (1993), which relied on mystical expression, proved highly influential. Omar Kavur studied film production at IDHEC in Paris, and developed an amazing visual style, which he used to narrate stories centred around (self-)investigation: *Yusuf and Kenan* (1979), *Oh Beautiful Istanbul* (1981), *A Broken Love Story* (1982), *The Merciless Road* (1985), *The Hotel Anayurt* (1986), and *The Secret Face* (1991).

The 1980s and 1990s saw several new tendencies emerge in the mainstream of Turkish cinema production. Throughout the 1980s, so-called 'women's films' were extremely popular. These mostly told the stories of marginal women (prostitutes) who do not actually live within accepted Turkish society. Towards the end of the decade the Turkish cinema began to produce films which have benefited from the country's traditional narrative forms, and visual and artistic culture. Innovative and promising examples of this trend are: Halit Refiğ's two most recent films, *The Lady* (1988) and *Two Strangers* (1990); several television mini-serials by Yücel Çakmakli and Salih Diriklik;

İsmail Güneş's *Drawing* (1990); Reha Erdem's *'A ... ay!'* (1990); Osman Sinav's *The Last Day of the Sultan* (1990); Ömer Kavur's *The Secret Face* (1991); Erdin Kiral's *The Blue Exile* (1993); and Yavuz Turgul's *Shadow Play* (1993).

A nation has to develop its own cinematography, its own film language, by relying on its visual culture, narrative traditions, and capacity for artistic experiments. Turkish film-makers have proved that they are beginning to discover a distinctive way of story-telling which will enable them to create a truly national cinema.

Bibliography

Armes, Roy (1987), *Third World Film Making and the West*.

Kaplan, Yusuf (1994), *Türk sinemasi: pathos ve retorik* ('The Turkish cinema: pathos and rhetoric').

Özön, Nijat (1968), *Türk sinemasi Kronolojisi: 1895–1966* ('The chronology of Turkish cinema: 1895–1966').

Scognamillo, Giovanni (1987–8), *Türk sinemasi tarihi* ('The history of Turkish cinema'), 2 vols.

Woodhead, Christine (ed.) (1989), *Turkish Cinema: An introduction*.

The Arab World

ROY ARMES

At the turn of the century, social and economic conditions throughout the Arab world were totally different from those in Europe and the United States, where the development of cinema had been closely linked to the growth of industrialization. The cinema was exploited in Europe and the United States as a commercial entertainment for a largely working- and lower middle-class audience now with money to pay for its entertainment needs, and, even when exported, it remained a secular, commercial entertainment quite unrelated to traditional forms of Arab leisure activity. In the Arab world the end of the nineteenth century was an era of colonization and European domination, so that many of the very early film showings were arranged by and for foreign residents.

Thus, in Egypt and Algeria, screenings of the Lumières' Cinématographe were organized as early as 1896 in the back rooms of cafés, but only in those cities with large numbers of foreign residents: Cairo and Alexandria, Algiers and Oran. Where screenings were arranged for a wider audience, those responsible tended to be local entrepreneurs with links to the west. In Tunisia, for example, Albert Samama, also known as Chikly, had already imported other western novelties, such as the bicycle, still photography, and the phonograph, when he introduced the cinematograph to Tunis audiences in 1897. Chikly, indeed, is a true pioneer, since he subsequently

directed the first Tunisian short film, *Zohra*, in 1922 and a first feature, *Ain al-Gheza* (*The Girl from Carthage*), in 1924. Both starred his daughter Haydée Chikly, who also appeared in Rex Ingram's 1924 feature *The Arab*, which starred Ramon Navarro and Alice Terry.

Elsewhere in the Arab world public screenings of films were delayed for social or religious reasons: the first public shows did not occur until 1908 in Aleppo, arranged by some Turkish businessmen, and 1909 in Baghdad, when films of unknown origin were shown at the al-Shafa house. Occasionally local scenes were shot by the Lumière operators, partly to add to the attraction of their programmes for local audiences, but principally to be offered as exotic novelties to western audiences. In time, screenings for an élite audience—foreign residents and members of a westernized bourgeoisie—came to be supplemented by film shows for a popular audience. A two-tier system of distribution—new imported films in luxurious but expensive air-conditioned cinemas and cheap trashy productions shown in poor conditions to the popular audience—remains common in many parts of the Arab world.

Usually in the Arab world the first film productions, like the first screenings, were the work of foreigners. In Egypt the Frenchman De Lagarne commissioned a foreign cameraman to shoot scenes in Alexandria in 1912. More authentic national productions usually followed within a few years, but overall film production remained low throughout the silent era of the 1920s. In addition to Chikly's pioneering efforts, the Egyptian Mohamed Bayoumi made a short film, *Al bash kateb* (*The Civil Servant*), in 1922. But subsequently in Egypt just thirteen silent features were made between 1926 and 1932, beginning with *Qubla fil-sahara* (*Kiss in the Desert*), directed by a Chilean émigré of Lebanese origin, Ibrahim Lama, and *Leila*, directed by Istaphane Rosti and Wedad Orfi and starring the stage actress Aziza Amir. While *Leila* is generally considered the first 'national' film (in that it was conceived and realized by Egyptians), the most important of these early features is generally agreed to be Mohamed Khan's 1930 adaptation of Mohamed Hussein Heykel's novel *Zeinab*. In addition two feature films—*Al-muttaham* (*The Innocent Victim*, 1928) and *Taht sama Dimashq* (*Under the Damascus Sky*, 1932)—were made in Syria, and just one, *Mughamarat Elias Mabrouk* (*The Adventures of Elias Marbrouk*, 1929), in Lebanon. By contrast, European film-makers made great use of some parts of the Arab world as film locations, with over sixty features shot in North Africa alone before the end of the 1920s.

THE 1930S

The coming of sound confronted Arab film-makers with fresh problems, such as higher production costs and greater technical demands, and the employment of foreign directors, mostly Italians, was common in early Egyptian sound cinema. Sound was also a problem for distributors, as differing languages and dialects fragmented previously unified markets. But sound also allowed the possibility of closer links with audiences, through the use of local languages and dialects and, above all, local music and song. Early Egyptian cinema was a cinema of genres rather than of *auteurs*: farces produced by Togo Mizrahi, the bedouin tales of love and adventure by the Lama brothers, and Yusuf Wahby's stage adaptations. What was to become the dominant genre, the Egyptian musical, made its first tentative appearance as early as 1932 with Mario Volpi's *Anshudat al-fuad* (*The Song of the Heart*). Gradually the conventions of stage musical performance were adapted for film-making and—aided by the scope of Egyptian radio—singers such as Mohammed Abdel Wahhab, Oum Keltoum (first seen in Fritz Kramp's first Misr production, *Wedad* in 1934), and, later, Farid al-Attrache acquired huge followings throughout the Arab world.

Though producers were usually seeking—in an unsophisticated way—to create a popular mass art imbued with national values, they remained very vulnerable to imported films. Far from giving support or offering tariff barriers, governments tended to see cinema simply as a source of tax revenue, usually at rates far higher than in the west. Even a comparatively successful film industry,

like that established in Egypt in the 1930s, found it hard to compete with films from the west, especially as these matched the tastes of élite audiences in the major cities, where most cinemas were located. But in Egypt the nascent film industry did receive substantial backing from the country's most powerful financial institution, the Bank Misr, which in 1935 opened the Misr studios, equipped with imported film-making material and staffed by foreign-trained technicians. In most parts of the Arab world production remained low in the period from 1930 to the end of the Second World War and beyond. In Tunisia Chikly's pioneering efforts found little echo and only two sound features were made in the period before independence in 1966. Abdel Hassine's 1935 feature *Tergui* was never shown and the specifically national film, the Tunisian dialect production *Majnun al-Kairouan* (*The Madman of Kairouan*, 1939), was directed by a Frenchman. In Lebanon, where cinema attendance was the highest in the Arab world, little progress was made after Julio de Bucci and Karim Bustany's pioneering sound film *Bayn hayakel Baalbek* (*In the Ruins of Baalbek*, 1935). Only seven other features were made in Lebanon before 1952—none with any lasting significance—and there was no production at all in Syria or Iraq before 1945.

Arab cinema became synonymous with Egyptian cinema, as Egyptian producers gradually came to dominate film markets throughout the Arab world. Initial progress was slow, however, and it was not until the mid-1930s, when the Misr studio opened, that Egyptian feature film output passed double figures for the first time, going on to reach a first peak of twenty-five films a year in 1945. The bulk of these films may have little lasting value individually, but they did establish a lasting film tradition in Egypt. Theatrical influence was very strong at this time, with three leading figures from the Egyptian stage—Georges Abyad, Yusuf Wahby, and Naguib al-Rihani—all becoming involved in cinema. Al-Rihani, best known for his stage persona as Kish Kish Bey, directed the first Franco-Egyptian co-production, *Yacout Effendi*—an adaptation of Marcel Pagnol's *Topaze*—in 1934. But critics are united in praising, as a first example of totally independent film making, *Al-azima* (*The Will*, 1939), the first film to look at all realistically at Egyptian life, which was directed by the short-lived Kemal Selim (1913–45).

After 1945 the basis of an industry was created in Iraq, where two Egyptian co-productions in 1945 were followed by a dozen or so 'national' productions in the years up to the 1958 revolution which finally put an end to British dominance. Critics have singled out two of these as being of particular note, Abdel Jabar Wali's *Man al-mas'oul?* (*Who is responsible?*, 1956) and Kameran Hassani's *Saïd Effendi* (1958). In Egypt, however, the immediate post-war period saw something of a boom in film production, as production levels rose to over fifty films a year, a total that

Abou Seif's *Lak yum ya zakem* (*Your Day Will Come*, 1951), based on Zola's *Thérèse Raquin*, which inspired a flood of Egyptian films based in a lower-class milieu

has been largely maintained into the 1990s. As a result, Egyptian films came to dominate the Arab film market and impose the Egyptian dialect as the 'natural' language for Arab films. Most of this output still comprised undemanding melodramas and farces, with a liberal helping of songs and dances, but from the early 1950s serious writers—among them the future Nobel prize-winner Naguib Mahfouz—began to involve themselves in filmmaking.

THE EGYPTIAN CINEMA

A number of major directors also made their appearance in Egypt from 1945 onwards. Salah Abou Seif originally studied commerce and worked in a textile factory, until his film journalism got him a job as editor at the Misr studios. From there he was sent on a study trip to Rome and Paris and, on his return, he worked as assistant to Kemal Selim on *The Will* (1939). He made various shorts before his feature début with *Daiman fi qalbi* (*Always in my Heart*, 1946), a version of *Waterloo Road*. During the next

two decades he made some two dozen films, which made him a dominant figure in the Egyptian film industry, and from 1963 to 1965 he served as head of the General Organization of Egyptian Cinema. His most characteristic work comprises lively and tightly scripted studio dramas, mostly with a realistic flavour, though on occasion—as with the expressionist thriller *Raya wa Sakina* (*Raya and Sakina*, 1953)—he explored other genres. Among his major films of the period are *Shabab imra* (*A Woman's Youth*, 1955), *Al-qahira thalathin* (*Cairo '30*, 1966), and *Al-Qadiya 68* (*Case 68*, 1968).

Youssef Chahine is a more cosmopolitan figure. He too began in the mainstream of Egyptian cinema, working initially as assistant director and making his début in 1950. His twenty films of the next two decades showed his mastery of the key genres of Egyptian cinema: the social drama with *Ibn al-Nil* (*Son of the Nile*, 1951); the melodrama with *Sira' fil-wadi* (*Struggle in the Valley*, 1954, which introduced Omar Sharif); the historical epic with *Al-nasir Salah al-din* (*Saladin*, 1963); and the peasant drama *Al-ard*

Youssef Chahine

(1926–)

Youssef Chahine was born in Alexandria in 1926, the son of a lawyer and supporter of the nationalist Waft Party. He was brought up a Christian and studied at the English-language Victoria College in Alexandria, before spending two years studying drama at the Pasadena Playhouse, near Los Angeles. His beginnings were in the mainstream of Egyptian cinema and he began work as assistant director immediately after his return from the United States. Throughout his career he was a totally professional film-maker, concerned to remain in touch with his audience. But at the same time he has treated a consistent set of themes, central to which is a concern with the psychology of the individual which, from the first, he has been at pains to locate socially. His output shows an increasingly keen perception of the contradictory interactions of the individual and society. At the same time, his work has grown in stylistic assurance, from the routine narrative structures of his early years as a director, through the compelling realism of the 1950s and 1960s to the more complex allegories and personal introspections of the 1970s and 1980s. His mature work combines cosmopolitanism with a strong sense of Egyptian identity in story structures that are increasingly complex and open-ended.

Chahine's début at the age of 24 with *Father Amin* (*Baba Amin,* 1950) came at a time of expansion for Egyptian cinema, and for a while he worked within its commercial confines. This was a period when serious writers were turning to the cinema, and Chahine worked with both Naguib Mahfouz and Abderrahmane Sharkawai on his film about the Algerian war, *Jamila* (*Jamila al-jazairiyya,* 1958), and his historical hymn to tolerance and Arab unity *Saladin* (*Al-nasir Salah al-din,* 1963). Central to Chahine's early work is *Cairo Station* (*Bab el hadid,* 1958), which, in its study of the poor and dispossessed, has many affinities with Italian neo-realism, and, like *Bicycle Thieves,* was rejected by those whose problems it addressed. It is the portrayal of the psychological breakdown of a crippled and sexually frustrated newspaper vendor, played with remarkable force and intensity by Chahine himself.

The historical epic *Saladin,* with its portrait of a great and magnanimous Arab conqueror, marked the summit of Chahine's commitment to the national revolution instigated by President Gamal Abdel Nasser. His later work, however, introduced a much more questioning note. *The Land* (*Al-ard,* 1969), Chahine's second realist masterpiece, was both a powerfully told story of peasant unity in defeat, and an implicit criticism of Nasser's policy towards the land. In total contrast, *The Choice* (*Al-ikhtiyar,* 1970) was a complex allegory which used elements of schizophrenia and the literary theme of the double to explore the uncertainties and confusions of the Egyptian intelligensia after the defeat of 1967. *The Sparrow* (*Al-'usfur,* 1973) was a directly critical examination of the Nasser era, attacking the corruption which Chahine sees as characteristic of the time, while celebrating the patriotism of the ordinary people, exemplified by the heroine, Baheya. The film's sharply critical tone was sufficient to get it banned for two years by the Sadat regime. Some twelve years after *Saladin* Chahine concluded a decade of social and political analysis with *The Return of the Prodigal Son* (*'Awdat al-ibn al-dall,* 1976), which was openly derisive of the aspiration and pretensions of the Egyptian *nouveaux riches.*

As Chahine's technical command has increased, he has allowed more and more of his intimate emotions to emerge. In the late 1970s he began what was to be a three-part autobiography: *Alexandria . . . Why?* (*Iskandariya leeh?,* 1978), *An Egyptian Story* (*Hadutha masriyya,* 1982), and *Alexandria: Again and Again* (*Iskandariya: kaman wa kaman,* 1990). Starting in the wartime Alexandria of 1942 with the young Yehia's dreams of escape, the trilogy, which mixes reconstructions, film clips, farce, and near-tragedy, paints a rich portrait of Chahine's commitments and enthusiasms. The trilogy does not comprise the whole of his output in the 1980s—he also directed a Franco-Egyptian historical epic, *Farewell Bonaparte* (*Alwida'a Bonaparte,* 1985), and an exuberant melodrama, *The Sixth Day* (*Al-yawm al-sadis,* 1987)—but it makes a fitting climax to one of the Arab cinema's most prestigious careers: perhaps the fullest self-portrait yet achieved by a Third World film-maker.

ROY ARMES

SELECT FILMOGRAPHY

Father Amin (Baba Amin) (1950); Jamila (Jamila al-jazairiyya) (1958); Saladin (Al-nasir Salah al-din) (1963); The Land (Al-ard) (1969); The Choice (Al-ikhtiyar) (1970); Cairo Station (Bab el Hadid) (1958); The Sparrow (Al-'usfur) (1973); The Return of the Prodigal Son ('Awdat al-ibn al-dall) (1976); Alexandria... Why? (Iskandariya leeh?) (1978); An Egyptian Story (Hadutha masriyya) (1982); Alexandria: Again and Again (Iskandariya: kaman wa kaman) (1990)

BIBLIOGRAPHY

Bosséno, Christian (ed.) (1985), 'Youssef Chahine l'Alexandrin'.

The Sparrow (*Al-'usfur,* 1973)

(*The Earth*, 1969). In a career extending into the 1990s he explored fresh areas of expression for Arab cinema—allegory and autobiography—in his later work.

Tewfik Saleh (born 1926), a graduate of literature, began his career in 1955 but found great difficulty in establishing himself in Egyptian cinema, with just four subsequent works in the 1960s, among which perhaps the most successful is *Al-mutamarridun* (*The Rebels*, 1966). But Saleh's social commitment made it difficult for him to obtain backing in Egypt and in 1972 he went to Syria to make a masterful version of Ghassan Kanafani's story of the plight of Palestinians in exile, *Al-makhdu'un* (*The Dupes*, 1972). Saleh's difficulties in the 1970s matched those of Chahine, whose three late-1970s features were made in co-production with the Algerian state production company, ONCIC, and Abou Seif, whose only feature of the early 1980s was the Iraqi-made *Al-qadissia* (1980).

During their period of critical dominance of Egyptian cinema from the 1950s, all three directors worked across a number of genres within the industry. But in the aftermath of Abou Seif's *Lak yawm ya Zalim* (*Your Day Will Come*, 1951—adapted by Naguib Mahfouz from Zola's *Thérèse Raquin*), they all made striking realistic studies of Egyptian lower- and middle-class life. Abou Seif went on to make *Al-usta Hassan* (*Foreman Hassan*, 1953), *Al-futuwa* (*The Tough Guy*, 1957—again from a Mahfouz script), and *Bayn al-sama wal-ard* (*Between Heaven and Earth*, 1959). Chahine made the celebrated *Bab al-hadid* (*Cairo Station*, 1958), and Saleh's first feature was an adaptation of Mahfouz's novel *Darb al-mahabil* (*Street of Fools*, 1955).

The virtual nationalization of the Egyptian film industry, after the establishment of the General Organization of Egyptian Cinema in 1961, served for a time to give some support to serious film-making in Egypt. Among the films produced by the State are most of the major films of the 1960s, works such as *Al-haram* (*The Sin*, 1965) by the prolific Henry Barakat (born 1914), and *Al-bustagi* (*The Postman*, 1968) by a newcomer, Hussein Kamal, as well as works by Saleh, Seif, and Chahine.

But nationalization was to prove a financial disaster. As a result, perhaps, Egyptian cinema did not experience the kind of renewal common in the Islamic world (and elsewhere) in the 1960s. The one major new film-maker to emerge at this time, Shadi Abdel-Salam (1930–86), was never able to create a real career for himself, though his sole feature film, *Al-momia* (*The Night of Counting the Years*, 1969), received international acclaim. Overall film production remained at a level of around fifty films a year, but in the 1960s many Egyptian producers moved abroad—followed by directors, for many of whom these were difficult times.

One destination was Lebanon where Egyptian film-makers (including, for a while, Youssef Chahine) continued to make 'Egyptian' films in exile. But the shift in location of Egyptian production in the 1960s did little to foster the emergence of a genuinely Lebanese cinema. It was not until the 1970s that a number of talented, western-trained Lebanese film-makers—Georges Chamchoum, Jocelyn Saab, and, especially, Heiny Srour and Borhan Alawiya—emerged and began to treat the social and political problems of their country in a number of features strongly influenced by documentary techniques. The output of Srour, one of the Arab cinema's few women directors, includes a study of the struggle in Oman, *Saat al-tahrir daqqat* (*The Hour of Liberation*, 1973), and a forceful analysis of the role of women in the Arab world, *Leila and the Wolves* (*Leila wal-dhiab*, 1984). Alawiya has made a striking documentary for Unesco, *La yakfi an yakoun allah maa al-fuqara* (*For God to Be on the Side of the Poor is not Enough*, 1976), and two impressive features, one on a Palestinian massacre, *Kafr Kassem* (1974), and the other on the plight of Lebanon, *Beirut al-liqa* (*Beirut: The Encounter*, 1982).

Egypt's nationalized film industry was dissolved in 1972, but the Higher Cinema Institute in Cairo has continued in operation. As a result, Egypt is the only Arab country to train its own film-makers locally. The generation, led by Mohamed Khan, which emerged in the late 1970s and early 1980s has shown itself very aware of the history and style of Egyptian film-making. In one of the more remarkable film developments in the Arab world, the so-called New Egyptian Realists—an informal group which also includes Atef al-Tayyeb, Bechir al-Dik, Khairy Beshara, and Doaud Abdel Sayed—have produced a series of films within the commercial structures of the industry which play with the genre conventions of film stories and star casting.

SYRIA TO THE GULF: THE EASTERN ARAB WORLD

Though the state film organization proved to be an expensive failure in Egypt, it provided a model for neighbouring Arab countries. In Syria, which, like Lebanon, became a site for expatriate Egyptian producers in the 1960s, a state sector was developed alongside the commercial industry. The policy of the General Organization for Cinema, which had produced some two dozen features by the end of the 1980s, was to offer state backing for talented young film-makers. This policy was rewarded with the emergence in the 1980s of two extremely talented newcomers, both born in 1945 and trained in Moscow: Samir Zikra with *Hadith al-nasf metr* (*The Half-Metre Incident*, 1983) and *Waqua'i' al-O'am al-muqbil* (*Events of the Coming Year*, 1986); and Mohamed Malass with *Ahlam al-madina* (*Dreams of the City*, 1984) and *The Night* (1992). Another Syrian-born film-maker to make an international reputation has been the French-trained documentarist Umar Amiralay, who, after an initial feature-length documentary, *Al-hayat al-yawmiyya fi qaria suriyya* (*Daily Life in a Syrian Village*, 1974), has

A scene from *Saat el tahrir dekkat* (*The Hour of Liberation*, 1973), Lebanese director Heiny Srour's study of colonialism and the People's Army's struggle for liberation in Oman

worked largely for television, both at home and in France (*Vidéo sur sable* ('Video on sand'), 1984).

In Iraq, by contrast, the private sector of film production failed to build on the base established before 1958. Nevertheless a number of films were produced, the best known of which were *Al haris* (*The Watchman*, 1968), directed by a leading actor, Khalil Shawqi, and *Al-zaniyun* (*The Thirsty People*, 1971), made by the British-trained Mohammed Shukry Jamil. The state-run General Organization for Cinema, which achieved autonomy in 1964, had produced some sixty documentaries when it turned to feature film production in 1977, beginning with Faisal al-Yassiry's *Al-*

ras (*The Head*). Subsequently, in the early 1980s, it pursued a policy of funding epic super-productions, all with multimillion-dollar budgets, some directed by Egyptian veterans such as Tewfik Saleh and Salah Abou Seif, others by Iraqi directors such as Sahib Hadd, al-Yassiry, and Shukry Jamil. The contradiction of telling national histories through the medium of international film co-productions is nowhere more apparent than in Jamil's *Al-masala al-kubra* (*Clash of Loyalties*, 1983), which uses British technicians to chronicle the Iraqi struggle for liberation from the British and even tells the story of this struggle from the viewpoint of the British colonizers (led by Oliver Reed). Despite such compromises, none of these works produced in Iraq achieved the international distribution sought by the General Organization for Cinema.

The mid-1960s also saw the emergence of highly talented individuals in many parts of the Arab world. In Kuwait, Khalid Siddick, who studied at the Pune Film and Television Institute in India, returned to make documentaries for television and for government departments, before finding backing for two interesting fictional features: *Bas ya bahr* (*The Cruel Sea*, 1971) and the Kuwaiti–Sudanese co-production *Urs Zayn* (*The Wedding of Zein*, 1976—from the novel by Tayeb Salih). The struggle of the Palestinian Arabs, which had earlier been the subject of numerous documentaries by Arab and foreign-born filmmakers, found an authentic local voice in Michel Khleifi. From a production base in Belgium, where he studied at the Belgian film school, INSAS, he made a documentary study of Palestinian women, *Al-dhikrayat al-khasibah* (*Fertile Memories*, 1981), the fictional feature *'Urs al-jalyl* (*Wedding in Galilee*, 1987), and *Nashid al-hijara* (*Song of the Stones*, 1988).

THE MAGHREB

In addition, new national cinemas came into being in the 1960s in the Maghreb, where distinctive voices found expression, though most of the film-makers were European-trained and the influence of France was all-pervasive. In Algeria the roots of the new cinema lay in the liberation struggle. At the time of independence in 1962 there were three organizations in existence. The first was the Centre Audio-Visuel, initially established in the 1950s within the context of the National Liberation Front by the Frenchman René Vautier, which was organized to produce agitprop material and remained in existence for six months. The second was the independent production company Casbah Film, run by Yacef Saadi, which specialized in international co-productions such as Gillo Pontecorvo's *The Battle of Algiers* (1966), in which Saadi played his own historical role in the liberation struggle, and Luchino Visconti's adaptation of Albert Camus's novel *The Outsider* (*Lo straniero*, 1967). The third centre was the newsreel organization the Office des Actualités Algériennes, founded by Mohammed Lakhdar Hamina, which also produced feature films and became the focus for the project to nationalize film production in 1964. By 1969 the Office National pour le Commerce et l'Industrie Cinématographique (ONCIC) had acquired a monopoly of importation and distribution as well as production.

Because of this state control, there is a remarkable homogeneity about early Algerian production. The first wave of films produced reflected the liberation struggle: the compilation film *Fajr al-mu'adhdhibin* (*The Dawn of the Damned*, 1965) by Ahmed Rachedi, and the fictionalized account of the struggle *Rih al-Awras* (*The Wind from the Aures*, 1966) by Mohamed Lakhdar Hamina. Both directors went on to reshape the narrative of liberation for a popular audience, Rachedi with *Al-afyun wal-Ôasa* (*The Opium and the Baton*, 1969) and Lakhdar Hamina with *December* (1972) and, especially, his epic production *Waga'i' sinin al-jamr* (*Chronicle of the Years of Embers*, 1975). In 1972 a series of films on rural reform was initiated, beginning with *Al-fahham* (*The Charcoal Burner*), the first feature of Mohamed Bouamari. But already by the late 1970s more diverse individual voices came to be heard. Merzak Allouache made a number of highly distinctive features beginning with *Omar Gatlato* (1976), and Mahmoud Zemmouri later turned a cynical eye on the politics of revolution in *The Mad Years of the Twist* (1983). Assia Djebbar, a novelist turned film-maker, brought a particular feminine vision to film-making with *The Nouba of the Women of Mont Chenoua* (1978) and *Zerda wa aghanial-nisyani* (*The Zerda and the Songs of Forgetfulness*, 1982). But by the mid-1980s the state monopoly had been broken up and even the pioneers offered idiosyncratic productions, among them Rachedi's *Tahunat al-sayyid Fabre* (*The Mill of M. Fabre*, 1982) and Bouamari's *Al-raft* (*The Refusal*, 1982).

In Tunisia the State had no such clear initial objectives as in Algeria, but there is a strong film culture, witnessed by the Arab film festival, the Journées Cinématographiques de Carthage, which has been held biennially in Tunis since 1968 and forms an important focus for Arab cinema. Output in Tunisia is largely the work of dedicated individualists, such as the self-taught Omar Khlifi who came to the fore with a number of action films in the 1960s. In the 1970s, Abdellatif Ben Ammar made a trio of distinctive features: *Such a Simple Story* (1970), *Sejnane* (1973), and *Aziza* (1980). Later Nouri Bouzid established a quite distinctive and controversial voice in Arab cinema with *Rih al-sadd* (*Man of Ashes*, 1986), *Safaith min dhahab* (*Golden Horseshoes*, 1989), and *Beznes* (1992), while the well-known critic Ferid Boughedir made an equally personal first fiction film, *Halfaouine* (1990).

Output in Morocco shows a similar mix. On the one hand those who seek commercial success, like Souhel Ben Barka who followed his excellent début film, *Alf yad wa yad* (*Thousand and One Hands*, 1972), with less controlled co-productions such as his García Lorca adaptation *Urs ad-dam* (*Blood Wedding*, 1977) and a confused view of South African politics, *Amok* (1982). On the other hand, Moumen Smihi has been consistently concerned with the expression of a specifically Moroccan reality and with formal innovation in *El chergui* (1975), *Forty-four, or Bedtime Stories* (1982), and *Quftan al-hubb* (*Caftan of Love*, 1988). Equally innovative have been the exploratory works of Hamid Benani—*Wechma* (*Traces*, 1970)—and Ahmed Bouanani—*Le Mirage* (1980).

In general the cinema of the Maghreb countries is not a popular cinema on the Egyptian model, and Maghrebi films receive more showings at foreign festivals than in local cinemas. Nevertheless they are evidence of the continuing vitality and variety of Arab cinema.

Bibliography
Berrah, Mouny, Lévy, Jacques, and Cluny, Claude-Michel (eds.) (1987), *Les Cinémas arabes*.
Cinema dei paesi arabi (1976), 'Pesaro: Mostra internazionale del nuovo cinema'.
Malkmus, Lizbeth, and Armes, Roy (1991), *Arab and African Film Making*.

The Cinemas of Sub-Saharan Africa

P. VINCENT MAGOMBE

Cinema as a form of entertainment has been in existence in Africa for over eighty-five years. The first films to be shown were documentaries originating from Europe and America. These were subsequently supplemented by films produced by the infamous Colonial Film Units and such short-lived projects such as the 'Bantu Cinema Film Projects'.

These colonial structures for cinema production and distribution have been criticized for their role in enhancing the forceful imposition of western ways, and the systematic dismantling of indigenous African cultures and traditions. Although a handful of their productions promoted modernization in a way sympathetic to African interests, the overall role of the Colonial Film Unit has been aptly summed up by African film historian Manthia Diawara (1992) in negative terms. The CFUs, he writes,

Sembene Ousmane

(1923–)

Sembene Ousmane is perhaps Africa's most highly respected film-maker. His pioneering role has inspired other directors in Senegal and throughout the continent, and his films have been screened and acclaimed throughout the world. He was an established novelist when he left Senegal in the early 1960s for a year at film school. When he returned he began adapting his own stories to film, working under incredibly difficult conditions, with little or no financial or technical support. Sembene takes great pride in portraying African traditions and culture in his films, and for this reason his cinema is sometimes referred to as 'folkloric'. However, while adapting and using traditional forms and images, he is also intimately involved with the problems and conflicts of modern Africa.

Sembene abandoned formal schooling at 14, and began to earn his living as a car mechanic, carpenter, and fisherman. Much of his spare time was spent attending performances of popular 'society-based' theatre groups and traditional storytellers, known as Griots. Later Sembene was to use this knowledge of Senegalese traditional culture in his own writing and films. For instance, in his short film *Niaye* (1964), Sembene uses a Griot to relate the story of a thirteen-year-old girl who is impregnated by her father, the village chief. This event leads to a string of tragedies for the villagers who, despite rejecting the young girl and her child, will not disclose their problems to the French colonial administration as this would diminish their dignity in the eyes of strangers. Sembene does not merely use the Griot as an uninvolved narrator, but places him within the complex play of the drama, allowing him to express his own feelings as a member of the traditional village society.

In *La Noire de …* (*Black Girl*, 1966), the first feature-length film made in Sub-Saharan Africa, Sembene draws on Senegalese 'mask traditions'. By using the image of the mask, which evokes a whole ritual of dance and music, Sembene seeks to find a film language that visibly relates to his own culture. *La Noire de …* revolves around the day-to-day experiences of an African housegirl, Diouana, whose employers take her back to France with them. Dreadfully lonely, Diouana finds comfort in the only thing that relates to her life back home in Africa, a mask. While the film is set in Europe, it is permeated with striking African imagery—the mask itself functioning as a powerful cultural symbol. Diouana kills herself, and the mask is returned to her family in Africa. The film closes with a dramatic sequence in which the dead girl's brother, wearing the mask, pursues the Frenchman out of the African residential area.

In the comedy *Xala* (1974), perhaps his best film, Sembene explores the role of the traditional healer or witchdoctor in a modern African context. A polygamous city businessman, El Hadji Abdoukader Beye, discovers

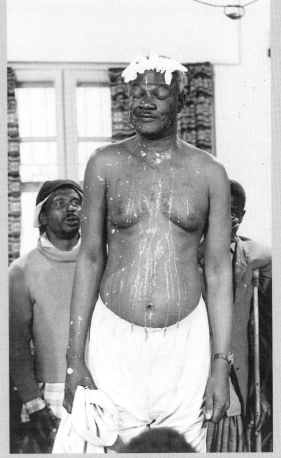

Thierno Leye as rich businessman El Hadji Abdoukader Beye subjecting himself to humiliating rituals in an attempt to regain his virility, in Sembene's masterpiece, *Xala* (1974).

that he is impotent and tries to find treatment by visiting various witchdoctors. Beye comes to believe that he has been cursed by a blind beggar whose land he has misappropriated. The beggar advises him to strip naked and be spat upon by all the local beggars in the hope of regaining his virility. Although the film ridicules the pride and hypocrisy of the rich business and political classes, Sembene is not nostalgic or sentimental about the practices of the witchdoctors, but allows the viewer to develop a critical view of some aspects of traditional African society.

Many of Sembene's films carry strong political and moral messages. His films are designed with an educational purpose; to be 'liberating art', fighting the evils of society, whether political, economic, or cultural. The short film *Taaw* (1971), for example, centres on an unemployed youth who cannot get a job at the harbour because he cannot afford to bribe the guard. When he finally gets the necessary money all the jobs are gone, and he learns the bitter truth about the contemporary social order; to survive one has to be a policeman, a paid informer, or a Member of Parliament. *Mandabi* (*The Money Order*, 1968) is a bitter comedy about a Senegalese civil servant whose daily survival depends on corrupt methods of working.

After the release of *Mandabi*, Sembene faced a barrage of criticism from the authorities for exposing the horrific levels of misery and poverty among the citizens of Senegal. Throughout his career Sembene has had to face this kind of official criticism and censorship. *Ceddo* (*The People*, 1977), which reflected the conversion of Senegalese people to Islam and the wretchedness of the political system, was considered offensive by the government, and banned for eight years. The film is set in the 17th century, and focuses on the conflict between traditional African customs and encroaching foreign cultures. It analyses the multi-dimensional reactions of African traditionalists to the advent of Islam, Christianity, and colonialism.

Like other sub-Saharan African film-makers, Sembene has not only experienced the censor's pressure within Africa, but from external backers as well, particularly the French, who have provided much of the technical and financial resources for the development of film in Francophone Africa. *La Noire de ...* was restricted and suppressed by the French Ministry of Co-operation because it drew attention to the exploitation of black migrants, in this case domestic servants. His 1972 film *Emitai* (*God of Thunder / Lord of the Sky*) was kept out of circulation for five years by the French, because of its critical portrayal of French colonial rule. When finally released, the ending was changed, with a blank screen substituted for the original shot of dead bodies in the wake of a massacre.

One of the first, and best, black African film-makers, Sembene has played a crucial role in the technical, artistic, political, and narrative development of sub-Saharan cinema, establishing its identity in the minds of African and European audiences alike.

P. VINCENT MAGOMBE

FILMOGRAPHY

Shorts
Borom Sarret (1963); Niaye (1964); Taaw (1971)
Features
La Noire de ... (Black Girl) (1966); Mandabi (The Money Order) (1968); Emitai (God of Thunder / Lord of the Sky) (1972); Xala (1974); Ceddo (The People) (1977); Camp de Thiaroye (1987)

BIBLIOGRAPHY

Diawara, Manthia (1992), *African Cinema*.

'treated everything African as superstitious and backward, and valorized Europe at Africa's expense, as if they needed to downgrade traditional culture in order to demonstrate European efficacy'.

The first practical attempts by Africans to make 'African films' in the Sub-Saharan region came about only in the mid-1950s. Master-minded by Senegalese documentalist and researcher Paulin Soumanou Vieyra, these early initiatives were greatly hampered by the lack of production facilities and technical know-how.

The films produced were of low quality, with naïvely tackled themes, and deserved no mention even in Vieyra's own filmographies. Unsuccessful though these pioneering efforts were, Vieyra and his friends are remembered for attempting to minimize the monopoly enjoyed by foreign firms and the Colonial Film Units in the production and distribution of films on the continent.

AFRICAN CINEMA IN THE FRANCOPHONE COUNTRIES

It was not until the early 1960s that a credible cinema industry began to emerge in Africa south of the Sahara. The man behind the new ambitious search for an indigenous African cinema was the well-known Senegalese novelist, Sembene Ousmane. In 1962 he returned to Senegal, having completed a one-year practical film-production course under the tutorship of experienced Russian film-makers, such as Mark Donskoi.

In 1963, with minimal financial and technical resources, and using non-professional actors and production staff, Sembene made his famous short film, *Borom Sarret*. Then in 1965 he made *La Noire de ...* ('Black girl'), the first feature-length film made in Sub-Saharan Africa. Soon, Sembene Ousmane was to become black Africa's most vibrant film-maker, his pioneering role inspiring many others, especially in the francophone countries of west Africa.

Sembene Ousmane's films won rapid international acknowledgement. *Borom Sarret* was judged best first film at the Tours Film Festival. *La Noire de ...* won several prizes, including the top prize at the Carthage Film Festival, and the Silver Antelope at the first World Festival of Black Arts in Dakar in 1966. Since the early 1960s, and in the period following the collapse of colonial rule, Senegalese film-makers have maintained a leading role in the development of Sub-Saharan African cinema. Besides Sembene Ousmane, there were other Senegalese film-makers whose qualitative and quantitative contributions highly enriched the continent's evolving film culture. These include Djibril Diop Mambety, whose films *Badou Boy* (1970) and *Parlons grandmère* ('Let's talk, granny', 1989) both won prizes at major African film festivals; Traore Mahama Johnson, director of *Diankhabi* ('Girl', 1969); Beye Bene Diogaye, whose feature *Seye Seyeti* ('A man, women', 1980) won a major prize at Ouagadougou; and Bathily

Moussa Yoro who gained international recognition for his 1981 film *Le Certificat d'indigence* ('Certificate of poverty').

Senegal also produced the first black African woman feature film director. Safi Faye, who studied ethnography and film-making in Paris, has made such films as *Kaddu Beykatt* ('Letter from my village', 1975) and *Fad Jal* (1979).

In the three decades since the early 1960s, a vibrant film production culture has developed in several other francophone countries, notably Burkina Faso, Niger, Cameroon, Upper Volta, and Mali, as well as in Algeria, Morocco, and Tunisia. These countries have provided African cinema with highly ambitious and productive film-makers, now internationally renowned for their talents and creative enterprise. Most notable are Idrissa Ouadraogo from Burkina Faso, whose work includes *Yaaba* (1989) and *Tilai* (1990), and, from Mauritania, Med Hondo, maker of *Soleil O* (1970). Souleymane Cissé from Mali, creator of *Yeelen* and *Finye* (1987), is the only African director apart from Sembene whose films have gained widespread distribution in the west. Overall the practice of film-making in francophone Africa remains more advanced than in English-speaking regions. More than 80 per cent of African films have been produced by francophone film-makers.

The success of francophone film-makers is something of a miracle given the very poor financial, technical, and human resource-base on which the practice has developed. There are a number of reasons for the success. The dynamism and creative initiative of individual African film-makers, like Sembene Ousmane, working against the odds in their own countries, have been important in establishing independent film ventures. At the same time, in such francophone African countries as Senegal, a fair amount of support has been given to film-makers by the state. This has helped alleviate the financial burden involved in the complex practice of film production, but it has also meant that the government censor has had a free hand in imposing limits on film production and distribution. The Senegalese government, for example, has been able to stop the production or circulation of certain 'unwanted' films.

Film production in francophone Africa has received a significant boost from the practical assistance offered by the governments of France and, to a lesser extent, Belgium. Unlike Britain, French colonial and post-colonial policies have been tendered around the concept of 'direct' rule, resulting in the direct participation of the French film establishment and, even more importantly, the French Ministry of Co-operation, in film production and distribution. France has been a major provider of financial resources to African film-makers, who have enjoyed the use of modern French studios for post-production processes. Many African film-makers and technical production staff have received training at the best French cinema schools, and African film-makers have often opted for joint-venture arrangements with the French Ministry of Co-operation, as well as individual French film-makers. Souleymane Cissé, for instance, routinely works with both French and African technical staff in his production crews.

Inevitably, assistance from abroad has come at a price. French Ministry of Co-operation officials and French film-makers with whom African film-makers have been co-operating are frequently accused of 'imposing their own aesthetic views of Africa as a way of judging films' (Diawara 1992). This imposition has been manifested in the form of control and censorship of film products by French authorities.

ANGLOPHONE AFRICA

The growth of film-making in anglophone Africa has been far slower than in former French colonies, even though from the very beginning film-makers from such anglophone countries as Ghana and Nigeria have enjoyed some rare privileges unattainable by their francophone counterparts. Under colonialism, anglophone Africa was better technically equipped for the development of what could have been an impressively viable cinema industry. The now infamous 'Bantu Film Projects' furnished Ghana and Nigeria with production studios and laboratories, a thing that did not happen in French colonies. Ghana is believed to have owned the best studios in Africa even before Sembene Ousmane made the first feature film in Africa. Meanwhile, Nigerian film-makers raised the standard of innovation as pioneers of what is referred to as the 'folkloric cinema'.

The so-called indirect colonial and post-colonial policies practised by the British are often blamed for the absence of a strong cinema industry in this part of Africa. The British colonial establishment lacked the enthusiasm to encourage the development of an indigenous African film industry. Unlike the French, who prepared Africans for such a process, the British trained few technical staff, and paid no attention to the education of African film directors, producers, and actors. The result of this colonial and post-colonial indifference by the British towards the development of cinema in Africa has been tragic. Today anglophone Africa remains far behind francophone in the production of feature films. The only recognized Anglophone film-makers are Haile Gerima (Ethiopia), Kwah Ansah (Ghana), Ola Balogun (Nigeria), Soa Gamba (Kenya), Abdulkader Said (Somalia), and one or two others. South Africa has produced several film-makers, notably Anant Singh, whose feature *Sarafina* proved both a critical and financial success.

With the collapse of the apartheid system in South Africa, and given the rich financial and technical resources available in the Republic (for so long controlled only by whites), there is great hope that the cinema of anglophone Africa will leap forward.

PROBLEMS OF TRAINING AND DISTRIBUTION

Throughout the history of African cinema African film-makers have faced enormous difficulties in their trade. These difficulties often looked so insurmountable that it is miraculous that so many films have been made.

One of the greatest handicaps faced by African film-makers is the lack of modern film training facilities and the resulting weak production and technical resource-base for the cinema. Many film producers use non-professional actors, and, with few technical support staff, the quality of films is sometimes pretty low. There have been some efforts to develop film training centres within Africa, most notably in Ghana and Burkina Faso, and, to a lesser extent, in Kenya and Tanzania, but these efforts have not always succeeded in establishing uninterrupted training possibilities for Africa's cinema professionals.

In Ghana the Ghana Film School was founded and developed with the encouragement of President Kwame Nkrumah himself, and, for a time, the school occupied a flagship position, offering training for students from all over Africa. However, economic collapse and other problems led to the weakening of the technical and human resource-base of the school. In Burkina Faso, the Ougadougou-based Institut Africain d'Éducation Cinématographique (INAFEC) had to close down because of the dire financial climate.

In these circumstances, African film-makers have become increasingly dependent on training institutions abroad. The main foreign cinema schools that have trained African film-makers are in Russia (Moscow Institute of Cinema), France (particularly IDHEC and the Conservatoire Indépendent du Cinéma Français), and Belgium. However, too much dependence on foreign training can limit the freedom and independence of African film-makers to develop their own approaches and attitudes to the medium.

African film-makers have always faced problems in

Souleymane Cissé combines social comment with sumptuous imagery in *Finyé* (*The Wind*, 1982), the story of two students and their roles in the rebellion at their university

distributing their films. Today, these problems are no easier, even within Africa itself. International monopolistic interference has meant that Africans cannot see films made by fellow Africans as often as they wish. The film markets are swamped by film products distributed by a few powerful foreign-owned distribution companies, from America, Europe, and the Indian subcontinent. Persistent efforts have been made by African film-makers to break this rigid monopoly. In 1969, the Fédération Pan-africaine des Cinéastes (FEPACI), an Africa-wide organization, was created to challenge directly the existing distribution monopolies. Since then, a number of locally controlled regional and national cinema organizations have been established, which have had a small but important impact on the processes of cinema production and distribution in Africa. In some countries, governments have intervened by nationalizing cinema screening halls and creating bodies to facilitate the distribution of film products by African film-makers.

As far as distribution in foreign markets is concerned, African cinema is still on the fringes, despite the growing and active presence of African films at international festivals and fairs. Most public cinemas in Europe and America have never screened an African film, and the stock of African films in educational and other institutions is embarrassingly poor. There is an urgent need for more equitable distribution practices in the African and international film markets.

Perhaps even more urgent is the need to improve on the quality of films produced in Africa, so as to enhance their competitiveness at home and abroad. There is no doubt that the scarcity of proper technical facilities and the acute lack of professionally trained production personnel has greatly limited the capability of African film-makers to compete.

FILM FESTIVALS

African film festivals held within and outside Africa have played a significant role in the promotion of the creative initiative and enterprise of African film-makers. The prizes offered for best film have always created healthy competition resulting in the production of more quality films. The festivals are effective forums for dialogue between professionals involved in film production, on one hand, and between film-makers and those who buy or watch their films, on the other. They are ideal platforms for the promotion of continental and regional co-operation, and also of the marketability of African films, by encouraging intra-African trade as well as export opportunities.

The biggest and most prodigious African film festival is the Pan-African Film and Television Festival (FESPACO), which has taken place annually in Ougadougou, Burkina Faso, since 1969.

In October 1993 the Southern Africa Film Festival was held in Harare, Zimbabwe. According to its director, Keith Shiri, the huge turn-out of film-makers and audiences from all over Africa signalled a new high-water mark of film activity in anglophone Africa. The success of the festival was a clear indication of a bright future for African cinema as a whole.

Bibliography
Diawara, Manthia (1992), *African Cinema*.
Rouch, Jean (1967), *Films ethnographiques sur l'Afrique noire*.
Shiri, Keith (ed.) (1993), *Africa at the Pictures*.

Iranian Cinema

HAMID NAFICY

THE SILENT ERA: 1900-1930

Up until 1930, when the first Iranian fiction feature film was made, Iranian cinema was entirely dominated by the production of non-fiction films. Before the First World War, most documentaries were sponsored and viewed by the Qajar royal family and the upper classes, creating a model of a private, sponsored cinema. The films themselves were 'primitive', consisting of footage of news events, actualities, and spectacles involving royalty, usually filmed in long shot.

The first Iranian non-fiction footage was shot in Ostend, in Belgium, on 18 August 1900, when a 'flower parade' of some fifty floats showered the visiting Shah with bouquets of flowers; the event was filmed by Mirza Ebrahim Khan Akkasbashi, the official court photographer, with a Gaumont camera he had bought by order of the Shah a few weeks earlier in Paris. Back in Iran, Akkasbashi filmed Moharram religious ceremonies and other spectacles such as the lions in the royal zoo. These films, along with French and Russian newsreels, were shown at the houses of dignitaries and the royal palace during weddings and birth and circumcision ceremonies.

The first public cinema in Iran was the non-commercial Soli cinema, set up in 1900 by Roman Catholic missionaries in Tabriz. But it was the entrepreneur Ebrahim Khan

Sahhafbashi-e Tehrani who first created the model for a public commercial cinema. He imported films from Europe and screened them in the backyard of his antique shop, and later, in November–December 1904, he opened a short-lived commercial cinema in Tehran.

Ethnic and religious minorities were instrumental in developing the nascent Iranian cinema. In addition, a number of the film pioneers were educated abroad and were connected to the ruling élite. Despite the rise of commercial venues, the cinema remained largely in the realm of the upper classes—in terms of both the content of the newsreels, and the sites of cinema screening. There are at least three chief reasons for the persistence of the private and sponsored cinema. The first has to do with the model set at the beginning, whereby the court or the government sponsored film-makers who showed their films privately to the upper classes. State sponsorship of documentaries has continued in the present-day Islamic Republic. The second reason was that the economic and technical infrastructures (such as labs, acting classes, technician training schools, and regulations) necessary to support an indigenous film industry had not yet developed. The third factor was the general social conditions and cultural attitudes which militated against the growth of a local industry. This included a high rate of illiteracy, a belief that film viewing led to moral corruption, and religious taboos against cinema-going and acting, especially for women. Calls for strict censorship of imports were not uncommon.

The first Iranian feature fiction film, *Abi va Rabi* ('Abi and Rabi', 1930), was directed by Avanes Ohanian, an Armenian-Iranian, and was a silent, black and white comedy depicting the adventures of two men, one tall and one short. Ohanian's next work, *Haji Aqa, actor-e sinema* ('Haji, the movie actor', 1932), was a technically sophisticated film which in a self-reflexive manner dealt head-on with the moral corruption charge against cinema. It tells the story of a traditional religious man (Haji) who is transformed from one who hates cinema to one who proclaims its values in improving the lot of Iranians.

THE SOUND ERA: 1930–1960

By the early 1930s foreign sound newsreels (Paramount, Metro, Movietone, Ufa, and Pathé) were playing in Iran. Iranian cinema benefited not only from the inter-ethnicity, immigration, and western education of its film-makers but also from exchanges with neighbouring countries. The first Persian-language sound newsreel, which was shown widely in Iran in 1932, was filmed by a Turkish photographer in Turkey. It showed the Iranian Prime Minister, Mohammad Ali Foroughi, conferring with Kemal Ataturk and delivering a brief speech in Persian, and it astonished audiences unaccustomed to hearing Persian spoken on the screen.

The first Persian-language sound feature, *Dokhtar-e Lor* ('The Lor girl', 1933), was written by the Iranian poet Abdolhosain Sepenta and directed in India by Ardeshir Irani. The film, a melodramatic love story which also extolled Iranian nationalism, was highly successful with Iranians, and from his base in India Sepenta went on to produce and export a succession of films based on Iranian folk-tales and epics. In their form and theme, these films resembled the Indian popular genre of 'epicals'. The first Persian-language feature produced inside Iran, *Tufan-e zendegi* ('The tempest of life'), was directed by Esma'il Kushan in 1948. A year later he directed a more polished film, *Zendani-e Amir* ('Prisoner of the emir', 1949). The success of Kushan's films produced at his Pars Film studio prompted a rejuvenation of the local industry, and a proliferation of new film studios. The growth of Iranian film production was also promoted by the stifling censorship of the early 1940s, which blocked the distribution of many foreign films. In 1940, for example, nearly 253 films were censored, 159 of which came from the United States, 32 from Germany, 31 from France, and 19 from Britain. Censorship was imposed on films showing revolutions, riots, and strikes, as well as indecency, pacifism, or anti-Islamic attitudes.

The global ascendancy of the United States in the wake of the Second World War was to have a profound impact on the development of the documentary film in Iran. As part of the US policy to win the hearts and minds of non-Communist countries, especially those like Iran which bordered the Soviet Union, the United States Information Agency began an ambitious project of film screening and production in these countries. Under its auspices, a group of American professors and film-makers (the Syracuse University team) visited Iran in the early 1950s to establish 16 mm. film-processing labs and train Iranians to make documentary and educational films. They also developed a pro-Shah, pro-American newsreel called Akhbar-e Iran (Iran News), 402 issues of which were shown in public theatres throughout the country.

THE MODERN ERA: 1960–1978

The 1960s were tumultuous years for Iran, bringing both the freedom which petro-dollars and globalization of capital promised and the restrictions which they actually produced in non-western countries. The political consolidation of Shah Mohammad Reza Pahlavi's regime involved the centralization and expansion of the state security apparatus (aided by the American CIA and the Israeli Mossad) and also the state's control over the film industry. Socially conscious films made by young, European-educated film-makers met with official disapproval and confiscation. For example, Farrokh Gaffary's *Jonub-e Shahr* ('South of the city', 1958), which realistically and critically depicted life in the poverty-stricken southern district of Tehran, was, according to the director, not only banned but also had its negative mutilated.

Even more damaging to the indigenous film industry was the regime's desire to modernize Iran along a western trajectory. This local ambition of the Shah and ruling élite fitted the globalized interests of the US film and television companies to expand their markets world-wide. Regional media influences in Iran were thus replaced by global interests. American companies began selling all kinds of products and services, from feature films to television programmes, from TV receivers to TV studios, from communication expertise to personnel training; in short, they sold not only consumer products but also consumer ideology. The development of the first television station in Iran provides an appropriate example. The station was established by Iraj Sabet, a graduate in business administration from Harvard, whose family was the agent for RCA and Pepsi-Cola. American firms assisted in planning and implementation of the station, which meant that, unlike many Third World countries, Iran's system of broadcasting would not be non-commercial and state-run but privately owned and commercially driven. RCA technicians trained the station's staff and US advertising agencies imported its programmes, the bulk of which consisted of MGM films and NBC TV series. In 1966 the government took over the Sabet station, consolidating its hold over broadcasting but at the same time retaining the commercial structure.

At the reception end, however, regional influences remained strong in Iranian cinema. Egyptian and Indian melodramas and song-and-dance films were very popular with movie-goers, and a thriving market for their songs intensified the hold of these films on the popular imagination. Record companies and radio stations, which promoted these songs, became part of a developing popular culture industry whose contents were highly influenced by western products.

At the end of the 1960s, the local film industry, which had been producing low-quality melodramas, comedies, and tough guy (*luti*) films, was suddenly jolted by the release of two films which set a new trend, later called the New Wave. Mas'ud Kimia'i's *Qaisar* (1969) polished the *luti* genre by developing a strong binary opposition of good guy vs. bad guy and by linking the good with Iranian tradition and culture and the bad with its violations (which in some circles was read as referring to the encroaching westernization and secularization). Thus, the tough guy genre's revenge plot, usually involving defending a kinswoman, was coded to be read as involving the defence of Iranian authenticity. Kimia'i also intensified the pacing of the genre by using an action-oriented filming style, dramatic camera angles, and stirring music. The other film that shook the local film industry and audiences alike was Dariush Mehrju'i's *Gav* ('The cow', 1969),

about a farmer who upon losing his cow, which is the source of his livelihood, begins to embody the cow in spirit and body. This film revived the social realist trend that Gaffary had begun over a decade before. *Gav*'s focus on villagers was seen as a return to roots, and its honest treatment of Iranian life and its sparse style, as a breath of fresh air. The film's use of a story by one of the leading contemporary writers, Gholamhosain Sa'edi, heralded a new alliance between film-makers and writers.

Gav also embodied a contradiction that became the hallmark of the New Wave movement: it was sponsored by the state (Ministry of Culture and Art, MCA) and was censored and banned (for one year) by the state (the same Ministry). This can perhaps be explained by the film's high visibility and critical acclaim at international festivals, which opened the way for government support of this type of cinema in the interest of gaining a positive international profile at the same time that it was being criticized by an increasingly vociferous population of Iranian students abroad. This uneasy alliance produced a succession of important films: Davud Mowlapur's *Showhar-e Ahu Khanom* ('Ahu's husband', 1966), Bahram Baiza'i's *Ragbar* ('Downpour', 1970), and Mehrjui's *Postchi* ('The postman', 1970).

The films of the New Wave gave impetus to, and were part of, a complex film culture which evolved between the late 1960s and the revolution of 1978–9. Both the MCA and the National Iranian Television and Radio (NIRT) were established, headed by trusted royal relatives and benefiting from increasing national oil revenues. Both supported documentaries and fictional cinema and heavily invested in cultural festivals of one type or another. State-sponsored and student-run university film clubs screened and discussed canonical films. Many festivals showcased and gave awards to local talent and exposed them to outstanding examples of foreign films, and the cultural arms of many foreign embassies also regularly exhibited important films from their countries. The Iranian government entered film-making through investment via state-run companies. This led to the production of some of the best films of the period: for example, The Institute for Intellectual Development of Children and Young Adults produced such important shorts as Amir Naderi's *Saz-e Dahani* ('Harmonica', 1973), as well as many of the finest animation films made in Iran; and Telfilm and the Film Industry Development Company produced many important features.

At the same time as these state-controlled developments, the film culture of Iran was given a boost by the emergence as a collective force of a group of foreign-trained film-makers, such as Hajir Dariush, Bahman Farmanara, and Farrokh Gaffary, who began collaborations with respected anti-government writers, such as Sadeq Chubak, Mahmud Dowlatabadi, Hushang Golshiri, and

Sa'edi. The films they produced moved away from traditional genres in favour of increased realism, individual character psychology, and higher technical quality. Film schools within Iran, and a Super 8 film-production network (Cinemay-e Azad/Free Cinema), were established and trained many new film-makers. Finally, an independent collective of New Wave film-makers unhappy with state intervention in cinema formed the New Film Group, which produced Sohrab Shahid Saless's *Tabi'at-e bijan* ('Still life', 1975) and Parviz Sayyad's *Bonbast* ('Dead end', 1979).

Many New Wave films were also produced independently or commercially, such as Baiza'i's *Gharibeh va meh* ('Stranger and the fog', 1975), but these were outnumbered by those supported by governmental and semi-governmental agencies. Despite such a remarkable flow of high-quality films, the New Wave represented only a small fraction of films produced in Iran during this period. The majority of the forty-five to seventy films made each year were escapist and formulaic.

Despite this apparently healthy film culture, by the mid-1970s the socio-economic basis of the film industry had begun to crumble. Import laws had made it more lucrative to import films than to produce them locally, and nearly a quarter of box-office receipts were lost in taxes. Inflation was pushing up the cost of raw stock, equipment, services, and salaries, while an imperial decree kept the ticket prices for this most popular form of entertainment deliberately low. Interest rates were high, and so even a short delay between a film's completion and its screening could drive the producer into bankruptcy, and the widespread censorship of political themes meant that completed films often had to wait for months, or even years, to obtain an exhibition permit. This not only jeopardized the financial health of the producers but also forced the directors to become timid in the issues they tackled. Ironically, the emergence of New Wave films had an indirectly adverse effect on local film production in that it fragmented the audience. Tired of formula song-and-dance films, a portion of the audience sought out the works of New Wave film-makers who, due to strict censorship, were often unable to meet their expectations. Unsatisfied by the heavily compromised films or by the abstruse filmic language some of them used to evade censorship, this audience turned back to foreign films. Also, direct government involvement in film-making added an extra level of competition, and undermined the healthy growth of an independent, commercially driven industry.

Faced with an industry in disarray, in 1976 the government took measures to revive Iranian film production, notably by raising cinema admission prices by 35 per cent, and investing in co-production deals with European and American companies. The changes created a short-lived resurgence in local production, but within a year the turmoil that would lead to a social revolution was under way; a turmoil in which cinema was deeply implicated.

POST-REVOLUTIONARY ERA: 1978–1994

Transition: 1978–1982

In the early days of revolution, cinema was condemned for what was widely perceived to be its support of the Pahlavi regime's westernization projects. Traditionalists particularly accused cinema of becoming an agent of cultural colonization of Iran by the west, and it became a favourite target of revolutionary wrath. In August 1978, nearly 400 spectators perished in a deliberate fire set in the Rex theatre in Abadan, after which burning cinemas became an integral part of the dismantling of the Shah's regime. By the time the Islamic government was installed in 1979, 180 cinemas nation-wide had been destroyed, creating a shortage of exhibition sites from which Iranian cinema still suffers. As part of this purification process, imports were curtailed, and those foreign films already in the country were reviewed, with the overwhelming majority failing to live up to the evolving Islamist values. Of a total of 898 foreign films reviewed in this period, 513 of them—the bulk from the west—were rejected. Likewise, of the 2,208 locally produced films reviewed, 1,956 were denied exhibition permits. Many films were made appropriate through strategic editing of scenes containing nudity or what was defined as immodesty. When cutting confused the narrative, the offensive body parts were blocked off with markers applied to each frame. The screenplays for new films were also subjected to the same rigorous process, with only 25 per cent being approved. Entertainers, actors, and film-makers were also subjected to 'purification', involving legal charges, incarceration, expropriation of their possessions, and various types of censorship including barring of their faces, voices, and bodies from the screen. Uncertainty about what was allowed led to a general absence of women from films.

Few films of quality were made during this period, but among them were Naderi's *Jostoju* ('Search', 1982) and Baiza'i's two films *Cherikeh-ye Tara* ('Ballad of Tara', 1980), and *Marg-e Yazd-e Gerd* ('Death of Yazd-e Gerd', 1982), which were banned.

Following the revolution some film-makers fled the country, and there has consistently been a large contingent of Iranian film-makers in exile. Even though they work in different countries, they have created what might be called an 'exile genre' of cinema—one concerned with the trauma and tragedy of displacement and the problematic of identity formation.

Consolidation: 1983–1986

The clerical leaders were not opposed to cinema *per se*; they were against what Ayatollah Khomeini called its 'misuse' by the Pahlavi regime to corrupt and subjugate Iranians. To ensure that it was used 'properly', in June 1982 the cabinet approved a set of landmark regulations governing the exhibition of movies and videos and charged the Ministry of Culture and Islamic Guidance (MCIG) with its enforcement. As before the revolution, political consolidation entailed consolidation of culture. In 1983, the Ministry created Farabi Cinema Foundation to streamline and control the import and export of films and to encourage local production. Many regulations codifying 'Islamic values' as well as encouraging the production of quality films were put into effect. The municipal tax for local films was reduced, ticket prices increased, importing equipment, film stock, and chemicals was calculated at the government-controlled exchange rate (instead of at the floating rate which was up to twenty times higher), and producers and exhibitors gained a voice in assigning their films to theatres. All

these measures centralized the regulative and enforcement authorities within the Ministry but also rationalized cinema, and in this period the number of films produced annually shot up almost threefold: in 1983 twenty-two features were produced, increasing to fifty-seven in 1986. A crop of new directors as well as some veterans of the Pahlavi era began making high-quality films. The highlights of the period included Baiza'i's *Bashu, gharibeh-ye kuchak* ('Bashu, the little stranger', 1985); Naderi's *Davandeh* ('Runner', 1985); Taqva'i's *Nakhoda Khorshid* ('Captain Khorshid', 1986); and Mehrju'i's *Ejarehneshinha* ('Tenants', 1986). Of the new post-revolutionary directors, Mohsen Makhmalbaf's works, such as *Dastforush* ('The pedlar', 1986), were the most controversial and versatile.

The presence of women in the cinema began to increase. Their representation was not simple or one-dimensional, but fraught with complex theological, ideological, political, and aesthetic considerations. A new grammar for

Amir Naderi's *Davandeh* (*Runner*, 1985)

filming developed, involving shot composition, acting, touching, and relay of the gaze between male and female actors. In essence, this grammar encouraged a 'modesty of looking and acting' and instituted an 'averted look' instead of the direct gaze, particularly one imbued with sexual desire.

Pains of maturity: 1987–1994

The commercial success of high-quality films led banks to offer long-term loans for film production, putting parts of the industry on a more secure financial footing. The MCIG put into place a film-grading system favouring higher-quality films; they were exhibited in higher-class theatres in prime seasons and for a longer period—all of which enhanced their box-office receipts. The government also encouraged sync-sound filming by selling film-makers who chose this method a third more raw stock at the cheaper government-controlled rate. This was designed to correct the tradition of the poorer-quality post-dubbing of dialogue. Locally made films were aggressively entered in international film festivals, many garnering praise, including Makhmalbaf's *Arusi-ye Khuban* ('Marriage of the blessed', 1988) and *Nasereddin Shah, aktor-e sinema* ('Once upon a time cinema', 1992), Sa'id Ebrahimian's *Nar O Nay* ('Pomegranate and the reed', 1988), Mas'ud Jafari Jozani's *Dar cheshm-e tond-e bad* ('In the wind's eye', 1988), Kimia'i's *Dandan-e mar* ('Snake's fang', 1990), Mehrju'i's *Madreseh-e keh miraftim* ('School we went to', 1989) and *Hamoun* (1990), Kiarostami's *Mashq-e shab* ('Homework', 1988), *Close-up* (1990), and *Zendegi va digar hich* ('And life goes on', 1992), and Baiza'i's *Mosaferan* ('Travellers', 1992).

Women moved from the background of the stories and the shots into the foreground. The restrictive filming grammar which curtailed their diegetic relations with men was liberalized. The averted gaze became more focused and direct, sometimes charged with sexual desires. More women directors of feature films emerged than in all the previous decades combined. Their best works include: Rakhshan Bani'etemad's *Kharej az mah-dudeh* ('Off limits', 1987) and *Nargess'* (1992), Puran Derakh-shandeh's *Parandeh-ye kuchak-e khoshbakhti* ('The little bird of happiness', 1989), and Tahmineh Milani's *Tazeh cheh khabar?* ('What's new?', 1992).

As in the Pahlavi era, however, censorship remained a big problem for film-makers. To receive an exhibition permit, all films had to undergo a four-phase approval process, involving approval of the film's synopsis, screenplay, cast and crew, and completed film. In 1989, for the first time in Iran the screenplay approval phase was removed, particularly for film-makers whose previous film had been given the highest quality rating. Although this procedure was intended to encourage quality films, its effect was insidious in that it moved the censorship from the outside to the inside, forcing film-makers to intern-alize its procedures and ideology and become their own censors. Because of conservatives' attacks on the nominal liberation that this method promised, the policy was reversed in 1992. Although political and social criticisms were not unknown in films, care was taken not to offend the clerical establishment or the religious doctrines and saints. This tended to be accomplished by the almost total erasure of official Islam from the bulk of high-quality post-revolutionary films.

During this period many of the financial, regulative, technical, and production infrastructures necessary for sustaining a high level of film output were put in place. However, the very success of these infrastructures, the doubling of the population in fifteen years to over 56 million, the relative cheapness of theatre tickets compared to other forms of entertainment, and the general popularity and prestige of cinema all highlighted the structural deficiencies existing in other sectors of the industry. Many of the theatres destroyed by revolutionary wrath were not rebuilt. Even if they had been, they could not accommodate the swelling population. At the start of 1993 there were 268 cinemas nation-wide, one for every 209,000 people. The conditions of the halls and the projection and sound equipment also deteriorated badly. The neglect of this sector of the industry has been so profound that even conservative clerical leaders, such as the Speaker of the Majles (parliament), have noted the necessity of urgent action. However, the need for allocating massive amounts of money to refurbish existing theatres and to build new ones came at a time when the national economy was in a tail-spin, forcing the country to borrow money, for the first time since the revolution, from foreign governments and the World Bank. In the aftermath of the Iranian war with Iraq (1980–8) and the Persian Gulf War (1990–1), the government attempted to rebuild the economy while still facing the continued North American-led boycott of Iran. These attempts created panic in the film industry, particularly the unification of the three-tiered exchange rate which removed the government's partial subsidy of the cinema. The long-term effects of these policies are yet to be seen.

The crisis, however, is deeper than the inadequacy of the exhibition and distribution systems. It is exacerbated by the availability of small, inexpensive satellite dishes which allow reception of multiple channels—some from neighbouring countries, such as Turkey, which are antagonistic to the Islamic government's policies. A variety of solutions are publicly debated, among them: rapid and massive construction of new cinemas and video cinemas, multiplexing of theatres, a more aggressive and wide-ranging advertising of films, and removal of the official ban on videocassette recorders and videos—a ban which was never very effective and which resulted in a thriving black market of poorly recorded videos from abroad. The broadcasting authorities, too, advocated using communication satellites for expanding their coverage nationwide (and also to the neighbouring regions, especially to central Asian republics), enhancing their channel capacity, and initiating a cable television system. Such a wide-ranging revolution in distribution, exhibition, and delivery systems for film, television, and video at a time of diminishing financial prowess of the country means the film industry must not only reach more and more of the swelling national population within the country but also create an international market for its products. This necessitates entering the commercial distribution of films abroad. Such a multifaceted scenario of change—which is tantamount to a veritable mass-media revolution almost

as profound as the anti-monarchy social revolution a dozen years earlier—can be realized only if the government and the film industry are able to muster sufficient foresight, political will, social stability, and economic growth to sustain the industry long enough for it to become self-sufficient. Recent history, however, has suggested that political will and social stability, like economic health, are fragile commodities in Iran.

Bibliography
Gaffary, Farrokh (1973), *Le Cinéma en Iran*.
Issari, Mohammad Ali (1989), *Cinema in Iran, 1900–1979*.
Naficy, Hamid (1979), 'Iranian Feature Films: A Brief Critical History'.
—— (1992), 'Islamizing Cinema in Iran'.

India: Filming the Nation

ASHISH RAJADHYAKSHA

In 1971 India overtook Japan to become the world's largest manufacturer of feature films, with a total of 431 titles. It had registered a fairly steady growth through the 1960s, but it fairly boomed in the next decade, topping the 700 mark in 1979. In 1975 a Unesco survey on film audiences showed that it was the only Third World nation to have a larger audience for indigenous cinema than for imported films. While foreign films remained relatively marginal to India's film distribution sector, and on two occasions the Motion Picture Export Association of America announced a boycott of the Indian market, its own foreign sales in North Africa, the Middle East, and the Far East (for example Malaysia) made it a cultural force equalling and sometimes outstripping Hollywood in these regions.

Inevitably the Indian cinema has come to mean many different things to different people. It developed as a cultural force largely independent of state support, surviving without subsidies (with the exception of the Karnataka, Andhra Pradesh, and Orissa regional governments) and facing a tax structure that hampered rather than assisted its growth. The mainstream cinema could hardly claim any 'official' cultural status, although it has had its political uses. And it has sustained a variety of ancillary industries: trade publications and fan magazines, the music recording industry, a fair portion of the popular fiction trade, the All-India Radio's only commercial 'light entertainment' channel Vividh Bharati, which was started in 1957, and now in the 1990s a variety of programming on Doordarshan (state-owned TV) and cable TV (especially the Hindi Zee-TV channel beamed on the STAR-TV network). And to the many *émigré* Indians whose only contact with the culture of their homeland

has been through the movies, it has been the dominant source for the language of cultural diaspora—in Britain, for instance, from Salman Rushdie's fiction to Apache Indian's music, Asian art has drawn from, commented on, and adapted its idioms for a variety of different cultural ends.

To a great extent, the Indian cinema megalith since 1960 has been effectively categorized in popular discourse as two things: the 'Hindi movie', and 'Satyajit Ray': the former being the song-dance-action stereotype made in over twelve languages and representing that most enviable of all national possessions, a cultural mainstream, and the latter a highly generalized category involving a variety of different directors generically celebrated as being culturally 'rooted' in their context. Both categories have been sustained as much by marketing strategies as by a committed and articulate brand of cinephilia accompanying each of them.

In both instances, it is obvious, a key component has been that of 'nation': and indeed, it is virtually impossible to speak of the Indian cinema without bringing somewhere into play that crucial cultural movement of Indian nationalism, and the shift or redirecting of nationalist utopia into other kinds of cultural practices after Independence was achieved and the promised 'nation' gave way to the Indian State.

POST-WAR TRANSFORMATIONS

India declared itself a sovereign democratic republic in 1950 and almost immediately instituted a series of measures to intervene in the movie industry that had been booming ever since the war had ended. The first was

Nehru's appointment of the S. K. Patil Film Enquiry Committee, which became the first official statement on the new independent freelance investment sector that had replaced the old pre-war studios. 'During World War II,' the Report observed:

the cinemagoing habit spread much further and faster among the population [following] a greater purchasing power among all classes. Within three months of the end of the War, the leadership of the industry had changed from established producers to a variety of successors. Leading 'stars', exacting 'financiers' and calculating distributors forged ahead. Film production, a combination of art, industry and showmanship, became in substantial measure the recourse of deluded aspirants to easy riches.

There were at least three separate trends on which the Patil Committee was basing its views. The first, its direct target of attack, was the new kind of money that was flowing into film. The second was the government's own evolving policy on the kind of cinema it should back: this included its propaganda wing, Films Division, as well as the cinema of the nationalist left which saw itself as the legitimate claimant of state backing after Independence. And the third was the genre question that surrounded cultural pan-nationalism, as represented by the Hindi cinema and replicated in region after region by a series of 'regional' production centres which sought the Hindi cinema's market while simultaneously extending the nationalist argument into a regionalist one, especially in south India.

By the mid-1950s, most of the major studios had closed down or transformed themselves into premises for hire: Prabhat, having never recovered from the loss of their premier director, V. Shantaram, made some panicky efforts to enter the Bombay mainstream with films like Yeshwant Pethkar's *Aage Badho* (1947: future Hindi star Dev Anand's début) before it closed its shutters in 1953. The New Theatres closed in 1955, while Bombay Talkies (Bombay) and Vauhini Studios (Madras) were replaced by veritable film factories in the Filmistan and Vijaya studios respectively. Meanwhile, the government withdrew state control on raw stock (imposed as a wartime measure in 1943), and production leapt from 99 films in 1945 to 199 in 1946 and 280 films in 1947. The year 1947 also saw the founding of the Udaya studios in Kerala, the dominant producer of Malayalam films for decades to come. The following year, 1948, S. S. Vasan's *Chandralekha* hit the screens all over the country, to become the first national mega-hit made outside Bombay and Calcutta. The year 1949 saw the birth of the Tamil regionalist Dravida Munnetra Kazhagam (DMK) Party, composed mainly of film people, which used the support of studios like the AVM Film Company (started in 1947) to present a political argument for popular regionalism. All over India, regionalist movements like the Maha-Gujarat, Samyukta Mah-arashtra, and Akhanda Karnataka *andolans* took hold and in many cases were the main cultural underpinning of the movie industry in the languages of Gujarati, Kannada, and Marathi.

THE IPTA

Many of the contending ideologies that inform the Patil Report are obviously of a post-Independence variety. Many of them deal, at some level, with arguments around authenticity: realist rootedness versus indigenous mass culture, nationalist utopia versus the regionalist components of nationalism. By this time, much of the moral high ground for setting the terms of the divide had effectively been appropriated by the influential Indian People's Theatre Association (IPTA), a Communist Party-backed theatre (and film) movement. The IPTA's ancestry, via the Progressive Writers Association, lay in the pre-war European anti-Fascist movements. Bijon Bhattacharya's play *Nabanna* (1944), a starkly realist documentary play staged by Sombhu Mitra and addressing the tragic Bengal famine that killed over 5 million people in 1943, launched the movement in a radically new direction. As the IPTA developed through large parts of India—including Assam, Kerala, Andhra Pradesh, Maharashtra, and Punjab—its simultaneous commitment to a localized people's art that merged folk traditions with a contemporary political address, and an avant-garde internationalism that saw the first experiments with Brecht and Piscator (as in Utpal Dutt's theatre), found it well placed to handle both postwar and post-Independence attitudes to market commodification as well as to the new ideas of authorship that were now introduced in tandem with a state film policy.

The IPTA entered film directly with K. A. Abbas's début *Dharti Ke Lal* (*Children of the Earth*, 1946), featuring its famous slogan 'People's Theatre Stars the People'. The film merged *Nabanna* with a novel by Krishen Chander to tell a story that became a virtual talisman for the nationalist realism to follow: the story of a family of Bengali migrants to the city, their struggles towards collectivity, and their faith in a socialist future. It was followed by Nemai Ghosh's seminal *Chinnamul* (*The Uprooted*, 1950) with a similar theme but a more sophisticated realism. Scripted with the informal assistance of Satyajit Ray and featuring Ritwik Ghatak as actor and assistant director, the film's crucial sequence shot the family of East Bengal refugees amid documentary footage of the thousands of migrants sleeping on Calcutta's Sealdah station. Hounded by official censorship, much of the film's rough-edged look consciously inscribed the extraordinarily difficult conditions under which it was made.

The most important cinema, both formally and as political address, to come out of the IPTA was that of Ritwik Ghatak and Mrinal Sen. Ghatak's début *Nagarik* (*The Citizen*,

Akeli mat Jaiyo (1963), a late film by the Hindi director Nandlal Jaswantlal

1952) directly continues from *Chinnamul* to tell the story of the proletarianization of a middle-class refugee family, but it goes formally much further actually to present something of the isolation of an economically deprived class that still defined itself in terms of feudal nostalgia, calendar art, and the rapidly eroding identity politics of the pre-war period. Both film-makers were fundamentally influenced by Brecht, and Sen in particular continued a vociferously anti-classical agitprop style through the next decade to comment on the breakup of the left, the peasant and student movements of the late 1960s, and the conditions of Indira Gandhi's rule that led to the 1975 Emergency.

Significant as it was, theirs was by no means the only impact the IPTA had on film. By the early 1950s, several major members of the IPTA and fellow-travellers of the CPI/Congress Socialist Left had moved into the mainstream of the Hindi cinema, and in various other languages had actually helped pioneer a local cinema movement. In Assam, Jyotiprasad Agarwala made the first ever film by erecting sets on his ancestral tea gardens and adapted Lakhindranath Bezbaruah's militant play to make *Joymati* (1955). More spectacularly, in Kerala several former members of the Kerala People's Arts Club (KPAC: the local affiliate of the IPTA) provided the industry with film-makers like P. Bhaskaran and Ramu Kariat, composers like Devarajan, lyric writers like Vyalar Rama Varma, and writers like Thoppil Bhasi (author of the KPAC's seminal play *Ningalenne Communistaki* (*You Made Me a Communist*), 1952) and Poonkunnam Varkey. Most of these figures had

680

established their considerable reputations during the turbulent history of pre-Independence Travancore (now part of Kerala), when the CPI's insurrection against the despotic Dewan Ramaswamy Aiyer culminated in the Punnapra-Vyalar uprising in the same year (1946) as the Telangana movement did in Andhra Pradesh. Bhaskaran and Kariat's début *Neelakuyil* (*The Blue Koel*, 1954) adapted a story by the novelist Uroob to critique Hindu caste oppression. Later films *Mudiyanaya Puthran* (*The Prodigal Son*, 1961) and *Chemmeen* (*The Shrimp*, 1965) not only continued the popular socialist critique of feudal systems but also provided Kerala with its first major commercial hits.

In Hindi, K. A. Abbas led the way. Sudhi Pradhan, author of the three-volume *Marxist Cultural Movement in India* (1979), speaks approvingly of Abbas's appointment as the IPTA's general secretary: 'In view of the political line the CPI was pursuing at the time he was admirably suited for the post, particularly when we had opted for the specialised groups of dancing and drama. His contact with the film world in Bombay enabled us to project our image in Indian cinema.' Having earlier scripted the Bombay Talkies hit *Naya Sansar* (1941), Abbas went on after making *Dharti Ke Lal* to write a series of classic melodramas. Among these were *Dr. Kotnis Ki Amar Kahani* (*The Immortal Story of Dr Kotnis*, 1946), directed by V. Shantaram, in which an Indian medical mission makes common cause with the Chinese in their fight against Japanese imperialism; and the Raj Kapoor blockbusters *Awara* (*The Tramp*, 1951) and *Shri 420* (*Mr 420*, 1955). Each of these was a crucial contribution to the updating of IPTA's realism into the era of cultural post-Independence statehood. In *Awara*, Kapoor plays the delegitimated son of a principled father, who has been raised by a bandit. He kills his foster father and nearly kills his real father as well, performing a double Oedipal act that is presented as something like a rite of passage into adulthood, modernity, and independence. Kapoor went even further in *Shri 420*: the poor but honest Chaplinesque tramp is inveigled by Bombay's corrupt rich into a scheme that will swindle the city's impoverished pavement dwellers. Wealth is equated with westernization, getting rich is akin to gambling, and the capitalists who have come into power with Independence are caricatures ripe for overthrow by infantile revolutionary 'collectivity'.

Abbas's pioneering efforts were followed by Bimal Roy's *Do Bigha Zameen* (*Two Acres of Land*, 1954), telling the story of a farmer who is forced to move to the city: the farmer was played by Balraj Sahni and the music was composed by Salil Choudhury, both important figures from the IPTA's theatre. The Navketan production house started by Chetan Anand, after he had made *Neecha Nagar* (1946), along with brothers Dev and Vijay Anand, then became dominant for the next two decades with musical melodramas and love stories that often demonstrated their moorings in post-

IPTA realism. Vijay Anand's classic *Kala Bazaar* (1960) has megastar Dev Anand play a petty black-marketeer who reforms, after an ironic opening in which he sells tickets for the première of Mehboob's *Mother India* (1957). The legendary 1950s director Guru Dutt was employed by Navketan before he became an independent producer and made his best-known film *Pyaasa* (*Eternal Thirst*, 1957). One of Indian cinema's most famous melodramas, *Pyaasa* has Dutt himself playing a lovesick poet, ignored and maltreated but made into a best-selling icon when he is believed dead—whereupon the hero denounces the world of 'palaces, thorns and crowns ... and broken hearts'.

In cinema, it was the IPTA's successful transition into a cinematic mainstream, rather than their early radical films, that proved to be the movement's most enduring legacy. Shantaram, Kapoor, Mehboob Khan, Navketan, Bimal Roy, and Guru Dutt were all major producers and most of them went on to develop their own studios or production concerns well into the 1960s, in a context characterized by the end of classic studio production and the pinnacle of the Patil Report's fly-by-night operators.

STATE POLICY

The epic melodrama of this period remains the closest India came to defining for itself an identifiable mass culture of nationalism: an indigenous and self-sustaining economy offering a cultural product that served to explain and make comprehensible the traumatic experiences of Partition, the mass migrations with the formation of Pakistan, an unrestrained urban expansion, and the religious and communal conflicts that ravaged almost every state in the nation. There were several reasons for the success of the merger of an erstwhile radical avant-garde with latter-day national policy: not least being the extraordinarily effective way in which its realist melodramas reflected some of the key conflicts around Independence. The dominant norm in Abbas, Kariat, or Guru Dutt was to use the paradigm for 'nation' to define community, family, and sometimes (as with Mehboob) the tribe, as principles of social legitimization and enfranchisement. With the affirmation of the new IPTA, the mainstream Swadeshi mythologicals of a Phalke, which were earlier the repositories of 'Indianness', came now to be placed in a genre of realism, and a lexicon of images—of the village, the worker, or the peasant—that were seen as more 'real' and thus more indigenously valid than other images.

Such an ideal of realism effectively became national cultural policy first with the founding of the Films Division, the documentary unit established in 1949 and the first government organization directly to enter filmmaking. Rooted in the war-propaganda featurettes of its predecessors, the Film Advisory Board and Information Films of India, and tracing thereby a link with the British documentary tradition of John Grierson and Basil Wright

Satyajit Ray

(1921–1992)

The Indian cinema's best-known director was born in Calcutta in a family that were among the prominent members of the social reformist Sadharan Brahmo Samaj. His grandfather was the writer and publisher Upendra Kishore Ray-Choudhury, who also created the fictional characters of Goopy and Bagha (later filmed by Ray in *Goopy Gyne Bagha Byne* (1968) and other films) in his children's journal *Sandesh*. His father was Sukumar Ray, a popular satirist and author of limericks and nonsense rhymes. Satyajit studied for a while in family friend Rabindranath Tagore's art institution Shantiniketan, being introduced there to the ideas of the Tagore/Nandalal Bose tradition of an Asiatic orientalism, of which he was to remain an adherent throughout his life.

His early career, however, was in advertising, and he became a noted illustrator by the early 1950s. At the same time he saw both American films and the European and Soviet films shown by the Calcutta Film Society (which he co-founded in 1947) and had several meetings with Jean Renoir during the shooting of *The River* (1951) in Bengal. But it was *Bicycle Thieves* (which he saw in London) that, he later said, effectively decided him to become a film-maker.

Pather Panchali (1955) adapted a renowned work of early twentieth-century Bengali fiction with a shooting style strongly influenced by the neo-realist commitment to location shooting and available light, and the well-chronicled difficulties he had in making the film included a major battle with the Indian cinema's studio-bound orthodoxy.

The film was a major success, notably in the way his realism extended a Nehruite, post-Independence rewriting of Indian history in the light of current programmes of industrialization and non-alignment. Nehru's *The Discovery of India*, published in 1946 and a foundational text for the entire nationalist enterprise, was part travelogue, part autobiography, and part history lesson, investigating 'that worthwhile something' that had allowed India to withstand foreign invasion and colonial rule. Ray's realism repeatedly, and in often uncanny fashion, evokes the tone of the book, especially in the way he symbolizes realism itself, as a vantage point from where to restage 'the past': to re-present memory in a land that could now, so to speak, celebrate the arrival of history.

He apparently followed Nehru's suggestion in making the two sequels of what came to be called the Apu Trilogy. Some of his classic 1960s films were located in the past, often the Bengal of the ninteenth and early twentieth centuries seen through the eyes of his mentor Tagore (the best known being *Charulata*, 1964, which he himself considered his best film). And his realism—in *Jalsaghar* (1958), *Devi* (1960), or *Teen Kanya* (1961)—became a mosaic of highly mannered gesture in painstakingly reconstructed sets, causing a major argument around whether

these films could ever be accessible to an audience unfamiliar with the highly encoded and understated evocations of his performances and scripts.

Beginning with *Kanchanjungha* (1962), his first original screenplay, he adapted the period motif in a series of tightly constructed scripts, usually featuring a small number of characters, each minutely defined down to the last detail, who undergo in a given time-frame a relatively insignificant experience that in some way changes them. In *Nayak* (1966) a movie star meets a journalist on a train ride that lasts twenty-four hours; in *Kapurush* (1965) a man accepts the hospitality of a stranger and meets his former lover; in *Aranyer Din Ratri* (*Days and Nights in the Forest*, 1969) a quartet from Calcutta go for a picnic to a forest. It was only with *Pratidwandi* (1970), the first of his Calcutta Trilogy, that the psychological-realist idiom expanded into a different realm. Those were the turbulent days of the Naxalbari peasant insurrection, student revolts in Calcutta crushed by police violence, and a new form of naked profiteering, corrupt bureaucracy, and chronic unemployment. Unlike Ray's noted contemporary Mrinal Sen, whose own Calcutta trilogy of the same time sought directly to participate in current politics, Ray's films (*Pratidwandi* was followed by *Seemabaddha*,

1971, and *Jana Aranya*, 1975) were disabused melodramas about the collapse of traditional values, critical of the political ruling élite while maintaining their distance from the left-wing radicalism of the Naxalite movement.

Ray had earlier made the first major commercial hit of his career, the children's film *Goopy Gyne Bagha Byne* (1968), and through the 1970s followed it with a series featuring the detective Feluda. One of the Goopy–Bagha series, *Hirak Rajar Deshe* (1980), was a barely disguised attack on Indira Gandhi's Emergency. At a time when the Ray idiom–or what was generally marketed as a 'Ray school' of regionalist realism–came increasingly to be adopted by Mrs Gandhi's government as the kind of 'authentic' Indian cinema the state would support, this decision to withdraw into the relatively uncontroversial area of commercially successful children's films was widely construed as his desire to keep away from the political establishment of the time.

He came out of a self-imposed semi-retirement, following a prolonged illness, to adapt Ibsen's *An Enemy of the People* (*Ganashatru*, 1989), and two melodramas (*Shakha Proshakha*, *Agantuk*). In his last years he scripted some films for his son Sandeep Ray, produced two TV series entitled *Satyajit Ray Presents*, and also published in book form some of his popular short fiction which had earlier appeared in *Sandesh* (which he had edited since 1961).

ASHISH RAJADHYAKSHA

SELECT FILMOGRAPHY

Pather Panchali (Song of the Little Road) (1955); Aparajito (The Unvanquished) (1956); Parash Pathar (The Philosopher's Stone) (1957); Jalsaghar (The Music Room) (1958); Apur Sansar (The World of Apu) (1959); Devi (The Goddess) (1960); Teen Kanya (Three Daughters; Two Daughters) (1961); Kanchanjungha (1962); Charulata (The Lonely Wife) (1964); Chidiakhana (The Zoo) (1967); Goopy Gyne Bagha Byne (The Adventures of Goopy and Bagha) (1968); Aranyer Din Ratri (Days and Nights in the Forest) (1969); Pratidwandi (The Adversary; Siddhartha and the City) (1970); Ashani Sanket (Distant Thunder) (1973); Sonar Kella (The Golden Fortress) (1974); Jana Aranya (The Middleman) (1975); Shatranj Ke Khiladi (The Chess Players) (1977); Joi Baba Felunath (The Elephant God) (1978); Hirak Rajar Deshe (The Kingdom of Diamonds) (1980); Ghare Baire (The Home and the World) (1984); Ganashatru (An Enemy of the People) (1989); Shakha Proshakha (Branches of a Tree) (1991); Agantuk (The Stranger) (1992)

BIBLIOGRAPHY

Das Gupta, Chidananda (1980), *The Cinema of Satyajit Ray*.
—— (ed.) (1981), *Satyajit Ray: An Anthology of Statements on Ray and by Ray*.
Ray, Satyajit (1976), *Our Films, their Films*.
Robinson, Andrew (1989), *Satyajit Ray: The Inner Eye*.

Opposite: Satyajit Ray's fable of India under the Raj, *The Chess Players* (1977)

(the latter worked with Films Division in the late 1960s), the organization grew into one of the world's largest documentary producers with an annual production of over 200 shorts, each multiplied into 9,000 prints and dubbed in 18 languages, to be released in every permanent movie theatre in the country. Films Division either made or sponsored a range of classic ethnographic documentaries (typically Paul Zils's *Martial Dances of Malabar*, 1958), or shorts celebrating a futuristic Nehruite iconography of industrialization (the classic instance of which is Harisadhan Dasgupta's 1956 *The Story of Steel*, written by Satyajit Ray, composed by Pandit Ravi Shankar, edited by Hrishikesh Mukherjee, and shot by Claude Renoir).

Then, in 1955, Ray made his *Pather Panchali*. He made it, as is well known, under extremely difficult conditions, on one occasion pawning his wife's jewellery to pay for shooting debts. It was eventually completed when the West Bengal government gave him finishing money, apparently from its road-building programme, being misled by its documentary look and by its title which translated into English as 'Song of the road'. The first cultural masterpiece of what historian Sumit Sarkar has called India's 'modest bourgeoisie', made in the same year as the epochal Bandung Conference that placed 'non-alignment' as the third global alternative, *Pather Panchali* represented an alternative ambition of the Nehruite intelligentsia to the Films Division-type ethnographic propaganda: it offered a new sense of the past against which post-war/post-Independence reconstruction could be attempted, presenting itself as an explicitly 'independent' cinema but nevertheless one that located Indian nationalism as itself a kind of Third World counterpart of western modernism.

Like its western counterpart, Ray's modernism—and the language of the Patil Report—located itself in its early years as distinct from and indeed in opposition to the mainstream commercial cinema. The mid-1950s were the years when the government, receiving the Patil Committee's proposals to start a Film Finance Corporation and a Film Institute, was faced with the sharpest divide yet between the commercial mainstream 'Hindi film' on the one side and 'Satyajit Ray' cinema on the other. *Chandralekha*'s nation-wide success in its Hindi dubbed version was followed through the 1950s with increasingly successful transplants of the Hindi cinema's formula on to the southern and eastern film industries. In Bengal the effervescent comedy featuring Uttam Kumar and Suchitra Sen, *Sharey Chuattar* (1953), launched the most successful screen stars in the history of Bengali film, and was followed by hits like Agragami's melancholy love tale *Sagarika* (1956). N. T. Rama Rao's mythological *Shri Venkateshwara Mahatyam* (1960), in which he plays the deity of India's richest temple shrine at Tirupati, effectively launched the 'living god' political career of the star (and future Andhra Pradesh Chief Minister). In Tamil and

Telugu, the L. V. Prasad school of film-makers led by K. Pratyagatma and T. Prakasha Rao perfected the genre of the low-budget domestic tear-jerker as well as a strategy of remaking films from south Indian languages into Hindi, with Hindi stars.

Meanwhile most of the IPTA's key artists had either been expelled or had left the organization, in the context of the ban on the CPI following the Telangana insurrection. Many of them moved into the commercial mainstream in Bombay and Calcutta.

Through the early 1960s, then, as the Film Finance Corporation came to define its priorities on the kind of cinema it should make, the earlier divisions between the different sectors of Indian cinema were gradually reconciled, even as a greater market-integratedness took place, helped by a greater standardization of plot and narrative structures and of conventions for sound mixing and other technical procedures. The foremost theoretician of this merger was Chidananda Das Gupta, a disciple of Ray, who spoke of an 'All-India film', a nationally integrative cultural-cinematic mainstream that took on a 'cultural leadership [reinforcing] some of the unifying tendencies in our social and economic changes...providing an inferior alternative [to a leadership that] has not emerged because of the hiatus between the intelligentsia, to which the leaders belong, and the masses'. Through the 1960s, and until the Naxalite movement challenged any naïve formulation of the 'masses' that was not determined by class, the Das Gupta-type argument of a kind of cultural organicity remained definitive of all state policy on the cinema, and indeed, after 1972, on television as well.

NEW INDIAN CINEMA

After Films Division, the second concrete film institution set up by the government was the Film Finance Corporation (1960), explicitly on the recommendation of the Patil Committee Report. For many years the sole funding alternative for independent Indian film-makers, its own chequered career, and its fluctuating priorities, are a good indication of the changing state attitudes to the film industry, and the enormous influence these have wielded on the Indian cinema in general. When it was started it was under the Ministry of Finance and was explicitly intended to provide institutional finance 'or other facilities for the production of films of good standard'. In 1964 it underwent its first personality change, when it was shifted into the Ministry of Information and Broadcasting, thereafter financing some fifty feature films, the best known being Satyajit Ray's work (*Charulata*, 1964; *Nayak*, 1966; and *Goopy Gyne Bagha Byne* (*The Adventures of Goopy and Bagha*), 1968).

The year 1964 was in many ways a landmark for India: Nehru died that year, and the disastrous 1962 war with China led to a cataclysmic split in the Communist Party. A major breakaway faction concentrated increasingly on creating extra-parliamentary peasant organizations. India was on the verge of a second war with Pakistan (1965), and major language riots raged through south India over the decision to adopt Hindi as the country's 'link' language.

As the Naxalite movement—an extra-parliamentary movement led by the CPI(ML), and named after the site of their first mass action, the Bengal village of Naxalbari—took hold in Bengal, Andhra Pradesh, Kerala, and Tamil Nadu, and an isolated and faction-ridden Congress Party regrouped under its new leader Indira Gandhi, the State itself turned in an increasingly socialist direction. Mrs Gandhi split the Congress in 1969, announced the nationalization of fourteen of India's leading banks, and also sponsored a brutal crackdown on the entire left, leading to numerous police and military 'encounters' with alleged 'Naxalites'.

It was under Mrs Gandhi's direct intervention during her brief reign as India's Information and Broadcasting Minister that the Film Finance Corporation undertook the most effective albeit short-lived programme in its history: granting loans for 'modest but off-beat films of talented and promising people in the field'. The new policy yielded instant results as a whole generation of new film-makers got the chance to make films and created what was later described as the New Indian Cinema. This movement is effectively chronicled, depending on two different retrospective histories, as having begun either with Mrinal Sen's *Bhuvan Shome* (1969), a Tati-esque comedy (and commercial success) involving a tyrannical Bengali bureaucrat and a Gujarati belle with whom he goes duck-shooting, or Mani Kaul's intensely formalist black and white experiment *Uski Roti* (*Our Daily Bread*, 1969).

Mrinal Sen's career, for all its unpredictability and dramatic formal shifts, remains the best example as well as the most consistent record of the turbulent political conditions that were inscribed into the New Indian Cinema. As already noted, his origins in the IPTA (he was a CPI member), and his early films *Neel Akasher Neechey* (*Under the Blue Sky*, 1958) and *Baishey Shravan* (*The Wedding Day*, 1960), were largely melodramas within the IPTA's political referents (the anti-Fascism of the CPI following the directives of the Communist International, the emphasis on rural activism and, the IPTA's leitmotif, the 1943 famine). In 1965 he claimed the influence of the French Nouvelle Vague in *Akash Kusum* (*Up in the Clouds*), and after 1970 made a series of Calcutta films, addressing as well as contributing to the Naxalite student movement, their future amid chronic unemployment and indiscriminate police brutality, and their anarchistic efforts to rewrite Bengal's and India's political history in the light of current conditions. His films *Interview* (1970) and *Calcutta '71* (1972) became political *causes célèbres*, the theatres where they ran became venues for rallying left activists, and screenings were repeatedly interrupted by police raids.

Ray himself made his own Calcutta Trilogy, presenting a slightly more disabused, if occasionally romanticized, account of the time. The example of Mrinal Sen was followed by Shyam Benegal, who located his record of Naxalite activity in Andhra Pradesh (the feudal systems recorded in *Ankur*, 1973, and the uprising against corrupt landlords in *Nishant*, 1975). *Ankur* especially was a major commercial success, and established the ideal of a self-financing brand of commercially viable independent cinema which, on Benegal's own account, was at the time considerably aided by the first boycott of the MPEAA and the withdrawal of foreign films and the consequent emergence of a ready-made élite middle-class audience for what later came to be called the 'middle-of-the-road' cinema.

In sharp contrast to this entire trend, Mani Kaul's *Uski Roti* inaugurated a polemic around the question of cinema itself, the first such investigation in Indian film's history since Phalke. His first three films were all adapted from literary sources, mainly from playwright Mohan Rakesh

and short-story writer Vijaydan Detha, and they engaged with a variety of classical musical, visual art, and theatrical traditions and aesthetic texts, in an attempt to reinvent the cinema and free it from what he saw as its parasitic dependence on other, more established art forms or, more importantly perhaps, from the dominant political rhetoric of the time. With *Satah Se Utatha Admi* (*Arising from the Surface*, 1980), a kind of non-fiction film text on the writings of Hindi writer Gajanan Madhav Muktibodh, Kaul increasingly emphasized for cinema the characteristics of Dhrupad music: an extraordinarily austere and formalist classical music, and in many ways the fountainhead of abstraction in Indian art. Improvisation, displacement, and abstraction remained his key formal devices in films that, in the 1980s, dealt variously with Dhrupad music itself (*Dhrupad*, 1982), terracotta artisans (*Mati Manas* (*Mind of Clay*), 1984), the Thumri form (*Siddheshwari*, 1989), and, in his recent return to fiction, the writings of Dostoevsky (*Nazar*, 1990, and *Idiot*, 1991).

Even more influential, although with fewer films, has been Kaul's erstwhile Film Institute colleague Kumar Shahani, who started his career shortly after Kaul did, very much in the New Indian Cinema context, with the

Mrinal Sen's *Ekdin pratidin* (1979), known in English variously as 'And Quiet Rolls the Dawn' and 'Quiet Rolls the Day'

Ritwik Ghatak
(1925–1976)

Ritwik Kumar Ghatak was born in Dacca in East Bengal (now Bangladesh), the son of an affluent magistrate and the youngest of nine children. He and his family moved to Calcutta just before millions of other refugees from East Bengal began to flood into the city, fleeing the terrible 1943 famine and the Partition of India in 1946. Identification with this tide of refugees was to define his practice, providing the overriding metaphor for cultural dismemberment and exile that marks his films.

His elder brother Manish Ghatak went on to become a well-known writer in the tradition of the Kallol literary group and much influenced by Maxim Gorky. Ritwik himself went to work in a textile factory as a teenager, an experience which he was able to draw on when he himself began to write short stories (notably *Raja*, published in 1948). He abandoned fiction, because 'it can reach out only to a handful of people', in favour of the theatre, joining the Indian Peoples' Theatre Association (IPTA), and participated in landmark plays like Bijon Bhattacharya's stage documentary *Nabanna* on the 1943 famine. He wrote, directed and acted in plays and translated Brecht and Gogol into Bengali, before he entered film with Nemai Ghosh's *Chinnamul* (1950) as actor and assistant director.

Chinnamul was followed two years later by Ghatak's first completed film *Nagarik* (1952), both major breakthroughs for the Indian cinema. Ghatak's early work sought theatrical and literary precedent in bringing together a documentary realism, a remarkable stylized

Ritwik Ghatak in the final scene of what was to be his last film, *Juki Takko Aar Gappo* ('Reason, debate and a story', 1974)

performance often drawn from the folk theatre, and a Brechtian use of the filmic apparatus. *Nagarik* shows a family of migrants from the east, victims of Partition, and their gradual descent into poverty. At the end the family moves out into a slum acknowledging its new identity as working class, as the Communist Internationale plays on the sound-track—Ghatak's only explicitly propaganda scene. *Nagarik* remained unreleased and for some years was believed lost. His second film, *Ajantrik* (1957), was a fable, where a taxi driver believes his decrepit vehicle to be alive and locates its identity in the ritual animism of the Oraon tribals of Bihar, while all around him a very different kind of mechanization intrudes on to the landscape. Ghatak's distinctive use of a wide-angle lens, firmly locating his character in a 'non-indifferent' nature—Eisenstein remained a major referent for much of his work—allowed him to redirect the urban realism of *Nagarik* into the historical processes of its formation, which here crucially included a sort of amalgam of tribal, folk, and classical forms and attitudes. This dialectic, a relay of exchanges central to India's epic tradition, largely suppressed by India's twentieth-century westernized modernists but emphasized by Marxist historians D. D. Kosambi and Debiprasad Chattopadhyay, remains even today a trademark of Ghatak's artistic approach.

His best-known films, *Meghe Dhaka Tara* (1960), *Komal Gandhar* (1961), and *Subarnarekha* (1962), a trilogy based in Calcutta and addressing the condition of refugeehood, proved controversial and prevented him from making features for the next decade. In all three films, he used a basic and at times starkly realist story-line, upon which he inscribed a range of mythic references through a dense overlay of visual and aural registers. *Meghe Dhaka Tara* centres on a working woman from a refugee family who ends up sacrificing her freedom and eventually her life for the survival of her family. Upon this story is overlaid a reference to a Bengali legend about the goddess Durga: the legend defines the actual means by which women are oppressed and thereby becomes also the means of political recognition. The landscape and the highly discontinuous merging of natural sound, that of human labour, with a gradually evolving classical music, a Tagore lyric, sounds of a whiplash, and a flute leitmotif directly relating to the Durga legend, create virtually parallel texts to transform the realist story-line. With *Subarnarekha* Ghatak carried this even further, to define, for the first time in his work and in the Indian cinema, the possibility of an epic idiom for the contemporary. The film's story chronicles the gradual disillusionment of an upright product of the Tagorean Bengal renaissance, especially when his young sister abandons him to marry a man from an 'untouchable' caste. However, most of its classic sequences—the abandoned Second World War airstrip where the childen play on a wrecked fighter, the sister's forced marriage and elopement, and the final sequence as the drunken hero sits in a night-club and quotes from the

Upanishads and from Eliot, while the music replays the striptease number from Fellini's *La dolce vita*—are a thick amalgam of quotation, political comment and epic construction.

Subarnarekha—and more so *Komal Gandhar*, which featured the internecine rivalries between two theatre groups and appeared as a retrospective comment on the much-revered IPTA—led to Ghatak's being driven out of the Bengal film industry. He moved briefly to Pune where he taught at the Film Institute, making his mark as a teacher to Mani Kaul, John Abraham, and others, but especially to Kumar Shahani, who was Ghatak's main inheritor in the 1970s and 1980s.

Ghatak returned to film-making only in the 1970s, when a Bangladeshi producer financed the epic *Titash Ekti Nadir Naam* (1973). Unavailable for public viewing until the mid-1980s, this extraordinary film, with a story set among the Malo fishermen living by the Titash river, has an iconographic rather than a narrative logic and carries over into film some of the quality of Indian sculpture. Kumar Shahani (1986) wrote of it: 'This wasn't transparent celluloid. Here is a film sculpted with light, with the cold pigmentation that has come down to us from the chiselling of granite and other rock yielding itself to elemental energy.'

His last film, and perhaps his most unusual, was the 'autobiographical' *Jukti Takko Aar Gappo* (1974): a picaresque featuring himself as a drunken intellectual who travels through Bengal to meet his estranged wife. He has an encounter with Naxalite youths in a forest, and in the morning dies when the police attack their hideout.

ASHISH RAJADHYAKSHA

SELECT FILMOGRAPHY

Nagarik (The Citizen) (1952); Ajantrik (The Unmechanical, The Pathetic Fallacy) (1957); Bari Theke Paliye (The Runaway) (1959); Meghe Dhaka Tara (The Cloud-Capped Star) (1960); Komal Gandhar (1961); Subarnarekha (1962); Titash Ekti Nadir Naam (A River Named Titash) (1973); Jukti Takko Aar Gappo (Reason, Debate and a Story) (1974)

BIBLIOGRAPHY

Bannerjee, Haimanti (1985), *Ritwik Kumar Ghatak*.
Bannerjee, Shampa (ed.) (1982), *Ritwik Ghatak*.
Ghatak, Ritwik (1987), *Cinema and I*.
Rajadhyaksha, Ashish (1982), *Ritwik Ghatak: A Return to the Epic*.
—— and Gangar, Amrit, (eds.) (1987), *Ritwik Ghatak: Arguments/Stories*.
Shahani, Kumar (1986), 'The Passion of Resurrection'.

movement's first (and eventually sole) full-scale experiment with colour: *Maya Daran* (*Mirror of Illusion*, 1972). Like Kaul, Shahani too addressed the formal propositions of Indian aesthetic theory, but politicized it to a greater extent with his use of the term Epic. Adapting the idea from Brecht (via his teacher, Ghatak), Shahani emphasizes the origins of the Epic in practice and tradition, and its crucial role in consolidating a discourse of civilization (including under that head technologies and modes of production). His key text in this has been the *Mahabharata*, which he adapted to make his biggest film, the melodrama *Tarang* (*The Wave*, 1984). *Tarang*, which tells the story of an industrial family riven with internal dissension, and that of a working class equally trapped in its own self-definitions, consciously attempted to comment on the history of Indian nationalism through the tradition of melodrama that became its cultural counterpart. *Tarang* also follows Mrinal Sen and Benegal in its references to the post-1964 period of Indian politics, but its alternative attitude to the contemporary—as a history in formation, rather than one to be referred to through given discourses and established oppositions—allowed for an unprecedented possibility for cultural intervention. This radical potential revealed by Shahani's work to some extent explains the vehemence with which the State disowned its own independent cinema programme so soon after it was instituted.

DOORDARSHAN AND MASS-COMMUNICATIONS POLICY

In 1971 Mrs Gandhi sent in troops to liberate Bangladesh, and returned to power with an unprecedented majority. Within two years, however, her socialist programme had turned authoritarian, following the declaration of presidential rule in Bengal and the constitutional amendments she sought that would make Parliament the supreme legal authority in the country. These amendments were defeated in the Supreme Court in 1973, and the following year the Nav Nirman student agitation in Gujarat and the opposition-supported movement in Bihar led by Jayaprakash Narayan created the pre-conditions for the declaration of the State of Internal Emergency (1975). In the four years that she exercised supreme power thereafter, having put her entire opposition into prison, Indira Gandhi sought to overcome the ossified political divides by a number of diversionary measures, one of which was a major investment in mass-communications technology.

In 1975 the Satellite Instructional Television Experiment (SITE) attempted for the first time the centrally broadcast national hook-up that was soon to become the Doordarshan television megalith. Much of SITE's programming adapted Benegal's type of ruralist realism into a quasi-documentary developmental style that has remained its staple form of assimilating the condition of

India's vast hinterland. In 1976, a Committee on Public Undertakings investigation violently attacked the Film Finance Corporation for its 'art film' policy, arguing, from the viewpoint of the forthcoming mass-communications network, that 'there is no inherent contradiction between artistic films of good standard and films successful at the box office'.

Ironically 'Satyajit Ray'-type realism became national communications policy, as the films henceforth to be supported had to follow the aesthetic criteria of 'human interest in theme', 'Indianness', and 'characters with whom the audience can identify'. The 80th Estimates Committee Report was even more vociferous, saying that 'it should have been apparent to the Corporation that films are primarily a means of entertainment and unless the films financed provide good entertainment they would not be acceptable to the masses'.

The year of the Emergency, 1975, was also the year in which two of the Indian cinema's biggest hits ever, Ramesh Sippy's 'curry' Western *Sholay* (*Flames of the Sun*), and a low-budget mythological *Jai Santoshi Maa* (*In Praise of Mother Santoshi*), were released. Earlier, a relatively fallow period had ended with Shakti Samanta's blockbuster love story *Aradhana* (*Dedicated Life*, 1969), introducing the star of the decade, Rajesh Khanna. *Sholay* effectively introduced his successor, and the biggest star in Indian film history, Amitabh Bachchan.

These successes, reiterating the cinema's continuing strength as a major cultural force, and its ability to handle the problems of a declining foreign market and the threat of video, was important for the mass-communications policy that the government was about to institute around its Doordarshan experiment. In 1969 the Indian scientist Vikram Sarabhai had outlined a utopian vision for a nation-wide TV hook-up that, he had argued, would in one fell swoop overcome the two major problems afflicting India's future: its size in terms of geographical distances and the relatively underdeveloped transportation and communications system; and its linguistic diversity—both claims obviously reinvoking the 'All-India film' argument of the 1950s refashioned to television distribution.

In 1980, when Mrs Gandhi returned to power, much of her earlier socialism had been replaced by a free market ideology: the major front on which she started her new policy of economic liberalization was television. In 1981, the year India accepted a massive loan from the International Monetary Fund and thus began its current crisis of extreme financial indebtedness, it also liberalized the import of colour TV sets, and set up the APPLE satellite. This, followed by the INSAT 1-B satellite in 1983, led to a new era in Indian cultural politics: the Special Plan for Expansion of Television was instituted, and forty-four new stations, and over 200 high- and low-power transponders, meant that geographically India could telecast to 70 per cent of its population. In 1985 Doordarshan offered this gigantic network to private-sector programming, especially appealing to the film industry to supply software, technical personnel, and equipment for its new commercialized evening slots.

Since 1985, when the commercial 'sponsored programme' was launched, television's domination has fundamentally affected the Indian film industry. Most of the major New Indian Cinema film-makers, like Benegal, Saeed Akhtar Mirza, Ketan Mehta, and even Mrinal Sen, moved to making TV films and TV serials, and several mainstream directors like *Sholay*'s creator Ramesh Sippy, Ramanand Sagar (with the *Ramayana*), and B. R. Chopra (with the *Mahabharata*) have done likewise. The use of Doordarshan as a publicity outlet—paralleling its unprecedented effectiveness as an advertising medium—meant a widespread formal change, as the Chitrahaar model (a programme stringing together song sequences from various films, and consistently the most popular genre on Indian TV in audience ratings) made it mandatory yet again that any major commercial success have at least one song hit. And this went along with the audiocassette revolution that saw (according to the *Financial Times* newsletter *Music & Copyright*) an astonishing fourteen-fold increase in record sales over just one year, from 1987 to 1988.

Pre-release sale of music rights, which since the late 1980s has generated income for the film industry equivalent to the distribution revenues from an entire 'territory' (India is divided into five 'territories' for distribution purposes), gave a new lease of life to the genre of the love story with the popular *Qayamat Se Qayamat Tak* (1988), as well as spawning a series of commercial successes beginning with N. Chandra's *Tezaab* (1988) and hits by the 1990s megastar Shah Rukh Khan (*Baazigar* and *Darr*, both 1992).

Perhaps the director who best exemplifies this trend is the most-discussed figure of recent Indian cinema, the Tamil film-maker Mani Rathnam. Having established himself, most unusually for a Tamil director, in a national market with *Nayakan* (*Hero*, 1987), a Kamalahasan crime movie based on *The Godfather*, he shifted into MTV-type rock video movies with *Agni Nakshatram* (1988) and *Anjali* (1990). Both films have extremely thin plot-lines—the former features a fight between two brothers, the latter has a middle-class family with a handicapped child—but are packed with songs, shot with flare lighting and diffused camera, and display an astonishing ability to replicate MTV editing with local references. *Anjali* was a hit in the dubbed Hindi version as well, and the director was thus a noted national figure long before he made his most recent, and most controversial movie yet, *Roja* (1992). In this film, a newly married Tamilian hero is sent by the Indian army to Kashmir, where he is abducted by pro-Islamic terrorists. In the context of the communal holo-

caust that has beset the country since the demolition of the Babri Masjid by Hindu fundamentalist mobs in 1992, this theme was topical to say the least. A westernized hero whose Hinduism is inscribed into all his behaviour from his marriage to a rural belle, to his 'patriotism' as a captive, was contrasted with a bunch of obviously Muslim and anti-Indian terrorists. The film, advertised as a 'patriotic love story', became one of the biggest hits of the year in both its original Tamil and its dubbed Hindi versions. This unprecedented success was due in equal measure to its politics, in which respect it belongs to a bunch of recent hits all feeding off recent 'Hindutva' militancy, and to its innovative use of music—notably its rap number 'Rukmini' with a chorus line of middle-aged Tamil matrons.

In the heyday of Indian cinema, many of the otherwise crass and deplorable forms of cinematic mass culture have stood the nation in good stead by rigidly maintaining the equation between nationalism and 'belonging', and by locating the nation as a 'secular' multi-cultural entity in opposition to the divisive challenge from the Hindu right. Even when promoting regional difference and even separatism, previous Indian cinema never set these differences at a religious-communitarian level. Two dangerous trends threaten the Indian cinema: one is political-commercial and stems from the compromises made with televisual neo-imperialism; and the other is more narrowly political and communitarian, deriving from the shattering of the national secular ideal. Should the latter prove definitive, it is the one more to be feared.

Bibliography

Barnouw, Eric, and Krishnaswamy, S. (1980), *Indian Film*.

Das Gupta, Chidananda (1968), 'The Cultural Basis of Indian Cinema'.

Patil, S. K. (1951), *Report of the Film Enquiry Committee*.

Pradhan, Sudhi (ed.) (1979), *Marxist Cultural Movement in India (1936–1947)*.

Rajadhyaksha, Ashish, and Willemen, Paul (eds.) (1994), *Encyclopaedia of Indian Cinema*.

Vasudev, Aruna, and Lenglet, Philippe (eds.) (1983), *Indian Cinema Superbazaar*.

Seema Biswas in *The Bandit Queen* (1994), a tale of epic revenge produced by S. S. Bedi and directed by Shakhar Kapur; its release was delayed by the Indian censors

Photo: S. S. Bedi

Indonesian Cinema

DAVID HANAN

In 1993 Indonesia had a total population of 186 million people made up of 300 ethnic groups (with over 300 languages and dialects) spread across the 13,000 islands that make up the Indonesian archipelago. The main population centre is the island of Java with over 100 million people. With the breakup of the Soviet Union, Indonesia became the world's fourth most populous nation.

Prior to independence, a small number of films were made in the Netherlands East Indies. About 110 films were produced between 1926 and 1950, mainly by Chinese companies, but also by the Dutch colonialists. An indigenous Indonesian cinema only began in earnest in the first year of independence from the Dutch in 1950. In the following decade, Indonesia produced an average of thirty-five features a year, mostly made in Jakarta, the national capital, in the national language, Bahasa Indonesia, a language similar to Malay.

MAJOR DEVELOPMENTS IN THE 1950S AND 1960S

The growth of Indonesian cinema after 1950 was led by the pioneering director Usmar Ismail, who made more than twenty-five films before his death in 1971. Usmar's first post-independence productions—*Darah dan doa'* ('The long march', 1950), *Enam djam di Djogdja* ('6 hours in Jogja', 1951), and *Lewat djam malam* ('After the curfew', 1954)—all celebrate the years of struggle for independence, but as post-revolutionary productions have an unusual scepticism, the very opposite of what was found in the Soviet Union in the 1920s. Instead, these films highlight, with a quiet understatement and considerable subtlety, the moral ambiguities produced by the revolutionary period. His most successful film, *Krisis*, now lost, was a comedy about the housing crisis in the early years of the republic; and in 1955 he made a brilliant and prophetic satire on the dangers of charismatic political leadership in Indonesia, *Tamu agung* ('Exalted guest'), which was released despite its implicit criticism of President Sukarno.

Usmar's production company, Perfini, provided a framework for the emergence of a number of other talented young directors. Most notably it supported Djayakusuma, who was interested in traditional cultures and regional diversity. He explored these issues in his 1953 film *Harimau Tjampa* ('The tiger from Tjampa'), which centred on the western Sumatran self-defence ritual *pencak silat*, and the Islamic philosophies of restraint that underlie it. Perhaps his most ambitious film was *Tjambuk api* ('Whipfire', 1959), a drama about villagers resisting oppression by the village head. The film mixed cultural traditions from different regional areas, attempting to prove that the Indonesian national motto, 'Unity in Diversity', could work as a formula for a feature film.

Other significant writer-directors to emerge under the Perfini umbrella were Asrul Sani—who was also a noted poet, and who scripted Usmar Ismail's *Lewat Djam Malam*—and Nya Abbas Akup, a director of comedies. Nya Abbas Akup's *Tiga buronan* ('Three fugitives', 1957) was a story about three bandits harassing the citizens of a quiet Islamic village. With a mild and easy wit, the film mixed the humour and style of *lenong Betawi* (a form of lyrical subversive theatre that evolved in the nineteenth century as entertainment for the indigenous population of Batavia under Dutch colonial rule) with a plot and visual style that also bear traces of the Hollywood Western, mocking in a gentle Indonesian way some of the conventions of Hollywood. Another major director who began work in the 1950s was Wim Umboh, whose best film, *Matjan Kemayoran* ('The tiger of Kemayoran', 1965), was a romantic portrait of resistance and collaboration in the colonial era, based on popular legends of the period.

The period of Guided Democracy (1957–65) saw a decline in local film production, and, when President Sukarno increased the power of the Communist Party, the government agency PAPFIAS (Committee to Boycott Imperialist American Films) ordered the banning of all American imports over a period of two years. The events of 30 September 1965, in which some leftist elements in the army massacred six leading army generals, resulted in the annihilation of the left in Indonesia and the emergence of a right-wing, military-backed government, known as the New Order, led by General Suharto, who remained in power for over three decades. Most of the films that had been made by left-wing directors such as Bachtiar Siagian and Basoeki Effendi were lost at this time, though some scripts have survived. New Order policies lifted restrictions on American imports and prioritized the emergence of a highly commercial indigenous cinema, which began to take off in the early 1970s.

THE INDUSTRY IN THE 1970S AND 1980S

In the 1970s and 1980s Indonesian film production averaged about sixty to seventy features per year. Throughout this period many of the producers were of Chinese or Indian origin, but most of the writers and directors were Indonesian (Javanese, Sumatran, Sulawesian, at least one Balinese). From 1967, the national industry was subsidized with money from imports, and in the mid-1970s a quota on imports was introduced. In the 1980s about 180 films were imported into Indonesia each year, and statistics show that over this period on average 35–40 per cent of viewers watched Indonesian films, 20–25 per cent watched American films, with films from Hong Kong and India gaining 15 per cent and 12 per cent of the audience respectively. However, because distributors screened the American films in the expensive urban cinemas where prices were almost equivalent to the west, the real profits were made on American films.

In the 1970s and 1980s, some Indonesian films were exported to Malaysia and Singapore, where they had a definite following, particularly among the Malay populations. The Singapore-based Malay cinema, which was popular in the 1950s in Indonesia, was not seen there after 1959 owing to new protectionist policies. However, in the 1990s, particularly with the development of an indigenous 'Bumiputera' cinema in Malaysia, there were some co-productions between Indonesia and Malaysia. In South-East Asia there was also a large Filipino commercial cinema, and a sporadically highly productive Thai cinema. However, all these national cinemas tended to operate primarily within the sphere of their own national languages.

In the early 1970s a new generation of talent emerged in the Indonesian cinema. Most notable were the Moscow-trained director Sjuman Djaya, who had begun writing scripts in 1956, and Teguh Karya, whose 'Teater Populer' collective proved to be an important training ground for new talent over the following twenty-five years. It was from Teguh's collective that director Slamet Rahardjo and multi-award-winning actress and entrepreneur Christine Hakim emerged.

Sjuman Djaya's dynamic early film *Si doel anak Betawi* ('Si Doel, Betawi lad', 1973) was a musical, celebrating the popular culture of Jakarta and its children, but his work also ranged from literary adaptations and history to films that engaged in political and social critique: *Atheis* (1974) was about the difficulties of reconciling Islam and Marxism; *R. A. Kartini* (1983) was a film biography based on the letters of a women's emancipationist; *Si mamad*, made in 1973, was an allegory about corruption in Jakarta; and *Kerikil kerikil tajam* ('Sharp gravel', 1985) dramatized the hazards for village women journeying to the big city. *Yang muda, yang bercinta* ('Young, in love', 1977), made at a time of student protest against New Order policies, starred the banned poet Rendra who recited poems in the film, and was never released in its full form.

In the 1970s Teguh Karya financed his collective by alternating production between popular commercial films—establishing major stars on the way—and special projects, such as his great historical film *November 1828* (1979). About the Java war, but also providing a cultural contrast between Javanese and western values and body language, *November 1828* was one of the first Indonesian films to become known abroad. His remarkable *Ibunda*

('Mother', 1986) criticized Jakartans for their treatment of minority groups in the Indonesian republic—in this case the Irian Jayans (i.e. Papuans), living in Jakarta. The film, mixing naturalistic family drama with an expressionistic folk opera, was an allegory about institutionalized political violence that ostensibly seems directed at Communism but can be read much more widely in its application. *Secangkir kopi pahit* ('Bitter coffee', 1985), like Sjuman Djaya's *Sharp Gravel*, explored the drift to the cities in the Third World, but told its story in both flashbacks and flashforwards with location shooting in the slums of Jakarta, producing an effect of both toughness and complexity.

Under the New Order, Indonesian films became subject to pre-censorship—censored at the script stage as well as at completion of production. The best Indonesian directors became adept at a certain approach to political allegory that did not infringe censorship requirements, but managed to make extended comment on the political and social system. In New Order Indonesia it was forbidden to criticize either the state ideology ('Pancasila'), or the government. Slamet Rahardjo's *Langitku, rumahku* ('My sky, my home'), about a friendship between two boys, one desperately poor, the other from a super-rich family, critiqued the widening gap between rich and poor that emerged in Indonesia during the 1970s. The film used the state ideology to raise this issue. The film passed the censors, but its restricted circulation by the leading exhibition conglomerate became a *cause célèbre* in Indonesian society in the early 1990s.

Other major directors of the period included Ami Priyono, whose *Roro Mendut* (1983) stylishly retold an old legend of female resistance to the overtures of a powerful general in the seventeenth-century Mataram empire; and Eros Djarot, a brother of Slamet Rahardjo, whose remarkable and poetic *Tjoet Nja' Dhien* (1988), starring Christine Hakim as the guerrilla leader in the mountains of Aceh in the early part of this century, was the first Indonesian film to be exhibited at Cannes. *Tjoet Nja' Dhien*, together with Asrul Sani's *Para Perintis Kemerdekaan* ('Pioneers of freedom', 1980), and *Nagabonar* (1987), set in Sumatra, kept alive the issue of regionalism in the Indonesian cinema.

POPULAR CINEMA IN THE 1970S AND 1980S

One of the strengths of the popular Indonesian cinema has been the way in which it has evolved several distinct genres that are not found in any other society in quite the same way. In the mid-1970s one of the most popular stars was the 'Betawi' comedian and singer Benyamin S., who in a string of films made very quickly and cheaply—*Raja Lenong* ('The king of Lenong'), *Benyamin jatuh cinta* ('Benyamin falls in love'), *Koboi Nungsi* ('Refugee cowboy'), *Tarzan pensiunan* ('Tarzan pensioned off')—developed what amounted to a critique of modernization. Sometimes

A scene from *November 1828* (1979), Teguh Karya's classic drama of resistance fighting during the Java War

Roro Mendut (1983): director Ami Priyono's adaptation of the Romeo and Juliet story, set in the 17th century

these films examined the new international business world of Jakarta that evolved rapidly in the 1970s and the shady land deals that accompanied this expansion, basing their critique on the loss of the Betawi values of reciprocity; sometimes they spoofed the images of western popular culture.

Another innovation was the 'Dangdut' musical. Dangdut is a highly rhythmic Indonesian popular music that exploded as a mass-culture phenomenon in the 1970s. It had some similarities with rock, but was highly melodious, and had a long line of evolution through Melayu 'kroncong' music, subtly mixed with elements of Indian and Arab music. Developed jointly with Elvy Sukaesih, it was very consciously given a further Islamic dimension by Rhoma Irama, in an attempt to discover an 'Eastern' style. Irama was banned from television for ten years because he espoused certain Islamic positions antithetical to the state, but his films did very well at the box-office. The dramas played out in these films are often rudimentary but the power of their music made them extremely popular, particularly among the poor.

A third genre that developed during this period was the 'Queen of the Southern Ocean' genre, based on legends about Nyi Roro Kidul, the mythical queen exiled to the bottom of the Southern Ocean, and her daughter, Nyi Blorong, who had the power to prey on the living, sometimes for good, more often for bad. This genre was related to the 'Crocodile Queen' films, and both were Indonesian variants of the 'monstrous feminine' or the ambiguous or negative mother image. Clearly there were strong influences from the Indian cinema in these films, but the matriarchal elements present in Javanese society made the genre popular, as well as the strength of pre-Islamic Hindu Buddhist mythology in the popular imagination.

Other codified genre films also proved extremely popular during the 1970s and 1980s; the Indonesian martial arts film (*silat*), the teenage film (*remaja*), the popular Islamic history film, usually about the coming of Islam to Indonesia, the Hindu Buddhist history film, the stories from the colonial period, and the government-funded political history film. In the 1980s a westernized group, known as 'Warung Coffee', emerged to produce films which delighted audiences with their slapstick humour and jokes in Jakarta dialect.

In the 1990s the viability of the national film industry has been put into crisis by the large-scale introduction of commercial television. However, the people of Indonesia have a great interest in their national cinema, with major directors more respected and better known than their counterparts in the west. Debates about film culture that in many western countries are limited to specialists are conducted openly in the daily press in Indonesia. The country has a National Film Council, a film school at the Jakarta Institute of the Arts (where students are taught by practitioners), and a film archive, Sinematek Indonesia. The National Film Council is a quasi-autonomous consultative body made up of artists, administrators, and businessmen, which has done much to raise the profile of the film industry. While censorship has restricted the range of issues that can be openly discussed in Indonesia, film culture has been used by artists to focus issues of national significance which might not otherwise have been raised.

Bibliography

Ardan, S. M. (1992), *Dari gambar idoep ke sinepleks* ('From early actualities to the multiplex cinemas').

Biran, Misbach Yusa (1982), *Indonesian cinema: lintasan sejarah* ('Indonesian cinema: a historical perspective').

Heider, Karl (1991), *Indonesian Cinema. National Culture on Screen.*

Said, Salim (1991), *Shadows on the Silver Screen: A Social History of the Indonesian Film.*

Sen, Krishna (1994), *Indonesian Cinema: Framing the New Order.*

China After the Revolution

ESTHER YAU

The history of cinema on the Chinese mainland after the Communist take-over in 1949 falls into four distinct periods. From 1949 to 1966, a national film base financed by the state produced Socialist Realist 'worker–peasant–soldier' films, in an attempt to build an indigenous 'revolutionary cinema'. Feature film production virtually stopped during the early years of the Cultural Revolution from 1966 to 1972, except for ten filmed operas ('revolutionary model operas'). In the years following the Cultural Revolution innovative efforts and 'exploratory films' dismantled the conventions of classical revolutionary realism and redefined the language of Chinese cinema. Then, in 1987, studios took up full financial accountability and started producing entertainment movies, prompting a gradual reversal to a market-driven commercial cinema.

THE REVOLUTIONARY CINEMA

1949–1956: politics and industry

After 1949, production, distribution, exhibition, and censorship of films fell under the purview of the Ministry of Propaganda and, later, the Film Bureau of the Ministry of Culture. Beginning in 1951, movies from Shanghai made before 1949 were banned, as were those from Hollywood and Hong Kong. In their place, films for and about workers, peasants, and soldiers (*gongnongbing dianying*) were shown, to support a socialist reconstruction of the country. With Soviet assistance, the industry soon achieved technological self-sufficiency. By 1959, ten feature film studios and an animation studio had been built in the major cities, and in the late 1950s small provincial studios also began producing newsreels and science education shorts.

National distribution of films was undertaken by the China Film Distribution and Exhibition Company which operated through provincial, city, and county offices. The Film Bureau also set up more exhibition units for the masses: from 646 theatres in 1949, exhibition units increased up to 20,363 in 1965, with 13,997 projection teams which serviced peasants in the countryside with 16 mm. projectors and slide projectors. Annual attendance grew from a total of 138,814,000 in 1949 to 4.6 billion in 1965. Beijing Film Academy, the country's only film school, was inaugurated in 1956 and offered formal training for prospective script-writers, directors, cinematographers, art designers, actors, and, later, for audio engineers and management personnel as well.

As early as July 1949, the First National Congress of film and literature professionals consecrated Mao Zedong's 'Talks at the Yan'an Forum' (1942) as the guiding principle for works in art and literature. The creation of new worker–peasant–soldier types in what Mao called revolutionary realism became an official mandate. The film-makers, however, were far from uniform in background and outlook; key members of the 1930s underground left-wing film movement, previously non-aligned employees of private Shanghai studios, and members of the theatre troupes from Yan'an and the army, they borrowed from various traditions. Hence, narrative and formal strategies used in traditional drama and literature, and in Soviet and Hollywood films of the 1930s and 1940s, often appeared together in orthodox versions of revolutionary history and class struggles. The film-makers' adherence to China's own theatrical and literary traditions was also revealed in their creation of 'opera film' and 'literary adaptations' (of modern Chinese literature) as new genres.

In October 1946, shortly after the Japanese retreat from Manchuria, Northeast Film Studio had begun production in Hegang, a coal-mining town north of Harbin. With equipment salvaged from the Japanese-owned Manchuria

Cinema Association and assisted by sympathetic Japanese technicians, it produced newsreels, translated Soviet films, and completed two animation films. On 1 May 1949 it released its first feature film, *Bridge*, written by Yu Min and directed by Wang Bin, who had worked in Shanghai before they joined Yan'an. Yu and Wang set the precedent for film professionals to 'immerse in real life' by living among the factory workers they depicted in the film.

From 1949 to 1950 the Northeast Studio produced about eighteen low-budget black and white films which were early models of revolutionary realism. They portrayed heroic figures and memorable episodes of the revolution, several of which, such as *Daughters of China* (*Zhonghua nuer*, 1949), *The White-Haired Girl* (*Baimaonu*, 1950), and *Zhao Yiman* (1950), told moving stories of women as fighters, victims, and martyrs. In these films, elements as diverse as documentary footage, folklore, traditional music, and hagiography enhanced the popular appeal of female figures of liberation and struggle.

After the Communist take-over, the private studios that remained in Shanghai, including Kunlun, Wenhua, Guotai, and Datong, were encouraged to make films for the transitional period. Between 1949 and 1951 they produced approximately forty-seven films, but they soon ran into political difficulties, as a result of which they gradually disbanded and were incorporated into an expanded Shanghai Film Studio in 1953.

The political criticisms of the output of the private studios focused on the film *The Life of Wu Xun* (*Wu Xun zhuan*, 1950), directed by Sun Yu. The film depicted a self-made educator who initially set up schools by literally begging on the streets. In a campaign which years later, in 1985, was officially denounced as 'partial, extreme and violent', it was accused of having misrepresented bourgeois reform as proletarian revolution and thus committed a grave political mistake. Following Mao Zedong's criticism of *The Life of Wu Xun*, the film circle underwent re-education and a Film Steering Committee was formed to censor scripts in a detailed manner. The harsh criticism launched against a single film not only ensured the Party's control over artists' interpretation of history and culture but also enabled the Yan'an faction to ride over veteran artists of Shanghai.

Standardization of administrative and censorship procedures took place in 1953. At the 2nd National Congress of All China Literature and Art Workers, Zhou Enlai declared that Socialist Realism in the Chinese context consisted of revolutionary realism and revolutionary romanticism. Though the formal and stylistic implications of these terms remained open for interpretation, their basic tenets remained the leadership of the proletariat in revolutionary struggles as guided by the CCP, and an idealistic rendering of the present and the future. Revolutionary realism, therefore, was grasped in its ideological rather than technical or formal sense. In formal terms, the films inclined towards classical realism as they took up traditional dramatic patterns and an organization of space and time according to the principle of verisimilitude. Nevertheless, motivation and behaviour as accounted for by the characters' class background and political attitude transformed the personal, psychological ground of 'bourgeois realism' into the collective, public, and struggle-oriented basis of 'revolutionary realism'.

During the 1950s new genres gained stability; the village film, the revolutionary history or war film, the thriller (or spy film), the national minority film, films with industrial subjects, and literary adaptation of works from the May Fourth movement of the 1920s. Through repetition, the visual and aural conventions of these genres established iconic significance. For example, lively folk-songs accompanied rural vistas and scenes depicting industrious and energetic peasants in the village film; brutal torture chamber scenes tested the Party member and a large red flag celebrated the triumphal ending in the revolutionary history film; exotic song-and-dance scenes underscored non-Han romances in the national minority film, and the presence of a male cadre as adviser and mediator represented the Party's position and policies in all genres. The European-style architecture and urbane life-styles which had symbolized China's modernity in films from the 1930s and 1940s were eliminated from the screens of the 1950s and replaced largely by Soviet-style buildings and the privileging of a rural and indigenous (i.e. non-westernized) orientation.

1956–1959: the 'Hundred Flowers' and Anti-Rightist periods

In May 1956 Mao Zedong launched the policy to 'Let a Hundred Flowers Bloom and a Hundred Schools of Thought Contend' 'Baihua qifang, baijia zhengming'. The film circle responded eagerly to the climate of openness by hinting at the negative impact of political pressures on film-making. Articles appeared, written by officials and film directors, which attributed the lack of interesting films to restrictions imposed on the creative process.

Connections with Europe were strengthened during this period as a five-member delegation attended the Cannes festival and visited Italy, England, and Yugoslavia to observe local productions. At home, Italian neo-realist films were shown in major cities, and studied by film-makers. Urban movie-goers were also able to see progressive films from Italy, Japan, India, and Mexico.

The search for connections between film and traditional opera, folk music, and literature also began. Discourse on the nationalization of film (dianying minzuhua) under-scored the cultural basis of revolutionary realism. Affirming the need to produce 'films with Chinese flavour' was a recognition of the tastes of Chinese artists and audiences and indicated a growing independence from Soviet models. Ways of merging the traditional arts and a Marxist-Leninist world-view were explored, exemplified by two early colour films: Liang Shanbo and Zhuyingtai (1954), an opera film based on a traditional love story, and New Year's Sacrifice (Zhufu, 1956), adapted by Xia Yan from Lu Xun's novella of the same name.

In the spirit of innovation, a number of films were made with anti-bureaucratic content. The satirical comedies of Lu Ban were sharpest in their criticisms: Before the New Director Arrives (Xinjuzhang daolai zhiqian, 1956) exposed the hierarchical relationship existing among cadres, and the three episodes in The Unfinished Comedy (Weiwancheng de xiju, 1957) hinted at the longevity of bureaucrats and dog-matists. Ethnic and gender bias became the focus in Cheng Yin's Young Women from Shanghai (Shanghai guniang, 1956). These films were not afraid to adopt an urban-based outlook and even to identify the wrongdoings of Party members.

In early 1957, director-centred production units were introduced in the Beijing, Shanghai, and Changchun studios. While the censorship system remained intact, the importance of the director was recognized in these units, which had more autonomy in selecting scripts and personnel, in budgeting and ensuring box-office returns. The Shanghai Studio branched into three substudios: Jiang-nan, Tianma, and Haiyen, each containing two or three director-centred production units.

Then, in August 1957, the Anti-Rightist movement hit the film circle. A large number of writers and film directors were designated as 'rightists', and publicly attacked for spreading 'bourgeois thinking'. Lu's Unfinished Comedy was labelled a 'poisonous weed', and Lu was never allowed to direct again. The Anti-Rightist movement moved to a new stage in April 1958, when Kang Sheng (later to become one of the Gang of Four) identified a number of films as 'white flags' that were against the spirit of worker–peasant–soldier films. All in all twenty-four films made during 1957 and 1958 were to be declared 'white flags' and banned from circulation.

In the two years following the Anti-Rightist movement, two major developments stimulated film output without lifting the repressive climate: in 1958, the national Great Leap Forward movement called for more films; in 1959, the occasion of the tenth anniversary of the PRC, better productions were demanded. In 1958, studios reduced budgets and shortened schedules. In response to Premier Zhou Enlai's call for more 'record-oriented films with an artistic character' (yishuxing jilupian), docu-dramas were made which combined documentary footage with re-enacted scenes to illustrate the workers' accelerated production during the year. Xie Jin's Huang Bao Mei (1958), which began with the model textile mill worker learning opera singing and ended with a dance around the textile mill in fairy costume, was hailed as the exemplary collaboration between workers, cadres, and artists. Most of the films produced in this year, however, were made to fulfil studio quotas and to break efficiency records. As a result, they appeared crude and dated; by 1962, many of them had been officially withdrawn from circulation.

The tenth anniversary of the PRC encouraged better-quality productions that celebrated the Party's achievements. While focusing on China's modern history, these films all shared an appealing human focus: Cui Wei and Chen Huaikai's *Song of Youth* (*Qingchun zhige*) traced the trials and triumphs of a young woman who was suffocated by the genteel May Fourth culture and ultimately found real liberation through participating in the Communist movement. Zheng Junli's *Lin Zexu* portrayed Commissioner Lin Zexu's anti-imperialist efforts during the Opium War. The film was meticulous in the recreation of period details, and its broad historical background was complemented by scenes that captured Lin's private moments. Wang Yan's *Our Days in the Battlefield* (*Zhanhuozhong de qingchun*) told the story of a young woman disguised as a male soldier who had to withdraw from the army after her sexual identity was revealed. These films stood out as capable works that successfully merged politics and art. Although box-office records were routinely boosted by bulk-buying from work units using state money, the 1959 record high of 4.17 billion annual movie attendance indicated that, after a decade's efforts, revolutionary cinema had earned a national audience base.

1960–1966: Classical revolutionary cinema

The early 1960s were a time of difficult social conditions, with widespread famine, Soviet withdrawal of financial and technological assistance, and the lingering effects of the Anti-Rightist movement. However, some of the best films of the classical revolutionary period were made in these years, with directors expanding the aesthetic possibilities of revolutionary realism/romanticism. Zheng Junli, director of *Lin Zexu*, made *A Withered Tree Meets Spring* (*Kumu fengchun*, 1962) to affirm the success of the combination of western and Chinese herbal medicine in healing peasants of schizotomaisis. The film, which extolled Chairman Mao's contribution to national healing, also beautifully incorporated codes of Chinese drama, scroll painting, and poetry in a heart-rending story of separation and reunion, death and survival. Xie Jin, who emerged as a new talent in the late 1950s, demonstrated exemplary skills in adapting traditional and Hollywood-type narrative and characterization strategies to revolutionary contexts. His military film *Red Detachment of Women* (*Hongse niangzijun*, 1960) incorporated thriller-type elements and exploited the 'exotic' details of southern China; while *Stage Sisters* (*Wutai jiemei*, 1964) was a finely crafted, melodramatic character study of two female opera singers.

Successful films of various genres appeared in the early 1960s. Two animated ink and wash films (*shuimo donghuapian*), *Where is Mama?* (*Xiaokedou zhao mama*, 1960) and *The Flute of the Cowherd* (1963), captured the art and poetry of Chinese brush painting. Xie Tieli's *Early Spring in February* (*Zaochun eryue*, 1963), adapted from a novella written by the May Fourth writer Rou Shi, dealt with emotional entanglements with an open story ending unusual for Chinese films of the time. Shui Hua's *A Revolutionary Family* (*Geming jiating*, 1960) and Ling Zifeng's *Red Flag Chronicle* (*Hong qipu*, 1960) traced the harsh trials faced by those committed to the revolution. National minority films, such as Su Li's *Third Sister Liu* (*Liu sanjie*, 1960), Wang Jia-yue's *Five Golden Flowers* (*Wuduo jinhua*, 1959) and Liu Qiong's *Ashma* (*A Shi Ma*, 1964), were popular for their folk tunes and vivid stories of romance which were acceptable in the non-Han contexts. Wang Ping and Dong Kena, the only women feature film directors of the period, completed *Lotus Tree Manor* (*Huaishu Zhuang*, 1962) and *A Blade of Glass on the Kunlun Mountains* (*Kunlunshanshang yikecao*, 1962) respectively. These films featured women protagonists whose strength and determination enabled them to overcome their own losses and complete demanding revolutionary tasks.

The Cultural Revolution

Attacks on drama and films served as the prelude to the Cultural Revolution. In June 1964 Mao Zedong indicated that many officials were verging on reformism, and a number of films, notably Shen Fu's *Jiangnan in the North* (*Beiguo Jiangnan*, 1963) and Xie Tieli's *Early Spring in February*, were shown in fifty-seven cities to generate a public critique of their 'bourgeois' ideology. By December 1964, another ten films were labelled 'poisonous weeds', including *A Revolutionary Family*, *Ashma*, and *Stage Sisters*. In the two years that followed, under the influence of Kang Sheng who had attacked the 'white flags' in 1957, a large batch of films made in the 1950s and early 1960s that were orthodox versions of the class struggle were labelled 'poisonous weeds', and many were either withdrawn from circulation or shown merely to generate public condemnation.

The political upheaval of the Cultural Revolution caused massive disruption to public and private life in China. The film industry suffered a major blow: several directors, writers, actors, and actresses were imprisoned and some died during the period, and most film professionals were dispatched to cadre schools and countryside work-camps. Almost all the films produced since 1949

Stylized representation and performance in the 1970 film version of Jiang Qing's (Madame Mao's) 'revolutionary model opera' *Taking Tiger Mountain by Strategy* (*Zhiqu Weihushan*), directed by Xie Tieli

were labelled 'anti-Party, anti-socialist poisonous weeds' and withdrawn from circulation. Many published materials and documents on film were permanently destroyed.

From 1967 to 1972, feature film production virtually stopped; later, it was partly resumed when a few specially selected directors were assigned by the 'Gang of Four' to film stage operas. The subsequent productions, *Geming yangbanxi* or 'revolutionary model operas', were subjected to close supervision by Jiang Qing (Madame Mao). They took an uncompromising stance in their condemnation of class enemies and celebration of poor peasant–worker–soldier types. Each energetic and stylized stage performance meticulously combined Beijing opera modes and western ballet dance steps, accompanied by choruses and symphonic music involving western and Chinese instruments. In the filmed versions, the placement of characters, the length, type, and angle of each shot, as well as the editing, carefully realized Jiang's principle of 'three prominences' (the prominence of positive figures, the prominence of heroic figures, and the prominence of a major heroic figure). Close-ups, frontal and low-angle shots, as well as a reddish lighting scheme (in colour films), were reserved for the major hero(ine), while long shots, more or less oblique and high-angle perspectives, and a greenish lighting scheme identified class enemies. The most famous operas were: *Taking Tiger Mountain by Strategy* (*Zhiqu Weihushan*, 1970) directed by Xie Tieli; *The Red Lantern* (*Hong Dengji*, 1970) by Cheng Yin; *The White-Haired Girl* (*Baimaonu*, 1970) by Sang Hu; and *The Red Detachment of Women* (*Hongse niangzijun*, 1971) by Pan Wanzhan and Fu Jie. The latter two were based on feature films of the same names made in 1950 and 1960, but in these new versions, the growth processes of the protagonists were eliminated to indicate that they were perfect class heroines from the very beginning. These productions formed a genre of their own; a unique stage hybrid, characterized by dense colours, long takes, and a binary approach in the visual presentation of class heroes and their enemies.

After 1973 feature film production slowly resumed, as film professionals returned from work-camps. Between 1973 and 1976 about eighty films were made, with the Changchun, Beijing, and Shanghai studios bearing most of the production load. Several classical opera films were adapted from folklore for their safe and presumably apolitical character, but many of them remained unreleased. Inevitably, stylistic inflections of 'revolutionary model operas' appeared in most films, and those which did not strictly follow Jiang Qing's 'three prominences' principle were immediately condemned. In 1975 and 1976 the Gang of Four commissioned several films including Xie Jin's *Chun Miao* and Li Wenhua's *Breaking with Old Ideas* (*Juelie*) which allegorized the Gang's political opponents within the Party as 'bourgeois' characters.

AFTER THE CULTURAL REVOLUTION

1977–1984: 'wound' or 'scar' films

In 1977 the Gang of Four's accusations were officially refuted and the rehabilitation of film-makers was accompanied by the exhibition of the once-condemned films made between 1949 and 1965. About fifty feature films, mostly anti-Gang of Four in content, appeared in 1977 and 1978, to the audiences' delight. Zhang Yi's *Upheaval in October* (*Shiyue fengyun*, 1977), which dramatized cadres and workers struggling together against the Gang's allies in an arms factory, was in circulation for fifteen months with attendances reaching 67 million. These anti-Gang films were, however, as schematic and clichéd in their approach as the pro-Gang ones, and soon they lost their audience.

Most of the films that were adapted from 'wound' or 'scar' literature were produced before 1983. They focused mainly on the disruption of relationships and careers by unjustified persecution before and during the Cultural Revolution. They used flashbacks and voice-over as narrative devices, and, overall, melodramatic and poetic approaches replaced didactic ones. These films were quite outspoken about political injustice, and 're-humanization' was their goal. For example, Yang Yanjin and Deng Yimin's *Troubled Laughter* (*Kunaoren de xiao*, 1979) centred on a journalist's frustration with bureaucratic pressure, Wu Yigong's *Evening Rain* (*Bashan yeyu*, 1980) contrasted the unsympathetic Red Guard with the human warmth of the common people, and Xie Jin's melodramatic *Legend of the Tianyun Mountain* (*Tianyunshan chuanqi*, 1980) presented a relentless picture of an intellectual's sufferings during the Anti-Rightist movement, recalled by a young woman who was pressured to jilt him for political reasons. The Party sanctioned these stark revelations of political persecutions; *Evening Rain* and *Legend of the Tianyun Mountain* won the first official Golden Rooster award in 1981, decided upon by a panel of officials and critics. The films of this period also saw a conscious redefinition of character types, in that they no longer eulogized peasants at the expense of intellectuals. For example, Wang Qimin and Sun Yu's *At Middle Age* (*Rendao zhongnian*, 1982) bemoaned the physical and mental exhaustion of a dedicated woman doctor, and Wu Tianming's *River without Buoys* (*Meiyou hangbiao de heliu*, 1983) dramatized workers' indifference to the 'model operas'. Overall, however, the genre of 'wound' or 'scar' films had run its course by 1984, as the imagination of writers and directors was captured by China's modernization.

1984: the process of modernization

Wu Tianming's 1984 film *Life* (*Ren Sheng*) was the first in a series of films that depicted an individual's struggle against his/her destiny in a conformist environment. In

Life, a young peasant who has obtained a high-school education bitterly rejects his family background. A claustrophobic setting visually reinforces his frustrations, and reverses the idyllic views of the countryside of the village genre film. The question of whether he is a sympathetic rebel or a ruthless opportunist remains open, as a triangular love relationship shows him ready to abandon his attachments in the countryside and leave the village through a romantic connection. In a similar spirit of youthful rebelliousness, the inquisitive high-school student in Lu Xiaoya's *Girl in Red* (*Hongyi shaonu*) refuses to accept her teacher's unreasonable chastisement. The delightful interplay of colours in this film invoked a new generation's innocence and vitality. In the early years of economic reform, engaging in private enterprise became a legitimate means of changing one's destiny, and this became the subject of many films of the period. Young entrepreneurs often felt isolated, as the sewing woman experienced in Chen Beichen's *Under the Bridge* (*Daqiao xiamian*); small businesses could rise and fall quickly, as the unemployed youths in southern China find out in Zhang Liang's *Yamaha Fish-Stall* (*Yamaha yudang*). Zhang's subsequent film, *Juvenile Delinquents* (*Shaonian fan*, 1985), caused a sensation by recruiting teenagers serving in juvenile disciplinary centres as actors to depict an aspect of Chinese society that had never appeared on film before. In many of the popular films of 1984, the thematic affirmation of individual desires was reinforced by a formal independence from generic conventions, and the pursuit of a more 'natural' style.

Two developments helped pave the way for the appearance of ground-breaking works in the 1980s. In December 1978 the historic 11th Plenary Session of the 3rd Central Committee of the CCP upheld an open-door policy as an integral part of economic reform, and inaugurated the second 'Hundred Flowers' period for art and literature. In 1979 a seminal article, 'On the Modernization of Film Language' ('Dianying yuyan de xiandaihua'), was published, written by woman director Zhang Nuanxin and writer Li Tuo. For the first time in three decades, narration, *mise-en-scène*, cinematography, sound, and rhythm were emphasized independently of their role in political edification. The essay sparked eager discussion on the nature of film (particularly the possibility of divorcing film from theatre), questions of aesthetics, authorship, and audience. In the early 1980s, production eagerly sought inspiration from translations of western film theory as directors steered away from revolutionary realism.

A new relationship between the Party/State, the film industry, and the audience also began to take shape in the early 1980s, caused by the policy of incorporating the market economy into the planned economy. The state withdrew financial backing for all but a few productions, and each studio was required to balance its own annual budget. Audiences' tastes gained a new status. Until 1993, however, box-office receipts were still only indirectly connected to studio profit, since distribution of films was monopolized by the China Film Distribution and Exhibition Company (CFDEC), whose local representatives would order a certain number of exhibition prints based on an estimation of a film's popularity and sometimes on decisions from another district. This practice had provided a financial buffer for studios in the years when prints were bought mostly on the basis of edifying needs. However, as both CFDEC's branch offices and local theatres had to balance their own budgets while annual movie attendance fell steadily from 1984, many films did not recoup their production costs as the selling of prints was no longer guaranteed. The conversion to an audience-based film market stimulated the massive production of entertainment movies, which hastened the demise of politically didactic films. However, the increasingly competitive entertainment market also proved to be detrimental to the formal experiments begun in the early 1980s.

The Fifth Generation

Until *One and Eight* (*Yige he bage*) appeared in 1984, attempts to modernize film language did not go beyond that of humanist realism. Director Zhang Junzhao and cinematographer Zhang Yimou, both 1982 graduates of the Beijing Film Academy, shocked everyone with the unprecedented handling of filmic space (specifically, close-ups and off-screen space to create tension between characters), a sparse and highly elliptical dialogue, as well as the creation of a masculinity so far absent from China's screens. The film has an unusual story, involving a chain-gang of prisoners held by Communists during the anti-Japanese war. Many changes had to be made before the film passed the censors, and it remained unreleased for quite some time.

In the same year, Chen Kaige, also a 1982 graduate of the Academy, made *Yellow Earth* (*Huang tudi*), again with Zhang Yimou as the cinematographer. The film impressed local critics but was considered too obscure by officials. It was not until *Yellow Earth* was shown at the Hong Kong International Film Festival and received praise from enthusiastic critics and audiences that its exceptional quality was properly acknowledged. *Yellow Earth* remained a seminal film with its critical insight into China's contemporary political culture through a deceptively simple story with sparse dialogue, involving four symbolic characters. Epic shots of the loess (silt) plateau of the Yellow River were created with a cinematographic style which, like that of a traditional Chinese painting, was austere yet rich in meaning; while local tunes underscored the film's ethnographic aspects.

Chen's next film, *The Big Parade* (*Dayuebing*, 1985), used military training as a metaphor for the society's repression of difference, and his obscure *King of Children* (*Haizi wang*, 1987) was a profound critique of the oppressive nature of China's symbolic order. Tian Zhuangzhuang, a classmate of Zhang and Chen, made *On the Hunting Ground* (*Liechang zhasa*, 1985) and *Horse Thief* (*Daoma zei*, 1986), situating his stories among the dignified Mongolians, and obliquely expressing a disdain for the dominant Han nationality and their ethnocentrism. His films caused noted documentarist Joris Ivens to declare that 'Chinese film has great hope'; but since they were thought to be too obscure for the Chinese audience, very few exhibition prints were bought by the distribution agents.

Though similar neither in theme or style, the experimental works by these young directors were identified by critics as 'exploratory films' and their makers as 'Fifth Generation directors'. The term 'exploratory' (*tansuo*) refers to an unprecedented use of modern film language, as well as an uncompromisingly critical outlook that later

was regarded as too élitist, especially since many of these films failed in their home box-offices while winning awards at international festivals. The Fifth Generation label acknowledged the previous generations' contribution to the development of Chinese film.

The young Academy graduates shared the experience of marginalization, exile from urban centres, and hardship during their adolescent years because of the Cultural Revolution, and they had no reservations in publicly expressing their disillusionment with their country. More importantly, the Fifth Generation movement enforced a rupture between itself and the types of realism so far established. In relentlessly dismantling the language and ideology of an established political culture, the Fifth Generation films renounced the dramatic patterns of both revolutionary and humanist realism; instead, their narrative and formal strategies were critique-oriented. In short, the Fifth Generation films refused to be appeased

Chen Kaige's *Yellow Earth* (*Huang tudi*, 1984), the seminal film of the Fifth Generation

with the official announcement of the coming of a 'new' era.

As mavericks, the Fifth Generation directors were far from being homogeneous in their output: Wu Ziniu's *The Last Day of Winter* (*Zuihou yige dongri*, 1986) centred on a prison labour-camp in the north-western desert; Hu Mei's *Army Nurse* (*Nuer lou*, 1985) focused on a young woman's feelings in a story of repressed love; Huang Jianxin's *Black Cannon Incident* (*Heipao shijian*, 1985) was a black comedy which exposed the debilitating aspects of China's political culture, and his *Dislocation* (*Cuo wei*, 1987) was a science-fiction fantasy; Zhou Xiaowen's *In their Prime* (*Tamen zheng nianqing*, 1986) staged scenes of the Sino-Vietnamese war to expose its bleak and tragic aspects; and Zhang Zeming's *Swan Song* (*Jue xiang*, 1985) traced the disappointments and betrayals in the life of a Cantonese musician. Though not considered a Fifth Generation director, Huang Jianzhong contributed towards the movement with his surrealistic experiment *Questions for the Living* (*Yige shizhe dui shengzhe de fangwen*, 1986).

While tragedy and satire had been largely absent from the didactic films of the classical revolutionary period, tragedy, absurdity, and ambiguity made their return in the Fifth Generation films, which consciously steered away from the established generic conventions. Though embraced by young critics in Shanghai and Beijing who admired their 'exploratory' path, from 1987 the Fifth Generation film-makers were subjected to increasing commercial pressure and criticism.

The mid-1980s saw the emergence of Zhang Yimou, from cinematographer to award-winning actor and director. Though a Fifth Generation member, Zhang cultivated a more sensuous and popular style than many of his classmates, and his stories of desire were captivating for their legendary and mythic dimensions. His art films' accessibility both internationally and locally marked the beginning of the end of the more austere and difficult 'exploratory films'.

The Fourth Generation

The so-called 'Fourth Generation' directors were more humanist in outlook than their younger counterparts, and thus were more accepted, even though they were as ambitious as the Fifth Generation in redefining China's filmic conventions. Given the label soon after the term 'Fifth Generation' appeared, the 'Fourth Generation' refers to those directors who completed their professional training before 1966, and whose careers were suspended by the Cultural Revolution. While diverse in subject and style, several of their films of the mid-1980s shared a thematic concern with the conflicts and frustrations arising from an individual's attempts to break with the established system. Huang Jianzhong's *A Good Woman* (*Liangjia funu*, 1985) incorporated Freudian imagery in its depiction

of the desires of a young woman who is married to a child husband, and has an affair with a farm labourer. Xie Fei and Wu Lan's *Girl from Hunan* (*Xiangnu xiaoxiao*, 1986) had a similar story but focused on the repression and internalization of feudal ideologies, which enabled such unreasonable arrangements to perpetuate. Yan Xueshu's *In the Wild Mountains* (*Ye shan*, 1985), winner of the year's Golden Rooster award, traced the changes between two peasant couples as one of them responds to the opportunities brought about by economic reform. Concerns with peasants encountering a different economic climate was also broached by Hu Binliu's *Country Folk* (*Xiang min*, 1986), whose village trilogies (which included *Call of the Home Village* and *Country Couple*) thematized the clash of traditional rural values with modern ones. Wu Tianming's *Old Well* (*Lao jing*, 1987) dramatized a village's desperate search for water and the sacrifices made by a young peasant who returned from the city to help the village and his own family. In many of these films, sexual love has a redemptive value, as it is expressive of individuality and desire to change.

The rise of Xi'an Film Studio to national prominence from the mid-1980s helped to develop the 'exploratory film' movement. Under the leadership of director Wu Tianming, Xi'an balanced its annual budgets with commercial hits like *Magic Braid* (*Shen bian*, 1986), and sponsored experimental works by the Fifth Generation directors. Wu undertook political and financial risks by producing *The Black Cannon Incident*, *Horse Thief*, *In their Prime*, and *King of Children*. Xi'an's goal, to 'make profit with one hand and take awards with another', was wonderfully realized when Zhang Yimou's *Red Sorghum* (*Hong gaoliang*, 1987) won the Golden Bear in the 1988 Berlin Film Festival and drew a large local audience as the result of its international reputation. Arguably, Wu's prolonged stay in the United States after 1989 also contributed to the demise of the 'exploratory film' movement.

COMMERCIALIZATION: INTO THE 1990S

Modern city films

In the late 1980s, economic reform hastened the disintegration of old ways and stimulated popular anticipation of living in an advanced society. In this atmosphere, the so-called city films, with urban settings and themes, flourished at the Chinese box-office. The Pearl River Studio in Guangdong produced films that explored the social and emotional implications of modernization for young people: Sun Zhou's *With Sugar* (*Gei kafei jiadiantang*, 1987) and Zhang Zeming's *Sunshine and Showers* (*Taiyang yu*, 1987) expressed ambivalence towards a culture of commodities which redefined the meaning of existence and human relationships. The escalation of insatiable desire was given full play in Zhou Xiaowen's action-oriented films

Zhang Yimou

(1952–)

Of the many talents to emerge among the 'Fifth Generation' of Chinese film-makers, Zhang Yimou is certainly the most versatile and arguably the most significant. With international awards for acting, cinematography, and direction, he is best known for five films he has made with Gong Li in the female lead: *Red Sorghum* (1988), *Judou* (1990), *Raise the Red Lantern* (1991), *The Story of Qiu Ju* (1992), and *Shanghai Triad* (1995).

Unlike contemporaries such as Chen Kaige who came from privileged backgrounds in the Communist Party intelligentsia, Zhang was an outsider. He was born in 1952 near Xi'an in the Shaanxi district featured in films such as *Yellow Earth* (1984) and *Red Sorghum*. His father's pre-revolutionary involvement with the Nationalist KMT that now runs Taiwan meant he could not find regular work and that his son was largely educated at home.

During the Cultural Revolution Zhang was sent to the countryside and later transferred to a cotton mill, where he took up still photography as a hobby. The legend of a career that almost never happened is well known; when the Beijing Film Academy reopened in 1978, Zhang's application was blocked because he was over the age limit, and he was only admitted after many special pleas. Even then, he was denied entry to his chosen department, direction, and was required to study cinematography.

However, Zhang's lack of political connections ultimately proved an advantage. Upon graduation in 1982, he was assigned to the fledgeling Guangxi Film Studio in Nanning, a remote south-western city whose location Zhang had to determine with the help of a map. However, such was the shortage of talent there that the new graduates were set to work straight away.

Determined to mark their films out from the existing Socialist Realist cinema, the young film-makers chose to question what was supposedly the most glorious period of Communist revolutionary history in *One and Eight* (1984) and *Yellow Earth*; the 1930s and 1940s. As cinematographer, Zhang complemented these challenging themes with an equally challenging look. The old Chinese cinema featured well-lit and centred, glossy compositions. Zhang designed dark, asymmetrical compositions in which humans were often small dots in enormous landscapes with a high horizon line. The result took the Chinese film world by surprise and was an enormous international success.

Zhang refined his cinematographic style in *Big Parade* (1985) and *Old Well* (1987), in which he also took the lead, and won the award for Best Actor at the Tokyo International Film Festival. In 1988, he made his directing début with *Red Sorghum*. This boisterous and lusty film, for which he discovered Gong Li, was an instant success with young people all over China; they identified with the unfettered sensuality of the lead characters, and whistled the folk-songs from the sound-track for months after the film's release. *Red Sorghum* also won Zhang the Golden Bear at the Berlin Film Festival, the first Chinese film to win such an honour.

Judou (1990)—another period piece, centred on a woman rebelling against feudal patriarchy, which won awards at Cannes and in Chicago—differed from *Red Sorghum* in two major respects. First, in the wake of the Tiananmen Square Massacre, the high spirits of *Red Sorghum* turned to apocalyptic rage and anger at old patriarchs in *Judou*. Second, facing political censorship and reduced funds, Zhang turned to co-production financing from overseas. This pattern was repeated with the powerful but bleak and despairing *Raise the Red Lantern*.

The release of *Judou* and *Raise the Red Lantern* was blocked in mainland China for some time. Zhang's most recent film has run into no such difficulties. *The Story of Qiu Ju* indicates a shift in Zhang's spirits, and a shift in his directing style that marks his versatility and command of the medium. A wry, ironic film with none of the grandeur and flamboyance of his previous works, *The Story of Qiu Ju* depicts a peasant woman's efforts to get justice out of China's complex legal bureaucracy. The camera is static, often in long shot, reminiscent of *cinéma vérité* documentary, as in the actors' improvised dialogue. For this new departure Zhang received the Golden Lion at Venice, and his partner Gong Li, who forsook her usual glamour to play Qiu Ju, won Best Actress.

CHRIS BERRY

SELECT FILMOGRAPHY

As cinematographer
One and Eight (1984); Yellow Earth (1984); Big Parade (1985); Old Well (1987).
As director
Red Sorghum (1988); Code Name Puma (1989); Judou (1990); Raise the Red Lantern (1991); The Story of Qiu Ju (1992); To Live (1994); Shanghai Triad (1995).

Zhang Yimou's leading lady Gong Li, here as Songlian in *Raise the Red Lantern* (1991).

Desperation (*Zuihou de fengkuang*, 1987) and *Obsession* (*Fengkuang de daijia*, 1988). These works stood out from among the many cheap imitations of Hong Kong action movies that Chinese studios were producing to fulfil the demand for films with an urban setting and modern theme.

By the late 1980s, it was quite obvious that socialism had become an empty signifier for most members of the Communist Party, especially since those that benefited first and foremost from economic reform were high officials and their families. The symptoms of a post-socialist era were vividly played out in Wang Shuo's novels, which captured the unique flavour of Beijing; its playful and piercing dialect and the political cynicism of its youth. Wang Shuo fever appeared in 1988 when four film adaptations of his novels were released; Huang Jianxin's *Samsara* (*Lunhui*), Xia Gang's *Half Flame, Half Brine* (*Yiban shi huoyan, yiban shi haishui*), Ye Daying's *Out of Breath* (*Da chuanqi*), and Mi Jiashan's *The Trouble-Shooters* (*Wanzhu*).

From 1989, disenchantment with the government was evident in bleak film versions of city life. Xie Fei's *Black Snow* (*Ben Mingnian*, 1989), winner of the Silver Bear at Berlin, charted the lonely days of a reformed ex-convict, finally ending in his murder. Zhang Nuanxin's *Good Morning, Beijing* (*Beijing nizao*, 1990) found solace in a young woman bus-conductor, trying to salvage a little dignity in her monotonous everyday routine.

Women directors

During the 1980s, approximately twenty women directors made their first features, and many remained active in the early 1990s. Commercial pressures aside, they had to establish themselves in a working environment still dominated by men, where male directors had for years appropriated the paradigm of female victimization for their own critical discourse, where feminism was rejected as 'foreign', and female leadership was associated with the unwelcomed authority of Jiang Qing. However, a 'woman's cinema' gradually emerged, which articulated female subjectivity and desire against social pressures to conform to conventional roles. Zhang Nuanxin, for example, refined her poetic and subtle approach in *Sha-O* (1983), *Sacrificed Youth*, and *Good Morning, Beijing*. Wang Shuqin, whose *Woman Demon Human* (*Ren gui qing*, 1988) was based on the life-story of a contemporary opera singer who played the role of a male ghost, continued to explore innovative ways to reveal the tension between a woman's familial experience and her artistic career. Her next film, *Huahun* (1993) which depicted Pan Yuliang, the legendary woman painter of the 1910s, was heavily censored for its scenes of nudity. Wang Junzheng's *First Woman in the Forest* (*Shanlinzhong touyige nuren*, 1987) and *Woman Taxi Woman* (*Nuren taxi nuren*, 1991) depicted vital and sexually active women who were resourceful partners and companions. Li Shaohong, a late starter for a 1982 Academy graduate, invoked the

1989 trauma as she analysed machismo in China's rural context in *Bloody Morning* (*Xuese qingchen*, 1990), which was adapted from a novella by Gabriel García Márquez. Her *Family Portrait* (*Sishi buhuo*, 1992) featured a middle-aged photographer, and had thought-provoking episodes which revived memories of the Cultural Revolution. Among the more elderly female directors, Wang Haowei was dedicated to well-made dramas in the traditional mode, including *Fascinating Musical Band* (*Miren de yuedui*, 1985) and *Oh! Sweet Snow* (*O! xiangxue*, 1989), which were especially welcomed by the government. By the early 1990s, however, many women directors could only find work in entertainment and action genre movies.

After Tiananmen: commercial cinema vs. the underground

In the two years after the Tiananmen Massacre of 1989, personnel changes in the government reflected the triumph of conservative factions. An 'anti-bourgeois liberalization' campaign was launched, though with little result. Meanwhile, studios kept churning out relentlessly commercial products, as they faced a host of worries: a shrinking annual movie attendance; increasing production costs; competition from western and Hong Kong movies on video; and the popularity of home musical entertainment and karaoke singing outlets.

In this climate the state financed several epic films, aiming to salvage the CCP's declining reputation. Ironically, these were packaged in a refined film language that benefited from the artistic and humanistic efforts of the 1980s. Examples included Wang Jun's *Childhood in Ruijin* (*Tongnian zai Ruijin*, 1989), Wang Jixing's *Jiao Yulu* (1989), and *The Decisive Engagement* (*Da juezhan*, 1991). The last film, said to have received an investment sum of RMB 20 million yuan from the government, was a trilogy made by six directors and featured three spectacular civil war battles fought between the CCP and the Kuomintang. These films, however, were exceptional, and studios continued to invest in cheap entertainment pictures that could be sold on violence and nudity.

The directors who undertook formal and stylistic experiments in the 1980s were pressured to make their films more accessible in the 1990s. Those that did not comply had their films censored or refused release. Among others, Tian Zhuangzhuang's *The Blue Kite* (*Lan fengzheng*, 1992), with a story set during the Cultural Revolution, remained shelved, as did Wu Ziniu's Sino-Vietnamese war film *Dove Tree* (*Gezi shu*, 1987).

In the early 1990s, a documentary movement quietly gained momentum among students of the Academy of Broadcasting. Shot in video format, these low-budget documentaries contained on-location interviews with college students who spoke openly on various topics. Wu Wenguang's *Bumming in Beijing, the Last Dreamer* (*Liulang Beijing, juihou de mengxiangzhe*, 1988), the first documentary of this kind, interviewed his classmates who were aspiring painters, photographers, writers, and drama directors. Whereas government-sponsored 35 mm. 'documentaries' were unanimously propagandistic, depending on prearranged scenes and enactments, Wu's video used few mediating devices but let the viewers directly encounter his subjects. In another video documentary, made by a 'Structure, Wave, Youth Cinema Experimental Group' and entitled *I Graduated! (Wo biye le!)*, about six or seven students talk to the camera about love, sex, career prospects, decisions to stay or leave the country, and the impact events in Tiananmen had had on their lives and outlooks. Made between 5 and 11 July 1992, the documentary began with hand-held shots and a voice-over which told the audience that the back-door entrance was the only one unchecked by the campus police of Beijing University. As well as the interviews conducted in the student dormitories, the film incorporated hidden camera shots of the campus police's intervention, departure scenes in the train station, and ended with a view of an empty Tiananmen Square at night accompanied by a sound-track that simulated the sound of gunshots and moving tanks. The video was personal and intense; the flexible documentary format set its makers free from indirect, allegorical ways of expression as often used in studio features.

No longer able to replicate the career paths of Fifth Generation directors in getting an early start through working in smaller studios, a number of 1989 graduates of the Beijing Film Academy began the difficult tasks of independent production. By producing commercials and music videos, the young film-makers saved enough to start production. With money borrowed from friends and technical help from fellow classmates and laboratories, these young film-makers made films with an average budget of under RMB 200,000 yuan (about US $2,000). Without a studio quota, their works remained 'underground' films that could not get distributed through official channels. Among the films completed this way in 1992 were Wang Xiaoshuai's *Days of Winter and Spring (Dong chun de rizi)*, Wu Di's *Golden Shower (Huangjin yu)*, and Zhang Yuan's *Mama*. Zhang Yuan sought international attention by entering his black and white feature *Mama* in about twenty film festivals. With awards from Nantes, Edinburgh, and Berlin, as well as an MTV award from the United States for a video on popular singer Cui Jian, Zhang financed part of his 1993 feature *Beijing Bastards (Beijing zazhong)* with a grant from the French Film Development Foundation.

As the self-described 'Sixth Generation' film-makers were scrambling around to finance their projects, the established Fourth and Fifth Generation directors continued to earn international acclaim and win overseas investment. In 1993 Chinese films swept the board at the European film festivals: Xie Fei's *Woman Sesame Oil Maker* (or *Xianghunnu*, also known as *Women in the Lake of Scented Souls*) won the Golden Bear award at Berlin; Zhang Yimou's *Story of Qiu Ju* took the Golden Lion award at Venice, and Chen Kaige's *Farewell my Concubine (Bawang bieji)*, financed by Taiwan money, was the first Chinese film to win the Palme d'Or at Cannes. However, these award-winning films seem tame when compared to the black and white independent works breaking through from the youthful underground video and film movement.

Bibliography
Bergeron, Régis (1984), *Le Cinéma chinois, 1943–1983*.
Berry, Chris (ed.) (1991), *Perspectives on Chinese Cinema*.
Browne, Nick, Pickowicz, Paul, Sobchack, Vivian, and Yau, Esther, (eds.) (1994), *New Chinese Cinema: Forms, Identities, Politics*.
Cheng Jihua, Li Xiaobai, and Xing Zuwen (1963), *Zhongguo dianying fazhanshi* ('History of the Development of Chinese Cinema').
Chen Kaige, Zhi Wan, and Rayns, Tony (1989), 'King of the Children' and the New Chinese Cinema').
Clark, Paul (1987), *Chinese Cinema: Culture and Politics since 1949*.
Leyda, Jay (1972), *Dianying: Electric Shadows*.
Rayns, Tony, and Meek, Scott (1980), *Electric Shadows: 45 Years of Chinese Cinema*.
Semsel, George S. (ed.) (1987), *Chinese Film: The State of the Art in the People's Republic*.

Popular Cinema in Hong Kong

LI CHEUK-TO

After 1949, mainland Chinese cinema came under the control of the Communists and became a state-financed propaganda arm that produced only 'socialist realist' films targeted at the 'worker–peasant–soldier' audience. Across the Strait in Taiwan, where no film industry had existed before 1945, cinema toiled under the Nationalist government's rigid control. Post-1949 Hong Kong cinema, however, became the most prolific and vigorous among the three Chinese communities. It initially adopted the classical tradition and many of the generic conventions of Shanghai cinema, and then gradually developed its own model in a relatively free business environment with few political taboos.

The history of Hong Kong cinema after the Second

World War can be divided into three distinct periods. From 1946 to 1970, the so-called classical period, the majority of both Mandarin (the official Chinese language) and Cantonese (the local dialect) film production was studio-based. An entertainment-oriented cinema developed, which opened its arms to genre influences from Hollywood and Japan. At the same time, local and overseas distribution networks were established, which have continued their operations to the present day. Then in 1971 Hong Kong cinema entered a transition period with the demise of Cantonese cinema. This period was marked by the dominance of kung-fu films, and the gradual formation of a local film culture, with Cantonese slowly reasserting itself as the language in local films. In 1979 Hong Kong cinema entered the modern period; a new generation took over, both behind and in front of the camera, and freed film production from the studio sound stages. As production qualities and marketing skills improved to international standards, Hong Kong cinema began to attract international attention and acclaim.

THE CLASSICAL PERIOD

Mandarin cinema

Although the films produced in Hong Kong in the 1930s were overwhelmingly in Cantonese, the most significant phenomenon in Hong Kong cinema after the Second World War was the large influx of film workers from Shanghai and the rise of a Mandarin film industry in Hong Kong. The majority of film-makers who migrated to Hong Kong after 1946 were already established names in the Shanghai film industry. Many had worked for the Japanese-controlled Huaying Studio during the Japanese occupation of Shanghai and were in danger of being blacklisted as traitors or collaborators after the war. Shunned by colleagues in the industry or prompted by fear of persecution, they went into voluntary exile in Hong Kong.

The founding of the Yung Hwa (Yonghua) Company by the Shanghai mogul Li Zuyong in 1947 further attracted talent from Shanghai, as China was torn by civil war. With an investment of US$3,750,000 and boasting the best modern film-making facilities, Li aspired to a studio that would equal or surpass the greatness of Lianhua and Mongxing in pre-war Shanghai. The plan was to produce Mandarin films in Hong Kong and distribute them on the Chinese mainland. The company's first 'million-dollar spectacle', *Soul of China* (*Guohun*, Bu Wancang, 1948), was a box-office success. Efforts were even made to sell expensive historical epics to western markets; and *Sorrows of the Forbidden City* (*Qinggong mishi*, Zhu Shilin, 1948) was shown at the Locarno Film Festival in 1950 to great critical acclaim. However, Li underestimated the speed with which the Communists would take over China, and when they did, the vital mainland market was lost forever. As the company became inactive with huge financial problems,

most of the talent it had recruited from Shanghai left the firm, but stayed on in Hong Kong, developing their own productions or joining other new companies. This group of film-makers maintained their cultural habits and insisted that only Mandarin be used in their films.

Most film-makers in exile were marked by a strong cultural chauvinism, expecting an early recovery of the mainland by the Nationalist government. This was reflected in their films. Even when dealing with realist subject-matters, the Hong Kong settings looked more like Shanghai, and the style and content of the films often evoked (or even directly remade) Shanghai films from before 1949.

For a Mandarin cinema to take root in a Cantonese-speaking community, it had to expand its market and enlarge its audience base. The nostalgia of many northern immigrants for their homeland provided a loyal audience in Hong Kong. There was also an expansion into the Taiwanese market. Taiwan had been ceded to Japan in 1895, and in the following fifty years imported Japanese films dominated the market. When the Second World War ended and the Nationalist (Kuomintang) government moved to Taiwan, the influx of mainland immigrants provided an audience base, and Hong Kong became the natural supplier of Chinese films.

Many small independent companies in Hong Kong could not survive without the Taiwanese market. However, the Kuomintang government was quick to exploit this situation for political aims. In 1953 it established an organization which became known as the 'Hong Kong–Kowloon Film and Drama Free Association' (Gangliu dianying xiju shiye ziyou zonghui). Only films made by members of the Association could be shown in Taiwan, and so almost all the independent companies in Hong Kong came under the influence of the Taiwanese government.

During the late 1940s, even the strongest independents had not been able to challenge the power of Yung Hwa, but in the early 1950s the strength of the independents grew. The most important were Xinhua under Zhang Shankun and Taishan under Bu Wancang. The only independents that maintained a distance from the Taiwanese Association were those which were 'left-wing', that is, financially supported by the Communist Chinese government. The largest of these was the Great Wall (Changcheng) Company, which, after its reorganization in 1950, joined together with two smaller 'left-wing' sister companies, Fenghuang and Longma, under the direction of Zhu Shilin, and trained a new generation of film-makers.

Melodrama, which bore the memory of suffering in the war years, became the mainstream genre. However, all the films, even the comedies, produced by these 'left-wing' and independent studios were didactic; preaching anti-feudalism, a quasi-feminist view on the sufferings of women, and even Marxist ideology of class struggle.

The early 1950s saw the rise of powerful socially conscious films. It was the immigrants' unbending nationalist sentiments that led them to support these productions. Untouched by the Hollywood tradition of escapist entertainment films, the classical realist tradition of 1930s Shanghai cinema was revived in Hong Kong, as economic recession hit in the wake of the Korean War and trade embargoes on China. The notable examples are *Flower Girl* (*Hua guniang*, 1951) and *Festival Moon* (*Zhongqiu yue*, 1953) by Zhu Shilin.

From the mid-1950s onwards, as the northern immigrants realized that their state of exile would be permanent, and a younger generation of Hong Kong filmmakers came of age (the most prominent being Tao Qin and Li Hanxiang), Mandarin cinema became more integrated into Hong Kong society, and more concerned with entertainment than didacticism. A larger variety of genres appeared. The Hollywood-influenced youth musical *Mambo Girl* (*Manbo nulang*, Yi Wen, 1957), which charts the heroine's search for her long-lost mother and her final return to her foster parents, can be read as the Shanghai director's love letter to Hong Kong.

Cantonese cinema

Despite the gradual integration of Mandarin cinema into Hong Kong culture, the basic fact remained that the majority of the immigrant population arriving in Hong Kong after 1949 came from the south, and about 80 per cent of the population spoke Cantonese. These immigrants needed inexpensive entertainment, and, as Cantonese films presented them with a familiar world and recognizable life-styles, they naturally became loyal supporters. Between 1946 and 1969, the total output of Cantonese films approximated 3,500 titles, more than three times the number of Mandarin productions.

This prodigious output, however, led to a sharp decline in the quality of the films produced; a large proportion were shoddy material dubbed 'seven-day wonders'. In 1952, in response to this crisis, nineteen concerned directors, producers, actors, and actresses founded Union Films Enterprises Ltd. (Zhonglian). The founding members pooled together a meagre initial capital of HK$62,000, and agreed to work for half or a third of their normal fees. Among the forty-four films it made from 1953 to 1964, twenty were adaptations from popular literary sources and other art forms, both contemporary and classical. *Family* (*Jia*, Wu Hui, 1953), *Spring* (*Chun*, Li Chenfeng, 1953), and *Autumn* (*Qia*, Qin Jian, 1954) were adapted from the renowned trilogy of contemporary Chinese novelist Ba Jin, and *Broken Spring Dreams* (*Chun can meng duan*, Li Chenfeng, 1955) was based on Tolstoy's *Anna Karenina*. Original screenplays were generally motivated by a concern with social problems of the time, and included the classics *In the Face of*

Demolition (*Weilou chunxiao*, Li Tie, 1953) and *Parents' Hearts* (*Fumu xin*, Qin Jian, 1955).

Zhonglian's many excellent productions engendered respect for Cantonese films as serious cinema both within Hong Kong and overseas. This revitalization in turn spurred a rapid increase in the output of Cantonese films from the mid-1950s onwards, as well as the formation of two important companies: Guanui in 1955, and Huaqiao in 1956. Together with Zhonglian and Xinlian they became known as the 'Big Four', comrades in their pursuit of high-quality film-making with serious themes.

Catering to a working-class audience with little education, the majority of Cantonese films chose character stereotypes and colloquial language (exploiting the dialect's complex tones and abundant whimsical slang) as their backbone instead of refined visual design. Plots were generally culled from opera stories, folklore, and popular anecdote. The most popular genres throughout the 1950s were Cantonese opera (e.g. Li Tie's *The Purple Hairpin* (*Zichai ji*, 1959), already a cult classic), martial arts films (such as the Huang Fei-hong series starring Kwan Tak-hing in seventy-five films from 1949 to 1970), comedies, and melodrama.

The 1960s: new audiences, new films

The flourishing Cantonese film industry reached its peak in 1960 when over 200 films were produced. Demographic changes largely accounted for this; the baby-boom generation, now approaching late adolescence, significantly boosted the size of the film-going public. Hong Kong itself was in the process of transforming itself from a commercial entrepôt to an industrial centre, and this transition provided cinema with many new themes and subject-matters.

The success of Qin Jian's *The Intimate Partners* (*Nan xiong nan di*, 1960) and *How to Get a Wife* (*Zhui qi ji*, 1961) spearheaded a rise of urban comedies about white- and blue-collar workers. To cater for the growing number of women working in factories, there were romantic fantasies, melodramas, and comedies aimed at them, such as *Factory Queen* (*Gongchang huanghou*, Mo Kangshi, 1963) and *The Chauffeur Was a Lady* (*Nu siji*, Wu Hui, 1965). The appearance of detective thrillers, musicals, and soft porn exemplified the influence of foreign films on this once parochial dialect cinema.

The new teenage audience led to the popularity of teen idols Chen Baozhu and Xiao Fangfang. Xiao, fashionably dressed and proficient in popular song and dance, gained the loyalty of the student audience, while Chen, as the girl-next-door, became the idol of lower middle-class girls entertaining rags-to-riches aspirations. Youth and higher living standards aside, the audiences were also more educated and westernized. This break from the past was reflected in cinema. Gone were family and social melo-

The popularity of Hong Kong martial arts films spread far beyond the colony: Bruce Lee in *Enter the Dragon* (1973), the first Hollywood kung-fu film

dramas, to be replaced by glossy imitations of Hollywood.

The Guangyi Film Company, managed by director Qin Jian, was perhaps most adaptive to these changes. From a staple of literary adaptations in the 1950s, the company quickly switched to urban comedies. Despite some successes, the modernization and westernization of Cantonese films ultimately failed. No matter how modern and stylish their décor and characters tried to be, the outlook of these films remained provincial. Western ideas had not been properly digested and integrated into local culture.

The output of Cantonese cinema took a rapid downward turn in the late 1960s, and the decade ended with only twenty-two films being made in 1970. Soon afterwards production ground to a virtual standstill. Decline was inevitable as market conditions worsened. Audience tastes in vital South-East Asian markets became more and more varied; production far exceeded demand; production costs soared with colour films; and free television emerged in 1967.

THE TRANSITIONAL PERIOD

While Cantonese film-makers struggled to keep pace with the times, Mandarin cinema began to turn its weakness into advantage. Mostly made by *émigré* directors from Shanghai, Mandarin films had once been too urbane for the Cantonese population, but in the 1970s it was precisely these qualities which became appealing. When Mandarin action-packed martial arts films began flooding the screen, Cantonese cinema—with its overworked themes

and outdated techniques—appeared even more anachronistic.

The new dominance of Mandarin cinema would not have been possible without two big corporations: the Motion Picture & General Investment (Dianmou) Company, and Shaw Brothers (Shaoshi). MP & GI had been founded in 1956, from the Singapore-based Cathay Organization (Guotai) which itself had bought the bankrupt Yung Hwa studio. The Shaw family had started film production in Shanghai as early as the 1920s, but had moved to Hong Kong during the Sino-Japanese War. They were the first company to move into distribution in Singapore and Malaysia, and reorganized in 1957 to challenge MP & GI, then the market leader. By 1961, Shaw Movietown, a huge studio complex, had been constructed in Clearwater Bay, and during its peak years Shaws boasted a staff of over 1,000, including 20 directors and 140 actors and actresses, and an annual film production of 40 to 50 features.

For several years, Shaw and MP & GI were locked in a game of ruthless rivalry, forcing each other to abandon projects by filming the same stories. But after the defection of many of MP & GI's directors and stars to Shaw Brothers in the early 1960s, the latter took control of the market while the former suffered a decline.

Both companies made films in many genres. MP & GI was famous for its comedies, especially those scripted by the famous writers Eileen Chang and Wang Liuzhao, as well as its romantic dramas. It also pioneered Chinese musical extravaganzas and its first colour film *Calendar*

Girl (*Long xiang feng wu*, Tao Qin, 1959) is a classic of its genre. Shaw Brothers' most notable films were romances and musicals, like *Love without End* (*Bu liao qing*, Tao Qin, 1960) and *Hong Kong Nocturne* (*Xiangjiang hua yue ye*, Inoue Umetsugu, 1967), but historical costume dramas remained its most lavish productions, while the *huangmei* operas set a trend for the next three years as *Love Eterne* (*Liangshanbo yu zhuyingtai*, Li Hanxiang, 1963) stormed Taiwan, taking over HK$1,200,000 at the box-office.

The kung-fu film in Taiwan and Hong Kong

Although *huangmei* opera films were popular and even Cantonese audiences were captivated by their glamorous spectacles, it was the new-style martial arts film that dealt the Cantonese cinema the fatal blow. In 1967, Chang Cheh's *One-Armed Swordsman* (*Dubei dao*) set a new box-office record, and, in the same year, King Hu grossed HK$2 million with his Taiwan production *Dragon Gate Inn* (*Longmen kezhan*). Fast-paced and sensational, the films excelled in an exuberant style of combat borrowed from Japanese *samurai* films and married to the Chinese martial arts tradition. It proved to be admirably suited to the needs of a rapidly developing Hong Kong.

The new-style martial arts film also had an important impact on Taiwanese cinema. In fact, the 1960s were Taiwan cinema's golden era as a large number of martial arts films and romantic dramas adapted from the popular writer Quiongyao were successfully exported to the Hong Kong market, changing the direction of film trade from one-way to two-way.

This process started in 1963 after the huge success of *Love Eterne*, when its director, Li Hanxiang, left Shaw Brothers to form his own company, Guolian, taking with him a contingent of Shaw technicians. To avoid a legal dispute about his contract with Shaws, Li left Hong Kong for Taipei with financial backing from the Cathay Organization (which MP & GI had become in 1965) and two film companies in Taiwan. Guolian succeeded in stimulating the increase in production of Mandarin films in Taiwan, from 10 in 1964 to 46 in 1967. In 1968 output leapt to 116, and by 1970 had reached 163, more than twice that of Hong Kong. This can only be explained by the popularity of the martial arts genre and the opportunistic nature of an industry unregulated by big studios.

However, this revitalization of Taiwan's film industry proved short-lived, and by the mid-1970s Hong Kong had replaced it as the producer of popular martial arts movies. Guolian had folded at the end of the 1960s, and Li Hanxiang was heavily in debt. This finally drove him back to Hong Kong to re-enter Shaw Brothers in 1972. The surprise return of the prodigal proved to be valuable in helping Shaws face the challenge posed by its most formidable defector, Raymond Chow. Chow had been the production manager at Shaws before he left with a group of Shaws

executives, film-makers, and actors, and started his own company, Golden Harvest, in April 1970. The new company soon had the backing of Cathay, which acted as its distribution arm in Singapore and Malaysia. This move eventually broke Shaws' monopoly of the market.

After a slow start, Golden Harvest's breakthrough came with Bruce Lee's *The Big Boss* (*Tangshan daxiong*, Luo Wei, 1971). The film brought in HK$3 million and set box-office history. It also shifted the emphasis to actors with authentic martial techniques. As a logical development of the new-style martial arts film, kung-fu films dominated the local screens for most of the 1970s, as well as making an impact on international markets. The popularity of this genre signified a fundamental and lasting change in Hong Kong cinema: action was valued over drama, and male stars replaced female stars as the main box-office appeal. Moreover, locally produced films proved continually more popular than Hollywood products and continued to have the largest share (between 50 per cent and 70 per cent) of the market into the 1990s.

Following the death of Bruce Lee in 1973, and as a result of excessive exploitation by opportunistic producers, the success of kung-fu films looked to be in decline. But the genre saw signs of rejuvenation with Chang Cheh's early work in Taiwan, *Heroes Two* (*Fangshiyu yu hong xiguan*, 1973) and *Shaolin Martial Arts* (*Hongquan yu yongchun*, 1974). In these films Chang introduced the legends of the Shaolin school of boxing, and filmed the combat styles and sequences in great detail. These elements were exploited to new heights when Liu Jialiang, Chang's martial arts choreographer, later turned to directing. Liu was probably the most accomplished film-maker in the kung-fu decade and the only *auteur* working under the studio system. He directed seventeen features before leaving Shaws in 1985, including classics like *Challenge of the Masters* (*Luacai yu huangfeihong*, 1976) and *Dirty Ho* (*Lantou he*, 1979). Another master of the martial arts genre, King Hu, found it easier to work in Taiwan, where he made his most accomplished works including *A Touch of Zen* (*Xianu*, 1972).

The revival of 'Cantonese' cinema

The dominance of the martial arts and kung-fu films from late 1960s to early 1970s can perhaps be explained by the fact that Hong Kong was entering the boom phase of all-out capitalist expansion and materialist development. It was natural for the population to indulge in the quest for excitement and pleasures of the senses. The stock market crash of 1973 marked a recession in the local economy, and a change in film tastes. *The House of 72 Tenants* (*Qishier jia fangke*, Chu Yuan, 1973), a satire on corruption dubbed in Cantonese, broke all the box-office records held by Bruce Lee's films, and helped revive the indigenous cinema.

Débuting in Shaws' *The Warlord* (*Da Junfa*, Li Hanxiang, 1972), Michael Hui moved to Golden Harvest, and became the most successful comedian in local film history. His directorial début *Games Gamblers Play* (*Guima shuangxing*, 1974) followed in the footsteps of *The House of 72 Tenants*, and set another new box-office record. Dubbing films into Cantonese became the new trend, and by the end of the 1970s, Mandarin was used in only 20 per cent of the films shown. Television was an important factor in this respect; during the few years when only Mandarin was heard at the cinemas, television maintained its broadcasting in Cantonese, thus keeping the potential market alive. Michael Hui started his career on TV on the *Hui Brothers' Show* (1970), and the gag-show format of the programme was to have a profound influence on the episodic structure and 'instant gratification' aspect of Hong Kong cinema in the 1970s.

Comic satires in Cantonese became another major trend beside the kung-fu action film. Ironically, this did not signal a revival of the old Cantonese cinema. All films were produced by the existing (previously Mandarin) system, and dialogues (whether Cantonese or Mandarin) were dubbed in later. There no longer existed different distribution networks or theatrical circuits for the two kinds of cinema, nor was there any difference in ticket price for Chinese and foreign films as in the previous decade. In other words, the dichotomy of Mandarin and Cantonese cinema after the Second World War almost disappeared, and there emerged a new breed of Hong Kong cinema which later blossomed in the 1980s. Gone were the didacticism and beliefs in cinema as a potential educational art form; cynicism was the prevalent attitude in the cinema of the 1970s behind the undisputed goal to entertain. Exploitation films with excessive sex and violence flooded the screens to a degree that horrified the critics. Chang Cheh might be rightly blamed for making blood and gore fashionable, but it was Li Hanxiang who introduced the sexploitation genre to Hong Kong cinema through his highly successful series of *fengyue* films, which started with *Legends of Lust* (*Fengyue qitan*, 1972), and were a mixture of soft porn, satire, and comedy. By foregrounding vulgarity as the basic human trait, the films of the series were seminal works that heralded the direction of Cantonese comedies to come, and set the tone for the film culture of the 1970s.

Towards the end of the decade, a popular new subgenre emerged that amalgamated kung-fu films with the social satires of the early 1970s: the kung-fu comedy. Following Liu Jialiang's lead, a number of martial arts instructors, like Sammo Hung and Yuen Woo-ping, turned into successful directors of this genre. Jackie Chan achieved stardom in Yeun's phenomenally successful *Drunken Master* (*Zui quan*, 1978). The kung-fu comedy combined spectacular and humorous action sequences with clever use of slang, puns, and television advertising slogans as in-jokes. Its heroes were ordinary characters driven only by opportunism and a sense of resignation. Mutual exploitation defined personal relationships in these films, which brought cynicism to a new peak.

Nevertheless, kung-fu comedies were still marked by the Chinese folk cultural background of their makers, many of whom had received rigorous training in the martial arts and Peking Opera as children, and started their careers playing extras in the old studio system.

THE MODERN PERIOD

The 'New Wave' phenomenon which burst on the scene in 1979 marked a new era, in which Hong Kong cinema established its identity and announced the coming of age of the indigenous culture, where artists and technicians travel freely across the spectrum from film to television and pop music. The 'New Wave' directors belonged to a new generation of film-makers born and educated in Hong Kong, who had undergone vocational training in film schools in the west, and displayed their talents in television before they entered the film industry. Although they did not establish a clean break with tradition, early works such as Ann Hui's *The Secret* (*Feng jie*, 1979), Tsui Hark's *Butterfly Murders* (*Die bian*, 1979), and Allen Fong's *Father and Son* (*Fu zi qing*, 1980) did display a more sophisticated visual style and a more westernized (yet typical of modern Hong Kong) consciousness than their predecessors.

The works of the 'New Wave' film-makers were generally marked by realism and technical competence. Most had modern settings and operated within highly popular genres like crime thrillers—for example Alex Cheung's *Cops and Robbers* (*Dian zhi bing*, 1979). The 'New Wave' can be seen as a successful replay of the 1960s failed experiment to modernize Cantonese cinema by adapting western genres. With little hesitation in exploiting violence and sensationalism, the 'New Wave' remained firmly in the grip of commercialism. By integrating itself into commercial mainstream cinema, it brought in new blood and a greater impetus for change. Its most important contribution was to raise the technical levels of the industry. A more professional approach by the film-makers helped define job responsibilities in the various departments, particularly art direction, which was often overlooked in the kung-fu decade.

In this respect, Tsui Hark is the most representative of the 'New Wave' directors. After three commercial failures, he joined the Cinema City Company, and made his first hit, *All the Wrong Clues (for the Right Solution)* (*Guima zhiduoxing*, 1981). The film developed the glamorous visuals and fast-paced editing which exerted significant influence on Cinema City's subsequent productions. The company excelled in big casts, high budgets, and the packaging of 'multi-genre' films plus over-the-top promotion campaigns. It prescribed collective script-writing, to accumulate 'selling points' and fully exploit every scene for comic effects. Its films, mostly comedies, combine spectacle (stunts), gimmicks, and verbal gags to attract the largest possible audience.

Cinema City's rapid rise to the top of the industry was spectacular. *Aces Go Places* (*Zuija paidang*, Eric Tsang, 1982) set a box-office record of HK$26 million, and four sequels were made over the next seven years. Suddenly, urban comedy in modern westernized settings replaced the kung-fu film (with historical or folk Chinese backgrounds) as the leading trend-setter. Other companies and film-makers were quick to cash in on Cinema City's success. Both Samm'o Hung (*Winners and Sinners* (*Qimou miaoji wu fuxing*), 1983) and Jackie Chan (*Police Story* (*Jingcha gu shi*), 1985) made the transition and established themselves in the new genre.

The industry

In terms of production, the 1980s saw the end of the old studio system, as Shaw Brothers closed down production in 1986. Production shifted into the hands of a more flexible production house system. However, major financing still came from the three big companies (Golden Harvest,

Golden Princess—the backer of Cinema City—and D. & B. Co., which took over Shaw's theatrical circuit) who maintained direct control over all distribution outlets for local production. As a result, the profit-sharing terms were weighted heavily in favour of these distribution companies (60 per cent of proceeds, with the advertising costs footed by the production companies). The size of all three theatrical circuits—each controlling over twenty theatres—fuelled the pressure on film-makers to produce only the most commercial mainstream films.

The situation did not improve even after the establishment of the fourth and fifth distribution outlets (Newport, founded in 1988, and Mandarin, 1993), as the number of theatres in Hong Kong drastically increased in the late 1980s. On the contrary, it got worse as film production rose and more mediocre or below-average productions flooded the market, dealing a serious blow to the audience's confidence. The average market share of each film shrank, and it became even harder for independent productions that strayed from the mainstream to make a profit in the 1990s.

This rise in the number of productions would not have been possible without the influx of foreign investment

Chow Yun-fat threatening Tony Leung in John Woo's stylized and ultra-violent *Hard Boiled* (1992)

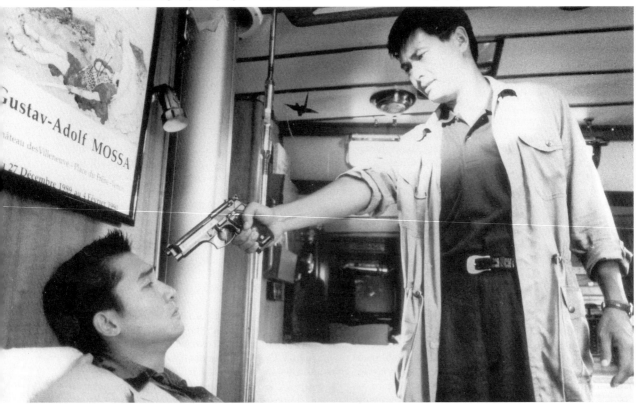

from Taiwan. The Taiwanese film industry was very small, and, with an economically resurgent Taiwan, opportunistic investors decided to pour money into Hong Kong movies as they were usually more profitable than their own. Thus, ironically, the gradual drop of annual attendance by 25 per cent from the recent peak of 66 million in 1988 was indirectly caused by the huge success that Hong Kong films achieved overseas in the 1980s.

New genres?

The valuable experience gained in making kung-fu films for nearly two decades, coupled with the introduction of special-effects hardware from the west, produced brilliant action stunts and flamboyant visual effects in the Hong Kong films of this period. These are best embodied in the work of Jackie Chan, Tsui Hark, and John Woo, which opened up new markets like Japan and South Korea, and received releases in Europe and America.

In terms of genre development, the modern period of Hong Kong cinema is a continuation of the major trends (kung-fu and comedy) of the 1970s. More polished visuals and urban settings aside, martial arts action and comic high jinks have remained the staples of Hong Kong movies.

The modern Hong Kong cinema is strongly characterized by genre combinations, where all subject-matters are game for comedy. This reflects the industry's ambitions to open up more markets and attract the widest audiences in the community; essential after the drastic rise in production budgets following Cinema City's lead. Comedies remain an overwhelmingly popular genre; the majority being farces which emphasize excess, chaos, a quick rhythm, and a preponderance of gags.

The evolution and adaptation of kung-fu into other genres has been complicated. The early works of the New Wave directors in the crime thriller genre were more heavily influenced by Hollywood, and succeeded in imparting a fresh feel to audiences by shooting in real street locations. When Jackie Chan turned to urban settings, he chose the same genre, but essentially just 'dressed up' traditional kung-fu acrobatics and combat sequences in modern clothes. The most important subgenre was the so-called 'hero film', initiated by John Woo's *A Better Tomorrow* (*Yingxiong bense*, 1986), which was a modern variation on the old martial arts movie. While gun-toting replaced sword-fighting, the emphasis on the kung-fu themes of honour, brotherhood, and male bonding remained unchallenged. Nevertheless, the successful adaptation of martial arts choreography into designing gun fights, explosions, and action stunts contributed to an aesthetics of stylized violence unrivalled anywhere in the world. Nowhere is this more apparent than in *Hard Boiled* (*Lashou shentan*, 1992), where the combined talents of director John Woo, art directors James Leung and John Chong, and cinematographer Wong Wing-heng produced a spectacle of quite dizzying proportions.

The ghost story movie emerged as a popular genre in the 1980s, encompassing all movies dealing with sprites and demons, superstitions, fatalism, and supernatural phenomena. The genre mixed horror, comedy, kung-fu, special effects, suspense, and melodrama. The rise of production standards with big investments in state-of-the-art special effects greatly benefited the rise of the ghost story movie. The most representative films were those of Sammo Hung; and Ching Siu-tung's *A Chinese Ghost Story* (*Qiannu youhun*, 1987).

The popular rise of the ghost story film in the early 1980s can be seen as a response to the uncertainties of the future. The prospect of the 1997 hand-over of Hong Kong to the Chinese has caused Hong Kong grief and anxiety. The spirits, demons, and superstitious fatalism that are inherent to the ghost genre mirror the fears of the people.

Bibliography
Teo, Stephen (1996). *Hong Kong Cinema: The Extra Dimension.*

Taiwanese New Cinema

JUNE YIP

The Taiwanese cinema is best known in the west for its kung-fu and other action films which for a time rivalled Hong Kong films in world-wide popularity. But Taiwan is also home to a movement known as 'Taiwanese New Cinema', of which the best-known representative is Hou Hsiao-hsien.

The New Cinema movement emerged in the early 1980s and has been seen as a culmination of the 'back-to-the-roots' cultural nationalism that swept Taiwan during the 1970s. A critical era of change for the island, the decade began with a series of embarrassing political set-backs for Taiwan—the forced severance of diplomatic ties with the USA, Japan, and other major nations, expulsion from the United Nations, and exclusion from the Olympic Games—

which precipitated a sense of national crisis. Taiwan entered a period of self-reflection that resulted, in part, in the awakening of nationalistic sentiments, a renewed interest in indigenous cultural traditions, and a blossoming of socio-political awareness most clearly evidenced by the emergence of *hsiang-t'u*, or nativist, literature. By insisting on 'making Taiwan the centre', *hsiang t'u* literature broke from the nostalgia literature of the mainland refugee writers, from the western-influenced literature of the educated élite, and from the escapist popular fiction of the era. It focused instead on the specifically Taiwanese experience of socio-cultural change during the post-war era.

Taiwanese New Cinema is, in many ways, the cinematic heir to this nativist tradition. One of the two portmanteau films that heralded the 'birth' of New Cinema, *His Son's Big Doll* (1983), is adapted from three short stories by Huang Ch'un-ming, a leading *hsiang-t'u* author. Like its literary predecessor, New Cinema marked a significant departure from established traditions. Taiwanese cinema of the 1970s was in a moribund state. Due in part to strict government censorship that discouraged socio-political analysis, the Hollywood-styled commercial studios did little more than churn out fantasy entertainment films—largely escapist swordsmen epics, martial arts films, formulaic melodramas, and teen romances. These were rapidly losing ground to imported films and videotapes from America, Japan, and Hong Kong, which not only crushed domestic films at the box-office, but also undermined public confidence in the native film industry. By the early 1980s, the desire to revitalize the industry and win back commercial success and critical respectability for Taiwanese cinema finally prompted the government to allow other, less rigid modes of film-making.

The chief beneficiaries of this cultural liberalization were the young Taiwanese men and women who, born in the late 1940s and early 1950s and educated in film schools in the USA, were, in the early 1980s, just beginning their careers in film-making. They seized the opportunity to make films that were not only technically more innovative, but also addressed the pressing social and cultural difficulties facing modern Taiwan. Born in 1947 in Kuangtung province on the Chinese mainland, Hou Hsiao-hsien fled to Taiwan with his family at the time of the Communist take-over in 1949. Like his New Cinema colleagues, therefore, he has grown up with the island, experiencing first-hand its emergence from fifty-one years of repressive Japanese occupation, its adjustment to Kuomintang (KMT) rule, and its transformation from a traditional agrarian society into a modern urban industrial power. Unlike the others, however, Hou did not study abroad. Instead, beginning in 1973, he followed a more conventional route of apprenticeship in the commercial studios, working as script-writer, production assistant, and as an assistant

director under several established directors. His first three films were commercial genre pieces and are not considered to be of any great significance.

With his fourth and breakthrough film, *His Son's Big Doll*, Hou finally freed himself from the constraints of potboiler film-making and began to find his own voice. In the films that followed, *The Boys from Fengkuei* (1983), *Summer at Grandpa's* (1984), and *A Time to Live and a Time to Die* (1985), Hou began to articulate a distinct cinematic style that was a far cry from the action-driven, fast cutting style of the commercial cinema. Hou is a laconic and oblique story-teller, downplaying the dramatic by offering leisurely observations of small, everyday occurrences. He favours meditative long takes with a minimum of camera movements, most often in medium or long shot. A favourite technique is to allow the camera simply to stare at an empty room that a character is about to enter or has just left, frequently making masterful use, through the soundtrack, of off-screen space. Like the Japanese director Yasujiro Ozu—to whom Hou is most often compared but whose influence he denies—Hou punctuates his films with shots of rural landscapes, abandoned corridors, lonely railway platforms, deserted pool halls, and empty dining-rooms. His cinematic style has been compared to classical Chinese poetry, to traditional landscape painting, and to Buddhist narrative scrolls.

Hou also found a central theme around which all his films revolve: what does it mean to be a modern Taiwanese? The autobiographical *A Time to Live and a Time to Die*, widely considered to be his first masterpiece, transcends its personal coming-of-age story to become an examination of the roots of modern Taiwanese life, a graceful and elegiac tracing of Taiwan's history from the KMT government's exile to Taiwan in 1949, through its decades of quasi-colonial rule on the island, to the gradual relinquishing of the dream of returning to the mainland. *The Boys from Fengkuei* and *Summer at Grandpa's*, like the later *Dust in the Wind* (1987), address the social tensions created by Taiwan's rapid urbanization, particularly the growing gap between the values and life-style of the industrialized metropolis and the rural villages. *Daughters of the Nile* (1987) is the only one of Hou's films set exclusively in the city, but, like the others, it depicts the problems faced by Taiwanese youth caught up in a society that is changing with bewildering speed. It raises important questions about the collapse of traditional values in the face of American and Japanese cultural imperialism.

In 1989 the ambitious *City of Sadness* won the Golden Lion at Venice, and cemented Hou's reputation both internationally and at home. The most overtly historical of Hou's films, it is the story of an extended Taiwanese family's experiences from 1945 to 1949, the violent and turbulent years of transition between the end of the Japanese occupation and the arrival of the Kuomintang govern-

A scene from *City of Sadness* by Taiwanese director Hou Hsiao-hsien. The film won the Golden Lion at Venice in 1989, but the Taiwanese flag could not be flown at the prize-giving because of protests from the Chinese government

ment from the mainland. It is also, however, a quest for national identity, an attempt to recover a period of Taiwanese history that, for Hou, is fundamental to an understanding of contemporary Taiwanese society, the frequently antagonistic relationship between the government and the people, and the continuing tensions between mainlanders and the native Taiwanese. The film generated controversy and debate in Taiwan because it dared to depict the corruption, greed, and brutality that accompanied the KMT take-over of the island, focusing on the infamous February incident of 1947—until recently denied by official history—in which native islanders protesting at the unfair policies of the KMT were savagely repressed. In the island-wide massacres which followed tens of thousands of Taiwanese were slaughtered, and a nascent Taiwanese nationalist movement wiped out.

City of Sadness forms the middle piece of Hou Hsiao-hsien's planned trilogy of films on Taiwanese history. *The Puppetmaster* continues his exploration of the island's past but precedes *City* in chronology. Part documentary and part fiction, it examines Taiwanese life during the Japanese occupation through the colourful life-story of Li Tien-lu, a master Taiwanese puppeteer who has appeared in all of Hou's films since *Dust in the Wind*. The film was co-winner of the Golden Bear award at the 1993 Berlin festival. The final film of the trilogy is to be called *A Man Named P'u-tao T'ai'lang*, and will tell a Rip-Van-Winkle-like tale about a political prisoner, goaled since the February 1947 incident, who suddenly finds himself released into Taiwanese society of the post-martial law 1980s. The story of his adjustment to the island's modern and multi-cultural urban society will bring Hou Hsiao-hsien's story of Taiwan up to date and, undoubtedly, further underscore his contribution towards helping to define a distinctive cultural identity for Taiwan and Taiwanese cinema.

Bibliography
Chiao Hsiung-p'ing (ed.) (1988), *T'ai-wan hsin tian-ying* ('Taiwanese New Cinema').
Li You-hsin (ed.) (1986), *Kang-t'ai liu-ta tao-yen* ('Six major directors from Hong Kong and Taiwan').
Stanbrook, Alan (1990), 'The Worlds of Hou Hsiao-hsien'.

The Modernization of Japanese Film

HIROSHI KOMATSU

From the mid-1930s, when sound film began to replace silent cinema in Japan, the Japanese studios modelled themselves on the Hollywood system. This was true not only of the institutions, but also of the form of the films produced, which were based around the unfolding of a narrative where all techniques were in the service of telling a story and eliciting particular emotions. This system dominated Japanese film production in the post-war period, but it was not monolithic or indestructible. Mizoguchi's films can be seen as deviations, and Kurosawa's *Rashomon* (Daiei, 1950) provided a decisive break. It did not simply portray the 'truth' of the narrative, but, by presenting multiple, conflicting views of the same event, made many interpretations possible and demanded active reading by the audience. *Rashomon* was the first film to introduce the concept of the modern into Japanese cinema.

Modernization first appeared in a change in the subject-matter tackled by film-makers. For example, Nikkatsu's *Taiyo no kisetsu* ('Season of the sun', Takumi Furukawa, 1956), adapted from the novel of Shintaro Ishihara, approached the subject of the anger of modern youth by directly depicting the rebellion of juveniles against the older generation. The film was not innovative in terms of film form, but by using the classical narrative mode drew attention to the challenge to tradition represented by new morals and behaviour. In the same year, Nikkatsu adapted Ishihara's new novel *Kurutta kajitsu* ('Crazed fruit', Ko Nakahira, 1956). This represented an attempt to establish the 'angry youth' film as a genre, after the model of Nicholas Ray's *Rebel without a Cause* and Ingmar Bergman's *Summer with Monika*. There was a bourgeois idealism inherent in the literature of Ishihara which was mirrored in these adaptations of his work. The films lacked any dimension of class-consciousness but represented rebellious youth in an imaginary world. This tendency towards a lack of realism of setting was to constitute an important element of Nikkatsu's youth films and action films for years to come.

In the 1950s, then, Nikkatsu tried to modernize Japanese cinema by establishing a new genre, aimed at and focusing on the younger generation. However, despite the popular success of many of these films the genre rarely produced anything other than standardized B movies of little lasting interest. This had much to do with the restrictions placed on film-makers by the studios. The genre did not attract eminent established directors, nor produce artists of its own. The one exception was Seijun Suzuki, who began his directing career making action films for Nikkatsu. He made a series of these films between 1956 and 1963 which were classed as B movies, but which stood out from those made by other genre specialists of the time. He ornamented the stereotyped story-lines of the genre with deliberately artificial images, and he pushed the most standard action film beyond the ordinary through the use of attractive shot composition and unique *mise-en-scène*. After 1964, promoted from low-budget B films, he turned his hand to adapting literature for the screen, but he continued to develop the style he had established on his action movies. Gradually Suzuki decreased the importance of a rational and logical story in his films. For example, in the gangster film *Koroshi no rakuin* ('The brand of killing', Nikkatsu, 1967), the plot, which generic conventions dictate should be clear, was transformed into a labyrinth. The increasing complexity and difficulty of his films finally led to his dismissal from Nikkatsu in 1968.

While Nikkatsu's youth films were set in imaginary bourgeois circumstances, Shohei Imamura, working in the same company, developed a very different milieu for his films. After working as the assistant director to Yasujiro Ozu at Shochiku, Imamura moved to Nikkatsu to work with Yuzo Kawashima. Since his début film in 1958 Imamura's concern had been with the world left behind by the development of Japanese bourgeois society, and the energetic people living in that world. His films were fundamentally different from the Nikkatsu action films, as they were not dependent on the method of realism. They included caricature-like depictions of strange people, blended with ethnographic and sociological concerns, and humour inherited from Kawashima. Many of his films from this period bore more resemblance to films made by independent companies than the output of a major studio like Nikkatsu. After *Nippon konchuki* ('Insect woman', Nikkatsu, 1963) Imamura's concerns gravitated towards issues of sex, and his films examined the sexual impulse that he believed existed at the root of all people.

Kiriro Urayama directed realistic films with a social message at Nikkatsu. He had been the assistant director to Imamura before making his first film in 1962, and he went on to work mostly in the youth film genre. However, films like *Kyupora no aru machi* ('The street with the cupola', Nikkatsu, 1962) and *Hiko shojo* ('The bad girl', Nikkatsu, 1963) were different from the stereotyped Nikkatsu films of the genre, as they contained political elements. By the late 1960s, both Imamura and Urayama had developed a metaphysical quality in their films. Urayama's last film at Nikkatsu, *Watashi ga suteta onna* ('The girl I abandoned', 1969) concentrated on the subjective experiences of a man who had abandoned a girl. However, this highly reflective film, which included some hallucinatory shots, was thought too abstract by the Nikkatsu executives. The film companies did not like to see their directors bring such experimental elements to their work. Directors were required to follow the norms of the genre and remain within the limits and rules laid down by their companies. Directors with a desire to experiment had to fight continually with the conservatism of the executives of their companies, and many found it an impossible task. Imamura realized that he could not make the films he wanted to at a major studio. After making *Akai satsui* ('Intentions of murder') in 1963 he left Nikkatsu to found his own independent production company.

During the 1950s most independent companies had been organized by groups with socialist sympathies. Directors like Tadashi Imai and Satsuo Yamamoto produced films with a political message. The independent sector, then, was not interested in the development of film form and could not be considered avant-garde. However, in the 1960s the situation changed. New independent companies began to be established to produce films that could not be made at the major studios but that were primarily concerned with extending the boundaries of Japanese film and not just with political messages from a specific party. Out of such newly founded independent companies, the so-called New Wave was born.

CRISIS IN THE STUDIOS

There were six major film companies in Japan in 1960: Nikkatsu, Daiei, Toho, Toei, Shochiku, and Shin Toho. Shin Toho produced only sensationalist films for which there

proved to be a limited market, and it went bankrupt in 1961, leaving five major studios throughout most of the 1960s.

From the late 1950s the bulk of Nikkatsu output had been genre staples such as the youth film and action film. The classics of Japanese cinema of the 1950s had been produced by Daiei: Kurosawa's *Rashomon*, Mizoguchi's *Ugetsu monogatari* (1953), *Chikamatsu monogatari* ('The crucified lovers', 1954), Naruse's *Inazuma* ('Lightning', 1952), Kinugasa's *Jigokumon* ('Gate of hell', 1953), and Kozaburo Yoshimura's *Yoru no kawa* ('Night river', 1956). The company had trained young directors like Yasuzo Masumura, and had let Kon Ichikawa develop his talent on a series of literary adaptations such as *Enjo* ('Flame of torment', 1958), *Nobi* ('Fires of the plain', 1959), and *Ototo* ('Younger brother', 1960) in order to fill the vacancy left in the field of artistic film by the death of Kenji Mizoguchi in 1956.

The Toei Company laid stress on the production of widescreen films after 1957. Its policy of attracting large audiences (especially men) to its entertainment *jidaigeki* (period drama) had been extremely successful, and by 1960 Toei had become the most profitable film company in Japan. The company relied on the regular and rapid production of standard and stereotypical genre films for this success, and so their widescreen *jidaigeki* were not of the highest artistic quality. Toei also produced highly artistic films by the masters of the pre-war era, like Daisuke Ito, Tomotaka Tasaka, and Tomu Uchida, but the company did not provide a place for young talent with innovative ideas.

The same was true of Toho, where the directors of the pre-war era, like Mikio Naruse and Shiro Toyoda, were able

A scene from *Kuratta kajitsu* ('Crazed Fruit', 1956), Ko Nakahira's film of affairs and revenge that attempted to popularize the youth genre in the Japanese film industry

Akira Kurosawa

(1910–)

In 1951 Akira Kurosawa's film *Rashomon* (1950) won the Golden Lion at the Venice Film Festival, thereby opening the doors of the western art circuit to Japanese cinema. *Rashomon* consists of four different versions of the same event, the attack on a nobleman by a bandit, and despite its Japanese setting is conceptualized around a very occidental theme; the relativity of truth. This combination of Japanese and western influences is a feature of Kurosawa's film-making, and has contributed to his continuing popularity in the West.

The dynamism of Kurosawa's method of story-telling through images has always gone hand in hand with a humanist treatment of his subjects. A fascination with social problems and human nature forms the constellation of Kurosawa's universe, and provides the link between his violent feudal epics and modern-day dramas. Kurosawa displays an unparalleled directorial power to create dense fictional worlds; a skill already evident in his first film *Sugata Sanshiro* (1943). The story composition of his films, which proceed toward their climaxes through a combination of realist description and occasional moments of romanticism, attains its classical completeness in films such as *Norainu* ('Stray Dog', 1949). This classical form is constituted by occidental style—a *mélange* of European and Hollywood modes. Many of the cinematic forms in Kurosawa's films have been based on western-style montage. Even when he employs Japanese classical performing arts like Noh and kabuki, they are articulated in the occidental mode, as in *Tora no o wo fumu otoko-tachi* ('They who step on the tiger's trail', 1945) and *Throne of Blood* (*Kumonosujo*, 1957), an adaptation of the story of Macbeth. A concern with non-Japanese themes is evident in Kurosawa's adaptations of western literary sources, including Dostoevsky, Gorky, and Shakespeare.

However, Kurosawa sought more than the intellectual world view of European literature. He also developed film as an entertainment form. He was deeply influenced by Hollywood movies, particularly those of John Ford. That which Ford expressed through the Western appeared in the form of *jidaigeki* (period films) in Kurosawa's films; *Shichinin no samurai* (*Seven Samurai*, 1954), *Kakushitoride no sanakunin* (*The Hidden Fortress*, 1958), *Yojimbo* (1961), and *Tsubai Sanjuro* (*Sanjuro*, 1962). The *samurai* films *Yojimbo* and *Seven Samurai* in turn inspired Sergio Leone's *A Fistful of Dollars* (1964) and John Sturges's *The Magnificent Seven* (1960); evidence of the cross-fertilization between Kurosawa, American genre movies, and the European art circuit.

Humanity lies at the centre of Kurosawa's themes, an approach which has formed the basis of his world view since his early works. It appears most clearly in *Ikiru* (1952), which was partly inspired by Goethe's *Faust*, and also in *Red Beard* (*Akahige*, 1965). While this concept of humanity is meant to be universal, it came to seem some-

The Seven Samurai (1954)

what anachronistic as a film theme in the agitated social situation of the late 1960s, when new Japanese directors were making innovative works, and numerous foreign films made by the new generation were imported into Japan. Kurosawa's film art came to be regarded as old-fashioned in this period. He appeared to reach a creative impasse; *Dodeskaden* (1970) reveals this perplexity in its form, and his artistic problems may have contributed to his attempted suicide in December 1971. However, with *Dersu Uzala*, made in the USSR in 1975, Kurosawa overcame these problems and developed his style further, in the form of the epic. *Kagemusha* (1980) and *Ran* (1985) were made on a massive scale in terms of length, theme, and spectacle, and remain among Kurosawa's most impressive work. He then turned to more personal visions, as seen in *Yume* ('Dream', 1990) and *Madadayo* (1993), an approach which had not been seen in his previous films.

HIROSHI KOMATSU

SELECT FILMOGRAPHY

Sugata Sanshiro (1943); Norainu (Stray Dog) (1949); Rashomon (1950); Ikiru (1952); Shichinin no samurai (Seven Samurai) (1954); Kumonosujo (Throne of Blood) (1957); Kakushitoride no sanakunin (The Hidden Fortress) (1958); Yojimbo (1961); Tsubai Sanjuro (Sanjuro) (1962); Akahige (Red Beard) (1965); Dodeskaden (1970); Dersu Uzala (1975); Kagemusha (1980); Ran (1985); Yume (Dream) (1990); Madadayo (1993)

BIBLIOGRAPHY

Desser, David (1983), *The Samurai Films of Akira Kurosawa*.
Richie, Donald (1984), *The Films of Akira Kurosawa*.

to develop their careers, but young directors found that they were highly restricted by the limitation of the studio. Eventually prominent new talents only emerged from the two oldest of the large companies: Nikkatsu and Shochiku. Together with several young directors working in the independent companies, they were to constitute the Japanese New Wave in the 1960s.

At Nikkatsu young film-makers who had developed their talents within the company (like Seijun Suzuki, Shohei Imamura, and Kirio Urayama) were leaving to further their artistic visions. A similar thing was happening at Shochiku. Shochiku was a very conservative company and they regulated and protected even the tone of their films. Yasujiro Ozu continued to make a film each year for the company, but apart from him only Keisuke Kinoshita had been given any kind of autonomy. Even he was not immune to interference from above. When he directed his rather bold film *Narayama bushi-ko* ('Ballad of Narayama', 1958), Shiro Kido, the principal of the company, criticized its violent content and objected to the adaptation of the story.

The conservatism of Shochiku prevented them from exploiting the rise of new genres like the action film which Nikkatsu and other companies were successfully producing. This policy precipitated the decline of Shochiku's fortunes at the box-office. As profits fell the company began to lose its place as one of Japan's major studios. Under pressure, Shochiku launched a new policy in 1960: while continuing to maintain the production of their traditional films, the company gave young directors the opportunity to make the films they wanted with a new degree of freedom. This strategy was aimed at capturing the attention of the young audience who had not been drawn to the company's products before. Thus the so called Shochiku New Wave directors Nagisa Oshima, Yoshishige Yoshida, and Masahiro Shinoda emerged on to the stage of Japanese film.

Oshima's *Seishun zankoku monogatari* ('A story of cruelty of youth', Shochiku, 1960) depicted young people's self-destruction with a harsh reality that had been absent from previous youth films. Produced in the middle of the campaign against the Japan–USA Security Treaty, political messages were woven into the drama. However, unlike the leftist party-political films of the independent companies, Oshima's message was directed toward the audience's own identity and independence, and it is this which gives the film its avant-garde edge. In *Nihon no yoru to kiri* (*Night and Fog in Japan*, Shochiku, 1960), which deliberately echoed the title of Resnais's 1955 film on concentration camps, *Nuit et brouillard*, political discussion was central to the film, reaching beyond the scope sanctioned by Shochiku's production policy. Oshima was forced to leave the studio and from this point worked outside the mainstream by founding his own production company.

Yoshishige Yoshida's *Rokudenashi* ('Good-for-nothing', 1960) was in many ways similar to Oshima's *Seishun zankoku monogatari*. *Rokudenashi* takes as its subject the crimes of four students, and in it Yoshida tried to achieve a new type of drama by deconstructing the traditional ideology of Shochiku. His next film *Chi wa kawaiteru* ('Dry blood', 1960) was also a crime film, but with an element of social concern evident in an attempt to deconstruct and examine the old moral order. Like Oshima and Yoshida's films, Masahiro Shinoda's *Kawaita mizuumi* ('Dry lake', 1960) also had college students as the protagonists. These three new Shochiku directors revealed the violent reality of the modern society in which they lived, through films focusing on the lives and behaviour of people of their own generation. This New Wave at Shochiku lasted a very short period because its central figure, Oshima, left the company shortly after making *Night and Fog in Japan*. In spite of this, Yoshida and Shinoda remained at Shochiku until the mid-1960s and both made interesting films within the limits of the company's policy.

Some New Wave directors appeared from outside the major companies. Susumu Hani had been working in the 1950s at Iwanami Eiga, the film-production section of a publishing company which made science and education films, and so his method of direction was completely different from that of those who studied film-making in the mainstream film companies. In 1961 he made his first feature *Furyo shonen* ('Bad boys'), using the mixed styles of documentary and fiction. In this film, which was based around the lives of boys in a reformatory, Hani did not use professional actors but improvised scenes with boys who had experience of such institutions. In his subsequent films Hani continued to use a documentary method of shooting which came to be seen as an alternative form of fiction film. It influenced other film-makers, for example Shohei Imamura, who used a similar method in *Ningen johatsu* ('A man vanishes', 1967).

Hiroshi Teshigahara was another influential film-maker who emerged from the independent sector. As in the case of Susumu Hani, Teshigahara's success lay in the unique film form he was able to develop from his position outside the major film companies. Like Hani he had made documentaries in the 1950s, which were the point of departure for his feature films. From his first feature, *Otoshi ana* ('The pitfall', 1962), he devoted himself to adaptations of Kobo Abe's literature. The visualization of existentialist stories was his main concern throughout the 1960s, *Suna no onna* ('Woman in the dunes', 1964) being the most successful work among these adaptations.

The creative films of the New Wave occurred at a time when mainstream Japanese film production was in crisis. In 1953 television broadcasting had begun in Japan, and the spread of television ownership had started to affect cinema attendances. The number of cinema-goers

Nagisa Oshima

(1932–)

Social critic, political agitator, and now a well-known television personality, Nagisa Oshima has always pursued a cultural strategy of which film-making is only a part. At the same time, Oshima's cinema itself does not remain within the domain of classical film art. In his best films he shows as interest beyond the illusionism designed for telling a fictional story. This attitude pushed him into the foreground of the Japanese avant-garde in the 1960s, and made him one of the most influential film-makers in Japanese history.

His first film *Ai to kibo no machi* ('A town of love and hope', 1959) was made at the Shochiku studio, and ought to have reflected the totally conformist ideology of that company. However, the completed film departed from the formula, and ended with the despair of a lower-class boy, quite contrary to the 'hope' in the title of the film. Oshima was not interested in producing the traditional film laid down by company policy, and it was not easy for him to remain at the studio and still make films which matched his ideals and ambitions. However, he made three films at Shochiku in 1960 that were closely connected to the contemporary political movement and its breakdown. He also made political statements outside his films, and, central though it is for him, cinema must be thought of as only one of his methods of expression.

Oshima's work is radically different from the official post-war political cinema that used only mediocre film form to present a particular party's policy. Oshima not only took a radically anti-Stalinist new left political stance, but his film form was also revolutionary. For example, the total number of shots in *Nihon no yoru to kiri* (*Night and Fog in Japan*, 1960) is less than fifty. Constituted by long takes and panning, and structured around an intense, lengthy political discussion, with complex flashbacks re-presenting the memories of characters, this was an avant-garde film that defied the entertainment demands made by the studio. It employed methods never before seen in Japanese cinema, and proved immensely influential on other young film-makers.

Oshima's films are responses to actual events, changes, and problems in Japanese society, and so each film inevitably holds a close connection with the time in which it was made. This can be seen in terms of form as well as content. Oshima does not cling to a consistency in film form, but uses and develops avant-garde techniques appropriate to the moment and the subject. Unlike *Nihon no yoru to kiri*, *Hakuchu no torima* (*Violence at High Noon*, 1966) is constituted by many shots. Even in the same year different subjects receive radically different treatments, as between *Death by Hanging* (*Koshikei*, 1968) and *Kaette kita yopparai* (*Three Resurrected Drunkards*, 1968).

Oshima was always sensitive to phenomena that were controversial and contemporary. *Etsuraku* (*The Pleasures of the flesh*, 1965) and *Hakuchu no torima* comment on the Japanese pornographic film (known as the 'pink film'), particularly the works of Koji Wakamatsu. Politics and sex are the most important themes for Oshima, and he directly challenged the system of film censorship that concealed sex and permitted violence by daring to make the hard core *Ai no corrida* (*In the Realm of the Senses*, 1976). He also challenged the institutional form of cinema by commenting on the so-called experimental and underground cinema in *The Man Who Left his Will on Film* (*Tokyo senso sengo hiwa*, 1970) and *Diary of a Shinjuku Thief* (*Shinjuku dorobo nikki*, 1969).

After completing the masterpiece *Gishiki* (*The Ceremony*, 1971) Oshima realized that his political message was losing its impact. He made one more film, *Natsu no imoto* (*Dear Summer Sister*, 1972) and broke up his independent company. Since 1976 he has been making films in collaboration with foreign companies, and has moved away from a direct cinematic involvement with the actualities of modern Japan. In films such as *Ai no borei* (*Empire of Passion*, 1977), *Merry Christmas, Mr Lawrence* (*Senjo no Merry Christmas*, 1982), and *Max mon amour* (1986), any political involvement or challenge to avant-garde film-making has virtually disappeared. In contemporary Japan, Oshima has become extremely famous for his activities as a commentator and a television personality, a fame that has come to overshadow his cinematic achievements.

HIROSHI KOMATSU

SELECT FILMOGRAPHY

Ai to kibo no machi (1959); Nihon no yoru to kiri (Night and Fog in Japan) (1960); Etsuraku (1965); Hakuchu no torima (1966); Koshikei (Death by Hanging) (1968); Kaette kita yopparai (1968); Shinjuku dorobo nikki (Diary of a Shinjuku Thief) (1969); Tokyo senso sengo hiwa (The Man Who Left his Will on Film) (1970); Gishiki (The Ceremony) (1971); Natsu no imoto (Dear Summer Sister) (1972); Ai no corrida (In the Realm of the Senses) (1976); Ai no borei (Empire of Passion) (1977); Merry Christmas, Mr Lawrence, (1982); Max mon amour (Max my Love) (1986).

BIBLIOGRAPHY

Oshima, Nagisa (1992), *Cinema, Censorship, and the State*.

The Ceremony (*Gishiki*, 1971)

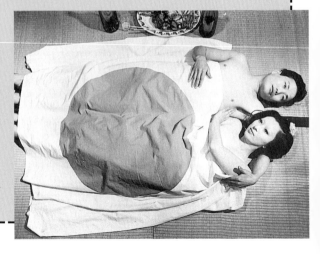

continued to increase to 1958, but thereafter gradually declined. The film companies tried to recapture audiences by producing films in colour and films featuring established stars. In 1957 the Toei production company shifted production practices to the manufacture of widescreen film, and the other major studios followed soon after. In 1962 Daiei produced the first Japanese 70 mm. film *Shaka* ('The life of the Buddha', directed by Kenji Misumi), which appealed to the audience's desire to see dramatic spectacle on a large screen.

Although the technology was new, there was a strong tradition of spectacles of this kind in Japanese cinema, and so there was a ready-made audience for these productions. For example, every summer the major companies released a ghost film, and in December, a new version of the dramatic story of the loyal forty-seven Ronin. Following the huge box-office success of *Gojira* ('Godzilla', Ishiro Honda) in 1954 Toho released many monster and science-fiction films every year. The production policies of big film producers exploited the custom for Japanese people to enjoy something individual and special in each season. From 1969 Shochiku produced the series *Otoko wa tsuraiyo* ('Tora-san', Yoji Yamada) for seasonal viewing. The policy of recycling a specific spectacle in a series of films had been a part of Japanese cinema since the silent years. These repeating spectacles had constituted an important part of Japanese film-making that co-existed with, but never crossed with, the creation of art cinema. The yearly repetition of a dramatic spectacle generally assured large box-office receipts. The plot of each film in a cycle was almost identical, but their popularity ensured that they were used as a last resort by the big companies to defend cinema audiences from erosion by television.

The monster film, the ghost film, and the Tora-san series were made specifically to be the spectacles of particular seasons. However, from the early 1960s when television audiences began to surpass those of the cinema, the five major companies each developed their own genre specialities. The *yakuza* (gangster) film genre from Toei, sold on the sensationalism of violence, is one of the most prominent examples. From the late 1960s and into the 1970s *yakuza* films were made continually. At Toho, monster films as well as wordy war films were made as seasonal spectacles, and for their regular programme Toho emphasized youth films and comedies. Shochiku also stressed the comedy, from which films like the Tora-san series were born. Nikkatsu and Daiei, however, could not penetrate such genre lines and their fortunes declined as a result.

SEX AND VIOLENCE

In 1971 Daiei went bankrupt and Nikkatsu took the dramatic step of turning to the production of soft-core pornography, called *roman poruno*. Sex films had been made

in Japan by independent companies since around 1963 under the name of *pink film*. At that time there had been some sex films which had drawn praise from mainstream critics, and the line between pornography and mainstream cinema was not rigid. For example, some of the sex films of Koji Wakamatsu had certain avant-garde elements and a political edge, and his work had been evaluated highly from early on. The works of Tetsuji Takechi were the most famous sex films before Nikkatsu launched the *roman poruno*. Takechi's films, unlike pink films, were released through mainstream companies and screened in ordinary theatres. Takechi's sex films *Hakujitsu mu* ('Daydream', 1964) and *Kokeimu* ('Scarlet daydream', 1964) are regarded as having artistic value, particularly in the use of hallucinatory sequences.

After November 1971 most films produced by Nikkatsu were sex films, resulting in the unique phenomenon of a major studio turning exclusively to the production of pornography. However, while the *roman poruno* was part of the sex film genre it was essentially narrative cinema with many sex scenes and different from the explicit pornography of the so-called *blue films*. In early *roman porunos*, directors like Tatsumi Kumashiro, Toru Murakawa, and Toshiya Fujita developed interesting films, and the genre soon became a place where young directors could learn the *mise-en-scène* of narrative film-making. Some of the directors who would later constitute the core of Japanese cinema learnt their craft from the *roman poruno*.

In the 1970s, with Daiei bankrupt, Nikkatsu making the *roman poruno*, and the three other major companies only manufacturing stereotyped genre films, there was little scope for the production of high-quality art cinema in Japan. Collaboration with the Arts Theatre Guild (ATG) provided the only opening for directors interested in this area. ATG had been founded with the aim of importing quality foreign films, both classic and modern, into Japan. In 1968 ATG began to produce films in collaboration with other independent companies. This provided a home for the directors of the New Wave who had been forced to leave the major companies, and ATG helped realize the further development of the work of Shohei Imamura, Nagisa Oshima, Masahiro Shinoda, and Yoshishige Yoshida. The company did not only help the New Wave directors of the 1960s, but also provided opportunities for younger film-makers like the television director Akio Jissoji, and the poet Shuji Terayama. However, the golden age of ATG did not last more than ten years, and by the late 1970s it was no longer the centre of creative Japanese cinema.

The degeneration of quality Japanese cinema became conspicuous in the late 1970s. In 1975 the yearly box-office profits of imported foreign films surpassed those of Japanese films. In this period the entrance fees at cinemas in Japan were the highest in the world and the numbers

Kazoku geemu ('Family Game', 1983), Yoshimitsu Morita's ironic dissection of the traditional family film genre

who would risk paying high prices to see Japanese films were steadily decreasing. Toei was still producing *yakuza* films and Nikkatsu was still making *roman poruno*, production policies which assumed (and ensured) that the primary audience was male. About half of the cinemas that showed Japanese films were never entered by women. Toei produced programmes for children as their seasonal spectacle in summer and winter, and so during the holidays the film theatres filled with children and their parents. This gave rise to the strange phenomenon of busy family seasons, sandwiched between times when films of sex and violence were shown to exclusively male audiences.

In the 1970s the major film companies seemed to have lost the ability to develop new talent for their products. This period did see the appearance of some talented directors like Kazuhiko Hasegawa and Mitsuo Yanagimachi, but these came from outside the major companies. In common with the New Wave of the 1960s, these young directors took violence as their point of departure. The depiction of violence seemed to open the way to new creative forms, sidestepping the stereotyped films of traditional of Japanese cinema. However, the shocking effectiveness of depictions of violence was lost by the 1980s.

In the late 1970s a new development added an edge to Japanese cinema. Young people in their teens and twenties began to make films with 8 mm. or 16 mm. cameras and exhibit them to general audiences. Among these amateur film-makers were some who would go on to give fresh power to the impoverished national cinema. The directors

Kazuki Omori, Nobuhiko Obayashi, and Sogo Ishii came from an amateur film-making background. Ishii's dynamic direction and his quasi-surrealistic stories had a character new to Japanese art cinema. The violent elements of his films are comical and it is in this that he can be distinguished from the other film-makers of the time who could not sever their links to the New Wave of the 1960s.

NEW DEVELOPMENTS

The significant Japanese films of the 1980s, however, were characterized by an absence of violence. Kohei Oguri adopted black and white and standard screen size for his début film *Doro no kawa* ('Muddy river', 1981), which was set in the 1950s. The nostalgia towards old film form resembled Kei Kumai's *Shinobu gawa* ('The long darkness', Toho, 1972). However, Oguri's method has more realism than Kumai's, and represents through poetic qualities the beautiful moments which Japanese people living in a modern society too often forget. Yoshimitsu Morita made a film using the traditional Japanese cinema theme of the family. In *Kazoku geemu* ('Family game', 1983) his ironic handling of the traditional family film genre and television drama showed that there are new possibilities to be found in the theme of the ordinary. The family film genre of Shochiku and the films of Yasujiro Ozu examined the attractiveness of images from daily life, a theme revived in the 1980s. Very subtle movements of the mind are seized in the description of daily life in *Taifu kurabu* ('The Typhoon Club', Shinzi Somai, 1985) and *Uhoho tankentai* ('An unstable family', Kichitaro Negishi, 1987). Com-

720

pared to these movies, Nagisa Oshima's *Merry Christmas, Mr Lawrence* (*Senjo no merii kurisumasu*, 1982), which depicted the realistic situation of men living by violence, seemed rather anachronistic.

In 1984 the actor Juzo Itami made his first film as a director, *Ososhiki* ('The funeral'). This film, based around an event frequently depicted in Japanese cinema, comically described people's behaviour at a funeral. Itami's starting-point lay in the concept of the manual. In modern Japanese society a manual is indispensable when embarking on anything new. If a new computer is bought the manual must be consulted first, and from Itami's ironic viewpoint, people cannot even conduct a funeral ceremony without the appropriate manual.

The popular comedian Takeshi Kitano made his début as the director of *Sono otoko kyobo ni tsuki* ('Beware the brutal man', 1989). From the late 1980s to the early 1990s, some TV stars and novelists made their own films as directors. Most of these films were amateurish and had no sense of film art, with the exception of the films of Takeshi Kitano.

Since the mid-1980s, many of the major companies' films had depended on *manga* (Japanese comics) as their story sources. By adapting the story of *manga* printed in weekly magazines, a certain measure of box-office profit is assured because of the already tremendous popularity of the story-line and characters. The power of *manga* is becoming nearly as influential as literature in Japanese cinema. However, there has yet to be a truly cinematic work based on a *manga* story.

Animated films have been made in Japan since the silent years. As early as the mid-1910s some excellent animated films were completed, including Noburo Ofuji's experimental series *Chiyogami Anime*. After the war Toei emphasized the production of feature-length animated films. Many animated films have been made for television in Japan, the majority for children. However, the situation changed in the 1980s, with feature-length animation for a broader audience being produced. One of the most important directors of this animation is Hayao Miyazaki, whose works, such as *Tonari no Totoro* ('Totoro, the neighbourhood ghost', 1988), constitute a definitive example of contemporary Japanese art.

Until the 1970s cinema was in close collaboration with television. All the major companies were making television films in parallel with their theatrical releases. In the 1980s the situation became more complicated on account of the diffusion of video. The film companies were the suppliers of films for television and the video market, but the more films the studios supply, the more the audiences are drawn away from the cinemas. Within a few months of its theatrical release, a film can be seen on the small screen, either on broadcast television or on videocassette. The videocassette extends the life and reputation of film classics, but the cheap rental fee of videos caused a decrease in the number of cinema patrons. The circulation of pornographic videos also struck a blow to the production of *roman poruno*. From the late 1980s Nikkatsu's box-office profits were diminishing each year, and in 1993 Nikkatsu, the oldest film company in Japan, went bankrupt.

In recent years several different genres have competed for popularity at the box-office. In the late 1980s, for example, films with animals in the leading roles enjoyed great success. Audiences also gathered to see the animation films of Hayao Miyazaki. Films that are made for a broad spectrum of the public, as well as films for children, are considered secure profitable subjects for the studios. It is true that some part of Japanese cinema has become infantile, but in order to attract audiences the film companies have been forced to produce such films. They made films using popular TV personalities to attract teenagers, the reverse of thirty years before, when people went to film theatres to see the actors who could not be seen on the television.

The condition of Japanese cinema in the 1990s is still unhealthy, with cinema attendances low. There is a danger that theatrical Japanese cinema may disappear altogether. The Tora-san series and animated films for families are still a guaranteed source of profit, but the situation has become so difficult that film can no longer be produced with the creative freedom enjoyed by directors of the New Wave.

Bibliography

Anderson, Joseph L., and Richie, Donald (1982), *The Japanese Film: Art and Industry*.
Desser, David (1988), *Eros Plus Massacre: An Introduction to the Japanese New Wave Cinema*.
Nolletti, Arthur, Jr., and Desser, David (eds.) (1992), *Reframing Japanese Cinema: Authorship, Genre and History*.
Sato, Tadao, *et al.* (eds.) (1986), *Koza Nihon Eiga*, vols. vi and vii.
Tanaka, Junichiro (1976), *Nihon Eiga Hattatsu Shi*, vols. iv and v.

New Australian Cinema

STEPHEN CROFTS

Since the 1970s Australian films have increasingly come to world attention. Critically acclaimed films such as *Picnic at Hanging Rock* (Peter Weir, 1975) and *My Brilliant Career* (Gillian Armstrong, 1979) have been followed by the major international successes of *Mad Max* (George Miller, 1979), *Crocodile Dundee* (Peter Faiman, 1986), and *Strictly Ballroom* (Baz Luhrmann, 1992). Then, in 1993, New Zealand-born Jane Campion became the first woman to win the Palme d'Or at Cannes, with the Franco-Australian production *The Piano* (1993), sharing the prize with Chen Kaige's *Farewell my Concubine* (1993). It is an impressive record for a country with a population of only 18 million, especially one whose feature film industry had been moribund throughout the 1960s.

THE 1960S

During the 1960s only fifteen features were made in Australia. Of these, eight were wholly or substantially financed and controlled by non-Australian interests. While there had been continuous documentary film-making throughout the post-1945 drought of features, cinema screens had long been dominated by Hollywood, and sporadically by British product. The 1960s' most significant films were the popular Italian immigrant–Australian girl love story of the UK co-production *They're a Weird Mob* (Michael Powell, 1966), and the self-consciously all-Australian *2000 Weeks* (Tim Burstall, 1969), heralding the feature renaissance.

The revival of Australian film in the 1970s was preceded by a quarter-century of such minimal production. There was another, more broadly historical legacy against which the resurrected feature production had to struggle. Australia's post-colonial history being dominional rather than post-revolutionary (like Canada's but unlike India's), the Australian cultural assertion embodied in the feature renaissance had to counter a long history of willing subservience to other countries' economic, political-strategic, and cultural interests.

1970–1975: THE AFDC PERIOD

In 1970, after years of lobbying by film cultural campaigners, notably commentators Tom Weir and Sylvia Lawson and film producer Antony Buckley, the Australian government made a move to establish infrastructural support for the feature film industry. The Prime Minister responsible, John Gorton, believed that the new Australian films could show the rest of the world that their country contained 'other things than avant-garde kangaroos or Ned Kellys'. However, this infrastructural support was provided in a form which highlighted the unequal balance of powers between Australian cultural nationalist drives and US/Hollywood interests. On the one hand, cultural nationalist assertion underpinned the 1970 establishment of agencies to fund production and training: the Australian Film Development Corporation (AFDC), the Experimental Film and Television Fund (EFTF), and the Australian Film and Television School (AFTS) handling film-production training. On the other hand, a certain cultural diffidence and failure of political will may be seen to underlie the key omission from that agenda, namely government intervention in the distribution sector dominated by Hollywood interests. Throughout the feature revival period, from 1970 to the present, Hollywood's box-office share has averaged about 80 per cent, higher than in almost all its other foreign markets, while Australian product has rarely exceeded 5 per cent, with some 70 per cent of films making a loss.

The principal funding agency of 1970–5 was the AFDC, which proclaimed a commercial and investor-oriented policy. In default of any feature film infrastructure, any regular production practices or generic traditions, or any pool of personnel or marketing expertise, its funding decisions were understandably hit-and-miss. The EFTF supported mostly short, experimental work such as cartoonist Bruce Petty's eighteen-minute *tour de force*, *Australian History* (1971), and Peter Weir's black comedy short *Homesdale* (1972). During this period the industry was enthusiastically amateurish, working with budgets below A$0.5m., with crew members often taking on multiple roles, and with relevant experience—if any—drawn only from television, documentary, or commercials.

Distributors were hostile to Australian product. Prior to *Alvin Purple* (Tim Burstall, 1973), feature producers routinely took their films direct to individual down-market city theatres, as the distributors, all dominated by American interests, preferred the proven track records and ready-made publicity packages of Hollywood imports. However, in 1973 the Tariff Board Report recommended 'legislative provision to adjust and regulate the ownership and control of cinemas', and although the recommendation was never implemented distributors and exhibitors felt threatened. Hence the 1973 Australia-wide release of *Alvin Purple*, and increasing subsequent investment in and support for Australian production by distributors. The lower-budget experimental sector, funded by the EFTF, fell way below the threshold of visibility in these calculations. The anomaly of government subsidy for producing films that went virtually unseen was often remarked upon, in this and subsequent phases of the revival, and in relation to features as well as to shorts.

Quite apart from the problems of distributors' reluctance to screen Australian product, the film-makers themselves had little clear conception of their audiences. The 1960s' avant-garde and documentary production and smattering of features afforded the revived feature industry few guidelines. The thirty features made in 1970–2 ranged wildly from student Godard *hommage* and experimental narratives to TV spin-off, social realism, and co-productions including *Ned Kelly* (Tony Richardson, 1970, starring Mick Jagger), *Walkabout* (Nicolas Roeg, 1971), and *Wake in Fright* (a.k.a. *Outback*, Ted Kotcheff, 1971). With such variable notions of style and address, it is little surprise that generic patterns did not emerge fully-fledged.

It was not until 1972 that the first genre began to emerge. *The Adventures of Barry McKenzie* (Bruce Beresford, 1972) confirmed the success of the cycle of 'ocker' comedies inaugurated by *Stork* (Tim Burstall, 1971), and became the film which decisively called attention to the rebirth of the feature film industry. The AFDC period was strongly characterized by this cycle of films. Drawing on theatrical traditions and TV comedy revues, the cultural phenomenon of the ocker celebrated male bibulous and sexual exploits, extolled the vulgar and the irreverent, was predominantly working-class and anti-intellectual, and insisted on the Australian vernacular as part of its cultural nationalist push against decades of servility to the British. *The Adventures of Barry McKenzie* is the *locus classicus*, with many of its colloquialisms devised by the co-script-writers, Barry Humphries and Bruce Beresford, *for* the film and *then* passing into the vernacular. The film simultaneously satirizes many British institutions and parodies Australian deference to the imperial centre with its 'shameless saga of a young Aussie in Pommieland ... shot in full-colour Chunderama' (Australian publicity for the film— 'chunder' being Australian slang for vomit).

The sexual dimensions of the 'ocker' comedy were boosted by the 1971 relaxation of the previously draconian censorship laws. New classifications opened up an adult market which Hollywood had not yet cornered, and, for a time, cult audiences had some clout. The ocker comedy appealed both as risqué titillation, and to the more middle-class permissive, libertarian counter-culture. Although decried by critics for their lack of clear moral stance or high-art seriousness, the ocker comedies tapped into culturally deep strains of humour, sexism, and a strident self-assertion sometimes undercut by self-deprecation. Their protagonists offered a range of forms of viewer attachment from empathic identifications to detached recognitions readily shading into disavowal. *Stork*, *The Adventures of Barry McKenzie*, *Alvin Purple*, and sequels proved that Australian films could be popular and profitable.

The soft-core sex feature, often documentary or quasi-sociological in style, was almost as popular at the box-office as the ocker comedy. Films such as *Number 96* (Peter Benardos, 1974), a spin-off from the lubricious television soap, and *Australia after Dark* (John Lamond, 1975) were very cheaply made, and highly profitable.

Tapping into less populist strains were several films exploring the underside of the ocker's brash openness and unthinking sexism. The most important of these were the co-production *Wake in Fright* (1971), which offered a trenchant critique of Australian masculinity through a story of a young schoolteacher trapped in an outback town, and the more experimental *Shirley Thompson versus the Aliens* (Jim Sharman, 1972) and *The Cars that Ate Paris* (Peter Weir, 1974). *Shirley* subverts the 'normality' of suburbia, while Weir's first feature locates its horror in the cannibalistic car culture of an outback town.

In the early 1970s there also emerged a group of films more closely resembling European art cinema. The strongest, *Between Wars* (Michael Thornhill, 1974), boldly essayed a range of issues from inter-war Australia—Fascism, psychoanalysis, cultural conservatism, and Australia's distance from the rest of the world—as seen through the disengaged consciousness of its protagonist.

The film which first achieved the success of a screening in Cannes's Director's Fortnight was the watershed *Sunday Too Far Away* (Ken Hannan, 1975). A period film using the 1955 shearers' strike as its backdrop, it rediscovered the Australian bush setting rarely seen in the cinema in the previous five years, as well as the male mateship central to the Australian bush myth. It had a narrative strength lacking in the episodic and pretextual plot-lines of the ocker comedies and sex features, and its virtually all-male dramatis personae and period setting anticipated many subsequent films.

While the 'Bazza' and 'Alvin' films re-established the Australian cinema's commercial viability, films such as *Between Wars*, *Shirley*, and *Cars* provided its cultural credentials. The profound critical disdain visited upon the ocker and sex films inaugurated a criticism/box-office split which obtained well into the 1990s. The manifest commercial success of the ocker and soft-core films and occasional biker film did not deflect widespread criticism of the AFDC's funding decisions. In fact, there was a certain embarrassment about the unflattering images of Australia generated by these commercial successes. This, combined with the cultural glow of overseas success and the criticisms of the AFDC, led to the establishment of the Australian Film Commission (AFC) to encourage a more culturally sensitive cinema.

1975–1980: THE AFC PERIOD

If *Sunday Too Far Away* was the watershed film which pointed the industry towards an art-film culture, it was

Picnic at Hanging Rock (1975) which clinched the official moves against the ocker comedies and sex features characterizing the AFDC period. For while soft-core films had continued box-office success, the period genre had the firm imprimatur of the new statutory body.

This was a phase of consolidation of the production industry, overseen and financed largely by the AFC. Although some distributors, notably the Greater Union Organization, did increase their investment in production, the distribution–exhibition sector of the industry continued to operate industrially, while the production sector continued to be artisanal. Yet regular patterns of funding, production, and distribution began to cohere. By the end of the 1970s, most features could rely on distribution by the majors, and many of the major creative personnel of the next decade emerged: amongst directors, Peter Weir, Gillian Armstrong, Fred Schepisi, Phil Noyce, George Miller, while the adaptable Bruce Beresford moved with ease from ocker comedies to period films. A marked overseas critical profile was achieved, and with it critical prestige at home. Budget sizes remained remarkably low by international standards—not least owing to enthusiastic cheap labour—averaging just over A$0.5m. through the period. Production rates, despite some fluctuations, gradually increased, peaking at twenty-one features in 1979.

Despite this success the AFC was caught in a dilemma which the AFDC had paradoxically avoided by supporting popular films. It had to discharge the dual responsibilities of nurturing an industry which was supposedly to be handed over eventually to the private sector, and simultaneously developing film as a form of cultural representation, as a way of showing the nation. The ocker option now discredited, the local variant on the quality art film, namely the period film instanced by *Picnic*, appeared to be the answer, especially given both the breathy rapture with which critics greeted it in 1975, and the fact that it recouped its costs within a year.

The period film, then, became the flagship genre of the second half of the 1970s. It constituted a reaction against the ocker comedy's relentless vulgarity, masculinism, and obsession with bodily functions, and frequently advanced strong, independent women and sidelined recessive, sensitive men. Often enjoying the cultural cachet of a literary source, these films blended the aesthetic protocols of European art film with those of British quality television drama, to project a polite gentility, a certain innocence, a middle-brow cultural worthiness, and a moral and political blandness. Character took precedence over action, and sensibility over issues of ethical choice. The narratives were largely episodic and inconclusive, often tracing tales of adolescent maturation. Camera movement and *mise-en-scène* languorously exposed Australian light, land, flora and fauna, and period costume and décor. Aestheticizing the uncanny desolation of the Australian landscape, often in the manner of the Heidelberg school of painting, the cinematography presented within Australia a sense of national cultural definition, of homeland.

As regards history, however, the period film was nostalgically unspecific. It relegated history to the aesthetic, to a meticulous *mise-en-scène* of costumes and antiques. Yet its historical settings were intriguingly fixated on the rebellious turn-of-the-century moment of Australia's nominal independence from Britain. In a phase of some political and moral uncertainty following the 1975 dismissal of the Whitlam government, the period film perhaps offered both escape from the present, and an assertion that white Australia had a history, a national past.

The period film faded quickly at the box-office, with many of its most prestigious productions failing to break even at home. But while the period film had lost its Australian audience, overseas markets, where its calculated innocence had marked appeal—a new 'national voice' on the world scene—sent back (much delayed) messages to produce more of the same. The period film was a thin seam to mine either aesthetically or in terms of clarifying any national identity, but it was one which the AFC was locked into by its conservative sense of commercial responsibility.

The finest justification for the etiolated life of the period film in this phase was *My Brilliant Career*, which did not appear until 1979. It stood as the most resonant of the period films, because of Gillian Armstrong's stylish direction and engagement with the subject, because of Judy Davis's performance in her first starring role, and because it tapped into contemporary strains of career feminism. It was itself the first Australian feature to have women in all major roles: Armstrong as director, Margaret Fink as producer, Eleanor Witcombe writing the script, and Davis. Other notable period films included *The Chant of Jimmie Blacksmith* (Fred Schepisi, 1978), whose violent black Australian anger broke open the confines of this respectably tame genre, but also did something of a disservice to Aboriginal representations in allowing readings of the 'mad black' variety.

By contrast to the period film, the historical film, which made a serious engagement with history, has been rare. Probably its finest instance is *Newsfront* (Phil Noyce, 1978). Scripted by Bob Ellis, it boldly links public and private by cross-cutting a social and political history of 1948–56, via newsreels, with the life of a newsreel cameraman. Len Maguire, avatar of left Labor Australian values, serves as an ethical touchstone in a period covering the sclerotic dominance of the Menzies Conservative government, its referendum to outlaw the Communist Party, and the country's seduction by American consumerist values and television. Where the period film cast its protagonists as

My Brilliant Career (1979): Judy Davis dreams of making a living by writing, in Gillian Armstrong's adaptation of the Miles Franklin novel

passive victims of history, *Newsfront* shows Len at least fighting its tide.

The second genre of this phase was the social realist film. A reaction against the studied elegance of the period film, it used urban, contemporary settings, centred on dispossessed characters—youth, women, migrants, addicts—and adopted an untidy, documentary style of framing quite the opposite of the period film's self-conscious lyricism. Though there had been forerunners, the genre consolidated with a certain urgency in the face of the period film. Important here were the fifty-minute films *Queensland* (John Ruane, 1976) and *Love Letters from Teralba Road* (Stephen Wallace, 1977), *The FJ Holden* (Michael Thornhill, 1977), and *Mouth to Mouth* (John Duigan, 1978). Made for only $129,000, Duigan's film detailed the developing relationships between four outcast teenagers eking out an existence in Melbourne, and stands as one of the best examples of Duigan's exceptional work with young actors.

Other generic groupings were much less firmly defined, and many of the period's most interesting films elude generic classification. *Backroads* (Phil Noyce, 1977) bracingly combined naturalistic vignettes of Aboriginal life with a road movie allegorizing black–white–foreigner and outback–coastal relationships in Australia. *The Night the Prowler* (Jim Sharman, 1978) follows up Shirley's struggle against the stifling norms of suburbia. In *Palm Beach* (1979), Albie Thoms, veteran avant-garde film-maker, presented a narratively inventive collage of four plot strands adding up to a subcultural essay on the northern beaches region of Sydney. This was a film which stretched the limited adventurousness of AFC funding.

Mad Max (1979) was arguably the most important film of this phase. Miller and producer Byron Kennedy were convinced—doubtless correctly—that the AFC would not fund this violent futuristic movie. In raising the money privately, and making such a successful film, they inspired those who wished to privatize the industry and had much influence on the subsequent development of Australian cinema. The film launched the career of that 1980s icon of male Australia, Mel Gibson. It also succeeded in connecting with strains of Australian masculinity which were compatible with action genres but with neither the period nor the social realist film.

1980–1988: THE '10BA' PERIOD

At the end of the 1970s, the failure of Australian films at the box-office, the disappearance of the period film, and the unexpected local and overseas success of the privately financed *Mad Max* combined to generate an atmosphere of change. Accountants Peat, Marwick and Mitchell were commissioned to report on the state of the production industry. One sentence summarizes that report: 'The AFC is in the money business, not the movie business.' Their proposals were accepted, and the AFC became a servicing organization, rather than an active agent in production. Stockbrokers now displaced cultural bureaucrats as principal arbiters of funding decisions, and an energetically commercialist ethos was introduced.

It was the tax incentives scheme called '10BA' after the relevant section of the Income Tax Assessment Act which gave its name to the period from 1980 until the 1988 establishment of the Film Finance Corporation. An instrument of privatization, the scheme replaced direct with indirect state funding, offering such generous tax concessions for investors that only a 10 per cent return was needed in order to break even, and money could follow

script with blithe unconcern for its quality. While the degrees of generosity of the tax breaks were progressively scaled down through the 1980s, the corollary financial and legal infrastructure became a fixed feature, especially for higher-budgeted productions: lawyers, financiers, executive producers with fees of up to $0.5m., brokerage fees, multiple insurances. Together with higher wages and a new blockbuster orientation, these contributed to a huge budget escalation: from an average of $599,000 per feature in 1980 to $2m. in 1982.

Given the small size of the domestic market, the escalating budgets and declining tax breaks of the 1980s obliged producers to seek overseas distribution guarantees and pre-sales. The key overseas market was the USA, which was not only thirteen times larger, but also anglophone. This resulted in medium-range US film or video distributors bargaining, and usually winning, on matters of casting, director, and plot changes, e.g. the casting of Meryl Streep in *Evil Angels* (also known as *A Cry in the Dark*, Fred Schepisi, 1988). The 10BA phase thus sharply focused the national versus international debates affecting many national cinemas operating in the shadow of Hollywood. The 10BA provisions on local content were in fact the same as those of the AFC and AFDC Acts, requiring of the films 'significant' Australian content and being made 'wholly or

War on the road: *Mad Max 2* (1981)

substantially' in Australia. The prime bulwark of cultural nationalism in these struggles was Actors' Equity, fighting for Australian actors, accents, mannerisms, and images.

The 10BA scheme unquestionably galvanized an atrophying industry. The inflow of private money more than quadrupled to $45m. in 10BA's first year, and led to sharply increased production rates: from averages of fifteen features per year in the 1970s to twenty-seven annually between 1981 and 1987.

The 10BA scheme underwrote a number of filmic successes, notably with the high-budget film, the financiers' preferred genre. The eight top-grossing Australian films in the home market as at 1988 were all big-budget spectaculars: *Crocodile Dundee* (1986), *Crocodile Dundee II* (1988), *The Man from Snowy River* (1982), *Gallipoli* (1981), *Mad Max II* (also known as *The Road Warrior*, 1981), *Phar Lap* (1983), *The Man from Snowy River II* (1988), and *Mad Max beyond Thunderdome* (1985). In that most important export market, the USA, the top eight Australian films were remarkably similar. Secured through distribution deals with US majors, these successes hugely increased US recognition of Australian cinema—previously virtually limited to the extended art-house successes of *My Brilliant Career* and *Breaker Morant* (Bruce Beresford, 1980)—and often had strong positive feedback effects in the local market. At the local box-office, all eight films cited above outstripped *all* the most popular Australian films of the preceding decade. The local successes reintroduced a popular Australian cinema not seen since the ocker and soft-core films, but reaching the broader demographic of 'the family'.

The prevailing image of Australia vouchsafed by these successful blockbusters drew on the bush myth. Aside from the losers of *Gallipoli* (Peter Weir, 1981), in which antipodean soldiers are sacrificed on the altar of the Empire, and of *Phar Lap*, the horse that is unstoppable until it goes to the USA, the *Crocodiles* and *Snowys* were Anglo-Celtic men of the outback who tame the intractable land and usually the heroine, and instance those stereotypically old Australian values of mateship (a club for white males) and larrikinism (cocking a snook at (colonial) authority), while the *Mad Maxes* posited a male narcissistic loner. That the settings remained non-urban testifies to the remarkable discursive tenacity of the bush myth in the world's second most urbanized nation—as well as to its overseas appeal. That heroes increasingly *succeeded* through this period may testify to a growing national confidence—or at least to film-makers being more prepared to invest in Hollywood assumptions. That only half of the eight films—and those are the most Hollywood-influenced—concluded in romantic coupledom may point to a continuing Australian resistance to that Oedipal aspect of Hollywood success stories.

A key factor in the success of five of the top eight—excluding, that is, *Gallipoli* and the *Mad Maxes*—was the television training of their directors, some of their producers, and star Paul Hogan. But while the populist touch appealed to audiences, television aesthetics rarely make for visually imaginative cinema. The early 1980s rise of 'quality' television, in the very significant form of the mini-series, and of television pre-sales for film enabled interpenetration between large and small screens of personnel, finance, and aesthetic forms on a markedly greater scale than previously.

The blockbuster policy, however, was not universally successful. *The Coolangatta Gold* (Igor Auzins, 1984), for instance, was a generic mishmash of youth, contest and running movie, domestic melodrama, rock musical, and love story; a film deploying genres as so many marketable components and targeting its audiences with the accuracy of a blunderbuss.

The financiers' second preferred form, the formula genre picture, was less successful than the blockbuster, both at the box-office and critically. It succeeded mainly in such non-theatrical markets as video and cable, which favour the formulaic modes encouraged by pre-selling. Vaguely targeted at both Australian and US markets, most of these films were culturally lost in the mid-Pacific, with either a complete erasure of Australian locale and culture, or a kitsch Australiana of theatrical-looking koalas and kookaburras. With American actors, and half-targeted at the US market, there were numerous plot-lines of Americans searching out lost relatives Down Under.

Aside from funding the blockbuster and formula genre piece, 10BA's lush liquidity enabled a diversification of aesthetic repertoires and genres of greater interest to the more culturally inclined in the industry. In the middle- and lower-budget ranges, it supported more modest, everyday, and culturally specific images than those of the formula genre pieces. And these lesser budgets often funded films as original and interesting as the first two *Mad Maxes*.

The social realist genre continued to serve as Australia's class—and increasingly, gender—conscience, at its best in the raw, street-wise *Hard Knocks* (Don McLennan, 1980) and the complex characterization of mother of three *Fran* (Glenda Hambly, 1985). The genre crossbred in the 1980s with other genres to produce three of the best films of the period: blending with the musical in the engagingly energetic *Starstruck* (Gillian Armstrong, 1982), with melodrama in *High Tide* (Gillian Armstrong, 1987), a richly metaphoric exploration of mother–daughter relationships, while *Shame* (Steve Jodrell, 1988) crossed social realism with the Western to produce a very powerful account of rape and the law in an outback town. Other films similarly 'Australianized' Hollywood genres, notably the first two *Mad Maxes* which inflected the road (movie) as site of murder.

Comedy was dominated by the genial, populist egalitarianism and knowingly self-deprecating humour of *Crocodile Dundee*, and by the humour of *Young Einstein*'s (Yahoo Serious, 1988) adolescent demographic. The comedy of this period generally divested itself of the ockerisms of the 1970s to embrace, for instance, a completely non-patronizing account of a gay doctor and a VD clinic in *The Clinic* (David Stevens, 1983), or the richly aesthetic black humour of *Man of Flowers* (Paul Cox, 1983), whose effete protagonist transforms a thoroughly obnoxious action painter into a statue in a park.

In the 1980s the period film briefly crossbred with the war film in *Breaker Morant* and *Gallipoli*, where two of the country's most competent directors touched a nationalist nerve by defining Australia positively against British pomposity, conniving, and incompetence. The period film later migrated to such mini-series as *Bodyline* (1984).

It was in the very low-budget feature and short film sectors, which rarely receive theatrical exhibition, that bolder issues and greater formal experimentation emerged. Supporting this vigorous independent sector in the 1980s were two divisions of the AFC, the Creative Development Branch (1978–90) and the Women's Film Fund (formalized in 1980, replaced by the Women's Program 1987), which between them helped fund some 600 films and videos. In the low-budget feature, the mix of documentary with fictional registers frequently foregrounded social/political issues, with varying degrees of experimentalism, from the docu-dramas of Bill Bennett's social issue films such as *A Street to Die* (1985), on Agent Orange, to *Traps*' (John Hughes, 1986) more demanding critique of mainstream politics. Elsewhere, this mix could de-dramatize narrative by disintegrating it into quotidian episodes, as in *With Love to the Person Next to Me* (1987), Brian McKenzie's existential meditation on lonely Melbourne lives.

Amongst short films in the independent sector in this period, women's films were the most consistently innovative. Two in particular make striking conceptual use of Brechtian techniques. *Serious Undertakings* (Helen Grace, 1983) urged a rewriting of Australian history and culture in terms of gender difference, and *Nice Coloured Girls* (Tracey Moffatt, 1987) a black, feminist reassessment of relations between Aboriginal women and white Australian men since white settlement.

Outside the 'official images department' of Film Australia, the documentary sector spent much of this period lobbying—eventually successfully—to have more of its films screened by the two state broadcasters, the Australian Broadcasting Corporation and the multi-cultural Special Broadcasting Service. The political compromises this would have entailed early in the 1980s were by the end of the decade less of a problem, as state television grew more pluralist, and class politics became less confrontational and its energy dispersed into other politics.

One effect of this mutual accommodation has been a remarkable auteurist consistency in the work of, say, Tom Zubrycki, best known in this phase for *Kemira: Diary of a Strike* (1984).

This curate's egg of a period produced many shady deals and shoddy films, but crucially it saw the consolidation of the revival of Australian film-making, its diversification, and its serious recognition locally and overseas. The period's blockbuster strategies also bequeathed Australian cinema one enormous benefit. Their assertiveness and success enabled subsequent films to think of themselves as films before thinking of themselves as Australian. The 1970s had seen films self-consciously carrying the burden of national self-definition, whether the ocker film's virulent anti-Britishness, or the period film's tasteful Europeanness. On the other hand, the formula genre picture had no such qualms, trying to outdo Hollywood at its own game and opting for an American-modelled transnational cultural limbo. The late 1980s saw the emergence of everyday, low-key Australian images that superseded the previous stultifying modes of populist ockerism and of European artiness. Films such as *Shame* and *High Tide* from this period are examples which, by linking Hollywood genres with local subjects, realistically acknowledge Australia's cultural hybridity.

SINCE 1989: THE FFC PERIOD

The rise of economic rationalism among Treasury bureaucrats in the mid-1980s sharpened awareness of 10BA's drain on tax revenue. Its replacement, the Film Finance Corporation (FFC), was set up in 1988 as a film bank with initial annual funding of $70m. to be gradually reduced in subsequent years, with the ideal scenario that it could eventually privatize itself out of any need for government subsidy. As part of its commercial, deal-driven policy, the FFC has required pre-sales of 35–50 per cent. As with 10BA, this has necessitated introducing some foreign actors, which has kept alive struggles between Actors' Equity and certain producers, notably over the casting of the American unknown Charlie Schlatter opposite Kylie Minogue in the Australian period-set *The Delinquents* (Chris Thomson, 1989). Probably in response to widespread criticism of its policy of sending scripts to Hollywood for vetting, the FFC set up an annual Film Fund. While its regular production budgets cost $5–13m., the Film Fund produced the fifteen films of its first four years at an average of $3.8m. each, with up to 85 per cent FFC funding, and guaranteed distribution from Australian companies specializing in overseas markets.

The AFC, meanwhile, has been 'slimmed down' to an annual budget hovering around $17m. It has functioned as development agency for film production, culture, and policy, as well as small-scale investment agency for work such as the world-famous *Proof* (Jocelyn Moorhouse, 1991).

Its funds are smaller than those of the old Creative Development and Women's Film Funds, but support larger proportions of fewer projects.

As in any national cinema, co-productions are the joker in the pack, confounding neat distinctions of the hermetic fictions of national identity. This may be all to the good in an era when cultural hybridity has more and more to be recognized as central to most people's lived experience. Economically, of course, co-productions broaden an audience without increasing the costs in proportion. As in the case of *Green Card*, they can reap a substantial profit which can be used to cross-subsidize other FFC films. Industrially, co-productions are displacing the often adversarial relationship obtaining between US interests and a prickly Australian nationalism defending jobs with formally co-operative international relationships. The USA, however, does still affect other countries' co-productions. For its ethnocentric domestic market is loath to view non-American locations and non-Hollywood actors, and that domestic market is popular enough to encourage, for instance, the New York location and casting of Andie MacDowell in *Green Card*, and the casting of Holly Hunter and Harvey Keitel in *The Piano*. Local cultural representations generally lose out to overseas stereotypes, as in the kangaroos conspicuously hopping in the foreground of the British co-production *No Worries*. On the other hand, a film like *Dingo* (Rolf de Heer, 1992) succeeds in neither denigrating nor romanticizing its outback, nor lionizing its Paris jazz settings.

Despite an apparent institutional entrenchment of discourses of art versus commerce, nationalist versus internationalist, low versus high budget with the separate establishment of AFC and FFC, there has in fact been a significant *rapprochement* between these formerly polarized discursive sets. This has been largely due to a weakened position of advocates of higher-budgeted films. State subsidy of films dropped by 50 per cent and the FFC Film Fund's lower funding tier gave respectability to films budgeted around $3m. With Hollywood's poaching of all the major name directors in Australia, the high-budget film has lost many of its most influential advocates. The majority of the expatriates have shown few signs of returning to Australia—Peter Weir, Bruce Beresford, Fred Schepisi, Phil Noyce, and George Miller—while others have divided loyalties: Gillian Armstrong, John Duigan, and George Miller 2. The blockbuster's last gasp was the failure of the FFC's two or three highest-budgeted aspirant blockbusters (each costing around $13m.): *Till there Was You* (John Seale, 1989) was unreleased; *Turtle Beach* (Stephen Wallace, 1992) a grave box-office failure; the $15m. *Reckless Kelly* (Yahoo Serious, 1993) gathered only a disappointing $5m. at the local box-office. The FFC's only high-budget box-office success has been *Green Card* (Peter Weir, 1991), a co-production directed by an expatriate name director, and

set overseas. The production slate has polarized into films budgeted at below $3.5m. for the domestic market, and above $6m. for the international market, but very few of the latter have been successful.

Meanwhile, the deregulatory atmosphere of the late 1980s and 1990s has encouraged the *rapprochement* between the cultural and commercial wings of the industry by uniting previously warring parties into pressuring government for continued funding and continued cultural protection measures. Film-makers have increasingly needed to seek funds from diverse sources—the AFC and FFC, subfederal support agencies such as Film Victoria, as well as pre-sales—and thus to be accountable to a broader range of interests than was usually the case under 10BA.

These factors have generated greater cohesion within the industry, and have contributed to making this arguably the most successful phase of the revival. So, too, has the exodus of major name directors to Hollywood, which has opened glorious opportunities to less experienced film-makers in Australia. Further, the virtual demise of the home-grown blockbuster has produced a degree of correlation between critical and box-office success missing since before the critical apoplexies that greeted the ocker comedy. Most notably, *Strictly Ballroom* not only won a Cannes prize, but also was the most profitable film exhibited in Australia (relative to its $3.5m. production budget) in the financial year 1992–3. *The Piano* (Jane Campion, 1993), in which the AFC invested development money, has become the first-ever art film in Australia to reach way beyond a traditional art-film audience, probably not just on account of its stars and its melodramatic force, but also because local chauvinism combined with the cachet of a top award at Cannes.

The FFC period's success can also be attributed to benefits accrued from twenty years of professional experience, and lessons learnt from 10BA. Compared with its fly-by-night quickies, many fine films of the subsequent era have been long in development: *Celia* (Ann Turner, 1989) for four years and *Proof* for six years, while *Phobia* (John Dingwall, 1990) went through sixteen rewrites. There has also been a stress on script development and on film-makers directing their own scripts, a policy which has paid off, most plainly with *Proof* and *The Piano*.

More broadly cultural factors have also contributed to the period's success, notably a growing cultural maturity, which has seen the country past *Crocodile Dundee*'s monocultural mix of Anglo-Celtic outback male and fantasies of marrying into the US media. This has been made possible by a deeper sense of historical understanding than the period film could ever allow. This was enabled by such widely seen mini-series as *The Dismissal* (1983) and *Vietnam* (1987), which dealt with two major recent historical traumas: the 1975 dismissal of Gough Whitlam's reformist Labor government by Queen Elizabeth II's representative in Australia, the Governor-General, and the nation's involvement fighting for the USA in Vietnam.

Other recent developments have urged the dominant national self towards reconciliation with its repressed female and black others. Feminist affirmative action policies have since the later 1980s achieved significant results in a previously strenuously male-dominated industry; the percentage of female directors in the feature industry rose from 6 per cent in 1985–6 to 23 per cent in 1990–1. A clear majority of this phase's strongest films have been directed by women: *Celia*'s beguiling historical fable about Cold War repressions, *Sweetie*'s (1989, Jane Campion) quirkily arty inversion of the domestic melodrama, the engaging teenage romantic/caper comedy of *The Big Steal* (Nadia Tass, 1990), *Proof*, with its fascinating hypothesis of a blind man who takes photographs and its (unconscious/ambivalent?) endorsement of male bonding, *Waiting*'s (Jackie McKimmie, 1991) witty comedy of manners, the mid-life crisis meditation of *The Last Days of Chez Nous* (Gillian Armstrong, 1992), and, arguably, the feminist melodrama of *The Piano*—which, with its Australian production base and crew, has been routinely claimed as Australian despite its French production finance, New Zealand-born director and lead, two American leads, and New Zealand settings. Comparably strong male-directed films have been the polished social realist *Return Home* (Ray Argall, 1990), *Phobia* (John Dingwall, 1990), a two-hander of Strindbergian intensity on the psychodynamics of co-dependency, *Flirting* (John Duigan, 1991), with its sophisticated treatment of a 1960s adolescence in a rural Australia isolated from world politics, *Strictly Ballroom*, one of the greater feelgood films, and *Romper Stomper* (Geoffrey Wright, 1992), the controversially violent social realist vision of a racist inner-city Melbourne.

As regards Aborigines, the best outcome of the chauvinist jamboree of 1988's Bicentennial (of white settlement) of Australia has been that it catalysed black resistance enough to advance Aboriginal land rights and black–white reconciliation. Aboriginal film-makers are now making significant inroads into feature film production. Building on the lead of such shorts as *My Survival as an Aboriginal* (Essie Coffey, 1979) and *Nice Coloured Girls* (Tracey Moffatt, 1987), 1993 has seen two black-directed features, *Black River* (Kevin Lucas, 1993), a bold adaptation of an Aboriginal opera, and *Bedevil* (Tracey Moffatt, 1993), a startlingly studio-set adaptation of three ghost stories, as well as the gutsy social realist, white-directed *Blackfellas* (James Ricketson, 1993).

In terms of ethnicities other than Aboriginal, this period appears to be marking a belated shift away from the Anglo-Celtic norm, a broader acceptance of the non-English-speaking background populations which form a very substantial proportion of the Australian people.

There had earlier been sporadic films representing ethnic experience from the inside such as *Promised Woman* (Tom Cowan, 1975) and *Silver City* (Sophia Turkiewicz, 1984). The present phase, though, sees ethnic awareness moving from the margins into the mainstream, and also away from an assimilationist towards a pluralist multi-cultural ethic. The Spanishness of *Strictly Ballroom* may be token tango stuff, but it *is* there, and serious social detailing is a rare commodity in this fairy-tale. Multi-cultural classrooms including Greeks, Italians, Vietnamese, and Cambodians are becoming familiar, as in *The Heartbreak Kid* (Michael Jenkins, 1993) and its TV spin-off *Heartbreak High*. *Romper Stomper*, meanwhile, is as agnostic on its Vietnamese gang as it is on its violence. Set in the 1950s, *Aya* (Solrun Hoaas, 1991) positively presents a Japanese war bride's view of Australia, whereas *Blood Oath* (Stephen Wallace, 1990), in exposing Japanese war crimes against Australians, finds it hard to be non-partisan.

In conclusion, the FFC period has achieved very creditable success, even if the name of the period is a misnomer given that the FFC has invested substantially in only three profitable films (*Strictly Ballroom*, *Green Card*, and *The Big Steal*) and has no policy for its investment beyond the insistently commercial. The Cannes awards, the local and overseas box-office triumphs, the openness of the industry to first-time directors, the withering away of the formula genre piece—all are cause for optimism, but the questions must be asked: How far are these developments structural rather than historically fortuitous? How much can policy, in a follower economy like Australia's, influence their future? Whereas the escalating Cannes successes of *Proof*, *Strictly Ballroom*, and *The Piano* in the last three years—with their subsequent box-office successes—point to a solid success story, Australia, with or without Jane Campion, could soon cease to be flavour of the month in the fickle world of international cinema, while at the local box-office Australian films' takings during 1988–91 fluctuated wildly between 23.8 per cent in 1988, with *Crocodile Dundee II* taking $36.6m., and 2.6 per cent in 1990, when the highest-rating Australian film, *The Big Steal*, took only $2.4m. The vast majority of the rest of the box-office takings went to Hollywood films. The question of the future may be formulated as: How many *Strictly Ballrooms* and *Pianos* can Australia produce?

Bibliography

Crofts, Stephen (1993), *Identification, Gender and Genre in Film: The Case of Shame*.

—— (1995), *Australian Cinema as National Cinema*.

Dermody, Susan, and Jacka, Elizabeth (1987), *The Screening of Australia: Anatomy of a Film Industry*.

—— (1988a), *The Screening of Australia: Anatomy of a National Cinema*.

—— (1988b), *The Imaginary Industry: Australian Film in the Eighties*.

Moran, Albert, and O'Regan, Jon (eds.) (1989), *The Australian Screen*.

New Zealand Cinema

BILL ROUTT

New Zealand cinema has never established a strong production base, but nevertheless has produced several distinguished film-makers who have had an important impact on world film culture. These range from Len Lye, who developed innovative animation practices in the 1930s, to Jane Campion.

Early feature film production in New Zealand was sporadic at best. From 1940 to 1970, for example, only three New Zealand features were made, all by John O'Shea, whose Pacific Films survived into the boom to come Interest, and production, picked up in the 1970s perhaps spurred on by the 'film renaissance' in Australia at the time. A film commission began operation in 1977 and tax incentives were introduced to stimulate production. The result was better than anyone would have predicted: features of exceptional quality from Roger Donaldson, Geoff Murphy, Vincent Ward, and others.

The original tax incentives were wound up in 1984, and production faltered but did not entirely cease. Latterly, the internationally prominent work of Ward and Jane Campion has been produced in a context which also supports a strong middlebrow liberal cinema in the work of Ian Mune, Sam Pillsbury, and Barry Barclay, the gore-comedies of Peter Jackson and a kind of poverty-row art film perhaps most easily recognized currently in Alison MacLean's *Crush* (1993). By the end of 1994, New Zealand had made a strong international impression with Jackson's fourth feature, *Heavenly Creatures*, and Lee Tamahori's first, *Once Were Warriors*.

If Jane Campion is currently the best-known New Zealand film-maker in the world, Ian Mune is the most important historically. Mune has acted, written, and directed with some distinction since 1977, but his actual significance lies in his tireless championing of film production in and of New Zealand, through which he has set himself the heart of the contemporary industry.

The future of a small industry is difficult to predict because so much depends on so few films. New Zealand's recent record of critical and box office success has thus been unexpected, but it is possible that exception rules this country's film industry.

Bibliography
Reid, Nicholas (1986), *A Decade of New Zealand Film: Sleeping Dogs to Came a Hot Friday*.
Sowry, Clive (1984), *Film Making in New Zealand*.

Canadian Cinema/Cinéma Canadien

JILL MCGREAL

Like the United States, the Canadian nation was formed by the dispossession of an original native population by successive waves of immigration from the sixteenth and seventeenth centuries onwards. But unlike its southern neighbour, Canada never successfully rebelled against colonial tutelage; nor (at least until recently) has it been a melting-pot of various ethnicities. It is principally composed of two distinct and erstwhile warring national elements—the French and the English—and the international conflicts of the past remain in the form of a bitter, internal division between the separatist-minded Quebec and the traditional, loyalist-minded rest of Canada. The repatriation of the Canadian Constitution, finally achieved in 1982, brought definitive independence from Britain but left Canada overshadowed by the neighbouring United States in a relationship described by Canada's former Prime Minister Pierre Trudeau as 'like sleeping next to an elephant'.

THE NATIONAL FILM BOARD AND THE DOCUMENTARY Within the Canadian context culture was wielded as a tool rather than a weapon, as exemplified in the mandate of the National Film Board of Canada (NFB) which was created in 1939 'to interpret Canada to Canadians and the rest of the world'. The NFB has been an unqualified success story. Set up after the virtual collapse of the Canadian film industry, wiped out by the powerful, vertically integrated, Hollywood machine, the NFB was the result of an inspired piece of federal legislation. Recognizing the impracticality of competing directly with Hollywood, the architects of the NFB instead created a national institution within which Canadians were able to develop a parallel and alternative film culture. Equally inspired was the first choice of Film Commissioner, John Grierson, whose work at the GPO and Crown Film Units in Britain in the 1930s had already established both him and the emerging documentary form as a new force in world cinema.

The first NFB Oscar came in 1941 for *Churchill's Island*. Part of a series of propaganda films, it was distinguished by the imaginative use of captured enemy footage and the genuinely uplifting sentiments conveyed by the first of many Lorne Greene voice-overs. Grierson's great energies and his capacity for mobilizing the talents of others had already begun to show. One of the young film-makers who had arrived in the early 1940s to join Grierson was fellow Scot Norman McLaren. McLaren's experiments in cameraless, frameless animation, in which he applied the technique of painting or scratching directly on to film, resulted in animation classics like *Hen Hop* (1942) and *Begone Dull Care* (1949). Later, McLaren pioneered his new pixillation technique (object animation) and in 1952 won an Oscar for his pacifist film *Neighbors*.

The early successes of the documentary and animation studios secured the NFB's future in terms of its film aesthetic and its continued funding. During the 1950s and 1960s the studios continued to flourish, developing the original Griersonian conception of film as a social document to include lyrical forms of documentary like Colin Low's *Corral* (1954) and *Pas de deux* (1967), McLaren's romantic experimentation with dance using the optical printer. The introduction of lightweight cameras and sound equipment in the early 1960s, together with the influence of television, saw the beginning of the direct cinema movement. Unit B, the documentary studio headed by Tom Daly, responded vigorously to the technological revolution with *The Candid Eye* film series. Intimate portraits using direct sound replaced the standard-issue information film with voice-over. Films from this period include *Lonely Boy* (1961), the acclaimed study of the pop star Paul Anka by Wolf Koenig and Roman Kroitor, and Terence Macartney-Filgate's *The Back-Breaking Leaf* (1959) about the working lives of the Ontario tobacco planters.

Also within the NFB, but working much more closely within the Griersonian tradition, was Donald Brittain. His first two films, *Fields of Sacrifice* (1963) and *Memorandum* (1965), tackled subjects that no other director at the NFB wanted to touch—Canadian war graves abroad and the Holocaust—and ended up as films that every director wished he or she had made. Brittain's genius was his ability to transform the standard NFB documentary into a work of spiritual consequence. His subject-matter thereafter was mainly biographical—well-known Canadian figures with legendary or heroic status whose inner characters Brittain's films aimed to reveal. At the same time, outside the NFB Allan King was making his own controversial documents on subjects shunned by other film-makers. In *Warrendale* (1967), which shared the Critic's Prize at Cannes, King explores the 'holding' therapy

Zac Wallace as the rebel warrior seeking revenge for the destruction of his community in *Utu* (Geoff Murphy, 1982)

being practised in a home for emotionally disturbed children in Toronto. As in many King films it is the intrusion of the camera as well as the subject-matter which is controversial. The result is both a film and a text for discussion.

The NFB moved its headquarters from Ottawa to its present premises in Montreal in 1952 but it was not until the late 1950s that the Québécois began agitating to improve their position in the organization. The lower rates of pay and lack of representation at senior levels suffered by the Québécois at the NFB mirrored the discrimination which had been endemic in Canada through much of its history. A further cause of discontent among the Québécois film-makers was the lack of representation of their own culture in the films themselves. The appointment of a Québécois Film Commissioner in 1957 and the victory of the Liberal party led by René Lévesque in the Province of Quebec in 1960, with its slogan of 'révolution tranquille', changed the old patterns. By 1962 there was a separate but parallel French studio within which film-makers like Michel Brault, Gilles Groulx, and Pierre Perrault were working.

The technological advances that had made direct cinema possible were now used to celebrate Quebec and its 'distinctness'. Despite opposition, Groulx's film *Les Raquetteurs* was released and became a manifesto for other Québécois film-makers. The film was shot at the annual congress of the raquetteurs (snowshoes) clubs in 1958, Michel Brault's camera itself a participant among the street celebrations and competitions. The principles of direct cinema—the roving camera, the refusal to enhance or idealize the subjects, the lack of commentary, the rejection of touristic or picturesque imagery, and the ideological rapport of the film-maker with his or her subjects—constituted a directly political approach to film-making which the Québécois came to regard as their own invention. Of the many films subsequently made at the NFB in this way none stands out more than Pierre Perrault's *Pour la suite du monde* (1963), in which Perrault, with cameraman Michel Brault, recorded the annual beluga fishing tradition on the Île-aux-Coudres. Perrault's 'cinéma de parole' was a development away from the cinema of simple observation to more immediate participation with the subjects and an emphasis on the importance of tradition as an expression of the collective life and will of a people.

The NFB has occupied a pivotal place in the history and development of Canadian film and television as a training ground for media personnel. Many senior film administrators and producers and many of Canada's leading film-makers began their careers at the NFB. Indirectly the UK benefited too: Sydney Newman, the doyen of British television in the 1960s, and several generations of animators have followed Richard Williams (*Who Framed Roger*

733

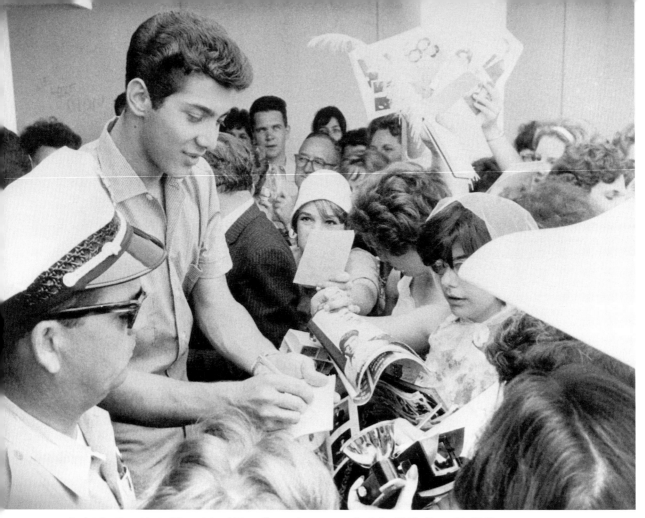

Paul Anka, the subject of the acclaimed Direct Cinema documentary *Lonely Boy* (1961), directed by Wolf Koenig and Roman Kroitor, and funded by the National Film Board

Rabbit, 1988) and George Dunning (*Yellow Submarine*, 1968) to the UK, many of them NFB trained. More importantly, however, the NFB has left its mark on the aesthetic of film-making in Canada, one which, interpreted broadly, has produced a recognizable national cinema.

FEATURE FILM-MAKING

In the 1920s Ernie Shipman operated a successful studio at Trenton making silent pictures often centring on the Canadian landscape and climate. However, his star players gradually began to leave for Hollywood. Mary Pickford, Fay Wray, Walter Pidgeon, and Norma Shearer set the pattern of southwards emigration for the future. (Jessica Tandy, Donald Sutherland, Geneviève Bujold, Dan Aykroyd, Michael J. Fox, Rick Moranis, John Candy, Norman Jewison, Ivan Reitman, and James Cameron would all follow them in time.) By the introduction of the talkies the Canadian motion picture industry had more or less collapsed. However, the early 1930s saw a fight-back against US penetration into the Canadian distribution and exhibition sector, led by an investigation of the practices of the Famous Players Corporation under the aegis of the Combines Investigation Act. But Famous Players were exonerated from the charge of pursuing practices detrimental to the public interest, and the motives for the investigation itself were unclear—was it culture or commerce that was being protected? In truth, the case failed because the business practices which it investigated were perfectly legal, merely the result of aggressive entrepreneurial strategies. The underlying problem, however, was not simply the aggressive distribution practices of the US companies, but the lack of Canadian films of either commercial or cultural value to compete in the market.

On the one hand Canada became a branch plant of the American film industry and on the other it was exploited by the British as a compliant host for the notorious 'Quota quickies'. Of the thirteen feature films known to have been made in Canada in the 1930s no prints remain. During the 1940s and 1950s a few features were made independently in Quebec but it was not until the 1960s that feature films returned significantly to the film-making agenda.

734

Don Haldane made *The Drylanders* at the NFB in 1963. Based on experiences of drought and depression among the farming community on the Canadian Prairies during the 1920s and 1930s, *Drylanders* faithfully and rather mechanically followed NFB documentary precepts. The result is a downbeat realism without the freshness of the realist cinema then being produced in the UK. But other features followed. Don Owen's *Nobody Waved Goodbye* (1964), shot from a thirty-page shooting script on light-weight cameras, dealt in an improvised and spontaneous way with teenage disaffections. Less ponderous, and with more attitude than anything that had gone before, *Nobody Waved Goodbye* was a success in New York, a breakthrough for Canadian theatrical releases. In the French studio, influenced by the French Nouvelle Vague, Gilles Groulx made *Le Chat dans le sac* (1964). More sophisticated than Owen's film in its attempts to confront issues of national identity and personal freedom, it was hailed instantly as a cultural landmark for Québécois cinema. Gilles Carle's first feature, *La Vie heureuse de Léopold Z*, was begun as a documentary short about snow-clearing during the Montreal winter and became a feature by default. Carle's feature film-making career progressed throughout the 1970s, with much of his work, including *La Mort d'un bûcheron* (1972) and *L'Ange et la Femme* (1977), featuring the actress Carole Laure through whose sensual beauty Carle developed his imaginative style of film-making.

QUEBEC

In the 1970s Sydney Newman returned to Canada from the BBC to become Film Commissioner. Newman was the last non-French-speaking Commissioner to be appointed at the NFB and his tenure there coincided with a new militant phase of Quebec nationalism. During the late 1960s the political situation in Quebec, inflamed by De Gaulle's famous 'Vive le Québec Libre' speech of 1967, had become volatile. The Parti québécois (PQ), led by erstwhile liberal René Lévesque, was formed in 1968 and the Front de libération du Québec (FLQ) had stepped up their campaign of demonstrations and minor skirmishes. The situation became more serious when, in 1970, the FLQ kidnapped a British commercial attaché and a Quebec minister. The minister was killed and the October Crisis began with Federal Government troops on the streets and the War Measures Act invoked. The political mishandling of this crisis by the ruling Liberal party in Quebec involved hundreds of arrests and the suspension of basic human rights, paving the way for the PQ victory in 1976.

These were golden years at the NFB for Quebec cinema. The films reflected, celebrated, documented, and dramatized the lives of the people. Michel Brault's *Les Ordres* (1974), which shared the director's prize at Cannes in 1975, stated the 'indépendentiste' case in its fictionalized account of five October Crisis arrests. Denys Arcand's *On est au coton* (1970, released 1976), a documentary film about the employment conditions of Quebec textile workers, provoked a scandalized reaction from the NFB administration, who banned it on the grounds of inaccuracy. Undeterred, Arcand went on to make the political feature *Réjeanne Padovani* (1973), in which he explored the corrupt world of the Quebec power élite. Jean Pierre Lefebvre was mid-career with his slow-paced, minimalist dramas: *Les Dernières Fiançailles* (1973), about the life of an elderly couple, and *L'Amour blessé* (1975), about a battered wife, both resist what Lefebvre has called the 'cultural mercantilism' and the 'industrialized production' of the private sector. But perhaps the most affectionately remembered film from these years is Claude Jutra's second feature *Mon oncle Antoine* (1971), a funny, nostalgic rites-of-passage film set in small-town, priest-ridden, 1950s Quebec during a typically snowy Christmas. Jutra's exploration of local colour made *Mon oncle Antoine* a success in Quebec and internationally, proving that the best national cinema can address both audiences simultaneously.

CFDC AND TELEFILM CANADA

In 1968, after many years of deliberation, the Federal Government set up the Canadian Film Development Corporation (CFDC), the function of which was to stimulate production in the private sector by investing public money in feature film projects. The legislation created a mini-goldrush, with non-Canadian companies, especially from the States, exploiting every legal loophole to claim the Canadian taxpayer's money. With the addition of the 100 per cent Capital Cost Allowance in 1974 and the new craze for making co-productions, the tax shelter years, as they came to be known, were born. Few films stand out from the indifferent mass but some of the later co-productions with France did well at the box-office including Jean-Jacques Annaud's dawn-of-man epic *Quest for Fire* (1981) and Louis Malle's *Atlantic City U.S.A.* (1980), in which Burt Lancaster plays an ageing petty crook rediscovering his self-respect. The one British co-production, Stuart Cooper's *The Disappearance* (1977), a confusing thriller with Donald Sutherland, is best forgotten. Two teen movies, Bob Clark's *Porky's* (1981) and Ivan Reitman's *Meatballs* (1979) with Bill Murray, became the top grossing Canadian movies of all time but were spurned as unworthy by critics in Canada. For director Ted Kotcheff the CFCD enabled him to return to Canada from a successful directing career in the UK to make *The Apprenticeship of Duddy Kravitz* (1974). But Kotcheff was only passing through on his way to the States where he subsequently made the first and best of the Rambo series, *First Blood*, in 1982.

However, the tax shelter years trained up a generation of private sector producers and crews in Canada and from the confusion emerged one great film-maker: David Cronenberg. His student shorts and early films already

David Cronenberg

(1943–)

David Cronenberg, a writer-director of some popular and cult following, emerged from Canadian state-subsidized cinema and the horror genre in the 1970s. He established a loose relationship with Hollywood which has allowed his eccentric and powerful films to acquire a significant reputation in the USA and world-wide.

Growing up in Toronto in a liberal Jewish but non-religious home, David Cronenberg's childhood was filled with books and music: his mother was a musician, and his father a journalist and avid book collector. As a child Cronenberg immersed himself in science fiction and horror comics. At the University of Toronto he switched majors from biochemistry to English, and his films provide an odd synthesis of these early scientific and literary concerns.

His early films *Stereo* (1969) and *Crimes of the Future* (1970) were underground hybrids of art film and science fiction. His affinity for the horror genre, however, together with the genre's popularity during the 1970s and 1980s, allowed Cronenberg, who might otherwise have remained in the avant-garde, to enter the mainstream. His first films to receive larger distribution in Canada—*Shivers / They Came from Within* (1975), *Rabid* (1977), and *The Brood* (1979)—were funded by the National Film Board of Canada. These films form a unified triptych in which Cronenberg creates metaphorical mutations of the human body which disrupt the individual's self-control as they successively threaten to disrupt society as well.

The suitability of the government funding for such horror films became the subject of parliamentary debate in Canada, but thanks to their success Cronenberg was able to move into purely commercial cinema. *Scanners* (1980) confirmed this shift, proving such a large-scale success that Cronenberg was able to receive his largest budget to date and secure distribution by Universal for his next film. *Videodrome* (1982) was a disturbing fantasy of televised violence and of the penetration of the medium into the human body as a means of political control. Although the film was not hugely popular, it secured Cronenberg's entrée into US film production. Ever since, he has been able to maintain the same loose rapport with Hollywood, securing distribution via a major company while continuing to film in Canada—a relationship Cronenberg has characterized as a dangerous 'deal with the devil'. He directed *Dead Zone* (1983) for Dino De Laurentiis, whose chronic insolvency almost scuttled the film, which was then rescued by 20th Century–Fox. His remake of *The Fly* (1986), about the technologically induced mutation of a scientist's body, was produced by Mel Brooks's company and distributed by Fox.

Subsequently Cronenberg shifted away from the horror genre proper, although his films retained their hallucinatory and horrifying atmosphere. *Dead Ringers* (1986) was based on the true story of the psychological disinte-

A scene from *Naked Lunch* (1992), David Cronenberg's extraordinary realization of the nightmare world of William Burroughs

gration of identical twin gynaecologists. Already heavily indebted to writer William S. Burroughs and his reflections on drugs, science, and mind control, Cronenberg adapted Burroughs's most famous novel to make *Naked Lunch* (1992). *M. Butterfly* (1993) is the adaptation of a successful play based on historical characters. In all these films, Cronenberg has continued to develop his favoured theme, the limits and definition of the human, as his heroes drift on isolated and gruelling voyages beyond the boundaries of the normal. He has continually explored cinematic technology in its potential to create unsettling and unreal effects in the consciousness of the viewer.

Critical reaction to his films continues to be violently divided. While Cronenberg, as well as many critics, sees his films as tragic and quasi-Shakespearian, other writers, such as Robin Wood, have seen in Cronenberg a revulsion for the body and for sexuality which they take to be politically reactionary. Perhaps this response stems from the fact that Cronenberg's films cannot be reconciled with a politics of liberation, sexual or otherwise. What is 'liberated' in Cronenberg's films is never simply benign, but is a play of forces at once personal and social, psychic and technological, in a society increasingly mechanized, rationalized, and yet deranged.

EDWARD R. O'NEILL

SELECT FILMOGRAPHY

Crimes of the Future (1970); Shivers / They Came from within (1975); Rabid (1977); The Brood (1979); Scanners (1980); Videodrome (1982); Dead Ringers (1986); The Fly (1986); Naked Lunch (1992); M. Butterfly (1993)

BIBLIOGRAPHY

Cronenberg, David (1992), *Cronenberg on Cronenberg*.
Handling, Piers (ed.) (1983), *The Shape of Rage: The Films of David Cronenberg*.

showed signs of the visceral universe to come. He made *Stereo* (1969) with a writing grant from the Canada Council but *Crimes of the Future* was made with an investment of $15,000 from the CFDC. Cronenberg's real début was *Shivers* (1975, also known as *The Parasite Murders*), produced by Ivan Reitman *et al.* and funded by the CFDC. The CFDC were repelled and disgusted by the script of *Shivers*; they had to be dragged 'kicking and screaming' into the investment and were vilified for so doing when the film was released. *Shivers* figures in a list compiled by Canadian critic Martin Knelman of the worst films made by the CFDC and was reviled across the board by opinion leaders in the Canadian film community. But *Shivers*, ostensibly a story about infestation in a Montreal apartment block, was distributed in forty countries and made $5 million, a massive profit on the original investment of $180,000 and the biggest financial success for the CFDC since it started trading. With the release of *Rabid* (1977) the imagery and the content of Cronenberg's films were provoking critical acclaim rather than small-town moralizing and his fan club was building, especially in France and the UK. The CFDC participated in the production of all his subsequent Canadian-made movies, including *The Brood* (1979), *Scanners* (1980), and *Videodrome* (1982).

In the early 1980s the Federal Government strengthened their commitment to the film industry by setting up Telefilm Canada with tighter controls on Canadian content and significantly more funds to invest. This time the protectionist policies were directed specifically at television. In the multi-channel broadcast environment in which a 20 per cent audience share (above 5 million viewers) constituted top ratings, revenue from advertising was insufficient for investment in Canadian programmes. One Canadian television drama might cost as much as the acquisition of several hours of similar American programming. If broadcast franchises were to be awarded on the basis of Canadian content then there had to be sufficient Canadian programming being made in the first place. So Telefilm Canada administered the Broadcast Fund which could be accessed by a producer with a broadcaster's letter of intent for his or her show. The Broadcast Fund facilitated production across all programming strands with a 49 per cent investment capacity.

During the transition from the former CFDC to Telefilm Canada Phillip Borsos made *The Grey Fox* starring Richard Farnsworth and Canadian actress Jackie Burroughs. The modest international success of Borsos's ballad-like drama about an ageing gentleman cowboy in turn-of-the-century Canada invigorated the industry at all levels. In the following years several movies were internationally released. Canadian director Daniel Petrie returned to Canada to make his rites-of-passage movie *The Bay Boy* (1984), which launched the young Kiefer Sutherland into his brat pack career in the States. In 1985 Sandy Wilson, working on the west coast, made her début feature *My American Cousin*, another rites-of-passage movie but one which turned the genre on its head by casting a cross little girl in the lead role instead of a gloomy, troubled boy. In 1985 John Paisz made *Crime Wave*, a low-budget Canadian Prairies version of punk culture, and Leon Marr made *Dancing in the Dark*, which was released in the UK to a blistering review by Derek Malcolm who later, in his *Guardian* column, publicly recanted and elevated it to his top ten films list for 1985.

In the mid-1980s Telefilm Canada's mandate was extended to feature films and the Film Fund was set up with producers' access coming through a distribution advance rather than a broadcast commission. The year 1986 saw the release of the three most significant Canadian films of this period: Patricia Rozema's *I've Heard the Mermaids Singing*, Denys Arcand's *The Decline of the American Empire*, and Atom Egoyan's *Family Viewing*. Rozema's film, which won the Prix de la Jeunesse at Cannes, is a whimsical exploration of lesbian love featuring Sheila McCarthy as Polly the wannabe photographer whose fantasies are shot in grainy black and white. Rozema has struggled to find the same form in subsequent movies. *White Room* (1990), also featuring Sheila McCarthy, was a disappointment despite the strong Canadian cast. McCarthy too wandered off course, appearing in *Die Hard 2* in an undemanding supporting role.

In contrast Arcand and Egoyan have consolidated their success: Arcand's *Jesus of Montreal*, a risky mix of theatre and religion, was given a standing ovation at the London Film Festival in 1989 and its star, Lothaire Bluteau, has since been fêted internationally for his stage performances. Egoyan's prolific output, including *Speaking Parts* (1989), *The Adjuster* (1991), and *Exotica* (1993), has confirmed his ability to manipulate the cinema medium to suit his unconventional approach to narrative and thematic content. Both Arcand and Egoyan deal controversially with contemporary issues, Arcand preferring to approach his themes of sexual mores or religious hypocrisy through the spectacle or epic form with large canvases and backdrops, Egoyan using a more cramped, interior style punctuated with video footage and other image distortions to achieve his dislocated and distanced interpretation of human relationships. Egoyan's work, more than Arcand's, comes out of the independent sector where traditional story-telling structures are not necessarily part of the film-making dynamic. Other directors, following closely behind the 1980s wave, occupy a similar space and have achieved a more modest international reputation. Bruce McDonald's hip *Roadkill* (1989) and *Highway 61* (1991), low-budget productions influenced by the rock music/road movie genres, promise an upcoming new talent.

The role of Telefilm Canada was crucial in the financing of all these films and has itself triggered the creation of separate provincial funding bodies like the Ontario Film Development Corporation (OFDC) and similar organizations in British Columbia, Nova Scotia, and Saskatchewan. In Quebec the Institut Québécois du Cinéma was established in the 1970s based on European models, and the Société Générale Cinématographique (SGC), later widened to include all Quebec cultural industries, was set up in 1981. Alberta, too, had created its own funding body, the Motion Picture Development Corporation, as early as 1981. Movie production during this fertile period was therefore not confined to the population centres of Montreal and Toronto. In the Prairies, Guy Maddin made the quirky, experimental *Tales from the Gimli Hospital* (1988), *Archangel* (1990), and *Careful* (1992) using a style and technique combination reminiscent of silent movies to tell mysterious northern folk legends. On the east coast Michael Jones, pursuing a very different agenda, satirized

provincial politics in his two Newfoundland farces *The Adventure of Faustus Bidgood* (1986) and *Secret Nation* (1991).

Meanwhile the NFB was also producing low-budget feature films which addressed contemporary Canadian issues. Giles Walker's *90 Days* (1985) and John M. Smith's *Welcome to Canada* (1989) both tackled the theme of immigration, Walker's film as gentle comedy in a story about a mail order bride and Smith's film more dramatically, focusing around an illegal landing of Tamil refugees off the Newfoundland coast. Smith also chose to address topical themes in *Sitting in Limbo* (1986) about the Montreal black population and *Train of Dreams* (1987) about poverty and delinquency. Most of the actors in these NFB films were non-professionals through whom the NFB directors were able to present a genuinely realistic form of cinema. But perhaps the most successful film of this period was Cynthia Scott's *Company of Strangers*, in which a group of

Denys Arcand's *Jesus of Montreal* (1988): Lothaire Bluteau achieved international acclaim for his performance as the actor whose life is profoundly affected when he takes the role of Christ in a passion play

elderly women is stranded in the Quebec countryside when their tour bus breaks down. Using non-professional octogenarian actresses Scott quietly extracts the drama of the situation as the women are thrown into each other's company and must practice self-reliance by pooling their resourcefulness.

ANIMATION

Throughout this period the NFB continued to produce a solid body of quality documentary films which were sold to television companies around the world. However, perhaps the NFB's greatest achievements have been in the field of animation. McLaren died in 1987 but his commitment to innovation and experiment lived on. Caroline Leaf joined the NFB in the early 1970s from the United States where she had made award-winning animations using sand on glass. Leaf used the same technique to tell an ancient Inuit legend in the 1974 *The Owl Who Married a Goose*, but to make *The Street* (1976) she used paint on glass to bring Mordecai Richler's short story to the screen. When the Los Angeles Animation Olympics were judged by a fifty-strong panel of international film-makers and critics in 1984 *The Street* came second only to Norstein's *Tale of Tales*. After a break from animation Leaf returned to make *Two Sisters* in the NFB French Animation Studio in 1990. Leaf spent a year and a half scratching directly on the 70 mm. film, the depth of the etching revealing the layers of colour beneath the emulsion. *Two Sisters* went on to win more than ten international awards.

Over the years the NFB has played host to many internationally renowned animators who have worked in a vast variety of techniques and styles. These influences have been absorbed into the NFB animation culture, ensuring that every year the work of both the French and English studios is represented at international festivals and animation events. NFB guest animators have included Alexander Alexeieff and Claire Parker, inventors of the pinscreen technique famously used in their 1933 *Night on a Bare Mountain*. At the NFB Alexeieff and Parker set up a second pinscreen, which was used by Jacques Drouin to make his award-winning *Mindscape* in 1976. Other animators like Paul Driessen and Co Hoedeman from Holland, Caroline Leaf from the United States, and Ishu Patel from India have spent much of their working lives in animation at the NFB, where their films have won numerous prizes. Recent award-winners include Richard Condie and Cordell Barker whose humorous animation, in *The Big Snit* (1985) and *The Cat Came Back* (1988) respectively, is classic NFB output. Alison Snowden and David Fine, now permanently based in the UK, were Oscar nominated for *George and Rosemary* (1987), a masterpiece of comic framing and timing.

Outside the NFB animation also flourishes, particularly in the commercial sector where animated series for children are big business. But one man, working alone outside the NFB, has dominated the international scene. Frédéric Back, based at the Société Radio-Canada, the French public broadcaster, won his first Oscar in 1982 for *Crac* and his second in 1989 for the magnificent *The Man Who Planted Trees*, an adaptation of a short allegorical story by Jean Giono. In 1993 Back presented his new work, *The Mighty River*, a shimmering, animated history of the St Lawrence Seaway—a lifetime's achievement.

THE EXPERIMENTAL FILM

Yet another source of public funding is available through the Canadian Council and its provincial equivalents for artist film-makers. Through this source a system of co-operative schemes and distribution centres and their client base is maintained. Best known of the Canadian experimental film-makers is Michael Snow, whose work in the 1960s and 1970s influenced a generation of structural film-making. His short film *Wavelength* (1967) is a crucial text in the avant-garde lexicon and established his international reputation. Snow's concerns centre on the camera and its position *vis-à-vis* the subject, both the seeing subject (the audience) and the filmic subject.

Canadian experimental film owes little to the painterly traditions of its colonial antecedents and eschews the Canadian landscape. Unlike the British landscape, which has fused with a consciously lyrical and romantic tradition in all the art-forms since the mid-eighteenth century, the Canadian landscape is a wild and awful presence prompting Michael Snow to attack it (and the viewer) in *La Région Centrale* (1971) with an angrily moving camera. But for the most part experimental and underground film-making ignores the mountains, forests, lakes, and seas and addresses itself to the more contemporary, urban issues of ethnicity and sexuality. But there is surprisingly little political content. Joyce Wieland's work is an exception. *Rat Life and Diet in North America* (1968) is a comic interpretation of political oppression in the United States and *La Raison avant la passion* ('Reason before passion', 1969), the title of which is taken from a speech by Canadian Prime Minister Pierre Trudeau, juxtaposes the sentiment of this speech with the raw passion and energy of the Canadian landscape itself and in so doing addresses the fundamental question of Canadian national identity. Few other films have explored this issue so dramatically. Both Snow and Wieland, contemporaries and sometime marriage partners, have also worked successfully in other area. Snow's sculptures have been commissioned all over Canada and Wieland's quilts and canvases have been exhibited internationally.

Subsequent generations of Canadian experimental film-makers have produced work of international repute. On the west coast David Rimmer, also working in the structural tradition, often with found footage, has been producing films over two decades, notably *Surfacing on the Thames* (1970). In the east, groups of film-makers centred around the Funnel and the Canadian Filmmakers Distribution Centre in Toronto have been working within a more personal context as in Phil Hoffman's *passing through/torn formations* (1990) about personal origin, or Midi Onodera's *Ten Cents a Dance* (1985) about sexual orientation. The latter theme is prevalent across all levels of film-making in Canada from mainstream features as in Léa Pool's *Anne Trister* (1986) through NFB documentaries like *Forbidden Love* (1992) by Lynne Fernie and Aerlyn Weissman, to the underground work of John Greyson, whose recent feature *Zero Patience* traces the origin of the AIDS virus in cult musical form.

THE FUTURE

In Canada today the Parti québécois has won another election victory and promises a second referendum on separation from the rest of Canada—*plus ça change ...*—and world recession has bitten deeply into cultural programmes. But the policies have not changed as the Federal Government continues to maintain its public subsidies for film through its organs Telefilm Canada, the National Film Board, and the Canada Council. Support for film is strong at all levels: for film festivals, for film exhibition programmes, for visiting film-makers, and, through the embassies and high commissions, for external film programmes and touring film packages in major cities throughout the world. The culture versus commerce debate, always a problem for protectionists where mass entertainment is concerned, has been resolved by hybridization—film is now part of a sector known as the cultural industries, its place in the political arena strengthened by the suggestion of an unquantifiable dollar value. As other national film industries collapse, as in the UK, or falter, as in France, the Canadian model, based on stubbornness of purpose and commitment, is one to watch.

Bibliography

Desbarats, Carole, *et al.* (1993), *Atom Egoyan.*

Garel, Sylvain, and Pâquet, André (eds.) (1992), *Les Cinémas du Canada.*

Handling, Piers (ed.) (1983), *The Shape of Rage: The Films of David Cronenberg.*

Lowder, Rose (ed.) (1991), *The Visual Aspect: Recent Canadian Experimental Films.*

Morris, Peter (1978), *Embattled Shadows: A History of Canadian Cinema 1895–1939.*

—(1984), *The Film Companion: A Comprehensive Guide to More than 650 Canadian Films and Filmmakers.*

New Cinemas in Latin America

MICHAEL CHANAN

In the late 1950s a new cinema began to appear in Latin America, carving out spaces for itself wherever it found the slightest chance, growing up even in the most inimical circumstances, indeed thriving upon them, for this was a cinema largely devoted to the denunciation of misery and the celebration of protest. In the space of ten or fifteen years, a movement developed which not only reached from one end of the continent to the other, but brought the cinema in Latin America to world-wide attention for the first time. It began with discrete and diverse initiatives in different countries, ranging from the Documentary Film School of Santa Fe in Argentina and the emergence of Cinema Novo in Brazil, to the creation of a new Film Institute in Havana. The dates and places are those of the recent history of Latin America. In Argentina and Brazil, growth and retrenchment have corresponded to the wax and wane of democracy. Cuban cinema is synonymous with the Cuban Revolution, Chilean cinema is another name for Popular Unity movement which elected Salvador Allende at the start of the 1970s. Ten years later came Nicaragua and El Salvador and the reflorescence of the idea of militant cinema which first developed in the 1960s, the decade of Che Guevara.

Some of the earliest initiatives occurred in out-of-the-way places, like Cuzco in Peru, where a film club was set up in 1955 and Manuel Chambi and others started making short documentaries on ethnographic and socio-cultural themes. The 1950s saw the spread of film societies throughout the continent, the proliferation of film-making courses and contests, and the publication of magazines. It was in the pages of titles like *Hablemos de cine* in Peru and *Cine al día* in Venezuela that in the 1960s and 1970s the movement debated its values and sense of identity.

Many of these groups were linked to social movements, like the cultural club Nuestro Tiempo run by the Young Communists in Havana in the early 1950s, which harboured several future Cuban directors. The first international meeting-place for the young film-makers was a film festival in Montevideo set up in 1954 by the SODRE, Uruguay's national radio station and a progressive cultural promoter. Among the film-makers attending in 1958, when John Grierson was the guest of honour, were Chambi from Peru, Nelson Pereira dos Santos from Brazil, and Fernando Birri from Santa Fe. A film by Pereira dos Santos, *Rio zona norte* ('Rio, north zone', 1957), established a new paradigm of fictional narrative, in the form of a neo-realist tale of the *favelas* (shanty towns) of Rio de Janeiro; in the years that followed, Pereira dos Santos became the presiding spirit and 'conscience', as Glauber Rocha put it, of Brazil's Cinema Novo. The film exhibited by Birri and his students, *Tire die* ('Throw us a dime'), a collaborative social inquiry into the shanty towns around the city of Santa Fe, later came to be celebrated as the founding social documentary of the new film movement. Known simply as the New Latin American Cinema (Nuevo Cine Latinoamericano), the term dates from a meeting in 1967 of film-makers from across the continent hosted by a film club in the Chilean seaside town of Viña del Mar, which had been running a festival of 8 and 16 mm. since 1963.

BRAZIL AND CINEMA NOVO

Several pioneers of the new Latin American cinema had studied film in Rome in the early 1950s, and, returning home, adopted the neo-realist principles of documentary-style location shooting with non-professional actors as the only practical solution for their situation. But they and others also took up neo-realism because they saw it as a critical aesthetic. As Birri explained, in Italy neo-realism was the cinema that discovered, amidst the rhetoric and outward show of development, another Italy, the Italy of underdevelopment. It was a cinema of the humble and the offended which Latin America cried out for.

In 1963, with *Vidas secas* ('Barren lives'), the Brazilian film-maker Nelson Pereira dos Santos carried the spirit of neo-realism deeper into new territory with a stark adaptation of a novel by Graciliano Ramos about the appalling conditions in rural north-east Brazil, a zone of underdevelopment within underdevelopment. The same aesthetic and the same locale served Ruy Guerra for *Os fuzis* ('The guns'), a drama of hunger in the *sertão* and violent confrontation between soldiers and peasants, while Carlos Diegues made *Ganga Zumba*, the story of the seventeenth-century maroon community of Palmares and thus the first film of Cinema Novo to tackle a historical theme.

These films, highly accomplished in themselves, were only a prelude. Wherever it was able to gain a niche, the new cinema quickly took off in new directions, creating new genres and exploring film language in radically new directions. *Ganga Zumba*, for example, initiates a genre of historical films about slavery in both Brazil and Cuba, where film-makers also explored the Afro-Brazilian and Afro-Cuban heritage both in the historical genre and in modern garb. Twentieth-century subjects included films like Joaquim Pedro de Andrade's *Macunaíma* (1969), an anarchic and picaresque comedy starring one of Brazil's most popular comedians, Grande Otelo, who also starred in *Rio zona norte* by Pereira dos Santos, where he plays an illiterate samba composer facing the corruption of the music business. Historical films included *Como era gostoso o meu francés* ('How tasty was my Frenchman', 1971) by Pereira dos Santos, a dark satire on the idyll of the noble savage, and T. G. Alea's dramatic *Una pelea cubana contra los demonios* ('A Cuban struggle against the demons', 1971). Both films explore the early centuries of the Conquest and adopt an experimental approach to the problem of historical truth. Alea also collaborated on the screenplay of *El otro Francisco* ('The other Francisco', 1973, directed by Sergio Giral) and then made a black comedy, *La última cena* ('The Last Supper', 1976); these two are slavery films set in the nineteenth century, the former an impressive piece of deconstruction of a nineteenth-century literary source.

All these films, whether comedy or tragedy, achieve an allegorical quality which becomes a distinctive trait of the entire movement: the ability to speak of subjects on more than one level at the same time, of the present while talking of the past, for example, or of politics while talking of religion. At the same time, the exploration of these themes quickly left the aesthetic of neo-realism behind, as directors and cinematographers sought to create a visual style which matched the legendary qualities of the subject-matter. Diegues himself made two more slavery films, *Xica de Silva* in 1976 and *Quilombo* in 1984, which show a striking progression from the sober black and white narrative of *Ganga Zumba* to the vivid colour, visual pyrotechnics, and powerful music of the style known as tropicalism, or at least one of its variants, which borrows directly from the carnivalesque at the heart of Brazilian popular culture. The first of these films recounts the rise and fall of an eighteenth-century slave possessed of magical and erotic powers who marries a colonial official, the second revisits the Palmares story, incorporating the results of new historical research. But Diegues is less concerned with objective narrative than with transposing to the screen the ritualistic forms through which Afro-Brazilian culture itself recounts its history, and the narrative form of these films is first cousin to the performances of the samba schools. Meanwhile Nelson Pereira dos Santos pursued his own highly original brand of allegory in films like *O amuleto de Ogum* ('The amulet of Ogum', 1974), where the invocation of Afro-Brazilian mythology effects a parody of the thriller. For other subjects, however, he retains a realist approach, as in the masterful *Memorias do carcere* ('Memories of prison'), an adaptation of the autobiographical novel by Graciliano Ramos about political repression, which won the Critics' Prize at Cannes in 1984.

While Diegues was the most popular of the Cinema Novo directors, the most notorious exponent of the

Glauber Rocha

(1938–1981)

Glauber Rocha was the shooting star of Brazilian cinema, and the *enfant terrible* of the Cinema Novo of the 1960s. Born in Bahia in north-east Brazil, he entered cinema through the film clubs when he was 16, studied law for two years, set up a production company, made a number of shorts, moved to Rio where he joined the group around Nelson Pereira dos Santos (whom he called the father of Cinema Novo), and directed his first feature in 1962.

Barravento ('The turning wind') was a basically realist portrait of religious mystification in a fishing community, but Rocha's treatment of the story gave it an allegorical dimension with a didactic political message in which the fundamental themes of his future work were already present, including his fascination with the social ambiguity of Brazil's popular semi-pagan religions. The film established its director's reputation as the leading figure of a new cinema that was made, as he himself put it, with 'an idea in the head and a camera in hand'.

In his 1965 manifesto 'The Aesthetics of Hunger', Rocha argued that the originality of Cinema Novo lay in its revelation that 'violence is normal behaviour for the starving' and 'the moment of violence is the moment when the colonizer becomes aware of the existence of the colonized'. Accordingly the aesthetics of hunger are directed against the values of the cinema of imperialism and in Rocha's hands the result is a style which eschews narrative clarity in favour of violent expressive imagery.

Combining the intellectual influence of the French *politique des auteurs* and the thinking of Che Guevara and Frantz Fanon, stylistically speaking Rocha's work bears strong relation to both Godard and Pasolini, with its jagged and abrupt montage, constant play of shifting oppositions, and often theatrical *mise-en-scène*; in Rocha's case this is partly Brechtian and partly ritualistic, inspired by Afro-Brazilian religion. These hallmarks are first found in *Deus e o diabo na terra do sol* (*Black God, White Devil*, 1964), a densely metaphorical story of a peasant couple in the *sertão*, the wilderness of the interior of the Brazilian north-east, who become involved with both a messianic religious leader (the Black God) and then a *cangaçeiro* or bandit (the White Devil).

With *Terra em transe* ('Land in anguish') three years later, Rocha shifted his ground to the city and the struggle for political power in a delirious allegory of the Latin American *coup d'état*, in particular that of Brazil in 1964, and the contradictions of a socially engaged artist forced to confront his own illusions. He then returned to the territory of the *sertão* for *Antonio das Mortes* of 1969 (which he originally called 'The Dragon of Evil against the Warrior Saint'). This was a kind of highly stylized inverted Western; the eponymous hero had already appeared in *Deus e o diabo* in his legendary role of killer of bandits and hireling of church and landlords. But here the symbol-

Antonio das Mortes (1969), Rocha's 'highly stylized, inverted western'.

ism of the earlier film is reversed, and Rocha extols the revolutionary zeal which blends social banditry with the ecstasy of messianic religion.

Following the second Brazilian coup in 1968, political repression intensified and in 1971 Rocha went into exile in protest. Most critics agree that the loss of contact with Brazilian reality weakened his work. He had already made two films outside Brazil, *Der leone have sept cabezas* ('The lion has seven heads') and *Cabezas cortadas* ('Heads cut off'). The former, inspired by Frantz Fanon's discussion of colonialism, was shot in Congo-Brazzaville in 1970 and explores the African roots of Brazilian culture, but imposes Rocha's own schematic allegorical structure. The latter, filmed in Spain immediately afterwards, casts Francisco Rabal as the dying ruler Diaz II but remains a piece of private mythology. The long documentary *Historia do Brasil* (1973) suggested for some critics a loss of ideological clarity, while a film for Italian television in 1975 called *Claro* failed to make any impression. Making his peace with the Generals and returning to Brazil in 1975, his last film was *A idade da terra* ('The age of the earth', 1980), a visually dazzling tapestry which preaches a utopian union of Catholicism, revolution and primitivism.

MICHAEL CHANAN

SELECT FILMOGRAPHY

Barravento (1962); Deus e o diabo na terra do sol (1964); Terra em transe (1967); Antonio das Mortes / O dragao da maldade contra o santo guerreiro (1969); Cabezas cortadas (1970); Der leone have sept cabezas (1970); Historia do Brasil (1973); A idade da terra (1980).

BIBLIOGRAPHY

Rocha, Glauber (1981), Revolucião do Cinema Nôvo.
—— (1983), 'The Aesthetics of Hunger'.

tropicalist style was Glauber Rocha (who died young in 1981). Playing the equivalent role of *enfant terrible* to Godard in France, Rocha argued for a politics of authorship that allowed the film-maker to probe historical contradictions and placed the author at the centre of an oppositional practice—the politicization, so to speak, of the *politique des auteurs*. In a manifesto widely reprinted throughout Latin America and known by two titles, 'The Aesthetics of Hunger' and 'The Aesthetics of Violence', he protested that people for whom hunger is a normal condition are suffering violence—the violence of the social system that makes them go hungry. We know, he said, this hunger will not be cured by moderate reforms, and its tumours are not hidden, but only aggravated, by the cloak of Technicolor.

His masterpiece *Antonio das Mortes* (1969) is set in northeast Brazil, with emblematic characters performing stylized actions, in a peculiarly Brazilian amalgamation of fact and legend, epic and lyric. For Rocha the mysticism of popular religion, a syncretistic fusion of Catholicism and the motifs of African religion transplanted with the slave-trade, constituted a double paradigm. He took it both as the expression of a permanent spirit of rebellion against unceasing oppression, a rejection and refusal of the condition in which the common people had been condemned to live for centuries, and as a model for the syncretism of his own film language. In Rocha, as Peter Schumann (1987) puts it, the exuberant torrent of images and the mix of mysticism and legend, cult and ritual, were married to surrealistic symbolism and achieved a visionary force.

THE CUBAN EXAMPLE

Cuba was the first country in Latin America where it became possible to envisage a new film culture, both popular and critical, of the kind imagined by Birri, on a national scale. Cinema was second only to music as the country's most popular form of entertainment when the revolutionary government of 1959 decreed the creation of a film institute (ICAIC—the Cuban Institute of Film Art and Industry), to take control of the movie business and become responsible for production and distribution. Under the leadership of Alfredo Guevara (no relation to Che but a close political comrade of Fidel Castro) ICAIC would become the most successful venture of its kind, bar one, anywhere on the continent, a model of state intervention in the film industry. The exception, by historical irony, was Embrafilme, the bureau set up by the Brazilian generals in the 1960s, which went bankrupt after the return to democracy in the 1980s and was disbanded in 1990.

Embrafilme was a political contradiction: created to advertise the Brazilian military miracle abroad, it ended up funding film-makers who, as Pereira dos Santos expressed it, were 'viscerally opposed to such regimes'.

The Cuban regime, however, enjoyed widespread support amongst artists and intellectuals, to whom, with the creation of institutions like ICAIC, it offered conditions which the country had never before enjoyed. ICAIC succeeded first of all in economic terms: a studio with control over distribution and a staff of 1,000, producing each year (until the country's economic collapse at the end of the 1980s) up to half a dozen features, a regular newsreel, and as many as four dozen documentaries, all for an annual production budget of around $10 million or less than half the price of a single Hollywood blockbuster. Communist egalitarianism and the absence of market competition combined to hold the costs of production down, enabling a cinema of poverty to flourish.

ICAIC also succeeded in artistic terms. The huge popularity of cinema in Cuba (television had been introduced in 1951 but reached only a limited audience until the 1970s) meant that ICAIC was rapidly catapulted to the very centre of Cuban cultural politics. As the Revolution took the road of Communism, Alfredo Guevara led the film-makers in arguing passionately against the narrow and restrictive orthodox ideology of Socialist Realism, and in favour of stylistic pluralism and artistic freedom. A few individuals, among them cinematographer Nestor Almendros, alienated from the national fervour, nevertheless called foul and departed; but they left behind a growing community of film-makers who began to feed off each other's enthusiasms. Aesthetically the most audacious was Santiago Alvarez, who headed ICAIC's newsreel unit, which he turned into a school for militant documentary. Progressing from short films like *Now* (1965), *Hanoi martes 13* ('Hanoi, Tuesday the 13th', shot in Vietnam in 1967), and *LBJ* (1968), to long documentaries like *Piedra sobre piedra* ('Stone upon stone') and *De América soy hijo . . .* ('I am a son of America')—shot in Peru in 1970 and Chile in 1972 respectively—he commandeered every different documentary genre, from the pamphlet to satire, by way of the reportage of war and peace. Employing every kind of visual imagery, from newsreel footage to stills, archive film to cuttings from magazines, combined with animated texts and emblematic musicalization, Alvarez amalgamated creative kleptomania with the skills of a *bricoleur* to reinvent Soviet montage in a Caribbean setting.

By the late 1960s, the experimental ethos had spread to fiction and produced an astonishing series of films which boldly transgressed the divisions between genres. Julio García Espinosa scored a great success with *Las aventuras de Juan Quin Quin* ('The adventures of Juan Quin Quin', 1967), which gives anarchic comedy a whole new dimension, while Humberto Solás reinvented the historical epic with *Lucia* in 1968, a portrait of three women in different historical periods—and different styles: Visconti-esque for 'Lucia 1895', the Hollywood of Elia Kazan for 'Lucia 1933', and Nouvelle Vague for 'Lucia 196-'; or rather, all of these

Tomás Gutiérrez Alea

(1928–)

Tomás Gutiérrez Alea's reputation as Cuba's leading director is inseparable from the story of the Cuban Revolution and the revolutionary cinema organization, ICAIC (Instituto Cubano de Arte y Industria Cinematográficos), set up at the time of the Revolution in 1959, of which he was a founder member.

Born in Havana, Alea graduated in law before going to Rome to study film directing at the Centro Sperimentale, where he met another Cuban film student, Julio García Espinosa. In common with other young Latin American film-makers, Italian neo-realism had fired their imagination as the aesthetic best fitted to the conditions in their own countries. Back in Cuba, the two collaborated on a clandestine documentary about charcoal workers in the Ciénaga swamp south of Havana called *El mégano* (1955), along with other members of a left-wing club called Nuestro Tiempo ('Our Times'); the film-makers were arrested by Batista's secret police and the film was banned. Four years later, the two would collaborate again, on the first documentary made after the triumph of the Revolution, *Esta tierra nuestra* ('This land of ours', 1959), about the need for agrarian reform. At the end of the 1960s García Espinosa was to argue the case for a committed form of film-making which made a strength of its economic limitations, in a polemic entitled 'For an imperfect cinema'. It was Alea who demonstrated in practice how accomplished such an 'imperfect cinema' could become.

His first four feature films alternated between neo-realist drama and comedy. After *Historias de la Revolución* (1960) came *Las doce sillas* ('The twelve chairs', 1962), a Cuban version of Ilf and Petrov's famous satire on the Soviet Revolution. This was followed by *Cumbite* (1964), a drama of underdevelopment set in Haiti and acted by Haitians living in Cuba, and by the black comedy *Muerte de un burócrata* ('Death of a bureaucrat'), which established Alea's name abroad when it took the Special Jury Prize at Karlovy Vary in 1966. Then in 1968 came the film whose originality both in form and content gave the idea of political cinema a completely new meaning: *Memories of Underdevelopment* (*Memorias del subdesarollo*), in which the doubts and alienation of a bourgeois intellectual are thrown into relief at the same time that they serve to provide a subtle commentary on the social upheavals produced by the Revolution.

From this point on almost every one of Alea's films combined either an experimental attitude towards film language, or else a spirit of improvisation in technique, with an independent critical attitude towards reality. *Una pelea cubana contra los demonios* ('A Cuban struggle against the demons', 1971), the first of two historical dramas of religious fanaticism, is set in the mid-seventeenth century; the second, *La última cena* ('The Last Supper', 1976), at the end of the eighteenth century. Both are based on historical incidents, and constitute paradigms of cinema's vocation for retelling history. The former becomes in the process an implicit critique of modern political dogma, and the most experimental of Alea's films, the first to be photographed by Mario García Joya, his collaborator ever since. The latter is a biting satire about hypocrisy and a celebration of Afro-Cubanism, with a brilliant performance by the Chilean actor Nelson Villagra. In *Los sobrevivientes* ('The survivors', 1978), another black comedy, the object of satire is both the mentality of those who oppose the Revolution and the politics of isolation. Five years later, in *Hasta cierto punto* ('Up to a point'), Alea turned his magnifying glass on the pretensions and contradictions of himself and his colleagues, in an ironic tale about Cuban film-makers.

In *Cartas del parque* ('Letters from the park', 1988), based on a story by Gabriel García Márquez, Alea allowed himself a romantic period piece without political overtones; a simple but curious love story set in the provincial town of Matanzas in the early years of the century. But critics who suggested that Cuba's political crisis had silenced even Alea's critical spirit stand corrected by *Fresa y chocolate* (1993), in which the story of a friendship between a gay photographer and member of the Communist Youth becomes a powerful and outspoken critique of political dogma and intolerance, the work of a film-maker at the height of his powers.

MICHAEL CHANAN

SELECT FILMOGRAPHY

Las doce sillas (1962); Cumbite (1964); Muerte de un burócrata (1966); Memorias del subdesarollo (Memories of Underdevelopment) (1968); Una pelea cubana contra los demonios (1971); La última cena (1976); Hasta cierto punto (1983); Fresa y chocolate (Strawberry and Chocolate) (1993); Guantanamera (1995)

BIBLIOGRAPHY

Chanan, Michael (1985), *The Cuban Experience*.
Fornet, Ambrosio (ed.) (1987), *Alea: una retrospetiva critica*.

Sergio Corrieri as the indecisive intellectual in Tomás Gutiérrez Alea's *Memories of Underdevelopment* (1968)

crossed with Cinema Novo in a highly original synthesis.

In the same astonishing year, when international revolutionary fervour was at its height, Alea made *Memories of Underdevelopment* (*Memorias del subdesarollo*, 1968), a subtle and complex study in the alienation of a bourgeois intellectual within the Revolution. The next year Manuel Octavio Gómez made *La primera carga al machete* ('The first machete charge'), and Manuel Herrera followed in 1972 with *Giron* ('Bay of Pigs'); the former reports an episode in Cuban revolutionary history dating from 1868 as if it were a contemporary documentary, the latter is a widescreen post-Brechtian dramatization of the defeat of the US invasion of 1961, with participants enacting their stories as they recount them in front of the camera. Then came *De cierta manera* ('One way or another'), a story of contemporary Havana by Sara Gomez (the release of the film in 1974 was delayed by her tragically early death) intermingling fictional characters with real people. All four films bring drama and documentary into powerful new relationships.

Julio García Espinosa summed up the trend which gave rise to these and other experiments in a polemic entitled 'For an Imperfect Cinema', widely reprinted and much misunderstood. Warning of the dangers of the technical accomplishment which after ten years now lay within the grasp of the Cuban film-makers, he argued that in the underdeveloped world technical and artistic perfection are false objectives. Not only is the attempt to match the production values of the big commercial movie a waste of resources, he said, but there is more to be gained by engaging the audience directly and with a sense of urgency, roughness included. The aim is what Umberto Eco, in another context, calls the open work, which refuses to fix its meanings and thus invites the active participation of the audience.

ACROSS THE CONTINENT

Cuban cinema was a major influence throughout the continent, although, because of the monopoly of the major distributors, less so with audiences than with film-makers, who were able to travel and encounter the films and each other at festivals and meetings. Cuban documentary, for example, animated a stream of films which attested to the conditions of life from Chihuahua to Tierra del Fuego. New paradigms of political documentary cinema appeared, combining the techniques of French *cinéma-vérité* and North American direct cinema, from the Brazilian Geraldo Sarno's *Viramundo* of 1964 to *Chircales* by the Colombian documentarists Marta Rodríguez and Jorge Silva in 1972, Paul Leduc's *Etnocidio: notas sobre Mezquital* ('Ethnocide: notes on Mezquital', 1976), or Ciro Durán's *Gamin* (1978). The first, an investigation into the migration of peasants from the drought-stricken north-east of Brazil to São Paulo, set a new standard for socially engaged reportage; the second is an analysis of the life of bricklayers on the outskirts of Bogotá, which achieves the fusion of politics, poetry, and visual anthropology; the film by Leduc, 'an A to Z of indictments against the modernising state' as John King (1990) calls it, confirmed its director as the foremost experimental film-maker in Mexico, while *Gamin* explores the world of the Bogotá street urchin in a provocative and interventionist version of direct cinema. At the same time, documentary realism also inspired films of fiction like Leon Hirszman's *São Bernardo* (1972), an allegory on the Brazilian miracle (and another adaptation of a novel by Ramos). Held back by the censorship board just long enough to bankrupt the production company, it must stand in here for the numerous films which have been banned for political offence in every country of the continent at one time or another.

In Argentina, where cinema in the 1960s was in retreat against political repression, the sense of political urgency was expressed with particular fervour by Grupo Cine Liberación, radical in both politics and film poetics, who in 1968 completed a mammoth three-part documentary running almost four and a half hours entitled *La hora de los hornos* (*The Hour of the Furnaces*). Constrained by the conditions of military rule after the coup of 1966, but bolstered by the growth of organized resistance, the film was shot clandestinely in conjunction with cadres of the Peronist movement. As Robert Stam (1990) puts it, it was made 'in the interstices of the system and against the system . . . independent in production, militant in politics, and experimental in language'.

Two of the film-makers, Fernando Solanas and Octavio Getino, followed up with a manifesto entitled *Towards a Third Cinema*, which they defined as a cinema of liberation 'whose moving force is to be found in the Third World countries'. In this scheme, however, First and Second Cinema do not correspond to the First and Second Worlds but constitute a virtual geography of their own. First Cinema is the model imposed by the American film industry, the Hollywood movie, wherever it is found—in Los Angeles, Mexico City, or Bombay; Second Cinema they identify with art or *auteur* cinema, which in turn is not just a European phenomenon, but is also found in places like Buenos Aires. Second Cinema is politically reformist but incapable of achieving any profound change. It is especially impotent in the face of the kind of repression unleashed by neo-Fascist forces like the Latin American military. The only alternative, they said, is a Third Cinema, films the system cannot assimilate, which 'directly and explicitly set out to fight the system'.

Several varieties of militant cinema appeared across the continent in the late 1960s, ironically, in some cases, as a result of support for film production on the part of reformist governments. In Bolivia, where Spanish was a minority language, Jorge Sanjinés and the Ukamau group were able

Blood of the Condor (*Yawar Mallku*, 1969), made in Bolivia by the Ukamau group, used the subject of the forced sterilization of Indian women as an example and metaphor for American imperialism

to make a number of indigenous-language films with non-professional actors. The group took their name, the Aymara word for 'the way it is', from the first of these in 1966, about the revenge of a man for the rape of his wife; they then went on to produce *Blood of the Condor* (*Yawar Mallku*, 1969), which recounts the response of a Quechua community to the sterilization of its women by an American Peace Corps maternity clinic. Hugely successful, the film forced the expulsion of the Peace Corps by the Bolivian government two years later. Nevertheless, the experience of exhibiting the film to peasant audiences prompted Sanjinés to question the efficacy of the style they were working in. *Ukamau* and *Blood of the Condor* still portrayed the protagonists as individuals. In *El coraje del pueblo* ('The courage of the people', 1971), the reconstruction of a massacre of miners in the town of Siglo XX in 1967, the protagonist is collective. The complex narrative built around flashbacks employed in *Blood of the Condor* is abandoned in favour of a linear structure and a tendency towards sequence shots. The style is thus adapted to the traditions of oral narrative: the players on the screen are the historical actors of the events portrayed, they are dramatizing their own experience; the use of long takes allows them

the greatest space to express their collective memory, and a new kind of popular cinema is born. A military coup while the film was being finished forced Sanjinés into exile, and his next productions along these lines were made in Peru and Ecuador.

In Chile, the new film-makers came together during the 1960s to support the coalition of left-wing parties known as Popular Unity. The years leading up to the electoral victory of Salvador Allende in 1970 saw a new wave in both fiction and documentary. The essays of the Experimental Film Group of the 1950s turned into a cinema of urgency, which combined political campaign films with innovation in filmic technique and language to denounce the marginalism inherent in underdevelopment. The same spirit fed a crop of features which appeared in the late 1960s, including *Tres tristes tigres* ('Three sad tigers', 1968) by Raúl Ruiz, an experimental socio-political comedy; *Valparaiso mi amor* ('Valparaiso my love', 1969) by Aldo Francia (the moving spirit behind the festival in Viña del Mar in 1967), a lyrical neo-realist drama of deprived children; and *The Jackal of Nahueltoro* (*El chacal de Nahueltoro*, 1969) by Miguel Littin, an agitated deconstruction of criminality; the last two are based on real incidents and characters.

Attempts to place this activity on a more secure footing were cut short by the infamous coup of 1973. The most extraordinary film to emerge from the latter part of this period is Patricio Guzmán's three-part documentary *The Battle of Chile* (*La batalla de Chile*, 1975), a record of the months leading up to the coup. A fertile mixture of direct cinema observation and investigative reportage, the footage was smuggled out immediately after Allende's fall and edited in Cuba at ICAIC. The result is a poignant work of historical testimony unique in the annals of cinema.

As in other countries which fell to the right, film-makers were among those who were forced into exile, or, if they did not escape, disappeared. Thanks to international solidarity, Chileans became the leading practitioners of a cinema of exile which grew up in the 1970s (according to one count, they made 176 films in the ten years 1973–83, 56 of them features). Some remained in Latin America, like Littin, who found a new base in Mexico. Here, amongst other films, he made *Actas de Marusia* ('Letters from Marusia', 1975), with the Italian actor Gian Maria Volonté and music by Mikis Theodorakis, in which the coup of 1973 is allegorized in the story of a massacre of miners in Chile in 1907. Nevertheless, the political imperatives of the Popular Unity period underwent a gradual transformation, as the overtly militant gave way to a more personal and ironic stance—especially in the impish work of Raúl Ruiz, now based in France, who became by the 1980s one of the leading figures of European avant-garde cinema. At the same time, the Chilean experience has contributed a new genre to the history of world cinema, as a number of films took the experience of exile as their subject-matter. The first of them, Ruiz's semi-documentary *Dialogo de exilados* ('Dialogue of exiles', 1974), was badly received in the exile community for its ironic, disrespectful portrait of life in exile. But later films, like Marilu Mallet's highly personal documentary *Journal inachevé* ('Unfinished diary', 1982) and Jorge Durán's dramatic feature *A cor de seu destino* ('The colour of his destiny', 1986), made in Canada and Brazil respectively, are remarkable expositions of the struggle to understand the exile's sense of identity. Perhaps the most extraordinary film of exile is *Tangos: el exilio de Gardel* ('Tangos: the exile of Gardel', 1985) by the Argentinian Fernando Solanas, an experimental musical set among the Argentine exile community in Paris.

INTO THE 1980S

The transformation of political thematics was not limited to the cinema of exile. Cuban directors during the 1970s developed a new brand of genre cinema, in films like *El hombre de Maisinicú* ('The man from Maisinicú') and *Río Negro* (Manuel Pérez, 1973 and 1977): macho adventure movies in which the good guys are revolutionaries and the bad guys counter-revolutionaries. A growing trend in the 1980s towards social comedy, marked by two films of

1984, *Los pájaros tirandole a la escopeta* ('Tables turned') by Rolando Díaz and *Se permuta* ('House swap') by Juan Carlos Tabío, represented a far more original development. Meanwhile the new cinema took root in several countries where state intervention for the first time created conditions for regular if limited levels of production, including Venezuela and Colombia.

In Venezuela, for example, Roman Chalbaud evolved new politically edged forms of old Latin American genres in films like *El pez que fuma* ('The smoking fish', 1977), which turns the world of the Mexican brothel film into a metaphor for power relations and corruption, or *Cangrejo* (1982), which turns the thriller into a denunciation of police corruption. Not always artistically successful, they nevertheless achieved top box-office ratings in their own countries, outgrossing all but the biggest Hollywood hits. Only US monopolization of international distribution prevented them reaching a wider audience. Nevertheless, by the time ICAIC launched the Havana Film Festival in 1979, it seemed at last as if a critical, national popular cinema was more than a dream in several countries.

The 1980s saw an assortment of developments including the renaissance of Argentinian cinema, the emergence of a women's cinema in a number of different countries (especially Mexico and Brazil), the revival of the Mexican film industry, and alternatives like the Super 8 movement in Venezuela. With the expanding variety of all these films, both aesthetically and politically, the idea of a movement generated in the 1960s, even one that was unified in its diversity, began to recede. But if the distinction between commercial cinema and committed cinema became blurred, it was mainly because of the recognition of different political realities. The tradition of a committed experimental cinema remained alive with directors like Mexico's Paul Leduc, in films like *Frida* (1984) and *Dollar Mambo* (1993). Discarding linear narrative in favour of mobile imagery, the former portrays the life and loves, painting and politics of Frida Kahlo as a series of interlocking and visually intoxicating *tableaux vivants*, while the latter tells the story of the US invasion of Panama in 1989 in the form of a wordless dance drama. *Frida* was produced by Manuel Barbachano Ponce, the producer of two of Buñuel's finest Mexican films (*Los olvidados* ('The forgotten') and *The Exterminating Angel*), and Jaime Humberto Hermosillo, better known as a director, and Mexico's leading exponent of gay cinema, with films like the banned *Las aparencias engañan* ('Appearances deceive', 1977) and *Doña Herlinda y su hijo* ('Doña Herlinda and her son', 1984).

Signs of a growing women's presence in Latin American cinema first appeared in Brazilian cinema in the late 1970s, with Ana Carolina's *Mar de rosas* ('Sea of roses', 1977), a carnivalesque deconstruction of the institution of marriage, and Tisuka Yamasaka's *Gaijin*, a story of

Japanese emigration to Brazil which places gender in relation to ethnicity and class. While the early 1980s saw the appearance of women's documentary groups in Brazil and Mexico, another strand is found in the feature work of the Argentinian María Luisa Bemberg (*Camila*, 1984) and the Venezuelan Fina Torres (*Oriana*, 1985), who both use feminist melodrama to tell the stories of individual women in different historical periods. The most extraordinary feature début of the time was *A hora da estrela* ('The hour of the star') by the 64-year-old Brazilian director Suzana Amaral, the gentle and penetrating portrait, moving and humorous, of a young woman from the northeast trying to survive in São Paulo.

In Argentina, as the grip of the military began to slacken, film-makers there too saw the opportunity for

revitalizing the genre movie. In 1981 Adolfo Aristarain came out with *Tiempo de revancha* ('Time for revenge'), which brilliantly adopts the format of a suspenseful thriller to tell a parable of power through the story of a worker taking revenge against his boss, or the exploiter exploited; a year later he made *Ultimos días del victima* ('Last days of the victim'), a *policial* and a parable of the death squads. When the military lost the Falklands/Malvinas War and fell, and cinema began to breathe the air of freedom, there followed films like *No habrá más penas ni olvido* (*A Funny, Dirty Little War*, 1983), Héctor Olivera's black comedy of Peronist militants in the early 1970s, and Luis Puenzo's powerful and harrowing 1986 Oscar winner *La historia official* ('The official version'), a character drama about the fate of the children of the Disappeared. That democracy

A woman who has cut her husbands throat flees with her daughter, in Ana Carolina Teixera Soares's *Mar de rosas* ('Sea of roses', 1977)

did not bring economic recovery, however, is revealed in another film of the same year, Carlos Sorín's wonderfully bathetic *La película del rey* ('A king and his movie'), which recounts a young film-maker's desperate attempt to make a costume drama while struggling against an inhospitable location, the desertion of the cast, and no money. Despite winning an award at the Venice Film Festival, the film failed to cover its costs—an ironic reminder of the truth of the comment by the Brazilian film critic Salles Gomes (1980) that, while the cinemas of North America, Europe, or Japan have never been underdeveloped, 'those of the Third World have never ceased being so'. This is not a question of volume or quality of production: the Indian and Egyptian film industries are among the largest in any continent, and Latin America since the 1950s has been pretty constantly in the vanguard of world cinema. But in cinema as in other regards, says Salles Gomes, under-development is not a stage or a step, but a state, a condition, and the films of the developed countries never went through this condition, while the others have a

tendency to remain stuck there. Hence the constant wonderment that, in Latin America, cinema refuses to die.

Bibliography

Burton, Julianne (ed.) (1986), *Cinema and Social Change in Latin America: Conversations with Filmmakers*.

—— (ed.) (1990), *The Social Documentary in Latin America*.

Chanan, Michael (ed.) (1983), *Twenty Five Years of the New Latin American Cinema*.

Johnson, Randal, and Stam, Robert (eds.) (1982), *Brazilian Cinema*.

King, John (1990), *Magical Reels: A History of Cinema in Latin America*.

—— *et.al.* (eds.) (1993), *Mediating Two Worlds: Cinematic Encounters in the Americas*.

Pick, Zuzana (1993), *The New Latin American Cinema*.

Salles Gomes, Paulo Emilio (1980), 'Cinema: trajetória no sub-desenvolvimento'.

Schumann, Peter B. (1987), *Historia del cine latinoamericano*.

Solanas, Fernando, and Getino, Octavio (1969), 'Towards a Third Cinema'.

Stam, Robert (1990), 'The Hour of the Furnaces and the Two Avant-Gardes'.

CONCLUSION

New Concepts of Cinema

GEOFFREY NOWELL-SMITH

As the cinema has changed, so have the ideas in terms of which it was discussed and written about. In the 1960s and 1970s there was a revolution in film criticism and theory. Starting in the world of specialist magazines, it went on to affect both journalistic and academic writing on the cinema and to influence many aspects of film-making, not only at the margins but also in the mainstream.

Like any such revolution, its effects were only partially irreversible. The bolder insights of the new writing failed to find general acceptance, while many originally radical ideas became routinized and academicized with the spread of film studies in the universities and the dwindling interaction between academic study and world outside.

To make sense of the revolution it is perhaps convenient to divide it into a number of distinct but overlapping stages. As each stage was consolidated so it became possible either to build on its achievements or to reject its limitations and head off a new direction. Events did not always precisely follow the order suggested here, and there were other tendencies at work, but a division into three or four stages demonstrates a certain logic in what, at the time, seemed a very confusing set of developments.

The first stage, beginning in the early 1960s, involved a general revaluation of the artistic values of mainstream cinema, and Hollywood in particular, stressing the contribution of individual *auteurs* and greatly extending the boundaries of what could be regarded as film art. This was followed, in the late 1960s and early 1970s, by a Marxist-influenced critique of that same cinema, downplaying the role of individual artists and seeing the cinema as a cracked ideological monolith, in which the cracks, interesting though they were, never seemed sufficient to challenge the general ideological character of cinema as a whole. Analysis of the ideological operations of cinema then in turn produced two contrasting developments. Acceptance of the ideological critique led to ideas of a 'counter-cinema', and of subversive practices within the mainstream, as a way of escaping the 'Hollywood–Mosfilm' monolith. Another school of thought, however, increasingly came to assert that the fissures were after all more important than the monolith and that the reception of

films was a more complex and open-ended process than the ideological critics maintained.

BEFORE THE REVOLUTION

Much of what passed for film theory in the 1940s and 1950s consisted of barely re-examined assumptions about film art inherited from the aesthetics of the silent period. The core of this theory was a notion of filmic specificity as located in the image, either singly or in juxtaposition through montage. The main difference of opinion concerned the status given to the photographic image. Some writers (and film-makers) saw it as inherently manipulable, so that the art of film consisted in the degree to which it could be transformed to produce new meanings and effects, while others located the specific difference of film in its subordination to the demands of reality as captured by the camera. Sound was seen as having added additional possibilities of counterpoint to basic imagistic values, but also, on the alternative view, as helping the cinema fulfil its inherent vocation for realism. Film theory was also very much oriented towards art practice, and to the idea of making films, in some nebulous way, more artistic. Emphasis was put on the effects the film-maker wanted to produce, rather than on the spectator's reading of them.

REVALUATION OF THE MAINSTREAM

Film theory as it existed in the 1950s tended to privilege films which were either self-consciously artistic or which used the supposed realism of the photographic image to psychological or social effect. It had relatively little to say about the great majority of mainstream films which were neither conspicuously arty nor systematically realistic. Critics admired Welles and Ford, but not Hawks or Preminger. Since individuality was prized, and the studio system was thought to value repetition and formula over originality, the qualities of genre films were often overlooked. A first stage in the critical and theoretical revolution, therefore, consisted in the affirmation of genre films in general and of directors working within a genre framework which disciplined and channelled their individuality. With this came a recognition of on the one hand the thematic richness of the Hollywood movie in general and on the other hand the subtler values of *mise-en-scène* to be found in the work of a number of studio directors with no obvious artistic pretensions. It was not long, however, before it was realized that there were, after all, limits within the system, not only to individuality, but to the range of ideas that could be expressed. The delirious over-valuations and over-interpretations found in *Cahiers du cinéma*, *Movie*, and other magazines gave way to more sober assessments of what Hollywood directors could and could not achieve.

MARXISM

In a seminal article, 'Tales of Sound and Fury', published in the British magazine *Monogram* in 1972, Thomas Elsaesser attempted to integrate the acquisitions of the new criticism in a broader intellectual framework and to show how the Hollywood melodrama of the 1950s was shaped by prevailing ideological assumptions, including the assimilation of Freud. By this time, however, *Cahiers du cinéma* had itself moved on and come under the influence of Marxist, psychoanalytic, and structuralist thought, while being politically radicalized by the ferment of May 1968. The new influences surfaced in Britain in the magazine *Screen* from 1974 onwards, spreading from there to the United States where they crystallized for a while into a new academic orthodoxy.

The *Cahiers/Screen* writers saw the cinema in general and Hollywood in particular as necessarily an instance of bourgeois ideology, both in its content and in its form. But unlike some Marxists, before or since, they were less interested in denouncing it than in exploring its contradictions and the complex articulations between economic determinations and the actual construction of meaning within the film. In their now famous analysis of John Ford's 1939 bio-pic *Young Mr. Lincoln*, the editors of *Cahiers* stressed the way the film does not hold together as a pure expression of ideology—whether as intended by the studio or in more general terms dictated by the crisis of capitalism during the Depression and its attempted restructuring under Roosevelt's New Deal. On the contrary, *Cahiers* argued, not only are there contradictions between the ostensible politics of the film and the input of Ford himself as director, but the way the film constructs meaning precludes any automatic translation of an ideological project into cinematic terms. Meaning in the cinema is both more complex and more precarious than straightforward Marxist interpretations make it out to be. It also has more to do with the way the film engages the spectator as subject than with the content as such.

PSYCHOANALYSIS

To account for the way films engage the spectator, the *Cahiers/Screen* writers turned to psychoanalysis, and

specifically to the reading of Freud proposed by the French writer Jacques Lacan. But whereas the choice of a particular school of Marxism—that of Louis Althusser—had mainly positive effects on the critical enterprise because Althusser specifically denied the self-sufficiency of Marxism and called instead for inputs from outside, the choice of Lacan was more controversial. Lacan is a notoriously difficult writer and the nature of his difference from orthodox schools of psychoanalysis is often obscure. Basically what film theorists got from Lacan, and would not have got from elsewhere, was a sense of the elusiveness of the knowing and perceiving subject and of the way the subject is constituted by its instinctual drives on the one hand and by its relation to the meanings offered to it by language and the structure of vision on the other. From this film theory formed the idea of a viewing subject positioned by the cinematic apparatus and specific mechanisms such as cross-cutting and the point-of-view shot and thus being bound into a particular way of reading the film and accepting its terms. Thus (in an extreme version) not only was the film itself 'bourgeois ideology', but the manner in which it put itself across to the spectator forced him or her to assume a restrictive range of positions, often apparently either neurotic or perverse. In practice, however, just as ideology was fissured and contradictory and expressed differently from film to film, so different films and film styles opened up a wide range of possible spectator positions. While Sternberg's films, for example, might impose on spectators regardless of gender a fetishistic experiencing of the female body, this was less true of other films; and while the use of shot/reverse-shot cutting in the majority of films might bind the spectator into an involuntary identification with the protagonists, Bresson's films, which do not use a shot/reverse-shot structure, allowed a greater autonomy of subject position. It was therefore possible, from a Lacanian position, both to criticize the ideological workings of cinema and to propose alternatives.

STRUCTURALISM AND SEMIOTICS

If Lacanian psychoanalysis offered a theory of how the meaning of a film worked on the spectator, it had to be shown that films were a vehicle of meaning in the first place. While it is obvious enough that films convey some sort of meaning to their spectators, it is by no means so sure that they operate as a structured set of significations which can be analysed with the precision applied by linguists to verbal language. A crucial step in the direction of a quasi-linguistic understanding of cinema came with the publication of Roland Barthes's *Elements of Semiology* in 1964. Following a line of thought first expressed by the Swiss linguist Ferdinand de Saussure at the beginning of the century, Barthes proposed that verbal language was

Jean-Luc Godard

(1930–)

Born into an upper middle-class Parisian family, Godard was educated in Switzerland (becoming a naturalized Swiss citizen during the Second World War) and in Paris. A student of ethnology at the Sorbonne, he spent the early 1950s watching films, globe-trotting, and supporting himself with a variety of odd jobs. In this period he helped found *La Gazette du cinéma* and contributed to *Cahiers du cinéma* and *Arts*, developed a passion for Hollywood and a critical sense of his own national cinema, produced a clutch of short films, and began to write screenplays. He was shortly to become a key figure in the French 'New Wave' cinema of the late 1950s and early 1960s alongside Truffaut, Chabrol, Rohmer, and Rivette.

His early feature films are innovatory genre pieces, generally crime stories and with a focus on the enigma of female sexuality. *À bout de souffle* (*Breathless*, 1959) is the anarchic and freewheeling story of a thief who guns down a policeman and goes on the run until he is betrayed by his girlfriend. *Bande à part* (1964) features two young men who plan an incompetent crime in order to impress the woman (played by Anna Karina) they are both in love with. Anna Karina, married to Godard 1960-5, also plays the stripper who longs for a baby in the upbeat widescreen musical *Une Femme est une femme* (1961—Godard's first film in colour), and the prostitute in *Vivre sa vie* (1962), a subdued story of everyday sexuality, shot in twelve severe tableaux.

Female subjectivity is at the heart of Godard's major commercial project of the early 1960s, *Le Mépris* (*Contempt*, 1963), which explores the breakup of a couple under the pressure of the husband's fateful attempt to rewrite *The Odyssey* for a director played by Fritz Lang. *Une Femme mariée* (*A Married Woman*, 1964) follows a day in the life of a woman who cannot tell whether she is pregnant by her husband or her lover. Other mid-1960s adventure films also centre on the heterosexual romance. *Alphaville* (1965) is both a stylized science-fiction adventure and a social myth about the competing claims of human love and new technology; set in the future, it was shot entirely on location in Paris, using high-contrast super-fast black and white film. *Pierrot le fou* (1965) offers a spectacular and tragicomic montage of colour and 'scope, in which a couple escape the capital for a zany and perilous life on the run in the south of France.

In the mid-1960s Godard's dilettantish politics (his early *Le Petit Soldat* was banned by the censor for three years for its sympathetic portrayal of a right-wing terrorist in the Algerian war) changed in the direction of a serious engagement with the left. The key work of the period is *2 ou 3 choses que je sais d'elle* (1966), which locates its story of a Parisian housewife's resort to prostitution within a wider treatise on the sociology of contemporary Paris. In *La Chinoise* (1967), a group of young French Maoists attempt to import the lessons of the Cultural Revolution. *Weekend* (1967) starts as a black satire on French bourgeois family life and then turns into an apocalyptic road movie which culminates in the take-over of the Paris region by a band of gun-toting, cannibalistic hippie revolutionaries.

In 1968 Godard's fictional concerns gave way to docu-

mentaries and essay films dealing with immediate political realities. In *Le Gai Savoir* (1968), a TV studio is the setting for a new political education in the languages of image and of sound, whilst *One Plus One* intercuts the Rolling Stones at work in the recording studio with fragmentary and tongue-in-cheek political motifs. In the aftermath of May 1968 Godard broke away from 'art' cinema, submerging individual authorship in the collective identity of the Dziga Vertov Group (essentially, Godard and Jean-Pierre Gorin) and turning to the production of experimental film essays about politics and ideology.

Vent d'est (1969) is the Group's experiment in fiction, a deconstructive Western starring Gian Maria Volonté. These initiatives—raw, inchoate, and often struggling to convince—find their most coherent expression in Godard's and Gorin's re-emergence in the mainstream context after Godard's motorcycle accident in 1971. The big-budget political romance *Tout va bien* (1972) stars Yves Montand and Jane Fonda in an engaging Brechtian study of the relationship between sexual, industrial, and representational politics which looks back at what has happened to France in the period since May 1968. The film is disturbingly contextualized by *Letter to Jane*, an essay film in which Godard and Gorin cruelly critique Fonda's relationship to the politics of representation and the Vietnam War.

Godard spent the remainder of the 1970s in a further shift towards the new medium of video, working in his experimental TV studio in Switzerland. With his new collaborator Anne-Marie Miéville, he produced a series of works exploring the possibilities of the new medium, most notably in the TV series *Sur et sous la communication* (also known as *Six fois deux*, 1976) and *France / tour / détour / deux enfants* (1978), and the feature *Numéro deux* (1975), whose multiple video images fill the film frame with complex representations of French working-class life, with particular reference to the relationship between work and sexuality.

Godard returned to narrative fiction cinema with *Sauve qui peut (la vie)* (1980), followed by *Passion* (1981). His films of the 1980s roam widely. They include the spoof thrillers *Détective* (1984) and the romantic murder story *Nouvelle Vague* (1990), an all-star reworking of *King Lear* (1967—with Norman Mailer, Woody Allen, Peter Sellers, Burgess Meredith, and Molly Ringwald), and the controversial *Je vous salue, Marie* (1983), which relocates the biblical story in contemporary Switzerland. Above all, however, the late films inscribe once more the now ageing film-maker himself as lost or fading visionary, or, concentrating once again on the institutional politics of representation, take the complex and illusionistic business of image-making and of film narration as their serious and sometimes comic central themes. Alongside the features he continues to produce a range of video works—an often neglected area of his work which was celebrated by an exhibition at the New York Museum of Modern Art in 1992.

Godard's is amongst the most political of cinemas, not simply in terms of subject-matter, but in terms of his insistence not just on making 'political films', but on 'making films politically'. His key themes are money, sexuality, politics, and cinema itself as representational machine. He is a materialist with powerful Romantic drives, and a Marxist with strong existential leanings. Steeped in the classicism of Hollywood cinema, his films are marked by a thoroughgoing European modernism which, at its best, creates intensely novel regimes of pleasurable looking and of listening. He is a radical anti-realist for whom the real remains a key priority. He is the narrator *par excellence* in a medium with too many tales to tell and un-tell, and the supreme semiotician of the cinema, with a lifetime's exploration of the complex links—and distances—between the sounds and images of cinema in its engagement with the human subject and the social.

PHILLIP DRUMMOND

SELECT FILMOGRAPHY

À bout de souffle (Breathless) (1959); Le Petit Soldat (1960); Une Femme est une femme (A Woman is a Woman) (1961); Vivre sa vie (It's My Life, 1962); Les Carabiniers (1963); Le Mépris (Contempt) (1963); Bande à part (The Outsiders) (1964); Une Femme mariée (A Married Woman) (1964); Alphaville: une étrange aventure de Lemmy Caution (1965); Pierrot le fou (1965); Masculin féminin (1966); Made in USA (1966); 2 ou 3 choses que je sais d'elle (Two or Three Things I Know about Her) (1966); La Chinoise, ou plutôt à la chinoise (1967); Weekend (1967); Un Film comme les autres (A Film Like the Others) (1968); Le Gai Savoir (1968); One Plus One / Sympathy for the Devil (1968); British Sounds (1969); Pravda (1969); Le Vent d'est (Wind from the East) (1969); Tout va bien (1972); Letter to Jane, or Investigation about a Still (1972); Ici et ailleurs (Here and Elsewhere, 1974); Numéro deux (Number Two, 1975); Comment ça va (1976); Sur et sous la communication / Six fois deux (1976); France/tour/détour/deux enfants (1978); Sauve qui peut (la vie) (Slow Motion) (1980); Passion (1981); Prénom Carmen (First Name Carmen) (1982); Je vous salue, Marie (Hail, Mary) (1983); Détective (1984); Grandeur et décadence d'un petit commerce de cinéma (Rise and Fall of a Little Film Company} (1985); Soigne ta droite (Keep your Right up, 1987); King Lear (1987); Nouvelle Vague (1990); Histoire(s) du cinéma (1994)

BIBLIOGRAPHY

Bellour, Raymond, and Bandy, Mary Lea (eds.) (1992), *Jean-Luc Godard: son + image 1974–1991*.
Brown, Royal S. (ed.) (1973), *Focus on Godard*.
Cerisuelo, Marc (1992), *Jean-Luc Godard*.
Godard, Jean-Luc (1980), *Introduction à une véritable histoire du cinéma*.
—— (1985), *Jean-Luc Godard*.
Lesage, Julia (1975), *Jean-Luc Godard: A Guide to References and Resources*.
MacCabe, Colin (1980), *Godard: Images, Sounds, Politics*.
Milne, Tom (ed.) (1973) *Godard on Godard*.
Roud, Richard (1970), *Godard*.

Opposite: Anna Karina with Claude Brasseur (left) and Sami Frey (right) in an impromptu dance in Jean-Luc Godard's *Bande à part* (1964)

only a special case (albeit a privileged one) of signifying codes used to communicate meaning. The idea of treating the cinema as a language had been put forward in the 1920s and 1930s, but had foundered on the difficulty—and sometimes absurdity—of assigning specific grammatical values to cinematic devices (a cut being like a comma or a fade like a semicolon, etc.). What Barthes argued was that the analogy between language and other communicative or signifying systems operated mainly at the level of a handful of general features necessary for structured communication. At this level it was necessary only for there to be a coded register of elements which could be put in a certain position in a communication, and an order, or syntax, in which they could be put. How meaning was conveyed—whether for example by denotation or connotation, by conventional symbols or by iconic resemblances—would depend on specific properties of the system in question.

Barthes's semiology can be seen as part of a wider structuralist enterprise, associated with the name of the anthropologist Claude Lévi-Strauss, which treated human culture as a whole—from myth, to poetry, to fashion—in terms of underlying structures of meaning. This was to have its influence on film theory in the 1960s, particularly in the analysis of genres like the Western. But the main application of semiology (or semiotics, as it later came to be called) was the attempt, initiated by Christian Metz, to map the signifying features of the cinema—its use of images, the spoken and written word, music, and natural sound—in as exhaustive and scientific manner as possible. Judged by the standards of linguistics the enterprise was never more than a partial success. The fluid and multiform character of film 'language', and the difficulty of pinning down the basic units with which it operates, meant that the results achieved were at best only provisional. Many would-be practitioners have therefore withdrawn from the systematic pursuit of a semiotics analogous with linguistics into an alternative discipline known as pragmatics, which deals with less structured and more context-determined forms of communication.

In spite of these disappointments, however, semiotics has had a real impact on writing about cinema, not just on film theory but on regular critical discourse as well. One of its effects has been to draw attention to the potential for meaning contained in details of phrase and gesture, and because it does so analytically, from the point of view of the spectator reading the film, rather than from the point of view of the film's makers, it has proved particularly applicable to the decoding of the routinized communications prevalent on television. Meanwhile its very failure to locate the elusive minimum units of film language encouraged a focus on the larger units of filmic construction, and particularly the analysis of narrative. The basic structuralist and semiotic ideas (derived in this case not from Saussure's linguistics but from the Russian Formalism of the 1920s) on how meaning is articulated by narrative have proved particularly useful in elucidating the deep structures (often strongly Oedipal) underlying many forms of popular narrative, from *Bambi* to *North by Northwest* to *Star Wars*.

COUNTER-CINEMA

The idea that the vast majority of films operated in much the same way, binding the spectator to a particular constellation of ideologically determined meanings, helped to accelerate the search for the terms of a counter-cinema which could communicate different meanings and offer the spectator a wider range of positions from which to assess them. A key influence here was the epic theatre of Bertolt Brecht, which set out to attract the spectator by means which avoided any form of identification with the action or the characters. Essential to Brecht's practice was the idea that the spectator should never lose the sense of being present at a spectacle, watching and listening to actors performing in a theatrical space. Just as Brecht had argued for an 'estrangement' (*Verfremdung*) between the actor and the audience, so the Russian Formalists in the 1920s had identified a similar form of 'making strange' (in Russian, *ostranenie*) in art and literature, sometimes seeing it as a distinguishing feature of art in general and sometimes as an effect to be aimed for.

Picking up on these antecedents, a number of film-makers and film theorists in the late 1960s attempted to elaborate a set of procedures which would enable the cinema to address the audience in a non-mystifying way. Film-makers such as Godard and Straub led the way, but the implications of what they were doing were spelt out in writings such as Peter Wollen's 'Counter-cinema: *Vent d'est*' (1972), which took one of Godard's most challenging films and both enumerated the procedures it used and offered a general critique of their applicability. While Wollen found much that was exemplary in *Vent d'est*, notably its consistent refusal to draw the spectator into a pretence that the spectacle being watched was real and therefore to be taken as an expression of truth, he also warned against Godard's aggression towards the spectator and his refusal to offer alternative pleasures to those of identification. Unfortunately these and similar warnings went unheeded by some of the succeeding generation of critics and film-makers, whose concern to resist the seductions of conventional cinema led them to make films which denied any form of pleasurable involvement on the part of the audience. For a while in the 1970s both the would-be political cinema and the artistic avant-garde suffered from a hypertrophy of theory which made them deeply unpopular.

Chantal Akerman

(1950–)

Born in Brussels of Jewish/Polish parents, Akerman's early aspirations to be writer were exchanged, on viewing Godard's *Pierrot le fou* (1965), for a career as a filmmaker. Her first 'explosive' short *Saute ma ville* (1968), in which she blows up a kitchen, set the agenda for an approach to cinema which would constantly stun, surprise, and confound expectations.

In her first feature *Je tu il elle* (1974) Akerman casts herself as the main visual presence and narrator. There is much evidence in this film of the strong personal style which was to earn her the label 'minimalist', including the use of a static camera and frontal framing, and a complete lack of either point-of-view shots or close-ups. Whilst her films have flirted with avant-garde, modernist, and structuralist forms, these early obsessions have been retained throughout.

Akerman's second film is her most (in)famous. *Jeanne Dielman 23 Quai du Commerce 1080 Bruxelles* (1975), which depicts roughly three days in the life of a housewife who is also a prostitute, was hailed as a masterpiece by feminists. Refusing the use of woman as seductive presence, *Jeanne Dielman* is shaped by Jeanne's own sense of ritual, time, and space. The meticulous recording of Jeanne's daily routine, and subsequent elision of that which is usually shown (the sexual act) disrupts the conventional hierarchy of importance in terms of both narrative and image. Thus, peeling potatoes is given as much screen time as the murder of a customer.

In *News from Home* (1976), the camera explores those parts of New York rarely captured on celluloid. In a series of tableau-like shots we are encouraged to look behind the myth, and enjoy the experience of various spaces: streets, subway stations, shop windows. With no narrative or characters, the look available in *News from Home* becomes one associated not with the masquerade of cinema, but with the possibilities the frame holds for looking, the emphasis being upon the properties of vision itself. Pleasure, meanwhile, is located largely in the camera's lingering gaze, which allows an intimacy to develop between viewer and image.

After *Les Rendez-vous d'Anna* (1978), in which Aurore Clément plays a (semi-autobiographical) Belgian filmmaker who journeys from Cologne to Paris, and *Toute une nuit* (1982), which uses genre (in the form of melodrama) for the first time, Akerman's films become increasingly playful, directly addressing the seductive aspects of classical narrative. *Golden Eighties* (1986), Akerman's biggest-budget film to date, is a musical whose setting in a shopping mall triggers an exploration of spectacle, artificiality, and performance, where love becomes something to be bought and sold, like a dress. Despite its charm and vitality the film was not a great success, which is perhaps the reason for Akerman's return to smaller-scale production with *Histoires d'Amérique* (1989).

The monotony of housework. Delphine Seyrig as the housewife/prostitute in *Jeanne Dielman, 23 Quai du Commerce 1080 Bruxelles* (1975)

Set, like *News from Home*, in New York, *Histoires* is based upon interviews and research which Akerman conducted throughout the city. Assembling an all-Jewish cast the film is simultaneously a celebration of Jewish culture and a lament for all that is displaced in the diasporic moment.

After *Nuit et jour* (1991), a playful love triangle set in Paris, Akerman returns to her eastern European roots with *D'est* (1993) a documentary which charts a journey through eastern Europe, concentrating upon gestures, faces, and daily routines. The attention which this film gives to its subject affirms Akerman's early project to film the 'images-between-images', and to address her cinema to the exclusion zones of dominant cinema. Hers is a cinema, then, which is resolutely marginal, yet which should not be marginalized, since its fundamental project is to challenge our perceptions of what cinema can or should be.

CATHERINE FOWLER

SELECT FILMOGRAPHY

Je tu il elle (1974); Jeanne Dielman 23 Quai du Commerce 1080 Bruxelles (1975); News from Home (1976); Les Rendez-vous d'Anna (1978); Toute une nuit (1982); Golden Eighties (1986); Histoires d'Amérique (1989); Nuit et jour (1991); D'est (1993)

BIBLIOGRAPHY

Atalier des Arts, 1 (1982).
Bergstrom, Janet (1977), 'Jeanne Dielman'.
Champetier, Caroline (1978) 'Les Rendez-vous d'Anna: rencontre avec Chantal Akerman'.
Mayne, Judith (1990), *The Woman at the Keyhole: Feminism and Women's Cinema*.

FEMINISM

Probably the most productive uses of the new theory were those made by feminism. For a while criticism of mainstream cinema by feminists (together with parallel criticism from ethnic and sexual minorities) concentrated on obvious things like the negative stereotyping of women characters and images of women as dumb blondes, hoydens, harridans—all seen as ways of putting women in their place in patriarchal society. But it soon came to be claimed that more was at stake than women's subordinate position in society and the way that this was variously mirrored and reinforced in particular films. Feminist writers like Claire Johnston, Pam Cook, and Laura Mulvey argued that the cinema as a whole was far more profoundly unequal in its representation of women and of sexual relations. It was not just that the majority of films took the form of heterosexual romance with a narrative resolution that put the woman in her place relative to the man (the same, after all, is true of much classic literature). Rather the means of representation produced a pattern of identification in which a masculine position dominated. Action was identified with masculinity, and women's bodies were spectacularized as the object of the male gaze and male desire—a procedure so prevalent and insistent that it overpowered any compensation offered by the creation of strong female characters or narrative resolutions in which the woman wins through undefeated.

This position had implications not only for the reading of mainstream cinema but also for feminist film-making and the idea of a feminist counter-cinema. The issue here was complicated by the realization that it was not enough to evade fiction (and its attendant dangers of spectacularization) in favour of fact. The factual, documentary image was in its way as contaminated as fiction, overlaid by conventions that had conspired to make women invisible throughout history. Unpicking historical representation became as important for film-makers as resisting the lures of fiction. Women film-makers tended, however, to be more accommodating to their audiences than some of their male counterparts and the political need to find allies generally prevailed over any impulse to bludgeon spectators into accepting the artist's ideas of what constituted a suitably deconstructive work.

In the 1980s feminist film theory continued to advance. The complex ambivalence of female spectatorship and the pleasures that women draw from cinema became the main object of attention. This led to a more sympathetic treatment of melodrama and the women's picture and a recognition that the masquerade of femininity widespread in the cinema is not a purely negative phenomenon. In feminist film theory, as elsewhere, more emphasis came to be put on what audiences read between the lines, or against the grain, and less on the ideological structuring that assigns women and femininity to a seemingly inevitable subordination.

QUEERNESS AND TRANSGRESSION

Central to the new theories has been the idea that the cinema is a mechanism which sets desire in motion and at the same time contains it. In itself this is not a new discovery, nor is its application confined to cinema. Flow and containment, frustration and satisfaction, are essential elements of musical form, and narrative theory has long maintained that all narrative proceeds by a movement from order to disorder and then to a new order being established. The content of narrative has also been traditionally seen as the channelling and shaping of desire in the interests of social cohesion, with couple formation, marriage, and reproduction as the explicit or implicit goal of stories the world over, and incest and homosexuality as the threats to be contained or warded off.

Nowhere has the heterosexual romance been so normative as in the cinema, or the temptation to transgression so great. Cinema is an erotic art which for much of its life has been uncomfortably strait-jacketed to the needs of family entertainment. The massive apparatuses of censorship and control of the cinema have as their object the regulation of images of the human body—in motion or frozen into poses—which are at all times potentially evocative of sexual disorder.

There is, however, nothing natural about the normativeness of the cinema, nor is it easily and comfortably achieved. Gay critics were not slow to note that, however normative the ostensible surface of the film, homosexual desire is not cancelled out but often remains present as a disruptive undercurrent in the work of directors as diverse as Eisenstein, Visconti, or Hawks. This proved to be a particularly fertile line of inquiry since previously gay criticism had been sidetracked by questions (which proved surprisingly hard to answer) of how homosexuals and homosexual activity were conventionally represented in cinema. The emergence in the late 1980s of a new broad concept of 'queer cinema' enabled critics to bring together in a single field a large number of manifestations of homosexuality in the cinema, from explicit to implicit, from pornography to the most respectable mainstream, all of which could be seen as in some way challenging the heterosexual norm.

An essential condition for the emergence of queer cinema was the liberalization and opening up of cinema which took place in America, Europe, and Japan from the late 1960s onwards and the affirmative political movements which flourished at the same time. A new cinema came into being, ranging from campaign films to gay and lesbian love stories to mainstream films which incorporated transgressive sexualities into their subject-matter. Elements of homosexual content began to appear more

Agnès Varda

(1928–)

A naturalized French film-maker, of Belgian and Greek parentage, Agnès Varda has made eleven features (five of which have won international prizes) and sixteen shorts or documentaries. She describes herself as an auteur and her work as an *artisanale* (small production craft work). Skills learnt and refined in her documentary work translate into her feature films in the form of a detached objectivity. Her detachment and skill in filmic experimentation also stem from her earlier experiences as photographer, painter, sculptor, and photo-journalist. Varda places her work at the interface between factual fiction and fictional fact, and speaks of filming the subjectivity of the individual as it relates to the objectivity of the environment. The individual is placed and viewed in the context of society, and so Varda's films are generally exceptionally topical (e.g. in the 1960s, cancer; in the 1970s, feminism; in the 1980s, social decline). Having seized upon an issue she proceeds to document it in a non-conflictual way. Consequently her films are non-ideological but replete with socio-realism.

Although each film for her is a new departure, there are several distinctive features to her film-making: use of counterpoint, distanciation, and what she terms *cinécriture* (cine-writing). Varda was the first to understand how to transcribe counterpoint (in the Faulknerian sense of sustaining two narratives side by side) into *the* cinematic form that would simultaneously express individual and social problems. Her detached contrapuntal editing style is unique and was one that the Nouvelle Vague film-makers adapted to their own work (especially Resnais and Godard). Both the subjective/individual and the objective/social must be observed impassively for a realism to emerge out of the collision of the two narratives. Hence Varda's frequent references to cinema in terms of violence.

Varda is equally detached from her characters. She does not supply them with any psychology, so they have no depth. This means that characters are not necessarily central—their story is as significant as the next person's. Hence the preponderance of titles referring to either places, general concepts, or movements.

Varda achieves her effect of distanciation through truncation of space, time, and narration. She subverts the codes and conventions of classical cinema, deconstructs genres to reconstruct them as other (e.g. *L'Une chante, l'autre pas*, 1977, a musical on women's reproduction rights). Her film practises counter spectator identification; held at a distance, it is for the spectator to evaluate the film. Similarly her *cinécriture* draws attention to the process of film-making. Varda sees it as closely allied to the technique of painting in its structural composition, texture, and tonality—and often refers to her work in painterly terms (in *Sans toit ni loi*, 1985, she talked of cinepainting the texture of solitude).

Varda is a feminist and most of her films address the way in which women are fixed in traditional cinema as eternal, unchanging, as spectacle, as object of and for the male gaze—and therefore as ahistoric, as other. Varda speaks of her film work in terms of asking questions and of doing so in disturbing ways. She uses cinematic language disruptively, intent on denaturalizing dominant male ideology, and opening up institutional myths. Since women are ahistoric, reified as other and therefore without subjectivity, she will render their non-existence visible (e.g. *Cléo de 5 à 7*, 1961). Since women are placed outside language she will show this by exposing and subverting the language that is available (e.g. *Sans toit ni loi*).

Thus, in her films, Varda shows that it is she who invents and controls the cinematic language. It is for this reason that some critics inveigh against her cold detachment and obsession with camera technique, something they praise in the work of Bresson or Resnais. To control language is to control the representation of reality and, since language is at present a male construct, how else to dismiss Varda's work than by accusing it of being 'unfemale'? Feminist critics are not of one voice; some perceive her work as perpetuating the European art cinema (i.e. male) style, but others argue that she continues the heritage of earlier French feminist film-makers, Guy, Dulac, and Epstein.

SUSAN HAYWARD

SELECT FILMOGRAPHY

La Pointe courte (1954); Cléo de 5 à 7 (1961); Le Bonheur (1965); Les Créatures (1966); Lion's Love (1969); Nausicaa (1970); Daguerréotypes (1975); Une minute pour une image (170 two-minute films, 1983); Sans toit ni loi (Vagabonde, 1985); Jane B. vue par Agnès V. (1987); Kung Fu Master (1987); Jacquot de Nantes (1991)

BIBLIOGRAPHY

Flitterman-Lewis, Sandy (1990), *To Desire Differently: Feminism and French Cinema*.
Hayward, Susan (1990), 'Beyond the gaze and into femme-film écriture: Agnès Varda's *Sans toit ni loi*'.

Corinne Marchand in Agnès Varda's *Cléo de 5 à 7* (1961)

boldly in the work of established European directors such as Visconti (notably *Ludwig*, 1972), Pasolini (*The Arabian Nights*, 1974), and Fassbinder (*Fox and his Friends*, 1974), while among the younger generation Pedro Almodóvar (*Law of Desire*, 1987) established his career around the deliberate flouting of gender conventions. For a long time Hollywood remained rather coy (Bob Fosse's 1972 *Cabaret* is a courageous early exception) and even in the 1990s films like Gus Van Sant's *My Own Private Idaho* (1991) exist only on the margins while the mainstream offers up the safe and unerotic *Philadelphia*.

Queer cinema, however, covers a much broader field than just films about homosexuals and homosexuality. It includes the homo-erotic subtexts in apparently straight films and the important phenomenon of 'camp' and other against-the-grain readings of films of many different types. It therefore points both to the textual properties of films and the way normative heterosexuality may be subverted in all sorts of unexpected places and to questions that have more to do with audience reception and with the appropriation that different audience groups may make of the same film. In this latter respect it is but one of many tendencies challenging the idea that meaning is something unequivocally present in the film text. For although many films lay themselves open to camp readings, the decision to read them that way—and therefore to draw from them distinct and unexpected pleasure—is one made by the audience, often against the grain of the film's intended meaning.

RECEPTION

The proponents of queer cinema are not alone in stressing the importance of audiences in deciding what the film meant for them. Feminist critics had already argued that the positioning of the female spectator was by no means as fixed as some of the 'structuralist' writers had maintained, while attempts to denounce the reactionary and racist stereotyping of Hollywood films such as Sylvester Stallone's Rambo series have often run foul of the fact that sections of the audience which seem to be negatively stereotyped have nevertheless developed their own way of discounting this stereotyping and enjoying the film. This ability of audiences to determine their own readings of films became a major focus of attention in the 1980s, drawing support from the more fluid theories of meaning associated with 'post-modern' thinkers like Jacques Derrida and Jean Baudrillard as well as from empirically based audience studies which showed wide differences in understanding between different components of the mass audience. Meanwhile audiences themselves have become increasingly segmented and, far more than in the classical period, films which aspire to mass appeal have to allow for all sorts of differential reading by spectators. In this respect the cinema has become post-modern because the

audience has made it so, with films like *The Last Action Hero* (1993) deliberately playing on audiences' preparedness to switch from one mode of reception to another.

FILM STUDIES AND THE CANON

With the expansion of higher education and the establishment of a new discipline of film studies, the locus of serious and scholarly writing has tended to shift away from the informal world of film enthusiasts to the more structured environment of the universities. This has been a mixed blessing. On the positive side, the writing of film history has become both more sophisticated and better resourced. Not only have film historians enjoyed fuller opportunities to practise their craft but they have been able to draw on intellectual developments in related disciplines such as economic and cultural history. Broader perspectives, supported by detailed work on a wide variety of sources, mean that the place of cinema in twentieth-century culture and in the world capitalist economy is much better understood than it was twenty or thirty years ago.

On the critical front, however, the situation is confused. Many of the film-theoretical revolutionaries of the 1970s were actively hostile to the idea of film criticism understood as a form of knowledgeable but subjective response to films, aiming to replace it by more refined and rigorous forms of film analysis. In the event, the practice of film criticism *is* in a state of general decline, but more because of the reluctance of literary editors of magazines to allow space for extended treatment of topical films than because of the cogency of the attacks on it. Meanwhile academic writing on films has become somewhat cocooned and obsessed with problems which (for all their claims to be political) have little influence on the world outside the academy. To some extent this is due to changes in the cinema itself. Compared with, say, the 1960s, relatively few films are being produced (or at any released) which seem to require the attentive aesthetic analysis given in its day to classic Hollywood or to European, Japanese, or Indian art cinema. If the mechanisms by which films form perception have become stale, and films which change perception have become rare, it is not surprising if the practice of film criticism has given way to breathless journalism on the one side and to academic nit-picking on the other.

The problem is compounded by the absence of a sense of canonical values. Up to 1960 there was a general agreement on what values were important and which films and film-makers best expressed them. The auteurist critics of the late 1950s and early 1960s attempted to change the canon of established values—putting Hawks above Ford, Rossellini above De Sica, Mizoguchi above Kurosawa, etc.—not to abolish the idea entirely. Subsequent writers have been suspicious of all forms of film canon, sometimes because their personal tastes took them in bizarre and definitely non-canonical directions, sometimes because they argued that the idea of a canon was by definition dangerously élitist.

This creates severe difficulties for a proper understanding of cinema. First, a canon continues to exist—but by default and determined more by the vagaries of fashion and the accidents of availability than by any form of reasoned argument. Secondly, in default of such argument the idea of the importance of cinema itself is undermined. If any film can be as important as any other, and if quasi-historical or idiosyncratically personal judgements take the place of aesthetic reasoning, it is open to anyone to challenge the purpose of taking films seriously in the first place. There has to be a sense of what the cinema has achieved over the past hundred years, and where to look to find the evidence of its achievement. This achievement takes the form of works which can endure, and which, having spoken in one way to audiences at one time, can pose new challenges to judgement now and in the future.

No canon, however, can be eternally fixed, nor should a film canon be allowed to degenerate, as the literary canon has tended to do, into an invocation of lists of authors—generally dead, white, and male—whose works are supposedly beyond challenge. Fortunately in the case of cinema this is unlikely to happen. For a start film studies has convincingly established the argument that cinema's achievement is not, or not solely, a matter of authors and that many key works, particularly in the classic Hollywood

cinema, are as much a product of the system as of any individual (both *Gone with the Wind* and *The Wizard of Oz* experienced changes of directors in mid-stream). Secondly the film-critical apparatus has always been internationalist, and critics have always striven—and hopefully always will—to promote the values of the alternative against the mainstream and the Third World against the industrial and cultural domination of the First.

The question of women's cinema is more problematic. Women's power in the cinema has always been more as consumers than as producers and establishing that women film-makers have had an important, if neglected, part to play in creating cinema has to a certain extent been an anti-canonical (or counter-canonical) exercise, in opposition to dominant values. But the argument put forward here in favour of canons is not an argument in favour of closing ranks around the status quo. Rather it is an argument in favour of argument, in favour of declaring and defending reasons for aesthetic and other choices.

Bibliography
Andrew, J. Dudley (1976), *The Major Film Theories*.
Barthes, Roland (1967), *Elements of Semiology*.
Cook, Pam, and Johnston, Claire (1974), 'The Place of Women in the Films of Raoul Walsh'.
Elsaesser, Thomas (1972), 'Tales of Sound and Fury'.
Metz, Christian (1971), *Language and Cinema*.
Mulvey, Laura (1975), 'Visual Pleasure and Narrative Cinema'.
Wollen, Peter (1972), 'Counter-cinema: *Vent d'est*'.
—— (1972), *Signs and Meaning in the Cinema*.

The Resurgence of Cinema

GEOFFREY NOWELL-SMITH

At various times and in various parts of the world since the 1960s it has often seemed as if the cinema was in a state of irreversible decline. The evidence was there in the form of dwindling attendances, less variety of films to be seen, and—most visibly—in the sad sight of former picture palaces boarded up, demolished to make way for parking lots, or converted to use as bingo halls, bowling alleys, or warehouses. Less visible, but equally disturbing, has been a sense that cinema has lost its centrality, particularly in Europe, yielding ground to other media and cultural forms.

Yet closer examination suggests that the decline is only apparent, both in quantity and in quality. The cinema has changed. It has changed character, and it has changed location. But having just completed its first century of existence, it is entering the second very much alive.

During this second century it will undoubtedly be very different, if only because its environment—that of television, video, and emerging forms of multimedia—is also changing. But certainly for the foreseeable future it will continue to survive and to develop as a distinct artistic and entertainment medium, offering irreplaceable forms of experience to audiences whether numbered in their thousands or in their millions.

THE CHANGING PATTERN OF EXHIBITION

To start with the most obvious signs of the cinema's reputed decline: it is certainly true that the number of theatres has been dwindling, particularly in the inner cities and (most sadly) in many small and even medium-sized towns which now have no cinemas at all. But the larger theatres that have survived have in many cases

TABLE 1. *Indigenous films' share of European national markets (%), 1995*

	1980	1981	1982	1983	1984	1985	1986	1987	1988	1989	1990	1991	1992	1993	1994	1995
Belgium	3.0	1.0	1.0	2.0	1.0	1.0	1.0	3.0	4.0	3.0	4.0	3.0	3.0	3.0	3.0	3.0
Denmark	23.0	25.0	20.0	20.0	23.0	19.0	25.0	21.0	19.0	17.0	10.0	11.0	12.0	13.0	13.0	14.0
France	47.0	50.0	53.0	47.0	49.0	45.0	43.0	34.0	38.0	34.0	38.0	30.0	35.0	35.0	32.0	33.0
Germany	9.0	19.0	12.0	14.0	17.0	23.0	22.0	18.0	23.0	17.0	9.7	11.0	10.0	10.0	11.0	11.0
Greece	28.0	30.0	33.0	30.0	25.0	12.0	12.0	11.0	10.0	9.0	8.0	7.0	6.0	5.0	5.0	6.0
Ireland	1.0	1.0	1.0	1.0	1.0	2.0	2.0	2.0	2.0	2.0	5.0	2.0	2.0	2.0	2.0	2.0
Italy	43.0	44.0	46.0	39.0	33.0	31.0	31.0	33.0	28.0	22.0	20.0	18.0	17.0	17.0	16.0	15.0
Luxembourg	3.0	3.0	3.0	3.0	3.0	3.0	3.0	3.0	3.0	6.0	2.0	3.0	3.0	3.0	3.0	3.0
Holland	8.0	13.0	13.0	14.0	19.0	4.0	14.0	21.0	12.0	5.0	3.0	2.0	3.0	3.0	3.0	4.0
Portugal	1.0	2.0	1.0	0.7	2.0	1.0	4.0	7.0	4.0	1.0	1.0	1.0	1.0	1.0	1.0	1.0
Spain	19.0	18.0	18.0	17.0	17.0	16.0	16.0	15.0	12.0	7.0	10.0	10.0	11.0	12.0	12.0	13.0
UK	15.0	15.0	14.0	13.0	12.0	15.0	15.0	10.0	15.0	19.0	18.0	17.0	18.0	18.0	19.0	20.0
EU	27.0	29.0	30.0	27.0	28.0	26.0	25.0	22.0	22.0	19.0	18.0	16.0	17.0	18.0	17.0	18.0

Source: Merged Database/BIPE.

TABLE 2. *US films' share of European national markets (%), 1995*

	1980	1981	1982	1983	1984	1985	1986	1987	1988	1989	1990	1991	1992	1993	1994	1995
Belgium	47.0	48.0	43.0	52.0	56.0	68.0	72.0	62.0	64.0	68.9	73.5	80.2	78.0	79.0	79.0	79.0
Denmark	44.5	49.0	50.0	53.0	51.0	61.2	61.0	55.8	60.0	63.6	77.0	83.0	82.0	80.0	79.0	77.0
France	35.2	30.8	30.0	35.0	36.8	39.1	43.3	43.8	45.9	55.3	56.9	58.7	58.0	57.0	58.0	58.0
Germany	52.0	52.9	55.4	60.4	65.8	59.0	62.6	58.3	64.4	70.0	74.8	76.4	82.9	79.0	76.5	75.0
Greece	58.0	56.0	51.0	56.0	63.0	77.0	79.0	81.0	85.0	86.0	87.0	88.0	88.0	89.0	88.0	87.0
Ireland	88.0	87.0	86.0	84.0	83.0	83.0	81.0	80.0	79.0	75.0	87.0	91.5	91.0	90.0	89.0	88.0
Italy	33.7	32.6	32.0	41.6	46.0	47.0	50.0	46.1	56.0	65.1	75.0	69.0	70.1	71.0	73.0	74.0
Luxembourg	60.0	60.0	62.0	62.0	64.0	65.0	65.0	65.0	65.0	68.0	78.0	84.0	82.0	83.0	84.0	85.0
Holland	49.0	46.0	51.0	59.0	60.0	72.0	74.0	63.0	76.0	77.0	86.0	93.0	91.0	90.0	89.0	88.0
Portugal	46.0	56.0	44.0	47.0	48.0	51.0	64.0	67.0	72.0	78.0	81.0	85.0	81.0	80.0	81.0	82.0
Spain	44.0	46.0	48.0	50.0	52.0	54.0	56.0	58.0	64.0	73.0	72.0	69.0	69.0	67.0	66.0	64.0
UK	80.0	80.0	81.0	82.0	83.0	80.0	80.0	89.0	77.0	79.0	78.0	80.0	79.0	77.0	76.0	75.0
EU	46.0	45.0	44.0	50.0	52.0	54.0	58.0	58.0	62.0	69.0	72.0	72.0	73.0	71.0	71.0	71.0

Source: Merged Database/BIPE.

'Art cinema' for the world? Bertolucci's Oscar-laden internationally acclaimed epic on Chinese history
The Last Emperor (1987)

doubled, tripled, or quadrupled their screens. This has sometimes led to a less attractive viewing experience as buildings were clumsily converted and projection quality slumped. But the multi-screen cinemas at least offer some choice to both mainstream and minority audiences, and both choice and comfort have been increased now that Europe has belatedly followed the US example and new multiplexes have been opened in suburban locations. Some of these are quite spectacular, and offer an enormous choice of films on a single site, enhanced by restaurants and other leisure facilities. At Kinepolis in Brussels, for example, in a sample week in early 1995, twenty-six different films were being shown spread over twenty-eight screens (the only duplication being due to the fact that Walt Disney's *The Lion King* was on show in French and Flemish versions and the latest Arnold Schwarzenegger vehicle, *Junior*, was on in both English and French).

The opening of the multiplexes suggests that the decline in cinema-going has been at least partly due, not to a lack of interest in films but to the fact that theatres were badly situated and offered inadequate facilities. Current indications are that the fall in box-office which was almost universal throughout the western world in the 1970s and 1980s has been stemmed. In Britain, where audiences in 1984 had dipped to 50 million (less than one visit to the cinema per year per member of the population), they have now gone back to around the 100 million mark; in other countries where the decline came later it seems to have bottomed out, while in the United States the figures have been remarkably stable for a number of years.

A more disquieting phenomenon from a European and indeed world perspective (though again its significance can easily be misinterpreted) is the growing dominance of Hollywood and quasi-Hollywood films in mainstream exhibition venues. The chief losers in the changing pattern of cinema exhibition have been old films (and the second- and third-run cinemas where they used to be shown), and foreign films. As the attached figures show (Tables 1 and 2), American films have now captured some 80 per cent of the market in most western European countries, with the rest of the market being taken up by indigenous films and only a negligible share going to films from other European or non-European countries. With the opening up of the market in eastern Europe the pattern there is somewhat similar. In Asia the situation is more complicated, since Chinese- and Hindi-speaking films maintain a strong international presence, and indigenous industries remain strong in countries such as the Philippines, Indonesia, and Iran. But even there a 'rationalization' of the market in favour mainly of Hollywood films is in progress and its effects cannot be long delayed.

The Hollywoodization of world cinema is not in itself a new phenomenon. Already in the 1920s Hollywood had acquired 80 per cent of the market in countries as far apart as Italy and Canada, and its market share throughout the west has never dropped below 50 per cent. But the market Hollywood first entered in the silent period was an expanding one and one in which there was considerable international circulation of non-American films. Also it was possible then for countries to close their markets selec-

tively, and many of them did. The coming of sound offered further respite for national industries and any hopes that Hollywood might have entertained for further unfettered expansion were checked.

What is new, and alarming, in the current situation is that there are now no checks on the exercise of market power by the major Hollywood companies and the room for manœuvre for other cinemas has become severely restricted, even in the United States itself. Hollywoodization is now an accomplished fact, and the survival of other cinemas, except in Asia, has become a matter of a complex symbiosis with the dominant power and the creation of small market niches. In many parts of the world the situation of national cinemas can be likened to that of the pilot fish in the jaws of the shark. Meanwhile the monopolization of the international market means that many films, particularly from small countries, are

Mr Orange (Tim Roth) and Mr White (Harvey Keitel) in the aftermath of a failed and bloody heist: Quentin Tarantino's *Reservoir Dogs* (1992)

only shown in their home country or at the occasional festival, making them hopelessly uneconomic to produce. The efforts of the European Union to create a 'common market' for European-produced films, and so enable them collectively to resist Hollywood competition, have not been conspicuously successful, at least as far as mainstream exhibition is concerned, but they have achieved important results in other areas.

At least as important as the symbiosis between Hollywood and the rest of world cinema is that between cinema and other media such as television and video, and here the picture is more encouraging. For a long time the film industry (especially, of course, the exhibitors) regarded television and video as hostile competitors. What has now emerged is a pattern of mutual dependence. The growth in the number of television channels has led to an increase in the demand for both new and old films. Television companies have purchased the languishing back catalogue of film studios and distributors (the most spectacular example being cable-TV mogul Ted Turner's acquisition of MGM and much of the Warner's catalogue) and are also major investors in new production, particularly in Europe. Far more films are now available to be seen on TV and video than were ever around in the cinema's heyday, and the total amount of film viewing (mostly on the small screen) is far greater than in the days when cinema-going as such was the world's most popular form of entertainment. Well over half of the revenue earned by the majority of films now comes from the 'secondary' markets of TV and video, aided by the 'tertiary' markets of music sales, multimedia, and rights on still images reproduced in various forms.

In 1993 the negotiations on the Uruguay round of the General Agreement on Tariffs and Trades (GATT) were more or less stalled on the question—or so it seemed—of the protection of the European (and in particular the French) cinema market from Hollywood competition. In fact the argument was not really about cinema exhibition at all, where Europe has already lost the battle. Rather it was about the markets which in cinema terms are secondary but which globally are of more value and where the battle is still very much alive. It is over the control of the airwaves and cable links—of television, video, digitized multimedia, and the 'information superhighway'—that the struggle is now focused. Both here and in the old (but still significant) markets of the film heritage and independent film exhibition, Europe, Japan, and the rest of the world are, for the moment at least, holding their own.

CINEMA AND OTHER MEDIA

Where does this leave the cinema? It can reasonably be objected that seeing films on the small screen is not cinema at all and that the films themselves are diminished by being made with small-screen viewing in mind. In fact, however, cinema in the pure sense remains central to the experience of the moving image even in the complex world of multimedia. Neither video nor television is a self-sufficient market for feature-length films. Although some films are 'made-for-TV' or 'straight-to-video' and can indeed be made electronically without recourse to celluloid, and although some films intended for the cinema never get beyond the small screen, theatrical release in 35 mm. is still a necessity for most films of any importance. It is through theatrical release that films acquire their reputation and it is in the cinema that they are seen (and heard) as they should be. Modern technology has made the cinema experience visually and aurally more powerful than ever before and it is this experience that continues to be treasured by audiences, even if their visits to the cinema are infrequent. In the new symbiosis, the much-heralded advent of High Definition Television (HDTV) needs to be seen much more as an extension of the values of cinema to the world of home entertainment than as a further encroachment of television on the world of cinema. The next phase of technological development, the digitization of film images for transmission by computer links, will increase the range of crossovers between media, but will still not challenge the role of cinema as the focal point and standard against which moving images are assessed.

In the new media symbiosis, the cinema is above all a showcase for the new and the spectacular (which in part accounts for the dominance of Hollywood on the big screen throughout the world). More and more the cultural, geographical, and historical variety of world cinema is reflected on the small screen rather than the large. At least in Europe and the United States, the number of old films available for theatrical or non-theatrical distribution has shrunk and the audience for big-screen presentation of films which are neither new, nor mainstream, nor spectacular (and which are liable to be in poor physical condition) has shrunk too. But these values count for less in small-screen presentation, and it is on television (though generally not in prime time) or through a visit to the video store that audiences come into contact with the extraordinary breadth of the accumulated culture of world cinema. Although there are bizarre gaps in what is available (often due to arcane rights disputes which prevent re-releases), access to knowledge of the cinema has never been so great or so widespread.

It is nevertheless worth pausing to consider the effects of a situation in which the shape of the cinema seems more and more to be that of a pyramid, with a wide base in the form of the many films viewable on television or video and a narrow peak composed of the far fewer films which now get full-scale theatrical release.

Martin Scorsese

(1942–)

Martin Scorsese grew up in the Sicilian neighbourhood of New York City's Little Italy, Elizabeth Street. His parents worked in the garment industry and were the children of immigrants. As a child, Scorsese's asthma prevented strenuous physical exertion, so he immersed himself in the movies, and a passion for and intimate knowledge of the films he saw in his childhood would profoundly mark his own work.

Scorsese studied for the priesthood, but switched to film-making at New York University, where he became an admirer of the French and Italian New Wave, and of the New York underground film-making of Shirley Clarke and John Cassavetes. As a student, and later instructor, at NYU he won recognition for his early short films, and raised the finance for his first feature *Who's that Knocking at my Door* (1969).

Like many directors of the era, Scorsese received his first commercial opportunity from Roger Corman, who hired him to direct the Depression-era crime saga *Boxcar Bertha* (1972). While working within the limits of a low-budget exploitation genre, Scorsese had considerable freedom to explore personal themes and styles.

With Corman's promise to distribute his next film, Scorsese made *Mean Streets* (1973), set in the Italian-American milieu of his childhood that he had already chronicled in his first feature and that he would return to throughout his career (in *Raging Bull*, 1980; *GoodFellas*, 1990; and a documentary about his parents, *Italianamerican*, 1974). *Mean Streets* is a violent, realist exploration of the neighbourhood and its characters, focusing on Charlie (Harvey Keitel) and his relationship with the reckless Johnny Boy (Robert De Niro in his first role for Scorsese). However, the film also contains sequences with experimental and stylized camera work—particularly long tracking shots and slowed-down action—and the ground-breaking use of contemporary music on the sound-track, edited closely to the images, to give the action a choreographed feel. (This effect was repeated in his later films, particularly in the boxing sequences in *Raging Bull*.) If *Mean Streets* showed the beginnings of a definite visual style, which would become more polished as his career progressed, the film also focused on themes that would prove recurrent in Scorsese's work; particularly religious notions of sin and redemption, here centred around the figures of priest and gangster. Like his visual style, these themes are an amalgam of semi-autobiographical realism, and the powerful influence of film history. Scorsese claimed that 'at the same time as giving this accurate picture of Italian-Americans, I was trying to make a kind of homage to the Warner Brothers gangster films'.

After finding commercial and critical success with *Alice Doesn't Live Here Anymore* (1975; unusually for Scorsese, a story centred around a woman) and the brilliant, violent *Taxi Driver* (1976), Scorsese suffered a string of box-office disappointments. These films later came to be considered among the best films of the 1980s: *Raging Bull, New York, New York* (1981), and *King of Comedy* (1983). Scorsese scaled himself down to fit within the industry's needs, making the dark comedy *After Hours* (1985) and even directing for TV, and finally winning commercial success with *The Color of Money* (1986), the sequel to *The Hustler* (1961). This success enabled Scorsese to secure the funding for a project he had been trying to make for many years (and which had gone into lengthy pre-production in 1983), an adaptation of Nikos Kazantzakis's *The Last Temptation of Christ*. Finally released in 1988, the film, about the conflict between the human and divine sides of Christ, suffered from protests by religious groups which prevented many exhibitors from showing it.

Scorsese's relationship with Hollywood has been mixed; skirting between commercial success and failure, he has been willing to direct studio movies (for in-

stance *The Color of Money* and *Cape Fear*, 1991) to secure the possibility of directing long-cherished personal projects. Scorsese's film-making methods also oscillate between an integration with commercial cinema and a more independent stance. In his first commercial experience with Corman, Scorsese meticulously planned every shot of *Boxcar Bertha*, a technique he would continue when working on the low-budget *Taxi Driver* for Columbia. On the other hand, Scorsese has also incorporated a looser approach by integrating actors' improvisation into his films. He tape-recorded improvisations for *Mean Streets*, *Alice Doesn't . . .*, *New York, New York*, and *King of Comedy*, then rewrote the improvisations into dialogue.

Scorsese's openness and sensitivity to actors' work has resulted in the powerful performances seen in his films. Ellen Burstyn, Robert De Niro, and Paul Newman have all won Oscars when directed by him. Scorsese repeatedly works with a coterie of actors, including Harvey Keitel and Joe Pesci, but it is certainly Scorsese's seven films with De Niro which will be most remembered, since, in films like *Mean Streets*, *Taxi Driver*, *Raging Bull*, *King of Comedy*, and *Cape Fear*, Scorsese gives De Niro the liberty to develop the monomaniacal characterizations which have become the actor's hallmark.

Although he is probably best known for his Italian-American films, Scorsese has worked within and renovated many traditional genres, making a concert film, a musical, a boxing film, a period costume drama, and a religious epic. In addition, his films are founded on his detailed study of and admiration for a wide range of films—and he has dedicated much of his time in between directing to campaigns for film preservation and support for other film-makers. Most notable are his efforts to revitalize the reputation of Michael Powell, whose films have had a profound influence on Scorsese's work. Scorsese is a director whose artistic aspirations are deeply attuned to the long tradition of film-making which is itself sometimes at odds with contemporary standards of aesthetic and popular success.

EDWARD R. O'NEILL

SELECT FILMOGRAPHY

Boxcar Bertha (1972); Mean Streets (1973); Alice Doesn't Live Here Anymore (1975); Taxi Driver (1976); The Last Waltz (1978); Raging Bull (1980); New York, New York (1981); The King of Comedy (1983); After Hours (1985); The Color of Money (1986); The Last Temptation of Christ (1988); GoodFellas (1990); Cape Fear (1991); The Age of Innocence (1993); Casino (1995)

BIBLIOGRAPHY

Kelly, Mary Pat (1991), *Martin Scorsese: A Journey*.
Keyser, Les (1992), *Martin Scorsese*.
Thompson, David, and Christie, Ian (eds.) (1989), *Scorsese on Scorsese*.
Weiss, Marion (1987), *Martin Scorsese: A Guide to References and Resources*.

Opposite: Robert De Niro as Max Cody, an ex-convict seeking revenge, in Martin Scorsese's *Cape Fear* (1991), a re-make of the 1960 J. Lee Thompson thriller.

HOLLYWOOD OR 'HERITAGE'?

Hollywood has not only captured most of the screen space for major new releases (twenty of the twenty-six films showing at Kinepolis referred to above were American), it has done so with a particular type of film. Gone are the days when Hollywood was artificially restrained by the Production Code while European films were freer in their representation of sexuality and deviant moralities (European films may still be more honest in these areas, but that is another matter). Although Hollywood still makes a handful of films for the shrinking 'family' audience, the vast majority are made principally for adolescent and young adult audiences and are liberal, to say the least, in their deployment of bad language, sex, and violence. This can no longer be interpreted as a move towards realism; on the contrary (as Linda Williams points out above) it constitutes a new rhetoric by which films affirm their character as racy, exciting, and above all as different from TV. Nor does this apparently transgressive rhetoric any longer have a power to shock, since what seems like excess has become a routine selling element to which regular audiences (if not external observers) have become inured. Often, too, behind the sex-and-violence rhetoric and the occasional grotesquerie, the new Hollywood films turn out to be quite conventional in their narrative forms and even in their moral values.

Most of the vitality in American cinema is to be found on the fringes—in independent productions which may or may not be picked up for mainstream distribution. A case in point is the work of Quentin Tarantino, whose *Reservoir Dogs* (1992) and *Pulp Fiction* (1994) draw on a mixture of cinematic sources and deploy the rhetoric of violence with exceptional intelligence, playfulness, and wit. Tarantino, however, draws inspiration not only from the American B picture and its successors (Monte Hellman, maker of off-beat Westerns and road movies in the 1970s, was one of the producers of *Reservoir Dogs*) but also from the French New Wave; *Pulp Fiction* does to Godard what Godard himself did to the American crime film of the 1950s. It is no accident that Tarantino's cult status is even greater in Europe than in the United States. Other young directors like Gus Van Sant have also been able to force their way into world-wide distribution with refreshingly open-minded treatments of non-mainstream subjects (junkies in *Drugstore Cowboy*, 1989; male street-hustlers in *My Own Private Idaho*, 1991), while Richard Linklater has boldly overturned Hollywood narrative convention as well as taking a fresh approach to his subject-matter in *Slacker* (1991) and *Dazed and Confused* (1993). Conversely, however, the circulation of non-American films in the United States itself is increasingly limited, depriving American audiences (and future film-makers) of the sort of cross-cultural fertilization which has always been so important to world cinema.

The fact that American films now have all the 'street' credentials with young audiences and have firmly reasserted their status as emblems of modernity is significant in two ways. On the one hand it shows that the American cinema is still capable of innovation and of responding to changes in audience demand. But it poses problems for producers in other countries. Should they (indeed can they?) compete? Are there possibilities of fusion between Hollywood and non-Hollywood styles and production modes? Or must producers elsewhere retreat into other areas and trade on qualities that American films cannot reproduce? The most aggressive response has come from Hong Kong, where directors like John Woo have developed a distinctly Chinese form of spectacle which also draws on European experience (notably the 'spaghetti' Western) to outdo Hollywood in the representation of stylized violence. Meanwhile in Italy the tensions of modern life, especially as experienced by young people, are reflected in the work of the director-performers known as the *nuovi comici* or New Comics, many of whom first developed their distinctive artistic personality on television or in theatre and cabaret. An urgency in dealing with contemporary problems of politics, morality, and life-styles is also apparent here and there elsewhere in Europe: in *cinéma beur* and in the work of young feminist film-makers in France, in the work of the writing–directing team of Hanif Kureishi and Stephen Frears in Britain and in films like Polish-born director Krzysztof Kieślowski's *Three Colours* trilogy—*Blue* (1993), *White* (1994), and *Red* (1994).

All too often, however, European directors and producers seem to have deserted the discontents of modern existence to seek refuge in the more comfortable world of the past. A new genre of film has been steadily emerging in the 1980s and 1990s, the 'Heritage movie'. In France and Britain in particular the cinema has turned increasingly to historical subjects and to adaptations of nineteenth- and early twentieth-century literature, from Émile Zola (*Germinal*, Claude Berri, 1995) to E. M. Forster (*A Passage to India*, David Lean, 1984). There is nothing intrinsically retrograde in this; where a rich past exists it is a pity not to draw on it, and history and literature have long provided sources for films. Moreover films with historical subjects are not necessarily cocooned irretrievably in the past and can be used (for good or ill) to provide allegories for the present. But, taken in conjunction with a number of successful films which have contemporary settings but approach their subject in a nostalgic and 'retro' manner (for example *A Fish Called Wanda* (1988) or *Four Weddings and a Funeral* (1994)), the current crop of heritage films is evidence of a worrying trend in European cinema. It is not just that most of them have little critical edge and that they are content to replicate an image of a nice past whose occasional nastiness we can complacently claim to have outgrown. More dangerous for the long-term future of European cinema is the temptation they provide to retreat into a kind of upmarket Disneyfication of Europe as a celluloid theme park from which the discontents of modernity have been comfortably banished.

HERITAGE FILMS OR FILM HERITAGE?

Meanwhile a serious ambiguity affects the recovery of the history of cinema itself. The richness of the cinematic past is widely recognized, but this recognition is reflected almost everywhere except at the box-office. Old films are on television and on video. They are seen by growing numbers of students taking courses in film studies. Alternatively they are to be found embalmed in a museum environment as monuments to a past state of culture with only scanty threads linking them to the present. This unsatisfactory situation is the direct result of one of the most distinctive features of the cinema as popular art. From the very beginning films have traded on newness. In the early days last year's—indeed last week's—films were almost routinely destroyed to make way for the next crop of releases. Now they are preserved—partly thanks to the efforts of archivists but increasingly because of their potential for continued earnings in secondary markets. But novelty remains the name of the game in the primary market of cinematic release, where all the publicity relating to films and the off-screen lives of the stars is centred. The popular cinema has never developed a 'repertory' or a sense of tradition (including a need to rebel against tradition) in the way that other arts like music, painting, and theatre have done. Even popular music is far more oriented to the recycling of a repertory (of songs or performance styles) than the cinema ever has been. To change this situation is certainly difficult, and will require a considerable effort of imagination on the part of the industry on the one side and the archives on the other. But in the changing media environment it is both possible and necessary. What have up to now seemed like straws in the wind—the occasional success of events like Kevin Brownlow and David Gill's restoration of Abel Gance's *Napoléon* for both live-orchestra and television presentation, or the dedication of directors like Martin Scorsese to the preservation of the classics—need to be turned into a more concerted programme of multimedia development which focuses attention simultaneously on film history and on its cinematic presentation. If the necessary effort is made, the cinema can afford to face its second century with confidence.

Bibliography

ABBAS, KHWAJA AHMED. *I Am Not an Island*. New Delhi: Vikas, 1977.

ABEL, RICHARD. *The Ciné Goes to Town: French Cinema, 1896– 1914*. Los Angeles: University of California Press, 1993.

—— *French Cinema: The First Wave, 1915–1929*. Princeton, NJ: Princeton University Press, 1984.

—— *French Film Theory and Criticism: A History/Anthology*. Vol. i: *1907–1929*. Princeton, NJ: Princeton University Press, 1988.

—— 'The Magnetic Eyes of Ivan Mozzhukhin'. *Griffithiana*.

—— 'Pathé's Stake in Early Russian Cinema'. *Griffithiana* 38/39 (Oct. 1990).

ABRAMSON, ALBERT. *The History of Television, 1880–1941*. Jefferson, NC: McFarland, 1987.

ADAMSON, JOE. *Bugs Bunny: Fifty Years and Only One Grey Hare*. New York: Henry Holt, 1990.

AGEE, JAMES. *Agee on Film*. New York: Grosset & Dunlap, 1969.

AGEL, GENEVIÈVE. *Hulot parmi nous*. Paris: Cerf, 1955.

AITKEN, IAN. *Film and Reform: John Grierson and the Documentary Film Movement*. London: Routledge, 1990.

AKRAMI, JAMSHEED. 'Cinema II: Feature Films'. In Ehsan Yarshater (ed.). *Encyclopedia Iranica*. Costa Mesa, Calif.: Mazda Publishers, 1991.

ALDGATE, TONY. 'Comedy, Class, Containment: The British Domestic Cinema of the 1930s'. In James Curran and Vincent Porter (eds.). *British Cinema History*. London: Weidenfeld & Nicolson, 1983.

ALEINIKOV, M. N. *Zapiski kinematografista* ('Notes of a film- maker'). Arkhiv TsGALI, no. 2734/1/21.

ALEKAN, HENRI. *Des lumières et des ombres*. Paris: Le Sycomore, 1984.

ALEXANDER, WILLIAM. *Film on the Left: American Documentary Film from 1931 to 1942*. Princeton: Princeton University Press, 1981.

ALLEN, JERRY C. *Conrad Veidt: From Caligari to Casablanca*. Pacific Grove, Calif.: Boxwood Press, 1987.

ALLEN, ROBERT C. 'The Silent Muse'. *Sight and Sound* 42 (1973).

ALTMAN, RICK. *The American Film Musical*. Bloomington, Ind.: Indiana University Press, 1987; London: BFI, 1987.

—— (ed.) *Genre: The Musical*. London: Routledge & Kegan Paul, 1981.

—— (ed.) *Sound Theory, Sound Practice*. New York and London: Routledge, 1992.

ANDERSON, GILLIAN. 'No Music until Cue: The Reconstruction of D. W. Griffith's *Intolerance*'. *Griffithiana* 38–39 (Oct. 1990).

ANDERSON, JOSEPH L., and RICHIE, DONALD. *The Japanese Film: Art and Industry*. Princeton, NJ: Princeton University Press, 1982.

ANDERSON, LINDSAY. *About John Ford*. London: Plexus, 1981

ANDREW, DUDLEY. *The Major Film Theories: An Introduction*. London and New York: Oxford University Press, 1976.

ANNINSKY, LEV. *Shestidesyatniki i my* ('The generation of the sixties and me'). Moscow: VTPO Kinocentr, 1991.

APRÀ, ADRIANO, and PISTAGNESI, PATRIZIA (eds.). *The Fabulous Thirties*. Milan: Electa, 1979.

ARDAN, S. M. *Dari gambar idoep ke sinepleks* ('From early actualities to the multiplex cinemas'). Jakarta: GPBSI, 1992.

ARIOTTI, PHILIPPE, and COMES, PHILIPPE DE. *Arletty*. Paris: Henri Veyrier, 1978.

ARLETTY. *La Défense*. Paris: Ramsay, 1971.

ARMES, ROY. *A Critical History of British Cinema*. New York: Oxford University Press, 1978.

—— *French Cinema*. London: Secker & Warburg, 1985.

—— *Third World Film Making and the West*. London and Berkeley, Calif.: University of California Press, 1987.

ARNHEIM, RUDOLF. *Film*. London: Faber & Faber, 1933.

—— *Film as Art*. Berkeley, Calif.: University of California Press, 1957.

—— 'A New Laocoön: Artistic Composites and the Talking Film'. In *Film as Art*. London: Faber, 1983.

ARROY, JEAN. 'Ivan Mosjoukine'. In *Des grands artistes de l'écran*. Paris, 1927.

Artes de México. Mexico City, 1988.

ASPINALL, SUE, and MURPHY, ROBERT (eds.). *Gainsborough Melodrama*. London: BFI, 1983.

ASTAIRE, FRED. *Steps in Time*. New York: Harper, 1959.

Atelier des arts, 1 (1982).

ATWELL, DAVID. *Cathedrals of the Movies*. London: The Architectural Press, 1980.

AUTY, MARTIN, and RODDICK, NICK (eds.). *British Cinema Now*. London: BFI, 1985.

BALÁZS, BÉLA. *Theory of the Film: The Character and Growth of a New Art*. London: Dennis Dobson, 1952.

BALCON, MICHAEL. 'Realism or Tinsel'. Paper presented to the Workers' Film Association, 1943.

BALIO, TINO. *History of the American Cinema*. Vol. v: *Grand Design: Hollywood as a Modern Business Enterprise, 1930–1939*. New York: Charles Scribner's Sons, 1993.

—— (ed.) *Hollywood in the Age of Television*. Boston: Unwin Hyman, 1990.

—— *United Artists*. Madison, Wis.: University of Wisconsin Press, 1976.

—— (ed.) *The American Film Industry*. Madison, Wis.: University of Wisconsin Press, 1985.

BANDY, MARY LEA (ed.). *Rediscovering French Film*. New York: The Museum of Modern Art, 1983.

BANNERJEE, HAIMANTI. *Ritwik Kumar Ghatak*. Pune: National Film Archive of India, 1985.

BANNERJEE, SHAMPA (ed.). *Ritwik Ghatak*. New Delhi: Directorate of Film Festivals, 1982.

BARBOUR, ALAN G. *Cliffhanger: A Pictorial History of the Motion Picture Serial*. Secaucus, NJ: The Citadel Press, 1977.

BARNES, JOHN. *The Beginnings of the Cinema in England*. London: David & Charles, 1976.

BARNOUW, ERIK. *Documentary: A History of Nonfiction Film*. New York: Oxford, 1974.

——, and KRISHNASWAMY, S. *Indian Film*. New York: Columbia University Press, 1963. (Revised edn. New Delhi: Oxford University Press, 1980).

767

BARR, CHARLES. *Ealing Studios*. London: Cameron & Tayleur and David & Charles, 1977. (Revised edn. London: Studio Vista, 1993.)

—— (ed.) *All our Yesterdays: 90 Years of British Cinema*. London: BFI, 1986.

BARSACQ, LÉON. *Caligari's Cabinet and Other Grand Illusions: A History of Film Design*. Boston: New York Graphic Society, 1976.

BARSAM, RICHARD. *Non-fiction Film*. Revised edn. Bloomington, Ind.: Indiana University Press, 1992.

BART, PETER. *Fade Out*. New York: William Morrow & Company, 1990.

BARTHES, ROLAND. 'Cher Antonioni'. *Cahiers du cinéma*, 311 (May 1980).

—— *Elements of Semiology*. London: Jonathan Cape, 1967.

BARTOŠEK, LUBOŠ. *Naš film: kapitoly z dějin, 1896–1945* ('Our [Czechoslovak] film: chapters from history'). Prague, 1986.

BATHRICK, DAVID, and HANSEN, MIRIAM (eds.). 'Special Issue on New German Cinema'. *New German Critique* 24–25 (Fall–Winter 1981–2).

BAUMERT, HEINZ, and HERLINGAUS, HERMANN (eds.). *20 Jahre Spielfilm*. Berlin: Henschel, 1968.

BAUSCHINGER, SIGRID, et al. (eds.). *Film und Literatur: literarische Texte und der neue deutsche Film*. Munich: Francke, 1984.

BAXTER, JOHN. *Hollywood in the Thirties*. London: Zwemmer, 1968.

BAXTER, PETER. *Just Watch! Sternberg, Paramount and America*. London: BFI, 1993.

BAZELON, IRWIN. *Knowing the Score: Notes on Film Music*. New York: Van Nostrand Reinhold, 1975.

BAZIN, ANDRÉ. 'The Destiny of Jean Gabin'. In Mary Lea Bandy (ed.). *Rediscovering French Film*. New York: The Museum of Modern Art, 1983.

—— 'The Evolution of the Language of Cinema'. In *What is Cinema?*, vol. i. Berkeley, Calif.: University of California Press, 1967.

—— 'The Evolution of the Western'. In *What is Cinema?*, vol. ii. Berkeley, Calif.: University of California Press, 1971.

—— 'The Virtues and Limitations of Montage', in *What is Cinema?*, vol. i. Berkeley, Calif.: University of California Press, 1967.

—— 'The Western or the American Film Par Excellence'. In *What is Cinema?*, vol. ii. Berkeley, Calif.: University of California Press, 1971.

—— *Jean Renoir*. Edited by François Truffaut. New York, Simon & Schuster, 1974.

—— *Orson Welles: A Critical View*. Foreword by François Truffaut. Profile by Jean Cocteau. New York: Harper & Row, 1978.

—— *What is Cinema?* 2 vols. Berkeley, Calif.: University of California Press, 1967 and 1971.

BECK, JERRY, and FRIEDWALD, BILL. *Looney Tunes and Merrie Melodies*. New York: Holt, 1989.

BEHN, MANFRED, and BOCK, HANS-MICHAEL (eds.). *Film und Gesellschaft in der DDR: Material-Sammlung*. 2 vols. Hamburg: Cinegraph/ Initiative Kommunales Kino e.V. 1988–9.

BELLOUR, RAYMOND. *L'Analyse du film*. Paris: Albatros, 1979.

—— (ed.) *Le Western*. Paris: Union Générale d'Éditions, 1966.

——, and Bandy, Mary Lea (eds.). *Jean-Luc Godard: Sound + Image, 1974–1991*. New York: Museum of Modern Art, 1992.

BELTON, JOHN. *The Hollywood Professionals*. Vol. iii: *Hawks, Borzage and Ulmer*. London: A. S. Barnes, 1974.

—— *Widescreen Cinema*. Cambridge, Mass.: Harvard University Press, 1992.

BENDAZZI, GIANNALBERTO. *Cartoons: One Hundred Years of Cinema Animation*. London: John Libbey, 1994.

BENSAIA, REDA. 'From the Photogram to the Pictogram: On Chris Marker's *La Jetée*'. *Camera Obscura*, 24 (Sept. 1990).

BENSON, THOMAS W., and ANDERSON, CAROLYN. *Reality Fictions: The Films of Frederick Wiseman*. Carbondale, Ill.: University of Southern Illinois Press, 1989.

BERG, SCOTT A. *Goldwyn*. New York: Knopf, 1989.

BERGER, JÜRGEN, et al. (eds.) *Zwischen Gestern und Morgen: Westdeutscher Nachkriegsfilm, 1946–1962*. Frankfurt am Main: Deutsches Filmmuseum, 1989.

BERGERON, RÉGIS. *Le cinéma chinois, 1905–1949*. Lausanne: Alfred Eibel, 1977.

—— *Le cinéma chinois, 1943–1983*. 3 vols. Paris: Harmattan, 1984.

BERGMAN, INGMAR. *Bergman on Bergman: Interviews with Ingmar Bergman by Stig Björkman, Torsten Manns and Jonas Sina*. London: Secker & Warburg, 1973.

—— *The Magic Lantern: An Autobiography*. London: Hamish Hamilton, 1988; New York: Viking, 1988.

BERGMAN, INGRID, and BURGESS, ALAN. *Ingrid Bergman: My Story*. London: Hamish Hamilton, 1980.

BERGSTROM, JANET. 'Asta Nielsen's Early German Films'. In P. Cherchi Usai and L. Codelli (eds.). *Before Caligari: German Cinema, 1895–1920*. Pordenone: Edizioni Biblioteca dell'Immagine, 1990.

—— 'Jeanne Dielman, 23, Quai du Commerce, 1080 Bruxelles by Chantal Akerman'. *Camera Obscura*, 2 (Fall 1977).

BERNARDINI, ALDO. *Cinema muto italiano, 1896–1914*. 3 vols. Bari: Laterza, 1980–2.

—— (ed.). *Archivio del cinema italiano*. Vol. i: *Il cinema muto, 1905–1931*. Rome: Edizioni Anica, 1991.

—— (ed.). 'I comici del muto italiano'. *Griffithiana* 24– 25 (Oct. 1985).

—— and GILI, JEAN A. (eds.). *Le cinéma italien*. Paris: Centre Georges Pompidou, 1986.

—— and Martinelli, Vittorio. *Il cinema italiano degli anni Venti*. Rome: Centro Sperimentale di Cinematografia, 1979.

BERNARDONI, JAMES. *George Cukor: A Critical Study and Filmography*. Jefferson, NC: McFarland, 1985.

BERRAH, MOUNY, LÉVY, JACQUES, and CLUNY, CLAUDE-MICHEL (eds.). *Les Cinémas arabes*. (*CinémAction*, 43.) Paris: Éditions du Cerf/Institut du Monde Arabe, 1987.

BERRY, CHRIS (ed.). *Perspectives on Chinese Cinema*. London: BFI, 1991.

BERTIN, CELIA. *Jean Renoir: A Life in Pictures*. Baltimore and London: Johns Hopkins University Press, 1991.

BERTRAND, INA (ed.). *Cinema in Australia: A Documentary History*. Kensington: New South Wales University Press, 1989.

BESSEN, URSULA (ed.) *Trümmer und Träume*. Bochum: Brockmeyer, 1989.

BEYLIE, CLAUDE. *Max Ophuls*. Paris: Lherminier, 1984.

BIRAN, MISBACH YUSA. *Indonesian Cinema: Lintasan Sejarah* (Indonesian cinema: a historical perspective). Jakarta: PT Perfin Pusat, 1982.

BISKIND, PETER. 'The Last Crusade'. In Mark Crispin Miller (ed.). *Seeing through Movies*. New York: Pantheon, 1990.

BITZER, BILLY. *Billy Bitzer: His Story*. New York: Farrar, Straus & Giroux, 1973.

BLAKE, MICHAEL F. *Lon Chaney: The Man behind the Thousand Faces*. New York: Vestal Press, 1993.

BLANK, LES, and BOGAN, JAMES (eds.). *Burden of Dreams: Screenplay, Journals, Reviews*. Berkeley, Calif.: North Atlantic Books, 1984.

BLESH, RUDI. *Keaton*. London: Secker & Warburg, 1967.

BOCK, HANS-MICHAEL, and TÖTEBERG, MICHAEL (eds.). *Das Ufa-Buch:*

die internationale Geschichte von Deutschlands größtem Film-Konzern. Frankfurt: Zweitausendeins and Verlag 2001, 1992.

BOGDANOVICH, PETER. *Fritz Lang in America.* New York: Praeger, 1969.

—— *The Cinema of Alfred Hitchcock.* New York: Museum of Modern Art Film Library, 1963.

—— *The Cinema of Orson Welles.* Garden City, NY: Film Library of the Museum of Modern Art and Doubleday, 1961.

—— *John Ford.* 2nd edn. Berkeley, Calif.: University of California Press, 1987.

BOGLE, DONALD. *Blacks in American Films and Television.* New York: Garland Publishing, 1988.

BÖHM-CHRISTL, THOMAS (ed.). *Alexander Kluge.* Frankfurt: Suhrkamp, 1983.

BONDANELLA, PETER. *The Cinema of Federico Fellini.* Princeton, NJ: Princeton University Press, 1992.

—— *Italian Cinema: From Neorealism to the Present.* New York: Continuum, 1990.

BORDWELL, DAVID. *The Cinema of Eisenstein.* Cambridge, Mass: Harvard University Press, 1993.

—— *The Films of Carl Theodor Dreyer.* Berkeley, Calif.: University of California Press, 1981.

—— *French Impressionist Cinema: Film Culture, Film Theory and Film Style.* New York: Arno Press, 1980.

—— *Ozu and the Poetics of Cinema.* London: BFI, 1988; Princeton, NJ: Princeton University Press, 1988.

——, Staiger, Janet, and Thompson, Kristin. *The Classical Hollywood Cinema: Film Style and Mode of Production to 1960.* London: Routledge, 1985; New York: Columbia University Press, 1985.

—— and Thompson, Kristin. *Film Art.* 4th edn. New York: McGraw Hill, 1993.

BOSSÉNO, CHRISTIAN (ed.). *Youssef Chahine l'Alexandrin. (CinémAction,* 33.) Paris: Éditions du Cerf, 1985.

BOURGET, JEAN LOUP. *Robert Altman.* Paris: Édilig, 1980.

BOUSQUET, HENRI (ed.). *Catalogue Pathé des années 1896 à 1914: 1907–1909.* Paris: By the Author, 1993.

BOWSER, EILEEN. *History of the American Cinema.* Vol. ii: *The Transformation of Cinema, 1907–1915.* New York: Charles Scribner's Sons, 1990.

BRANDO, MARLON. *Songs My Mother Taught Me.* London: Century, 1994.

BRIGGS, ASA. *The History of Broadcasting in the United Kingdom.* Vol. iv: *Sound and Vision.* London: Oxford University Press, 1979.

BRODE, DOUGLAS. *The Films of Jack Nicholson.* New York: Citadel Press, 1990.

BROSNAN, JOHN. *Future Tense: The Cinema of Science Fiction.* New York: St. Martin's Press, 1978.

BROWN, ROYAL S. 'Herrmann, Hitchcock, and the Music of the Irrational'. *Cinema Journal,* 21/2 (Spring 1982).

—— *Overtones and Undertones: Reading Film Music.* Los Angeles: University of California Press, 1994.

—— (ed.). *Focus on Godard.* London: Prentice-Hall, 1973.

BROWNE, NICK (ed.). *Cahiers du cinéma.* Vol iii: *1969–1972: The Politics of Representation.* London: Routledge, 1990.

—— PICKOWICZ, PAUL, SOBCHACK, VIVIAN, and YAU, ESTHER (eds.). *New Chinese Cinemas: Forms, Identities, Politics.* London: Cambridge University Press, 1994.

BROWNLOW, KEVIN. *The Parade's Gone by.* London: Secker & Warburg, 1968.

—— *The War, the West and the Wilderness.* New York: Knopf, 1979; London: Secker & Warburg, 1979.

BRUNETTA, GIAN PIERO. *Cent'anni di cinema italiano.* Rome/Bari: Laterza, 1991.

—— *Storia del cinema italiano.* Vol. i: *1905–1945.* Rome: Editori Riuniti, 1980.

—— *Storia del cinema italiano.* Vol. ii: *Dal 1945 agli anni ottanta.* Rome: Editori Riuniti, 1982.

BRUNETTE, PETER. *Roberto Rossellini.* New York: Oxford University Press, 1987.

BUCHSBAUM, JONATHAN. *Cinema Engagé: Film in the Popular Front.* Urbana: University of Illinois Press, 1988.

BUNCHKA, PETER. *Augen kann man nicht kaufen: Wim Wenders und seine Filme.* Munich: Hanser, 1983.

BUÑUEL, LUIS. *My Last Sigh.* New York: Knopf, 1983. (Published in UK as *My Last Breath,* London: Jonathan Cape, 1983.)

BURCH, NOËL. *To the Distant Observer: Forms and Meaning in the Japanese Cinema.* Berkeley, Calif.: University of California Press, 1979; London: Scolar Press, 1979.

BURGESS, MURIEL, and KEEN, TOMMY. *Gracie Fields.* London, 1980.

BURTON, JULIANNE (ed.). *Cinema and Social Change in Latin America: Conversations with Filmmakers.* Austin, Tex.: University of Texas Press, 1986.

BURTON, JULIANNE (ed.). *The Social Documentary in Latin America.* Pittsburgh: University of Pittsburgh, 1990.

BUSCOMBE, EDWARD (ed.). *The BFI Companion to the Western.* London: André Deutsch, 1993.

BUTLER, GEORGE. *Arnold Schwarzenegger: A Portrait.* New York: 1990.

CABARGA, LESLIE. *The Fleischer Story.* New York: Da Capo Press, 1988.

CALDER-MARSHALL, ARTHUR. *The Innocent Eye: The Life of Robert J. Flaherty.* New York: Harcourt, Brace, World, 1963.

CALLOW, SIMON. *Charles Laughton: A Difficult Actor.* London: Methuen, 1987.

CAMERON, IAN (ed.). *Movie Reader.* London: November Books, 1972.

—— *A Pictorial History of Crime Films.* London: Hamlyn, 1975.

CANEMAKER, JOHN. *Felix: The Twisted Tale of the World's Most Famous Cat.* New York: Pantheon Books, 1991.

—— *Winsor McCay: His Life and Art.* New York: Abbeville Press, 1987.

—— (ed.). *Storytelling in Animation.* Los Angeles: American Film Institute, 1988.

CANTRIL, HADLEY, with GAUDET, HAZEL, and HERZOG, HERTA. *The Invasion from Mars: A Study in the Psychology of Panic.* Princeton, NJ: Princeton University Press, 1940.

CANUDO, RICCIOTTO. *L'Usine aux images.* Geneva: Office Central d'Édition, 1927.

CAREY, GARY. *Cukor & Co.: The Films of George Cukor and his Collaborators.* New York: Museum of Modern Art, 1971; Greenwich, Conn.: New York Graphic Society, 1971.

CARNEY, RAYMOND. *American Dreaming: The Films of John Cassavetes and the American Experience.* Berkeley, Calif.: University of California Press, 1985.

CARRÈRE, EMMANUEL. *Werner Herzog.* Paris: Édilig, 1982.

CARRICK, EDWARD [Edward Craig]. *Art and Design in the British Film.* London: Dennis Dobson, 1948.

CARRINGER, ROBERT L. *The Making of Citizen Kane.* Berkeley, Calif.: University of California Press, 1985.

—— and Sabath, Barry. *Ernst Lubitsch: A Guide to References and Resources.* Boston: G. K. Hall, 1978.

CASETTI, FRANCESCO. *Bernardo Bertolucci.* Florence: La Nuova Italia, 1975.

CAUGHIE, JOHN. 'Broadcasting and Cinema 1: Converging Histories'. In Charles Barr (ed.). *All Our Yesterdays: 90 Years of British Cinema*. London: BFI, 1986.

CAWELTI, JOHN. *The Six-Gun Mystique*. Bowling Green, Oh.: Bowling Green University Popular Press, 1970.

CERISUELO, MARC. *Jean-Luc Godard*. Paris: Éditions des Quatre-Vents, 1992.

CHAMPETIER, CAROLINE. '*Les Rendez-vous d'Anna*: rencontre avec Chantal Akerman'. *Cahiers du cinéma*, 288 (May 1978).

CHANAN, MICHAEL. *The Cuban Image*. London: BFI, 1985.

—— *The Dream that Kicks: The Prehistory and Early Years of Cinema in Britain*. London: Routledge & Kegan Paul, 1980.

—— (ed.). *Twenty-Five Years of the New Latin American Cinema*. London: BFI and Channel 4, 1983

CHAPLIN, CHARLES. *My Autobiography*. London: The Bodley Head, 1964.

CHATMAN, SEYMOUR. *Antonioni: The Surface of the World*. Berkeley, Calif.: University of California Press, 1985.

CHENG JIHUA, LI XIAOBAI, and XING ZUWEN. *Zhongguo dianying fazhanshi* ('History of the development of Chinese cinema'), Vols. i and ii. Beijing: China Film Press, 1963.

CHEN KAIGE, ZHI WAN, and RAYNS, TONY. *'King of the Children' and the New Chinese Cinema*. London: Faber & Faber, 1989.

CHERCHI USAI, PAOLO. *Burning Passions: An Introduction to the Study of Silent Cinema*. London: BFI, 1994.

—— and CODELLI, LORENZO (eds.). *Before Caligari: German Cinema, 1895–1920*. Pordenone: Edizioni Biblioteca dell'Immagine, 1990.

——, CODELLI, LORENZO, MONTANARO, CARLO, and ROBINSON, DAVID (eds.). *Silent Witnesses: Russian Films 1908–1919*. London: BFI, 1989; Pordenone: Edizioni Biblioteca dell'Immagine, 1989.

CHIAO HSIUNG-P'ING (ed.). *Tai-wan hsin tain-ying* ('Taiwanese New Cinema'). Taipei: Jen-chien Books and China Times Publishing, 1988.

CHION, MICHEL. *Jacques Tati*. Paris: Cahiers du cinéma, 1987.

CHIRAT, RAYMOND, and ICART, ROGER (eds.). *Catalogue des films français de long métrage: films de fiction, 1919–1929*. Toulouse: Cinémathèque de Toulouse, 1984.

—— and Le Roy, Eric (eds.). *Le cinéma français, 1911– 1920*. Paris: La Cinémathèque Française, 1994.

CHOLODENKO, ALAN (ed.). *The Illusion of Life: Essays on Animation*. Sydney: Power Publications and the Australian Film Commission, 1991.

CHOUDHURY, ASHIM. *Private Economic Power in India*. New Delhi: People's Publishing House, 1975.

CHRISTIE, IAN. *Arrows of Desire*. Revised edn. London: Faber & Faber, 1994.

—— (ed.). *Powell, Pressburger and Others*. London: BFI, 1978.

CIMENT, MICHEL. *Conversations with Losey*. London and New York: Methuen, 1985.

—— *Kubrick*. Paris: Calmann-Lévy, 1980.

Cinema dei paesi arabi. Pesaro: Mostra Internazionale del Nuovo Cinema, 1976.

CLAIR, RENÉ. *Cinema Yesterday and Today*. New York: Dover Publications, 1972.

CLARENS, CARLOS. *George Cukor*. London: Secker & Warburg, 1976.

CLARK, PAUL. *Chinese Cinema: Culture and Politics since 1949*. New York: Cambridge University Press, 1987.

CLINCH, MINTY. *Burt Lancaster*. London: Arthur Barker Ltd., 1984.

CLOVER, CAROL J. *Men, Women and Chain Saws: Gender in the Modern Horror Film*. Princeton, NJ: Princeton University Press, 1992.

COISSAC, G. MICHEL. *Histoire du cinématographe: de ses origines jusqu'à nos jours*. Paris: Cinéopse, 1925.

COMITO, TERRY (ed.). *Touch of Evil*. New Brunswick, NJ: Rutgers University Press, 1985.

COMOLLI, JEAN-LOUIS. 'Machines of the Visible'. In Teresa de Lauretis and Stephen Heath (eds.). *The Cinematic Apparatus*. New York: St. Martin's Press, 1980.

CONVENTS, GUIDO. *À la recherche des images oubliées: Préhistoire du cinéma en Afrique, 1897–1918*. Brussels: OCIC, 1986.

COOK, PAM, and JOHNSTON, CLAIRE. 'The Place of Women in the films of Raoul Walsh' (1974). Repr. in Constance Peuley (ed.). *Feminism and Film Theory*. New York: Routledge, 1988.

COOKE, ALISTAIR. *Douglas Fairbanks: The Making of a Screen Character*. New York: Museum of Modern Art, 1940.

COOPER, MERIAN C. *Grass*. New York: G. P. Putnam's Sons, 1925.

COPLAND, AARON. *Our New Music*. New York: McGraw-Hill, 1941.

CORMAN, ROGER. *How I Made a Hundred Movies in Hollywood and Never Lost a Dime*. New York: Random House, 1990.

CORRIGAN, TIMOTHY. *New German Film: The Displaced Image* Austin, Tex.: University of Texas Press, 1983.

—— (ed.). *The Films of Werner Herzog: Between Mirage and History*. New York and London: Methuen, 1986.

COSANDEY, ROLAND, GAUDREAULT, ANDRÉ, and GUNNING, TOM (eds.). *Une invention du diable? Cinema des premières temps et religion* [An Invention of the Devil? Religion and Early Cinema]. Quebec: Sainte-Foy Les Presses de l'Université Laval, 1992; Lausanne: Éditions Payot Lausanne, 1992.

COURTADE, FRANCIS, and CADARS, PIERRE. *Le Cinéma nazi*. Paris: Losfeld, 1972.

COUTARD, RAOUL. 'Light of Day'. *Sight and Sound* 35 (Winter 1965– 6).

COWIE, PETER. *Ingmar Bergman: A Critical Biography*. 2nd edn. London: André Deutsch, 1992.

COWIE, PETER. *The Cinema of Orson Welles*. South Brunswick, NY: A.S. Barnes, 1978.

COYLE, WALLACE. *Stanley Kubrick: A Guide to References and Resources*. Boston: G. K. Hall, 1980.

COYLE, WILLIAM (ed.). *Aspects of Fantasy: Selected Essays from the Second International Conference on the Fantastic in Literature and Film*. London: Greenwood Press, 1981.

CRAFTON, DONALD. *Before Mickey: The Animated Film, 1898–1928*. Chicago: University of Chicago Press, 1993.

—— *Émile Cohl, Caricature and Film*. Princeton, NJ: Princeton University Press, 1990.

CRANE, ROBERT DAVID, and FRYER, CHRISTOPHER. *Jack Nicholson Face to Face*. New York: M. Evans & Co., 1975.

CRIPPS, THOMAS. *Slow Fade to Black: The Negro in American Film, 1900– 1942*. New York: Oxford University Press, 1977.

CROCE, ARLENE. *The Fred Astaire and Ginger Rogers Book*. New York: Galahad Books, 1972.

CROFTS, STEPHEN. *Australian Cinema as National Cinema*. Oxford: Oxford University Press, forthcoming.

—— *Identification, Gender and Genre in Film: The Case of Shame*. Melbourne: Australian Film Institute, 1993.

CRONENBERG, DAVID. *Cronenberg on Cronenberg*. Edited by Chris Rodley. Toronto: Knopf Canada, 1992.

CROWTHER, BRUCE. *Burt Lancaster: A Life in Films*. London: Robert Hale, 1991.

CULHANE, SHAMUS. *Talking Animals and Other People*. New York: St Martin's Press, 1986.

CUNNINGHAM, STUART. *Featuring Australia: The Cinema of Charles Chauvel*. Sydney: Allen & Unwin, 1991.

CURRAN, JAMES, and PORTER, VINCENT (eds.). *British Cinema History*. London: Weidenfeld & Nicolson, 1983.

CURTIS, DAVID. *Experimental Cinema*. London: Studio Vista, 1971.

CURTISS, THOMAS QUINN. *Von Stroheim*. New York: Farrar, Straus & Giroux, 1971.

DALL'ASTA, MONICA. *Un cinéma musclé: le surhomme dans le cinéma muet italien (1913–1926)*. Crisnée: Éditions Yellow Now, 1992.

DAS GUPTA, CHIDANANDA. *The Cinema of Satyajit Ray*. New Delhi: Vikas, 1980.

—— (ed.). *Satyajit Ray: An Anthology of Statements on Ray and by Ray*. New Delhi: Film India and Directorate of Film Festivals, 1981.

—— 'The Cultural Basis of Indian Cinema'. In *Talking About Films*. New Delhi: Orient Longman, 1981.

DAVIS, BETTE. *The Lonely Life: An Autobiography*. New York: G. F. Putnam's Sons, 1962.

DAWSON, JAN. *Wim Wenders*. New York: Zoetrope, 1976.

DAZAT, OLIVIER. *Alain Delon*. Paris: Seghers, 1988.

DE BEAUVOIR, SIMONE. *Brigitte Bardot and the Lolita Syndrome*. London: André Deutsch and Weidenfeld & Nicolson, 1961.

DEGRAZIA, EDWARD. *Girls Lean Back Everywhere: The Law of Obscenity and the Assault on Genius*. New York: Random House, 1992.

DELAHAYE, MICHEL. 'Carl Dreyer'. In Andrew Sarris (ed.). *Interviews with Film Directors*. New York: Avon, 1967.

DE LAURETIS, TERESA, and HEATH, STEPHEN (eds.). *The Cinematic Apparatus*. New York: St Martin's Press, 1980.

DELLUC, LOUIS. *Cinéma et cie*. Paris: Grasset, 1919.

DELMAR, ROSALIND. *Joris Ivens: Fifty Years of Film making*. London: BFI, 1979.

DE LOS REYES, AURELIO. *Cine y sociedad en México, 1896–1930*. Mexico City, 1983.

'Delon/Borsalino'. *The Little Film Gazette of NDW* 4 (Aug. 1973).

DEMILLE, CECIL B. *The Autobiography of Cecil B. DeMille*. Englewood Cliffs, NJ: Prentice-Hall, 1959.

DENNING, MICHAEL. *Mechanic Accents*. London: Verso, 1987.

DERMODY, SUSAN, and JACKA, ELIZABETH. *The Screening of Australia: Anatomy of a Film Industry*. Sydney: Currency Press, 1987.

—— *The Screening of Australia: Anatomy of a National Cinema*. Sydney: Currency Press, 1988.

—— *The Imaginary Industry: Australian Film in the Eighties*. Sydney: Australian Film, Television and Radio Board, 1988.

DESAI, A. R. *Social Background of Indian Nationalism*. Bombay: Popular Prakashan, 1948

DESBARATS, CAROLE, RIVIÈRE, DANIÈLE, LAGEIRA, and VIRILIO, PAUL. *Atom Egoyan*. Paris: Éditions Dis Voir, 1993.

DESSER, DAVID. *Eros Plus Massacre: An Introduction to the Japanese New Wave Cinema*. Bloomington, Ind.: Indiana University Press, 1988.

—— *The Samurai Films of Akira Kurosawa*. Ann Arbor, Mich.: UMI Research Press, 1983.

DIAMANT-BERGER, HENRI. *Le cinéma*. Paris: La Renaissance du Livre, 1919.

DIAWARA, MANTHIA. *African Cinema*. Bloomington, Ind.: Indiana University Press, 1992.

DICKINSON, MARGARET, and STREET, SARAH. *Cinema and State: The Film Industry and the Government, 1927–1984*. London: BFI, 1985.

DIORIO, AL, JR. *Barbara Stanwyck*. New York: Coward McCann, 1983.

—— *Little Girl Lost*. New Rochelle, NY: Arlington House Publishing, 1973.

D'LUGO, MARVIN. *Carlos Saura: The Practice of Seeing*. Princeton, NJ: Princeton University Press, 1991.

DOMARCHI, JEAN. *George Cukor*. Paris: Seghers, 1965.

DOVZHENKO, ALEXANDER. *Alexander Dovzhenko: The Poet as Filmmaker*. Edited and translated by Marco Carynnyk. Cambridge, Mass.: MIT Press, 1973.

DROUZY, MAURICE. *Carl Th. Dreyer né Nilsson*. Paris: Éditions du Cerf, 1982.

DRUMMOND, PHILLIP, DUSINBERRE, DEKE, and REES, A. L. (eds.). *Film as Film*. London: Arts Council of Great Britain/Hayward Gallery, 1979.

DUBERMAN, MARTIN. *Paul Robeson: A Biography*. New York: Ballantine Books, 1989.

DUMONT, HERVÉ. *Frank Borzage: Sarastro à Hollywood*. Milan: Edizioni Gabriele Mazzotta and Cinémathèque Française, 1993.

DURGNAT, RAYMOND. *Jean Renoir*. Berkeley, Calif.: University of California Press, 1974.

—— and Kobal, John. *Greta Garbo*. New York: E. P. Dutton, 1965.

DU YUNZHI. *Zhongguo Dianyingshi* ('History of Chinese Cinema'). Taipei: Commercial Press, 1972.

DWOSKIN, STEPHEN. *Film Is*. London: Peter Owen, 1975

DYER, RICHARD. *Heavenly Bodies: Film Stars and Society*. London: Macmillan, 1986; New York: St Martin's Press, 1986.

—— and VINCENDEAU, GINETTE (eds.). *Popular European Cinema*. London and New York: Routledge, 1992.

EATON, MICHAEL (ed.). *Anthropology – Reality – Cinema: The Films of Jean Rouch*. London: BFI, 1979.

EBERTS, JACK, and ILOTT, TERRY. *My Indecision Is Final: The Rise and Fall of Goldcrest Films*. London: Faber & Faber, 1990.

EDERA, BRUNO. *Full Length Animated Feature Films*. New York: Hastings House, 1977.

EISENSCHITZ, BERNARD. *Nicholas Ray: An American Journey*. London: Faber & Faber, 1993.

EISENSTEIN, SERGEI. *Film Form: Essays in Film Theory*. Edited and translated by Jay Leyda. New York: Harcourt, Brace, 1949.

—— *Towards a Theory of Montage*. Edited by Richard Taylor and Michael Glenny. Translated by Michael Glenny. London: BFI, 1992.

—— *Writings, 1922–34*. Edited and translated by Richard Taylor. London: BFI, 1988; Bloomington, Ind.: Indiana University Press, 1988.

—— *The Film Sense*. Translated and edited by Jay Leyda. New York: Harcourt, 1970 (reprint of 1947 edn.).

EISNER, LOTTE. *Fritz Lang*. London: Secker & Warburg, 1976. (Revised and augmented edn. Paris: Éditions de l'Étoile/ Cinémathèque Française, 1984.)

—— *The Haunted Screen*. London: Thames & Hudson, 1969; Berkeley, Calif. and Los Angeles: University of California Press, 1969.

—— *Murnau*. London: Secker & Warburg, 1973; Berkeley, Calif.: University of California Press, 1973.

ELLIS, JACK. *The Documentary Idea: A Critical History of English-Language Documentary Film and Video*. Englewood Cliffs, NJ: Prentice Hall, 1989.

ELSAESSER, THOMAS. *New German Cinema: A History*. London: Macmillan, 1989.

—— 'Tales of Sound and Fury'. *Monogram*, 4. (1972)

—— 'Vincente Minnelli'. In Rick Altman (ed.). *Genre: The Musical*. London: Routledge & Kegan Paul, 1981.

—— (ed.). *Early Cinema: Space, Frame, Narrative*. London: BFI, 1990.

EMERY, WALTER B. *National and International Systems of Broad-*

casting. East Lansing, Mich.: Michigan State University Press, 1969.

ENGBERG, MARGUERITE. *Dansk Stumfilm*. Copenhagen: Rhodos, 1977.

EPSTEIN, JEAN. *Bonjour cinéma*. Paris: Éditions de la Sirène, 1921.

—— *Le Cinématographe vu de l'Etna*. Paris: Les Écrivains Réunis, 1926.

ERDMANN, HANS, and BECCE, GIUSEPPE. *Allgemeines Handbuch der Film-Musik*. 2 vols. Edited by Ludwig Brav. Berlin-Lichterfelde and Leipzig: Schlesinger, 1927.

ESSER, MICHAEL. 'Poeten der Filmarchitektur: Robert Herlth und Walter Röhrig'. In *Das Ufa-Buch*. Frankfurt: Zweitausendeins, 1992.

ESTÈVE, MICHEL. *Wim Wenders*. Paris: Seghers, 1989.

EVANS, GARY. *In the National Interest: A Chronicle of the National Film Board of Canada from 1949–1989*. Toronto: University of Toronto Press, 1991.

EYLES, ALLEN. *John Wayne*. London: The Tantivy Press, 1979.

EYMAN, SCOTT. *Five American Cinematographers*. Metuchen, NJ: Scarecrow Press, 1987.

—— *Mary Pickford: From Here to Hollywood*. Toronto: Harper Collins, 1990.

FALDINI, FRANCA, and FOFI, GOFFREDO. *L'avventurosa storia del cinema italiano raccontato dai suoi protagonisti, 1935–1959*. Milan: Feltrinelli, 1979.

—— *L'avventurosa storia del cinema italiano raccontato dai suoi protagonisti, 1960–1969*. Milan: Feltrinelli, 1981.

—— *Il cinema italiano di oggi, 1970–1984: raccontato dai suoi protagonisti*. Milan: Mondadori, 1984.

FANO, MICHEL. 'Film, partition sonore'. *Musique en jeu*, 21 (Nov. 1975).

FASSBINDER, RAINER WERNER. *The Anarchy of the Imagination: Interviews, Essays, Notes*. Edited by Michael Töteberg and Leo A. Lensing. Baltimore and London: Johns Hopkins University Press, 1992.

—— *Filme befreien den Kopf: Essays und Arbeitsnotizen*. Edited by Michael Töteberg. Frankfurt and Main: Fischer, 1984.

FBI file on Paul Robeson (on microfilm). Wilmington, Del.: Scholarly Resources, 1987.

FELDMAN, SETH. *Dziga Vertov: A Guide to References and Resources*. Boston: G. K. Hall, 1979.

FELL, JOHN L. *Film and the Narrative Tradition*. Berkeley, Calif.: University of California Press, 1986.

—— *Film before Griffith*. Berkeley, Calif.: University of California Press, 1983.

Fellini on Fellini. New York: Delacorte Press, 1976.

FENIN, GEORGE N., and EVERSON, WILLIAM. *The Western from Silents to the Seventies*. New York: Penguin, 1973.

FESCOURT, HENRI. *La Foi et les montagnes*. Paris: Paul Montel, 1959.

FEUER, JANE. *The Hollywood Musical*. London: BFI, 1982; Bloomington, Ind.: Indiana University Press, 1982.

FIAF. *Le Cinéma français muet dans le monde, influences réciproques*. Perpignan: Institut Jean Vigo, 1989.

FIELDING, RAYMOND (ed.). *A Technological History of Motion Pictures and Television: An Anthology*. Berkeley, Calif.: University of California Press, 1967.

FIELDS, GRACIE. *Sing as we Go*. London, 1960.

15th Hong Kong International Film Festival. *Hong Kong Cinema in the Eighties*. Hong Kong: Hong Kong Urban Council, 1991.

Film in Norway. Oslo: Norsk Filminstitutt, 1979.

Films and Filming, 329 (May 1987).

FINKELSTEIN, NAT. *Andy Warhol: The Factory Years*. London: Sidgwick & Jackson, 1989.

FINLER, JOEL. *The Hollywood Story*. New York: Crown, 1988.

—— *Stroheim*. London: Movie Paperbacks, 1968; Berkeley, Calif.: University of California Press, 1968.

FISCHER, LUCY. *Jacques Tati: A Guide to References and Resources*. Boston: G. K. Hall, 1983.

FISCHER, ROBERT, and HEMBUS, JOE. *Der neue deutsche Film, 1960–1980*. Munich: Goldmann, 1981.

FISCHETTI, RENATE. *Das neue Kino: acht Porträts von deutschen Regisseurinnen*. Dülmen: Tende, 1992.

FITZGERALD, F. SCOTT. *The Collected Short Stories*. London: Penguin, 1986.

FLAHERTY, ROBERT J. *My Eskimo Friends*. New York: Doubleday, 1924.

FLITTERMAN-LEWIS, SANDY. *To Desire Differently: Feminism and French Cinema*. Urbana: University of Illinois Press, 1990.

FOFI, GOFFREDO. 'The Cinema of the Popular Front in France (1934–8)'. *Screen* 13/4, Winter 1972–3.

—— *Totò: l'uomo e la maschera*. 1977.

FONER, PHILIP S. (ed.). *Paul Robeson Speaks: Writings, Speeches, Interviews, 1918–1974*. New York: Brunner & Mazel, 1978.

FORBES, JILL. *The Cinema in France after the New Wave*. Basingstoke: Macmillan, 1992.

—— 'France: Modernization across the Spectrum'. In Geoffrey Nowell-Smith (ed.). *The European Experience*. London: BFI, 1989.

FORD, DAN. *Pappy: The Life of John Ford*. Englewood Cliffs, NJ: Prentice Hall, 1979.

FORDIN, HUGH. *The World of Entertainment*. New York: Equinox, 1975.

FORGACS, DAVID (ed.). *Rethinking Italian Fascism: Capitalism, Populism and Culture*. London: Lawrence & Wishart, 1986.

FORNET, AMBROSIO (ed.). *Alea: una retrospetiva crítica*. Havana: Editorial Letras Cubanas, 1987.

FORSLUND, BENGT. *Victor Sjostrom. His Life and his Work*. New York: Zoetrope, 1988.

FOUCAULT, MICHEL. *History of Sexuality*. Vol. i: New York: Random House, 1978.

FRANCE, RICHARD. *The Theatre of Orson Welles*. Lewisburg, Pa.: Bucknell University Press, 1977.

FRANK, GEROLD. *Judy*. New York: Harper & Row, 1975.

FRANKLIN, JAMES. *New German Cinema: From Oberhausen to Hamburg*. Boston: Twayne, 1983.

FRAYLING, CHRISTOPHER. *Clint Eastwood*. London: Virgin Publishing, 1992.

—— *Spaghetti Westerns: Cowboys and Europeans from Karl May to Sergio Leone*. London: Routledge & Kegan Paul, 1981.

FREIBERG, FREDA. 'Genre and Gender in the Wartime Japanese Cinema'. *Historical Journal of Film, Radio and Television*, 12 (1992).

—— *Women in Mizoguchi Films*. Melbourne: Japanese Studies Centre, Monash University, 1981.

FRIEDEN, SANDRA, et al. (eds.). *Gender and German Cinema: Feminist Interventions*. 2 vols. Providence, RI: Berg Publishers, 1993.

FRIEDLÄNDER, SAUL. *Reflections of Nazism: An Essay on Kitsch and Death*. Translated by Thomas Weyr. New York: Harper & Row, 1984.

FURHAMMAR, LEIF, and ISAKSSON, FOLKE. *Politics and Film*. London: Studio Vista, 1971.

GAFFARY, FARROKH. *Le Cinéma en Iran*. Tehran: Le Conseil de la Culture et des Arts et Centre d'Étude et de la Coordination Culturelle, 1973.

—— 'Cinema I: History of Cinema in Persia'. In Ehsan Yarshater (ed.). *Encyclopedia Iranica*, vol. 5. Costa Mesa, Calif.: Mazda Publishers, 1991.

GALLAGHER, TAG. *John Ford: The Man and his Films*. Berkeley, Calif.: University of California Press, 1986.

GAREL, SYLVAIN, and PÂQUET, ANDRÉ (eds.). *Les Cinémas du Canada*. Paris: Centre Georges Pompidou, 1992.

GARRI, A. *I.I. Mozzhukhin*. Moscow and Leningrad: Kinopechat, 1927.

GAUTEUR, CLAUDE, and VINCENDEAU, GINETTE. *Anatomie d'un mythe: Jean Gabin*. Paris: Éditions Nathan Université, 1993.

GEDULD, HARRY M. *The Birth of the Talkies*. Bloomington, Ind.: Indiana University Press, 1975.

GEIST, KÄTHE. *The Cinema of Wim Wenders*. Ann Arbor, Mich.: UMI, 1988.

GERBER, JACQUES. *Anatole Dauman: Pictures of a Producer*. London: BFI, 1992.

GHATAK, RITWIK. *Cinema and I*. Calcutta: Ritwik Memorial Trust and Rupa, 1987.

GIDAL, PETER. *Andy Warhol: Films and Paintings*. New York: Dutton, 1971.

GIFFORD, DENIS. *American Animated Films: The Silent Era, 1897–1929*. Jefferson, NC: McFarland, 1990.

— *British Animated Film, 1895–1985: A Filmography*. Jefferson, NC: McFarland, 1987.

GILDER, GEORGE. *Wealth and Poverty*. New York: Basic Books, 1981.

GINZBURG, SEMION. *Kinematografiya dorevolyutsionnoy Rossii* ('The cinema of pre-revolutionary Russia'). Moscow: Iskusstvo, 1963.

GIRARD, JEAN. *Le Lexique français du cinéma, des origines à 1930*. Paris: Centre National de la Recherche Scientifique, 1958.

GISH, LILLIAN. *The Movies, Mr. Griffith and Me*. Englewood Cliffs, NJ: Prentice-Hall, 1969.

— *Dorothy and Lillian Gish*. London: Macmillan, 1973.

GODARD, JEAN-LUC. *Jean-Luc Godard*. Paris: Éditions de l'Étoile, 1985.

— *Introduction à une véritable histoire du cinéma*, vol. i. Paris: Éditions Albatros, 1980.

GOLDBERG, JUDITH N. *Laughter through Tears: The Yiddish Cinema*. London and Toronto: Fairleigh Dickinson University Press, 1983.

GOLDMAN, ERIC A. *Visions, Images and Dreams: Yiddish Film Past and Present*. Teaneck, NJ: Ergo Media, 1988.

GOMERY, DOUGLAS. *The Hollywood Studio System*. New York: St Martin's Press, 1986.

— *Movie History: A Survey*. Belmont, Calif.: Wadsworth, 1991.

— *Shared Pleasures: A History of the Movie Presentation in the United States*. Madison, Wis.: University of Wisconsin Press, 1992.

— (ed.). *The Will Hays Papers*. Frederick, Md.: University Publications of America, 1986.

GORBMAN, CLAUDIA. 'Music as Mirror: *Cleo from 5 to 7*'. *Wide Angle*, 4 (1981).

— 'Music as Salvation: Notes on Fellini and Rota'. *Film Quarterly*, 28 (Winter 1974–5).

— *Unheard Melodies: Narrative Film Music*. Bloomington, Ind.: Indiana University Press, 1987; London: BFI, 1987.

GORHAM, MAURICE. *Television: Medium of the Future*. London: Percival Marshall, 1949.

GÖTTLER, FRITZ, GRAFE, FRIEDA, JACOBSEN, WOLFGANG, PATALAS, ENNO, and ULLMANN, GERHARD. *Friedrich Wilhelm Murnau*. Munich: Carl Hanser Verlag, 1990.

GOULDING, DANIEL J. (ed.). *Post New Wave Cinema in the Soviet Union and Eastern Europe*. Bloomington, Ind.: Indiana University Press, 1989.

GRAFE, FRIEDA, PATALAS, ENNO, PRINZLER, HANS HELMUT, and SYR, PETER. *Fritz Lang*. Munich: Carl Hanser Verlag, 1976.

GRAHAM, COOPER C. *Leni Riefenstahl and Olympia*. Metuchen, NJ: Scarecrow Press, 1986.

GRAHAM, PETER (ed.). *The New Wave: Critical Landmarks*. London: Secker & Warburg, 1968; Garden City, NY: Doubleday, 1968.

GRANT, BARRY KEITH. *Voyages of Discovery: The Cinema of Frederick Wiseman*. Urbana, Ill.: University of Illinois Press, 1992.

— *Film Genre Reader*. Austin, Tex.: University of Texas Press, 1986.

GRAY, MARIANNE. *Depardieu: A Biography*. London: Warner Books, 1992.

GREEN, STANLEY, and GOLDBLATT, BURT. *Starring Fred Astaire*. New York: Dodd, Mead & Company, 1973.

GREENE, GRAHAM. *The Pleasure-Dome*. London: Secker & Warburg, 1972.

GRIERSON, JOHN. *Grierson on Documentary*. Edited by Forsyth Hardy. London: Faber & Faber, 1966.

GROB, NORBERT. *Wenders*. Berlin: Volker Spiess, 1991.

GROBEL, LAWRENCE. *The Hustons*. New York: Scribner's, 1989.

GUARNER, JOSÉ LUIS. *Rossellini*. London: Studio Vista, 1970.

GUBACK, THOMAS. *The International Film Industry: Western Europe and America since 1945*. Bloomington, Ind.: Indiana University Press, 1969.

GUIBBERT, PIERRE (ed.). *Les Premiers Ans du cinéma français*. Perpignan: Institut Jean Vigo, 1985.

Guide du cinéma et de l'audiovisuel en Europe centrale et orientale. Paris: Institut d'Études Slaves, 1992.

GUNNING, TOM. 'The Cinema of Attractions: Early Film, its Spectator and the Avant-Garde', *Wide Angle*, 8 (Fall 1986). Reprinted in Thomas Elsaesser (ed.). *Early Cinema: Space, Frame, Narrative*. London: BFI, 1990.

— *D. W. Griffith and the Origins of American Narrative Film: The Early Years at Biograph*. Chicago and Urbana, Ill.: University of Illinois Press, 1991.

HACKETT, PAT. *The Andy Warhol Diaries*. New York: Warner Books, 1989.

HAINING, PETER. *The Legend of Garbo*. London: W. H. Allen, 1990.

HALAS, JOHN. *Masters of Animation*. Boston: Salem, 1987.

HALL, STUART. 'The Whites of the Eyes'. In George Bridges and Rosalind Brunt (eds.). *Silver Linings*. London: Lawrence & Wishart, 1981.

HALLIDAY, JON. *Sirk on Sirk*. London: Secker & Warburg, 1971.

HALLIWELL, LESLIE. *The Dead that Walk*. London: Grafton, 1986.

HAMBLEY, JOHN, and DOWNING, PATRICK. *The Art of Hollywood: Fifty Years of Art Direction*. London: Thames Television, 1978.

HAMES, PETER. 'Czechoslovakia: After the Spring'. In Daniel J. Goulding (ed.). *Post New Wave Cinema in the Soviet Union and Eastern Europe*. Bloomington, Ind.: Indiana University Press, 1989.

HAMMEN, SCOTT. *John Huston*. Boston: Twayne, 1985.

HAMMOND, PAUL. *The Shadow and its Shadow: Surrealist Writing on the Cinema*. London: Polygon, 1991.

HAMPTON, BENJAMIN B. *A History of the Movies*. New York: Covici Friede, 1931.

HANDLING, PIERS (ed.). *The Shape of Rage: The Films of David Cronenberg*. Toronto and New York: General Publishing Co. Ltd. and Zoetrope, 1983.

HANDZO, STEPHEN. 'A Narrative Glossary of Film Sound Technology'. In Elisabeth Weis and John Belton (eds.). *Film Sound: Theory and Practice*. New York: Columbia University Press, 1985.

HANSEN, MIRIAM. *Babel and Babylon*. Cambridge, Mass.: Harvard University Press, 1991.

—— 'Deadly Scenarios: Narrative Perspective and Sexual Politics in Pre-Revolutionary Russian Film'. *Cinefocus*, 2/2 (Spring 1992).

HARDING, JAMES. *Jacques Tati: Frame by Frame*. London: Secker & Warburg, 1984.

HARDT, URSULA. *Erich Pommer: Film Producer for Germany*. Los Angeles: University of California Press, 1993.

HARDY, PHIL. *The Western*. London: Aurum Press, 1983.

HARVEY, STEPHEN. *Directed by Vincente Minnelli*. New York: Cambridge University Press, 1993.

HARVEY, SYLVIA. *May '68 and Film Culture*. London: BFI, 1978.

HASUMI, SHIGUEHIKO. *Kantoku Ozu Yasujiro* ('Director Yasujiro Ozu'). Tokyo: Chikuma Shobo, 1983.

HAYMAN, RONALD. *Fassbinder Filmmaker*. London: Weidenfeld & Nicolson, 1984.

HAYS, WILL H. *The Memoirs of Will H. Hays*. Garden City, NY: Doubleday, 1955.

HAYWARD, SUSAN. *French National Cinema*. London: Routledge, 1993.

—— 'Beyond the gaze and into femme-film écriture: Agnès Varda's *Sans toît ni loi*'. In Susan Hayward and Ginette Vincendeau (eds.). *French Film, Texts and Contexts*. London: Routledge, 1990.

—— and Vincendeau, Ginette (eds.). *French Film, Texts and Contexts*. London: Routledge, 1990.

HEATH, STEPHEN. 'Film and System, Terms of Analysis'. *Screen* 16 (1975).

HEIDER, KARL. *Indonesian Cinema: National Culture on Screen*. Honolulu: University of Hawaii Press, 1991.

HEIN, BIRGIT. *Film im Underground: von seinen Anfängen bis zum unabhängigen Kino*. Frankfurt am Main: Ullstein, 1971.

HEMBUS, JOE. *Der deutsche Film kann gar nicht besser sein*. Munich: Rogner & Bernhard, 1981.

HENDRYKOWSKA, MAŁGORZATA. 'Was the Cinema Fairground Entertainment? The Birth and Role of Popular Cinema in the Polish Territories up to 1908'. In Richard Dyer and Ginette Vincendeau (eds.). *Popular European Cinema*. London: Routledge, 1992.

—— *Śladami tamtych cieni: Film w kulturze polskiej prze omu stuleci, 1895–1914* ('In search of distant shadows: film in Polish turn-of-the-century culture'). Poznan: 1993.

HEPWORTH, CECIL. *Came the Dawn: Memories of a Film Pioneer*. London: Phoenix House, 1951.

HERLTH, ROBERT. 'Dreharben mit Murnau'. In Lotte Eisner (ed.). *Murnau*. Frankfurt: Kommunales Kino, 1979.

HERZOG, WERNER. *Screenplays*. New York: Tanam, 1980.

HIGASHI, SUMIKO. *Cecil B. DeMille: A Guide to References and Resources*. Boston: G. K. Hall, 1985.

HIGHAM, CHARLES. *Bette*. New York: New England Library, 1981.

—— *Cecil B. DeMille*. New York: Charles Scribner's Sons, 1973.

—— *Hollywood Cameramen: Sources of Light*. London: Thames & Hudson, 1970; Bloomington, Ind.: Indiana University Press, 1970.

—— *Brando: The Unauthorized Biography*. London: Sidgwick & Jackson, 1987.

HIGSON, ANDREW. 'Addressing the Nation: Five Films'. In Geoff Hurd (ed.). *National Fictions: World War Two in British Films and Television*. London: BFI, 1984.

HILL, JOHN. *Sex, Class and Realism: British Cinema, 1956– 1963*. London: BFI, 1986.

HILLIER, JIM (ed.). *Cahiers du Cinéma*. Vol i: *The 1950s*. London: Routledge and Kegan Paul, 1985.

—— (ed.). *Cahiers du Cinéma*. Vol ii: *The 1960s*. London, Routledge and Kegan Paul, 1986.

—— and Lipstadt, Aaron (eds.). *Roger Corman's New World*. London: BFI, 1981.

HILMES, MICHÈLE. *Hollywood and Broadcasting: From Radio to Cable*. Urbana, Ill.: University of Illinois Press, 1990.

HIRANO, KYOKO. *Mr. Smith Goes to Tokyo*. Washington, DC: Smithsonian Institution Press, 1992.

HIRSCHHORN, CLIVE. *The Hollywood Musical*. London and New York: Octopus Books and Crown Books, 1981.

HOBERMAN, JIM. *Bridge of Light: Yiddish Film between Two Worlds*. New York: The Museum of Modern Art and Schocken Books, 1991.

HOCKINGS, PAUL (ed.). *Principles of Visual Anthropology*. The Hague: Mouton Publishers, 1975.

HODGKINSON, ANTHONY W., and SHERATSKY, RODNEY E. *Humphrey Jennings, More Than a Maker of Films*. Hanover, N. H. and London: University Press of New England, 1982.*

HOLM, BILL, and QUIMBY, GEORGE IRVING. *Edward S. Curtis in the Land of the War Canoes: A Pioneer Cinematographer in the Pacific Northwest*. Seattle: University of Washington Press, 1980.

HOLMAN, L. BRUCE. *Puppet Animation in the Cinema, History and Technique*. London: The Tantivy Press, 1975.

HOLMAN, ROGER (ed.). *Cinema 1900–1906: An Analytic Study by the National Film Archive (London) and the International Federation of Film Archives*. Brussels: FIAF, 1982.

HOPEWELL, JOHN. *Out of the Past: Spanish Cinema after Franco*. London: BFI, 1986.

HORTON, ANDREW, and BRASHINSKY, MICHAEL. *The Zero Hour: Glasnost and Soviet Cinema in Transition*. Princeton, NJ: Princeton University Press, 1992.

HOUSEMAN, JOHN. *Front and Center*. New York: Simon & Schuster, 1979.

HUETTIG, MAE D. *Economic Control of the Motion Picture Industry*. Philadelphia: University of Pennsylvania Press, 1944.

HUFF, THEODORE. *Charlie Chaplin*. London: Cassell, 1952.

HUGHES, ROBERT. *Culture of Complaint*. New York: Oxford University Press, 1993.

HUGUES, PHILIPPE D', and MARTIN, MICHEL. *Le Cinéma français: le muet*. Paris: Atlas, 1986.

HUNNINGS, NEVILLE MARCH. *Film Censors and the Law*. London: Allen & Unwin, 1967.

HURD, GEOFF (ed.). *National Fictions: World War Two in British Films and Television*. London: BFI, 1984.

HUTCHINSON, TOM. *Horror and Fantasy in the Movies*. New York: Crescent Books, 1974.

ICART, ROGER. *La Révolution du parlant, vue par la presse française*. Perpignan: Institut Jean Vigo, 1988.

INDIANA, GARY. 'Getting Ready for the Golden Eighties: A Conversation with Chantal Ackerman'. *Artforum* (Summer 1983).

INSDORF, ANNETTE. *Indelible Shadows: Film and the Holocaust*. New York: Random House, 1983.

ISSARI, MOHAMMAD ALI. *Cinema in Iran, 1900–1979*. Metuchen, NJ: Scarecrow, 1989.

—— and PAUL, DORIS A. *What is Cinema Verité?* Metuchen, NJ: Scarecrow, 1979.

Istoriya sovietskogo kino v chetyryokh tomakh ('A history of the Soviet cinema in 4 volumes'). Vol. i: *1917–1931*. Moscow: Iskusstvo, 1969.

IVENS, JORIS. *The Camera and I*. Berlin: Seven Seas, 1969.

JACKSON, KEVIN (ed.). *The Humphrey Jennings Film Reader*. Manchester: Carcanet Press, 1993.

JACKSON, MICHAEL. 'Cinema versus Television'. *Sight and Sound* (Summer 1980).

JACOB, GILLES. 'Chris Marker and the Mutants'. *Sight and Sound* (Autumn 1966).

JACOBS, LEA. *The Wages of Sin: Censorship and the Fallen Woman Film, 1928–1942*. Madison, Wis.: University of Wisconsin Press, 1991.

JACOBS, LEWIS (ed.). *The Documentary Tradition*. 2nd edn. New York: W. W. Norton, 1979.

JACOBSEN, WOLFGANG. *Erich Pommer: Ein Produzent macht Filmgeschichte*. Berlin: Argon, 1989.

—— (ed.). *Babelsberg: Ein Filmstudio 1912–1992*. Berlin: Argon, 1992.

—— (ed.). *Conrad Veidt: Lebensbilder*. Berlin, 1993.

——, KAES, ANTON, and PRINZLER, HANS HELMUT (eds.). *Geschichte des deutschen Films*. Stuttgart: Metzler, 1993.

JAMES, C. VAUGHAN. *Soviet Socialist Realism*. London: Macmillan, 1973.

JAMES, DAVID. *Allegories of Cinema: American Film in the Sixties*. Princeton, NJ: Princeton University Press, 1989.

—— (ed.). *To Free the Cinema*. Princeton, NJ: Princeton University Press, 1992.

JANSEN, PETER W., and SCHÜTTE, WOLFRAM (eds.). *Film in der DDR*. Munich: Hanser, 1977.

—— (eds.). *Rainer Werner Fassbinder*. Frankfurt am Main: Fischer, 1992.

—— (eds.). *Werner Herzog*. Munich: Hanser, 1979.

—— (eds.). *Wim Wenders*. Munich: Hanser, 1992.

JARRATT, VERNON. *The Italian Cinema*. London: Falcon Press, 1951.

JARVIE, IAN C. *Window on Hong Kong*. Hong Kong: University of Hong Kong, 1977.

—— *Hollywood's Overseas Campaign: The North Atlantic Movie Trade, 1920–1950*. Cambridge, Mass.: Cambridge University Press, 1992.

JEANCOLAS, JEAN-PIERRE. *Le Cinéma des Français: La Ve République (1958–1978)*. Paris: Stock, 1979.

—— *D'un cinéma à l'autre: notes sur le cinéma des années cinquante*. Paris: Centre Georges Pompidou, 1988.

JEANNE, RENÉ, and FORD, CHARLES. *Histoire encyclopédique*. Vol. i: *Le Cinéma français*. Paris: Robert Laffont, 1947.

—— *Victor Sjöström*. Paris: Éditions Universitaires, 1963.

JENKINS, STEPHEN (ed.). *Fritz Lang*. London: BFI, 1980.

JENNINGS, HUMPHREY. *Pandaemonium*. London: André Deutsch, 1985.

JENNINGS, MARY-LOU (ed.). *Humphrey Jennings: Film-maker, Painter, Poet*. London: BFI, 1982.

JOBS, GERTRUDE. *Motion Picture Empire*. Hamden, Conn.: Archon, 1966.

JOHNSON, RANDAL, and STAM, ROBERT (eds.). *Brazilian Cinema*. Toronto: Associated University Presses, 1982.

JOHNSON, SHEILA. *Wim Wenders*. London: BFI, 1981.

JOHNSON, VIDA T., and PETRIE, GRAHAM. *Tarkovsky: A Visual Fugue*. Bloomington, Ind.: Indiana University Press, 1994.

JONES, CHUCK. *Chuck Amuck*. New York: Farrar, Straus & Giroux, 1989.

JOSSÉ, HARALD. *Die Entstehung des Tonfilms: Beitrag zu einer faktenorientierten Mediengeschichtsschreibung*. Freiburg: Alber, 1984.

JOUSSE, THIERRY. *John Cassavetes*. Paris: Éditions de l'Étoile and Cahiers du Cinéma, 1989.

JOWETT, GARTH. *Film: The Democratic Art*. Boston: Little, Brown and Co., 1976.

Jump Cut, 31 (Mar. 1986).

Jump Cut, 34 (Mar. 1989).

KAEL, PAULINE. *The Citizen Kane Book*. New York: Bantam, 1974.

KAES, ANTON. *From Hitler to Heimat: The Return of History as Film*. Cambridge, Mass.: Harvard University Press, 1989.

KAGAN, NORMAN. *American Skeptic: Robert Altman's Genre-Commentary Films*. Ann Arbor, Mich.: Pierian, 1982.

—— *The Cinema of Stanley Kubrick*. New York: Holt, Rinehart & Winston, 1972.

KALBUS, OSKAR. *Vom Werden deutscher Filmkunst: der Tonfilm*. Altona-Bahrenfeld: Cigaretten-Bilderdienst, 1935.

KALINAK, KATHRYN. *Settling the Score: Music and the Classical Hollywood Film*. Wisconsin Studies in Film. Madison, Wis., and London: University of Wisconsin Press, 1992.

KAPLAN, YUSUF. *Turk sinemasi: pathos ve retorik* ('Turkish cinema: pathos and rhetoric'). Istanbul: Agaç, 1994.

KARLIN, FRED. *Listening to Movies: The Film Lover's Guide to Film Music*. New York: Schirmer Books, 1994.

—— and Wright, Rayburn. *On the Track: A Guide to Contemporary Film Scoring*. New York: Schirmer Books and Macmillan, 1990.

KATZ, ROBERT. *Love is Colder than Death: The Life and Times of Rainer Werner Fassbinder*. New York: Random House, 1987.

KEATON, BUSTER. *My Wonderful World of Slapstick*. London: Allen & Unwin, 1967.

KELLY, MARY PAT. *Martin Scorsese: A Journey*. New York: Thunder's Mouth Press, 1991.

KEMP, PHILIP. *Lethal Innocence: The Cinema of Alexander Mackendrick*. London: Methuen, 1991.

KENDRICK, WALTER. *The Secret Museum: Pornography in Modern Culture*. New York: Viking Press, 1987.

KENEZ, PETER. *Cinema and Soviet Society, 1917–1953*. Cambridge, Mass.: Cambridge University Press, 1992.

KEPLEY, VANCE. *In the Service of the State: The Cinema of Alexander Dovzhenko*. Madison, Wis.: University of Wisconsin Press, 1986.

KERMABON, JACQUES. *Les Vacances de M. Hulot*. Crisnée: Yellow Now, 1988.

KERR, WALTER. *The Silent Clowns*. New York: Knopf, 1975.

KERSTEN, HEINZ. *Das Filmwesen in der Sowjetischen Besatzungszone Deutschlands*. 2 vols. Bonn and Berlin: Bundesministerium für gesamtdeutsche Fragen, 1963.

KEYSER, LES. *Martin Scorsese*. New York: Twayne, 1992.

KEYSSAR, HELENE. *Robert Altman's America*. New York: Oxford University Press, 1991.

KHANZHONKOV, ALEXANDER. *Pervyie gody russkoi kinematografii: vospominaniya* ('The first years of Russian cinema: memoirs'). Moscow and Leningrad: Iskusstvo, 1937.

KHRENOV, NIKOLAI. *Sudba Ivana Mozzhukhina: Iz istorii kino*. Moscow: Iskusstvo, 1977.

KINDEM, GORHAM (ED.). *The American Movie Industry*. Carbondale, Ill.: Southern Illinois University Press, 1982.

KINDER, MARSHA. *Blood Cinema: The Reconstruction of National Identity in Spain*. Berkeley, Calif., and London: University of California Press, 1993.

—— 'Pleasure and the New Spanish Mentality: A Conversation with Pedro Almodóvar'. *Film Quarterly* (Fall 1987).

KING, JOHN. *Magical Reels: A History of Cinema in Latin America*. London: Verso, 1990.

——, LOPEZ, ANA M., and ALVARADO, MANUEL (eds.). *Mediating Two Worlds: Cinematic Encounters in the Americas*. London: BFI, 1993.

KINNARD, ROY. *Fifty Years of Serial Thrills*. Metuchen, NJ: Scarecrow Press, 1983.

KIRIHARA, DONALD. *Patterns of Time: Mizoguchi and the 1930s*. Madison, Wis.: University of Wisconsin Press, 1992.

KITSES, JIM. *Horizons West*. London: Thames & Hudson, 1969.

KLOTMAN, PHYLLIS RAUCH. *Frame by Frame: A Black Filmography*. Bloomington, Ind.: Indiana University Press, 1979.

KNIGHT, JULIA. *Women and the New German Cinema*. London and New York: Verso, 1992.

KOCH, STEPHEN. *Stargazer: Andy Warhol's World and His Films*. London: Calder & Boyars, 1973.

KOLKER, ROBERT PHILLIP. *Bernardo Bertolucci*. London; BFI, 1985; New York: Oxfrod University Press, 1985.

—, and BEICKEN, PETER. *The Films of Wim Wenders: Cinema as Vision and Desire*. New York: Cambridge University Press, 1993.

KOPPES, CLAYTON R., and BLACK, GREGORY D. *Hollywood Goes to War: How Politics, Profits and Propaganda Shaped World War II Movies*. New York: Macmillan, 1987.

KORDA, MICHAEL. *Charmed Lives*. London: Allen Lane, 1980.

KOSANOVIĆ, DEJAN. *Poceci kinematografija na tlu Jugoslawije, 1896–1918* ('The beginnings of cinema in Yugoslavia, 1896–1918'). Belgrade: 1986.

KOSZARSKI, DIANE KAISER. *The Complete Films of William S. Hart: A Pictorial Record*. New York: Dover Publications, 1980.

KOSZARSKI, RICHARD. *History of the American Cinema*. Vol iii: *An Evening's Entertainment: The Age of the Silent Feature Picture, 1915–1928*. New York: Charles Scribner's Sons, 1990.

—— *The Man You Loved to Hate: Erich von Stroheim and Hollywood*. New York: Oxford University Press, 1983.

KOVÁCS, KATHERINE S. 'Berlanga Life Size: An Interview with Luis García Berlanga'. *Quarterly Review of Film Studies* (Spring 1983).

KRACAUER, SIEGFRIED. *From Caligari to Hitler*. Princeton, NJ: Princeton University Press, 1947.

KREIMEIER, KLAUS. *Die Ufa-Story: Geschichte eines Filmkonzerns*. Munich and Vienna: Hanser, 1992.

KUENZLI, RUDOLF E. (ed.). *Dada and Surrealist Film*. New York: Willis, Locker & Owens, 1987.

KULIK, KAROL. *Alexander Korda: The Man Who Could Work Miracles*. London: W. H. Allen, 1975.

KÜNTZEL, UWE. *Wim Wenders: Ein Filmbuch*. Freiburg: Dreisam, 1989.

LACASSIN, FRANCIS. *Louis Feuillade*. Paris: Seghers, 1964.

—— *Pour une contre histoire du cinéma*. Paris: Union Générale d'Éditions, 1972.

LACOMBE, ALAIN (ed.). 'Cinéma et musique (1960–1975)'. *Écran 75* (Sept. 1975).

LAHUE, KALTON C. *Continued Next Week: A History of the Moving Picture Serial*. Norman, Okla.: University of Oklahoma Press, 1964.

—— *Kops and Custard*. Norman, Okla.: University of Oklahoma Press, 1967.

—— *World of Laughter*. Norman, Okla.: University of Oklahoma Press, 1966.

LAMBERT, GAVIN. *On Cukor*. New York: Putnam, 1972.

LAMPRECHT, GERHARD. *Deutsche Stummfilme, 1903–1931*. Berlin: Deutsche Kinemathek, 1976–80.

LAMSTER, FREDERICK. *Souls Made Great through Love and Adversity*. Metuchen, NJ: Scarecrow Press, 1981.

LÄNGSFELD, WOLFGANG (ed.). *Filmarchitektur Robert Herlth*. Munich: Deutsches Institut für Film und Fernsehen, 1965.

LANGTON, MARCIA. *'Well, I Heard It on the Radio and Saw It on the Television'*. Sydney: Australian Film Commission, 1993.

LANT, ANTONIA. *Blackout: Reinventing Women for Wartime British Cinema*. Princeton, NJ: Princeton University Press, 1991.

LAPIERRE, MARCEL. *Les Cents Visages au cinéma*. Paris: Grasset, 1948.

LAWDOR, STANDISH. *The Cubist Cinema*. New York: New York University Press, 1975.

LAWTON, ANNA. *Kinoglasnost: Soviet Cinema in our Time*. Cambridge and New York: Cambridge University Press, 1992.

LEAB, DANIEL J. *From Sambo to Superspade: The Black Experience in Motion Pictures*. London: Secker & Warburg, 1975.

LEAMER, LAWRENCE. *As Time Goes By*. New York: Harper & Row, 1986.

LEAMING, BARBARA. *Bette Davis, A Biography*. London: Weidenfeld & Nicholson, 1992.

—— *Orson Welles: A Biography*. New York: Viking, 1985.

LEBEDEV, N. A. *Ocherk istorii kino SSSR: Nemoye kino, 1918–34* ('An outline history of cinema in the USSR: silent cinema, 1918–34'). Moscow: Iskusstvo, 1965.

LEE, SPIKE, *et al*. *Five for Five: The Films of Spike Lee*. New York: Stewart, Taboti & Chang, 1991.

LEES, DAVID, and BERKOWITZ, STAN. *The Movie Business*. New York: Vintage, 1981.

LE FANU, MARK. *The Cinema of Andrei Tarkovsky*. London: BFI, 1987.

LEFF, LEONARD J., and SIMMONS, JEROLD L. *The Dame in the Kimono: Hollywood Censorship and the Production Code from the 1920s to the 1960s*. New York: Grove Weidenfeld, 1990.

LE GRICE, MALCOLM. *Abstract Film and beyond*. London: Studio Vista, 1977.

LENT, JOHN A. *The Asian Film Industry*. London: Christopher Helm, 1990.

LEPROHON, PIERRE. *The Italian Cinema*. London: Secker & Warburg, 1972; New York: Praeger, 1972.

LESAGE, JULIA. *Jean-Luc Godard: A Guide to References and Resources*. Boston: G. K. Hall, 1975.

LEUTRAT, JEAN-LOUIS. *Le Western*. Paris: Armand Colin, 1973.

LEVIN, G. ROY. *Documentary Explorations: 15 Interviews with Filmmakers*. Garden City, NY: Doubleday, 1971.

LEVY, EMANUEL. *John Wayne: Prophet of the American Way of Life*. Metuchen, NJ: Scarecrow Press, 1988.

LEWANDOWSKI, RAINER. *Die Oberhausener: Rekonstruktion einer Gruppe, 1962–1982*. Dieckholzen: Regie, 1982.

LEYDA, JAY. *Dianying: Electric Shadows, an Account of Films and the Film Audience in China*. Boston: MIT Press, 1972.

—— *Kino: A History of Russian and Soviet Film*. London: Allen & Unwin, 1960; New York: Macmillan, 1960. (Revised edn. Princeton, NJ: Princeton University Press, 1983.)

—— and Voynow, Zina (eds.). *Eisenstein at Work*. New York: Pantheon, 1982.

LIEHM, MIRA. *Passion and Defiance: Film in Italy from 1942 to the Present*. Berkeley, Calif.: University of California Press, 1984.

—— and Liehm, Antonin J. *The Most Important Art: Eastern European Film after 1945*. Berkeley, Calif.: University of California Press, 1977.

LIESEGANG, FRANZ PAUL. *Moving and Projected Images: A Chronology of Pre-Cinema History*. London: The Magic Lantern Society of Great Britain, 1986.

LIKHACHEV, BORIS. *Kino v Rossii* ('Cinema in Russia'). Moscow, 1926.

LIMMER, WOLFGANG. *Rainer Werner Fassbinder, Filmemacher*. Reinbek: Rowohlt, 1981.

LINDER, MAUD. *Les Dieux du cinéma muet: Max Linder*. Paris: Éditions Atlas, 1992.

LIPTON, LENNY. *The Super 8 Book*. San Francisco: Straight Arrow Books, 1975.

LI YOU-HSIN (ed.). *Kang-tai Liu-ta Tao-yen* ('Six major directors from Hong Kong and Taiwan'). Taipei: Tzu-li Evening Post Publications, 1986.

LONG, CHRIS. *Australia's First Films*. Melbourne: Oxford University Press, 1994.

LOW, RACHAEL. *The History of the British Film*. Vol. ii: *1906- -1914*. London: George Allen & Unwin, 1949.

—— *The History of the British Film*. Vol. iii. *1914–1918*. London: Allen & Unwin, 1950.

—— *The History of the British Film*. Vol. iv: *1918–1929*. London: Allen & Unwin, 1971.

——, and Manvell, Roger. *The History of the British Film*. Vol. i: *1896– 1906*. London: George Allen & Unwin, 1948.

LOWDER, ROSE (ed.). *The Visual Aspect: Recent Canadian Experimental Films*. Avignon: Archives du Film Expérimental, 1991.

LYONS, BRIDGET GELLERT (ed.). *Chimes at Midnight*. New Brunswick, NJ: Rutgers University Press, 1988.

LYONS, TIMOTHY J. *Charles Chaplin: A Guide to References and Resources*. Boston: G. K. Hall, 1979.

MCBRIDE, JOSEPH. *Hawks on Hawks*. Berkeley, Calif.: University of California Press, 1982.

——, and Wilmington, Michael. *John Ford*. New York: Da Capo, 1975.

MACCABE, COLIN, MULVEY, LAURA, and EATON, MICK. *Godard: Images, Sounds, Politics*. London: Macmillan, 1980.

MCCABE, JOHN. *Charlie Chaplin*. New York: Doubleday, 1978.

MCCAFFREY, DONALD W. *Four Great Comedians*. London: Tantivy Press, 1968.

MCCANN, GRAHAM. *Rebel Males: Clift, Brando and Dean*. New York: Viking Press, 1991; and London: Hamish Hamilton, 1991.

—— *Marilyn Monroe*. New Brunswick, NJ: Rutgers University Press, 1988.

MACCANN, RICHARD DYER. *The People's Films: A Political History of US Government Motion Pictures*. New York: Hastings House, 1973.

MCCARTHY, TODD, and FLYNN, CHARLES (eds.). *Kings of the 'B's*. New York: E. P. Dutton, 1975.

MCCARTY, CLIFFORD. *Film Composers in America: A Checklist of their Work*. New York: Da Capo, 1972.

MCCORMICK, RUTH (ed.). *Fassbinder*. New York: Tanam, 1981.

MCDONALD, KEIKO. *Mizoguchi*. Boston: Twayne, 1984.

MACDONALD, KEVIN. *Emeric Pressburger: The Life and Death of a Screenwriter*. London: Faber & Faber, 1994.

MACDONALD, SCOTT. *Avant-Garde Film*. Cambridge: Cambridge University Press, 1993.

MCGILLIGAN, PATRICK. *George Cukor: A Double Life*. New York: St Martin's Press, 1991.

—— *Robert Altman: Jumping off the Cliff*. New York: St Martin's Press, 1989.

MCROBBIE, ANGELA. 'Passionate Uncertainty'. *Sight and Sound* (Sept. 1992).

MCSHINE, KYNASTON (ed.). *Andy Warhol: A Retrospective*. New York: Museum of Modern Art, 1989.

MAGLIOZZI, RONALD S. (ed.). *Treasures from the Film Archives: A Catalog of Short Films Held in FIAF Archives*. Metuchen, NJ: Scarecrow Press, 1988.

MAHIEU, JOSÉ AGUSTIN. *Breve historia del cine argentino*. Buenos Aires: Editorial Universitaria, 1966.

MALKMUS, LIZBETH, and ARMES, ROY. *Arab and African Film Making*. London: Zed Press, 1991.

MALTBY, RICHARD. 'The Production Code and the Hays Office'. In Tino Balio (ed.). *Grand Design: Hollywood as a Modern Business Enterprise*. New York: Charles Scribner's Sons, 1993.

MALTIN, LEONARD. *The Art of the Cinematographer*. 2nd edn. New York: Dover Publications, 1978.

—— *Of Mice and Magic: A History of American Animated Cartoons*. New York: New American Library, 1980.

MAMBER, STEPHEN. *Cinema Verite in America: Studies in Uncontrolled Documentary*. Cambridge, Mass.: MIT Press, 1974,

MANCINI, ELAINE. *Luchino Visconti: A Guide to References and Resources*. Boston: G. K. Hall, 1986.

MANCINI, HENRY, with LEES, GENE. *Did They Mention the Music?*. New York: Contemporary Books, 1989.

MANVELL, ROGER, and HUNTLEY, JOHN. *The Technique of Film Music*. Focal Press Library of Communications Techniques. New York: Hastings House, 1975 (2nd edn., revised and enlarged by Richard Arnell and Peter Day).

MARCUS, MILLICENT. *Italian Film in the Light of Neorealism*. Princeton, NJ: Princeton University Press, 1986.

MARGOLIT, E. Y. *Sovietskoie kinoiskusstvo: Osnovnyie etapy stanovleniya i razvitiya* ('Soviet film art: the main stages of its growth and development'). Moscow: Vsiesoyuzniy Zaochniy Narodniy Universitiet Iskusstv, 1988.

MARKER, CHRIS. *Commentaires*. Paris: Éditions du Seuil, 1961.

MARKS, MARTIN. *Music and the Silent Film: Contexts and Case Studies, 1895–1924*. New York: Oxford University Press, 1996.

MARTIN, LÉONA BÉATRICE, and MARTIN, FRANÇOISE. *Ladislas Starewitch*, JICA (Annecy Film Festival), 1991.

MARTINELLI, VITTORIO. 'Il cinema muto italiano, 1915–1931', *Bianco e nero*, 41 (1980), 42 (1981), 50 (1989), 51 (1990), and 52 (1991).

MASI, STEFANO, and FRANCO, MARIO. *Il mare, la luna, i coltelli: per una storia del cinema muto napoletano*. Naples: Pironti, 1988.

MAST, GERALD. *Howard Hawks, Storyteller*. New York: Oxford University Press, 1982.

—— *A Short History of the Movies*. New York: Macmillan, 1986.

MAXWELL, RICHARD. *The Spectacle of Democracy: Spanish Television, Nationalism and Political Transition*. Minneapolis: University of Minnesota Press, 1994.

—— (ed.). *Focus on Howard Hawks*. Englewood Cliffs, NJ: Prentice-Hall, 1972.

MAYNE, JUDITH. *The Woman at the Keyhole: Feminism and Women's Cinema*. Bloomington, Ind.: Indiana University Press, 1990.

MEEKER, DAVID. *Jazz in the Movies: A Guide to Jazz Musicians, 1917– 1977*. New York: Da Capo, 1981.

MERRITT, RUSSELL, and KAUFMAN, J. B. *Walt in Wonderland: The Silent Films of Walt Disney*. Berkeley, Calif.: University of California Press, 1994.

MICHALEK, BOLES LAW. *The Cinema of Andrzej Wajda*. London: Tantivy Press, 1973.

—— and TURAJ, FRANK. *The Modern Cinema of Poland*. Bloomington, Ind.: Indiana University Press, 1988.

MILNE, TOM (ed.). *Godard on Godard*. London: Secker & Warburg, 1973.

MILNE, TOM. 'Victor Sjöström'. In Richard Roud (ed.). *Cinema: A Critical Dictionary*, vol. ii. London: Secker & Warburg, 1980.

—— (ed.). *Losey on Losey*. Garden City, NY: Doubleday, 1968.

MINNELLI, VINCENTE, with ARCE, HECTOR. *I Remember It Well*. London: Angus & Robertson, 1975.

MITRY, JEAN. *Histoire du cinéma*. Vol. i: *1895–1914*. Paris: Éditions Universitaires, 1967.

—— *Histoire du cinéma*. Vol. ii: *1915–1923*. Paris: Éditions Universitaires, 1969.

—— *Histoire du cinéma*. Vol. iii: *1923–1930*. Paris: Éditions Universitaires, 1973.

—— 'Ivan Mosjoukine'. *Anthologie du cinema*, no. 48 (Oct. 1969).

—— *Max Linder*. Paris: L'Avant-Scene, 1966.

MIX, PAUL E. *The Life and Legend of Tom Mix*. South Brunswick, NY, and New York: A.S. Barnes, 1972.

MODLESKI, TANIA. *The Women Who Knew Too Much: Hitchcock and Feminist Theory*. New York: Routledge, 1989.

MÖHRMANN, RENATE. *Die Frau mit der Kamera: Filmemacherinnern in der Bundesrepublik Deutschland; Situation, Perspektiven; Zehn exemplarische Lebensläufe*. Munich and Vienna: Hanser, 1980.

MOLEY, RAYMOND. *The Hays Office*. Indianapolis: Bobbs-Merrill, 1945.

MONACO, PAUL. *Cinema and Society: France and Germany during the Twenties*. New York: Elsevier, 1976.

MONTGOMERY, JOHN. *Comedy Films: 1894–1954*. London: George Allen & Unwin, 1954.

MONTY, IB. *Portrait of Carl Theodor Dreyer*. Copenhagen: Danish Government Film Foundation, 1965.

MORAN, ALBERT, and O'REGAN, JON (eds.). *The Australian Screen*. Ringwood: Penguin, 1989.

MORIN, EDGAR. *The Stars*. New York: Grove Press, 1960.

MORRIS, MICHAEL. *Madam Valentino*. New York: Abbeville Press, 1991.

MORRIS, PETER. *Embattled Shadows: A History of Canadian Cinema, 1895–1939*. Montreal: McGill–Queens University Press, 1978.

—— *The Film Companion: A Comprehensive Guide to more than 650 Canadian Films and Filmmakers*. Richmond Hill, Ont.: Irwin Publishing, 1984.

MOUSSINAC, LÉON. *Naissance du cinéma*. Paris: Povolovsky, 1925.

—— *Panoramique du cinéma*. Paris: Le Sans Pareil, 1929.

MUELLER, JOHN. *Astaire Dancing: The Musical Films*. New York: Knopf, 1985.

MULVEY, LAURA. 'Visual Pleasure and Narrative Cinema'. *Screen* 16 (1975).

MUNSTERBERG, HUGO. *The Photoplay: A Psychological Study*. New York: Appleton, 1916.

MURPHY, ROBERT. 'Rank's Attempt on the American Market'. In James Curran and Vincent Porter (eds.). *British Cinema History*. London: Weidenfeld & Nicolson, 1983.

—— *Sixties British Cinema*. London: BFI, 1992.

MURRAY, BRUCE. *Film and the German Left*. Austin, Tex.: University of Texas Press, 1990.

MURRAY, SCOTT (ed.). *Australian Film, 1978–1992: A Survey of Theatrical Features*. Melbourne: Oxford University Press, 1993.

MUSSER, CHARLES. *Before the Nickelodeon: Edwin S. Porter and the Edison Manufacturing Company*. Berkeley, Calif.: University of California Press, 1991.

—— *History of the American Cinema*. Vol. i: *The Emergence of Cinema: The American Screen to 1907*. New York: Charles Scribner's Sons, 1990.

——, with NELSON, CAROL. *High Class Moving Pictures: Lyman H. Howe and the Forgotten Era of Traveling Exhibition, 1880–1920*. Princeton, NJ: Princeton University Press, 1991.

NAFICY, HAMID. 'Iranian Feature Films: A Brief Critical History'. *Quarterly Review of Film Studies*, 4 (1979).

—— 'Islamizing Cinema in Iran'. In Samih K. Farsoun and Mehrdad Mashayekhi (eds.). *Iran: Political Culture in the Islamic Republic*. London: Routledge, 1992.

NAREMORE, JAMES. *The Films of Vincente Minnelli*. New York: Cambridge University Press, 1993.

—— *The Magic World of Orson Welles*. New York: Oxford University Press, 1978.

NEALE, STEPHEN. *Cinema and Technology: Image, Sound, Colour*. London: Macmillan, 1985.

—— *Genre*. London: BFI, 1980.

NELSON, THOMAS ALLEN. *Kubrick: Inside a Film Artist's Maze*. Bloomington, Ind.: Indiana University Press, 1982.

NESTEBY, JAMES R. *Black Images in American Films, 1896–1954: The Interplay Between Civil Rights and Film Culture*. Lanham, Md.: University Press of America, 1982.

NEWMAN, KIM. *Nightmare Movies: A Critical History of the Horror Film*. London: Bloomsbury, 1988.

NICHOLS, BILL (ed.). *Movies and Methods: An Anthology*. Berkeley, Calif.: University of California Press, 1980.

—— *Movies and Methods, Volume II: An Anthology*. Berkeley, Calif.: University of California Press, 1985.

—— *Newsreel: Documentary Filmmaking on the American Left*. New York, 1980.

—— *Representing Reality: Issues and Concepts in Documentary*. Bloomington, Ind.: Indiana University Press, 1991.

NIPPON HOSO KYOKAI. *The History of Broadcasting in Japan*. Tokyo: NHK and Radio & TV Culture Research Institute, 1967.

NIZHNY, VLADIMIR. *Lessons with Eisenstein*. Translated and edited by Ivor Montagu. New York: Hill & Wang, 1962.

NOAKE, ROGER. *Animation: A Guide to Animated Film Techniques*. London: Macdonald, 1988.

NOAM, ELI. *Television in Europe*. New York: Oxford University Press, 1991.

NOLLETTI, ARTHUR, JR., and DESSER, DAVID (eds.). *Reframing Japanese Cinema: Authorship, Genre and History*. Bloomington, Ind.: Indiana University Press, 1992.

NORIEGA, CHON A., and RICCI, STEVEN (eds.). *The Mexican Cinema Project*. Los Angeles: UCLA Film and Television Archive, 1994.

NOWELL-SMITH, GEOFFREY. 'Beyond the Po Valley Blues'. *Pix*, 1 (1993).

—— *Visconti*. Revised edn. London: Secker & Warburg, 1973; New York: Viking, 1973.

—— (ed.). *The European Experience*. London: BFI, 1989.

NUSSINOVA, NATALIA. *Koster pylaiushchii Ivana Mozzhukhina: vybor ivorcheskogo puti kak poisk novoi rodiny Kinovedcheskie zapiski*. Moscow: VNIIK, 1989.

OBERHOLTZER, ELLIS P. *The Morals of the Movies*. Philadelphia: Penn Publishing Co., 1922.

OGLE, PATRICK L. 'Technological and Aesthetic Influences upon the Development of Deep Focus Cinematography in the United States'. *Screen*, 13 (1972).

OMS, MARCEL. *Alexandre Dovjenko*. Lyons: Premier Plan, 1968.

On Film, 14 (Spring 1985).

O'PRAY, MICHAEL (ed.). *Andy Warhol: Film Factory*. London: BFI, 1989.

OSHIMA, NAGISA. *Cinema, Censorship, and the State: The Writings of Nagisa Oshima*. Cambridge, Mass.: MIT Press, 1992.

—— *Écrits, 1956–1978: Dissolution et jaillissement*. Paris: Gallimard, 1980.

OZIMEK, STANISLAW. *Film polski w wojennej potrzebie* ('Polish film under the stress of war'). Warsaw, 1974.

ÖZÖN, NIJAT. *Türk Sinemasi Kronolojisi: 1895–1966* ('The chronology of Turkish cinema: 1895–1966'). Ankara: Bilgi, 1968.

PALMER, CHRISTOPHER. *The Composer in Hollywood.* London and New York: Marion Boyars, 1990.

PALMIERI, EUGENIO FERDINANDO. *Vecchio cinema italiano.* Venice: Zanetti, 1940.

PANDIAN, M. S. S. *The Image Trap: M. G. Ramachandran in Film and Politics.* New Delhi: Sage, 1992.

PAOLELLA, ROBERTO. *Storia del cinema muto.* Napoli: Giannini, 1956.

PARISH, JAMES ROBERT. *The Tough Guys.* New York: Arlington House, 1976.

PARK, JAMES. *British Cinema: The Lights that Failed.* London: Batsford, 1990.

PARKER, JOHN. *The Joker's Wild: The Biography of Jack Nicholson.* London: Anaya, 1991.

PASOLINI, PIER PAOLO. *Heretical Empiricism.* Bloomington, Ind.: Indiana University Press, 1988.

PASSEK, JEAN-LOUP (ed.). *Le Cinéma russe et soviétique.* Paris: Centre Georges Pompidou, 1981.

PATHÉ, CHARLES. *De Pathé-frères à Pathé-cinéma.* Lyons: SERDOC, 1970.

PATIL, S. K. *Report of the Film Enquiry Committee.* New Delhi: Government of India Press, 1951.

PAYNE, STANLEY. 'Spanish Fascism'. *Salmagundi*, 76–77 (Fall–Winter 1987–8).

PEARSON, GEORGE. *Flashback: The Autobiography of a British Filmmaker.* London: Allen & Unwin, 1957.

PEARSON, ROBERTA E. *Eloquent Gestures: The Transformation of Performance Style in the Griffith Biograph Films.* Berkeley, Calif.: University of California Press, 1992.

PECORI, FRANCO. *De Sica.* Florence, La Nuova Italia, 1980.

PENSE, HANS. *Seastrom and Stiller in Hollywood.* New York: Vantage Press, 1969.

PÉREZ TURRENT, TOMÁS, and DE LA COLINA, JOSÉ. *Objects of Desire: Conversations with Luis Buñuel.* New York: Marsilio, 1992.

PERKINS, V. F. *Film as Film.* Harmondsworth: Penguin, 1972.

PERRY, GEORGE. *Forever Ealing.* London: Pavilion and Michael Joseph, 1981.

—— *The Great British Picture Show.* London: Pavilion, 1985.

PETERSON, BERNARD L., Jr. 'The Films of Oscar Micheaux: America's First Fabulous Black Filmmaker'. In *The Crisis of 86.* 1979.

PETLEY, JULIAN. *Capital and Culture: German Cinema 1933–45.* London: BFI, 1979.

PETRIC, VLADA. *Constructivism in Film: The Man with the Movie Camera: A Cinematic Analysis.* Cambridge: Cambridge University Press, 1987.

PETRIE, DUNCAN. *Creativity and Constraint in the British Film Industry.* London: Macmillan, 1991.

—— (ed.). *New Questions of British Cinema.* London: BFI, 1992.

PETRO, PATRICE. *Joyless Streets.* Princeton, NJ: Princeton University Press, 1989.

PFLAUM, HANS GÜNTHER. *Rainer Werner Fassbinder: Bilder und Dokumente.* Munich: Edition Spangenberg, 1992.

—— and PRINZLER, HANS HELMUT. *Cinema in the Federal Republic of Germany: The New German Film, Origins and Present Situation: A Handbook.* Bonn: Inter Nationes, 1983.

—— *Film in der Bundesrepublik Deutschland: der neue deutsche Film, von den Anfängen bis zur Gegenwart: mit einem Exkurs über das Kino der DDR. Ein Handbuch.* Bonn: Inter Nationes, 1992.

PHILIPE, ANNE. *No Longer than a Sigh.* London: Michael Joseph, 1962.

PHILLIPS, KLAUS (ed.). *New German Filmmakers from Oberhausen through the 1970s.* New York: Ungar, 1984.

PICK, ZUZANA. *The New Latin American Cinema: A Continental Project.* Austin, Tex.: University of Texas Press, 1993.

PICKFORD, MARY. *Sunshine and Shadow.* Garden City, NY: Doubleday, 1955.

PIKE, ANDREW, and COOPER, ROSS. *Australian Film, 1900–1977: A Guide to Feature Film Production.* Melbourne: Oxford University Press and Australian Film Institute, 1980.

PILLING, JAYNE (ed.). *Women and Animation: A Compendium.* London: BFI, 1992.

PINES, JIM. *Blacks in Films.* London: Studio Vista, 1975.

PINTER, HAROLD. *The Proust Screenplay: À la recherche du temps perdu.* New York: Grove Press, 1977.

PIOTROVSKY, A. *Teatr, Kino, Zhizn* ('Theatre, cinema, life'). Leningrad: Iskusstvo, 1969.

PIRIE, DAVID. *A Heritage of Horror: The English Gothic Cinema, 1946–1972.* London: Gordon Fraser, 1973.

PLUMMER, THOMAS *et al. Film and Politics in the Weimar Republic.* New York: Holmes & Meier, 1982.

POAGUE, LELAND. *Howard Hawks.* Boston: Twayne, 1982.

POITIER, SIDNEY. *This Life.* London: Hodder & Stoughton, 1980.

POLLITT, ELIZABETH. *Our Gracie.* Rochdale, 1978.

PORTER, VINCENT. 'The Context of Creativity: Ealing Studios and Hammer Films'. In James Curran and Vincent Porter (eds.). *British Cinema History.* London: Weidenfeld & Nicolson, 1983.

Positif, 223 (Oct. 1979).

Positif, 224 (Nov. 1979).

POWELL, MICHAEL. *A Life in Movies.* London: Heinemann, 1986.

—— *Million Dollar Movie.* London: Heinemann, 1992.

PRADHAN, SUDHI (ed.). *Marxist Cultural Movement in India (1936–1947)*, vol. 1. Calcutta: Santi Pradhan/National Book Agency, 1979.

PRATLEY, GERALD. *The Cinema of John Huston.* London: Tantivy Press, 1977.

PRÉDAL, RENÉ. *La Photo de cinéma.* Paris: Éditions du Cerf, 1985.

—— *La Société française (1914–1945) à travers le cinéma.* Paris: Armand Colin, 1972.

PRENDERGAST, ROY M. *Film Music, a Neglected Art: A Critical Study of Music in Films.* 2nd edn. New York: W. W. Norton, 1992.

PRINZLER, HANS HELMUT, and PATALAS, ENNO (eds.). *Lubitsch.* Munich and Lucerne: Bucher, 1984.

PUTTNAM, DAVID. 'Filmmaker in Wonderland'. In Brian Wenham (ed.). *The Third Age of Broadcasting.* London: Faber & Faber, 1982.

PYE, MICHAEL, and MYLES, LYNDA. *The Movie Brats.* New York: Holt, Rinehart, & Winston, 1979.

QUAGLIETTI, LORENZO. *Storia economico-politica del cinema italiano, 1945–1980.* Rome: Editori Riuniti, 1980.

QUIQUEMELLE, MARIE-CLAIRE, and PASSEK, JEAN-LOUP (eds.). *Le Cinéma chinois.* Paris: Centre Georges Pompidou, 1985.

QUIRK, LAWRENCE J. *The Films of Ingrid Bergman.* New York: Citadel Press, 1970.

RADVANYI, JEAN (ed.). *Le Cinéma géorgien.* Paris: Centre Georges Pompidou, 1988.

—— *Le Cinéma d'Asie centrale soviétique.* Paris: Centre Georges Pompidou, 1991.

—— *Le Cinéma arménien.* Paris: Centre Georges Pompidou, 1993.

RAINSBERGER, TODD. *James Wong Howe, Cinematographer.* New York: A.S. Barnes, 1981; London: Tantivy Press, 1981.

RAJADHYAKSHA, ASHISH. *Ritwik Ghatak: A Return to the Epic.* Bombay: Screen Unit, 1982.

—— and GANGAR, AMRIT (eds.). *Ritwik Ghatak: Arguments/Stories.*

Bombay: Screen Unit and Research Centre for Cinema Studies, 1987.

—— and WILLEMEN, PAUL (eds.). *Encyclopaedia of Indian Cinema*. London: BFI, 1994.

RAMIREZ BERG, CHARLES. 'The Cinematic Invention of Mexico'. In Chon Noriega and Steven Ricci (eds.). *The Mexican Cinema Project*. Los Angeles: UCLA Film and Television Archive. 1994.

RANVAUD, DONALD, and UNGARI, ENZO. *Bertolucci by Bertolucci*. London: Plexus, 1987.

RAPÉE, ERNO (comp. and ed). *Motion Picture Moods*. New York: G. Schirmer, 1924.

—— *Encyclopedia of Music for Pictures*. New York: Belwin, 1925.

RATHBUN, JOHN B. *Motion Picture Making and Exhibiting*. Chicago: Charles C. Thompson, 1914.

RAUH, REINHOLD. *Wim Wenders und seine Filme*. Munich: Heyne, 1990.

RAY, SATYAJIT. *Our Films, their Films*. New Delhi: Orient Longman, 1976.

RAYNS, TONY (ed.). *Fassbinder*. 2nd ed. London: BFI, 1976.

—— and MEEK, SCOTT (eds.). *Electric Shadows: 45 Years of Chinese Cinema*. London: BFI, 1980.

REDI, RICCARDO. *Ti parlerò... d'amor: cinema italiano fra muto e sonoro*. Turin: RAI, 1986.

REEVES, NICHOLAS. *Official British Film Propaganda during the First World War*. London: Croom Helm, 1986.

REFIĞ, HALIT. *Ulusal Sinema Kavgasi* ('The struggle for a national cinema'). Istanbul: Hareket, 1971.

REID, MARK A. *Redefining Black Film*. Berkeley, Calif.: University of California Press, 1993.

REID, NICHOLAS. *A Decade of New Zealand Film: Sleeping Dogs to Came a Hot Friday*. Dunedin: John McIndoe Ltd., 1986.

REITZ, EDGAR. *Liebe zum Kino: Utopien und Gedanken zum Autorenfilm, 1962–1983*. Cologne: Verlag KÖLN 78, 1984.

—— and STEINBACH, PETER. *Heimat: eine deutsche Chronik*. Nördlingen: Greno, 1985.

RENAN, SHELDON, *An Introduction to the American Underground Film*. New York: Dutton, 1967. (Published in the UK as *The Underground Film: An Introduction to its Development in America*. London: Studio Vista, 1968.)

RENOIR, JEAN. *Renoir, my Father*. Boston: Little, Brown & Co., 1962.

—— *My Life and my Films*. New York: Atheneum, 1974.

RENTSCHLER, ERIC. *West German Film in the Course of Time: Reflections on the Twenty Years since Oberhausen*. Bedford Hills, NY: Redgrave, 1984.

—— (ed.). *German Film and Literature: Adaptations and Transformation*. New Brunswick, NJ: Rutgers University Press, 1986; New York and London: Methuen, 1986.

—— (ed.). *West German Filmmakers on Film: Visions and Voices*. New York and London: Holmes & Meier, 1988.

Report of the Indian Cinematograph Committee, 1927–28, Calcutta, 1928.

RHODE, ERIC. *A History of the Cinema*. London: Allan Lane, 1976.

RICH, B. RUBY. 'Nobody's Handmaid', *Sight and Sound* (Dec. 1991).

RICHARDS, JEFFREY. *The Age of the Dream Palace: Cinema and Society in Britain, 1930–1939*. London: Routledge & Kegan Paul, 1984.

—— 'British Imperial Cinema in the 1930s'. In James Curran and Vincent Porter (eds.). *British Cinema History*. London: Weidenfeld & Nicolson, 1983.

—— 'Gracie Fields: The Lancashire Britannia', *Focus on Film*, 33 (Summer 1979) and 34 (Winter 1979).

RICHIE, DONALD. *The Films of Akira Kurosawa*. Berkeley, Calif.: University of California Press, 1984.

—— *Ozu*. Berkeley, Calif.: University of California Press, 1974.

RICHTER, HANS. *The Struggle for the Film*. London: Scolar Press, 1986.

RICHTER, ROLF (ed.). *DEFA-Spielfilm-Regisseure und ihre Kritiker*. 2 vols. Berlin: Henschel, 1983.

RIHOIT, CATHERINE. *Brigitte Bardot: un mythe français*. Paris: Livre de Poche, 1986.

RINGGOLD, GENE, and BODEEN, DEWITT. *Chevalier: The Films and Career of Maurice Chevalier*. Secaucus, NJ: The Citadel Press, 1973.

RITTAUD-HUTINET, JACQUES. *Le Cinéma des origines: les frères Lumière et leurs opérateurs*. Seyssel: Éditions du Champ Vallon, 1985.

RIVA, MARIA. *Marlene Dietrich by her Daughter*. New York: Alfred A. Knopf, 1993.

ROBINSON, ANDREW. *Satyajit Ray: The Inner Eye*. London: André Deutsch, 1989.

ROBINSON, DAVID. *Buster Keaton*. London: Secker & Warburg, 1969.

—— *Chaplin: His Life and Art*. London: Collins, 1985.

—— *The Great Funnies: A History of Film Comedy*. London: Studio Vista, 1969.

ROCHA, GLAUBER. *Revolução do cinema novo*. Rio de Janeiro: Alhambra/Embrafilme, 1981.

—— 'The Aesthetics of Hunger'. In Michael Chanan (ed.). *Twenty Five Years of the New Latin American Cinema*. London: BFI and Channel 4, 1983.

RODDICK, NICK. 'The British Revival'. In Gilbert Adair and Nich Roddick (eds.). *A Night at the Pictures: Ten Decades of British Film*. London: Columbus, 1985.

ROHDIE, SAM. *Antonioni*. London: BFI, 1990.

—— *The Passion of Pier Paolo Pasolini*, London: BFI, 1995.

ROHMER, ERIC. *L'Organisation de l'espace dans le 'Faust' de Murnau*. Paris: Union Générale d'Éditions, 1977.

—— and CHABROL, CLAUDE. *Hitchcock: The First Forty-Four Films*. New York: Frederick Ungar, 1979.

ROSENTHAL, ALAN. *The New Documentary in Action: A Casebook in Film Making*. Berkeley, Calif.: University of California Press, 1980.

ROSSELLINI, ROBERTO. *Quasi un'autobiografia*. Milan: Arnoldo Mondadori, 1987.

ROSSI, PATRIZIO. *Roberto Rossellini: A Guide to References and Resources*. Boston: G. K. Hall, 1988.

ROSTEN, LEO. *Hollywood: The Movie Colony*. New York: Harcourt, Brace, 1941.

ROUCH, JEAN. *Films ethnographiques sur l'Afrique noire*. Paris: UNESCO, 1967.

ROUD, RICHARD (ed.). *Cinema: A Critical Dictionary*. 2 vols. London: Secker & Warburg, 1980

—— *Godard*. Revised edn. London: Secker & Warburg, 1970.

RÓZSA, MIKLÓS. *Double Life: The Autobiography of Miklós Rózsa*. New York: Hippocrene Books, 1983.

RÜLICKE-WEILER, KÄTHE (ed.). *Film und Fernsehkunst der DDR: Traditionen, Beispiele, Tendenzen*. Berlin: Henschel, 1979.

RUSSELL, SHARON A. *Semiotics and Lighting: A Study of Six Modern French Cameramen*. Ann Arbor, Mich.: UMI Research Press, 1981.

RUSSELL TAYLOR, JOHN, and JACKSON, ARTHUR. *The Hollywood Musical*. London: Secker & Warburg, 1971.

RUSSET, ROBERT, and STARR, CECILE (eds.). *Experimental Animation: Origins of a New Art*. New York: Da Capo, 1988.

RYALL, TOM. *Alfred Hitchcock and the British Cinema*. Urbana, Ill.: University of Illinois Press, 1986.

RYAN, PAUL. *Marlon Brando: A Portrait*. London: Plexus, 1991.

SADOUL, GEORGES. *Dictionary of Filmmakers*. Berkeley, Calif.: University of California Press, 1992.

— *Dictionary of Films*. Berkeley, Calif.: University of California Press, 1992.

— *Gérard Philipe*. Paris: Seghers, 1967.

— *Histoire générale du cinéma*. Vol. iii: *Le Cinéma devient un art, 1909–1920 (l'avant-guerre)*. Paris: Denoël, 1951.

— *Histoire générale du cinéma*. Vol. iv: *Le Cinéma devient un art, 1909–1920 (la première guerre mondiale)*. Paris: Denoël, 1974.

— *Histoire générale du cinéma*. Vol. v: *L'Art muet (1919–1929)*. Paris: Denoël, 1975.

— *Histoire générale du cinéma*. Vol vi: *L'Art muet (1919- -1929)*. Paris: Denoël, 1975.

SAID, SALIM. *Shadows on the Silver Screen: A Social History of the Indonesian Film*. Jakarta: Lontar Foundation, 1991.

SALLES GOMES, PAULO EMILIO. *Cinema: Trajetória no sub-desenvolvimento*. Rio de Janeiro: Editorial Paz e Terra and Embrafilme, 1980.

SALT, BARRY. *Film Style and Technology: History and Analysis*. London: Starword, 1983. (Revised edn., 1992.)

— 'Schiave bianche e tende a strisce. La ricerca del "sensazionale"'. In *Schiave bianche allo specchio: le origini del cinema in Scandinavia (1896–1918)*. Pordenone: Studio Tesi, 1986.

SAMPSON, HENRY T. *Blacks in Black and White: A Source Book on Black Films*. Metuchen, NJ: Scarecrow Press, 1977.

SANDERS-BRAHMS, HELMA. *Deutschland, bleiche Mutter: Film-Erzählung*. Reinbek: Rowohlt, 1980.

SANDFORD, JOHN. *The New German Cinema*. New York: Da Capo, 1980.

SANNWALD, DANIELA. 'Continental Stranger: Conrad Veidt und seine britischen Filme'. In G. Dunkhase and Jörg Schöning (eds.). *London Calling*. Munich: CineGraph, 1993.

SANTNER, ERIC L. *Stranded Objects: Mourning, Memory and Film in Postwar Germany*. Ithaca, NY, and London: Cornell University Press, 1990.

SARRIS, ANDREW. *The John Ford Movie Mystery*. London: Secker & Warburg, 1976.

— (ed.). *The American Cinema: Directors and Directions, 1929–1968*. New York: E. P. Dutton, 1968.

— (ed.). *Interviews with Film Directors*. New York: Avon, 1967.

SATO, TADAO, *et al.* (eds.). *Koza Nihon Eiga*. 7 vols. Tokyo: Iwanamishoten, 1985–6.

SAVIO, FRANCESCO. *Ma l'amore no: realismo, formalismo, propaganda e telefoni bianchi nel cinema italiano di regime (1930–1943)*. Milan: Sonzogno, 1975.

SCANNELL, PADDY, and CARDIFF, DAVID. *A Social History of British Broadcasting*. Vol. i: *1922–1939*. Oxford: Basil Blackwell, 1991.

SCHARY, DORE. *Heyday*. Boston: Little, Brown & Co., 1979.

SCHATZ, THOMAS. *The Genius of the System*. New York: Pantheon, 1988.

— *Hollywood Genres: Formulas, Filmmaking and the Studio System*. New York: Random House, 1981.

SCHENK, ROLF (ed.). *Das zweite Leben der Filmstadt Babelsberg: DEFA Spielfilme 1946–1992*. Berlin: Henschel, 1994.

Schiave bianche allo specchio: le origini del cinema in Scandinavia (1896–1918). Pordenone: Studio Tesi, 1986.

SCHICKEL, RICHARD. *D. W. Griffith: An American Life*. New York: Simon & Schuster, 1984.

— *Brando: A Life in our Times*. London: Pavilion, 1991.

— and FAIRBANKS, DOUGLAS, JR. *The Fairbanks Album*. Boston: New York Graphic Society, 1975.

SCHIFANO, LAURENCE. *Luchino Visconti: The Flames of Passion*. London: Collins, 1990.

SCHNEIDER, STEVE. *That's All Folks!* New York: Henry Holt, 1988.

SCHNITZER, LUDA, and SCHNITZER, JEAN. *Alexandre Dovjenko*. Paris: Éditions Universitaires, 1966.

SCHRADER, PAUL. *Transcendental Style in Film: Ozu, Bresson, Dreyer*. Berkeley, Calif.: University of California Press, 1972.

SCHUMANN, PETER B. *Historia del cine latinoamericano*. Buenos Aires: Editorial Legasa, 1987.

SCHYGULLA, HANNA. *Bilder aus Filmen von Rainer Werner Fassbinder*. Munich: Schirmer & Mosel, 1981.

SCOGNAMILLO, GIOVANNI, *Turk sinemasi tarihi* ('The history of Turkish cinema'). 2 vols. Istanbul: Metis, 1987–8.

SELEZNYOVA, T. *Kinomysl 1920-ykh godov* ('Cinema thinking in the 1920s'). Leningrad: Iskusstvo, 1972.

SEMSEL, GEORGE S. (ed.). *Chinese Film: The State of the Art in the People's Republic*. New York: Praeger, 1987.

SEN, KRISHNA. *Indonesian Cinema: Framing the New Order*. London: Zed Books, 1994.

SESONSKE, ALEXANDER. *Jean Renoir: The French Films, 1924–1939*. Cambridge, Mass.: Harvard University Press, 1980.

SETON, MARIE. *Sergei M. Eisenstein: A Biography*. London: John Lane, The Bodley Head, 1952.

SEYDEL, RENATE, and HAGEDORFF, ALLAN (eds.). *Asta Nielsen: ihr Leben in Fotodokumenten, Selbstzeugnissen und zeitgenössischen Betrachtungen*. Munich: Universitas Verlag, 1981.

SHEPHERD, DONALD. *Jack Nicholson: An Unauthorized Biography*. New York: St. Martin's Press, 1991.

—, and SLATZER, ROBERT, with GRAYSON, DAVE. *Duke: The Life and Times of John Wayne*. London: Weidenfeld & Nicolson, 1985.

SHIRI, KEITH (ed.). *Africa at the Pictures*. London: BFI, 1993.

SHIRLEY, GRAHAM, and ADAMS, BRIAN. *Australian Cinema: The First Eighty Years*. Revised edn. Sydney: Currency Press, 1983.

SHLAPENTOKH, DMITRY, and SHLAPENTOKH, VLADIMIR. *Soviet Cinematography 1918–1991: Ideological Conflict and Social Reality*. New York: Aldine de Gruyter, 1993.

SHMERUK, CHONE. *Historia literatury jidisz* ('History of Yiddish literature'). Wroc aw, 1992.

SIEGEL, JOEL E. *Val Lewton: The Reality of Terror*. London, Secker & Warburg, 1973; New York: Viking, 1973.

SILVERMAN, KAJA. *Male Subjectivity at the Margins*. London: Routledge, 1992.

SINCLAIR, ANDREW. *John Ford: A Biography*. New York: Dial, 1979.

SINGER, BEN. 'Fictional Tie-ins and Narrative Intelligibility, 1911–18'. *Film History*, 5/4 (Dec. 1993).

SINYARD, NEIL. *The Films of Steven Spielberg*. London: Bison Books, 1987.

SITNEY, P. ADAMS. *Visionary Film*. New York and London: Oxford University Press, 1974.

SIVATHAMBY, KARTHIGESU. *The Tamil Film as a Medium of Political Communication*. Madras: New Century Book House, 1981.

SKLAR, ROBERT. *Film: An International History of the Medium*. New York: Abrams, 1993; London: Thames & Hudson, 1993.

— *Movie-Made America*. New York: Vintage, 1976.

—, and MUSSER, CHARLES (eds.). *Resisting Images: Essays on Cinema and History*. Philadelphia: Temple University Press, 1990.

SKORODNIKOVA, SVETLANA. 'Ivan Ilich Mosjoukine'. In P. Cherchi Usai *et al.* (eds.). *Silent Witnesses: Russian Films, 1908–1919*. London: BFI, 1989; Pordenone: Biblioteca dell'Immagine, 1989.

781

SLIDE, ANTHONY. *The Big V: A History of the Vitagraph Company*. Metuchen, NJ: Scarecrow Press, 1987.

—— *The Griffith Actresses*. New York: A. S. Barnes, 1973.

SLOTKIN, RICHARD. *Gunfighter Nation: The Myth of the Frontier in Twentieth Century America*. New York: Atheneum, 1992.

SLUSSER, GEORGE, and RABKIN, ERIC S. (eds.). *Shadows of the Magic Lamp: Fantasy and Science Fiction in Film*. Carbondale, Ill.: Southern Illinois Press, 1985.

SMITH, ALBERT. *Two Reels and a Crank*. New York: Doubleday, 1952.

SMITH, ELLA. *Starring Miss Barbara Stanwyck*. Revised edn. New York: Crown Books, 1985.

SMITH, PAUL. *Clint Eastwood: A Cultural Production*. Minneapolis: University of Minnesota Press, 1993.

SMITH, PAUL JULIAN. *Laws of Desire: Questions of Homosexuality in Spanish Writing and Film, 1960–1990*. Oxford: Clarendon Press, 1992.

SNYDER, ROBERT L. *Pare Lorentz and the Documentary Film*. Norman, Okla.: University of Oklahoma Press, 1968.

SOBCHACK, VIVIAN. *Screening Space: The American Science Fiction Film*. New York: Ungar Publishing Co., 1987.

SOLANAS, FERNANDO, and GETINO, OCTAVIO. 'Towards a Third Cinema' (1969). In Michael Chanan (ed.). *Twenty Five Years of the New Latin American Cinema*. London: BFI and Channel 4, 1983.

SOLOMON, CHARLES. *Enchanted Drawings: The History of Animation*. New York: Knopf, 1987.

SONTAG, SUSAN. 'Fascinating Fascism'. In *Under the Sign of Saturn*. New York: Vintage, 1981.

—— *On Photography*. New York: Farrar, Straus & Giroux, 1977.

SORLIN, PIERRE. *European Cinemas, European Societies, 1939–1990*. London: Routledge, 1991.

SOUTO, H. MARIO RAIMONDO. *The Technique of the Motion Picture Camera*. 3rd edn.. New York: Hastings House, 1977.

SOWRY, CLIVE. *Film-Making in New Zealand*. Wellington: New Zealand Film Archive, 1984.

SPOTO, DONALD. *Blue Angel: The Life of Marlene Dietrich*. New York: Doubleday, 1992.

—— *The Dark Side of Genius: The Life of Alfred Hitchcock*. Boston: Little, Brown & Co., 1983.

—— *Marilyn Monroe: The Biography*. London: Chatto & Windus, 1993.

SQUIRE, JASON E. (ed.). *The Movie Business Book*. New York: Simon & Schuster, 1992.

STAIGER, JANET. 'Individualism versus Collectivism'. *Screen*, 24 (Autumn 1983).

STAM, ROBERT. 'The Hour of the Furnaces and the Two Avant-Gardes'. In Julianne Burton (ed.). *The Social Documentary in Latin America*. Pittsburgh: University of Pittsburgh, 1990.

STANBROOK, ALAN. 'The Worlds of Hou Hsiao-hsien'. *Sight and Sound* (Spring 1990).

STEAD, PETER. *Film and the Working Class: The Feature Film in British and American Society*. London: Routledge, 1989.

STEDMAN, RAYMOND WILLIAM. *The Serials: Suspense and Drama by Installment*. Norman, Okla.: University of Oklahoma Press, 1977.

STEELE, JOSEPH H. *Ingrid Bergman: An Intimate Portrait*. New York: David McKay Co., 1959.

STEEN, MIKE. *Hollywood Speaks: An Oral History*. New York: Putnam's, 1974.

STERNBERG, JOSEF VON. *Fun in a Chinese Laundry*. New York: Collier Books, 1965.

STETTNER, PETER. *Von Trümmerfilm zur Traumfabrik: die 'Junge Film-Union', 1947–1952*. Hildesheim, Zurich, and New York: Olms, 1992.

STITES, RICHARD. *Revolutionary Dreams: Utopian Vision and Experimental Life in the Russian Revolution*. Oxford: Oxford University Press, 1989.

—— *Soviet Popular Culture: Entertainment and Society in Russia since 1900*. Cambridge: Cambridge University Press, 1992.

STOLLER, PAUL. *The Cinematic Griot: The Ethnography of Jean Rouch*. Chicago: University of Chicago Press, 1992.

STUDLAR, GAYLYN. 'Valentino, "Optic Intoxication" and Dance Madness'. In Steven Cohan and Ina Rae Hark (eds.). *Screening the Male*. London: Routledge, 1993.

—— *Von Sternberg, Dietrich and the Masochistic Aesthetic*. Urbana, Ill.: University of Illinois Press, 1988.

—— and Desser, David (eds.). *Reflections in a Male Eye: John Huston and the American Experience*. Washington, DC: Smithsonian, 1993.

SUROWIEC, CATHERINE A. *Accent on Design: Four European Art Directors*. London: BFI, 1992.

SUSSEX, ELIZABETH. *The Rise and Fall of British Documentary: The Story of the Film Movement Founded by John Grierson*. Berkeley, Calif.: University of California Press, 1975.

SYBERBERG, HANS JÜRGEN. *Der Wald steht schwarz und schweiget*. Zurich: Diogenes, 1984.

—— *Die freudlose Gesellschaft*. Munich and Vienna: Hanser, 1981.

—— *Hitler: A Film from Germany*. Translated by Joachim Neugroschel. New York: Farrar, Straus & Giroux, 1982.

SYKES, CHARLES J. *A Nation of Victims*. New York: St Martin's Press, 1992.

TABORI, PAUL. *Alexander Korda*. London: Oldbourne, 1959.

TALON, GÉRARD. 'Cinéma français: la crise de 1928'. In *Synchronismes: 1928*. Paris: Éditions du Signe, 1975.

TANAKA, JUNICHIRO. *Nihon Eiga Hattatsu Shi*. 5 vols. Tokyo: Chuei Koron, 1957–76.

TAYLOR, PHILIP M. (ed.). *Britain and the Cinema in the Second World War*. London: Macmillan, 1988.

TAYLOR, RICHARD. *The Politics of the Soviet Cinema, 1917–29*. Cambridge: Cambridge University Press, 1979.

——, and CHRISTIE, IAN (eds.). *The Film Factory: Russian and Soviet Cinema in Documents*. London: Routledge & Kegan Paul, 1988.

TEO, STEPHEN. *Hong Kong Cinema: The Extra Dimensions*: London, BFI, 1996.

TESSIER, MAX. 'Yasujiro Ozu'. *Anthologie du cinéma*, 64 (July–Oct. 1971).

THARRATS, JUAN-GABRIEL. *Los 500 films de Segundo de Chomón*. Zaragoza: Prensas Universitarias, 1988.

THOMAS, BOB. *Brando: Portrait of the Rebel as an Artist*. New York and London: W. H. Allen, 1973.

THOMAS, HANS. *Die deutsche Tonfilmmusik: von den Anfängen bis 1956*. Neue Beiträge zur Film und Fernsehforschung 3. Gütersloh: Bertelsmann, 1962.

THOMAS, TONY. *Film Score: The Art and Craft of Movie Music*. Burbank, Calif.: Riverside Press, 1991.

THOMAS, FRANK, and JOHNSTON, OLLIE. *Disney Animation: The Illusion of Life*. New York: Abbeville, 1981.

THOMPSON, DAVID, and CHRISTIE, IAN (eds.). *Scorsese on Scorsese*. London: Faber & Faber, 1989.

THOMPSON, KRISTIN. 'Boredom on the Beach: Triviality and Humor in *Les vacances de M. Hulot*'. In *Breaking the Glass Armor: Neoformalist Film Criticism*. Princeton, NJ: Princeton University Press, 1988.

—— *Exporting Entertainment: America in the World Film Market, 1907–1934*. London: BFI, 1985.

—— 'Late Spring and Ozu's Unreasonable Style'. In Breaking the Glass Armor: Neoformalist Film Criticism. Princeton, NJ: Princeton University Press, 1988.

—— 'Play Time: Comedy on the Edge of Perception'. In Breaking the Glass Armor: Neoformalist Film Criticism. Princeton, NJ: Princeton University Press, 1988.

—— and BORDWELL, DAVID. Film History: An Introduction. New York: McGraw-Hill, 1994.

THOMSON, VIRGIL. 'A Little about Movie Music'. Modern Music, 10 (Nov. 1932–June 1933).

TOEPLITZ, JERZY. Geschichte des Films, 1895–1933. Munich, 1987.

—— Historia sztuki filmowej ('History of film art'). Vol. v. Warsaw, 1970.

TOLAND, GREGG. 'Realism for Citizen Kane'. American Cinematographer (Feb. 1941).

TOROPTSEV, SERGEI. Ocherk istorii kitaiskogo Kino, 1896–1966 ('Essays on the history of Chinese cinema'). Moscow: Nauka, 1979.

TRAUBERG, L. Z. Leonid Trauberg et l'excentrisme. Edited by Natalia Noussinova. Brussels: Yellow Now – STUC, 1993.

TRAUDISCH, DORA. Mutterschaft mit Zuckerguss? Frauenfeindliche Propaganda im NS-Spielfilm. Pfaffenweiler: Centaurus, 1993.

TRUFFAUT, FRANÇOIS. 'A Certain Tendency of the French Cinema'. In Bill Nichols (ed.). Movies and Methods. Berkeley, Calif.: University of California Press, 1976.

—— with SCOTT, HELEN G. Hitchcock. New York: Simon & Schuster, 1984.

TSIVIAN, YURI, 'Some Preparatory Remarks on Russian Cinema'. In P. Cherchi Usai et al. (eds.). Silent Witnesses: Russian Films 1908–1919. London: BFI, 1989; Pordenone: Edizioni Biblioteca dell'Immagine, 1989.

TUDOR, ANDREW. Monsters and Mad Scientists: A Cultural History of the Horror Movie. Oxford: Basil Blackwell, 1989.

TULLOCH, JOHN. Legends on the Screen: The Narrative Film in Australia 1919–1929. Sydney: Currency Press, 1981.

TURCONI, DAVID, and BASSOTTO, EMILIO. Cinema scritto: il catalogo delle riviste italiane di cinema, 1907–1944. Edited by Riccardo Redi. Rome: Associazione Italiana per le Ricerche di Storia del Cinema, 1992.

TURNER, GEORGE. 'Xanadu in Review: Citizen Kane Turns 50'. American Cinematographer (Aug. 1991).

TURNER, FREDERICK JACKSON. The Frontier in American History. New York: Holt, Rinehart & Winston, 1962.

TUROVSKAYA, MAYA. Tarkovsky: Cinema as Poetry. London: Faber & Faber, 1989.

TUSKA, JOHN. The Filming of the West. Garden City, NY: Doubleday, 1976.

TYLER, PARKER. Magic and Myth of the Movies. London: Secker & Warburg, 1971.

UKADIKE, NWACHUKWU FRANK. Black African Cinema. Berkeley, Calif.: University of California Press, 1994.

URICCHIO, WILLIAM, and PEARSON, ROBERTA E. Reframing Culture: The Case of the Vitagraph Quality Films. Princeton, NJ: Princeton University Press, 1993.

UUSITALO, KARI. 'Finnish Film Production (1904–1918)'. Facts about Film in Finland, 1 (1975).

VASEY, RUTH. Diplomatic Representations: The World According to Hollywood, 1919–1939. Madison, Wis.: University of Wisconsin Press, 1995.

VASUDEV, ARUNA, and LENGLET, PHILIPPE (eds.). Indian Cinema Superbazaar. New Delhi: Vikas, 1983.

VERTOV, DZIGA. Kino-Eye: The Writings of Dziga Vertov. Edited and introduced by Annette Michelson. Berkeley, Calif.: University of California Press, 1984.

VERTREES, ALAN. 'A Singular Vision: David O. Selznick and the Film Production of Gone with the Wind'. Ph.D. dissertation, Columbia University, 1991.

VIANO, MAURIZIO. A Certain Realism: Making Use of Pasolini's Film Theory and Practice. Berkeley, Calif.: University of California Press, 1993.

VINCENDEAU, GINETTE. 'Hollywood Babel'. Screen, 29/2 (1988).

VIRILIO, PAUL. Guerre et cinéma 1: logistique de la perception. Paris: Éditions de l'Étoile, 1984.

VISHNEVSKY, VIENIAMIN E. Khronologicheskiie tablitsy i stat'i po istorii sovetskogo kino ('Chronological tables and articles on the history of Soviet cinema'). Gosfilmfond Manuscript Archive no. 27.

——, and FIONOV, P. V. (eds.). Sovetskoie kino v datakh i faktakh, 1917–69 ('Soviet Cinema dates and facts, 1917–69'). Moscow: Iskusstvo, 1974.

VRIELYNCK, ROGER. Le Cinéma d'animation avant et après Walt Disney. Brussels: Meddens, 1981.

WALKER, ALEXANDER. Greta Garbo: A Portrait. London: Weidenfeld & Nicolson, 1980.

—— Hollywood, England: The British Film Industry in the Sixties. London: Harrap, 1986.

—— National Heroes: British Cinema in the Seventies and Eighties. London: Harrap, 1985.

—— The Shattered Silents: How the Talkies Came to Stay. London: Harrap, 1986.

—— Valentino. London: Penguin, 1976.

WARHOL, ANDY. Blue Movie. New York: Grove Press, 1970.

—— The Philosophy of Andy Warhol: From A to B and Back Again. New York: Harcourt Brace Jovanovich, 1975.

WARSHOW, ROBERT. 'The gangster as tragic hero'. The Immediate Experience. New York: Doubleday, 1962.

WEINBERG, HERMANN G. The Lubitsch Touch: A Critical Study. New York: Dover Publications, 1977.

WEIS, ELISABETH, and BELTON, JOHN (eds.). Film Sound: Theory and Practice. New York: Columbia University Press, 1985.

WEISS, MARION. Martin Scorsese: A Guide to References and Resources. Boston: G. K. Hall, 1987.

WELDON, MICHAEL. The Psychotronic Encyclopedia of Film. New York: Ballantine Books, 1983.

WELLES, ORSON. Orson Welles on Shakespeare: The WPA and Mercury Theatre Playscripts. Edited by Richard France. New York: Greenwood Press, 1990.

——, with BOGDANOVICH, PETER. This is Orson Welles. Edited by Jonathan Rosenbaum. New York: Harper Collins, 1992.

WENDERS, WIM. Emotion Pictures: Reflections on the Cinema. Translated by Sean Whiteside. London: Faber & Faber, 1989.

—— The Logic of Images: Essays and Conversations. London: Faber & Faber, 1991.

WENDERS, WIM, SHEPARD, SAM, and CARSON, L. M. KIT. Paris, Texas. New York: Ecco, 1990.

WERNER, GÖSTA. Den svenska filmens historia ('History of Swedish film'). Stockholm: P. A. Norstedt & söners, 1978.

—— Mauritz Stiller: ett livsöde ('Mauritz Stiller: a biography'). Stockholm: Bokförlaget Prisma, 1991.

WEXMAN, VIRGINIA WRIGHT, and BISPLINGHOFF, GRETCHEN. Robert Altman: A Guide to References and Resources. Boston: G. K. Hall, 1984.

Wide Angle, 11 (1989).

WILLEMEN, PAUL (ed.). 'Andaz'. In Wimal Dissanayake (ed.). *Melodrama and Asian Cinema*. Cambridge: Cambridge University Press, 1993.

—— (ed.). *Ophuls*. London: BFI, 1978.

—— (ed.). *Pasolini*. London: BFI, 1977.

WILLIAMS, ALAN. *Max Ophuls and the Cinema of Desire*. Ann Arbor, Mich.: University Microfilms International, 1977.

—— *Republic of Images: A History of French Filmmaking*. Cambridge: Harvard University Press, 1992.

WILLIAMS, LINDA. *Hard Core: Power, Pleasure and the Frenzy of the Visible*. Berkeley, Calif.: University of California Press, 1989.

WINDELER, ROBERT. *Burt Lancaster*. London: W. H. Allen, 1984.

WINKLER-BESSONE, CLAUDE. *Les Films de Wim Wenders: la nouvelle naissance des images*. Berne, New York, and Frankfurt am Main: Peter Lang, 1992.

WITTE, KARSTEN. 'Filmkomödie im Faschismus'. Dissertation, Johann Wolfgang Goethe-University of Frankfurt, 1986.

—— 'Gehemmte Schaulust: Momente des deutschen Revuefilms'. In Helga Belach (ed.). *Wir tanzen um die Welt: deutsche Revuefilm, 1933–1945*. Munich and Vienna: Hanser, 1979.

WOLLEN, PETER. 'Counter-cinema: *Vent d'est*'. *Afterimage*, 4 (1972).

—— *Readings and Writings: Semiotic Counter-Strategies*. London: Verso, 1982.

—— *Signs and Meaning in the Cinema*. Revised edn. London: Secker & Warburg, 1972.

WOOD, NANCY. 'Towards a Semiotics of the Transition to Sound: Spatial and Temporal Codes'. *Screen*, 25 (1984).

WOOD, ROBIN. *Hitchcock's Films Revisited*. New York: Columbia University Press, 1989.

—— *Howard Hawks*. London: BFI, 1981.

—— *Ingmar Bergman*. London: Studio Vista, 1969.

—— 'An Introduction to the American Horror Film'. In Bill Nichols (ed.). *Movies and Methods*. Berkeley, Calif.: University of California Press, 1985.

WOODHEAD, CHRISTINE (ed.). *Turkish Cinema: An Introduction*. London: Centre of Near and Middle Eastern Studies, SOAS, Apr. 1989 (Occasional Paper 5).

WRIGHT, WILL. *Sixguns and Society*. Berkeley, Calif.: University of California Press, 1975.

WYVER, JOHN. *The Moving Image: An International History of Film Television and Video*, Oxford: Basil Blackwell, 1989.

YAMAGUCHI, YOSHIKO, and FUJIWARA, SAKUYA. *Ri Ko Ran: Watashi no Hansei*. Shincho Bunko, 1987.

YOUNGBLOOD, DENISE JEANNE. *Soviet Cinema in the Silent Era, 1918–1935*. Ann Arbor: UMI Research Press, 1985.

ŽIŽEK, SLAVOJ. *Everything You Always Wanted to Know about Lacan (but Were Afraid to Ask Hitchcock)*. London: Verso, 1992.

ZMIJEWSKY, STEVE, ZMIJEWSKY, BORIS, and RICCI, MARK. *The Complete Films of John Wayne*. Secaucus, NJ: Citadel Press, 1983.

ZORKAYA, NEYA. *The Illustrated History of Soviet Cinema*. New York: Hippocrene Books, 1991.

—— *Ivan Mozzhukhin*. Moscow: Znanie, 1990.

ZWERENZ, GERHARD. *Der langsame Tod des Rainer Werner Fassbinder*. Munich: Schneekluth, 1982.

Index

Notes:
1. Entries in *italics* indicate **captions** to illustrations. In some cases there are also textual references on these pages
2. Page numbers in **bold** indicate special features in boxes
3. Dates are occasionally added to distinguish different films with the same or very similar names
4. Films with non-English titles from Western Europe are entered in both languages; films from the rest of the world are mainly given in English, where it has been supplied

C

F

INDEX

INDEX

List of Picture Sources

Unless otherwise stated, all photographic material in the book was obtained from the British Film Institute. While every effort has been made to secure permissions, we may have failed in a few cases to trace the copyright holder. We apologize for any apparent negligence. The editor and publisher would like to thank Vicki Reeve and Diana Morris for their assistance in permissions clearance of the illustrations throughout this book, and the following companies and individuals who have kindly given permission to reproduce the illustrations on the following pages:

26 © Danish Film Museum. **30** © Museum of Modern Art, New York. **34** Photo: Kobal Collection. **40** Photo: Kobal Collection. **44** © Turner Entertainment Co. All Rights Reserved. **49** © 1930 Turner Entertainment Co. All Rights Reserved. **54** © 1919 by Universal City Studios, Inc. Courtesy of MCA Publishing Rights, A Division of MCA Inc. All Rights Reserved. **64** © 1927 Twentieth Century Fox. **69** © 1925 Twentieth Century Fox. **72** © 1996 DACS, London. **75** © Felix the Cat Productions Inc. **76** © 1928, Saturn Film. **83** © Pathé Television. **84** © Chaplin Films. **91** © Fox/Europa. **92** © Mosfilm. **97** © 1996 DACS, London. **99** © Pathé Television. **102** © Palladium, Denmark. **120** (*bottom*) © Pathé Television. **133** © By courtesy of the Rank Organisation Plc. **138** © Rohauer Pendemis. **140** © Still courtesy of CTE and the Samuel Goldwyn Co. **142** © Friedrich-Wilhelm-Murnau-Stiftung. **146** © Friedrich-Wilhelm-Murnau-Stiftung. **148** © Friedrich-Wilhelm-Murnau-Stiftung, MGM Costume Dept. **152** © Svensk Filmindustri. **155** © Svensk Filmindustri. **156** © Svensk Filmindustri. **168** © 1944 Mosfilm. **169** © 1937 Mosfilm. **173** © 1929 Sovkino. **176** © 1936, Greenfilm. **190** © 1928 Turner Entertainment Co. All Rights Reserved. **200** © 1927 Turner Entertainment Co. All Rights Reserved. **206** © 1939 Turner Entertainment Co. All Rights Reserved. **208** © 1927 Turner Entertainment Co. All Rights Reserved. **212** (*top and bottom*) © BIP. **215** © 1952 Turner Entertainment Co. All Rights Reserved. **216** © 1928 Paramount Pictures. **222** © 1938 Turner Entertainment Co. All Rights Reserved. **224–5** © 1943 Warner Brothers. **228** © 1944 Turner Entertainment Co. All Rights Reserved. **231** © 1949 Excelsa Film/Renzo Rossolini. **232** © Still courtesy of CTE and the Samuel Goldwyn Co. **240** © 1932 by Universal City Studios, Inc. Courtesy of MCA Publishing Rights, A Division of MCA Inc. All Rights Reserved. **244** © 1933 Universal Elekta Film. **246** © 1934 Turner Entertainment Co. All Rights Reserved. **251** © By courtesy of The Rank Organisation Plc. **254** © 1938 Turner Entertainment Co. All Rights Reserved. **256** © Range/Bettmann/UPI. **262** © 1941 Turner Entertainment Co. All Rights Reserved. **264** © 1953 Twentieth Century Fox. **269** © 1944 Turner Entertainment Co. All Rights Reserved. **271** © 1949 Warner Brothers. **278** © 1944 Turner Entertainment Co. All Rights Reserved. **281** © 1946 Turner Entertainment Co. All Rights Reserved. **282** © 1940 Turner Entertainment Co. All Rights Reserved. **284** © 1944 by Universal City Studios, Inc. Courtesy of MCA Publishing Rights, A Division of MCA Inc. All Rights Reserved. **287** © 1923 Paramount. **288** © 1946 Twentieth Century Fox. **290** © 1949 Turner Entertainment Co. All Rights Reserved. **292** © 1950 by Universal City Studios, Inc. Courtesy of MCA Publishing

Rights, A Division of MCA Inc. All Rights Reserved. **295** © 1933 Turner Entertainment Co. All Rights Reserved. **296** Photo: Kobal Collection. **298** © 1936 RKO Pictures Inc. Used by permission of Turner Entertainment Co. All Rights Reserved. **302** © 1955 Turner Entertainment Co. All Rights Reserved. **305** © 1931 Turner Entertainment Co. All Rights Reserved. **307** © 1939 Ste UGC. **308** © 1947 RKO Pictures Inc. Used by permission of Turner Entertainment Co. All Rights Reserved. **310** © 1960 by Universal City Studios, Inc. Courtesy of MCA Publishing Rights, A Division of MCA Inc. All Rights Reserved. **311** © 1972 by Universal City Studios, Inc. Courtesy of MCA Publishing Rights, A Division of MCA Inc. All Rights Reserved. **314** © 1935 Turner Entertainment Co. All Rights Reserved. **317** © 1931 by Universal City Studios, Inc. Courtesy of MCA Publishing Rights, A Division of MCA Inc. All Rights Reserved. **318** © 1943 Turner Entertainment Co. All Rights Reserved. **320** With thanks to Pandora and to the C.L.T. © Visionlight. **323** © 1935 British Gas Sponsored. **324** Resettlement Administrative Unit. **238** Crown copyright. Reproduced by Permission of the Controller of HMSO. **331** Mme Loridan Ivens/Capi Films. **336** © Still courtesy of CTE and the Samuel Goldwyn Company. **338** © Les Grands Films Classiques, Paris. **341** © 1936 by Universal City Studios, Inc. Courtesy of MCA Publishing Rights, A Division of MCA Inc. All Rights Reserved. **346** © Ste UGC. **347** © 1945 Pathé Television. **348** © 1953 VGC. **349** © 1951 Les Films Ariane. **351** Caday/Discina. **354** 1937 ENIC. **359** 1951 Janus. **360** 1948 MOMA, NY. **364** © By courtesy of The Rank Organisation Plc. **366** © 1934 Lumière Pictures Ltd. **368** © By courtesy of The Rank Organisation Plc. **371** © 1951 Lumière Pictures Ltd. **373** (*top*) © By courtesy of The Rank Organisation Plc. (*bottom*) © Hammer Films/Lumière Pictures Ltd. **378** © Friedrich-Wilhelm-Murnau-Stiftung. **380** © Courtesy of the Rank Organisation. **386** 1936 Barrandov Studios. **388** © Stefan Themerson Estate, 1996. Themerson Archive, 12 Belsize Park Gardens, London NW3 4LD. **391** 1937 Lenfilm. **392** 1934 Lenfilm. **410** © Twentieth Century Fox. **418** 1939 Daiei Film Productions. **430** © Courtesy of Clasa Films Mundiales. **432** 1961 UNICI. **434** 1957 Argentina Sono Film. **438** 1946 Excelsa Film/Renzo Rossolini. **439** © Lumière Pictures Ltd. **440** 1954 Janus/Lux. **444** © 1951 Warner Bros. **447** © 1948 RKO Pictures Inc. Used by permission of Turner Entertainment Co. All Rights Reserved. **448** © By courtesy of Romulus Films. **452** 1963 Seven Arts/Joel/John Frankenheimer. **454** Internaccional Films Espanola. **457** © 1955 by Universal City Studios, Inc. Courtesy of MCA Publishing Rights, A Division of MCA Inc. All Rights Reserved. **458** © 1961 Turner

Entertainment Co. All Rights Reserved. **460** © 1975 Warner Bros. **469** © Hammer Films. **470** 1977 Twentieth Century Fox. **472** 1964 Eastwood. **476** © Paramount. **478** © Orion Pictures Corp. **481** © 1979 Metro Goldwyn Mayer Inc. **482** © 1982 by Universal City Studios, Inc. Courtesy of MCA Publishing Rights, A Division of MCA Inc. All Rights Reserved. **487** 1961 Rome–Paris/Euro International. **492** © Ste Les Films Ariane. **493** © Warner Bros. **494** Janus. **499** Courtesy of the Edward Mapp Collection. **501** © 1939 Turner Entertainment Co. All Rights Reserved. **503** © Twentieth Century Fox. **504** © 1967 Metro Goldwyn Mayer Inc. **506** © Warner Bros. **508** UIP/Forty Acres and a Mule Filmworks. **510** © 1975 The Saul Zaentz Company. All Rights Reserved. **512** © Orion Pictures. **514** © Warner Bros. **517** © 1981 by Universal City Studios, Inc. Courtesy of MCA Publishing Rights, A Division of MCA Inc. All Rights Reserved. **520** © 1972 by Universal City Studios, Inc. Courtesy of MCA Publishing Rights, A Division of MCA Inc. All Rights Reserved. **524** © 1981 Lucas Film Ltd. **525** © Warner Bros. **529** © Les Films du Jeudi. **530** © Ste Argos Films. **533** 1968 ICAIC. **534** 1980 Clarity Educational Productions. **535** © 1990 J & M Entertainment Ltd./Miramax Film Corp. **538** MOMA, New York. **544** The Andy Warhol Foundation for Visual Arts. Photo: John Chamberlain. **556** © 1976 Bruno Bozzetto. **560** © Ste Artedis. **563** © Warner Bros. **565** © Apple Corps Inc./Walter Shenson. **568** 1962 Interopa-Cineriz, Paris Film. **571** © UGC DA. **572** © Svensk Filmindustri. **577** © Ste AFMD. **579** © Ste Pathé Cinema. **581** © 1950 Robert & Mylène Bresson. **583** © Gaumont/Walt Disney (France) SA. **585** © Gaumont/Walt Disney (France) Ltd. **587** © MOMA, New York/Film Stills Archive. **588–9** 1975 PEA/UA. **591** 1963 CCC/Concordia. **593** 1970 Mars/Marianne/Maran. **595** 1958 Vides. **598** 1981 Emiliano Piedra Produccion/Edificio Luna. **599** © El Imar Cine y TV SA. **600** Photo: Mimmo Catarinich/El Deseo SA. **605** © Woodfall Films. **606** © By courtesy of the Rank Organisation plc. **610** 1968 Warner Brothers. **611** © 1982 BFI/Channel 4. **615** © 1968 Kairos Films. **618** © Filmverlag der Autoren. **620** 1972 Hessischer Rundfunk. **624** 1974 Film Verlag der Autoren. **626** © 1977 Bioskop Film. **629** 1946 DEFA. **634** 1958 Film Polski. **638** © Euro London Films Ltd. **639** 1989 Film Polski/Tor. **642** © 1959 Mosfilm. **645** 1971 Lenfilm. **646** 1979 Mosfilm. **649** 1970 Lenfilm. **653** 1968 Armenfilm. **655** 1978 Uzbekfilm. **659** 1983 Contemporary/Guney Prod/MKZ Prod/TFI Films. **671** 1982 Les Films Cissé. **676** 1985 Institute for the Intellectual Development of Young Children and Young Adults, Teheran. **682** 1977 Devki Chitra. **689** 1994 Mainline/Kaleidoscope/Channel 4. **700** Guangxi Film Studio. **702** 1991 Century Communications Ltd. **707** © 1973 Warner Bros. **710** Still courtesy of Video Tartan.